lonely planet

Nicaragua & El Salvador

Paige R Penland

Gary Chandler, Liza Prado

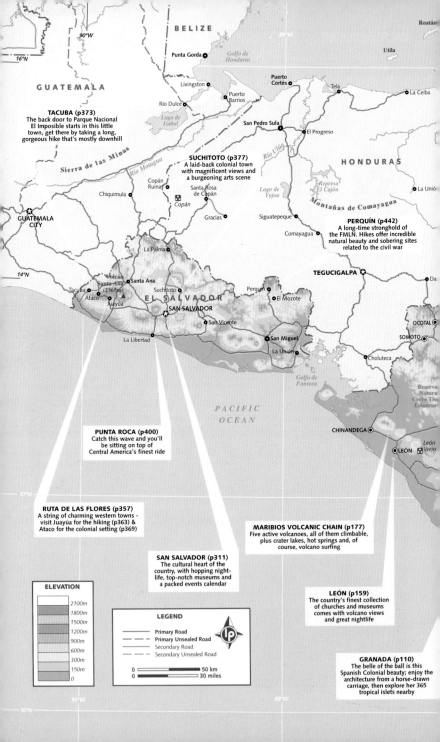

TACUBA (p373)
The back door to Parque Nacional El Imposible starts in this little town, get there by taking a long, gorgeous hike that's mostly downhill

SUCHITOTO (p377)
A laid-back colonial town with magnificent views and a burgeoning arts scene

PERQUÍN (p442)
A long-time stronghold of the FMLN. Hikes offer incredible natural beauty and sobering sites related to the civil war

PUNTA ROCA (p400)
Catch this wave and you'll be sitting on top of Central America's finest ride

RUTA DE LAS FLORES (p357)
A string of charming western towns - visit Juayúa for the hiking (p363) & Ataco for the colonial setting (p369)

MARIBIOS VOLCANIC CHAIN (p177)
Five active volcanoes, all of them climbable, plus crater lakes, hot springs and, of course, volcano surfing

SAN SALVADOR (p311)
The cultural heart of the country, with hopping nightlife, top-notch museums and a packed events calendar

LEÓN (p159)
The country's finest collection of churches and museums comes with volcano views and great nightlife

GRANADA (p110)
The belle of the ball is this Spanish Colonial beauty; enjoy the architecture from a horse-drawn carriage, then explore her 365 tropical islets nearby

ELEVATION

	2100m
	1800m
	1500m
	1200m
	900m
	600m
	300m
	150m
	0

LEGEND

———— Primary Road
– – – – Primary Unsealed Road
———— Secondary Road
– – – – Secondary Unsealed Road

0 ————— 50 km
0 ————— 30 miles

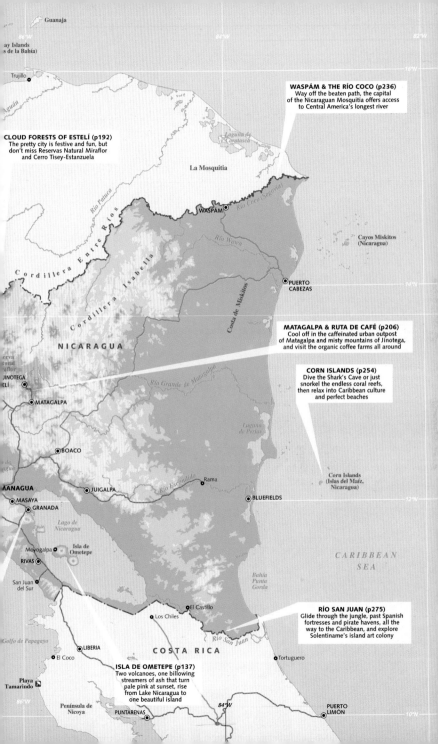

WASPÁM & THE RÍO COCO (p236)
Way off the beaten path, the capital of the Nicaraguan Mosquitia offers access to Central America's longest river

CLOUD FORESTS OF ESTELÍ (p192)
The pretty city is festive and fun, but don't miss Reservas Natural Miraflor and Cerro Tisey-Estanzuela

MATAGALPA & RUTA DE CAFÉ (p206)
Cool off in the caffeinated urban outpost of Matagalpa and misty mountains of Jinotega, and visit the organic coffee farms all around

CORN ISLANDS (p254)
Dive the Shark's Cave or just snorkel the endless coral reefs, then relax into Caribbean culture and perfect beaches

RÍO SAN JUAN (p275)
Glide through the jungle, past Spanish fortresses and pirate havens, all the way to the Caribbean, and explore Solentiname's island art colony

ISLA DE OMETEPE (p137)
Two volcanoes, one billowing streamers of ash that turn pale pink at sunset, rise from Lake Nicaragua to one beautiful island

Destination Nicaragua & El Salvador

These two brave nations – united less by geography than by their shared volcanic topography and violent, tumultuous past – stretch vast and sandy along the undulating Pacific. Sea turtles and surfers alike come to nest amid the thundering crash of waves; though these countries remain Central America's least touristed republics, each year more travelers rise to the challenge, climbing the fuming volcanic craters and jungle-clad granite peaks that pierce this misty realm of cloud forests. There one can sit back with a cup of rich organic coffee just outside some sweet Spanish colonial town brimming with artisan goods and ancient myths, and wonder why only the staccato memories of these nations' shared recent histories are what reverberate more than a decade on.

Two civil wars – separate, but equally bitter – brought these countries into the Cold War's brutal endgame, but both small nations have since found peace, rebuilt and healed. In many ways, it seems that all that their warriors once struggled for – democracy, social justice and some measure of prosperity – is finally coming to pass. Surprisingly sophisticated El Salvador has become Central America's economic tiger (well, jaguar), while Nicaragua is one of the safest destinations in the hemisphere and is working to conserve almost one-fifth of its landmass as national parks and reserves.

Nicaraguans and Salvadorans have gleaned intensity and wisdom from their turbulent histories on the outer fringes of the Maya empire and at the heart of the Spanish Conquest. Their colorful folklore and art, and their treasured wilderness and wildlife, are all finally opening up to the world, beckoning visitors to explore what has flowered along these sparkling shores, amid the ashes of volcanoes and history.

MARGIE POLITZER

It's a Wild World

Thousands of hawks can be seen filling the skies over Lago de Suchitlán (p177) in El Salvador

OTHER HIGHLIGHTS

Hike through the mist up Volcán Maderas (p139) on Isla de Ometepe, Nicaragua

Approach the rumored entrance to hell at Parque Nacional Volcán Masaya (p100), Nicaragua

MARGIE POLITZER

Trek out to the deep, cold Laguna Verde crater lake (p367), El Salvador

ALFREDO MAIQUEZ

Volcanic activity formed the unusual Los Tercios Waterfall (p379) in El Salvador

Get in amongst the early-morning bustle in La Unión (p412), El Salvador

MARGIE POLITZER

Building a Culture

In Suchitoto, El Salvador, murals immortalize Archbishop Óscar Romero (p305), martyr to the country's poor

Literacy rates in Nicaragua soared under the literacy campaigns of the 1980s (p56)

ERIC L WHEATER

Migration to the cities is on the rise, but many Nicaraguans still follow the harvest around the country (p59)

ERIC L WHEATER

Much-loved poet Rubén Darío (p35) is memorialized in Managua, Nicaragua

El Salvador's Monumento a la Revolución towers outside the Museo de Arte de El Salvador (p323) in San Salvador

ANTHONY PLUMMER

The Color of Life

See where it all began - prehistoric rock carvings
in San Salvador's Museo Nacional de Antropología
David J Guzmán (p323), El Salvador

Buy intricately woven traditional
textiles in the markets of San
Salvador (p340), El Salvador

Dancers and music make for lively festivals (p285) in Nicaragua

ANTHONY PLUMMER

Shop in the markets of San Salvador (p340), the most colorful in the country

The hammock salesman does his rounds of San Salvador's markets (p340)

ANTHONY PLUMMER

ERIC L WHEATER

Join the locals and enjoy the tasty produce of Nicaragua (p67)

Take Action

Catch some of the world's best surf (p45) in Nicaragua

PAUL F

Take the plunge on Little Corn
Island (p258), Nicaragua

MARGIE POLITZER

Hop a boat ride to 'las isletas' (p118), the islands of Lago de
Nicaragua in Granada, Nicaragua

MARGIE PO

Contents

Regional Map Contents

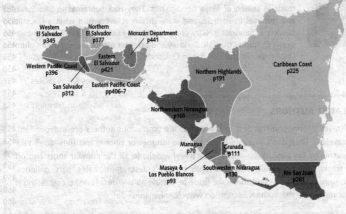

Western
El Salvador
p345

Northern
El Salvador
p377

Morazán Department
p441

Western Pacific Coast
p396

Eastern
El Salvador
p421

San Salvador
p312

Eastern Pacific Coast
pp406–7

Northern Highlands
p191

Caribbean Coast
p225

Northwestern Nicaragua
p160

Managua
p70

Granada
p111

Masaya &
Los Pueblo Blancos
p93

Southwestern Nicaragua
p130

Río San Juan
p261

The Authors

PAIGE R PENLAND
Coordinating Author

Paige R Penland is a freelance writer currently based in Liberia, Costa Rica, just 80km south of the Nicaraguan border. She is the co-author of Lonely Planet's *Costa Rica 6,* and author of many other books and articles including Iguanacaste Publishing's *A Week or Two in Southwest Nicaragua*.

My Favorite Trip

Crossing the border from Costa Rica, I've grown especially attached to Isla de Ometepe (p137), though the Archipiélago de Solentiname (p266) may prompt me to cross via Los Chiles more often. I love witchy Diriomo (p104); Managua (p68), which grows on you; and León (p159), with wonderful volcanoes. While the whole of the Northern Highlands are enchanting (and refreshingly cool), Jinotega (p217) is the nation's most spectacular unsung gem. But the great joy of this job is taking a Blue Bird school bus past massive ceiba trees and tiny, red-roofed Moravian churches into Reserva de Biosfera Bosawás (p230), where I just have to return.

GARY CHANDLER

Gary Chandler has covered El Salvador three times now, including a trip for Lonely Planet's *Central America on a Shoestring* in 2003. This project, co-authored with Liza Prado, was by far the biggest of the three. Research took Gary and Liza to glittery black-sand beaches, through balsam forests with torch-toting men dangling from the branches, and down leafy horse-roads in search of Maya petroglyphs. They had Supremas in San Salvador and pupusas in Perquín, and were shown at every turn what a fascinating country El Salvador is. Gary grew up in a ski-town near Lake Tahoe, has a BA in ethnic studies from UC Berkeley and a master's in journalism from Columbia University. He and Liza live in Oakland, CA.

LONELY PLANET AUTHORS

Why is our travel information the best in the world? It's simple: our authors are independent, dedicated travelers. They don't research using just the Internet or phone, and they don't take freebies in exchange for positive coverage. They travel widely, to all the popular spots and off the beaten track. They personally visit thousands of hotels, restaurants, cafés, bars, galleries, palaces, museums and more – and they take pride in getting all the details right, and telling it how it is. For more, see the authors section on www.lonelyplanet.com.

LIZA PRADO

Liza Prado first visited El Salvador in 2003; the trip was only hours old when a passenger punched a flight attendant and the plane was turned around. This time, Liza arrived two days after El Salvador's largest volcano erupted and 24 hours before Hurricane Stan caused flooding and mudslides. Despite this, Liza and co-author Gary Chandler were continually reminded of the spirit and camaraderie of everyday Salvadorans, not to mention the joys of fording roads-turned-rivers in a rental car. A graduate of Brown University and Stanford Law School, Liza traded corporate lawyerdom for the glory (and muddy shoes) of travel writing and has never regretted it. This is her third assignment with Lonely Planet.

Getting Started

Where to go and what to do? Nicaragua and El Salvador offer everything from homestays and hiking trails through chilly cloud forests to relaxation and a fair amount of decadence in luxury beachfront resorts. If you're headed to San Salvador or Managua, you may want to pack a snazzy outfit or two; if you're more interested in getting into the uncharted jungle interior, malaria pills and a water purifier are perhaps in order.

But – unless you consider this part of the fun – this is one region where planning ahead isn't absolutely necessary, as crowds are thin, except during Semana Santa (Holy Week), and there are things to see and do all year round. This chapter offers an overview of your options.

WHEN TO GO

See Climate Charts (p467) for more information.

With the exception of Semana Santa, when Nicas and Salvadoreños pack the beaches and hotels, you really don't have to worry about tourist season prices or crowds in either destination – yet. The exceptions are Granada and Southwestern Nicaragua, both easily accessible from Costa Rica, and La Libertad in El Salvador, beacon to the surfing faithful, which observe the traditional Central American high season (late November to mid-March) with more gusto (and higher prices) each year.

The reason why tourists flood the rest of Central America this time of year is the excellent weather – *verano* (literally summer; dry season) falls between November and May, and is the best time for back-country hiking and driving on dirt roads into the interior, not to mention sunbathing on the Pacific beaches. The Caribbean Coast of Nicaragua is less predictable (not to mention wetter) but it's worth checking to see if the sun's out on the other coast if you're trying to decide which way to head.

Check for travel advisories at either the UK Foreign & Commonwealth Office (www.fco.gov.uk) or the even more alarmist, and therefore entertaining, US State Department (www.state.gov).

Invierno (winter; the rainy season) runs roughly from May to November. Expect afternoon downpours for a couple of hours and higher humidity (especially in lowland areas), not to mention beautiful greenery in the usually dry tropical forests of the Pacific coast. Uninterrupted days of rain and flooding do occur, but with less frequency. The entire Caribbean Coast braces itself for hurricane season, technically from June to November, with the worst storms blowing through in October and November: not a good time to plan that Corn Islands diving jaunt.

COSTS & MONEY

Both Nicaragua and El Salvador are inexpensive, and serious budget travelers who limit time in pricier destinations (including San Salvador, Granada and the Corn Islands) can realistically travel on US$15 per day in Nicaragua and US$20 per day in El Salvador. Prices rise if you want little luxuries like private bathrooms, sit-down meals and guided tours.

El Salvador (like Ecuador and Panama) uses the US dollar as its official currency, so expect prices to remain more stable. In Nicaragua US dollars are the alternate currency, although using the Nicaraguan córdoba is usually cheaper and easier. Traveler's checks are being phased out in both countries, and it's more convenient to bring debit and credit cards. For more advice on the financial scenes in each country, see p287 and p459.

DON'T LEAVE HOME WITHOUT...

- A flashlight (torch) for exploring caves, and your room when the electricity fails (as it often does); candles are a more romantic option.
- A mosquito net, if you plan an extended jungle adventure or will be sleeping in cheap rooms without screens.
- Insect repellent containing DEET (p488) for wet-season travels. You may want to take medication against malaria, too (p486).
- A towel; Douglas Adams knew what he was talking about.
- An alarm clock for those early-morning departures.
- Bathing suit, snorkeling gear, flip-flops (thongs) and a sarong for the coast; light jacket or sweater, and warmish pants (eg denim) for the highlands.
- A small Spanish–English dictionary and/or Lonely Planet's *Latin American Spanish Phrasebook*.
- Water purifier or iodine tablets if you're headed into the wild, wild east.
- Documents; in addition to photocopying your passport, make copies of all your important documents, including airline tickets, and stash them in at least two places (try your backpack frame, camera bag or 'secret' pocket in your favorite pants).
- A prescription for any medication you might need – hey, what if you decide to extend your vacation for a few months?
- Contact-lens solution, tampons, sunscreen and any premium-brand toiletries, all of which can be hard to find.
- Photos from home, coloring books for kids and other portable bridges between cultures.

Sleeping

Budget travelers can find a clean, basic room with shared bathroom for US$3 to US$5 per person in most of Nicaragua, and US$10 per person in Granada, San Juan del Sur or the Caribbean Coast; dorms usually run to about US$3 per person. In El Salvador the only dorm-style options are in San Salvador and Santa Ana (US$6 to US$8 per person); elsewhere budget rooms cost US$8 to US$15, single or double.

Midrange travelers pay US$20 to US$40 per room (single or double) in most of Nicaragua, but in El Salvador very comfortable hotels start at around US$18 per night, some US$12 per person, a good option for solo travelers. Luxury hotels can cost US$80 to US$400 per night, a good deal for that sort of thing.

Eating

Shoestringers can order up a huge *comida corriente* (set plate) for US$1.50 to US$3 in either country, or try a simple *fritanga* (roadside barbecue; US$1) or a few pupusas (US$0.30 to US$0.50 each) for even less. Sit-down meals are US$2 to US$4 for a steam-table buffet or simple fare, jumping to US$5 to US$15 per person for fancier or international cuisine. A 10% gratuity is usually added to the bill (but rarely the menu) in both countries.

Transportation

Buses cost US$0.50 per hour in El Salvador and US$1 per hour in Nicaragua; *expresos* (express buses) and minivans are a bit more. Rental cars start at about US$30 per day in both countries, more for 4WD, and gas US$3.50 to US$4 per gallon. Internal flights in Nicaragua run to about US$90 a pop.

READING UP

English-language books (as well as your guidebooks and phrasebooks) are hard to find once you're there, so get them ahead of time.

Books

If you read Spanish, both countries are famed for their literature (see p61 and p305), in particular their poetry.

Before the Volcano Erupted: The Ancient Cerén Village in Central America, by Payson Sheets, tells how one evening in AD 595, Joya de Cerén (see p356) was buried by Volcán Laguna Caldera; they call it Central America's Pompeii.

History junkies will get a kick out of the dry, heartbreaking yet somehow still hillarious Iran-Contra Report (www .fas.org/irp/offdocs /walsh); don't skip the Caspar Wienberger section.

Blood of Brothers: Life and War in Nicaragua by Stephen Kinzer is out of print but worth finding. This insightful book, by the *New York Times'* man in Managua during the Contra War, is recommended by the Peace Corps to its Nicaragua volunteers.

In *The Country Under My Skin: A Memoir of Love and War* by Gioconda Belli, a Managua debutante starts working undercover for the Sandinistas while discovering her own poetic and sexual power. Remarkable.

The wisdom of the beautiful Islas Solentiname, in a far-off corner of Lake Nicaragua, is translated for the world in *The Gospel of Solentiname* by Ernesto Cardenal (see the boxed text, p267).

Massacre at El Mozote, by Mark Danner, tells how the people of El Mozote (see p448), caught in the crossfire of the bloody Salvadoran civil war, thought that their neutrality would save them. They turned out to be wrong.

Our Own Backyard: The United States in Central America 1977–1992, by William M LeoGrande, almost exclusively covers Nicaragua and El Salvador with a detailed, readable history and analysis of US involvement during (and leading up to) the civil wars.

Salvador by Joan Didion is a book-length essay that describes the dark, terrifying early years of the war; it's a slice of life and death during 1982.

And We Sold the Rain: Contemporary Fiction from Central America, edited by Rosario Santos, lets local voices explain indigenous political movements and activity.

Follow guerrilla DJs through the mist in *Rebel Radio: The Story of El Salvador's Radio Venceremos,* by Jose Ignacio Lopez Vigil et al, as they instruct and inspire the Farabundo Martí National Liberation Front (FMLN), one step ahead of the military.

When the catcalls start to grate, pull out *Women & Guerrilla Movements: Nicaragua, El Salvador, Chiapas, Cuba* by Karen Kampwirth, featuring lovely ladies no one would mess with in a dark alley.

Websites

There are more website listings for El Salvador on p458 and Nicaragua on p286.

El Salvador in Images (www.4elsalvador.com) Excellent website with tons of photos, organized in galleries, virtual tours and more in Spanish and English.

El Salvador Music (www.musica.com.sv) This awesome website has five categories of 'metal,' seven of 'electronic' and so much more.

Guanaquín (www.guanaquin.com) New Spanish speakers will love this kids' website covering El Salvador with detailed and easy-to-read info and maps.

Latin America Bureau (www.latinamericabureau.org) An excellent UK-based research organization and publisher dedicated to human rights; check out its booklist online.

Latin American Network Information Center – Nicaragua (www1.lanic.utexas.edu/la
/ca/nicaragua) An excellent portal with academic and tourism-oriented offerings.
Manfut (www.manfut.org in Spanish) A cornucopia of photos, history, myth, articles,
important phone numbers and much, much more, at this huge, messy, wonderful site covering
every corner of Nicaragua.
Nicaragua Béisbol League (www.ibw.com.ni/~beisnica in Spanish) Keep up with the
schedules and stats of Nicaragua's national pastime.
Vianica.com (www.vianica.com/transportation) Log onto this interactive map and click on
your route to find Nicaraguan road conditions, travel-time estimates, bus fares and more.

Central American key-
boards often access the
all-important *aroba* (@)
by pressing 'alt gr' and '2'
at the same time; or 'alt,'
'6' and '4.' Otherwise
just cut and paste, or ask
'¿Cómo se hace aroba?'

MUST-SEE MOVIES

Unfortunately not much of either country has been captured in quality
celluloid, but there are still a few movies to see.

Fire from the Mountain, based on the book by the same name, is
an award-winning documentary about the Contra War that includes
interviews with Omar Cabezas (the book's author) and others.

Noche Inocente (Innocent Night) is an excellent, low-budget 2005
film covering child soldiers in the Salvadoran civil war.

Romero is a heartbreaking and sometimes graphic movie with Raul
Julia in the title role. It traces the archbishop's path to liberation
(see the boxed text, p305).

The Oliver Stone classic *Salvador,* starring James Woods, received two
Oscar nominations for its story of a reporter covering the assassination
of Archbishop Oscar Romero, and getting entangled in the war along
the way.

Under Fire, a box-office sleeper starring Nick Nolte and Gene Hack-
man, does the Hollywood version of the revolution, built up around the
murder of ABC journalist Bill Stewart by President Somoza's National
Guard, which was captured on film.

Men with Guns, written and directed by indie legend John Sayles,
is an allegorical tale set in an unnamed, war-torn Latin American
country, where one doctor comes to terms with conflict's physical and
psychological carnage.

The World is Watching is a documentary covering the media feeding
frenzy during the Contra War; the makers went back in 2003 to make
When the World Stopped Watching, to document what happened when the
reporters took off for the next war.

FESTIVALS & EVENTS

Nicaragua and El Salvador both celebrate **Semana Santa**, or Holy Week,
the week before Easter Sunday, with barbecues, trips to the beach and
fiestas across both countries – know where you want to be and be
sure to have reservations, especially if you're headed to the beach.
More of the major festivals are listed on p285 (Nicaragua) and p457
(El Salvador).
Feria Gastronómica (weekly; Juayúa, El Salvador) Fill up on tasty Salvadoran treats at this
almost entirely edible handicrafts fair.
Palo de Mayo (May; Bluefields, Nicaragua) Dancing around the maypole probably isn't this
enticing in your home country.
San Jerónimo (September 30; Masaya, Nicaragua) Three months of dancing, fireworks and
men in drag; for more Masaya mayhem, see p96.
Festival de Hamacas (November; Quezaltepeque, El Salvador) Easily one of the most relaxing
festivals in Central America.
La Gritería (Día de la Purísima Concepción) (December 7; celebrated all over Nicaragua)
You'll finally find out what causes so much happiness around here.

RESPONSIBLE TRAVEL

Look for the 'Red Sostenible' (Sustainability Network) sign – with a volcano and humming-bird – in Nicaragua for quality, locally owned, community-friendly businesses.

In both Nicaragua and El Salvador, where tourism is only beginning to gain a firm foothold – and where people are eager to show off their beautiful 'sliver of the world' for what it is, instead of what was on TV during the 1980s – you're already using developed-world *dinero* (money) in a democratic way. Educating yourself on where to spend your money – on local, green or otherwise proactive businesses (see below) – is a great way to take it further.

As part of the tourism vanguard, industry professionals and community leaders are watching your habits and preferences closely. If you can, make the effort to visit a national park or reserve (see p63 and p307), try some unconventional tourism (see the boxed text, p244), take a tour through the past (p317), or go all out and help campesinos (farmers) harvest organic coffee (p206). Other tips for treading lightly include the following:

- Take a week of survival Spanish (see p284 and p455 for courses) or bring a phrasebook. Language is your passport to the real Central America.
- If you already speak Spanish, consider volunteering; there are scads of worthy causes around (see p289 and p461).
- Just chat folks up. Outside La Libertad and the Granada zone, you're something of a novelty and people want to meet you. Accept that invitation for coffee and *rosquillas* (baked corn snacks), even if you're worried that your host can't afford it; you'll have fun.
- Get off the beaten track. This isn't for everyone, but if you've got the time, energy and inclination, step away from the crowds, share the wealth and take a piece of people's lives back home with you.
- Never litter. One of Nicaragua's tourism slogans says that 'a clean Nicaragua attracts more tourists,' and you don't want to be the one who spoils it. Pack up all trash when camping, put butts where they belong and never, ever toss garbage from bus windows.
- Stay away from the cocaine – if there's a potential tourism disaster waiting to happen in these regions, it's this one. Besides, that shit will kill you.
- Buy directly from craftspeople or artisan cooperatives; it's a great excuse to get off the beaten path.
- Avoid souvenirs (or meals) made from endangered plants or animals.

Internet Resources

International Ecotourism Society (TIES; www.ecotourism.org) Links to businesses devoted to ecotourism.

Planeta.com (www.planeta.com) Ron Mader's outstanding ecotourism website.

Tourism Concern (www.tourismconcern.org.uk) UK-based organization dedicated to promoting ethical tourism.

Transitions Abroad (www.transitionsabroad.com) Eponymous website of the magazine focusing on immersion and responsible travel.

Books

For more on how not to dent the lands we visit (as well as listings of ecotour groups), read *The Good Alternative Travel Guide* or Mark Mann's outstanding *The Community Tourism Guide*.

Itineraries
CLASSIC ROUTES

THE CLASSIC NICARAGUA & EL SALVADOR   One Month to One Lifetime

Fly into **Managua** (p68) and take in the view from **Sandino's Silhouette** (p74) and the markets of **Masaya** (p99), then head south for sunny **San Juan del Sur** (p148), Nicaragua's best beach town; **Isla de Ometepe** (p137), a volcanic lake island; and **Granada** (p110), a graceful colonial beauty whose northern neighbor, **León** (p159), offers an unrivalled collection of churches and poets, plus volcanoes. Then dive into the revolutionary culture and cloud forests of **Estelí** (p192), the peaceful beauty of **Jinotega** (p217) and the urban bustle of **Matagalpa** (p206). The Caribbean Coast offers jungle-covered Spanish fortresses along the **Río San Juan** (p275), along with the awesome diving and white-sand beaches of the **Corn Islands** (p254).

From Managua, fly or book an international bus to San Salvador – or stop in **Ocotal** (p201), and see the pine forests of **Jalapa** (p203); or cross closer to the canyon of **Somoto** (p205). Surfers and sea-turtle lovers can stretch out on the sands of **Playa El Cuco** (p417) and the wild eastern beaches, while history buffs may climb to former FMLN stronghold **Perquín** (p442) and **Ruta de la Paz** (p447). Stop in sweet **Alegría** (p429) on your way back to **San Salvador** (p311), where wonderful nightlife and cultural attractions await.

Surfers should visit **La Libertad** (p396) and the western beaches, while culture (and flower) lovers can investigate **Ruta de las Flores** (p357), paying particular attention to **Juayúa** (p363). Hikers can indulge in **Parque Nacional Los Volcanes** (p353) and **Parque Nacional El Imposible** (p375), or head north to **Parque Nacional Montecristo-El Trifinio** (p360) and **Cerro El Pital** (p392), taking time for handicrafts in **La Palma** (p389) and the artsy scene in **Suchitoto** (p377).

Roll through both countries, indulging yourself on Nicaragua's almost-forgotten coast, or just dallying as you explore Nicaragua's misty Northern Highlands. From there you can enjoy the undeveloped beaches of Eastern El Salvador. Stepping off the beaten path is one of this 1500km route's greatest pleasures.

CLASSIC EL SALVADOR
Two Weeks to One Month

Start in **San Salvador** (p311), where you can take your pick of museums – anthropology (see p323) for the history buffs or modern art (see p323) for the cool kids – but don't skip the poignant memorials to Archbishop Oscar Romero (p323). No matter what you do, finish your day at San Antonio Abad's (see p329) collection of restaurants and nightlife options.

Stop and smell the flowers along **Ruta de las Flores** (p357), 36 pretty kilometers winding through El Salvador's high-altitude heartland, where you'll discover lined stands selling *artesanías* (handicrafts) and, of course, flowers – plus one beautiful orchid garden. **Juayúa** (p363), with its weekend food fair and excellent hiking, is one tiny town you won't want to miss.

From here hikers can get their fix in **Tacuba** (p373), featuring the back way into **Parque Nacional El Imposible** (p375), or up the dosage a bit at **Parque Nacional Los Volcanes** (p353), with three impressive peaks, two of them active; one erupted at the time of research.

Take one of the most beautiful rides in the country up to **Metapán** (p358), with access to El Salvador's most important park for wildlife, **Parque Nacional Montecristo-El Trifinio** (p360); **La Palma** (p389), nearby, lets you combine outdoor activities with handicrafts shopping.

Surfers will head to **La Libertad** (p396) for some of the best surfing in the world, while adventurers will go northeast to **Perquín** (p442), the FMLN headquarters during the war and home to the best museums and monuments on the subject. Stop in **Alegría** (p429) for more flowers, plus hot sulfur springs, and commune with sea turtles and sea birds; or just catch some rays at **Playa El Cuco** (p417). Be sure to leave a couple of days for **Suchitoto** (p377).

> Relish tiny El Salvador's short distances as you ramble about 500km, stopping to smell the flowers (or rappel down the waterfalls) and hike across volcanoes or the northern mountains. Surfing is served up from La Libertad to the Guatemalan border.

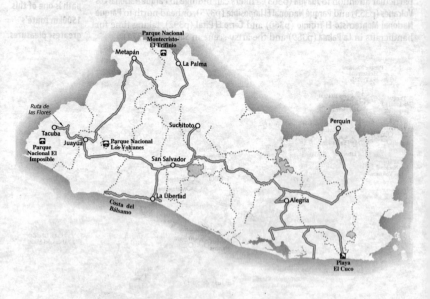

CLASSIC NICARAGUA: SOUTHERN LOOP   10 Days to Three Weeks

Long popular with the 'escape from Costa Rica' set, this ride begins on the beaches around **San Juan del Sur** (p148), with nesting sea turtles at **Refugio de Vida Silvestre La Flor** (p157) from July to January and plenty of perfect waves at beaches like **Playa Madera** (p156), all the way from the border to **Playa Guasacate** (p135).

Then it's time for some culture in charismatic, colonial **Granada** (p110), with museums, churches and art galleries; spend the day kayaking through its 365 islets or hiking **Volcán Mombacho** (p128). Take a day trip (at least) to **Masaya** (p92) and **Pueblos Blancos** (p103) – **Catarina** (p104) is the most popular, but **Diría** (p104) is more festive – or even spend the night next to **Laguna de Apoyo** (p102). Then hop the ferry to **Isla de Ometepe** (p137) for a day or week.

Your next stop: **San Carlos** (p262). If the nine-hour ferry ride across sounds rough, you could take the plane, which gives you an excuse to investigate **Managua** (p68). Enjoy the view from **Sandino's Silhouette** (see p74) and the perspective offered by **Huellas de Acahualinca** (p76).

Check the boat schedules in San Carlos and decide where you want to go first. It's a bit tricky to get out to the isolated island–art colony of the **Islas Solentiname** (p266), which has some of the most scenic souvenir shopping you'll ever enjoy, not to mention one very pretty church. Then it's down the mighty Río San Juan, through some of the wildest rain forests remaining in Central America, to the Spanish fortress at **El Castillo** (p278); real adventurers could take it all the way to **San Juan del Norte** (p280).

This 500km tour takes you to the less touristed beaches of Southwest Nicaragua, then to Spanish colonial Granada for the culture portion of your vacation. From there, tropical lake islands await, or head down Río San Juan before crossing back over the border.

CLASSIC NICARAGUA: HEARTLAND TOUR   10 Days to Three Weeks

Start with an abbreviated version of the Southern Loop, but instead of crossing Lago de Nicaragua, come back to **Managua** (p68) for a day or two, then grab a bus to **León** (p159), a culture-junky haven of museums and churches – and don't miss the original churches at **León Viejo** (see the boxed text, p175). Climb a **volcano** (p177) or hit **Playa Poneloya** (p174); heck, get way off the beaten track at isolated **Playa Jiquilillo** (p188), where sea turtles nest nearby.

From León, go east to **Estelí** (p192), perhaps stopping in **San Jacinto** (p179) for a mud facial or **El Sauce** (p179) for an amazing church en route. After your cigar tour in Estelí, you'll have to decide which cloud forest to visit: **Reserva Natural Cerro Tisey-Estanzuela** (p198), with volcanic views and goat cheese, or **Reserva Natural Miraflor** (p197), where you can stay in a farmhouse and help make breakfast. Adventurers headed north to El Salvador will want to see newly discovered **Somoto Canyon** (p205) or the wonderfully chilly wilderness around **Jalapa** (p203).

Take the dirt road to **Jinotega** (p217), the beautiful City of Mists, being sure to stop in scenic **San Rafael del Norte** (p221). Wend your way back down the mountains to **Matagalpa** (p206), enjoying **Ruta de Café** (see the boxed text, p210) as well as the city's more urban attractions, before heading back to Managua, with a stop at **Museo Precolobiano de Chagüitillo** (p214).

And if you're going to do Nicaragua right, hop on a plane – or better yet, take the **Road to El Rama** (p239) – to the **Corn Islands** (p254) where you can recover Caribbean-style.

In this 600km itinerary, head north from cosmopolitan Managua to intellectual León's museums and volcanoes, investigating quiet beaches and Spanish colonial treasures. Then it's up to the cloud-forest scenery and quetzals of the Northern Highlands.

TAILORED TRIPS

VOLCANOES & VOLCANIC CLIMBS

El Salvador and Nicaragua have almost 50 known volcanoes. Start with Izalco (1910m), the 'Lighthouse of the Pacific,' part of **Parque Nacional Los Volcanes** (p353). It was closed at press time due to the erupting Ilamatepec (2381m); you could still cool off nearby in **Lago de Coatepeque** (p352).

Keep climbing in **Juayúa** (p363), with 'wet rappelling' down a waterfall, or take on **Cerro El Pital** (2730m; p392), El Salvador's highest point; neighboring Cerro Montecristo (2418m), in **Parque Nacional Montecristo-El Trifinio** (p360), is tougher, but there's camping. Head east to **Chichontepec** (2182m; p435), with a helipad and great views, or **Chaparrastique** (2130m; p424), a much tougher climb to its incredible crater.

You can see **Volcán Cosigüina** (849m; p189), Nicaragua's northernmost cone, and perhaps the **Maribios chain** (see p177), with five active – and climbable – craters. Awesome nonvolcanic hiking in the misty Northern Highlands is centered around Estelí, Matagalpa and Jinotega, with **Cerro Musún** (see the boxed text, p242) a standout volcano in the nation's center.

Continue southwest for the active **Volcán Masaya** (p100), the swimmable **Laguna de Apoyo** (p102) and/or the cloud forest–topped **Volcán Mombacho** (p128). You'll need a boat for the spectacular volcanoes on **Isla Zapatera** (see p129) and **Isla de Ometepe** (p137), which also offer sunbathing.

INDIGENOUS NICARAGUA & EL SALVADOR

Amateur archaeologists will get their kicks from the petroglyphs on **Isla de Ometepe** (p137) or **Isla Zapatera** (p129). Granada's finest treasures are at **Convento San Y Museo Francisco** (p116). **Juigalpa** (p243) has even better statues, while **Museo Precolobiano de Chagüitillo** (p214) offers petroglyph hikes.

Modern indigenous cultures are strong in **Barrio Monimbó** (p97) in Masaya, **Barrio Subtiava** (p168) in León, and in **San Marcos** (p107), which has spectacular *fiestas*. On the **Caribbean Coast** (p224) the Miskito and Mayangna peoples are largely autonomous, while smaller populations of Garífuna and Rama are working to maintain their own cultures.

There's an excellent museum in **Condega** (p200), then see **Cacaopera** (p449), for cliff paintings and Maya culture, and the modest ruins at **Quelepa** (p429) or **Cihuatán** (p385).

Impressive ruins include **San Andrés** (p356), with grassy pyramids; **Joya de Cerén** (p356), suddenly buried Pompeii-style; and **Tazumal** (p357), El Salvador's finest, close to **Casa Blanca** (p358), an old ceremonial site. **Parque Nacional El Imposible** (p375) has ancient Maya writing, while **Nahuizalco** (p362) and **Izalco** (p354) have modern Maya culture. Learn more in San Salvador at one the country's best museums, **Museo Nacional de Antropología David J Guzmán** (p323).

SHOPPERS & LUXURY LOVERS

Sure, you'd love to shop Nicaragua and El Salvador, but will there be hotels with room service, or at least hot water? Book a suite in San Salvador's posh **Colonia Escalón** (p330) and browse the **art galleries** (p320) and more. Just east, **Ilobasco** (p438) has famed – and infamous – handicrafts, while **Ruta de las Flores** (see the boxed text, p357) offers a swish resort in **Apaneca** (p366), food festivals in **Juayúa** (p363) and handicrafts shopping galore.

Suchitoto (p377) also offers upscale offerings, plus easy access to handicrafts in **Concepción de Quezaltepeque** (p388) and **La Palma** (p389); head to **Guatajiagua** (p452) for black pottery.

Need to tan? Try **Los Cóbanos** (p404) or **Costa del Sol** (p407) in El Salvador; or **Playa Aserradores** (p187), **Montelimar** (p90) or **El Ostional** (p158) in Nicaragua. For Spanish colonial elegance, León's **Hotel El Convento** (p171) and Granada's **Hotel Gran Francia** (p123) are hard to beat, but **Boaco** (p239) has hot springs.

The pinnacle of Nicaraguan shopping is Masaya's **Mercado Artesanías** (Old Market; see p99), or tour **Los Pueblos Blancos** (p103). Stay in top hotels in **Granada** (p123) or **Managua** (p68). Head to the Northern Highlands, with more wonderful handicrafts at places like **San Juan de Limay** (p199); the major towns all have plush lodging, too. Or head east for fabulous tarpon fishing in **San Juan del Norte** (p280) and the world's most scenic shopping in **Islas Solentiname** (p266).

TOUGH TRAVELERS

You're not into shopping, but you enjoy vacationing in old war zones with infrastructure issues because…well…you're not sure why. Anyway, start at **Sandino's Silhouette** (see p74) in Managua, where you can contemplate **Volcán Momotombo** (p177), the toughest volcano climb in Nicaragua. After a few more Maribios peaks, take in the revolutionary collection of monuments and museums in **León** (p159). Then it's up to **Estelí** (p192) for a drink at **Bar-Restaurant Rincón Legal** (p196), a Sandinista shrine, plus more museums and murals. Sadly **Cerro Mogotón** (p202), Nicaragua's highest point, is still landmined, so it's **Matagalpa** (p206) for the Carlos Fonseca Museum and hikes following the footsteps of armies and refugees.

Explore alternative tourism in **Santa Lucia** (p241) and organic agriculture in **Nueva Guinea** (p247), then it's **Reserva de Biosfera Bosawás** (p228) – pick up your machete in **Bonanza** (p228). Cross the border at **Waspám** (p236), with one of very few Contra memorials, then hack your way across Honduras to El Salvador's FMLN stronghold **Perquín** (p442), its museums and monuments beginning **Ruta de la Paz** (see the boxed text, p447).

Just south, **Volcán San Miguel** (p424) is El Salvador's toughest volcano climb, while **Suchitoto** (p377) combines hiking and war tourism. Perhaps include **Arcatao** (p388) as a side trip. Finally, get a nice room in **San Salvador** (p311), with more thought-provoking sites.

Snapshots

CURRENT EVENTS

For two countries so strongly linked by history and poetry, El Salvador and Nicaragua are pretty much polar opposites within the narrow context of Central America. El Salvador has the highest population density in the region, a cramped 288 people per sq km, while Nicaragua's is the lowest, only 35 people per sq km – compare these to the regional average of 65. That basic inequity seems to underlie many other sharp contrasts.

El Salvador has become an economic engine over the past decade, with a rapidly rising minimum wage and standard of living. Infrastructure is solid in most urban areas, and improving elsewhere. The country is also experiencing a crime wave, largely because of gangs (see p302).

Nicaragua keeps threatening to have an economic boom, but according to most rankings remains the second-poorest country in the hemisphere (after Haiti), its economy relying heavily on small farms and self employment. Infrastructure is good on the country's Pacific side, but head into the untamed east, and really abject poverty becomes apparent. Despite the privations, crime for crime (not including most narcotrafficking on the Caribbean Coast), Nicaragua is also the safest country in Central America.

But for all their differences, the two neighbors are inextricably linked, their peninsulas stretching across the Gulf of Fonseca in a volcanic high five. Both use the informal 'vos' tense when they talk, and both speak the language of poetry. The scars of war remain: both populations are young – with an average age of around 21 – and majority female. Both have high rates of emigration, with émigrés ranging from wealthy political refugees in Miami to hunched-over coffee pickers in Costa Rica – many of whom send significant amounts of money home

One of the best portals for El Salvador, Nicaragua and the rest of the region is the University of Texas Latin American Network Information Center (lanic .utexas.edu/subject /countries.html).

Look for *Wani* magazine, 'The Voice of the Caribbean,' with excellent and insightful articles about Caribbean Nicaragua – in Spanish and Miskito.

FIVE GREAT SMALL TOWNS

You've got to go to Granada – Juayúa is waiting – and it'd be difficult to avoid Managua or San Salvador even if you wanted to. But what about the *pueblocitos*, or little towns, that the tourist trail has missed?

- Ataco (p369) Has Spanish colonial hotels, cobblestone sidewalks, crosses overlooking El Salvador and a swimmable waterfall – all without the crowds of Coast Rica or Cancún.

- El Castillo (p278) Famed for its picture-perfect Spanish fortress overlooking the languid Río San Juan, but it also makes a great base for all manner of rainforest adventures.

- San Rafael del Norte (p221) A high-altitude, easy-access sparkler with an awe-inspiring church, the best Sandino museum in Nicaragua, and much more.

- San José de los Remates (p242) Amid the granite peaks of Nicaragua's Central Highlands, this is an inspiring opportunity to experience Nicaragua's alternative tourism (p244) at its best.

- Suchitoto (p377) A colonial-era indigo boomtown, which is the perfect base for wilderness hikes and war memorials, plus it has arts festivals and an impressive cultural center.

TIMELINE	6000 BC	AD 400
	Clam shells left at Monkey Point, Nicaragua; among the oldest remains left by humans in Central America	Construction of cities, including Tazumal, begins in El Salvador

Watch as the Nicaraguans (with backup from Salvadoran troops) take on William Walker in the critically panned and somewhat hallucinogenic movie *Walker*, directed by Alex Cox (*Sid and Nancy*, *Repo Man*), filmed on location in 1986.

to Nicaragua and El Salvador. The respective diasporas also enrich both countries with a cosmopolitan outlook you might not expect from such small nations, which may have convinced both to gamble on Cafta (see the boxed text, p32).

They are also examples of countries successfully undergoing the trasition from paramilitary conflicts to peaceful participatory democracies. In El Salvador, the FSLN (Farabundo Martí National Liberation Front) remains an important popular voice from the left, and it did well in the past two congressional elections. The Sandinistas are now a center-left party that won about 60% of the last municipal elections, while many prominent former Contras run on the Yatama ticket.

IRAN-CONTRA

On July 19, 1979, the Nicaraguan revolution marched to victory, its martyrs vindicated and its enemies in flight. The Junta of Five (p56), including FSLN leader Daniel Ortega, made ready to take power. The world cheered; even US president Jimmy Carter extended his congratulations and a generous aid package.

Two hours south of the border, Costa Rican observers had already videotaped the first US troops arriving.

In Our Back Yard

As the left-wing Sandinistas consolidated power, many of their achievements, including celebrated literacy and health-care initiatives, continued earning international accolades. Other acts, including the nationalization of more than 300 companies, convinced international observers that the FSLN – known allies of Castro's Cuba – were headed down the communist path. Finally, when the CIA confirmed that the Sandinistas were supplying leftist rebels in El Salvador, newly elected US president Ronald Reagan cut all ties with Daniel Ortega's regime and began supporting former government troops and other allies of the fallen Somoza regime.

This group called themselves the Contras, and were lauded by Reagan as 'the moral equivalents of our founding fathers.' The USA increased aid to them and to the surrounding countries, where military bases, training grounds and other support was available to the rapidly growing resistance. Reagan's goal? To protect democracy by keeping communism out of America's back yard.

After Daniel Ortega won the 1984 elections, Contras stepped up attacks on farms and crops, coordinated with a US blockade of all food and medicine. Ortega responded by expanding the Sandinista military, graciously retooled by the Soviet Union, with a hated draft. It had become a war of attrition, with well over 100,000 casualties. By the time Ortega signed the Arias Peace Accords in 1987, Nicaragua had been at war for more than a decade. Regardless, calls for a ceasefire were answered, in part because the Contras were suddenly out of bullets.

Busted

In October 1986, Sandinistas shot down a Contra supply plane originating in Ilopango, El Salvador – with an American pilot. This was in spite of the fact that in 1984, after learning that the CIA had illegally mined El Corinto Port, the US Congress had banned Reagan from spending taxpayer dollars 'for the purpose of overthrowing the government of Nicaragua.'

Two weeks later, with Reagan's spin doctors already working overtime, Lebanese newspaper *Al-Shiraa* revealed that National Security Advisor Robert McFarlane, and the then-unknown Colonel

1000	1524
Maya and Aztec migration to Central America follows the collapse of those empires	Granada, León and Suchitoto founded by the Spanish conquistadors

Both nations, of course, spent the 1980s locked in battles that were, in many ways, just white-hot expressions of the so-called Cold War.

HISTORY

Nicaragua and El Salvador have been in regular contact since trade links were established up and down the Central American isthmus – probably around 2000 BC. Though El Salvador seems to have been the southernmost border of the Olmec and Maya civilizations, both countries were using variations of Aztec Náhuatl (among other languages) at the time of the Spanish conquest, indicating a migration from what's now southern Mexico.

Oliver North, had made an arms-for-hostages deal with the revolutionary Islamic government of Tehran.

The two stories would prove to be closely linked.

After Congress shut down Contra support in 1984, McFarlane and North had begun looking for alternative funding sources by soliciting third-party donations, from Saudi royals, the Sultan of Brunei and $5 million from Saudi arms dealer Adnan Khashoggi, who later told his story on US television.

After Islamic Lebanese terrorists took seven US hostages, Iranian arms dealer Manucher Ghorbanifar (who resurfaced in 2002 with 'proof' that Saddam Hussein had yellowcake uranium) informed McFarlane and North that Iran could help – in exchange for HAWK anti-aircraft and TOW anti-tank missiles. 'America will never make concessions to terrorists,' said President Reagan on February 18, 1985. 'To do so would only invite more terrorism.'

Reagan's uncharacteristic prescience notwithstanding, more than 1500 weapons were sold to Iran over the next two years, though only one hostage was released. McFarlane and North arranged the fateful Tehran meeting to see what was wrong, where Iranian officials, surprised, said they knew nothing about a hostage deal.

As the flummoxed twosome headed home, North played the optimist, reassuring McFarlane that profits from the missiles were at least being funneled to the Contras.

It was then that McFarlane realized how deep things had gotten. 'Oh shit,' he thought, according to transcripts from the Iran-Contra hearings.

The Teflon President

Reagan denied that the meeting had occurred, but recanted a week later, still saying there was no arms-for-hostage deal. Only 14% of Americans believed him.

One administration official after another refused to testify. Reagan could 'not recall' authorizing the arms sales. Luckily, Israel had kept signed receipts, but ranking House Republican Dick Cheney felt an impeachment trial 'wouldn't be good for America.' Vice President Bush refused to turn over his diary until 1991; when the log's contents, including a passage reading 'I'm one of the few people that know fully the details…It is not a subject we can talk about,' was reviewed, it justified re-opening the case.

'On…the question of the hostages,' he had written in 1986, 'I'm one of the few people who knows the details.' His notes implicated McFarlane and other close friends, but on the eve of their trials, Bush pardoned six of them, effective ending the investigation before he or General Colin Powell (who had signed off on the missiles) could testify.

'George Bush's misuse of the pardon power made the cover-up complete,' wrote Iran-Contra independent counsel Lawrence Walsh.

1821	1853
Central America becomes independent from Spain on September 15	William Walker arrives at the forefront of US imperialism

CAFTA: A FREE-TRADE AGREEMENT OF SORTS

After several years of heated protests, fearmongering and spin-doctoring, the US–Central American Free Trade Agreement (Cafta) took effect rather uneventfully in 2006.

Cafta, a much-anticipated and little-understood trade pact between the United States, the Dominican Republic, Guatemala, El Salvador, Honduras and Nicaragua (with Costa Rica invited to the dance but yet to RSVP), was originally set to start on January 1, 2006.

But due to the last-minute insistence of Uncle Sam, who suffers sleep anxiety over first-world issues such as intellectual property rights, all the participating Central American countries were told several weeks before the planned start date that they would first have to pass new legislation to protect copyright, patents and the rights of authors.

El Salvador was quick to comply, and entered Cafta with the United States on February 1 2006. The other countries were then let in on a rolling basis, with Nicaragua joining in March.

Meaningful public discourse about what was actually being negotiated was almost nonexistent in both countries, and in Nicaragua both sides indulged in shameless fear campaigns.

The pro-Cafta camp, led by the business sector, warned Nicaraguans that failure to ratify Cafta would be like returning to the US economic embargo of the 1980s. The con side, led by the Sandinistas, warned Nicaraguans that free trade with the United States would only lead to 'misery, unemployment and death.'

Probably neither side is correct.

Cafta will be good for a few select sectors of the economy – mostly the textile factories, sugar growers and peanut farmers. Also, under Cafta, Nicaragua received preferential textile-quota options that were not extended to the other Central American countries ('free trade', you see, is not really free trade, it's just trade under different rules and quotas).

Those preferential quotas, coupled with the lowest wages in Central America, led the Minister of Foreign Trade recently to announce that Nicaragua was on its way to becoming the 'textile capital of Central America.' Look out, world.

Tim Rogers Editor, 'Nica Times'

The agricultural revolution swept through around 300AD, bringing with it the basis of the modern regional diet: maize (or corn), beans and yucca. With reliable food and imported technology, a wave of creative expression followed, with impressive stone cities like Joya de Cerén (see p356) being erected in El Salvador, and less technically advanced, but still cool, petroglyphs (see the boxed text, p140) and statues (see the boxed text, p117) popping up in Nicaragua.

The Spanish conquest got off the ground in the late 1520s. Nicaragua and El Salvador were administrated as separate units by Antigua, Guatemala. In tiny, tidy El Salvador, with more manageable boundaries and a single coast, the conquest was efficient and ruthless, leaving the modern population light-skinned and very European. In vast Nicaragua, however, indigenous groups put up waves of resistance, retaining some autonomy even on the Pacific side and effectively stopping the Spanish incursion at the Central Highlands. The British also played an important role, settling the Atlantic Coast of Nicaragua (see the boxed text, p113).

After independence from Spain in 1821, the original five Central American nations (Belize, as a British colony, and Panama, then part of Colombia, were counted separately) remained linked as a series of

The disturbing 1988 documentary *Coverup: Behind the Iran-Contra Affair* lets you flashback to the Reagan years, complete with cocaine, landmines and aborted back-alley deals with Iran's fundamentalist factions.

1979	1990
Sandinista revolution is victorious in Nicaragua; President Carlos Humverto Romero overthrown in El Salvador	Violeta Barrios de Chamorro beats Daniel Ortega in Nicaraguan elections; Contra War and US-led economic embargo end

federations and organizations, though dreams of a unified Central America never panned out. El Salvador and Nicaragua were often allies, and worked together when, for example, a foreign mercenary army (see the boxed text, p55) disturbed the peace.

Their informal political alliances caused a bit of a stir in the United States, where they inspired a shadowy collection of international double deals that remain largely veiled in history, as perpetrators lied under oath. Their informal political alliances caused a bit of a stir in the United States, where they inspired a shadowy collection of international double deals that remain largely veiled in history, as perpetators lied under oath, received convenient presidential pardons and even died of sudden brain tumors (seriously, CIA director William J Casey – google it) right before going to trial.

PEOPLE

Both Salvadorans and Nicaraguans, rarely treated to the easiest lives, are known for their impressive work ethic, poignant literature and colorful crafts. And – this is perhaps the defining feature of recent decades – both are willing to stand up for themselves.

Lifestyle

In both countries, the income gap is tremendous; development rarely hits a nation all at once. In the capitals and major cities, an upper class – young, mobile, wired and usually English-speaking – fuels opulent malls and discos, or zips up to Miami to visit friends. The vast majority, however, live hand to mouth, with around 30% of Salvadorans and 50% of Nicaraguans surviving below the international poverty line. In the cities, begging, glue sniffing and rising crime rates seem to radiate from shanty towns, often built on ground that's geologically unstable, just waiting for the next earthquake.

In rural areas, the poverty is worse on paper, but it's mitigated by gardens, hunting and family close by. Tiny wooden shacks with no electricity or running water are common, and most employment is agricultural – ie seasonal and unstable. Consider visiting a coffee collective (see p210), just to meet the people on the other side of your latte.

Emigration

Approximately 20% of both countries' populations live abroad, often illegally. Wealthy and connected families immigrated to the USA (principally Miami and Los Angeles) during the wars. Poor Salvadorans fled to Honduras or Mexico, while Nicaraguan refugees headed south to Costa Rica.

Many longtime expats are now returning home, some for the first time as adults. Others are coming involuntarily – a notable instance was when the USA deported thousands of California gang members to El Salvador, resulting in dramatic social problems (see the boxed text, p302). This can be something of a boon to travelers, who may be in some totally untouristed corner of the country, when a local will ask, in perfect Miami English, 'So, what do you think of my little town? I live here.'

SPORTS

Both Nicaragua and El Salvador, as part of Latin America, have football (soccer) teams. El Salvador's often wins; the Nicas wouldn't know, however, since they're all busy watching (or playing) baseball (see the boxed text, p60).

Courtesy counts! *'Buen provecho'* before a meal, *'con permiso'* when squeezing past on a bus, or *'mucho gusto'* upon introduction are all pleasantries to practice.

TEN WHO SHAPED NICARAGUA & EL SALVADOR

Nicaraguan President Violeta Barrios de Chamorro (president 1990–1996) The first female president in the hemisphere pulled together a fractured nation.

Carlos Henriquez Consalvi Also known as 'Santiago,' this Venezuelan journalist founded the FMLN's Radio Venceremos and now runs the Museo de Imagen y Palabra (p320) in San Salvador.

Cacique Nicarao Along with Cacique Nagrandano (for whom the Llanura Nagrandano, or northwestern plains, are named) and Cacique Diriangén (still remembered on La Meseta), wise Nicarao gave the nation his name.

Nicaraguan President Daniel Ortega (president 1984–1990) Today he is mostly a political albatross around the neck of the moderate FSLN, but Ortega's finest moment was his hardest, conceding the presidency in 1990 without becoming the *caudillo* (military dictator) that he could have been.

US President Ronald Reagan (president 1981–1988) Together with political philosopher Jeanne Kirkpatrick, Secretary of State Alexander Haig Jr and Fox TV personality Oliver North, he came up with the brilliant idea of arming the Ayatollah Khomeini to fight communism.

El Salvador Archbishop Óscar Romero (archbishop 1977–1980; see the boxed text, p305) The bravest name in Liberation Theology begged US president Jimmy Carter and Pope John Paul II to support the Salvadoran military, which in the end assassinated him.

Joaquin Villalobos This fearless, complex Salvadoran *guerrillero* led the ERP faction in Morazán and reportedly ordered the death of leftist poet (and accused CIA informant) Roque Dalton in 1975.

Sandino (see the boxed text, p222) His somber silhouette still dominates the Managua skyline, and his refusal to take any shit dominates the Nicaraguan collective consciousness.

The Somozas A dynasty of Nicaraguan dictators, the first installed by the United States military, and the last deposed more than four decades later by popular revolution.

William Walker (see the boxed text, p55) The Tennessean who thought he could take on Central America, but ended up in front of a Honduran firing squad.

If you enjoy playing either sport, not to mention basketball or almost anything else, look around for pickup games in area parks in the evening and represent for your home country. There's no better way (especially for visitors with limited Spanish) to make friends.

RELIGION

Both Nicaragua and El Salvador are predominantly Catholic, with figures ranging from 55% to 70% for Nicaragua, and around 80% for El Salvador. Accurate statistics are hard to find because of the recent (over the past decade or two) mass conversion to more than 100 forms of Protestantism, collectively known as '*evangelismo*.' There are at least two million converts watching famous-name US evangelists on TV (or healing live at the soccer stadiums), blasting accessibly upbeat hymns from storefront churches and passing out flyers at bus stations. It was only a matter of time until the backlash – look for stickers saying 'We are Catholic here…our parents were Catholics and we will be Catholics forever. We will not change our religion, please don't insist.' Public-nuisance laws are also forcing churches to turn down the music, or at least stop singing by 9pm.

Most converts are poor and/or indigenous, and see Protestantism as more democratic, compared to Catholicism's rigid hierarchy and association with the Spanish conquest. Not that Central American Catholicism has ever been particularly pure: indigenous rites have been interwoven with Christian festivals (see the boxed text, p97) since day two of the Spanish Conquest; the Liberation Theology movement, which supports armed struggle by the poor, never really got the Vatican's blessing; Ernesto Cardenal (see the boxed text, p267) was defrocked for his involvement with the Sandinistas; and newly elected Pope Benedict XVI

According to *Ometepe en el Siglo XX*, by Hamilton Silva Monge, many Catholic saints also represent old Náhuatl deities: for instance, San Isidro, Patron of Farmers, is also Quiateot, God of Harvests.

The best of Óscar Romero's inspiring orations from 1977 to his death in 1980, are collected in *The Violence of Love: The Pastoral Wisdom of Archbishop Oscar Romero*.

was one of Liberation Theology's most vehement critics under Pope John Paul II, which sends a message.

ARTS

'Poetry will exist as long as there is a problem of life and death,' wrote Rubén Darío, which may explain why Nicaragua and El Salvador are tied together not only by their recent history of revolution, but also their long tradition of poetry. Both also have other cultural riches, some touched on here, that you can learn more about in the Arts sections on p61 and p305.

Literature

Nicaragua – certainly among the most prolific countries, person per person – produced (to its never-ending pride) at least one poet on par with Shakespeare: Rubén Darío (see the boxed text, below), founder of Latin American Modernism and legend of 'immoderation.' His mentor was Francisco Gavidia, perhaps El Salvador's favorite poet. For a rundown on other important Nicaraguan and Salvadoran authors, see p61 and p305.

Both Nicaragua and El Salvador are also home to the peculiar cultural archetype of 'warrior poets,' folks who choose to go with both the pen and the sword. Among the most famous of Nicaragua's warrior poets are Leonel Rugama Rugama, who held off the National Guard while hero Carlos Fonseca escaped; Rigoberto Lopez Perez, who assassinated the original Somoza in León; liberation theologian Ernesto Cardenal; and former Sandinista undercover agent Gioconda Belli. Meanwhile, over in El Salvador, Roque Dalton wrote rather Marxist verse that almost earned him a death sentence from the military government of the day.

Learn more about what so inspired Óscar Romero and Ernesto Cardenal in a Concise History of Liberation Theology (www.landreform .org/boff2.htm).

RUBÉN DARÍO

Comparable only to Mozart, Nicaragua's favorite son and Latin America's most important poet began reading at age three and had published his first poem by the time he was 12. Dubbed El Niño Poeta (the poet child) by Nicaragua's verse-obsessed media, Rubén Darío – for whom his birthplace (Ciudad Darío; p215), the national theater (Teatro Nacional Rubén Dario; p84) and Cordillera Dariense mountain range are all named – was denied a scholarship in Europe because his work was too 'anti-religious.'

Thus stymied, the resourceful young poet instead made his way to El Salvador, where he became apprentice poet to Francisco Gavidia (see p305), who introduced him to French poetry's rhythmic structure, which would remain a cornerstone of Darío's work. Later, Darío would visit Chile and discover racism, which would also heavily influence his verse.

After Darío's first wife died, he went on a bender that barely hit a speed bump when an ex-girlfriend, Rosario Murillo, set him up – her brother 'discovered' them in bed together. Darío remembered nothing, married her anyway, and continued boozing his way through mistresses and muses, adventures and day jobs. All the while, he was writing some of the most beautiful poetry in the world, peaking after 1903, when Darío was named ambassador to Paris.

In 1914, Darío was both awarded his first major medal – from the Hispanic Society of America – and went bankrupt, thanks to an ill-timed bout of pneumonia. It was his fellow poets who banded together to raise enough money to pay the doctor and get Darío back home to León, where he died two years later at age 49.

Poesía en Español (luis.salas.net/indexrd.htm) has most of Rubén Darío's poems available online, while English-language **Dariana** (www.dariana.com), a Rubén Darío tribute site, has 11 of his poems translated into English by fellow legendary Leónese poet, Salomón de la Selva.

Colonial Architecture

The success of the Spanish conquest let the motherland finally break free of French architectural forms, such as Gothic architecture, and experiment with homegrown styles both at home and in the Americas.

Some of the earliest New World churches are a Moorish-Spanish hybrid called *mujédar*, with squat silhouettes, wooden roofs and geometric configurations. Influenced by Islam as well as the Italian Renaissance, are *plateresque*, or elaborate silver filigree, on alters like that in El Viejo (p184).

Baroque hit big in the mid-1600s, and was the most popular choice for major buildings over the next century. Primitivist Baroque, featuring graceful but unadorned adobe and wood columns, and common in smaller colonial towns, was followed by full Spanish Baroque style, with extravagant design (stone grapevines wending up massive pillars, for example) sometimes called *churriguera*.

The most famous examples of Spanish Colonial architecture can be found in Granada and León in Nicaragua, and in El Salvador, such as in accessible Santa Ana or adorable Ataco, with its intriguing Gothic cathedral and striking *alcaldía* and municipal theater. But Spanish colonial gems are scattered throughout both countries.

To see the original, never-bombed models, visit the original León, buried by Volcán Momotombo in 1610, or the previous site of San Salvador (see p377), occupied for only 17 years (1528–45).

Arts & Crafts

Although Guatemala gets all the press for its arts and crafts, both Nicaragua and, to a lesser extent El Salvador, are known for their beautiful, and clever, *artesanías*. El Salvador's most famous painter, Fernando Llort (see the boxed text, p306), has inspired a cottage industry with his simple, colorful scenes of pastoral Salvadoran living, while Nicaragua's most famous painters are based on the island art colony of the Solentiname Archipelago (p266).

Both countries are also justly famed for hammocks: Nicaragua's favorite place to recline is Masaya, while they even throw a hammock festival every year in El Salvador's Concepción de Quezaltepeque (see p388).

Although it's always cheaper and more fun to find handicrafts in the regions where they originate, more convenient souvenir shopping can be had at the National Artesanías Markets in San Salvador and Masaya, or Mercado Huembes in Managua. For a rundown of what to buy, check the arts and crafts sections on p62 and p307.

ENVIRONMENT

This is perhaps the greatest difference between the two countries. El Salvador is the most densely populated country in the continental Americas, and only about 6% of its original forest cover still stands. Most of this is preserved as part of 12 federally protected reserves and parks, most with 'shared use' – usually this involves organic coffee or another relatively low-impact agribusiness. A handful of other private reserves and low-profile conservation initiatives, including sea-turtle operations (see the boxed text, p48), are beginning to take hold. But it's already too late for species including the jaguar and giant red macaw, both of which are extinct in El Salvador.

Nicaragua, on the other hand, is much larger and less densely populated. It's managed to preserve 18.2% of its landmass, or 21,000 sq km, roughly the same area as El Salvador. There are 76 different protected areas in nine

Rock and roll with websites devoted to seismic activity in Nicaragua (www.sinapred.gob .ni/Noticias/Terremotos .html) and El Salvador (www.terremotoelsalvador .org.sv).

Get ecological at sites including www.garrobo .org, with a focus on Central America, or more general www .conservation.org and www.foe.co.uk.

Glittering Santa Ana, Morazán, San Miguel and La Unión in El Salvador, and RAAN, the Northern Highlands and Sierra Amerrisque in Nicaragua, all have gold deposits.

categories, most of them reserves (with light protection) augmented by a wide variety of municipal parks and private reserves. Just the sprawl, however, makes most of the system impossible to protect from poachers, loggers, squatters and economic migrants just looking for a place to grow some corn. But the government has committed serious resources to enforcing the national parks in the past, mainly because of the ecotourism dollars and euros they're hoping to see someday.

The Land

Tiny El Salvador is the only country in Central America without a Caribbean coastline, and its ecosystems are therefore very similar to those of the Nicaraguan Pacific. Both have broad coastal plains (narrowing as you head northwest) and relatively long, pronounced dry seasons, when most of the vegetation turns dry and brown. Most of El Salvador's original forest is gone, as it has better soil, and is therefore more attractive to farmers than the humid tropical forest soils to the north and east.

The region's appeal to early colonists increased as they realized that the soil was further enriched by the region's most striking geological feature: a volcano chain that stretches from northern Panama to central Mexico, with some of the most dramatic cones in the world looming over El Salvador. Volcán Santa Ana (p346) exploded while this book was being researched, destroying coffee *fincas* (farms) and claiming two lives. Earthquakes and volcanoes are a part of life along the borders of the Caribbean and Coco (see the boxed text, p65), and you'll find very few authentic colonial buildings that haven't been touched up since the 1500s.

In El Salvador's north, and running down the center of Nicaragua like an opening zipper, the mountains rise to their greatest heights as a metamorphic, granite mountain chain contiguous with the Rocky Mountains and the Andes. Topped with cool cloud forests above 1200m, these refreshing regions are home to some of the best national parks in both countries.

In addition, Nicaragua has the two largest lakes in Central America: Lago de Managua is badly polluted, but Lago de Nicaragua – more than a third the size of El Salvador – is surprisingly clean, thanks to underdevelopment. Surrounded by protected wetlands and home to the world's largest lake island, it drains to the Caribbean along one of the country's four major Atlantic lowlands river systems.

The Atlantic Coast is worlds apart, geologically as well as culturally, from the dryer, more developed Pacific side. A vast eroding plain of rolling hills and ancient volcanic plugs, around 90% of the country's rainfall ends up here. This is the region with the wildest protected reserves and worst access – and don't forget your mosquito net. The Caribbean Coast, with very few exceptions, is difficult and relatively expensive to travel, as most transportation is by boat.

Wildlife

El Salvador has about 800 animal species, mostly birds and butterflies, while Nicaragua has some 18,000 vertebrates and 30,000 species in total, including almost 700 birds. While Nicaragua is clearly the much better choice for wildlife viewing, neither country can match the bounty of neighboring Costa Rica, where peace and prosperity have kept endangered species off the menu for half a century.

Animals are slowly working their way northward, a migration of densities that will one day be facilitated by the Meso-American Corridor, a proposed aisle of shady protected rainforest stretching from Panama to

Two companies want to revive Nicaragua Canal schemes: one wants to dredge the Río San Juan, the other wants to build a 'dry canal,' or high-capacity freight railroad connecting the coasts.

In the late 1990s, ENRON wanted to build a wind farm in Nicaragua's Sierra Amerrisque, but the Alemán government was too corrupt even for them.

Wildlife watchers flocking south could read L Irby Davis' *Field Guide to the Birds of Mexico & Central America* or Adrian Forsyth's *Tropical Nature: Life & Death in the Rainforests of Central & South America*.

PUPUSAS, OVERPOPULATION AND THE FOOTBALL WAR

There are few foods as richly invested with nationalistic pride as the pupusa, though Nicaragua's *gallo pinto* (see the boxed text, p57) comes close. Every afternoon at around 4pm, in El Salvador and throughout the strongholds of the Salvadoran diaspora, pupusas are patted out.

Make Delicious Pupusas at Home

If you don't have a Salvadoran barrio (neighborhood) nearby, you can still make pupusas yourself. Begin with prepared tortilla flour, such as Maseca, and follow instructions for *masa*, or dough. For simple cheese *pupusas de quesillo*, use soft *quesillo*, or substitute three cups of shredded mozzarella mixed with cream cheese or ricotta. Add four tablespoons heavy cream and one cup of *loroco*, an edible flower native to El Salvador, or substitute chopped green pepper or scallions. Salt to taste and mix to a paste.

For *pupusas de chicharrón*, traditionally made with wild boar, sauté one cup of bacon with garlic, tomatoes and green pepper; for *pupusas mixtas*, make your favorite pot of beans, then mix with all of the above.

Pat two balls of *masa* (about two tablespoons each) to 1cm thick, then add a dollop of filling on top of one and press the other on top. Lightly grease a large frying pan and set at 350°F, then cook (this could take several flips) until lightly browned and crispy. Serve with a thin tomato sauce, some *curtido* (pickled cabbage), and enjoy the taste of Old El Salvador in your own home.

Honduras & The Football War

Old El Salvador? As with so many regional foods, the origin of the Salvadoran national snack is controversial. Some in neighboring Honduras also claim pupusas (though they freely attribute delicious *loroco* to El Salvador), and furthermore say the dish only crossed the border in the wake of the 1969 Football War.

Mexico. Other countries in on the agreement are just getting started on the project, but Nicaragua's two enormous Unesco biosphere reserves, Bosawás and Southeast Nicaragua (Río San Juan), make a significant chunk.

ANIMALS

Most people are looking for monkeys, and there are three natives: big smart spider monkeys, smaller howler monkeys (with their reverberating roar), and capuchins, which will steal your lunch while you snap photos. Pizotes, elsewhere called coatis, are the long-tailed, toothy-smiled rodents that are particularly bold on the Rivas peninsula – feed them at your own risk. Several cats – puma, jaguar and others in Nicaragua, the diminutive tigrillo in El Salvador – survive, but you probably won't see them. Baird's tapirs, 250kg herbivores, are another rare treat. At night you'll see hundreds of bats, including, if you're very lucky, vampire bats – which usually stick to livestock.

Birders are discovering Nicaragua, in particular the wild east coast's estuaries, where migratory birds flock, starting in August and packing places like the Río San Juan and Solentiname Islands by September and October. Kingfishers, swallows, scarlet tanagers and Tennessee warblers are just a few of the birds that make their winter homes around here. Local birds are even more spectacular, including the red macaw, the yellow-chested oropendola (which hangs its ball-shaped nests from the trees in oddly beautiful sacks), the three-wattled bellbird of the cloud forests, with its distinctive call, and of course the resplendent quetzal, a resident of both Nicaragua and El Salvador.

There are lots of reptiles, including five kinds of sea turtles, two kinds of iguanas, and several snakes, including the poisonous coral snake and

Get inspired by the BBC's reality series Beyond Boundaries I (www.bbc .co.uk/ouch/tvradio /beyondboundaries), which followed 11 disabled people across Nicaragua (using machetes for part of it), including up the side of a live volcano.

Throughout the 1950s and 1960s, El Salvador's burgeoning overpopulation problem was already spilling over into Honduras, to the tune of 300,000 illegal immigrants, stressing the already impoverished country. Social tensions mounted, with Hondurans demanding that land go to citizens, and Salvadorans complaining of abuse by Honduran authorities.

The qualification stages for the football World Cup, usually a good outlet for frustrated nationalism, then ensued – with three matches between the teeth-gnashing neighbors planned. Round one in Tegucigalpa saw Honduras win, one–nil. El Salvador took their home game by halftime, three–nil. Which is about when the rioting started. Visiting Honduran fans were attacked in the stadium; Honduras threatened to retaliate by repatriating every last Salvadoran immigrant. El Salvador invaded, bombed the Tegucigalpa airport, and occupied the country for 100 hours.

Honduras unsurprisingly continued with land reforms, replacing Salvadoran immigrants with Honduran campesinos, and deporting tens of thousands of people. This sent both economies into a tailspin that eventually crashed the US-led Central American Common Market. And, unknown to the Honduran government, some of those returning Salvadorans carried with them the secrets of pupusa perfection.

Snack Attack

Though the war was a draw, with about 1000 dead on either side, El Salvador won the final qualifying match, in Mexico City. And there, as all over the world, pupusas are being readied right now in ramshackle stands and glittering restaurants, almost all owned and operated by proud, and probably homesick, Salvadoreños. Heck, most Hondurans now consider pupusas authentically Salvadoran. Other unforeseen consequences of the six-day war included centralizing power with both nations' increasingly autonomous militaries, paving the way for the bloody wars of the 1980s.

Can't believe it? Learn even weirder details about this and other absurd international conflicts in *The Soccer War*, by Ryszard Kapuscinski

the cascabel, also poisonous but a danger mostly to cattle. The most famous fish in Nicaragua is the world's only freshwater shark, the bull shark (see the boxed text, p149).

Insects, of course, make up the vast majority of species, including over 1000 species of butterflies shared between the countries. Tarantulas are common, but not deadly (just shocking!), and keep your eyes open for leaf-cutter ants, which raise fungus for snacks beneath massive anthills the size of VW Beetles. Acacia ants are hidden inside the hollow thorns of acacia trees – shake one of them and you'll see several hundred swarming reasons why the plant goes to all the trouble. And the weird-looking woody balls in the trees? Termites.

PLANTS

Tropical dry forests are home to more than 30 species of hardwood, including precious mahogany. Some of the most dramatic species in the region's dominant ecosystem include: strangler figs, which start out as slender vines and end up entombing the host tree in a dramatically buttressed encasement; the wide-spreading guanacaste of the endless savannahs; and the pithaya, a branch-dwelling cactus with delicious edible fruit. El Salvador and Nicaragua, along with Honduras, share the largest mangrove forest in Central America.

Farther up and east, tropical humid forest is home to the multi-story green canopies most people think of as classic rainforest. Conditions here are perfect for all plant life; almost no nutrients are stored in the soil, but there is a vast web just beneath the fallen leaves of enormous ceibas, formed of tiny roots, fungus and other assorted symbiotes that devour every stray nutrient as soon as it hits the ground.

This, of course, does not hold true on regularly fertilized (with ash!) volcanic slopes, where the jungle has more often than not been cut down for timber and replaced with (hopefully) organic coffee. In the metamorphic highlands, the farms last a few years, and then become scrubland useless for anything except grazing a few head of cattle.

Atop the highest volcanoes and peaks are cloud forests, easily the most impressive (and rarest) biome, with some 800 species of orchids shared between the countries. There are also scores of different epiphytes and bromeliads, a variety of high-humidity plants that grow in the branches of other trees; houseplant aficionados will recognize lots of their favorites.

FOOD & DRINK

Neither El Salvador nor Nicaragua is known for its cuisine, with a few (mostly fried) exceptions. The standout is El Salvador's pupusa (see the boxed text, p38), which is also common throughout Nicaragua. For a breakdown of national dishes and local favorites, check out the Food & Drink sections for El Salvador (p310) and Nicaragua (p67).

Both Nicaraguans and Salvadorans usually eat three meals per day. *Desayuno* (breakfast) in both countries is usually eggs with rice and beans – refried in El Salvador, whole in Nicaragua. *Almuerzo*, or lunch, is the big meal of the day, and if you're on a shoestring budget it will be yours, too. Simple Nicaraguan restaurants offer *comida corriente*, a heaping set plate with a couple of choices of meat, while in El Salvador it's all served separately – soup, salad, meat and sides – and it's cheap. *Cena* (dinner) is more of an afterthought – in El Salvador a few pupusas, in Nicaragua a stop at the nearest *fritanga*, where cooks renowned throughout the neighborhood sell traditional favorites, including grilled meats and all things deep fried.

Where to Eat & Drink

Both El Salvador and Nicaragua have decent sanitation systems and drinking and washing water in some cities, but most of both countries require a bit of care. Remember that personal hygiene plays as important a role as watching what you eat – wash you hands before meals and after touching animals or anything else a bit sketchy.

Bottled water is cheap and available almost everywhere (discarded water bottles litter every beach and river), and many restaurants – even those not geared to tourists – use purified water (*agua purificada*) to make ice cubes and *frescos* (but ask). As you travel farther from major population centers and tourist havens, you should become pickier about your food – trust your gut, literally. If a town strikes you as unsanitary, or just has less infrastructure in general (and remember, the public water supply can be tainted by storms and flooding), skip the cheap *comedor* (basic eatery) at the market and pay for a real meal somewhere nice.

Groceries aren't always a great way to save money on meals (compared to cheap eateries), but they do provide some welcome variety. Be sure to skip the bland, sliced bread and stop by a *panadería* (bakery) for something more interesting. Many hotels and *hospedajes* (guesthouses) have kitchens you can use, perhaps for a small price.

Get far off the beaten track and small *pulperías*, or teeny tiny convenience stores, may or may not have something other than ramen noodles and chicken bullion in stock. Plan ahead and pack a few power bars or tins of sardines for the road.

Vegetarians & Vegans

Tell the waiter '*soy vegeteriano/a*' (I'm vegetarian), and you'll probably get what everyone else does (rice, beans, salad, plantains), without the meat. Steam-table buffets, or '*comida a la vista*' places usually have lots of vegetarian options that you can mix and match. *Gallo pinto* is light on beans, if that's your planned source of protein, so vegans in particular should stock up on healthy snacks in Managua, Granada, León or San Salvador before heading out.

Eating with Kids

Most travelers rate Latin America one of the best regions in the world to travel with children, and these countries are no exception. Food is already fairly bland, and sweetened exotic fruit juices (*refrescos*) go over well with the kid in everyone. Don't expect high chairs or kids menus, though.

Food Glossary

For staples and regional specialties, see p67 (Nicaragua) and p310 (El Salvador).

DISHES, FOODS & DRINKS

agua purificada	*a*•gwa pu•ree•fee•*ka*•da	purified water
arroz chino/cantonés	*a*•ros chee•no/kan•to•*nes*	fried rice
arroz	*a*•ros	rice
café …	ka•*fe*(a)	coffee
con leche	kon *le*•che	with milk (probably more than you're used to)
de grano	de *gra*•no	ground ('real') coffee
instantáneo	in•stan•*ta*•ne•o	instant coffee crystals (blech)
sin azúcar	seen a•*soo*•kar	without sugar (unless you like your coffee and fresco very sweet)
camarones	ka•ma•*ro*•nes	shrimp
carne/pollo en salsa	*kar*•ne/*po*•lyo en *sal*•sa	beef/chicken stewed in tomato sauce
chayote	cha•*yo*•te	green, pear-shaped squash used in soups
chicharón	chee•cha•*ron*	fried pig skins
chilero	chee•*le*•ro	jar of hot pickled chilies, carrots, onions and more (for your table)
cuajada	kwa•*kha*•da	fresh, salty, crumbly cheese served with tortillas
ensalada	en•sa•*la*•da	salad, usually made with cabbage, tomatoes and vinegar, but also with boiled veggies; potato salad could fall into this category
frijoles	free•*kho*•les	beans
gallo pinto	*ga*•lyo *peen*•to	rice and beans, cooked separately and fried together, served at breakfast
gaseosa	ga•se•*o*•sa	soft drink
huevos de paslama	*hwe*•vos de pas•*la*•ma	turtle eggs
huevos del toro	*hwe*•vos del *to*•ro	bull testicles
leche	*le*•che	milk
melón	me•*lon*	cantaloupe
pescado	pes•*ka*•do	fish
pithaya	pee•*tha*•ya	a cactus fruit related to the prickly pear, made into drinks; also called dragon fruit
plátanos	*pla*•ta•nos	fried plantains, a starchy relative of the banana
plato surtido	*pla*•to sur•*tee*•do	a mixed platter of fabulous food, usually for groups of four
pollo	*po*•lyo	chicken
postre	*pos*•tre	dessert

queso	ke•so	cheese
refresco	re•fres•ko	fruit juice beverage whipped with water or milk, plus lots of sugar
sandía	san•dee•a	watermelon
yuca	yoo•ka	cassava; manioc; a starchy root vegetable similar to potatoes, but stringier

COOKING METHODS & STYLES

a la criolla	a la kree•o•lya	cooked with a tomato, sweet chili and onion sauce
a la jalapeña	a la kha•la•pe•nya	cooked in a spicy pepper sauce
a la plancha	a la plan•cha	broiled
al lado	al la•do	on the side
al vapor	al va•por	steamed
empanizado/a	em•pa•nee•sa•do/a	breaded and fried
encebollado/a	en•se•bo•lya•do/a	grilled with onions
gratinado	gra•tee•na•do/a	baked with cheese (au gratin)
frito/a	free•to/a	fried
picante	pee•kan•te	spicy hot
rostizado/a	ros•tee•sa•do/a	roasted
salsa agridulce	sal•sa a•gree•dool•se	sweet-and-sour sauce
salsa de ajillo	sal•sa de a•khee•lyo	garlic sauce

USEFUL WORDS & PHRASES

algo sano	al•go sa•no	something healthy
algo dietético	al•go dye•te•tee•ko	something low calorie
comida a la vista	ko•mee•da a la vee•sta	literally 'food that you can see;' a steam-buffet
comida casera	ko•mee•da ka•se•ra	at very small restaurants, usually the one dish on offer
comida corriente	ko•mee•da ko•ryen•te	the day's set plate, usually rice, beans, meat,salad, plantains and a tortilla; usually better at lunch
comida rápida	ko•mee•da ra•pee•da	fast food
para llevar	pa•ra lye•var	to go; take-away
servicio al domicilio	ser•vee•syo al do•mee•see•lyo	delivery service
Tengo alergía a ...	ten•go a•ler•khee•ya a ...	I'm allergic to ...
Soy vegetariano/a. (m/f)	soy ve•khe•ta•rya•no/a	I'm vegetarian.
¡Buen provecho!	bwen pro•ve•cho	bon apetit, said when you walk in on (or out on) someone eating.

Nicaragua & El Salvador Outdoors

Kept pristine by conflict, even heavily populated El Salvador has more than its fair share of parks, protected areas and privately owned reserves, crisscrossed with trails and laced with waterfalls just waiting to be experienced. Much-less-populated Nicaragua is even more wide open for wilderness adventure, with unscaled cliffs, unrafted rapids and plenty of other opportunities to make history, if that's your game.

And for those who prefer their trails (freshly?) blazed, there are plenty of ways to get out there and enjoy all those cloud forests scented with orchids, dirt roads echoing with howler monkeys and long lazy rivers flowing through steamy jungle – and, one mustn't forget, volcano surfing (see p178).

BOATING

With its rivers, wetlands and oceans – not to mention the two biggest lakes in Central America – Nicaragua is probably where most canoe and kayak aficionados will head. El Salvador also has several intriguing options.

Kayaking on Lago de Nicaragua is easy – paddle through the Isletas de Granada (p118) or around Isla de Ometepe (p137), both of them easily accessible and easily arranged as guided tours. Reserva Natural Isla Juan Venado (p176) also offers kayak tours, but you'll need to go in a wooden canoe (or a comfy *panga,* or motorized skiff) down the Río San Juan (p278). You can rent wooden canoes all over the Caribbean Coast; just ask.

You can also take rowboats around Lago de Managua (p177) or high-altitude Lago de Apenas. El Salvador also has plenty of rowboats you can take for a spin: explore Embalse Cerrón Grande from San Francisco Lempa (p387), or San Luis del Carmen (p387). Suchitoto (p377) has the best access to the islands, plus lots of other outdoor adventures.

Recover from all that activity in La Unión (p412), where a booze cruise takes you around Golfo de Fonseca and lots of little islands, from which you can wave hello to Nicaragua.

TOP FIVE UNREAL EXPERIENCES

Who needs hallucinogens when you've got Nicaragua, El Salvador and a pair of hiking shoes (or reef booties)?

Diving Los Cóbanos (p404) Cliffs, cool volcanic formations and at least four shipwrecks (plus whales in December and January) make this El Salvador's best diving.

Surfing Punta Roca (boxed text, p400) The best wave in Central America awaits – fast, strong and long enough for 15 maneuvers or more – all just an hour from San Salvador.

Gazing into Volcán Masaya (p100) Watch parakeets – mysteriously immune to the tons of poisonous gases pouring from an active crater – return to nest above visible pools of lava.

Strolling to the Reserva Natural Cerro Tisey-Estanzuela overlook (p198) Gaze, shivering in the cloud forest, across the 60km gash in the earth that is the Maribios Chain, to the Cosigüina Peninsula.

Canoeing the Río San Juan (p278) Take on the rapids that stymied pirates on the plunder, from an old Spanish fortress into the pristine Indio-Maíz jungles, alive with egrets and macaws.

CYCLING & MOUNTAIN BIKING

With wide shoulders, fresh pavement and friendly people, both El Salvador and Nicaragua get thumbs up from distance cyclers doing the great American dream trip. There are not many places to rent equipment (or buy high-quality equipment), so consider bringing your own. And always feel free to ask at your hotel or the *alcaldía* (mayor's office) to see about renting a bike from a friend.

Some of the easiest and most rewarding spots to arrange mountain-bike adventures include the beautiful mountains around Juayúa (p363), where outfitters can also offer great guided tours; Tacuba (p373) and Suchitoto (p377) are other scenic options with rental bikes.

In Nicaragua, Isla de Ometepe (p137) has rentals and a 35km ring road around Volcán Maderas; in San Juan del Sur (p148) dirt roads stretching up and down the coast make for a great adventure.

There are also excellent opportunities for road biking. Western El Salvador offers Ruta de Las Flores (boxed text, p357), which wends its way through colonial mountain towns, indigenous strongholds and flower nurseries, while Nicaragua's classic bike tour is through Los Pueblos Blancos (p103), another colorful collection of charismatic villages, known for sweets, crafts and more flowers.

DIVING & SNORKELING

Diving is only just getting off the ground, but there are some awe-inspiring sites.

Diving is only just getting off the ground in Nicaragua and El Salvador – unless you count the very non-PADI-certified lobster-diving opportunities out there, which we most certainly do not. Neither country can really match Honduras, but if you want to check out the wildlife under the waves there are certainly plenty of awe-inspiring places to do it.

El Salvador's top dive sites include Los Cóbanos (p404), not a reef, but thousands of rocky heads scattered like birdseed during a long-ago volcanic eruption and today covered in coral. You can also dive two crater lakes: though Lago de Coatepeque (p352) is prettier topside, Lago Ilopango (book dives through dive shops in San Salvador; see p317) has thermal steamers.

You can also dive Nicaragua's Laguna de Apoyo (p102), then take the short trip across the isthmus to San Juan del Sur (p148), with always good, sometimes spectacular, Pacific dives. But the best place in either country – and certainly comparable to the Bay Islands, especially if you like cave dives – are the Corn Islands (p254), in the middle of the sapphire Caribbean.

HIKING & TREKKING

Thanks to an unlikely environmental consciousness (the Nicaraguan and Salvadoran governments both found time to protect dozens of wilderness areas during the turbulent 1980s) and the wars, which probably did more to save the rain forests than Unesco did in most countries, there's a lot of fairly pristine forest out there to see. Even better, there are often excellent trail systems – sometimes built by the warriors themselves, as in Perquín (p442) – many of which offer the opportunity to see old war relics or follow old evacuation trails, as in Matagalpa (p209), quite possibly the hiking capital of Nicaragua.

If you're headed into the serious outback, for instance, Reserva Natural Cordillera Dipilto y Jalapa (p202), with Nicaragua's highest mountain, Cerro Mogotón (2106m), be sure to educate yourself about landmines (see p474); sure, both countries are officially almost mine-free, but

---

TREKKING TIPS

Hikes in Nicaragua and El Salvador range from easy interpretive trails to trail-free bushwalking – don't forget your machete! Here are a few tips for making the most of any walk in the woods.

- Spring for a guide (and bring snacks to share). Even on easy hikes, guides can almost always find things you never would; where they're recommended or required, there's usually a very good reason. In smaller towns, ask about guides at the *alcaldía* (mayor's office), usually right on the central park, or the *juez* or *wihta* (judge) in Mayangna and Miskito communities.

- The best hikes, hot springs and secret cove beaches are often (and understandably) secrets guarded closely from guidebook writers. Ask around.

- Morning and late afternoon are the best times to see animals. Don't just hike – stop and stay very quiet for a while, perhaps close to a watering hole, and see what happens.

- Remember: rain forests are often rainy, and cloud forests may be cloudy (and cold!); dress accordingly.

- Be careful crossing rivers, particularly during rainy season, when you could lose your footing or even the trail. Coastal river crossings may be low tide only; sometimes it's just better to wait.

- The dazzling array of tropical wildlife is one wonderful reason why we hike, and also why we shouldn't put our hands anywhere we haven't looked first.

---

sometimes it's just smart to stay on trails. Happily, El Salvador's highest point offers access to Cerro El Pital (2730m; p392). It's an easy hike, since you can drive most of the way up. And hikers *have* to take on a volcano while they're down there; it's just the done thing.

Check each country's activity section (p282 and p454) for more ideas on great hikes, but don't miss Juayúa (p363), El Salvador's hiking hot spot with lots of waterfall access and coffee plantations – not to mention an option to descend a 70m waterfall in about 20 refreshing minutes; they call it 'wet rappelling.' And in addition to Matagalpa, Nicaragua's hiking havens include Estelí (p192) and, for adventurers, the Central Highlands (p243).

SURFING

El Salvador's surf scene is divided into two areas: the long-popular west and the up-and-coming 'wild east.' The western region is based at and around La Libertad (p396), a none-too-pleasant city a short drive south of San Salvador that's home to what's arguably the best wave in Central America, Punta Roca. The eastern scene is based near the popular Playa El Cuco (p417). The west is more developed, with hotels, surf shops and more surfers, while the east is mainly visited by multiday surf tours.

The waves line up like ducks and there are virtually no days when at least one spot isn't on.

The only problem with El Salvador (other than less-than-appealing La Libertad) is a chronic lack of lefts. But the rights are epic: perfect shape, perfect set-ups and as mechanical as a skate park. Rides of 50m to 150m are standard, and 200m not unheard-of. Good hollow barrels form at a number of spots, and rocky bottoms make for strong fast waves, but the bread and butter here is consistency: the waves line up like ducks and there are virtually no days when at least one spot isn't on.

The epicenter of Nicaraguan surfing remains San Juan del Sur (p148), giving rise to a wave of surf camps and strongholds spreading northward to the holy grail of Nica waveriding, Popoyo (see p135), past flawless beach breaks, scary-fun lava point breaks and lots of barrels, when conditions are right. North of Popoyo, despite some excellent surfing, services are thin; surfing on the Caribbean Coast is possible, but there's no infrastructure and not much information available.

SURFING IN NICARAGUA & EL SALVADOR

SURFING				
Acajutla	1 A1	Playa El Zonte (Right Break)	15 A1
Atami	(see 3)	Playa Guasacate/Popoyo	16 F4
Barra de Santiago	2 A1	Playa Huehete	17 F4
El Cocal	(see 13)	Playa La Paz	18 B1
El Palmarcito	3 A1	Playa Las Flores (Right Break)	19 C2
El Sunzalito	(see 6)	Playa Majahual	20 B1
Km.59 (Right Break)	4 A1	Playa Mizata	21 A1
Km.61	5 A1	Playa Pie de Gigante	22 F4
La Bocana	6 B1	Playa San Blas	(see 13)
La Bocanita	(see 6)	Playa Shalpa	(see 5)
La Flor	(see 9)	Playas Madera & Marsella	23 F4
La Perla	(see 5)	Poneloya/Las Piñitas	
La Vaca	7 C2	(Right Break)	24 D3
Los Cóbanos	8 A1	Puerto Sandino to El Velero	25 E3
Lucky Man's	9 C2	Punta Bongo	26 C2
Masachapa & Pochonil	10 E4	Punta Coco	(see 4)
Paso Caballos (Left Break)	11 D2	Punta Mango	(see 26)
Playa Aserradores	12 D2	Punta Roca (Right Break)	(see 18)
Playa Conchalía	13 B1	Punta Sunzal (Right Break)	(see 6)
Playa El Tunco	14 B1	San Juan del Sur	27 F4
		Toro de Oro	28 C2

Nicaragua's best breaks often require boats to get to, not just because they're offshore, but as housing developments plaster themselves along the coast, blocking land access. To make up for it, southern Nicaragua is caressed by an almost constant offshore wind, perhaps caused by the presence of Lago de Nicaragua and Lago de Managua.

Both countries have great waves year-round. The rainy season (March to November) is considered the best time to surf, with the biggest waves usually in March, April and October (consistently 1m to 2m, frequently 3m to 4m). November to March is the dry season, with smaller waves (averaging under 2m) but better weather – this is the best time for beginners. Water temperature averages in the mid-20s year-round, but from December to April upwelling offshore means that the water's temperature can drop; consider bringing a long-sleeve wetsuit top.

Booties and rash vests are nice to have for those rocky landings. Other items that are worth packing include some extra leashes, tropical-formula wax, board bag, bladders, rail guards and some fins if you like to body surf.

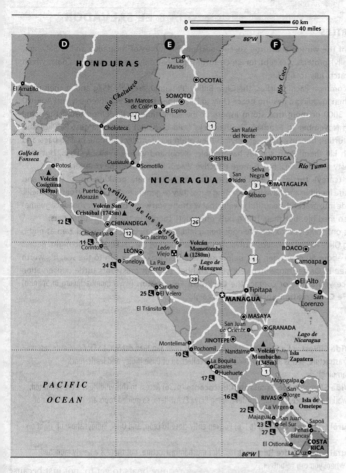

You can buy, sell and rent boards in La Libertad and San Juan del Sur, but it's generally better to bring your own board (consider selling it when you leave). But don't leave anything on the beach: backpacks, shirts, sandals and even bag lunches are all liable to be stolen, whether on crowded town beaches or isolated spots with seemingly no one around. Even locals bring only what they can carry on their bodies.

If you're just learning, be sure that your instructor explains the etiquette of surfing and about *localismo*, where certain waves are considered off-limits to foreigners, especially beginners, out of respect for local surfers.

Numerous surfing outfits offer everything from one-on-one instruction to week-long all-inclusive surf packages. Listings are provided in the closest city to the waves, or log onto **Surf Maps** (www.surfmaps.com; per map US$8) for the best maps to the waves in either country. The newest edition of Mike Parise's *Surfer's Guide to Costa Rica* includes coverage of Southwest Nicaragua. Here are some favorite waves, which we've listed northeast to southwest.

SEE SEA TURTLES

At least five of the world's sea turtle species nest on the shores of Nicaragua and El Salvador, all (theoretically) protected except for green turtles, present only on the Atlantic Coast, which are legal to catch July to April.

The most common Pacific turtles, the Olive Ridley (Paslama), are only 45kg and at their most impressive when invading a nesting beach (July to December, peaking in September and August) in flotillas of 3000 or more that storm ashore at the same time to lay. Often using the same beaches from November to February, leatherbacks (*tora* or *baula*) are the largest (450kg) and rarest of the turtles; because they eat jellyfish they often accidentally consume plastic bags and bottles, which kill them. Both species have edible, illegal and widely available eggs, but they aren't very tasty and, besides, much more effective Viagra is sold over the counter.

Hawksbill (carey) turtles – which nest May to November, peaking in October and September – are inedible and have lousy-tasting eggs; they're generally caught only for their shells, which are made into graceful, beautiful jewelry that we hope you won't buy. Loggerhead (caguama) turtles are also inedible, but their 160kg bulk often gets caught in the green-turtle nets.

Most tours only take you to see the eggs being laid, usually between 9pm and 2am at night, except during Olive Ridley *arribadas* (arrivals), when the beaches are packed day and night. Babies usually hatch about 60 days later, just before sunrise, then make their run to the sea; it's worth camping to see it. Or get more involved; you can hook up with grassroots turtle conservation initiatives once you arrive, or contact the **Cocibolca Foundation** (www.mombacho.org in Spanish) or the **Wildlife Conservation Society** (www.wcs.org).

Nicaragua

Refugio de Vida Silvestre La Flor (p157) Easily accessible from San Juan del Sur, La Flor's wildlife reserve has the best infrastructure, access and protection for their collection of Olive Ridley and leatherback turtles – plus camping!

Refugio de Vida Silvestre Río Escalante Chococente (p136) Access to this wildlife reserve is limited, but it's within walking distance from rapidly developing Playa El Astillero, so guided tours are just a matter of time.

Reserva Natural Isla Juan Venado (p176) Conveniently close to León, and Olive Ridleys show up right on time.

Reserva Natural Estero Padre Ramos (p188) Not much infrastructure, but there is a newly launched turtle program where you can volunteer.

Pearl Keys (p254) This group of expensive-to-access Caribbean islands hosts hawksbill turtles. Other nesting sites on the Atlantic Coast include: the Miskito Keys (p234), even more difficult to get to; and Río San Juan Wildlife Preserve, where green, hawksbill and leatherback turtles nest, can only be reached via San Juan de Nicaragua (p280), a challenge in itself.

El Salvador

Bahía de Jiquilisco (p410) This beautiful bay has some of the best beaches in El Salvador – and a fledgling turtle program to protect its most precious visitors. Isla de Méndez has the prime nesting grounds.

El Cuco (p417) Privately owned Rancho de Amor in eastern El Salvador has its own turtle-rescue project in the works.

Corral de Mulas (p411) With another turtle nursery in the works at Playa El Icacal, just west, this region may develop into a successful marine-turtle sanctuary.

Barra de Santiago (p405) It's got a research lab, and Olive Ridley and leatherback turtles; there were hawksbills up until a few decades ago.

El Salvador

All breaks are rights, unless otherwise specified.

Km 59 (p400) Short, hollow and fun – and if don't mind tramping across private property, all yours.

Playa El Zonte (p404) Reliable right with less traffic, especially after the day-trippers head back to the capital. Two excellent surf camps make for quick access and easy living.

Playa El Tunco (p402) Four big breaks and plenty of small hotels make this a popular spot. El Sunzal and El Sunzalito are good rights for beginners, longboarders and when everything else is flat; La Bocana and La Bocanita are reliable left and right river breaks, but are usually for locals only. Playa El Tunco is 7km from La Libertad, also reachable from Casa de Mar and Playa El Sunzal.

Playa San Blas (p401) Not the best wave in the country, but one of few reliable lefts and a decent beach to boot. It's 4km west of La Libertad.

Punta Roca (see the boxed text, p400) La Libertad's pride and joy isn't just the best wave in El Salvador, it's the best wave in Central America. A world-class right that's fast, strong and mechanical – fasten your seatbelt.

> Punta Roca is the best wave in Central America - it's fast, strong and mechanical.

Playa Las Flores (p417) The best surfing in Eastern El Salvador is 5km west of El Cuco, where the water is cleaner and the waves are mainly boat access. It has two world-class waves: Las Flores, a fast, sandy point break; and Punta Mango, shorter and more aggressive.

Nicaragua

All of these beaches are on the Pacific Coast; the only accessible Atlantic beach where there's rumored to be surfing is Tuapí, south of Bilwi (p234).

Playa Aserradores (p187) Just northeast of Chinandega, the beach is also called 'boom-wavos' for the powerful, hollow beach break making all that noise. There's another left five minutes offshore and plenty more waves around.

El Corinto (p186) One of the best waves in the country goes almost unsurfed out there beyond Playa Paso Caballos, but it's boat access only; just north is a rivermouth break with left-breaking peaks.

Poneloya/Las Peñitas (p174) Only decent surfing, but the easiest access on Nicaragua's North Pacific, just 20km from León.

Puerto Sandino (p176) The stretch from Puerto Sandino to El Valero has half-a-dozen reef and rocky-bottomed beach breaks, including one spectacular left.

Masachapa & Pochomil (p88) Just an hour from Managua are no less than eight quality breaks in the vicinity of Masachapa and Pochomil, including Montelimar, a hollow right reef break, and Quizala, a beach break right in front of Masachapa.

Playa Huehete (see p110) Now is that golden time between when the road is paved and when the gated communities go up: check out the point, beach and rivermouth break now!

Popoyo (see p135) This collection of sandy-floored surf lodges may be Nicaragua's next bona fide surf town, with at least four named waves: Popoyo, a right and left point break; aggressive Bus Stop; fast and rocky-floored Cobra; and the best wave in the region, Emergencias, with a left for the longboards and hollow right for short boards.

Playa Pie de Gigante (p134) Accessing another handful of named waves, most of them a boat ride away, it's no wonder that surf lodges are springing up all over this beautiful beach.

Playa Madera (p156) Sometimes called Los Playones, this excellent surf spot with easy access from San Juan del Sur has a slow wave with two rights and two lefts that's perfect for beginners, and much more challenging Panga Drops; boat access only.

San Juan del Sur (p148) Ground zero for Nica surfing, the beach break's only so-so, but the town provides access to a dozen waves nearby and more through any of its many surf-tour operators.

SWIMMING

From sunny Pacific beaches to cool crater lakes, and lots of rivers and waterfalls, you'll always find places to put your bathing suit to work. Ladies, use your best judgment: going topless is almost never acceptable, and in rural areas you may want to swim in shorts and a T-shirt.

The sparkling blue crater lake of Lago de Coatepeque (p352) is watched over by the twin sentinels of Cerro Verde and Santa Ana. Swim from the youth hostel pier or take a boat ride to nearby islands. In Nicaragua there are eight major crater lakes, with excellent swimming at Laguna de Apoyo (p102), surrounded by lodging options; or undeveloped Laguna de Asososca (p178), near León. Lago de Nicaragua is refreshingly clean (well, away from Granada), but Lago de Managua has a way to go.

El Salvador is heaven to waterfall lovers, with falls of all sizes easily reached from the towns of Juayúa, Tacuba, Suchitoto, Tacuba and Perquín.

WILDLIFE WATCHING

Though the wars helped preserve untold hectares of forest, they played havoc with anything edible, though wildlife populations are rebounding. The best spots to see big animals are along Nicaragua's southern border, where critters coming from peaceful, well-fed Costa Rica are moving into Refugio de Vida Silvestre los Guatuzos (Los Guatuzos Wildlife Reserve; p274), along the Río San Juan (p275) and anywhere on the Rivas Peninsula, which has been thoroughly colonized by howler monkeys.

One of the rarest ecosystems in the world is the cloud forest, a cool, misty tropical rain forest above 1200m, offering opportunities for seeing wildlife, most famously colorful quetzals and orchids. Some of the easiest to see are Volcán Mombacho (p128), with easy access from Granada, and Cerro Montecristo (p360), on the Guatemalan border – and you can stay overnight atop either with advance arrangement.

Dramatic shorelines include the world's largest remaining mangrove forest, around Golfo de Fonseca (Gulf of Fonseca), shared by Honduras, El Salvador and Nicaragua. It's also a haven for nesting turtles (see the boxed text, p48) and sea birds, in particular pelicans that populate the Farallones de Cosigüina (cliff-sized splinters of rock cast from an exploding volcano; see p189), Isla Montecristo (p409) and Bahía de Jiquilisco (p410).

Birders will also be drawn to sweet-water wetlands, including Río Escondido (see p248), a scenic transportation option in Nicaragua, or the more isolated Archipiélago de Solentiname (see p266), in the southeastern corner of Lago de Nicaragua. In El Salvador, Barra de Santiago (p405) is another protected estuary.

Even surfers have options when the waves aren't working: Parque Nacional Walter T Deininger (p397), close to La Libertad, has an 18km trail through dry tropical forest populated by endangered *tepezcuintle* (paca) and *torogoz* (blue-crowned motmot), El Salvador's national bird. And close to San Juan del Sur, you've got to try to catch the sea turtles nesting at nearby La Flor (see the boxed text, p48).

Golfo de Fonseca is a haven for nesting turtles and sea birds.

Nicaragua

Smoking Volcán Concepción and her almost perfect cinder cone rise from silvery, pure Lago de Nicaragua to pierce the cloudy sky. 'Land of Lakes and Volcanoes' indeed, you think, as the rolling waves of Cocibolca (an ancient indigenous name for this 'Sweet Sea') rock your suddenly tiny ferry into unspeakable admiration. For these symbols of the nation – wind over water, fire from the earth – convey the elemental significance of Nicaragua's most powerful passions, poetry (don't get them started, unless you want to) and revolution.

For visitors of a certain age, just the name Nicaragua – taken from a tribal chief of such wisdom and power that he may never fade from this nation's collective memory – evokes grainy footage of camouflage-clad guerrillas, punctuated by gunfire and a 1980s soundtrack. Despite having ended more than 15 years ago, leaving Nicaragua one of the safest countries in the Americas, the Contra War is too often our collective memory of the land of Nicarao.

But you'll see so much more. If you climb Concepción you'll look out over gorgeous colonial Granada and her hundreds of tiny tropical *isletas* (islets), across the slender isthmus pockmarked with crater lakes to where the Pacific breaks hollow on sandy cove beaches. Beyond, red-and-black Volcán Momotombo towers above Lago de Managua – its counterpoint is Sandino's massive iron silhouette, conscience of the nation and solemn defining feature of the Managua skyline.

Proud León also beckons with its churches and museums, while the cloud forests, frothing waterfalls and incredible coffee of the cool, green Northern Highlands may tempt you upwards. Here, in the mountains and lakes, Central America's mightiest rivers begin their journey across the autonomous, indigenous-owned rolling hills of the Caribbean lowlands, to the sea.

FAST FACTS

- **Area** 129,494 sq km (largest in Central America)
- **Capital** Managua
- **Country Code** ☎ 505
- **Money** córdoba; US dollar widely used
- **Number of Animal Species** 1400
- **Phrases** *Nica* (Nicaraguan guys and gals); *vos* (you); *tuanis* (right on)
- **Population** 5,465,100 (least densely populated in Central America)
- **Shoreline** 1040km
- **Visa** US$25 for citizens of 40 countries; US$7 entry (no visa needed) for everyone else; see p288

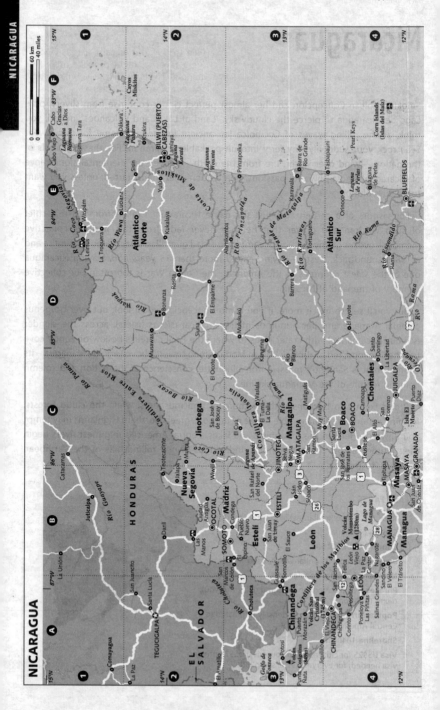

NICARAGUA

0 — 60 km
0 — 40 miles

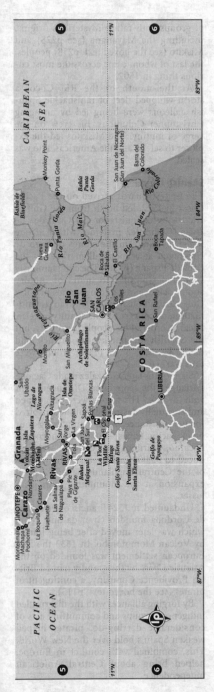

HIGHLIGHTS

- **León** (p159) and **Granada** (p110) Choosing a favorite might provoke these two colonial rivals, with the country's best museums and architecture
- **Río San Juan** (p275) Take a riverboat ride into the rain forest, then visit the art colony of the Archipiélago de Solentiname
- **Isla de Ometepe** (p137) Nicaragua's ecological crown jewel has two volcanoes, one active and both with stunning lake views
- **Jinotega** (p217) Colonial treasure surrounded by steep jungled mountains, with Matagalpa's hip scene close by
- **Waspám** (p236) Get off the beaten track and into the indigenous-owned Mosquitia and its lifeline, Central America's longest river

CLIMATE & WHEN TO GO

Nicaragua has a range of microclimates, and it's always worth checking the weather to see where you want to go first. On the Pacific side, *invierno* (winter), or rainy season, runs May to November, at its rainiest in September and October when sea turtles nest 3000-strong to a beach. *Verano* (summer), or dry season, is November to April, the best time for hiking, camping and partying, as it coincides with high tourist season (December to March), most pronounced along the Costa Rican border. As *verano* desiccates to a close, the Pacific forests lose their leaves and lake levels drop revealing sandy lake beaches that you'll put to good use as temperatures soar from the normal high 20s into the mid-30s or worse.

And then there are the mountains, from the islands of cool cloud forests atop each volcano to the monolithic granite peaks of the central highlands, where the seasons become blurred in the chilly misty mornings, with temperatures between 12°C and 24°C. On the Atlantic side rainy and dry seasons are almost entirely academic, so check the weather; along the Río San Juan, one of the wettest places on earth, always pack a raincoat.

HISTORY

Monkey Point, south of Bluefields, has evidence of one of the earliest human encampments in the Americas, perhaps

NICARAGUA

HOW MUCH?

- **Surfboard rental** per day US$10-15
- **Museum admission** US$2
- **2-hr bus ride** US$2
- **Internet access** per hr US$0.70
- **Típica breakfast** US$1.50

LONELY PLANET INDEX

- **Gallon of gas** US$3.50
- **1L bottled water** US$0.70
- **Servico of Flor de Caña rum** US$5
- **Sandino T-shirt** US$5
- **Quesillo with extra onions** US$1

8000 years old, marked by clam shells. More impressive, however, is a site in Managua, where a family left their footprints in the volcanic mud about 6000 years ago.

By 1500 BC, Nicaragua was broadly settled, and though much of this history has been lost, at least one ancient treaty between the Nicarao capital of Jinotepe and its rival Chorotegan neighbor, Diriamba, is still celebrated as the Toro Guaco (see p107).

The agricultural revolution arrived around 450 BC, when domesticated corn, yucca, beans and other crops were introduced. By AD 300, trading partners as far away as modern-day Colombia and the United States were providing new technology like *matates* (corn-grinding stones) and tough obsidian tools capable of carving soft volcanic basalt.

By AD 800, petroglyph and statue fever was sweeping across Nicaragua, and many designs, including an Aztec calendar and representations of the deity Quetzalcóatl, heralded the arrival of one of Nicaragua's most important migrations.

With the collapse of the Aztec empire, a tribe of Náhuatl-speaking refugees seeking a prophesied lake island settled Isla de Ometepe in the early 1000s, although some archaeologists question this official story. Colonies of possible Maya origin had already settled the central highlands of Matagalpa, Chontales and Juigalpa, while the Atlantic Coast was home to a number of groups with rather mysterious origins, including the Mayangna (see p228) and Miskito (see the boxed text, p238) peoples, the last of whom came across the most curious thing in 1502.

At the mouth of the Río Coco, a storm-whipped fleet of ramshackle Spanish galleons were being led by an aging Christopher Columbus, his crew on the verge of mutiny. The Miskitos led the explorer to safety, and the Americas' fate was sealed.

Spanish Conquest

The first Spaniards arrived on the Pacific Coast in 1522, led north from the Gulf of Nicoya by conquistador Gil González de Ávila. González first met with Cacique (chief) Nicarao on the shores of Lago de Nicaragua at a spot still marked by the Cruz de España (p136). The chief famously subjected González to hours of inquiry about science, technology and history; González famously gave Nicarao an ultimatum: to convert to Christianity, or else. Nicarao ordered his people to comply, but the Spanish did not live up to their end of the bargain; other native groups were thus warned.

Six months later González made Cacique Diriangén the same offer; Diriangén went with 'or else.' His troops were outgunned and eventually destroyed, but they inspired further resistance. After conquering four main Pacific tribes – 700,000 Chorotega, Nicarao, Maribios and Chontal were reduced to 35,000 in 25 years – the nations of the Central Highlands halted Spanish expansion at the mountains, with grim losses.

Undaunted, in 1524 Francisco Fernández de Córdoba founded Granada and León, which was later moved after being buried by Volcán Momotombo. In 1633 the first European settlement was founded on the Atlantic Coast by the grandly named British Providence Company, a contingent of pirates (see the boxed text, p113).

By forging alliances with the disgruntled indigenous groups and committing acts of considerable derring-do, pirates helped weaken Spain's hold on the New World. This, combined with conflict in Europe, helped bring about Central American independence.

Nicaraguan Independence & Civil War

Nicaragua won independence from Spain in 1821, and the resulting power vacuum led to civil war. Conservative Granada had long played rival to the colonial capital, Liberal León – and with independence, its position was suddenly vulnerable. The compromise – naming the fishing village of Managua as national capital in 1852 – only interrupted hostilities.

Desperate, León hired filibusterer William Walker (see the boxed text, below) to help, naïvely failing to realize that the Tennessee mercenary had his own agenda. After Walker was finally defeated and León completely humiliated, the conservatives took power for 30 years of peace, if not prosperity. Their cozy relationship with the US became an emotional issue, and when Liberal General José Santos Zelaya took power in an 1893 coup, he rejected a US proposal to build the interocean canal through Nicaragua out of hand.

When the USA began construction in Panama instead, Zelaya tried to backtrack, approaching Great Britain, Germany and Japan about another canal. His reforms – for instance, repealing laws requiring unemployed campesinos (farmers) to pick plantation coffee for subsistence wages – had already alienated the upper classes, thus Zelaya was politically weak when US marines arrived.

For the next two decades the USA dominated politics in Nicaragua. In 1914 the Bryan-Chamorro Treaty was signed, granting the USA exclusive rights to a canal that it had no intention of building, just to shut out the competition. The occupation's casual brutality – torture, political killings, dragging the bodies of dead rebels through city streets – intimidated most Nicaraguans and inspired one teenage boy, Augusto C Sandino (see the boxed text, p222).

Sandino & the Somoza Dynasty

The Liberals mounted a noble, if ineffective, resistance to the US occupation, which wilted completely in the late 1920s. But Sandino – by now commander of his own personal army – continued fighting. Although domestic pressure forced the US

WILLIAM WALKER

It's a cliché to accuse Nashville, Tennessee-born William Walker of a Napoleon complex – at 5ft 2in he'd suffered childhood taunts of 'missy' while caring for his ailing mother. His social life thus lacking, by age 22 he spoke several languages and had degrees in medicine and law.

Quite progressive at the outset of his career, Walker became editor of the left-wing *San Francisco Herald*, where he spoke out against slavery. After the deaths of his young wife and beloved mother, however, and after the 1848 Treaty of Guadalupe where Hidalgo ceded half of Mexico to the United States – leaving the other half tantalizingly independent – Walker decided to change careers.

Filibustering, a word derived from an old Dutch term for pirate, had become the Spanish verb for invading another country as a private citizen, then unofficially receiving aid from your home government. Walker's first filibustering gig attacked La Paz, Mexico, where he pulled off a stunning, if short-lived, victory against the larger, better equipped (but totally unprepared) Mexican army. Walker raised the flag of the Republic of Sonora and declared himself president, then was chased back over the border; only 10 of the original expedition survived. The venture played well in the press, however, and Walker was offered a job by the town of León.

Dubbed 'The Immortals' by the tabloid press, Walker's army landed in San Juan del Sur and easily took Granada – but didn't cede control to the Leónese. Walker was instead elected president by the largest margin in Nicaraguan history, and US president Franklin Pierce was the first to recognize the not-at-all suspicious new government. Walker reinstituted slavery, declared English the official language and launched an attack on Costa Rica, a cholera-ridden debacle that saw both armies decimated by disease. Other Central American armies fell on Walker, forcing him into retreat and, as he passed his old home he set it alight, leaving behind the sign 'Here was Granada.'

Despite his defeat, Walker returned to the USA a hero and easily raised enough cash for two return trips. The first ended with his capture by US troops, who returned him home, the second with his capture by the British Navy, which turned him over to Honduran authorities, who had Walker executed by firing squad in 1860.

military to pull out of the country as the Great Depression ground on, they trained the National Guard, under the command of loyal bureaucrat Anastasio Somoza García, as an insurance policy.

In February 1934, after a dinner party celebrating peace accords with the new Liberal president Sacasa, Sandino and his men were murdered outside the Presidential Palace. Somoza, a guest at that party, would go on to overthrow Sacasa in 1937. His US-backed dictatorship, veneered with fraudulent elections and puppet governments, allowed Somoza to amass landholdings equal to all of El Salvador.

After his 1956 assassination in León, Somoza was succeeded by his elder son, Luis Somoza Debayle, the best of the Somozas. His innovative projects were supported by the US Kennedy administration, which in return graciously granted full use of Puerto Cabezas for launching its disastrous 1961 invasion of Cuba. Somoza called for actual elections shortly afterwards, lost handily to Liberal Renée Schick, then quietly retired. His younger brother, Anastasio Somoza Debayle, was not as eager to give up his birthright.

Luis died in 1967 and Anastasio assumed the presidency. The West Point graduate used the National Guard ruthlessly, stifling a growing call for democracy. An increasingly militant group of university students calling themselves the Sandinistas tried to counter him, but few thought them a viable alternative.

A 6.3 earthquake in the early morning of December 23, 1972 changed all that. Fifteen square kilometers of Managua's city center were reduced to rubble; 6000 people were killed. The world, moved by the holiday devastation, donated aid on an unprecedented scale; Somoza diverted almost everything to family and friends.

The Sandinistas were, with one powerful betrayal, legitimized. Nicaraguans from every walk of life threw in their support, and over the next five years the nation became ungovernable. The National Guard destroyed entire cities and assassinated *La Prensa* editor Pedro Joaquín Chamorro, still somehow failing to win the hearts and minds of the people. Almost every country in the Americas and Europe cut ties with the Somoza regime...except the US.

The revolution marched to victory on July 19, 1979 and Somoza fled the country. He was assassinated shortly afterwards in Paraguay.

Revolutionary Government & the Contra War

The Sandinistas inherited a country in shambles. Poverty, homelessness, illiteracy and staggeringly inadequate health care were just a few of the widespread problems. Some 50,000 people had been killed in the revolutionary struggle and 150,000 were made refugees.

The FSLN (Sandinista National Liberation Front) and prominent anti-Somoza moderates (including Violeta Barrios de Chamorro, widow of the martyred Pedro Joaquín Chamorro) set up a 'Junta of Five' to administer the country. The constitution was suspended, congress was dissolved and the National Guard was replaced by the Sandinista People's Army. Health-care reforms and a widely lauded Literacy Crusade, which cut illiteracy from more than 50% to 13% in two years, earned the revolutionary government accolades on the world stage.

But the junta was rigged: two of the supposed moderates were secretly aligned with FSLN commander Daniel Ortega, and the other two – Chamorro and businessman Alfonso Robelo – resigned within the year. Unchaperoned, S andinistas nationalized more than 300 businesses and passed the Agrarian Reform Law, nationalizing 'nonproductive lands' larger than 500 *manzanas* (blocks of 350 hectares). Though the number of landowners went from 10,000 to 30,000, such reforms did little to quell international concerns about all those Soviet and Cuban advisors, or allegations that the Sandinistas were providing arms to leftist rebels in El Salvador.

In January 1981, just days after taking office, US president Ronald Reagan cancelled Nicaragua's aid package and publicly committed his administration to helping the National Guard regroup and re-arm as the Contras, whose mission to overthrow the Sandinista-led Nicaraguan government would last a decade. Reagan constructed bases for Contras in Honduras and Costa Rica, providing millions in training and material aid.

TICOS, NICAS & THE GALLO PINTO WARS

Like so many Central American conflicts, this, too, can be reduced to basic grains: both Costa Rica and Nicaragua claim to have invented *gallo pinto*, that breakfast treat involving rice, beans, oil and salt. In Costa Rica they usually use black beans; in Nicaragua, red. And if anyone, in either country, asks which you prefer, don't answer. It's a trap.

Both countries have won awards for their version of the breakfast dish. A year after Costa Rica earned a spot in the *Guinness World Records* for cooking the largest batch of *gallo pinto* in human history, clearly a direct challenge to Nicaraguan nationalistic pride, Pharaoh's Casino in Managua decided to pick up the glove. For 16 hours four chefs and 30 cooks stirred the mix with shovels in a Humvee-sized basin. The result was 18,400 servings exactly, making Costa Rica's *gallo pinto*, with only 13,000 servings, look like, well, a hill of beans.

'The idea arose after Costa Rica announced that this typical Nicaraguan dish would be theirs if they cooked a lot of it,' explained Pharaoh's manager Héctor García, hopefully in jest. 'Nicaragua has now done the same, even surpassing our goal in the response and defense of our national dish.' Perhaps coincidentally, Costa Rica took the Río San Juan dispute (see the boxed text, p276) to the World Court at the Hague one month later.

The civil war between the Contras and government forces intensified after Daniel Ortega won apparently free and fair elections in 1984. He declared a state of emergency, shut down the press and initiated a military draft, his troops graciously retooled by the Soviet Union. Contras then targeted the food supply, and over half of the year's wheat and bean crops were lost. In 1985, the US implemented a full economic blockade, including food and medicine. More than 60,000 soldiers – roughly half from each side – and 50,000 civilians died.

In 1987, Costa Rican President Oscar Arias asked five Central American presidents to sign a desperate peace plan, which also aimed to stop the horrific civil wars tearing apart El Salvador and Guatemala. Among other things, it called for an end to all military aid, specifically from the US and Soviet Union.

All of them signed. Arias was awarded the Nobel Peace Prize. Reagan criticized the treaty as 'deeply flawed' and, according to Arias, his administration did everything it could to undermine the process. It failed. By 1993 Central America was at peace for the first time in generations.

Nicaragua at Peace

The Arias accords succeeded not only because both sides truly thirsted for peace, but because both were having problems with their arms dealers. The Soviet Union, months away from collapse, was mired in its own political upheaval, while the

Reagan administration had just been busted in an embarrassing debacle known as the Iran-Contra Affair (see p30).

In accordance with the Arias accords, Ortega lifted press censorship, enforced a ceasefire and called for general elections to be held in 1990. His second presidential bid was opposed by a coalition, the Unión Nacional Opositora (ONU; National Opposition Union), united only in their opposition to the FSLN, the embargo and the war. Their candidate, former Junta leader and *La Prensa* publisher Violeta Barrios de Chamorro, became the first female head of state in the Americas. Conservative commentators speculated that Ortega would refuse to step down, but the transition of power was relatively peaceful, although there were some lovely parting gifts (farms, islands) to the Sandinista faithful, a move known as 'La Piñata.' The USA finally called off the embargo, but the country was in ruins.

Although Chamorro had been perceived as a weak candidate, she rose to the office. Two of her children had been Sandinistas, two of them Contras, thus all Nicaraguans understood that national reconciliation was no abstraction to her. She decentralized the government, brought the police and military under civilian control, and cut the military's numbers from almost 95,000 at the war's peak to less than 20,000. Her best efforts were thwarted by unpleasant realities – poverty, hunger and continued US interest in the region – but for all the compromises she was forced to make she constructed a stable foundation upon which the nation could rebuild.

Chamorro's replacement, who handily beat Ortega (despite the FSLN's new, less threatening campaign color – pink!), was a blast from the dictatorial past: corpulent Liberal Arnoldo Alemán, voted one of the world's 10 most corrupt politicians by the UN Human Rights subcommission. Alemán siphoned some US$100 million from government coffers, which may be chump change where you're from, but not in Nicaragua. Even after Hurricane Mitch savaged the country in 1998 – killing 4000 people and destroying a surreal 70% of the infrastructure – he stayed on the take. When current (at research time) president Enrique Bolaños, also of the Liberal Party, took office in 2001, he promised to put Alemán in jail. To everyone's surprise Bolaños actually did it. But it was too late, in a way.

Current Events

In 1999 perennial FSLN presidential candidate Daniel Ortega, honing in on Arnoldo Alemán's post-scandal political weakness like a bull shark in a kiddy pool, joined with the disgraced president in El Pacto. The secret (for 10 minutes) agreement has effectively ensnared the country in a two-party electoral system while simultaneously keeping Alemán out of prison, a neat trick if you can pull it off.

Despite these Machiavellian manipulations Ortega lost the 2000 presidential elections, though his influence remains at least equal to President Bolaños': the Central American Free Trade Agreement (Cafta; see the boxed text, p32) couldn't pass until the two had a long, probably symbolic, meeting behind closed doors. The real upset was in the Región Autónoma del Atlántico Norte (RAAN; North Atlantic Autonomous Region) where the Yatama political party, blocked from running for office, called on its almost entirely indigenous constituency to boycott the elections. A Sandinista candidate won in Bilwi – a bit shocking in the Contra stronghold – and the World Court ruled that elections were tainted. In the 2005 municipal elections Yatama returned to the ballot and won three major towns.

Banking on similar international pressure against the pact, current presidential candidate Herty Lewites, a much-loved former Managua mayor and the brains behind Hertylandia theme park, has founded his own political party: Alianza Herty. Lewites, a former Sandinista gunrunner and member of the FSLN's inner circle, mistakenly believed that there were primaries for his party's presidential candidates. Daniel Ortega wasted no time correcting Lewites, excommunicating him from the FSLN and forbidding him to use red and black (and, presumably, pink) in his campaign.

Lewites went with baby blue and regularly appeared with the man who should have been his top political rival, Eduardo Montealegre, the Liberal stalwart who refused to play puppet to the not-quite-incarcerated Alemán, and was forced to found Alianza Liberal Nicaragüense – Partido Conservador (ALN-PC) to make his bid for the presidency.

In the meantime, at the time of going to print, most Nicaraguans are just hoping that they get through the November 2006 elections peacefully, if only to keep rising tourism revenues flowing in. There is the sense that if Ortega wins or, worse, if there are violent protests, international investment will flee the country. Regardless, the pluralistic process, and an economy that continues to expand no matter what intrigue is on in Managua, keeps things optimistic on the home front.

THE CULTURE
The National Psyche

Nicaragua has a fierce cultural streak and prides itself on home-grown literature, dance, art, music and cuisine, consciously resisting gnawing globalization at its borders. This spiritual independence is a holdover not only from the revolution and Contra War, it goes back to Spanish colonization when indigenous nations won limited autonomy at enormous personal cost, which was considered worth it.

Nicaragua also still suffers from a bit of post-traumatic stress disorder. Spanish speakers will hear plenty of stories involving tanks, explosions and aerial bombings, not to mention 'the day the family cow wandered into the minefield' stories. Former Sandinistas and Contras work, play and take communion together, however, and any tensions you might expect seem to have been addressed and worked through. Opinions differ about the Sandinista years, but both sides will always agree to a good debate. Jump in and you'll learn more about the political scene than you ever would by reading a paper.

Of course attitudes differ from place to place. Residents of the English- and Miskito-speaking Atlantic Coast rarely consider themselves part of Nicaragua proper, and many would prefer to be returned to the British Empire than suffer further oppression by the 'Spaniards' on the other side of the country. The cattle ranchers of the Central Highlands resist interference from the federal government, while coffee pickers in Matagalpa or students in León are willing to walk to Managua to complain to the government if they perceive that any injustice has been done.

Lifestyle

Nicaragua is a country in motion. One in five Nicas live outside the country, most in the United States, Costa Rica and Honduras. Waves of migration to the cities, which began in the 1950s, have left more than 55% of the population urban. Most internal immigrants are young women, and most go to Managua; men tend to follow the harvest into rural areas and the surrounding countries. Regular jobs are difficult to find, and more than half of employed Nicaraguans are in the 'informal sector' – street vendors, maids, artisans – with no benefits and no job security.

Wealth is distributed unequally, with the moneyed elite living much as they would in Miami or elsewhere, hanging out at the malls, talking on cell phones and driving in SUVs that here, at least, occasionally see a dirt road. For the vast majority of Nicaraguans, however, just putting food on the table is a daily struggle, with 50% living below the international poverty line and perhaps a third of the country subsisting on two meals or less per day; almost one fifth of children are at risk of problems relating to malnourishment.

Women, especially in rural sectors, are likely to work outside of the home, and do half of all agricultural labor. This stems in part from ideals espoused by the Sandinistas, who considered women equal play-ers in the remolding of the country, but also from necessity, as many men died or were maimed during the wars, and later emigrated to find work; after the Contra War, the country was more than 55% female. The strong women's movement is fascinating; check out **Boletina** (www.puntos .org.ni in Spanish) to learn more.

Population

With 5.5 million people spread across 130,000 sq km, Nicaragua is the least densely populated country in Central America, but it's uncommonly diverse. The CIA World Factbook estimates that 69% of the population is mestizo (mixed indigenous and white), 17% white, 9% black and 5% indigenous. Ineter (Nicaraguan Institute of Territorial Studies) claims that almost 500,000 people are indigenous: Miskito (150,000), Mayangna/Sumo (13,500) and Garífuna (7000), all with some African heritage, occupy the Caribbean Coast alongside the Rama (1350), and all are thought to have originated in South America. In the Central and Northern Highlands, the Cacaopoeras and Matagalpas (97,500) may be Maya in origin, while the Chorotegas (82,000), the Subtiavas (40,500) and the Nahoas (19,000) have similarities to the Aztecs.

European heritage is just as diverse. The Spanish settled the Pacific Coast, with a wave of German immigrants in the 1800s leaving the Northern Highlands surprisingly *chele* (white, from *leche,* or milk). Many of those blue eyes you see on the Atlantic Coast can be traced back to British, French and Dutch pirates.

The original African immigrants were shipwrecked, escaped or freed slaves who began arriving almost as soon as the Spanish. Another wave of Creoles and West Indians arrived in the late 1800s to work on the banana and cacao plantations of the east coast. Mix all that together, simmer for a few hundred years, and you get an uncommonly good-looking people who consider racism a bit silly.

SPORTS

It's just not a weekend in Nicaragua without the crack of a baseball bat, but there really are other sports in Nicaragua, though you may have to look.

Football, or soccer, is growing in popularity and the **National Fútbal League** (www.fenifut .org.ni in Spanish) has a website with schedules and stats. The Mexican government, clearly shocked by Nicaraguan indifference to the sport, is building a new 20,000-seat stadium in Managua, which may one day fill.

Cockfighting is another popular spectator sport, where beautiful alpha roosters with knives strapped to their feet slash each other apart in teeny tiny bullrings; it may be fun if you can stomach it. If you can't, check out *Gente de Gallos* magazine, which includes breeding tips, detailed photos and a special history feature in each of its issues.

Bullfights, which take place during *fiestas patronales* (saints days), are considerably less gory as it's illegal to kill the bull. This leaves the exhibition somewhat point-free, but watching drunks try to ride the exasperated bulls is always good fun.

Many towns have pickup soccer, baseball, volleyball and basketball games, and foreigners are more than welcome to join in. Hey, it's an opportunity to interact with the locals without worrying about the subjunctive tenses.

RELIGION

Although Nicaragua's majority religion is Catholic – between 55% and 70% of the country – Nicaraguan Catholicism retains many indigenous elements, as the décor and ceremonies in such churches as San Juan Bautista de Subtiava and Masaya's María Magdelena make clear. Liberation theology also made its mark on Nicaraguan Catholicism, influencing priest and poet Ernesto Cardenal (see the boxed text, p267) to advocate armed resistance to the Somoza dictatorship. Though he was publicly chastised and later defrocked by Pope John Paul II, Cardenal remains a beloved religious leader. Nicaragua's incredible selection of Catholic churches and fascinating *fiestas patronales* remain highlights of the country.

On the Atlantic Coast, Moravian missionaries from Germany began arriving in the early 1800s, and today their red-and-white wooden churches are the centerpieces of many Miskito and Mayangna towns. More recently, over 100 Protestant sects, most US-based and collectively referred to as *evangelistas*, have converted at least 15% of the population; in fact, many of the foreigners you'll meet in rural Nica-

---

TAKE ME OUT TO THE BEISBALL GAME

The best afternoon out in all Nicaragua is appreciating Nicaragua's national pastime: baseball. Americans may want to brush up on the rules, as tourists from other countries will want you to explain what's going on.

Despite the urban myth, Nicaraguan baseball pre-dates the arrival of the United States Marines in 1909, although their presence certainly gave the game a boost. The first recorded baseball series in Nicaragua took place in 1887, when two Bluefields teams – Southern and Four Roses – played a seven-game set. Baseball made its official Pacific Coast debut in 1891, and the first national championship took place in 1915.

The Atlantic and Pacific leagues battled separately for decades, but came together in 1932; an Atlantic team won the season 40-3. Nicaragua would nevertheless rise to become a baseball power, on par with Cuba, the Dominican Republic and the USA, and has produced at least five major-league legends: Tony Chevez, Albert Williams, David Green, Porfirio Altamirano and, of course, Hall of Famer Denis Martinez, for whom the national stadium is named.

The **National Baseball League** (www.ibw.com.ni/~beisnica in Spanish) begins the season November 14 with the *primera vuelta* (first flight) and *segunda vuelta* (second flight), which pit all seven teams – Estelí, Chinandega, León, Granada, Managua, San Fernando (Masaya) and Costa Atlantica (Bluefields) – against each other. The top four go to the semifinals, played between mid-February and March 25. The winners go for seven games March 26 to April 4, when the national champion takes the crown.

Of course, there's no reason to pay extra to see a pro team unless you want to. Municipal and department leagues have free or cheap games almost year-round at stadiums and parks across the country, which is almost more fun.

ragua are missionaries, who may try to convert you too.

Most of Nicaragua's tiny Jewish community fled in 1979, when the country's one synagogue was abandoned and destroyed, but Judaism is beginning to make a comeback, perhaps inspired by current renegade presidential candidate Herty Lewites, son of Jewish immigrants who fled Eastern Europe during WWII. Perhaps most interesting, almost 10% of Nicaraguans say they are atheist or agnostic, unusual in Latin America and a huge relief if you're one too.

ARTS
Literature
Nicaragua, as any book will tell you, is the only country in the world that celebrates literature, particularly poetry, with appropriate passion, revering its writers with a fervor reserved (in more developed countries) for people like Paris Hilton. Both major daily papers run a literary supplement in their Friday editions, high-school kids form poetry clubs, and any campesino picking coffee in the isolated mountains can tell you who the greatest poet in history is: Rubén Darío (see the boxed text, p35), voice of the nation. They will then recite a poem by Darío, quite possibly followed by a few of their own.

The nation's original epic composition, the Nica equivalent to Beowulf or Chanson de Roland, is El Güegüense, a burlesque dating from the 1600s. A morality play of sorts, it pits an indigenous Nicaraguan businessman against corrupt and inept Spanish authorities; using only his sly wit and a few multilingual double entendres, the Nica ends up on top.

León has been home to the nation's greatest poets, including Darío, Azarias H Pallais, Salomon de la Selva and Alfonso Cortés, the last of whom did his best work while going insane in Darío's childhood home. A Rubén Darío tribute site (www .dariana.com) has biographies and bibliographies of major Nicaraguan writers. The most important modern writers include Pablo Antonio Cuadra, a former editor of La Prensa, and Ernesto Cardenal.

One of the few Nicaraguan writers regularly translated into English is Giaconda Belli (www.giocondabelli.com in Spanish),

who was working undercover with the Sandinistas when she won the prestigious Casa de las Americas international poetry prize. Her internationally acclaimed work is both sexual and revolutionary, and is the best way to get a chick's-eye view of Nicaragua in the 1970s.

Music & Dance
Folkloric music and dance received a huge boost from the revolution, which sought to mine Nicaraguan culture for cultural resources rather than import more popular options, quite possibly at great cost. As a result, you'll probably be able to see a musical or dance performance during even a short visit, the most convenient being Noches Verbenas held every Thursday evening at the National Artisans Market in Masaya. Also check at cultural centers, close to the parque central (central park) in most larger towns, or at the municipal theaters in Granada, León and Managua, to see what's on. Fiestas patronales are a good time to catch a performance, which in the Northern Highlands will likely have a polka component.

Polka lovers should keep an eye out for Don Felipe Urrutia's La Flor de Tuna; his native Valle de Tunosa de Estelí is famed for polka masters like Guilbaldo Sosa and Carlos Benavides. Other artists to keep an eye out for include Alejandro Vega Matus, sometimes credited with writing the music for the national anthem; Luis A Delgadillo, founder of the National School of Music and Symphony Orchestra; and Camilo Zapata, known for Solar de Monimbó.

Perhaps the most important musical form is marimba, usually played on xylophones made of precious wood with names like 'The Lovers,' 'Dance of the Black Woman,' and 'Fat Honey,' which you'll enjoy over a cold glass of chichi (mildly alcoholic corn beverage) at some shady parque central. The guardians of this and other traditional forms of Nicaraguan music are the **Mejía Godoy brothers** (www.mejiagodoy.org in Spanish), who you can (and should) catch live in Managua. For the latest in the Nica rock scene, check out popular program **El Expreso Imaginario** (www.ibw.com.ni/~expreso in Spanish) or **Radio Pirata** (pirata.tk). These are radio stations whose websites have lots of info on the music scene.

NICARAGUA

Theater

Traditional music, dance and theater are difficult to separate; all are mixed together with wild costumes to create spectacles that generally also have a religious component plus plenty of fireworks. Pieces you'll see performed by streetside beggars and professional troupes include *La Gigantona*, with an enormous Spanish woman and teeny tiny Nicaraguan guy; the lady in question was probably real. Another common piece is *The Dance of the Old People*, in which an older gentleman woos a sexy grandma, but once she gives in, he starts chasing younger women in the audience.

Modern theater is not well developed in Nicaragua, and only major towns have performance spaces. One of the most successful recent shows has been *El Nica* (see the boxed text, p85), a monologue about being a migrant worker in Costa Rica.

There's also a growing independent film scene, and you can catch very low-budget, usually documentary films, usually with overtly feminist or progressive themes, at cultural centers – but never movie theaters, which show mostly attempted Hollywood blockbusters.

Sculpture & Painting

The oldest artistic tradition in Nicaragua is ceramics, dating from about 2000 BC, with simple, functional vessels, developing into more sculptural representations by around AD 300. By the time the Spanish arrived, Nicaraguan ceramics were complex, artistic and often ceremonial, and indicate a pronounced Aztec influence in both design and decoration. Remember that it's illegal to remove pre-Colombian ceramics from Nicaragua – they can theoretically put you in jail for it.

Today, top-quality ceramics are most famously produced in San Juan de Orient, which is known for colorfully painted fine white clays and heavier, carved pots; in Mozonte, near Ocotal; and at Matagalpa and Jinotega which are renowned for their black ceramics.

Almost as ancient an art, stone carving probably became popular around AD 800, when someone realized that the soft volcanic basalt could be shaped with obsidian tools imported from Mexico and Guatemala. Petroglyphs (see the boxed text,

p140), usually fairly simple, linear drawings carved into the surface of a stone, are all over the country, and it's easy to arrange tours from Isla Ometepe, Granada and Matagalpa.

Stone statues (see the boxed text, p117), expressive and figurative, not to mention tall (one tops 5m) are rarer, but also worth seeing; the best museums are in Granada and Juigalpa. Much finer stone statues are being produced today, using polished, translucent soapstone worked in San Juan de Limay; some of the best examples are in the nearby Estelí cathedral.

Painting apparently arrived with the Spanish (though there's evidence that both statues and petroglyphs were once more vividly colored), the earliest works being mostly religious in nature; the best places to see paintings are in León, at the Museo de Arte Sacre and the Ortiz-Gurdían Foundation.

The latter also traces Nicaraguan painting through the present, including the Romantic and Impressionistic work of Rodrigo Peñalba, who founded the School of Beaux Arts, and the Praxis Group of the 1960s, led by Alejandro Arostegui and possessed of a heavy-handed social realism, depicting hunger, poverty and torture.

In the 1970s, Ernesto Cardenal founded an art colony on the Archipiélago de Solentiname, an isolated group of islands in the southeast corner of Lago de Nicaragua, today internationally renowned for the gem-toned paintings and balsa-wood sculptures that so colorfully (and accurately) capture the tropical landscape. If you can't get to the islands yourself, try the Masaya markets, or any of the art galleries in Managua or Granada.

Murals are another art form that took hold in the 1970s and 1980s, and all over the country (standout cities include León, Estelí and Managua) you'll find incredible pieces; check out www.muralesdeoctubre.com (in Spanish) for a sneak peak at what's going on now. A more venerable form of the art is on display every Semana Santa in the Subtiava neighborhood of León, when 'sawdust carpets,' scenes painstakingly rendered in colored sawdust, are created throughout the neighborhood, then swirled together as religious processions go by.

ENVIRONMENT

About 18.2% of Nicaragua is federally protected as part of 76 different wildlife areas with nine different levels of management. The system is not even close to perfect, and problems with poaching and deforestation are rife. But the government, perhaps inspired by the ability of neighboring Costa Rica to sell a walk in the woods for US$14 per person, has deemed it worth fighting for, and in 2005 it even committed Navy vessels to help save the baby sea turtles (see the boxed text, p48).

Marena (Ministry of Environment & Natural Resources; www.marena.gob.ni) administrates most wildlife areas, often through other public and private organizations. There's a Marena office in most major towns, and while tourism is not its main job, staff may be able to find guides, transportation and lodging for more-difficult-to-access parks. They can at least point you toward folks who can help, which could be, for example, a women's organic coffee collective. Have fun!

The Land

The formation of the Central American Isthmus began about 60 million years ago, only connecting the two massive American continents for the first time three million years ago. Marking the volcanic crush of the Cocos and Caribbean tectonic plates, the Maribios Volcanic Chain is one of the most volcanic places in the world. There are 58 major volcanic formations, including 28 volcanoes and eight crater lakes, including Reserva Natural Laguna de Apoyo, with hotels and a Spanish school, Laguna Tiscapa in downtown Managua, and Laguna Asososca, with no development at all.

Nicaragua's highest mountains, however, are metamorphic, not volcanic, and contiguous with both the Rocky Mountains and Andes; they go by several names, including Cordillera Dariense (after Rubén Darío), and inspired the name of this book's Northern Highlands section. Two of the most accessible reserves up top are Reserva Natural Miraflor, close to Estelí, and Reserva Natural Cerro Apante, a hike from Matagalpa. Or go deeper, to Reserva Natural Macizos de Peñas Blancas, actually part of the largest protected swath of rain forest north of the Amazon, Bosawás (see the boxed text, p219).

La Reserva de Biosfera Bosawás (Bosawás Biosphere Reserve; from Río BOcay, Cerro SAslaya and Río WASouk), 730,000 hectares of humid and tropical and subtropical forest, is also accessible by the largest river in Central America, the Río Coco (560km). The Caribbean lowlands, remarkable for their dry pine savannas and countless wetlands, have four major river systems, and the easiest way in is along the Río San Juan (p275), a Unesco Biosphere reserve.

Nicaragua also has the two largest lakes in Central America, Lago de Managua (1064 sq km) and Lago de Nicaragua (8264 sq km), a freshwater echo of the Caribbean Sea with more than 500 islands, some protected, including the petroglyphs of Isla Zapatera (p129), as well as wonderful wetlands, like Refugio de Vida Silvestre los Guatuzos (Los Guatuzos Wildlife Refuge; p274).

Wildlife
ANIMALS

Nicaragua is home to about 1800 vertebrate species, including 250 mammals, and 30,000 species in total, including 688 bird species (around 500 resident and 150 migratory). While Nicaragua has no endemic bird species, 19 of Central America's 21 endemics are represented here. Nicaragua's spectacular national bird, the turquoise-browed mot-mot, has a distinctive notched tail. Other birds people come to see are the uracas, or huge bluejays, of Isla de Ometepe, the canaries who live inside the fuming crater of Volcán Masaya and beautiful waterfall of Reserva Natural Chocoyero-El Brujo, and beautiful waterfowl of the Río San Juan.

Other visitors are more interested in the undersea wildlife, which on the Pacific side includes tuna, rooster fish and snook. From May to September, you can try for wahoo and dorado, while sailfish bite through to October. Note that deep-sea fishing is more work, as the continental shelf lies further offshore (more than 50km) in Nicaragua than other places. Lago de Nicaragua and the Río San Juan have their own scaly menagerie, including sawfish, the toothy-grinned gaspar, mojarra, guapote, and most importantly, tarpon, as well as the only freshwater sharks in the world.

NICARAGUA'S PARKS & PROTECTED AREAS

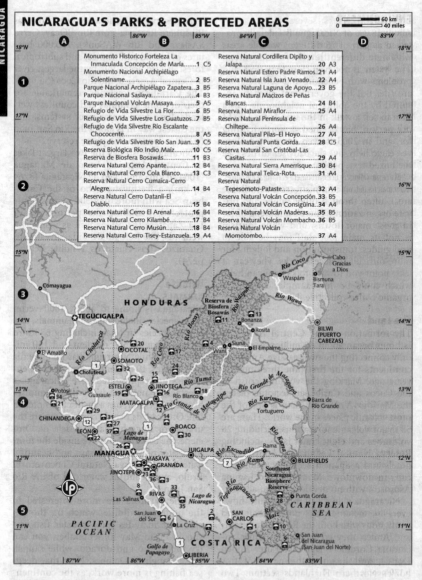

Monumento Historico Fortaleza La Inmaculada Concepción de María......**1** C5	Reserva Natural Cordillera Dipilto y Jalapa..................................**20** A3	
Monumento Nacional Archipiélago Solentiname...............................**2** B5	Reserva Natural Estero Padre Ramos...**21** A4	
Parque Nacional Archipiélago Zapatera..**3** B5	Reserva Natural Isla Juan Venado......**22** A4	
Parque Nacional Saslaya.................**4** B3	Reserva Natural Laguna de Apoyo.....**23** B5	
Parque Nacional Volcán Masaya........**5** A5	Reserva Natural Macizos de Peñas Blancas..................................**24** B4	
Refugio de Vida Silvestre La Flor.......**6** B5	Reserva Natural Miraflor................**25** A4	
Refugio de Vida Silvestre Los Guatuzos..**7** B5	Reserva Natural Península de Chiltepe...............................**26** A4	
Refugio de Vida Silvestre Río Escalante Chococente.............................**8** A5	Reserva Natural Pilas–El Hoyo.........**27** A4	
Refugio de Vida Silvestre Río San Juan..**9** C5	Reserva Natural Punta Gorda...........**28** C5	
Reserva Biológica Río Indio Maíz........**10** C5	Reserva Natural San Cristóbal–Las Casitas.................................**29** A4	
Reserva de Biosfera Bosawás............**11** B3	Reserva Natural Sierra Amerrisque.....**30** B4	
Reserva Natural Cerro Apante...........**12** B4	Reserva Natural Telica-Rota............**31** A4	
Reserva Natural Cerro Cola Blanco......**13** C3	Reserva Natural Tepesomoto-Pataste..................**32** A4	
Reserva Natural Cerro Cumaica-Cerro Alegre.................................**14** B4	Reserva Natural Volcán Concepción..**33** B5	
Reserva Natural Cerro Datanlí-El Diablo.................................**15** B4	Reserva Natural Volcán Consigüina....**34** A4	
Reserva Natural Cerro El Arenal.........**16** B4	Reserva Natural Volcán Maderas.......**35** B5	
Reserva Natural Cerro Kilambé..........**17** B4	Reserva Natural Volcán Mombacho....**36** B5	
Reserva Natural Cerro Musún............**18** B4	Reserva Natural Volcán Momotombo..................**37** A4	
Reserva Natural Cerro Tisey-Estanzuela..**19** A4		

Endangered Species

Nicaragua has about 200 species on the endangered list, including four types of sea turtles (see the boxed text, p48) and two types of iguanas, both traditional food sources, as well as boa constrictors and alligators, which will feed your family in a pinch. Golden frogs and blood frogs, like amphibians across the globe, are also dwindling. Endangered birds include quetzals, peregrine falcons and macaws, with two of Central America's last viable population in Reserva Natural Volcán Cosigüina and Reserva Indio-Maíz. Several endangered or threatened mammals also make their homes here, including howler, white face and spider monkeys; several kids of cats, including jaguars and mountain lions; as well as aquatic species like manatee and dolphins. Offshore fisheries are being, or have been, depleted of oysters, lobster, green turtles and all manner of fish.

PLANTS

Nicaragua has four major life zones, each with very different ecosystems and plant life. Dry Tropical Forests are perhaps the least impressive but also the rarest, as their location – below 500m, often right by the beach – and seven-month dry season make them perfect places to plant crops and build resort hotels. Most plants lose their leaves by January, except in the largest remaining mangrove stand in the world, partially pre-served as Reserva Natural Isla Juan Venado and Reserva Natural Estero Padre Ramos.

The North-Central Subtropical Forests vary widely in altitude (100m to 2107m), temperature and rainfall (800mm to 2000mm), with three main classifications: Subtropical Dry Forest, with sandy acidic soils and four species of pine trees (this is their southernmost natural border) can be seen in the RAAN and Segovias, including Jalapa, with access via private reserves; Humid Tropical Forests, with poor soils that make for lousy farming and are there-fore still intact; and Cloud Forest, above 1200m, with epiphytes, mosses, lichens and lots of orchids, which you can see at Reserva Natural Cerro Datanlí-El Diablo, among many other places.

WHEN THE EARTH MOVES   Robert Olson

Geology doesn't often move fast, but when it does, as in Nicaragua, it can be devastating. The greatest hazard in Nicaragua is landslides, which can and have buried entire villages. Volcanoes produce unstable slopes, and when heavy rains come the slopes give way. The worst is called a *lahar*, a river of mud that that can remove bridges, towns and roads; this was the cause of most deaths during Hurricane Mitch, when the crater lake of Volcán Casita gave way, killing 3600 people. But volcanic eruptions, tsunamis and earthquakes are also issues.

So what causes all of this exciting geology? Plate tectonics. Nicaragua, like most of Central America, is on the Caribbean Plate, which is stationary. The Cocos Plate, to the west, is moving east and colliding with the Caribbean Plate. (The velocity of this collision is about 10cm per year, or about four times as fast as your fingernails grow). Since something must give way, the Cocos Plate descends beneath the Caribbean Plate, a process called subduction.

The Cocos Plate, which has been detected 40km below the surface, is composed of rock that is less dense than that of the Caribbean Plate, and saturated with seawater. When this rock reaches a depth of a few kilometers, it melts and rises through the overlying rock, reaching the surface as volcanoes. Nicaragua has 28 volcanoes, some rising to nearly 1800m, and all within about 50km of the Pacific coast. Most are considered inactive, but that is a relative term.

Plate motion creates other interesting geology. Just west, on the Cocos Plate, are remnants of ocean floor spreading centers with pillow lavas and black smokers. Because some of the Cocos Plate is being scraped off to pile up on top of the Caribbean Plate, the West Coast of Nicaragua is littered with recognizable pillow lavas, which look like pillows, but can be as large as automobiles! These can be hard to find because only geologists care about them, but keep your eyes open.

The process of subduction causes stress to build up in the plates, and it is relieved by earth-quakes. Because many of the earthquakes occur beneath the Pacific, they cause tsunamis. The earthquake and tsunami of September 1992 caused waves up to 10m to strike the coast. At least 170 people died and 13,000 were left homeless. Earlier tsunamis occurred in 1854 and 1902.

Earthquakes have shaped Nicaragua as well. Not only did the 1972 earthquake devastate Managua, but a 1931 quake had already initiated discussion about relocating the city. And in 2000, two earthquakes in two days destroyed villages to the southeast.

Plate motion also created Lago de Nicaragua which, with an area exceeding 9000 sq km, was once a part of the Pacific. It was separated from the Pacific by uplift of the land which now forms the coast, and by accumulation of volcanic deposits. It gradually became a freshwater lake, but still contains some saltwater fish species.

PARKS & RESERVES IN NICARAGUA

Major park or natural area	Features	Activities
Parque Nacional Volcán Masaya (p100)	most heavily venting volcano in Central America, possibly gateway to hell; lava tunnels; parakeets	driving to the edge of an active crater, bird-watching, hiking
Reservas Natural Volcán Concepción and Volcán Maderas (p138)	one island, two volcanoes: gently smoking Concepción and dormant Maderas, crowned in cloud forest	hiking, petroglyph hunting, swimming, kayaking
Refugio de Vida Silvestre Río San Juan (p260)	epic riverboat ride, stunning Spanish fortress, island art colony, macaws, trees full of egrets, giant tarpon	canoeing, kayaking, shopping, hot springs, fishing, horseback rides
Reserva de Biosfera Bosawás (p228)	largest reserve in Central America, gold mines	testing your limits, trail-less hikes, shopping
Reserva Natural Cerro Musún (p242)	quetzals, cloud forests, huge waterfalls, real trails	hiking, birdwatching, swimming
Reserva Natural Miraflor (p197)	cloud-forest reserve innovatively managed by agricultural cooperative: it's nature and culture!	milking cows, hiking, swimming in waterfalls, admiring orchids
Reserva Natural Cerro Tisey-Estanzuela (p198)	cloud forests, views across the Maribios volcanic chain, goat cheese	hiking, swimming, eating cheese
Reserva Natural Tepesomoto-Pataste (p205)	the Río Coco is born – in the 'Grand Canyon' of Nicaragua	Hiking, rock scrambles, freezing cold water
Reserva Natural Isla Juan Venado (p176)	Sandy Pacific barrier island; mangroves, sea turtles, lagoons	boating, surfing, camping, swimming
Parque Nacional Archipiélago Zapatera (p129)	isolated islands covered with petroglyphs, ancient statues, small volcano, rustic accommodations	climbing, hiking, boating, pretending you're an archaeologist
Refugio de Vida Silvestre La Flor (p157)	leatherback & Olive Ridley turtles, primary dry tropical forest, beaches	surfing, camping, sea turtle ogling
Reserva Natural Volcán Mombacho (p128)	volcanic views of Granada and Cocibolca, dwarf cloud forest, 100 species of orchids, fumeroles	hiking, camping, riding in military transport, butterfly garden
Reserva Natural Volcán Cosigüina (p189)	5 reserves, 6 active volcanoes, hot springs, crater lakes, macaws, archaeological sites, boiling mudpits	volcano surfing, hiking, camping, swimming, facial mud masks

The Central Subtropical Forests of Boaco and Chontales have been largely devoured up by cattle ranches, and while there are a few reserves, including Reserva Natural Sierra Amerisque, access to these areas is limited. Just to the east are the Caribbean lowlands, where there are swamps and thick, dense foliage that you can see on the riverboat ride from El Rama.

Endangered Species

Nicaragua has lost about 90% of its original forest since the 1930s, although the revolution and Contra War put a halt to much of the harvest. But as the mines have been cleared and paramilitary groups captured, the logging companies have begun moving in fast – there were only 22 timber companies in 1992, compared to 600 in 1995.

The Indio Maíz and Bosawás Biosphere Reserves are two of the largest preserved tracts of rain forest in the world, forming the core of the proposed Mesoamerican Biological Corridor, which will one day (hopefully) allow species to pass freely through wild jungle between North and South America. Unfortunately, illegal logging operations seem unstoppable, and the mysterious five-year moratorium on a ban on exporting mahogany, a slow-growing precious wood, threatens even more forests.

But what seems unstoppable is the migration eastward of small farmers hoping to carve out a subsistence living from the natural reserves. Since the Somoza era, these unpopulated lands have been considered a 'political safety valve,' one not yet shut off. As the land often occupied is usually humid tropical forest, which keeps most of its nutrients as biomass tied up in trees and plants, the soil usually only has enough oomph for two or three harvests, when the would-be farmer has to slash and burn another farm from the jungle.

FOOD & DRINK

Although Nicaraguan food lacks the sophisticated complexity of French or Peruvian cuisine, not to mention the spices of Mexican food (although there's usually a homemade *chilero,* jar of pickled peppers, carrots and onions, on the table), it's good, cheap and healthy. Granada, Managua and San Juan del Sur all have international eateries, which are a wonderful thing if you need a break from rice and beans, but they tend to be expensive and only OK. But if you prefer a taste of the local culture, there are plenty of places to start.

Staples & Specialties

Most Nicaraguans start and finish every day with *gallo pinto,* rice and beans cooked separately and then fried together (on the Atlantic Coast, in coconut milk). Granada's light signature dish, *vigarón,* is made with yucca and cabbage salad, and topped with a big *chicharon,* or pork skin, while heftier *quesillos* are like mozzarella cheese, sautéed onions and sour cream burritos – yum.

Güirílas hail from the Matagalpa highlands; they're rich pancakes made with fresh corn and griddle fried, then served with *cuijada,* a soft crumbly cheese. Tripe soup, also called *mondongo,* is a Central Meseta specialty, but also keep an eye open for *sopa huevos del toro,* or 'eggs of the bull soup,' made from another surprisingly appetizing part of the bull.

Nacatamales, often only available on Sundays, pack a banana leaf with cornmeal *masa,* potato, pork, tomato, onion and sweet chilies steamed to greasy perfection. *Tamal rellenos* have a sweet cheese filling, *tamugas* use sticky rice instead of cornmeal, while *yoltamals* are made with fresh corn, and usually come in their own husk. *Baho* (pronounced bow), what's steaming in those kettles at parks and markets, is another weekend specialty involving plantains, yucca, cassava and other vegetables steamed together with spicy pork, topped with cabbage salad.

The Caribbean Coast may have better food, most famously *rondon,* a slow-cooked seafood-and-coconut stew you should order well in advance . Don't miss coconut bread, usually sold fresh from private homes, or the enormous river shrimp of the Río San Juan. The Miskito and Mayangna people's signature dish is *wabul,* made with mashed plantains, milk and perhaps cacao, and is served hot.

Rosquillas are simple corn bread rings, made to be served with coffee, which can be seasoned with cheese, spices or cinnamon for desert. Other sweets include *bunuelos,* a Semana Santa tradition made with fried cassava stuffed with cheese and sugar, topped with hot syrup; *cajetas* made by combining fruit, milk, sugar, cinnamon and perhaps some grated coconut; and *picos,* common triangle-shaped sweetbreads stuffed with sticky-sweet *cuajada* cheese, sugar and cinnamon.

Drinks

Believe it or not, the coffee may be your big disappointment. Though Nicaragua produces some of the best coffee in the world, most places outside the Northern Highlands and tourist zones serve Presto instant. Sigh. Note that a *café con leche* may be a cup of hot milk that you stir the coffee crystals into.

Rum drinkers, on the other hand, will love Flor de Caña rum, usually ordered by the half liter with a bottle of Coke, tub of ice and bowl of sliced limes, and called a *servicio completo*. The same company also makes the country's two major beers, Victoria and Toña.

Pinol is so beloved by Nicaraguans that they call themselves *pinoleros*, but this beverage, made of toasted corn powder, should be sweetened or taken with cacao (chocolate) as *tiste* the first time. *Chicha* is the bright pink corn beverage, and if it's called *chicha bruja* (witch chicha) or *chicha fuerte* (strong chicha), it's been fermented into an alcoholic beverage, an indigenous tradition.

Refrescos, also called *naturales* or *batidas,* are fruit drinks blended with either water or milk (sometimes yogurt or orange juice), served sweet unless you specifically request it *sin azucar* (without sugar). Be sure to try bright purple *pithaya* and creamy, rich *semilla de jícara.*

Where to Eat & Drink

Comedors are very basic eateries that usually serve eggs and *gallo pinto* for breakfast and a cheap (US$1.50 to US$3) *comida corriente* (set plate) the rest of the day, usually consisting of rice, beans, fried plantains (*tostones* are the hard-fried savory ones, *repochetas* are the sticky-sweet brown ones), cabbage salad and some type of meat. *Sodas* are more of a Costa Rican term for small restaurant with a menu, but you'll still find them near the southern border. *Fritangas* are temporary stands that set up each evening and sell inexpensive grilled meats, fried foods and (surprise) rice and beans, sometimes on a banana leaf in Granada or a plastic bag at bus stations everywhere. Steam-table buffets let you point and choose from an array of mains and sides, but try to go as early during mealtime as possible.

Vegetarians & Vegans

The biggest problem vegetarians will have in Nicaragua won't be staying full – that's a cinch (well, as long as you don't inquire too deeply into the origins of the grease your

gallo pinto was cooked in). It'll be boredom. Love rice and beans? Good. Because that's what you'll be eating pretty much every day, along with a scrambled egg, fried plantains, hunk of cheese, cabbage-based salad and tortilla. Don't be jealous; your carnivorous pals are eating the same thing, but with the added option of stewed or fried meat.

Steam-table buffets are another good option, where you can point to several vegetarian sides and make your own meal. Vegans will have a hard time getting enough protein, so take advantage of city grocery stores to stock up on snacks.

Eating with Kids

Although few restaurants actually have children's menus, all will try (unless they're extremely busy) to accommodate finicky kids. Nicaraguan cuisine is fairly bland, and you're usually safe with *gallo pinto* and *refrescos.* Nicaraguans also seem much more accommodating of unruly behavior than in North America and Europe, and will make a community effort to entertain distressed young diners.

MANAGUA

pop 1,400,000 / elevation 90m

Sprawling along the silvery edges of Xolotlán, broad Lago de Managua, this is the nation's capital and nerve center, an admittedly unlovely urban expanse of unsigned, tree-lined boulevards and uninspired modern monoliths that almost never seduce visitors into spending more time here than is absolutely necessary.

Yet this sultry and seismic 'Daughter of War' and 'City of Peace' is beloved with a proud ferocity by its 1.4 million inhabitants, and its volcanic skyline and cosmopolitan charms have inspired a library's worth of poems. Aren't you curious as to why?

Start by ascending Loma de Tiscapa to Sandino's famous silhouette, with views from the ancient crater lake to monumental Volcán Momotombo (not to mention the wacky cathedral). And around you the city pulses, with great nightlife, excellent restaurants and, most importantly, thousands of families rebuilding their nation, *poco a poco* (little by little), into all that

NAVIGATING MANAGUA

As in other Nicaraguan cities and towns, only Managua's major roads are named. Large buildings, *rotondas* (traffic circles) and traffic lights serve as de facto points of reference, and locations are described in terms of their direction and distance, usually in *cuadras* (blocks) from these points. Many of these reference points no longer exist, and thus addresses may begin with something like *'de donde fue Sandy's'* (from where Sandy's used to be...).

From the reference point, a special system is used for the cardinal points, whereby *al lago* (to the lake) means 'north' while *a la montaña* (to the mountains) means 'south.' *Arriba* (up) is 'east' toward the sunrise, while *abajo* (down) is 'west,' and sunset. Thus one might hear: *'del antiguo Cine Dorado, una cuadra al lago y dos cuadras arriba'* ('from the old Cine Dorado, one block toward the lake and two blocks up').

Confused? So are we. Most listings in this chapter give the 'address' in Spanish, so you can ask locals for help or just let the cab driver figure it out.

their poets and revolutionaries, campesinos and visionaries, once promised.

HISTORY

A fishing encampment as early as 6000 years ago (see p76), Managua has been an important trading center and regional capital for at least two millennia. When Spanish chronicler Fernandez de Oviedo arrived in 1528, he estimated Managua's population at around 40,000; most of these original inhabitants fled to the Sierritas, the small mountains just south, shortly after the Spanish arrived. The small town, without even a hospital or school until the 1750s, didn't really achieve any prominence until 1852, when the seemingly endless civil war between Granada and León was resolved by placing the capital here.

The clever compromise might have worked out better had a geologist been on hand: Managua sits atop a network of fault lines that have shaped its history ever since. The late 1800s were rocked by quakes that destroyed the new capital's infrastructure, with churches and banks crumbling as the ground flowed beneath their feet. In 1931 the epicenter was the stadium, which killed dozens during the big game; in 1968 a single powerful jolt right beneath what's now Metrocentro Mall destroyed an entire neighborhood.

And on the evening of December 23, 1972, a series of powerful tremors rocked the city, culminating in a 6.2 quake that killed 11,000 people and destroyed 53,000 homes. The blatant siphoning of international relief funds by President Somoza touched off the Sandinista-led revolution, which was followed by the Contra War, and the city center, including the beautiful old cathedral, was never rebuilt.

ORIENTATION

The Interamericana (Pan-American Hwy) enters Managua from the southwest, via Jinotepe, as Carr Sur, and exits to the northeast, past the airport toward Matagalpa and El Rama, as Carr Norte. Running southeast from Metrocentro and Rotonda Rubén Darío is Carr Masaya, along which Managua's swankiest discos, restaurants and malls can be found. Heading west are Carr Nueva and Carr Vieja (New and Old Hwys) to León. Managua has hundreds of neighborhoods stretched between these highways, and not even the kamikaze *taxistas* (taxi drivers) know them all (although they will assure you that they do).

Zona Monumental, on the lakefront site of Managua's pre-1972 downtown, is home to the Museo Nacional, Casa Presidencial (Presidential Palace) and Teatro Rubén Darío. It's connected by Av Bolívar, a major thoroughfare, to the Plaza Inter shopping mall, Loma de Tiscapa and Barrio Martha Quezada, with most services for budget travelers. To the southwest are Barrio Balonia, with midrange accommodations, and Plaza España, next to Rotonda El Güegüense, with banks, travel agencies and airline offices.

To the southeast is Managua's modern commercial center, a 2km strip of Carr Masaya extending southeast from Metrocentro Mall and Rotonda Rubén Darío through the cluster of glittering restaurants and bars known as Zona Rosa, as well as swish Los

NICARAGUA

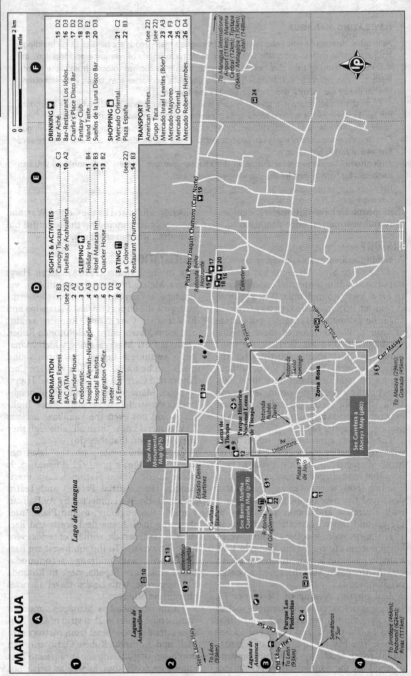

MANAGUA

INFORMATION
American Express	**1** B3
BAC ATM	(see 22)
Ben Linder House	**2** A2
Credomatic	**3** C4
Hospital Alemán-Nicaragüense	**4** A3
Hospital Bautista	**5** C3
Immigration Office	**6** D2
Ineter	**7** D2
US Embassy	**8** A3

SIGHTS & ACTIVITIES
Canopy Tiscapa	**9** C3
Huellas de Acahualinca	**10** A2

SLEEPING
Holiday Inn	**11** B4
Hotel Maracas Inn	**12** B3
Quacker House	**13** B2

EATING
La Colonia	(see 22)
Restaurant Churrasco	**14** B3

DRINKING
Bar Aché	**15** D2
Bar-Restaurant Los Idolos	**16** D3
Charlie's Place Disco Bar	**17** D2
Fantasy Club	**18** D2
Island Taste	**19** E2
Sueños de la Luna Disco Bar	**20** D3

SHOPPING
Mercado Oriental	**21** C2
Plaza España	**22** B3

TRANSPORT
American Airlines	(see 22)
Grupo Taca	(see 22)
Mercado Israel Lewites (Boer)	**23** A3
Mercado Mayoreo	**24** F3
Mercado Oriental	**25** C2
Mercado Roberto Huembes	**26** D4

0   1 mile
0   2 km

Lago de Managua

Laguna de Acahualinca

Laguna de Asososca

New León HWY
To León (93km)

Old León Hwy
To León (93km)

Carr Sur

Parque Las Piedrecitas

To Jinotepe (46km); Pochomil (62km); Rivas (111km)

Semáforos 7 Sur

Cementerio Occidental

Estadio Denis Martínez

Cranshaw Stadium

Rotonda El Güegüense

Plaza 19 de Julio

Loma de Tiscapa

Parque Histórico Nacional Loma de Tiscapa

Av Universitaria

Rotonda Rubén Darío

Rotonda Santo Domingo

Zona Rosa

Rotonda Bello Horizonte

Cemetery

Pista Pedro Joaquín Chamorro (Carr Norte)

El Bypass

Pista Portezuelo

Carr Masaya

To Masaya (29km); Granada (45km)

See Carretera a Masaya Map (p80)

See Area Monumental Map (p75)

See Barrio Martha Quezada Map (p78)

To Managua International Airport (11km); Marena Central (12km); Tipitapa (26km); Matagalpa (133km); Estelí (148km)

MANAGUA IN ...

One Day

If you wake up in Barrio Martha Quezada, you can just walk to the top of **Loma de Tiscapa** (p74) and the unmissable silhouette of **Sandino** (see the boxed text, p222). Then grab a cab (negotiating your fare beforehand!) to **Huellas de Acahualinca** (p76) for ancient history, then **Zona Monumental** (p74) for the modern version. If nothing's on at **Teatro Nacional Rubén Darío** (p84) that night, enjoy a mellow evening of live music at **La Casa de los Mejía Godoy** (p84) or dance the night away at **Hipa Hipa** (p84).

Three Days

After communing with Sandino and Momotombo, you'll even have time to take the **Tiscapa Canopy Tour** (p74), then really enjoy the museums and monuments, grabbing tickets for **El Nica** (see the boxed text, p85) at Teatro Nacional Rubén Darío; discuss afterward at **Bar La Cavanga (p84)**. The next morning, check out the beaches of **Pochomil** (p88) or the mountains of **Montibelli Reserva Privada** (p91), then show off your tan on the **Zona Rosa** that night. Day three is shopping: grab souvenirs at **Mercado Roberto Huembes** (p85) or resupply for the hinterlands at the markets and malls. After lunch in exclusive Altamira, perhaps **Ola Verde** (see the boxed text, p81), stop by the **Nueva Catedral** (p76), then have a nap before hitting **Bello Horizonte** (see the boxed text, p83) for your last night out.

Robles and Altamira, two of Managua's most exclusive neighborhoods. West of Rotonda Rubén Darío is Universidad Centro America (UCA) with left-wing bookstores and microbuses to most major regional cities, including Granada and Masaya.

Mercado Israel Lewites, where there are buses to northwest Nicaragua and Carazo, is about 3km west of UCA on Pista de la Resistencia, while Mercado Roberto Huembes, with great souvenir shopping and buses to Granada and southwest Nicaragua, is southwest of Metrocentro. Further west still is Mercado Mayoreo, where there are buses to northwest Nicaragua and the Caribbean Coast. Managua International Airport is 11km west of town on Carr Norte.

MAPS

Free maps of Managua are widely available at Intur and most hotels, but none of them are particularly detailed. If you're headed out into wilder Nicaragua, pick up topos and maps of Nicaragua's major protected areas at **Marena Central** (☎ 263 2830; www.marena.gob.ni; Km 12.5 Carr Norte; ☼ 8am-4pm Mon-Fri), or check out **Ineter** (Nicaragua Institute for Territorial Studies; Map p70; ☎ 249 2768; frente Imigración Extranjera; ☼ 8-11:30am & 1-4pm Mon-Fri), which has excellent maps of the entire country.

INFORMATION

Managua is a modern city that's (arguably) designed for the automotive age, as opposed to a strollable colonial town. It's also hot and sticky: daytime temperatures hover between 30°C and 34°C most of the year, only dipping into the 20s in December and January, and cooling off with afternoon showers during the May to September rainy season. Moreover, Managua has big-city problems, including plenty of crime and a bus system that's not exactly user friendly. Unless you're a committed shoestringer or have a rental car, chances are you'll be getting to most of these destinations in a taxi.

Bookstores & Libraries

Managua has a great selection of bookstores – if you can read Spanish. There are better selections of English-language books in San Juan del Sur and Granada. UCA and UNAN (see p73) both have excellent libraries.

Biblioteca Banco Central de Nicaragua (☎ 265 0131; Km 7 Carr Sur, 150m este) Also has art openings and other events.

Casa de los Tres Mundos (Map p80; La Marseilles, 2½c norte; ☼ 8am-5pm Mon-Fri) Artsy and lefty Spanish-language books.

El Parnaso (Map p80; ☎ 270 5178; ☼ 9am-6pm Mon-Fri, 9am-3pm Sat) Across from the UCA, this lefty bookstore also has a great selection of magazines.

La Colonia (Map p70; Plaza España; Rotonda Jean Paul Genie 1c sur, Carr Masaya) This upscale grocery chain has a big selection of books and magazines; the Plaza España outlet is great.

Librería Hispamer (Map p80; ☎ 278 3923; www .hispamer.com.ni) One block east, one block south of UCA, Hispamer has the country's best selection of Nicaraguan and Latin American literature, history and poetry, plus local news and arts periodicals.

Plaza Inter (Map p78; Plaza Inter; ☒ 9am-9pm) Near Barrio Martha Quezada, the parking-lot level at the mall has a stand selling beat-up paperback thrillers and old lefty lit – in English.

Cultural Centers

Ben Linder House (Map p70; ☎ 266 4363; www .casabenlinder.org; Monseñor Lezcano, de donde fue el Banco Popular, 2c al lago, 2c arriba) Named for an American engineer and unicycle clown who was killed by Contra forces in 1987, this cultural center primarily serves the English-speaking volunteer community, with weekly presentations and discussion groups Thursday at 8:30am, but stop by anytime to see the amazing murals and chat.

Centro Budista Bodhichita (Map p78; ☎ 268 2541; centrobudistanic@yahoo.com.mx; Estatua Montoya 1c abajo, ½c al lago) Meditation and related classes.

Centro Cultural Managua (Map p75; ☎ 222 5291) One block south of the Plaza de la República, with changing art exhibits, concerts and dances, plus handicrafts fairs the first Saturday of the month.

Códice Espacio Cultural (Map p80; ☎ 267 2635; www.galeriacodice.com; Hotel Colon 1c sur, 2½c arriba) Not just the hippest progressive art exhibition space in the country, its mix of openings, unusual performances and other offbeat offerings make this the place to hook up with Managua's creative elite.

Emergency

Ambulance (Cruz Roja; Red Cross; ☎ 128)
Fire (☎ emergency 115, ☎ 222 6406)
Police (☎ emergency 118, ☎ 249 5714)

Immigration Office

Immigration office (Direccion de Migración y Extranjeria; Map p70; ☎ 265 0014; ☒ 8-11:30am & 1:30-3pm Mon-Fri) Stays can be extended for up to three months for US$25 per month. The office is 200m north of the Tenderí traffic signal near the Ciudad Jardín area. There's a US$1.50 per-day fine for overstaying your allotted period (three months for US citizens, one month for most others, which is just odd).

Internet Access

Internet access is fast and plentiful, averaging US$0.70 per minute at cafés all over town. Internet cafés in Barrio Martha Quezada include:

In Touch Internet (Map p80; per hr US$0.70) Close to Hotel Colón.

Internet Posada de Ruth (Map p78; per hr US$0.70; ☒ 8am-10pm) Across from Shannon Bar.

Kafe Internet (Map p78; per hr US$0.70; ☒ 8am-8pm Mon-Sat, 9am-6pm Sun) Pay for half-hour increments in advance.

Plaza Inter (Map p78; per hr US$2.50; ☒ 10am-10pm) Ground floor, offers plush seats.

Laundry

Laundry services are sadly lacking here, but most hotels offer laundry (in cheaper places, by hand, so allow time to dry). If your hotel doesn't do laundry, try the one next door.

Media

Six major TV channels arebased in Managua; the most popular is **Canal 2** (www.canal2tv .com), with trusted news. Scores of radio stations, mostly play reggae, Mexican *norteños*, Shakira or soft rock of the '70s and '80s, but be sure to tune into **Radio Sandino** (AM 740; www .lasandino.com.ni), with left-wing news, views and folk music; **Radio Ya** (FM 90.1; www.nuevaya.com.ni), the popular FSLN station; and **Radio Pirata** (FM 99.9; http://pirata.tk), a heavy-metal, blues and grunge antidote to Air Supply overload.

MAGAZINES

Between the Waves Ignore the gorgeous, scantily clad cover model (or don't), this great English-language quarterly has tourist information, bus schedules and in-depth stories about Nicaragua's neatest destinations.

Magazine Published weekly by *La Prensa,* this glossy magazine is free for subscribers and worth hunting down by anyone else for articles like 'Daniel Ortega and Arnoldo Alemán in High School.' (They were both mediocre students with discipline problems, if you were wondering.)

Nicaragua's Best Guide (www.guideofnicaragua.com) A slick online magazine with lots of reviews, articles and free downloadable maps.

NEWSPAPERS

El Mercurio It's never available anywhere remotely respectable, but you can practice your Spanish with brutally illustrated car-accident stories or soft-core porn that may begin, 'When I first joined the revolutionary army, I didn't realize it was co-ed...'

El Nuevo Diario (www.elnuevodiario.com.ni) Once upon a time the FSLN mouthpiece, the more sensationalistic (this is a good thing) and still left-wing daily also has a fine Sunday humor edition, *El Alacran*, which adds excellent captions to the week's news photos, as well as a competing Thursday entertainment insert.

La Prensa (www.l aprensa.com.ni) Nicaragua's blue-chip, right-wing newspaper is worth picking up on Thursday for *Viernes Chiquito,* an entertainment supplement, and on Sunday for *El Azote,* with political cartoons and *Muro de Fermin,* a sharp 'funny' featuring a witty Nica couple who live in a one-room shanty, corrugated tin roof secured by an old tire, with their (at least) nine kids.

Medical Services

There are scores of pharmacies, some open 24 hours (just knock), and nine hospitals in Managua, including:

Hospital Alemán-Nicaragüense (Map p70; ☎ 249 3368; Km 6 Carr Norte) Has some German-speaking staff and modern equipment.

Hospital Bautista (Map p70; ☎ 249 7070, 249 7277) This was Managua's best hospital, and still has much of the country's top health-care facilities; some staff members speak English.

Hospital Metropolitano Vivian Pellas (☎ 255 6900; www.metropolitano.com.ni; Km 9.75 Carr Masaya) This new, US$23 million state-of-the-art hospital is Central America's most advanced, with one of the best child burn units in the world. Pellas, matriarch of Nicaragua's wealthiest family – Flor de Caña rum, Toña and Victoria beer, Toyota, Dollar, Credomatic, BAC, and that's just for starters – was burned on over 40% of her body in a horrific 1991 plane crash that killed 150 people, and decided to make sure that others in her situation would get the best treatment possible.

Money

Also thanks to the Pellas family (see above) and Credomatic (Map p70), you can probably use Visa, MasterCard and Amex more often in Nicaragua than back home. Traveler's checks, basically useless elsewhere in the country, can be changed at either **Banco America Central** (BAC; Map p70; www.credomatic.com /nic; Plaza España) or the **American Express office** (Map p70; ☎ 266 4050; Viajes Atlántida office; ⏰ 8:30am-5pm Mon-Fri, 8:30am-noon Sat). Managua has scores of banks and ATMs, most on the Visa/Plus system. BAC, with machines at Metrocentro Mall (Map p80), the international airport, Plaza España (Map p70) and the Esso station (Map p78) just north of Plaza Inter, accepts MasterCard/Cirrus debit cards and gives US dollars and córdoba. Any bank can change US dollars. *Coyotes,* black-market moneychangers, are generally honest (but you should know roughly how much to expect back) and use the same exchange rates as the bank; try Plaza España.

Post & Telephone

Enitel is adjacent to Palacio de Correos. More convenient and cheaper are the millions of Internet cafés with inexpensive international calls, or using Enitel phone cards, available at *pulperías* (convenience stores) everywhere, for local and national calls. Private rental phones (available at many shops and hotels) are convenient but expensive.

Palacio de Correos (Map p75; ⏰ 8am-5pm Mon-Fri, 8am-1pm Sat) Two blocks west of the Plaza de la República is the main post office (the former Enitel building). *Lista de correo* (poste restante) mail goes here and is held for up to 45 days. An Express Mail office is also here.

Tourist Information

Intur Central (Map p78; Nicaraguan Institute of Tourism; ☎ 222 3333; www.intur.gob.ni; Crowne Plaza 1c sur, 1c oeste) The flagship office of Nicaragua's official tourist info organization, in Barrio Martha Quezada, has heaps of flyers and other useful info, and can point you to hotels and other services in Managua and throughout the country. There's another office in the international terminal at the airport.

Marena Central (Ministry of the Environment & Natural Resources; ☎ 263 2830; www.marena.gob.ni; Km 12.5 Carr Norte; ⏰ 8am-4pm Mon-Fri) Bring ID to the inconveniently located headquarters (out past the airport, a US$6 taxi ride) to access maps, flyers and management plans for most of Nicaragua's 82 protected areas.

Universities

Universidad Centro America (UCA; Map p80; www .uca.edu.ni) Founded in 1960 as a Jesuit school, this is one of Nicaragua's premier universities, with a science and alternative-technology-heavy curriculum, Che Guevara sculptures and vegetarian eateries out front. Worth a wander, in particular the Centro Historia Militar, with relics from Sandino to the Sandinistas, if you're beginning to worry that the revolution is over.

Universidad Nacional Autónoma de Nicaragua (UNAN; Map p80; ☎ 278 6769; www.unan.edu.ni; Enel Central 2 Km al sur) The Managua branch of Nicaragua's oldest university (the original is in León, the former capital) was founded in 1958 and has more than 24,000 students.

DANGERS & ANNOYANCES

Managuans seem almost proud that the city is dangerous; strangers will warn you constantly to watch your bag and back, not realizing their own friendly concern is the norm. Statistically, Managua is the safest Central American capital (though it sure doesn't feel like it); most travelers have no problems.

Still, as a 'rich foreigner' you will be targeted, so be smart. Around Tica Bus, Barrio

Martha Quezada and Plaza Inter Mall, just assume that you are being watched. Stay alert, walk confidently, and leave backpacks, purses, passports and important documents in your hotel. ATM machines are under constant surveillance – see those adorable tots on bicycles? Yeah, them. Take a taxi after banking or shopping, not to mention after dark, even if it is just a few blocks. The unlit streets between the mall and Barrio Martha Quezada are particularly dangerous.

'Guides' and taxi drivers (see the boxed text, below) who meet the international buses will do anything to steer you toward hotels that give them a cut. Just tell them (politely – they're friends with all the muggers) that you have reservations.

SIGHTS & ACTIVITIES

Managua's sights are few and, with the exception of the often deserted Zona Monumental, far between. Even shoestringers should consider taking taxis.

Barrio Martha Quezada & Around

Since the days of the *internacionalistas* (idealistic visitors who came during the revolutionary years in the 1980s) Barrio Martha Quezada has been the city's budget travel headquarters. It has a great mall, most international buses and lots of cheap food and lodging. It's also convenient to a handful of sights.

TAXI SCAMS

Driving a Managua taxi is an art – a scam art. Here are some favorite techniques:

■ The Runaround: Look at the Barrio Martha Quezada map – your hotel is probably just a few blocks from the bus station. So why was it a 10-minute, US$20 ride?

■ The Bait & Switch: After quoting you a price (25!), they'll tell you that it was 25 each, or worse, 25 dollars (instead of 25 córdoba, which would have been a deal).

■ The Back Scratch: The hotel is closed? It's changed names? It's filled with rats? No. But the other hotel he's recommending gives him a cut.

PARQUE HISTORICO NACIONAL LOMA DE TISCAPA

Home to what's easily Managua's most recognizable landmark, Sandino's somber silhouette, this **national historic park** (Map p70; ☯ 8am-8pm Tue-Sun) was once the site of the Presidential Palace where Sandino and his men were executed in 1934; what looks like a dilapidated parking structure was for decades one of Nicaragua's most notorious prisons. You can see Sandino, hastily erected by the departing FSLN government after its electoral loss in 1990, from almost anywhere in town; begin your ascent at the Crowne Plaza. You'll pass **Monumento Roosevelt**, constructed in 1939 with lovely lake views, which is today a memorial to those killed in the revolution.

The top of the hill is actually the lip of Volcán Tiscapa's beautiful little crater lake, with incredible views of the city, both cathedrals and Volcán Momotombo, plus **Canopy Tiscapa** (Map p70; ☎ 893 5017; canopytiscapa@yahoo.com; US$11.50), a small but fun 1.2km, three-platform, 25-minute tour. There's a cave just hidden by the lake's surface where you can evidently take snacks for the spirits of those who have drowned here, who will then reward you with gold; but keep in mind that the lake is polluted with untreated sewage.

ARBORETUM NACIONAL

These modest **gardens** (National Arboretum; Map p78; US$0.30/0.06 adult/student; ☯ 8am-5pm Mon-Fri), inconveniently located halfway between Barrio Martha Quezada and the Plaza Monumental on Av Bolívar (well, it's convenient if you're making the hot 40-minute walk between them), features more than 200 species of plants divided into Nicaragua's five major life zones, of which only the Dry Tropical Forest and Central Lowlands look happy; that was one sad coffee plant. Your fee includes a guided tour, where you'll see a *madriño*, the national tree, and *sacuanjoche*, the national flower. Enjoy the shade.

Zona Monumental & Malecón

This quiet collection of pre-earthquake and postrevolutionary monuments, pretty parks, museums and government offices was once the pulsing heart of Managua; the *malecón* (pier), a pleasant stroll from the Zona Monumental, once overlooked a living lake lined with restaurants and festivities. Then came the 1972 earthquake, and two decades of war and privation, and the center was all but abandoned.

But slowly – little by little, as they say in Nicaragua – it is being resuscitated. Government buildings have been rebuilt; trees replanted; and ramshackle restaurants once again host cheerful after-church crowds on the lakefront. Heck, ex-President Alemán's pork-barrel extravaganza **Fuente Audiovisual** here offers a Vegas-style light-and-sound spectacular involving 'dancing' fountains, Strauss waltzes and *cumbias* (Colombian dance tunes) at 6pm and 9pm most nights.

The hollow shell of Managua's **Old Cathedral** (Map p75) remains Managua's most poignant metaphor, shattered by the 1972 earthquake and, despite promises, never restored. Though still beautiful and serene, attended by stone angels and dappled in golden light, it is empty and off-limits; the cathedral without a heart, in the city without a center.

Adjacent to the cathedral, the 1935 **Palacio Nacional de la Cultura** (Map p75; ☎ 222 2905) houses the **Museo Nacional** (admission US$2; ⏰ 8am-5pm). The timeline starts only 500 million years ago, as Nicaragua is one of the newest places on earth, and takes visitors through the formation of the lakes and volcanoes – not to mention gold mines – before getting to pre-Columbian statuary (see the boxed text, p117) and one of the best pottery collections in the country, all well signed and explained.

Other exhibits whiz through the Spanish colonial period before landing in the Sandino, then Sandinista, eras. Above the main staircase is a mural of revolutionary movements in the Americas by Mexican artist Arnold Belkin, and there's also a room tracing 500 years of art (most from the 1970s). Admission includes a 30-minute guided tour in Spanish.

Opposite is the brand-new **Casa Presidencial** (Map p75), the offices (but not the home) of the current president, rebuilt during the Alemán years with the help of the Taiwanese government. Directly south of the plaza is the old Grand Hotel, now the **Centro Cultural Managua** (Map p75; ☎ 222 5291) – see p72 for details of programs. In the center of it all is shady **Plaza de la**

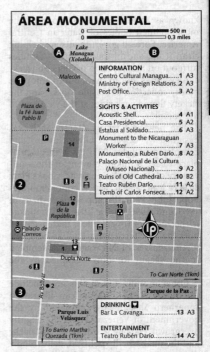

ÁREA MONUMENTAL

0   500 m
0   0.3 miles

Lake Managua (Xolotlán)

Malecón

Plaza de la Fé Juan Pablo II

Plaza de la República

Palacio de Correos

Dupla Norte

Av. Bolívar

To Carr Norte (1km)

Parque de la Paz

Parque Luis Velásquez

To Barrio Martha Quezada (1km)

INFORMATION	
Centro Cultural Managua........1	A3
Ministry of Foreign Relations..2	A3
Post Office...........................3	A2

SIGHTS & ACTIVITIES	
Acoustic Shell......................4	A1
Casa Presidencial.................5	A2
Estatua al Soldado...............6	A3
Monument to the Nicaraguan Worker.............................7	A3
Monumento a Rubén Darío....8	A2
Palacio Nacional de la Cultura (Museo Nacional)..............9	A2
Ruins of Old Cathedral........10	B2
Teatro Rubén Darío.............11	A2
Tomb of Carlos Fonseca......12	A2

DRINKING 🍸	
Bar La Cavanga...................13	A3

ENTERTAINMENT	
Teatro Rubén Darío.............14	A2

República, inaugurated in 1899 by national hero and original anti-American General José Santos Zalaya, and called José Dolores Estrada Park. Snacks and poorly lit benches for young lovers are attended by enterprising children hoping to sell nifty little insects (US$0.06) crafted from local palm fronds. On the northeast of the plaza rests the tomb of Sandinista commander **Carlos Fonseca** (Map p75). See p207 for more on Fonseca.

On the lake side of Plaza de la República, the **Monumento a Rubén Darío** (Map p75) was recently refurbished after the original 1933 statue fell into graffitied disrepair. A group of artists did a guerrilla installation, veiling the city's shame from public view and demanding poetic justice. In 1998 the cash-strapped government bowed to public opinion and, with Texaco Oil's help, restored the likeness of Nicaragua's favorite son. Toward the lake is the oblong **Teatro Nacional Rubén Darío** (Map p75; ☎ 266 3630) – see p84 for entertainment details.

The *malecón* is a bit depressing on off days, especially if you're pondering almost beautiful Lago de Managua, more properly known as **Xolotlán**, since 1927 one of the most polluted bodies of water in Central America. Foreign governments are helping clean it up, and in the meantime families turn out on Sundays and partiers on weekend evenings, not to swim but to enjoy the quirky collection of seaside kiosks, and the rickety theme park rides at the west end of the complex.

The new and trippy **Acoustic Shell** was designed by US artist Glen Howard and completed in July 2005; it's a spectacular place to see a folkloric event of the anniversary of the revolution. It overlooks **Plaza de la Fé Juan Pablo II**, which commemorates Pope John Paul II's appearances here in 1983 and 1996. On a little hill opposite is the *ranchito* (open-sided, thatch-roofed hut) that sheltered John Paul as he spoke to the masses of Nicaraguans assembled in the vacant lot now occupied by the plaza.

Other monuments in this area include the statue of Latin American liberation superhero **Simón Bolívar**, donated by the government of Venezuela in 1997; slightly overgrown **Plaza de la Cultura de Guatemala**; and the unabashedly political, disturbingly disproportionate **Estatua al Soldado** (Nameless Guerrilla Soldier; Map p75) on the west side of Av Bolívar, catercorner from the Centro Cultural Managua. 'Workers and campesinos onward till the end,' reads the inscription, which explains the pickax, if not the assault rifle with a Sandinista flag sticking out of it. A block away, another uncomfortably contorted sculpture, this one commissioned by the Liberals, celebrates the **Nicaraguan Worker** with a bronzed, rather hunchbacked couple who look like they need a vacation and decent health care.

From here, you can see the lighthouse, a symbolic beacon for a country torn apart, of the 1990 **Parque de la Paz** (Peace Park; Map p75), perhaps the most interesting monument of all. The reflection pool has been drained and the light rarely shines, but what remains are weapons – machine guns, pistols, even a tank – forever encased in concrete by former President Violeta Barrios de Chamorro. It's sort of like Mad Max meets Rollerball, not pretty or comfortable, but it is the monument most worth seeing.

Around Managua
HUELLAS DE ACAHUALINCA

Take a taxi (US$3 per person) to what's perhaps Managua's most intriguing site, the **Footprints of Acahualinca** (Map p70; ☎ 266 5774; admission US$2, photos US$1.25; ☻ 8am-5pm Mon-Fri, 9am-4pm Sat). Discovered by miners in 1874, these fossilized tracks record the passage of perhaps 10 people – men, women and children – as well as birds, raccoons and deer across the muddy shores of Lago de Managua some 6000 years ago. Despite early speculation that they were running from a volcanic eruption, forensics specialists have determined that these folks were in no hurry – and oddly enough, were fairly tall, between 145cm and 160cm.

The excavation was undertaken by the Carnegie Foundation in 1941 and 1942, and unearthed 14 layers, or 4m, of earth. They found some later Chorotega ceramics (about 2m down) and other intriguing artifacts, though there's no money to take it further. There is, however, a nifty on-site museum, with human skulls, a fossilized bison track and lots of ceramics, and your fee includes a Spanish-language tour of the whole shebang. Don't skip this one, it's an international treasure.

NUEVA CATEDRAL

Just north of the Metrocentro Mall is an unforgettable Managua landmark, and the hemisphere's newest **cathedral** (Map p80; ☎ 278 4232), an architectural marvel that leaves most visitors, well, scratching their heads. It's not a mosque, really: the 63 cupolas (or breasts, or eggs; speculation continues) symbolize Nicaragua's 63 Catholic churches, and also provide structural support during earthquakes – a good thing, since it sits astride a fault line. The interior is cool, heartfelt and unspectacular, although the shrine on the northwest side is nice. Of the US$45 million used to construct the cathedral, US$3.5 million was donated by avid pro-Lifer Tom Monaghan, owner of Domino's Pizza.

COURSES

At **La Academia Nicaragüense** (Map p80; ☎ 277 5557), just north of the UCA gates, you can take Latin dance classes, among other offerings (ballet for kids, for example) for about US$20 per month.

FESTIVALS & EVENTS

In addition to enthusiastic celebrations of national events, Managua has its own parties.

Annual Taxi Grand Prix (Last week in March) Drivers modify a licensed taxi's exhaust system, don a helmet and seat belt, then head to the pit at the Old Cathedral. The roads of central Managua are closed off and dozens of five-car, five-lap races scream through the city, but only one will win a brand-new cab.

Day of the Revolution (July 19) You'll finally understand why people still love Daniel Ortega when you see the master work a crowd of 100,000 red-and-black flag-waving faithful.

Festival of Santo Domingo de Guzman (August 1–10) Managua's *fiestas patronales* (patron saint parties) feature a carnival, sporting events, *hípicos* (horse parades) and a procession of *diablitos*, which takes Santo Domingo to his country shrine at Sierritas de Managua, followed by music and fireworks.

SLEEPING

Most budget travelers stay in Barrio Martha Quezada, about 10 square blocks of fairly strollable streets, although crime is on the rise (see p73). But there are other options, from the posh boutique hotels of the Centro Commercial to more modest midrange options in Boloñia, convenient to Barrio Martha Quezada's collection of backpacker-oriented businesses.

Barrio Martha Quezada

Better known to *taxistas* as 'Ticabus,' the international bus terminal upon which the barrio (district) is centered, Martha Quezada's been hosting shoestringers for a generation.

BUDGET

Casa Vanegas (Map p78; ☎ 222 4043; casavan egas@cablenet.com.ni; s US$6, s/d with bathroom US$10/12; ✗) Exceptionally clean and comfortable, this friendly family-run spot is a great budget choice offering spotless nonsmoking rooms, hammocks and great security.

Apartamentos Vanegas (☎ 249 8707; unfurnished/furnished apt US$400/500) Long-term visitors can ask at Casa Vanegas about these beautiful apartments in convenient Barrio Boloñia.

Guest House Santos (Map p78; ☎ 222 3713; r per person US$4) This cheap and funky backpackers hot spot hosts international shoestringers and jewelry-selling locals in its randomly shaped and occasionally cleaned

rooms. The equally grungy annex, Casa Azul, is quieter.

Hospedaje La Quintana (Map p78; ☎ 254 5487; claudiaquintana@cablenet.com.ni; r per person US$5, d with bathroom US$12; 🖳) A good deal on a somewhat dark but very clean room in a comfortable family home, this fine spot also has Internet.

Posada de Ruth (Map p78; ☎ 222 4051; s/d with fan US$10/12, with air-con US$20/22; ✗) Across from Shannon Bar, clean, recently remodeled rooms are brightly painted, and offer easy access to the best Internet around.

Casa Gabrinma (Map p78; ☎ 222 6650; s/d/tr per person US$10) Relaxed and homey guesthouse has a variety of different rooms arranged around a garden, with rudimentary bedding, private bathroom, fan and large screened windows, plus access to the excellent library.

There are other perfectly acceptable budget options, including:

Hospedaje El Viajero (Map p78; ☎ 228 1280; s/d US$8/12) West of Tica Bus, has six rooms with rattling fans and private bathrooms, featured a little prominently in each room.

Hospedaje El Dorado (Map p78; ☎ 222 6012; r per person US$6) Small rooms, tiny showers, wonderful owners and a no-drunks policy; ask about group rates.

MIDRANGE

Hotel-Apartamentos Los Cisneros (Map p78; ☎ 222 3535; paginasamarillas.com/hotelyapartamentosloscisneros .htm; s/d with fan US$20/30, with air-con US$35/45; 🅿 ✗) A great deal on quirky, colorful, relative luxury, it's got hot water, phones, art, hammocks and potted plants everywhere; for US$5 more you basically get an apartment, including kitchen.

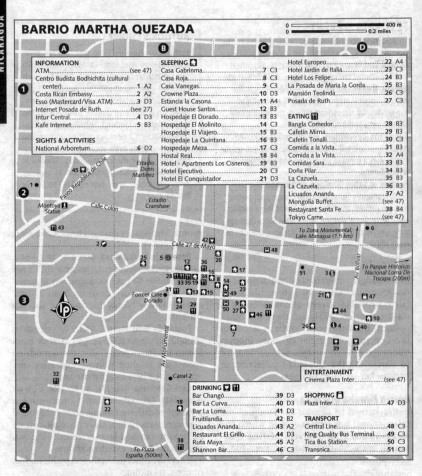

BARRIO MARTHA QUEZADA

INFORMATION	
ATM...(see 47)	
Centro Budista Bodhichita (cultural	
center)..**1** A2	
Costa Rican Embassy..............................**2** A2	
Esso (Mastercard/Visa ATM)...................**3** D3	
Internet Posada de Ruth...................(see 27)	
Intur Central...**4** D3	
Kafe Internet...**5** B3	
SIGHTS & ACTIVITIES	
National Arboretum................................**6** D2	

SLEEPING	
Casa Gabrinma.......................................**7** C3	
Casa Roja..**8** C3	
Casa Vanegas..**9** C3	
Crowne Plaza...**10** D3	
Estancia la Casona..................................**11** A4	
Guest House Santos................................**12** B3	
Hospedaje El Dorado..............................**13** B3	
Hospedaje El Molinito............................**14** C3	
Hospedaje El Viajero..............................**15** B3	
Hospedaje La Quintana..........................**16** B3	
Hospedaje Meza.....................................**17** C3	
Hostal Real...**18** B4	
Hotel - Apartments Los Cisneros............**19** B3	
Hotel Ejecutivo......................................**20** D3	
Hotel El Conquistador............................**21** D3	

Hotel Europeo.......................................**22** A4	
Hotel Jardin de Italia.............................**23** C3	
Hotel Los Felipe.....................................**24** B3	
La Posada de Maria la Gorda..................**25** B3	
Mansión Teolinda...................................**26** C3	
Posada de Ruth.......................................**27** C3	
EATING	
Bangla Comedor.....................................**28** B3	
Cafetín Mirna...**29** B3	
Cafetín Tonalli..**30** C3	
Comida a la Vista....................................**31** B3	
Comida a la Vista....................................**32** A4	
Comidas Sara..**33** B3	
Doña Pilar..**34** B3	
La Cazuela..**35** B3	
La Cazuela..**36** B3	
Licuados Ananda....................................**37** A2	
Mongolia Buffet...............................(see 47)	
Restayrant Santa Fe................................**38** B4	
Tokyo Carne.....................................(see 47)	

DRINKING	
Bar Changó..**39** D3	
Bar La Curva..**40** D3	
Bar La Loma...**41** D3	
Fruitilandia..**42** B2	
Licuados Ananda....................................**43** A2	
Restaurant El Grillo................................**44** D3	
Ruta Maya..**45** A2	
Shannon Bar..**46** C3	

ENTERTAINMENT	
Cinema Plaza Inter.............................(see 47)	
SHOPPING	
Plaza Inter...**47** D3	
TRANSPORT	
Central Line...**48** C3	
King Quality Bus Terminal......................**49** C3	
Tica Bus Station.....................................**50** C3	
Transnica...**51** C3	

Hotel Los Felipe (Map p78; ☎ 222 5622; www
.hotellosfelipe.com; s/d with fan US$15/20, with air-con
US$25/30; ⓟ ✹) With four monkeys, 22
parrots and lots of weird yard art around
the pool, you may not spend time in
your well-kept room with cable TV and
hot-water bathroom. Fun for kids.

La Posada de Maria la Gorda (Map p78; ☎ 268
2455; www.posadamarialagorda.com; Iglesia del Carmen 1c
sur, 25m oeste; s/d incl breakfast US$30/37; ✹) Away
from Martha Quezada's hustle and bustle,
this place has colorful lounging areas complete with a fountain, and large rooms with
air-con.

Hotel El Conquistador (Map p78; ☎ 222 4789;
www.hotelelconquistdor.com; s/d US$40/46; ⓟ ✹)
Located closer to the mall, restaurants and

bars than Martha Quezada proper, this spot
shows attention to detail, with pretty murals in the cavernous downstairs lounge and
spacious, nicely decorated rooms.

El Hostel de Regina (☎ 254 4909; Rotonda El
Güegüense 3c oeste, 1c sur, .5 oeste; s/d US$25/35, deluxe
US$35/45, all incl breakfast; ▯) Potpourri-scented
rooms come in different shapes and sizes,
with varying amenities (one has a hot-water
Jacuzzi), and a kitchen you can use.

TOP END
Mansión Teodolinda (Map p78; ☎ 228 1050; Intur 1c
sur, 1c oeste; s/d incl breakfast US$65/70; ▯) This ab-
solute gem has a darling pool, super-swish
rooms hung with original art, wireless Internet and other luxuries.

The latest upscale franchise to inhabit the landmark neo-Aztec pyramid by the mall, **Crowne Plaza** (Map p78; www.cpmanagua.com) was in the middle of a full-scale remodel at press time; let us know how it turns out.

Barrio Boloñia

Between Martha Quezada and Plaza España, this more upscale residential neighborhood has a handful of relaxed boutique hotels. Directions are usually given from Canal Dos (Canal 2; see Map p78).

Estancia La Casona (Map p78; ☎ 266 1685; www .estancialacasona.com; esquina norte Canal 2 2½c abajo; 🏵 🖳) Adorable and has all the amenities you'd expect – hot water, air-con, cable TV, free Internet – but the clincher is a big thatch-roofed *ranchero* in the gardens out back that makes a good lounge or conference room.

Hotel Maracas Inn (Map p70; ☎ 266 8612; www .maracasinn.com; Hopital Militar 1c norte, 1½c oeste; r incl breakfast US$50-75; 🏵 🖳) Cute rooms in pastel colors come with all the amenities, excellent service and, best of all, a pool.

Hostal Real (Map p78; ☎ 268 1438; www.hostalreal .com.ni; Rotonda El Güegüense 1½c al lago; s/d incl breakfast US$60/65; 🅿 🏵 🖳) The area's most luxurious option has big windows, beautiful antiques and hot-water bath*tubs*. Impressive.

Centro Comercial & Carretera Masaya

Although this cluster of upscale neighborhoods includes Metrocentro Mall and Managua's busiest intersection, walking around these shady side streets is rather nice, plus it's convenient to the country's best hotels and discos. Of course, you'll pay for it.

BUDGET

Hotel Ideas D Mamá (Map p70; ☎ 278 2908; www.hotelideasdemama.com.ni; Rotonda Santo Domingo 5c sur, 2½c abajo; r per person with fan/air-con incl breakfast US$12/20) This beautiful, if budget, B&B has pastel rooms with romantic lighting and a tropical garden out back. A good deal.

MIDRANGE

Hotel Sol y Luna (Map p80; ☎ 277 1009; solyluna@ cablenet.com.ni; La Marseilles, 50m abajo; s/d incl breakfast US$57/73; 🅿 🏵 🖳) This is one of Managua's snazzier boutique hotels, with

large, attractively furnished, Internet-wired rooms, tiny personal patios and a sunken circular couch thing in the main area. It's soothing.

Hotel Colón (Map p80; ☎ 278 2490; hcolon@ hcolon.com; de Edificio BAC 2c arriba; s/d US$52/67; 🅿 🏵 🏵) Clean and pastel, with breezy causeways, lots of wrought iron and a vaguely Roman theme.

Hotel El Almendro (Map p80; ☎ 270 1260; www .hotelelalmendro.com; de Metrocentro 2c oeste, ½c sur; r incl breakfast US$46-59; 🅿 🏵) The whole place is sort of stylish, but it's a good deal because of the in-room kitchens, and there's a nice patio, too.

TOP END

Real Intercontinental Metrocentro (Map p80; ☎ 278 4545; www.grupoeal.com; r US$140-160; 🅿 🏵 🏵 🖳 🏵) The fanciest hotel in town, period, this place has amazing rooms, great views, flawless service, various buffet restaurants, gym, business center, 24-hour Internet, boutique stores and maybe 10 mysterious little bottles of attractively packaged toiletries in the gigantic bathrooms. Oh, yes.

Seminole Plaza Hotel (Map p80; ☎ 270 6496; www.seminoleplaza.com; Bancentro Carr Masaya 1c oeste, 1c sur; s/d US$85/95; 🅿 🏵 🏵 🖳 🏵) Business class gone baroque-crazy means gold gilt accents and art with your flawless concierge service – all at half the price of the Intercontinental. Even better, it's all part of a slightly scandalous business venture by Florida's Seminole Tribe, which has invested US$10 million into Nicaragua since the late 1990s. Perhaps unsurprisingly, the US$14 lunch buffet rocks.

Hotel Princess (Map p80; ☎ 270 5045; www .hotelesprincess.com; d US$95-195; 🅿 🏵 🖳 🏵) More elegant, with attractive rooms that don't take decorating risks, it's also got a five-star lunch buffet and beautiful pool.

Holiday Inn (Map p70; ☎ 270 4515; www .holidayinn.com.ni; Pista Juan Pablo II; r US$75-80, ste US$105-150; 🅿 🏵 🖳 🏵) Just like back at home, but more expensive; the suites are huge, some with kitchens, and have great views.

Around Managua

Quaker House (Centro de los Amigos, Casa Cuaquera; ☎ 266 3216; friends@ibw.com.ni; Hospital Lenin Fonseca, 5c al lago, 75 varas arriba; dm volunteer/traveler US$5/8;

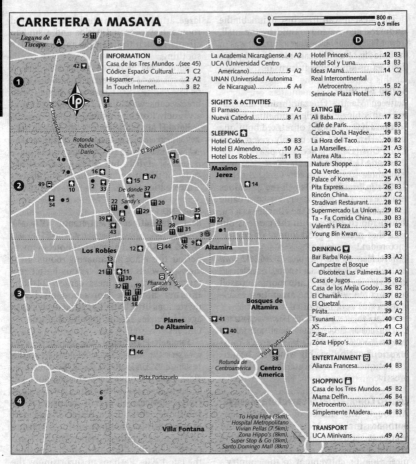

CARRETERA A MASAYA

0   800 m
0   0.5 miles

INFORMATION
Casa de los Tres Mundos ..(see 45)
Códice Espacio Cultural.......1 C2
Hispamer.............................2 A2
In Touch Internet................3 B2

La Academia Nicaragüense..4 A2
UCA (Universidad Centro
  Americano)......................5 A2
UNAN (Universidad Autonima
  de Nicaragua)..................6 A4

SIGHTS & ACTIVITIES
El Parnaso.........................7 A2
Nueva Catedral..................8 A1

SLEEPING
Hotel Colón.......................9 B3
Hotel El Almendro............10 A2
Hotel Los Robles..............11 B3

Hotel Princess..................12 B3
Hotel Sol y Luna...............13 B3
Ideas Mamá.....................14 C2
Real Intercontinental
  Metrocentro..................15 B2
Seminole Plaza Hotel........16 A2

EATING
Ali Baba...........................17 B2
Café de Paris....................18 B3
Cocina Doña Haydee........19 B2
La Hora del Taco..............20 B2
La Marseilles....................21 A2
Marea Alta.......................22 B2
Nature Shoppe.................23 B2
Ola Verde........................24 B3
Palace of Korea................25 A1
Pita Express....................26 B3
Rincón China....................27 C2
Stradivari Restaurant........28 B2
Supermercado La Union....29 B2
Ta - Fa Comida China.......30 B3
Valenti's Pizza..................31 B3
Young Bin Kwan...............32 B3

DRINKING
Bar Barba Roja.................33 B3
Campestre el Bosque
  Discoteca Las Palmeras....34 A2
Casa de Jugos.................35 B2
Casa de los Mejía Godoy...36 B2
El Chamán.......................37 C2
El Quetzal.......................38 C4
Pírata.............................39 A2
Tsunami..........................40 C3
XS.................................41 C3
Z-Bar.............................42 A1
Zona Hippo's...................43 B3

ENTERTAINMENT
Alianza Francesa..............44 B3

SHOPPING
Casa de los Tres Mundos...45 B2
Mama Delfin....................46 B4
Metrocentro....................47 B2
Simplemente Madera........48 B3

TRANSPORT
UCA Minivans..................49 A2

(**P**) In quiet, residential Las Brisas, this Friends House caters to witness trips and work brigades but happily accepts travelers, with kitchen, washing machine, telephone and limited parking.

Hotel y Restaurante César (☎ 265 2728; www .hotelcesar.com; Km 8.5 Carr Sur; s/d US$59/65; **P** ⊠ 🖵 🖳) The best reason to stay on the outskirts of town is the big pool surrounded by beautiful gardens overlooked by a neat outdoor bar. Rooms come with air-con, hot water, cable TV and in-room Internet, and the restaurant makes its own cheese.

El Camino Real (☎ 263 1381; www.caminoreal .com.ni; r US$95-195; **P** ⊠ 🖳 🖳 🖳) About 1.5km west of the airport, El Camino has pools, pool tables, convention centers, glittering

shops etc, but the reason you're here is the huge 24-hour, Egyptian-themed, Las Vegas–style Pharaoh's casino next door.

EATING

Go budget in Barrio Martha Quezada or up-scale on Carr Masaya, but whatever you do, enjoy Managua's variety of cuisines before you head out into the *campo* (countryside).

Barrio Martha Quezada & Boloñia

This area caters to businesspeople and back-packers, so prices are good.

BUDGET

Cafetín Mirna (Map p78; pancakes US$1.50; ⏰ 6am-3pm Mon-Fri, 6:30-11am Sat & Sun) Everyone loves a big breakfast here, with fluffy pancakes, fabulous fresh juices and a good lunch buffet, too. It's a tradition.

Doña Pilar (Map p78; dishes US$2-4; 6-9pm Mon-Sat) Get mouthwatering *típico* (regional) fare at this popular evening *fritanga* (sidewalk grill). Chicken or enchiladas are served with *gallo pinto* (rice and beans), chopped pickled cabbage and plantain chips.

Comidas Sara (Map p78; dishes US$2.50-4; 4pm-1am) Perhaps the best chicken curry (veggie curry also available) with mango sauce in Managua is served at this fabulous four-table hole-in-the-wall.

Cafetín Tonalli (Map p78; dishes US$2-6; 7am-6pm Mon-Fri, 7am-12:30pm Sat) Enjoy yogurt and granola, fresh-baked bread or vegetarian lasagna in the lovely garden in back of this pleasant café, run by a women's co-op.

Comida a la Vista (Map p78; dishes US$2-5; 11am-3pm Mon-Sat) Easily the best of the barrio's half-dozen steam-table buffets is this popular restaurant, with another location in Bolonia (Map p78). It serves a variety of salads and meatless entrées in addition to the usual beef and chicken.

Licuados Ananda (Map p78; healthy mains US$1-4, lunch buffet US$2.25; 6am-9pm Mon-Sat) Enjoy vegetarian goodies and 50 different kinds of *licuados* (sugary fruit and veggie juices; US$1) on this spacious patio overlooking lush gardens; the lunch buffet is held from 11am to 3pm.

MIDRANGE

La Cazuela (Map p78; mains US$3-12; 8am-9:30pm) There are two outlets of this seafood restaurant in the neighborhood, the first more upscale, the second a bit cheaper, with a great seafood lunch buffet that's only US$3, including a drink.

In addition to the dozen or so cheapo restaurants in the food court, Plaza Inter has two Asian restaurants: **Tokyo Carne** (Map p78; noon-3pm & 6-10pm) and **Mongolia Buffet** (Map p78; noon-3pm & 6-10pm). Choose to grill your own meat and veggies at the table (US$2 to US$12) or indulge in the very complete, and not entirely Asian, buffet (US$8).

TOP END

Restaurante Santa Fe (Map p78; 268 9344; Canal 2 2c sur; mains US$4-12; noon-10pm) Despite the name, there's no green chili at this quality Tex-Mex spot, with a huge bar, good enchi-

ladas and renowned steak. Make reservations on weekends.

Restaurant Churrasco (Map p70; mains US$6-15; noon-midnight) Across the street is this other date-night favorite, specializing in slabs of flame-broiled meat.

Palace of Korea (Map p80; 266 8968; del Hospital Militar 1c abajo; mains US$8-20; 11am-10pm) Satisfy your kim chi craving surrounded by marble columns and alongside Korean-style sushi, table-top barbecues and a potent chicken soup with ginseng. One room has traditional seating.

Centro Commercial & Carretera Masaya

There are probably 50 restaurants lining this strip, including plenty of Nicaraguan and US chains (TGI Fridays, anyone?), not to mention the massive food court at Metrocentro.

BUDGET & MIDRANGE

La Hora del Taco (Map p80; de donde fue Sandy's, Carr Masaya 1c arriba; dishes US$2-8; noon-11pm) This may be the best Mexican food in Nicaragua, and enchiladas, tacos and *chiles rellenos* are reasonably priced, too.

Cocina Doña Haydee (Map p80; mains US$3-8; 7am-10pm) One block east of Pharaoh's, this spot does rustic right down to the traditional costumes and classic menu, from *gallo pinto* to *guiso de chilote* (cheese soup with baby corn) to steak with all the trimmings.

Pita Express (Map p80; Sinsa 75m sur Calle Altamira; mains US$3-6) Take a pillow and grab a hookah (flavored tobaccos available), then relax with a delicious pita packed with hummus, shwarma or falafel.

Valenti's Pizza (Map p80; Lacmiel 2c este; mains US$3-6) Good pizza and great atmosphere at

---

AUTHOR'S CHOICE

Ola Verde (Map p80; Pharaohs 2c abajo, ½c al lago; 9am-7:30pm Mon-Fri, 9am-3pm Sat) This combination whole-foods store, deli and upscale vegetarian restaurant in the shady Altamira neighborhood is a real treat, with a beautiful dining area and even lovelier food, from curried tofu and veggie soups to the wonderful daily specials, all designed by a PhD nutritionist who knows how to cook.

the heart of a neighborhood packed with restaurants catering to business lunchers, sometimes called 'Zona Cero.'

TOP END

Alí Babá (Map p80; meals US$5-10; ☾ 6pm-late Tue-Sat) Also in Zona Cero, this hot spot is famed for its shwarma, shish kebabs and other Middle Eastern treats with a Libyan flavor, not to mention the disco it turns into after-hours.

Rincón China (Map p80; meals US$5-8; ☾ 11:30am-9:30pm) Considered one of the city's best Asian restaurants, it has huge US$4 lunch specials.

La Stradivari Restaurant (Map p80; meals US$6-15; ☾ 6-11pm daily, noon-3pm Mon-Sat) Also in Zona Cero but more upscale than Valenti's, La Stradivari is known for its fresh pasta and pizza; try anything in spinach sauce.

Marea Alta (Map p80; ☎ 278 2459; meals US$6-18; ☾ noon-midnight) A tourist tradition since the US ambassador was kidnapped here in the 1970s, the menu is in English, the beef is USDA, the seafood is absolutely spectacular and comes with a wine list from Argentina, Italy, Spain, France and so on – and it delivers.

Young Bin Kwan (Map p80; Calle Principal Los Robles; mains US$6-60; ☾ 11am-10pm) The city's most exclusive sushi joint has a menu in Japanese (ack!) and also specializes in exotic soups.

Ta-Fa Comida China (Map p80; ☎ 278 4967; mains US$4-35; ☾ noon-10pm Tue-Sun) The other contender for best Chinese food in Nicaragua, most dishes are a reasonable US$4 to US$6; with the much pricier Peking duck and shrimp-ball soup you'll need to order ahead.

La Marseilles (Map p80; ☎ 277 0224; Calle Principal Los Robles; ☾ Mon-Sat) The gold standard of Managua cuisine is a landmark, with other fine dining options clustering around its tastefully art-bedecked walls, outstanding wine pairings and authentic French cuisine. Make reservations.

Café de Paris (Map p80; ☎ 278 3267; meals US$8-30; ☾ noon-3pm & 6-11pm Mon-Sat) Less renowned but just as good as La Marseilles, this intimate dining option involves lots of forks, delicious crepes and a very French chef who recommends the lobster with mushrooms in cognac sauce. Be sure to make reservations.

Groceries

Managua is the best place to stock up in the country. Supermercado La Unión (Map p80) is convenient to Metrocentro and Zona Cero hotels.

La Colonia (Map p70; Plaza España, Rotonda Jean Paul Genie 1c sur, Carr Masaya) The poshest supermarket chain, with organic veggies, imported liquor and all the brands you miss from back home, plus one of the best selections of books (in Spanish) in the city. The one at Plaza España is the nicest, and close to Boloñia and Barrio Marta Quezada; the HyperColonia on Carr Masaya is huge.

Super Stop & Go (Km 8 Carr Masaya; ☾ 8am-9:30pm) Expats in the know hit this hidden spot for Nicaragua's best selection of gringo grub – caviar, curry paste, eight kinds of barbecue sauce and more. Don Pan, with gourmet baked goods, and Bavaria Delikatessan, with imported meats and cheeses, are nearby.

Nature Shoppe (Map p80; ☎ 270 2822; naturalshoppe@hotmail.com; ☾ 8am-7pm Mon-Sat) Close to Valenti's Pizza, this natural grocer has all the vitamins and mysterious holistic treatments you need, plus the organic cookies you want. It also arranges massages, acupuncture and other treatments by reservation.

DRINKING

Managua is far and away the country's nightlife capital. Check entertainment listings in *Esta Semana*, the Thursday supplement to the newspaper *El Nuevo Diario*, or *Viernes Chiquito*, the competing Thursday supplement from *La Prensa*, and keep an eye open for *Diversión Total*, a free entertainment zine covering Managua, Masaya and Granada. **Nicaragua Tonight** (www.nicaragua2night.com) and **Nicaragua Bacanal** (www.bacanalnica.com) have lots of photos and some information.

Nonalcoholic Beverages

In addition to **Licuados Ananda** (Map p78; ☾ 6am-9pm Mon-Sat), there are several options for healthy drinking.

Casa de los Jugos (Map p80; juices & snacks US$1.50-4; ☾ 8am-8pm) In Zona Cero, serves fresh juices and healthy snacks on a nice porch.

Frutilandia (Map p78; Calle 27 de Mayo; snacks US$1-2; ☾ 8am-3pm Mon-Fri, 8am-5pm Sat) With fruity beverages, healthy sandwiches and light breakfasts.

Bars & Pubs

There are several spots for a cold one around Barrio Martha Quezada.

Shannon Bar (Map p78; www.shannonbar.com; ⊙4pm-2am) The classic bar in this area, this Irish pub is an expat gathering spot and one of the only places in town where you can get a cold Guinness tallboy, Old Holburn rolling tobacco, and big plate of *bocadillo Irlandes* (US$3), aka bangers 'n' mash.

Bar La Curva (Map p78; Av Bolívar) South of the Crowne Plaza hotel, there's live music on weekends at this open-air bar, with its mellow globe lights and tropical ambience, just oozing a laid-back vibe.

El Chamán (Map p80; ☎278 6111; cover US$2) Young scenesters gather at this popular dance club near Metrocentro. Live music on Thursday.

Zona Hippo's (Map p80; www.zonahippos.com; ⊙noon-2am) Wanna go where everybody knows your name? Globalization has arrived and it's called Hippo's Grill & Tavern, with nine different burgers, next door to affiliated Woody's Sports Bar, with 15 different types of hot wings. Both have Caesar salads, plenty of 'flair,' nonthreatening rock music and very full bars. There's another outlet by the Santo Domingo mall.

Pírata (Map p80; seafood US$10-30; ⊙noon-2am) Next door to Hippo's but not affiliated, Pírata has live music on Friday, tasteful Cuban music most other days, expensive cocktails, an outdoor bar and an elaborate pirate theme (see the boxed text, p113) that includes booths inside a Spanish galleon and fountains with fake treasure and real turtles. It's upscale; the US$30 signature *boca* (appetizer) is lobster baked in a pineapple with cheese, served with white wine.

Tsunami (Map p80; ☎267 1009; Lacmiel, 15 varas este) In Zona Cero, off Carr Masaya, this big, conversational, outdoor sports-type bar gets a good meat-markety crowd, with several similar watering holes nearby.

Just south of La Curva, set back from the street, Bar La Loma (Map p78) attracts a young 20s crowd, with music ranging from rock to hip-hop. One block west of La Curva, there is evidently food at Restaurant El Grillo (Map p78), this spot's most recent hard-partying incarnation, but the crowd still goes all night. Close to El Grillo, you can dance all night at Bar Changó (Map p78), a Cuban-themed disco which sometimes screens movies in the early evening. For special events, it may charge US$2 cover.

Gay & Lesbian Venues

The gay and lesbian scene is hidden, but you can find it. There are a few gay clubs in Managua, which is a few more than you'll find anywhere else in the country. Most Nicaraguan gays and lesbians hook up with friends through http://gay.com or www.gaydar.co.uk, so log on and see if anyone's found better places than these.

Somos (González Paso 1c al lago) Gay and lesbian, but straight friendly, this gay disco has live shows and sometimes a cover. Nearby, try Le Bistro.

Pacu's (Puente del Edén 1c al lago, ½c arriba) A bit mellower, this bar and disco has a restaurant and pulls in a youthful crowd some nights. Gays and lesbians are welcome.

Tabú (Hospital Militar 3c norte, 1c oeste) The dance floor gets going on weekends.

BELLO HORIZONTE

Arguably the best night out in Managua, this traffic circle in the northeast corner of town has grown into an epicenter of mariachi madness and magnet for party people from all over the country. With an unrivalled and oh-so-strollable collection of fast food and *fritangas,* discos and dive bars, plus one legendary pizza joint holding it all together, this is the place to be.

Bar-Restaurant Los Ídolos (Map p70; medium pizza US$4-7; ⊙9am-5am) A small, dark, and impossibly hip restaurant, fronted with the aforementioned idols and packed to the wide and sparkly brim with mariachi musicians on their tequila break, this is the rock upon which Bello Horizonte's party scene was built. The pizza's good, too.

From there, your options really are endless. You could get your groove on Charlie's Place (Map p70) or Sueños de la Luna (Map p70) disco-bars, catch a quiet brew or some great live music at Bar Aché (Map p70), play pool, watch the big game, or just pour your spare change into any of several casinos; Fantasy Club (Map p70) has a 'No Mariachi' policy, which you may appreciate at some point in the evening. Or just hang out in the traffic circle with a bottle of rum and Managua's underage cool kids, and enjoy the vibe.

Nightclubs

Remember, those cute heels take up much more space than they're worth in your backpack. Well, unless you're coming to Managua.

XS (Map p80; ☎ 277 3086; Km 5 Carr Masaya; ☽ Wed-Sat) XS draws 20-something clubheads, eager to dance away their worries in this sleek mirrored space.

Hipa Hipa (Carr Masaya; cover US$3) Not just a club, but *the* club, with a dress code, Euro styling, imported DJs and 'a better class of people' (between 18 and 22), as one pudgy scenester suavely put it.

El Quetzal (Map p80; ☎ 277 0890; Km 5 Carr Masaya) Near Rotonda de Centroamérica, El Quetzal has had one of the city's largest and liveliest dance floors for years. Salsa, *merengue* and cumbia are in heavy rotation at this cavernous club.

Island Taste (Map p70; ☎ 240 0010; Km 6.5 Carr Norte) On weekends the Caribbean crowd packs the floor to soca (defined by fast beats and calypso-like undertones) and reggae grooves at this spot on Carr Norte.

Live Music

La Casa de los Mejía Godoy (Map p80; ☎ 270 4928; Plaza El Sol 2c sur; cover US$8-15; ☽ Thu-Sat) Living legends Carlos and Luis Enrique Mejía Godoy, whose folk music explorations into the heart of Nicaraguan culture have become church hymns and revolutionary standards since they first started laying down riffs in the 1960s, have their own intimate venue. Here you can watch them and similarly inclined friends play. Make reservations.

Bar La Cavanga (Map p75; ☎ 228 1098; Centro Cultural Managua; cover US$4; ☽ from 9:30pm Thu-Sat) Take a taxi out to this 1950s-era gem, which stages live folk and jazz shows in the sketchy neighborhood near the old cathedral.

Ruta Maya (Map p78; ☎ 266 0698; Estatua Montoya 1.5m este; cover US$1-5) Look around for flyers with monthly listings of the happenings at this thatch-roofed venue, which range from Bee Gees cover bands to Caribbean *palo de mayo* to *son nicaragüense* (traditional Nicaraguan folk music). Traditional Nicaraguan food is served buffet style at lunch.

Campestre el Bosque Discoteca Las Palmeras (Map p70; semáforos antigua 1c norte, ½c oeste; ☽ 4pm-midnight) Party like the locals at this shady spot with a pool and live (think folksy Nica) music after 8pm.

Bar Barba Roja (Map p80; Rotonda Darío 1c sur, 10 varas oeste; cover US$2-5) Proving that you don't need a garage to play garage rock, bands come to this bar from all over Nicaragua to show what they can do with three chords.

ENTERTAINMENT

There are dozens of venues around town that occasionally have live music, folkloric dance, alternative theater, poetry readings and other cultural offerings; check the Thursday edition of *La Prensa* or *El Diario* for listings.

If you can, try to catch something at Instituto de Nicaragua y Centroamerica, a good excuse to hang out at UCA (see p73), or **Biblioteca Banco Central de Nicaragua** (☎ 265 0131; Km 7 Carr Sur, 150m este), with wonderful art shows and offbeat performances in a beautiful building.

La Academia de Danza (Map p80; ☎ 277 5557; frente UCA) At the UCA, this place often has performances, and also teaches classes if you'll be in town for a while.

Cinemas

Alianza Francesa (Map p80; Mexican embassy in Altamira) Free unusual movies, usually in French, at 8pm Wednesday and Saturday.

Cinema Plaza Inter (Map p78; US$2) At Plaza Inter close to Barrio Martha Quezada, has eight screens of (mostly) Hollywood's finest.

La Sala de Teatro Justo Rufino Garay (☎ 666 3714; contiguo al Parque de las Palmas; US$2) Artsy movies at 7pm Wednesday.

Metrocentro Cinemark (Map p80; US$2.50) At the bigger, better mall, an even plusher six screens, playing the same blockbuster movies.

Theater

One of the few Managua buildings to survive the 1972 earthquake, groovy **Teatro Nacional Rubén Darío** (Map p75; ☎ 266 3630; Zona Monumental) often has big-name, international offerings on the main stage. It's worth trying to catch some experimental jazz or performance art in the smaller Sala Experimental Pilar Aguirre, which usually has a lower cover charge and more interesting work. Shows and schedules are listed in the paper.

NICARAGUA

EL NICA: A MONOLOGUE BETWEEN TWO CULTURES

Like 500,000 Nicas living and working in Costa Rica, José Mejía went there to build a better life for his family, but for him it didn't work out. After being ridiculed by his Costa Rican co-workers for his supposedly humble origins, he returned home for a lengthy discussion of Costa Rican–Nicaraguan relations with his tabletop crucifix.

El Nica (www.elnica.org), a two-hour monologue by writer and actor César Meléndez, who plays José Mejía, has gone from a labor of love performed in schools and basements to being one of the biggest theatrical hits in Central America. It's a biting critique of Tico nationalism, but is not afraid to poke fun even at Sandino: 'Now that kid even had the nerve to put together an army to kick out the foreign invader…so well, that foreign investment has been afraid of coming to Nicaragua ever since!'

Meléndez' family came to Costa Rica as migrant workers when he was only five years old, and he has lived his life between the two cultures. 'When you have an emergency in life, you always turn to your nearest brothers. Isn't that right?' Mejía asks his tormenters. And this play's success on both sides of the border proves that there's still love underneath it all.

Sports

Estadio Denis Martínez (Map p78) is the national baseball stadium, and is absolutely packed between mid-November and early April, when Nicaragua's seven professional teams, including the Managua Bóers, go for the national championships. Get stats, schedules and more at **Beisbal Nica** (www.ibw.com.ni).

Cranshaw Stadium, the smaller soccer stadium nearby, is currently being replaced by a brand-new 22,000-seat beauty close to UNAN; the **Nicaraguan Football Association** (www.fenifut.org.ni) will have the latest.

SHOPPING

Boutiques are clustered in Altamira, with standouts being Mama Delfina (Map p80), with top-quality *artisanías* (handicrafts) and a cute café up top, and Simplemente Madera (Map p80), a fascinating place to browse even if you don't go home with the organically shaped wood furniture, much of it made from already fallen trees.

Casa de los Tres Mundos (Map p80; La Marseilles, 2½c norte; 8am-5pm Mon-Fri) In the Zona Rosa/Zona Hippo, this is Ernesto Cardenal's (see the boxed text, p267) home turf, selling not only his sleek, modernistic sculptures but also a great selection of top-quality naïve paintings from the Archipélago de Solentiname, books and DVDs (most in Spanish, all leftist).

Galería Solentiname (277 0939; Enel Central sur 600m) If you can't make it out to the islands, this attractive gallery featuring top-of-the-line work will make you want to figure out a way.

Markets & Malls

Mercado Roberto Huembes (Map p70) This is more than just the southbound bus terminal; it has the best selection of souvenirs in Managua, from all over the country.

Mercado Oriental (Map p70) Stash your cash in a couple of places (sock, bra) and try to find a local guide for Central America's largest market and scariest shopping experience. But it's so cheap, and probably the only place in town with live hand grenades…

Plaza Inter (Map p78) Adjacent to Barrio Martha Quezada, it's convenient, with a movie theater, lots of US$1 shops, a couple of department stores and solid food court.

Metrocentro (Map p80) Watch young, rich Managuans mate and date at more than 50 glittering boutique shops and department stores, dainty cafés and beauty salons; there's also a cinema and food court.

Santo Domingo Mall (Km 8 Carr Masaya) The biggest, newest and, at press time, emptiest shopping center.

GETTING THERE & AWAY
Air

Managua International Airport (MGA; 233 1624/28; www.eaai.com.ni; Km 11 Carr Norte) is a small, manageable airport that is getting more business as tourism and business travel to Managua increases, but it still has that small-country charm. There's a BanPro Visa/Plus ATM, Internet access (per hour US$2), souvenir shops and crappy food in the main terminal; don't expect to lounge over a good meal. **Intur** (8am-10pm) has an office inside the international terminal where English-speaking staff can recommend hotels, confirm flights and share flyers. The airport also has the best selection of English-language magazines in the country.

The smaller, more chaotic domestic terminal is just west of the main building. Departure tax for domestic flights is US$2, for international flights US$32, payable in US dollars or córdoba only.

Aerocaribbean (☎ 270 4134; Bosques de Altamira, frente el Cine 158) One Saturday flight to Havana, Cuba.

American Airlines (Map p70; ☎ 266 3900; www .aa.com; Plaza España 3c sur) Two flights daily to Miami.

Atlantic Airlines (☎ 222 5787; www.atlanticairlines .com.ni; Bust José Martí 2½c este) International flights to Tegucigalpa on Monday, Wednesday and Friday; and daily domestic flights to Bluefields and the Corn Islands.

Continental Airlines (☎ 278 7033; www.continental .com; Ofiplaza bldg, 2nd-level bldg 5) One daily flight to Houston.

Copa Airlines (☎ 267 3976; www.copaair.com; Km 4.5 Carr Masaya, Tip Top ½c oeste) Daily flights to Guatemala City, Managua, San José, San Salvador and Panama City.

Grupo Taca (Map p70; ☎ 266 6698; www.taca .com; Plaza España) Daily flights to Miami, Los Angeles and several Latin American cities.

La Costeña (☎ 263 2142; www.flylacostena.com) The major internal carrier has regular service to Bluefields, the Corn Islands, Las Minas, Bilwi and Waspám.

Bus

Managua is the main transportation hub for the country, with four major national bus and van terminals, plus a handful of international bus lines, most grouped in Barrio Martha Quezada.

INTERNATIONAL BUSES

Tica Bus (Map p78; ☎ 222 3031) is in a newly re-modeled terminal at the heart of Barrio Martha Quezada.

Costa Rica US$12, 10 hours, 5:45am, 7am and noon; for Liberia and San José

Guatemala US$33, 30 hours, 5am; there is a continuing service to Tapachula, Mexico (US$48, 48 hours)

Panama City US$36, 34 hours, 5:45am and 7am

San Salvador US$25, 11 hours, 5am

Honduras US$20, seven hours, 6am; there is a continuing service from Tegucigalpa to San Pedro Sula (US$28, 11 hours)

King Quality (Map p78; ☎ 228 1454), across from Tica Bus, has in-flight…er, in-ride meal service and less intense air-conditioning.

Costa Rica US$16, eight hours, 2:30pm

Guatemala US$51, 32 hours, 3:30am; for Guatemala City

El Salvador US$27, 10 hours, 5am and 3pm; for San Salvador

Honduras US$24, 10 hours, 5am; for Tegucigalpa

Transnica (Map p78; ☎ 270 3133; 1c west of Esso), in convenient new digs in Barrio Martha Quezada, also offers luxury service.

Costa Rica US$12, nine hours, 5:30am, 7am and 10am; there's a luxury bus (US$20) at noon; for San José

San Salvador US$25, 11 hours, 5am

Honduras US$20, 10 hours, 5am; for Tegucigalpa

Del Sol Bus (☎ 270 2547) has one bus leaving for San Salvador (US$25) from Managua's Holiday Inn (Map p70) at 6am daily.

Central Line (Map p78; ☎ 254 5431; 3c west of Esso) offers services to San Salvador (US$25, 10 hours, 5am) and San José, Costa Rica (US$12, eight hours, 10am), with stops in Masaya and Liberia.

NATIONAL BUSES & MINIVANS

Buses leave from three main places: Mercado Roberto Huembes (for Granada, Masaya and southeast Nicaragua); Mercado Israel Lewites (for León and the Northern Pacific); and Mercado Mayoreo (for the Caribbean Coast and the Northern Highlands). Some also leave from the Mercado Oriental (Map p70), mainly to rural destinations not covered in this book. It's faster, more comfortable and a bit more expensive to take minivans from **UCA** (pronounced 'ooka'; Map p80). Minivans leave when full for León, Granada, Masaya, Rivas, San Jorge, Ticuantepe, Jinotepe, Masatepe and all of the Pueblo Blancos (White Villages).From Mercado Roberto Huembes (Map p70) microbuses leave when full to Ticuantepe, Santo Domingo and most of the Pueblos Blancos, among others. Regular buses and micro-buses leave for destinations including:

Granada US$0.75, one hour, 5am to 10pm, every 15 minutes

Jinotepe microbus US$1.25, one hour, depart when full

Masatepe US$1.10, 5am to 6pm, every 20 minutes; also serves San Marcos

Masaya US$0.60, 40 minutes, 5am to 8pm, every 20 minutes

Naindame US$1.50, one hour, 6am to 8pm, every 15 minutes

Rivas *expreso* US$2.10, two hours, 4am to 6pm, every 30 minutes; *ordinario* US$1.50, 2½ hours, 4am to 6pm, every 30 minutes; microbus US$2.50, 1½ hours, depart when full

San Juan del Sur US$3.50, 2½ hours, 9am and 4pm

Sapoá/Costa Rica US$3.50, 2½ hours, 6am to 5pm, every 30 minutes

From **Mercado Israel Lewites** (Bóer; Map p70; ☎ 265 2152) microbuses leave when full to Chinandega, La Concha, Corinto, Jinotepe, León, Masatepe, Nagarote, Puerto Sandino and El Sauce, among others. Regular buses run to destinations including:

Carazo US$0.80, one hour, 4:30am to 6:20pm, every 20 minutes; serving Diriamba and Jinotepe

Chinandega/El Viejo US$2, 2½ hours, every 30 minutes; bus stops in León

El Sauce US$3, 7:45am and 2:45pm

La Paz Centro US$.90, one hour, 6am to 5pm, every 30 minutes

León *expreso* US$1.25, 1¼ hours, 5am to 4:45pm, every 30 minutes; via New Hwy and La Paz Centro

León *ordinario* US$1, two hours, 5am to 4:45pm, every 20 minutes; via Old Hwy and Puerto Sandino

León microbus US$1, 1¼ hours, depart when full

Nagarote US$0.70, 45 minutes, 6am to 5pm, every 30 minutes

Pochomil/Masachapa US$0.70, 1½ hours, 6am to 6pm, every 20 minutes

Mercado Mayoreo (Map p70; ☎ RAAN 233 4729, Rama 233 4533) serves both the Northern Highlands and RAAN and the road to Rama, including San Carlos. Destinations include:

Boaco US$1.75, one hour, 4am to 6:30pm, every 30 minutes

El Rama *expreso* US$9, 5½ hours, 2pm, 6pm and 10pm; *ordinario* US$7, eight hours, 4am, 5am, 6am, 7:30am, 8:45am and 11:30am

Esquipulas US$3, 2½ hours, 6:25am, 8:20am, 12:25pm, 1:25pm, 2:50pm and 3:50pm

Estelí US$3, 2½ hours, 5:45am to 5:45pm, every 30 minutes

Jinotega US$3.50, three hours, 4am to 5:30pm, almost hourly; the 3pm bus serves San Rafael del Norte (US$3.75)

Juigalpa US$1, two hours, 5am to 4:45pm, every 20 minutes; transfer to San Carlos, Nueva Guinea and El Rama buses

Matagalpa US$3, two hours, 3am to 6pm, every 30 minutes

Ocotal US$3.75, 3½ hours, 3:20am to 4:15pm, almost hourly; the 3:20am, 10:15am and 3pm buses serve Jalapa (US$6, five hours)

Río Blanco US$5, four hours, 4am to 3pm, almost hourly

San Carlos US$9, 12 hours, 5am, 6am, 7am, 9:15am, 10:15am, 1pm and 6:30pm

Siuna US$9,10 to 12 hours, four daily

Somoto US$3.75, 3½ hours, 7:15am, 9:45am, 11am, 12:45pm, 1:45pm, 2pm, 3:45pm and 4:45pm

Car

INSURANCE

By law, you must get basic insurance (US$10 per day) with car rental, which usually has a US$1500 deductible and does not cover flat tires. For another US$10 to US$15 per day, you can get supplemental insurance that will cover the deductible. Chances are, your credit card already provides supplemental insurance for at least the first two weeks of your rental, so call your card company and ask.

RENTAL

Renting a car is relatively inexpensive, thanks to pro-tourism tax laws. You need a driver's license from your own country (valid for one month after you arrive in Nicaragua) and a credit card; you must be over 25 years old, but ask around if you're not. Renting a car at the airport costs you a hefty 15% extra, so consider taking a taxi to an off-site office. Rental-car companies will wait for you at the Peñas Blancas border, and some companies, including Hertz, will let you take your rental car to Costa Rica with prior arrangement; it doesn't work the other way around.

Budget (☎ in Managua 266 6226, in the US & Canada 800-758 9586) has excellent service and consistently lower rates than the other guys, but Dollar also gets rave reports. Other possibilities:

Alamo (☎ airport 233 3718, Managua 270 1939; alamo@cablenet.com.ni)

Avis (☎ airport 233 3011, Barrio Boloñia 268 1838; avisnic@cablenet.com.ni)

Best (☎ 263 3242) Airport only.

Dollar (☎ 266 3620; www.dollar.com.ni) Has deals that include rooms at several Managua hotels, including El Conquistador and La Casona.

Exotic (☎ 233 4695; www.exoticrentacar.com.ni; Km 9.5 Carr Norte) At flashy Hotel Camino Real, specializes in limos and other fabulous rides.

Hertz (☎ airport 233 1237; www.hertz.com.ni)

Lugo (☎ airport 263 2368, Managua 277 0582; www.lugorentacar.com.ni)

National (☎ 270 1968; www.nationalnicaragua.com)

Nicaragua (☎ Barrio Boloñia 250 2114, Bello Horizonte 244 1051; www.nicarentacar.com) Managua-based company that will accept a US$200 deposit in lieu of a credit card.

Payless (☎ airport 233 1329, Managua 278 1825; www.payless.com.ni)

Targa (☎ reservations 222 4824, airport 233 1176, Managua 222 4881; rentacar@ibw.com.ni)

World (☎ 263 1011; worldrentacar@cablenet.com.ni) Avoid the airport tax by running across the street to the office at Best Western Las Mercedes.

GETTING AROUND
To/From the Airport

The airport is 11km from town and has its special, more expensive taxis (US$15 to US$20 to most Managua destinations) which don't pick up passengers. At night this is worth it, but during the day you can just run across the very busy Carr Norte to the bus stop, where *colectivo* taxis cost US$5 to go into town.

Bus

Local buses are frequent and crowded. They're also known for their professional pickpockets, though the warnings are probably overblown – stay alert and you'll be fine. Routes run every 10 minutes from 4:45am to 6pm, then every 15 minutes until 10pm. Buses do not generally stop en route – look for the nearest bus shelter. The fare is US$0.35. Useful routes include:

No 109 Plaza de la República to Mercado Roberto Huembes, stopping en route at Plaza Inter.

No 110 Mercado Israel Lewites (Bóer) to Mercado Mayoreo, via the UCA, Metrocentro, Rotonda de Centroamérica, Mercado Roberto Huembes and Mercado Iván Montenegro.

No 116 Montoya statue, Plaza Inter, Mercado Oriental and Rotonda Bello Horizonte.

No 118 From Parque Las Piedrecitas, heads down Carr Sur, then east, passing by the Mercado Israel Lewites (Bóer), Rotonda El Güegüense (Plaza España), Plaza Inter and Mercado Oriental on its way to Mercado Mayoreo.

No 119 From Lindavista to Mercado Roberto Huembes, with stops at Rotonda El Güegüense and the UCA.

Car & Motorcycle

Driving in Managua is not recommended at night – even if you have a rental car, consider getting a taxi, and make sure your car is in a guarded lot. Night drivers should keep their windows rolled up and stay alert.

Taxi

Most taxis in Managua are *colectivos*, which pick up passengers as you go. There are also more expensive private taxis based at the airport, Metrocentro Mall, Mercado Roberto Huembes and other places. These are safer, but regular taxis also always congregate close by. Licensed taxis have red plates and the driver's ID above the dash; if yours doesn't, you're in a pirate taxi. This is probably OK, but don't go to the ATM, and beware of scams (see the boxed text, p74) no matter what kind of taxi you're in.

Fares are US$1 to US$4 per person within the city. From Barrio Martha Quezada, taxis go to the airport (US$10/10/15 for one/two/three people), Mercado Roberto Huembes (US$3/4 for one/two people), Mercado Israel Lewites (US$2/3), Mayoreo (US$5/6), Zona Rosa (US$2/3) and Huellas deAcahualinca (US$3/4). Prices rise at night.

AROUND MANAGUA

LAGUNAS DE XILOÁ & APOYEQUE

Half a dozen crater lakes lie near Managua. The best for swimming is **Laguna de Xiloá**, on the Península de Chiltepe, about 20km northwest of Managua off the ro ad to León. Xiloá is also suitable for windsurfing and diving, with clear waters holding at least 15 endemic species. Though crowded on weekends, the lagoon remains quite peaceful during the week.

It's a steep 30-minute hike from Laguna de Xiloá to less accessible but more picturesque **Laguna de Apoyeque**, deep within a steep crater. Small alligators can be spotted basking beside its sulfurous waters. Take bus 110 from the UCA to Ciudad Sandino, where you can catch an onward bus to the lagoons.

EL TRAPICHE

This natural *balneario* (thermal spa), **Los Baños Termales y del Club Náutico de Río Tipitapa** (admission US$2.30), is 22km from Managua in the town of Tipitapa, with therapeutic waters surrounded by gardens and restaurants. Buses to Tipitapa depart from Mercado Central/Roberto Huembes.

PACIFIC BEACHES

Not even 50km from Managua are some of the most beautiful beaches in Nicaragua.

Masachapa & Pochomil

Although the three square blocks of restaurants, bars and hotels have largely supplanted the original fishing village of

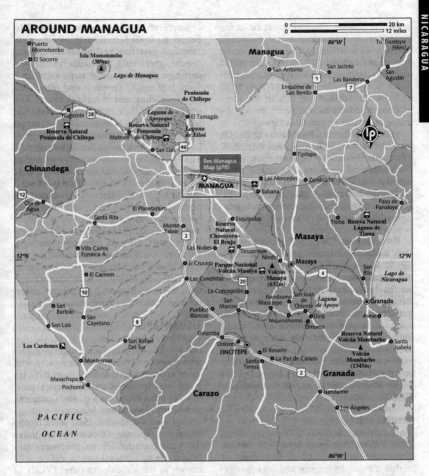

AROUND MANAGUA

Machapa (now located just north), it's still the only organically grown town around. **Cyber & Restaurant GLC** (Internet per hr US$1; 6am-10pm) has hamburgers (meals US$1 to US$4) and Internet access. There are no banks in Masachapa but Montelimar has an ATM (p90).

There's great surfing – a left point break just north of Montelimar, and a hollow right reef break to the south; Quizala, a beach break, is closer to Masachapa. South to Pochomil there are scores of smallish, predictable peaks that would be perfect to learn on, if someone had a surfing school around here. In fact, no one even rents boards, though you could rent a **private lancha** (small motorboat; per hr US$12-20).

Buses and pedicabs ply the 2km **Centro Turístico Pochomil** (car/pedestrian US$1/free), between Masachapa and the government-operated tourist center. This one has about 30 businesses, mostly waterfront restaurants and bars, almost all with *palapa* (thatched) roofs, fronting a truly spectacular beach. Come for the day or stay at **Hotel Alta Mar** (269 9204; tr with fan/air-con US$15/25;), with small, clean, wood-paneled rooms that are more than adequate.

Hospedaje Flipper (d US$6) is the cheapest accommodations in town, with OK cement rooms and cleanish private bathrooms; it caters to couples on a beach break. Right on the water, **Hotel Summer** (269 7754; s/d US$30/40;) has a big pool and classy rooms with cable TV, and if you eat at the restaurant, nonguests can swim (adult/child US$3/1.50) here too. Next door, you could rent a **private home** (☎ 266 7975; house US$150) right on the beach – it's a big, yellow, five-room wooden house. **Hotel Vista al Mar** (☎ 269 0115, 244 0736; d US$30-40; P 🞫), in the same cluster, is closest to the water; go for the more expensive rooms, with views.

Just south, cheerful **Hotel Bahía** (☎ 254 5128; www.hotelbahia.com; s/d/tr incl all meals US$35/60/75; P 🞫) is threadbare but somehow nicer, with pretty cabins, words of wisdom, and a woodsy lot. Meals are served family-style.

Several beachfront bars cater more to local fishermen than tourists; give Comacho's Disco Bar, on the road to Montelimar, a whirl.

Hotel Vistamar (☎ 265 8099; www.vistamarhotel .com; d with/without 3 meals, beer & rum US$155/81; P 🞫 🞫) is one of the nicest hotels on the Nicaraguan Pacific. Try to stay upstairs in the breezy two-story beach bungalows arranged around two pools, with great porches and outdoor seating scattered around the premises. Rooms aren't enormous, but could certainly sleep a family of four.

Buses run from Pochomil and Masachapa to Managua's Mercado Israel Lewites (US$1.25, one hour) every 20 minutes from 7am to 5:30pm.

Montelimar

Formerly the Somoza's summer home, **Barceló Montelimar Beach Resort** (☎ 269 6769; www.barcelo.com; P 🞫 🞫 🞫 🞫) does it right: it's got 88 rooms and 204 bungalows, stocked with coffeemakers, hairdryers, DirectTV, Internet access and more, plus four huge pools, tennis courts, discos, restaurants, beauty parlors, and even miniature golf. Prices are all-inclusive – food, beer, rum and most activities – and if you're into this sort of thing are a good deal. Day-trippers can visit the casino for free, or pay US$50 per person for use of all facilities. If you just want to use the ATM, tell the gatekeeper 'casino.' Works like a charm.

Close by is **Montelimar Cave**, with several petroglyphs that show traces of red and blue pigment still apparent, suggesting that all these monochromatic carvings were once a bit showier.

North of Montelimar, **Los Cardones Hotel Ecológico** (☎ 887 5225, 222 6887; www.loscardones .com) has just five pretty *cabinas* (cheap hotels), great food and some of the best surfing in Nicaragua just steps away from your hammock. Owners also offer fishing, snorkeling and horseback riding, and sea turtles lay their eggs on the beach. The whole operation is not only low impact (solar energy, composting) but also family friendly, with breaks for kids under 12. They want you to stay at least two nights, with single/double packages including three meals starting at US$150/200; a week surfing package is US$450/600. An expert left point break, a right reef point, and beach breaks just offshore make this a surfing paradise. From Managua, head toward the beach until California, then follow the signs 15km to Los Cardones. Or, take the bus from Managua's Mercado Israel Lewites to San Cayetano (US$0.70, one hour, 4am to 9pm, every 45 minutes), get off in California and stick your thumb out.

TICUANTEPE
pop 30,000 / elevation 360m

Just 19km from Managua, Ticuantepe is a refreshing escape from the sweltering city, with temperatures ranging from 22°C to 28°C. It's on the western rim of the Complejo Ventarrón Volcanic (Ventarrón Volcanic Complex), across from Nindirí and Masaya.

Occupied for at least 2500 years by the Matagalpa Indians, Ticuantepe is today the service center for an enormous and productive agricultural region, colloquially known as the Valle de las Piñas (Valley of Pineapples). The closest thing to a tourist attraction in town is the **Museo Arqueológico Municipal Raúl Rojas** (admission free), next to the *alcaldía* (mayor's office), with more than 50 stone and ceramic pieces dug up in the immediate era, plus an actually impressive mural of Ticuantepe c AD 1200. If it's closed, ask at the mayor's office if they'll let you in. There's also a quiet **trail** climbing dormant Cerro Ventarrón: go southeast on the dirt road by Comedor Bianca for about an hour on foot, then enjoy the views of Masaya.

One of the most important petroglyphs in the region, tantalizingly entitled **Pared de Serpientes** (Wall of Snakes), has more than 25 beautifully preserved, serpent-related drawings, and is evidently within easy walking distance of town. Unfortunately, it's on private property (ask Cantur, downtown, about guides) and surrounded by trash, including open sewage.

Parque Zoológico Edgar Lang Sacasa (adult/child US$0.70/0.30; ⏱ 8:30am-5pm Tue-Sun), at Km 16 on the Masaya Hwy, is your basic developing-world zoo, featuring local wildlife and a few African species lounging listlessly in smallish enclosures; the nutria sure are cute, though. If you do drop by, bring insect repellent.

There's no lodging in town, but you can eat at Comedor El Chanchito, two blocks north of the post office) and specializing in pork dishes, or Comedor Bianca (half a block south of the *alcaldía*), where the focus is on *carne asada*. Two more upscale and outdoorsy eateries are right on the highway: **El Parador** (Km 18 Carr Masaya; dishes US$2-8), with prim gardens and some Salvadoran food, including pupusas (cornmeal mass stuffed with cheese or refried beans); and **Mi Viejo Ranchito** (Km 17.5 Carr Masaya; ⏱ 7am-8:30pm), a thatch-roofed spot, open later on Fridays for 'Romantic Nights,' which could include *quesillos* and *tiste* (corn liquor) *au deux*.

Microbuses to Managua (Mercado Roberto Huembes; US$0.70) and San Marcos (US$0.50) leave from the parque central (central park) when full (about every 20 minutes). You can catch a taxi or *moto* (motorcycle) to the area reserves.

Reserva Natural Chocoyero-El Brujo

This deep, Y-shaped valley encompassed by a small, 184-hectare **natural reserve** (☎ 864 8652; admission US$4), 23km south of Managua and visited by 10,000 people visit each year, was originally protected to safeguard almost one-third of Managua's water supply. Then some astute soul noticed that these aquifers are exceptional. **El Brujo** (The Wizard) is a waterfall that seems to disappear underground, separated by a 400m cliff from **El Chocoyero** (Place of Parakeets), the less immediately impressive cascade. But show up at around 3pm and you'll see bands of parakeets come screaming home for their evening gossip.

Start at the Interpretive Center, with displays about the park's five different parakeet species, then the two trails leading to the waterfalls, both of which could take all afternoon, if you're slow. It may just have the most comfortable public campsites in Nicaragua (per person US$4), and you can rent a small tent for just US$10 more.

The reserve is 7km away from where the Managua–La Concepción bus drops you off, so it's much easier to get a cab in Ticuantepe (about US$10). After going 14km on the main road, turn west to Ticuantepe and La Concepción, and at Km 21.5 a dirt road goes to the entrance.

Montibelli Reserva Privada

Make reservations at least three days in advance to visit one of Nicaragua's best **private reserves** (☎ 270 4287; www.montibelli.com; d cabinas US$40; ⏱ Tue-Sun), tucked into a quiet corner of humid tropical forest along the Meseta's flattened spine. It has excellent birding, almost 40 species of butterfly, great food and wonderful guided hikes. On **Los Balcones Trail**, you can see yellow and brown orependola birds, best known for their unique nests that swing like mossy pendulums from the trees. **Mirador Trail** offers spectacular views of Volcán Masaya, Cerro Ventarrón and Mombacho.

The reserve also organizes package deals geared toward students and scientists, including camping (per person US$35) for groups of at least 10 people, including five meals, guided hikes and other activities. To get here, take a *moto* (US$2) from the Ticuantepe bus stop. The well-signed turnoff for the reserve is at Km 19 of Carretera Ticuantepe–La Concepción (or La Concha); it's another 2.5km to the reserve.

MASAYA & LOS PUEBLOS BLANCOS

This is the *meseta central,* the central plateau, a patchwork panorama of crater lakes and active volcanoes, colorful colonial cities and brilliant green *fincas* (plantations). It is in many ways the heart and soul of Nicaragua, as densely populated as El Salvador and home to a disproportionate number of myths, traditions and wild *fiestas patronales,* holy days that at heart seem less Catholic, revealing rather something that the Spanish were never quite able to tame.

Masaya, the 'Cradle of Nicaraguan Culture,' is the regional capital and home to the national *artesanía* (handicraft) market, where folkloric dance takes place at least once a week, if nothing more exotic is on.

To the south and west are Los Pueblos Blancos, or White Towns, a colorful collection of indigenous sites and Spanish cities, each with its own claim to fame. Further west still are Carazo's coffee-topped highlands, which suddenly slope down the continental shelf to broad and sandy Pacific beaches that international visitors almost never explore.

Climate & Geography

The relatively hot, low-altitude cities of Masaya and Nindirí actually sit on the rim of what may be the largest crater in the Americas, El Ventarrón, whose rim also encompasses Ticuantepe, Masatepe, the Laguna de Masaya and Parque Nacional Volcán Masaya (p100), a must-see attraction.

Heading west, the landscape rises to the *meseta*, a cool central plateau with peaks as high as 600m and a refreshing median temperature of 20°C to 24°C, then even higher past San Marcos, in the Carazo department. Coffe e, citrus and other relatively cool-weather crops carpet slopes that still harbor some of the region's original semihumid tropical savanna, which eceives a moderate 1300mm of rainfall annually. The ridge of this volcanic crinkle runs parallel to the Pacific, dropping fast and steep just 20km to the hot and sandy Carazo beaches.

In addition to Volcán Masaya, there are two important and accessible natural reserves nearby: Laguna de Apoyo (p102), an enormous, ancient, clean crater lake, with several hotels and regular busservice; and tiny Reserva Natural Chocoyero-El Brujo (p91), with a waterfall and lots of parakeets, most easily seen with your own transportation.

Getting There & Around

Masaya is the regional transportation hub, with regular buses to Managua, Granada, Rivas and the Costa Rican border, as well as throughout the Pueblos Blancos and Carazo towns. Jinotepe is the western transportation center. Roads are excellent throughout the region, with the exception of beach access, and fleets of minivans run regularly from village to village.

One of the best reasons to travel this region is the opportunity to ride in a *moto*, a tiny three-wheeled taxi that uses a motorcycle (or riding mower) engine and maxes out at about 40km/h, going downhill. They're everywhere. The smoothly paved and gently rolling hills also make for remarkable cycling – there used to be a place in Masaya's Mercado Artesanías (Mercado Viejo) to rent bicycles; ask around to see if it's reopened.

MASAYA

pop 118,000 / elevation 240m

Masaya has been a center of art and culture since long before the Spanish arrived, its Chorotegan roots showing throughout its extravagant annual events calendar and at every religious event, not to mention in the residents' mastery of traditional indigenous handicrafts.

Most international visitors come for two reasons: Volcán Masaya, fuming madly overhead, and the Mercado Artesanías, a square-block, Gothic, Spanish-fortress-themed edifice built more than a century ago, and today packed with some of Central America's best souvenirs (see (p99). Nicaraguan tourists, by the way, always make sure their visit coincides with one of Masaya's many spectacular festivals (see p96).

Despite the excellent shopping and perfect location (between Granada and Managua), Masaya isn't exactly a tourist mecca. Its authentic Spanish colonial architecture still shows wear and tear incurred during the massive 2000 earthquake, and the hotel and restaurant scene leaves a bit to be desired. Regardless, compared to Granada, Masaya's lack of pretensions and its cultural attractions make it a less glamorous, but perhaps more authentic, base from which to explore this rich region.

Orientation

Masaya, the smallest department in the country at only 590 sq km, is 29km southeast of Managua and 16km northwest of Granada. The city sits at the edge of Laguna de Masaya, beyond which rises Volcán Masaya, and is the economic and transportation hub for the region.

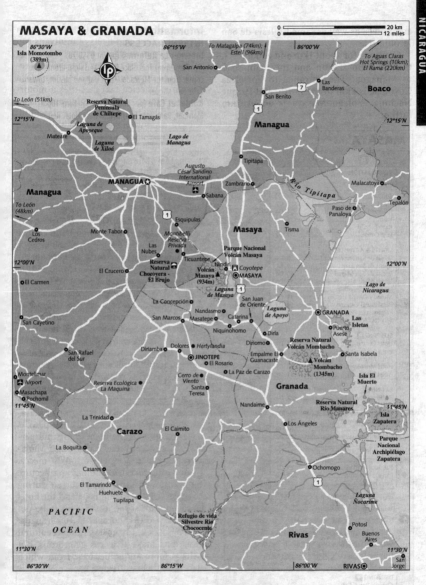

There are several parques central (central parks), remnants of when Masaya was a group of small communities, but today the most important central plaza is the one that fronts Iglesia La Asunción, two blocks west of the Mercado Artesanías. From La Asunción, the lagoon and baseball stadium are seven blocks to the west. Five blocks to the south are Barrio Monimbó and Iglesia San Sebastian. The Mercado Municipal (Mercado Nuevo) and main bus station are about six blocks to the east of Parroquia La Asunción, past the Mercado Artesanías.

The neighborhood north of La Asunción contains most of Masaya's restaurants and hotels, as well as famed Iglesia de San Jerónimo.

Continue for about 1km and you'll reach the old train station and the main road to Managua. The entrance to Forteleza Coyotepe is 2km to the north, and Parque Nacional Volcán Masaya is about 7km further.

Information

INTERNET ACCESS

Internet La Reform@ (per hr US$0.70; 🕑 7am-9pm) This place is fast and right around the corner from the Mercado Municipal and bus lot, toward Calle San Miguel.

Kablenet Café (per hr US$0.70; 🕑 8am-10pm Mon-Sat, 9am-3pm Sun) Across from Hotel Regis.

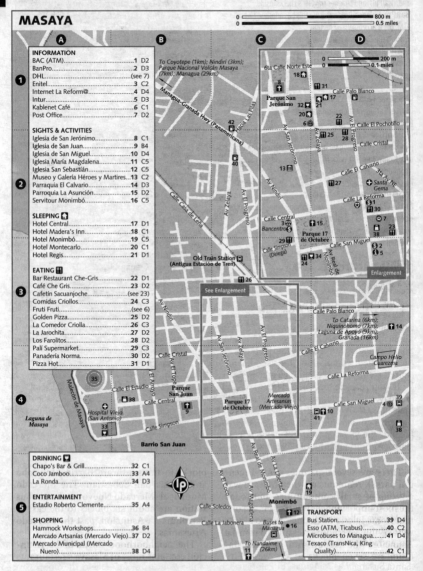

MASAYA

INFORMATION		
BAC (ATM)	1	D2
BanPro	2	D3
DHL	(see 7)	
Enitel	3	C2
Internet La Reform@	4	D4
Intur	5	D3
Kablenet Café	6	C1
Post Office	7	D2
SIGHTS & ACTIVITIES		
Iglesia de San Jerónimo	8	C1
Iglesia de San Juan	9	B4
Iglesia de San Miguel	10	D4
Iglesia María Magdalena	11	C5
Iglesia San Sebastián	12	C5
Museo y Galería Héroes y Martires	13	C2
Parraquia El Calvario	14	C2
Parroquia La Asunción	15	D2
Servitour Monimbó	16	C5
SLEEPING		
Hotel Central	17	D1
Hotel Madera's Inn	18	C1
Hotel Monimbó	19	C5
Hotel Montecarlo	20	C1
Hotel Regis	21	D1
EATING		
Bar Restaurant Che-Gris	22	D1
Café Che Gris	23	D2
Cafetín Sacuanjoche	(see 23)	
Comidas Criollos	24	C3
Fruti Fruti	(see 6)	
Golden Pizza	25	D2
La Comedor Criolla	26	C3
La Jarochita	27	D2
Los Farolitos	28	D2
Palí Supermarket	29	C3
Panadería Norma	30	D2
Pizza Hot	31	D1
DRINKING		
Chapo's Bar & Grill	32	C1
Coco Jamboo	33	A4
La Ronda	34	D3
ENTERTAINMENT		
Estadio Roberto Clemente	35	A4
SHOPPING		
Hammock Workshops	36	B4
Mercado Artsanías (Mercado Viejo)	37	D2
Mercado Municipal (Mercado Nuero)	38	D4
TRANSPORT		
Bus Station	39	D4
Esso (ATM, Ticabus)	40	C2
Microbuses to Managua	41	D4
Texaco (TransNica, King Quality)	42	C1

To Coyotepe (1km); Nindiri (3km); Parque Nacional Volcán Masaya (7km); Managua (29km)

Managua-Granada Hwy (Panamericana)

6ta Calle Norte Este

Parque San Jerónimo

Calle Palo Blanco

Calle Cristal

Calle El Calvano

Santa Gema

Calle La Reforma

Calle Central

Bancentro

Parque 17 de Octubre

Calle Simpson (Dinega)

Calle San Miguel

Enlargement

Old Train Station (Antigua Estación de Tren)

See Enlargement

Calle Casa de Teña

Calle Palo Blanco

To Catarina (6km); Niquinohomo (7km); Laguna de Apoyo (9km); Granada (16km)

Campo Hélio Cuarezma

Calle La Reforma

Calle Cristal

Calle El Calvano

Parque San Juan

Parque 17 de Octubre

Mercado Artsanías (Mercado Viejo)

Calle San Miguel

Malecon de Masaya

Calle El Estadio

Calle Central

Calle Simpson

Hospital Viejo (San Antonio)

Laguna de Masaya

Barrio San Juan

Monimbó

Calle Soledos

Calle La Jabonera

Buses to Managua

TRANSPORT

To Nandaime (26km)

MEDICAL SERVICES
Hospital Hilario Sanchez Vásquez (☎ 522 2778; Calle San Miguel) Has emergency room services.

MONEY
Banco America Central (BAC) With a 24-hour ATM next to the Mercado Artesanías, it accepts MasterCard/Cirrus and Visa/Plus, and changes traveler's checks inside.
BanPro A block away from BAC, this has another 24-hour ATM, but it accepts Visa/Plus only.
Esso At the *empalme* (three-way intersection) with the main Granada–Managua highway. Use Visa/Plus or Master-Card/Cirrus debit cards at this ATM, which offers US dollars or córdobas.

POST & TELEPHONE
Enitel For international calls. It faces Parque 17 de Octubre.
Post office & DHL Both conveniently inside the Mercado Artesanías. Depending on how fast you want that hammock on your porch back home, DHL is open Saturday mornings.

TOURIST INFORMATION
Intur (☎ 522 7615) This well-funded office with English-speaking staff sells a fairly useful, if distorted, map (with lots of factoids in English) and has broad information about the region.

Sights & Activities
Most people visit Masaya to shop; if that describes you, skip ahead to p99.

One of the best ways to see the town is in a **horse-drawn carriage**, about US$2 per person for the grand tour. Skinny horses may dissuade some would-be riders, but note that Granada's burgeoning tourist industry (ie horrified, complaining tourists) has inspired some serious equine weight-gain.

If you're here between Thursday and Sunday, consider taking the cute little **tourist train** (US$2, 40 minutes) from Hotel Madera's Inn on a guided tour of Masaya. Highlights include the *malecón* (waterfront), Iglesia de San Jerónimo and the old **1926 train station** (Av Zelaya), which unfortunately remains closed to the public.

CHURCHES & PLAZAS
There are 12 major barrios (neighborhoods) in Masaya, all of which were once separate communities with their own churches, plazas and identities: Monimbó, San Jerónimo, Santa Teresa, Villa Bosco Monge, Aserrio, Santa Susana, Las Malvinas, El Palomar, La Ceibita, Cerro Fortaleza El Coyotepe, Sylvio Renazco and Cerro la Barranca

At the center of it all is the 1750 **Parroquia de La Asunción**, an attractive but scarred late-Baroque beauty that the Spanish government has offered to help repair. It watches over the parque central, formally known as **Parque 17 de Octubre** in honor of the 1977 firefight that pitted local residents (armed with explosive homemade weapons) against Somoza's National Guard.

Monimbó is Masaya's most famous neighborhood, its ancient center now marked by the 1935 **Iglesia San Sebastián**. Perhaps more important, **Iglesia María Magdalena**, sort of the female counterpart to San Sebastián, is where many of Monimbó's most important festivals begin or end.

Although **Iglesia San Juan** is usually closed to the public, check out the surrounding neighborhood strung between La Asunción and the lake, with more than a dozen hammock workshops and factories. Other churches worth seeing include more modern **Iglesia de San Miguel**, whose resident San Miguel Arcángel makes the rounds during the procession of St Jerome, and 1848 **San Juan Bautista**, small, simple and much nicer inside than out.

Parroquia El Calvario, seven blocks northeast of the parque central on Calle El Calvario, is a squat colonial structure with no spire, most remarkable for the extragory statues of Jesus and the thieves being crucified, right at the entrance. Those are original – the rest had to be remodeled after the earthquake of 2000.

Among the major buildings worst hit by the earthquake, which also destroyed about 80 homes, was 1928 **Iglesia de San Jerónimo**, the spiritual heart of Masaya and one of the most recognizable silhouettes on the skyline. But that hasn't stopped anyone from celebrating the longest *fiestas patronales* in Nicaragua, with their epicenter, as always, right here.

THE MALECÓN & LAGUNA DE MASAYA
Just seven blocks west of the parque central, past hammock factories and Iglesia San Juan, is one of the most inspiring views in a region famed for the same, across Laguna de Masaya to the smoking Santiago crater. The still attractive, if crumbling, *malecón* was constructed in 1944, when you could still swim, drink or fish in the impressive

lagoon. Things have changed. Several trails carved into the volcanic crater millennia ago still lead from a humble collection of restaurant/bars down to the water, but hardly anyone ever uses them anymore.

MUSEO & GALERÍA HÉROES Y MARTIRES

Inside the *alcaldía* (mayor's office), this **museum** (☎ 552 2977; suggested donation US$1; ⌚ 8am-noon & 2-5pm Mon-Fri) honors Masayans who gave their lives during the revolution. There are walls of photos and interesting displays of bomb-building materials and weapons, as well as personal effects including musical instruments and a few Chorotegan funeral urns. It's poignant.

FORTELEZA COYOTEPE

Built in 1893 atop Cerro de los Coyotes, the eerie **Forteleza Coyotepe** (admission US$0.70; ⌚ 8am-6pm) witnessed the last stand of Benjamín Zeledón, the 1912 hero of resistance to US intervention. The marines managed to take the fortress, watched all the while by a young man named Sandino, who vowed his revenge. In the end it would also be the National Guard's last stronghold, overrun during Sandinista's final 1979 offensive.

It's worth the climb just for the view: Laguna de Masaya, Lago de Managua, Volcán Mombacho and, if it's clear, Volcán Momotombo, rising red and black above Managua. But your entrance fee, a donation to the Nicaraguan boy scouts, also includes a Spanish-language tour of the underground prison, detailing each daily atrocity.

You can walk 2km north on the Interamericana (Pan-American Hwy), but it's worth getting a Managua-bound bus (US$0.30) or taxi (US$1) to avoid the scary traffic. Taxis charge extra to take you up the steep hill, otherwise it's a sweaty half-hour hike.

Tours

Most people organize tours from Granada (see p119), but there is one homegrown Masaya outfit, **Servitour Monimbó** (☎ 522 7404, 623 5689). Across from Iglesia San Sebastián, it offers inexpensive tours of local crafts workshops, as well as trips to Aguas Clara hot springs (p241) and Reserva Natural El Chocoyero-El Brujo (p91). Most trips are geared toward larger groups.

Festivals & Events

Every Thursday night at about 5pm, **Jueves de Verbena** has food, music and ballet *folklorico* at the Mercado Artesanías; most Granada tour outfits offer this as a weekly add-on to their regular Masaya trips.

La Virgen de la Asunción (March 16) Better known as the Virgin of the Burning Finger or Festival of the Cross, the town's top Virgin is taken to the lake for a blessing of the waters and a good look at the slender protrusion of lava that threatened the town during the 1772 eruption, until she stopped it.

Jesús del Rescate (April 3) Scores of *carretas* (oxcarts) begin their journey from Masaya to San Jorge (p136).

San Lázaro (week before Palm Sunday) Includes a procession of costumed dogs.

Día de la Virgen de la Asunción (August 15) Everyone's favorite patron saint, María Magdalena, is hoisted atop the shoulders of revelers for her annual tour of Monimbó; fireworks are involved.

San Jerónimo (September 30) Officially eight days of festivities, folks have stretched out Nicaragua's most famous festival to three months. The patron saint (in the guise of a bearded campesino named 'Tata Chombó,' or 'Doctor of the Poor') is taken from the San Jerónimo church altar and borne around Masaya while traditional dances are performed, including Mozote y Verga, a mock battle that ends with peacemaking ceremonies to commemorate the September peace treaties of 1856, 1912 and 1979. Fireworks, marimbas, parades, drag queens and more make this a fiesta to remember.

Noche de Agüizotes (last Friday in October) Not to be confused with Halloween or Day of the Dead, this spooky festival features legends come to life and ghosts of the dead, plus the costumed living parading through the streets.

El Toro Venado (last Sunday of October, third Sunday of November) This dance involves a mythical creature which is half-bull, half-deer (read: half-Spanish, half-indigenous), and whose mission is to make fun of the rest of the fair.

Baile de los Diablitos (last Sunday of November) Little devils dance in honor of Mephistopheles and San Jerónimo.

Sleeping

Most budget lodging is clustered about four blocks north of Parroquia La Asunción, along Av Zelaya. Nicer hotels are on the Carretera Masaya, interspersed with lots of love hotels. A good rule of thumb: if there's a hiding place for your car, chances are rates will be hourly.

Hotel Regis (☎ 522 2300; cmolinapalma@hotmail.com; old/new r per person US$3/6) Three and a half blocks north of the main plaza, Hotel Regis offers small, tidy rooms in aquamarine cement for

'MONIMBÓ IS NICARAGUA!'

Masaya may have been declared the 'Cradle of National Folklore,' but the folklore of Masaya is the folklore of Monimbó. Once the region's most important indigenous city, this famous Masaya neighborhood, centered around Iglesia San Sebastián, is still populated mainly by people of Chorotegan descent.

Though a vital part of Masaya and Nicaragua, in many ways Monimbó remains a world apart: indigenous government structures such as the Council of Elders are still in place, if largely relegated to ceremonial status.

One reason for Monimbó's cultural autonomy is its celebrated history of almost continuous rebellion against the Spaniards and other occupiers. Most recently, in 1977, the people of Monimbó famously attacked Somoza's feared National Guard, using homemade weapons – contact bombs, machetes and lances – produced by their own artisans and craftspeople. They held the barrio for a week.

After the battle, the Monimboseños donned traditional Spanish masks, borrowed from folkloric dances that ridiculed those occupiers, and denounced to the newspapers the abuses and atrocities of the National Guard. Those who participated are proud to note that masks, both as symbols and disguises, have been used ever since in revolutionary movements across Latin America and the world.

The country was inspired by the barrio's spectacular resistance, and streets across the nation echoed with the battle cry, 'Monimbó is Nicaragua!' Ernesto Cardenal (see the boxed text, p267) wrote that the masked Monimboseños had declared their barrio 'Free Nicaragua.' And in the end, Masaya and Monimbó were the first cities to be liberated.

Monimbó has also fought to protect its traditions and folklore, in particular its very traditional way of celebrating religious events. During the festivals for **St Lazarus**, one week before Easter, Iglesia María Magdalena is attended by devotees and their dogs, which are dressed up as children, witches, space aliens and more. A special mass is followed by food and corn liquor for all.

Los Agüizotes is another important celebration, featuring spirits of the dead and characters from indigenous horror stories (many originating during the Spanish conquest). The Headless Priest and La Carreta Nagua (Chariot of Death) are used throughout the year to scare children into better behavior, but on the last Friday in October make their way through the streets of Monimbó and Masaya.

Costumes are prepared the night before in a ceremony called **La Vela de Candil** (Vigil of the Candle). They are placed on a table with a large candle in the middle, and those watching over it throughout the night keep themselves awake with fireworks, live music, alcohol and dancing, after which everyone prepares for the annual procession.

The Barrio of Monimbó organizes festivals and events throughout the year; ask at **Intur** (☎ 522 7615) or your hotel if anything is on while you're in town.

Monimbó native Ruth Danelia López Gaitan wrote her 'Sustainable Tourism' thesis for the University of Nicaragua about the cultural traditions of Monimbó. Contact her through **Landcruiser Tours** (☎ 645 5702; www.landcruisertours.com).

---

cheap prices, or newer, nicer rooms with more light for a bit more. They're arranged around a pleasant courtyard, at the end of which are several clean, shared bathrooms. The couple who run the place are especially helpful, and maintain a solid information board.

Hotel Central (☎ 522 2867; horacio_perez boza@hotmail.com; d with/without bathroom US$8/6) Almost next door to Regis, this place is super-basic, but you get a TV. There's one tiny, windowless single under the stairs for US$3.

Hotel Monte Carlo (☎ 522 2927; tr with fan/air-con US$10/20; 🖵) Across the street and a step up, clean bathrooms are still shared (with only one other room, though). Still, rooms are nice, and the wicker furniture and lush plants give it a sort of rustic jungle ambience.

Hotel Madera's Inn (☎ 522 5825; hmaderas@ibw .com.ni; Av Zelaya; s US$15, q US$20-30; 🖵) This homey and colonial family-run hotel has doubles with air-con and direct TV and bathroom or small rooms with firm bunk beds and separate bathrooms. Cozy common areas are strategically arranged throughout the rambling mansion, breakfast is US$2, and there is a Budget and Alamo desk where you should reserve cars at least two hours in advance (they need to be driven down from Managua).

Hotel Monimbó (☎ 522 6867; r US$10-25; ♨) Around the corner from San Sebastián, in the heart of Monimbó, this brand-new spot has spacious, immaculate, modern rooms with cool tiling, air-con and bathroom, plus pickups at Managua international airport and other little luxuries you'll appreciate.

Madonna Inn y Restaurant (☎ 522 6363; lunaz@munditel.com.ni; d US$30-35; ℗ ♨) Just north of Texaco on the Carretera, this is a great option if you just need a real hotel: super-clean, pretty furniture, great mattresses, hot-water bathrooms, air-con, the works. There's even an attached Mexican restaurant open 24 hours (meals US$3 to US$8) downstairs.

Eating

Masaya isn't known for its cuisine, but you can get by on the cheap.

RESTAURANTS

Comidas Criollas (lunch buffet US$2-3; ♨ 9:30am-7pm) Right on the park, this impressive steam-table buffet serves huge portions of great food with a few solid vegetarian options.

La Comedor Criolla (Av Zelaya; ♨ 7am-3pm) Not to be confused with Comidas Criollas, this place is close to the budget hotels and also does a good steam-table buffet.

La Jarochita (Av Zelaya; dishes US$2-3; ♨ 11:30am-late) A block north of the main plaza, Jarochita is well known throughout the region as one of the (if not the) best Mexican restaurants in Nicaragua. It is very good, with Vera Cruz–style tacos, spicy *posole* (rich hominy stew) and good seafood; it doesn't skimp on the cheese.

Bar Restaurant Che-Gris (mains US$3-7) Around the corner from Hotel Regis, this popular spot has a selection of meat, seafood and vegetarian meals; a *comida corriente* (mixed plate of different foods typical of the region) is US$2.50. It's considered one of the best restaurants in town, which may be true, but don't get all excited.

Pizza Hot (♨ 10am-10pm) In addition to decent pizza, this franchise location also offers fried chicken and spaghetti.

Los Farolitos (mains US$2-5; ♨ 6:30am-midnight) This narrow restaurant/bar serves breakfasts with a backpacker-friendly gimmick: you pay for each item (toast, fried plantains, *gallo pinto* – blended rice and beans) separately, each never costing more than US$0.50. Creative salads (try the broccoli and chicken) and other snacks come all or nothing.

Aeropuerto 79 (Km 31.5 Carr Masaya; dishes US$2.50-8; ♨ 10am-11pm) Just south of Masaya on the main road, this fairly spectacular spot – colorful tilework, beautiful gardens, sculptures of large-breasted women – has well-prepared typical food, and specializes in exotic meat, such as armadillo, rabbit or deer. It was a Sandinista military depot during the revolution, and a nearby plane crash in 1979 inspired the peacetime name.

CAFÉS & QUICK EATS

Inexpensive *comedores* (basic eateries) cling to the outside of the Mercado Municipal, away from the buses, where plastic baggies of *vigarón* (mashed yucca topped with coleslaw and pork rinds), fruit salad and *gallo pinto* can be had for less than US$1, a sit-down meal with a drink for around US$2.

Mercado Artesanías (Mercado Viejo; mains US$2-4; ♨ 10am-6pm) Has a handful of slightly more expensive cafés with less hectic ambience, longer menus and ice cubes made of purified water. Café Che Gris gets the raves, but most local business owners order their food from Cafetín Sacuanjoche, with a cheap set plate at lunch.

Fruti Fruti (Av Zelaya; snacks US$2-6; ♨ 7am-10pm) Fruit smoothies (and not the healthy kind) plus cold sandwiches, salads and snacks make this a fine stop.

Golden Pizza (☎ 522 4601; Av Zelaya; slice/pie US$0.70/4) It's not the best pizza on earth, but it delivers.

Panadería Norma (♨ 8am-8pm) One block north of the Mercado Artesanías, this outlet of Nicaragua's best bakery has a variety of cakes, buns and pastries, plus real, brewed coffee for just US$0.15 a cup.

GROCERIES

Palí (♨ 7:30am-8pm Mon-Sat, 8am-6:30pm Sun) Opposite the park, you can put your own meal together, then indulge in Eskimo ice cream.

Drinking

Masaya actually has a great – and evidently gay-friendly – party scene. **Viva Masaya** (www .vivamasaya.com) has photos and up-to-date information for party people.

La Ronda (🕑 noon-midnight Tue-Sun) This rather tranquil and elegant spot right on the park has a good happy hour and popular Wednesday karaoke night.

Coco Jamboo (🕑 9pm-3am Fri-Sun) Danceheads opt for this big club at the south end of the *malecón*, where a cheesy good time can usually be had.

El Toro Loco (cover US$2.50; 🕑 Thu-Sun) gets packed on reggae nights, while Chapo's Bar & Grill, the new hot spot, serves steak, allows smoking in the open-air bar and hosts all-night reggae parties on weekends, conveniently right next to the budget hotels.

Entertainment

Enjoy a soda or beer at one of the very basic eateries on the *malecón* or, better, take yourself out to a ball game at the wonderfully rustic, red-brick-and-masonry Estadio Roberto Clemente, with lagoon views and professional baseball games between January and May, with local leagues getting a workout in the off season.

Shopping

Masaya's main claim to fame is shopping, and savvy buyers come here to find great deals on Nicaragua's finest handicrafts. Tours and taxi drivers drop you off at the 1888 **Mercado Artesanías** (National Artisans Market, Mercado Viejo or Old Market), a somewhat incongruous, black-basalt Gothic structure with a Spanish-fortress motif, including turrets, towers and oversized gates. Despite a major fire in 1966, it was used as a regular market until 1978, when Somoza's National Guard all but leveled it. The building, which covers an entire city block, was abandoned until renovations began in 1994.

Today it is a wonderful place to stroll, with attractive booths separated by wide and breezy walkways, showcasing the highest quality crafts in the country. Thursday nights are *Noches Verbenas*, when free folkloric dance exhibitions, marimba performances and traditional foods make this the best party in town. If you run out of money, there are two ATMs across the street; if you run out of space, there's a post office *and*

DHL office inside the building. They're serious.

Public buses drop you off in the massive bus lot behind the huge, chaotic Mercado Municipal (Mercado Nuevo), a more typical market with unrefrigerated meat counters, colorful vegetable stands, toiletries and a wide selection of somewhat lower-quality handicrafts, cigars, handmade shoes and fun souvenirs at discount prices crammed under the hot, busy tents. Pay attention, watch your backpack and wallet, and have fun.

Can't stop shopping? There are handicrafts workshops all over town. Hammock factories congregate in Barrio San Juan, between La Asunción and the lagoon, while wood and leather workshops are hidden throughout Monimbó. **Servitour Monimbó** (☎ 522 7404, 623 5689) can arrange guided walks through the best of them.

Getting There & Around

Agencia Ticabus (☎ 522 3697; Av Zelaya) is operated out of a private home, so knock if it doesn't appear to be open. Buses depart from the Esso station at the junction for San José, Costa Rica (US$12.50, nine hours, 6am and noon); San Salvador (US$25, 4am); and Panama City (US$37.50, 4am). Transnica and King Quality buses stop at Texaco, across the Carretera. Taxis and horse-drawn carriages both charge around US$0.75 for a ride across town. **Hotel Madera's Inn** (☎ 522 5825; hmaderas@ibw.com.ni) has a Budget and Alamo desk, but vehicles need to be driven down from Managua.

Minivans to Managua (UCA; US$0.80, 30 minutes) leave the park in front of Iglesia de San Miguel when full, about every hour. Other buses and minivans arrive and depart from the eastern side of the Mercado Municipal.

Carazo (San Marcos, Diriamba and Jinotepe) US$1, 1¼ hours, 5am to 6pm, every 20 minutes

Catarina, Diriomo and Diría US$0.80, 40 minutes, 6am to 5pm, every 20 minutes

Catarina, San Juan de Oriente, Niquinohomo, Masatepe and San Marcos US$0.80, 1¼ hours, 5am to 6pm, every 20 minutes

Granada US$0.80, 40 minutes, 5am to 6pm, every 20 minutes

Laguna de Apoyo rim US$0.35, 20 minutes, 5am to 5pm, every 20 minutes; bottom US$0.70, 30 minutes, 5:30am, 10:30am and 3:30pm

Managua US$0.50, one hour, 4:30am to 5:10pm, every 20 minutes

MASAYA & MESETA ARTS & CRAFTS

Let's face it: you didn't come to Masaya for the food. This is where you can find *artesanías* (handicrafts) from throughout Nicaragua, all within an hour of the airport. Heck, if you check out the factories, you may even be able to get some of this stuff emblazoned with 'Mexico,' 'Guatemala,' or 'Pura Vida Costa Rica,' just to confuse your friends and coworkers.

Masaya itself has been famed since long before the Spanish arrived for its excellent craftsmanship, including leather, woodcrafts and so much more, on display alongside work from all over the country.

The prices given are for items of average quality – a spectacular piece may warrant a spectacular price tag.

■ Hammocks (US$10 to US$20 for the simple ones, US$25 to US$50 for the nice ones) Bulky but beautiful, Nicaragua's signature craft is made right here in Masaya, and yes, you'll be kicking yourself for not struggling home with one on the plane.

■ Naive paintings and balsawood carvings (US$5 to US$200) Glowing colors and tropical subjects are a window on the exotic Islas Solentiname (see p266).

■ Black ceramics (US$3 to US$20) Typical of Matagalpa and Jinotega (see p217), smooth, heavy ceramics are specially fired for a deep black sheen.

■ Natural fiber weavings (US$3 to US$10) Whether it's the light, flexible jipi japa hats of Camoapa (see p241), the elaborately patterned reed mats from Masatepe (see p106), or even the woven palm-leaf crickets (US$0.06, or 1 córdoba) that every enterprising eight-year-old in Nicaragua has on offer, you'll find it here.

■ Carved jícara shells (US$1 to US$5) You've probably seen the shiny green seeds hanging from the rangy-looking trees, one of the first plants ever domesticated – not for food, but for the shell. Carvings on durable cups and bowls range from simple to stunning, and are priced accordingly.

■ Che Guevara memorabilia (Give what you can, take what you need) Some claim you can find more variation on Che Guevara–related items – jewelry, stash boxes, coffee brands, soapstone carvings, T-shirts with images other than 'pensive Che' – in Nicaragua than anywhere else in the world, including Cuba. Let the communist in your life know you care.

■ Caribbean woodcarvings (US$5 to US$25) Several indigenous groups, including the Garífuna and Miskito (see p253), make small, detailed woodcarvings in precious hardwood, generally with nautical themes like canoes, lobsters and fish.

■ Organic coffee (US$3 to US$6) If you can't make it to the Northern Highlands (see p210) or Isla de Ometepe (p147), be sure to pick a couple of bags of premium high-altitude brew here.

■ Soapstone sculptures (US$20 to US$50) They don't take up much space, but these sensually smooth marmolina sculptures from San Juan de Limay (see p199) will weigh you down.

Matagalpa US$1.30, 1½ hours, 5:30am and 6am
Ticuantepe US$0.70, 45 minutes, 6am to 5pm, every 20 minutes

PARQUE NACIONAL VOLCÁN MASAYA

The Spaniards said this was the gate to hell, and put the Bobadilla cross (named for the priest who planted it) atop a now sadly inaccessible cliff. **Volcán Masaya** (☎ 522 5415; admission US$4; ⏰ 9am-4:45pm) is the most heavily venting volcano in Nicaragua, and there is no way, in a more litigation-happy nation, that you would ever be allowed to drive up to the lip of a volcanic cone as volatile as the Santiago crater.

There's always lava bubbling at the bottom (you probably won't see it, though), and a column of sulfurous gases rising above; in 2001 an eruption hurled heated rocks 500m into the air, damaging cars and narrowly missing people. The brochure explains that this is 'adventure tourism,' with risks, and recommends limiting your visit to 20 minutes or so.

But you have to go. Masaya is already inside the volcano, an enormous and ancient crater called El Ventarrón, with a barely perceptible rim that runs from Ticuantepe (see p90) to Masatepe, and around the Laguna de Masaya. Don't you want to see this open gateway into the earth's mantle, which has inspired human sacrifices and Catholic exorcisms? Try to arrive in the afternoon, when the crater's thousands of *chocoyos* (parakeets) return to their nests in the crater walls, apparently unharmed by the billowing toxic gases.

There are more than 20km of hiking trails. Shorter, most accessible treks require **guides** (per group US$0.70, plus tips), which you pay for with your admission. **Sendero Los Coyotes** (1.5km) meanders through lavastrewn fields and dry tropical forest; **Sendero El Comalito** (2km) takes you to a smaller cone surrounded by fumaroles; and **Sendero Las Cuevas** (1½ hours) lets you explore the very cool lava tunnels of Tzinancanostoc, with bats.

There are also longer hikes (5km to 6km) that don't require guides (although you could certainly arrange them) to lookout points and large rocks. If you speak Spanish, ask your guide to show you around the attractive **museum**, at the visitors center, with impressive natural history displays and beautiful murals, and a new **butterfly garden**.

The **park entrance** is 7km north of Masaya. You'll pay for your entry and guided hikes at the booth, and receive a surprisingly handy brochure with a map and useful information in Spanish and English. It's 5km of paved road to the crater and **Plaza de Oviedo**, which honors the intrepid priest who went down into the volcano with a sample dish, to find out whether or not the lava was (as he suspected) pure gold. It wasn't, but folks were still impressed enough with the feat to name the parking lot after him.

There's no camping, but **Hotel Volcán Masaya** (☎ 522 7114; r with 1/2 beds US$27/37), right by the park entrance, has bare but comfortable rooms complete with screened-in porches. It only serves breakfast (US$2) and snacks, and restaurants are a long walk along the busy road; consider bringing food with you. About 3km south, **El Raizón Hotel** (☎ 279 8520; www.hotelraizon.com; r incl breakfast US$20-40; P ⌘ ▢) is inconvenient unless you have a rental car, in which case it's a good deal. There are a variety of rooms (some with

air-con), hammocks strewn around pretty gardens, tasteful furnishings and on-site Internet, plus a restaurant andminimarket.

Any Managua-bound bus from Masaya or Granada can drop you at the entrance, but it's a steep, hot climb to the crater; hitching is definitely possible. Consider taking a round-trip taxi from Masaya (US$8) or Granada (US$15), including an hour's wait at the top. Most tour outfits in Granada come here as part of a Masaya day trip, including the markets and Catarina overlook, for around US$15 per person.

NINDIRÍ
pop 35,700

Only 3km north of Masaya, the much more adorable (and cleaner) town of Nindirí may have been even more important than Monimbó during the Chorotega era. Archaeological treasures abound, as you'll see at tiny **Museo Tindirí** (donations accepted; ☽ 8am-noon & 2-5pm Mon-Fri). Vast quantities of priceless ceramics, ancient sculptures and colonial-era artifacts (3000 in all) have been crammed into this cheerfully painted building, one block from the attractive parque central.

If the lady who runs the museum is out, you could check out the 1529 Catholic **church**, which has been left in adobe simplicity by subsequent renovations. It's home to Cristo del Volcán, credited with stopping a lava flow from destroying the town during the 1772 eruption that opened the Santiago crater.

Adventurous souls could take the short hike to **Cascadas Cailagua** and **petroglyphs**. Start at the cemetery close to the Nindirí *empalme:* take the road through the cemetery until you get to the three green crosses; make a right and follow the trail through the gap in the fence and across the field. The waterfall would be more attractive without the litter (and raw sewage), but check out the wall of petroglyphs nearby.

Unfortunately, there are no hotels in Nindirí, but tour operator **Harold Ramos** (☎ 522 5979, 611 8196; Del Parque de Nindirí 21/2c oeste Colegio Oreana Teresa) can arrange lodging in the city (per person US$5) or country (US$4). Meals cost US$3 extra. Ramos also leads guided city tours in pedicabs (US$3) and visits to indigenous communities (US$10) around Nindirí, as well as hiking trips at a private reserve. He's a member of the Red de Turismo Sostenible (RTS; Sustainable Tourism Network).

There are two great restaurants close to the Nindirí *empalme*. **Nika Pollo** (dishes US$2-3; ☼ 7am-11pm), a huge diner and international truckers refuge, has 11 massive breakfasts and excellent wooden playground. Call ahead if you want an entire pig roasted. **Bucaneros** (meals US$5-13; ☼ 10am-midnight) is also a bar, but serves good food alongside great volcano and lagoon views, with live music on weekends and pool all week long.

RESERVA NATURAL LAGUNA DE APOYO

This 200m-deep, 200-centuries-old crater lake is said to be the country's cleanest and deepest, with warm undersea fumaroles that feed the refreshing, purportedly healing and slightly salty waters. A vision in sapphire set into a thickly forested, steeply walled volcanic crater, the whole place echoes with howler monkeys at sunrise. And the reason why Laguna de Apoyo is Nicaragua's easiest reserve to enjoy is because it's so poorly protected.

The lagoon falls into several Marena (Ministry of the Environment & Natural Resources) jurisdictions, some of which can apparently be talked into ignoring flagrant abuse of fuzzy 'integrated ecosystem management' regulations, as you'll see. It's not paradise lost (yet) but this fragile environment has been developing rapidly. Please tread as lightly as you can here.

Many visitors are content with just taking in the view from Catarina or Diría, Mombacho rising like a distant lover above the far rim. But it's worth making your way to the bottom for one of the finest swims you'll ever enjoy.

Activities

Real serious adventure-sports addicts – the ones who have their own equipment and don't mind paying to drag it all over Central America – have been hitting this place for years. Parasail off the crater rim, windsurf across the surface, but please don't use any sort of motorboat or jet-ski (they are available), as it's illegal and probably bad karma as well.

A tiny, increasingly touristy town lies at the bottom of the paved road into the crater, accessible via an often unsigned turnoff about 15km north of Granada, halfway to Masaya. There's a free **beach** at the bottom of the road; look for the trail just to the right of where the road splits. Otherwise, pay a few dollars to any of the hotels for day-use privileges at their docks.

Spanish School Laguna de Apoyo (☎ 825 1409, 882 3992; www.guegue.com.ni/eco-nic; dm US$7.50, s/d/tr without bathroom US$16/19/22, r with bathroom US$25) runs 20-hour per week tuition for US$190/700 per week/month with room and board, US$20 extra to guarantee individual instruction. Rather than stay with a host family, you can stay and eat at its cozy hostel with pleasant, if rustic, rooms. Note that one of the shared bathrooms has a great little waterfall. It also serves good family-style meals (US$3) at 7:30am, 12:30pm and 6:30pm; guests can use the kitchen at any other time.

This is also an ecological research station, and hosts scientists studying the region's endemic fish population – which means it also offers **crater dives** (1/2 tanks US$35/45). The way the crater so suddenly plunges into murky darkness is worth a look, as are fumaroles and a brownish endemic species (one of four) nicknamed 'chancho.' You must be PADI certified. The school also rents kayaks (US$10 for four hours) and bikes (US$5 per day).

San Juan del Sur Diving School (☎ 279 8628; www.abucear.com), based in San Juan del Sur (p148), also offers Laguna de Apoyo dives.

Sleeping & Eating

There are lots of options for staying at the bottom of the crater, or check out Masatepe (p106) and Catarina (p104) if you're more interested in the view. Your dining options are very limited; consider bringing groceries.

A handful of very basic bar/restaurants have been squatting here illegally over cheap beer and fried food for years, but may soon be pushed out by more upscale developments, which are also probably illegal. They're generally deserted except on Sunday afternoon, when half of southwestern Nicaragua turns out to drink and swim.

Monkey Hut (☎ 887 3546; www.thebeardedmonkey .com; dm US$10, r US$16-24, cabañas US$30-40; P) Operated by Granada's popular Bearded Monkey hostel, this waterfront property has a beautiful dock, lots of toys (including free kayaks), beer on the honor system and a swimming hole the size of a volcanic crater. It sells snacks, but bring your own grub. You can come as a day-tripper for US$5, plus US$1 transport from Granada.

Hospedaje Crater's Edge (☎ 895 3202; www .craters-edge.com; dm US$10, d US$20-35, q US$40; P ⊗) In a cool, tiled house about 500m from the *empalme*, this new entry has rocking chairs right by the water, a 12-bed dorm with lake views and breezes, and five double rooms with different combinations of bathroom and air-con. The quads are larger with two double beds each. Hostal Oasis (p121) in Granada runs a minivan to here at 10am and 4:30pm daily.

Hospedaje Las Clarineros (s/d US$7/11) This 1940s beach house has a shared bathroom, nice porch, a kitchen you can use, and is within convenient stumbling distance of all the bars. If they'd just wipe everything down, it'd be OK.

La Orquidea (☎ 872 1866; dm US$10, r US$15-35; P) With B&B ambience and outstanding backyard, this winner has a variety of rooms including one 2nd-story US$15 option with windows on all sides, which may be just for you. Guests can use the full kitchen. It's a bit past the Spanish school.

Norome Resort & Villas (☎ 883 9093; www .noromevillas.com; d US$65-75, villas US$90-180; P ⊗ ⬜ ⬛) More popular with packaged tourists, this swanky spot offers beautiful wooden homes (some three-bedroom) with all the amenities, including Internet access, artfully arranged around the bottom of the crater. You can also visit for the day (US$3), and take advantage of its nice dock. Like it? They'll sell you a timeshare.

Getting There & Around

You can walk here from Granada: take the dirt road northeast of the cemetery for about two hours through a poor but pretty region, and bring everything you'll need to eat and drink, as there are no services at this end of the lake. Once you reach the crater rim, ask local farmers for permission to cross their land. Steep trails also begin at the *miradors* (viewpoints) in Catarina and Diría, more or less a 1½-hour round-trip.

Buses run every half-hour between the crater rim and Masaya (US$0.30, 6am to 6pm). Only three buses, which read 'El Valle de la Laguna,' descend all the way to the waterfront (US$0.70, 6:30am, 11:30am and 4:30pm), returning from Masaya at 5:30am, 10:30am and 3:30pm. The half-hour, 2km descent isn't a bad walk, but going uphill is just hot.

Hitchhiking is common on this stretch, but taxis are not (except on Sunday). Taxis from Granada (US$10) and Masaya (US$6) may charge less to drop you off at the top. The Bearded Monkey Hostel and Hostal Oasis (both in Granada, see p120) charge US$1 for the trip.

LOS PUEBLOS BLANCOS

Drenched in local color, it's no wonder that the White Towns often use the tagline 'Meseta de los Pueblos' (Little Plateau of the Towns) instead. Originally built from the chalky, pale volcanic tuff upon which this pastoral scene is spread, these rural communities – not to mention the roads between them – once shimmered a blinding white indeed, amid the pale green patchwork of pasture and jungle.

Today the centuries-old buildings have been painted, and the shady roads are paved, most days lined with stands selling vividly painted *artesanías*. Each town has its specialty: hand-crafted ceramics or homemade sweets, wooden furniture or freshly cut flowers. Cool breezes (an average 23°C) blowing in off the crater lakes keep these colonial gems crisp and clean, but it is their myths and legends that make them so appealing.

Festivals & Events

With a pantheon of saints and virgins celebrated with an almost pagan vigor, the Masaya *meseta* claims some of the most colorful fiestas in the country.

San Silvestre Papa (Catarina; December 31–January 1) Hey, you've got to do New Year's somewhere, and this parade is famous for its bouquets of flowers.

Virgen de la Candelaria (Diriomo; February 2–8) Wake up early – the fireworks will help – to see the Virgin off on her annual trip to nearby Los Jirones.

Domingo de Trinidad (Masatepe; mid-May) Forty days after Semana Santa, this is the biggest *hípica*, or horse parade, in Nicaragua; festivities peak on May 23 but keep going for another month.

María Auxiliadora (Pío XII; May 24) There's rarely much reason to visit this little town, unless you want to see the Baile del Viejo y Vieja (Dance of the Old Couple) done right.

San Pedro (Diría; June 17 through July) Diría celebrates its patron saint with some dances celebrating Cacique Diriangén, and with others involving dried bull penises.

San Juan Bautista (Catarina; June 24) Coincidentally falling on the summer solstice, this wild festival features dances, ceremonial fights and music.

Santa Ana (Niquinohomo; July 26) Ballet *folklorico*, fireworks and parades make this one of the country's biggest celebrations for this popular saint.

Santa Catalina de Alejandría (Catarina; November 25–26) Ballet *folklorico* and a parade.

Catarina

pop 7100

At the crossroads of Los Pueblos Blancos, Catarina is known for its *viveros* (greenhouses), displaying in the misty altitude bright tropical plants that visitors take home to gardens across Nicaragua.

Its real claim to fame, however, is the **mirador** across the startling blue waters of Laguna de Apoyo, to Granada and Cocibolca all the way to Ometepe. Today lined with inexpensive restaurants and souvenir shops connected by windy walkways, this spot is rumored to have been youthful Augusto C Sandino's favorite place to meditate, and appropriately so, for this is also the grave site of Benjamín Zeledón, whose burial Sandino witnessed. There's a half-hour trail to the water, with excellent views.

The town itself is sparkling clean and beautiful, a Spanish colonial gem with two of the nicest budget hotels on the *meseta*. **Hospedaje Euro** (☎ 558 0045; r per person US$3) has rather cavernous turquoise rooms sleeping three, with fans, volcano art and clean shared bathrooms. **Hotel Jaaris** (☎ 558 0020; s/d US$9/12) has a cool, tiled porch with rocking chairs, hammocks and a large dog; OK rooms all have bathrooms. The hotels are next to each other, one block downhill from the church.

It's easy to visit Catarina, and almost any regional tour from Masaya or Granada includes a quick stop at the top of the volcanic crater. If you're driving, note that there's a US$0.70 fee to park at the *mirador*. There are microbuses for destinations throughout the *meseta*, while buses run regularly between the *mirador* and destinations including:

Granada US$0.80, 30 minutes, 6am to 6pm, at least every hour

Managua Mercado Roberto Huembes US$0.60, 50 minutes, 6am to 6pm, every 30 minutes; microbus (UCA) US$0.80, 40 minutes, depart when full

Masaya US$0.70, 30 minutes, 6am to 6pm, every 30 minutes

San Juan de Oriente

pop 3100

Also known as San Juan de los Platos, this very attractive colonial town has been in the pottery business since before the Spanish conquest. While production of inexpensive and functional pottery for local consumption is still important, most of the cheerful shops lining the hilly cobblestone roads are selling decorative pieces – vases, wind chimes, wall hangings, that sort of thing – which you probably won't want to carry for weeks and weeks in your backpack.

The most famous workshop is **Cooperativa Quetzalcóatl**, but there are dozens of places where you can find your masterpiece, and probably watch the artisans at work. After the pieces are thrown on the wheel, they are partially dried. Then the designs are carved by hand from the cool, moist clay, and painted to be fired a final time. Many artisans feared they had lost their livelihood in July 2000 when earthquakes shattered their kilns, but Nicaraguan business groups came to their rescue, donating almost 200 new kilns to the community.

Diría & Diriomo

pop 26,000

These twin towns are located right across the road from one another (a US$0.70 *moto* ride) and both are well worth visiting.

Diría boasts Mirador el Boquete, the mellower, less touristed overlook of Laguna de Apoyo, where views include a handful of **bar-restaurants** (✪ noon-midnight Mon-Thu, noon-2am Fri-Sun) that get packed with *fiesteros* on weekends.

From the lookout, there's a steep, half-hour trail to the bottom, where a muddy little beach offers access to the bright blue water for swimming. This viewpoint is no more difficult to visit than Catarina: from Granada, take any Niquinohomo-bound bus (US$0.50, every 30 minutes), which will stop in front of 1650 Parroquia San Pedro, in the city center. It's a 2km walk or US$0.30 *moto* ride to the lookout.

This unassuming **church**, by the way, marks the spot where Cacique Diriangén, chief of the Dirian peoples at the time of the Spanish conquest, first met conquistador Gil González Dávila, on April 17, 1523. Unlike Nicarao, Diriangén didn't trust the newcomers and opted to ignore their three-day deadline to become a Christian, instead choosing 'or else.' Diriangén attacked, which in retrospect was the best course of action, and today both of these towns – as well as Diriamba in Carazo – are named for the indomitable *cacique* (chief). In one corner of the shady park, there's a sculpture of the man, always ready. See p54 for more on Cacique Diriangén.

Enchanting **Diriomo** has a world-class claim to fame, and even officials at the *alcaldía* would like to stress that it has long been known (this reputation evidently predates the Spaniards) as the **Witch Capital of the Meseta**. Although the entire region is well known for its *curanderos* (folk healers), Diriomo remains proud of them, even after centuries of oppression.

Most healers work out of their homes, which are unsigned. If you're looking for love potions, hoping to attract wealth, or simply want your fortune told, ask at the *alcaldía*, or look for Professor William Mena, Antonio Castellon or Andrea Peña, three of the better-known practitioners. Most Granada-based tour companies can also arrange an audience.

Diriomo is also famous for its *cajetas*, rich fruit-flavored sweets most famously available at **Casa de Cajetas** (US$1-2; 6am-noon & 1-8pm); the day's flavors are posted on the wall. They're also sold elsewhere in town and along the highway. The town is also known for its *chicha bruja* (an alcoholic corn beverage) and even stiffer *calavera del gato* ('skull of the cat'; drink at your own risk). **Iglesia Nuestra Señora de Candelaria** is the perfect centerpiece for this witchy place, with rather Gothic stone walls and an extra-interesting collection of saints.

There's no lodging in either town, and while there are simple *comedores* in both, the best restaurants are on the freeway between them: Los Robles, a block before the Diría *empalme*, and El Aguate, about 200m past the turnoff, are both beautiful *rancheros* (thatch-roofed, open-air structures) with upscale Nica dining. You can check your email at **Cyber Conexion** (per hr US$1).

Buses leave almost hourly from the parque central for Managua (US$0.80), via Naindame, and every 40 minutes for Masaya (US$0.60).

Niquinohomo
pop 13,500

This quiet, 16th-century Spanish colonial village is the birthplace of General Agusto César Sandino, who did indeed appreciate the fact that the name is Náhuatl for 'Valley of the Warriors.' The church is lovely and there's all sorts of attractive architecture all over town, but you've probably come all the way out here to see the man's birthplace, now **Agusto C Sandino Library** (9am-noon & 1:30-5pm Mon-Sat). Well, there is a small room off to the side with a couple of artifacts, displayed beneath a taped-up English-language biography that someone downloaded from the Internet.

If you want to stay, you could make reservations at **Rancho Ebenezer** (☎ 884 9452; www.ranchoebenezer.com; dm US$3; P), 3km from town. The *finca* is run by a Christian group, but anyone is welcome if there's space. The family-style meals are US$3 each, farm tours US$30 per group. There's Internet (US$3 per hour) but no flush toilets. They may be able to arrange transportation from town.

Closer to town, you can grab a good meal in the gardens of **Estancia El Bosquecillo** (meals US$1-6; 10:30am-4pm & 5:30-9pm), right by the park; try the chicken tacos (US$1.25). Check your mail two blocks from the park at **Cyber Esquina** (per hr US$1).

Nandasmo
pop 7900

On a spur road, the small village of Nandasmo is best known for its tiny arts and crafts – itsy-bitsy wooden furniture and tableware, doll-house scale. Unlike the other towns in the region, roadside stands and adorable shops aren't really in evidence, though it might be different during the high season. Most of the miniatures are actually sold in Mexican, Costa Rican and Guatemalan handicraft markets, which then pass on the markup to you.

There's also an undeveloped **overlook of Laguna de Masaya** several kilometers north of town along a rough dirt road.

NICARAGUA

Masatepe
pop 25,500

Photogenic and fabulous, this undiscovered colonial gem has a wonderfully well-kept downtown, great food, better views of the volcano than Masaya (not to mention better furniture than Catarina and sticky-sweet *cajetas* that one might compare favorably with those in Diriomo, if one weren't afraid of being jinxed) and one truly marvelous guesthouse in the countryside.

There's not a whole lot to do, although Masatepe's old railway station has been reincarnated as one of the best **artisan markets** (⏱ 9am-6pm) in the country. Unfortunately for backpackers, the focus here is furniture – from wonderful cane-woven rocking chairs and brightly colored cabinets – all of which is ridiculously cheap, until you factor in the cost of shipping it back home. Sigh.

There are two websites that cover the city: **Masatepe Online** (www.masatepe.org), with more of a focus on events and the arts, and **M-City** (www.masatepecity.com), with more commercial listings.

For a celluloid glimpse of the city, check out the film *Los Gallos no Lloran* (The Roosters Don't Cry; gallosnolloran.com), a low-budget romance involving the bitterly competitive Nicaraguan cockfighting scene, which was filmed right here.

Towering over Masatepe's attractive central plaza, **Iglesia San Juan Bautista** is home to El Cristo Negro de La Santísima Trinidad, whose feast days mean a month of parties between mid-May and mid-June, and features nationally famous folkloric dances like La Nueva Milpa, Racimo de Sacuanjoche and Masatepetl. The sweeping adobe makes a fine colonial centerpiece, but it's the views from its gates, of fuming Volcán Masaya, that add depth to your prayers.

Casa de Cultura Zoila (admission free; classes per month US$9), in one of Masatepe's oldest extant buildings, is just downhill from the church. It has pool and ping-pong tables you can use, as well as the occasional painting or folkloric dance exhibition; it also offers classes in art, Latin dance and pastry making. **Cyber Compa** (per hr US$0.85) is two blocks toward the main road from the park.

There's one place to stay in town – actually a 4km downhill walk or US$2 *moto* ride from town, and well worth the trouble.

Beautiful **Centro Ecoturístico Flor de Pochote** (☎ 885 7576; www.flordepochote.com; dm per person US$4, cabins US$20; Ⓟ) actually lies within the Reserva Laguna de Apoyo. Enjoy excellent views of the lake and volcano, fuming right overhead (OK, 6km away, but that's close enough), from the porch of your basic dorm or beautiful cabin – all made of local materials. You're welcome to wander the 14-*manzana finca* or go on a number of guided hikes (US$3, horses extra US$2), including a walk to Laguna de Masaya. There's also an alternative trail from near here to the Santiago crater; it's currently off-limits, but ask. Day-trippers are welcome to stop by, especially if they spring for a guided hike or great meal at the restaurant (US$2 to US$4), with lots of Zvegetarian options and an outstanding view.

Disco Masatepe, on the freeway, gets going on weekends only.

The reason why most people come to Masatepe, however, is the food. It's best known for delicious, steaming bowls of *mondongo* (tripe soup), a source of serious regional pride. Yes, tripe is indeed cow stomach, but it's not only been cleaned, it's been marinated with bitter oranges and fresh herbs, then simmered with garden vegetables for hours.

There are several spots to try this or other, less threatening, local specialties. **Mondongo Veracruz** (dishes US$2-6; ⏱ noon-9pm), three blocks north of the church, is the classic, where soup (with its traditional side, Flor de Caña) has been served at noon sharp for half a century. **Mi Terruño** (dishes US$3-8; ⏱ 9am-10pm), 4km west of town, is the more attractive and upscale option, serving *mondongo* and other regional specialties, including *peli-buey* (a tasty and adorable cross between a sheep and goat), in luxuriant gardens alongside *tiste* or local fruit wines in traditional jícaro (a hard-shelled fruit traditionally used to make cups and bowls) gourds; it's even got its own-brand coffee beans.

Even shoestringers need to check out the other local specialty, *tamugas* – like a *nacatamale* (banana-leaf-wrapped bundles of cornmeal, meat, vegetables and herbs), but made with sticky rice instead of cornmeal. Pick up yours at **Leonor Barquero Tamugas/Nacatamales** (large/larger US$0.75/0.90), just half a block from the park, then finish it off with some of Masatepe's famous sweets from Dulcería Chepita, half a block west of the train station.

Buses leave the parque central every half-hour for Masaya (US$0.60) and Managua (US$1.30, one hour), while minivans make the run to Jinotepe (US$0.50, 15 minutes) when full.

San Marcos
pop 25,900 / elevation 600m
On the site of what's thought to be the oldest human settlement in Nicaragua, San Marcos has a pronounced and festive student presence thanks to bilingual **Ave Maria College** (www.avemaria.edu.ni). San Marcos' *fiestas patronales* (April 24 to 25) are some of the most impressive in the country.

This would make a fine place to spend the night, if it weren't for the lousy hotel situation. But it's almost worth it just to enjoy slurred political commentary including 'I hope the Sandinistas win everything and kick all of the gringos out!' (from an American exchange student) or 'President Somoza wanted to get out of politics, but the old man, he didn't want to hand the country to the communists, so he hung in there…he hung in there!' (from a recently returned Nicaraguan).

There's no statue for San Marcos' most famous native son – Anastasio Somoza García, the original dictator. This might make Sandino feel better about that lousy excuse for a museum in Niquinohomo.

Bancentro, on the main road just west of the park, has a 24-hour ATM (Visa/Plus only). If you're on the MasterCard system, go south two blocks for the BAC ATM. There are lots of Internet cafés, but the most convenient is **SuperCyber** (per hr US$0.70), right on the park.

Unfortunately, the hotel situation is irritatingly expensive for what's on offer. **Casa Blanca** (☎ 535 2717; d/tr US$35/45), three blocks east of the parque central, has big, nice rooms with hot-water bathrooms, but no TV or air-con, which you might expect at this price. **El Portal** (☎ 432 2276; d US$25; ✷), across from La Casona, does have TV, air-con and even refrigerators, but is sort of grimy.

Hotel y Restaurante Lagos y Volcanes (☎ 883 4060; www.resortlagosyvolcanes.com; r US$35; P ✷ ✷), 2km south of San Marcos in La Concha,

has attractive cabañas strung with hammocks, an on-site restaurant and a pool with Jacuzzi. Cabañas have hot-water bathrooms, and the pool has volcano views.

Day-trippers must stop by for a stroll around the park and a fabulous gourmet coffee beverage at **La Casona Coffee Shop** (snacks & drinks US$2-5; ☯ 10am-midnight Tue-Sun, 4pm-midnight Mon), which has huge burgers and sandwiches, and lots of other excellent coffee-shop grub. It's also a good place to have a beer or six after dark.

Other popular spots include **Cafeteria Paladar** (dishes US$1-3), a basic *comedor* at the corner of the park, and a good *fritanga* (sidewalk barbecue) that sets up at dusk in front of Farmacia Inmaculada, also by the park. There are lots of bars (and better house parties), but up-and-coming grunge bands get their workout at La Fabrica, a warehouse space catercorner from Casa Blanca.

San Marcos lies at the border of the Masaya and Carazo departments, and you'll probably have to changes buses or minivans here to get between them. Minibuses leave when full from the parque central to Managua (US$1, one hour), Jinotepe (US$0.30, 20 minutes), Masaya (US$0.60, 45 minutes) and other destinations all day long.

CARAZO
This department, blessed with beautiful mountains reaching 870m (bring a sweater) and wide, sandy beaches (bring your swimsuit) – separated by only 35 steep kilometers – is central in Nicaraguan history and myth. This is not only where the first Nicaraguan coffee was sown, but also where the nation's most famous burlesque, *El Güegüense,* was anonymously penned in the late 17th century. The comedy, which pits Nicaraguan ingenuity against Spanish power, always gets a laugh. It was written (and is still performed) in Náhuatl, Spanish and Mayangna.

Regional relations apparently predate the Spanish conquest, as Carazo's four major towns still celebrate an interesting ritual called the **Toro Guaco**: La Concepción brings out her patron saint, the Black Virgin of Montserrat, to meet Santiago, patron of Jinotepe, the old Nicarao capital; San Sebastián from its ancient Chorotegan rival, Diriamba; and San Marcos, from the university town of the same name. Four times throughout the year – the saints' feast days – the saints pay ceremonial visits to each other, an event livened up with striking costumes and masks displayed in dances, mock battles and plays that satirize their Spanish invaders. The biggest bash is on April 24 to 25, in San Marcos (see p107).

Diriamba

pop 51,191 / elevation 576m

Already a bustling Chorotega town when the Spanish arrived, Diriamba has a reputation for the revolutionary (Cacique Diriangén's sculpture welcomes you to town), as well as some truly terrible roads. It was also, as architecture buffs will note, an early benefactor of the coffee boom, and remains the repository of some fairly spectacular European-style architecture from the late 19th century and early 1900s – and check out that clock tower.

Museo Ecológico Trópico Seco (☎ 534 2129; museoeco@ibw.com.ni; admission US$1; ☼ 8am-noon Mon-Sat, 2-5pm Mon-Fri), four blocks south of the park, was Nicaragua's first natural history museum (sort of), with informative, if low-budget, displays that focus primarily on the ecosystem of the Río Grande de Corazo and turtles of the Refugio de Vida Silvestre Río Escalante Chococente (see p136). Your fee includes a Spanish-language tour, which really brings the rain forest mural to life.

There are two budget hotels in town, **Hospedaje Diriangén** (☎ 534 2428; s/d US$7/9; **P**), just east of the Shell station, with bathrooms and a parking lot; and **Casa Hotel Diriamba** (☎ 534 2523; d US$12), even more basic, just east of the clock tower.

Closed at press time, **Abundance Farm** (www .abundancefarm.com) offered inexpensive lodging at an organic farm; check the website to see if it's reopened. Or, try brand-new **Finca San Gregorio** (greenokstu@hotmail.com; dm US$2; 🖳), with a dormitory, tent sites, a pool (!) and great meals for US$2.

Jardín y Vivera Tortuga Verde (☎ 534 2948; www.ecolodgecarazon.com; r US$30-40) is perhaps the most luxurious lodging on the *meseta*. This verdant spot has just three rooms, all hewn from beautiful precious woods in different configurations (the largest has a kitchen and sleeps five), with hot water, cable TV and bathrooms. Better, it's on the grounds of one of the most elaborate garden-greenhouses you've ever seen, with

little paths weaving between an entire jungle's worth of tropical plants and flowers. It also rents out a little house by the shore in Casares.

There are several simple *comedores* clustered close to the market, or go upscale at **Rancho Mi Bohio** (meals US$3-8; ☼ lunch & dinner) three blocks east of the clock tower, specializing in *churrasco* (roasted meats), lobster and other goodies.

Jinotepe is the main transportation hub, and you can get a Jinotepe microbus (US$0.30, 15 minutes) any time at the market in front of the clock tower. A few buses and microbuses do leave from this station, including:

La Boquita microbus US$0.80, 45 minutes, 6am to 6pm, every 30 minutes

La Boquita/Casares US$0.40, 1½ hours, 5am to 5pm, every hour

Managua US$1.25, 1¼ hours, 5am to 6pm, every 20 minutes

Jinotepe

pop 38,000 / elevation 600m

Historically separated from its eternal rival by the Río Grande de Carazo (which is predictably too polluted for swimming, but worth a wander if you're here), proudly Nicarao Jinotepe is the capital of Carazo and the most city-like of any town this side of Masaya.

INFORMATION

Bancentro Right on the parque central, has a Visa/Plus ATM.

Cyberland (per hr US$0.70) Internet cafés are everywhere, but Cyberland, next to Pizza to Go, is fast and comfortable.

Intur (☎ 412 0298; carazo@intur.gob.ni) Conveniently inside a tiny arts-and-crafts market across from Palí, it can recommend hotels and offer information for all of Carazo.

Jinotepe Online (www.jinotepenicaragua.com) Check out this site for a rundown of the area's attractions in English (scroll down).

SIGHTS & ACTIVITIES

The Spanish-colonial-style city is centered on the requisite impressive church, **La Iglesia Parroquial de Santiago**, with excellent stained glass, and perpetually bustling **Parque Los Chocoyitos**.

The oddest attraction has to be **Hertylandia** (☎ 532 3081; www.hertylandia.com), Nicaragua's first and only theme park, built by perpetual optimist and popular former Managua mayor (and perhaps, by the time you read this, president) Herty Lewites. The former Sandinista gun runner become Minister of Tourism during the 1980s, and his few less-than-spectacular private projects, including this and those drowned *rancheros* along Lagunas Xiloá and Apoyeque (see p88), have clearly convinced him to go back into public service.

Hertylandia has fared fairly well, and its aging stucco turrets (like Disney, there's a castle theme) holds two options for diversion: a **water park** (per person US$3.50), with a pool and several decent waterslides, and the **dry park** (admission US$1.25, per ride less than US$1), with mellow kids rides. It's a 1km, US$0.30 cab ride from Jinotepe.

SLEEPING

There are a handful of cheap hotels, some unsigned, close to the parque central, but the best of the bunch is very clean **Hospedaje Colson, Casa Huéspedes** (r per person US$5), two blocks south of the old cinema, with flush toilets, windows, fans and mattresses that don't have a life of their own.

Hotel Casa Grande (☎ 532 2741; casagrande@nicarao.org.ni; basic/deluxe d US$35/55) This, on the other hand, is one of the nicest hotels on the *meseta*. The rather plush property has hot water, laundry service, cable TV and even an in-room phone, all located right downtown.

Cerro de Viento (marcial_jaen@hotmail.com; admission US$0.70, camping per person US$3, cabaña US$10) About 5km south of Jinotepe, near the town of Santa Teresa, is some home-grown sustainable tourism. The pretty property has with trails, swimming holes and an outstanding view to the Pacific Ocean. It belongs to Marciel Umaña, who offers guided hikes and horseback rides (US$5). There are six cabañas with bathroom set out in the forest, and *comida típica* (cooked over a wood fire) costs US$2 a plate. Camping includes shower and toilets.

EATING & DRINKING

The parque central is packed with food stands and *fritangas* all day long, or eat at permanent Cafetín Tunng Yeun, with cheap Nicaraguan and Asian dishes in a friendly kiosk. There's also an early-morning coffee stand, a favorite of expats.

El Coloseo (mains US$3-6; ⏱ noon-10pm Tue-Sun) One block north of the church, El Coloseo may have the best pizza in Nicaragua, or at least on the *meseta*.

Pizza to Go (medium pie US$3.50) Shoestringers will note that, just down the street, Pizza to Go is pretty darned good and about half the price of El Coloseo.

Restaurant El Sardina (meals US$3-8; Km 49.5 Carr Sur) In a spacious thatched-roof *ranchero*, on the main road, this place has the best seafood in town.

There's an enormous Super Palí, one block from the parque central, which is the best grocery store in the region. Keep an eye open for a Seventh Day Adventist health-food store that allegedly has fresh wholewheat bread.

La Academia was the most popular disco at press time, with reggae and karaoke nights.

GETTING THERE & AROUND

Jinotepe is a transportation hub, and the big, messy terminal is just north of the parque central, on the Interamericana. To get to the beaches take a microbus to Diriamba (US$0.30, 15 minutes), leaving every few minutes. Buses leave Jinotepe for destinations including:

Granada US$1.25, 1½ hours, three daily
Managua bus US$1.25, 1¼ hours, 5am to 6pm, every 20 minutes; microbus US$2, one hour, 6am to 6pm, every hour
Masaya US$0.40, 1¼ hours, 5am to 5pm, every 30 minutes; with stops in San Marcos, Masatepe and Catarina
Rivas US$2, two hours, 6am to 3pm, every hour; with stops in Santa Teresa and Nandaime
Ticuantepe US$1, one hour, six daily

La Maquina

About halfway between Diriamba and the beaches, take a break from dodging potholes at this excellent roadside attraction. **Reserva Ecológica La Maquina** (☎ 887 9141; admission US$1.25; ⏱ Tue-Sun) is a respected private reserve and a fine place for a swim.

There's an on-site **restaurant** (meals US$2-5), or you're welcome to have a picnic at the reasonably spectacular waterfalls just a few minutes from the road. Displays note that, according to an ancient legend, the water has Viagra-like properties.

There's also **camping** (per person US$3) and three trails that explore the 154-hectare property, mainly primary dry tropical forest and a few bonus waterfalls and big trees, including huge strangler figs. Buses between the beaches and Diriamba pass every 40 minutes.

La Boquita

Make a right when you hit the sand for the nicest of the government tourism complexes that pepper the Pacific coast: **Centro Turistico La Boquita** (pedestrian/car US$0.10/1.25). Enjoy the broad white-sand beach at any of 11 restaurants, all serving cold beer and US$6 lobster plates, or in one the two hotels.

Hotel Palmas del Mar (☎ 887 1336; d US$40; P ✗ ⚑), open in high season only, is a relatively swish spot with private pool, cable TV and room service. **Hotel-Restaurant Suleyka** (☎ 854 9733; tr US$20), open year-round, has basic rooms that sleep three, including fans and musty bathrooms – try to get room 4, which is bigger and has more light. The restaurant is solid.

This is more of a swimming than a surfing beach, but if swells are big, waves can get a nice peak; some restaurants rent boards.

Casares

If Boquita seems too synthetic, head south to Casares, a real fishing village, with three seafood restaurants that do brisker business in adult beverages; Doña Paulina seems to be the favorite for food.

The only accommodations in town are at the fairly luxurious **Hotel Lupita** (☎ 552 8708; lupita41@ibw.com.ni; tr US$45; P ✗ ⚑), which doesn't really have a beach, just waves crashing into the cliffs far below the swimming pool (which is actually sort of nice). Rooms are fine, with air-con, TV and flagstone floors, but the whole place seems isolated and a bit creepy.

The often-impassable road south to **Playa Huehete** was being paved at the time of research; considering that this is Carazo's best **surf beach** – with a point, beach and rivermouth break – and already a favorite spot for vacation homes among Jinotepe's hoity-toity crowd, expect more development soon. There is a road, sort of, between Casares and El Astillero (p136), but it's 4WD-only in dry season. Be sure to check water depth before crossing any streams.

GRANADA & AROUND

pop 90,000 / elevation 40m

Granada is Nicaragua at its most photogenic, a city of graceful adobes and elegantly proportioned porticoes drenched in rich tropical colors, Volcán Mombacho rising ragged above and shimmering Cocibolca (Sweet Sea; Lago de Nicaragua) arranged at her feet. But the beauty overlooking the lake is more than just a pretty facade: behind the city's carved wooden doors, arranged around beautifully restored courtyards, you'll find an eclectic bar and restaurant scene, wonderful hotels and other little luxuries that offer a taste of Nicaragua's historic wealth and power.

This Spanish colonial masterpiece, arguably the oldest European city on the American mainland, has become the epicenter of a lively expat scene that has furnished its new home with creature comforts from sushi to a Reiki massage. So put away your water purification tablets, slip into your nicest (or cleanest) clothes and flag down one of the horse-drawn carriages plying the city's lively boulevards, and just enjoy.

GRANADA

Nicknamed 'the Great Sultan,' in honor of its Moorish namesake across the Atlantic, Granada was founded in 1524 by Francisco Fernández de Córdoba, and is the oldest city in the New World. It was constructed as a showcase city, the first chance that the Spanish had to prove they had more to offer than bizarre religions and advanced military technology, and it still retains an almost regal beauty, each adobe masterpiece faithfully resurrected to original specifications after every trial and tribulation.

A trade center almost from its inception, Granada's position as the mistress of Lago de Nicaragua became even more important when the Spanish realized, in the 1530s, that the Río San Juan was navigable from the lake to the sea. This made Granada rich – and vulnerable. Between 1665 and 1670, pirates sacked the city three times (see the boxed text, p113), and that was only the worst of it.

Undaunted, Granada rebuilt and grew even richer and more powerful, a conservative cornerstone of the Central American

NICARAGUA

GRANADA

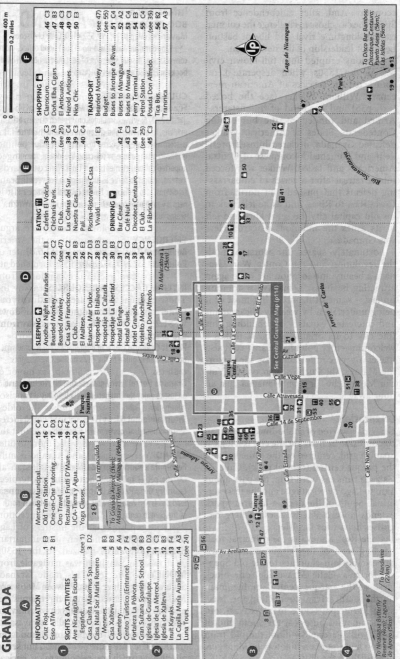

0   400 m
0   0.2 miles

Lago de Nicaragua

economy. And, after independence from Spain, the city chose to challenge the colonial capital, longtime rival and liberal bastion León, for leadership of the new nation.

Tensions erupted into full-blown civil war in the 1850s, when desperate León contracted the services of American mercenary William Walker (see the boxed text, p55) and his band of 'filibusterers.' Armed and funded by the burgeoning Confederate States of America, Walker defeated Granada, declared himself president and launched a conquest of Central America – and failed. Walker was forced into a retreat after a series of embarrassing defeats that pushed him north, from Costa Rica to Rivas, and as he fell back to his old capital city, he set it afire and left in its ashes the infamous placard: 'Here was Granada.'

Fortunately spared the worst of both the revolution and the Contra War, Granada's beauty and location are once again attracting business. A massive restoration project – some of it public, but most of it being undertaken by wealthy Nicaraguans and interested expats – is rebuilding this fine city to its original glory. It makes a welcoming entry point to Nicaragua. It also makes a very comfortable base for exploring Masaya, the Pueblos Blancos and Volcán Mombacho, or even Managua, just an hour away.

Orientation

Granada's warren of adobe-lined streets can be confusing at first, but the city is a logical Spanish grid, centered on the cathedral and the parque central (central park). Calle La Calzada runs eastward from the park about 1km to Lago de Nicaragua and the ferry terminal. South of the dock, a lakefront park extends toward Puerto Asese, where day cruises depart for Las Isletas.

Calle Real Xalteva is the principal road heading west of the parque central, past three important churches to the old Spanish fortress. Calle Atravesada, one block west of the parque central, is the main north–south artery, connecting the Mercado Municipal (close to the Rivas- and Masaya-bound buses) at the south end of town with Parque Sandino, the old train station and the main highway to Managua, just north of the city.

Information

BOOKSTORES

Mavericks (Map p114; ☎ 552 4120; Calle El Arsenal; ✆ 9am-6pm Tue-Sat, 10am-noon Sun) Good coffee, great conversation, a solid selection of new magazines and used books in English and other languages.

CULTURAL CENTERS

Fundación Casa de los Tres Mundos (Map p114; ☎ 552 4176; www.c3mundos.org) French classes, art exhibits, free movies and cheap musical and theatrical performances are all geared to diversifying influences on Nicaraguan culture by rejecting the idea of 'forcing imported cultural elements on a Third World country. Instead, it aims to serve as a connection between these traditions…to rediscover buried cultural heritage and to help a young nation search for a unique identity.' Which seems to be working.

EMERGENCY

Ambulance (Cruz Roja; Red Cross; ☎ 552 2711)
Police (☎ 552 2977, 552 2929)

INTERNET ACCESS & RESOURCES

Those colonial adobes are packed with Internet cafés, most charging about US$1 to US$1.25 a minute, less if you get away from the plaza.

Find It Granada (www.finditgranada.com) A somewhat more complete guide to the city's business, restaurants and hotels.

Granada Portal (www.granada.com.ni) Worth logging on just to enjoy the inspired introduction, but actual information is light.

InterKa@fe.net (Map p114; per hr US$1.10; ✖) Very air-conditioned, across from Hotel Colonial.

LAUNDRY

Fernanda Laundry Service (Map p114; Calle La Calzada; per 1-5kg US$2.50) Next to Zoom Bar.

Laundry Olga Padilla (Map p114; Calle Consulado; per load US$4; ✆ 7am-9pm) It's one and a half blocks north of the parque central.

MEDICAL SERVICES

Hospitals (☎ 552 2719)

MONEY

Several banks have Visa/Plus ATMs, while MasterCard/Cirrus customers have BAC and the Esso station. *Coyotes* (moneychangers) can be found along Calle Atravesada, one block west of the park, or around the market. They are generally honest, but know about how much you're going to get back.

PIRATES OF LAKE NICARAGUA!

It was one of the most daring exploits in pirate history, a career coup even for dashing, up-and-coming buccaneer Henry Morgan and his band of rum-soaked merry men: the sacking of Central America's crown jewel, Granada.

It couldn't have been done in a full-size sailing vessel – if you follow Morgan's path up the Río San Juan you'll see how those rapids would tear a regular ship apart. But this crafty band of quick thinkers appropriated six 12m wooden canoes (after their regular pirate ships were impounded by Spanish authorities) following an equally spectacular sacking of Villahermosa, Mexico. The atypical craft proved more than adequate for further pillaging along the Caribbean coast, which gave the 30-year-old Morgan an idea.

The crew battled the currents of the Río San Juan at night and hid their canoes during the day, then made their way across the great lake. The June 1665 attack caught complacent Granadinos completely off guard: the pirates occupied the city for 16 hours – just like the Disney ride, but more violent – then stole all the ammunition, sank all the boats and sailed off to a warm welcome, as heroes and legends, to Port Royal, Jamaica.

Buccaneers had been a part of Caribbean culture since the late 1500s. They were bands of escaped slaves, indentured servants and deported criminals who lived off livestock, and (so the legend goes) stretched the skins on 'buccans,' hence the name. When other European powers, envious of Spain's newfound riches, decided to set up shop in the sunny Caribbean, they contacted the buccaneers and began making deals.

In 1655 the English made their move and, with buccaneer support and intelligence, took the island of Jamaica and transformed it into a British colony – a colony of ex-convicts and street toughs. Among them was Henry Morgan, who quickly climbed the ranks from co-pirate, sacking such hot spots as Santiago, Cuba, to a pirate commander with the successful Granada expedition under his belt. By the time Sir Henry Morgan drank himself to death in 1688, he had been made Pirate King (technically, Lieutenant Governor of Jamaica) and Knight of the British Empire.

He had also influenced a generation. Between 1665 and 1670, Granada was sacked three times, even as Morgan took more pirate canoes up the Río Coco, where he made powerful allies of the Miskito Indians (see the boxed text, p238). With their help, pirates sacked Ciudad Antigüa and Estelí, where Morgan himself stayed for a while, and founded several of the surrounding towns.

Pirates actually founded more cities in Nicaragua than they ever sacked, including Pueblo Viejo and several surrounding towns in the Segovias, Bilwi, on the Caribbean Coast, and most famously Bluefields, named for founder Abraham Blauvelt, a Dutch pirate who worked the waters from Rhode Island to Panama. Heck, pirate William Dampier, a trained scientist and veteran of the 1665 sacking of Granada, filed the report on the earliest historic eruption of San Cristóbal in 1685.

Although the 1697 Treaty of Ryswick guaranteed that England, Spain, France and Holland would respect each others' property in the New World, the pirates (for whom legality was not a huge concern) continued to try for Granada; in 1769, 17-year-old Rafaela Herrera was forced to command Spanish forces at El Castillo against pirates trying to sack Granada yet again. And she won, even as the age of pirates on the sweet sea slipped into history.

Banco America Central (BAC; Map p114) With the most services for tourists of any bank, it also has a 24-hour ATM (Visa/MasterCard/Plus/Cirrus) that gives US dollars and córdobas.

Esso (Map p111) An ATM (Visa/MasterCard/Plus/Cirrus) is available at the gas station on the main highway, 11 blocks north of the center.

POST & TELEPHONE

Post office (Map p114; Calle Atravesada; ⏲ 8am-noon & 1-5pm Mon-Fri, 8am-noon Sat) Opposite the Cine Karawala.

TOURIST INFORMATION

Intur (Map p114; ☎ 552 6858; www.intur.gob.ni; ⏲ 8:30am-12:30pm & 1:30-5pm Mon-Sat) The Granada branch of the national tourist office is predictably professional, with up-to-date transportation schedules, a good city map (US$1) and lots of information and flyers. It's half a block south of Iglesia San Francisco.

Mavericks (Map p114; ☎ 552 4120; Calle El Arsenal; ⏲ 9am-6pm Tue-Sat, 10am-noon Sun) The bookstore has a good bulletin board out back with information about area busin esses and events.

NICARAGUA

CENTRAL GRANADA

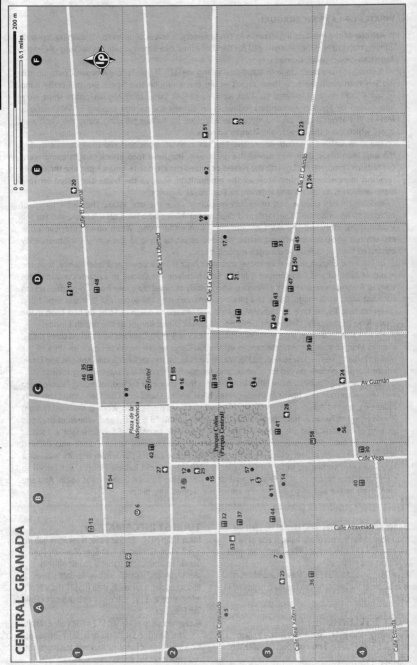

Sights & Activities

Although Granada is one of those places you'll want to capture on film forever, please keep an eye open for camera snatchers.

GRANADA WALKING TOUR

Too tired? Take a **horse-drawn carriage** (see p119), about the same price as a taxi, to any of these locations (at least between the city center and the lake) or ask for a city tour, around US$12 for a maximum of five people.

Beribboned horses line up alongside the fine parque central, also called **Parque Colón**, pleasantly shaded by mango and malinche trees. The **Cathedral de Granada** (Map p114), on the east side of the plaza, was originally built in 1583 but has been destroyed countless times since. This most recent version, built in 1915, has four chapels; a dozen stained-glass panels are set into the dome.

On the park's southeast corner, the beautifully restored Hotel Gran Francia (see p123) was formerly the home of William Walker, and is now a fine place for a drink, if only to ogle the gorgeous pool and shady green courtyard across the street. On the west side of the park, **Palacio**

de la Cultura Joaquín Cuadro Pasos (Map p114), named after the Granadino poet who wrote *Canto de Guerra de las Cosas* (War Song of Things), a surrealist masterpiece of 20th-century Spanish verse, is worth a wander, then head north to **Plaza de la Independencia**, also known as the 'Plaza de los Leones.' The obelisk is dedicated to the heroes of the 1821 struggle for independence, while the Cruz de Siglo was erected in 1900 to mark the new century.

On the east side of this plaza is the **Casa de los Leones** (see p117), named for the carved lions on the stone portal, the only part of the original structure that survived Walker's 1856 retreat. Rebuilt as a stately private home in 1920, it is currently home to Casa de los Tres Mundos, which often shows movies right on the plaza and has other cheap or free cultural events.

Head one block east on Calle El Arsenal for the awesome blueberry facade of **Convento y Museo San Francisco** (see p116), best captured on film close to sunset (but the museum closes at 5:30pm). From here, head south on Calle Cervantes, passing all manner of beautiful colonial mansions – keep an eye out for ceramic historical markers embedded in the walls – until you get to Calle La Calzada. This is where the carriage would be handy – it's a hot kilometer through the featureless new neighborhoods (built as the lake retreated from its much higher waterline in the 1500s) to Lago de Nicaragua, passing 1626 **Iglesia de Guadalupe** (Map p111), originally built as a fort.

The ferry terminal is on your left, but make a right through the green Spanish fortress (US$0.12) for the **Centro Turistico** (see p118), a lazy lakeside park with restaurants, bars, playgrounds, beaches, kayaks and Puerto Asese, where you can catch boats and explore a year's worth of volcanic lake islands, the **Isletas de Granada** (see p118).

Grab a cab, unless you're enjoying the heat (and Granada is not a 'dry heat'), back to the park, where you can fortify yourself with a plate of *vigarón* (a pile of mashed yucca topped with a tangy cabbage salad and big pork rind served up on a washed banana leaf) and a tall glass of *chicha* (a creamy, bright pink corn-based drink), perhaps purchasing a ceramic whistle from one of the cute kids wandering around. From here, you could head four blocks south on Calle Atravesada to the overflowing and fun (if not particularly good for souvenir shopping) 1892 **Mercado Municipal** (Map p111), a neoclassical building that may be beautiful, though there's really no way of knowing until somebody gets up there and scrubs down the facade.

Or, head west on Calle Xalteva, which once connected the Spanish town of Granada to its much older indigenous neighbor, Xalteva. You'll pass **Iglesia de La Merced** (Map p111), four blocks west of the parque central, considered the most beautiful of Granada's churches. A handful of art galleries and antique shops are clustered nearby. Just south of the main road is the poorly signed **Casa Natal Sor María Romero Meneses** (Map p111), where a small collection of artifacts and original writings mark the birthplace of Central America's first official saint.

The old indigenous neighborhood, now wholly assimilated, is marked by **Iglesia de Xalteva** (Map p111), the dilapidated but attractive 19th-century church that houses La Virgen de la Asunción. Across the street is shady Parque Xalteva, with rough stone columns and overgrown ambience, perfect for a picnic lunch. Continuing west, you'll pass another gorgeous little church, **La Capilla María Auxiliadora** (Map p111), closed for remodeling as of December 2004, but worth a look for its beautiful pastel interior.

If you've come this far, it's only four more blocks to 1748 **Fortaleza La Polvora** (see opposite), where you can climb to the top of the guard tower for the best view in town.

CONVENTO Y MUSEO SAN FRANCISCO

The oldest church in Central America and the most striking building in Granada (that is to say, Nicaragua) boasts the big robin-egg-blue birthday cake facade of **Iglesia San Francisco** (Map p114; ☎ 552 5535; admission US$2; ⊙ 8:30am-5:30pm Mon-Fri, 9am-4pm Sat & Sun), which, incidentally, houses the best museum in the region. Originally constructed in 1585, it was subsequently burnt to the ground by pirates and later William Walker, rebuilt most recently in 1868 and restored in 1989.

The museum is through the small door on the left, where guides (some of whom speak English) are available for tours; tips are appreciated. Museum highlights include top-notch primitivist art, a scale model of the city and a tribe of papier-mâché Indians cooking, relaxing in hammocks and swinging on *comelazatoaztegams,* a sort of a 360-degree see-saw.

The reason why you're here, however, is the Zapatera statuary, two solemn regimens of black basalt statues, looming above large men and possessed of 10 times their gravity, carved between AD 800 and 1200, then left behind on the ritual island of Zapatera (see p129). Most were discovered by US diplomat Ephraim Squier and Swedish scientist Carl Bollivius in the late 1880s and gathered in Granada in the 1920s.

IGLESIA DE LA MERCED

Arguably the most beautiful church in the city, this landmark (Map p111), four blocks west of the parque central, is fronted by a plaza popular with young lovers and players after dark. Originally completed in 1539, it was razed by pirates in 1655 and rebuilt with its current baroque facade between 1781 and 1783. Damaged by Walker's forces in 1854, it was again restored with the current elaborate interior in 1862. Although Catholics come to see an important image of the Virgen de Fatima, anyone can enjoy climbing the **bell tower** (admission US$1). The

THE STATUARIES OF NICARAGUA

Although Nicaragua has yet to be adequately explored by trained archaeologists, at least four important statuary sites have been unearthed. The figurative pieces range from 1m to 4m high, were probably carved between AD 800 and 1200 using obsidian tools (technology imported from Mexico in about AD 300), then sanded to a smooth finish, and possibly painted. While the different 'schools' of sculptors clearly influenced each other, sites reveal unique artistic styles.

Chontales Statuary

Several sites throughout Boaco, Matagalpa and Zalaya produced finely detailed statues with expressive faces, much taller and thinner than elsewhere. Archaeologists hypothesize that they were used as columns for buildings, and you can see for yourself at Juigalpa's incredible Museo Arqueológico Gregorio Aguilar Barea (see p243).

Isla de Ometepe statuary

The island is known for its squat and realistic figures, thought to represent chiefs and other historic people, but portrayed as half-human, half-animal. Although other sites are likely entombed in the ashes of Concepción's eruptions, only a few excavated examples are on display on the island, most behind the church in Altagracia (see p145).

Isla Zapateria Statuary

The best-known statuary, with excellent examples on display at Granada's Convento y Museo San Francisco (see opposite), also includes sites on the ceremonial islands of Pensacola, Zonzapote, Punta de las Figuras and Las Cañas. Considered the best artistically, archaeologist Frederik W Lange called the sculptors 'poets of rock.' Human-animal hybrids, or animals with human heads in their mouths, probably refer to legends that humankind emerged from beneath the ground.

León Statuary

Least known is this statuary, which includes the Isla de Momotombito (see p177), where Ephraim Squier reported some 50 statues still standing in 1854. Sadly, most of the statues overlooking Lago de Managua island seem to have disappeared.

caretaker usually takes people up at around 11am, but you can ask anytime.

CASA DE LOS LEONES & FUNDACIÓN CASA DE LOS TRES MUNDOS

Founded in 1986 by Ernesto Cardenal (see p267), **Fundación Casa de los Tres Mundos** (Map p114; ☎ 552 4176; www.c3mundos.org; adult/child US$0.70/0.30; ⏱ gallery 8am-6pm) moved to elegant 1720 Casa de los Leones in 1992. At the entrance, a board lists special events, which are frequent, cheap and usually interesting: poetry readings, classical ballet, folkloric dance and free movies on the 'Cube of Light,' a fabric screen where foreign and artsy films are shown for free on the plaza. During regular business hours, your entrance fee buys you a look at a beautiful mansion (the facade is original) and a few art displays.

MI MUSEO

This brand-new **museum** (☎ 552 7614; cnr Calles El Arsenal & Atravesada; admission free; ⏱ 8am-noon Mon-Sat, 1:30-5pm Mon-Fri) displays an incredible private collection of ceramics dating from at least 2000 BC to the present. Hundreds of beautifully crafted pieces were chosen with as much an eye for their artistic merit as their archaeological significance, and displayed in the grand old adobe with the same aesthetic awareness.

NICARAGUA BUTTERFLY RESERVE

About 4km from Granada on the dirt road that leads from the cemetery to Laguna de Apoyo, this new **mariposario** (☎ in English 895 3012, in Spanish 863 2943; www.backyardnature.net /nbr; admission US$7) offers tours through the butterflies, and also rents cabinas for US$20, including a tour.

FORTALEZA LA POLVORA

Originally called the **Fortaleza de Armas** (Map p111; donations appreciated; ⏱ 8am-5pm) when it was constructed in 1748, this lavishly turreted Spanish fortress still has the best view in town, over ancient, water-stained church domes all the way to Lago de Nicaragua.

You can also check out a roomful of paintings, some for sale, a couple of artifacts worth poking around, not to mention one of the better public toilets (it's hexagonal!) in Nicaragua.

ANTIGUA ESTACIÓN DEL FERROCARRIL

Nine long blocks north of town along Calle Atravesada, you'll find shadeless Parque Sandino, next to the **old train station** (Map p111), now a technical vocational school. Built in 1882 and operational in 1886, the US marines remodeled it in 1912. There's lots of playground equipment, some with train themes, and a few well-preserved railroad cars are on display nearby.

GRANADA CEMETERY

Used between 1876 and 1922, some of Granada's wealthiest decades, this beautiful cemetery (Map p111) has lots of picturesque mausoleums and tombs, including those of six Nicaraguan presidents. Most people come to see the 1880 neoclassical stone **Capilla de Animas** (Chapel of Spirits), a scale replica of the French chapel of the same name. Close by is another rather mysterious replica, of Notre Dame cathedral. No one knows who built it, as the names have been chiseled away. This is also the starting point for the two-hour walk (or much quicker bike ride) to the back of Laguna de Apoyo (see p102).

CENTRO TURISTICO

Enter through the green **mock Spanish fortress** (Map p111; admission per person/car US$0.12/1) to a 2km stretch of lakefront with shady paths, sandy beaches, trees that seem designed for hammocks, restaurants, picnic areas and playgrounds, and free mangoes (if you can beat the parrots and street kids to 'em) all over the place starting in late February. Before jumping into the water with all the smiling families, take a good look at the river draining into the lake right there. Luckily, **Piscina-Ristorante Casa Vivaldi** (☎ 552 7567; Calle El Caimito; ☯ 9am-9pm) has a clean pool for US$3 just up the street.

There are probably a dozen restaurants, most of the 'fried fish and cold beer' variety, but the standout is **Restaurante Frutti D'Mare** (Map p111; seafood US$6-12; ☯ 10am-10pm), with Italian-style seafood and a good wine list. More famously, the Centro is home

to some of the town's top youth-oriented discos – see Drinking, p125.

If you come during the day, you can arrange a trip to Las Isletas in a motorized *panga* (small covered boat) at **Puerto Asese**, almost 3km from the entrance (see below).

LAS ISLETAS

One of the most beautiful ways to pass the time is touring this miniature archipelago of 365 (OK, maybe fewer) tiny tropical islands, topped with rare birds and colorful flowers, mansions hung with hammocks, and a handful of hotels and restaurants where you're most cordially invited to sit back and enjoy it all for a while. There's even a Spanish fortress, 1784 **Castillo San Pablo**, with great views of Granada and Volcán Mombacho, plus a fine swimming hole nearby, and **Isla de los Monos** (Monkey Island), where the residents are friendly, but may run off with your picnic lunch.

Formed 10,000 years ago when very visible Volcán Mombacho exploded into its current ragged silhouette, these islands were once one of the poorest neighborhoods in Granada, and some are still home to impoverished families, who in general have no official property rights. They are being gradually supplanted by the beautiful homes of folks like the Pellas (Flor de Caña, Credomatic) family, former President Chamorro, and lots of expats in paradise. Want to join them? There are plenty of 'For Sale' signs, and your guide knows all the prices.

Most tour companies run trips to Las Isletas, or do it yourself with **Inuit Kayaks** (Map p111; ☎ 614 0813, 608 3646), about 1km from the Centro Turistico entrance, which runs several guided tours (about US$10 per hour) and also rents tents – camping is free in the Centro Turistico. Inuit Kayaks also plans to offer sailboats and windsurfing soon.

You can hire a boat at either **Puerto Asese** (☎ 552 2269; www.aseselasisletas.com) or **Marina Cocibolca** (☎ 228 1223); there may also be cheaper collective boats, so ask. Private *pangas* seating at least 12 cost about US$15 per hour, so try to get a group together. Binoculars and sunscreen are a good idea.

There are several places where you can ask your driver to stop for lunch, including **Isleta Cifar**, about 15 minutes from Puerto Asese, where María Teresa Marenco has a pool and serves her famous fried fish platter (US$10). A bit further in, **Isla Punta Correviento** has two pools, a kid's playground and another seafood restaurant, also locally owned.

You could stay a while on Isla La Ceiba at **Hotel Isleta La Ceiba** (☎ 552 2100, 882 3928; www.nicaraolake.com.ni; all-inclusive r per person US$55; ❄ ▨) with a package deal that includes a pretty air-con cabin with hot-water bathroom, three meals, drinks and round-trip transportation to Puerto Asese, not to mention access to the pool, rowboats and kayaks. You can stop in for lunch or visit on a day trip. A collective boat (US$10 return) leaves Puerto Asese at 10am, noon, 2pm and 4pm daily, returning at 11:30am, 1:30pm, 3:30pm and 5:30pm.

Hotel Isleta El Roble (☎ 894 6217, in France 06 08 93 56 96; www.nicadescanso.com; d/tr incl 3 meals US$80/90; ❄ ▨), almost an hour from Puerto Asese, is a beautiful French-owned hotel that limits visitors to 12 per day, including day-trippers who can come as part of a tour (US$35, including lunch). There's also a pool, kayaks and multiday deals that save you a bundle.

MASSAGE & THERAPIES

After all that sightseeing, don't you need to pamper yourself with a massage (US$40), facial (US$45) or perhaps some reflexology? Try **InterConnection Wellness Center** (Map p114; ☎ 552 7954, 880 0438), upstairs from Cafe DecArte.

Or you could get a massage (US$10 to US$20) from Roxanne, at **Roxanne Massage** (Map p114; ☎ 829 9184; roxven26@yahoo.com; Calle El Caimito), who's also a home decorator; there's also **Casa Clarita Maximus Spa** (Map p111; ☎ 552 8422; www.casaclarita.com; Calle El Arsenal), behind Iglesia San Francisco, with facials (US$25), massages (US$40 to US$50) and more.

Courses

There are loads of freelance Spanish teachers, most with experience at one of the schools listed, who will come to your hotel for US$5 per hour, and may be able to arrange homestays. Check bulletin boards in backpacker hotels, or try **Ruth Abea** (☎ 552 5866; per 1/12/20hr US$5/35/50), one and a half blocks north of Iglesia de Xalteva; **Bayardo Corea Cuadra** (☎ 552 4684); or **Maycor**

José García (☎ 898 5768; granadaspanishtutor@yahoo .com).

Ave Nicaragüita Escuela Español (Map p111; ☎ 605 5092, 806 4974; www.avenicaraguita.com; Calle La Calzada; per 10/20/30hr US$87/157/197) Professional operation works with (and at) the Red Cross; classrooms could get hot by the afternoon.

Casa Xalteva (Map p111; ☎ 552 2436; www.casa xalteva.com; Calle Real Xalteva 103) Next to the church of the same name, Casa Xalteva also runs a children's shelter. It can get hot during afternoon classes.

La Gran Sultana Spanish School (Map p111; ☎ 898 5768; granadaspanishtutors@yahoo.com; per 1/10/20hr US$5/45/80) Homestays (one has a mom who speaks French) are US$60 extra, including all meals, and you pay the family directly. It's one block south of Iglesia de Xalteva.

One-on-One Tutoring (Map p111; ☎ 552 6771; www.1on1tutoring.net; Calle La Calzada; per 10/20hr US$50/95) With guaranteed private classes arranged around a beautiful leafy patio, this is a good option. Homestays with meals cost US$60 per week.

OTHER CLASSES

Mosaics Workshops (Map p114; US$3) Janet Gallagher at Cafe DecArte regularly offers classes; the fee includes all your materials, which will (hopefully) become a beautiful bowl; she also teaches local kids as part of the Muchachos de Mosaico program, and you can buy their work here.

Painting Classes (per day/month US$1.25/7) Ask at Casa de los Tres Mundos about twice-weekly classes at Fortaleza El Polvora.

Yoga Classes (Map p111; ☎ 834 5884; helenkaye@ yahoo.com; Calle Cuiscoma; US$4; ◷ 8am Mon, Wed & Fri) Travel is about stretching yourself, right?

Tours

The classic Granada tour takes a **horse-drawn carriage** (up to 5 people US$12) from the park for an hour-long whirl past churches, the cemetery, the *malecón* (waterfront) and more with your Spanish-speaking guide. These guys know how to give a tour, too: this has been a family business since 1868, when carriages were first introduced here and in Masaya. They'll also wait at Puerto Asese for the other classic Granada trip, a boat ride through Las Isletas (see opposite), and wait. You can arrange trips all over the country from Granada, which is the epicenter of Nicaragua's nascent tourist industry, with recommended splurges including the Granada City Tour (per person US$15 to US$25), Reserva Natural Volcán

Mombacho (with/without canopy tour US$65/40) and Masaya Market and Volcano (US$30 to US$50, including Catarina).

Prices are lower for larger groups, so solo travelers should shop around to see who is already going; reputable operators include:

Amigo Tours (Map p114; ☎ 552 4080; www.amigo tours.net) This is fancier than the others, it's inside Hotel Colonial.

Eco Expedition (Map p114; ☎ 552 2727; www .discoverynicaragua.com; Calle Real Xalteva) On the pricey side.

JB Funtours (Map p114; ☎ 552 6732; jbfuntoursni@ yahoo.com) Located in a souvenir shop on the parque central.

Paradise Tour (Map p114; ☎ 841 9285) One block east of the cathedral, this is a budget option.

Tierra Tour (Map p114; ☎ 862 9580; www.tierra tour.com) Across the street from Paradise Tour, this is a recommended company.

Other operators include:

Blue Mountain Horseback Riding (Map p114; ☎ 552 5323, 838 4487; per person US$20) Offers one tour: horseback rides through the lakes and volcanoes begin at 10am, stop for a lunch buffet in a little town, and return at 5pm.

Land Cruiser Tours (☎ 895 5244; www.land cruisertours.com; from per person US$50) See the country on a custom tour in a super-plush Land Cruiser; co-owner Ruth López Gaitan is an expert on Masaya's fascinating Barrio Monimbó (see the boxed text, p97).

Mombotour (Map p114; ☎ 552 4548; www.mom botour.com) In Centro Comercial Granada, this recommended outfitter is part of the Mombacho Canopy Tour (US$40), which you can combine with other active options like guided hikes up Reserva Natural Volcán Mombacho, kayak trips through Las Isletas and bike rides to Laguna de Apoyo.

Nicaragua Adventures (Map p114; ☎ 883 7161; www.nica-adventures.com) This outfit is the most expensive – and exclusive – tour operator of them all, dahlings.

Oro Travel (Map p111; ☎ 552 4568; www.orotravel .com; Calle Corral) Reputable outfitter, half a block west of the San Francisco convent, offers good-value trips all over the country.

Festivals & Events

Granada hosts a variety of interesting events and festivals throughout the year; check out the website **Casa de los Tres Mundos** (www.c3mundos.org) for what's on during your visit.

International Poetry Festival (February; www .festivalpoesianicaragua.org.ni) This festival brings together wordsmiths from all around the country and Latin America.

Fiestas de Agosto (third week of August) Granada celebrates the Assumption of Mary with fireworks, concerts in the park, bullfights (although it's illegal to kill the bull in Nicaragua), horse parades and major revelry by the lakefront.

Inmaculada Concepción (Purísimas; November 28–December 7) Neighborhoods bear elaborate floats through the streets in honor of Granada's patron saint, the Virgen Concepción de María. You'll hear them signaling their arrival by blowing in conch shells to drive the demons away.

Sleeping

These are all low-season prices, which at pricier hotels increase around 15% during the high season (December to May). Make reservations and expect to pay more around Christmas, Semana Santa, the mid-August *fiestas* and Independence Day (September 15).

Granada was undergoing a time of explosive growth at the time of research, with several hotels under construction. While this sort of overdevelopment can be frustrating for guidebook publishers, it's great for travelers – don't be afraid to bargain.

BUDGET

Bearded Monkey (Map p111; ☎ 552 4028; www .thebeardedmonkey.com; Calle 14 de Septiembre; hammock/dm/s/d/tr US$2/4/9/11/14) Make sure you make reservations for the popular Bearded Monkey, managed by a British-American couple, in a cavernous colonial home containing co-ed dormitories with foam-pad bunks and several private rooms. The pleasant café/bar here serves outstanding international cuisine – don't miss the burritos or Thai food – and gets lively in the evening, making it a good spot to chat with other travelers. Those interested in working or volunteer opportunities should check out the extensive message board. The owners rent out bikes, screen English-language movies and run several cheap tours, including one to their Laguna de Apoyo–side dream home, the Monkey Hut (see p102).

Hospedaje Cocibolca (Map p114; ☎ 552 7223; www.hotelcocibolca.com; d with fan/air-con US$13/29;

RURAL TOURISM WITH UCA-TIERRA Y AGUA

Originally formed in 1984, the **Union of Agricultural Cooperatives** (es.geocities.com/ucatierrayagua) was about the only tour operator in the country, helping the eager and idealistic *internacionalistas* (politically motivated foreign tourists) of the 1980s arrange food, lodging and entertainment. It was low-tech: visitors would stay in a home, eat (and perhaps learn to cook) traditional foods with the family, and tour farms, rural development projects and nature areas that weren't too dangerous.

Today it's called UCA-Tierra y Agua (more upbeat than the previous 'UCA-Heroes and Martyrs of Nandaime), and along with its sister program in Estelí, UCA-Miraflor (see p198), is going stronger than ever. There are four community-based ecotourism opportunities available within a few hours in Granada, three with lodging and all with guided hikes (per day US$7), horseback rides (per hour US$3), boat trips and basic restaurants. Begin by visiting **UCA's Granada office** (Map p111; ☎ 899 2927; ucatierrayagua@yahoo.es; ☒ 8am-4pm Mon, Wed & Fri) in the unsigned green and white house one block west of Shell Palmira; a mural on the corner has a map and directions. They'll help arrange transportation and lodging:

Albergue Nicaragua Libre (dm incl 3 meals US$12) Easiest to reach, it's a 1km walk from where the bus drops you on the Granada–Nandaime road, and the lodge has electricity, running water and guided trips through organic coffee farms and horseback rides to San Juan de Oriente (see p104).

La Granadilla (dm incl 3 meals US$10) A bit further down the same road, La Granadilla is more rustic and electricity is iffy, but you're only 20 minutes from the entrance of Volcán Mombacho. You can arrange guided hikes up the mountain, or for farms in the area.

Isla Sonzapote (dm or campin g per person US$3, incl 3 meals US$10) On spectacular Isla Zapatera (see p129), dorms have a simple restaurant, solar electricity, running (but not drinking) water, and access to the petroglyphs, fishing trips and the three-hour hike to the top of the volcano (629m). UCA will help you catch the public boat.

La Nanda There's no lodging, but there is a restaurant, and a three-hour hike to otherwise inaccessible Reserva Natural Lagunetas de Mecatepe (US$4 per group), with five cute lagoons.

☒ ☐) This is a great choice for couples, an excellent option with attractively furnished rooms, cozy hangout spots, a guest kitchen and Internet access (per hour US$1), all done with an eye for detail and cleanliness.

Hostal Oasis (Map p111; ☎ 552 8006; oasis granada@hotmail.com; Calle Estrada; dm/s/d US$6/14/22; ☐ ☒) It's a bit more expensive – and totally worth it – for the beautiful dorm with gorgeous polished-wood furniture (where you can lock up your pack) and there's a beautiful little swimming pool. Besides, you can make up the difference by using the fast and free Internet, or by making a complimentary 15-minute phone call (value US$3) to the USA or Canada. Hotel staff can arrange stays at Hospedaje Crater's Edge (see p103), at Laguna de Apoyo.

Hostal Esfinge (Map p111; ☎ 552 4826; esfingehostal@yahoo.com; s/d without bathroom US$6/9, with bathroom US$9/12, r with air-con US$35; ℗ ☒) Never mind the scruffy neighborhood

across from the market; this beautiful old house has been colorfully painted and has good security, a gracious hostess, a guest kitchen and new mattresses – but circa early-1970s furniture – plus guarded parking. There are good vine-covered hangout areas out the back. Groups get better deals here.

Hospedaje La Libertad (Map p111; ☎ 552 4117; hospedaje_lalibertad@hotmail.com; Calle La Libertad; dm US$6, r per person with/without bathroom incl breakfast US$25/10; ☐) In an elegant colonial mansion across from the El Club hotel, this is a new hostel that takes care of you, with free Internet, a guest kitchen and very clean dorms, all decked out in super-cool furniture.

Hostel San Angel (Map p114; ☎ 552 6373; myvcay@hotmail.com; s/d with fan US$10/18, d with air-con US$28; ☒) Granada's best deal on Spanish colonial elegance, just half a block south of the parque central, is this homey spot. There are good, clean rooms that have lots of little amenities –

showers, towels and soap – plus a kitchen you can use, free coffee all day and a nice TV hangout area.

Hotelito Mochilero.com (Map p111; dm/d/tr US$3/7/10) Mochilero means 'backpacker' and the .com is just randomly tacked on, but this is still the cheapest decent bed in town, with cleanish rooms, a guest kitchen and a big dirt lawn out back with hammocks. Walls almost hit the ceiling.

Hospedaje La Calzada (Map p111; ☎ 552 6736; s/d without bathroom US$6/9, with bathroom US$8/12) Big, clean, tiled rooms with thin mattresses surround a huge cement courtyard with a ping-pong table and a kitchen that guests are welcome to use – a good deal.

Another Night in Paradise (Map p111; ☎ 552 7113; donnatabor@hotmail.com; apt US$20) Home of Granada's very own 'Mother Teresa with a potty mouth,' Donna Tambor's fabled *hospedaje* (guesthouse) is mostly closed, but you can still rent one fully furnished little house at back. Donna is a great contact person for hooking up volunteer opportunities, so feel free to get in touch if you're interested in helping out.

Hospedaje Central (Map p114; ☎ 552 6044; dm US$3.25, r US$5-16) The wonderful original owner of this longtime travelers' favorite recently passed away, and both the restaurant and hostel have gone straight downhill since then. Too bad.

Marina's Hostel (Map p114; ☎ 552 8340, 887 6035; marinashostel@yahoo.com; dm US$6-10, s/d with fan US$21/26, with air-con & cable TV US$32/36; 🔊) Newly remodeled, with clean, decent rooms, good beds and a cute little pool, plus free coffee all day, this place is just fine.

MIDRANGE

El Club (Map p111; ☎ 552 4245; www.elclub-nicaragua .com; Calle La Libertad; s US$35, d US$45-65; 🔊) Decorated in an impeccable minimalist groove, with beds on platforms that rise from the floor, this is one of the coolest options in town. Fresh flowers every day, attention to lighting, air-con and a great courtyard for lounging are even better if you stay in the upstairs rooms.

Posada Don Alfredo (Map p111; ☎ 552 4455; alfredpaulbaganz@hotmail.com; d US$25-35, extra with air-con US$10; 🔊) In what Alfredo claims is the fifth-oldest European house in the Americas, huge, gorgeous rooms sprawl around a miniature jungle garden that you

can enjoy in hammocks or over a big German breakfast (US$5 to US$8). Most rooms have shared bathroom (building codes), but there's hot water. Bikes (per day US$6) can be rented.

Estancia Mar Dulce (Map p111; ☎ 552 3732; www.hotelmardulce.com; small s/d US$25/35, large r US$40; 🅿 🔊 🔊) Rooms – especially the big ones, with two double beds – are cute, air-conditioned and decorated with an awesomely ticky-tacky vibe, but it's really all about the pool, a serious project in creative tilework that may be one of Granada's great architectural wonders.

Hotel Cocibolca (Map p114; ☎ 552 8219; www .hotelcocibolca.com; Calle El Caimito; d with fan/air-con US$18/30; 🅿 🔊 🔊) A brand-new option opened by the superstars at Hospedaje Cocibolca, this sterile spot has a big Spanish courtyard and US chain-motel styling: small pool, two double beds, nightstand with lamp, little soaps, the whole thing – which makes this a great deal close to the city center.

Hospedaje La Pergola (Map p114; ☎ 552 4221; lapergolanic@yahoo.com; Calle El Caimito; d US$40; 🅿 🔊) Around the corner from the Cocibolca and also brand-new, with similar style and amenities, this hotel is a bit more expensive and not quite as nice; but it's still OK.

Casa Naranja (☎ 880 0438; redwarriorwon@msn .com; r per day/week US$25/140; 🅿 🔊) Two blocks south of Calle La Calzada, this cute little orange house has air-conditioning, hot water, a pretty private garden and even coffee in the morning. Talk to Cafe DecArte for more information.

Casa Doña Pilar (www.granadanicaraguahotel.com; r incl breakfast US$29-42; 🅿 🔊 🔊 🔊) With only four attractive rooms, this British-owned guesthouse on the outskirts of town (a US$0.70 taxi ride from downtown), with its *palapa*-lined swimming pool, secure parking and amenities including satellite TV, free Internet and laundry service, is well loved.

Casa Capricho (Map p114; ☎ 552 8422; www .casacapricho.com; s/d incl breakfast US$35/50; 🅿 🔊 🔊) This attractive option has sophisticated and creatively decorated twofloor suites (and smaller, but still cool, one-floor options for solo travelers) plus hot water, air-con and a neat brick arch over the small pool outside.

El Maltese (Map p111; ☎ 552 7641; www.nicatour .net/en/elmaltese; r US$22-50; P 🞩) The best option for staying right on the lake, this peaceful spot has good, clean rooms, air-conditioning and good views. There's a restaurant on-site, and bikes and canoes can be rented.

Hospedaje El Italiano (Map p111; ☎ 552 7047; italianrick@latinmail.com; s/d with bathroom US$25/32; 🞩) Spotless and air-conditioned rooms surround a tranquil patio. The café in the lobby serves tasty Italian gelato.

Hotel Granada (☎ 552 2974; info@hotelgranada nicaragua.com; s/d US$25/30; 🞩) Venerable and inconvenient Hotel Granada always held promise, and new owners have finally painted and fumigated the spacious rooms and furnished them with mismatched wicker, making this a decent midrange option.

TOP END
Hotel Gran Francia (Map p114; ☎ 552 6000; www.lagranfrancia.com; d incl breakfast US$80-140; P 🞩 ▢ ▣) With adobe-walled amenities suitable for a self-crowned king, William Walker's former home, right off the parque central, has been reconstructed according to his specifications – precious woods, beautiful tiles, shady courtyards – with all the modern amenities. The architecture is soaring, service impeccable and the cheap rooms are really small. Go ahead and spend the extra US$20 to upgrade to a 'Junior Suite,' with a couple of sofas and a balcony. With all this architectural beauty, it's well worth dropping by for a drink at the upstairs bar overlooking the street scene.

Casa San Francisco (Map p111; ☎ 552 8235; www.casasanfrancisco.com; d incl breakfast US$40-60; P 🞩 ▣) Perhaps even better, if you love a luxurious bathroom, this vine-draped and mosaic-tiled Spanish colonial mansion has been lovingly restored and finely furnished – Turkish lamps, hand-carved beds – plus modern amenities like air-con, cable TV and a pool. Some rooms have balconies, others patios, and some can be connected to make family rooms. There's a great Latin-fusion restaurant downstairs, plus one of the better selections of souvenirs in town.

Hotel Alhambra (Map p114; ☎ 552 2035; d/ste US$80/100; P 🞩 ▢ ▣) Serving Granada for more than half a century, this recently remodeled, fairly luxurious property has a five-star location on the parque central and 60 rooms, including the high-ceilinged suites (worth the extra US$20) with refrigerator, air-con, cable TV, two terraces, fresh flowers and room for four – there's even an OK pool downstairs. Other rooms are still nice.

Hotel Colonial (Map p114; ☎ 552 7299; www .nicaragua-vacations.com; s/d US$55/70, ste US$80-100; P 🞩) Another quality luxury property, in a Spanish colonial dream home just off the parque central. The 2nd-floor suites are fabulous, with little balconies, kitchenettes and lots of light; note that some of the luxuriously appointed bottom-end rooms don't have windows.

Eating
The classic Granada dining experience is relaxing over a light meal in a shady corner of the parque central. Four cute **kiosks** (vigarón US$2; 🕑 9am-9pm) anchoring the plaza serve *vigarón*, best washed down with *chicha*.

RESTAURANTS
El Zaguán (Map p114; ☎ 552 2522; meals US$4-10; 🕑 11am-11pm) Right behind the cathedral, the best restaurant in town does succulent fire-grilled meats, wonderfully prepared *guapote* (rainbow bass) from the lake or sea bass from the Pacific, all in a cozy dining room where dueling mariachi trios descend at sunset. Make reservations in the high season.

Rosticería J3 (Map p114; Calle Atravesada; típica US$1-4; 🕑 8am-9pm) Inside this mini mall, enjoy outdoor tables and excellent service over big plates of typical food; the chicken in salsa is great.

Tercer Ojo (Map p114; ☎ 552 6451; meals US$2-7; 🕑 10am-10pm Tue-Sun) Consider making reservations for one of the scarf-draped tables in this beautiful trippy-gypsy gourmet restaurant, where international offerings range from sushi to curries to big salads, lots of imported wines and a gourmet grocery in front.

Cafe DecArte (Map p114; dishes US$3-6; 🕑 7am-10pm Wed-Mon) This restaurant serves fresh, healthy cuisine, including a recommended Caesar salad and tuna pita sandwich, plus daily vegetarian specials and fresh soups, not to mention a pretty darned spectacular breakfast buffet (US$4). The owners also offer mosaics classes to adults as well as local kids, who sell their stuff right here (see p119).

Nuestra Casa (Map p111; ribs US$4-7; 🕑 8am-close) This homey spot serves some of the best baby back ribs anywhere – no joke, the owner is from Alabama and knows his craft – plus other mostly meaty specials. There's live music on weekends.

Doña Conchi (Map p114; Calle El Caimito; dishes US$4-10; 🕑 9am-10pm) Excellent Spanish cuisine is served in a lovely garden, lit by candles in the evening. Prices aren't cheap, but the ambience and sangria (iced punch made from red wine, fruit juice and soda water) are unbeatable, and from time to time Conchi breaks out her castanets to dance for the lucky few.

Mona Lisa (Map p114; meals US$3-8; 🕑 5pm-midnight Mon-Fri, noon-midnight Sat & Sun) The best pizza in town is served at this upscale joint, which is also a popular bar.

Restaurante Mediterránio (Map p114; ☎ 552 6764; tapas US$4-6, mains US$8-12; 🕑 11am-3pm & 6-10pm Mon-Fri, 11am-10pm Sat & Sun) This beautiful restaurant, set around a big, leafy courtyard, has romantic music, great service and top-quality Spanish cuisine.

Piscina-Ristorante Casa Vivaldi (Map p111; ☎ 552 7567; meals US$3-15; Calle El Caimito; 🕑 9am-9pm; 🖳) Winning 'best perk' in the Mediterranean category, however, is this Italian restaurant specializing in fresh pasta, tiramisu espresso beverages and fine wine served beneath a vine-draped patio. But really it's all about the pool (US$3 just to swim). Hotel rooms are also being built.

Casa San Francisco (Map p111; dishes US$2-6; 🕑 7am-2:20pm & 6-10pm) Around the corner from the eponymous church, San Francisco serves 'pan-Latin' cuisine, including moles (spicy sauce made with chilies, chocolate and served with meat), nachos, pupusas (a cornmeal mass stuffed with cheese or refried beans) and fajitas (marinated and grilled strips of meat served with a flour tortilla and savory fillings), plus a good happy hour with US$2 margaritas and a fabulous Sunday brunch (10am to 3pm) for nursing your hangover.

Las Colinas del Sur (Map p111; Calle Atravesada; mains US$4-8) Out past the Mercado Municipal, it's best to take a taxi (US$0.70) to this locally revered hole in the wall, with delicious *guapote*, at reasonable prices.

El Club (Map p111; Calle La Libertad; mains US$3-8) This attractive restaurant/bar does excellent international cuisine, from Italian lasagna to Indonesian satay, in cool Euro styling; it's a great place to meet friends.

Tequila Vallarta (Map p114; mains US$3-8; 🕑 10am-10pm) The chef is actually from Puerto Vallarta, and the Mexican food – enchiladas, moles – is actually spicy. And there's a full bar with lots of tequilas!

Taquería La Jarochita (Map p114; mains US$3-8; Calle El Caimito; 🕑 11:30am-10:30pm) The Masaya institution has opened another one of its fine Mexican restaurants here in town.

CAFÉS

Kathy's Waffle House (Map p114; dishes US$2-3; 🕑 7am-2am; 🖳) With one of the best views in town (right across from the Convento San Francisco), this cheerful café has seven different kinds of waffles and lots of other great breakfasts, plus good coffee and wi-fi (!).

Café Blue (Map p114; meals US$2-3; 🕑 7am-5pm) Not wanting to let expats make all the money off the pancake-loving backpacking crowd, these local ladies have started serving all your international faves under a cane roof, but consider going for the Nica breakfast instead.

Nica Buffet (Map p114; Calle Estrada; breakfast US$3; 🕑 6am-noon) It's not actually a buffet, but it does have some of the best Western-style pancakes in town.

Restaurant Los Portales (Map p114; meals US$2-6; 🕑 7am-10pm) Right on Plaza de la Independencia with ringside seats to all the action, you can enjoy a healthy selection of Mexican food, big salads, great service and Presto coffee on a porch across from Casa de los Leones.

Cafetín El Volcán (Map p111; quesillos US$0.50-2; 🕑 7am-8:45pm) Get your *quesillos* (see the boxed text, p181) and *tiste* (toasted corn beverage) at this cheapie, close to Hostal Oasis.

Chichería Paris (Map p111; snacks US$1-2; 🕑 10:30am-8pm) If you need a snack after climbing all those guard towers at La Fortaleza, stop here for *vigarón* and other traditional treats.

QUICK EATS

Granada has excellent street food, with bags of fruit salad (with fork US$0.30) and other goodies on sale between the parque central and Mercado Municipal in the morning. Just before sunset, **fritangas** (sidewalk barbecues; snacks US$1-3) set up in the parque central and Calle La Calzada, dishing up barbecue, *gallo pinto* (rice and beans) and all things fried, onto washed banana leaves for you to enjoy.

Melbar & Los Hijos del Maíz (Map p114; set plate US$1.25; ☺ 11am-10pm) Melba, the best-dressed woman in Granada, serves *comida corriente* (a mixed plate of different typical foods) and 13-córdoba (US$0.76) *cerveza* (beer) in her five-star location, right around the corner from the cathedral.

Restaurant Don Daffa (Map p114; meal US$3-5; ☺ 11am-7pm) This steam-table buffet, right on the park, may be a bit on the pricey side, but that's because it rocks.

Tele Pizza (Map p114; ☎ 552 4219; Calle El Arsenal; slice/pie US$0.30/3) The excellent hand-tossed pizza may not be gourmet, but good prices, speedy delivery and carrot cake for dessert make this a local favorite.

Hot Dogs Connection (Map p114; hot dogs US$1-3; ☺ 11am-8pm) In the same mini mall as Rosticería J3, it does lots of different dogs, including Don Perro Italiano, with mozzarella, oregano and olives.

It's worth checking out the cheap 'n' traditional steam-table buffet at **Las Bocaditas** (Map p114; dishes US$2-6; ☺ 8am-10pm), to see if anything looks good. **Comedor-Fritanga Doña Cruz** (Map p114; dishes US$2-4; ☺ 7am-10pm), the steam-table buffet next door, seems to have more fried items. There's also **Sophie's Deli Sandwiches** (Map p114; Calle Atravesada; 6-/12-inch sub US$1.50/3; ☺ 10am-10pm), in the Centro Commercial Granada, which does submarine sandwiches.

GROCERIES

There are two grocery stores: Supermercado Lacayo (Map p114), one and a half blocks east of the parque central, with a better selection and cigarette rolling papers; and Palí (Map p111), across from the Mercado Municipal, with better prices and a tiny Musmanni bakery.

Drinking

The Centro Turistico is home to several discos, including Bar César (Map p111), close to the entrance, Discoteque Centauro (Map p111) and Disco Bar Bamboo (Map p111), a bit further in. Always use cabs between the Centro Turistico and central Granada at night.

Café Nuit (Map p111) features live music on Friday and Saturday, and has a lush outdoor courtyard with round tables beneath the palms. Inside, the old colonial home has been transformed into a lounge, enjoyed largely by a Nica crowd. Granada's hottest dance spot, La Fábrica (Map p111), was closed at press time – if it's reopened, slip into your sexiest outfit and get ready to party into the wee hours.

Jazz-Bar Restaurant (Map p114; no cover, mains US$3-12; ☺ music from 7:30pm) Hotel Colonial's low-key restaurant/bar serves French cuisine and has live jazz on Friday and Saturday evening at least.

El Quijote (Map p114; snacks US$1-3) This new place with a sports-bar atmosphere and cheap *tragos* (shots) has some definite meat-market potential.

Mi Tierra Bar & Restaurant (Map p114; cnr Calles Real Xalteva & Atravesada; ☺ 10am-late) The disco goes especially late on Saturday and Sunday, but Fridays are Noches Bohemias, with drink specials and live music. Giant video screens, a very full bar and cheap food round out your night.

Redford's (Map p114; Calle El Caimito; fast food US$2-6; 4pm-midnight) Big-screen TV, burgers and pasta even come with a few OK rooms out back for US$8 a pop.

El Club (Map p111; ☎ 552 4245; www.elclub -nicaragua.com; Calle La Libertad) A stylish space without pretensions, El Club attracts a good mix of Nicas and travelers basking in the mellow vibe. If you're in town on the first Saturday of the month, be sure to hit one of its rotating parties, often featuring DJs from outside the region.

You can order up a hamburger and cold brew at Zoom Bar, then kick back for some NFL action at Granada's original expat hangout. Also keep an eye open for Pitbull Production 'Bar Tours' of Managua, which takes you to Hipa Hipa (see p84) and a few other clubs.

Entertainment

Cine Karawala (Map p114; Calle Atravesada; tickets US$1.50) Granada's popular cinema shows mostly Western films on one of its two screens.

Bearded Monkey (Map p111; ☎ 552 4028; www .thebeardedmonkey.com; Calle 14 de Septiembre; tickets

US$1) Everyone's favorite hostel screens indie and foreign films at 6pm and 8pm nightly.

Shopping

Casa de los Tres Mundos (Map p114; ☎ 552 4176; www.c3mundos.org) The foundation here sells a very good lefty selection of books, magazines and other souvenirs, including *Wani* magazine, 'the voice of the Caribbean Coast,' and *Gente de los Gallos,* your cockfighting resource.

Mavericks (Map p114; ☎ 552 4120; Calle El Arsenal; ☽ 9am-6pm Tue-Sat, 10am-noon Sun) In addition to stocking a great selection of books and magazines, your cheerful hostess Nadene is committed to supporting local art cooperatives, including Escuela Especial de Artesanías Populares, which teaches kids with disabilities how to make handicrafts that are on sale right here.

Nica Chic (Map p111; Calle La Calzada; ☽ 8am-6pm Mon-Fri, 10am-5pm Sat & Sun) Cool clothes, handmade furniture and an oddball selection of affordable art make this worth a stop – there's also a book exchange with titles in English and German.

Doña Elba Cigars (Map p111; ☎ 552 3217) If you aren't getting up to Estelí (see p193) this trip, stop by here for a cognac-cured taste of Nicaragua. It's one block west of Iglesia de Xalteva.

Sultan Cigars (Map p114; ☽ 8am-7pm) A half-block east of the parque central on Calle La Libertad, watch folks hand-roll Estelí and Ometepe's finest into stronger *capa maduras* or smoother *sumatras.*

Al Anticuario (Map p111; ☎ 552 4677; ☽ 8am-10pm) Selling off unbelievably beautiful antiques, some several hundred years old, this is the place to find a cathedral-quality saint (US$50 to US$80 for smaller saints/virgins, US$550 full size) or hand-carved mahogany furniture. It's a couple of blocks north of Iglesia de La Merced.

Harold Antiques (Map p111; ☎ 881 4975; haroldsandino@hotmail.com; ☽ 8am-6pm) Located just north of Iglesia de La Merced, Sandino began collecting beautiful antiques and high-quality replicas when he was hired to find props for the movie *Walker;* today this place is packed to the brim with beautiful stuff.

Claroscuro (Map p111; ☎ 895 3836; galleria_claro scuro@hotmail.com; ☽ noon-6pm Mon-Sat) Next door to Harold's, this Cuban-run gallery represents about 35 Nicaraguan artists, some of them amazing, and periodically has openings where you can meet them.

Getting There & Around

Granada is not actually on the Interamericana (Pan-American Hwy), but instead is linked to the Costa Rican border and Managua by two spur roads. This means that Managua-bound buses from Rivas bypass Granada, so have the driver drop you off at Nandaime, which marks the turnoff to Granada, where regular Granada-bound buses arrive every 15 minutes or so.

AIR

Tiny **Granada International Airport** (☎ 233 2791), about 3km from the city center, has one flight daily to La Ceiba, Honduras, at 11:30am.

Nature Air (www.natureair.com) flies to Liberia, Costa Rica (US$65/130 one way/return, 40 minutes), with a continuing service to San José (US$120/240, two hours). Flights leave Granada at 8:15am and 5pm on Wednesday and Friday, and 5pm only on Sunday. Flights leave San José at 6:15am and 3pm on Wednesday and Friday, 3pm only on Sunday. The same planes leave Liberia one hour later.

BICYCLE

While bicycling in town might require nerves of steel, there are several mellow bike rides from town, including Laguna de Apoyo, Peninsula de Asese north of the Centro Turistico, and for strong bikers any of the Pueblos Blancos. The **Bearded Monkey** (Map p111; ☎ 552 4028; www.thebeardedmonkey .com; Calle 14 de Septiembre) rents bikes (US$5 per day), as do **Bicicletería** (Map p114; bikes US$9), half a block south of the park, **Tierra Tour** (Map p114; ☎ 862 9580; www.tierratour .com), **Posada Don Alfredo** (Map p111; ☎ 552 4455; alfredpaulbaganz@hotmail.com), and other hotels.

BOAT

Ferries leave the **ferry terminal** (Map p111; ☎ 552 2966; ☽ 10am-5pm) at the end of Calle La Calzada at 3pm Monday and Friday, stopping at Altagracia (Isla de Ometepe; US$2, three hours), San Miguelito (nine hours) and San Carlos (US$6/3 1st/2nd class, 13 hours). First-class seats, on the upper deck, have padded chairs and access to the TV, which will be on all night. Stake out a sleeping spot early and don't forget your seasickness medication.

Puerto Asese (☎ 552 2269; www.aseselasisletas .com), about 2km southeast of town, has boats for the Isletas de Granada (see p118) and Parque Nacional Archipiélago Zapatera (see p129).

BUS

Both **Transnica** (Map p111; ☎ 522 661; www .transnica.com), with buses at 6:20am, 8am and 11am, and **Tica Bus** (Map p111; ☎ 552 4301; www .ticabus.com), with buses at 7am and 1pm, have offices located on Av El Ena Arellano; they both have daily buses to San José (US$12), Costa Rica. For other international services, you'll need to go to either Rivas or Managua.

Granada does not have one central bus terminal. Buses to Managua's Mercado Roberto Huembes (Map p111; US$1, one hour, 4am to 7pm, every 15 minutes) depart from near the old hospital. Microbuses leave for Managua UCA (US$1.20, one hour, 4:20am to 6pm, every 25 minutes) from two places: the convenient lot (Map p111) just south of the parque central on Calle Vega, and Parque Sandino, near the old train station (Map p114). Buses for Masaya (Map p111; US$0.40, 30 minutes, 5am to 6pm, every 30 minutes) leave from two blocks west of the market, around the corner from Palí.

The main lot (Map p111) for southbound buses is one block south of the market, across from the Shell station. Normally no direct buses go to the border at Peñas Blancas (but ask during the Christmas rush from the border), so you'll need to change buses in Rivas.

Carazo US$0.70, 50 minutes, 6am to 5:05pm, every 20 minutes; for San Marcos, Diriamba (with connections to the Carazo Beaches) and Jinotepe

Catarina & San Juan de Oriente US$0.50, 30 minutes, 5am to 5:50pm, every 20 minutes; also serves Niquinohomo

Nandaime (Reserva Natural Volcán Mombacho) US$0.60, 20 minutes, 5am to 6pm, every 30 minutes

Pueblos Blancos/Carazo US$0.40-0.70, 5:50am, 8:30am, 2:10pm and 5:10pm; for Diriomo, Diría, Catarina, Niquinohomo, Masatepe, San Marcos and Jinotepe

Rivas US$1.10, 1½ hours, 5:45am, 6:30am, 7:10am, 8am, 9:30am, 12:30pm, 1:30pm and 3:10pm; catch the 1:30pm bus to make the last boat to Isla de Ometepe

---

THE FAST BOAT TO SAN CARLOS

Visiting the Río San Juan and Islas de Solentiname didn't always require a 14-hour ferry ride (or 12-hour bus ride, or inconvenient flight) across vast Lago de Nicaragua. During the 1980s it only took five hours, thanks to four already ancient but still speedy hydrofoil boats donated by the USSR, with several strings attached. Only Soviet technicians were allowed to maintain the machines, and also rather secretively supplied all the spare parts. Then the Soviet Union fell, the technicians were recalled, and one by one the hydrofoils were docked forever.

But they're still around – and two of them still run, sort of. There's always talk of resurrecting these old fast boats, which once crossed Cocibolca at a breezy 50km/h, and it seems likely that by the time you read this that state-of-the-art 1950s Soviet technology will be riding again. Keep your fingers crossed, and wear a life jacket.

RENTAL CAR

It's generally cheaper to rent cars in Managua, where your rental is probably parked right now – so be sure to allow a couple of hours for it to arrive. This region has good roads, and many attractions, including Los Pueblos Blancos, make excellent road trips. Although you can take cars to Isla de Ometepe (see p141), it's an expensive hassle.

Alamo (Map p114; ☎ 552 2877; www.alamo nicaragua.com) At Hotel Colonial.

Budget (Map p111; ☎ 552 2323; www.budget.com.ni) At the Shell station.

Dollar (Map p114; ☎ 552 2947; www.dollar.com.ni) At Hotel Gran Francia.

Hertz (Map p114; ☎ 552 8103; sergiouca@yahoo.com) At Eco Expedition Tours.

TAXI

Taxis are plentiful and quality varies – choose a nice one if you're taking a trip of any distance. Always agree on a fare before getting in the taxi, which should be US$0.50 per person during the day and US$0.70 at night in the city. Always take a taxi between the beach bars and downtown. Horse-drawn carriages (Map p114), available at the parque central, are a more romantic, if recently more expensive, way around the city.

It's inexpensive and convenient to take taxis to other destinations, including Masaya (US$10/15 market/volcano), Laguna de Apoyo (US$10), Rivas (US$20), San Juan del Sur (US$25) and Managua (US$30), keeping in mind that fares vary according to gas prices and your bargaining skills.

RESERVA NATURAL VOLCÁN MOMBACHO

It's been a few decades since this 1344m volcano, the defining feature of the Granada skyline, has acted up, but it is still most certainly active and sends up the periodic puff of smoke, just to keep the locals on their toes. It's easy to get to the crown of cloud forest, steamed up with fumaroles and other volcanic bubblings beneath the misty vines and orchids.

Reserva Natural Volcán Mombacho (☎ 552 5858, 624 0625; www.mombacho.org; adult/child US$9/3; dm US$12; ☉ 8am-5pm Thu-Sun) is managed by the very professional Fundación Cocibolca, which since 1999 has been building trails and running an ecomobile (think refurbished military jeeps seating 25) up the 40% grade up to 1100m. Get there early (especially if you have kids) to take the short trail through the **organic coffee farm**, or check out the **mariposario** (butterfly garden; adult/child US$0.70/0.30) and **orchid garden** (adult/child US$0.70/0.30) close to the parking lot.

Once you get to the top, where troops of three species of monkeys, 168 bird species and over 100 types of orchids are just part of the jungle canopy this park is intent on preserving, you have a choice of two trails: **Sendero del Cráter**, a 1.5km jaunt to the fumaroles, plus great views of Granada and Las Isletas; and **Sendero la Puma**, a steeper 4km trek around the lip of the crater, with even better views. Guides, many of whom speak English, are available at the entrance and run US$5 per group (six maximum) for Sendero del Cráter, which you can also do on a self-guided tour, and US$10 for Sendero la Puma, for which guides are mandatory.

You can also make reservations to sleep dorm-style in the **biological station**, with 10 beds and latrines outside, for US$30 per person – this seems steep, but includes your entrance fee, transportation, a night tour, breakfast and dinner. Anyone can grab a simple meal at the cafeteria for US$3.

Although the park is only open Thursday to Sunday, groups can make arrangements to visit on Tuesday or Wednesday, when it's less crowded. Time your arrival to coincide with an ecomobile departure, at 8:30am, 10am, 1pm and 3pm. If you have 4WD, you can drive for an extra US$12 – plus US$2 for every adult and US$1 for every child in the car (it's discouraged). Public transportation is inconvenient. Take any Nandaime bus from Granada and ask to be let off at the entrance. From here, you'll walk two steep kilometers (stay left where the road splits) to where the jeep picks you up.

Several operators in Granada arrange tours to Mombacho, but try **Mombotour** (Map p114; ☎ 552 4548, 860 2890; www.mombotour.com; canopy tour adult/student/child US$30/20/15), with offices in Granada's Centro Comercial. Part of Mombacho Canopy Tour, this local outfitter does guided hikes of Volcán Mombacho, coffee tours and a combo deal where you'll see the reserve and do the best zip-lines in the country, with 17 platforms and more than 1500 cables through the treetops.

The closest hotel is excellent: **Brisas de Mombacho** (☎ 561 2312; d US$30; ❖), at the Nandaime *empalme* (three-way junction), is a very comfortable spot to spend the night, with very clean rooms with good beds, cable TV and air-con, and lots of Louis XIV sorts of accents. The **Drive Inn La Cabaña** (meals US$2-11), the *rancho* (thatch-roofed, open-air structure) on the other side of the parking lot, is considered the best restaurant in town.

Aguas Termales La Calera

The beautifully maintained, 45°C **hot springs** (☎ 552 6330; osorio@invernic.com), replete with sulfur, calcium and other minerals quasi-scientifically proven to keep you radiant and healthy, are hidden away on Finca Calera, inside the reserve and right by the lake. They're easiest to visit on a day trip from Granada (about US$15 per person, including transport and entry); try **Tierra Tour** (Map p114; ☎ 862 9580; www.tierratour.com). You can also call or write ahead, then arrange the boat trip yourself.

Reserva Silvestre Privada Domitilia

A great place to take a break from the Granada scene and get back to nature is this **private wildlife reserve** (☎ 881 1786; info@domitilia

.org; dm US$45, r per person US$65, incl 3 meals), which borders the Reserva Natural Volcán Mombacho. It's pricey for what you get (no fans, composting toilets, but all the free fruit juice you can drink), but this protected patch of dry tropical forest is home to lots of howler monkeys, 165 species of bird and thousands of butterflies which take the place over like so many snowflakes on acid right at the end of rainy season, December or so. As dry season wears on, trees lose their leaves and you'll be able to see even more wildlife from the 20km of trails; bring sunscreen.

The reserve is 35km from Granada and not accessible via public transportation. Most Granada tour outfits run day trips (around US$30 per person, including lunch). Or, drive here yourself (head east at Km 71½ on the Interamericana), then pay the US$5 entry fee and mandatory guide fee (US$5 per hour), and have fun.

PARQUE NACIONAL ARCHIPIÉLAGO ZAPATERA

Isla Zapatera, a dormant volcano rising to 629m from the shallow waters of Lago de Nicaragua, is an ancient ceremonial island of the Chorotega Indians and male counterpart to more buxom Isla de Ometepe, whose smoking cone can be seen after you take the three-hour hike to the top. The 45-sq-km island and surrounding archipelago of 13 islands are part of Parque Nacional Archipiélago Zapatera, designated to protect not only the remaining swaths of virgin tropical dry and wet forest remaining, but also the unparalleled collection of **petroglyphs** and **statues** left here between 500 and 1500 years ago.

A handful of archaeologists have worked these sites, including Ephraim Squier, who shipped several of the 15 statues he discovered here in 1849 to the US, where they are displayed at the Smithsonian Museum, and Swedish scientist Carl Bollivius, who discovered more statues, many of which are displayed at Convento y Museo San Francisco (see p116) in Granada.

Perhaps the most impressive expanse of petroglyphs is carved into a 95m by 25m expanse of bedrock at the center of **Isla El Muerto** (Island of Death), where many statues have also been found. Several of the other islands also have petroglyphs and potential archaeological sites. But, as in the rest of Nicaragua, there simply aren't funds to dig further.

About 500 people live here quasi-legally, fishing and subsistence farming and hoping that no one puts pressure on Marena to do anything about it. Fortunately for them, the government isn't doing much of anything with these islands, which means infrastructure is basic and access is inconvenient. You can camp for free on the island, but bring your own food and water; there's one restaurant, as well as a simple lodge, both run by UCA-Tierra y Agua in Granada (see the boxed text, p121). They can help arrange passage on one of the public boats (US$3) that leave irregularly from Puerto Asese, and may be able to arrange cheap transportation at other times.

Otherwise, you'll need to sign up for a pricey day-long **tour** (per person US$50-80) offered by almost every operator in Granada, or hire a private *lancha* (small boat) seating 12, about US$150 round-trip, including a five-hour wait. You may be able to hitch a ride come November, however, when the Guapote Fishing Tournament of Isla Zapatera and Isla Muerto sends scores of fishing skiffs southward in search of the biggest *guapote* and grand prize – a motorboat.

SOUTHWESTERN NICARAGUA

This is the point where Nicaragua narrows to an isthmus, a slender land bridge of low mountains and sandy beaches stretched between the mighty Pacific Ocean and tranquil Lago de Nicaragua. These two massive bodies of water play a trick of light every evening, as the sun sets and paints the skies between them a fierce swirling violet and orange.

You may never forget your first sight of Isla de Ometepe in this light, rising from the shimmering lake to two volcanoes, one of them among Central America's most active, at press time murmuring threats of eruption. Fringing the isthmus from top to bottom are beautiful beaches that are only just now being discovered.

Their discovery may unnerve some travelers; the half-moon bay of San Juan del Sur may be the most touristed spot in

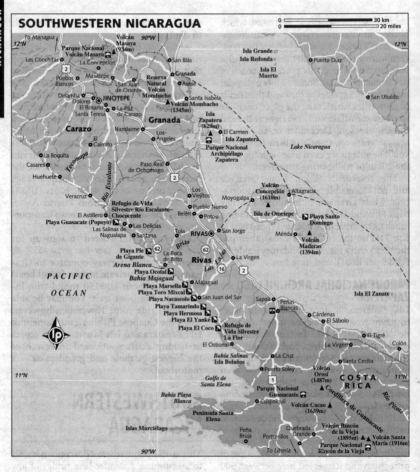

SOUTHWESTERN NICARAGUA

Nicaragua, so come psychologically prepared. But if you're in the mood – or just looking for a way to ease yourself into Nicaragua – San Juan's well-developed infrastructure makes this region a vacation in every sense of the word.

Climate & Geography

The Rivas Peninsula shares the same sedimentary shelf, deposited over the eons atop ancient, forgotten volcanoes, with Costa Rica's Nicoya Peninsula; both are far older than much of the surrounding countryside. The sunny, dry climate that makes the beaches perfect along here also hosts dry tropical forest, which wilts to brown and loses its leaves as the dry season (November

to May) wears on. On the upside, you can come here when the rest of the country is drenched, and still count on at least a couple of hours' sunbathing each morning.

Isla de Ometepe, the world's largest lake island, is the country's crown jewel. It is formed of two beautiful volcanoes, one of which seemed ready to erupt at the time of research (see the boxed text, p138).

Getting There & Around

Rivas is the regional travel hub, and its enormous, chaotic bus lot (which may be a bit of a shock if you're arriving from orderly Costa Rica; see p133) connects the region to Granada, Masaya and the rest of the country. It's usually easier to take *colectivo* taxis to San Jorge, where the main ferry terminal to Isla de Ometepe is located. You can also get to Ometepe via ferry from Granada (see p126).

Regular buses also serve the beach towns, but for some, including Bahía Majagual and Playa Pie de Gigante, you'll still require an alternate form of transportation. The region is developing fast, though, so keep an eye out for more options.

RIVAS

Most visitors just come here to change dollars or buses, barely noticing as they navigate the raised, tiled sidewalks that this is a well-preserved Spanish colonial town, right down to the outstandingly kitschy parque central (central park) and fine collection of churches. It's not exactly like Granada – its horse-drawn carriages use regular old car tires instead of more photogenic wagon wheels, for example. But this regional capital, which administrates the country's wealthiest department, is too busy hustling and bustling to bother with inefficient traditions.

Rivas' obvious potential and proximity to Granada, Ometepe and San Juan del Sur are encouraging more cutting-edge investors to look at property here, but as yet, the town remains simply the easiest-to-reach spot off the beaten path.

Orientation & Information

Rivas has the biggest market, best groceries, cheapest Internet and widest choice of banks and businesses in southwest Nicaragua. Stock up!

Banco America Central (BAC) Three blocks west of parque central; it has an ATM, changes traveler's checks and gives advances on credit cards.

Café Internet This cybercafé (three blocks west of parque central's southwestern corner) and a dozen other cafés charge US$1 per hour.

Intur (☎ 563 4914; rivas@intur.gob.ni) This friendly Intur outpost, northeast of parque central, has the usual selection of flyers and information on not only Rivas but also San Juan del Sur and Ometepe.

Rivas, Nicaragua (www.rivasnicaragua.com) A city website geared to locals more than tourists, with good information on doctors, businesses and services.

Sights

The main reason that Rivas is worth taking a two-hour layover between buses is the **Museo de Antropología** (admission US$1; ⏰ 8:30am-noon & 2-5pm), four blocks northwest of the park. The building itself, Hacienda Ursula, is an 18th-century architectural treasure and site of William Walker's decisive defeat. After his troops, limping home after an embarrassing route by the Costa Rican military, took control of the hacienda, a school teacher named Emmanuel Mongalo y Rubio (who has his own monument two blocks south of the Texaco), set the fortress on fire. Most of the men were shot or captured as they fled the burning building. See the boxed text, p55 for more on William Walker.

Inside, the obviously underfunded museum has some moth-eaten taxidermy, a wall of myths and legends and, best of all, a well-signed (in both English and Spanish) collection of pre-Columbian artifacts, many of them recently discovered by the Santa Isabela Archaeological Project. This Canadian-Nicaraguan team is excavating what it believes to be Chief Nicarao's ancient capital of Quauhcapolca, just north of San Jorge. The site was occupied between AD 1000 and 1250, and the 400,000 artifacts they have uncovered there include tools, blow guns, jewelry, funeral jars and cookware, as well as a fertility goddess complex and representations of the Aztec deity Quetzalcoatl. One thing they haven't found are *comales* (Aztec tortilla griddles), which has convinced the crew that this region had contact with, but was never colonized by, the Aztecs.

Architecture buffs could also check out the **Biblioteca Pública de Rivas**, which may be the oldest extant building in Nicaragua. The 1863 **Iglesia Parroquial de San Pedro**, on the east side of the park, is also worth a look for its attractive classical facade and a great fresco in the cupola showing a battle at sea, with communism, Protestantism and secularism as burning hulks, and Catholicism as a victorious ship entering the harbor. Four blocks west is 1778 **Iglesia de San Francisco**, a beautiful wooden church notable for several well-carved saints and the mysterious underground tunnel connecting it to the parque central.

The **baseball stadium**, just south of town on the Interamericana (Pan-American Hwy), hosts one of the most competitive leagues in Nicaragua.

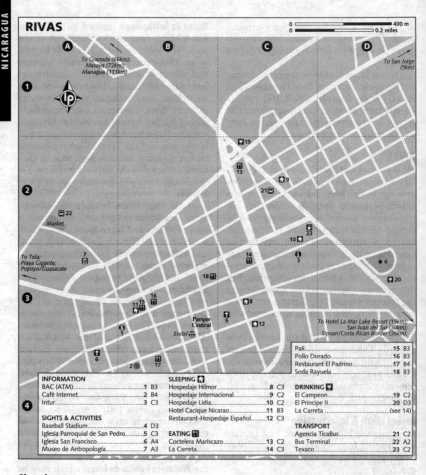

RIVAS

0 ———————— 400 m
0 ———————— 0.2 miles

To Granada (66km);
Masaya (72km);
Managua (111km)

To San Jorge
(5km)

Market

To Tola;
Playa Gigante;
Popoyo/Guasacate

Parque
Central

Enitel

To Hotel La Mar Lake Resort (15km);
San Juan del Sur (30km);
Sipoan/Costa Rican Border (36km)

Sleeping

Also check out the sleeping options in San Jorge (see p137).

Restaurant-Hospedaje Español (☎ 453 0006; r per person US$10) At the corner of the church, this solid budget option has four rooms with attractive hardwood floors, all with separate twin beds. The restaurant here (meals US$3 to US$6, open 9am to 10pm Monday to Saturday) does a fabulous *tortilla española*, plus lots of other Iberian goodies.

Hospedaje Lidia (☎ 453 3477; r per person US$5, with bathroom US$10) Opposite Intur, this amiable, family-run operation offers great budget lodging, with well-scrubbed rooms and thin mattresses. Breakfast (US$2), served family style, is worth it.

Hospedaje Internacional (☎ 453 3652; r per person US$4, with bathroom US$10) Of all the roadside cheapies along the Interamericana, this is the best, with clean rooms ranging from tiny and basic to large and oddly shaped with TVs and other amenities.

Hotel Cacique Nicarao (☎ 453 3234; s/d/tr US$35/45/55; 🖵) This hotel has little rooms of painted brick that come with air-con, hot water, cable TV and breakfast. The attached restaurant (meals US$3 to US$10, open 6am to 10pm) has a nice dining room where you can watch Palí shoppers try to hail cabs. It's a block northwest of the park.

Hotel La Mar Lake Resort (☎ 453 0021; www .lamarlakeresort.com; d US$45-85) Denis Martínez had a dream. And when you're already in the Baseball Hall of Fame and have had the national stadium of your home country named after you (see p85) your dreams can be a little bit quirky. Martínez has transformed an old Sandinista prison into a lakeside resort with some of the finest Ometepe views anywhere. It's a half-hour, US$5 taxi ride from either Rivas or the border, and almost worth it just for a drink or meal out on the breezy patio restaurant/bar (meals US$4 to US$11, open 7am to 10pm). Comfortable, if unexciting, rooms are flawlessly furnished down to the little bottles of shampoo, and there are two pools, kayak and bicycle rentals (US$3 per hour), plus a popular Sunday barbecue (US$8).

Eating

Rivas has plenty of cheap eats, with the very cheapest clinging to the outside of the chaotic market, next to where the bus pulls in – keep an eye on your stuff. The biggest grocery store in the region is **Palí** (⏰ 7:30am-7:30pm Mon-Sat, 7:30am-3pm Sun), a couple of blocks northwest from the park.

Pollo Dorado (dishes US$2-3; ⏰ 10am-9pm) It gets raves for the ceviche (seafood marinated in lemon or lime juice, garlic and seasonings), jalapeño chicken and very cold beer.

Soda Rayuela (dishes US$2-4) This clean, friendly restaurant north of the park has Rivas' best *tacos al pastor* (slow-cooked pork served on corn tortillas) and good chicken fajitas (grilled, marinated meat and vegetables served with a flour tortilla), too.

You can go upscale right downtown with a cold beer or a plate of buffalo wings at Tex-Mex La Carreta, east of Soda Rayuela, with dancing on weekends.

Restaurant El Padrino (dishes US$2-3; ⏰ 10am-3pm) This solid steam-table buffet offers lamb on Friday and seafood all week long, in addition to rice, beans, plantains, chicken dishes, salads and whatever else is fresh.

Coctelera Mariscazo (dishes US$2-6; ⏰ 11am-10pm) Some say it's the best restaurant in town, and you can indulge in one of its renowned fish dishes or go for the inexpensive set plate at lunch.

Drinking

Rivas isn't what you'd call a party town, but **El Príncipe II** (⏰ Thu-Sun), by the stadium, is a popular 'family-style' disco with karaoke on Thursday, dance music on Friday and Sun-

day, and mixed music on Saturday. The food here is also very good. El Campeon and La Carreta both have dancing on weekends.

Getting There & Around

BUS

Rivas is the regional transport hub. Both **Transnica** (☎ 453 6619) and **Tica Bus** (☎ 453 4301) have offices in town and daily buses to San José, Costa Rica (US$10); Tegucigalpa, Honduras (US$20); San Salvador (US$20); and Managua (US$10). Both stop at the Texaco station.

The **bus terminal** (☎ 453 4333) is adjacent to the market, about 10 blocks west of the Interamericana. You can catch more luxurious long-distance buses (most headed to Managua, not Granada) at the bus stop just north of the exit to San Jorge.

Granada US$1.50, 1½ hours, 6:30am, 7:25am, 11:20am, 12:15pm, 1:15pm, 3:20pm and 4:25pm; or take any Managua-bound bus and change at Nandaime

Managua US$1.50, 2½ hours, 4:30am to 6pm, every 25 minutes

Refugio de Vida Silvestre La Flor & El Ostional US$2.50, two to three hours, 5am, 7:30am and noon

Salinas & Tola Beaches US$1.70, two hours, 9:10am, 11am, 12:50pm, 2:30pm, 4pm and 4:30pm; returns at 5am, 6am, noon, 7pm and 7:30pm

San Jorge US$0.30, 20 minutes, every 30 minutes

San Juan del Sur US$0.75, 45 minutes, 6am to 6pm, every 30 minutes; with continuing service to La Flor and El Ostional at 11:30am, 3pm and possibly 4pm

Sapoá/Peñas Blancas, Costa Rica US$0.50, 45 minutes, 5am to 6pm, every 30 minutes

Southern beaches US$2.50, two to three hours, 11am, 3pm and 4:30pm; service to San Juan del Sur, Playa el Coco, La Flor and El Ostional

TAXI

Colectivo taxis run regularly to San Jorge (US$1.50) and San Juan del Sur (US$4), but you'll have to charter your own for the Costa Rican border (US$10), Granada (US$35) or the Tola Beaches. Pedicabs and horse-drawn carriages are usually less expensive (and more fun) for shorter trips; the usual cost is US$1 per kilometer per person.

TOLA & THE TOLA BEACHES

pop 20,000

It was too good to last, what with the perfect weather, pale beaches, excellent surfing and cheap land. But it's happened. The

NICARAGUA

Tola Beaches, once almost inaccessible and totally wild, now have a landowners association with an English-language newsletter and even a tagline: the Pacific Riviera. And you should see plans of all the fabulous gated communities they're going to build.

But as yet, only a few tastefully toned retirement resorts have actually gone up. Right now most of them are busy improving the roads (this is a good thing) and surfing forces are slowly carving out appealing, if sometimes rustic, claims in the sand; so there are plenty of beaches where you can still lounge on a shoestring.

There are no banks, real grocery stores, Internet cafés or cell phone signals in this region, so do what you need to do before you hit the trail.

Getting There & Around

Bus access is reliable but inconvenient, though it is improving along with the atrocious roads. The road is paved to Tola, then turns into an OK dirt road that can become impassable after particularly heavy rains; it's on the short list to be paved, however.

Buses leave Rivas for Las Salinas at 5:30am, 6am and 8:30am, and return at noon and 2pm. Note that Playa Pie de Gigante is a 7km walk from the bus stop.

El Astillero and Refugio de Vida Silvestre Río Escalante Chococente (Río Escalante Chococente Wildlife Refuge) are more accessible by bus from Managua, or you can catch a US$10 cab from Salinas.

Taxis from Rivas make the run to Playa Pie de Gigante (US$10), Santana (US$30), Las Salinas (US$35) and El Astillero (US$40). If you take the bus to Tola, cabs cost about US$3 less.

Tola

pop 23,200
Tola, whose name means 'the land of the Toltecs,' is rapidly developing into a service town for the construction, and eventually workers, for the big resort communities. The main reason to come here is to save a few dollars and catch a taxi to the beaches. There are no signed hotels, although you could arrange homestays. There is, however, a great restaurant, **El Naranjito** (dishes US$2-6), serving excellent *plato típico* (a mixed plate of various foods typical of the area) and cheap beer.

Playa Pie de Gigante

This glorious white crescent of sand snuggled into the wildly forested mountains is almost worth the 7km hike from the bus stop, but consider taking a taxi. Playa Pie de Gigante has long been famed for cheap lobster, best enjoyed with a *servicio* of rum at one of the ramshackle seaside restaurants, and great surfing.

The popular sandy beach break right in front of 'town' gets hollow and fun when conditions are perfect, and has reliable peaks year-round. There's an endless tube about 45 minutes north that's also good for beginners. Special-name waves include Chiggers and Outer Chiggers, close to a rocky reef, and Hemorrhoids – this tube is for serious surfers, as it dumps you right onto gravel.

You'll need to hire a boat to most of the breaks, including the point break at Punta Manzanillo, just south, also called Punta Reloj. Ask the driver to take you past the 2m-long 'footprint' left in the rocky headlands that gave the beach its name, 'Giant Foot Beach.' Boats cost about US$30 per hour; try Julian Martínez at Bar Mary Mar, who can also supply fishing poles and bait, or any of the surf camps.

SLEEPING & EATING

Most accommodations options are at surf camps, although you're always welcome to string up a hammock at **Bar y Comedor La Gaviota** (hammocks per person US$3; ☺ 7am-10pm), a big wooden seafood restaurant (meals US$1 to US$6). Most prices quoted below are for surf packages that include boat tours, meals and more, but just show up and you will find room and board. During rainy season, some businesses are closed or keep shorter hours.

Giant's Foot Surf Camp (www.giantsfoot.com; per week per person US$1000; ☒) This comfortable camp has two beachfront lodges. All rooms are air-conditioned and have bathroom, plus big TVs, screened-in lounges and more. The environmentally conscious crew is also planning working with a Spanish school in San Juan del Sur.

Hidden Bay Surf Lodge (www.nicasurf.com; per week per person US$888, maximum 6) Surfer Dale Dagger is basically a legend. You can either arrange trips with him from San Juan del Sur, or stay here in Gigante in this plush oceanfront pad, with big-screen TVs with DVD player, a gourmet chef in the kitchen and a boat ready to go when you are.

Reserva Ecológica Zacatan (www.zacatan.org; camping per person US$3) This privately owned, 12-hectare swath of secondary tropical dry forest, 2km from the beach, is being developed by a University of Texas-Austin professor as a low-impact ecotourism destination. At press time there were already campsites with basic facilities and rough trails, with plans to have waterproof *rancheros* (thatch-roofed, open-air structures) and other creature comforts by the time you read this.

Hotel Brio (www.hotelbrio.com; r for 1 person US$20, extra person US$5) The same folks who run Reserva Ecológica Zacatan are also building this guesthouse and restaurant closer to the beach. Check the website to see if it's open.

There are a handful of ramshackle restaurants on the beach. Try **Bar y Restaurant Blue Sol** (dishes US$2-6) for a pretty dining room. Or, for something completely different, try the **Restaurant** (dishes US$4-10), where classically trained chef Maria Esperanza knows how to work with local ingredients. It can get crowded when the waves aren't breaking.

No less than nine enormous 'tourism complexes' are being constructed in the area, with condominiums, hotels, infinity pools, golf courses and more. Heck, **Arenas Bay** (www.arenasbay.com) even wants to change the name of the beach. Come soon.

Santana

The only way to walk to three of the prettiest beaches around – Playa Dorada, Playa Escondida and Playa Rosada – is if you're a guest or resident of plush **Rancho Santana** (☎ 887 4343; www.ranchosantana.com; d US$80, casitas US$150, house US$250, 7th night free). Easily the most successful resort village on the block, it's got clubhouses, rental homes, pools, horses, tennis courts, a helipad and more. Fully furnished casitas have two bedrooms; houses have up to four (maximum two people per bedroom), with private pools. If you're tired of rice and beans, the swanky restaurant here (meals US$4 to US$10) is open to the public; consider wearing your cleanest shirt.

The most famous of the three beaches is Playa Rosada, with pretty pink sand, great

surfing and the **Jaro de Leche blowhole**, an odd hydrogeological formation that shoots ocean water several meters into the waves. You'll only see it if you stay here or come in a boat. But the owners are pretty cool, and if you ordered a nice meal at the restaurant and wore your cleanest shirt, maybe you could sweet-talk them into a stroll. Or, you could just tour the condominiums.

A very rough dirt road (4WD only in rainy season) to the coast begins from a signed turnoff about 1km past Rancho Santana and leads to **Santana Surf** (hammocks US$2, r per person US$5). There's also a small cluster of *pulperías* (stores) and *comedores* (basic, cheap eateries) at the corner, should you need to resupply.

Las Salinas de Nagualapa y Playa Guasacate

Home to one of the most storied waves in Nicaragua, the little town of Las Salinas de Nagualapa, named for the salt evaporation ponds you'll pass on the way in, is beginning to feel a bit like a beach town. You'll also see a large barn –it's actually the **hot springs** (admission US$0.30), where you could soak away surfing-related soreness or wash your clothes.

Most people continue 4km past town to Playa Guasacate, where a shallow lagoon and slow river shift through the long sandy beach. It's often called Playa Popoyo in honor of the famed beach break, with right and left point breaks that break huge and hollow over the outer reef when conditions are right. Other named waves include Bus Stop – fast, powerful and unpredictable, it ends in shallow water with a rocky bottom. Cobra, nearby, is another fast wave, breaking left on more rocks. Emergencias, considered the best wave in the region, has a long, smooth left for longboarders and a short, fast, hollow right for shortboarders.

At **Hospedaje Mendoza** (aka 'La Tica II,' or 'Mendoza's Tiltin' Hilton'; hammock/camping per person US$2/3, d US$10, with 3 meals US$15) you can stay in either the gently leaning one-story house or the newer two-story building; meals often involve fresh seafood, but don't miss the awesome pancakes.

Popoyo Surf Lodge (☎ in the US 888-899 8823; www.surfnicaragua.com; per week US$960-1770) is about 2km back toward Salinas. This relatively plush surf camp has cheerfully painted, two-story cement cabins arranged around the manicured grounds. Packages here include meals, transportation from the airport and trips out to the waves every day.

If you're a dedicated surfer, but ever since the company went public you just don't mind splashing out on a really nice place every once in a while, try **Hotel Punta Teonoste** (☎ 267 3008; www.hotellosrobles.com/en /playa; r per person US$70, 2 people US$85; ⊠)), associated with Managua's swanky Los Robles: thatched-roof, bamboo-accented cabinas have playfully plush interiors and overlook a fierce spire of rock jutting past Playa Conejo's pink-sand beaches. It even has plans for a spa – massages, gym, steambaths, the whole thing.

El Astillero

This picture-perfect fishing and lobstering village, inhabiting the dramatic headlands above a gently scalloped white-sand beach, doesn't have any hotels. But grab a whole fish with all the fixings at Bar Miramar, where fresh seafood comes with a view of the fishers mending their nets. This is also where you can arrange fishing boats to breaks offshore.

There's a beach break, too, a long left close to the mouth of Río Escalante, which gets hollow and powerful when swells top a meter, and crowded when neighboring surf camps get there first. There's also a fairly easy point break.

The folks who brought you Rancho Santana in Santana are planning **Astillero Beach Resort** (www.astilleroland.com), with con-dos, time-shares, an 18-hole golf course and even a synthetic Granada-esque 'colonial village.' But it's not built yet.

Refugio de Vida Silvestre Río Escalante Chococente

Much less visited than Refugio de Vida Silvestre La Flor (see p157), this wildlife refuge also gets *arribadas* (flotillas) of more than 3000 nesting Olive Ridley tur-tles at one time, as well as more solitary leatherback turtles, which make their nests here between July and December (peak-ing in August and September). The refuge protects five species of turtles, as well as 4800 hectares of dry tropical forests and mangrove swamps.

There's currently no public transporta-tion, and no regularly offered organized tours to the refuge, but if you have a 4WD there are two signed entrances from the In-teramericana; Ochomogo, closer to Rivas, is the better road, and winds 35 rocky kilo-meters to the sea. Or, you could walk along the shore 4km from El Astillero, which may have lodging before this book is updated. You can camp at the park for US$4.

SAN JORGE

Just 15 minutes from the bustle of Rivas are the beaches of San Jorge, lined with in-expensive seafood restaurants and rollick-ing bars, not to mention the country's best views of Isla de Ometepe. It gets packed during Semana Santa and on sunny sum-mer weekends with revelers from all over the region.

International tourists, however, tend to just roll through en route to the island, stop-ping at the ferry terminal just long enough to wonder if those delicious breezes might be worth enjoying a moment more.

Orientation & Information

San Jorge is inconvenient to stroll around, but the beachfront – with the ferry termi-nal, several restaurants and most of the bars – is a featureless 1km walk past a faux Spanish fortress on the main road. Take taxis after dark.

Cybercafé San Jorge (per hr US$1) A half block east of the park.

Ometepe Tours (☎ 563 0665) Part of Bar El Navigante, right at the ferry terminal, this brand-new guide service offers island tours, hotel reservations and more.

Online Internet (per hr US$1) One block north of the park.

Sights & Activities

Ask your taxi driver to point out the **Cruz de España**, suspended from a gleaming half-arch above the traffic, which allegedly marks the exact spot where conquistador Gil González Dávila and Cacique Nicarao first met, October 12, 1523. Brightly colored statues of both men flank the monument.

The breezy, volcano-gray **beach** (voted Nicaragua's cleanest in 2003) stretches 20m into the water during high season, when it boasts a busy boardwalk feel and free camp-ing. During rainy season (June–November), lake levels rise and reduce the beach to a slender strand, and many of the restaurants keep limited hours. There are excellent windsurfing conditions here November to April, as well as in La Virgen, about 10km south of town on the Interamericana.

San Jorge's eccentric selection of churches includes the squat, 19th-century Catholic **church** that welcomes you to downtown, and the humble blue-and-white **Iglesia de las Mercedes**, one of the oldest churches in the hemisphere; it may have been built in the late 1500s. It's rarely open to the public; religious holidays are your best bet for seeing inside.

Nuestra Señor de Rescate is the most striking church, repainted a brilliant purple with a mix that uses *huevos de amor* (fertilized chicken eggs) donated by parishioners; an equally colorful sculpture of a *carreta* (oxcart) is out front. It's a national historic landmark, and the destination of an annual caravan of some 150 *carretas* from Masaya each year. They arrive April 23, the anniversary of San Jorge's miraculous appearance on the coast of Lago de Nicaragua. The ensuing **fiestas patronales** include parades, rodeos and several ceremonial dances, including a much-celebrated dance between the city's two images of San Jorge.

Sleeping

You can camp at the beach, close to the restaurants and bars, for free, although there's not much beach during rainy season. Restaurants offer showers for a small fee.

Hostal Azteca (☎ 563 0759; dm US$3, r US$10-15; P ❷ ⌘) The 46-bed, thatched-roof dorm actually offers some privacy (really) thanks to brightly colored curtains and partial walls. There are also cute private rooms, some with air-con, as well as an excellent restaurant (dishes US$3 to US$5) worth checking out even if you aren't staying here. But the real reason to stay, or at least drop by, is the incredible pool surrounded by murals, some with Canadian themes. It's a 15-minute walk or US$0.30 taxi ride from the ferry terminal, and is well signed from the main road, two blocks west of the mock Spanish fortress.

Hotel Hamacas (☎ 453 0048; www.hotelhamacas .com; s/d with fan US$15/20, with air-con & cable TV US$20/35; P ❷ ⌘) Just a block from the beach, surprisingly nice, spotless rooms have big windows that open onto the shady courtyard/parking area, lined with the promised hammocks and a tiny pool.

Breakfast is complimentary, and other meals can be arranged in advance.

Eating

Bar-Restaurant Ivania (dishes US$2-4; ⊙ 6am-11pm) Two blocks from the parque central, this spot does good fish soup and *típico*, and has a rollicking bar scene at night. El Coralito, a block away, has similar offerings with a cowboy theme.

Los Ranchitos (dishes US$2-10; ⊙ 11am-10pm Mon-Sat) The best restaurant in town specializes in steaks and seafood served in a lovely *ranchero*. Hungry? Try the enormous and recommended *plato típico* (US$12), which comes with enough rice, beans, avocado salad, sausage, pork and more for four people. There's a full bar.

The restaurants lining the beach are convenient if you're waiting on your ferry. Most are open 11am to 10pm, and serve mid-price seafood (US$3 to US$10) on breezy, palm-thatched patios. *Sopa de mojarra* (a fish soup made with coconut milk) is the local specialty. The best recommended beach spots are El Refugio and Restaurant el Ancle del Sur, south of the dock, or Sol y Arena, just north.

In town, there's a great **fritanga** (sidewalk barbecue; snacks US$1-2; ⊙ evenings) half a block west of the turnoff to Hostal Azteca; it sets up in the garage next to Carniceria San Jorge. A hamburger shack occupies the kiosk in the parque central starting at around dusk. One of the better pastry shops anywhere is Pandería San Martin, half a block west of the park.

Getting There & Around

Buses (US$0.30) leave for Rivas almost hourly from the ferry terminal, passing by the parque central. *Colectivos* (US$0.30 in town, US$1.25 to Rivas) roam the streets.

The road ends at the ferry terminal, where there's inexpensive guarded parking for your car and regular boat service to Moyogalpa on Isla de Ometepe; see p141 for schedules and other information.

ISLA DE OMETEPE

pop 35,000

Nicaragua's dramatic candidate for 'Eighth Wonder of the World,' Isla de Ometepe is exquisite: two volcanic peaks rise from the hazy blue expanse of Cocibolca, 'the

Sweet Sea' (Lago de Nicaragua), and form an hourglass of beaches and jungles cinched to a sinuous isthmus between them.

It seems unsullied, and spectacularly so, protected from so many of the world's follies, including a lot of tourist infrastructure, by a cool, clean moat. But it's most certainly worth roughing it a bit to see primary forests trade off with organic farms in the folds of the volcanoes' fertile skirts, teeming with howler monkeys and parrots, and hiding a wealth of archaeological treasures.

Orientation & Information

Isla de Ometepe's 78km main road runs in a rough barbell shape, circling each volcano and running along the northern shore of the isthmus between them. The Concepción side of the island is more developed, and the major port towns of Moyogalpa and Altagracia are connected by a newly paved road. Charco Verde is on this side of the island, as is the best boat access to Isla de Quiste and Isla Grande.

Playa Santo Domingo, with the best hotels and most popular beach, is on the isthmus; the road splits upon arriving on the less developed Volcán Maderas side of the island, going right to Mérida and the San Ramón waterfall, left to Balgüe and Finca Magdalena.

No banks provide credit card or debit card transactions, although you can change US dollars. Internet access tends to be slow and unreliable; at press time it was available only in Moyogalpa, Altagracia and a few hotels, but look for that to change.

Hacienda Mérida (☎ 868 8973) Cashes traveler's checks and euros (5% commission).
Hospital (☎ 569 4247) In Moyogalpa.
Police station (☎ 569 4231) In Moyogalpa.

Activities

Many of Ometepe's tourist attractions are hard to find or even a bit dangerous – take that active volcano, for example. Sometimes it's just worth hiring a guide. A handful of Moyogalpa-based tour companies have offices near the ferry terminal, but hotels can arrange almost any tour for you. You should almost always tip your guide. See also Tours, p141.

VOLCANO CLIMBS

Náhuatl-speaking colonists came because their legends foretold an island with two *(ome)* peaks *(tepetl)*: gently smoking Concepción (1610m) and inactive Maderas (1394m), carpeted in cloud forest, both of which are great climbs. Seriously consider taking a guide; tourists die on these volcanoes every year, usually after falling into a ravine, breaking something, then starving to death, which gives you plenty of time to feel like a dumbass for wanting to save US$3.

THE EXPLOSIVE MOOD SWINGS OF VOLCÁN CONCEPCIÓN

She knows she's special: the star of the largest lake island in the world, Volcán Concepción is Central America's most symmetrical and arguably loveliest volcano, not to mention one of its most active and dangerous. Concepción roared back to life the same year that Krakatoa blew, in 1883, after centuries of hosting gentle cloud forests around her now gray and smoking craters. The event's thick and streaming lava invoked her ancient name, Mestlitepe, 'The Menstruating Mountain.'

And indeed, the fiery flow seems cyclical. In 1921 ash gave way to glowing red, and the following year lava and glowing boulders were tossed out with explosions heard in Granada. In 1944 ashfalls as far as Rivas were just a warning; six month later lava flows consumed hectares of crops. In 1957 tongues of flame 15m high leapt from the summit following months of ashy exhalation. And although no lava burst forth, ashes inaugurated another two years of activity between 1983 and 1985.

In late 2005, in her first tantrum since the revolution, Concepción was showering ashes over Rivas and guides were excitedly explaining that it 'smelled like lava' at the top. It's worth noting that in 1957, when Concepción last bellowed fire and rock, President Somoza sent boats to evacuate. Not one person left – and not one person died. As Concepción seemed to be indulging her PMS at press time, locals were watching with anticipation – nervous, but excited – wondering whether their mountain was about to put on a show.

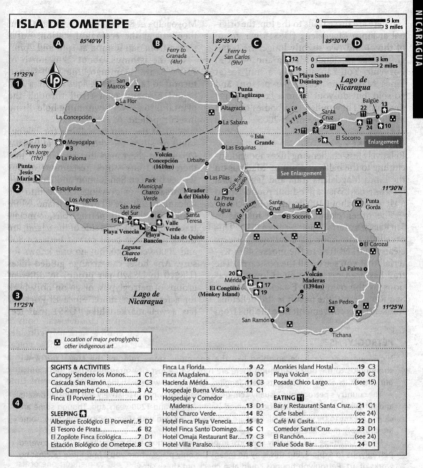

ISLA DE OMETEPE

SIGHTS & ACTIVITIES		
Canopy Sendero los Monos	1	C1
Cascada San Ramón	2	C3
Club Campestre Casa Blanca	3	A2
Finca El Porvenir	4	D1
SLEEPING		
Albergue Ecológico El Porvenir	5	D2
El Tesoro de Pirata	6	B2
El Zopilote Finca Ecológica	7	D1
Estación Biológico de Ometepe	8	C3
Finca La Florida	9	A2
Finca Magdalena	10	D1
Hacienda Mérida	11	C3
Hospedaje Buena Vista	12	C1
Hospedaje y Comedor Maderas	13	D1
Hotel Charco Verde	14	B2
Hotel Finca Playa Venecia	15	B2
Hotel Finca Santo Domingo	16	C1
Hotel Omaja Restaurant Bar	17	C3
Hotel Villa Paraíso	18	C1
Monkies Island Hostal	19	C3
Playa Volcán	20	D1
Posada Chico Largo	(see 15)	
EATING		
Bar y Restaurant Santa Cruz	21	C1
Cafe Isabel	(see 24)	
Café Mi Casita	22	D1
Comedor Santa Cruz	23	D1
El Ranchón	(see 24)	
Palue Soda Bar	24	D1

Volcán Concepción (guide per person US$12-20) is a serious 10- to 12-hour hike up loose volcanic stone, so be in good physical condition and bring water, snacks and real hiking shoes. Most hikes leave from either Moyogalpa or Altagracia. Get started as early in the morning as possible, and remember that there's no shade above the tree line, it's even steeper than it looks, and it can get windy and cold, particularly if it's cloudy, at the top. And it's almost always cloudy at the top, which means your chances of seeing the fuming craters and awesome views over the lake and across Central America's volcanic spine are slim, even during dry season. But they're zero everywhere else.

There are three main trails to the top: La Concha and La Flor (the most popular trail) are both a short bus ride from Moyogalpa, while the trailhead for La Sabana is walking distance from Altagracia.

Volcán Maderas (guide per person US$5-20) is much more accessible. It's a muddy seven- to eight-hour slog (four to five hours of climbing) to a misty cloud forest ending with a steep crater descent to a chilly jade-green lake. This climb has been tested and approved by overweight chain smokers, only some of whom took the cold and muddy swim. Though there aren't any views from the top, the halfway point of the Finca Magdalena trail, with benches, offers the money shot of Concepción.

There are three trails to the top: the original at Finca Magdelena (US$15 per group of three) and two slightly longer trails beginning at Hacienda Mérida and Finca El Porvenir. You can also pay a trail fee at Finca Magdelena (US$2 per person) and go solo, but do your mom a favor and get the guide. They pulled two bodies out of a muddy ravine in November 2005.

OTHER HIKES

Relatively less-challenging hikes abound, including to the halfway point up Maderas on the Finca Magdelena trail, and **Tour al Floral** (guide per person US$10), a five-hour round-trip to a viewpoint about 1000m up Concepción.

The other classic Ometepe hike is to **San Ramón waterfall** (guide per person US$2). This excellent four-hour hike follows a steep, clearly marked trail to the mossy, 40m waterfall that you see on all the postcards. The trail has been ravaged a bit at lower elevations by the owners of Estación Biológica San Ramón, but the payoff is still delicious. Bus service is convenient: take the bus from Moyogalpa at 8:15am or Altagracia at 9am, then exit at the ecological station. Buses return from San Ramón at 1pm and 2pm.

On the isthmus, about 2km north of Playa Santo Domingo, the well-signed turnoff to **La Presa Ojo de Agua** (admission US$1) begins a shady 1km stroll through the plantains to a lovely swimming hole. Bring insect repellent.

A great day trip is walking (or biking) some or all of the **circumference of Maderas** (35km) on the rough dirt road (note that there aren't any stores, restaurants or bus service between San Ramón and La Palma).

Petroglyphs, or drawings carved into the volcanic basalt, are all over the island. More than 1700 known petroglyphs, concentrated on the Maderas side of the island, are thought to have been carved between 800 and 2000 years ago, but no one knows for sure. Any hotel can arrange guided hikes (US$10 to US$20 per group) to different groups of petroglyphs, or go on horseback for a few dollars more. Finca El Porvenir has a well-marked hike (US$1 trail fee)

PETROGLYPHS

Nicaragua may not have anything like the enormous stone ruins of the Maya and Aztec strongholds to the north (although there are rumors of a lost city somewhere near San Carlos), but even if its ancient architects were lagging, their artists were working overtime.

The country's petroglyphs, usually 1cm-deep linear engravings in relatively soft volcanic basalts and tuffs, are thought to have been carved between 800 and 1200 years ago. Though some are clearly meant to be very special, they are not always imbued with deep spiritual meaning; some are probably more like graffiti.

Isla de Ometepe has arguably the most impressive collection, with more than 1700 discovered petroglyphs to explore. But this is by no means the only place where you'll find these fascinating works of art. Petroglyph hounds could also check out these sites:

- Isla Zapatera, Ometepe's 'male' counterpart, and neighboring Isla del Muerto (see p129), were even more intensely sculpted into ceremonial centers.
- Museo Precolombino de Chagüitillo (see p214) is an amazing museum with photos on-site; or book a cheap guided hike to see this huge mural in real life.
- Río Blanco (see the boxed text, p242) is where artisans with a sense of humor left a big snake on a rock that's only visible when the river runs low.
- Isla Momotombito (see p178); dedicated fans may make it to Momotombo's mini-me, once a ceremonial center in Lago de Managua.
- Cailagua waterfall (see p101) has Masaya's most famous petroglyphs, which could stand to be cleaned up a bit.
- La Cueva del Duende (see p273) is the famed Islas Solentiname cave that is only above water during the dry season, when you'll see more than 160 drawings.
- San Juan del Sur (see p150): it's not quantity, it's quality that matters – and SJDS's petroglyphs are doozies.

through about 20 petroglyphs, including a sundial sometimes taken as proof that vacationing extraterrestrials think this place is pretty special, too. Don't miss the two small archaeological museums (US$1) in Altagracia or Moyogalpa, which also have archaeological treasures on display.

SWIMMING

While it's sad that the freshwater bull shark (see the boxed text, p149) is almost extinct, take advantage of these beaches now, as the species is staged to make a comeback. Keep in mind that Lago de Nicaragua rises dramatically in the rainy season, shrinking the beaches to thin strands. By the end of the dry season in April, however, some 20m of gray volcanic sand may stretch out to the water.

The most popular beach is **Playa Santo Domingo**, on the windy east side of the isthmus and home to some of the island's best accommodations. **Playa Bancón** and the other beaches around Charco Verde are greener and perhaps prettier. **Punta Jesús María** is a spectacular jetty that stretches more than 1km into the lake during the dry season, just a few minutes south of Moyogalpa. There's no beach in Moyogalpa (though there is a fine pool), but Altagracia has a small sandy cove. There are other untouristed beaches around the island, all of which would make a fine destination for a bicycle ride.

KAYAKING

Kayaking is a great way to visit El Cogüito (Isla de los Monos, or Monkey Island), Isla de Quiste and the Río Istiam. Kayaks are available at **Hacienda Mérida** (☎ 868 8973; www.lasuerte.org) and **Hotel Charco Verde** (☎ 887 9302; charcoverde22@yahoo.es), but ask around to see if anyone else has them.

BIKING

The island's little-used roads, particularly the rough, dirt 35km loop around Maderas, are perfect for mountain bikes, or just pick one of the off-the-beaten-track beaches and go. Most population centers have a place that rents mountain bikes, but note that quality varies widely. **Hotel La Isla Vista** (per hr US$1) in Moyogalpa, **Hotel Finca Playa Venecia** (☎ 887 0191; www.islaometepe.com; per hr US$1), **Hotel Finca Santo Domingo** (☎ 820 2247; hotel_santo_domingo@yahoo.com; per hr US$2) and **Hacienda Mérida** (☎ 868 8973; www.lasuerte

.org; per hr US$8) in Mérida all rent bikes, or ask at your hotel.

HORSEBACK RIDING

Horses remain Ometepe's most common form of transportation, and any hotel can hook you up with rides (US$2 to US$5 per hour), plus a guide for US$10 to US$20 more, if you need one.

Tours

Just about any hotel can organize **horses** (per hr US$2-5, guides per group US$10-20 or more) and tours. Guides are highly recommended for **Volcán Concepción** (per group US$20-30) and **Volcán Maderas** (per group US$15-20), as well as for trips to the various **petroglyphs** (per person US$5-40). Always be sure to tip your guide.

Guides are not really necessary for San Ramón waterfall, La Presa Ojo de Agua or Reserva Charco Verde, although it's always easier to have someone else arrange transportation. Air-conditioned **island tours** (per person US$20-30) are much easier, but also more expensive, than doing the scenic figure eight on a public Bluebird school bus (US$2 to US$4).

Most tour companies keep offices close to the docks, and all employ roughly the same pool of experienced guides.

Exploring Ometepe (☎ 647 5179, 873 7714; www.exploringometepe.com) Professional, English-speaking, knowledgeable guides with tons of experience offer a variety of treks, from volcano climbs to custom trips with a scientific bent – birding, ecosystems, ecology and, of course, geology. Berman Goméz, one of the founders, was selected as expedition leader for the BBC TV show *Beyond Boundaries*, where a group of 'disabled' Brits made their way from one end of Nicaragua to the other. 'It was the first time anyone got to the top of Concepción in a wheelchair,' beams Berman. So, what's your excuse?

Ometepe Expeditions (☎ 873 1599, 825 2290; www.ometepeexpeditions.com) A Río San Juan and Solentiname specialist.

Ometepe Tours (☎ 563 0665) With guided hikes and a few other services, located at the ferry terminal in San Jorge.

Getting There & Away

The most convenient way to get to Isla de Ometepe is the one-hour, 17km boat ride from San Jorge to Moyogalpa. There are two classes of boats: smaller, less stable **lanchas** (motorboats; one way US$1.80) and larger, less frequent **ferries** (☎ 277 5354, 278 8190; ferry@ibw.com.ni; one way US$2.25), which can also transport bicycles (US$0.70), motorcycles (US$1.50) and, with 72 hours advance notice, cars (US$16.50).

Between November and February, winds can make the sea rough, particularly in the afternoon; consider taking the ferry. Fewer boats make the run on Sunday.

Moyogalpa to San Jorge 5:30am, 6am, 6:30am, 6:45am (ferry), 7am, 11am, 11:30am, 12:30pm (ferry), 1:30pm and 4pm (ferry)

San Jorge to Moyogalpa 7:45am, 9am, 9:30am, 10:30am (ferry), 11:30am, 12:30pm, 1:30pm (ferry), 3:30pm, 4:30pm and 5:30pm (ferry)

ALTAGRACIA TO GRANADA & SAN CARLOS

The *lancha* **Mozorola** (one way US$2) usually leaves Altagracia at 11am Tuesday and Friday, returning from Granada at 11am Wednesday and Saturday; it's not reliable and not recommended for those prone to seasickness.

Larger, more reliable ferries cross the lake between Granada and San Carlos twice weekly, stopping in Altagracia (unless the weather is really bad) en route. First-class tickets get you a padded seat, less-crowded floor space, and access to the TV, which will not be turned off all night long.

Altagracia to Granada US$3, four hours, 11pm Tuesday and Friday

Altagracia to San Carlos US$6/4 1st/2nd class, nine hours, 8pm Monday and Thursday; also serves San Miguelito

Granada to Altagracia US$3, four hours, 3pm Monday and Thursday

San Carlos to Altagracia US$6/4 1st/2nd class, nine hours, 2pm Tuesday and Friday

Getting Around

The big news is that the southern loop between Moyogalpa and Altagracia, the island's two major towns, has been paved. All other roads remain atrocious. Remember when asking for directions that most locals really do consider a 3km, uphill hike in shadeless 45°C weather 'right over there.'

BUS

Bus service is solid, but schedules change frequently, and fewer buses run on Sunday. There are two routes between Moyogalpa and Altagracia: the scenic northern loop, via San Marcos, which is shorter but takes much longer; and the paved southern route, with speedy, hourly bus service. All buses from Moyogalpa to the Maderas side of the island stop in Altagracia about one hour later, then head down the isthmus past Playa Santo Domingo.

At Santa Cruz, buses go right (south) to Mérida and San Ramón, and left (east) to Balgüe, perhaps continuing to La Palma. Buses do not serve the southeastern portion of the island, between San Ramón and La Palma, at all.

Altagracia south to Moyogalpa US$0.75, one hour, 5:30am to 6:45pm, every hour

Balgüe to Altagracia US$1.10, one hour, 5am (Moyogalpa), 7am, 5:45am, 6:20am, 10am, 11:15am, 1:15pm (Moyogalpa) and 5pm

Mérida to Altagracia US$1, 1½ hours, 4am (Moyogalpa), 8:45am (Moyogalpa), 3pm (Moyogalpa) and 5pm

Moyogalpa south to Altagracia US$0.75, one hour, 5:30am to 6:45pm, every hour

Moyogalpa to Balgüe US$1.10, two hours, 10:30am and 3:45pm

Moyogalpa to La Flor & San Marcos US$0.30 and US$0.40, 30 minutes, 8am, 10:30am, 12:45pm and 4:45pm, 11 daily; buses continue to Altagracia

Moyogalpa to Mérida US$1.25, 2½ hours, 8:30am and 4:45pm

Moyogalpa to San Ramón US$1.10, 2½ hours, 8:30am

San Ramón to Altagracia US$1, 2½ hours, 1pm and 2pm

CAR & MOTORCYCLE

There were no rental-car places on the island at press time, although that's almost certain to change. Contact **Hotel Ometepetl** (☎ 569 4276; www.hotelesenometepe.com) to get the latest. You can rent motorcycles (US$4 per hour) at **Hotel Castillo** (☎ 552 8744) in Altagracia, and *motos* (small all-terrain vehicles; for US$5 per hour) from **Exploring Ometepe** (☎ 647 5179, 873 7714; www.exploringometepe.com) in Moyogalpa.

If you have your own car, consider leaving it in the inexpensive guarded parking lot by the San Jorge ferry terminal, particularly if you don't have 4WD. Ferries (see p141) can transport your car; make reservations well in advance.

TAXI

Taxis are rare and expensive, and they're all minivans with 4WD. They meet all buses and ferries, but otherwise you should have your hotel make arrangements with a driver at least a few hours in advance. From Moyogalpa, expect to pay at least US$15 to Altagracia, US$20 to Playa Santo Domingo, and US$40 to either Balgüe or Mérida. There are lots of excellent drivers, including **Sergio Rodríguez** (☎ 832 3220) at Los Ranchitos in Moyogalpa.

Moyogalpa

pop 6700

Not just the ferry terminal for hourly boats from the mainland, Moyogalpa is the nerve center for Ometepe's nascent tourist industry, with several hotels and restaurants and the fastest Internet on the island. It's also home base to most of the island's tour companies, and base camp for the climb up Volcán Concepción.

ORIENTATION & INFORMATION

The ferry terminal is at the bottom of Moyogalpa's main street; almost all services are within one block of this street. Buses and taxis stop at the dock after 8:30am; before 8:30am, they leave from the Catholic church at the top of the street. Go left for the dirt road to La Flor and San Marcos, right for the paved road to Charco Verde, Playa Santo Domingo and Volcán Maderas.

Connections at @rcia Cyber Café, Sala Archaológica and Cyber Ometepe can be slow and unreliable. All charge US$1.25 per hour. Minisuper Martínez, at the top of the street, is your last chance to buy film on the island.

SIGHTS & ACTIVITIES

Moyogalpa is the most popular base camp for summiting **Volcán Concepción**, which you can examine more carefully at the **Ometepe Fountain**, right by the docks, a colorful not-quite-to-scale model of the island that used to spew water from the craters. There's a pleasant park and **Catholic church** at the top of the main road or make a right for Club Campestre Casa Blanca, with a casino and **rooster fights** (admission US$0.70; 🕒 3pm Sat & Sun).

The past meets the future…well, the present, anyway, at **Sala Archaológica & Cyber Ometepe** (☎ 569 4225; museum US$1; 🕒 8am-9pm), a combination Internet café (US$1.25 per hour) and family-operated museum. Your fee includes a Spanish-language guided tour of *metates* (flat stones on which corn is ground) and lots of beautiful ceramics, including what may be the best collection of ceramic funeral jars in Nicaragua, emblazoned with bats, snakes and other emblems.

How did they fit whole people inside those itsy-bitsy funeral jars? Well, the creepy answer is that they didn't – they're just for the bones. So what happened to the…erm…meat? That's something of a mystery. The most popular (and least likely) explanation is cannibalism, a charge probably invented or exaggerated by the Spanish conquistadors. The second sounds time-consuming: locals buried the bodies, waited six years or so for them to decompose, dug them back up, put the bones in the jars, then reburied them. The most intriguing explanation, however, is that they wrapped the bodies in nets, lowered them into the water at the perhaps mythical 'Beach of the Dead,' and let the sharks (see the boxed text, p149) clean up the bones for them. But nobody knows for sure.

See p141 for details on swimming, and p141 for mountain bike rentals.

Exploring Ometepe (☎ 647 5179, 873 7714; www.exploringometepe.com) rents *motos* for US$5 per hour.

FESTIVALS & EVENTS

Moyogalpa's **fiestas patronales** (July 23 to 26) are famous for the Baile de las Inditas, a celebration of both Spanish and indigenous culture, as well as several ceremonies timed with the solar calendar that have nothing at all to do with Catholicism. Patron Santa Ana leads a long walk to Punta Jesús María, where there are fireworks and drinking.

SLEEPING

These are just a few of the perfectly acceptable hotels in town.

Hotelito y Restaurante Aly (☎ 569 4196; hotelitoaly@yahoo.com; r per person with/without bathroom US$6/5, q with air-con US$30; Ⓟ ❄) One block up from the ferry terminal, this fine hotel has rooms in different shapes and sizes, all clean and comfortable, and arranged around an attractively lit courtyard with hammocks, tables and pretty darned good food (US$2 to US$5).

Hospedaje Central (☎ 569 4262; hammocks US$1.50, dm US$3, r with fan/air-con US$10/17; ❄) This colorful, backpacker-friendly option is three blocks up from the dock and one block south. Rooms are clean and basic, and there's a decent restaurant in front.

Hotel Ometepetl (☎ 569 4276; www.hotel esenometepe.com; d with fan/air-con US$15/25; P ❄ ☲) One of the island's plushest properties, Hotel Ometepetl has colorful new rooms featuring Direct TV, hammocks, a huge swimming pool and excellent service.

Casa Familiar (r per person US$9) and **Hotel Bahía** (☎ 569 4116; r per person US$3) also rent out basic rooms.

EATING

Almost everything grown on Ometepe is organically farmed (or close to it), simply because fertilizers are unnecessary in the rich volcanic soil, and pesticides prohibitively expensive. Their rice and beans are considered the country's best, and the papayas are certainly among the largest.

Casa Familiar (fish dishes US$3) Two blocks up from the dock, this pleasant little *rancho* serves great steamed fish and also rents rooms.

Hotel Bahía (☎ 569 4116; dishes US$1-3; ❧ 7am-midnight) On the main road, this volcano-kitsch restaurant/bar serves excellent soups and fish dishes beneath the twinkling Christmas lights.

Los Ranchitos (mains US$2-5; ❧ 7am-9:30pm) On the same block as Casa Familiar, the restaurant here also offers inexpensive open-air dining. Portions are huge – a 'medium' fish served with rice and *tostones* (thick, deep-fried plantain slices) will feed two.

Carne Asada Peli-Buey (mains US$1.50-2.50; ❧ 5pm-9pm) On the main drag, this classic *fritanga* specializes in deliciously grilled *peli-buey*, the adorable short-haired sheep you've seen gamboling about the island.

Chido's Pizza (medium pizza US$4) Half a block north of Casa Familiar, Chido's Pizza conveniently rents videos, but isn't quite as good as the Chido's in Altagracia.

Pandería y Reposteria Balestro (snacks US$0.30-2; ❧ 6:30am-9pm Mon-Sat) Half a block from the church, this is the best (only?) bakery on the island.

Around Volcán Concepción

This has been the more populous side of the island (despite the looming, active volcano overhead) since the Chorotega arrived, and remains so today.

ALTAGRACIA VIA SAN MARCOS

There are no real tourist facilities along the northern route between Moyogalpa and Altagracia, although the trailheads for both La Concha and La Flor, which summit Concepción, leave from the towns of the same name. La Flor also has a nice beach. Several archaeological sites, partially excavated from the volcanic ash, are rumored to be located near San Marcos.

PUNTA JESÚS MARÍA

About half an hour by bicycle from Moyogalpa, this well-signed sand spit stretches out into the lake for more than 1km at the height of the dry season, when lake levels drop and reveal what was once a natural dock for indigenous fishermen. It's still used the same way today, with the addition of a few ramshackle restaurants that may or may not be open.

Finca la Florida (☎ 822 9713; ligiamados@yahoo .com; cabinas US$10-20; P) is a tobacco farm that also offers three simple cement cabinas with bathrooms and a basic restaurant serving US$2 set plates. It also rents horses (US$5 per day) and bikes (US$3 per day).

CHARCO VERDE & ISLA DE QUISTE

On the south side of Concepción lies a lush, less windblown clutch of beaches, centered around **Reserva Charco Verde** (admission US$0.30). This fine green pond is accessible from a short hiking trail that begins at Hotel Charco Verde. Not only is this a lovely spot for swimming, but also the home of Chico Largo, a tall, thin and ancient witch who often appears swimming or fishing in the lagoon. His primary duty is to protect the tomb and solid-gold throne of Cacique Nicarao, buried on the banks of the water. He may also offer you a life of luxury in exchange for your soul, which would then become a cow on Isla de Ometepe. This may actually sound OK, but check out the mural at Museo de Ometepe (opposite) before you decide. Incidentally, Chico Largo doesn't like people to take pictures of his pond, either. Just so you know.

Just offshore, **Isla de Quiste** is within swimming distance of the beach, or any of the area's hotels can arrange boat service and perhaps rental tents, as it's a prime camping, fishing and birding spot.

The most comfortable hotel around here is **Hotel Finca Playa Venecia** (☎ 887 0191; www

.islaometepe.com; d US$10-35; (P) (X)), right on the beach with several different clean cabinas, all of them adorable. More expensive ones have air-con. The restaurant serves good inexpensive meals, and the owners can arrange trips, rent horses (US$5 per hour, including guide) and bikes (US$1 per hour).

Posada Chico Largo (☎ 886 4069; camping per tent US$3, dm US$3.50), a budget spot, is next door. It has five-bed dorms, dinner buffets (when there are enough guests), and access to Mirador del Diablo, the hill in between the two volcanoes. The hill – originally called 'Cinacupa,' Náhuatl for the 'Bat Cave' – has been featured in documentaries about vampire bats. It's a half-hour climb to views clear to the Pacific, featuring what owner Ramiro del Diablo says is the most beautiful sunset in Nicaragua. You can camp on top (no facilities) or just come for the full moon parties.

On another fabulous beach, **Hotel Charco Verde** (☎ 887 9302; charcoverde22@yahoo.es; r per person US$5, d cabina with fan/air-con US$25/45; (X)) has older, beautiful wooden rooms (stay upstairs), and a growing collection of large, modern cabinas, only some of which have a beach view. There's no price difference, so ask.

El Tesoro de Pirata (☎ 832 2429; camping US$2, tent US$5, dm US$3, q cabinas with fan/air-con US$25/30; (X)) is a 1km walk from the bus stop down to Valle Verde (Green Valley), an even mellower spot with excellent restaurant and basic, concrete cabinas with porches overlooking a precious beach. The owners can set you up with food, tents and transport to Isla de Quiste (US$20), and can arrange fishing trips.

LAS ESQUINAS

All buses headed to Playa Santo Domingo and Volcán Maderas stop in Altagracia, adding perhaps half an hour to your trip. If you're headed to Playa Santo Domingo, consider getting off at Las Esquinas (El Quino); it's a downhill, 4km walk to the beach.

Altagracia
pop 11,191

With more natural protection from Concepción's occasional lava flow than Moyogalpa, this is the original indigenous capital of Ometepe, and still the island's most important town. Its parque central is much more central, and comes alive in the cool of the evening with barbecue grills, young lovers and sometimes even live music.

ORIENTATION & INFORMATION

Buses stop at the attractive parque central. The museum and all services are within three blocks of here. To get to the ferry terminal, head north along the road in front of Chido's Pizza and Comedor Nicarao for another 2km. Taxis make the run for US$0.30 during the day, US$0.60 at night.

Hotel Castillo and Su Tienda de Fashion offer unreliable Internet access (US$2 per hour). The latter also has a book exchange and the best selection of souvenirs in town. There is a pharmacy at Posada Cabrera.

SIGHTS & ACTIVITIES

This is base camp for the other trailhead to Concepción, called **La Sabana**, which begins about 2km from town. Both Hotel Central and Hotel Castillo can arrange guides.

The main attraction, **Museo de Ometepe** (admission US$1; 🕘 8am-4pm Mon-Sat), is a block from the park. This is Ometepe's official museum, packed with information (in Spanish) about the island. Non-Spanish-speakers will still appreciate the amazing scale model of the volcanoes (much more accurate than the Moyogalpa fountain) as well as a few stone sculptures, petroglyphs and lots of pottery thoughtfully displayed as part of a timeline. There are also photos of Concepción's crater, in case it was cloudy the day you went, and a fairly spectacular painting of the legend of Chico Largo (see opposite).

Another place to see some of the finest remaining ancient excavated statues on Ometepe is beside the Altagracia church, close to the parque central, where a handful of softly eroding monoliths still stand sentry.

There is not much else to see in town except a small beach, **Playa Paso Real**, about 1km from town. Head toward the ferry dock, and after about 20 minutes you'll see a trail veer off to the right, marked by a blue sign; it's another 10 minutes to the water. Hotel Castillo rents **mountain bikes** (per hr US$1).

Close to Altagracia, **Isla Grande** is rarely visited despite being a fantastic place for bird-watching. No one offers a tour to the island, basically a plantain *finca* (farm) gone feral, but you could certainly arrange a custom trip.

FESTIVALS & EVENTS

Altagracia's **fiestas patronales** (November 12 to 18) honor San Diego, whose feast day is coincidentally the same as that of Xolotl, the ancient city's original patron deity. The party's most famous dance, Baile del Zompopo (Dance of the Leaf Cutter Ant), was clearly choreographed long before the Christians got here. San Diego also visits the outlying towns, where believers stay up all night as part of a vigil.

SLEEPING & EATING
All the hotels have restaurants except the Posada Cabrera. The cheapest eats, as usual, are served up at the central park – during the day, a couple of kiosks serve snacks, and starting at dusk several *fritanga* (barbecue) type set-ups offer roast chicken, *tamales* (boiled or steamed cornmeal filled with chicken or pork, usually wrapped in a banana leaf), *baho* (a meat, plantain and vegetable stew) and more, until 9pm or so.

Hotel Central (☎ 552 8770; r per person with/without bathroom US$5/4; cabins per person US$7) Located two blocks south of the park, this attractive option has bathrooms with river-pebbled accents in the front rooms, arranged around a pretty garden. The cabinas out back are super-cute, and the hotel restaurant serves cheap and good Nica food.

Hotel Castillo (☎ 552 8744; r per person with/without bathroom US$5/4; 🖳) Around the corner from Hotel Central, popular Castillo has quiet, airy rooms with screened windows. The restaurant (dishes US$2 to US$4) is excellent, and serves real coffee. Informative owner Julio César Castillo offers Internet access and can arrange custom tours with local guides.

Posada Cabrera (☎ 552 8753; anamariacabrera@ yahoo.com; r per person with/without fan US$3/2) Right on the park, the narrow rooms are drywall topped with tin and charm-free, but cheap and clean.

Hospedaje Kencho (☎ 820 2246; r per person with bathroom US$3, s/d with bathroom US$5/6) The shared bathroom at this shabby spot is actually much nicer than the private one.

Playa Santo Domingo
Windswept (sometimes a little too windswept) beaches and the island's finest accommodations lie southeast of Altagracia, on the long and lovely lava isthmus that cradles Playa Santo Domingo.

SIGHTS & ACTIVITIES
The main attraction is the **beach**, a 30m expanse of gray volcanic sand that retreats almost to the sea wall at the height of the rainy season. It's known for always having a cool breeze v some of the highest windspeeds anywhere in Nicaragua – which is why the windsurfers have been eyeing it.

Also on the isthmus is a pleasant stroll through banana plantations to the well-signed **La Presa Ojo de Agua** (admission US$1), a shady swimming hole about 1.5km north of Playa Santo Domingo. The clear, deep pool was made by partially damming the refreshing Río Buen Suceso, which at 3km is the island's longest river.

Río Istiam, on the southern side of the isthmus, shimmers as it snakes through the island's swampy lava valley. It used to be possible to cross the isthmus entirely by canoe, in the rainy season at least, back in the late 1800s. See p141 for details of kayaking and p141 for bike rental.

If you're in the mood for more modern ecotourism, **Canopy Sendero Los Monos** (per person US$10), across from Hotel Finca Santo Domingo, offers six platforms and 500m of zip-lines constructed by a reputable company. It's small, but these things have a tendency to grow.

SLEEPING & EATING
Make reservations for Finca Santo Domingo and Villa Paraíso well in advance during the high season. The following businesses are listed north to south.

Hospedaje Buena Vista (r with/without bathroom US$10/8) The best budget spot on the beach has a marvelous patio surrounded by lovely gardens and lined with hammocks, all overlooking clean Cocibolca. Rooms are basic but clean, there's free coffee in the morning, and a simple restaurant in the high season.

Hotel Finca Santo Domingo (☎ 820 2247; hotel_santo_domingo@yahoo.com; r with fan US$15-23, with air-con US$20-35; 🅿 🕱) A variety of rooms, all immaculate and richly painted, are just up a rickety spiral staircase in the charming and breezy converted farmhouse; the cement cabinas across the road are air-conditioned, but further from the water. The owners can arrange all types of tours, and the restaurant may be the best on the beach.

Villa Paraíso (☎ 563 4675; www.hotelvillaparaiso .com; d US$18, ste US$40-55; P ✕ ▢) Ometepe's first hotel geared to tourists and still the best, the pleasantly rustic rooms have fan and shared bathroom, while elegant cabañas arranged throughout the gardens have air-con, direct TV and hammock-strewn terraces; some have kitchens. The excellent staff will arrange tours; there's Internet access and a fantastic restaurant.

Around Volcán Maderas

The lusher, wilder side of the island is even less developed than Concepción's realm, and petroglyphs are much more common. They were perhaps left behind by a race of tall, elegant people who occupied Maderas as late as the 1870s, but have since drifted away.

SANTA CRUZ TO BALGÜE

The Santa Cruz split is marked by a small store. It's a pleasant 3km, downhill walk to Balgüe from here, if you're on a Mérida-bound bus.

Just past the split, **Comedor Santa Cruz** (dishes US$2-3) serves fish dishes and ceviches on an outdoor patio surrounded by lovely gardens. **Café Mi Casita** (dishes US$1-2; ◷ 6am-10pm), a bit further along, has fresh-brewed organic coffee from Finca Magdalena, typical breakfasts and cheap set plates.

To reach **El Zopilote Finca Ecológica** (www .ometepezopilote.com; hammocks US$1.25, dm US$2, r per person US$6), on the inland side of the road, follow the trail to the left of the concrete house, then 200m up to the clutch of traditionally constructed thatched-roof huts on the grassy hillside. This Italian-run spot is super-basic, but you've got to love the amazing wooden *mirador* (lookout) and outdoor shower curtained with mammoth grasses. Cook on the wood-fired stove or purchase homemade yogurt, bread, jam and even chocolate, among other goodies, all available along with a few *artesanías* (handicrafts). It's worth stopping by to check out the *mirador* as well. You can volunteer on the farm from 6am to 10am, six days a week, and learn lots about organic farming techniques; but you don't get free lodging or food.

Balgüe, about 1km further, has a cluster of good cafés, including cozy **Palue Soda Bar** (dishes US$2-3; ◷ 7am-7pm), with spaghetti

and a full bar, and excellent **Cafe Isabel** (dishes US$1-3; ◷ 6am-8pm), featuring a huge fixed plate with your choice of meat. **El Ranchón** (dishes US$2-5; ◷ 9:30am-9:30pm) has a nice, thatch-roofed dining room, and serves typical food and cold beer.

Hospedaje y Comedor Maderas (☎ 882 3553; r per person US$2; ◷ 6:30am-8pm), at the base of the driveway to Finca Magdalena, has basic rooms that aren't quite as basic as its famous neighbors, and clean shared bathrooms, fans and walls that go all the way up to the ceiling. Pork chops are the restaurant's specialty (meals US$1 to US$3).

The Ometepe classic, **Finca Magdalena** (☎ 880 2041; www.fincamagdalena.com; hammocks or camping per person US$1.50, dm/r US$2/2.50, cabañas US$30-40), isn't just a place to stay, it's an experience. Rooms and dorms are ultra-basic (the cabañas are pretty sweet, though), but the rambling 19th-century farmhouse has everything you need – sweeping island views, fresh organic coffee, a cheap restaurant serving farm-fresh goodies, and a handful of petroglyphs scattered around the farm, all operated by a communally owned coffee collective going strong since the 1980s.

Well known among hikers as a trailhead to Volcán Maderas, climbers started showing up here even before the Contra War was over, and often asked about food and shelter after the hike. The business began informally, but today tourism represents half the collective's revenues. You can also purchase bags of organic coffee and honey produced right here. Note that it's a 1.5km climb to the *finca* from the bus stop.

Buses are beginning to serve the region all the way to La Palma, passing the tiny town of El Corozal, where a local cooperative and US-based NGO are building **Finca Vista El Corozal** (www.paradisewithapurpose.org), a community-conscious resort – check the website to see how it's coming along.

SANTA CRUZ TO MÉRIDA & SAN RAMÓN

Just past the Santa Cruz split, **Bar y Restaurant Santa Cruz** (meals US$1.25-3; ◷ 6am-8pm), in a thatched-roof *ranchero* overlooking the bus stop, serves great jalapeño chicken and cold beer.

Almost across the road is the entrance to **Albergue Ecológico El Porvenir** (☎ 855 1426;

r per person US$5; (P)). This sunny hilltop lodge and restaurant is a great deal, and uses solar electricity, has great volcano views and petroglyphs amid attractive gardens, and a restaurant serving organic grub grown right here. Several trails (trail fee US$1) include a two-hour trip through about 20 petroglyphs; a four-hour trail to La Chorrera waterfall, where you can swim; and the eight-hour round-trip up Volcán Maderas. It's managed by Hotel Central in Altagracia, which is a good thing.

About 1km before Mérida, look for a sign to **Playa Volcán** (☎ 871 8303; www.playavolcan.tk; hammock or camping US$1, dm US$1.50), a student-run, tin-roofed, dirt-floored experiment in ecotourism that's super-basic and super-cheap. Cook on the wood-fired stove or order simple meals (US$1 to US$2), or even take Spanish classes (US$4 for three hours).

Hacienda Mérida (☎ 868 8973; www.lasuerte.org; camping per person US$1.50, dm US$3-4, r US$6; P 🖵) is a backpacker resort that uses a wonderful dock originally built by the Somozas. It has clean and spacious rooms with well-maintained shared bathrooms. You pay once to use the Internet (US$3), great bikes (US$8) and OK kayaks (US$5) for the duration of your stay. The food gets raves. This is also the trailhead for the steepest ascent up Volcán Maderas; you'll descend via Finca Magdalena.

It's worth the climb to **Hotel Omaja Restaurant Bar** (☎ 855 1124; dm per person US$4-10, r with fan/air-con US$25/50; P 🍴), a new, upscale entry with gorgeous wooden cabinas featuring Direct TV, air-con and incredible views of both volcanoes from the private porches; even the dorms are beautiful. There's an excellent restaurant, a swimming dock across the road and plans for a pool.

Monkies Island Hostal (☎ 844 1529; r per person US$2.50) is about 500m south. This wonderful place is much more basic, with simple rooms, lots of hammocks and a relaxed, thatched-roof restaurant serving inexpensive typical food (US$1 to US$3), rum and beer. The friendly family who run the place are well loved within the close-knit Ometepe community, and the hostel has received the most reader recommendations of any business in this book. It's sort of like a homestay with the nicest family ever.

Estación Biológica de Ometepe (☎ 563 0875; www.lasuerte.org; dm per person US$12, ste US$85; 🍴)

claims to be a center for research in tropical ecology, which may be true. Four bed dorms are pretty nice, and the immaculate suites have air-conditioning, huge Direct TVs and Jacuzzis. The restaurant (meals US$2 to US$4, open 6am to 7pm) is the star of the show, however, so make plans to eat here after your hike.

Any hotel on this stretch will organize tours past the island of **El Cogüito**, now called Isla de los Monos or Monkey Island, home to the descendants of four spider monkeys (Ateles geofroyi). Spider monkeys aren't present anywhere else on the island (howler and white face monkeys are) so these guys are pretty much alone. Be careful kayaking by, as they do bite.

Also worth seeing is **Cascada San Ramón** (admission US$3, free for station guests), a stunning 40m waterfall that is one of the jewels of the island. It's a steep four-hour round-trip on an easy-to-follow trail that's lost some of its charm since lots of trees were cut down. But it's still mossy and beautiful at the top.

SAN JUAN DEL SUR
pop 13,000

This golden sand-fringed, half moon of a cove, hemmed in by stunning cliffs and filled with boats in repose, may be the most touristed destination in Nicaragua – something you should keep in mind when planning your time here. It's easy to understand why San Juan del Sur (SJDS) is so popular. The gateway to some of Nicaragua's best and most accessible beaches, it offers the same white-sand geology, excellent surfing and sunny, dry resort weather as Costa Rica's Nicoya Peninsula, an hour south, where folks like Madonna shack up at the Four Seasons.

But this collection of beautiful beaches, 14 of them named and all of them within a few kilometers by dirt road or boat taxi, have been built up with the budget tourist in mind. Sure, there are plenty of posh pads around these days, including one of the most beautiful hotels in Central America. But here, despite the relative crowds, you're still able to walk along stretches of almost pristine shoreline and find yourself a hammock, and some rice and beans served by the beach, which is sometimes all you need.

Orientation & Information

Wrapped around a crescent bay, SJDS is easy to explore on foot, and flanked by at least six other cove beaches on a single 40km stretch of coast, all connected by a rough dirt coastal road that can be 4WD-driven mostly in the rainy season, and gets much rougher north of Majagual. If you're walking to the northern beaches, save 2km by walking along the shore (instead of the road) and taking the tiny boat (US$0.12) across the river.

BDF Has a 24-hour Visa/Plus ATM, but does not do credit-card withdrawals; there's a MasterCard-friendly BAC ATM at Hotel Casa Blanca.

Biblioteca Móvil (☽ 8am-6pm Mon-Fri, 9am-4pm Sat) This lending library lets visitors browse its magazine and book collection, with lots in English.

Casa Oro Hostel (☎ 458 2415) This private information center wants to sell you a variety of tours, but it can also point you toward independent Spanish instruc-

tors and hiking trails and surfing lessons. It can also change traveler's checks, euros and other currency for a stiff fee.

Cyber Leo's (per hr US$1.25; ☽ 8am-10pm) The cheapest Internet in town; others charge US$1.70 but may be less crowded.

El Gato Negro Coffee & Book Exchange New and some used books in English and other languages; also check Ricardo's Bar and Big Wave Dave's.

Lavandería (per load US$4; ☽ 9am-4:30pm Mon-Sat) Drop-off service only.

Police (☎ 453 3732)

Post office/Enitel At the western end of the beachfront drive.

San Juan del Sur Info (www.sanjuandelsur.org.ni) English-language, traveler-savvy site that has links to several area businesses.

Tesorera Cantur (☎ 458 2473; www.cantur.org.ni; ☽ 9am-5pm) The official tourist information office makes hotel and tour reservations, and sells a pretty, if useless, map (US$1) of the region.

BULL SHARKS, FIN SOUP & A TALE OF OVERFISHING

There was a time when the people of Lago de Nicaragua, then called Cocibolca (Náhuatl for the Sweet Sea), did not learn how to swim. From the gulf of the Río San Juan to Granada's shores, the bull shark, the world's only freshwater shark, ruled these waters, and had a taste for human flesh.

Carcharhinus leucus is among the Caribbean's most ferocious sharks, not enormous but strong, with an appetite for anything terrestrial that might fall into its realm. Small eyes, adapted to the silty water of the river mouth, are useless, but it can smell blood from 100m away. Its flattened tailfin is perfect for the punishingly shallow rapids of rivers which it, unlike any other shark, can penetrate well inland.

All sharks can modify salts in their bloodstream, to sink and float at will, but the bull shark, alone, can urinate these salts away as it heads upstream, and find equilibrium in places where they are not expected.

The shark, always itself hunted, became a major cash earner as the 20th century began. By the 1930s Chinese buyers were paying as much as US$70 a kilogram for the fins, a legendary 'restorative.' As the market grew, Nicaraguans found buyers for the shark's liver, rich in vitamin A, and the skin, which can be prepared as fine leather. This shark's meat, however, rots too quickly to export. The bulk of this brutal catch was ground to fertilizer or dog food, or simply thrown away.

In 1969 the Somoza family decided to take full advantage of this renewable natural resource, and built a shark processing plant in Granada. By some estimates, 20,000 sharks flowed through during the decade it churned. More than 100 boats fed the facilities, even as the sharks became rarer, perhaps endangered, and ever more difficult to catch. The revolution coincided with this unprofitable decline, and the entire operation was shut down in 1979. It has never recovered.

The bull shark has not entirely abandoned these waters, however, make no mistake. Its bulk is still spotted with alarming regularity not a person's length from potential prey…but it does not bite. Some say it doesn't like the noise motorboats make, or has simply learned to avoid human settlements – this is, after all, a most adaptable creature. But you've got to wonder, as you swim these once forbidden waters, if it remembers the taste.

A great book about Nicaraguan bull sharks is the page-turner *Savage Shore: Life and Death with Nicaragua's Last Shark Hunters*, by the amazing Edward Marriot.

Dangers & Annoyances

As everywhere, flocks of tourists are attended by charming predators. Don't lend money that you can't afford to lose to your new friends, don't leave unattended valuables on the beach, double-check your bill and count your change. And remember, there's never any reason to give dealers your cash up front. Ever.

Although most tourists never experience these problems, note that the trail to Playa Remanso is well known for muggings and best avoided; at least leave your camera at the hotel. Always be alert when walking between beaches, and go in groups if possible. The beach in front of the SJDS bars can be unsafe at night, and sexual assaults have occurred on 'party' beaches.

Sights

SJDS's several square blocks of souvenir shops and businesses are worth a wander; drop by **Iglesia San Juan Bautista**, with a shady park right out front, for your cultural pit stop.

Activities

SURFING

The best surfing is generally April to December, but waves are less crowded in the off season. There's a **beach break** on bigger swells at the northern end of the beach, but most surfers hire boats or stay at the beaches north and south of town. It's always cheaper to rent your board in SJDS, where several places charge about US$7 per day. Almost anyone with a boat can take you to the breaks.

Arena Caliente (☎ 824 1152; www.arenacaliente .com) Everyone loves this locally owned and operated shop, which rents boards and arranges inexpensive group transportation to the best breaks. It also offers budget surf packages where prices vary depending on your choice in lodging (or camping) and other options.

Nica Surf International (www.nicasurfinternational .com; per week per person US$990, maximum 6) Perhaps the most professional surfing operation in Nicaragua, Nica Surf sets you up at a swish hotel and runs a gamut of tours during your week's stay.

Surf Nicaragua (☎ 838 3808; www.localtreasureinter national.com) In Hotel Estrella, offers three-hour surf tours for up to eight people for US$180.

SWIMMING & DIVING

The beach right in town is only OK; head to the northern end for the best swimming.

But for real, untrammeled beauty, you'll want to visit beaches north and south of town. It's always easier to go by boat taxi; ask at Arena Caliente if you can hitch a ride with a surf group for a few dollars.

Pelican Eyes (half/full day US$5/9) If you need a break from the waves, enjoy the stunning view at this luxury hotel's pool – no typo on those prices.

San Juan del Sur Diving School (☎ 279 8628; www .abucear.com) This dive shop offers PADI certification courses, and trips into the bay and beyond, where you'll see lobsters, moray eels, dolphins, turtles and more. Owner Fidel López Briceño also arranges diving trips to Laguna de Apoyo (see p102).

HIKING

Unfortunately, the popular 3km hike to the **old lighthouse** crosses land tied up in a property battle, which means you are currently forbidden to take the obvious trail that begins up at the fishing port, continuing uphill every time it forks, to the spectacular views all the way to Costa Rica.

Instead, try the **Antennas Trail**: ask the driver of any Rivas-bound bus to let you off at 'Bocas de las Montañas.' Follow the dirt road through jungle and pasture up to the radio antennas, from where you have similarly stunning views.

There's a **spectacular petroglyph** not far from town; if you do Da Flying Frog canopy tour (see Other Activities, p152), ask to be taken by. Otherwise, walk toward Rivas, passing the Texaco station, and make a left after the bridge. Pass a school and then a gate on your right. Continue to the old farmhouse; if anyone's around, you should ask permission to cross the land. Otherwise, follow the irrigation pipes to the river, where you'll find the stone, showing an enormous and elaborate hunting scene carved perhaps 1500 years ago. If you continue upstream, you'll come to a small waterfall.

BIKING

Both **Hospedaje Elizabeth** (☎ 458 2270) and **Hotel Colonial** (☎ 458 2539) rent mountain bikes (US$5 per day), which are perfect for the dirt roads heading to the northern and southern beaches. You can take your bike on buses that run between SJDS and El Ostional, as well as the little river ferry at the northern end of the SJDS beach.

Both Big Wave Dave's and Zapata Vive restaurant rent *motos*.

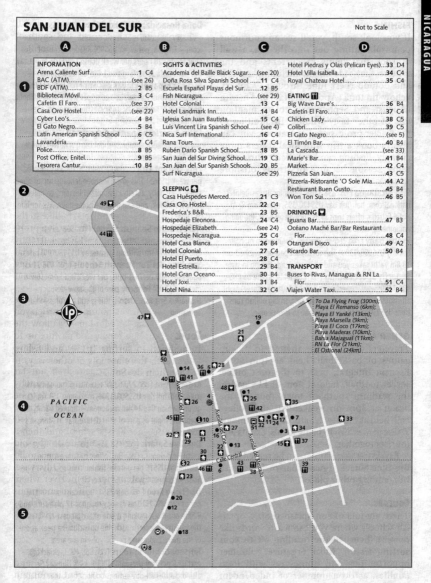

SAN JUAN DEL SUR

Not to Scale

INFORMATION
Arena Caliente Surf...........................1 C4
BAC (ATM)......................................(see 26)
BDF (ATM)..2 B5
Biblioteca Móvil................................3 C4
Cafetín El Faro...............................(see 37)
Casa Oro Hostel.............................(see 22)
Cyber Leo's.......................................4 B4
El Gato Negro...................................5 B4
Latin American Spanish School 6 C5
Lavandería...7 C4
Police...8 B5
Post Office, Enitel.............................9 B5
Tesorera Cantur..............................10 B4

SIGHTS & ACTIVITIES
Academia del Baile Black Sugar......(see 20)
Doña Rosa Silva Spanish School 11 C4
Escuela Español Playas del Sur.........12 B5
Fish Nicaragua................................(see 29)
Hotel Colonial.................................13 C4
Hotel Landmark Inn.........................14 B4
Iglesia San Juan Bautista..................15 C4
Luis Vincent Lira Spanish School.....(see 4)
Nica Surf International......................16 C4
Rana Tours......................................17 C4
Rubén Darío Spanish School............18 B5
San Juan del Sur Diving School........19 C3
San Juan del Sur Spanish Schools....20 B5
Surf Nicaragua...............................(see 29)

SLEEPING
Casa Huéspedes Merced..................21 C3
Casa Oro Hostel..............................22 C4
Frederica's B&B...............................23 B5
Hospedaje Eleonora.........................24 C4
Hospedaje Elizabeth......................(see 24)
Hospedaje Nicaragua.......................25 C4
Hotel Casa Blanca...........................26 B4
Hotel Colonial.................................27 C4
Hotel El Puerto................................28 C4
Hotel Estrella..................................29 B4
Hotel Gran Oceano..........................30 B4
Hotel Joxi.......................................31 B4
Hotel Nina......................................32 C4

Hotel Piedras y Olas (Pelican Eyes)...33 D4
Hotel Villa Isabella..........................34 C4
Royal Chateau Hotel........................35 C4

EATING
Big Wave Dave's..............................36 B4
Cafetín El Faro.................................37 C4
Chicken Lady...................................38 C5
Colibrí...39 C5
El Gato Negro...............................(see 5)
El Timón Bar....................................40 B4
La Cascada....................................(see 33)
Marie's Bar......................................41 B4
Market..42 C4
Pizzería San Juan.............................43 C5
Pizzería-Ristorante 'O Sole Mia........44 A2
Restaurant Buen Gusto.....................45 B4
Won Ton Sui....................................46 B5

DRINKING
Iguana Bar.......................................47 B3
Océano Maché Bar/Bar Restaurant
  Flor..48 A2
Otangani Disco.................................49 A2
Ricardo Bar......................................50 B4

TRANSPORT
Buses to Rivas, Managua & RN La
  Flor..51 C4
Viajes Water Taxi.............................52 B4

PACIFIC
OCEAN

To Da Flying Frog (300m);
Playa El Remanso (6km);
Playa El Yankê (13km);
Playa Marsella (9km);
Playa El Coco (17km);
Playa Maderas (10km);
Bahía Majagual (11km);
RN La Flor (21km);
El Ostional (24km)

TURTLE WATCHING

Between July and December – peaking in August and September – some 30,000 female Olive Ridley turtles, and a few hundred very endangered leatherback turtles, visit **Refugio de Vida Silvestre La Flor** (La Flor Wildlife Reserve; see p157) to nest. And you just have to see turtles laying eggs on the beach, not to mention tiny baby turtles making their death-defying run for the water, at least once in your life. Several San Juan del Sur hotels, including Hotel Nina and Casa Oro Hostel, run night-time tours, including transportation, for around US$12. Don't forget to bring your insect repellent.

FISHING

If you look south, you'll see an enormous peninsula jutting out into the sea, a wall of rock that hems in currents and the critters that ride them, including sailfish and dorado (best June through October), yellow-fin tuna (April and May) and marlin (August and September), not to mention lots of other tasty wildlife. In addition to the pricier professional operations, you can always book a trip with local fishers more cheaply. Fishing can be difficult during the rainy season because of strong offshore winds.

Fish Nicaragua (☎ 838 3808; www.localtreasureinter national.com; half/full day US$420/595, maximum 8) At Hotel Estrella, offers trips in its 10m diesel boat, including equipment, lunch and beer.

Pretty Baby (☎ 266 3620; www.fishing.com.ni; half/ full day US$900/1300) This totally souped-up, plushed-out 13.8m yacht takes you and all your friends fishing in style.

Superfly Sport Fishing (☎ 884 8444, in the US 888-331 7489; www.superflynica.com) A four-day, three-night all-inclusive fishing package focusing on big billfish runs from US$2500 to US$5500 for one to four people.

OTHER ACTIVITIES

Travelers are cordially invited to pickup games of basketball, held at 4pm at La Escuela Integral, next to the post office; soccer/football, held at 4pm at El Cuadro, the stadium south of town (but on the beach at 3pm on weekends); and volleyball, held at the beach Saturday and Sunday. These games aim to bring locals, expats and tourists together.

Kayaks (per hr around US$3) can be rented from Big Blue Safaris, Iguana Bar or Landmark Inn, among other places.

Courses

There are lots of sun-splashed SJDS Spanish schools where you can learn words like *cerveza* (beer) before heading off to your surfing lesson. Most organize volunteer opportunities and homestays with local families, as do a number of independent teachers, who generally charge less and come to your hotel. Check the bulletin boards at **Casa Oro Hostel** (☎ 458 2415) and **Tesorera Cantur** (☎ 458 2473; www.cantur.org.ni; ◷ 9am-5pm).

Academia del Baille Black Sugar (Black Sugar Dance Academy; ☎ 458 2255, 877 7957; naomi300@hotmail .com) Offers dance classes in the Casa de Cultura.

Doña Rosa Spanish School (☎ 621 8905; spanish _silva@yahoo.com – Spanish, spanish_jorvine@yahoo .com – English; per week US$90) Reader recommended, your fee for 20 hours per week doesn't include homestay, but does include surfing and Latin dance lessons.

Escuela Español Playas del Sur (☎ 568 2233; escuelaplayasdelsur@yahoo.com; per week with/without homestay & 3 meals US$145/95) Offers one-on-one instruction.

Latin American Spanish School (☎ 832 4668; www.latinamericanspanishchool.com) A newer choice with happy students.

Luis Vincent Lira (☎ 872 1645; lvl1948@yahoo.es; per week US$65) This jovial independent instructor offers three-hour daily, totally customized lessons, complete with workbook, and can arrange homestays. Ask for him at Cyber Leo's.

Rubén Darío Spanish School (☎ 568 2594; darionicspanishschool@yahoo.com) Has hourly (US$6) and weekly (with/without homestay US$180/95) rates.

San Juan del Sur Spanish Schools (☎ 458 2115; pages.prodigy.net/nss-pmc; per week incl homestay & meals US$195) Formerly part of the now-defunct Nicaragua Spanish Schools, this is still a professional operation.

Tours

In addition to surfing (p150) and fishing tours (left), there are lots of other ways to see San Juan del Sur.

Argonautica (☎ 270 6825; reception@morgansrock .com; half/full day US$600/1200, maximum 15) You can go upscale on this 14.4m mahogany-trimmed yacht, or spend the night as part of your deluxe stay at Morgan's Rock (see p156).

Big Blue Safaris (☎ 458 2527; puravida2201@yahoo .com) Next door to Casa Oro, offers custom excursions, starting at US$15 per person; fishing trips cost US$25 per hour. Also rents kayaks (US$10 per day).

Da Flying Frog (☎ 568 2351; tiguacal@ibw.com.ni; per person US$25) This canopy tour has 17 platforms and 2.5km of cables, making it one of the biggest zip-lines in the country. The horseback ride up includes a peek at one of the more impressive petroglyphs in the area.

Horseback Riding Tours (☎ 868 4003; eblackb@ earthlink.net; per person US$30) Rosie's Laundry Service also organizes all-day outings on horseback that include a swim on gorgeous Playa El Coco and lunch in the village of Cangrejo.

Pelican Eyes Sailing Adventures (☎ 568 2110; www.sanjuandelsur.org.ni/pelicaneyes; per person from US$65) Offers full- and half-day adventures on a 14m sailboat including drinks and a barbecue lunch.

Rana Tours (☎ 877 9255; per hr for 6 people US$30) In addition to a water-taxi service, arranges private surfing, fishing or sightseeing expeditions, including snacks, for four hours or more.

Festivals & Events

San Juan del Sur is *de rigueur* for wealthy Managuans during Christmas and Semana Santa; make reservations and expect prices to double.

St John the Baptist (June 24) SJDS's patron offers another excuse to party.

Procession of the Virgin of Carmen (July 16) The Virgin – patron saint of fishers – is taken aboard a local ship at 2pm, placed on an altar decorated with fishing nets and poles, and taken on a sailing trip around the bay to bless the boats; seafood and mariachi music are involved.

Sleeping

This is one of the few destinations in Nicaragua with pronounced seasonal rates: prices rise dramatically during the December to March high season and double for Semana Santa and Christmas. Bargain for deals during the rainy season.

BUDGET

There are lots of sandy-floored, shared-bathroom cheapies around town; these are just a few favorites.

Hospedaje Nicaragua (☎ 568 2134; r with/without bathroom US$20/12) Light, airy, furnished and almost OCD-clean, this place is a deal for couples or groups; the wonderful upstairs rooms (with bathroom) have a breezy balcony.

Hotel Estrella (☎ 568 2210; r per person US$5) The romantic option, this high-ceilinged (higher than the walls), century-old landmark is basic, but has balconies with beautiful views. Bathrooms are downstairs, in the backyard.

Hotel Nina (☎ 458 2302; r US$10) Wonderful, spotlessly clean rooms with lots of light – try to stay upstairs, next to the rooftop patio – and kitchen access make Nina a solid budget choice for couples, and a good midrange option for solo travelers.

Casa Oro Hostel (☎ 458 2415; dm US$5, r with/without bathroom US$15/12; 🖵) This backpacker stand-by has all the amenities – great information center, discount Internet, kitchen, lounge areas – but could stand to be gussied up a bit.

Hospedaje Elizabeth (☎ 458 2270; r per person without bathroom US$5, s/d with bathroom US$12/15) Packed with party people, this popular joint offers rooms that vary in size and comfort; breezy upstairs rooms facing the ocean are the best.

Hospedaje Eleonora (☎ 458 2191; r per person with/without bathroom US$6/4) Nearby, this is the best of a string of smaller budget spots.

MIDRANGE

Hotel El Puerto (☎ 823 5729; hotel-el-puerto@gmx .net; s/d US$18/23) Brand-new fan-cooled rooms have tasteful wooden furnishings, spotless bathroom and decent views.

Hotel Joxi (☎ 458 2483; casajoxi@ibw.com.ni; r per person US$15; ✵) A crowd-pleaser with lots of return clients and European flavor. Cute rooms come furnished with air-con, cable TV, attention to lighting and a decent restaurant downstairs.

Casa Huéspedes Mercedes (☎ 458 2564; r per person US$10) Off the main strip, this family-run spot has a kitchen for guests' use and comfortable, individually decorated rooms, some with independent entrances.

Royal Chateau Hotel (☎ 568 2551; s/d with fan US$20/25, with air-con US$30/35; 🅿 ✵) Huge, clean and unadorned rooms have TV and bathroom, plus a little balcony outside overlooking the grassy parking lot.

Hotel Gran Océano (☎ 458 2539; hgoceano@ibw .com.ni; s/d incl breakfast US$45/50; ✵) Much closer to the beach and painted in juicy colors, this tropical hideaway has lots of wicker, air-conditioning and cable TV in all the rooms.

TOP END

Hotel Colonial (☎ 458 2539; www.hotel-nicaragua. com; s/d incl breakfast US$44/50; ✵) This plush spot is a surfing fave despite smallish rooms, which are elegantly attired in Spanish antiques and outfitted with all the modern amenities.

Frederica's B&B (☎ 847 8019; rapido1@ibw.com.ni; d with fan/air-con US$50/55; ✵) Enjoy Southern-style hospitality and personal attention in one of two gorgeous (one more colorful, one classier) rooms, with all the amenities.

Hotel Villa Isabella (☎ 568 2568; www .sanjuandelsur.org.ni/isabella; d incl breakfast US$45-100; ✖ ✵) This beautifully furnished, nonsmoking hotel is a dream, with all the amenities – except that cheaper rooms share a bathroom with one other room. More expensive suites have kitchenettes and more.

Hotel Piedras y Olas (☎ 458 2110; www .piedrasyolas.com; d US$75-100; ✕ ☒) With sweeping bay views and fairly fabulous cabinas, featuring mini kitchens, terraces and all the trimmings, you may not want to leave. Luckily, it has a stunning pool and arguably the best restaurant (meals US$5 to US$15) in town, well known for its breakfast buffet (US$6).

Eating

The best meals in town are served in SJDS's tidy **market** (dishes US$2-4; ✕ 6am-4pm), where four small eateries serve Nica standards and lots of options (fruit plates, granola, veggie dishes) designed to appeal to the backpacking set.

RESTAURANTS

There are several charming, thatched-roof restaurants lining the beach, all with spectacular sunsets, full bars and solid seafood, running US$4 to US$8 for fish, more for shrimp and lobster. Two of the best are **Restaurant Buen Gusto** (✕ 7am-10pm), where you'll want everything in the garlic sauce, and the landmark **El Timón Bar** (dishes US$5-16; ✕ 7am-midnight), beacon for local business and political heavyweights, who come to have their egos stroked over excellent seafood and plenty of Flor de Caña rum.

El Colibrí (dishes US$3-8; ✕ 5pm-late Wed-Sun) Serves scrumptious veggie options, organic treats, handmade bread and meatier Mediterranean fare in the beautiful gardens; there's sometimes live music.

Pizzeria San Juan (☎ 568 2295; slice/pie US$0.75/5.75; ✕ 5:30-10pm) Taste for yourself why they call this the best pizza in town, on the relaxed patio out back or phone in for delivery.

Big Wave Dave's (dishes US$5-8) The classic expat joint serves famously good breakfasts and wonderful comfort food – big burgers, bigger organic-leaf salads and more – all day.

Marie's Bar (dishes US$4-7; ✕ from 5:30pm Tue-Sun) Marie's spices up the usual seafood platters with eclectic variations, and the cappuccinos and espressos here are tops. Save room for the tasty dessert crepes (US$2.25).

Pizzeria-Ristorante 'O Sole Mio (mains US$4-10; ✕ 5:30-9:30pm Tue-Fri, 11:30am-9:30pm Sat & Sun) Dripping with fine-dining ambience and serving up good wine, fresh pasta (gnocchi is a specialty) and, of course, pizza, this is a good spot to propose. It's open shorter hours in the low season.

La Cascada Restaurant (meals US$6-25; ✕ 7am-9:30pm) This is the fanciest fine dining in town, atop Pelican Eyes' perch above the bay, where you can relax over aged USDA-quality steaks, lobster in garlic sauce or the enormous breakfast buffet.

CAFÉS

El Gato Negro (http://elgatonegronica.com; light meals US$1-6; ✕ 7am-3pm Wed-Sat, 5-8pm Wed, 9:30am-6pm Sun) With what may be the best selection of English-language books in Nicaragua, you'll have plenty of excuses to linger over real espresso beverages and yummy pastries, sandwiches and other light meals in the comfortable dining room.

Cafetín El Faro (items US$0.50-2; ✕ 7am-10pm) Run by the youth center, this is also the best bakery in town. Enjoy delicious fresh bread, cinnamon rolls, pizza and real coffee in the pleasant *palapa* (thatched-roof) dining area, or inside over a game of ping-pong.

QUICK EATS

Won Ton Sui (dishes US$2-6; ✕ 11am-10pm) Show up at meal times for the freshest choices at this Chinese steam-table buffet.

Chicken Lady (roast chicken US$3; ✕ 4-9pm) This local legend sells delicious roast chicken from her green and yellow house on the west side of the parque central.

Drinking

Start your evening at one of the waterfront bars, or check out Big Wave Dave's happy hour, with 10-córdoba (US$0.70) beers. Ricardo's Bar, a beachfront expat institution with great gringo grub and a book exchange, is a fine place to kick back with a cold one and meet the neighbors. There are free movies on Monday and Thursday at 8pm, DJs on Wednesday, and live music when it comes around.

Another classic beachside hangout is Iguana Bar. It hosts All Those Wasted Mangos live every Tuesday night (no cover).

A late-night place is Maché Bar (it's signed Bar-Restaurant Flores), which gets packed for Tuesday's open mic; but show up anytime for a decent steak, cold brew and good conversation. This is where the city's other bartenders relax after their last call.

Otangani Disco (☻ Fri-Sun) The original SJDS disco, the mirrored balls and colored lights start spinning at 9pm, but the in-crowd doesn't show up until at least 11pm, primed for an all-night party.

Getting There & Around

Getting to the beaches north and south of town can be expensive, so ask at the surf shops if they have a boat going with extra space for you. Majagual usually sends a truck (US$3) to the market at 11am to bring you back to the beach.

BUS

The newly implemented bus service to the northern beaches (US$2.50, open 6:50am and 12:50pm), serving Toro Mixcal, Nacascolo, Marsella, Los Playones, Maderas, Majagual, Ocotal and Rivas, had been suspended at press time, but should be running again by the time you read this. There is regular bus service from the bus stop in front of the market to destinations including:

Managua *expreso* US$3.30, 2½ hours, 4:30am, 5am, 5:30am, 6am and 7am; *ordinario* US$2.50, four hours, 8am to 6:15pm, at least hourly

Rivas US$0.70, 40 minutes, 3:30am to 7pm, every 25 minutes

Southern beaches US$1, two hours, 11am, 3pm and 4:30pm; service to Empalme de Remanso, Playa el Coco, Reserva La Flor, El Ostional; returning buses leave El Ostional at 5am, 7:30am and noon

TAXI

The Taxi Cooperative of San Juan del Sur charges US$0.70 to anywhere in town, US$1.25 for *colectivo* taxis to Rivas. Each driver has a list of set rates for other destinations, including Morgan's Rock (US$10), Majagual (US$15), Playa El Coco or Reserva La Flor (US$30), El Ostional (US$40), the Costa Rican border (US$15), Masaya or Granada (US$40) and Managua (US$75). Taxis congregate close to the market.

WATER TAXI

Viajes Water Taxi (☎ 877 9255), part of Rana Tours, has boats leaving from Hotel Estrella (US$8 return, departing 10am) to Majagual, stopping at the beaches along the way, and returning at 5pm daily. It may also offer service to the southern beaches, depending on demand.

BEACHES NORTH OF SAN JUAN DEL SUR

If buses still aren't serving the northern beaches and you don't won't to shell out for a taxi or boat, you can always walk (hitching is common) or bike the 8km dirt road to Bahía Majagual or Playa Madera, but don't expect beach views.

Playa Nacascolo & Playa Toro Mixcal

Although access to Playa Nacascolo is privately owned, cooler than average **Nicaragua Properties** (www.realestatenicaragua.com) actually allows visitors onto the property to cross (for now); ask at the entrance and guards will give you directions to Las Miradores waterfall.

Finca Forestal El Toro Mixcal (www.zonanica.com/toromix) is a private, Marena-recognized reserve that protects a nice stretch of coastline and dry tropical forest. There are short trails, good bird-watching and no other infrastructure for tourists; contact it for more information.

On the main road (well away from the beach), **Cabinas Miramar** (☎ 278 4658; camping per person US$3) doesn't have cabinas yet (it's all part of the plan), but does offer camping and outdoor showers.

Playa Marsella

There are two rather upscale spots to stay on this beautiful beach, about 8km north of SJDS and easy walking distance to the next two beaches. Although the best surfing is just north, at Playa Madera, there's a good estuary break right here.

El Nido Bed & Breakfast (☎ 862 5344, 879 7062; paslynch@comcast.net, cherylserra@yahoo.net) is on a hill overlooking the bay. This pleasant spot has two rooms sitting on 10 *manzanas* (blocks) of tropical dry forest, with stone-walled gardens and a great cool pool.

One mellow option, but closed for renovations at press time, **Marsella Beach Resort** (☎ 887 1337; www.marsellabeachresort.com; bungalow d US$60, extra person US$10, house US$200; 🏊) has long been a good deal on comfortable, modern rooms with a pool and restaurant, as long as you don't mind the gated community ambience.

Playa Madera

This stunning beach, with rocky expanses that offer excellent tidepooling and wide, wonderful sandy stretches for sunbathing, is famed for having one of the best beach breaks in the country. Sometimes called Los Playones (which is a bit rude), it's a slow wave in fairly deep (2m) water, good for beginners, with two right and two left breaks that get hollow on a rising tide. It becomes unpleasantly crowded with locals on weekends.

If swell is really big on a low to medium tide, there's a faster, intermediate level reef break between Madera and Majagual called Panga Drops, accessible by boat only, that offers an awesome ride before dumping you onto the rocky shallows. It gets choppy and you can be caught in the shore break, so watch the wind; it also gets sneaker sets, so stay alert. Waves get big – as do crowds, and it doesn't hold a crowd well.

Surfers – locals and visitors alike – love **Madera Surf Camp** (camping/hammocks per person US$2, r US$3), just steps away from one of the country's best breaks. Basic meals are available, and the owners are cool. A few steps up the beach is the entrance to the **Hideout** (r per person US$2.50), where there's a 'no service,' but there is a good spaghetti dinner on Saturday nights.

Buena Vista Surf Club (www.buenavistasurfclub .com), more upscale, is about five minutes from the beach on the only dirt road. It has an absolutely stunning house for rent; contact it for rates. It also rents surfboards for US$15 per day.

A beloved family-run option in between Maderas and Majagual, **Matilda's** (☎ 862 5727; camping per person US$3, dm US$7, r US$20) rents campsites and tents, or go for the basic dorms. Relatively fancier private rooms with bathroom are also available. There's no food service, but a poorly stocked *pulpería* nearby helps keep body and soul together.

Parque Maderas (www.parquemaderas.com) is the sort of new-agey housing development that may let you trade hard work for beachside accommodations.

Bahia Majagual

This beautiful bay is perfect for swimming (watch the rip current, though), but only has OK surfing – you'll need to walk all of 10 minutes to the big breaks. It's best known as the home of **Bahia Majagual** (☎ 886 0439; majagual@ibw.com.ni; camping per person US$2, s/d tents US$6/8, hammocks per person US$4, dm US$5-6, s/ d cabins US$18/24), a backpacking and beach-bum institution.

This colorful spot has everything you need – a good restaurant, beer, lots of hammocks, surf lessons and rentals, book exchange, board games, horseback rides – all of which will be added to your running bill, which you should go over *before* waking and baking, dude. You can check your tab any time, and have 24 hours to contest any charges you're not sure about. Note that room rates rise dramatically in the high season, recently hitting US$80 per cabin. It's still the best party spot on the beach, though.

Playa Ocotal

The best way to visit this shady cove beach is by booking a cabin at the very best hotel in Nicaragua, **Morgan's Rock** (☎ 506 296 9442; www.morgansrock.com; s/d in high season US$240/340). Yes, that's ridiculously expensive, but you're staying in the poshest dream cabin ever, gleaming with precious woods dappled in the forest light, which filters through the parrot- and monkey-filled jungle canopy right into your screened-in porch. Crashing waves reverberate from the beach just below, which, by the way, gets nesting sea turtles. *And* you have to cross a hanging bridge through the jungle canopy on the little trail to your cabin (some trails are much shorter than others). Great service, excellent food and environmental awareness (which means no air-conditioning), and you could also get a package spending the night on its old-school yacht, the *Argonautica* (see p152).

If you don't have hundreds of dollars to blow, you can rent a boat taxi or walk to the still very public beach, which is much better for swimming than surfing. Follow the signs to Majagual and turn right after passing a black and yellow gate; continue until you get to the beach.

Arena Blanca

With some of the clearest water and whitest sand on the Pacific coast, this little inlet is only accessible by rented boat or along a very rough dirt road across very private property – ask permission. At the northern end of the beach is Punta Manzanillo, also called Punta Reloj, a point break that may work around midtide if swells are big enough.

BEACHES SOUTH OF SAN JUAN DEL SUR

Although there is regular bus service between SJDS and El Ostional, you'll still need to walk several kilometers from the bus stop to most of the beaches; only Playa El Coco and La Flor are close to the road. If you have a group, water taxis are generally cheaper and easier than regular taxis, and may be the only way to access private beaches as they become gated off with increasing frequency each passing month.

Playa Remanso

The most accessible in a cluster of pretty beaches, this crescent of white sand has OK surfing, interesting caves and good swimming and tidepooling. The smallish beach break would be good for beginners, if it weren't so crowded. But it is beautiful; heck, Spanish luxury chain Barceló is planning a resort nearby.

Remanso Beach Resort (☎ 458 2498; www .remansobeach.com) sprawls across much of the area, but happily lets visitors cross its private property to the beach. It rents rooms and houses at prices that vary, but may drop rates if you're interested in purchasing a retirement home.

The walking path to Remanso is known for muggings at machete point, so go in groups and leave valuables back at the hotel.

Playa Tamarindo & Playa Hermosa

The next beach south, Playa Tamarindo, a half-hour walk from Playa Remanso, is generally less crowded; surfers come with the rising tide to try for a long wave with right and left breaks, which can get hollow coming off the rock wall when swells are under 1m. It's another half-hour's walking to Playa Hermosa with another smallish, consistent beach break; it's less crowded, as only surfers usually get this far.

Playa El Yanké

Several kilometers further along, this gentle crescent of sand, spectacularly bounded by rocky points, used to have a rustic hotel. That's closed, however, and the stucco

announcement of a brand-new gated community had just gone up at press time.

There's a decent beach break on the rising tide; the right dumps you onto the rocks, but there's a mellower left on the southern end of the beach.

Playa El Coco

This is a world-class beach, a spectacular stretch of sparkling white sand punctuated by cliffs so pretty that they grace about half of the country's tourist literature. The river crossing is generally OK for regular cars, but ask ahead in the rainy season.

Parque Maritimo El Coco (☎ 892 0124; www .playaelcoco.com.ni; bungalows US$50-400; P ⊠ 🖵), right on the water, is a great, laid-back luxury option that's fairly affordable if you're in a big group. Several different-sized and priced houses have kitchens, separate bedrooms, little porches with hammocks – the works. Prices drop for long-term stays, and go through the roof at Christmas and Semana Santa. It also rents bikes, organizes tours, sells condos, offers on-site Internet and has good food at the attractive beachfront restaurant, Puesto del Sol (meals US$2 to US$10).

Across the road and up the hill, **Casa Canada** (☎ 877 9590; billhayes46@hotmail.com; s/d US$10/15) serves excellent pizza and ceviche with a great view, and the two simple rooms come with a complimentary boogieboard.

Just south is a free, unofficial campsite long used by turtle-egg poachers. It's best to be polite, as the poachers have machetes.

Refugio de Vida Silvestre La Flor

One of the principal laying grounds for endangered Olive Ridley and leatherback turtles, La Flor Wildlife Refuge, managed by **Fundación Cocibolca** (☎ 277 1681, 458 2514; fcdeje@ibw.com.ni; adult/child US$12/6, camping per tent US$30), is 20km south of San Juan del Sur by a rough road; pay your entrance fee at the farmhouse. It's easy to visit on a **guided tour** (per person US$12) from San Juan del Sur, or you can stay in the attractive campsite for a whopping US$30 per tent – bring the biggest tent you've got. Park guards sell water and soft drinks, but there's no food or insect repellent, so come prepared.

Turtles lay their eggs here, usually between 9pm and 2am, between July and

January, peaking in September and October. Leatherbacks usually arrive solo, but Olive Ridleys generally come in flotillas or *arribadas*, when more than 3000 of them pack the beaches at a time. Some people time these arrivals by moon cycles, but no one really knows for sure until the ladies arrive; call the ranger station if you want to be sure.

Until recently, beaches just north of the reserve were packed with black plastic tents, where turtle-egg poachers collected their hauls unmolested. In October 2005, all that changed. Earlier that year, a long-standing federal law that set aside 10% of turtle eggs for human consumption was overturned. Finally able to enforce turtle conservation initiatives, Marena sent in some 25 eco-cops to patrol the reserve, with the navy standing by offshore. Dozens of poachers were caught and informed that their eggs were no longer part of the legal 10%, and more than 30,000 nests survived to hatching.

When there aren't any turtles around, the park still has an attractive, undeveloped beach and a few short trails; there's a decent beach break (right and left) at the north end. It's off-limits during turtle season.

El Ostional

This fishing village, practically a stone's throw from the Costa Rican border, has an attractive beach with a well-known point break called 'Los Senos' (the Breasts), that's best at midtide with decent-sized swells. The area is evidently being eyed by several luxury hotels, but in the meantime you can arrange accommodations with a home-grown, community-based ecotourism initiative, **Coop Genaro Pizarro Community Tours** (☎ 883 6753; s/d US$14/27). It also offers a variety of tours, including visits to La Flor and small, indigenous fishing communities, as well as guided hikes and horseback rides.

Buses leave from the parque central to Rivas (US$2.50, two to three hours) at 5am, 7:30am and noon.

LEÓN & NORTHWESTERN NICARAGUA

Steamy, volcanic and intellectual, the northwest is home to Nicaragua's best museums, oldest universities and finest churches, including the grandest cathedral in Central America (not to mention the refinery of one of the world's best rums).

Even better, if you've ever wondered what two tectonic plates smashing together looks like in real time, the Cordillera de los Maribios is this region's smoking backbone: some 60 unbroken kilometers of undulating lava and ash, from the red and black sands of Volcán Momotombo to smoking San Cristóbal's smooth, gray cone. The cordillera rises from the sweaty plains to cool crater lakes, delicious hot springs and more than a dozen peaks, five of which have erupted in the last century, and all of which can be climbed.

Bounded by more than 150km of shoreline – sandy beaches with solid surfing, to lush mangrove wetlands – and peppered with colonial towns, indigenous villages and archaeological sites, Nicaragua's northwest is one of the most accessible undiscovered treasures you'll ever find.

Climate & Geography

This is the hottest part of the country, with daytime temperatures in the low 30°Cs almost year-round, spiking in sweltering April and dipping into the relative cool mid-20°Cs in December. The Llano Nagrandana (Nagrandana Plains), which stretch from Nagarote to the Cosigüina Peninsula, are carpeted in dry subtropical forest that loses its leaves during the long November-to-May dry season, revealing the uncompromising geology beneath.

This is one of the most volcanic regions on earth, and if you look on any map (or, better, the 'flying' function on Google Earth), you'll appreciate how the steaming 60km Maribios Chain marks a great crack in the planet's crust. Volcán Cosigüina, separated by 50 relatively flat kilometers from the group, is not considered part of the chain. Its most recent eruption in 1835, which had residents believing it was Judgment Day, hurled the striking Farallones de Cosigüina, some of the oddest islets you'll ever see, into the great brown Golfo de Fonseca.

Getting There & Around

This region is relatively untouristed, despite its wealth of attractions, because it's separated from the tourist-packed Granada zone by big, bad Managua.

BORDER CROSSING: TO SAN JOSÉ, COSTA RICA

If you've booked an international bus from Rivas or Managua, the border crossing between Sipoá, Nicaragua, and Peñas Blancas, Costa Rica, will be a snap, as they do everything but hold your hand. Make reservations in advance during the high season. It's often cheaper and more convenient, however, to take local buses and cross on your own.

The 1km-long, enclosed border is fairly simple, although the sudden (and strategic) crush of 'helpers' can be intimidating. Pedicabs (US$1) not only roll you through, they also protect you from the masses. Banks on either side exchange local currency for US dollars, while moneychangers (called *coyotes* for a reason) exchange all three currencies freely, but may try to rip you off; look for folks wearing identification badges. Exchange as little money as possible here, know about how much you're supposed to get back, and note that 1000-córdoba bills from the Sandinista administration are out of circulation and worthless.

On the Nicaraguan side, get your passport stamped at a window in the large, poorly marked cement building just east of the main road. It costs US$7 to enter Nicaragua, US$2 to exit, payable in córdobas. The Municipality of Sipoá charges US$1 extra to enter or exit the border zone. There are three duty-free shops on the Nicaraguan side, but no restaurant or bathroom.

Leaving or entering Costa Rica is free. Immigration has a good restaurant, clean restrooms and a bank with an ATM. Everyone entering Costa Rica technically needs a ticket leaving the country, which is rarely asked for. If it's your unlucky day, Dendu Transport and Transnica, both located right outside, sell US$10 tickets from San José to Managua.

Sipoá has no real lodging, other than a few dodgy unsigned guesthouses, and Peñas Blancas has none at all, so don't plan on spending the night. Although the border is open 24 hours, buses only run between 6am and 6pm, after which taxis triple their fares.

Buses from Sipoá run at least hourly to Rivas (one hour, US$10) between 6am and 5:30pm, where you can make connections throughout Nicaragua. *Taxistas* (taxi drivers) may tell you Nicaraguan buses aren't running, or are unsafe, but they are lying.

Transnica runs buses from Peñas Blancas to San José (five hours, US$8) at 5:15am, 7:30am, 9am (direct), 10:45am, noon, 1:30pm, 3:30pm and 6pm. Pulmitan de Liberia goes to Liberia (two hours, US$2) at 6:30am, 8:30am, 9:30am, 12:30pm, 2:30pm and 5:30pm.

It's always faster and easier to take a taxi, which may be prohibitively expensive on the Costa Rican side (US$45 to Liberia), but much more reasonable from Sipoá to Rivas (US$10), San Jorge (US$12), San Juan del Sur (US$15) and Granada (US$40). Find other tourists to share your taxi while you are still inside the border zone, and bargain hard.

Fear not! Take any minibus from asaya or Granada to Managua's Universidad Centro America (UCA) bus lot, where you can catch another minivan for the short, sweet trip to León. Or take a regular bus to Managua, then grab a cab to Mercado Israel Lewites, where buses and minivans leave regularly for León, less frequently for Chinandega.

Both León (92km from Managua) and Chinandega (37km north of León) are transportation hubs. Buses to more remote beaches and volcanoes can be inconvenient, with perhaps only one bus a day.

You can rent cars in both León and Chinandega; hire a 4WD in rainy season, if you plan to do much exploring. The roads of the Cosigüina Peninsula are some of the country's worst, and beach access can be a muddy mess by October.

LEÓN
pop 182,000 / elevation 110m

Refined, intense and politically progressive, León would be mildly offended if you referred to it as 'Nicaragua's second city.' Formally known as Santiago de León de los Caballeros, the country's original capital was founded by Francisco Fernández de Córdoba on June 15, 1524 – almost two months after arch-rival Granada, which has never let León forget it, and 242 years before the (ahem) quaint little fishing village of Managua was handed the prize.

León remains what many frustrated isitors are looking for in the capital: cultural center with mind-blowing churches, thriving universities, fabulous art collections and historic sites. Its thick-walled colonial architecture has yet to receive the

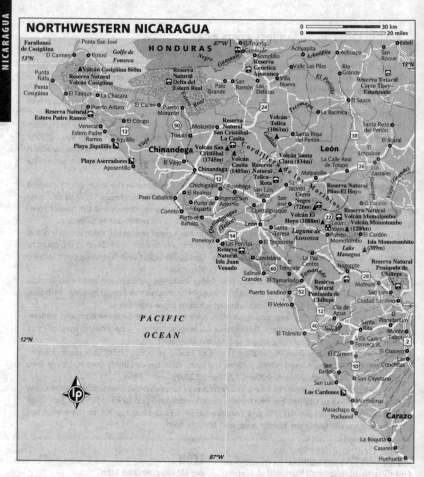

NORTHWESTERN NICARAGUA

makeover Granada is currently enjoying (there are still bullet holes leftover from the 1970s), but this is actually the more authentically Spanish city, having been burned to the ground only a fraction of the times of its oft-sacked southern adversary.

Originally located on the slopes of Volcán Momotombo, León committed some of the Spanish conquest's cruelest excesses; even other conquistadors suggested that León's punishment was divine retribution. When the mighty volcano reduced León (see the boxed text, p175) to rubble in 1610, the city was moved, saint by saint, here, next to the existing indigenous capital of Subtiava.

The reprisals did not end there. Eager to win the civil war with Granada, which had, since independence, been contesting the colonial capital's continuing leadership role, in 1853 León invited US mercenary William Walker (see the boxed text, p55) to the fight. After the Tennessean declared himself president (and Nicaragua a US slave state), he was executed; the nation's capital was moved to Managua, and Granada's conservatives ran the country for the next three decades.

Finally, in 1956, Anastasio Somoza García (the original dictator) was assassinated in León by Rigoberto López, a poet in waiter's clothing. The ruling family never forgot, and when the revolution came, their wrath fell on this city in a hail of bullets and bombs whose scars have still not been erased.

León has remained proudly Liberal, even a bit aloof, through it all, a Sandinista stronghold and political power player that has never once doubted its grand destiny. To hear what this sort of self-confidence sounds like set to a tune, ask any troupe of mariachis to play the city's theme song, *'Viva León Jodido'* (the word *jodido* has a PG rating in Nicaragua), then climb on top of Central America's largest cathedral and contemplate anew this most volcanic of views.

Orientation

León actually has a system of clearly signed and logically numbered *calles* (streets) and *avenidas* (avenues), allowing anyone to pinpoint any address. Unfortunately, no one actually uses it, preferring the old reliable '2½ blocks east of the Shell station' method instead.

Just for kicks, this is how it works: Av Central and Calle Central Rubén Darío intersect at the northeast corner of the parque central (central park), forming the city's northeast, northwest, southeast and southwest quadrants. Calles running parallel to Rubén Darío are numbered NE (Calle 1 NE, Calle 2 NE) north of the cathedral, SE to the south. Av 1 SO (*suroeste*, or 'southwest'), one block from Av Central, forms the park's western boundary, paralleling Av 2 SO, and so on.

Calle Central Rubén Darío is the city's backbone, and runs east from the cathedral to striking Iglesia El Calvaro, and west almost 1km to Barrio Subtiava, continuing another 20km to the Pacific. The majority of tourist services are within a few blocks of the cathedral, with another cluster of museums and churches in Barrio Subtiava.

Information

BOOKSTORES & LIBRARIES

Libraría Don Quijote (Calle Central Rubén Darío; 8:30am-6pm Mon-Sat, 9am-1pm Sun) Load up on lefty texts or dog-eared paperbacks (some in English, German and French) at this quaint used bookstore.

CULTURAL CENTERS

Casa Cultural de Subtiava (Iglesia San Juan Bautista 2c norte; 8am-noon & 2-5pm Mon-Fri) Look for the faded mural at the headquarters for area indigenous communities and home to Museo Adiáct, in Subtiava.

La Casa de Cultura (☎ 311 2116; Iglesia Merced 2c oeste; Mon-Fri) Come by for the inexpensive restaurant, open 8am to noon, and stay for the art collection, or perhaps sign up for Latin dance classes.

EMERGENCY

Ambulance (Cruz Roja; Red Cross; ☎ 311 2627)
Fire Station (☎ 311 2323)
Police (☎ 311 3137)

INTERNET ACCESS & RESOURCES

Fever Nov@ (per hr US$1) Fairly expensive, but faster than others.
León Online (www.leononline.net) Useful Spanish-language portal to all things Leónese, including hotels and attractions.

LAUNDRY

Clean Express Lavandería (cnr Av Central & Calle 4 NE; 7am-7pm) Do-it-yourself machines wash (US$2) and dry (US$1.25 per 20 minutes) your clothes, or pay a little extra to have it done for you.

MEDIA

In addition to the free, bilingual *León & Chinandega Visitors Guide* available from Intur, which has a good León city map, Spanish-language *ServiGuia de León* (US$1) is a bimonthly tourist magazine worth a look; old issues are probably stacked in a corner of your hotel.

MEDICAL SERVICES

Clínica de Terápias Naturales y Orientales (9am-3pm Mon-Fri) Offers natural remedies, acupuncture, reflex therapy and a US$3, 45-minute massage.
Hospital San Vicente (☎ 311 6990) Out past the bus station, the region's largest hospital is a 1918 neoclassical beauty that attracts architecture buffs as well as sick tourists.

MONEY

Several banks have ATMs that accept Visa/Plus debit cards.
Banco America Central (BAC) Next to La Unión supermarket, has 24-hour ATMs also on the Master Card/Cirrus system, and gives either US dollars or córdobas.

POST & TELEPHONE

FedEx (☎ 311 2426) Inside the Western Union.
Llamadas Internacionales (Calle Central; 8am-9:30pm) Just one of several spots with ultra-cheap calls to the USA and Canada (US$0.06 per minute), Europe (under US$0.15 per minute) and elsewhere.

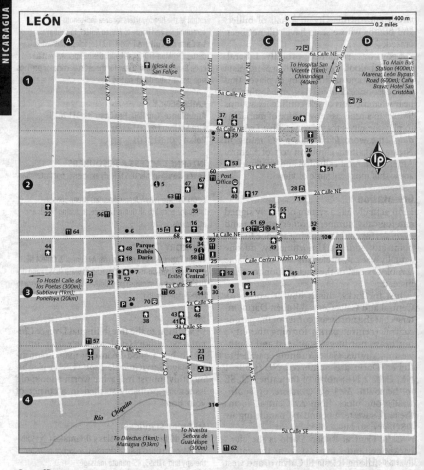

LEÓN

Post office (1a Av NE) Opposite the Iglesia de La Recolección.

TOURIST INFORMATION

Intur (☎ 311 3382; leon@intur.gob.ni; 2a Av NO; ☺ 8am-12:30pm & 2-5pm Mon-Fri) Helpful and knowledgeable staff have lots of flyers, a great free city guide, and a cutesy, distorted city map (US$2); they can recommend hotels and services.

Marena (Ministry of the Environment and Natural Resources; ☎ 311 3776; mareleon@ibw.com) Inconveniently across from the Shell station at the southern entrance to the León bypass road, it administers three volcanic national reserves: Telica-Rota, Pilas–El Hoyo and Momotombo; and nonvolcanic Isla Juan Venado. It offers general information, but your best bet for guides is going directly to the Isla Juan Venado ranger station in Las

Peñitas (see p174), or one of the private tour companies for the volcanoes.

Oficina de Información Turística León (☎ 311 3528; Av Central; ☺ 8:30am-noon & 2-6pm Mon-Fri, 9am-5pm Sat & Sun) Operated by UNAN tourism students, it has more information, better maps (Stadtsplan; US$2) and can book reservations at hotels, Ticabus and other businesses, arrange city tours (US$15 per group) and find guides for almost any other adventure.

UNIVERSITIES

In 1999, León was officially declared Nicaragua's 'University City.' It has three major and several minor universities, which explains the hot nightlife; note that students are on vacation in July, December and January.

Universidad Cristiana Autónima de Nicaragua (UCAN; www.ucan.edu.ni) Pricey private school offers degrees in law, international relations and tourism (oddly enough, one of the most expensive degrees to get at any university in Nicaragua). **Universidad de Ciencias Comerciales** (UCC; www.ucc .edu.ni) Architecture, engineering and interior design, plus tourism-related degrees.
Universidad Nacional Autónoma de Nicaragua (UNAN; www.unanleon.edu.ni; continguo Iglesia de la Merced) Nicaragua's first and most important university was founded in 1812, and today has six separate León schools with more than 6000 students; the main campus is considered one of the city's loveliest collection of buildings.

Sights & Activities

León is the most culturally rich of Nicaragua's cities; architecture and museum buffs will want to spend a few days exploring.

LEÓN WALKING TOUR

Begin at the recently refurbished **parque central**, a fine place for people-watching, purchasing a souvenir Sandino T-shirt and enjoying that most Leónese of treats, *raspados,* where small wooden carts open

to reveal a block of ice, which is shaved (with a rasp) into a cup, then topped with your choice of sticky fruit syrups.

Enjoy your treat in front of the eternal (more or less) flame at the **Mausoleo de los Héroes y Mártires** (p167), on the north side of the park, where a phenomenal and heartbreaking mural traces Nicaraguan history from the Spanish conquest to the most recent revolution, complete with smoking volcanoes. If you lose your appetite, street children back at the plaza will take any remaining *raspado* off your hands.

Dominating the plaza is **Basílica de la Asunción** (p165), Central America's largest cathedral; take your **rooftop tour** early for the clearest views of the Volcáns Maribios. Most of the thick-walled old adobe homes you're surveying were originally topped with wooden roofs and coated in *tapial,* a colored adobe that once gave León its signature hues. These Leónese-style homes are called **casas pinariegas**; as you stroll through town, look for ceramic plaques noting those with historical significance.

On the south side of the cathedral, the 1679 **Colegio La Asunción**, the first theological college in Nicaragua, was partially destroyed by fire in 1935 and rebuilt in its current Gothic style. Next door is **Palacio Episcopal** (Bishop's Palace), designed by Marcelo Targa and one of the first buildings to display Leónese neoclassical architecture. In this same group of buildings, **Archivo Histórico Dicesano de León** has documents dating back to 1674.

Continuing on around the cathedral, 1680 **Colegio de San Ramón** educated revolutionary hero Miguel Larreynaga, who drafted the first Central American constitution. It was rebuilt in 1752, and housed the Universidad Autónoma, Nicaragua's first university. Though it's been a high school since 1945, paintings of all León's bishops are still on display. Around the corner, two-story, adobe **Casa Salud Debayle** was originally constructed in 1814 as a bank, then became the first private health clinic in Central America.

Head west on 2a Calle SE one block, then south two blocks on Av Central to visit **La XXI** (pronounced 'la ventay uno'), an old military garrison that's today home to the truly fabulous **Museo de Leyendas y Mitos** (p167); check out the mosaic tilework at the entrance. Across the street are the photogenic **Ruinas San Sebastián**; the church was bombed almost into oblivion in 1979.

Backtrack through clean and pleasant **Mercado Central** then make a right on Calle Central Rubén Darío to the early-18th-century **Iglesia El Calvario** (p166), famed for its comic-book-style facade. Close by, the **Antiguo Reformatorio de Menores** (Old Reform School) is a rare, almost all original *casa pinariega*–style building. The squat adobe has *tejas* (ceramic half-pipe ceiling tiles), plus classic corner double doors, a clever architectural trick that allows owners to adjust sunlight throughout the day without letting in too much heat.

Make another right on Av 3 NE, stopping to see if the **Museo Entomológico** (p167) is open to the public yet. Then it's on to somewhat scruffy 1625 **Iglesia de San Juan**, rebuilt in 1860 in the modernist neoclassical style. Close by is Mercado San Juan and the **old train station**, constructed in 1882 with austere lines and simple, utilitarian design.

Backtrack two blocks to 2a Calle NE and make a right for unmissable 1786 **Iglesia de La Recolección** (p166), the ornate, ultra-baroque masterpiece one critic called 'the most important monument to passion in Nicaragua,' which is saying something.

Two blocks west on 2a Calle NE is the flagship campus of UNAN, with several beautiful buildings, and a collection of cheap restaurants and festive bars that form the heart of the student scene. **La Esquina El Movimiento** (p172) has espresso beverages if you're losing steam, and interesting *artesanías* (handicrafts) if you're not.

Make a left on Av 1 NO for the 1615 **Iglesia de La Merced** (p166), another of León's signature churches, then west on 1a Calle NE to the **Galería de Héroes y Mártires** (p167), with photos of the revolution's fallen. Continue south, stopping into **La Casa de Cultura**, with its excellent art collection (including a portrait of former US President Ronald Reagan that you'll want to photograph), then make a left on Av 3 NO.

Tired? Fortify yourself at **Hotel El Convento** (p171), with an amazing collection of colonial-era religious art and good, if pricey, restaurant. Attached **Iglesia San Francisco** was badly damaged during the revolution, but will soon be restored to its former glory.

Allow at least two hours to appreciate the best art museum in Central America, **Museo de Arte Fundación Ortiz-Guardián** (p167), then head two blocks south and one block east to see if anything's on later that night at 1885 **Teatro Municipal José de la Cruz Mena** (p173). Finally, backtrack to Calle Central Rubén Darío for the poet's home and national museum, **Museo-Archivo Rubén Darío** (p166), the city's pride and joy.

Walk (or take a taxi) 1km to Barrio Subtiava (p168) to see the hodgepodge of archaeological treasures at **Museo Adiáct**, then check if the ruins of **Iglesia Santiago**, around the corner, are open. Close by is León's other 'cathedral,' **Iglesia San Juan Bautista**, heart of indigenous Barrio Subtiava – check out the not-especially-Catholic sun god emblazoned on the roof. Next door is the 1544 **Museo de Arte Sacro**, rebuilt in 1752, that's home to a small but impressive collection of colonial-era religious masterpieces.

From here, walkers could take the 2.5km hike south to **El Fortín de Acososco** (not recommended if you have valuables on you), catch a bus to **Playa Poneloya**, or just head back to León proper for a well-deserved nap.

CATHEDRAL

Formally known as the **Basílica de la Asunción**, León's cathedral is the largest in Central America, its expansive design famously, and perhaps apocryphally, approved for construction in much more important Lima, Peru. Leónese leaders originally submitted a more modest but bogus set of plans, and then architect Diego José de Porres Esquivel, the Capitan General of Guatemala (also responsible for San Juan Bautista de Subtiava, La Recolección and La Merced churches, among others), pulled the switcheroo and built this beauty right here.

This is the cathedral's fourth incarnation. The 1610 original was replaced in 1624 with a wood and adobe structure that pirate William Dampier burned to the ground in 1685. Another adobe was used until work began on this enormous 'Antigüeño,' Central American baroque-style masterpiece in 1747. Construction, done primarily by indigenous laborers from Subtiava and Posoltega, went on for more than a hundred years.

The cathedral is a sort of pantheon of Nicaraguan culture. The tomb of Rubén Darío, León's favorite son, is on one side of the altar, guarded by a sorrowful lion and the inscription, 'Nicaragua is created of vigor and glory, Nicaragua is made for freedom.' Nearby rest the tombs of lesser-known Leónese poets Alfonso Cortés and Salomón de la Selva, as well as Miguel Larreynaga.

THE CHURCHES OF NICARAGUA

Nicaragua hasn't always been this poor – in the 1960s Costa Ricans were sneaking across the border to work here. From the first days of the Spanish conquest through the late 1800s, when Nicaragua controlled the only warm-water route between the world's two great oceans, this little country was a major power broker.

With cash to spare and a Catholic population to impress, this country has churches even devout atheists will enjoy. León may be the nation's pinnacle of religious architecture, but here are a few other must-sees:

- Cathedrals of Managua (p74): The poignant, burnt-out husk of Managua's original cathedral is off-limits, but you're welcome to ponder the new cathedral's ultramodern domes: cooling towers for a divine nuclear reactor? Homage to Islam? Eggs hatching into a peaceful tomorrow?

- Basílica de Nuestra Señora de la Inmaculada Concepción (p184): Even Pope John Paul II visited the beautiful Virgen del Trono, patron saint of Nicaragua and mistress of La Gritería, the nation's most important religious event.

- El Templo de El Sauce (p179): Quite literally a pilgrimage-worthy destination, every January thousands come to see El Señor de Esquipulas, the Black Christ.

- Moravian Church in Bluefields (p250): Faithfully rebuilt to its Victorian-era specs after Bluefields' utter destruction during Hurricane Juana, it's not just lovely, it's a symbol of hope and perseverance.

- Iglesia Catedral San Pedro (p207): This baroque 1874 beauty, known for its twin bell towers, remains one of the country's most elegant churches despite a desperate need for renovation.

- Templo Parroquial de San Rafael Arcángel (p221): This is religion as sensory overload, with beautiful architecture and truly amazing murals by Australian John Fuchs Holl.

- Nuestra Señora de Solentiname (p268): Ernesto Cardenal and the Solentiname community built this heartfelt and humble adobe church, its murals designed by children.

- Iglesia San Francisco (p116): This 1529 convent's soaring blueberry facade is one of Granada's definitive buildings.

Among the magnificent works of art within are the Stations of the Cross by Antonio Sarria, considered masterpieces, and El Cristo Negro de Pedrarias, possibly the oldest Catholic image in the Americas, brought here in 1528. Marble statues inside are beautifully crafted, most notably the elaborate Inmaculada Concepción de María. The interior is also noted for the strategic skylights, ingeniously oriented to catch sun throughout the day, then sent reverberating across the white marble interior.

If it's clear, take the **roof tour** (admission US$0.70; 8am-noon & 2-4pm Mon-Sat), with a spectacular view of the city and smoking volcanoes beyond.

IGLESIA DE LA RECOLECCIÓN

Three blocks north of the cathedral, the 1786 **Iglesia de La Recolección** (1a Av NE) is considered the city's most beautiful church, a Mexican-style baroque confection of swirling columns and bas-relief medallions that portray the life of Christ. Dyed a deep yellow accented with cream and age, the lavishly decorated facade may be what makes the cover of all the tourist brochures, but be sure to stop inside and admire the slender mahogany columns and ceiling decorated with harvest motifs.

IGLESIA DE LA MERCED

Home to León's patron saint, **La Virgen de La Merced**, this less immediately enchanting gray edifice (albeit with a glittering and ornate interior) is considered the city's second-most important church. The image, originally from Barcelona, was brought to León's original church (see the boxed text, p175) in 1528. After Volcán Momotombo erupted and forced the city's evacuation, the Leónese built a new church here in 1615, replaced with the current building in the early 1700s. The virgin's feast day, September 24, is one of León's biggest religious bashes.

IGLESIA DULCE NOMBRE DE JESÚS EL CALVARIO

A hodgepodge of neoclassical and baroque styles, 18th-century **El Calvario** stands at the top of Calle Central. The interior is nice, with predictably gory, full-sized statues of Jesus and the thieves being crucified, but you're here for the brightly painted facade

between the red-brick bell towers, with brightly colored bas-relief biblical scenes that resemble comic-strip panels.

OTHER CHURCHES

With more than 16 places to pray, including several more in Barrio Subtiava (p168), the city tourist board is lobbying to have León officially declared 'The City of Churches.'

The 1639 **Iglesia de San Francisco** is one of the oldest in the city, a national heritage site with lots of gold, a gorgeous nave, and rather rococo interior. It was abandoned between 1830 and 1881, then refurbished with two elaborate altarpieces for San Antonio and Our Lady of Mercy.

Nuestra Señora de Guadalupe, built in 1743, is León's only church oriented north–south, and historically connected to the city by the 1850 Puente Guadalupe, built across the Río Chiquito. And don't let the dumpy, modernist neoclassic exterior of 1625 **Iglesia San Juan de Dios** fool you – when it's open, the interior is one of the city's prettiest, with lots of precious wood and a very human scale.

Convent San Francisco, founded in 1639, was badly damaged during the 1979 Battle for León. Most of the church, which still has two of the original altars, is being renovated, but you can check out what used to be the convent at Hotel El Convento (p171).

For something completely different, swing by ultra-Gothic 1884 **Iglesia Zaragoza**, one of the best spots for film students to stage a vampire flick. They could also use one of the several ruined churches around town, including **Ruinas Veracruz** and **Iglesia Santiago** in Barrio Subtiava, and **Ruinas San Sebastian**, near La XXI.

MUSEO-ARCHIVO RUBÉN DARÍO

Of all the museums and monuments dedicated to the poet that are scattered across his doting homeland, **Museo Rubén Darío** (Calle Central; admission free; 9am-noon & 2-5pm Tue-Sat, 9am-noon Sun) seems like the one where you'd be most likely to run into his ghost. Exhibits are displayed throughout the house where he lived until he was a teenager, ranging from everyday items – more a window into well-to-do Nicaragua in the late 1800s – to handwritten manuscripts of Darío's famous works. His Bible, the bed where he died 'an agonizing death' and the fancy duds he wore as the Ambassador to Spain (as well as for his most famous portrait) are just highlights among the historic bric-a-brac.

Another poet, Alfonso Cortés, also lived here during the 1950s and 1960s; much of that time he was chained to the bed, stark raving mad, writing poetry that, while very good, would for all eternity be compared with the home's previous resident. Which would drive anyone crazy.

Other Darío monuments in the area include **Parque Rubén Darío**, with a statue of the master, but only busts of other, lesser Leónese poets, including Alfonso Cortés (1893–1969), Azarias H Pallais (1884–1954) and Salomon de la Selva (1893–1959), all accompanied by verses. Darío's final resting place is the León cathedral.

MUSEO DE ARTE FUNDACIÓN ORTIZ-GUARDIÁN
Probably the finest contemporary art museum in all of Central America, the **Ortiz-Guardián Collection** (centrodearte@hotelelconvento. com.ni; adult/student US$0.80/0.50; ☺ 10:30am-6:30pm Tue-Sat, 11am-7pm Sun) has spilled over from its original home in Casa Don Norberto Ramiréz, refurbished in 2000 to its original Creole Civil style, with Arabic tiles and impressive flagstones. It and another beautiful old home across the street are now packed with artwork; a Spanish-speaking guide costs an extra US$1.25, which is well worth it.

Begin surrounded by the luxurious realism of the Renaissance and spare beauty of the colonial period, then wander through romanticism, modernism, postmodernism and actually modern pieces by Cuban, Peruvian and other Latin American schools. Rubens, Picasso, Chagall and other big names make an appearance, but it's the work by Latin American masters – Diego Rivera, Rufino Tamayo, Fernando Botero, Roberto Matta and more – that define the collection. If you can't get enough, grab a coffee at nearby Hotel El Convento, owned by the same family, which displays many of their nicest religious pieces.

LA XXI & MUSEO DE LEYENDAS Y MITOS
León's most entertaining and eclectic museum is now housed in La XXI (the 21st Garrison), the **Museum of Myths & Legends**

(admission US$0.50; ☺ 8am-noon Tue-Sun, 2-5pm Tue-Sat). What makes this museum opposite Ruinas San Sebastián unmissable is the striking contrast of its main subjects: a quirky collection of life-size papier-mâché figures from Leónese history and legend, handmade by founder Señora Toruña (also represented in glorious papier-mâché), and murals graphically depicting methods the National Guard used to torture prisoners.

You're led from room to room, each dedicated to a different aspect of Leónese folklore, from La Gigantona – the giant woman who represents an original colonist still ridiculed by a popular ballet *folklorico* – to La Carreta Nagua (Chariot of Death), which picks up the souls of those foolish enough to cross intersections catercorner.

And between each rundown of local legends, your Spanish-speaking guide will cheerfully shift gears to describe the gory human-rights abuses – stretching on racks, beatings, water tortures etc – that took place here regularly until June 13, 1979, when Commander Dora María Téllez successfully breached Somoza's defenses and secured La XXI for the Sandinistas, releasing all prisoners. It's highly recommended.

GALERÍA DE HÉROES Y MÁRTIRES
Monuments to León's more recent history include the **Galería de Héroes y Mártires** (1a Calle NE; donation US$1; ☺ 7am-5pm Mon-Sat), run by mothers of FSLN veterans and fallen heroes. There's some signage in English and Spanish, but you're here to look into the eyes of more than 300 revolutionaries, mostly pimply faced teens with feathered disco haircuts, and wonder if you would be willing to make the ultimate sacrifice to free your country from dictatorship. A small craft shop supports the gallery.

MAUSOLEO DE LOS HÉROES Y MÁRTIRES
Another monument to the local heroes, the eternal flame of the **Mausoleum of Heroes & Martyrs** rests within a small plaza just north of the parque central, surrounded by the city's best murals.

MUSEO ENTOMOLÓGICO
Still not open to the general public at press time, biologists Jean Michel Maes and Joan Tellez have big plans to display the

largest collection of Nicaraguan insects in the world. In the meantime, you can visit the **museum** (☎ 311 6586; jammaes@ibw.com.ni; admission free) by appointment only, although you may have to root through stacks of bug trays to find your favorite insect. The specialty is *Lucanidae*, a genus of beetles where males usually display ferocious-looking pincers, but there are also heaps of butterflies and other more charismatic critters to peruse.

EL BARRIO SUBTIAVA

A regional capital long before León moved in, the barrio of Subtiava takes its name from a Chorotega tribe who still count themselves apart from León, and Nicaragua, as a whole. After refugees from León Viejo arrived in 1610, the two separate towns co-existed as equals until 1680. Flexing their rebuilt military muscle, the Spanish forced 12,000 indigenous inhabitants of Subtiava to become part of León, basically relegating them to slave labor. Tensions simmered for two generations, until a police crack-down in 1725 inspired a revolt. Although the insurrection was violently shut down by the Spaniards, Barrio Subtiava was able to remain a separate entity until 1902, when it was finally, officially, annexed to the city. The key word being 'officially.'

About 1km west of the León cathedral, the neighborhood is centered on **San Juan Bautista Subtiava** (13 Av SO), better known as 'Catedral Subtiava,' the oldest intact church in the city. Built in the 1530s and reconstructed in 1710, its relatively plain beige facade and precious wood interior is largely unadorned; even the struts are there to stabilize the structure during earthquakes. With two exceptions: spirals outside, and an extraordinary sun icon mounted to the typical arched timber roof, pay homage to deities far older than the Spanish conquest.

Far simpler, the **Ermita de San Pedro**, two blocks east and one block south of San Juan Bautista, was constructed between 1706 and 1718, and is considered one of the best examples of primitive baroque style in Nicaragua. This means that it's almost unadorned, save for three brick crosses inlaid into the adobe.

Other Subtiava churches haven't fared quite as well. **Ruinas Iglesia Santiago**, well signed one and a half blocks awawy from San Juan Bautista, was (according to local legend) cursed by *duendes* (fairies), and by the looks of it the curse worked. Enter through the corrugated tin gate and ask the family there if it's OK to cross their front yard; they may ask for a few córdoba. The architecture is still obvious – and the bell tower still standing – and makes for an interesting wander.

A few blocks west are the ruins of 16th-century **Iglesia Veracruz**, destroyed by a volcanic eruption in 1835. It remains a spiritual center, and as the indigenous counterpoint to La Gritería on December 7, people gather here for a pre-Columbian festival involving torches and the sun deity on the roof of San Juan Bautista.

Call ahead to make sure the intriguing **Museo de Arte Sacro** (☎ 311 8288; frente Iglesia San Juan Bautista; admission US$0.70; ☺ 8am-noon Mon-Sat, 2-5pm Mon-Fri) is open, as the curator and founder, Monsignor Ricardo Clemente Juárez Soza, sometimes needs to run errands during the day. You've probably noticed this neighborhood's churches are in some disrepair, a situation that inspired Juárez to preserve the region's absolutely beautiful 16th- and 17th-century religious art right here, where it would be safe. Faithfully detailed wooden saints (including one of the first Virgins of Guadalupe) to more ostentatious examples of baroque overkill, including lots of gold and silver artifacts, have been packed in the original Casa de Cultura Subtiava, built in 1544.

Museo Adiáct (admission US$0.70; ☺ 8am-noon Mon-Sat, 2-5pm Mon-Fri), around the corner, is a beautifully (if faded) muraled building that also houses the neighborhood's government; you may need to ask them to open this interesting little museum. Funeral urns, ceramic tableware, stone statues and more are on display, with very little signage or attempt at a timeline. Old copies of *La Voz de Adiáct* magazine, with news and views about the history of Barrio Subtiava, are piled on shelves toward the front.

The fine **Museo Insurreccional Luís Manuel Toruño** (Casa El Buzón; donations accepted; ☺ Sat only) was recently relocated from León proper to this smaller Subtiava Sandinista stronghold, two blocks east and one and a half blocks south of San Juan Bautista. Also called El Buzón (Big Mailbox), this building was a secret weapons depot during the revolution. Curator 'El Chanclazo' has kept the faith and displays his enormous collection of revolutionary mementos, newspaper clippings, and communist memorabilia; if it's not open, ask around.

El Tamarindón (Iglesia San Juan 3c sur, 2c oeste) is a huge tree where Adiáct, *cacique* (chief) of the Subtiava tribe during the Spanish conquest, was unceremoniously hung so his people would see him as weak. It didn't work, and today 'The Big Tamarindo' is a rallying point for indigenous locals, who placed a plaque there in 2003 that declares 'This tree was the cross of he who is our light,' and they sure as heck weren't talking about Jesus. There are a few benches underneath and a market every third Sunday in April.

It's a solid 20-minute walk or US$0.70 taxi ride to Subtiava from the León cathedral, or you can take one of the covered trucks (US$0.18) plying the streets. Catch a Subtiava-bound truck at the southwest corner of the parque central (in front of Sandinista headquarters) and yell 'Catedral Subtiava' as they haul you inside, probably while the truck is still moving. Hang on!

EL FORTÍN DE ACOSOSCO

The National Guard's last holdout in León, **El Fortín** can be reached by the 2.5km dirt road that begins on the west side of Guadalupe cemetery, on the southern border of Barrio Subtiava. The large, squat gray building was originally constructed in 1889 to take advantage of great city views. It was abandoned until the 1950s, when the Somozas realized that they needed to keep an eye on León itself. They lost the fort on July 7, 1979, and the Sandinistas still have a parade every July to celebrate.

The fortress is next to a smelly garbage dump; you'll need to ask for permission to enter. Muggings are common on this stretch, so go in a group and leave your camera and other valuables at the hotel.

Courses

Vía Vía (☎ 311 6142; www.viaviacafe.com; 2a Av NE) and **Hostel La Clínica** (☎ 311 2031; mary111994@yahoo .es; 1a Av SO) are good places to inquire about private tutors (about US$5 per hour). Vía Vía also offers salsa classes (per hour US$7).

Latin American Spanish School (☎ 311 5421; www .latinamericanspanishschool.com; parque central 2c oeste,

1c sur) In the big yellow house, this new school also offers classes, homestays and field trips, and teachers are willing to come to your hotel.

León Spanish School of Nicaragua (☎ 865 3579; jdflores28@yahoo.com; contiguo a Restaurant Cactus; class per week US$175) This school was in a temporary facility at the time of research, so call ahead. Instruction is professional, materials are available, there are lots of field trips, cultural activities and volunteer opportunities. Your weekly fee includes homestay and three meals daily. It also rents bicycles.

Tours

Volcano surfing, just so you know, involves hauling yourself to the top of steaming Cerro Negro (see p178), then riding a surfboard, mattress or cardboard box down its black gravel 50-degree slopes. Hold on!

Knowing Nicaragua (☎ 866 6814; fparajon2003@ yahoo.es, Lenin_obando@yahoo.com) Leónese operator Flavio Parajón offers tours to all places covered by other operators, plus Casitas, San Cristóbal, Laguna de Asososca and kayak tours of Reserva Natural Isla Juan Venado. Ask about surfing tours.

Quetzaltrekkers (☎ 843 7647; www.quetzaltrekkers .com; frente Iglesia El Calvario) This outstanding operator offers recommended climbing tours of the area's volcanoes, including public transportation, big meals and camping. Try Volcán Momotombo (two days, US$42 per person), Volcán Telica (two days, US$32), Volcán Cosigüina (three days, US$53), and a two-day Cerro Negro tour that takes in El Hoyo and Laguna de Asososca. There's also a monthly full moon climb (one night, US$24 per person). There's usually a two- or three-person minimum, but solo travelers can check its offices or Vía Vía on ☎ 311 6142 or www .viaviacafe.com to see what's coming up. All profits go to Las Tias, a charity that helps problem kids learn to build their own lives; volunteers are very welcome.

Sampson Expeditions (☎ 311 3306; rsampson@ibw .com.ni; Calle Central Rubén Darío) Headquartered at Hostel Calle de los Poetas, Rigo Sampson speaks fluent English and offers personalized and athletic tours of volcanoes and kayaking in Reserva Natural Isla Juan Venado (US$25). He also offers oddball trips, including a three-week 'Footprints of William Walker' tour, and can also arrange visits to Las Minas and Bosawás.

Servitour León (☎ 311 1927; hectournica@yahoo .com; catedral ½c norte) Offers city tours (US$15 per person), a Cerro Negro/Laguna de Asososca combo day trip (US$40) and several other tours, usually with a two-person minimum.

Va Pues Tours (☎ 277 4628, 611 8784; vapuestours@ hotmail.com; frente Iglesia El Calvario) In addition to volcano tours and Reserva Natural Isla Juan Venado, this tour operator, at CocinArte, offers city tours of León and treks to León Viejo and Matagalpa; it can also organize sunset barbecue parties at Poneloya, returning via El Pelón, the open-air disco bus (see p172).

Festivals & Events

Every Saturday, from early afternoon till midnight, the parque central comes alive for the *Tertulia Leonesa*, inviting everyone outside to eat, drink and dance to music played by local combos. León's annual celebrations include:

Semana Santa (late March or early April) The Leónese Semana Santa is something special, with Barrio Subtiava's colorful sawdust 'carpets,' temporary and beautiful images that the funeral procession for Jesus walks over, and a sand-castle competition in Poneloya.

Masacre del 23 Julio 1959 (July 23) One afternoon in 1959, local school children staged a demonstration against Somoza. As they chanted 'Freedom! Freedom!', the National Guard fired into the crowd, killing four students and wounding several others. Those wounded, some in wheelchairs, still lead a parade, right after every single marching band from the area has announced that their generation will not forget.

La Griteria Chiquita (August 14) This celebration began in 1947, as an erupting Cerro Negro threatened to bury the city in ashes. The volcano suddenly halted its activity after an innovative priest, Monseñor Isidro Augusto Oviedo, vowed to initiate a preliminary *griteria*, similar to December's but changing the response to *¡La asunción de María!* ('The ascension of Mary!').

Día de la Virgen de Merced (September 24) León's saint's day is solemnly observed, but the preceding day is more festive: revelers don a bull-shaped armature lined with fireworks, called the *toro encohetado*, then charge at panic-stricken onlookers as the rockets fly.

Carnaval Mitos y Leyendas (November 1) See the papier-mâché crew from the Museo de Leyendas y Mitos on a parade from the cathedral and Barrio Subtiava, for this Halloweenesque fiesta.

Día de la Purísima Concepción (December 7) Celebrated throughout the country, this celebration of Nicaragua's patron saint is the occasion for the *griteria* (shouting), enjoyed here with unusual vigor.

Sleeping

With tourism on the rise and hostels packed to overflowing, many local families are jumping on the gravy train and offering rooms in their own Spanish colonial dump…er, fixer-upper, at backpacker prices.

BUDGET

Vía Vía (☎ 311 6142; www.viaviacafe.com; 2a Av NE; dm/s/d US$3/10/12) If you're looking for back-packer central, you've found it at this hotel, complete with a book exchange, bulletin board accompanied by stacks of tourist information and updated list of Quetzal-trekkers' upcoming hikes. There's also a popular restaurant/bar (mains US$2 to US$5, open 8am to 11:30pm) with pool tables, vegetarian options, live music on Friday and karaoke on Wednesday, which light sleepers should keep in mind. Don't leave your stuff laying around in the dorm.

Big Foot Hostel (www.bigfootadventure.com; dm/ s/d US$4/7/10; Ⓟ) Right across the street, the brand-new competition has fewer beds in the dorms and cheaper private rooms, but ambience was still a work in progress. The helpful English-speaking owners serve simple food and drink, organize surfing trips to Poneloya and Las Peñitas, and also offer volcano climbs and other tours.

Hostel La Clínica (☎ 311 2031; mary111994@yahoo.es; 1a Av SO; dm US$3.75, d with/without bathroom US$6/5) The friendly, family-run La Clínica has clean rooms and a pleasant vibe. It's popular, with a good mix of travelers and long-term guests.

Hospedaje El Garage (1a Av SO; ☎ 311 4195; d with/without bathroom US$6/5) Next door to La Clínica, this spot is extremely clean and compact, and has an upstairs study loft.

Casa Ivana (☎ 311 4423; 2a Calle SE; s US$5, d US$7-9) Centrally located beside the Teatro Municipal, Casa Ivana is a little threadbare, but has a pretty interior garden, wicker rocking chairs and a photo gallery of old León. Rooms are neat and simple with overhead fans and decent bathrooms.

Casa Iguana (☎ 881 3493; cinquegrana@hotmail.com; Parque San Juan 75 varas este; s/d/tr US$10/15/20) In a huge, echoing Spanish colonial mansion, its courtyard hung with hammocks and flanked by a row of toilets and showers shared by guests staying in the enormous, slightly musty rooms, this place is perfect for large groups.

Hospedaje Colibrí (☎ 889 1891) Two blocks around the corner, the owners of Casa Iguana have a house in Poneloya and an annex, which doesn't have a cavernous common area, but does have a kitchen.

Casona Colonial (☎ 311 3178; Parque San Juan ½c abajo; s/d US$10/15; ✕) On the same row of colonial mansions near Iglesia San Juan as several pricier hotels, this architectural jewel has very attractively furnished rooms with bathroom and fan, great beds and a comfortable family-style common area, with rocking chairs and a TV. Recommended.

MIDRANGE

Hotel Colonial (☎ 311 2279; 1a Av NO; s/d without bathroom US$10/15, with bathroom US$30/35; ⓟ ⌧) Two and a half blocks north of the plaza, this fading beauty surrounds a lovely palm-lined inner courtyard with two floors of dingy but elegant wooden rooms. First-floor rooms with air-con are a bit overpriced, while the expansive upstairs cheapies, with rapidly deteriorating wooden floors, cleanish shared bathrooms and wonderful porch, seem almost nicer.

Hostel Miriam (☎ 311 0870; Museo Rubén Darío 1c oeste, ½c norte; s/d without bathroom US$15/20, with bathroom & air-con US$25/30; ⌧) Quite possibly the cleanest hotel in León, this spot has small, neat rooms and a colorful common area with a fully stocked kitchen and great security.

Calle de los Poetas (☎ 311 3306; rsampson@ibw .com.ni) On Calle Central Rubén Darío, two blocks west of Museo Rubén Darío, this popular property offers spacious rooms surrounding attractive gardens; make reservations in advance.

Hotel San Juan de León (☎ 311 0547; www .hsanjuandeleon.com; frente Iglesia San Juan; tr with fan/ air-con incl breakfast US$30/40; ⓟ ⌧ ⌨) This tidy Spanish colonial gem has lovely common areas with interesting murals and other art, wireless Internet (also machines on-site) and a kitchen you can use, but rooms are only comfortable, not spectacular.

Posada del Doctor (☎ 311 4343; www .laposadadeldoctor.com; Parque San Juan ½c oeste; s with fan US$25, d with fan/air-con incl breakfast US$30/40; ⓟ ⌧ ⌨) Close by and under the same ownership, this colonial mansion also has a kitchen and wireless Internet, but is even nicer, with a manicured courtyard and bigger, more nicely furnished rooms.

Hotel Los Balcones (☎ 311 0250; www .hotelbalcones.com; esquina de los bancos 1c este; r US$40-55; ⌧) This fairly luxurious property inhabits a Spanish colonial mansion furnished with attractive antiques and lots of old religious art. Rooms are small, but the ones upstairs (well worth the higher price) are great, with gleaming wooden floors and the promised balconies.

La Casa Leonesa (☎ 311 0551; www.lacasaleonesa .com; Catedral 3c norte, 15 varas este; s/d US$35/45, ste US$55, incl breakfast; ⌧ ⌨ ⌦) Colonial Leónese luxury with a bit more attention to detail, this attractive old home's 10 converted rooms have patterned tiles, high ceilings and religious-themed art, plus air-con and a small pool in the central gardens.

TOP END

San Cristóbal (☎ 311 1606; www.sancristobalhotel .com; s/d US$40/50, ste US$55; ⓟ ⌧ ⌨ ⌦) Away from it all on the bypass road (but close to several good restaurants), this attractive property has clean, modern rooms, a popular Italian restaurant, and a to-die-for pool surrounded by thatch-roofed *rancheros* where you can enjoy a cold beer.

Hotel Austria (☎ 311 1206; www.hotelaustria .ni; catedral 1c sur, ½ abajo; s/d/tr r US$36/50/59, s/d/tr ste US$45/59/70, incl breakfast; ⓟ ⌧ ⌨) The most convenient place to stay in town, modern and comfortable with all the amenities – cable TV, hot-water bathroom, phones and air-con. Suites have kitchenettes and come with a full breakfast. German is spoken.

Hotel El Convento (☎ 311 7053; www .hotelelconvento.com.ni; continuo Iglesia San Francisco; s/d/ ste incl breakfast US$69/87/111; ⓟ ⌧ ⌨) Not just the best hotel in León, but one of the best in the country, this architectural dream surrounds impressive, almost English gardens with spacious rooms replete with amenities; the suites are much nicer, with huge windows. You're surrounded by precious paintings and carvings (the owners also operate Museo de Arte Fundación Ortiz-Guardián), some of it among the finest colonial religious art you're ever likely to see. The fancy on-site restaurant, El Victoriano (mains US$4 to US$12, open 11am to 11pm), is predictably pricey, but may be worth a cappuccino just so you have an excuse to check this place out.

Eating

The best place to eat on the cheap or buy fresh veggies is the beautiful, clean **central market** (⏱ 6am-5pm), with several inexpensive eateries serving *comida corriente* (a mixed plate of different foods typical of the region) made from whatever's fresh that day. After-hours, two of the best *fritangas* (sidewalk barbecues) in town set up right outside, on the corner closest to the cathedral, where you can enjoy a huge meal for around US$2.

RESTAURANTS

CocinArte (frente Iglesia Laborío; mains US$2-4; ⏰ 11am-10pm) Worth the trek across a pretty part of town, particularly for falafel lovers, this wonderful spot has traditional Nica food, real coffee, plus all sorts of vegetarian options, good juices and a beautiful wooden table with an oversized, built-in chessboard. Try the spinach empanadas for a treat.

El Sesteo (Calle Central; dishes US$3-5; ⏰ 11am-10pm) A León institution, you can't beat the location (although you can beat the prices) of this pleasant plaza-side café, with spectacular people-watching, fresh-brewed espresso beverages, a very full bar and a long menu of carefully prepared Nica classics.

Italian Pizza y Comida Lebanesa (pizza US$5-7, Lebanese dishes US$7-10) Half a block north of the cathedral, this Lebanese-owned restaurant makes good pizza, but travelers aching for quality Middle Eastern grub (vegetarians take note) will be stoked on the great hummus and babaghanoush.

Mediterraneo Ristorante Pizzeria (☎ 882 4924; Iglesia Guadalupe ½c norte; meals US$5-10; ⏰ 3pm-late) Consider making reservations at this more authentic Italian restaurant, with an attractive outdoor dining area and live music on weekends, including bands from all over the country.

Casa Vieja (3a Av NO; meals from US$5; ⏰ 4-11pm) *Churrasco* (grilled meat) is the specialty at this romantic old bohemian haunt, where the fine bar and candlelit ambience attracts an eclectic mix of people.

Taquezal (2a Av SO; dishes US$3-6; ⏰ 4pm-late) Opposite the Teatro Municipal, many people think this relaxed restaurant/bar has the best food in town, with signature salads, Mexican specialties and the 'Taquezal cocktail,' which involves whisky, vodka, coffee liquor and orange. Drink specials on Monday and Tuesday nights guarantee a crowd.

Los Pescaditos (Iglesia San Juan Bautista 1c Sur, 1½ oeste) This Subtiava landmark, close to the Poneloya buses, may look like a modest, unassuming, moderately priced seafood restaurant, but it's famous throughout the country as the best place to eat in León.

CAFÉS & QUICK EATS

Plaza Siglo Nuevo (⏰ 11am-midnight; dishes US$1-5) This strip-mall-style eatery is home to Tip Top, with fast chicken, and Eskimo, with ice cream and burgers.

Hollywood Pizza (☎ 311 0636; slice US$1, pie US$4-6) Eat in at Plaza Siglo Nuevo, or have delivered for a US$0.70 fee.

La Esquina El Movimiento (buffet US$2-3; ⏰ 7am-10pm) Run by a youth collective, this interesting shop has *artesanías* on sale out front, plus a decent steam-table buffet at mealtimes, and an espresso machine, which your server may or may not feel like bothering with.

Puerto Cafe Benjamín Linder (1a Av NO & 2a Calle; comidas corrientes US$1; ⏰ 10am-11pm Mon-Sat) This lively, breezy café serves decent coffee, *comida corriente* and cold drinks. A large indoor mural depicts the life of Ben Linder, an American volunteer who built small hydroelectric dams and entertained children on his unicycle – until the Contras gunned him down in 1987.

GROCERIES

Supermercado Salman (1a Calle NE) Just west of La Casa de Cultura, Salman is half grocery store, half superstore, with everything you need and lots you don't, plus the cheapest cup of (Presto) coffee in town – US$0.12!

La Unión Supermercado (1a Calle NE) The best supermarket in town, this place has more gringo brands than anywhere else in the Pacific Northwest.

Panadería El León Dorado (⏰ 6:30am-1pm & 1:30-6pm) Delivering delicious starches since 1958, this well-known bakery sells great sweet stuff plus sandwiches and other savory goodies as well.

Drinking

Even more so than Granada, León is a party town, thanks to all those university students, plus it's much easier and safer to bar-hop here than in Managua.

El Bus Pelón (US$0.50; ⏰ 6pm-late) Follow the thumping disco beat to find 'The Bald Bus,' its classic Bluebird styling enhanced by having the entire roof torched right off, all the better to share its impressive sound system with the people. Adult beverages are also available. You can catch it at the parque central, or as it runs around the city until the wee hours.

Don Señor (☎ 311 1212; 1a Calle NO; cover US$1-3) One block north of the plaza, this place is more than just a hot nightspot – it's three.

There's a disco upstairs, a relaxed bar (with dance floor) downstairs, and the restaurant pub El Alamo around the corner. It's open till 4am.

Payitas Bar & Cafetín (1a Calle NO) Catercorner from Don Señor, this after-hours drinking spot is a landmark and tradition, and has a terrace with a view. Fried food that may be several days old is also available.

Disco Bohemio (6pm-late Wed-Sun) Almost always packed, this hot spot, close to Don Señor, is popular with locals and tourists alike. Nearby, Salon Estrella may be an Old West–themed casino, complete with staff in ten-gallon hats, but mosey on past the slot machines to the popular bar in the back.

Caña Brava (Pista de Circunvalación León; cover US$3-10) Out on the ring road toward Chinandega, this elegant spot claims to have the best steak in town, and the 'filete bravo,' in chili sauce, may convince you. There's live music and dancing on the weekends, and outdoor seating if that's a bit much for you.

El Matchico (catedral 2½c norte; admission free; 8pm-2am) A comfortable, relaxed spot to get your drink on, with a 'What if the Aztecs discovered Europe first?' theme. Jazz music, sometimes live, and French *bocas* keep things interesting.

Dilectus (311 5439; cover US$2) The fanciest spot to see and be seen, this place has expensive drinks, a killer dance floor, mariachi Thursdays and sometimes celebrity DJs and/or live music.

Entertainment

Teatro Municipal José de la Cruz Mena (2a Av SO) Check the board in front of this attractive 1885 theater to see what's on during your visit. It's been impressively restored, and for less than US$2 you may be able to catch anything from Salvadoran rock groups to art films to the national ballet on the very accessible stage. Hey, 14-year-old Rubén Darío did his first poetry here; who knows what sort of up-and-comers you'll catch. The board often lists other cultural events going on in the city.

La Casa de la Cultura (contiguo Iglesia Merced) often has folk music and other events, while **Plaza Siglo Nuevo** (1a Calle NE; tickets US$3), León's cinema, shows mostly big-budget American films.

Shopping

There are a few souvenir stores in town, but this isn't exactly Masaya.

La Esquina El Movimiento (7am-10pm) For politically correct gifts, including certified *artesanías* and a selection of books.

Las Tejedoras Manuales de León (nhleon@tmx.com.ni; Ermita Dolores 1c norte, ½c abajo) Pick up an all-cotton, vegetable-dyed tapestry at this women's collective, which makes all manner of woven goods on big wooden looms, some dating from the Spanish colonial era.

Enterprising area teens sell poems (US$0.70 each) on the street, often illustrated with hearts and unicorns, the perfect gift for the nonmaterialist in your life.

Getting There & Away

There are several international bus agencies, including **Ticabus** (Calle 6a NO; daily) and **King Quality** (311 2426; cnr 2a Calle NE & 3a Ave NE). There are three main bus lots.

MAIN TERMINAL

Most buses leave from León's chaotic **bus station** (311 3909; 6a Calle NE), about 1km northeast of the center.

Chinandega bus US$0.80, 1½ hours, 4:30am to 6pm, every 20 minutes; microbus US$1, 50 minutes, 5am to 7pm, depart when full

Corinto US$1, 1½ hours, 4:30am to 6pm, every 30 minutes

El Sauce US$2, 2½ hours, 6am to 4pm, hourly

Estelí US$3, 2½ hours, 5:20am and 12:45pm

Hervideros de San Jacinto US$0.50, 40 minutes, 4am to 5:30pm, every 30 minutes

Las Paz Centro US$0.50, 40 minutes, every 45 minutes

Malpaisillo US$0.80, one hour, 4am to 5pm, hourly

Managua microbus US$1.30, 1¼ hours, 4:30am to 8pm, depart when full

Managua (Carr Nueva, via La Paz Centro) *expreso* US$1.50, 1¼ hours, 5am to 4pm, almost hourly

Managua (Carr Vieja, via Puerto Sandino) *ordinario* US$1.25, 1¾ hours, 5am to 6:30pm, every 20 minutes

Matagalpa US$3.59, three hours, 5am and 3pm

Nagarote US$0.90, one hour, every 45 minutes

San Isidro US$2, 2½ hours, 6am to 5:30pm, every 30 minutes; with connections to frequent Matagalpa and Estelí buses

MERCADO SAN JUAN

This much smaller bus lot hosts *ordinario* buses to destinations including:

Las Salinas Grandes US$0.60, two hours, 5:15am, 8:30am, 11:30am, 1:30pm and 4pm

Playa Astillero US$0.70, 2½ hours, 12:30pm and 4pm

Rota (Cerro Negro) US$0.60, 2¼ hours, 5:50am, 11am and 3:30pm; Rota is 5km from the base of the volcano

THE BEACHES
Buses to Poneloya and Las Peñitas (US$0.65, 40 minutes) depart hourly 6am to 7pm from El Mercadito in Subtiava. Day-trippers take note: the last bus returns at 6:40pm.

Getting Around
The city is strollable, but big enough that you may want to take **taxis** (☎ 311 1043; per person day/night US$0.70/1), particularly at night. You can also get taxis to Poneloya (US$15), San Jacinto (US$20) and Managua (US$40).

PACIFIC BEACHES NEAR LEÓN
The most accessible beaches from León are Poneloya and Las Peñitas, both an easy 20-minute bus ride from Mercadito Subtiava in León. The road splits at the sea: go right for Poneloya proper, left for more developed La Peñitas and Reserva Natural Isla Juan Venado.

Several wilder, less accessible beaches further south are a bit more difficult to reach, including Las Salinas Grande (not to be confused with Las Salinas de Nagualapa, the surfing beach further south), with regular bus service from León and its own access to Reserva Natural Isla Juan Venado. A group of three even less explored beaches can be reached from the fractured but passable Old Rd to Managua: Puerto Sandino, El Velero and El Tránsito.

Poneloya
Although this beach has the famous name – it's highly praised in the 'Viva León Jodido' theme song – it's actually less developed than its twin. Be sure to visit during Semana Santa for the annual **Sand Castle & Sculpture Building Contest**, which makes a nice break from the sawdust carpets. There's one small cluster of hotels, all with seafood restaurants, in sight of a rocky outcropping called **Peña del Tigre**.

Hotel Locayo (r per person US$3), a dark and dilapidated wooden hotel, may not survive the next hurricane, and who knows what's living in those mattresses, but you can basically spit from your rapidly disintegrating 2nd-story balcony into the sea. **La Terraza**

(dm/d/tr US$6/15/20) has a great view, a small dorm and one cramped room with bathroom. A meal on the oceanfront terrace, spectacular as promised, would be great if the restaurant were open.

Across from the beach, **Posada de Poneloya** (☎ 317 1378, 311 4812; posadadeponeloya.com; d US$25; P ⊠) is much more comfortable than the other two, with newly remodeled rooms (some with wheelchair access) with hot-water bathroom and air-con. There's a big, tiled porch area with hammocks out back.

La Bocanita, about 1km north, offers a collection of thatched-roof seafood shacks at the edge of an estuary. This is where you can hire a private *panga* (small motorboat) seating four (US$60 to US$90) up to **Corinto**, or just to explore the coastline. Meet buses to León (US$0.65, 40 minutes, 5:40am to 6:40pm, every 50 minutes) at the *empalme* (three-way junction).

Las Peñitas
When people say they're headed to Poneloya, they usually mean the lazy beach town of Las Peñitas, a wide, sandy stretch fronted by a fine collection of hotels and restaurants. It offers the easiest access to the turtles and mangroves of Reserva Natural Isla Juan Venado (p176), and there's also good, if not spectacular, surfing here, with smallish regular waves that are perfect for beginners. Both Barco de Oro and Hotelito Oasis, as well as **Big Foot Hostel** (www.bigfootadventure.com) in León all rent surfboards and offer lessons and expeditions. Swimmers and surfers alike need to watch that undertow; people die here every year.

While it's a fine place to spend the night, you're always welcome at the restaurant/hotels lining the shore, where showers, shade and hammocks are happily provided, as long as you buy a snack. Tough life, isn't it? Just remember that the last bus back to León is at 6:40pm. The following businesses are listed north to south.

SLEEPING & EATING
Suyapa Beach (☎ 854 2699; www.suyapabeach.com; r with fan/air-con US$21/25; P ⊠ ⊠) The swankiest address in town, this spot was obviously on the cutting edge of luxury accommodations a couple of decades ago. Air-conditioned rooms are much nicer overall, large and comfortable if a bit worn.

DETOUR: LEÓN VIEJO

For centuries it was just another lost city. One of Spain's most important colonial capitals, León was first founded in the thickly forested skirts of a sleeping Volcán Momotombo, convenient to Lago de Managua and the indigenous city of Imabite (where they presumably realized Momotombo was Náhuatl for 'The Boiling Mountain'). In 1580 the mountain awoke.

For the next 30 years, Spanish settlers held on, though 'the city would appear a lake of lava and ashes.' In 1610 a series of eruptions darkened the sky to a perpetual burning night, and the colonists, huddled together against an almost biblical rain of smoke and fire, took the Virgin of Merced from her altar and, led by Pedro de Muniguía y Mendiola, carried whatever they could to the new home he'd found for them. When the curious returned from what's now León, to see what, if anything, remained, they found nothing but ashes.

León Viejo (admission US$2, video/camera US$2/3; ⊗ 8am-5pm) had all but passed into legend during a four-century lapse of human memory, linked to fanciful tales of lost basilicas beneath the surface of placid Lago de Managua, or indigenous curses exacting a more final retribution. Some scientists, however, thought the city might be rather more accessibly hidden, near the tiny town of Puerto Momotombo.

In 1967 UNAN archaeologists finally located Old León, their excavations revealing the original cathedral and main plaza – and underneath, the headless remains of Francisco Fernández de Córdoba, founder of both León and Granada. According to legend, he had been beheaded 'for treason against the crown,' on orders of jealous octogenarian overlord Pedrarias Dávila, the first governor of Nicaragua. And myth was suddenly made history.

In 2000 Unesco declared the complex a World Heritage Site, and you could easily spend several hours roaming around the partially excavated city. Admission includes a Spanish-language guided tour, but detailed signs are also in English. The best time to visit is the second Sunday in November, when the Virgin of Merced leaves her comfortable new church and, leading a procession of the faithful from La Paz Centro, revisits her first home in the New World.

Almost every tour outfit in León (as well as several in Managua and Granada) arranges visits to León Viejo, which can be combined with a hike to the top of Cerro Negro, and/or a cool swim in Laguna de Asososca, both nearby. But it's easy to visit on your own. Buses run every 50 minutes between León and La Paz Centro (US$0.80, 45 minutes), meeting buses to Puerto Momotombo (US$0.50), less than 1km from the site. Driving, the turnoff is 3km east of La Paz Centro on the new León–Managua highway. From there it's a 15km drive along a cobblestone road; make the poorly signed right to the ruins when you get into town.

If you continue straight through Puerto Momotombo, however, you'll quickly come to a less-than-appealing beach scene on Lago de Managua, where a handful of disposable-looking restaurants and a playground enjoy a truly awesome view of Volcán Momotombo, the hydroelectric plant steaming eerily against its naked red and black slopes, and Isla Momotombito; you could rent a boat for US$30 per hour and paddle around.

The restaurant (meals US$3 to US$10, open 7am to 7pm) is considered the best on the beach, and specializes in paellas (US$30 for four people) that you'll need to order a few hours in advance.

Hostel La Palmera (☎ 317 0279; s/d US$20/25; P ☒) Across the road and giving the Suyapa a run for its reputation, La Palmera has great rooms, a huge barbell-shaped pool, excellent service...but it's the only hotel not right on the beach. Only some rooms have TVs, so ask.

Mi Casita (☎ 894 6467; inter_monsal@yahoo.com; d US$12-15) This is a great place for lounging day-trippers, with a comfortable, sandy-floored bar/restaurant serving excellent seafood (mains US$2 to US$5). There are also cramped but cheerfully painted rooms upstairs; ask for No 3.

Hotelito y Cafetín Oasis (☎ 839 5344; patrick426@caramail.com; dm/s/d/tr US$5/10/12/15) Catering to surfers and backpackers, this super-clean spot has a great *palapa* (thatched-roof), hammock-hung restaurant serving soups, salads and seafood (dishes US$1.50 to US$7), all overlooking the waves. Or stay a while in one of the immaculate rooms, with small windows and foam mattresses but still somehow very comfortable. It must be the feng shui. It rents surfboards for US$5 per day.

Barco de Oro (☎ 317 0275; www.barcodeoro.com; s/d/tr US$10/14/18, d with air-con US$25; ❷) The old stand-by has fine rooms with shell art, mosquito netting and fans; the ones with air-con are freshly painted. The owners organize tours of Isla Juan Venado, have a book exchange and pool table, and rent surfboards, kayaks (per day US$5), bikes (per day US$6), and arrange massages (per hour US$8).

Hotel-Casa Patricia (☎ 641 9904; d with/without bathroom US$18/12) In a beautiful brick building just a bit further down the beach, this German-run operation is a dream in progress, with beautiful rooms – you want the more expensive ones, upstairs and facing the water – gardens, and hammocks on the terrace. Surfing lessons are offered.

GETTING THERE & AROUND

Buses leave from the clutch of restaurant/bars just north of Barco de Oro for León (US$0.65, 5:40am to 6:40pm, every 50 minutes). You can also arrange private boats seating at least four to Salinas Grande (US$70), including a tour of the reserve.

Reserva Natural Isla Juan Venado

This 18km-long, sandy barrier island (in some places only 300m wide) has swimming holes and lots of wildlife, including nesting turtles and mosquitoes galore. On one side of the island you'll find long, wild, sandy beaches facing the crashingly surfable Pacific; on the other, red and black mangroves reflected in emerald lagoons. Best of all, it's very easy to visit.

Several hotels, including Barco de Oro (which has an English-speaking guide), set up guided boat tours of the reserve, but it's generally cheaper to go through the reserve itself. You can get here by boat from less-developed Las Salinas, where you'll need to ask around for park rangers Ramón Hernandez and Vilal Espinosa, who organize three-hour **guided boat tours** (for 15 people US$50-60). Make reservations, if possible, or just show up at the **ranger station** (☎ 861 9099, in León 311 3776; infocomap@apcomanejo.com; admission US$2). It's actually much easier to go through Las Peñitas, which has a ranger station and is closer to the turtle nesting sites.

During turtle laying season, which runs July through January, peaking in September and October, thousands of Olive Ridley, careys and leatherbacks lay their eggs in El Vivero, close to the Las Peñitas entrance; nighttime turtle tours can be arranged. You can also go fishing here, in Casa de las Peñas. But no matter what you do, just remember your swimsuit, sunscreen and mosquito repellent.

Puerto Sandino

Originally called Puerto Somoza, Puerto Sandino is, as the name suggests, a hard-working port town. It overlooks a pretty bay studded with shipping equipment and lined with salt evaporation ponds. The reason you're here is to surf.

'Hawaii-sized waves' may just be part of the promotional material, but there are a few misleadingly named breaks: 'Poneloya,' which is not actually in Poneloya (look for it at Playa Diamante), has a rocky bottom and reliable waves. The most photogenic break is at the mouth of the port, but isn't always working. The best wave around, sometimes called Miramar (although it's not actually in Miramar), is about 6km south of Puerto Sandino, a hollow, powerful left that can go well over 2m high. At low tide, there's a reliable reef break just south.

The other big reason to come is for **Hotel Yeland** (☎ 312 2256; www.hotelyeland.com; s/d incl breakfast US$35/45; Ⓟ ❷ 🖵), a beautiful guesthouse owned by Doña Yelba Rancé. Big rooms come with air-con, bathroom and on-site Internet. Staff can organize anything from surfing trips to city tours, and run the excellent Restaurante Chango (mains US$3 to US$7), specializing in Caribbean-style seafood (including *rondón*, slow-cooked seafood stew, if you're lucky).

Buses leave for León (US$0.70, 30 minutes) and Managua (US$1.40, one hour) at least hourly.

El Velero

The excellent dirt coastal road continues south to El Velero, lined with the stuccoed entrances to future gated communities, as yet just untouched coastal scrub. Finally, you come to a fence with follow-through.

El Centro Turistico El Velero (☎ 312 2270; pedestrian/car US$0.12/2.50; cabaña US$41; ☾ Wed-Sun; ❷), operated by the social security administration, could be held up as proof that Nicaragua did, at some point, go communist. A handful of soulless corrugated tin cabins (sleeping seven uncomfortably) rust, alone and unloved, out there on one of the prettiest beaches you'll ever see. Don't count on the restaurant being open, either. On the other hand, it is a gorgeous beach with no one around…

From León, take a Puerto Sandino bus and get off at the gas station, where pickup trucks run hourly to El Velero (US$0.50).

El Tránsito

If El Velero seems too synthetic, head south on the increasingly rough coastal road to El Tránsito, a fishing village with beaches carpeted with abandoned plastic water bottles. It may have been quaint before the 1992 tidal wave wiped out the town, who knows. The one *hospedaje* (guesthouse) has closed.

If you do make it here – and there's good surfing at either end of the beach – head straight to fabulous **Bar Primavera** (mains US$2-5; 😊 daily), with great seafood and *nacatamales* (banana-leaf-wrapped bundles of cornmeal, meat, vegetables and herbs), where the friendly owner can help you arrange lodging or boats. The beach has a strong undertow, but to the south, near the lava flows, there are protected swimming holes.

Buses to Managua (US$1, 1½ hours) leave at 5am, 6am and 7am, and return from Managua's Mercado Oriental at 2pm, 4pm and 5pm daily.

THE VOLCANOES

It's more than 60km from Volcán Momotombo, which dominates the Managua skyline, to Volcán San Cristóbal, the most dramatic volcano in León's vast collection. These mark the Maribios Chain, epicenter of one of the most active volcanic regions on earth, and a rare glimpse into the subterraine where the Cocos and Caribbean plates collide.

The chain is named for the Maribios nation, who famously wore the skins of sacrificial victims inside out to do battle with the Spaniards, scaring them senseless. Which is rather fitting, considering the nature of the geology. Four natural reserves, none more than 10% federally owned, protect 12 distinct volcanoes, several hot springs and

crater lakes, and lots of other interesting activity along the chain.

Park management is split between two Marena offices: **Marena León** (😊 311 3776; mareleon@ibw.com) manages Reserva Natural Momotombo, Reserva Natural Telica-Rota and Reserva Natural Pilas–El Hoyo, which includes Cerro Negro; **Marena Chinandega** (😊 344 2443; lider@ibw.com.ni) keeps tabs on Reserva Natural San Cristóbal-Casita and Reserva Natural Volcán Cosigüina.

Marena offices have excellent information about the reserves, but don't actually organize tours. The easiest and safest way to visit the volcanoes is a guided hike, arranged by several outfitters in León (see p169) and elsewhere, but there's always a way to get there on your own.

Reserva Natural Volcán Momotombo

The perfect cone of **Volcán Momotombo**, destroyer of León Viejo and inspiration for its own Rubén Darío poem, rises red and black 1280m above Lago de Managua, and is the country's most beautiful threat. It is a symbol of Nicaragua, and has furnished at its base itself in miniature, the lake island of Momotombito (389m), sometimes called Isla Rosa or just 'The Child.'

There are several other structures worth seeing in the reserve, including the 4km-diameter, 200m-deep **Caldera Monte Galán**, tiled with five little lagoons (alligators included) reflecting theoretically extinct **Cerro Montoso** (500m), but you'd need to arrange a custom tour for that sort of adventure.

Most people come to climb Momotombo, a serious eight-hour excursion that can be done in one day, though most outfitters offer an overnight involving hot springs at a nearby private *finca* (farm).

To enter, you first need a permit from **Ormat Momotombo Power Company** (😊 270 5622; Róger Arcia Lacayo, de donde fue El Sandy's Carr Masaya 1c este, Centre Finarca, módulo 10, Managua), the geothermal plant steaming away at the volcano's base. The Israeli-owned plant, which supplies about 10% of Nicaragua's electrical power, saves around 90,000 tons of fossil fuels, offsetting 120,000 tons of CO_2 annually.

You could just show up at its gates with your hiking boots on – it's 14km on a good dirt road from Km 54 on Carr Nueva a León – but management can be famously irritable about letting unannounced guests onto its property. In addition to operators in León, guides with the required permits include:

Cooperativo Pilas el Ojo en León (☎ 885 0844, 878 0283) Mario Muguia charges US$25 to do the climb, which is a deal.

Ecotours de Nicaragua (☎ 222 2752; turismo@cablenet.com.ni; per person US$45, minimum 7) Drive from Managua one-third of the way up Volcán Momotombo in a Unimog truck (a sort of mega-jeep), from where it's just two hours up the lava-strewn landscape to the crater.

Isla Momotombito is most conveniently (hah!) accessible from Puerto Momotombo, just around the corner from the ruins of León Viejo (see the boxed text, p175), on the shores of Lago de Managua. The basaltic cone has long been a ceremonial site, and a few remaining petroglyphs and statues are still visible on it and the surrounding islands. Rangers who live on the island may be able to take you on a tour once you get out there.

Although it's possible to visit the islet, it's not cheap or easy. A private boat seating four costs at least US$100 to make the 9km trip, over sometimes very choppy water. Boat operators hang around the handful of disposable-looking restaurants at the lakeshore, all serving beer and *comida corriente,* or you could call **Miguel Narváez** (☎ 868 6279) to arrange a boat in advance.

Reserva Natural Pilas–El Hoyo

Most people come to this reserve to see the volcano that doesn't even get second billing: **Cerro Negro** (726m…and growing), one of the youngest volcanoes in the world. It first erupted from a quiet cornfield in 1850, and its pitch-black, loose gravel cone has been growing in spurts ever since. In 1992 a 6000m column of ash collapsed roofs in León and destroyed crops for kilometers around; in 1995 fountains of lava spewed forth. More recently, in 1999, an eruption following heavy rains that had collapsed the main crater opened three more craters at its base.

Almost every guide in León offers a guided hike to the top, a shadeless, two-to three-hour climb into the eye-watering fumes of the yellow streaked crater. Then – inspired by French cyclist Eric

Barone, who broke the world mountain bike speed record (not to mention his bicycle frame) in May 2002, clocking a cool 172km/h – your outfitter will offer a faster way down. **Volcano surfing** is offered on not only surfboards, but old mattresses, cardboard boxes and more. Be careful!

Other structures worth climbing include the dormant **Volcán Pilas**, which last had gas in 1954; and **El Hoyo** (1088m), the park's second-most active peak, basically a collapsed crater with fumaroles. Then it's time to relax in deliciously cool **Laguna de Asososca** (818m; also called Ajusco or El Tigre), a jungle-wrapped crater lake that's poorly signed and on private property, and therefore difficult to visit on your own. But if you book a tour climbing Cerro Negro (or are visiting León Viejo, nearby), definitely try to get this as an add-on.

Reserva Natural San Cristóbal– La Casita

This is the one that probably caught your eye, **Volcán San Cristóbal** (1745m), the tallest volcano in Nicaragua, streaming gray smoke from its smooth cone. Summiting this beauty is a serious hike, six to eight hours up, three hours down. A guide is highly recommended, as access is difficult, dangerous and requires crossing private property.

If you're game, however, rent a 4WD and head to Posoltega, then take the rough dirt road to Finca Bella, where you'll be charged a US$2 trail fee. Ask to be pointed toward **Volcán Casita** (1405m), an eight-hour climb past fumaroles, to amazing views over Managua. From there, the trail to San Cristóbal's smoking crater should be clear.

Most tour operators in León arrange the hike, as does the **Chichigalpa alcaldía** (☎ 343 2303, 343 2232; alchichi@ibw.com.ni), where you'll take a trail that begins in the municipal park. Or check out **San Cristóbal las Finca Rojas** (☎ 341 0325, 341 0021), the coffee *finca* closest to the top, which can arrange guides and meals. There's currently hammock and tent space, plus plans for a hotel. **Hotel Casa Grande** (☎ 341 0325) in Chinandega can make reservations.

There are several other volcanic structures worth seeing, including **El Chonco** (715m), an inactive volcanic plug contiguous with San Cristóbal, and **Moyotepe**

(917m) close by, a small lagoon accessible from the Chinandega–Somotillo road.

HURRICANE MITCH MEMORIAL

Difficult to visit unless you have your own car, this sobering memorial on the slopes of Volcán Casita is 6km from the well-signed exit off the León–Chinandega road. You can tell which volcano is Casita from the highway; look for the denuded strip of earth, torn from the crater lip to the base. In October 1998, Hurricane Mitch (see p55) devastated Nicaragua; almost 4000 people lost their lives in the inundation. The vast majority of those are buried here, beneath a 3m-high tidal wave of volcanic mud that swept away the towns of Posoltega, El Porvenir and Rolando Rodríguez.

This is their headstone, a quiet pyramid of smooth rock topped with a simple white cross and surrounded by gardens. The memorial has wonderful views of San Cristóbal and, of course, Casita, once known as Apastepe, 'The Mountain of Water.'

Reserva Natural Telica-Rota

This very active, 9052-hectare complex peaks at **Volcán Telica** (1061m), whose twin craters are a mere 9km north of León. Also called the 'Volcano of León,' Telica is active in four- to five-year cycles; the last really big eruption was in 1765. Most eruptions these days involve gases and a few pyroclastic belches.

There are several 'extinct' cones around the base, including **Cerro Agüero** (744m), **Loma Los Portillos** (721m) and **Volcán Rota** (832m), which still has constant fumaroles. There are big plans for this park, which is considered a potential ecotourism gold mine, due to its easy access from San Jacinto.

SAN JACINTO

The only town of any size on this stretch of the Ring of Fire, San Jacinto is base camp for climbs up **Volcán Telica** (1061m; six to eight hours), **Volcán Rota** (three to five hours), with great views of Telica, and **Volcán Santa Clara** (three to five hours). If you're up for it, you can walk to Cerro Negro from here. Views from San Jacinto are at once inspiring and unsettling, with volcanoes fuming away on all sides.

Organized tours invariably stop at the famous **Hervideros de San Jacinto** (admission US$1; ☺ 7am-5pm), an expanse of bubbling mud puddles. They shift in size and location after a good rain, so put more faith in your pint-sized **guide** (per child US$0.30-0.60) than the rickety fence. While you admire the simmering soil, consider asking one of the kids to grab you some fresh mud for a facial mask. You can wash it off about six blocks away at **Aguas Termales San Jacinto** (San Jacinto Hot Springs). Though not steaming hot, or even particularly scenic, this thermal cascade forms several natural pools that locals use for bathing and laundry, and it's free. You'll particularly appreciate the hot springs if you spend some time at **Hostel La Ceiba** (☎ 266 1018; nir@nicaraolake.com.ni; dm incl breakfast US$9.20; **P**)), a simple cement structure with three six-bed dorms and shared cold-water bathrooms, operated by **Nicarao Lake Tours** (☎ in Rivas 266 1018; www .nicaraolake.com.ni). There's an on-site restaurant, and it also rents bicycles and horses.

La Ceiba can locate guides for climbing the volcanoes, or ask around for Delvin Castillo, half a block north of Colegio Sarah Maria Parrales. Guides may also be able to arrange tours of the **San Jacinto-Tizate Proyecto de Energia Geotermica**, about 1km north of town.

Buses leave for León (US$0.50, 40 minutes) every half-hour between 4am and 5:30pm.

EL SAUCE

pop 30,000

Once a bustling and important link on the national railway, today scenic El Sauce is just a sleepy mountain town – except on the third Sunday in January. Pilgrims from all over Nicaragua, Guatemala and beyond make there way here to pay their respects to **El Señor de Esquipulas**, or the Black Christ.

The image, to which all manner of miracles have been attributed, arrived in El Sauce in 1723 from Esquipulas, Guatemala, and refused to move another centimeter upon arriving at this lovely spot. The beautiful, if not flashy, 1828 **Templo de El Sauce** was declared a national sanctuary in 1984, but burned in 1999. But the Black Christ was saved, and all El Sauce pitched in to rebuild the sanctuary.

Perhaps fittingly, the town's most important products are milk and honey, and most visitors would agree that it is uncommonly blessed. The gateway to the Cordillera Dariense, El Sauce is surrounded by cool green mountains strewn with waterfalls, and several **hiking trails** begin in town.

Hotel Blanco (☎ 319 2403) arranges guided hikes, or just ask around for the trailhead to the year-round green of the forest to **La Piedra de San Ramón**, which starts about 3km north of town. If you're looking for more excuses to stay, you could check out **Iglesia Calvario**, the city's other church, which is interesting for its A-frame construction, or take a taxi 6km from town to the **Río Grande**, with a swimming hole. There are no banks, although there is an **Internet café** (per hr US$1) two blocks from the Templo.

Around the corner from the sanctuary, **Bar-Hotel El Viajero** (☎ 319 2325; r with/without bathroom US$5/2.50) is a huge, once luxurious but now dilapidated adobe, with simple rooms with thin mattresses. **Hotel Blanco** (☎ 319 2403; s/d US$6/9; P ⚡), two blocks downhill from the sanctuary, is a cozy spot with modern and comfortable, if not luxurious, rooms with new mattresses and plans to add a few air-con rooms. Conveniently, it's also the best restaurant in town. Owner Francisco Blanco can arrange guides for (or just point you toward) a variety of hikes, including La Piedra de San Ramón.

Finca Campestre Cárdenas (☎ 319 2329; harcaco@hotmail.com; P ⚡ 🏊) is a tourist *finca* with a small petting zoo, pool and private rooms with air-conditioning and bathroom, walking distance from town. It's also a *vivero* (plant nursery), and brings in a local crowd for their Sunday afternoon barbecue.

In addition to the hotels, other recommended eateries include Cafetín El Saucero and Comedor Falkis, both near the sanctuary.

Buses to León (US$2.25, 2½ hours, 5am to 4:30pm, six daily) leave from the market, downhill from the sanctuary. Note that although the 28km road from the León–San Isidro highway is beautifully paved, the El Sauce–Estelí road (shown as the same 'level' of road on most maps) is 4WD-only in the dry season, if you're lucky.

NAGAROTE
pop 32,100

Not exactly a tourist attraction, this adobe enclave's main claim to fame is having been awarded 'Cleanest City in Nicaragua' three years running. But there are a few other excuses to make the pleasant

side trip, an easy 45-minute bus ride from León.

Originally called Nagrand Otle by its Chorotega founders, Spanish conquistadors changed the name to Nagarote in the late 1520s. They could do pretty much whatever they wanted at that point, having successfully secured the major intertribal trading town of the Dirian, Niquira, Chorotega and Subtiava nations. They even tastefully left the body of Cacique Nagrandano hanging from the branches of the town's largest tree, El Genízaro, to ensure that the locals would never forget.

They haven't, and **El Genízaro** is still here, surrounded by benches and looking a bit the worse for wear. In 1964, at between 700 and 1300 years old, the big tree was finally made a national monument by President Rene Schick Gutiérrez, who grew up here. It's fronted by a fallen branch (bigger than most trees) carved into a rather compelling monument, **Indito de Nagarote**.

Sightseers (hire a pedicab to take you on the grand tour for US$1) could also take in **El Templo Parroquial Santiago**, a lovely 1600s adobe that claims to be the only church in Nicaragua with four images of the same saint. More importantly, you can buy delicious *quesillos* (see the boxed text, opposite) from the cart rolling around the pleasant parque central out front.

One block from the park is **Casa Cultura y Sala Museo El Genízaro** (⏱ 7:30am-noon & 2-6pm Mon-Fri), with Latin dance and cooking classes, and a museum filled with more statues and art carved from the branches of El Genízaro, one depicting the *cacique* with a noose around his neck. The cultural center can tell you where to find **petroglyphs**, under a bridge across Río Zayulapa, close to town.

There are no guesthouses in Nagarote, but you could grab another *quesillo* at El Guayacan, a spacious restaurant/bar about two blocks from the big tree, or Quesillos Acacia, near the main road. Buses leave the parque central every 45 minutes to León (US$0.90, 45 minutes) and Managua (US$1.25, one hour).

LA PAZ CENTRO
pop 36,770

You'll be changing buses here if you're headed to León Viejo (see the boxed text, p175), so why not take a long layover, just to wander around a typical Nicaraguan town, and eat *quesillos.*

La Paz Centro is a *tejas*-making center, and several families make and fire these sunset-colored half-pipe ceramic shingles, for which Spanish colonial architecture is known. Most are actually sold in Costa Rica, where wealthy homeowners (primarily expats) have been buying them to top off their dream homes. The **alcaldía** (mayor's office; ☎ 314 2247) can arrange visits to *tejas* factories, with pit kilns so huge that they could bake paint onto a Cadillac.

Mercado de Artesanías (⊙ 9am-7pm), on the highway across from the bus station, offers work by 14 ceramicists, who apparently got tired of making *tejas* and started on these heavy and appealing pots and sculptures, depicting Nicaraguan daily life. If you're up for an adventure, you could also take the one bus daily to the banks of **Río Tamarindo**, where you can't swim, but can go fishing or enjoy a big shrimp meal. The bus leaves at 6am and returns at 3pm.

There's one place to stay, **Hospedaje Familiar** (☎ 314 2340; d US$8), two blocks from the *empalme*, with simple rooms and shared bathrooms. There are several places to eat, but only one matters: **Quesillos Guiligüiste** (quesillos US$1; ⊙ 6:30am-7pm), the original and still the best, right at the entrance to the city and conveniently close to the bus stop.

Buses leave across from the *empalme* to León (US$0.80, 45 minutes, 6am to 6pm, every 50 minutes), Puerto Momotombo and León Viejo (US$0.50, 30 minutes, every 50 minutes), and Managua (US$1.25, one hour, every 45 minutes).

CHINANDEGA

Winning the title of 'Hottest City in Nicaragua' (and not in the metaphorical sense), Chinandega is primarily a service town for the country's only deepwater port, El Corinto, and a fertile agribusiness region taking advantage of all that rich, volcanic soil. Most visitors come because it's convenient to volcanoes, beaches and wetlands, but end up enjoying their time here.

Lots of lit-up signage and a healthy dose of groovy 1960s architecture give the old adobes a more modern feel, but architecture lovers needn't fret. Instead, take a tour of the country's most colorful collection of churches (again, not in the metaphorical sense), then relax with the alligators in the parque central.

Orientation & Information

Chinandega is on a logical Spanish grid, but note that the *alcaldía* is actually five blocks east of the natural city center at Parroquia Santa Ana.

Costa Rican consulate In the Intur shopping center.
FedEx In the Intur shopping center.

QUESILLO CONTROVERSY

It's no wonder that this is a point of pride: *quesillos,* Nicaragua's rich and refined answer to the common burrito, are the best food ever. Unless you're trying to beat high blood pressure, in which case you should still have a bite.

A thick, steaming corn tortilla is topped with a pancake of mozzarella-like cheese, then loosely rolled into a cylinder and fitted into a special plastic bag. A smiling cook will ask if you want the spicy onion chutney (you probably do), which is ladled into the tortilla's center along with a thick sour cream sauce. *Quesillos* go for around US$1 a pop, are available alongside every paved road in the country and should not be missed.

Two towns have a legitimate claim as the *cuña,* or cradle, of *quesillo* culture: Nagarote, birthplace of innovator and originator Señora Socorro Munguía Madriz; and La Paz Centro, where she came up with the culinary triumph. In 1912, along with the Rueda sisters, she began selling *quesillos* – at both the Nagarote and La Paz Centro train stations, further confusing the issue.

As *quesillos* proliferated across the country, this original crew opened what's now an almost pilgrimage-worthy destination, Quesillos Guiligüiste (pronounced *kayseeyos wilee weestay*), so popular that it has its own freelance car-parking personnel out front. This, of course, is in La Paz Centro. But, as Nagarote natives note, Doña Dalila Lara, another early *quesillo* adherent, moved to Nagarote in the 1970s, where she opened Quesillos Acacia, also pilgrimage worthy, especially if you're still hungry.

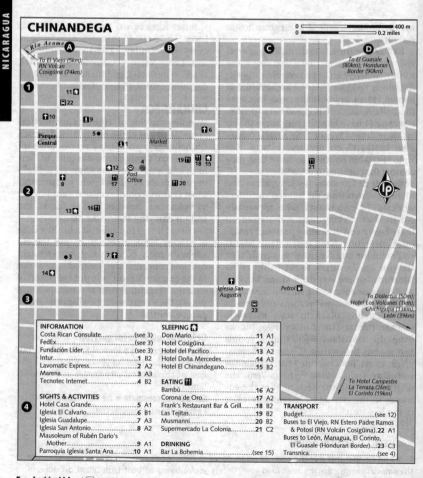

CHINANDEGA

Map labels:
- Río Acome
- To El Viejo (5km); RN Volcán Cosigüina (74km)
- To El Guasale (80km); Honduran Border (90km)
- Parque Central
- Market
- Post Office
- Iglesia San Augustin
- Petrol
- To Dialectus (50m); Hotel Los Volcanes (1km); Chichigalpa (13km); León (39km)
- To Hotel Campestre La Terraza (2km); El Corinto (19km)

INFORMATION	
Costa Rican Consulate	(see 3)
FedEx	(see 3)
Fundación Lider	(see 3)
Intur	1 B2
Lavomatic Express	2 A2
Marena	3 A3
Tecnotec Internet	4 B2

SIGHTS & ACTIVITIES	
Hotel Casa Grande	5 A1
Iglesia El Calvario	6 B1
Iglesia Guadalupe	7 A3
Iglesia San Antonio	8 A2
Mausoleum of Rubén Darío's Mother	9 A1
Parroquia Iglesia Santa Ana	10 A1

SLEEPING	
Don Mario	11 A1
Hotel Cosigüina	12 A2
Hotel del Pacifico	13 A2
Hotel Doña Mercedes	14 A3
Hotel El Chinandegano	15 B2

EATING	
Bambú	16 A2
Corona de Oro	17 A2
Frank's Restaurant Bar & Grill	18 B2
Las Tejitas	19 B2
Musmanni	20 B2
Supermercado La Colonia	21 C2

DRINKING	
Bar La Bohemia	(see 15)

TRANSPORT	
Budget	(see 12)
Buses to El Viejo, RN Estero Padre Ramos & Potosi (RN Volcán Cosigüina)	22 A1
Buses to León, Managua, El Corinto, El Guasale (Honduran Border)	23 C3
Transnica	(see 4)

Fundación Lider (☎ 344 2381; www.turismo consiguina.com) The main office is in El Viejo, but there's a representative in the Chinandega Marena who can help arrange your trip to Volcán Cosigüina.

Intur (☎ 341 1935; chinandega@intur.gob.ni) Much more helpful and organized than average, Intur Chinandega keeps its collection of flyers and handy information-packed scrapbooks in a shopping center one and a half blocks west of the market. The staff here say that Granada is almost as hot, 'and often feels hotter' than Chinandega.

Lavomatic Express (per load US$3) Does your laundry for you. It's one block north of Iglesia Guadalupe.

Marena (☎ 344 2443; lider@ibw.com.ni) Exceptionally friendly and helpful, this office keeps tabs on Reserva Natural San Cristóbal-Casita, Reserva Natural Volcán Cosigüina and Reserva Natural Estero Padre Ramos, all

with reasonable access; and Reserva Natural Delta de Estero Real, where you're on your own. Staff also keep an eye on Reserva Genetica Apacunaca (Apacunaca Genetic Resource Reserve). Marena can point you toward guides and other services, but doesn't generally arrange trips itself.

Tecnotec Internet (per hr US$0.70; ⏱ 8am-10pm; ❄) Just one of several super-speedy Internet spots, all with frosty air-conditioning.

Sights & Activities

Like many municipalities in Nicaragua, Chinandega has an enormous collection of archaeological treasures, including several jade pieces, but no real space to display them. At press time, the tentatively named **Museo de Arte Pre-Columbiano** had just been approved; ask at your hotel to see whether it's open.

In the meantime, Chinandega really does have some seriously striking churches. Grab a bottle of water and a camera before heading to the vivid blueberry 1878 **Santuario de Nuestra Señora de Guadalupe**, which despite the radiant and rather grandiose colonial-style facade has a simple precious wood interior with an exceptionally lovely Virgin. Four blocks to the north and two blocks west, **Iglesia San Antonio**, its dramatic facade steeped in a more sedate pastel yellow, has delightful Easter egg–blue and yellow columns and arches inside.

Next, it's 1586 **Parroquia Santa Ana**, three blocks north, Chinandega's most important church, with a splendid Stations of the Cross, lots of gilt and some Russian Orthodox styling that earn this one 'Best Interior in Town.' A richer yellow with white trim, it stands watch over what may be Nicaragua's best parque central, featuring **live alligators** (and turtles) in decorative cement enclosures. There's sometimes ballet *folklorico* and live music in the central kiosk. The **mausoleum of Rubén Darío's mother** is just one block east.

It's seven blocks east to **Iglesia El Calvario**, with a rust-red, rather Art-Deco exterior with a very nice bell tower, its otherwise simple interior hung with chandeliers.

Sleeping

Even Managuans complain that Chinandega is hot. Consider paying extra for air-con and keep an eye on kids to make sure they're drinking enough water.

Don Mario (☎ 341 4054; Entel 170 varas norte; s/d with fan US$12/16, with air-con US$26/32; P ⌘) The extremely nice rooms with high ceilings, cable TV and excellent art by the English-speaking owner are wrapped around a pleasant courtyard and a kitchen that you can use.

Hotel Doña Mercedes (☎ 341 3201; s with bathroom US$4, s/d with bathroom & cable TV US$7/9) This hotel's clean and cheap, basic wooden rooms come with a fan and TLC; the immaculate shared toilets have puffy comfort seats.

Hotel Cosigüina (☎ 341 3636; www.hotelcosiguina .com; esquina de los bancos; s/d US$30/40; P ⌘) This relatively plush property has hip 1960s accents, cable TV, hot-water bath-

rooms and even air-con so you can enjoy them.

Hotel del Pacífico (☎ 341 3841; hotelpac@ibw .com.ni; BAC 1c abajo, ½c sur; s/d incl breakfast US$26/30; P ⌘) Even nicer, attractive, modern rooms are on the small side but have hot-water bathrooms and other amenities. It's the comfortable *ranchero* backyard (suitable for weddings, seriously), perfect for breakfast or hanging out, that makes this spot special.

Hotel Campestre La Terraza (☎ 341 3827; hotelcampterraza@lycos.com; s/d with fan US$12/18, with air-con US$26/30; P ⌘ ⌘) Run by the same owners as Hotel del Pacífico, right outside of town, this has equally nice rooms and a pool; for US$1.25, you can visit on a day trip.

Hotel El Chinandegano (☎ 341 4800; raulbaca@ hotmail.com; Esso El Calvario 1½c arriba; r with 1/2/3 beds US$25/30/35; P ⌘ ⌘) Contender for the nicest spot in town, this place has free Internet, tasteful furniture, cable TVs and phones, plus one of the nicest restaurant/bars in the city. Avoid room Nos 1 and 2, which are right by the macaws.

Los Volcanes (☎ 341 1010; www.losvolcaneshotel .com; s/d incl breakfast US$53/73; P ⌘) About 3km from town, this swanky spot has the custom toiletries, attractive lighting, fancy restaurant and Budget car-rental desk, but no pool.

Eating

The best cheap eats set up at dusk in the parque central, lined with hamburger stands. There are two great *fritangas* beside the basketball court just beyond.

Musmanni (snacks US$1-2; ⏱ 5am-9pm) Everyone's favorite chain bakery serves up sweet and savory starchy snacks around the corner from the market, next to the *alcaldía*.

Las Tejitas (mains US$2; ⏱ 6am-10:30am, 11am-2:30pm & 5-10:30pm) An institution, this *fritanga* gets packed breakfast, lunch and dinner – and mariachis could show up at any time. It's a solid steam-table buffet with a nationwide reputation.

Frank's Restaurant Bar & Grill (mains US$4-10; ⏱ 11am-10:30pm) This is Chinandega's fine-dining date night out, with white tablecloths and long-stemmed glasses. The specialty is steak with all sorts of fine imported wines on the side. It's next to Hotel El Chinandegano.

Corona de Oro (mains US$3-5; ⏲ 11am-10pm) Right in the thick of things, this spot serves large portions of decent Chinese food.

Bambú (BAC 75 varas norte; juices US$1; ⏲ 10am-11:30pm) This tiny café juices all sorts of good stuff – sugarcane, carrot, pineapple, spinach – right in front of you, with pastries, sandwiches or healthy snacks on the side.

La Colonia supermarket, five blocks east of La Bohemia, is the best place to resupply on the peninsula.

Drinking

Bar La Bohemia (⏲ 5pm-midnight; ⏲) In Hotel El Chinandegano, serves quality food and 'the coldest beer in town,' which is a draw. It's also air-conditioned to the point where you'll want a sweater.

There are two popular discos, and both serve food: Montserrat, on the ring road around town, gets the youth vote with reggae and Latin dance; Dialectus, even more opulent than its sister disco in León, attracts a more mature crowd. Thursday is mariachi night at both of them.

Getting There & Around

You can rent a car at **Budget** (☎ 341 1663; ⏲ 8am-5pm Mon-Sat), at Hotel Cosigüina, or **Dollar** (☎ 341 2303), across from La Colonia supermarket. Taxis charge US$0.50 in town, and also make the runs to El Viejo (US$3) and Corinto (US$6). There are two places to catch a bus: the big and relatively well-organized Mercado Bisne, and the more chaotic Mercadito, close to Parroquia Santa Ana. Transnica has an office in the Intur shopping center.

MERCADITO

El Viejo microbus US$0.23, 10 minutes, 5am to 6pm, depart when full; bus US$0.18, 20 minutes, 5am to 6pm, every 15 minutes

Machapa US$1.30, two hours, 2:30pm

Playa Jiquilillo & Reserva Natural Estero Padre Ramos US$0.75, 1½ hours, 7am, 10am, 11:20am, 3pm and 4:30pm; the 7am bus meets collective boats to Venecia Wednesday, Thursday and Saturday

Potosí (Volcán Cosigüina) US$1.50, 3½ hours, 6am, 11:10am and 2:20pm

Punta Ñata US$1.50, 3½ hours, 12:10pm

MERCADO BISNE

Chichigalpa microbus US$0.20, 15 minutes, 5am to 6pm, depart when full

Corinto bus US$0.40, 40 hours, 5am to 6pm, every 15 minutes; microbus US$0.60, 25 minutes, 5am to 6pm, depart when full

El Guasale (Honduran border) bus US$1.25, 1¾ hours, 6am to 6pm, every 25 minutes; microbus US$2, one hour, 6am to 6pm, depart when full

León bus US$0.70, 1½ hours, 4am to 7pm, every 15 minutes; microbus US$1.10, one hour, 5am to 7pm, depart when full

Managua bus US$2.15, three hours, 5am to 4pm, every 30 minutes; microbus US$3, two hours, 5am to 4pm, depart when full

AROUND CHINANDEGA

El Viejo

Just 5km from Chinandega is the ancient indigenous capital of Tezoatega, today called El Viejo and among the most symbolically important of the colonial cities. This is the site of **Basílica de Nuestra Señora de la Inmaculada Concepción de la Virgen María**, home of Nicaragua's patron saint and mistress of its biggest national religious event, La Gritería, when troupes of *fiesteros* shout the question *¿Quién causa tanta alegría?* ('Who causes so much joy?') to receive the response, *¡La concepción de María!* ('The conception of Mary!').

The most dedicated pilgrims show up to her beautiful church a few days early for the Lavada de la Plata (Polishing of the Silver) on December 5 and 6. The devout use cotton to clean the church's spectacular silver filigree altar, and the offerings (also usually silver) left throughout the year. The work is meditative but fun, with mariachis serenading the faithful at their brilliant task.

There's not much else to do in this tiny town, other than check email at Ciber Center, behind the *alcaldía*, but El Viejo is home to two organizations that work together to arrange recommended guided trips to Reserva Natural Estero Padre Ramos and Reserva Natural Volcán Cosigüina; Selva offers accommodations here in El Viejo.

Fundación Lider (☎ 344 2381; www.turismo consiguina.com) caters primarily to larger groups, and offers two-day (per person US$80) and three-day (US$90) trips to the volcano, including transportation, food and lodging. **Parque Ecológico Tzesuatega** (☎ 344 2381; lider@ibw.com.ni; Portón Inatec 1c norte, 1c oeste; r per person incl breakfast US$10) has comfortable bamboo and thatch huts open to anyone, but is usually used as an overnight orientation for the conservation organization **Selva** (Somos Ecologistas en la Lucha por la Vida y Ambiente; We Are Ecologists Fighting for Nature – *selva* is Spanish for 'forest'). It offers recommended package tours to Reserva Natural Estero Padre Ramos and Reserva Natural Volcán Cosigüina, with an emphasis on sea turtle conservation during laying season, which peaks in September and October. The 'park' sits on 1.5 *manzanas* (1.1-hectare blocks) just outside El Viejo, which isn't a bad place to be.

You could also stay in town at the very basic but clean adobe **Hostel San Joaquín** (☎ 893 5480; r with/without bathroom per person US$5/3), two and a half blocks downhill from the basilica, with thin mattresses and walls that almost touch the ceiling. It also sells cheese.

There are a few *fritangas* fronting the market, or go upscale at **Bar-Restaurant Tezoatega** (mains US$4-6; ☺ 11am-midnight), two blocks from the basilica, with seafood and a dance floor, or **Restaurant Piscina Olímpica** (mains US$3-6; ☺ 11am-11pm), around the corner, which is a bit cheaper and really does have a huge pool, though it's usually empty.

Drivers should note that this is the last chance for gas on the peninsula. All buses headed north from Chinandega to Potosí or the Cosigüina beaches stop at the El Viejo *empalme* about 20 minutes after leaving Chinandega. To Chinandega, you can get buses (US$0.18, 20 minutes, every 15 minutes) and minivans (US$0.23, 10 minutes, leaving when full) from in front of the basilica. A taxi to Chinandega costs US$3.

Chichigalpa

The town with the cutest name in Nicaragua is best known as the source from which all **Flor de Caña rum** flows, in 12 beloved shades running crystal clear to deepest amber. Chichigalpa is also home to **Ingenio San Antonio**, the largest sugar refinery in the country, and cane fields carpet the skirts of **Volcán San Cristóbal**, which rises from the sweaty lowlands a mere 6km from the city center.

There's no Intur, but the **Chichigalpa alcaldía** (☎ 343 2303, 343 2232; alchichi@ibw.com.ni), about two blocks from the exceptionally nice parque central, has a Commission of Culture that can arrange guided tours of

Flor de Caña (not open to the general public); city tours that take in the ruins of **Iglesia El Pueblito**, and guided hikes to the top of San Cristóbal via **Parque Ecológico Municipal**. This smoking city park, about 10km from town and accessible by 4WD only, preserves 50 *manzanas* of mostly primary forest including a trailhead to the top of the volcano. Guides cost US$12 per group.

Other than the automotels at the *empalme*, there's the ultra-basic **Hospedaje Imperial** (d US$3) two blocks west of the park, with cement rooms, cleanish shared bathrooms and an odd smell, or very nice **Hotel La Vista** (☎ 343 2035; jbarker@nicaraguasugar.com.ni; s/d US$25/35; ℗ ⌗), where you get what you pay for: super-clean, modern rooms with tile floors, tasteful paint jobs, cable TV and air-conditioning. And the balcony does indeed have a fine volcano view.

There are lots of good places to eat. Try **Rincón Criollo** (meals US$6-8; ☺ daily), around the corner from the park, specializing in *churrasco* and barbecued chicken, or **Cafetín Los Antojitos** (dishes US$2-4), right on the park, with a great lunchtime steam-table buffet.

Microbuses to Chinandega (US$0.20, 15 minutes) depart from the market when full, 5am to 6pm.

To Somotillo & El Guasale (Honduras Border)

It's a smooth, paved 80km through mostly empty grazing land to the border town of Somotillo, though you will see signs for **Reserva Genetic Apacunaca** (Apacunaca Genetic Resource Reserve). There's no tourist infrastructure, which is sort of the point. It protects one of four known caches of *teosinte*, or wild corn, in the world, only discovered here in the late 1990s.

Corn, long a Nicaraguan staple food, has rather mysterious origins. *Teosinte* has a very hard outer shell, rendering it almost inedible except as popcorn – an odd choice for domestication. It, like modern maize, employs a type of photosynthesis most common in cacti and other dry-weather plants, but its roots are actually modified branches, an adaptation more common in swamps.

Both adaptations are common in epiphytes, however – tree-dwelling plants usually associated with the cloud forest. But there are also tropical dry forest epiphytes, such as pithaya (made into a bright purple drink), which is closely related to prickly pear cactus; perhaps corn started up in the trees. But no one knows, and the cache at Apacunaca is key to this genetic sleuthing: while other *teosinte* stocks grow in dry, high-altitude areas, fast-growing *Zea luxurians* thrives at an elevation of 10m, surviving in standing water during the six-month rainy season.

If you're not deeply interested in corn, however, it's on to sunny Somotillo, more a place to get stuck than to visit. If this happens to you, hire one of the 7000 pedicabs to take you on a grand tour, perhaps of the two **churches**. You could also check your email at **CiberCafe San Lorenzo** (per hr US$1; 8am-10pm), next to the big, dirty market.

A cluster of hotels on the main road are the real attraction, however. **Hotel Fronteras** (346 2264, 602 5088; d with fan/air-con US$10/15;) is the most comfortable, with attractive furniture, cable TV and a nice restaurant. Acceptable **Hotel Nelson** (346 2579; d with fan/air-con US$6/12;) comes in a distant second. The best restaurant in town is Comedor Oasis de Julia, on the main road, but there are several others near the market.

COSIGÜINA PENINSULA BEACHES

The Cosigüina Peninsula is well on its way to becoming an island, worn away on two sides by brilliant estuaries and fringed with sandy beaches, ranging from the pearl grays of Jiquilillo to coal black at Playa Carbón.

These aren't the easiest beaches to visit in Nicaragua, but you'll be rewarded with impressive stretches of sand interrupted only by fishing villages, sea turtles and mangrove swamps. The surfing is great, but largely unexplored; hotels are few and far between. If you make it here, once you're settled in, tanned and relaxed and ready, consider climbing what was until very recently the tallest volcano in Central America.

El Corinto
pop 20,000 / elevation 10m
Nicaragua's only deep-water port, El Corinto actually inherited the job from a much older town, Puerto El Realejo, founded on February 26, 1522, and subsequently attacked by such famous-name pirates as William Dampier and John Davis. As the centuries passed and sand filled in the estuary, the barrier island of Punto Icaco became the port, where El Corinto was founded in 1858.

This was the port that US President Ronald Reagan illegally mined in 1983, inspiring his horrified congress to pass a law specifically forbidding the use of taxpayer dollars for overthrowing the Nicaraguan government, and thus marking the beginning of the Iran-Contra Affair (see the boxed text, p30).

Today, just 19km from Chinandega, El Corinto's 19th-century wooden row houses, narrow cobbled streets and broad beaches score high on the 'adorability potential' scale, although actual adorability ratings are much lower. It's sort of sad; although some 65% of the nation's imports and exports flow through, very little of the money stays here, mostly in the dark bars and massage parlors that surround

---

DIY: PUERTO MORAZÁN & DELTA DEL ESTERO REAL

If you love wetlands, you're going to be disappointed: there's no tourist infrastructure at all for enormous Reserva Natural Delta del Estero Real, about 20km – two hours by bus on this terrible road – north of Chinandega in the desperately poor town of Puerto Morazán.

The worst part is that this monumental river delta, luxuriating along the Honduran border, is beautiful, with alligators lounging alongside the lush, mangrove-lined shores, views to Volcán Cosigüina and natural lagoons all aflutter with migratory birds. And threatened: its inaccessibility has emboldened poachers, loggers and dirty shrimping operations. This wetlands needs tourist.

Should you choose to accept this mission, head out early for a day trip to Puerto Morazán, or pack your mosquito net and ask at the **alcaldía** (342 2580) if anyone is renting rooms or hammock space in town. Fishing boats holding four, plus your Spanish-speaking guide, ask about US$20 for a four-hour tour of the reserve. There are seven buses daily from the Chinandega Mercadito (US$1, two hours).

BORDER CROSSING: TO CHOLUTECA, HONDURAS

This painless, uncrowded border crossing begins about 200m from the bus stop, with clean bathrooms (US$0.30). Walk or take a pedicab (US$0.70) about 1km total between the two border posts, separated by two duty-free stores, a Bancentro and a pool hall.

It costs US$5 to enter Nicaragua, US$2 to leave; Honduras charges US$3 to enter, you exit free of charge. The post is open 24 hours, but buses stop running and other services are curtailed after 6pm. You can drive across this border; Nicaragua charges US$12 to enter, while Honduras has a sliding scale; cars with US plates pay the maximum US$32 to enter.

On the Honduran side, microbuses (US$1.25, 6am to 6pm, every 15 minutes) run regularly to Choluteca, with hotels, restaurants and regular bus service to Tegucigalpa and the Salvadoran border. From the Nicaraguan side, buses serve Chinandega (US$1.25, 1¾ hours, 6am to 6pm, every 25 minutes) and Managua (US$4, five hours, 11am, 1:30pm, 3pm and 4pm), and there is one *directo* to León at 11am daily. If it's late, Somotillo is just a US$0.70 cab ride away.

the massive docks. Cruise ships arrive in February and March, but customers are whisked away to more scenic spots.

The **parque central** is downright audacious, however, a concrete confection of fountains and turtles with a striking nautical-themed clock tower. **Alfonso Cortes-Corinto History Museum, Library & Auditorium** (admission by donation; 7:30am-noon & 1:30-6pm), in the bright blue former train station, has a handful of informative displays about Corinto's once and future greatness arranged around a few railroad artifacts, gathering dust in the grinding reality of the present.

Across the street, a squat, green Catholic church is the final resting place of poet **Azarías H Pallais**, although most literature ignores him, noting instead that **Isla El Cardón**, just offshore, inspired Rubén Darío's poem 'A Magarita Debayle.'

The **beaches** close to town are dirty, but walk just a few minutes north to find cleaner **Paso Caballos**, with a string of thatched restaurant/bars, a terrible rip current and **good surfing**. Between El Corinto and Paso Caballos, a big, hollow left is supposed to be one of the best waves in the country, but it's boat access only. North of Paso Caballos is a river mouth break and some peaks break left. The protected bay also offers world-class **windsurfing**, if you've brought your own equipment – big swells roll in toward the estuary when the tide changes, good for jumps.

El Corinto actually does get packed the first weekend in May for the **Fiesta Gastronomica del Mar**. It begins with a fishing competition and ends with every chef in the department turning out top-quality seafood

dishes for the crowd. Cultural activities, parades, beauty contests and lots of dancing help you work it off.

Stay a while at downscale **Hospedaje Luvi** (342 2637; d US$6), a block from the parque central, with basic rooms, decent shared bathrooms and a couple of hammocks strung up inside. Better, shell out for **Hotel Central** (342 2380; s/d US$30/40; P), across from the port, with huge rooms featuring c 1965 furniture, somewhat newer air-conditioning and cable TV.

Most restaurants are on the water. Costa Azul brings in movers and shakers from León for its shrimp dishes, while El Peruano also has great seafood for under US$5 a plate. At either one, you can hire boats for about US$30 to take you on a **sightseeing tour** of the islands, some of them (including Isla El Cardón; sorry, Darío fans) private and off-limits.

At Puente Paso Caballos (not to be confused with the beach further north) on the road to Corinto, **Restaurante Español** (342 8055; meals US$2-8; 11am-9pm) overlooks the estuary and serves good-quality seafood and paella. The owners' goals include a hotel with windsurfing classes.

Buses (US$0.40, 40 minutes) and microbuses (US$0.60, 25 minutes) depart the parque central every 15 minutes or so for Chinandega.

Playa Aserradores

Worth the bumpy ride from the well-signed exit off the Chinandega–Potosí highway, this long, smooth stretch of sand has two good lodging options, seafood *ranchos* in high season and excellent surfing. The name of the wave is Boom-wavos (The Boom), and it's worth checking Chancletas' website to see it for yourself.

Hotel Chancletas (☎ Apr-Oct 894 4669, Nov-Mar 305 858 1914; www.hotelchancletas.com; d US$30; ⚡) is a comfortable surfers spot offering clean rooms (some with air-con), camping space and an excellent hammock-to-guest ratio. In the end, however, it's all about the view: this grassy hill overlooks the breaks at Boom-wavos, named for the powerful, hollow beach break making all that noise. There's also a left five minutes offshore and a few other good breaks around.

Marina Puesto del Sol (☎ 276 0323; www .marinapuestodelsol.com; d US$110-190, ste US$400; P ⚡ ⚡), another 1km along the road, is a five-star, Santa Barbara–style yacht club offering great views of smoking San Cristóbal from the infinity pool, and even better ones from the enormous, fully equipped (fluffy robes, sofa beds, coffeemakers) rooms, close to the fancy sailboats in the glittering marina. Sure, the amazing private beach is really public, by law, but you won't care as you're shuttled to the oceanfront restaurant in complimentary air-conditioned vans.

The club hosts an international fishing tournament in December, and organizes yacht tours up and down the coast. Upscale outfitter **Kilambé Nature Travel** (☎ 266 9391; www.kilambetours.com) does a yoga retreat here, which would probably be pretty sweet.

Playa Jiquilillo

This endless pale gray beach (pronounced *heekeeleeyo*) frames what you thought existed only in tales that begin 'You should have seen it back when I was first here…' The picture-perfect fishing village fronts a dramatic rocky point, where tide pools reflect the reds and golds of a huge setting sun, Cosigüina's ragged bulk rising hazy and postapocalyptic to the north. The region remains largely undeveloped, despite its beauty and accessibility, because a devastating 1992 tsunami wiped this village out completely.

But it's so perfect right now. Clean and shady, there's no real rip current in the calm cove. Just beyond is a good river-mouth break, with regular peaks where you can almost always carve out a few turns; bring your own board. Most people are here to see **Reserva Natural Estero Padre Ramos**, where you can also arrange lodging. Jiquilillo has two official places to stay, but locals are used to visitors and many have a room they'll rent cheap. Water and electricity are unreliable.

Let Nate know you're on your way to **Hospedaje Rancho Esperanza** (☎ 862 1004; hospedaje_rancho_esperanza@yahoo.com; dm US$4, cabaña s/d/tr/q US$6/10/14/18), a quiet collection of bamboo huts scattered across a grassy field where you can hear the waves crash. The dorm is on stilts above the common area, where meals (US$1 to US$3) and hammocks are available. Horseback rides, turtle tours, area hikes and even the climb up Cosigüina can all be arranged right here; there are discounts for long-term stays. It's just north of the bus stop – ask for 'El Rancho de Nato.'

Originally a health-care volunteer, Nate decided to stay on after his NGO went bellyup. He arranges all manner of volunteer opportunities, and if you have a useful skill (cutting hair, making handicrafts, baking bread) there may be people eager to learn; if you're in marketing, the Children's Club will still take you. Musicians and Spanish-language books are always welcome.

A couple of kilometers north is **Hotel Los Zorros** (☎ 860 3433; s/d US$6/9), in the community of Los Zorros, fronting a picturesque estuary. Cabinas were basic to begin with and have run way down since then; showerheads are decorative. There's an on-site restaurant that may be open.

There are several seafood shacks in Jiquilillo proper, all serving set plates for US$1 to US$3; seafood specials for up to US$10. Standouts include Padre Ramos, Don Rocky and, right before the speed bump, Doña Isabelle. About 200m north of Hospedaje Rancho Esperanza, fancier (cement!) **Gemellos** (mains US$4-9; ⚡) has a swimming pool and ocean views, plus well-prepared seafood.

Buses to Chinandega (US$0.80, 1½ hours) leave at 6:15am, 7:30am, 9:30am, 1:30pm and 3:30pm, returning from the Chinandega Mercadito at 7am, 10am, noon, 3pm and 4:30pm, with continuing service to Los Zorros and Padre Ramos.

Reserva Natural Estero Padre Ramos

A few minutes north of Los Zorros is the community of Padre Ramos, one of 16 small towns inside the federally protected wetlands of **Reserva Natural Estero Padre**

Ramos. The river delta is part of the largest remaining mangrove forests in Central America, and is key in the proposed Reserva Biologica Golfo de Fonseca (Gulf of Fonseca Biological Corridor), a wetlands conservation agreement between Nicaragua, Honduras and El Salvador.

The **ranger station** in Padre Ramos offers access to a boats-only system. Rent boats with local guides or do it yourself in a dugout canoe, and explore these 8800 hectares of mangroves inhabited by alligators, ocelots, all manner of birds and an epic number of mosquitoes. You can visit Isleta Champerico, where the real Padre Francisco Ramos once lived; Isla La Tigre, with swimming beaches; or La Loma Chichihualtepec, a good spot for bird-watching.

Olive Ridley and other sea turtles lay their eggs here between July and December, peaking in October and November, when **Selva** (☎ 884 9156; selvanic@hotmail.com), based in El Viejo, arranges turtle tours and accepts volunteers. It also offers package tours of Estero Padre Ramos year-round, including comfortable bamboo huts with real beds (and mosquito nets!) in paradise, all transportation and food. Huts are in three picturesque spots: Padre Ramos, where the bus drops you off; in Machapa, with bus access from Chinandega; and Venecia, with boat access only. Packages run US$90 for two days, including food, transportation and guides, or you can just show up and stay at any of its outposts for US$10 per person, with meals available for US$3 to US$5 each.

There's other food and lodging in Padre Ramos, including **La Tortuga Boluda** (r per person US$4), a family-run spot with shared bathrooms; they can arrange guided boat tours. Tour prices vary according to the type of boat, running from US$30 for a motorized canoe to US$90 for a plush 10-person *lancha* (small boat). Bargain hard. There are **collective boats** (US$2) from Padre Ramos to Venecia and other inland villages on Wednesday, Thursday and Saturday only.

Buses to Chinandega (US$0.80, 1½ hours) leave at 5:50am, 7am, 9am, 1pm and 3:30pm, returning from the Chinandega Mercadito at 7am, 10am, noon, 3pm and 4:30pm. There's one bus to Machapa daily, leaving the Chinandega Mercadito at 2:30pm.

RESERVA NATURAL VOLCÁN COSIGÜINA

It was once the tallest volcano in Central America, perhaps more than 3000m high, but all that changed on January 20, 1835. In what's considered the Americas' most violent eruption since colonization, this hot-blooded peninsular beauty blew half her height in a single blast that paved the oceans with pumice, left three countries in stifling darkness for days and scattered ash from Mexico to Colombia.

Today, what remains of Volcán Cosigüina reclines, as if spent, the broad and jagged 872m heart of the peninsula. It's now a very manageable (if blisteringly hot) three-hour climb up one of two trails to the top: **Sendero La Guacamaya**, which starts at the ranger's station near El Rosario; and **Sendero el Jovo**, which descends to more developed Potosí. The rare dry tropical forest, home to one of the continent's last sustainable populations of huge red macaws, as well as pumas, spider monkeys and plenty of pizotes, loses its leaves by January.

You can do the trail as a loop, and go on foot, horseback or even in a truck. Whichever way, when you arrive at the lookout you'll be able to gaze out over a 2000m-diameter, rainwater-filled crater lake, dyed a rich blue-green by continuing volcanic activity. Or descend, if you know what you're doing and have real equipment, 700m to the waterline.

And beyond all that lies the **Golfo de Fonseca**, bordered by the largest mangrove stand left in the Americas, shared by three nations whose volcanoes represent them right here: Cosigüina, Volcán Conchagua in El Salvador and Volcán Amapala in Honduras. The majestic rocky islands rising so steeply from the rich and brackish gulf, alive with squawking pelicans and frigate birds, are called the Farallones de Cosigüina; they are all that's left of Cosigüina's mighty peak.

After you come back down, you could hire a boat in Potosí to inspect the islets and Punta San José, or if you have a car you can drive along the shore – and this is a transformative experience – another 15 rocky kilometers further into no-man's-land. In the other direction, around the volcano's back, Punta Ñata overlooks cliffs that plunge 250m into the Farallones-studded sea.

Or relax at one of the many beaches, all in varying shades of dark volcanic sand. The sea turtles love this shoreline, and four Pacific species nest at pitch-black Playa Carbón. Contact **Selva** (☎ 884 9156; selvanic@hotmail.com) in El Viejo for information on volunteering along with University of León students in turtle season.

Sore muscles? Head to the hot springs; you have some choices. In Potosí, **Centro Ecoturistico Potosí** offers hot springs with shade and food service, or go wild at one of several undeveloped springs that locals will happily point out.

Tours

Several outfitters in León (see p169) also offer tours. No matter who you trek with, just remember the mosquito repellent.

Fundación Lider (☎ 344 2381; www.turismo consiguina.com) Offers all-inclusive tours, including transportation from Chinandega or El Viejo, food, lodging and horses; two days and one night run US$60, three days and two nights US$90. The main office is in El Viejo, but there's a representative in the Chinandega Marena (see p182).

Petrona Perez & Yuritzia Zeas (☎ 842 2007, 865 2229; aidepc2004@yahoo.com) Based in El Viejo, these guides go to the top on foot (US$10 per group) or horseback (US$5 extra per person) and arrange homestays (US$10 per person) in the community of Los Laureles, about 2km from the base of the volcano. Sleep in a hammock, share flush toilets and enjoy homemade meals (US$2 to US$3).

Sleeping & Eating

Fundación Lider can arrange a dorm bed or hammock (US$3 per person) at the ranger station in El Rosario, or just show up. Other guide services can arrange homestays in Potosí or El Rosario. In Potosí, you could also stay at Hospedaje Brisas del Golfo, next to the dock, with cement rooms, fans and shared bathroom.

Hotel Cosigüina (☎ 341 2878; www.hacienda cosiguina.com.ni;dm/s/d/tr/q US$20/25/40/60/80; P ⊠) The best of the accommodations around are at this hacienda 65km north of Chinadega. The *finca* was originally founded in 1775, and 55 families still work tgether raising peanuts, sesame and sorghum. You'll stay in a century-old, precious hardwood cheese barn with a partially thatched roof that's been remodeled into comfortable, air-conditioned

rooms. Your hosts offer several tours, including a trip up the volcano in a truck (US$22 per person), horseback rides (US$15), guided hikes (US$7) and hot-spring treks (US$10).

Getting There & Away

It used to be two hours by ferry from Puerto Potosí to La Unión, El Salvador, and there's talk of reinstating the route, which hasn't run regularly since the Contra War. So far, however, it's just talk. Any tour office in León or Chinandega will be able to give you the latest.

There are at least three buses daily to Chinandega (US$1.50, 3½ hours). One bus leaves Chinandega daily for Punta Ñata (US$1.50, 3½ hours) at 12:10pm, returning in the early morning.

NORTHERN HIGHLANDS

Nicaragua's scenery soars into the misty cloud forests of the Northern Highlands, where three ancient mountain chains conspire to fold away, into their thickly forested skirts, cathedrals and quetzales and tumbling waterfalls, not to mention some of the world's best coffee and tobacco.

The cities here are ancient, founded long before the gracefully fortified adobes were erected (as often by British pirates as by Spanish colonists), and many of them still go by their old names. The ridges and valleys between them gave local hero Augusto César Sandino the chance to start building his vision when he made his base here among the pines in the 1920s and '30s. And later, the Contras and Sandinistas who fought in his name, would bury too many of their own in these granite hills.

This is where the Río Coco is born, flowing from the cloud forest to the steaming Caribbean, past campesino coffee cooperatives and indigenous villages, and into the mighty Bosawás.

Climate & Geography

This is the region with the best climate in Nicaragua, assuming you enjoy the all-natural air-conditioning of the Cordillera Dariense, topped with cloud forests over 1200m, where 12°C isn't unusual. If

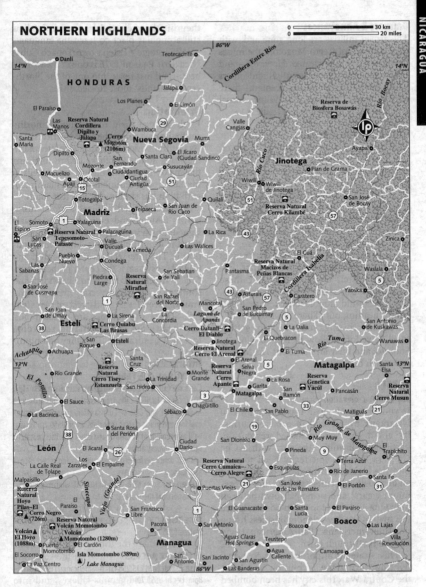

NORTHERN HIGHLANDS

you have your heart set on a hot tropical vacation conducive to tanning, it might not be for you. It's green and muddy in rainy season (May to December), and desiccated and warmer in dry season (January to May), when things get dusty and brown.

The Segovias are Nicaragua's highest mountains, soaring up to 2106m Cerro

Mogotón, the highest point in Nicaragua and one of the last spots (unfortunately) still landmined. Sierra Dipilto-Jalapa, the Segovian Mountains and Cordillera Isabelia are all limestone and granite with acidic soils, hence the four species of pine, evergreen oaks found here, and orchids galore.

NICARAGUA

Dangers & Annoyances

The armed militias are long gone and, with the exception of Cerro Mogotón, the mines have been officially cleared. However – and this really only affects scientists and others headed away from population centers – there are still mines out there. Always hire a local guide and stay on established trails.

Getting There & Around

Bus connections in the region are excellent, and both transportation hubs, Estelí and Matagalpa, are around 2½ hours by bus from Mercado Mayoreo in Managua. There is a daily service to León, as well, but it's usually easier to take buses to San Isidro and change to a León bus there. There's a regular service to Estelí and Matagalpa until 5:30pm.

Many roads are graded dirt that ranges from excellent (Estelí to Jinotega) to impassable (Estelí to El Sauce), but these conditions can change with heavy rains. Drivers should double check with locals before heading out. There are two Honduras border crossings convenient for getting to El Salvador: mellow El Espino, close to Somoto; and busy and efficient Las Manos, just north of Ocotal.

ESTELÍ

pop 85,000 / elevation 856m

If you're one of those travelers drawn to Nicaragua by more than a bit of curiosity about the Sandinista-led revolution, particularly if you're the sort with a Che Guevara T-shirt, you really need to stop into the highland stronghold of Estelí. It's an agribusiness center (specializing in premium cigars) and principal town between Managua and the Honduran border, hence the strip of trucker-friendly business lining the Interamericana (Pan-American Hwy) as it blasts through town.

This strategic importance led to heavy fighting during the revolution and later, the Contra War; this city has been bombed too many times. Regardless, then, as now, it remained one of the Sandinista's strongest support bases in the country. This sentiment is expressed all over town, from murals and bars to the several Spanish schools that were once the first stop of the *internacionalistas* (idealistic young volunteers who came during the 1980s) before

they hit the collectivized farms. Estelí is still a popular place to learn the language, smoke a stogie – Estelí's own Tobaco Cuba-Nica Serie Padrón 1926 is one of the world's best – and just relax into one of the Northern Highlands' most storied cities.

Orientation

Estelí has two main roads running north-south through town, the Interamericana and Av Central, which runs parallel to the Interamericana some 25 blocks before rejoining the major road. The turnoff to Jinotega is marked by a monument on the main road, with both bus stations located just south.

Atypically, Estelí utilizes a street numbering system, and every block is clearly signed; this system is so universally ignored that the official city maps don't even mention it. The intersection of Av Central and Calle Transversal is the center of the system. *Calles* (streets) ascend in number north and south of Calle Transversal; *avenidas* (avenues) ascend east and west of Av Central. Streets and avenues are suffixed 'NE' (northeast), 'SO' (southwest) etc, according to which quadrant of town they belong to.

Information

CULTURAL CENTERS

Casa de Cultura Leonel Rugama Rugama (☎ 713 3021; cnr Av 1a NE & Calle Transversal) Next to El Museo Archeologica, this Casa de Cultura offers a variety of dance, cooking and music classes (per class/week US$0.70/3), as well as evenings of live music and other activities, notably the *peña cultural*, an evening of folkloric dance performed by its students and other activities.

Ixchen (cnr Av 3a NE & Calle 3a NE) This women's center is just north of the market.

EMERGENCY

Police (☎ 118)

INTERNET ACCESS

Casa Estelí (☎ 713 2584; Interamericana; ◷ 8am-8pm; per hr US$0.70)

MEDICAL SERVICES

Cruz Roja (Red Cross; ☎ 713 2330)
Hospital (☎ 713 6303)

MONEY

Banco America Central (BAC; esquina de los bancos) Has a MasterCard/Cirrus/Visa/Plus ATM. Several other banks nearby, including BanCentro and BanPro, have Visa/Plus ATMs

POST & TELEPHONE
Enitel (Calle Transversal) Two blocks east of the post office.
Post office (cnr Calle Transversal & Av Central)

TOURIST INFORMATION
Casa Esteli (☎ 713 2584; Interamericana; ☻ 8am-8pm) Associated with Turicentro Estelimar (p195), this information outlet, right on the highway, has stacks of flyers, a good city map (US$1), lots of information and an Internet café, and arranges tourist packages.
Fider (Foundation for Rural Investigation & Development; ☎ 713 3918; fiderest@ibw.com.ni) The office is 1½ blocks east of PetroNic. Takes care of visitors to Reserva Natural Cerro Tisey-Estanzuela.
Intur (☎ 713 6799; cnr Calle 3 NE & Av 3 NE) This friendly Intur outlet has flyers and other general information about the area.
Marena (Ministry of the Environment & Natural Resources; ☎ 713 2302; delestel@ibw.com.ni) This office manages several reserves, including (nominally) Reserva Natural Miraflor and Reserva Natural Cerro Tisey-Estanzuela, which have good access, and Reserva Natural Cerro Quiabú-Las Brisas, Reserva Natural Mesas de Moropotente and Reserva Natural Cerro Tamabú, which don't. It wasn't geared to tourists at press time, but the Fider office looks after visitors to Reserva Natural Cerro Tisey-Estanzuela and the UCA Miraflor office can arrange everything for Reserva Natural Miraflor.
Unión de Cooperativas Agropecuarias de Miraflor (UCA; ☎ 713 2971; www.miraflor-uca.com; Calle 9a NE; ☻ 8am-noon &12:30-5:30pm Mon-Sat) Looks after visitors to Reserva Natural Miraflor. The office is one block west of the Interamericana, actually inside the schoolyard. Look for the helpful mural.

Sights & Activities
Although Estelí's most impressive attractions are in the mountains surrounding the 'Diamond of the Segovias,' the 1823 **Estelí Cathedral** is worth a wander, and the murals surrounding the parque central (central park) are interesting as well. Several of the parks display **petroglyphs** that were brought down here from the mountains in the early 1900s, many of which are now badly damaged.

Be sure to stop by the **Galería de Héroes y Mártires** (☎ 713 3753; Av 1a NE; donations appreciated; ☻ 9am-5pm Mon-Sat), devoted to fallen revolutionaries, with walls of faded photos and personal effects, from clothing to weaponry, on display. There are spe-

cial exhibits (with a bit of signage in English) about Leonel Rugama Rugama, the warrior-poet whose last line was his best: when he and Carlos Fonseca were surrounded by 300 National Guard, with tanks and planes, they told him to surrender. 'Surrender, your mother!' he famously replied, which is one, quite literally, for the history books.

Next door, **Museo de Historia y Arqueología** (☎ 713 3753; Av 1a NE; donations appreciated; ☻ 8am-noon) has a small collection of pottery shards, shells and other miscellanea that could keep you entertained for a few minutes longer.

A good excuse for a 2km walk toward Jinotega, **Turicentro Estelimar Science Museum & Pools** (☎ 713 7453; www.asdenic.org; admission US$1.25; ☻ 8am-4pm) has a small science museum with some fabulous solar- and pedal-operated dinosaurs made out of old car parts, plus displays involving alternative energy, gears and hydraulics. There are also three attractive pools where you can relax afterward.

About 1km south of town, **Cecalli** (☎ 713 4048; ☻ 8am-5pm) is an organic farming cooperative specializing in medicinal plants; it has a small museum with dried and fresh herbs that is well worth visiting. You can also check out the selection of herbal teas, organic shampoos, *pomada Don Juan* and other herbal remedies, or get a massage (US$5, 30 minutes), have acupuncture, or just talk to a doctor about whatever ails you. No appointment is necessary, and it's about US$6 per treatment. Afterward, La Casita café (p196) is right next door.

Courses
Ananda Yoga (per class US$0.30; ☻ 5pm Mon-Fri) Yoga classes are offered at the Yoga Y Licuaudos Ananda health-food restaurant next to the Casa de Cultura.
CENAC Spanish School (☎ 713 2025; www.ibw .com.ni/~cenac; per week US$140, incl homestay) Also teaches English to Nicaraguans, if you'd like to volunteer. It's 50m north of Cotran Sur.
Escuela Horizonte (☎ 713 4117; www.ibw.com.ni/u /horizont; Av 2 btwn Calles 9 & 10 SE; per week US$165, incl homestay) This well-established program uses its extensive contacts with local development groups to get students involved in the community.

Tours
Both the Spanish schools and Intur can help arrange guides to any of the attractions, or to the wilderness just outside town.

NICARAGUA

ESTELÍ

0 ————————— 400 m
0 ————————— 0.2 miles

To Hotel-Restaurant
La Campiña (5km);
Paradise Discoteque
(5km); Somoto (68km);
Ocotal (78km)

To Miraflor,
La Tunoza (5km)

To Turicentro
Estelimar (1.5km);
Concordia (33km);
Jinotega (66km)

Río Estelí

Calle 9a NE

Calle 8a NE

Av 1a NO
Av Central
Av 1a NE
Av 2a NE
Av 3a NE
Av 4a NE

Calle 3a NE

Calle 2a NE

Parque
Central

Calle 1a NE

Interamericana (Pan-American Hwy)

Calle Transversal

Calle 1a SO

Calle 1a SE

Calle 2a SO

Calle 2a SE

Calle 3a SO

Calle 3a SE

Calle 4a SO

Calle 4a SE

Petrol

Calle 5a SO

Calle 5a SE

Calle 6a SO

Calle 6a SE

Calle 7a SO

Calle 7a SE

Calle 8a SO

Calle 8a SE

Playground

Calle 9a SO

Calle 9a SE

Calle 10a SO

Calle 10a SE

Calle 11a SO

Calle 11a SE

Petrol

Calle 12a SO

Calle 13a SO

Calle 14a SO

To Hospital (500m);
La Casita (1km);
Cecalli (1km); Salto
Estanzuela (5km);
Santa Cruz (10km);
Managua (148km)

INFORMATION

BAC ATM	1 A3
BanCentro ATM	2 A4
BanPro ATM	3 A3
Casa de Cultura Leonel Rugama Rugama	4 B3
Casa Estelí	5 C2
Enitel	6 B3
FIDER	7 B4
Intur	8 B3
Ixchen	9 B6
MARENA	10 B4
Post Office	11 A3
UCA Miraflor	12 C1

SIGHTS & ACTIVITIES

CENAC Spanish School	13 C6
Escuela Horizonte	14 B5
Estelí Cathedral	15 B3
Galería de Héroes y Mártires	(see 16)
Museo de Historia y Arqueología	16 B3
Yoga y Licuados Ananda	17 B3

SLEEPING

Hospedaje Familiar	18 A4
Hospedaje Sacuanjoche	19 B4
Hotel El Mesón	20 B3
Hotel Los Arcos	(see 34)
Hotel Miraflor	21 B3
Hotel Nicarao	22 B3

EATING

Café-Arte Tipiscayan	23 B2
Casa del los Hamburguesas	24 B3
Juventus Centro Cultural	25 A3
La Gran Via	26 A3
Pizza Hot	27 B3
Repostería España	28 B3
Restaurant Casa Italia	29 B4
Restaurant Las Brasas	30 A3
Rincón Pinareño	31 B3
Supermercado Las Segovias	32 A4
Tacomex	33 A3
Vuela Vuela	34 B3

DRINKING

Bar - Restaurant Rincón Legal	35 A5
Studio 54	36 C4
Tabú	37 C1

ENTERTAINMENT

Cinema Estelí	38 B3

SHOPPING

Artesanía Nicaragüense	39 B3
Market	40 B6

TRANSPORT

Agencia Ticabus	41 A3
Cotran Norte	42 C5
Cotran Sur	43 C6
Del Sol Buses	(see 20)
King Quality & TransNica Buses	44 B4

Cigar tours are worth doing. Estelí produces some of the world's finest tobaccos, and if you still haven't quit smoking then you really need to try one, if only to make the rest of us jealous. Most of the seeds are original Cuban stock, as are many of the curing and rolling techniques you're able to see firsthand. Tobacco is harvested March through April and *porros* (cigars) are rolled all year long. In general, you should make arrangements to visit a cigar factory at least 48 hours in advance; guides are always your best bet. **Tobaco Cuba-Nica** (☎ 713 2383), **Empresa Nica Cigars** (☎ 713 2230), **Tobacalera Perdomo** (☎ 713 6227; www.perdomocigars.com) and the huge **Estelí Cigar Factory** (☎ 713 5688; etelici@ibw.com.ni) can all arrange tours.

Casa Estelí (☎ 713 7453; Interamericana; ⏰ 8am-8pm) offers several all-inclusive 'Portal to the Northern Highlands' packages (per person US$50 to US$70, two days) in conjunction with two of the region's plushest hotels, El Pantano (p205), in the highland enclave of Jalapa, and Hotel Frontera (p202), visiting your choice of amazing outdoor attractions that are otherwise very difficult to see.

There's an Estelí Ruta de Café in the works, a grand tour of area coffee producers that will eventually take in the beans at Finca Solidaridad, Culitlán, Estelimar, Lindos Ojos, El Higo, La Garnacha and perhaps others in the area; ask at Intur for more information.

Festivals & Events

Virgen del Carmen (July 16) *Fiestas patronales* with fireworks, fiestas and masses.

Virgen de Rosario (October 7) An annual event since 1521, this was originally celebrated in Villa de San Antonio Pavía de Estelí, too close to the river and those pesky pirates, and moved here with the Virgin in the late 1600s.

Virgen de Guadalupe (December 12)

Sleeping

Very basic budget options abound in the market area; you can save money if you don't need a shower or flush toilets.

BUDGET

Hospedaje Sacuanjoche (☎ 713 2482; Av 1a NE & Calle 2a SE; r per person US$4) Tranquil and an excellent deal on simple but very livable rooms with shelves and personal touches, this clean spot also has a quiet courtyard, paneled

TV area and dining room where breakfast (US$1.25, including coffee) is served.

Hotel Nicarao (☎ 713 2490; Av Central; s/d without bathroom US$10/12, s/d with bathroom US$15/20) Clean and colorful, this lovely spot's charm is hidden behind the storefronts, but come inside to see the pleasant courtyard, murals and attractive rooms, some of which have TVs.

Hotel Miraflor (☎ 713 2003; Av Central; r per person US$7) It's got a friendly owner, fans, foam mattresses and *comida corriente* (mixed plate) served in the thatched-roof restaurant right next door.

Hospedaje Familiar (☎ 713 3666; Av 1a NO; r US$6-15) The sentimental favorite has deep Sandinista roots, and is an OK deal on clean rooms right next to a restaurant with lots of vegetarian options.

MIDRANGE

Hotel El Mesón (☎ 713 2655; Av 1a NE & Calle 3a NE; barlan@ibw.com.ni; s/d/tr with fan US$12/17/23, s/d with air-con US$25/29; P ⁂) The best value in this price range for comfortable rooms with hot-water bathroom and cable TV (test them both) arranged around a grassy courtyard with guarded parking.

Turicentro Estelimar (☎ 713 7453; d US$25, ste sleeping 5 US$35; P 🖳 🖳) On the unpaved edge of town, a US$1.25 cab ride toward Jinotega, Estelimar is isolated but interesting, with an on-site science museum (p193), three pools, Internet and big cabañas that are a good deal for groups and families.

Hotel-Restaurant La Campiña (☎ 610 3510, 855 5105; r per person US$20; P 🖳) Also inconveniently located (or ultra conveniently, depending on your point of view), this attractive hotel, ideal for conferences, is 5km north of town, not far from a cluster of discos and bars. The modern hotel is built to colonial specs, but spacious rooms come equipped with Direct TV, Internet access and hot water. The great restaurant (dishes US$1 to US$5, open 7am to 8pm) has homegrown coffee, fruit juices and healthy snacks, plus a steam-table buffet at mealtimes.

TOP END

Hotel Los Arcos (☎ 713 3830; hotelosarcos@hotmail.com; d with fan/air-con US$35/45; P ⁂ 🖳) The best hotel in town, Los Arcos has the dream location one block north of the cathedral, and lots of beautiful brick arches and colorful rooms that are on the small side but attractively decorated, with quality hot-water bathrooms and free candy. There's a stylish restaurant with stunning views and free Internet on-site.

La Posada Cuaulitlán (☎ 713 2446; s/d incl breakfast US$32/42; P) Worth stopping in for a cup of coffee just to see the place, this shady spot offers beautiful, fully furnished cabinas and a great restaurant, which is a good thing since you're at the south end of town away from everything else.

Eating

The market has the cheapest meals, but the excellent sit-down *fritangas* (barbecue stalls) that set up on the parque central are a much better choice. Self-caterers can visit **Supermercado Las Segovias** (cnr Calle 4a SO & Av 1a NO), a half block from PetroNic, a solid supermarket with great deals on gourmet coffee.

RESTAURANTS

Rincón Pinareño (Calle Transversal; dishes US$2-6; ☻ 8:30am-9pm) Almost worth the trip from Managua – in an *ordinario* – this Cuban restaurant serves up crusty pressed sandwiches that skimp on nothing, truly delicious soups and more in a cozy dining room that can get packed at lunch.

Vuela Vuela (Calle 3a NE; mains US$3-6) One of Estelí's best restaurants, serving delicious roasted meat, good salads and sandwiches, and big breakfasts (*presto* 'coffee' though… hmmm). Not the cheapest place, but worth the splurge if you've OD'd on *gallo pinto*.

Restaurante Casa Italia (Av 1a NE; mains US$3-7; ☻ 5-10pm) Not only does the friendly owner create eight kinds of spaghetti, lasagnas and pizzas, plus good antipasti, from Italian family recipes, he also teaches Italian classes, if you need to brush up.

La Gran Via (Calle 1a SO; dishes US$3-7) Chinese food comes hot, fresh and in large portions; the soups are great. Lunch specials are a better deal.

CAFÉS

La Casita (snacks US$1-4; ☻ 9am-7pm Tue-Sun, 2-7pm Mon) Hidden about 1km south of town along the Interamericana, just past Cecalli (US$0.70 in a cab), La Casita is surrounded by gardens framing a mountain stream, where you can relax amid all the jungly

loveliness over chai tea, homemade yogurt or the signature *mariedas,* a small loaf of whole-wheat bread with different toppings (veggies, hummus, cheese, whatever), then peruse the little shop selling spices, seeds, top-quality handicrafts and other interesting items in front, or (better) wander out back and enjoy the *finca* (farm).

Café-Arte Tipscayan (hearty snacks US$1-3; ☻ 11am-11pm Wed-Mon) The family of San Juan de Limay soapstone sculptor Freddy Moreno serve ultratraditional fare (there's a menu category for 'lukewarm drinks') like *güirílas* and cheese curd, *montucas* and grilled meats, as well as excellent coffee in this amazing space, packed with gleaming art. It's well worth seeing: Freddy sculpted the cathedral's baptismal font, the Stations of the Cross and several secular public pieces displayed throughout the region, plus he's very friendly.

Juventus Centro Cultural (Calle 1a NE; ☻ 9am-6pm Mon-Sat) The open-air patio offers sweeping views of the mountains to the west, making a fine setting for the excellent coffee, *licuados* and sandwiches served.

Casa de Cultura (Calle Transversal; dishes US$1-3) Vegetarian offerings and tasty juices (along with teas, fresh yogurt and pancakes) are served in this pleasant outdoor café.

QUICK EATS

Look for Estelí's signature *montuca,* like a *nacatamale* but with *masa* made of fresh corn and a meaty center with rich mole. Too tired? **Pizza Hot** (Calle 3a NE; ☎ 713 5899) and **Casa del los Hamburguesas** (cnr Calle Transversal & Av 2a NE; ☎ 713 5264) both deliver.

Tacomex (Av 1a NO; dishes US$1-3; ☻ 10am-8pm Sun-Fri) Tex-Mex fast food comes blunted for the sensitive Nic araguan palate but tasty nonetheless; try the 'gringa,' like a quesadilla, with salsa inside.

Reposteria España (Av Central; snacks US$0.50-3) The best bakery in town also serves fresh fruit juices and salads.

Drinking & Entertainment

Bar-Restaurant Rincón Legal (Av 1a NO & Calle 9a SO; ☻ 8pm-late) A beer-soaked shrine to all things Sandinista, plus 'The Wall of Che' for you *internacionalistas* out there, Estelí's best bar is decorated in red and black, and hosts great live music, political commentary and more.

Studio 54 sprawls beside the Interamericana and has a good dance floor plus billiards and a bar. La Hacienda and Tabú can also be fun. About 5km north of town, a group of discos and bars, including fairly swanky Paradise Discoteque, brings in folks from all over the countryside.

Cinema Estelí (Calle 1a NE; admission US$2.25), next door to Recreativo Las Segovias, is Estelí's quaint single screen, showing Hollywood hits.

Shopping

The must-have souvenir of Estelí is a box of cigars, best purchased after a cigar tour (see p193). The region is also renowned for high-quality leather work, including saddles, boots and wallets, which you can find in shops along Av 1a NO and Av Central.

Artesanía Nicaragüense (Calle Transversal) is among the largest of several souvenir shops clustered right here, with the area's incredible pottery and crafted leather items.

La Tunoza Cooperative (☎ 844 7996), in the community of La Tunoza, about 5km north of Estelí, is a women's cooperative that makes paper out of natural fibers like tuza, rice and pine needles.

The big, bustling **market** (Calle 12a SO) is a fine place for fresh veggies, cheap thongs and much, much more.

Getting There & Away

Estelí is a transportation hub, and its easy access to two major border crossings with Honduras makes it an ideal place to catch a bus to El Salvador.

King Quality and **TransNica** (☎ 713 6574, 843 0757 on Sunday) operate out of the same office, half a block north of PetroNic. TransNica buses go to Costa Rica (US$25, 9:30am) and Tegucigalpa (US$20, 4pm); King Quality serves San Salvador (US$28, 7am) and Tegucigalpa (US$25, 7am).

Del Sol Bus (☎ in Estelí 713 3099, in Managua 270 2547, in San Salvador 503-2257 0505) has one bus that leaves for San Salvad or at 8am daily (US$25).

Ticabus (☎ 713 7350; Av Central) offers daily buses to Tegucigalpa and San Pedro Sula (Honduras), Managua and Costa Rica.

Estelí has two beautiful bus terminals, Cotran Norte and Cotran Sur, located at the south end of the city on the Interamericana.

COTRAN NORTE

This very comfortable terminal had a live DJ mixing smooth 1980s soft-rock hits at the time of research.

Jalapa US$3, 2¾ hours, 4:10am and 2pm

Jinotega (via Concordia) US$2, one to two hours, 4:45am, 7:30am, 8:30am, 1:30pm and 4pm

La Branza (Miraflor) US$1, one hour, 5:30am and 12:30pm

Managua expreso US$3, two hours, 4:45am to 3:15pm, hourly; ordinario US$2.25, 1½ hours, 3:30am to 4:30pm, every 30 minutes

Masaya US$2.50, 2pm and 3pm

León US$2.50, 2½ hours, 5:15am, 6:45am and 3pm; microbus US$2.75, two hours, depart when full; alternatively, take the Matagalpa bus and change at San Isidro

Ocotal US$1.50, 1½ hours, 4:10am to 5:35pm, hourly; for border crossing at Las Manos

Pueblo Nuevo US$1.75, two hours, 7:45am to 6:30pm, almost hourly

Quilalí US$3, 3¼ hours, 3am, 4am, 5am, 6:05am, 7:35am, 11:30am and 1pm

San Juan de Limay US$2, two to three hours, 5:30am, 7am, 10am, 12:15pm, 2pm and 3pm

Somoto US$1.50, 1½ hours, 5:30am to 6:10pm, hourly; for border crossing at El Espino

Wiwilí US$4, five to six hours, 3am, 4am, 5am, 7:35am and 8:40am

Yalí (via Venecia) US$1.60, 1½ hours, 5:15am to 4:30pm, almost hourly

COTRAN SUR

Coyolito (Miraflor) US$0.70, 1¼ hours, 5:45am and 12:45pm; returns 8:20am and 3:45pm

La Rampla (Miraflor) US$1, 1¾ hours, 6am, noon and 3:30pm; returns 7am, 11:30am and 4:15pm

Managua ordinario US$2.25, 1½ hours, 3:30am to 6pm, every 30 minutes; expreso US$3, 2 hours, 5:45am to 3:15pm, almost hourly

Matagalpa ordinario US$1.25, 1¾ hours, 5:30am to 4:50pm, every 30 minutes; expreso US$1.30, 1½ hours, 8:05am and 2:35pm

Murra US$3, 3½ hours, 4:45am

San Nicolás (Reserva Natural Cerro Tisey-Estanzuela) US$1, one hour, 7am, noon, 2pm, 3pm and 4:30pm

Sontule (Miraflor) US$1.20, two hours, 2:15pm; returns 8:10am

Yalí (via Venecia) US$1.25, 1½ hours, 5:15am

RESERVA NATURAL MIRAFLOR

Named for the enchanting lake at its heart, Reserva Natural Miraflor was officially declared a nature reserve in 1996, but is privately owned and communally managed. Remarkably, this haven for orchids and trogons is very accessible thanks to the **Unión de Cooperativas Agropecuarias de Miraflor** (UCA; ☎ 713 2971; www .miraflor-uca.com; Calle 9a NE; ◷ 8am-noon & 12:30-5:30pm Mon-Sat) in Estelí. There are basically three different population centers equipped to handle guests.

Sights & Activities

La Rampla has access to trails that climb to 1400m – past amazing scenic overlooks, waterfalls and whatnot – well within the quetzal zone. Convenient buses (US$1, 1¾ hours) run three times daily from Estelí Cotran Sur at 6am, noon and 3:30pm, returning from La Rampla at 7am, 11:30am and 4:15pm.

Sontule is closest to archaeological sites such as Cuevas Apagüise, and surrounded by coffee farms worked by a collective of 25 women, who'll show you around. One bus (US$1.20, two hours) leaves Estelí Cotran Sur at 2:15pm, returning from Sontule at 8:10am the next morning; it may not run during rainy season.

Coyolito is the warmest and closest to Estelí, with the region's loveliest collection of waterfalls, brilliant bird-watching, English-speaking guides and trails into the cloud forest. Make reservations for accommodations through the UCA office in high season. Buses (US$0.70, 1¼ hours) leave Estelí at 5:45am and 12:45pm, returning from Coyolito at 8:20am and 3:45pm.

Local **guides** (per day US$10, horses per person US$7) can take you on 20km of trails 800m to 1450m above sea level, covering a range of habitats from tropical savanna to cloud forest, with mossy oaks, monkeys galore, toucans and a few barnyard friends. Some residents charge a small fee (US$0.30 to US$1) to cross their land.

Sleeping & Eating

There are several choices of accommodations within the reserve, all of which need to be booked through the UCA office in Estelí. **Cabañas** (per person US$17) have more privacy; **farmhouse rooms** (per person US$13) allow more interaction with the people who run the cooperative, should you want to, say, milk the cows. Both options are rustic. You can also **camp** (per person US$1.20) December to April only; bring your own tent and remember, there's no cooking.

Meals (US$2 to US$3) are served family style.

RESERVA NATURAL CERRO TISEY-ESTANZUELA

Smaller, less developed and some say just as beautiful as Reserva Natural Miraflor, the *other* cloud-forest natural reserve, just 10km south of Estelí, is finally developing its own tourist infrastructure. It's a bit dryer and lower altitude, ranging from 700m to 1500m, with acid soils just perfect for those murmuring pines.

Fider (Foundation for Rural Investigation & Development; ☎ in Estelí 713 3918, in Managua 249 6039; fiderest@ibw .com.ni), with offices in central Estelí, manages the reserve and offers a one-night, two-day package tour (per person US$60) including lodging and guided trips to the park's many attractions. This is convenient, as sites are spread out all over the park's 9344 hectares and only accessible by different entrances. You pay the US$2 entrance fee to the reserve at the Fider office.

The main entrance, near the tiny town of Garnacha, has the ranger station and lodge, and accesses the 1.2km **Mirador Trail**, with a view clear to the Cosigüina Peninsula; slightly longer, interpretive **Woodpecker Trail**; and the two-hour trail to **Cuevas de Cerro Apaguaji**, where you can see the Cave of the Duendes and Cave of La Mocuana.

About 10km from the station is the beginning of the more rugged trail to the **Mirador Segoviano**, with views over Estelí and the mountains, and **Galería de Arte El Jacalate**, where a local artisan began carving rock to help overcome his alcohol addiction, and ended up creating cliffs full of wonderful crosses and creatures, including foxes and snakes and other woodland animals.

On the other side of the park, **Salto Estanzuela** (admission free) is an amazing 36m waterfall pouring into a perfect swimming hole; it's probably the park's most visited attraction. The road to the falls starts about 1km south of town, just past the hospital, and heads about 5km southwest on a lousy dirt road to the community of Estanzuela. It's a beautiful walk, or take the Estanzuela bus from Cotran Sur (6:30am and 1:30pm). There are *pulperías* (small grocery stores) on the way, but pack a picnic just in case.

Other attractions to ask your guide about include La Tunoza Cooperative (see p197), El Quebracho's soapstone mines and, most inaccessible of all, Cuevas de la Queserita, near El Pastoreo, with petroglyphs and an abandoned archaeological dig nearby.

Sleeping & Eating

Fider offers basic wooden **dorms** (per person per night/week US$5/25) and **camping** (per person per night/week US$8/40, tent per night US$2).

In addition to the ranger station, you can stay right where the bus drops you off, at **Rancho Don Luis** (no phone; cabins 1/2 beds US$10/15). It's 5km from the park, in a beautiful property with its own incredible view over the Maribios Chain, plus two attractive wooden cabins (and plans for more) with hammocks on the porch, latrines out back, meals (*típica* US$2 to US$3) and – sweet – cable TV inside.

The community of La Garnacha, right by the park entrance, is a small dairy cooperative that makes artisenal Swiss and Italian-style goat cheeses. You can grab a calcium-rich snack or even stay at **Casa Pablo Patricio** (no phone; dm US$5), a rustic dorm with goats next door, OK shared bathrooms, two private rooms, and set meals for US$2 each.

Getting There & Away

Take any San Nicolás bus from Estelí Cotran Sur, and have them drop you at Rancho Don Luis. Buses return to Estelí at 8am, 9am, 10am, 2pm and 4pm. Drivers can go 12km south of Estelí to the turnoff in Santa Cruz, then continue 13km south to Rancho San Luis. Turn right and continue 5km to La Garnacha and the park entrance.

PUEBLO NUEVO

One of the oldest cities in the department, Pueblo Nuevo sits close to ruins that may be evidence of a long-theorized Maya incursion into Central America, as well as one of the oldest paleontological sites in the Americas. Of course, there's no money to investigate either, right now.

Sitio Paleotológico El Bosque was discovered by Rubén Olivas in 1974, just as these woods (about 11km from Pueblo Nuevo) were getting dangerous. Excavations go on sporadically when interested parties find funding, and to date people have found the bones of mastadons, bison, giant armadillos, marine turtles (up here!) and other long-extinct critters dated to between 18,000 and 32,000 years old. There are plans for a museum, someday, but in the meantime you can arrange tours of partially excavated fossils under plastic.

In town, tourist sites are limited. The ultra-Gothic 1922 Catholic **church** is decorated with the year's harvest on May 14, for the festival of San Isidro. **Casa de Cultura Calmecatle** (admission free; ☻ 8am-5pm Mon-Fri) has great murals and a teeny-tiny museum displaying a handful of treasures from nearby San Antonio, including one real jewel: **La Princesa de Pueblo Nuevo**, a probably very pretty young lady who was between 20 and 25 years old sometime between AD 600 and 800, when she died. She was uncovered in 1997 and her skeleton has been the town's pride and joy ever since.

There's not much tourist infrastructure, but the **alcaldía** (☎ 719 2504, 719 2527; alcpun@yahoo.com) will happily help arrange guided tours, horses, lodging and trips to El Bosque. At press time, you could stay in the basic home of **Doña Selina** (no phone; r per person US$3), two blocks from the church, with meals (US$2) provided and guides to El Bosque arranged. **El Chino Restaurant** (mains US$2-4) was building a *hospedaje* (in spite of the name, the food is Nicaraguan). You could also eat at Eskimo, with burgers and ice cream, or Rosti-Cafetín el Viajero, serving *comida corriente* on the park.

In the even tinier town of La Virgen, **Auxilio Mundial** (☎ 275 0066, 275 3430) has a *finca* famous for its excellent blackberries and interesting petroglyphs, and can arrange food and lodging with advance notice.

Buses take the beautiful paved road back to Estelí (US$1.75, two hours) almost hourly from 7:45am to 6:30pm.

SAN JUAN DE LIMAY

On the brisk and breezy outskirts of **Reserva Natural Cerro Quiabú-Las Brisas**, which doesn't have much tourist infrastructure, San Juan de Limay is known for its marmolina, or soapstone, sculptures. The rock itself, a heavy, lustrous stone that seems to glow like alabaster in certain light, is mined at Cerro Tipiscayán and worked by artists all over town. You're welcome to peruse the galleries and workshops, just 44km from Estelí down a lousy road which can be closed in

NICARAGUA

rainy season. There's shrimp cultivation in the rivers and an iguana farm. Buses leave the central park for Estelí (US$2, two to three hours) six times daily.

CONDEGA
pop 8650

Condega, usually translated from Náhuatl as 'the place of the potters,' has been a ceramics production center since long before the Spanish incursion, and remains home to some of the most important factories in the country. But not to worry, non-shopaholics: even if you have no interest in terracotta past and present, Condega's top attraction, a Somoza-era bomber downed during the strafing climax of the 1979 revolution, almost always gets a grin.

Sights & Activities

You can see classic designs at the excellent archaeological museum, or the latest models at the famed **Ducualí Ceramic Factory**, a collective of 13 women who sell their fine work all over the country, just 3km from Condega. Take any bus north. Even closer to town is the **Guacamayo Workshop**, a cooperative where they make beautiful (and more transportable) wooden crafts.

Museo Arqueológico Julio César Salgado (admission US$0.30; 8am-noon & 1:30-4:30pm Mon-Fri) is a surprisingly good museum, right on the park. It is absolutely packed with informatively displayed ceramics, including many examples in a style popular around AD 800, when pots, bowls and incense burners were studded, like an old punk-rock jacket's shoulder. A map to some 60 unexcavated or partially excavated archaeological sites in the area is tucked into the corner, and they plan to offer tours to Sitio San Diego, 3km from town. There's also a room covering more recent Condegan history and culture, and a small library.

Condega's main claim to fame is **Airplane Park**, housing a twin-engine plane used by the FAN (Nicaraguan Air Force) to bomb the region. It was on a reconnaissance mission and flew too low and got shot down on April 7, 1979, much invigorating the desperate struggle in the mountains. This is where couples come to make out.

While the 1962 **El Templo Parroquial de Condega** isn't the prettiest church in Latin America, it gets packed December 11 and

12 for the **Virgin of Guadalupe**. Come a few days later for the **Feria del Patio**, when local women dress up as Mother Nature – in dresses made of corn husks and medicinal plants – and there's a huge party.

Sleeping & Eating

Hospedaje Framar (611 5447, 715 2393; r per person US$3), right on the parque central, is a fine budget option with clean painted-brick rooms, thin foam mattresses and good shared bathroom. English-speaking owner Francisco Centeno has information about everything in Condega, and you can check your email next door at Cybercafé Condeg@net (US$0.70 per hour).

La Granja (715 2521; r with/without bathroom per person US$10/7), about 300m across the highway from town, is an outstanding lodging option with beautiful gardens surrounding a huge pool (per adult/child US$1/0.70) and three high-ceilinged, wooden rooms with fans and mosquito nets; the one with private bathroom is great. The on-site restaurant (dishes US$1 to US$5) will serve you out by the pool.

Lateas Guacal (quesillos US$1; lunch & dinner) serves *tiste* and *quesillos* right by the highway, or sit down at **Restaurant Lindo Vista** (US$2-6), just out of town on the road to Estelí. This sprawling restaurant has a pretty view, which you can enjoy in any number of colorful nooks and crannies over great soups or better barbecue – they bring the sizzling hot plate right to the table.

Getting There & Away

Buses leave Condega's parque central regularly for the following destinations:

Estelí US$0.70, 30 minutes, 6am to 7pm, every 20 minutes

Managua *expreso* US$2.60, 2½ hours, 4:45am and 8:30am

Ocotal US$1, one hour, 7am to 6:30pm, every 30 minutes

Pueblo Nuevo US$0.70, 30 minutes, 8:45am, 9:45am, 10:45am, 11:45am, 12:45pm, 2:40pm, 4:10pm and 7:30pm

Somoto US$1, one hour, 7:30am to 7:10pm, every 30 minutes

Around Condega

Twenty-two kilometers east of Condega, toward the town of San Sebastian de Yalí, tiny, picturesque **Venecia** is home to **Parque Ecológico Cantagallo**, a private, community-managed reserve with a comfortably rustic lodge. **Albergue Venecia** (☎ in Estelí 713 2584; dm US$8), operated by a local farming co-operative with deep Sandinista roots, offers clean, wooden four-bed dorm rooms, family-style meals for US$2 to US$3 (including excellent coffee) and eight gorgeous kilometers of trails that head through the 1500m cloud forest to Laguna Venecia. Guides cost US$1 per hour, horses US$2 more, or take a boat out into the lake for US$3 per hour. Buses (US$1, one hour) leave Condega at 2:30pm and 3pm daily, returning from Venecia at 6am and 8am the next morning.

Just south of Condega is the old indigenous capital of **Totogalpa**, today better known for its incredibly detailed corn-husk dolls. Arrange tours or lodging through **Raúl Sevilla** (☎ 829 4655; puebloindigenachorotegatotogalpa@ yahoo.es), at the Comunidad Indígena de Totogalpa offices on the Totogalpa parque central. Take any bus heading south to Estelí from the Condega parque central.

OCOTAL

pop 32,000 / elevation 650m

Long known as La Sultana del Norte (Sultan of the North), Ocotal is perhaps better described by its modern moniker, 'City of Pines,' a homage to the ocote pines that surround the highland city. This is the capital of the storied Segovias, strewn with wildflowers and bristling with pillars of rock, which once tempted pirates up the Río Coco in search of gold and treasure.

It is more famed, however, for its 1927 liberation by Sandino's 'Crazy Little Army,' which seized control from federal forces and suddenly earned the undivided attention of its neighbors to the north. Ocotal would become the first city in history to be bombed by fighter planes, courtesy of the United States Marine Corps.

Sandino adapted to this revelation in warfare with surprising ease. He became a pioneer of guerrilla warfare hidden beneath the jungle canopy, and would regain control of Ocotal and all of the Segovias before his death.

Orientation

Built on a classic Spanish grid, Ocotal is easy to navigate, and most services are located within a few blocks of the cathedral and stunning parque central, or on the access roads connecting the city center to the highway.

The bus station is beside the highway at the south end of town, just north of where the road splits. The left branch bypasses town to the west, while the right branch heads straight north through the center. The paved road to Jalapa leaves the highway right before the Shell station and Hotel Frontera.

Information

Internet services are available all over town for US$0.70 per hour.

BanPro Opposite the municipal market, BanPro has a Visa/Plus ATM. If you're on Cirrus/MasterCard, you're out of luck.

Cruz Roja (Red Cross; ☎ 732 2485)

Hospital (☎ 732 2491) Ocotal has the region's biggest hospital.

Intur (☎ 732 3429; ocotol@intur.gob.ni) Across from Palí supermarket, one block west of the parque central. It has information about the surrounding Segovian communities, including Jalapa, and may also be able to arrange tours of the Ocotal's nascent Ruta de Café (coffee route), visiting Finca Los Cipreses, Los Jardines and other organic and fair-trade farms.

Police (☎ 732 2333)

Sights & Activities

In the center of town, baroque-neoclassical hybrid **El Templo Parroquial de Ocotal** (1803–69), with a new tower built in 2003 and saints from Antigüa, Guatemala, is a nice enough church, but you're really here for what's considered Nicaragua's finest **parque central** (☸ 6am-10pm). Former mayor Fausto Sánchez was both a botanist and avid gardener, and today more than 100 types of tropical plants, including magnolias, roses, orchids and birds of paradise, scent the air between cypress and pine trees that are more than 100 years old.

Around the corner, **Casa de Cultura** is a graceful 1890 structure whose slender wooden columns once oversaw a US Marine base, and today frame the public library. Continue west three more blocks to 1945 **Monument to San Francisco**, with a photogenic spire and great views all around. Also interesting is 1919 **Hermita San José**, with an onion dome that must have made visiting Soviets stationed along the border somewhat misty-eyed. **Parque Mirador de la Cruz**, on top of the hill with the crosses on it, is a 45-minute walk or US$0.30 cab ride to the top.

Festival de La Virgen de la Asunción, in mid-August, is the best time to show up, when Ocotal's ranching gentry show off their horsemanship through the streets and around the plaza. Or from Thursday through Sunday, after 11pm or so, you can check them out at Discoteca Infinito, four blocks north of the cathedral, or Disco Sky Dancing, close to the Esso.

Sleeping

Hotel Francis (☎ 732 2244; r per person US$2.50) This family-run spot, two blocks south of the park, is the city's best cheapie, with super-clean shared bathrooms, decent rooms with fans and neat little gardens.

Hotelito Familiar (☎ 847 5567; r per person US$2.50) Across the street from the Francis, this one's a bit grungier, but will do in a pinch.

Hospedaje Segovia (☎ 732 2617; r per person US$2) Even cheaper than the Francis or the Familiar, and in a family home two blocks north of the park, it makes lumpy mattresses and shared baths seem for some reason sort of cozy.

Hotel Frontera (☎ 732 2668; nofrosa@ibw.com.ni; s/d with fan US$20/25, s/d/tr with air-con US$43/54/66; P ⊠ ⧏) Behind the Shell station, all the huge rooms at Ocotal's premier hotel have TVs and hot water, and the air-con rooms have telephones and little balconies overlooking the alley and mountain; nonguests can use the pool (per child/adult US$2/3). It's not centrally located, though.

Eating & Drinking

Llamarada Cafetín del Bosque (dishes US$1-3) On the south side of the park, this steam-table buffet gets raves, and justly so – if they're cooking up a big bowl of *baho* (plantain, meat and vegetable stew), you've got to stop by.

Donde La Lucilita (snacks US$1-3; ❀ 8am-noon & 2-9pm) A very nice coffee shop four blocks south of the park, this spot makes its juices with filtered water and serves espresso beverages with light meals.

Hotel y Restaurant Deportiva (☎ 732 2009; mains US$3-7) The hotel four blocks east of the parque central was being remodeled at press time, but the pretty thatched-roof restaurant/bar, with wine, dancing, good steaks and seafood, was tops.

La Yunta (dishes from US$5) One block west and two blocks south of the park, La Yunta

serves Nicaraguan dishes on a pleasant outdoor patio.

Getting There & Away

Buses depart from the **main terminal** (☎ 732 3304), 1km south of the parque central. Border-bound buses stop to pick up passengers by the Shell station at the north end of town.

Ciudad Antigua US$1, 40 minutes, 5am and noon
Estelí *ordinario* US$1.50, 2¼ hours, 4:45am to 6pm, every 45 minutes; *expreso* US$2, 1¾ hours, 4:15am
Japapa US$2, 2½ hours, 4:30am to 4:20pm, every 1¼ hours
Jícaro (Ciudad Sandino) US$2, 2½ hours, 6:15am, 10:45am, 3:20pm and 5pm
Las Manos (Honduran border) US$0.75, one hour, 5am to 4:40pm, every 30 minutes
Macuelizo US$1, one hour, 6am and noon
Managua *expreso* US$4, 3½ hours, 4am to 3:30pm, 10 daily
Murra US$3, 3½ hours, 5:15am, 7am, 8:45am, 12:30pm and 1:25pm
Quilalí US$3, three hours, 5am, 7:45am, noon and 2pm
Santa Maria US$2, 2¼ hours, 12:30pm
Somoto US$0.80, 1¼ hours, 5:45am to 6:30pm, every 45 minutes

DIPILTO

pop 263 / elevation 880m

This tiny mountain town 20km north of Ocotal isn't just any old roadside attraction; it's home to **Santuario de la Virgen de la Piedra,** where the Virgin of Guadalupe gazes down on her adoring masses from the top of a very large rock. It's a pilgrimage site surrounded by lovely gardens, and the spring nearby may have healing properties. December 12, the Virgin's feast day, is a party – and a serenade.

While we would never recommend it, this is a good place to begin inquiring about **Cerro Mogotón** (2106m), the highest point in Nicaragua and centerpiece of difficult-to-access Reserva Natural Cordillera Dipilto y Jalapa. It's also home to one of the last minefields left in Nicaragua; locals sometimes hear 'the explosions of large animals.' But we've heard that it's possible to climb.

Parador Turistico La Cascada (☎ 732 2620, 855 0238; US$2-8), a few hundred meters north of the shrine, has good beef dishes and great coffee (Finca El Dipilteño; it's amazing). It can also arrange a hiking tour: two people minimum (US$5 per person) leave Ocotal at 6am for the top of 1867m El Volcán, covered with cloud forest and quetzals – so wear long pants. As part of the tour you can spend the night at **Finca San Isidro** (r per person incl dinner & breakfast US$15), a coffee plantation with a few spare rooms. **Distribuidora Mantugales** (Banco DF, 75 varas norte) in Ocotal, a dry-goods shop signed 'El Barratillo del Mercado' around the corner from Intur, also arranges the trip – and sells bags of that amazing coffee.

Take any bus bound for the Las Manos border crossing (they stop at the Shell station in Ocotal) and ask the driver to let you out in Dipilto; buses run south to Ocotal and beyond every half-hour or so.

OCOTAL TO JALAPA

The smooth 65km paved road into the alpine loveliness of Jalapa traverses beautiful mountains holding any number of interesting sites, most easily accessible with a guide or your own vehicle. This is the heart of the Segovias, so count on spur roads to be 4WD only in rainy season. Buses from Ocotal serve most of these locations several times daily.

About 3km north of Ocotal, **Mozonte** is most famously home to **Colectivo de Artesanías de Mozonte** (ceramics collective; 8am–5pm), where you can watch the artisans at work using a variety of different techniques, then buy your favorites, cheap. You can arrange a tour of less well-known ceramicists and other local sites, including **La Gruta de Guadalupe** (another rooftop shrine to the Mexican Virgin) or, for adventurous souls, **Reserva Nacional Cordillera Dipilto y Jalapa**, where you really should have a guide. Ask at the ceramics collective (right across from the park entrance) about guides, or contact **José Fermin Torres** (896 2169, 732 2872; puebloindigenademozonte@yahoo.com).

There's a well-signed turnoff to **Ciudad Antigua**, a Spanish colonial masterpiece about 5km from the main road. Founded in 1536 and under almost constant attack from local indigenous groups for the next century, it was sacked in 1654 by pirate Henry Morgan, who had come up the Río Coco in a canoe. The city's main claim to fame is beautiful **Santuario de los Milagros**, with a Christ figure brought from Austria in 1665 and backed with a facade of Spanish ships sailing up the Río Coco,

today just a trickle of its former self. Attached **Museo Segoviano** has a few fossils and pre-Columbian ceramics, plus a fairly good assortment of colonial artifacts and pirate lore. Other attractions include the ruins of Convento la Merced and 'the best baseball stadium in Nueva Segovia.'

Back on the main road, continue through the speedbumps of **San Fernando**, with a great parque central, and consider making a left turn for the 13km road to **Salto San José**, the highest-altitude major waterfall in Nicaragua, falling from the Cordillera Dipilto into the coffee zone. Cerro Mogotón is less than 20km from town.

About 10km past San Fernando, you can make a right onto the recently graded and excellent dirt road to **El Jícaro (Ciudad Sandino)** and **Murra**, with what may be the highest and most amazing waterfall in the country. Pass **Santa María**, with beautiful Laguna Fría and the Las Brisas hot springs. Next is El Jícaro, where Minas San Albino were mined by Sandino's military for gold. There are two cheap *hospedajes*, **El Segoviano** (735 2411), close to the El Jícaro entrance, and **Maryfer** (735 2243), and a few simple restaurants.

Eventually, you'll come to the community of **Murra**, undulating between 820m and 1300m above sea level, where the *alcaldía* (no phone) can arrange lodging and transport 24km northeast to the municipality of **El Rosario**. Tiny Murra is home to **Finca Santa Rita**, which sits on 200 hectares of land that include the singularly spectacular Salto el Rosario waterfall, with three sections in rapid succession that total more than 200m.

About 15km south of Jalapa is the turnoff to **El Limón** and the smaller town of **Aguas Calientes**, with hot springs. Great for the skin (if a bit hard on the nose), these hot springs are saturated with sulfur and are far too hot to enter close to the source; try the pools next to the river.

JALAPA

pop 13,266 / elevation 687m

This wonderful mountain town was long isolated by a lousy, if scenic, dirt road. That's all been paved (well, cobblestoned), and today the tropical highland town of Jalapa, in the foothills of several peak stopping 1500m, is the gateway to a rare wilderness only recently opened to the casual tourist.

September is the **Feria de Maiz**, or the Corn Festival, when corn clothing, altars and culture all come together for corn contests, theater and dances that tell the history of corn. Also on offer are tamales, *rosquillos*, *montucas*, *elotes*, *güirílas* and more.

In addition to one bank, ProCredit, with no tourist services, Jalapa has three Internet cafés, all charging US$1 per hour, near the park.

Sights & Activities

Access to the wilderness isn't easy, but both the *alcaldía* and El Pantano hotel (opposite) can find guides (around US$10 per day), some of whom may speak English, Russian and/or German. The *alcaldía* also manages **La Jungla Municipal Reserve**, 40 hectares of primary rain forest right on the border, accessible by vehicle in dry season and a 3km hike from Teoticacinte in muddy season, when you should really tip the guide extra.

Other possible treks include visits to a couple of beautiful coffee *fincas* with little tourist infrastructure. **Las Nuberones**, close to El Limón, has coffee plantations, a pine forest and guides who speak English, while **Finca Selva Verde** is a huge property with waterfalls and coffee and is trying to develop into a tourist attraction. Ask about **La Cueva del Tigre**, with a petroglyph calendar.

La Esperanza is a women's cooperative that makes handicrafts out of pine needles, which are sewn into bundles and made into Dr Seuss–style containers and sculptures. Some 70 women spread across five communities belong to the co-op, and also support one another with a variety of undertakings, from *fritangas* to farming.

Near Jalapa, the road is paved all the way to **Teoticacinte**, right on the border (with no official crossing), where ruins of a 1500-year-old town are being excavated. There are also two more wild **hot springs**, in Santa Barbara and El Porvenir, nearby; the latter is medicinal.

Tours

You can arrange guided tours through Casa Estelí (p193) in Estelí, which works with the region's best hotel, El Pantano (opposite). El Pantano's owner, Wim van der Donk,

---

BORDER CROSSING: EL ESPINO & LOS MANOS

From Estelí, there are two major border crossings to Honduras, convenient to getting to El Salvador.

El Espino, 20km west of Somoto, is the least used and mellower of the two, and the scenery isn't bad either. From Somoto, buses (US$0.40, 30 minutes) leave for the border hourly from 5:15am to 4:15pm. It costs US$5 to enter Nicaragua, US$2 to leave; Honduras charges US$3 to enter, and exiting is free. Most services, including buses, only operate 7am to 5pm. You can drive across this border; Nicaragua charges US$12 to enter, while Honduras has a sliding scale; cars with US plates pay the maximum US$32 to enter.

On the Honduran side, microbuses (US$0.60, 7am to 5pm, every 30 minutes) run regularly to San Marcos, with hotels, restaurants and regular bus services on to Tegucigalpa (US$3, 4½ hours, almost hourly). From the Nicaraguan side, buses serve Somoto (US$0.40, 30 minutes, every 15 minutes) and Managua (US$4, four hours, 7am to 5pm, hourly). Somoto is a 20km, US$4 per person cab ride away.

Las Manos, about 15m north of Ocotal, is the major Honduras–Nicaragua border crossing, and mountains are even more dramatic. This is a true 24-hour border, though bus service only runs 6am to 6pm. All crossing fees are the same as at El Espino. This crossing has two tiny duty-free stores, a *casa de cambio* on the Honduran side, and *coyotes* offering lousy exchange rates – know how much you should get back ahead of time. There's even lodging on the Nicaraguan side, **Hospedaje/Comedor Los Laurales** (☎ 840 4198; r US$3), with very nice owners and terrible cement rooms.

Microbuses to the Honduran town of Paraíso (US$0.70, 30 minutes) run every half-hour 6am to 6pm, from where you can catch a bus to Tegucigalpa (US$3, 2½ hours, five daily), or more convenient Danlí (US$2, 1½ hours, 6am to 5:45pm, almost hourly), with hotels and other services. In Nicaragua, buses run to Ocotal (US$0.75, 30 minutes) every half-hour.

speaks Dutch, Spanish and English, and can arrange guides to all the sights as well as specialty tours of cigar factories and Finca Cerro de Jesús (1793m), in the community of El Escambray, with 600 *manzanas* of organic coffee, a nature reserve and an 8m waterfall. The *alcaldía* can also help with tours.

Sleeping & Eating

El Pantano (☎ 737 2231; hotelelpantano@yahoo.com; s/d US$10/17). Cabins spread across the wilderness, about six blocks from the city center (look for signs down the dirt side roads), are cute and clean. Warm up over amazing coffee at the restaurant (dishes US$2 to US$6, open 7am to 11pm) serving good *típica*, including the house specialty, '*boca* Pantano,' which might be better known as *bitter ballen*. Two-day all-inclusive packages have a two-person minimum and cost US$50 to US$70 per person, depending on your plans.

Hotelitón No 1 (☎ 737 2229; d without bathroom US$4, d with bathroom US$10-20; ❇ Ⓟ) Truckers love this sprawling hotel, where rooms with private bathroom are much nicer. Some come with air-con and cable TV.

Hotel Jonatan (☎ 737 2210; s US$10, d US$7-15; Ⓟ) This spot spoils its guests with a variety of very clean, well-kept rooms surrounding the guarded parking lot. For a little extra, you get cable TV and more natural light.

Típico del Norte (dishes US$2-5; ⏰ lunch & dinner) Across from Hotel Jonatan, this local fave does good, meaty mains and a brisk trade in beer after dark.

Restaurant Luz de Luna (dishes US$3-8) One block from the park, this is a relatively upscale dining option, serving Nica classics, that turns into a disco after dinner.

Getting There & Away

Although the dream trip to Jalapa would end with a rapid bicycle descent down the smooth paved road, you'll probably be taking the bus; the station is just south of town, near the cemetery.

El Jícaro (Ciudad Sandino) US$1.25, 1½ hours, 6am to 4pm, hourly; meets buses to Murra
El Porvenir US$0.80, 45 minutes, six daily
Estelí US$4, 4½ hours, 3:45am and 10am
Managua US$7, 5½ hours, 4am, 9am and 2pm
Ocotal US$2, 1½ hours, 5am to 4pm, hourly
Teotecacinte US$0.60, 30 minutes, 5am to 5pm, hourly

SOMOTO

pop 28,000 / elevation 705m

Somoto was once just another quaint colonial border town, a little bit war-torn but friendly, your last stop for a big plastic bag of delicious *rosquillos* (cornbread rings) before entering Honduras. Then, in 2003, a pair of Czech scientists working for Ineter (Nicaragua Institute for Territorial Studies) stumbled across the discovery of a lifetime: a mere 75 million years after these solid granite peaks were first forced up from the sea, Europeans laid eyes on appropriately inspiring **Somoto Canyon**, where the Río Coco, Central America's largest river, is born.

Powerful from the get-go, the young mountain stream is currently wearing away a ribbon-thin canyon – 3km long, sometimes 160m tall and less than 10m wide – from the solid granite heart of Namancambre Canyon. The town's original inhabitants probably knew all about it: Somoto is the Spanish corruption of Tepesomatl, or 'Mountain of Water.'

Today protected as part of **Reserva Natural Tepesomoto-Pataste**, the gorge is phenomenal, with steely gray cliffs and graded peaks carved from the dry forest and pockmarked with caves. It's a 3km hike into the canyon from a trailhead that leaves from a well-signed exit 15km north of Somoto. A taxi can take you there for US$4. **Guides** (US$6-10) are highly recommended, because the hike is slippery and the water tricky, but they're not required. You need to be in good physical condition for this hike. Nearby, in the community of Macuelazo, there are also the **Hervideros de Macuelazo**, basically bubbling mud springs.

Somoto itself, the capital of the Madriz department, is a small, easily navigable Spanish colonial grid, centered on the graceful 1661 **Iglesia Santiago**, a pretty adobe with a Black Christ inside, fronting a shady parque central.

Information

BDF Less than a block from the park, the only bank in town changes only US dollars.
Cybernet Sylva (per hr US$0.80) Next to Hotel Colonial.
Hospital (☎ 722 2247)
Marena (☎ 722 2431) Tourist infrastructure is still pretty seat of your pants, but Somoto's Marena, a block and a half south of the church, can help you find

information, guides and, perhaps, *burros*. Any hotel should be able to help, too.

Police (☎ 722 2359)

Sleeping

Hotel Panamericano (☎ 722 2355; r with/without bathroom per person US$10/3; ℗) Even if you don't stay here, right on the plaza, staff can arrange guides to the canyon, and there's a solid souvenir shop. There's a range of rooms, from super-simple boxes with shared hot-water bathrooms to spacious, better private rooms, some with refrigerators and/or TVs.

Hospedaje La Providencia (☎ 722 2089; r per person US$3.50) This family-run budget option has lots of doves, a parrot and a cat, plus simple, very clean rooms (with shared bathrooms) with thin mattresses, hammocks out front and winning hostesses.

Hotel Colonial (☎ 722 2040; s/d/tr US$18/24/30; ℗ 🖭) As close to luxury as this town gets, they've gone all out gold satin bedspreads, with mock–Louis XIV furniture, hot-water showers and a pool, right around the corner from the church.

Finca La Virgen (☎ 719 2445; cabañas US$15) You could stay closer to Reserva Natural Tepesomoto-Pataste at this cooperative (day admission US$5) close to Pueblo Nuevo Macuelizo, with trails through coffee plantations, neat cabañas and guided treks on foot and horseback into the canyon.

Eating

Carne Asada el Buen Gusto (meat dishes US$1-2) Across from Marena, this tiny purple spot has cheap, good *típica* and better pork plates.

Don Chu (US$4-10) Go upscale one block west at Don Chu, with real tablecloths and good steak and fish dishes.

Bar y Restaurant El Almendro (US$3-9) Everyone's favorite, across from Hotel Colonial, with high-quality *típica* and a festive vibe.

Somoto is most famous for *rosquillas*, which at their simplest are crusty cornbread rings, hard baked and served with black coffee. You may have sampled them elsewhere, but even if your experience was a bit gritty and tasteless, it's time to try again. In Somoto, somehow richer *rosquillas* are baked plain, with cheese and/or herbs, or sweetened with cinnamon and molasses. They come in different shapes and sizes (with different names like *rosettes* and *tostaditas*, though all will eventually answer to *rosquilla*). The best *rosquilla* restaurants are roadside cafés, inconvenient to town, but you can buy a baggie of those babies anywhere – try the Somoto bus station.

Getting There & Away

The bus station is on the Interamericana, a short walk from the center of town.

El Espino (Honduran Border) US$0.40, 30 minutes, 5:15am to 4:15pm, hourly

Estelí US$1.25, 1¾ hours, 5:20am to 4pm, every 45 minutes

Managua *ordinario* US$4, 4½ hours, 4am to 5pm, almost hourly; *expreso* US$4.25, four hours, 5am, 6:15am, 7:30am, 2pm, 3:15pm and 3:45pm

Ocotal US$0.70, one hour, 3:45am to 4:30pm, every 45 minutes

MATAGALPA

pop 105,000 / elevation 650m

This is the gateway to Nicaragua's most impressive mountain range, and as such one might think this would be a misty and untouched mountain village. Nope – that'd be Jinotega, just up the road. Matagalpa, Náhuatl for 'Ten Cities,' is a bustling and cosmopolitan regional capital, a sea of urban sprawl straining against the natural reserves and mountain barriers that hem it all in. Cars honk and sidewalks bustle in the cool mountain air as rural visitors run their big-city errands. This is the nerve center for Nicaragua's vital and gourmet coffee-growing industry, and these are the people who make sure you get your fix.

If it's all a little too overcaffeinated for you, wild nature – and lots of it – is just a short hike away. Matagalpa makes a very comfortable, even sophisticated, base for cloud-forest reserves and coffee-related tours, including one organization that will put you up in a grower's home so you can see firsthand what that few cents extra for a cup of Fair Trade coffee really buys. And when you come back to the big city, you'll appreciate the great restaurants, hotels and nightlife even more.

Orientation

Bordered on its western edge by the Río Grande de Matagalpa, the city sprawls between two principal plazas, Parque Morazán on the north side and the scruffier Parque Rubén Darío to the south. The cathedral faces Morazán; budget accommodations are concentrated around Darío. The two main bus stations lie at either end of the city, almost 2km apart.

Information

EMERGENCY
Police (☎ 772 3870)

INTERNET ACCESS
Internet access is available for around US$0.70 per hour at Internet cafés all over the city.
Cyber Moagüina (per hr US$1; ⏲ 9am-8pm) More expensive, but has big screens, great coffee and fruity beverages.
Downtown Cyber (per hr US$0.70) Close to Hotel Apante.

MEDICAL SERVICES
Hospital (☎ 612 2081)
Cruz Roja (Red Cross; ☎ 772 2059)

MONEY
BanPro and BanCentro, both with Visa/ Plus ATMs, are clustered with several other banks two blocks south of Parque Morazón.
BAC With an ATM on both Visa/Plus and Cirrus/MasterCard networks, half a block east of Parque Morazón, across from the Toyota dealership.

POST & TELEPHONE
The Enitel office is a block east of the cathedral. There is a post office one block south of Parque Morazón and another opposite Parque Darío.

TOURIST INFORMATION
CIPTMA (Center for Tourist Promotion of Matagalpa; ⏲ 8am-12:30pm & 2-7pm) The Museo de Café (p209) operates a CIPTMA desk, which can make hotel reservations and has information about visiting area coffee plantations.
Intur (☎ 612 7060; matagalpa@intur.gob.ni) Two blocks north of Parque Darío, this unusually professional Intur outlet has flyers and information on tour guides, hotels and coffee fincas. It sells a useful map for US$3, and also has a good, free, bilingual visitors guide.
Marena (☎ 772 3926) Despite managing easy-to-access Reserva Natural Cerro Apante and Reserva Natural Cerro El Arenal, as well as undeveloped Reserva Natural Guabule, Reserva Natural Cerro Pansacán, Reserva Natural Cerro Sierra Quirriagua, Reserva Natural Fila Cerro Frio-La

Cumplida and Yucúl Genetic Reserve, this Marena was not particularly useful for tourists at the time of research. The Secretaria de Ambiental office, around the corner, may also have information.

Sights & Activities

The 1874 **Iglesia Catedral San Pedro** is considered one of the country's most beautiful buildings. It's a solid neoclassical structure that has simply seen one too many bombing runs. Originally founded by the Jesuits, who were later run out of the country, this fading beauty fronts **Parque Morazón**, where most of the city's public events take place. Across the street, 1938 **Palacio Episcopal** is architecturally interesting and now houses the high school.

Iglesia San José was originally constructed in 1751 and used as a jail for indigenous rebels in the late 1800s, then rebuilt to its current glory in 1917 by Franciscan friars. It fronts **Parque Rubén Darío** and has a nice baroque altar. The 1751 **Iglesia Molagüina**, in the center of town, is the plainest of the churches but has nice gardens.

Just east of the city are two outstanding cemeteries, if you're into that sort of thing; the **Foreigners Cemetery** and the **National Cemetery**. There are great views, a break from the traffic and the headstone of Benjamin Linder, an American hydroelectric engineer and unicycle clown who was killed by Contra forces in 1987.

CASA MUSEO COMANDANTE CARLOS FONSECA
This low-budget but heartfelt **museum** (donations appreciated; ⏲ 9am-noon & 2-5pm Mon-Fri) honors Commander Carlos Fonseca, the intense and bespectacled architect of the Sandinista Movement. He grew up in this humble adobe with his single mother and four siblings, like Sandino, caught between abject poverty and relative wealth after his coffee-scion father finally admitted paternity when Carlos was in grade school.

At age 19, in 1955, Fonseca joined the PSN (Nicaraguan Socialist Party) and started publishing Marxist tracts. After the 1959 Cuban Revolution he was invited to a journalists' convention in Havana, where he ended up staying to host Sandino discussion groups. This sort of thing didn't sit well with the Somozas, who had him jailed

NICARAGUA

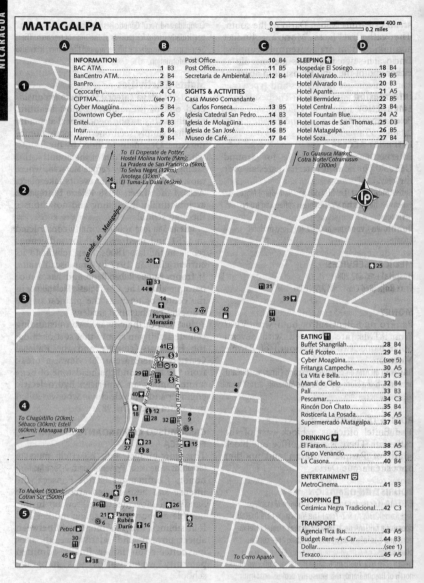

MATAGALPA

0 — 400 m
0 — 0.2 miles

INFORMATION
BAC ATM...............................1 B3
BanCentro ATM......................2 B4
BanPro.................................3 B4
Cecocafen............................4 C4
CIPTMA..........................(see 17)
Cyber Moagüina.....................5 B4
Downtown Cyber.....................6 A5
Enitel..................................7 B3
Intur...................................8 B4
Marena................................9 B4
Post Office...........................10 B4
Post Office...........................11 B5
Secretaria de Ambiental............12 B4

SIGHTS & ACTIVITIES
Casa Museo Comandante
    Carlos Fonseca.................13 B5
Iglesia Catedral San Pedro........14 B3
Iglesia de Molagüina...............15 B4
Iglesia de San José................16 B5
Museo de Café.....................17 B4

SLEEPING
Hospedaje El Sosiego..............18 B4
Hotel Alvarado.....................19 B5
Hotel Alvarado II...................20 B3
Hotel Apante.......................21 A5
Hotel Bermúdez.....................22 B5
Hotel Central.......................23 B4
Hotel Fountain Blue................24 A2
Hotel Lomas de San Thomas......25 D3
Hotel Matagalpa....................26 B5
Hotel Soza..........................27 B4

To El Disperate de Potter;
Hostel Molina Norte (5km);
La Pradera de San Francisco (5km);
To Selva Negra (12km);
Jinotega (32km);
El Tuma-La Dalia (45km)

To Guanuca Market;
Cotra Norte/Cotramusun
(300m)

Río Grande de Matagalpa

Parque Morazán

To Chagüitillo (20km);
Sébaco (30km); Estelí
(60km); Managua (130km)

EATING
Buffet Shangrilah..................28 B4
Café Picoteo.......................29 B4
Cyber Moagüina..............(see 5)
Fritanga Campeche................30 A5
La Vita é Bella.....................31 C3
Maná de Cielo......................32 B4
Palí..................................33 B3
Pescamar............................34 C3
Rincón Don Chato..................35 B4
Rosticería La Posada...............36 A5
Supermercado Matagalpa.........37 B4

DRINKING
El Faraon...........................38 A5
Grupo Venancio....................39 C3
La Casona...........................40 B4

ENTERTAINMENT
MetroCinema.......................41 B3

SHOPPING
Cerámica Negra Tradicional......42 C3

TRANSPORT
Agencia Tica Bus..................43 A5
Budget Rent -A- Car...............44 B3
Dollar...........................(see 1)
Texaco..............................45 A5

To Market (500m);
Cotran Sür (500m)

Parque Rubén Darío

Petrol

To Cerro Apante

---

when he returned, forcing him to sit still long enough to write the widely published letter, 'From Jail I Accuse the Dictator.' After a few years of exile in Costa Rica, Fonseca returned to the fight. In 1976, during a National Guard ambush in the tiny town of Zinica, Matagalpa, Fonseca was gunned down.

But, as with Che Guevara and Obi-Wan Kenobi, killing Fonseca only made him stronger. He was already the revolution's semiofficial philosopher; his heroic death made it its face (which is good PR, considering it could have been Ortega). His childhood home is dominated by his most famous image, a painting of him looking every inch the disco swinger that he absolutely was not. If you can read Spanish, you'll appreciate the two rooms full of newspaper clippings and water-stained original documents that chronicle this remarkable man's life; anyone can contemplate his glasses and typewriter. And machine gun. Curious? The best biography available in English is *Sandinista: Carlos Fonseca and the Nicaraguan Revolution*, by Matilde Zimmermann.

MUSEO DE CAFÉ

There's a lot of information in this **museum** (Av José Benito Escobar; admission free; ☺ 8am-12:30pm & 2-7pm), almost all of it in Spanish, and very little actually pertains to coffee. Staff, however, who also operate a tour desk, are highly caffeinated, offer free cups of coffee, and also sell bags of the stuff. This is actually more of a Nicaragua and Matagalpa history museum. It begins with a nice archaeology display, then segues into high-school-quality exhibitions about the city and region, from photos of beauty-contest winners past and present through a list of Latin America's great liberators, from Bolívar to Martí.

HIKING

Hiking maps (US$1.50 each) with maps and precise instructions ('after going under the barbed-wire fence, take the small path to the left of the big bend in the stream…') are sold by Centro Girasol café (p213). Routes include:

Ruta Cerro El Toro (three to six hours) See the bull-shaped rock (really!) and wonderful city views.
Ruta de Cafe (2½ to seven hours) Climb up into the organic coffee farms in the mountains around town.
Ruta de la Guerra 1978 (1½ to five hours) When Matagalpans fled the city in 1978, they hid at Cerro Buena Vista and Cerro Apante; there are fine views.
Ruta de la Guerra 1979 (1½ to four hours) The National Guard later retreated to scenic Cerro El Calvario, along paths now lined with pottery studios and forests.
Ruta Santuarias de Chagüitillo (two to seven hours) Keep going when the museum's petroglyph guide turns around.

RESERVA NATURAL CERRO APANTE

This must be among the easiest-to-access reserves in Nicaragua, with walking access (for hearty souls) right from town. Or, you could even hitch most of the way to the top of the cool, misty 1442m peak on the access road.

Either Intur or Marena may be able to find guides, if you'd prefer, and Matagalpa Tours (below) offers guided hikes (US$10 to US$16, five hours) to the top.

There are two other entrances to different sectors of the park; one is just north of town on the road to El Tuma, the other on the road to Guadalupe–Samulali, off the Matagalpa–Muy Muy road.

Tours

Matagalpa Tours (☎ 772 4581; www.matagalpatours.com) does rural community tourism, and takes you to tiny towns (perhaps on mountain bikes?), such as the indigenous community of El Chile, known for its beautiful fabric arts. Among other offerings, it arranges one- to six-day guided hikes through the mountains; gold-mine tours (US$25 per person) and a Matagalpa City Tour (US$16); it has English- or Dutch-speaking guides, too. Spanish lessons are also offered.

Festivals & Events

Anniversary Party (February 14) This may be the biggest party in the Northern Highlands, a fireworks-splashed extravaganza with live music, parades, beauty contests and lots of *chicha bruja* (fermented corn liquor). The region's biggest handicrafts festival, Fair Nicamer, takes place in the weeks leading up to the event.
Fiestas Patronales (September 24) Rather more sedate festivities and *hipicas* (horse parades) honor the Virgin of Merced.
Festival of Polkas, Mazurkas and Jamaquellos (mid-October) It's sort of like Oktoberfest, but with *chicha bruja* instead of beer and *güiilas* instead of sausages. More traditional Oktoberfest celebrations go on at Selva Negra (p215), where there's also a coffee harvest celebration later in the month.

Sleeping

There are a handful of *hospedajes* near Cotran Norte where privacy and security, not to mention flush toilets, are nonexistent, with beds for under US$2 per night.

BUDGET

Hotel Apante (☎ 772 6890; s/d without bathroom US$6/9, d/tr with bathroom & air-con US$12/15; ✺) This excellent budget choice has clean, simple rooms with high ceilings, lots of light and great security – and free coffee all day. Some of the better rooms with private bathroom also have cable TV, and the bubbly owner knows a lot about the region.

There are two inexpensive options by the river: claustrophobic **Hotel Soza** (☎ 772 3030; r per person US$5), with clean, if institutionally furnished units with private bathrooms; and more basic, but much more spacious, **Hospedaje El Sosiego** (no phone; d US$6), with big, wonderful beds inside dark, cool, cement rooms that may make you feel like you're

in a castle – the haunted kind. Shared bathrooms use bucket-flush technology.

Hotel Bermúdez (☎ 616 7073; s/d US$3/5) This somewhat smelly entry, east (up a steep hill) of Parque Rubén Darío, prides itself on being the cheapest place in town – grab a sagging mattress and make a deal.

Hotel Matagalpa (☎ 772 3834; d with/without bathroom US$6/4) One block east of Parque Rubén Darío, thin walls and fan-cooled

---

COFFEE ROADS OF THE HIGHLANDS

La Ruta de Café

There must be a dozen *Rutas de Café* (Coffee Trails) promoted throughout the Northern Highlands. Matagalpa's is the best developed, and you can do it on your own with help from Intur or the Museo de Café, or go through Matagalpa Tours (p209). Coffee is harvested between October and February, when beans are picked, soaked, cleaned, dried and prepared for roasting; come in April to enjoy the tiny white blossoms. Plantation tours are usually followed with free samples or a visit to a 'cupping room.'

There are several official members of the Ruta de Café, all offering slightly different angles on coffee tours. Two of the best-organized options, easy-to-visit Selva Negra (p215) and award-winning Finca Esperanza Verde (p216), are covered later. Others include:

Finca La Ponderosa (bookings through Intur or the Museo de Café) Four kilometers north of Matagalpa, this ecological *finca* offers horseback tours through organic coffee, after which you can swim beneath a chilly waterfall.

Finca Shamballa (☎ 772 3195, 852 5424) Located inside Reserva Natural Cerro El Arenal (p216), this swish spot offers tourist packages from US$12 to US$20 per day that include not just food and horseback riding, but also aromatherapy and massage.

Finca la Leonesa (☎ 772 2049) This San Ramón *finca* has camping, lodging and horseback rides to abandoned gold mines. You can explore 1500m-long tunnels, so bring a flashlight.

Finca San Antonio (☎ 772 3819) There's a simple, four-room *hospedaje* on this dairy and coffee farm, which has some of the best access to Reserva Natural Cerro El Arenal, including a waterfall on Río El Ocote.

Cecocafen & the Fair-Trade Coffee Trail

Like the Ruta de Café without the luxurious haciendas, this community-based initiative for small-scale, sustainable tourism arranges visits and homestays in small coffee-producing villages. **Cecocafen** (Organization of Northern Coffee Cooperatives; ☎ 772 6353; turismo@cecocafen.com), three blocks east and one block south of the Museo de Café, not only arranges tours, but also supports women's groups and builds schools while it promotes Fair Trade coffee. Homestays cost US$5 per person, plus US$2.50 per meal.

Although it can work with individuals, Cecocafen is set up for large groups, who usually contact them well ahead of time about visiting communally operated coffee producers, who work small family plots (averaging only five *manzanas*), such as Cooperative El Roblar, a women's organic coffee and veggie-growing collective. You can do this as a day trip for around US$25 per person, meeting the growers, enjoying homemade *nacatamales* (corn masa formed around a savory meat filling then wrapped in banana leaves and steamed) and folkloric music for lunch, then testing coffee in the 'cupping laboratory' of SolCafe Dry Mill. Or stay on for a while in family homes, where you'll bathe in *pelas* (cement washbasins), use latrines and perhaps do some work, particularly if you're here during harvest time. You'll also walk untried trails, swim in wild waterfalls and finally meet the folks you've been thinking about every time you opted for the more expensive cup of joe.

rooms (better ones are upstairs) offer decent value for the money; soap and fresh towels are included. It may be moving, so call ahead.

Hotel Alvarado I (☎ 772 2830; s/d without bathroom US$7/9, d with bathroom US$12) Downright frilly, with doilies on the tables and skirts on the beds, this adorable budget option has OK rooms with clean shared bath, and spacious, pretty rooms with private bath, all upstairs by the TV nook and terrace overlooking the park.

Hotel Central (☎ 712 3140; Av José Benito Escobar; s/d without bathroom US$6/9, d with bathroom US$14) Right in the middle of town, this hotel is better than it looks outside, with clean, colorful rooms scattered around an attractive courtyard. The owner, Lupe, speaks English and is hysterical.

MIDRANGE

Hotel Fountain Blue (☎ 772 2733; s/d without bathroom US$9/15, d with bathroom US$17-21, incl breakfast; P) This excellent-value, 11-star property has simple rooms of varying sizes (some with windows) with great beds that share a clean hot-water bathroom, plus several much better rooms with private bathroom, cable TV and other amenities. The delightful owner provides free sweetbread and coffee in the morning, but can serve full breakfasts with advanced arrangement.

Hostel Molino Norte (☎ 865 2519; s/d incl breakfast US$20/30; P) About 5km north of Matagalpa on the road to Jinotega, comfortable modern rooms have little extras like furry floral toilet covers in the private hot-water bathrooms, and huge cable TVs. Meals are available for US$3, which is a good thing, since there's not much else around except for the two *manzanas* of coffee planted right out back and several trails worth wandering into the mountains. From town, it's a US$0.18 bus ride until 7pm, a US$3 cab ride after 7pm.

Hotel La Pradera (☎ 772 4365; s/d US$15/18; P) This hotel next to the Girasol café was so new that you could smell the paint drying in the brightly colored rooms. Hot water, cable TV and new beds – can't complain.

TOP END

Hotel Lomas de San Tomas (☎ 772 4189; www .hotellomassnthomas.com; d incl breakfast US$35-45; P 💻) A huge step up, this place is un-

missable. Several hundred meters above the city, it has spacious, airy rooms, the more expensive ones with balconies, and an upscale ambience that is surprising given the very reasonable prices. The on-site restaurant is great and has the best view of town around.

Eating

Matagalpa has a few good restaurants, but you'll need to look to the smoky booths that set up at sunset just north of Palí and the cathedral for the regional specialty, *güirílas*. Made with a fresh corn *masa*, they are sweeter and thicker than your average tortilla; a *servicio* includes a hunk of crumbly, salty *cuajada* cheese and *crema*, or cream sauce and costs about US$1. For self-caterers, there are two grocery stores. Supermercado Matagalpa is near Parque Darío, and has a better selection; Palí, close to Parque Morazón, has better prices.

RESTAURANTS

La Vita é Bella (☎ 772 5476; pasta dishes from US$4; ☽ 2-11pm Tue-Sun) If you can't find it, take a taxi; if they can't find it, tell them 'Parañas Billares,' which is at the entrance to the narrow alley where this hidden gem serves up tasty Italian and vegetarian specialties in an intimate setting. Try the pizza (some of it on focaccia) or spaghetti vitabella, with a bacon and mushroom white sauce with olives, but start with a bruschetta and finish with an espresso beverage.

Rosticería La Posada (dishes from US$3.50) Half a block west of Parque Darío, this popular eatery specializes in chicken dishes, like the tasty *pollo en salsa jalapeño* (chicken in jalapeño sauce).

Pescamar (dishes US$3-6; ☽ 11am-10pm) Excellent seafood – the soups are impressive – is served on a great porch overlooking the city.

La Hora del Taco (dishes US$2-6; ☽ 11am-11pm) Serving the same great Mexican food as its sister restaurant in Managua – it uses spices! – one can only hope that this place becomes a full-blown chain. Just south of town on the highway to Managua.

El Pullazo (dishes US$3-8; ☽ 10am-11pm) A see-and-be-seen spot for Matagalpa's upper crust, this place serves the spectacular and eponymous cut of marinated beef and delicious steaks, served alongside fresh *güirílas*.

FAIR TRADE & CAFFEINE DREAMS

More fiercely traded than any global commodity other than oil, black coffee makes up half of Nicaragua's exports and is the jittery engine upon which the economy turns. Until 1989, coffee prices were regulated by the International Coffee Organization (ICO), after a drought in Brazil doubled prices several years before. But the USA pulled out of the ICO about the same time that Vietnam and other new producers were beginning to flood the market with beans. By 1999 coffee prices had dropped from a spike of more than US$3 to only US$0.42 per pound, less than it cost to produce.

In Nicaragua, small farmers abandoned their land; of Matagalpa's 25 major haciendas, 20 of them closed, putting 36,000 people out of work. Some went to Costa Rica or other parts of the country to work; most were stuck here, begging for change by the sides of the road. A union, ATC (Rural Workers Association) formed, and former coffee workers shut down the highway four times until the government fell back on an old Sandinista tactic and agreed to give each family a plot of land, for which they would need to pay half.

Some farmers, with the help of international organizations, began growing organic coffee. It was relatively easy to become certified in Nicaragua, as agriculture has never relied on fertilizers and pesticides (because farmers couldn't afford them). It was expensive, however. No single organization certifies coffee 'organic' or 'Fair Trade.' Starbucks, for example, has its own certification program, but there are dozens of others, including Rainforest Alliance and Utz Kapeh. A cooperative of 150 farmers pays around US$2500 per year to be certified, which is still a good deal considering how much more the coffee earns.

Organic coffee, however, is still subject to volatile market forces, and could easily glut in the future. In the past decade, Fair Trade coffee has been guaranteeing these farmers a set price independent of supply or demand, around US$1.25 for conventionally grown coffee and US$1.40 per pound for organic. About one-third of that goes back into the Fair Trade cooperative, for certification fees and other communal expenses.

Despite the fact that Fair Trade basically asks consumers to voluntarily pay extra (who thought that would work?), it's now the fastest-growing segment of the coffee market. Some 800,000 farmers in 40 countries are working Fair Trade plots. In Nicaragua, communities often still work together as Sandinista-style cooperatives, making group decisions and encouraging women to participate. These often work in conjunction with NGOs, which provide support like microcredit from international banks and help coordinating the vital 'wet processing' stage, when the red, pulpy fruit is removed from the coffee bean, which must be done immediately, at the farm, before shipping.

But farming is something like gambling, and one major problem that even Fair Trade can't solve is that producers in Costa Rica pay two or three times what the average picker in Nicaragua makes, which means that there's often a labor shortage right around harvest time. In 2005 the situation – exacerbated by roads being washed out by Hurricane Stan – became so desperate that President Bolaños ordered the army to pick coffee, which they did, probably just happy that they weren't in Iraq with the Salvadoran military.

It's not as though these growers are getting fat off Fair Trade – most make around US$2 per day. But in a desperately poor region where electricity and running water are luxuries, a better and more reliable price for their coffee means three meals a day – by no means universal in Nicaragua – plus the chance to plan for the future.

It's just south of town on the highway to Managua.

La Pradera de San Francisco (mains US$2-8; 10am-10pm) This elegant spot is at once out of the way, at the *empalme* to San Ramón, and also easy to get to, just a US$2 taxi from Matagalpa (or US$0.30 bus ride).

Restaurante El Disparate del Potter (Km 142; mains US$2-5; 9am-9pm) On the road to Jinotega, this ridge-top restaurant marks the spot where driven road builder Charles Potter blasted his way through a wall of solid rock. Renowned for its onion *quesillos* and *repochetas* (a corn and cheese torta), the real reason you're here is the view. If it's a clear day, pay the US$0.30 to climb the spire of rock and check out the mountaintop view.

CAFÉS

Rincón Don Chato (batidos under US$1, mains US$1-3; ⏲ 7:30am-8pm Sun-Thu, 7:30am-5pm Fri) It looks like a regular formica diner on the main drag, but this nifty nitch has the best *batidos*, or fruit shakes, in town – the pineapple and celery in orange juice is amazing. Also on the menu are Nica classics with your choice of meat, plus veggie burgers and other vegetarian options. Good breakfasts.

Centro Girasol (☎ 612 6030; snacks US$1-3; ⏲ 6:30am-9pm) More than just an outstanding source of great coffee, fabulous baked goods and sweet treats, the Girasol is part of Familias Especiales Julia Biliarte, an organization that supports disabled kids and their families. Around the corner, Casa de Yogurt has fresh, frozen and/or flavored yogurt for the same great cause.

Café Picoteo (dishes US$2-4; ⏲ 10am-10pm) This cozy wood-paneled hangout is a Matagalpa classic, serving espresso beverages alongside affordable Nica snacks like *nacatamales*, *vigarón* (mashed yucca topped with coleslaw and pork rinds) and the excellent *enchiladas suizas* (with ham and cheese).

Cyber Moagüina (snacks US$1-3; ⏲ 9am-8pm) Named for one of the original 10 indigenous settlements of the valley, this cybercafé's coffee, *batidos* and pastries are so good that it's almost worth the slightly higher Internet prices to enjoy them. Or just come for the coffee and surf elsewhere.

QUICK EATS

Buffet Shangrilah (☎ 612 3074; mains US$2-4; ⏲ 7am-8pm) Show up at regular mealtimes for the best selection at this solid steamtable buffet, with a better-than-average salad bar and selection of vegetarian entrees. Bonus: they deliver.

Maná de Cielo (Av Central Don Bartolomé Martínez; meal US$3-4; ⏲ 7am-9pm) This popular steam-table buffet is even better than Shangrilah's (but doesn't have the salad bar), with lots of meaty entrees.

Fritanga Campeche (US$1-3; ⏲ sunset-sunrise) The best spot for grease to counter all the alcohol is this all-night *fritanga*, which sets up across from the Texaco.

Drinking & Entertainment

Grupo Venancio (☎ 772 3562; ⏲ Fri & Sat) When you tell your taxi driver 'Grupo Venancio,' three blocks east and three blocks south of Parque Morazán, he may ask why you want to hang out with lesbians and witches (*brujas*). But there are so many reasons! One of Matagalpa's best nights out, this women's collective runs an excellent bar and restaurant which shows movies, has live music and hosts all manner of woman-empowering events. It's usually only open Fridays, with movies and a quieter crowd, and Saturdays, which get packed if the band is good; there's usually no cover. This is a good place to start looking for Matagalpa's thriving gay and lesbian scene, but respectful heterosexual men can and have scored here, too.

MetroCinema (Av Central Don Bartolomé Martínez; movie US$1.25) This cheap, air-conditioned theater changes movies (probably to another Hollywood action flick) on Thursday, but only charges US$1 to see it on Monday and Tuesday.

La Casona has live music on Friday nights, while Gran Faraon, a block from the Texaco, lets you put on the show with its karaoke machine.

Shopping

Keep an eye open for brightly colored, almost Guetamalan-style fiber arts from El Chile, an indigenous village 12km east of town, where four workshops sell this stuff all over Central America.

Matagalpa, along with Jinotega, is known for its smooth, heavy black pottery, an effect achieved by specially preparing the volcanic clay, firing it until red hot, then removing bowls and pots with tongs and tossing cedar ashes over them. Cerámica Negra Tradicional, two blocks east of the cathedral, offers pieces by Doña Ernestina Rodríguez, including jewelry and tiny tea sets. There are several other shops nearby.

La Vita é Bella (p211) and Centro Girasol (left) also have a carefully chosen collection of high-quality *artisanias*.

Getting There & Around

There's a **Budget Rent-A-Car** (☎ 772 3041; budgetmt@ibw.ni) close to the cathedral, and another desk at **Hotel Apante** (☎ 772 6890).

There's a **Dollar Rent-A-Car** (☎ 772 4645) two blocks south of Parque Morazón.

Make reservations at **Agencia Tica Bus** (☎ 612 4502) for buses from Matagalpa to San Pedro Sula, Honduras (US$10, 6:40am); you'll need to head back to Managua for Costa Rica, Panama or Guatemala.

There are two main bus terminals in Matagalpa, Cotran Sur and Cotran Norte/Cotramusun.

COTRAN SUR

Clean, well-organized **Cotran Sur** (☎ 772 4659), attached to the main market, is about 800m west of Parque Rubén Darío, and in general serves Managua and points south.

Chinandega US$3, 3½ hours, 2pm

Estelí *ordinario* US$1.25, 1¾ hours, 5:15am to 5:45pm, every 30 minutes; *expreso* US$1.40, 1½ hours, 10am and 4:30pm

Jinotega US$1.25, 1½ hours, 5am to 7pm, every 30 minutes

León US$2.75, 2½ hours, 6am; alternatively, take any Estelí-bound bus and transfer at San Isidro

Managua *ordinario* US$2, 2¾ hours, 3:35am to 6:05pm, every 30 minutes; *expreso* US$3, 2¼ hours, 5:20am to 5:20pm, hourly

Masaya US$3, three hours, 2pm and 3:30pm

Sébaco & Ciudad Darío US$1, one hour, 5:30am, 7:30am, 10:25am, 11am, 11:25am and 12:55pm

COTRAN NORTE/COTRAMUSUN

Much sloppier, this is your basic market-side bus lot, with buses for destinations including:

Cerro Colorado US$4, 2½ hours, 5:30am, 7:45am, 11:45am and 1:30pm

Escipulas US$1.50, 1½ hours, 5:30am, 7am, 8am, 9am, noon, 1:30pm, 3pm, 4:30pm and 5:30pm

Río Blanco US$3, four hours, 4am to 4:30pm, at least hourly; *expreso* 11:15am and 2:15pm

San José de Bocay US$4, six hours, 4am to 3:30pm, almost hourly

San Ramón US$0.40, 30 minutes, 5am to 7pm, every 15 minutes

Waswah US$3.50, 5½ hours, 3am to 2pm, hourly; *expreso* 5:30am and 3:45pm

SOUTH TO MANAGUA

The smooth paved road from Matagalpa to Managua drops from stunning peaks into the epic lowlands of lakes and volcanoes, passing an excellent museum, two historic sites and three lovely lagunas.

Chagüitillo

Just 20 smooth kilometers south of Matagalpa is Chagüitillo, with the very worthwhile **Museo Precolobiano de Chagüitillo** (☎ 775 2151; adch@ibw.com.ni; admission US$2), a striking stucco that would seem more at home in California than this rural community. The museum itself is pretty typical, with a room dedicated to a local Sandinista farming co-operative, lots of Chorotegan pottery, and an exhibit on local hero Domingo Sánchez Salgado, aka 'Chagüitillo.' Construction worker and leader of the CGT (Confederation of General Workers), a union that won its members vacation time and basic social security, Chagüitillo founded the Socialist Party of Nicaragua in 1945. He was arrested by the Somozas more than 130 times, inspiring a generation – including his son, Efrain Sanchez, one of the original Sandinistas.

But the reason you're here is to take a guided stroll through two incredible **petroglyph sites**, one right in town, one 1.5km away. The one further out, Santuario Sitio el Mico, is downright epic, 3m long and 2m high, a swirly sort of calendar with moons, snakes and dancers. Make reservations for hikes in advance, if possible, at the museum.

There are no hotels or restaurants in Chagüitillo, but ask at the museum about **homestays** (r per person US$7.50, incl all meals) and a local swimming pool that's open on weekends. **Comedor Popular** (dishes US$1-2) serves fried favorites close to the parque central. Any Managua-bound *ordinario* from Matagalpa (or vice versa) stops in town. If you're driving, make a right at the arrow for 'Pre-Columbian Art.' It's the modern yellow building that looks hopelessly out of place.

Sébaco

The economic engine of the Northern Highlands, this agricultural stronghold was an important trading town long before the Spanish arrived. It's still a bustling town, with plenty of lit-up signage and convenient banking. There are a few decent *hospedajes* and plenty of simple *comedores*, but no reason for most travelers to stay.

Still, the 'City of Onions' does have its charms, including the colorful vegetable stands for which it is famous. Attractive wooden **Church of Immaculate Concepción** has a small museum with pottery, *metates* and literature that talks about the town's copious historical mythology, including information about a lost temple to Cihua Coalt (Serpent Woman), a Chorotega goddess, at the bottom of Laguna Tecomapa.

On June 25, the curious tradition of **Santigüito de Sébaco** takes place. The saints are taken to the city's humblest homes, and the rest of the neighborhood prays for them to enjoy a harvest – which benefits everyone in this agribusiness powerhouse.

The mountains behind Sébaco appear to many people to have a distinctly feminine silhouette, and with good reason. These are said to be the remains of Oyanka, an indigenous princess who in 1590 fell in love with a Spanish soldier named Joseph de Canterero, who dumped her. She was so depressed that she collapsed into the mountains behind town.

Ciudad Darío

This pretty town, originally known as Metapa, lies well off the main road, in a crease of the Cordillera Dariense carved out by the Río Grande de Matagalpa.

You're probably here to see **Casa Natal Rubén Darío** (☎ 776 3846; admission US$0.70; ⏰ 8:30am-4:30pm), where Rubén Darío was born. It's actually the house of Darío's aunt, which was as far as his mother got en route to León before the contractions started. Although the baby poet didn't spend more than a few weeks here, the museum is worth a look, furnished with mid-1880s kitchenware and a tiny wooden altar. There's also a chronology of Darío's life (in Spanish), plus a pretty outdoor auditorium that hosts the occasional poetry reading and other events. There's a pretty park in front with a statue of Darío as Orpheus.

The parque central, fronted by the fairly impressive Spanish colonial **Iglesia San Pedro**, has another statue of Darío, as Ambassador to Spain, atop a green, sort of abstract fountain. The park also has a better-than-average playground. There's a third bronze Darío statue at the southern entrance into town.

La Casa de Agricultor (☎ 776 2379; r per person US$2; P) has basic, clean cement rooms with very firm beds (cement pedestals with foam mattresses), but only some with private bathrooms. There's a handful of restaurants and *fritangas*, most close to the park or bus stop, but fancier Los Gamelos has dance parties some weekend. Buses for Managua and Matagalpa leave the bus station, two blocks downhill from La Casa de Agricultor, every half-hour.

Continuing south, you'll drop back into the steaming lowland plains, passing three lagoons, **Las Playitas**, **Moyoá** and **Teconapa**; a trail leads from a cluster of fried fish restaurants, if you want to explore. Bring insect repellent.

Further along, you'll pass lots of folks vending everything from parakeets to truly amazing wooden birds, the last worth pulling over for if you're in your own car.

Hacienda San Jacinto

You've got to be a committed history buff to appreciate this tiny **national monument** (admission US$2; ⏰ 8am-4pm), isolated and inconvenient, a shadeless 3km walk from the closest bus stop. It commemorates the Battle of San Jacinto, when William Walker's filibusterers (see the boxed text, p55) and León Liberals were met by stiff resistance from the southern Conservative crew. Most famously, a 23-year-old Granadino by the name of Andrés Castro ran out of ammunition, but undaunted, began throwing rocks instead, killing one of the filibusterers. Walker lost the battle, and later the war, and this gorgeous early-1800s Spanish hacienda has a couple of murals depicting the event, plus a few busts depicting the participants and a handful of artifacts.

Hacienda San Jacinto is about 25km south of Ciudad Darío. Any bus can drop you off at the entrance.

SELVA NEGRA

One of the most comfortable ways to experience Nicaragua's vast and largely untamed cloud forests, hung with bromeliads and rare orchids, is **Selva Negra** (☎ 612 3883; resort@selvanegra.com; admission US$3). Named after Germany's Black Forest, Selva Negra was founded in the 1880s by German immigrants who came at the invitation of the Nicaraguan government to grow coffee, and their descendants still manage the 850-hectare estate, over half of which is protected rain forest.

Day trippers can do coffee tours at 9am and 3pm, or just hike several kilometers of trails, and visit the museum and 'terrocarril' (a rail-less train that ran between Corinto and Matagalpa in the early 1900s). Black coffee and a pastry are included with your fee, or enjoy a meal with lots of German options. The hotel may be overpriced (US$10/40/62.50 per dorm bed/single/double), particularly the dorms, but the Bavarian-style cottages (US$100 to US$150) have charm to spare, with miniature forests growing out of the roof and Saxon interior styling, and you can't beat the backyard.

Take any bus heading north from Matagalpa and get off at the signed turnoff, 12km north of town, marked by an old military tank. From there it's a pleasant 1.5km walk.

RESERVA NATURAL CERRO EL ARENAL

Despite its proximity to Matagalpa and Jinotega, this tiny (575 hectares) reserve remains a relatively difficult park to access. The easiest way is to organize a tour through Selva Negra (p215), whose property abuts the park; guests or visitors can hire a guide (US$12). Finca San Antonio (p210) also has lodging and guided tours of the park.

If you're feeling adventurous and have a 4WD, head 8km north of Matagalpa on the road to La Dalia, where there's a signed turnoff to the park entrance. A good road leads through the *fincas* and past the San Antonio coffee-processing facility, abandoned except during the coffee season. This is a good place to park in rainy season, when the rest of the road is impassable. It's another 1km to the tiny town of San Antonio, with *pulperías* and a couple of *comedores* where you can ask about guides up the 3km trail to the top of El Arenal. Matagalpa Tours (p209) leads a two-day trek up the mountain.

FINCA ESPERANZA VERDE

About 35km east of Matagalpa toward the town of San Sebastian de Yalí, sitting on 100 cool green *manzanas* at 1190m, this is the official edge of the cloud forest, a peaceful **preserve** (☎ 772 5003; www .fincaesperanzaverde.org; camping per person US$6, s/d/tr US$30/45/60; **P**) and organic coffee *finca* that in 2004 was named the world's best ecolodge by *Smithsonian* magazine. You can visit for the day and hike three short but lovely **trails** (admission US$1.25; guides per group US$4). Or stay in one of the ultracomfortable lodges, with hot-water private bathrooms and hammocks where you can watch the sun set over the impossibly pretty mountainscape.

In addition to guided hikes and horseback tours they'll take you to **Río Wabul** (US$100 per group), in otherwise inaccessible Reserva Natural Guabule. There is also a great on-site restaurant (dishes US$5 to US$6), where musicians from nearby Yucúl are invited to perform for US$35 extra per diner.

Reservations are needed in dry season, when birders book the place weeks in advance. Staff may be able to arrange transportation from San Ramón, but most likely you'll be hiring a taxi from San Ramón or taking any Río Blanco–bound bus and getting off in Yucúl, home to **Yucúl Genetic Reserve**, with a rare species of pine but no tourist infrastructure. It's a steep 3km climb from the *empalme* to the reserve itself, which really is worth it.

EL TUMA-LA DALIA

If the potholed road from Matagalpa to La Dalia starts getting too hot, get off the bus (or pull over) at Km 149, the community of Santa Emilia, and ask about **Balneario Santa Emilia** (US$1). A short, steep hike from town, this is a fine 15m waterfall that may be OK for swimming, and most certainly makes a good photo op.

But the reason you're probably coming all the way out here is to see amazing **Reserva Natural Macizos de Peñas Blancas** (☎ 772 5746; admission US$2, guide US$6). If you won't be staying at the lodges, talk to Marena (p207) in Matagalpa about arranging a guided hike to the unforgettable peak of La Cordillera Isabelia, an enormous mesa rock surrounded by sheer 100m cliffs. You'll need to have (or pay for) a group of three people to warrant a guide. This is high-altitude exploring in intact primary cloud forest, where some 48 discovered waterfalls pour from the mists into swimming holes; at least one of them is almost 50m tall. Matagalpa Tours (p209) arranges a three-day guided trek into the reserve, all inclusive, from Matagalpa.

There are a couple of very basic *hospedajes* in La Dalia, and one fabulous hotel. **La Sobra Eco-Lodge** (☎ 772 3733, 846 3500;

sombra-ecolodge@yahoo.es; per person incl 3 meals US$40; Ⓟ), associated with Finca Esperanza Verde (opposite), has opened this gorgeous place with 220 *manzanas* of forest and coffee *finca* right on the border of Bosawás. Daytrippers (admission US$10) can use the 3km of trails past to lovely waterfalls, El Edén and El Gavilán, or just ask about arranging guides further into the park.

Nearby, the much more basic, less-developed **San Rafael Private Reserve** (☎ 772 2229) offers bird-watching tours and other guided hikes into Peñas Blancas; you can camp or arrange to stay in the main house, about 7km from La Dalia proper, in the even smaller town of Yasika Norte.

La Canavalia (d US$45-60), a rural development organization 19km from Matagalpa toward El Tuma, offers comfortably rustic cabañas with private bath, as well as several trails and a variety of nature tours, as well as horses and bicycles for rent. Meals are available for US$2 to US$3. To find this place you really have to just turn up and ask around.

Buses leave La Dalia for Matagalpa (US$1.25, 1½ hours) almost hourly 6am to 6pm.

JINOTEGA

The City of Mists, this is one of those places kept pristine by conflict, where high-altitude forests have hidden warriors within their dramatic ridges and gorges since at least AD 596, when the first Náhuatl-speaking people arrived. They called this valley Xinotoga, the Place of Refuge, the Eternal City, embraced in green and granite peaks ascending another 200m into the sky all around.

First settled by the Spanish in the 1500s, Jinotega's architecture remains well preserved, if pockmarked by bulletholes here and there; it saw some of the heaviest fighting in the revolution and Contra War. But when the mists flow through the cobbled streets, blurring the harsh lines of reality, it is almost as though there was always peace in this most poignantly beautiful of places.

Peace *has* arrived, and Jinotega is beginning to receive a trickle of visitors from the steaming lowlands to this rarified world, with good hotels and restaurants at the gateway to an almighty swath of almost untried nature.

Orientation & Information

Jinotega's nickname, City of Mists, is a gentle reminder to bring a jacket and pants – the average temperature is a chilly 20°C and it can get 2600mm of rain annually. The ride up here from Matagalpa is stunning; it's worth hopping off the bus at the high-altitude pass to pick up some produce from one of the colorful stands, and continue north on the main road to San Rafael del Norte and Wiwilí. Jinotega sprawls a bit, with most services (but not all) within a few blocks of the parque central. BanCentro and BanPro banks both have Visa-plus ATMs, while BAC accepts MasterCard debit cards.

Hospital ☎ 782 2626
Intur (☎ 782 4552; jinotega@intur.gob.ni) This branch, right on the parque central, not only has English speakers on staff and a fine collection of flyers, it also helps organize trips to ecological *fincas*, finds guides for Reserva Natural Dantalí-El Diablo and offers information about the entire department.
J&M Internet C@fe (per hr US$1) Internet's pretty darned slow in Jinotega, at this shop one block from the parque central, and at several other cafés in town.
Jinotega (www.jinotega.8k.com) This helpful city website has promise.
Marena (☎ 782 2719; sinap@ibw.com.ni) nconveniently located 2km from the town center on the road to San Rafael, this Marena isn't really set up for tourists yet. It may be able to arrange guides for Reserva Natural Dantalí-El Diablo.
Police (☎ 782 22150)

Sights & Activities

The Jinotega **archaeology museum** closed several years ago, but the collection is currently in storage, awaiting the restoration of heroic former president Benjamin Zeledón, here it will hopefully be displayed before this guide is on the shelves. Ask at Intur for up-to-date information.

Jinotega's 1805 **Cathedral San Juan** suffers a bit because it's in competition with heavyweight churches in San Rafael del Norte and Matagalpa, but the arched white interior is quite literally lined with beautiful saints – including a very nice Virgin of Guadalupe – and several subtle artistic paeans to both Russian Orthodox and indigenous beliefs. **Iglesia de los Angeles**, on the other side of town, is also pretty, but run-down.

Across the plaza from the church, fading **murals** on the walls of the old Somoza jail (now a youth center) serve as reminders of the revolutionary years. One portrays coffee pickers with rifles slung over their shoulders; another depicts young people at war.

CERRO LA CRUZ

This town's top tourist attraction and can't-miss hike is up to the gently glowing cross (it was illuminated a couple of years back, and floats rather eerily in the nighttime mists), from a trail that starts by the cemetery. Originally placed here in 1703 by Franciscan Fray Margíl de Jesús, it's become the focus of Jinotega's biggest party, **Fiestas de la Cruz** (April 30 to May 16), which peaks on May 3 when everyone and their grandmother scales the mountain en masse. There are trails to the top of most of these hills, too, if you need another challenge.

Tours

SOPPEXCCA COFFEE COOPERATIVE

The same concept as Cecocafen (see the boxed text, p210), this **coffee cooperative** (Society of Small Coffee Producers, Exporters & Buyers; ☎ 782 2617; www.soppexcca.org/en) offers a variety of tours throughout the area, as well as homestays, horseback rides and more. The group is consistently recognized for growing some of the highest-quality coffee in the world, and some of its best comes from **Cooperative Luis Hernandez** (r per person incl 3 meals US$20), with lodging in pastoral San Pedro de Buculmay, about 12km from Jinotega. The Soppexcca office is north of Cotran Norte.

ECOLOGICAL FINCAS

Jinotega has a handful of 'ecological *fincas*,' offering a variety of different tours and services on the misty fringes of the department. Two of the most professional are listed under Reserva Natural Datanlí-El Diablo (p221), or you can have Hotel Sollentuna Hem (p220) arrange an 8km guided trek (hiking/horseback per person US$15/25) through the coffee fields to **Finca El Laurel**. You'll climb the ring of mountains around town then descend to the shimmering lakeshore, where you'll be picked up for the drive home – or not. There are two basic,

DIY: WIWILÍ, BOCAY & RESERVA DE BIOSFERA BOSAWÁS

Jinotega offers access to two routes into Reserva de Biosfera Bosawás (Bosawás Biosphere Reserve; see the boxed text, p230), neither of them simple or easy. But if you're game, head either to Wiwilí, about 100km north of Jinotega on a rocky dirt road, or through El Cuá and San José de Bocay (the 'Bo' in Bosawás), accessible on an even worse road headed northeast.

Wiwilí is the youngest city in Nicaragua (1989), and is actually two neighboring cities on either side of the Río Coco, with the same name. At just 300m, it can get hot, but it's still a mountain town, in the shadow of Cerro Cantagallo (1485m). It has a couple of *hospedajes* and one good hotel, clean **Hotel Central** (no phone; r with/without bathroom per person US$4/8). Around the corner is excellent Faisan Dorado restaurant, the best of several *comedores*. Either of these places can find you guides and boats for the Río Coco; Wiwilí is about five or six hours by boat to the Honduran border. The Wiwilí *alcaldía* can also arrange guides; it doesn't have a phone but a nearby house (☎ 273 3209) does, and will call over someone from the *alcaldía*.

The tiny town of **El Cuá** is actually inside Bosawás itself, and is the closest population center to Reserva Natural Macizos de Peñas Blancas (p216). The town itself has a couple of *hospedajes* and simple eateries, as well as **Guardianos del Bosque** (no phone; cabinas per person US$6), a cooperative with simple lodging, or just come on a day trip and hire a guide from the cooperative for the 'Waterfalls of Peñas Blancas Trail.'

There's a ranger station further up the road at **San José de Bocay**, closest to **Reserva Natural Cerro Kilambé**, preserved for its incredible cliffs and profusion of waterfalls, which feed the Yakalwas, Pijinero and Wamblam Rivers. At 1750m, Kilambé is the tallest mountain in the department and covered with pine trees up to about 900m; this cloud forest and dwarf cloud forest is where you may see resplendent quetzals.

How adventurous do you feel? About 50km northeast of San José de Bocay, from a trail starting at the Tunowalan Ranger Station, is the **Cuevas Belén de Tunowalan**, an incredible riverside cave system that may be developed for adventure tourism. At present, it's just an adventure; in San José de Bocay, ask around for Henry Taylor, a Miskito guide who speaks some English; he has hats and lamps, as well as a boat for the 5km trip up river to the cave, which has petroglyphs and bats, and according to some legends may be home to the devil himself.

---

concrete rooms with private bath (US$6 per person), and meals are provided for US$2 each. The hike itself is a four-hour trip, and they may be able to find a guide who speaks English. Sollentuna Hem also arranges city tours and other trips.

Lácteos Santa Martha (☎ 782 4063; lactosam@ibw .com.ni) has been making great cheese and other dairy products since 1993, and can take you on a tour. You can arrange it with them or Intur.

Festivals & Events

Festival de la Cruz (May 3) One of Nicaragua's most athletic fiestas, since 1703 visitors have been shamed into climbing to the cross by area octogenarians. Breath…

San Isidro Laborador (May 15) Both Jinotega and Condega honor the patron saint of farmers by building altars out of fruits and veggies.

Fiestas Patronales (June 24) Solemn processions, rodeos, beauty queens and more celebrate the feast day of San Juan Bautista.

Festival de Musica Vernacula (mid-October) This folk-music festival brings in bands and dance troops from throughout the region, showcasing polkas, mazurkas and other colorfully warped German traditions at venues all over town.

Sleeping

There are a number of very simple US$2 *hospedajes* geared toward campesinos right around Hotel La Fuente and Cotran Norte; don't expect flush toilets.

Hotel Bosawás (☎ 782 3311; r per person US$4) Besides offering the best deal in town on big, clean, tiled rooms with nice bedspreads and a hot-water shared bathroom, owner Lenin Castro is absolutely in love with Reserva Bosawás and can offer tips on visiting via Wiwilí. Breakfast can be arranged for US$2.

Hotel Central (☎ 782 2063; s/d US$10/12; P ⊠) Pretty fabulously remodeled large rooms have private hot-water bathroom and cable TV; ask about cheaper rooms that have yet

NICARAGUA

to get the full makeover. The location is great, and it's excellent value for couples.

Hotel Rosa (☎ 782 2472; s/d US$2/4) Among the dingy but clean cheapies, Rosa deserves special mention: Jinotega's oldest hotel is charmingly rustic or appallingly run-down, depending on your point of view.

Hotel Primavera (☎ 782 2400; s without bathroom US$3, d with bathroom US$9) Simple singles have limited floorspace and walls that don't hit the ceiling, and the ultra-clean doubles have TV and fans. It's a good deal, but note that the door shuts at 10pm sharp.

Hotel Sollentuna Hem (☎ 782 2334; s without bathroom US$8, s/d/tr with bathroom US$11/18/21; P) This pleasant hotel has the feel of a country inn, and warm blankets are supplied. Rooms range from cozy singles to roomier doubles with cable TV, private bathroom and hot water. It also organizes a variety of tours, including guided hikes to Finca El Laurel, close to the lake, and a city tour.

Hotel Milagro (☎ 610 6967; r with/without bathroom US$9/7) Across the street from Sollentuna Hem, the Milagro has a few dark but cheerfully painted cement rooms, one with TV.

Hotel Café (☎ 782 3249; s/d incl breakfast US$40/50; P ✕ 🖳) Almost luxury rooms have beautiful furnishings, big cable TVs, attractive hot-water bathrooms with little soaps, and even air conditioning, as if you'd need it. Its Restaurant Borbon (dishes US$3 to US$10) is gourmet and very good (try the herb-rubbed filet mignon, US$10). The owners have hookups with Finca Kilimanjaro (opposite), and can arrange package deals.

Eating

Most Nicas head straight to the lake (opposite) for fried *guapote* (rainbow bass), one of the main reasons to come to Jinotega.

Soda El Tico (☎ 782 2059; buffet US$2-4; ✕ 7:30am-10pm) A Jinotega tradition, this cozy restaurant gets a cast of thousands for its impressive lunch and dinner buffets, not to mention menu items – including *casados* – and it even delivers. It also sells landscape paintings from local artists. Soda El Tico II, by Cotran Sur, is much more basic.

Bufet El Buen Sazón (dishes US$1.50-3; ✕ lunch & dinner) Dueling buffets! This winner, across the street, has fewer choices, costs less, tastes great and comes with free coffee.

Sopas El Chipotle (dishes US$2-5; ✕ 11am-8pm) About 3km from the city center on the road to San Rafael, this locally revered spot serves up big bowls of delicious soup and other traditional fare in the attractive gardens.

La Colema (dishes US$4-10; ✕ 10am-10pm) Candlelight dining, formal jackets on the waiters and even separate salad forks (!) almost make you forget that you're in an otherwise pretty typical Nicaraguan restaurant. The steak is melt-in-your-mouth, the fish is fresh from the lake and there's a private dining room if you're afraid your husband might walk in.

Restaurante Borbón (US$4-10; ✕ 6am-10pm) Inside lovely Hotel Café, this restaurant doesn't quite have La Colema's cachet, but may have better food – try *pollo a la crema*, lean chicken breast smothered in a parsley and garlic white sauce.

Drinking & Entertainment

Monkey's Jungle Discoteque (✕ 8pm-3am Sat & Sun) City lights dim when this place gets going: a huge dance floor, petroglyphs on the wall and a monkey swinging from the ceiling.

Discoteque Oriental (✕ Thu-Sun) This disco attracts a more mature crowd, and also serves Chinese food.

Getting There & Around

There are two bus stations. Cotran Norte is on the highway east of town, while **Cotran Sur** (☎ 782 4530) sits near the town's southern entrance.

COTRAN NORTE

This easy-to-navigate bus station is in the very nice market, a good place to stock up on high-altitude veggies if you're headed back to the flatlands.

Estelí US$2.50, 1¾ hours, 7am, 9am, 1pm, 2:45pm and 3:30pm

La Pita US$4, four to five hours, 7:30am, 9am, 11am and 2:30pm

Pantasma (Lago de Apanás) US$2, 1½ hours, 4am and 5:30am

San José de Bocay US$4, four to five hours, 4am, 6:30am, 10am and noon; stops in El Cuá

San Rafael del Norte US$1, 30 minutes, 6am to 6pm, every 30 minutes

Wiwilí US$3.50, four to five hours, 4am, 6:30am, 8:45am, 11am and 1:15pm

Yalí US$2, two hours, 6am, 8:30am, noon and 2:30pm

COTRAN SUR
Managua *expreso* US$4.25, 3½ hours, 4am, 5am, 5:30am, 6:10am, 7:30am, 9am, 10:45am, noon, 1:30pm, 3pm and 4pm; *ordinario* US$3.25, 4½ hours, 5am to 6:15am, every 30 minutes; stops in Matagalpa

RESERVA NATURAL DANTALÍ-EL DIABLO

With very little tourist infrastructure, this is a rewarding (if muddy) climb up into the quetzal zone at 1650m where the misty chill hovers at around 20°C. While Jinotega's **Marena** (☎ 782 2719; sinap@ibw.com.ni) may be able to arrange guides, such as **Aldea Global** (☎ 782 2237), it's actually much easier to go through one of the private *fincas* that are part of the reserve.

There are two entrances to the park. The southern entrance is 12.5km down a lousy dirt road from the signed turnoff 'Km146' on the Matagalpa–Jinotega road. Stay straight until you get to **Finca La Esmeralda** (no phone; r per person incl 3 meals US$10; típica US$2.50), with one of the most impressive orchid gardens you'll ever see. You can hire a guide (US$6 per group) for trails that include the park's most impressive discovered waterfall. One bus daily leaves Cotran Norte in Matagalpa for 'Las Nubes,' stopping close to the *finca*.

If you continue through Jinotega and make a well-signed right turn on the somewhat better dirt road, continuing 20km toward El Cuá, you come to the northern entrance, close to two ecological *fincas* that offer tours.

Above the clouds at 1300m, **El Jaguar** (☎ 279 9219, 886 1016; www.jaguarreserve.orgbienvenidos.htm; per person incl breakfast & dinner US$30) has the nicest lodging and easiest access to the reserve's best trails: Sendero La Bujona, an easy, family-friendly 1.5km loop; Sendero Quétzal, a 3.5km climb to a chilly overlook; and Sendero El Congo. El Jaguar itself sits on 45 *manzanas*, some primary cloud forest where more than 138 species of bird have been seen. There are two beautiful, if fairly basic, lodges, one separated into apartments with kitchens that sleep four, another for large groups.

Finca Kilimanjaro (☎ 782 2113, 838 9418; andres8820000@hotmail.com), about 32km from Jinotega, arranges tours and overnights through Hotel Café in Jinotega (opposite). A full day trip, including transportation,

horseback riding, cow milking, swimming and more, costs US$50 per person. They don't have a lodge yet, but you're welcome to camp with reservations.

LAGO DE APANÁS-ASTURIAS

The third largest body of water in Nicaragua is artificial, formed in 1964 when the Mancotal dam was built on the Río El Tuma, just 6km north of Jinotega. It's actually two lakes, much larger Lago de Apenás (54 sq km) and its smaller, northern brother, Lago Asturias (3 sq km), and they are locally known for producing some of the best *guapote* in the country, on sale at lots of rickety-looking *rancheros* lining the lakeshore. If you'd prefer to catch your own, fishermen will take you out on the lake for around US$3 per hour in a rowboat, US$10 per hour with the motor running.

This is a hydroelectric dam, and Planta Cetroamérica produces about 50,000kw and usually holds about 324 million cubic meters of water; during Hurricane Mitch it held back 756 million cubic meters, just barely. Although it's an artificial body of water, this is one of the last remaining habitats of *nutria*, a really big rodent, left in Nicaragua. Buses leave Matagalpa for Pantasma and Lago de Apanás (US$2, 1½ hours) at 4am and 5:30am.

There's not really anywhere to stay on the lake, but the brand-new **Carlos Augusto Private Reserve** (☎ 240 0477; carlosaugustoreserv@hotmail.com) has big plans. At press time, you could bring your own tent or just come for the day.

SAN RAFAEL DEL NORTE

pop 14,066 / elevation 1062m

In a region of peaks, this beautiful city sits the highest, buoyed by chill jungles more than a crisp, clear kilometer above the seas. Founded in the 1600s, but a backwater until the last century, there are a few five-star reasons to make your way to the very top of Nicaragua.

Sights & Activities

Templo Parroquial de San Rafael Arcángel was made a National Artistic Monument in 2000, and is one of the most beautiful churches in a country known for the same. A labor of love by Father Odorico

SANDINO: PROPHET OF THE SEGOVIAS

Born in 1895 to a wealthy Niquinohomo landowner, Gregorio Sandino, and an indigenous servant girl, Margarita Calderón, Augusto César Sandino was always painfully aware of class differences. He spent his childhood in poverty until his mother abandoned him, and the Sandinos unenthusiastically took him in.

The family eventually entrusted him with overseeing the farm, but after he almost killed the son of a prominent local Conservative politician in a gun duel, Sandino had to leave that life and flee the country. He traveled and worked in Guatemala, Honduras and Mexico, discovering yoga, communism and Seventh Day Adventism along the way, even becoming a Freemason. For seven years he primed himself for a higher path, and when the statute of limitations ran out on his attempted murder charges, he returned to Nicaragua, which was by now embroiled in civil war.

Sandino offered his services to the Liberal forces, who refused to arm the untried newcomer. A group of prostitutes loaned Sandino the money instead, and he began a tireless guerrilla campaign, attracting mostly campesino and indigenous followers, getting financial backing from Mexico, and ignoring other Liberals.

In 1927 more than 2000 US marines arrived with a treaty and orders to enforce it. 'All my men surrender,' said the Liberal commander during the formalities, tired of war and now hopelessly outgunned. 'Except One.'

On 15 July 1927 Sandino attacked the Marines in Ocotal; the US responded with aerial bombing, which worked. Realizing that traditional warfare was out of the question, Sandino retreated to the mountains and began a six-year, low-intensity war with US occupiers and the National Guard. But although he had a near-fanatical following in the mountains of Nueva Segovia, broader urban and international support was drying up.

Throughout the early 1930s, Sandino's army went from ratcheting up hit-and-run victories to controlling almost half the country. Sandino declared himself the incarnation of Caesar, saying that a horrific Managua earthquake was proof of his divinity, and delivering the *Manifesto of Light and Truth*, which revealed that Nicaragua would be the final staging ground in the battle between good and evil. Things had gone way beyond ridding Nicaragua of US imperialism.

By 1933, despite Sandino's position as the *de facto* president of half of Nicaragua, the writing was on the wall: international support was gone, popular moderate Juan B Sacasa had just been elected president, and Sandino dreamt that he had to either make peace or commit suicide immediately. Sacasa gave the Sandinistas 36,000 sq km to homestead near Jinotega, which they operated as a commune, and Sandino seemed to settle down. But the US military, which had to pull out due to domestic pressures, suspected he still had a secret cache of weapons.

As an insurance policy, the United States began providing substantial military support to Anastazio Somoza García, a water-company official married to a niece of President Sacasa, who spoke fluent English. He was among the guests at an official dinner party celebrating the big peace treaty with the Sandinistas on February 20, 1934.

After dinner, as they left the presidential palace, Sandino and his supporters were abducted and shot, not far from where Sandino's enormous silhouette commands the Managua skyline. The bodies were never found.

'Our banner is red over black,' Sandino once explained. 'Black is death and red is resurrection.' Check out www.sandino.org to learn more.

D'Andrea (see the boxed text, opposite), construction began atop the site of a much older church in 1955, and today the church boasts a soaring interior with Italian marble, an exquisite altar and, most importantly, a series of inspiring murals set to a remarkable sky blue, painted by Australian professor John Fuchs Holl in 1967 and 1968. The story of the Bible and the temptation of Christ, not to mention that Virgin of Guadalupe, are striking, but be sure to check out the Last Supper tile mosaic, too.

Father Odorico himself is buried a few hundred meters away, at the **Santuario Cerro Tepeyac**; it is a landmark that covers a mountainside, modeled after the Shrine to the Virgin of Guadalupe in Mexico. And

NICARAGUA

FATHER ODORICO D'ANDREA

Father Odorico D'Andrea was born in Italy in 1916, and anointed as a Franciscan friar in 1942. He found his way to San Rafael 12 years later, where he not only constructed the magnificent temple, but also got the first roads, running water, schools and clinic into the region. His efforts never sat well with the government; in 1959 he had to flee Somoza's forces, and he later became an outspoken critic of the Sandinistas, though he always worked for peace. And he lived to see it, just barely. On May 3, 1989, in La Naranja, he gave the Eucharist to Sandinistas and Contras together. He would die peacefully a year later.

although September 29 is the feast day for San Rafael del Norte's patron, those fireworks and festivities pale in comparison to the devotion offered here, between March 5, Odorico's birthday, and March 22, the anniversary of his death, where he was mourned by more than 10,000 people at his funeral.

Museo Sandino (no phone; donations appreciated), around the corner from the church and open 'when it's open,' is the best museum in Nicaragua to Augusto César Sandino. It's in his in-laws' home, later used as a telegraph house, and is run (one assumes Sandino would approve) without government funding or support by one devoted man, Tomás Herrera-Zeledon, who deserves a medal for pulling this place together. This tidy museum has Sandino's typewriter and guns, lots of original documents and copies of just about every existing photo of the man and his 'Crazy Little Army,' who were based right here. It's also got a library of lefty required reading, from Lenin to Brezhnev to Rugama. The anniversary of Sandino's wedding to local gal Blanca Aráuz, which took place here on May 18, 1927, is still one of the biggest annual parties in town.

Do you need more excuses to hang out around here a little longer? The **alcaldía** (☎ 652 2209) can help find guides to **Salto de El Salitre**, an area waterfall that drops 10 glorious meters into a perfect swimming hole not far from town. Further afield are a 21m waterfall, **Salto Santa María**, the

Cuevas del Hermitanio, and pine-covered, climbable **Volcán Yalí** (1542m).

About 15km north of San Rafael on a rough dirt road, **San Sebastián de Yalí** has outstanding petroglyphs in the parque central, but it's 10km further north to **La Pavona**, with the really good petroglyphs, a huge scene carved into the rocks near Cerro la Cruz.

Sleeping & Eating

Casita San Payo (☎ 784 2327; r US$9-14) This great hotel in San Rafael features very clean, comfortable rooms with lots of natural light and private hot-water bathrooms. For a few dollars more, you get cable TV and more space. The restaurant (dishes US$2 to US$4) has a solid baked-goods selection.

Hospedaje Aura (r without bathroom per person US$4) Across the street, this is a much more basic option.

Getting There & Away

A bus runs from the parque central to Jinotega (US$1) hourly 5:30am to 6pm. Microbuses run to Estelí (US$1.25) from the *empalme* until 3:30pm.

THE ROAD TO ESTELÍ

The back road to Estelí, on a smooth, graded dirt road (better, at any rate, than the patched and potholed stretch between Matagalpa and Jinotega), has got to be one of the most beautiful drives in the country. It's just high-altitude beauty, with one town, **La Concordia** (899m), almost exactly 33km from Jinotega and 33km from Estelí.

There are two restaurants: **Restaurant Casona** (set plate US$2; 🕑 7:30am-8:30pm), right on the road, serving decent *típica* in an enormous and probably ancient adobe; or, if you head into town, Comedor Mary, also serving set plates.

If you want to stretch your legs, you could check out the rock altar, which predates the attractive 1851 **Iglesia Nuestra Señora de Lourdes** by at least a few hundred years, or ask a local kid to show you the town's locally famous **petroglyphs**, located right outside of town. They're outstanding, carved into a cliff face at least 4m high above the river, with six huge drawings and a human handprint.

NICARAGUA

THE CARIBBEAN COAST

There are so few places left on this ever less lonely planet so beautiful and yet so untouched. This enormous region of bubbling hot springs and soaring ceiba trees, white-sand Caribbean islets and endless tropical rivers makes up roughly 70% of Nicaragua's total landmass. It is another world in so many ways, where tiny townships of Miskito and Mayangna Indians are raised from the jungle on slender wooden stilts, centered on their red-roofed and incongruously Germanic churches. From the cloud-forested peaks of the soaring Serranía Amerrisque to the wide and humid Río Coco, Central America's largest river, you may encounter more challenges than usual exploring Nicaragua's Caribbean Coast, but there are some vacations destined to become adventures.

Climate & Geography

The Caribbean Coast is a broad alluvial flood plain, washed down from the central highlands by four major – and countless minor – river systems. The Río Coco, or Wangki (Miskito for 'Big River),' is Central America's mightiest waterway and forms the border with Honduras. The other three, from north to south, are the Río Prinzapolka, Río Grande de Matagalpa and Río Escondido, which you'll take between El Rama and Bluefields, because there's no road.

More than 90% of Nicaragua's rainfall ends up on the Atlantic side, between 2000mm and 5000mm annually, depending on where you are, so pack accordingly. The Serranías de Amerrique, which form the dramatic backdrop to Boaco and Juigalpa, can be brisk, but for most of this region you'll be wearing light, fast-drying clothes. Other impressive peaks include Cerro Musún (1438m) and Cerro Saslaya (1651m), both relatively accessible

---

ENDANGERED TURTLES

Please refrain from eating endangered sea turtles, or buying tortoiseshell jewelry, made from the shells of inedible hawksbill turtles.

---

and protected as natural reserves. Lowland tropical rain forest covers most of the immense region east of the mountains (except where it's been clear cut), but the northeastern corner of the country, the Miskito Savanna, is light and dry, with acidic clay soils and pine trees that can reach 30m into the cobalt sky.

Boaco and Chotales, covered here under 'The Road to El Rama' (p239), are politically and culturally part of mainstream Nicaragua; east of the mountains, things change. This huge region has been divided into the RAAN (North Atlantic Autonomous Region) and RAAS (South Atlantic Autonomous Region) since 1987, and is largely independent of the federal government in Managua. English is spoken as often as Spanish in some spots and in many areas people speak only Miskito, Mayangna, Rama or various Creoles. See the boxed text, p491, for some handy phrases. The autonomous regions are sparsely populated, with 650,000 people sharing 60,000 sq km, an area significantly larger than Costa Rica. Visitors often remark that the Caribbean Coast is almost a separate country, to which residents most heartily agree.

Dangers & Annoyances

The regions covered in this chapter are poorer and have less infrastructure than the rest of Nicaragua, which is saying something. Bring a flashlight and candles for electrical outages and be prepared to use buckets to both shower and flush.

Narcotic traffickers smuggle cocaine throughout the RAAN and RAAS, but the last thing they want to do is hurt a tourist and call attention to themselves. Regardless, stay alert and stick to big city rules: take taxis at night, watch your valuables closely, don't get too wasted, and travel in groups when possible. These are not amateurs and this is not the place for your holiday binge.

This region is conservative, and, apart from the Corn Islands, women should consider swimming in shorts and a T-shirt, as bathing suits attract a crowd.

Getting There & Around

This chapter covers two of the three overland passages from Managua to the Caribbean Coast; the third is along the Río San

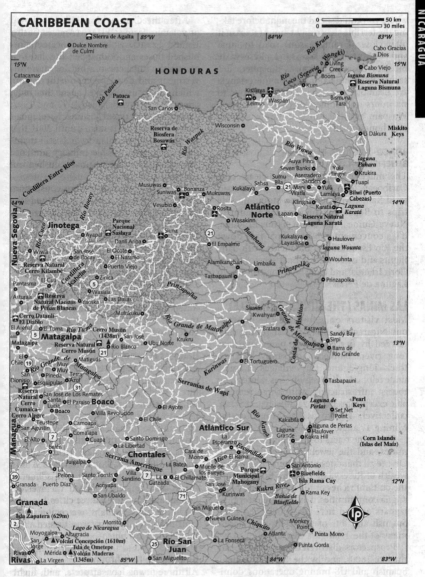

CARIBBEAN COAST

Juan (p275). Most visitors take convenient and inexpensive flights, however, as there are airstrips in Bilwi, Waspám, Bluefields, Big Corn Island and all three mining towns. Note that there is no regular passenger service up and down the Caribbean Coast, although you can arrange private transport or find cargo ships. But if you want to see

the scenery, the two overland routes, diverging in Boaco, are your best option.

LAS MINASO–BILWI (PUERTO CABEZAS)–WASPÁM & RÍO COCO

The grueling journey north begins with a 10- to 12-hour bus ride from Managua, paved until Reserva Natural Cerro Musún, where you could spend the night before taking the terrible six- to eight-hour (at least; it often closes in rainy season) 'road' to Siuna and Las Minas, with access to La Reserva de Biosfera Bosawás (Bosawás Biosphere Reserve). Bus connections within the Triangle are bearable, and from Rosita it's four to six hours on another lousy road to Bilwi. Waspám and the Río Coco are a smooth four hours north.

BOACO–JUIGALPA–EL RAMA–BLUEFIELDS–CORN ISLANDS

The much easier trip to the clear, blue Caribbean follows the freshly paved road to El Rama, with refreshing mountain side trips to Boaco and Juigalpa, or a jaunt to Nueva Guinea, just south. From El Rama, it's a convenient two-hour boat ride down the Río Escondido to Bluefields, with daily flights and twice-weekly boat service to the Corn Islands, and daily boat connections to Laguna de Perlas.

LAS MINAS (THE MINING TRIANGLE)

Most visitors only fly over the mysterious Nicaraguan interior: vast rolling hills pierced by fierce volcanic plugs, and lazy long rivers banked with sandy beaches, thick jungle and tiny villages. Largely undeveloped, this region has almost no tourist infrastructure, with three remarkable exceptions: Bonanza, Rosita and Siuna, collectively known as Las Minas, or the Mining Triangle.

The name refers to gold mines, not landmines, and the jewelry shopping is great. Or, see all that does not glitter – the natural wealth of Reserva de Biosfera Bosawás and the cultural riches of the Miskito and Mayangna communities. Tourists are rarer than jaguars around here, so you'll need basic Spanish and lots of persistence to access many of the Triangle's treasures.

Prospectors discovered gold here during the late 1800s, and by the 1930s Canadian, Spanish and US mining operations dominated the region's economy and politics. The Sandinistas nationalized the whole shebang in 1979, and whatever the former owners couldn't take with them, they sabotaged. Soviet technicians failed to get the mines up and running again, and the once relatively wealthy region became a backwater, with 80% unemployment and no rule of law.

After the Contra War ended, a group of veterans formed FUAC (Andrés Castro United Front), which ran cocaine, ambushed buses and kidnapped the children of wealthy ranchers in a bid for more investment and development in the region, which might not have been the most effective strategy. Between 1992 and 1997, almost no one risked visiting Nicaragua's heart of gold, and it wasn't until 2001 that the federal government (which still maintains a huge and visble military presence throughout the region) finally flushed out the last FUAC faithful.

Since the Canadian mining consortium Hemconic (now Hemsa) reopened the Bonanza mine in 1994, jobs and money have been flowing into the region. Although (as workers' rights groups note) most profits flow out of the country, and (as conservancy groups note) cyanide and other industrial pollutants flow in. Regardless, this newfound prosperity, compounded by Unesco's 1997 recognition of Reserva de Biosfera Bosawás, has offered the first hope these hills have seen in a generation.

Dangers & Annoyances

Although the region is allegedly landmine and paramilitary free, it's always smart to hire a guide and stay on trails and roads. Infrastructure in Siuna and, to a lesser extent, Rosita, is just atrocious: bring a flashlight and be prepared for bucket showers. No businesses in the Triangle take credit cards, including La Costeña airlines. Banks change US dollars, but don't have ATMs, nor do they facilitate credit card advances. Bring cash or send it ahead via Western Union, available in all three cities.

On the upside, this is one region where your flashy gold jewelry won't merit a second glance. Go nuts.

Getting There & Around

All three towns have airports, with flights Monday through Saturday only. Make reservations in advance and try to avoid checking bags, which will be weighed. The 12-seat plane leaves Managua International (US$70 one way, one hour) at 9am, stops in all three towns if necessary, then continues to Bilwi (Puerto Cabezas). To catch the Bilwi flight (US$70 one way, 30 minutes) be at the airstrip by 11am. Planes leave Bilwi for the Triangle at 1:15pm, continuing to Managua as early as 2:15pm. There's another plane to Managua at 10:30am.

Road access is scenic but terrible, and the Río Blanco–Siuna stretch of the 12-hour ride from Managua is considered the country's worst road, and may be closed in rainy season. Rosita is a more manageable four- to six-hour ride from Bilwi, and involves a river crossing by barge and lots of ceiba trees. Although roads are 4WD-accessible in dry season, driving through this poor, sparsely populated region is never, ever recommended for casual tourists – those school buses have seriously modified suspensions. The Triangle is linked by OK dirt roads with regular bus service, and you can take taxis between Bonanza and Rosita.

Siuna

pop 20,000 / elevation 150m

Not only is this the easiest access to Reserva de Biosfera Bosawás, it's also access to its utterly untamed, undeveloped, wild nucleus at Parque Nacional Saslaya with real campsites and trails. In addition to the park, Siuna has the requisite abandoned mine surrounded by gorgeous mountain scenery, and hot springs outside of town. It's also got the Minas' best selection of hotels and restaurants, a branch of Urracan University, and what's got to be Nicaragua's most photogenic landing strip.

Siuna is also extremely poor, and only gets running water for a few hours each week, so make sure your hotel has water tanks or enjoy your bucket bath. Electricity can flicker out at any time, so carry a flashlight.

ORIENTATION & INFORMATION

If you arrive by plane, you land right in the middle of town. To your left, take the stairs up Siuna's small hill to the alcaldía (mayor's office), Western Union and Hotel Siu; a road then loops to the right, around the hill and down past the bus station, market, abandoned mine, several restaurants and hospedajes (guesthouses), then returns to the airstrip.

Bosawás office (⊙ 8am–noon, 1:30–4:30pm) The helpful staff can arrange authorized guides and transportation to Parque Nacional Saslaya. The office is to the plane's right, on the paved road sloping slightly downhill.

Urrican University (per hr US$1.25; ⊙ 8am–8pm Mon-Fri, 8am–noon Sat) About 2km away, has the fastest Internet in the Triangle.

SIGHTS & ACTIVITIES

Most people come to visit fairly pristine **Parque Nacional Saslaya**, the wildest part of the Reserva de Biosfera Bosawás. There are two campsites: the town of Hormiguero is the trailhead for the three-hour hike to **Camp Salto Labú**, with a stunning swimming hole that has a cave, canyons and petroglyphs; and Rosa Grande is the trailhead for the four-hour trek to **Camp Piedra Colorada**, on a lagoon surrounded by pristine forest. You can visit either on a day trip.

Guides are US$6 per day, per group; horses US$5 extra per day, per person. There's unpurified water at the campsites, but bring your own food. A *pulpería* (corner store) in Siuna sells large plastic sheets that work as tents in a pinch. You can also arrange guides for the four-day hike up **Cerro Saslaya** (1651m), the three-day climb to **Cerro El Toro** (1652m) and overnight trip up **El Revenido**.

Humboldt Center (⊙ 8am–5pm Mon-Fri), close to Enitel, has maps and information about Bosawás and the surrounding area. There are several swimming holes close by: **Río Wani** has a sandy beach about 11km from town; taxis charge US$10 round-trip, including a two-hour wait. Or, head to the **hot springs**: have a taxi take you to 'la bomba' (US$1.50), then follow the obvious trail about 1½ hours across a private *finca* (farm) to the springs.

SLEEPING & EATING

Hotelito Los Chinitos (☎ 794 2038; s/d/tr without bathroom US$6/10/12) This bright-yellow hotel is a great deal on small but comfortable spotless rooms with cable TV, fans and mosquito screens; bathrooms have 24-hour water. The well-loved *comedor* (basic, cheap eatery; dishes US$1.25 to US$3, open 7am to 9pm) downstairs serves recommended Nica (not Chinese) classics.

Other cheapies include clean, secure **Hospedaje Rivas** (r per person US$3), just uphill from the bus station, with cement jail-cell ambience and mosquito nets, and **Hospedaje Costeño** (s/d US$3/4), close to Los Chinitos, a creaky wooden structure that's the oldest hotel in town. The owner speaks English.

NICARAGUA

Hotel Siu (794 2028; hotel_siu@yahoo.com; r without bathroom per person US$8, s with bathroom US$15-20, d with bathroom US$20-25;) Siuna's best hotel is at the end of a shady sidestreet near the *alcaldía*, and has cozy, nicely decorated rooms with cable TV and 24-hour water, plus a porch where you can linger over breakfast (US$2). Cheaper rooms with shared bathroom and no TV are also nice.

Refresquería Siuna (US$1.25-2; 6am-10pm) Across the street from Los Chinitos, serves cheap, simple meals.

Fritanga (set plate US$1.25) This excellent place is in front of the minimarket, just downhill from the bus station.

Restaurant Hoiming (mains US$4-8; 11am-11pm) Come here for the best Chinese food in the Triangle.

DRINKING
Disco Mia, close to the airstrip, is downscale and family oriented, while discoteca la Secreta, close to Urracan, gets the university crowd; both run Thursday to Sunday.

GETTING THERE & AWAY
La Costeña (794 2017; 8am-1pm) has offices in the 'Bienvenidos a Siuna!' building, right by the airstrip. Buses leave from the market to destinations including:
Managua US$9, 10 to 12 hours, 5am, 3pm, 5pm and 8pm
Río Blanco US$5, five to seven hours, 5am, 7am, 10am, noon and 2pm
Rosita US$3, two to three hours, 5:30am to 3pm, hourly

Bonanza
pop 15,000 / elevation 200m
The crown jewel of the Mining Triangle, Bonanza is the wealthiest and most beautiful of the matched set, an architectural gem of brightly painted wooden homes threaded with cobblestone streets, all displayed in one of Central America's most impressive bezels: the emerald green mountains of Bosawás.

The whole scene, so perfect and pretty in the right light, may offer the impression of some 'Ye Olde Mining Town' theme-park confection, but note that charming shops sell subsistence goods, not souvenirs (unless you count gold jewelry as a souvenir, which your mother really wishes you would), while quaint taverns may have bleeding drunks passed out in their doorways. It's authentic.

So richly blessed above and below, Bonanza is one of the loveliest towns in Nicaragua, and could one day be a real tourist attraction. As yet, however, this brilliant stopover remains the realm of more intrepid adventurers, a diamond in the rough.

ORIENTATION & INFORMATION
Bonanza is 29km north of Rosita on a spur road, well within Bosawás. It is compact, with three paved roads forming a small triangle around which almost all services are located. The bus terminal is 1km south of town on the road to Rosita; the Bosawás office is 2.5km north of town, past the airport on the road to Musuwas.
Hemsa (free; 7am-4pm Mon-Fri) The gold mine, on the road to the bus terminal, offers Bonanza's only Internet, primarily for residents.

SIGHTS & ACTIVITIES
The **alcaldía** (794 0001) can theoretically arrange guides all over the mountains, and will at least be able to point you in the right direction. Persistence!

Reserva de Biosfera Bosawás
The **Bosawás office** (794 0109), 2km from town towards Musuwas, has maps and information about guides and transportation to two sectors of the reserve. Much easier to visit, **Reserva Natural Cerro Cola Blanca** has one main trail, Sendero Tesoro, which starts 4km from Bonanza in the community of Panamá. The Bosawás office also maintains a **teaching finca** 12km south of Bonanza that borders the reserve. Organically grown fruit trees, a babbling brook and trails that lead into the reserve's primary rain forest are free for day trippers by advanced arrangement, and there are plans to add cabins and a restaurant; contact the Bosawás office to find out more. Any Rosita-bound bus can drop you off at the entrance.

Bonanza is also the gateway to one of Bosawás' great cultural treasures, the **Mayangna Heartland**. There are only about 9000 Mayangna (also called Sumo, the less politically correct, but more common, term) Indians left in the world, most concentrated in this cluster of about 20 very poor indigenous communities centered on the de facto Mayangna capital of **Musuwas**, about 30km north of Bonanza on a terrible dirt road. Like all Mayangna towns, Musuwas maintains a community shelter where travelers can stay and arrange simple meals; bottled water and other supplies may also be available, but don't count on it. From here, you can take canoes down Río Pis-Pis and Río Waspúk, climb Cerro Cola Blanca, or ride horses to smaller Mayangna communities.

Recommended guides include Arecia Generon, president of Masaku, a Mayangna organization with offices about 200m up the unpaved road from Hotel B y B (veer left at Monedero Peter's); and Professor Orlando Salamán Justo, at the Bonanza *alcaldía*. Or, you could take a truck 15km north to the Mayangna community of Suniwas (halfway to Musuwas), and look for guides Fidencio Devis and Rodolfo Amador. Bring water purification technology, trekking equipment and extra food; consider taking malaria pills. Including your guide, transportation, meals and lodging, count on spending around US$70 per day for a group of four.

Other Outdoor Attractions

Cerro la Cruz, the big hill with the cross on it, is a 45-minute climb from downtown, but the best view around is a 1.5-hour hike or US$4 taxi ride to **El Chiquero**, 1500m above sea level. It's a 4km walk or US$4 taxi to **Aguas Claras**, a riverside beach and swimming hole. **El Salto Grande**, 7km from town along the road to Suniwas, has a swimming area, waterfall and hydroelectric plant. **Siempre Viva** is the region's most impressive waterfall: take the bus 17km to Vesubio, then walk the last 2km.

Gold Mines

Hemsa (☎ 794 0066, ext 789; elmomendoza@hemconic .com in Spanish, amilkarramos@hemconic.com) is the most important gold mine in Nicaragua, and harvests 24,000 troy ounces annually from 14 tunnels worked by almost 500 miners – 12% of whom are female. In addition to providing gold and jobs (and waste cyanide), Hemsa offers free tours over hanging bridges, past processing equipment and into a tunnel 250m underground – using stairs, so be in good physical condition. Reserve two weeks in advance, with the dates you'll be in town, number of people (six maximum), and reason for your visit.

The *alcaldía* can arrange trips to artisanal mining operations, including small

strip and pit mines, and streams where you can pan for gold. You can also visit one of three gold-processing cooperatives, where more than 6000 artisanal miners, working more than 1000 claims, process their ore. Guides run about US$10 per group, per day, not including transportation.

SLEEPING & EATING

Hotel y Restaurant B y B (☎ 794 0017; s/d without bathroom US$4/5) Bonanza's best-loved landmark is this bright blue-and-yellow place next to the market, with small, freshly painted rooms with mosquito-proofed windows and clean bathrooms. Neither B involves breakfast (Bayardo and Bustillo were the original owners), but it has Bonanza's best restaurant (meals US$3 to US$7, open noon to 10pm), a casino, pool hall and Eskimo.

Hotel Bonanza (☎ 794 0177; r per person with bathroom US$11) Across from the *alcaldía*, this hotel has modern, tiled rooms with cable TV and gleaming plastic furniture. The annex (room per person without bathroom US$5), across the street, is also clean and pleasant.

Hospedaje Claudia (r per person US$2) Very basic, unsigned *hospedajes* catering to miners include Claudia, just uphill from the *alcaldía*, with tiny wooden rooms, shared bucket-flush toilets and a friendly owner.

Himacar (set plate US$2; ☺ 7am-7pm Mon-Sat, 7am-noon Sun) Have breakfast here with its solid set plates and a cozy dining room.

Restaurant El Encuentro (US$3-6; ☺ 11am-close) Have dinner in this big lavender Victorian, a block uphill from B y B (make a right at Monedero Peter's), with a great view and recommended wild boar in salsa.

DRINKING & ENTERTAINMENT

You won't go thirsty in Bonanza, and you can dance at Diskoteck El Ranchón, on the south side of the market, or join the Karaoke craze at rowdy Bar-Restaurant Serrania, nearby.

Tropical Market Video (US$0.40) One block from B y B, this place shows movies in air-conditioned comfort on its big screen TV at 6pm nightly.

SHOPPING

With all this fresh gold everywhere, it's no wonder so much beautiful jewelry is available, dirt cheap. Keep an eye out for the delicate gold filigree work for which the Caribbean Coast was once famous, very different from the heavy colonial styles of the Pacific. Hotel y RestaurantB y B has a great selection, or stop by one of the workshops in town.

Just uphill from Hotel y Restaurant B y B, Casa de las Mujeres offers weekend classes where you can watch women (and men) learn goldsmithing.

Across from Iglesia Santa Teresita, an unmissably Gothic airplane hangar of a church, Joyeria Rivera turns out fine gold jewelry all week long.

RESERVA DE BIOSFERA BOSAWÁS

Supported by three neighboring reserves in Honduras (Río Patuca National Park, Tawhaka Anthropological Reserve and Río Plátano Biosphere Reserve), **Reserva de Biosfera Bosawás** (Bosawás Unesco Biosphere Reserve; ☎ in Managua 233 1594; www.tmx.com.ni/~bosawas/reserva.htm) is the largest protected expanse of rain forest north of the Amazon, clocking in at 20,000 sq km, more than 14% of Nicaragua's national territory.

Named for three geographical features that delineate the reserve – the Río BOcay, Cerro SAslaya and Río WASpúk – enormous Bosawás is also home to more than 200,000 people, including 30,000 Mayangna and Miskito Indians, who have some claim to this land. The reserve loses 120 to 175 hectares of forest per year to farms, and more to illegal lumber operations. A 1.2 million-hectare, multi-use 'amortization area' aims to protect Bosawás by promoting sustainable economic development, such as collecting wild plants to sell, organic *cacao* (cocoa) and coffee *finca*s, and, of course, tourism.

That's the trick. Access to the reserve's 800,000-hectare wild and undeveloped nucleus, which includes Saslaya and Cerro Kilambé national parks, and Peñas Blancas and Cerro Cola Blanca reservas naturals, ranges from challenging to almost impossible, and is never cheap or risk-free. Come prepared: someone in your group (don't do this alone) should speak a fair amount of Spanish, and consider taking malaria pills for longer adventures. Water purification technology is necessary for most of the reserve. But the real key to access is persistence – you can get in, just don't count on it happening on your timetable, and expect to be following leads like: 'find Jaguar José at the *pulpería* near the *empalme* of (something unpronounceable), he's got a truck that can get through.'

During the reserve's February to April dry season, rivers (read: the freeway system) may be too low to travel, unless you help carry the canoe around the rapids.

Luckily, it's usually raining, and some spots (for instance, the Río Waspúk region) get 3200mm of rain per year – regular roads may be impassable most of the year. Temperatures average a sweaty 26.5°C, but bring a jacket for Cerro Kilambé (1750m).

You can begin inquiries at the Bosawás office at Marena Central in Managua (p73), or any of the satellite offices located in most large towns bordering the reserve, where they can arrange guides and transportation, or at least point you in the right direction. It's often easiest to access the reserve through lodges or private organizations, however, so ask around. Here are some points of entry:

- El Tuma-La Dalia (p216): an ecolodge can arrange guided trips to the stunning clifftop mesa of Peñas Blancas.
- Siuna (p227): park rangers guide you to campsites in Parque Nacional Saslaya.
- El Cuá (p219): a women's collective runs hikes to the 'Waterfalls of Peñas Blancas' trail.
- Waspám & Río Coco (p236): take a riverboat ride into the waterfall-strewn wilderness, spending the night in a jungle paradise.
- Wiwilí (p219): hire a boat down the Río Coco, or climb lush Cerro Kilambé (1745m).
- Musuwas (p228): head from Bonanza into the heart of the Mayangna nation.
- San José de Bocay (p219): take a boat ride to mysterious Cuevas Belén de Tunowalan.
- Reserva Natural Cola Blanca (p228): these waterfall-strewn highlands were named for the white-tailed deer teeming on its forested slopes. The Bonanza Bosawás office can get you there.

GETTING THERE & AROUND

The airstrip is about 3km from town; head toward Musuwas and make a right at the stadium. **La Costeña** (☎ 794 0023; ☉ 8-9am & 4-5pm) has offices half a block uphill from the *alcaldía*.

Taxis cost US$0.70 anywhere in town and US$20 to Rosita. The Blue Bus (US$0.30) runs between El Coco (the Bosawás office) and Santa Rita, passing the bus terminal, about 1km south of town, throughout the day. Regular buses leave for destinations including:

Managua US$13, 13 to 15 hours, 10am and 2:30pm; via Rosita (US$2, 1½ hours) and Siuna (US$8, four to five hours)

Rosita US$2, 1½ hours, 7:30am, 11:30am, 1:30pm and 4:30pm

Salto Grande & Suniwas US$1.25, 1½ hours, 8am and noon; meeting trucks to Musuwas

Vesubio US$2, two hours, 7am and 1:30pm

Rosita

pop 17,000

With potential as a stand-in for Dodge City – should Hollywood ever want to film a Western really, really cheap – this very multicultural town not only has the late-1800s clapboard architecture with horses tied up out front, and mustachioed, ten-gallon-hatted cowboys (with sidearms) sauntering around; it's got a country music soundtrack, twanging from all sides.

ORIENTATION & INFORMATION

The dusty frontier town is stretched along one roughly east–west road running from the hospital (east) to the police station (west), with the market and bus station in the middle. Both lagunas are located about 1.5km east of the hospital. **Colegio Santa Rosa** (per hr US$3; ☉ 1-3pm & 5-8pm Mon-Fri) offers Internet access.

DANGERS & ANNOYANCES

Rosita is a cocaine shipping hub, and the neighborhood right behind the police station (ahem) may be unsafe after dark. The main road is patrolled and safe for strolling until the wee hours.

SIGHTS & ACTIVITIES

Sonia Garcia at the *alcaldía*, about one block west of the bus station, contiguous with the police station, can help organize tours to Miskito, Mayangna and Creole communities, down beautiful rivers, and up Yakalwás Mountain and Risco de Oro, a hill honeycombed with abandoned gold mines.

FURCA (Foundation for Unity & Reconstruction of the Atlantic Coast; ☎ 794 1045, in Managua 249 7801; furca@sdnnic.org.ni), a block from the *alcaldía*, can arrange trips to area indigenous communities with guides Juan McKenzie and Mateo Salinas. Trips usually visit Wasa King (Wasakín), with a cool new suspension bridge and river access along the Río Bambana in rainy season. Prices vary, but run around US$60 for four people. If the office is closed, feel free to call director Brenda Jarkin-Manzares (☎ 794 1190) at home.

In town, you could enjoy the view from **Santa Rosa Catholic Church**, on the hill (stairs provided) behind Colegio Santa Rosa. A **trail** past rusting mining equipment leads to the top of the mountain, beginning about one block east of the church. Take a taxi (US$0.70, 1.5km) to Bar Campestre La Laguna Verde, overlooking an allegedly pristine lake, where you could go for a swim or just enjoy a beer under one of the dilapidated *rancheros*.

There's another **laguna** near Bar 2000 (2km, taxi US$0.70), a steely gray expanse of utterly poisoned water surrounded by huge mine tailings and rusting mining equipment;

DIY: ALAMIKANGBAN & PRINZAPOLKA

The isolated towns of Alamikangban, about 70km southeast of Rosita, and Prinzapolka, another two hours by boat along the Río Prinzapolka to the Caribbean Coast, don't get many visitors. They both have a couple of super-basic *hospedajes* and simple *comedores*, but the real reason to go is the river. It marks the southern boundary of natural pine forest that phases into tropical rain forest, with wetlands that are a haven for all sorts of birds.

Buses leave Rosita (US$3, four hours) at 8am and 1pm daily for Alamikangban, where you can hire a private boat to Prinzapolka. Both towns, as well as the smaller communities lining the river, have indigenous government structures, so ask for the *wihta* (judge) or *síndico* (resource manager) when trying to find guides or lodging – and just hope that someone speaks Spanish.

more machinery rises ominously from the lifeless water in dry season. It's pretty at sunset, in a post-apocalyptic way.

SLEEPING & EATING

Rosita has lots of mosquitoes, so make sure to ask your hotel for a net. Basic hotels cluster around the bus station.

Cecap (☎ 794 1003; r per person US$3) This is a great deal. In the unsigned, two-story Victorian next to the hospital, it houses medical students and travelers-in-the-know with comfortable, very clean wooden rooms, a fine porch and shared bucket showers.

Hospedaje el Sol (☎ 794 1129; s/d with bathroom US$2.50/4) Much nicer than average, with small, clean rooms and tidy shared bathrooms. There's also a TV nook with swinging chairs that overlooks the street scene.

Hotel Los Ensueños (☎ 794 1004; r with fan/aircon per person US$10/20; 🔀) There's one really nice hotel in town, half a block north of the *alcaldía*, with spotless, attractively furnished modern rooms and the option of cable TV and air-con, all surrounding manicured gardens and a parking lot. Breakfast (US$2) is served on the patio.

The cheapest eats are at the outdoor *comedores* close to the bus station.

Bar-Restaurant El Escorpión (mains US$2-6; 🕙 10am-11pm) Big-hatted ranchers prefer this place, featuring porkchops, seafood and Mexican *norteños*.

Restaurant & Video Bar Martinez (mains US$3-7; 🕙 5pm-2am) Everyone loves Martinez, with steak, lobster and several TVs.

Bar Campestre La Laguna Verde (set plate US$1.25; 🕙 all day) Take a taxi (US$0.70) out to the lake for a meal overlooking the water.

GETTING THERE & AWAY

If **La Costeña** (☎ 794 1015), across from the *alcaldía*, is closed, make flight reservations at Eskimo Ice Cream, in the same building. The airstrip is a US$1.25 taxi ride from town. Buses leave from the market to destinations including:

Alimikamba US$3, three hours, 8am and 1:15pm
Bonanza US$2, 1½ hours, 7:30am, 11:30am, 1:30pm and 4:30pm
Puerto Cabezas US$8, four to six hours, 6:30am, 9:25am and 11:45am
Siuna US$3, four to five hours, 5:30am to 5pm, hourly

BILWI (PUERTO CABEZAS)

pop 39,800 / elevation 30m

Although the capital of the enormous Northern Atlantic Autonomous Region (RAAN) has been officially renamed Bilwi, most residents still refer to their isolated tropical stronghold as they have for almost a century, Puerto Cabezas, or just Puerto. Or just Port.

Neither name is the original, however. Founded in 1690 by a trio of pirates who called it Bragman's Bluff, it only later came to be known as Bilwi. The port town was officially renamed in 1925 to honor General Rigoberto Cabezas, who helped put the largely indigenous and English region under full control of the Nicaraguan government in 1894 – never really appreciated by the locals.

Even after the English were forced out, English-speaking companies like banana empire Standard Fruit, which built the 1km dock in 1823, helped keep federal interference in the region minimal. The same dock was used in the 1960s to launch the failed, US-backed invasion of Cuba that has come to be known as the Bay of Pigs. Heck, most people in Bilwi still speak some English – as well as Creole, Mayangna, Miskito and Spanish – and do brisk business selling lobster tails, pine lumber and shrimp to the USA.

And there are also still plenty of pirates. Bilwi (Mayangna for 'snake leaf') is a major cocaine transit point. Keep your nose clean, take taxis at night and through Barrio El Cocal (between the city center and Restaurant Kabu Payaska) even during the day, and avoid going to beaches alone. Port has a terrible water supply, which runs for a few hours three times a week, and that water is green. Don't even use it to brush your teeth.

Information

BanPro Changes money and does cash advances on Visa credit cards.
Bilwinet (per hour US$2; 🕙 8am-9pm Mon-Sat, 3-6pm Sun) Fast computers are a half block north of the park.
Hospital (☎ 453 3301)
Intur In a dingy upstairs office at the Gobierno Regional complex, staff are just happy to see you. Resources are geared toward building area businesses, but they'll still help you out.
Marena (Ministry of the Environment & Natural Resources; ☎ 792 2201, 282 2366) One block west and three blocks south of Supermercado Monter, this helpful

office manages Reservas Nacionales Laguna Pahara, Yulu, Klingna and Laguna Karatá, as well as the Miskito Keys, but Amica (p234) is your best bet for arranging guided trips to any of them.

Police (☎ 282 2257)

Sights & Activities

The **parque central** (central park) is a little scruffy, although the giant Indian sculpture is impressive, but there's a much prettier park two blocks east, overlooking the Atlantic, with playground equipment. Across the street, enormous **Parroquia San Pedro Apostol** is worth a look for its giant murals and unusual construction.

Casa Museo Judith Cunningham (☎ 792 2225; admission US$1; ☺ daily), two blocks north and one block west of the Moravian church, is perhaps the best museum about regional history and Miskito culture, and was put together by Judith Cunningham, a local legend who recently passed away. In 1981 she and her family had to cross to Waspám and the Río Coco to avoid the Sandinistas, then returned after the RAAN won its autonomy in the late 1980s. You can still see

photos and artifacts chronicling her experiences from Laguna de Perlas all the way up the Caribbean Coast to Honduras; 62 of her paintings are also on display. See p235 for accommodations at the museum.

Four blocks northwest of the park, tiny **Museo Lakia Tara** (admission US$1) has photos, woodwork displays and books about Miskito language and culture, plus a workshop downstairs where you can watch people make clothing and other crafts from *tuno*, a type of plant fiber – and you can buy it here, cheap. It also has excellent budget lodging (p235).

You could also stroll down to the disintegrating **Old Pier**, where both Sandino and the Contras received arms smuggled in from abroad and where you can watch people haul in their catches...including endangered sea turtles, which are kept on their backs, alive, with their little flippers pierced crucifixion style and tied together. Don't get all mushy: one tourist paid US$100 to free one of them, and the fisher obliged, then recaptured it 20 minutes later. *Pangas* (small motorboats) for hire congregate just south of the pier.

BILWI (PUERTO CABEZAS)

0 ————— 400 m
0 ————— 0.2 miles

To Kabu Payaska (1.5km); Airport (2km); Comedor Mirasol (2km); La Bocana (4km)

⊕ Hospital

Central Park

Park

Estadio Municipal Ernesto Hooker

To Bus Station (2km); Waspám (138km); Rosita (145km); Managua (536km)

To Immigration (300m); Old Pier (400m); Tuapi (8km)

CARIBBEAN SEA

Beaches south of the pier may one day be beautiful, but at press time were just trashed. Instead, head to **Kabu Payaska** restaurant (opposite), where you can use the clean, safer stretch of sand as long as you order something. North of town is **La Bocana**, at the mouth of the river, an old pirate hangout with broad sandy beaches and modern-day security issues – come in groups, preferably with a local.

Tuapí, a small community eight unsigned kilometers south of Bilwi on a good dirt road through a pine tree farm, is the area's best, safest beach, with OK surfing (but nowhere to rent a board) and good swimming, but watch out for the undertow. A cab costs around US$20, with a few hours' wait, not including a US$0.70 bridge toll. Public trucks (US$1) run a few times daily from the bus lot. There's a café open Sunday, otherwise bring a picnic.

If you're feeling especially adventurous, **Alejandro Arouse** (☎ 844 8337) is a renowned hunting and fishing guide who can also arrange very non-PADI-certified lobster dives.

MISKITO KEYS BIOLOGICAL RESERVE

Just 50km, but a world, away, the Miskito Keys are a group of beautiful Caribbean islands surrounded by houses built on stilts out over lobster-infested coral reefs and crystal-blue water. The historic first meeting between the British pirate Captain Sussex Camock and his future Miskito allies took place here in 1633. It's still a pirate haven, so if you see any boats with Colombian plates, don't take photos.

There are no hotels or restaurants in the keys, and while you can rent a hammock in a private home (through Marena or Amica, or just ask around), you should bring your own food and water. Anyone with scientific credentials can visit with advance approval from Marena, while Amica arranges overnight visits for around US$500 per group.

Otherwise, you'll need to rent an expensive private *lancha* (small motorized boat) or make arrangements with a lobster fisherman, which is sketchy. There are rumors that you need a permit, but neither Marena nor the Navy have details. It's two hours to the keys on a fast boat, perhaps five on a lobster vessel.

AMICA

The easiest way into area natural reserves and indigenous communities is through the **Association of Indigenous Women on the Atlantic Coast** (Amica; ☎ 792 2219; asociacionamica@yahoo.es; ⊗ 8am-noon Mon-Sat, 2-5:30pm Mon-Fri), 1½ blocks southwest of the stadium. In addition to working to stop domestic violence and promote indigenous rights, it can arrange fishing trips, expeditions to turtle-nesting sites, Tuapí (US$80, six people), the Miskito Keys (US$500, eight people overnight) and more, and has a few English-speaking guides. Arrange tours for two to six people in advance, if possible. Other destinations include the following:

Karatá & Wawa Bar (per person US$40-50) This scenic Miskito village 17km south of Bilwi, at the mouth of Río Wawa, has a beautiful lagoon packed with migratory birds and alligators plus a sandy oceanfront beach with restaurants, campsites and hiking trails. Karatá has one pretty four-room hotel with good mattresses and a seafood restaurant. You could also rent a private *panga* (day trip/overnight US$100/150) and visit on your own.

Haulover (per group US$200-500) The first Morovian missionaries arrived here, 30km south of Port, in 1860, and named it in honor of the sand bar that boats had to cross to enter the lagoon. Protected by Reserva Natural Laguna Kukalaya and Reserva Natural Layasiksa, the town has comfortable cabinas with running water and beautiful views, and your tour includes a performance of the 'King Pulanka' dance.

Krukira (prices vary) About 20km north of Bilwi, this is the gateway to Reserva Natural Laguna Pahara, with lots of wildlife, in particular huge tarpon. Although campers are welcome and meals can be arranged, there are currently few services for visitors.

Festivals & Events

Different facets of Bilwi's multicultural population have each taken a day (or month) and made it their own.

Dance of El King Pulanka (January 6–mid-February) First performed in the late 1700s, the dance of El Rey and La Reina is today performed throughout the Mosquitia. Two groups of dancers wearing 18th-century costumes represent the king's allies and enemies, and stage a mock battle using arrows, machetes and 'triki trakas,' or firearms. The good guys win, there's a barbecue, and poets, artists and other folkloric dance troops keep the party going all month long.

Emancipation (August 28) The Creole and Afro-Caribbean population puts on a wild show – parades, floats, costumes, food – while the schools have special history classes and workshops in the Creole language.

Día de la Hispanidad (October 12) Called Día de la Raza in most of Nicaragua, this is the occasion for Bilwi's Spanish population to shine.

Día de la Autonomia (October 22) Celebrates the day the RAAN was finally rid of those Spaniards in Managua! Well, sort of.

Sleeping

Even in the best hotels, you may have to resort to bucket showers and toilets.

Hospedaje Tininiska (dm US$5-6) Run by Museo Lakia Tara, this pretty wooden house has several spacious dorm rooms with one to four beds in each, all with mosquito nets. Very clean bathrooms with flush toilets are shared; this is a fabulous place for backpackers.

Casa de Huéspedes Pelican (☎ 792 2336, 828 8646; s/d without bathroom US$9/12) Two blocks east of the parque central, simple rooms with skylights share a wonderfully muraled back porch with rocking chairs and Caribbean views.

Casa Museo Judith Cunningham (☎ 792 2225; casamuseojudithkain@hotmail.com; s/d without bathroom US$9/12, tr with bathroom US$24; P ✖ ☐) In the same mahogany dream home as the museum, beautiful rooms come with fans, Internet access and a conference room; some have air-con and TVs.

El Cortijo (☎ 792 2340; s/d US$24/27) This beautiful wooden farmhouse, one block south of the *alcaldía*, is so nice that the Sandinistas used it as their East Coast base for 10 years, something that still irritates Doña Aura. She's repaired the damage, and the attractively furnished, high-ceilinged rooms have views of the lovely gardens and fountain. Cheaper downstairs rooms (double room US$20) have lower ceilings and private bathrooms. El Cortijo II, two blocks north, only has double beds and is super romantic, with a lovely wooden walkway right to the pretty beach; try to get one of the two rooms with porches and hammocks overlooking the backyard.

Eating & Drinking

Lobster and shrimp are the region's main (legal) business; enjoy the fruits of that labor for around US$6 a plateful. If you're pinching pennies, the scruffy parque central is surrounded by unappealing food stands, as well as **Junior Fast Food** (US$1-4), with a brisk business in *bocas* (appetiz-

ers) and beer, and Rosti Pollos, with roast chicken, nearby.

Comedor Mirasol (US$1-5; ⏰ 7:30am-9pm) Across from the airport, this place has great, inexpensive burgers and *comida corriente* (mixed plate of local food). At press time a group of festive English-speaking expats had plans to open an information center inside, but if they haven't gotten around to it, stop by and ask for 'Miskito' Alan, who can tell you anything you need to know, particularly if you're buying the next round.

Dragon Chino (US$5-9; ⏰ 11am-11pm) Everyone's favorite, this Chinese place two blocks to the northeast of the parque central does great fried rice and chow mein, but try the grilled lobster, on the menu's upper end.

Restaurant Wah May (US$4-7; ⏰ noon-midnight Tue-Sun) This place is the new Chinese restaurant; try the chop suey. It's close to the parque central.

Kabu Payaska (fast food US$2-3, seafood US$5-10; ⏰ 10:30am-11pm) The best restaurant in town has a breezy dining area, great service, fabulous seafood and piped-in Miskito music, all overlooking a lovely stretch of sand. To get here, head north from town toward the airport, but make a left at the gas station and continue another 1km; this neighborhood is considered unsafe, so take a taxi (US$.70) even during the day.

Two good seafood restaurants closer to town double as the town discos: **Bar-Restaurant El Malecón** (US$2-6; ⏰ 10am-midnight) serves lobster, seafood soups and *bocas* within view of the old dock; while **Disco-Bar Miramar** (US$3-7; ⏰ 11am-late) has better food and a more mature dance floor.

Enormous Discoteque Jumbo, close to the parque central, doesn't have food but it does have pool tables.

Supermercado Monter (⏰ 8am-8pm Mon-Sat, 8am-1pm Sun), across from the stadium, and Kupia Kumi grocery store, half a block south of the parque central, are your last chances for real groceries before Honduras.

Entertainment

Cinema Ubieta (US$2) Around the corner from Parroquia San Pedro Apostol, you could catch the latest (well, three months ago) Hollywood blockbuster here.

Getting There & Away

Although you can theoretically catch a cargo vessel to Prinzapolka and Bluefields, most people come by plane. Once the longest airstrip in Central America, it was specifically built to launch air support for the invasion of Cuba at the Bay of Pigs, which never actually arrived. Today both La Costeña (LC) and Atlantic Airlines (AA) offer regular flights to Managua, Bluefields and the Mining Triangle. Note that while RAAN does not use daylight savings time, the airlines do.

Bluefields US$90/140 one way/return, one hour, 12:10pm (LC), Monday to Saturday

Managua US$100/150 one way/return, 1½ hours, 8am (AA), 8:20am (LC), 12:10pm (AA), 12:20pm (LC) and 1:15pm (LC); Monday to Saturday service to Las Minas

BUSES

Take a taxi to the bus station, 2km from town. There are no services at the bus lot, though vendors do sell snacks. Buses leave for destinations including:

Managua US$18, 20 to 24 hours, 10am and 1pm; stopping in Río Blanco (US$15, 16 to 18 hours) and Boaco (US$16, 18 to 20 hours)

Rosita US$7, six to 10 hours, 7am and 12:45pm

Siuna US$10, eight to 12 hours, 8:30am

Waspám US$6, four hours, 7:30am and 7:30am

WASPÁM & THE RÍO COCO

pop 35,000

Waspám is the de facto capital of 116 communities lazing along the languid lifeline of the Río Coco, around here known as the Wangki, or 'Big River,' – the cultural, geographic and economic heart of the Mosquitia. During the rainy season, it flows a fast muddy brown; in summer months, it runs crystal clear, and sandy beaches appear on either side. The longest river in Central America also forms the border between Nicaragua and Honduras, a distinction most Miskitos ignore. But if you'll be crossing into Honduras, get your passport stamped at **Bilwi Immigration** (☎ 792 2258; Bilwi; ☻ 8am-noon Mon-Sat, 2-5pm Mon-Fri),located two blocks from the old pier.

If you are coming to Waspám from Bilwi, you'll immediately feel more relaxed in this indigenous river town. Waspám isn't nearly as coked up as the rest of the coast, and women will be relieved that the Miskito culture doesn't require men to whistle at anything with breasts. Oh, and there's 24-hour water and electricity here – go figure.

Mosquitoes are the big drawback, and if you're going to be here for more than a couple of days, particularly during rainy season (June to October), seriously consider taking antimalarials. No matter what, wear long sleeves and pants at dusk, topped with DEET and a mosquito net (or hermetically sealed rooms) at night.

Orientation & Information

Waspám is fairly small and most services are located within three blocks of the parque central and Río Coco, which is a good thing, since the town's two taxis are nowhere to be found. If you'll be exploring, remember that although the region was declared mine-free in 2004, it's always best to stay on trails.

Bosawás office In the little white house behind the market, staff can help you arrange treks into the biosphere reserve, recommending guides and destinations, and helping arrange boats.

Enitel Has one phone in the center of town.

Wangkinet (per hour US$2; ☻ 8am-9pm) Across from the airstrip, it may have the best name of any Internet café anywhere.

Sights & Activities

Other than the fabulous river views, the attractions here are scant: there's the oddly constructed **Iglesia San Rafael**, while the rather barren parque central has the requisite **war monument** – but here, it's for fallen Contras.

The town's top attraction is a 10-minute walk along dirt roads curving away from the river; just ask anyone for the fabulous Dr Dionisio Melgara Brown and his **Museo Auka Tangki** (brownmelgara@hotmail.com; donations accepted; ☻ daily), across from INKA. The small but informative museum sells what may be the only Miskito-Spanish dictionary (US$18) available, plus lots of photos and cultural artifacts, including tortoiseshell jewelry, traditional fishing nets, musical instruments and *Miskito batana,* a type of hair pomade made from the African palm oil. You'll also see those big, wooden mortar-and-pestle sets up close, used for making *wabul,* a very traditional Miskito power shake consisting of plantains or other starchy fruits mashed with coconut milk and/or cow milk, and a

---

BORDER CROSSING: WASPÁM TO PUERTO LEMPIRA, HONDURAS

This is a total adventure border crossing, and begins by getting your US$2 exit visa (US$7 to enter) at **Bilwi Immigration** (☎ 792 2258; Bilwi; ◷ 8am-noon Mon-Sat, 2-5pm Mon-Fri), located two blocks from the old pier. Then it's up to Waspám to find a *colectivo* motorized canoe (US$6, two hours) to the border crossing at Leimus. You can also get to Leimus by 4WD taxi or private *panga*, both of which are much more expensive.

There's a Honduran border post in Leimus where they will process your passport (US$3 to enter, free to exit). Then you catch a pickup truck (US$9, three hours) through the jungle to the capital of the Honduran Mosquitia, Puerto Lempira. There are a handful of dining and sleeping options here; try basic **Santa Teresita** (d US$6) or relatively swish **Hotel Yubaiwan** (d US$25), with TV and air-con. There are regular flights and an inconvenient boat service from Puerto Lempira to La Ceiba, gateway to the Bay Islands.

---

variety of flavorings, often *cacao*. It can be served hot or cold.

Perhaps because the traditional Miskito diet doesn't include many vegetables, *yumuh*, or constipation, is a cultural preoccupation. Healers use special massages, or you can boil a *yumulah*, a smooth rock that sometimes appears when lightening hits a tree, as part of a special tea that should take care of it. Long-term visitors could consider bringing along a fiber supplement instead.

Hotel El Piloto (☎ 273 3794) can arrange horse (US$4 per hour) and bicycle (US$2 per hour) rental, and can find guides for area attractions, none of which are developed for tourism. Ask about **Indio Watla**, a petroglyph cave about four hours from town on horseback, in the community of Wisconsin. In dry season, El Piloto can also get you to **Bismuna**, about 70km east of town on a terrible road, with a beach, food and lodging, and lots of tarpon. From here you can get a boat to **Cabo Viejo**, a lagoon with horrible sand fleas and lots of oysters, which is a haven for migratory birds, or even **Cabo Gracias a Dios**, at the mouth of the Río Coco, one of the most remote destinations anywhere. By river, Cabo Gracias is a four-day round-trip that will cost at least US$1200 for four people.

They can also arrange shorter tours of the Miskito communities of Ulwas, Sowpuka and Bilwas Karma by car, or visits to **Kum** (accessible by 4WD in dry season, river only in rainy season), where the former Miskito royal family still resides. If you want to see the Dance of El King Pulanka done right, this is the place.

RESERVA DE BIOSFERA BOSAWÁS

The Río Coco forms the northern boundary of the Bosawás biosphere reserve, and the park can be relatively easily accessed using scenic river routes that will cost you plenty. You can start at the Bosawás office (see opposite), in a white house one block from the bus station, or go through Hotel El Piloto, where owner Barry Watson speaks perfect English. The classic trip takes you 135km upriver to **Salto Yaho**, an enormous waterfall on the Río Waspúk, a tributary of the Wangki that forms the northeastern border of Bosawás. Always wear a life jacket when swimming under the falls. The deal includes an overnight stay at **Hotelito Ruth** (r per person US$5) in San Carlos, with simple rooms, a good restaurant and boat tours further into Bosawás. Bring bottled water, just in case. El Piloto charges US$150 for a group of up to six people.

Emserta Transports, located at the larger dock just east of the bus station, can arrange private *pangas* and guides to locations up and down the river, which is not cheap. In addition to fishing trips (US$12, four hours), including all equipment, and an overnight Salto Yaho (135km, US$300 for four people) tour, you could try Los Raudales (the Rapids, 280km, US$700 for four people), a canyon with a waterfall and lots of petroglyphs. Keep in mind that you'll be running serious rapids in a tiny wooden canoe with no life jackets. Travel upstream to Wiwilí can theoretically be arranged, but you'll be carrying canoes around the white water.

Independent operators here and at the other dock (which has smaller, cheaper motorized canoes) may be less expensive.

NICARAGUA

THE MOSQUITIA

Some legends say that the Miskito Nation, which for two centuries controlled more territory than any other indigenous group in American history (after the Maya), originated in the Miskito Keys and only then took control of the Miskito Coast of Nicaragua and Honduras, more properly known as the Mosquitia. The keys first appeared on a European map in 1630, labeled the Musquitu Islands, '14 leagues from Cabo de Gracias,' where the Miskitos first made contact with pirate captain Sussex Camock in 1633.

The Miskitos quickly grasped the potential for firearms, and in return for the new technology aided in the sacking of Spanish strongholds up and down the Río San Juan and Río Coco. In 1687 the English monarchy was pleased enough to help found the Miskito monarchy, and by the mid-1800s most of the Caribbean territory between Central Honduras and Limón, Costa Rica, was under Miskito and British control. And when the Crown hosted King Jeremy in England, his tutors were surprised that he looked more African than Indian.

Miskito culture has historically embraced outsiders, and not always figuratively. Most trace their obviously African roots to a Portuguese slave ship that wrecked on the keys in 1640, though waves of escaped slaves and West Indian banana workers are almost certainly part of the mix. Other important outside influences include the German Moravian church, whose missionaries arrived in 1849, and built pretty red-roofed wooden churches that are now at the physical and cultural heart of most Miskito communities. To this day many Miskito festivals and handicrafts have a distinctly Saxon flavor.

The Mosquitia did not submit willingly to Nicaraguan rule in 1894, and their discontent at domination by the 'Spaniards' in Managua was brought to a head by one of the most horrific chapters of Sandinista rule. President Somoza had been popular since 1960, when Miskito refugees poured into the country following a border dispute – instead of turning them away, Somoza ordered houses and churches built. Regardless of this, few appreciated the apartheid system Somoza maintained, which required Miskitos to obtain a passport before traveling to the Pacific Coast, where the jobs were.

Sleeping

Hotel El Viajero (r per person US$3) Located right on the park, simple clapboard rooms come with mosquito nets and fans, shared working showers and bucket-flush toilets.

Hospedaje Waspám (r per person US$4) A cheapie with small, dark rooms at least have a sweet little porch with hammocks overlooking the river.

Hospedaje La Cabañas (cabinas per person US$5, r per person US$9; P) Popular but unsigned behind a red and white house four blocks from the docks, this place has bamboo huts on the verge of collapse and a modern, cement building with four better rooms.

Hotel El Piloto (☎ 273 3794; d/q with bathroom US$18/24; ❄) Just one block up from the docks and bus stop, this hotel is as luxurious as it gets, and its large, immaculate rooms have lots of light. There's an onsite restaurant and free coffee all day, and the English-speaking owners here can arrange tours, boat transportation and other activities.

Eating

Although authentic Miskito cuisine is hard to find, keep an eye out for delicacies like *wabul*, *pihtu talla laya* (fermented pineapple-rind drink), *twalbí* (corn liquor), *takrú* (fish and yucca baked together in banana leaves) and *auhbi piakan* (Miskito for 'mixed together'), which involves plantains, meat and coconut. The Central Market should at least have a few stands selling coconut bread, fresh fruit and bags of lukewarm rice with meat.

Coco Bar (meal US$3-5; ❧ 10am-10pm) Half a block from the airport and often referred to as 'La Negra,' Coco Bar serves good Chinese food and even better curried chicken.

There are two riverfront restaurants: popular **El Ranchito** (set plate US$3; ❧ 6am-10pm), where you walk through the owners' living room to get to the screened-in dining area with great views of the Big River and little boats, and an outstanding hot sauce; and **Bar y Comedor Linda Vista** (set plate US$2-3; ❧ 8am-close), which also has fine views.

Thus the Miskitos' loyalty was split, though when the revolution triumphed many joined the FSLN-backed group Misurasata (MIskito, SUmo, RAma, SAndinista & AslaTAlanka), hoping to help with the literacy campaign. Volunteers were soon informed, however, that the Sandinista-led government had decreed Spanish the official language, which few people spoke, much less read. The FSLN then declared the Mosquitia's natural resources to be public property, 'to be exploited efficiently and reasonably.' Tensions built.

At the same time, Somoza's National Guard was regrouping in the Mosquitia. The Sandinistas got intelligence that they would be meeting in San Carlos on December 23, 1981, and put two and two together. Some 7000 troops received their orders: evacuate the people, burn the houses, kill the animals and destroy the wells. No one had time to pack, or think, just flee the columns of smoke rising from the riverbanks and the squeals of dying animals. Every single town on the Río Coco was burned to the ground, and no one knows how many civilians died. It is remembered as Red Christmas.

Some 20,000 people became refugees, moving to Honduras, Bilwi and San José de Bocay, and what's now known as Tasba Pri or 'Free Land,' the impoverished string of towns clinging to the road from Rosita to Bilwi. Many others joined the Contras.

The Sandinistas backpedaled and apologies were issued, but it was too late. In 1987 the National Autonomy Law granted the RAAN and RAAS official independence in response to local pressure, though in reality the central government continued to exploit the region's natural resources without providing federal infrastructure. Unemployment hovered at 50%, and the regions remained the poorest in the nation.

Shortly after autonomy, former Contras and Misurasata members formed Yatama (Yapti Masrika Nani, or 'Descendants of Mother Earth'), a political party that probably gets about 90% of the indigenous vote in every election. Barred from participating in the 2000 elections because of The Pact (p58), Yatama called on its constituency to abstain, and a Sandinista actually became mayor of Bilwi. The World Court ruled that the elections were tainted, and in 2005 Yatama got on the ballot and won big, taking the mayorships of Waspám, Prinzapolka and Bilwi. It was a historic victory, and one that matters, as the Mosquitia rises once again.

Drinking & Entertainment

Japanese-themed Discoteca Kufu is currently the more popular of the two discos, both of which are open Thursday to Sunday.

Video Bar Freddy (snacks US$2-4; 🕑 noon-midnight) Shows DVDs on its big-screen TV, and if you're nice you may be able to choose the movie.

Getting There & Away

La Costeña is open on flight days only, right across from the airstrip, which means that it is difficult to make the recommended reservations. The flights leave from here for Managua (US$90/160 one way/return, 70 minutes) at 12:10pm on Tuesdays, Thursdays and Saturdays, and 10:40am on Fridays.

Buses (US$6, four hours) leave for Bilwi at 6:30am and 7:30am daily, a surprisingly pleasant trip through the pine savanna on a smooth graded road, with latrine break at the halfway point.

THE ROAD TO EL RAMA

This region is much cheaper and easier to visit than most destinations in this chapter, as it's connected to Managua by a smooth, perfect strip of cement that takes about six hours – in an *ordinario* (slow bus) – from the capital to the river port of El Rama, with boats to the real Caribbean Coast. A rental car or even bicycle would be a fine way to explore Boaco and the Chonatales, which, unlike the two autonomous regions, is part of Nicaragua proper and shares the dominant culture's history and Spanish language.

Boaco

pop 45,000 / elevation 390m

It calls itself 'The City with Two Floors,' because two communities, each with its own beautiful church, have grown together from the hill and valley, intersecting in such a way that it could be better named 'The City of Stunning Views.' The town sprawls into the shallower valley to the south (the 'lower floor') and continues to grow. And to the north and west the upper floor is perched at the edge of a 400m drop into the deeper and more beautiful valley below.

But more than anything, Boaco is a cowboy town; really, *the* cowboy town, and if you're lucky, some enterprising farmer will bring his or her cow right to the green and breezy parque central to sell fresh-squeezed milk, almost direct from the udder to you.

ORIENTATION & INFORMATION
Boaco is easy to get around – once you figure out the whole 'two floors' thing. Most tourist services are concentrated on the upper floor. The town does sprawl but most services are within three blocks. A handful of restaurants and discos are located just out of town; take a cab.

BanCentro, If you arrive by bus, at the main market, head downhill then back up, toward yellow Santiago Apóstol Church; you'll pass this bank with a Visa/Plus ATM on the way. The road passes Hotel Alma on the right; take the stairs and end up at the parque central.

Centro de Internet (per hr US$0.70) Across from the park.

Hospital (☎ 842 2301) Located just out of town; take a cab.

Marena (☎ 843 1677) Two blocks north of the *El Bailante* statue, this very helpful office manages Reserva Natural Cerro Cumaica–Cerro Alegre, with relatively easy access via Santa Lucia and San José de los Remates (p242); and Reserva Natural Cerro Mombachito-La Vieja and Reserva Natural Filas de Masigüe, which have ecotourism projects in the works. Marena can tell you the latest, and point you toward guides for the hike to La Cebadilla, a nearby mountaintop shrine, and other outdoor activities.

SIGHTS & ACTIVITIES
If you're driving, it's worth a stop in **Boaco Viejo**, the original, one-floor site of Boaco, which was an indigenous stronghold (hence the relocation) but still has a beautiful old church housing La Virgen Auxiliadora.

Other than the **mysterious mushroom statue** in the parque central (perhaps homage to what's growing beneath the cow patties?), Boaco's not exactly teeming with tourist attractions. There are very nice Catholic churches: classic and very yellow **La Parroquia de Santiago Apóstol**, on the upper floor, and, perhaps more interesting, Russian Orthodox-style (but still very Catholic) **Parroquia de Nuestra Señora del Perpetuo Socorro** downstairs.

Museo Antropológica Arturo José Suarez Miranda (admission free; ☽ afternoons), two blocks west of the park, has a handful of archaeo-

logical treasures, photos of several Boaco mayors, and adult reading classes at night.

Time is better spent taking in the views from **Parque El Cerrito del Faro**, two blocks north and 1½ blocks west of the parque central, with the climbable 1895 'lighthouse' above the city; you'll see a pretty hill rising from the other side of town, with a farmhouse at the base, where a breezy, popular 45-minute climb begins (ask permission).

A block west (uphill), then north, of Marena, the street ends at **Paseo de los Poetas**, which honors Boaco's four Rubén Darío Literary Prize winners – Antonio Barquero, Julian Guerrero, Hernan Robleto and Diego Sequeira – with an appropriately romantic vista. Nearby, the statue of *El Bailante*, a dancing clown, is a reminder to show up for Boaco's biggest party, the **Procession of Santiago Apóstol** (July 24–25), when all the men dress like that.

Cooperativa San Isidro (☎ 542 1822; snisidro@ibw .com.ni), located one block north of Entel, can arrange free guided tours, including transport, visiting members of its 152-strong cooperative of small organic coffee growers (with advance notice). Nearby, in Teustepe, **Comunidad Asiento Viejo** (☎ 542 2609; per person US$7) offers all-day tours of area caves, petroglyphs and wild hot springs.

SLEEPING
Hotel Alma (☎ 542 2620; r without bathroom US$6, r with bathroom US$9-12; ℗ ⊠) On the road between the floors, this place is super clean, and a few extra dollars buys a TV and/or air-con; the US$9 rooms have awesome views.

Hotel Santiago (☎ 829 0671; r without bathroom US$7-9) Two blocks from the park, this big, cool, clean, tiled colonial has huge rooms with lovely shared bathroom and a TV area that the English-speaking owner, Carlos Obando, had just started remodeling. He had plans to add a tourist information desk, so stop by.

Hotel Bosquesa (☎ 542 1675; dm US$4, r with bathroom US$10; ⊠) Take a taxi to the rain forest and great rooms – air-con, TV – plus pool and recommended restaurant.

EATING
Boaco is a beef town, with cheese on the side; vegans can consider themselves warned.

El Paladar (US$1-4; ☽ 9am-midnight) This popular spot serves all your meaty favorites including the Plato Paladar: ham, cheese and beef wrapped in a thick flour tortilla and arranged over mashed potatoes, all smothered in a mushroom-cream sauce. With a salad.

El Borbonne (US$2.50-4; 10am-9:30pm) Across from Marena, this is the other favorite, with a mellower atmosphere and more meaty entrees.

Take a taxi to recommended Chinchilla Restaurant and Restaurante La Bosquesa, both serving steak and other beefy meals beneath *palapas* (thatched-roof huts) in the woods.

GETTING THERE & AWAY

Boaco is actually 12km from the Empalme de Boaco, on the main Managua–El Rama highway; to get to Juigalpa, Nueva Guinea, San Carlos or El Rama, you'll need to take any Managua-bound bus to the *empalme* and flag an east-bound bus from there. Buses leave from the market to destinations including:

Camoapa US$1, one hour, 6:30am to 5:15pm, almost hourly

Managua *ordinario* US$2, three hours, 3:45am to 5:25pm, every 30 minutes

Managua minivan US$2.50, two hours, every 1½ hours or so, depart when full

Río Blanco US$3.25, 2½ hours, 5:30am to 5:45pm, every 45 minutes

San José de los Remates US$2, 1½ hours, 8:15am; returns 2:15pm

Santa Lucia US$1, one hour, 10:30am, 12:10pm, 1:15pm, 4pm and 5pm

Aguas Claras Hot Springs

This region may not be the easiest place to travel, but **Aguas Claras** (244 2916; adult/child US$1.25/0.70; 9am-6pm Wed-Sun;) is waiting to sooth those volcanoes away. Nicaragua's premier hot spring resort is a relatively inexpensive place to stay – air-con rooms (US$29) with hot showers, and use of a couple of guest-only pools, sleep three comfortably. The Hawaiian-shirted crew provides impeccable service, the 10 pools are spotlessly clean and food (US$4 to US$6), served anywhere beneath the *palapa* ranchos, is excellent. Although the water – with assorted healing properties – isn't absolutely boiling, there are two small 'therapeutic pools,' that you're welcome to fill with fresh, steaming volcano juice on demand, about as hot as

you'll want in this climate (elderly or infirm visitors have dibs on these, however).

From Managua, take almost any east-bound bus from El Mayoreo (US$1.50, 45 minutes, every 15 minutes) and ask the driver to let you off; the springs are right by the highway. Taxis charge US$4 from Boaco. Make reservations, especially on weekends.

Santa Lucia

Just 12km north of Boaco, at the heart of a 1000-year-old volcanic crater surrounded by rain-forested peaks, the lovely Spanish colonial town of Santa Lucia is part of **Reserva Natural Cerro Cumaica–Cerro Alegre.**

The **alcaldía** (273 3600; santaluciaalcaldia@yahoo .com) makes visiting a cinch. Contact Mayor Adiel Obregón in advance to set up **guided tours** (US$6 per group, horses extra) to rivers, waterfalls and more attractions including a difficult 4km hike to 15km-deep **Cueva Santo Domingo**, an old Sandinista stronghold with rusting military equipment, plus scores of petroglyphs left by the previous residents. **Homestays** (per person including all meals US$6) are included. There are more petroglyphs at **Piedra de Sapo**, at the top of the volcanic rim, from where you can see Masaya, Managua and the lakes on a clear day. Less arduous adventures include tours of area *fincas*, medicinal plant hikes, and tortilla-making (and eating) demonstrations.

Camoapa

pop 32,300

The rough-and-tumble cow town of Camoapa is best known for producing an excellent souvenir: flexible, woven **pita hats**. If you've got a hat, no problem – pita handbags, dolls and other crafts are also available.

The parque central has excellent park benches and pre-Columbian statues, and **CyberCafé Camoapa** (per hr US$0.80; 8am-2pm Mon-Fri) is next door.

The reason why you're probably here is to access **Cerro Mombachito-La Vieja Reserve**, with hikes up awesome **Cerro Mombachito**, **Cerro La Vieja** and **Cuisaltepe Peak**, perhaps the most dramatic outcropping in the range. Theoretically, you can arrange guides in Camoapa; ask at **Hotel Las Estrellas** (549 2240; r with fan/air-con US$10/20;), which at the very least has comfortable, modern rooms featuring great beds, private hot-water bathrooms, cable TV and a well-loved on-site restaurant (dishes US$3 to US$9), where the specialty is bull testicle soup.

Other good spots include recommended **Restaurant-Discotek Atenas** (US$3-6), a block from the church, where a sign warns, 'Absolutely no guns allowed inside.' Just so you know.

San José de los Remates
pop 2000

Impossibly scenic, peacefully pastoral and light years from anything you're used to,

San José de los Remates has relatively easy access to **Reserva Natural Cerro Cumaica–Cerro Alegre**, and probably the country's best developed, most easily accessible, experiment in alternative tourism.

Begin at the **alcaldía** (☎ 542 2359; geosan jose@yahoo.com, geosanjose@hotmail.com), where the youthful mayor Jorge Isaacs and his team of fresh-faced government officials have put together six different one-day **tourist packages** (per person US$14-20), which

---

DETOUR: RÍO BLANCO & RESERVA NATURAL CERRO MUSÚN

Although Cerro Musún is actually closer to Matagalpa, the road from Boaco is newly paved and much faster, breezing by Muy Muy, with a handful of nice *campestre* restaurants, then through the rapidly growing town of Matiguás, also not a tourist mecca, though **Hotel Dulce Sueños** (r per person US$4) would work in a pinch. About 3km from Río Blanco, you'll pass thatch-roofed **Güirilaria** (*servicio* US$0.80) which serves one thing: two of the best *güirilas* (thick, fresh and aromatic tortillas made with fresh corn) on Earth, a hunk of *cuajada* cheese, a bowl of thick cream and a tiny cup of over-sweetened coffee.

Thus fortified, enter **Río Blanco**, a town of 26,000 dwarfed by the enormous volcano that it claims is Nicaragua's geographical center (maybe), and which does mark the end of the paved highway system and beginning of the wild, wild RAAN.

Reserva Natural Cerro Musún (☎ 278 3041; fundenic@ibw.com.ni, infocomap@apcomanejo.com) has almost a dozen peaks over 1400m and as many dramatic waterfalls. Head uphill from the Texaco *empalme* to find the excellent **Marena** (per hr US$1), which in addition to offering Internet access can arrange guides (US$3 to US$6 per day) with one days' notice. A two-day package, including guided hikes, one night at its biological station and all meals, costs US$34 per person.

Two short trails lead into primarily secondary lower-elevation humid tropical forest, Sendero Río la Golondrina (1.2km), with great views and a nice swimming hole, and Salto Los Valles, with cascading 5m tall falls. More ambitious hikers are rewarded with Cascada Bilampi, a 40m high waterfall with neat geological formations in the cave behind it, or seven-hour round-trip Sendero Mojón, which wends its way through the wilderness to the highest point (1438m) in the park. A camping area was also in the works. The park is walking distance from Marena.

While in Río Blanco check out the **Catholic Church**, topped with what appears to be a map of the world, but is actually just Nicaragua, with a three-dimensional concrete Cerro Musún rising from its geographic center, not exactly to scale. You can ask to climb the bell tower. In the dry season, ask about the short hike to the confluence of the Río Adalia and Río Viejo, where several **petroglyphs**, including a huge snake, rise from the water.

Hotel Musún (☎ 778 0103; s/d without bathroom US$4/6) has simple, tin-roofed rooms with a fabulous, cheap steam-table buffet at mealtimes, but neighboring **Restaurant Musún II** (mains US$5-10; 10am-1am) is considered the best restaurant in town, specializing in *churrasco* (Brazilian-style barbecue) and other hearty dishes, and seats – no joke – 1500 people. Just in case.

Hotel Bosawás (d US$15;) has the best rooms in town, with cable TV and hot water, surrounding its loud, flashy restaurant/bar; it's probably a 'love hotel' (see the boxed text, p282).

Try **Disco-Bar El Atlantico** (US$2-4; 6am-10pm, disco goes later), serving great food on the outskirts of town. Women traveling solo should avoid this and all bars at night. It's on the eastern edge of town, about 1km east of the Texaco *empalme*.

The bus station is about 1.5km east of town; take a taxi (US$0.50) to catch buses for destinations including the following:

Boaco US$3, two hours, 6am to 4:20pm, every 1½ hours
Managua US$5, four hours, 3:30am to 5pm, almost hourly
Siuna US$5, five to seven hours, six daily

include three meals, a homestay and various guided tours that you can mix and match over the length of your stay.

The **Ruta de los Chorros** takes you past three 50m waterfalls (one of which you can see from town), to a *mirador* (lookout point) with views clear to the Pacific Ocean. The **Río Santa Cruz** visits a swimming hole with canyons, petroglyphs and a natural rock slide. Or try **Community Agrotourism**, which includes an organic coffee farm. They also arrange visits to **local schools** and **development projects**, and for an extra fee will teach you how to ride horses, cook Nicaraguan food and make wood carvings.

What inspired this unusual venture? Several years ago, the land around the local watershed was purchased by a Boaco-based cattle rancher, threatening the water supply. The townspeople mobilized, convinced the rancher to grow sustainable organic coffee instead, and reforested much of the property themselves. The plan required the community to come up with US$6000 – 10 times the average Nicaraguan's annual salary – to pay off the rancher. More land is being purchased every year and is protected as a municipal park, **Reserva Ecológica Vida Silvestre Llanos de las Mesas**, adjacent to the national reserve.

There's one bus to Boaco (US$2, 1½ hours) at 2:15pm; four buses to Teustepe (US$1, one hour); and regular minivans (US$0.70) to Esquipulas.

The Back Road to Matagalpa

From San José de los Remates, you can take the scenic back road to Matagalpa, a string of rural communities with strong Chorotega roots. Regular buses ply this back road, but it's much easier in a private vehicle.

Small, scenic Esquipulas, less mountainous and a bit bigger than San José, doesn't have any tour packages, but **El Hotelito** (☎ 772 9132; r per person US$6) will hook you up. Very attractive rooms (No 4 is the best) have lovely furniture, fans, soap and towels surrounding a tree-filled courtyard, and share a very nice bathroom and on-site restaurant (dishes US$1 to US$3). Enterprising owners Theresa and Adacila Alcantara will happily locate guides for the 2½-hour hike to **Cerro Santa Maria**, with virgin rain forest, swimming holes and views

of Boaco; **Finca de Juan Gea**, with cheese; **El Cerro del Padre**, with orchids; and **La Cueva de la Mocuana** – hey, every other town in this part of Nicaragua has one, why not Esquipulas?

You could also stay at **Hotel Central** (r per person US$3), a row of clean, windowless, one-person rooms with shared latrines. Pollo El Campero specializes in (surprise) chicken, while better **Bar-Restaurant Quelite** (US$1.50-3) has a menu; go for anything in the jalapeño sauce. All are close to the park.

From here, it's a long and winding (and not bad, for dirt) road through volcanoes that are draped in a patchwork of farms and *fincas*, their rocky spines still cloaked with tropical dry forest left intact because you just can't plant beans at that angle. **San Dionisio** is the biggest city on this stretch of road, with two basic *hospedajes*, and then it's on to **El Chile**, known for its brightly colored textiles worked into handbags and dolls. You can visit any of the four workshops, after which it's just 12km to Matagalpa.

Juigalpa

pop 50,800 / elevation 117m

Juigalpa is blessed with well-preserved Spanish-colonial architecture that predates its 1669 foundation, and an incredible mountain backdrop, so you may be surprised to have such a lovely spot to yourself. The almost untouristed capital of Chontales department also boasts an excellent museum and a fine church with colorful mosaics that spill over from the shrine and throughout the shady parque central, not to mention all manner of adventures just outside the city.

INFORMATION

On the southeast side of the park, a brand-new Intur was just getting started; it can recommend hotels and has big plans for organizing guided tours to the Salinas Caves, El Monolito de Cuapa and undeveloped hot springs.

BanPro Next door to Intur, with a 24-hour Visa/ Plus ATM.

Hospital (☎ 812 2332) Chontales' biggest hospital is outside of town.

Llamadas Heladas (☽ 8am-10pm) Cheap, international calls, around the corner from BanPro.

SIGHTS & ACTIVITIES

The main reason why it's worth getting off the bus for at least a couple of hours is to visit **Museo Archaológico Gregorio Aguilar Barea** (☎ 512 0784; admission US$0.70; ☺ 8am-noon & 2-4pm Mon-Fri, 8am-noon Sat), two and a half blocks east of the park, and right around the corner from the bus station. The outdoor hangar houses the most important collection of stelae in the country, with more than 120 examples of these basalt statues, probably carved between AD 800 and 1500, some reaching 5m tall. *La Chinita*, recognizable by her early 1990s Madonna-style brassiere, is also known as the 'Mona Lisa of Chontales,' and has appeared at the Louvre.

Originally organized by the namesake Professor Aguilar (or 'Goyito') and a group of his students in 1949, the museum's current structure went up on January 8, 1967, Rubén Dario's 100th birthday. In addition to the stelae, it contains hundreds of pre-Columbian pots, incense burners, funeral jars, art objects and the largest *metate,* or corn grinder, ever found. Paintings of famous locals, stacks of old cash registers, and (Ripley, eat your heart out) *two* two-headed calves – not to mention a seven-legged bull, a one-eyed pig and a one-eyed human fetus that one hopes is a hoax – round out the collection.

Museo de Arte Taurina (donations appreciated; ☺ afternoons), across from Supermercado San Antonio, is a roomful of cattle-related art, rusting mess kits and news clippings involving all things bovine.

One of two zoos in the nation, the predictably depressing **Jardín Zoológico Thomas Belt** (admission US$0.30; ☺ 8am-6:30pm) has lots of local wildlife and a few non-native species, including a lone chimpanzee caged next to a sign that more humanitarian smokers may want to ignore: 'please don't give this species cigarettes.'

Juigalpa has two excellent parks. Get your shoes shined at the **parque central** next to La Lustrador, better known as 'Chaco,' the beloved statue of a shoe-shine boy; El Templo de Cultura, the kiosk in the center, occasionally hosts live music and poetry readings. **Palo Solo** park, five blocks east, has a good restaurant and one of the best views in Nicaragua of the Serranía Amerrisque and broad valley below.

It's a US$2 taxi or US$0.30 bus ride to **Pozo el Salto**, 4km north on the road to Managua. This absolutely stunning, partially dammed swimming hole framed in clean cascades of water has been popular with picnickers for generations; on weekends and during Semana Santa there may be a US$1 entry fee.

FESTIVALS & EVENTS

Juigalpa's **fiestas patronales**, held from August 11 to 18, are nationally known for their *hípicas*, or horse parades and shows, and are definitely worth making a special trip for.

WANTED: AN UNCONVENTIONAL TOURIST

Intur calls ecotourism that is off the beaten track in this part of the country 'Unconventional Tourism,' and it is truly your welcome to the unroamed delights of the region.

Despite access to everything from 70m waterfalls and 1200-year-old petroglyphs to 15km-deep caves and loads of luxuriant hot springs, the majority of Nicaraguan towns simply don't have the resources to develop normal tourist infrastructure. Which means they can't bring in tourist dollars. It's a feedback loop.

Enter Unconventional Tourism. Basically, entire backwoods towns are working together cooperatively to offer tour packages, usually through their *alcaldía*. It's low-tech, with guided hikes and horseback rides to the petroglyphs and gold mines, and homestays and home cooking in between. It's never air-conditioned and often physically demanding, but you could well see wilderness never captured in photographs; or find cliffs that have never been climbed. Better, your money goes straight to Nicaraguan communities that need it the most.

This sort of tourism isn't for everyone. In general, you should be in good physical condition, speak at least survival Spanish, have a high tolerance for *gallo pinto* (rice and beans) and potentially uncomfortable beds (or hammocks). But the infrastructure, while basic, is ready and waiting – they just need unconventional tourists.

SLEEPING

Several budget options in the city center and on the road to Puerto Díaz function as bordellos and are best avoided.

Hotel Casa Country (☎ 512 2546; r with fan/air-con US$15/20; ✦) With a great location across from Palo Solo park, this is easily the best hotel in town, with attractive wood furnishings, hot water and cable TV.

Hospedaje El Nuevo Milenio (☎ 512 0646; r without bathroom per person US$4, s/d with bathroom US$12/15; ✦) This family-run option one block east of the church has OK tiled rooms; the ones with private bathroom also have air-con and cable TV.

Hotel El Bosque (☎ 512 2205; r with/without bath US$15/8; P ✦) Right on the highway, this nice spot has clean little rooms and a central garden that absorbs most of the car noise; the more expensive rooms also have air-con and cable TV.

La Quinta (☎ 512 0920; r with fan US$10-15, r with air-con US$16-20; ✦) Also on the main road, this place has small, dark, overpriced cement rooms with easy access to a good restaurant and the best disco in town.

EATING & DRINKING

Several good *fritangas* (sidewalk barbecues) are set up around the parque central.

Casa de Queso/Restaurante 24/7 (☎ 812 2295; mains US$2-8; ✦ 24hr) A popular, loud and reliable spot for fast food, Chinese cuisine, espresso beverages and even upscale seafood dishes served to your plastic booths. Dine in or call for delivery, and be sure to check out the dozens of different local cheeses on sale out front.

La Embajada (US$2-5) The classic cheapie is this tiny place close to the cemetery, with grilled meat, served by weight, tortillas and cheese.

Palo Solo (US$4-6; ✦ 10am-10pm) The unmissable meal with a view in Palo Solo park, where you can dine on slightly overpriced steak and other upscale offerings.

Restaurante El Chupis (mains US$2-4; ✦ 10am-10pm) Five blocks north of the park, it's worth the walk for *pupusas*, bull testicles in garlic sauce, foosball and air-hockey.

For fine dining, it's **La Quinta** (mains US$4-10; ✦ 7am-late) or **Restaurante Tacho** (US$2-6; ✦ 10am-11pm), with great grilled chicken and sometimes live music, both on the highway.

There are two supermarkets here: **Supermercado San Antonio** (✦ 8am-8pm), one block west of the parque central, has a better selection and local goodies like homemade jams from Hermanas Trapenses; while **Palí** (✦ 7:30am-8pm), close to the market, is bigger, cheaper and has an Eskimo.

Party with the locals at popular **La Quinta** (✦ Thu-Sun), or slightly more downscale Hotters, both on the highway.

GETTING THERE & AWAY

Managua-bound minivans (US$3, 2½ hours) leave from beside the church at 10am, noon and 5pm, arriving at the Mayoreo bus terminal in Managua. Buses leave from the local market, less than one block from the archaeology museum. Destinations include:

El Rama US$4, six hours, 7am, 8am, 9am, 10:30am, 11:45am and 2:30pm

Managua US$7, four hours, 4am to 6pm, hourly

Nueva Guinea US$3, four hours, 6:30am, 7:30am, 8:45am, 10am, 11am, noon, 1:05pm and 3:15pm

Puerto Díaz US$1, one hour, 9:30am, 11am, noon, 1pm and 2pm

San Carlos US$7, seven to nine hours, 8:05am, 9am, 1:15pm, 1:30pm and 2:45pm

San Miguelito US$6, five to seven hours, 2:15pm

Santo Domingo US$3, 2½ hours, every 1½ hours

Puerto Díaz

pop 300

Just 28km from Juigalpa, the lakefront village of Puerto Díaz doesn't have a beach right in town, but you can swim in the cement pools of **Mirador Vista Linda** (☎ 512 2699; adult/child US$0.70/0.30; ✦ sunrise-late), on the hill just above. This friendly spot serves fish (US$3 to US$6) any way you want, and offers spectacular views of Isla de Ometepe's back side (check out Concepción's crater from this angle!) and the Nancital Archipelago, three of the least-visited islets in the lake. Vista Linda also rents the only room (US$12) in town, a huge, bare cement space with one double bed, but feel free to pack in the whole gang. There are plans for more.

The village and port are just downhill, where a handful of restaurant/bars serve rum and fish dishes. You can easily arrange a private *panga* seating six people to the three islands of the archipelago for about US$90. **Isla Redonda** is the most appealing destination, with sandy beaches, lots of wildlife and private homes where they'll rent you a hammock for the night. Bring bottled water and food, just in case. **Isla Grande** and **Isla El Muerte** are both home to tiny farming communities.

About 20km further north along the lakeshore, a fairly luxurious resort-style hotel, **La Bocana Mayal** (☎ 512 1766, 512 2322; www.ameriquetour.com.ni), with several well-appointed individual cabins, was being finished at the time of research. Contact the hotel for the latest.

Buses (US$1, one hour) run to Juigalpa at 4:30am, 5am, 7am, 3pm and 4:30pm. If you're driving, the good dirt road leaves the highway just south of Hotel El Bosque in Juigalpa.

La Libertad & Santo Domingo

A good excuse for spending some time among the granite peaks of the Serranía Amerrisque is visiting these two century-old gold-mining towns, connected to Juigalpa by a decent dirt road and regular bus service.

La Libertad, the 'Birthplace of Religious and Historical Figures,' is hometown of famed Archbishop Miguel Obando y Bravo, who has at least two statues, and perpetual Sandinista presidential candidate Daniel Ortega, who doesn't have a statue yet, though the life-size likeness of Sandino in the pleasant parque central is something of a stand-in. The town always votes Liberal. There are no services for tourists, but this is your last chance for gas.

At a crisp, cool 1000m, the Santo Domingo *alcaldía* offers several guided tours (US$6 per group) through the mountains; guide Santiago Urbina-Sosa is highly recommended. The 2.5km hike to **Peñas Blancas**, a spire of white rock rising from the cattle ranches, is a must for the incredible views; unscrupulous guides may take you elsewhere. This hike is not recommended on windy or rainy days.

Santo Domingo Mine, less than 1km from town (listen for the grinding rocks), produces 60 grams of gold per day using machinery from 1913. Ask for Modesto Allestas, who'll show you the sluices and *rastras* – a centuries-old technology involving flat boulders on chains being dragged across moist ore. You need a guide to visit the other mine, which is next to a stunning, if polluted, 70m cascade; you'll get to the mine via a 30m mining tunnel drilled through the rock beneath the falls.

Reserva Montañosa Santo Domingo is actually the private property of Raúl Valenzuela, who will take you on a tour of his organic coffee farm, swimming hole and some allegedly virgin forest. It's gorgeous, and camping can be arranged.

There's one pleasant hotel in town, **Bar Hotelito San José** (☎ 855 6217; r per person without bathroom US$4), with simple rooms; the ones by the second-floor balcony have windows – plus a good restaurant (dishes US$1.50 to US$4) that's known for its jalapeño steak. Soda-Café Mama Lila, by the park, does good burgers.

Buses return to Juigalpa (US$3, 2½ hours) almost hourly.

Cuapa
pop 11,000

This small mountain town is a pilgrimage-worthy destination for two reasons. The first is the miracle of the **Virgin of Cuapa**, whose statue, currently enshrined a scenic 2km walk from town, began glowing and then appeared five times to local tailor Bernardo Martínez in 1980, telling him that all Nicaragua would suffer without peace (read the entire transcript, in English or in Spanish, at www.apparitions.org/cuapa .martinez). This, of course, turned out to be true. Pilgrims pack the place the first week in May, when they make the relatively easy and scenic hike to the shrine en masse.

The other reason people come is to climb **El Monolito de Cuapa**, a strenuous, three-hour, nontechnical hike that begins in town and ends up on top of that enormous rocky outcropping you saw from the highway.

Note that any single man who successfully climbs the monolith will be enchanted into marrying a Cuapeña woman and live the rest of his days in this gorgeous mountain enclave, which doesn't sound too bad. The Monolito is also well known for its tribe of *duendes* (elves), who fell for a pretty little girl named Florita back in the 1930s, like Snow White and the Seven Dwarves, but creepier. They put the family donkey on top of El Monolito, refusing to return it until the parents promised them Florita. Frustrated, they agreed – but decided to flee with the donkey and their daughter.

They made their escape, when the mother realized she'd forgotten something, and turned around. And there were the *duendes,* missing items in hand, who smiled maliciously: 'Don't worry, ma'am, we didn't forget anything.'

Ask about reliable guides at the **alcaldía** (☎ 812 3206) or **Hospedaje la Maravilla** (r without bathroom per person US$4), with good-sized cement rooms.

Nueva Guinea

pop 80,000 / elevation 184m

As you continue toward El Rama, you'll see a cluster of vegetable stands and cheap *comedores* on your right, marking the turnoff for San Carlos (see p262). It's another 50km to **El Chillamate**, with more vegetable stands and basic eateries, plus the turnoff to Nueva Guinea.

The good paved road heads southeast, past very groovy **El Coral Central Park**, with excellent snake art, about 20km along. **Puente El Rama**, another 35km further, has refreshing cascades and swimming holes close to the road. It's just a few more minutes to the town of Nueva Guinea, which really is brand-new, founded in the 1960s as part of a federal homesteading initiative with the unfortunate acronym Prica.

The Somoza government successfully directed the refugees of the 1972 Managua earthquake and 1973 Cerro Negro eruption to this isolated experiment, over a month's journey from Managua in ox-carts. The homesteaders, no slouches, got busy razing pristine rain forests to graze cattle, an economic success and 'agricultural disaster.'

In 1984 Prica decided to transform the region into a 'Cradle of Nicaraguan Alternative Agriculture' and started La Esperanzita, a teaching *finca* where unconventional crops, organic agriculture and alternative technologies were researched and taught to area campesinos. It has been joined by a handful of other alternative agriculture experiments, and Nueva Guinea also offers rather difficult access to surrounding natural reserves founded to protect the remaining wilderness.

ORIENTATION

Nueva Guinea sprawls along Calle Central, about 12 blocks that run from the highway turnoff to the one-*manzana* (block) market, where the blue-and-white 'monument' is the landmark from which all area addresses are measured.

INFORMATION

At the Marena, ranger Abel Torrez Hernandez can help organize guides and transportation to Reserva Biológica Indio-Maíz (Indio-Maíz Biological Reserve), which isn't easy. Take a truck to Puerto Principe (US$1.50, twice daily) – you may need to walk the last two muddy kilometers in rainy season. From there, catch a boat to Atlanta (US$3, 6.5km), with food, lodging and boats further into the reserve. There's also access from Fonseca, 20km south of Nueva Guinea, but this involves a two-day horseback ride. Both Finca Esperanzita and Auxilio Mundial can arrange trips into the reserve; make reservations in advance.

Bancentro Two blocks from the monument; changes dollars but has no other tourist services.

CyberCafé Nueva Guinea (per hr US$1; ⌚ 8am-9pm) One block from the monument.

Marena (☎ 575 0220) Two blocks north and three east from the monument.

ACTIVITIES

The main attraction in Nueva Guinea is alternative agriculture. The *alcaldía* may be able to find guides, or locate **Marisol Robles-Jarquin** (☎ 575 0090; jlmoreno2004@yahoo.es) at Hotel Nueva Guinea (p248), who can arrange guided tours of the *fincas* for around US$25 per day, per group, including transportation.

La Finca Esperanzita (☎ 575 0174, 843 5010; esperanzita84@yahoo.com), a 13km, US$3 taxi from town, is the original teaching *finca* and best prepared for ecotourism, with packages that include tortilla-making classes, hiking 5km of trails and getting a good look at organic valerian and pepper, and an underground tank that turns cow manure into natural gas, used to cook your *gallo pinto* if you spend the night. It can also arrange tours into the Indio-Maíz. Packages are designed for groups; it's US$42/62 for two-/three-day packages including dorm beds, food and tours, for up to 15 people. It can accommodate individuals, too, but make advanced arrangements.

Auxilio Mundial (☎ 275 0066, 275 3430) is a beautiful (and cattle-free) 716-*manzana* demonstration *finca* and has some 30,000 plants, including weird stuff from Australia, Ecuador and other exotic spots, as well as a Brazilian aphrodisiac called *borrojo* (ahem; did we mention Auxilio Mundial was a Christian organization?). All are being tested for climate adaptability and economic viability. There's also a reforestation project, hydroelectric dam, trails and a swimming hole, and it can arrange guided hikes throughout the region, including Indio-Maíz. Auxilio Mundial has an office two blocks from the monument, near Llamas del Bosque, where you can make reservations.

Several regular private farms hoping to get in on the ecotourism tip offer tours and camping, at least theoretically:

Finca Pedrito Figuera Has rustic camping, guided tours of pineapples, oranges and spice trees, for tips only.

Finca El Verdún (☎ 854 0589) Has similar services, plus a shower and a reforestation project (also with camping) about 15km from town.

Lecheria Zapote (☎ 844 8265) Offers free tours of its cheese-making facility from 8am to 9am only; make reservations.

SLEEPING & EATING

Nueva Guinea is a business center, so make hotel reservations in advance. Try to arrive on the first or third Friday of the month for the big organic vegetable market.

Hospedaje Central (☎ 620 8949; r per person without bathroom US$2) The best cheapie, right at the market, has tiny singles and much nicer doubles, all super clean with lots of murals and a kiosk outside with cable TV.

Hotel Nueva Guinea (☎ 575 0090; s/d with fan US$7/12, d with air-con US$40; ❄ P) The best hotel in town, it's got big, clean rooms sleeping three, with little tables and chairs, cable TV, plans for a pool and a solid restaurant (dishes US$4-6, open 6am to midnight); there's also an annex across the street with tiny, US$3 rooms with shared bathroom and no mosquito screens.

El Peñon (pizza slice US$1, set plate US$2; ❧ 6am-7pm Mon-Sat) On the main drag, sells pizza slices, set plates, and baked goods for pennies.

Pizza Hot (☎ 575 0109; pizzas US$3-7; ❧ 9am-10pm) This place delivers.

Llamas del Bosque (US$4-6; ❧ 10am-midnight) Two blocks from the monument, this spot is everyone's favorite place for steak and shrimp, and becomes the town's hottest disco after 8pm, sometimes with live music.

Ristorante Las Brisas (US$3-7; ❧ 11am-11pm) In the *palapa* at the turnoff from the main road, it also gets raves for steak and fish.

GETTING THERE & AWAY

The airport shown on most maps is primarily decorative, a war relic that still sees the occasional helicopter. The road from Managua is beautifully paved (watch those speed bumps, though) and the bus station is at the market.

Juigalpa US$3, four hours, hourly

Managua *expresso* US$10, six hours, 7:30am, 9:30am, 11:30am and 1:45pm; *ordinario* US$8, seven hours, 2am to 9pm, every two hours

San Carlos US$7, seven to nine hours, four daily

EL RAMA

At the confluence of the Río Rama and Río Escondido, an international thoroughfare that empties into Bluefields Bay, this beautifully paved road was recently improved for a reason other than tourism: the newly inaugurated Rama International Port will ship some 2000 containers in 2006, 10 times that by 2010. This is Nicaragua's first heavyweight Atlantic port, despite over 80% of imports coming from Europe and the USA's East Coast. These goods currently come through expensive Costa Rica and Honduras, which is just about to change.

El Rama is getting itself all gussied up for the event, with newly paved streets and a refurbished church, as well as infrastructure for visiting **Parque Municipal Mahogany**, halfway to Bluefields. Most people are just passing through, of course, but it's an

---

CAUTION ON THE CARIBBEAN COAST

Remember that El Rama is a port town, with lots of young men, thus women traveling solo should stay alert. Several of the cheapest hotels cater to young workers and pretty prostitutes, many of whom may be hanging around in your hotel lobby looking for easy marks; men traveling solo should also stay alert. And remember, no matter how cool you are back home, it's OK to wear your life jacket on the riverboat ride to Bluefields.

interesting place to spend the night, if only to enjoy that misty-morning *panga* ride through the jungle.

Orientation & Information

El Rama hugs the riverbank, forming a rough 'L,' with the Catholic Church at the curve. Everything is located within five blocks of the church, except the international port, which is 1.5km east.

Bancentro Behind the church, changes dollars but provides no other services.

Cyber Café (per hr US$1.25; ⏰ 7am-9pm Mon-Sat) Four blocks east of the church.

Sights & Activities

There's no tourist office, but look for river guides (US$6 per hour, plus gas) at the *alcaldía* or municipal dock. In town, the humble, wooden **Catholic Church**, about two blocks east of the main bus stop, with nifty stained-glass windows, was being renovated at press time, as was the parque central. The big hill just east of town, **La Loma** or **Cerro de Rama**, is definitely climbable (through some very poor neighborhoods); ask anyone where the one-hour round-trip walk begins. You could also take a canoe (US$0.30) from Hotel Amy's dock across the Río Rama to the tiny, strollable, muddy town of **La Palmera**, with lots of cows and wildlife.

About 5km west of town in the community of El Recreo, a big ecotourism project – hanging bridges, guided rainforest hikes to the waterfalls of **Salta Mataka** and accommodations – was in the works.

Eco-Hotel El Vivero (see right) arranges guided tours of Mahogany Tropical Reserve (US$500 for eight people) and Laguna Perlas (US$700, US$30 extra to stay overnight).

Sleeping & Eating

New Hotel Oasis de Caribe (☎ 517 0264; r with fan US$6-12, r with air-con US$20-30; 🍴 🅿) Several configurations of clean, modern rooms, with TVs, air-con, different sizes of beds etc, are all cheerfully painted; secure parking and a breakfast (US$2) nook are just bonuses. It's one block north of the main drag, close to the bus station.

Hospedaje García (d US$9) In a big, white Victorian one block west and just south of the main bus station, this spot's clean and simple, but safe wooden rooms are just fine.

Hotel Johana (☎ 817 0066; d with fan/air-con US$8/16; 🍴) A big step down, larger cleanish wooden rooms share somewhat less clean bathrooms, plus a few bored-looking but buxom gals in the restaurant.

Eco-Hotel El Vivero (☎ 517 0330; teknisa@ibw.com.ni; s/d with bathroom US$12/15) A 3km, US$1 taxi west of town, big, pleasantly rustic wooden cabinas have porch and mosquito nets all sitting on a very pretty 164-*manzana* plantation, which you can tour on a day trip for US$20 per group.

In town, the market has the cheapest eats. **Pollo El Fogón** (US$2-5), a standout cheapie, serves up yummy roasted chicken and lots of sides, while **Comedor La Mita** (US$2-3), across the street, has cheap, good set plates.

Locals are split on which is El Rama's best restaurant. **El Expresso** (US$3-6; ⏰ all day) is a big open-air place located two blocks north of the main drag; it's known for its huge servings, steak and the seafood stew. Meanwhile, **Casa Blanca** (mains US$1-7; ⏰ 11am-midnight), located on the riverfront, has great fish dishes as well as karaoke on weekends.

Getting There & Around

Getting around El Rama is a stroll, but consider taking a pedicab (US$.30) the 1.5km to **Rama International Port** (☎ 517 0315). Primarily for cargo shipping, you can still catch the *Captain D* to Bluefields (US$9, seven hours) at 1pm Monday, with continuing service to El Bluff, Big Corn, and perhaps Prinzapolka and Puerto Cabezas. *Ferry 1* leaves for Bluefields (passenger/car US$9/60, eight hours) at 8am Monday, Wednesday and Friday, with continuing service to Big Corn Island.

The **Municipal Dock** (☎ 517 0073), close to the *expreso* buses, has a faster, more convenient collective *panga* service to Bluefields (US$11, 1½ hours); boats leave 'when full,' almost hourly in the morning and less often as the day wears on.

BUS

The road to El Rama has finally been paved, cutting travel time dramatically, but bus schedules still seem designed for a 12-hour ride. Check for new bus schedules at Managua's Mayoreo. *Expresos* leave from in front of Hotel Amy, *ordinarios* two blocks inland.

Juigalpa US$4, six hours, 5am to 3pm, hourly
Managua *expresso* US$9, five hours, 9pm and 10pm; *ordinario* US$7.50, eight hours, 7:30am and 9am

BLUEFIELDS
pop 39,208

As with Bilwi and the RAAN, the South Atlantic Autonomous Region (RAAS) has no official capital, but Bluefields is the largest city, the seat of both regional and indigenous governments, and until El Rama International gets up and running, Nicaragua's principal Caribbean port.

Bluefields is no beauty; the town's prim Victorian charm was blown away in 1988 by monster Category IV Hurricane Juana.

'What neighborhoods were affected?' a journalist asked one survivor, after phone lines were restored.

'There are no neighborhoods,' the witness replied. 'Everything is gone.'

The city was rebuilt with little thought for aesthetics, and visitors may feel a sense of unease walking its gritty streets. But with comfortable hotels, great restaurants and a very multi-ethnic party scene, it makes a good base for visiting the very rainy (up to 4400mm per year) rain-forest reserves surrounding the city on all sides. Most locals also speak English.

Named after the Dutch pirate Blewfeldt, who made his base here in the 1700s, Bluefields is still home to plenty of shady characters. Big city rules apply: avoid going to bars solo and don't walk around with valuables at night.

Orientation & Information

Most of Bluefields' commerce, *hospedajes* and restaurants are found in a nine-square-block area between Parque Reyes and the Caribbean. The airport is about 3km south of downtown. There are several banks; unofficial moneychangers are found near the banks.

Bancentro With a Visa/Plus ATM.
Central Computer Service (per hr US$1; 9am-10pm) Around the corner from Intur, this is just one cybercafé of several.
Intur (☎ 822 0221) One block west of the Moravian church, this helpful outlet can make reservations for hotels and airplanes.
Marena (☎ 572 2324) Next door to Intur, has basic information for people organizing trips to Reserva Natural

Cerro Silva and Reserva Natural Punta Gorda, neither of which has much tourist infrastructure.
Police (☎ 822 2298)
Post office Two blocks south, 1½ blocks east of Entel.

Sights & Activities

Activities in town are sparse, but do stop by the **Moravian church**, built to the exact specifications of the 1849 original, which was destroyed in Hurricane Juana. Friendly and simple with nice columns, it has the typical stained glass of the order, depicting a chalice. But chances are, you're eager to explore the constellation of wilderness areas and other attractions just a boat ride from town.

Come to **El Bluff International Port** for enormous oil tanks and some interesting machinery; all just a US$3 boat ride from town. Hot and sort of sad, El Bluff's one **hotel** (d US$6) is dark and dirty, and the town restaurant is open afternoons only.

Parque Municipal Mahogany (www.eco-index.org/ong/agcoma-ni-esp.html; admission US$10) is on the curvy Caño Negro, a tributary of Río Escondido as it runs between El Rama and Bluefields. This 278 sq km reserve is a convenient side trip as you travel between them. Either town's **alcaldía** (☎ in El Rama 517 0316; in Bluefields 822 5202) or, better, **Bluefields Indian & Caribbean University** (BICU; ☎ 572 1116, ext 40; gonzalrojas@yahoo.com), can arrange tours through the Volunteer Park Rangers Association. A boat seating six plus a guide will cost around US$100. The park, which is contiguous with both Reserva Natural Punta Gorda and the Indio-Maíz, is boat access only, and has waterfalls, several species of migratory birds and lots of other wildlife – including tarpon and bass. Fishing is definitely allowed.

Rama Key, a barbell-shaped island 15km southeast of Bluefields, inside the bay, is home to around 800 people – over half of all remaining Rama Indians. Isolated by the dominant Miskito culture, they still speak their own language and use their traditional government structures. **Casa Historia** (donations appreciated) may be the only museum that chronicles their story. But the real reason to come is **Hotel Surpise Dream** (☎ 572 1116, ext 34, 628 1112; castrofrancis@hotmail.com, otobeloto@hotmail.com; per person all-inclusive US$80), a hotel and eco-tourism project run by the Rama Nation in conjunction with BICU. The package deal

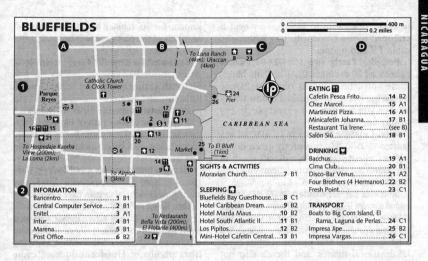

BLUEFIELDS

0 ———————— 400 m
0 ———————— 0.2 miles

To Luna Ranch (4km); Uraccan (4km)

Catholic Church & Clock Tower

Parque Reyes

To Hospedaje Kaorha View (200m); La Loma (2km)

Pier

CARIBBEAN SEA

To Airport (3km)

To Restaurants Bella Vista (200m); El Flotante (400m)

Market

To El Bluff (1km)

EATING 🍴
Cafetín Pesca Frito..............**14** B2
Chez Marcel..........................**15** A1
Martinuzzi Pizza...................**16** A1
Minicafetín Johanna.............**17** B1
Restaurant Tia Irene.............(see 8)
Salón Siú..............................**18** B1

DRINKING 🍷
Bacchus................................**19** A1
Cima Club.............................**20** B1
Disco-Bar Venus...................**21** A2
Four Brothers (4 Hermanos)..**22** B2
Fresh Point...........................**23** C1

SIGHTS & ACTIVITIES
Moravian Church...................**7** B1

SLEEPING 🛏
Bluefields Bay Guesthouse......**8** C1
Hotel Caribbean Dream...........**9** B2
Hotel Marda Maus.................**10** B2
Hotel South Atlantic II...........**11** B1
Los Pipitos...........................**12** B1
Mini-Hotel Cafetín Central....**13** B1

TRANSPORT
Boats to Big Corn Island, El
  Rama, Laguna de Perlas....**24** C1
Impresa Jipe.........................**25** B2
Impresa Vargas.....................**26** C1

INFORMATION
Bancentro..............................**1** B1
Central Computer Service.......**2** B1
Enitel...................................**3** A1
Intur.....................................**4** B1
Marena.................................**5** B1
Post Office............................**6** B2

---

includes transportation from Bluefields, three meals and guided tours, which could include trips to Wairu Cay for crab catching, or canoeing to Gwilling Cay Creek. There's currently no regular boat service to Rama Key, so independent travelers can choose a pricey private *panga* (US$80 return) or try to hitch a ride with a Rama fisher, who may or may not speak Spanish.

Reserva Silvestre Greenfields (☎ 268 1897; www .greenfields.com.ni; s/d two days all-inclusive US$184/247), a privately managed, 284-hectare wildlife reserve near Kukra Hill, offers a variety of pricey but plush package deals that get better as you add people and days. You can go canoeing, swim on virgin beaches, hike through the orchids and butterflies, or just relax at the pool. A real road to Kukra Hill is currently being built.

Fundeso (☎ 572 0617; eahodgeso@yahoo.com, fun deso@ibw.com.ni) arranges guided trips to Reserva Natural Cerro Silva and indigenous communities around Laguna de Perlas. Take a taxi to Barrio New York to find this small white house. Guides and lodging (in ridiculously tiny bamboo cabins) are organized for **Orinoco** (p253) and **Kakabila**, a beautiful little community just across a sandy inlet from the town of Laguna de Perlas. Fundeso can also find guides for climbing 635m **Cerro Silva**, about the only way into the natural reserve.

Collective boats leave El Bluff to points north twice weekly, stopping in **Tasbapauni**, a kilometer-wide strip of sand with one

hospedaje and beaches on either side; **Sandy Bay Sirpi**, a Miskito-speaking community that also has a *hospedaje;* and Rio Grand Bar, Caraguala, Cara, Tazapapone, San Nivel (which may have a *hospedaje*) and finally Set Net Point, the cheapest place to find a boat to the Pearl Keys.

Festivals & Events

Palo de Mayo (Maypole Festival) is one of the biggest events in Nicaragua – all 30 neighborhoods compete to create the most extravagant street show, with scantily clad dancers, floats, live music, you name it; and a dance party that goes for weeks in May. The centerpiece is, of course, the maypole, but you've never seen spring celebrated like this. Hotels can be booked weeks in advance as the month-long festival comes to a climax on May 31.

Other big parties are on October 11, Bluefields' birthday, and the *fiestas patronales* between September 30, for San Jerónimo Doctor, and October 5, for la Virgen El Rosario.

Sleeping

Los Pipitos (☎ 572 1590; d with fan US$15, s/d with air-con US$18/25; ❄) About 1½ blocks west of the market, this is a good deal on four clean, livable rooms with desks, nice lamps, and discounts for long-term stays.

Mini-Hotel Cafetín Central (☎ 572 2362; d with bathroom and fan/air-con US$12/25; ❄) At the rear of a lively and much loved café (dishes US$2 to US$6, open 8am to 10pm), very neat if cramped rooms come with tiny bathroom, cable TV and phone.

Hospedaje Kaorha View (☎ 572 0488; r without bathroom and 1/2 double beds US$13/16) This handsome hotel, three blocks north of Parque Reyes, has beautiful furnished rooms with a kitchen you can use, and a great porch. Try to stay upstairs.

Hotel Caribbean Dream (☎ 822 0107; s/d with bathroom US$25/30; ✖) In a pretty green house with excellent security two blocks south of the Moravian church, super-clean and cool tiled rooms have air-con.

Bluefields Bay Guesthouse (☎ 572 2143; kriolb@ hotmail.com; dm US$20, s/d with bathroom incl breakfast US$28/45; ✖) Homey-feeling but spacious, the relaxing common area has shipwreck views, a book exchange and photos of most black US historical figures, and there's also hot water, air-con and a kitchen. Breakfast is included at attached Restaurant Tia Irene.

Eating

Almost no one comes to Nicaragua for the food, but that's because almost no one knows about the Caribbean Coast. Fresh seafood, particularly lobster and shrimp, is inexpensive and exquisitely prepared, most famously as *rondo;* a one-pot meal in which seasoned fish is steamed atop plantains and vegetables, letting the flavor 'run down,' then coconut milk, the Caribbean Coast's secret ingredient, is added halfway through cooking. Coconut milk, considered the key to good health and digestion in these parts, is added to bread, *gallo pinto,* and almost any other dish on your mind.

Minicafétin Johanna (US$3-5; ✖ 8am-9pm) Up the street from the Moravian church, this spot has the cheapest shrimp cocktail in town and good fried-fish dishes.

Bella Vista (US$2-8; ✖ 10am-10pm) Overlooking the waves at the south end of town, this joint is one of the best spots for shrimp, done your way, in town. And what a view.

Restaurante El Flotante (meals from US$5) Four blocks south of the Moravian church, where the bayside street meets the water, El Flotante has dining on a covered patio with a marvelous view of the bay.

La Loma (mains US$3-6; ✖ 11am-1am) Across from BICU on a hill overlooking the city, this thatch-roofed, open-air restaurant is known for its lobster and shrimp almost as much as the party scene it becomes after dark (8pm or so).

Restaurant Tia Irene (US$4-8; ✖ noon-9:45pm), At Bluefields Bay Guesthouse, try the fish filet with a sauce made from vegetables and little shrimps here.

Chez Marcel (mains US$5-11; ✖ 11:30am-3pm & 5:30-10pm) One block south of Parque Reyes, this is the swankiest date night in town, specializing in lobster cocktails and great service.

Pizza Martinuzzi (medium pizza US$5-7; ✖ 11am-2pm, 4:30-10pm) Chez Marcel's lower-key sibling next door also gets rave reviews.

Luna Ranch (US$2-8; Barrio Pancasan, frente Urracan; ✖ 10am-10pm) Take a taxi (US$.70) if you want to splash out at a really neat place; an outdoor *palapa* decorated with everything from photos of Hurricane Juana (before and after) to costumes for *El Macho Ratón.* Choose from cheap fast food or full seafood plates, and try to come on Sunday at noon, when it hosts ballet *folklórico* (cover US$0.70 per table).

Drinking

Discos and bars can be rough, so go in groups and try not to get too plastered. La Venus and Bacchus, both just south of the park, are *the* discos, with lots of security and a good mix of people.

Four Brothers (✖ Thu-Sun) Six blocks south of the park, Four Brothers has a big wooden dance floor pounding reggae and calypso till late.

Fresh Point is unsigned (look for Bodega Transport Acuatico) but worth seeking out for a great patio overlooking several shipwrecks, which turns into an outdoor dance floor when the music strikes.

Getting There & Away

Take a taxi (US$0.70) to the Bluefields Airport, where **La Costeña** (LC; ☎ 822 2500) and **Atlantic Airlines** (AA; ☎ 822 1299) both have daily flights to Managua and Big Corn Island; La Costeña also flies to Bilwi.

Big Corn Island US$60/90 one way/return, 20 minutes, 7:40am (LC), 8am (AA), 3pm (LC) and 3:25pm (AA)

Bilwi (Puerto Cabezas) US$90/140 one way/return, 50 minutes, 12:10pm (LC), Monday to Saturday

Managua US$90/125 one way/return, 70 minutes, 7:30am (LC), 9:10am (AA), 9:30am (LC), 12:10pm (LC), 3pm (LC) and 4:35pm (AA)

BOATS

The international port is in El Bluff, with cargo ships that you could theoretically take to Prinzapolka and Bilwi, but not San Juan de Nicaragua. The municipal dock has collective *pangas* to El Rama and Laguna de Perlas, larger boats to the Corn Islands and private *pangas*. The smaller docks behind the market also have private *pangas*, and this is where you may be able to hitch a ride to Rama Key.

Both **Impresa Vargas** (☎ 572 2247; Municipal Dock) and **Impresa Jipe** (☎ 572 1879, 607 3702; Market Dock) offer private *pangas* seating eight to Laguna de Perlas (US$200), Sandy Bay Sirpi (US$500) or the Corn Islands (US$1000), among other destinations. A four-hour fishing trip for up to six people, not including equipment (which can be easily arranged), runs about US$90. Several independent operators offer similar deals. Public boats leave the municipal dock (unless otherwise noted) to:

Corn Islands US$10/5 adult/child, four hours, Wednesday 9am, returning Thursday 9am

Corn Islands Ferry 1; US$12, 10 hours, 10pm Friday and maybe 2pm Wednesday

El Bluff US$4, 30 minutes, hourly

El Rama (☎ 572 2247) US$10, two hours, *colectivos* leave when full, and definitely at 6am and 3pm to connect with Managua buses

Laguna de Perlas US$7, two hours, *colectivos* leave when full (10 people), and you can count on one before 7am daily – get there early; stops in Kukra Hill (US$4), with continuing service to Orinoco (US$12)

Sandy Bay Sirpi US$18 one way, 80km, *colectivos* leave El Bluff at 9am Wednesday and Friday, returning Thursday and Monday

LAGUNA DE PERLAS

pop 1500

Laguna de Perlas (Pearl Lagoon) forms where the Río Kurinwas meets the sea, about 80km north of Bluefields. Along its mangrove-lined and sandy-shored perimeter, 18 small indigenous communities make a living off abundant fish, shrimp and lobster. You could easily spend a few days getting away from it all up here, walking to nearby beaches, visiting fishing villages and enjoying the best country and reggae music in the world in Pearl Lagoon's ramshackle collection of restaurant/bars.

And if you find yourself longing for the clear, blue Caribbean instead of the admittedly murky lagoon, just off the coast are the beautiful Pearl Keys, with white-sand beaches, coconut palms and turtle nesting sites, all with very little development and lots of fairly healthy coral reef. Getting here isn't cheap, but this is one picnic that you'll never forget.

There are no banks or other services in Pearl Lagoon, though there is an **Entel** (☎ 822 2355; 🕒 8am-noon & 2-5pm Mon-Fri).

Sights & Activities

Take a *panga* for a few dollars or walk about 45 minutes north of town to **Paisaje de Awas**, the best swimming beach near Pearl Lagoon. Waves are small, water is clear, and there's a sandy beach with tiny bamboo huts (US$2) that get packed around Semana Santa. Green Lodge Guesthouse (p254) rents bikes for US$1 per hour.

Endangered hawksbill turtles nest from May to November in the Pearl Keys, peaking in August and September. Traditionally hunted by the locals for their shells, as opposed to the meat of their tastier cousins, hawksbills are now also under pressure because of developers that have compromised their laying grounds. **Wildlife Conservation Society** (WCS; ☎ 572 0506; clagueux@wcs.org) is helping, by hiring fishermen to help watch turtle nests, which seems to be working – from their estimations, egg poaching now takes about 10% of the total, as opposed to 97% six years ago. WCS does not formally organize outings for visitors, but may be able to offer advice for seeing the lovely ladies on your own. It's worth dropping by the WCS office, close to the dock, just to learn more.

Pearl Lagoon Snorkeling & Sport Fishing Alliance (☎ 821 8047, contact person Kelvin Bernard) is a newly formed group of local boat owners that can find boats and guides for fishing, snorkeling or combo trips in the lagoon or keys.

Make a right as you get off the boat to find professional, American-owned **Atlantic Adventures** (☎ 572 0367), with guided trips that include a deep jungle hike (US$45 to US$60) and trips to Kukra Hill (US$20 to US$30), with waterfalls; per person prices drop as groups grow.

You can rent private *pangas* and visit other villages around the lagoon, and one of the most interesting is **Orinoco**, a Garífuna stronghold so isolated that it was discovered during the National Literacy Campaign of the early 1980s. There are 450,000 Garífunas, a mix of African and Native American cultures and bloodlines, in the world; most live in the USA and Canada, but about 7000 live here and still practice cultural traditions more closely related to those of the Yoruban people of Nigeria than anything from this continent. It's a US$90 *panga* (seating six) round-trip, and Fundeso (see p251) offers very basic lodging.

And then, you could charter a private *panga* (about US$120 for six people) to the **Pearl Keys**, 18 perfect tropical islands, with sand as white, water as clear and coral reefs as packed with stripy little fish as you'd want, all communally owned by the Miskito Indians. Technically. At least one of the islands has been developed into a resort-style hotel, which is hard to recommend not only because the WSC says it's built on top of an important hawksbill turtle nesting site, but also because the whole operation is embroiled in a legal suit and is not open for business. Nicaraguan law guarantees that all the Pearl Islands are communally owned by Miskito people, in perpetuity. Not that this has stopped anyone from selling the islands online (www.tropical-islands.com), without mentioning to potential buyers that their deeds will be subject to vicious legal battles, in perpetuity.

Sleeping & Eating

Green Lodge Guesthouse (☎ 572 0507; r without bathroom per person US$4-5) Three rooms have TVs, and there's a shady courtyard with hammocks, but Green Lodge is more than just a pleasant guesthouse – manager Wesley Williams is a knowledgeable source of information on local history and culture. You can get breakfast (US$2), too.

Hotel Estrella (☎ 572 0523; s without bathroom US$5, d without bathroom US$7-9) This fine spot, with different room configurations that could include twin beds and/or TVs, all have fans. At the time of research, competing beauty queens had booked the hotel during their pageant; if it's good enough for them, it's probably good enough for you.

Casa Blanca (☎ 572 0508; s/d without bathroom US$15/20) Laguna de Perlas' premier lodging is two long blocks inland from the cellular tower, and is a lively household headed by

a Danish-Nica couple with probably the best restaurant (most dishes US$2 to US$4, lobster US$7) in town. Double rooms have screened windows and woodwork crafted in the proprietors' own shop.

Getting There & Away

Boats run to Bluefields (US$7) at least once each morning before 7am; after that, it's all luck. Wake up with the chickens and get your name on the list at the dock.

CORN ISLANDS

Once a haven for British buccaneers (and still a frequent stopover for Colombia-based pirates), Big and Little Corn Islands are now low-key vacation spots in an isolated corner of the Caribbean. The two Islas del Maíz retain in many ways the magic associated with the Caribbean – clear turquoise water, white sandy beaches fringed with coconut palms, excellent fishing, phenomenal coral reefs to explore and an unhurried, peaceful pace, as yet uncluttered with Cancún-style resorts. Little Corn in particular lives up to this elusive image.

Christopher Colón breezed through in 1502, but it wasn't until 1660, when a French pirate by the name of Jean David Nau arrived, that continuous contact was made with the local Kukras-Mayangna Indians. In the 1700s British pirates and African slaves arrived, and both groups mingled with the Kukras. Although the British were asked to leave the islands in 1786, as part of a treaty with the Spanish, they returned in 1841 after independence from Spain; an event still celebrated after August 27 with crab soup and dancing.

Dangers & Annoyances

The Corn Islands are ports of call for Colombian drug boats, which combined with a history of bare-bones law enforcement and a growing, youthful tourist industry, has led to serious problems. Petty theft is common, and muggings, hotel break-ins and even sexual assault have been reported. Solo female travelers should get a hotel room (as opposed to a bamboo shack) with real locks and doors. Anecdotally, crime happens mostly to tourists who have purchased cocaine earlier; your cool new friends know you're high and have money.

Police presence was radically increased in late 2005 in response to these problems, and many issues were being resolved at press time. Regardless, be careful and ask locals for the latest.

Diving & Snorkeling

Both islands have excellent diving and snorkeling, with some coral damage and lots of wildlife, including 40 species of coral and, in December and January, hammerhead sharks. Most diving sites are within 20 minutes of shore and fairly shallow (well under 30m), normally with 30m to 50m visibility. The world-class cave diving on the east side of Little Corn is sometimes too windy to dive.

Big Corn Island
pop 5970

Bigger and more urbane (this is, of course, all relative), Big Corn makes a good choice for people who want more upscale accommodations and more island to explore on bicycle or on foot. You'll arrive at the small town of Brig Bay, and while there's OK swimming and lodging right here, there are many more options around the island, with some of the most secluded beaches stretched between the North End and Southwest Bay.

Collective taxis cost US$0.70 per person regardless of distance traveled, and there's also a bus (US$.30) that makes the loop of the island.

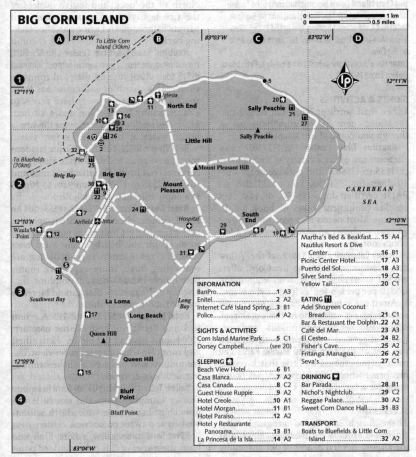

BIG CORN ISLAND

INFORMATION	
BanPro	1 A3
Enitel	2 A2
Internet Café Island Spring	3 B1
Police	4 A2

SIGHTS & ACTIVITIES	
Corn Island Marine Park	5 C1
Dorsey Campbell	(see 20)

SLEEPING	
Beach View Hotel	6 B1
Casa Blanca	7 A2
Casa Canada	8 C2
Guest House Ruppie	9 A2
Hotel Creole	10 A1
Hotel Morgan	11 B1
Hotel Paraíso	12 A2
Hotel y Restaurante Panorama	13 B1
La Princesa de la Isla	14 A2
Martha's Bed & Breakfast	15 A4
Nautilus Resort & Dive Center	16 B1
Picnic Center Hotel	17 A3
Puerto del Sol	18 A3
Silver Sand	19 C2
Yellow Tail	20 C1

EATING	
Adel Shogreen Coconut Bread	21 C1
Bar & Restauant the Dolphin	22 A2
Café del Mar	23 A3
El Cesteo	24 B2
Fisher's Cave	25 A2
Fritanga Managua	26 A2
Seva's	27 C1

DRINKING	
Bar Parada	28 B1
Nichol's Nightclub	29 C2
Reggae Palace	30 A2
Sweet Corn Dance Hall	31 B3

TRANSPORT	
Boats to Bluefields & Little Corn Island	32 A2

NICARAGUA

ORIENTATION & INFORMATION

Big Corn is located 70km from El Bluff and measures about 6 sq km. The airport and main dock for the Corn Islands are located on Big Corn. It's a 40 minute *panga* ride to Little Corn.

May 15 to September 15 is the rainy season, when it rains almost every afternoon and is muddy all day. There are no ATMs or banks with credit card withdrawals, and very few businesses accept credit cards; bring lots of cash. Almost everyone speaks English.

Atlantic Airlines Airport desk does Visa card advance (7% commission).

BanPro Changes dollars but has no other services for tourists.

Big Corn Island (www.bigcornisland.com) Good English-language website with tips, listings and links for Big Corn.

Internet Café Island Spring (per hr US$2; ☉ 10am-10pm Mon-Fri, 2-10pm Sat & Sun) Just north of the dock on Big Corn.

Intur Has a booth at the airport with a handy bulletin board.

Police (☎ 575 5201)

SIGHTS & ACTIVITIES

Other than work on your tan or get into the water, there are few attractions, *per se*, though you could climb **Mount Pleasant**.

Nautilus Dive Center (☎ 575 5077; www .divebigcorn.com) offers a variety of diving tours (US$35 to US$65) and package deals – get 10 dives for US$250. You could also get PADI certified for US$250, or just rent snorkel equipment, bikes or book a fishing trip. Most hotels also rent snorkel gear and can probably arrange horses with a few hours' notice.

Dorsey Campbell (☎ 575 5059), at the Yellow Tail guesthouse (right) on Big Corn, offers guided snorkeling trips, with equipment; US$10 per person for 'as long as you want.'

Anastasia's by the Sea, an overpriced restaurant on stilts above the coral reef, rents snorkeling equipment and offers a suggested swimming path through the reef at the **Corn Island Marine Park**. The route is punctuated by little thatch-roofed platforms where you can climb out of the water for a bit.

SLEEPING

These hotels are listed geographically, clockwise around the island, beginning at the airport. Several decent, if not charming, budget options geared toward fishers clustered in Brig Bay may offer long-term rates.

Hotel Paraíso (☎ 575 5111; cabañas US$35-55; ✗) Excellent thatched-roof bungalows are paired with good food in the lively restaurant bar. Larger, more expensive options include two beds and air-con, but everyone can rent snorkel gear, horses or just hang out with the resident spider monkey, Irma, and her pet tabby cat.

Casa Blanca (s/d without bathroom US$8/10) This breezy budget option in a neat green-and-white clapboard house has simple rooms with mosquito nets, big windows, and a couple of hammocks strung up next to the decent bathrooms.

Hotel Creole (☎ 848 4862, r per person US$9) North of the dock, the festive owners of the Creole have small rooms, some with private bathroom, and a fine porch for kicking back.

Nautilus Resort & Dive Center (☎ 575 5077; www.divebigcorn.com; r per person without bathroom US$10, house US$45) Just up the road from the Creole, this charming old house has three spacious rooms and guests have access to a large, sunny living room and a kitchen. Make reservations in advance for the whole house, a steal at this price.

Best View (s US$20, d US$25-30) Clean, modern rooms have good beds and a fine view of the coral reef out front. The attached restaurant (dishes US$5 to US$7, open 9am to 10pm) is a popular local watering hole.

Hotel Beach View (☎ 575 5062; r US$5-20) The small, cement cheap rooms are rough, but make fine budget lodging if you just want to sleep on the beach; bring your own mosquito net. Across the road, owners are renovating huge, more expensive rooms with quirky extras – cement dolphins, mahogany ceilings etc – that should be ready by the time you read this.

Hotel Morgan (☎ 575 5502; r US$35) A vision in Pepto Bismal-pink, sterile but comfortable rooms have all the modern amenities, and room No 6 has a great sunset view. The compound also has a pleasant restaurant/bar with sunset views.

Yellow Tail (☎ 575 5059; US$10) Snorkel guide Dorsey Campbell rents this one little yellow cabina in paradise, with a kitchen, double bed and sweet ocean view.

Silver Sand (campsite US$7, tr US$20) Everyone loves the owner of this palm-studded point on the north end of Long Bay, where rustic, high-ceilinged cabins with private flush toilets sit just a stone's throw from the water's edge. There's country music in the laid-back bar.

Casa Canada (☎ in the USA 306 861 9224; www .thecornislands.com; r US$60-75) It had to happen: the Corn Islands' first real resort, with beautifully furnished 278 sq meter condos overlooking the infinity pool, was almost completed at press time.

Martha's Bed & Breakfast (☎ 835 5930; d/tr US$45/55; ✹) This potpourri-scented and family-run option has homey rooms with cable TV and little desks, generators for 24-hour electricity, and your choice of a manicured backyard or a breezy porch where you can pass the time just gazing out over the Caribbean. But there's no breakfast.

La Princesa de la Isla (☎ 854 243; www.la princesadelaisla.com; d US$40, bungalow US$55) At secluded Waula Point, close to the airport, this really special spot is constructed with local rocks, shells and timber that fell during Hurricane Juana. Rooms are beautiful and eclectic, the mahogany honeymoon bungalow (make reservations) is outstanding, and there's also food and real coffee. You can rent canoes or snorkeling gear (there's a fine reef right out front).

EATING

Several of the Big Corn Island hotels also have restaurants. On both Corn Islands, tipping is as common as in the USA and service as slow as the sea turtles on the menu.

Fritanga Managua (set plate US$2-3; ✹ evenings) This place oOffers cheap and greasy *comida corriente* while waiting for your *panga* to come in.

Bar & Restaurant The Dolphin (set plate US$1.25-2; ✹ 10am-close) Across from the dock, this place has the cheapest food in town, and bubbly staff won't blink if you order a beer with breakfast.

Fisher's Cave (seafood US$4-7) Slow service and great seafood come standard at this breezy restaurant overlooking the bay.

Seva's (US$3-5) Another highly recommended restaurant, on the other side of the island, this spot serves hearty breakfasts and bowls of lobster soup none too quickly.

Adel Shogreen Coconut Bread (per loaf US$2) About 100m north of Seva's, Adel sells fresh-baked coconut bread and other goodies out of her house; look for the spider monkey.

DRINKING

Bar Parada, near Nautilus, is a colorful space that offers nights of live music. On the weekends, islanders crowd the dance floor at Reggae Palace, a sweaty hot spot on Brig Bay.

Island Style Tiki Bar holds open-air dance parties on weekend nights and on Sunday afternoons, while Nichol's Nightclub, on Long Beach, gets going on on Sunday.

DIVING NICARAGUA

With 1040km of coastline, most of it untainted with overdevelopment, it's no wonder that people are interested in getting all wet. The best Pacific diving is between December and April, but the Caribbean's clear anytime – and don't forget those crater lakes! Here are a few options if you're eager to dive right in:

Dive Little Corn (www.divelittlecorn.com) Get PADI certified in underwater caves!

Dive Nautilus Nicaragua (☎ 575 5077; www.nautilus-dive-nicaragua.com) Go for it on Big Corn.

Abucear (☎ 279 8628; www.abucear.com) San Juan del Sur's best (only?) dive shop does the Pacific Coast and Laguna Apoyo.

Spanish School Laguna de Apoyo (☎ 825 1409; www.guegue.com.ni/eco-nic) Dive Laguna Apoyo while learning the subjunctive tense.

Oceanica Dive Center (☎ 278 4022; www.diveoceanica.com; Los Robles Etapa II 56, frente a Pastelería Margarita) Managua dive center puts together custom tours with all sorts of activities.

Scuba Dive Nicaragua (☎ 882 2067; Clinica Tiscapa ½c abajo) Also based in Managua, this outfitter does both coasts and Laguna Apoyo.

Little Corn Island

pop 515

This tiny *isleta*, as it's also known, is thickly jungled at its heart and fringed in lovely, deserted white-sand beaches interspersed with rocky coves lining the eastern shore. In the center of the island a climbable tower affords fine panoramic views of the tiny settlements below, shaded with palms and mangoes.

Don't let the *tranquillo* vibe lure you into complacency, however. Big-city security rules definitely apply: watch your stuff, watch your back and travel in groups, especially at night. Caribe Town, just north of the village, is a bit sketchy.

ORIENTATION & INFORMATION

Little Corn is located 85km from El Bluff and is to the northeast of Big Corn. It's only about 1.5 sq km, and you can walk end to end in an hour. It's a 40-minute *panga* ride to Big Corn.

See p256 for more information about services on the Corn Islands.

Internet Café (per hr US$12; 8am-midnight) At Casa Iguana (see opposite).

Police (575 5201)

SIGHTS & ACTIVITIES

The highest point on Little Corn has a nifty, climbable **mirador** where you can risk vertigo for an awesome view.

In the village, the recommended **Dive Little Corn** (www.divelittlecorn.com; 8:30am-5:30pm) has similar prices to Nautilus (p256), with deals if you're coming from Honduras' Bay Islands. It also rents snorkel gear (US$5 per day) and kayaks (US$15 per day).

SLEEPING & EATING

You can either stay in the village, which is convenient and offers most restaurant and nightlife options, or in one of the more secluded bits of paradise hidden around the island. Most businesses have signs in the village telling you which path to take.

The Village

The cluster of businesses around here includes a handful of hotels as well as several inexpensive dining options, such as Sweet Oasis and Café Alejandro, both of which serve up inexpensive local favorites and seafood.

Lobster Inn (r with bathroom US$20) Stuffy rooms come with a double bed, thoughtfully furnished with a condom.

Hotel Sunshine (836 4589; d US$40;) A huge step up, this almost luxurious spot has pretty, modern rooms with good beds and cable TV – one has a DVD player. The restaurant (dishes US$3 to US$10, open 8am to 9pm) gets good reviews.

Hotel Los Delfines (892 0186; hotellosdelfines@hotmail.com; s/d/tr with bathroom US$30/40/45;) Larger, equally comfortable rooms with all the amenities – air-con, hot-water bathrooms, TV, good beds – fronted by little porches with rocking chairs. Attached Cueva Los Lobos is the hottest disco on the island.

Cuban Restaurant (mains US$6-10) Little Corn's standout restaurant, this is the place to splurge on lovingly prepared shrimp and lobster dishes; you'll need to order Cuban classics like the recommended roast pork and *ropa vieja* (spicy shredded beef combination served over rice) in advance.

Garret Point

The northeastern corner of the island has a cluster of budget accommodations and some of the island's best dining. It's a solid 40-minute hike from the village.

Derek's Place (huts US$15-25) A backpacker favorite that's headed a bit upscale, Derek's offers pretty bamboo huts and better wooden houses on stilts scattered around a grassy, isolated point. Energy is solar, hammocks are provided and snorkeling equipment is available. Let them know if you'll want breakfast (US$3) or a tasty dinner (curries and pastas US$7 to US$10).

Ensueños (dm or hammock US$5, cabaña d US$15, house d with bathroom US$25) Hidden in the forest, this groovy budget spot has architecturally fascinating cabañas and houses, the latter with kitchenette. The shared bathroom is especially fabulous, with a trippy outdoor shower. There's snorkel gear available, and they'll prepare meals (US$6 per person) with advanced arrangement.

Farm Peace & Love (www.farmpeacelove.com; d/tr US$40/50, cottage q US$65) Make reservations in advance (drop by or have Iguanas or the Dive Shop radio ahead) for a fabulous traditional Italian meal (per person US$12) – the menu depends on what's ripe in owner Paola Carminiani's garden, and vegetarians are happily accommodated; a

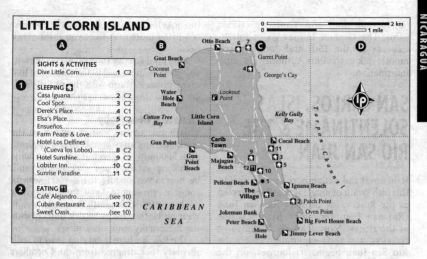

LITTLE CORN ISLAND

SIGHTS & ACTIVITIES	
Dive Little Corn....................1	C2

SLEEPING	
Casa Iguana........................2	C2
Cool Spot............................3	C2
Derek's Place.......................4	C1
Elsa's Place.........................5	C2
Ensueños............................6	C1
Farm Peace & Love............7	C1
Hotel Los Delfines	
(Cueva los Lobos)............8	C2
Hotel Sunshine...................9	C2
Lobster Inn........................10	C2
Sunrise Paradise................11	C2

EATING	
Café Alejandro...............(see 10)	
Cuban Restaurant 12	C2
Sweet Oasis..................(see 10)	

Otto Beach
Goat Beach
Coconut Point
Garret Point
George's Cay
Water Hole Beach
Lookout Point
Cotton Tree Bay
Little Corn Island
Kelly Gully Bay
Gun Point
Carib Town
Cocal Beach
Gun Point Beach
Majagua Beach
Pelican Beach
The Village
Iguana Beach
Jokeman Bank
Patch Point
Oven Point
Peter Beach
Big Fowl House Beach
Moss Hole
Jimmy Lever Beach

CARIBBEAN SEA

good wine selection is extra. Too stuffed to leave? Paola rents a beautiful room with private entrance and a fully equipped cottage.

Cocal & Iguana Beaches

This beautiful stretch of beach offers a cluster of budget lodging with bamboo restaurant bars where security may be an issue, so be careful.

Sunrise Paradise (☎ 820 2923; cabañas with/without bathroom US$20/15) Pleasant, green, tin-roofed wooden shacks seem like they might get hot, but they do lock.

Elsa's Place (r without bathroom US$5-8, per month US$50) A backpacking fave, Elsa's place has a great restaurant, a kitchen you can use and simple rooms.

Casa Iguana (no phone; www.casaiguana.com; cabañas d US$25-80) South of the crowd and atop the rocky headline, this is the classic Corn Islands experience. This largely self-sufficient ecolodge has more sophisticated facilities than the other places. Perched on a cliff with incredible sea views, it features two simple cabins with shared bathrooms and six luxury cabins equipped with flush toilets and showers. The restaurant serves fresh-cooked, family-style meals. It's often booked; don't expect to stay without reservations, which are accepted only by email.

Getting There & Around

Both islands are eminently strollable, but on Big Corn you might get tired. Take a collective taxi (day/night per person US$.70/

US$1.50) or cute little bus (US$.30), which blasts roots reggae as it zips counterclockwise around the island. Nautilus (p256) rents bikes (US$6/10 half/full day). The only vehicles navigating Little Corn's jungle trails are wheelbarrows.

AIR

At press time, Big Corn's airport had just been approved for international flights, and locals were looking forward to connections with Miami and Houston as early as November 2006 – but they've been promised that for years.

In the meantime, the small airport is served by **Atlantic Airlines** (☎ 575 5055) and **La Costeña** (☎ 575 5131), which run flights to Bluefields (US$65/100 one way/return, 20 minutes), with continuing service to Managua (US$110/180 one way/return, 70 minutes), at 8:10am (LC), 8:35am (AA), 3:40pm (LC) and 4pm (AA).

BOAT

Collective *pangas* between the islands (US$6, 40 minutes) leave from Big Corn at 10am and 4:30pm; if you're staying on the far side of Little Corn, you need to take the morning boat. Boats leave Little Corn at 7am and 2pm, meeting each round of flights. It can get choppy. The main dock on Big Corn is 1.5km from the airport; take a taxi.

Boats make the four- to six-hour trip to Bluefields Sunday (US$12, 9am), Tuesday

(US$6, morning) and Thursday (US$9, 9am). The *Captain D* may go to Puerto Cabezas on the 15th and 30th of each month; talk to the Port Authority for more information.

SAN CARLOS, ISLAS SOLENTINAME & THE RÍO SAN JUAN

Rain forest and wetlands, rivers and islands: this lush swath of jungle is wholly protected as the Reserva de Biosfera Río San Juan (Río San Juan Biosphere Reserve), one of the richest ecosystems on Earth. Most travelers start their exploration where the Río San Juan begins its journey, on the shores of Lago de Nicaragua, beneath the Spanish fortress of San Carlos. Though it's not Nicaragua's most photogenic town, it offers comfortable accommodations and easy access throughout this new biosphere reserve.

Much of it is inviolable, and visitors are forbidden to enter the realm of massive red macaws that is the Indio-Maíz. Other regions are preserved for their cultural wealth, including the tropical artists' colony of the Archipiélago de Solentiname and 1724 El Forteleza, above scenic El Castillo, where a teenage girl once held a fleet of British pirates at bay.

The Río San Juan may seem almost mythic, a vast jungle river where pirates and conquistadors once battled for the hemisphere, surrounded by human-eating sharks. But today, it and the Archipiélago de Solentiname are among the easiest places to navigate in Nicaragua, with inexpensive collective boats running fairly regularly through one of the world's last wild places.

Information

This is basically a cash-only destination. Some of the nicer hotels take credit cards, but San Carlos' sole bank offers no services other than changing US dollars. This region has Nicaragua's best souvenirs plus relatively expensive lodging and food, including monster lake shrimp – bigger than some lobsters, topping a cool kilogram

(no joke) – that you'll probably need to try. Bring more cash than you think you'll need.

Pricey but reliable Internet access is available in San Carlos and El Castillo. Note that many phones (those with the prefix '506') are on the Costa Rican system.

Climate & Geography

This is one of the wettest regions in the world, getting anywhere between 2500mm and 5000mm of precipitation annually, including at least one day when you'll be here. Even during the dry(er) season, roughly February to April, make sure your pack is lined with plastic bags and you're wearing clothes that will dry quickly during the usually sunny mornings.

The Río San Juan is carving away at sedimentary rock dragged from the Cordillera Chantaleña, and deposited atop the remains of ancient volcanoes. This geological layer cake is thickly frosted in humid tropical jungle comprising 19 separate ecosystems, all of which were recognized in 2003 as the Reserva de Biosfera Río San Juan.

The biggest, wildest area is the Reserva Biológica Indio-Maíz (Indio-Maíz Biological Reserve), with one of the two remaining macaw populations in the country (the other is in Reserva Natural Volcán Cosigüina; see p189).

Other protected areas within the reserve include: Monumento acional Archipiélago de Solentiname, home to Nicaragua's most famous art colony; Monument Histórico Forteleza La Inmaculada, at 375 sq hectares the smallest piece; and Refugio de Vida Silvestre los Guatuzos (Los Guatuzos Wildlife Refuge) and the Refugio de Vida Silvestre Río San Juan (Río San Juan Wildlife Refuge), which run along the border with Costa Rica. Despite its protected status, the reserve's human population has grown from 21,000 in 1970 to more than 70,000 today.

Almost 70% of Nicaragua's bird species can be found right here: toucans, trogons, hummingbirds, parrots, anhingas, jacanas, egrets, great blue herons, striped tiger herons with their impressive neck ruffs, and the massive black-billed and white-bodied jabiru are just the most impressive. Huge tarpon, ancient gaspar fish and gigantic river shrimp (wait until you see their

RÍO SAN JUAN

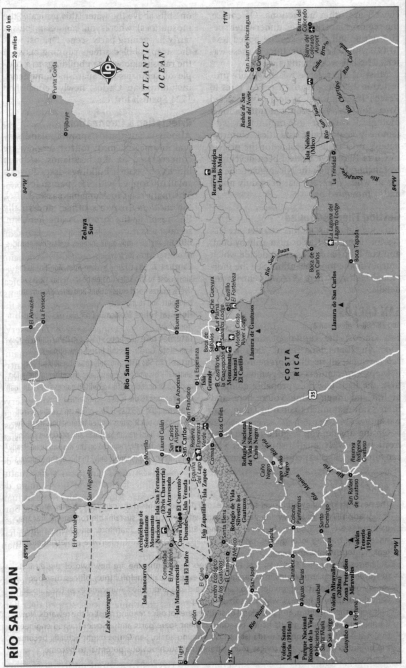

claws!) are other attractions. Of course, the region's most famous underwater species is the bull shark (see the boxed text, p149), which is almost extinct in these waters. The key word being almost.

Most of the reserve was originally protected in 1990 as part of SI A PAZ ('Yes to Peace'; International System of Protected Areas for Peace), a proposed international biological corridor in conjunction with famously ecological Costa Rica. Unfortunately, most lands set aside for the project in Costa Rica have instead been developed by ranchers, though the Nicaraguan side remains wild. The irony has been duly noted and commented on.

Getting There & Around

Most destinations in this chapter are accessible from San Carlos primarily by boat, and you'll be hard-pressed to decide which journey is the most beautiful. See the individual Getting There & Away entries for details.

SAN CARLOS

pop 28,600 / elevation 40m

San Carlos, the capital of the isolated Río San Juan department, gets a bad rap – which, all in all, is probably OK, as it keeps expectations manageably low. So first, the bad news: it's probably going to be hot and muggy while you're here, and there's not that much to do other than swat mosquitoes.

On the upside, you've got a festive lakefront lined with small fishing boats you can hire for lake expeditions, restaurants on stilts above the water (this mitigates the mosquitoes) where you can relax, plus a fairly happening party scene. Or, just walk the steep cobbled streets running between the ramshackle wooden buildings to a couple of centuries-old Spanish monuments, including San Carlos' newly refurbished 1724 Spanish fortress.

Orientation & Information

Although San Carlos sprawls inland several kilometers, most tourist services are concentrated on the headlands, a dozen blocks of wooden buildings draped over a small hill topped with the Spanish fortress. The main road to Managua passes Enitel, the *alcaldía* (mayor's office) and finally the hospital; the airport is another 2km, so take a taxi.

BDF The region's only bank changes dollars but provides no other services for travelers.

Cantur (☎ 583 0126; ☼ 8am-5pm Mon-Fri) In the kiosk close to the Solentiname boats, it has stacks of flyers, makes hotel reservations and arranges private transport and tours.

Hospital Felipe Moncada (☎ 583 0238) About 1km from town.

Internet café (per hr US$1.50; ☼ 8am-10pm) Across from Hotel Carelhys is this brand-new business.

Intur (☎ 583 0301; riosanjuan@intur.gob.ni) This unusually helpful office has flyers and other information, and can book tours with accredited guides from San Juan de Nicaragua to the Islas Solentiname.

Marena (☎ 583 0296) This office isn't really geared for tourism, but it offers limited information about the Reserva de Biosfera Río San Juan and processes fishing licenses, technically required on the Río San Juan. Ready? Apply in writing (Spanish only) to this or the Managua

---

AURACARIA

The best economic news this river's had since they decided to build the canal in Panama, Auracaria is a Spanish-Nicaraguan development program with a focus on sustainable tourism. Auracaria, named for a type of flower, has been working with the Río San Juan Intur and Marena offices since 2003, training local guides, printing up maps and flyers, and otherwise professionalizing regional tourist infrastructure.

The result? The Río San Juan and Archipiélago de Solentiname are now two of the easiest-to-travel-around destinations in Nicaragua, with exceptionally helpful Intur offices that book a variety of great tours with guides who carry first-aid kits and radios. Auracaria even fixed up San Carlos' old Spanish fortress, which is sort of fitting.

It's all rather inspiring, and small local businesses are for once reaping most of the rewards. Now, if only Auracaria could get its hands on some ancient spare parts and a Soviet-trained engineer to get the fast boats from Granada (see p127) running again, San Carlos might actually become the brightly colored, sort of cheesy tourist trap it has such obvious potential to become.

SAN CARLOS

0 ————————— 200 m (Approx)
0 ————————— 0.1 miles

INFORMATION
Alcaldía..................................1 C1
BDF..2 B3
Cantur Kiosk..........................3 B3
Enitel....................................4 B1
Immigration...........................5 C3
Internet.................................6 A2
Intur......................................7 B3
Marena..................................8 B3
Monte Cristo Office.................9 B3
Post Office............................10 B3

SIGHTS & ACTIVITIES
Forteleza de San Carlos.........11 B2
Market..................................12 C3
Tropic Tours.....................(see 7)

SLEEPING
Hospedaje Peña.....................13 A3
Hotel Carelhys......................14 A3
Hotel San Carlos...................15 B3
Hotel-Cabinas Leyko..............16 A2

EATING
Comedor Alondra...................17 C2
El Grenadino.........................18 B3
Restaurant Mirador...............19 A3
Restaurant Mirasol................20 A3

TRANSPORT
Boats to El Castillo, San Juan de
  Nicaragua...........................21 C3
Boats to Los Chiles, Costa
  Rica...............................(see 5)
Boats to Solentiname.............22 B3
Bus Terminal.........................23 C3
Ferries to San Miguelito, Isla
  Ometepe, Granada................24 C3
La Costeña............................25 B3

To Hospital
Felipe Moncada
(1km); Airport (3km);
San Miguelito (60km);
Managua

Parque
Central

Lake Nicaragua

Río San Juan

Marena office (see p73), noting when and where you'll be fishing, what equipment you'll be using, and which species you plan to catch. If your documents are in order, Marena will have your free fishing permit ready within three weeks or so. Or, just pay a guide.

Police (☎ 583 0397)

Sights & Activities

The main tourist activity in San Carlos is waiting for your ship, or *panga* (small motorboat), to come in; consider bringing a book. The **market** is worth a wander, and there are a handful of stores along the *malecón* (waterfront) selling sexy clothes, rubber boots and a small selection of Solentiname handicrafts.

Yep, San Carlos has a Spanish fortress, too, even if 1724 **Forteleza de San Carlos** (admission free; ⌚ 24hr) monument isn't quite as photogenic as El Castillo. It does have fantastic views, of the Río San Juan and Río Frío flowing into Lago de Nicaragua, and the Islas Solentiname. Those volcanoes illuminated in the radiant San Carlos sunsets aren't Isla de Ometepe, by the way. That's Costa Rica, the volcanoes being from west

to east Rincón de la Vieja, Miravalles, Tenorio and smoking Volcán Arenal.

Now a cultural center, the *fortaleza* is ringed with covered benches overlooking the river and lake, all connected by pleasant stone walkways lined with informative displays about natural and human history, with a focus on pirates. There are occasionally ball games and ballet *folklorico* exhibitions here, and there's a small selection of *artesanías* (handicrafts; from Masaya) that you can peruse. There's another old **Spanish observation post**, with cannons, at Restaurant Mirador.

Restaurant Mirasol (p264) can arrange **artisanal fishing trips** (US$10-20, extra person US$5) using *barritas* (hand lines) or homemade nets, which your Spanish-speaking 'guide' will attempt to teach you to use. The restaurant will cook your catch and serve it up with all the fixin's for US$3.

In September, however, step aside for the professionals, who have come from all over the globe annually since 1955 for the **San Carlos International Sportfishing Competition**, in search of the elusive 100kg tarpon.

Tours

Both Intur and Cantur keep a list of dependable tour guides and *panga* operators, or ask around at the docks, where you'll have more room to bargain.

José Miguel Bermudez (☎ 839 7469, 848 0505) Private tours of San Miguel and the lake beaches, Los Guatuzos, Solentiname and the Río Frío.

José Piñeda (☎ 506-301 880; gsolentiname@amnet.com.ni) Look for this excellent, Solentiname-based guide at the San Carlos docks or Hotel Cabañas Paraíso on Isla San Fernando.

San Juan Express (☎ in Nicaragua 505-823 5233, in Costa Rica 506-842 7672) Based at La Esquina del Lago jungle lodge in Los Guatuzos, provides private transport and specializes in tarpon fishing.

Tropic Tours (☎ 583 0010; www.tropictours.net in Spanish) One of the most professional outfits in town; make reservations at Intur.

Viajes Turisticos A Ortiz (☎ 283 0039) Runs tours to El Castillo, Río Papaturro and the Centro Ecológico de Los Guatuzos, Solentiname and the Reserva Biológica Indio-Maíz.

Sleeping

San Carlos has unreliable water and electricity, so shower when you can and keep candles or a flashlight handy.

Hospedaje Peña (☎ 583 0298; r per person US$2) Humble but clean and pleasant, make sure your spring mattress hasn't already sprung, then grab a rocking chair and relax with the friendly owners and their assorted tabby cats. Shared bathrooms have bucket-flush toilets.

Hotel San Carlos (☎ 583 0265; r per person US$6) It's got a back porch over the water and a front porch over the street scene, plus a row of large, spotless wooden rooms with shared bathrooms; Nos 3 and 4 have windows.

Hotel-Cabinas Leyko (☎ 583 0354; leyko@ibw.com.ni; d with/without bathroom & fan US$15/11, s/d/tr with air-con US$30/40/50; Ⓟ Ⓧ) Excellent service and a variety of clean, polished-wood rooms make this a winner. Larger, upstairs rooms with shared bathroom are rather nicer than the expensive rooms. The owners also arrange visits to Reserva Esperanza Verde in Refugio de Vida Silvestre los Guatuzos.

Hotel Carelhys (☎ 583 0389; d US$12) Spacious tiled rooms, great mattresses and spotless bathrooms (but not 24-hour running water) make this San Carlos' most comfortable option. Storing your backpack here costs US$0.70 per night, a service other hotels provide for free.

Eating & Drinking

The cheapest eats in town are at the popular *comedores* (basic eateries) right by the bus station; try **Comedor Alondra** (set plate US$1.25; ☺ 7am-10pm), with a solid *comida corriente* (mixed plate of typical food), while you wait for your bus.

Restaurant Mirasol (seafood US$2-4; ☺ 10am-midnight or later) Jutting out over the water, with a cool breeze and an occasionally used dance floor, this place specializes in *bocas* (appetizers), fried food, good music and cold beer. If you catch a fish, they'll clean, cook and serve it with side dishes for US$3.

Restaurant Mirador (mains US$3-5; ☺ 10am-10pm Mon-Sat) Atop an old Spanish overlook of the Río San Juan leaving the Sweet Sea, complete with strategically placed cannons, this restaurant serves pretty darned good seafood and tasty pork chops.

El Granadino (mains US$3-8; ☺ 10am-midnight or later) Considered the best restaurant in town, El Granadino has an amazing mural, good music, cold beer and an incredible fish filet in garlic sauce. Steak, chicken and other dishes are priced according to size, and cooked to order. Have another beer.

This being a port town, there's plenty of nightlife – much of it scary, so take care – in the string of basic bars lining the waterfront between the docks and market.

Getting There & Away

San Carlos is isolated from the rest of Nicaragua, unless you book a fairly pricey flight, take a nine-hour ferry, or suffer the bumpy 12-hour bus ride from Managua. But keep in mind that it's a smooth, 3½-hour, US$8 bus ride from San José, Costa Rica, to the border at Los Chiles; from there it's a gorgeous two-hour riverboat trip up the Río Frío to San Carlos. If you're coming from Costa Rica, consider starting your adventure right here.

AIR

The San Carlos airport is a 3km, US$1 cab ride from downtown San Carlos, but you can make reservations in town at the **La Costeña office** (☎ 283 0271; ☺ 7:30am-noon & 1-5pm Mon-Fri, 7:30am-noon Sat). Flights leave for Managua (US$80/120 one way/return, 45 minutes) at 9:15am Monday through Saturday, 2:30pm Sunday through Friday. Flights leave Managua for San Carlos at 8:30am Monday

---

BORDER CROSSING: TO LOS CHILES, COSTA RICA

One of the simplest and most scenic border crossings in Central America, this could almost be listed as an attraction. Begin at friendly **San Carlos Immigration** (🕒 8am-5pm), one and a half blocks from the municipal docks.

Collective boats (US$10, two hours, 10:30am and 4pm Monday to Saturday, noon and 4pm Sunday) leave directly from behind the Immigration office; a 1:30pm boat may be added if there are at least nine passengers, but don't count on it. You can rent a private boat seating eight to Los Chiles for about US$120.

It costs US$7 to enter Nicaragua, US$2 to exit. Entering or leaving Costa Rica is free. When you arrive in Los Chiles, go to customs first, one block from the dock, to have your bags searched, then another building about two blocks away to have your passport stamped. The mellow river town has several hotels and restaurants.

Buses leave from the terminal, about five blocks east of the dock, to San José (US$8, 3½ hours, 5am to 6pm, hourly) and less frequently to Parque Nacional Caño Negro (US$3, one hour, 5am and 2pm). There are also boats from Los Chiles to Caño Negro, where you can find food and lodging, for US$25 per person, including a two-hour wildlife tour.

---

through Saturday, 1:30pm Sunday through Friday.

Flights should be reserved as far in advance as possible, particularly during the rainy season, when the road may be closed. Get to the airport early, as flights are always overbooked.

BUS

The road from Juigalpa to San Carlos is one of the worst in the country, and never recommended for casual tourists in rental cars. If you must, it's 4WD-only in dry season, and pack a spare tire – or two.

Buses (which are modified to deal with these conditions) take seven to nine hours to grind 100 bladder-bouncing kilometers from Juigalpa to San Carlos, and may not be able to make it in the rainy season. The one bathroom break involves bushes by a plastic-bag-strewn river – you go in the open or not at all. Buses leave from opposite the San Carlos market for the following destinations:

Juigalpa US$7, seven to nine hours, 9am, 10am, 11am, 12:40pm, 1:30pm and 2:30pm

Managua US$10, 10 to 12 hours, 2am, 6:30am, 8am, 11:45am, 6pm, 8pm and 10pm

Nueva Guinea US$7, seven to nine hours, 4am, 11:50am, 2pm and 5:15pm

San Miguelito US$3, two to four hours, 1pm, 2:20pm and 4:30pm

BOAT

Your hotel or any tourist office can arrange private boats seating around six from San Carlos to the Islas Solentiname (US$110,

one hour), Boca de Sábalos (US$160, one hour), El Castillo (US$180, 1½ hours) and San Juan de Nicaragua (US$900, seven hours).

Granada, Isla de Ometepe & San Miguelito

Promises of a fabled 'fast boat' between Granada and San Carlos (see the boxed text, p127) may have been fulfilled before you read this, but at press time your only option was the slow ferry. A private *panga* from San Carlos to San Miguelito costs around US$40 and takes about an hour.

Show up at the San Carlos ferry terminal, half a block from the market, for boats leaving at 3pm Monday and Friday to San Miguelito (US$2, two hours), Altagracia (Isla de Ometepe; US$6/3 1st/2nd class, nine hours) and Granada (US$6/3 1st/2nd class). First-class seats, on the upper deck, have padded chairs and access to the TV, which will be on all night. Stake out a sleeping spot early and don't forget your seasickness medication. Ferries return from Granada at 3pm Monday and Thursday, stopping in Altagracia (except during very rough weather) at 7pm.

SAN MIGUELITO

About 60km from San Carlos (and much closer by boat, although you can take the bus) is one of Nicaragua's newest and least visited refuges, the **Sistema de Humedales de San Miguelito** (San Miguelito Wetlands). Fronted by a fishing village, the wetlands' main claim to fame is the enormous number of birds, many of them migratory, and reptiles – in particular, loads of alligators.

Three rivers meander through the reserve – Río Tepenaguazapa, Río Camastro and Río Tule – but the best swimming hole in the area is right offshore on **Isla El Boquete**, a sandy spot popular with the locals. You can also visit **Los Guanabanos**, a private *finca* (farm) with a beautiful old hacienda and an iguana farm, plus spectacular lake views.

There's one hotel geared to tourists, the Italian-owned **Hotel Cocibolca** (☎ 552 8803; hotelcocibolca@yahoo.com; r per person US$12), with 16 comfortable rooms featuring fans, mosquito nets and awesome views of the back of Ometepe, plus breakfast service in the morning. The owners can arrange private transport and tours throughout the wetlands, as well as to Solentiname and down the Río San Juan.

Getting There & Away

See p265 for details on taking a boat to San Miguelito.

You can also take the bus. It's an 8km walk to town from the San Carlos–Managua road, so take a direct bus from Managua (US$9, nine to 11 hours, 6:30am) or one of three daily from San Carlos (US$3, two to four hours, 1pm, 2:20pm and 4:30pm), delivering you right to the dock and hotel.

ISLAS SOLENTINAME

pop 800 / elevation 40–250m

Almost forgotten for 500 years, and almost destroyed in a single day, the Archipiélago de Solentiname does not seem entirely of this world. Isolated by the cleanest, purest waters of Lago de Nicaragua – an epic translucence that somehow amplifies each sunset – the beauty of these ancient volcanic islands has been famously captured, in luminous full color, by the work of its world-famous art colony.

Until the 1960s, the Islas Solentiname didn't even appear on Nicaraguan maps. Metal tools for hewing wood seemed impossibly expensive to these families of subsistence farmers and fishers; homes and churches were made of palm thatch. Then, in 1966, an idealistic young poet priest named Ernesto Cardenal (see the boxed text, opposite) arrived on the islands, built

a church, and recorded the remarkable *La Misa Campesina,* or Peasants' Mass, when the islanders themselves stood up and spoke the word of God.

Largely because of Cardenal's socialist leanings, in 1977 a group of Sandinista supporters attacked San Carlos, and failed. On October 3, as retribution, the National Guard burned every structure on the islands to the ground. Survivors fled to Costa Rica, leaving the archipelago all but abandoned.

When the revolutionary government took power, the islanders returned and rebuilt, raising a new church, and began painting and sculpting again. And Solentiname, for so long a commune in the purest sense, remains more staunchly committed to the most extreme ideals of the revolution than perhaps anywhere else in the country. 'It's just hard to get used to capitalism,' explained one artist.

Orientation & Information

There are 36 islands in the Archipiélago de Solentiname, most arranged in a graceful arc about 17km west of San Carlos. Tiny Islas Zapote and Zapotilla are closer to the mainland, with easy access to Los Guatuzos Wildlife Refuge, while Isla Zanata is about 25km northwest, almost halfway to Isla de Ometepe.

Most tourist services are located on Islas Mancarrón and San Fernando (officially Isla Elvis Chavarría). There are also services on Islas Mancarroncito, Atravesada and Venada (officially Isla Donald Guevara). Note that while everyone misses, and remains very proud of, revolutionary martyrs Elvis Chavarría and Donald Guevara, they usually use those islands' Spanish names.

Auracaria (see the boxed text, p262) plans to build an Intur kiosk at the Mancarrón dock, with information on tours and homestays. In the meantime, your hotel or the San Carlos **Intur** (☎ 583 0301; riosanjuan@intur .gob.ni) and **Cantur** (☎ 583 0126) offices can find guides and transportation.

Most hotels offer two prices: just lodging, or a package deal including meals. Light eaters can save by bringing snacks, or purchasing them at the poorly stocked *pulperías* (corner stores), and buying meals separately. Many families offer **homestays** (per person US$5–10) in their spare rooms – which vary widely in quality and may be full of

NICARAGUA

half-carved balsa toucans when you arrive. Plan on giving your hosts a couple of hours to clean up. Many families also offer meals (US$3 to US$5) with advance notice.

Getting There & Around

You need time or money to visit the archipelago, as inexpensive public boats only run three times a week, leaving San Carlos at 2pm Monday (US$2) and 1pm Tuesday and Friday (US$3.50), with stops at San Fernando and Mancarrón. They leave Mancarrón, stopping about 15 minutes later at San Fernando, at 5am Monday (US$2), 4am Tuesday and Friday (US$3.50).

If that doesn't work with your schedule, you'll need to hire a private boat (seating at least six) for around US$100 between San Carlos and the islands; hotels will try to find cheaper transportation if you ask ahead of time. You'll also need to hire private *pangas*

ERNESTO CARDENAL & REVOLUTIONARY CULTURE

As a poet, his subject matter ranges from theoretical physics to Marilyn Monroe; as a sculptor, from the creatures of the jungle to the life of Christ. A Trappist monk originally committed to nonviolence, Ernesto Cardenal came to fully support the Sandinista-led revolution, by any means necessary. He was Nicaragua's original liberation theologian, the revolutionary government's Minister of Culture, and remains its unofficial ambassador of the arts.

Like many Marxists, **Ernesto Cardenal** (www.ernestocardenal.org in Spanish) was well born and well educated, at the University of Mexico and University of Columbia in New York City. After the failed 1954 'April Revolution' against Somoza, he felt called to a Trappist monastery in Kentucky, where he found peace in meditation and silence. He returned to Nicaragua in 1966, to Solentiname, perhaps seeking the same solitude.

Instead, he found a community all but forgotten by the modern world, impoverished, poorly educated, but where a special wisdom had been born. Cardenal helped erect the islands' first simple adobe church, where he gave Mass. Here, the people of Solentiname interpreted the Scripture through their own eyes and lives, a living word of Christ, which Cardenal recorded and published as *El Evangelio de Solentiname* (Gospel of Solentiname). It would later be rendered in song by legendary artist Carlos Mejía Godoy (see p84) as *La Misa Campesina* (Peasants' Mass).

One day, a grateful islander named Eduardo Arana presented Cardenal with an elaborately decorated jícara shell, which impressed the priest into giving the young man paints and a canvas. Those first few paintings, some on display in the Biblioteca y Sala Archaeologica on Mancarrón (p268), launched Nicaragua's Primitivist Art Movement, internationally recognized for the vibrant colors and expert lines that so accurately capture this tropical paradise. One artist, Ufredo Argüello, began applying the same saturation of color to balsa-wood carvings, which also caught on.

Throughout the late 1960s and early 1970s, families worked together painting and sculpting, sending their work to market in Managua. There, trouble was brewing, and even this peaceful hippy haven could not isolate itself. In October 1977, inspired by Cardenal, the islands rebelled; retribution by the National Guard was swift and complete. Solentiname was abandoned and Cardenal was denounced as an outlaw.

When the Sandinistas took power in 1979, however, they appointed Cardenal the Minister of Culture, a position he used for almost a decade to successfully preserve and enrich Nicaraguan arts and folklore.

The Catholic Church was not happy with its wayward son; in 1983 Pope John Paul II publicly chastised the prostrate priest on the tarmac of the Managua airport; many Nicaraguans sided with Cardenal. In his recent book, *The Lost Revolution*, Cardenal writes that 'The people lacked respect for the Pope, it's true, but it's because the Pope first lacked respect for the people.' In more recent years, he's even fallen out of favor with the Sandinistas, after he criticized frontman Daniel Ortega's 'Stalinist' control of the party.

At 80 years old, Cardenal still works and travels, and remains on the board of directors for Casa de los Tres Mundos in Granada (see p117) and Managua (see p117).

And when he grows tired of his wandering, this is where he returns. Islanders point out the tidy wooden house with pride, saying simply 'that's where Ernesto Cardenal comes to write.'

between the islands; it's at least US$6 between San Fernando and Mancarrón.

Note that Refugio de Vida Silvestre los Guatuzos is closer and cheaper (US$45) to Solentiname than San Carlos, so consider doing this as a triangle, springing for one private *panga* between the archipelago and Río Papaturro, and taking public boats to and from San Carlos.

If you've been waiting for that one rewarding splurge, a boat tour of Solentiname (prices vary widely according to what you want to see) is highly recommended. You'll never look at those paintings as being at all abstract again.

Mancarrón

The largest of the islands cradles the archipelago's most famous historic treasure: **Nuestra Señora de Solentiname**. The original thatch-roofed, bamboo church was first constructed in 1935, then replaced in the late 1960s with a sturdy adobe built by communal effort. It was here that each person would stand and speak on Sunday, their thoughts recorded by the priest, Ernesto Cardenal, as *La Misa Campesina*.

The church was destroyed, like everything else, in October 1977. With the end of the war two years later, however, the people returned to rebuild what you'll see right here. There is no gold, not much in the way of earthly riches at all. Just one beautiful cross above a simple altar, both designed by Cardenal, and dirt floors, wooden beams and imperfect adobe walls. These are covered with brightly colored drawings of birds and fish, mothers and trees, which were originally children's paintings, reproduced by painters Róger Peréz and William Agudelo where the Stations of the Cross might have hung instead.

Behind the church, there's a nice **beach** (during dry season) and in front a well-equipped **playground** that centers on a plain gray boulder, often covered with wilting bouquets of flowers. This is the **Memorial to the Martyrs** of that one terrible day in 1977, and brass plaques record words from Masses given so long ago by the fallen.

About 100m uphill is the **Biblioteca y Sala Archaeologica** (admission free; ⏰ 8am-noon & 1-5pm Mon-Sat), which most folks prefer to the official museum on San Fernando. It's a library where schoolchildren gather each day, but packed with archaeological treasures including metates, ceramics and one good-sized idol, most accidentally excavated by locals.

The highest concentration of **craft workshops** on the islands are just inland in **Comunidad El Mancarrón** (also called El Refugio). Feel free to wander and watch as families work together, some hewing balsa into rough forms, which children sand smooth and the most trusted adult paints. Wooden animals cost US$1 to US$6, a painting for as little as US$10, but prices rise with size and quality.

SLEEPING

Hotel Mancarrón (☎ in Costa Rica 506-393 9612, 505-583 0083; hmancarrun@ibw.com.ni; r per person US$8, ind 3 meals US$35) Closest to the church, this hotel offers large, simple accommodations in a sprawling, whitewashed complex. Rooms are furnished with fans, bathroom and art, and management organizes tours and private transport, and rents canoes and kayaks.

Hospedaje Buen Amigo (r per person incl 2 meals US$12) Further up the dirt path into town, this friendly spot has five small, colorful rooms, which share clean bathrooms that usually work. There are rocking chairs and locals carving balsa-wood animals out front, and you can choose which two meals you want.

San Fernando (Elvis Chavarría)

With even fewer people, tranquil San Fernando has some of the nicest accommodations on the islands and two attractions you should make an effort to see even if you're staying elsewhere.

SIGHTS & ACTIVITIES

Museo Archipiélago Solentiname (Musas; admission US$2; ⏰ 8am-noon & 2-5pm) is worth visiting just for the view and gardens, which attract all manner of bird and insect life; you may have to ask around town for the curator, if you want to go in. Actual information is a little thin, but the natural-history displays feature smiling balsa-wood subjects; the turtle-hatching exhibit is just adorable. There's a selection of archaeological treasures, plus illustrations of the famed petroglyphs of La Cueva del Duende (under water and inaccessible most of the year). Better yet, there's a map to more petroglyphs, well off the tourist trail, scattered throughout the islands.

(Continued on page 273)

ERIC L WHEATER

Church walls, Archipiélago de Solentiname (p266), Nicaragua

Girl with papayas, Granada (p110), Nicaragua

MARGIE POLITZER

LOU

Young boy, El Salvador (p295)

ERIC L WHEATER

Dressed for a festival (p120),
Granada, Nicaragua

El centro (p318), the centre of San Salvador, El Salvador

ANTHONY PLL

ANTHONY PLUMMER

Bar patrons, San Salvador (p311), El Salvador

Waiting for the ferry, Nicaragua

MARGIE POLITZER

Back streets of San Miguel (p422), El Salvador

CHARLOTTE HIN

MARGIE POLITZER

Iglesia de La Recolección (p166),
León, Nicaragua

Playa El Cuco (p417), El Salvador

ALFREDO MAIQ

(Continued from page 268)

Next door, the **Union de Pintores y Artesanos de Solentiname 'Elvis Chavarría'** (☎ in Costa Rica 505-277 0939; ☽ 8am-noon & 2-5pm) gallery features the work of about 50 of the islands' top artisans, including some real top-of-the-line, museum-quality paintings (US$40 to US$250). If you don't have that kind of cash, you should still check this place out – the view is incredible and the impressive selection of balsa-wood animals is much more affordable. And you have to see the murals.

Some smaller **galleries** and **workshops** are strung along the strand of homes between Musas and Albergue Celentiname. Residents are considering putting up signs along the rest of their extensive **walking trail** network, but until they do, don't go on your own – it's easy to get lost. Any local kid will happily show you around for a few córdoba. For more extensive tours, contact guides José Piñeda at Hotel Cabañas Paraíso or Olivia Guevara at Albergue Celentiname.

SLEEPING & EATING

Hotel Cabañas Paraíso (☎ 506-301 8809; gsolentiname@amnet.com.ni; r per person with/without bathroom US$12/10, incl 3 meals US$25/20) With incredible views – older, simpler rooms with shared bathroom actually have better ones – these are the most comfortable accommodations in the archipelago, with excellent food and service. You can also contact the talented owner, painter Elena Piñeda, at her Managua art gallery, Galería Solentiname (☎ 277 0939).

Albergue Celentiname (☎ 506-377 4299; r per person US$10, incl 3 meals US$25) Just northwest of the main dock, these remarkable gardens envelop six cute cabañas (one family-sized) with wood floors and huge bathrooms, connected by paved paths lit up with lots of tiny solar lanterns. The 32-*manzana* property has its own short hiking trail to a private petroglyph, but it may be hard to leave the comfy porch.

Mancarroncito

Mancarroncito is locally known for producing potent fruit wines – guava, pineapple – that you can pick up for about US$1.25 per bottle. This is also where they grow those soccer-ball-sized avocados you saw on sale in San Carlos.

Mancarroncito, separated from Mancarrón by a slender channel, is also home to what are probably the last primary forests left on the islands; others were all but grazed into oblivion and replanted over the past two decades. At the time of research, **Fundación del Río** was building a biological station and research station with trails and lodging. Ask at the San Carlos **Intur** (☎ 583 0301; riosanjuan@intur.gob.ni) to see if it's open.

Isla Venada (Isla Donald Guevara)

Most of this island is owned by a Sandinista VIP, but the northwestern shore is also home to one of the most important painting families, the Aurellanos. In addition to selling truly remarkable work, they theoretically rent out one room (US$10 per person), which was packed solid with art supplies at the time of research.

You'll need a boat to see the most important attractions, only visible during dry season (February–April). A system of caves at the water line honeycombs the island; you can allegedly walk from one end to the other underground. On the northern shore, **La Cueva del Duende** holds the most famous petroglyphs on the island, 161 separate drawings including dancers, animals and a female fertility figure. Another enormous rock dome called **El Convento** is so big that you can fit an entire *panga* inside during the dry season.

Isla Atravesada

It's not the 'naughty island,' but so named because it's the only one oriented north–south, rather than east–west like the rest of the archipelago. It's famed for its enormous alligators, some reaching five ferocious meters, and is where you'll probably be taken on your night-time alligator tour.

The most luxurious hotel on the islands should be opening here soon – big rooms with enormous windows, a lovely porch and beautiful paved trails crisscrossing gorgeous gardens, plus an infinity pool looking over the water. Just keep a close eye on the kids, OK?

Other Islands

There are at least 36 islands in the archipelago, many privately owned and most without much to interest the casual visitor. Just north of Mancarrón, a group of several small islands, the largest of which are **Santa Elena**, **Santa Rosa** and **Ciguëna**, are known for excellent fishing – but check out that sunken Spanish galleon, the prow of which may be visible in the dry season.

You will at least hear the residents of **Isla El Padre**, between Mancarrón and San Fernando, named for yet another priest who long ago sought solitude in these tranquil waters. Today, it's inhabited by a troupe of howler monkeys and a few families who never, ever get to sleep in.

Isla la Sevilla, just west of Mancarroncito, is a haven for bird-watchers, with thousands of cormorants, tiger herons and pelicans – not to mention the excellent fishing they're here to enjoy.

Real birders won't want to miss tiny **Islas Zapote** and **Zapotillo**, with Nicaragua's highest concentration of birds, most famously flocks of roseate spoonbills that nest in February and March. Migratory birds of all kinds converge here between December and April – more than 30,000 nests were counted in 2004. These islands are 12km from the rest of the archipelago, but a visit could easily be tacked on to a day trip to Refugio de Vida Silvestre los Guatuzos, nearby.

Landing a boat is risky business at **Isla Zanata**, a solid hour away by *panga*. But dedicated fishers are willing to risk the rocks and waves for the privilege of camping here for days on end to enjoy the best freshwater fishing in Central America.

REFUGIO DE VIDA SILVESTRE LOS GUATUZOS

Like so many national treasures, Los Guatuzos Wildlife Reserve, a 44,000-hectare band of river-streaked wilderness and wetlands wedged between the Costa Rican border and Lago de Nicaragua, was conserved quite by accident. The earliest inhabitants, the Guatuzos, were sold into slavery, their lands co-opted by farmers whose crops (rubber and cacao) could not survive without the natural shade. Just as those crops failed, inviting in the timber companies, revolution and war hit hard along the border, leaving this region as pristine as only a minefield can be. (It was declared mine-free in 2001.)

By the time it was safe for people to return to the rich ecosystem, the federal government had already taken pains to protect it. This lush band of nature inviolate, say scientists, may well be what keeps Lago de Nicaragua so clean and healthy – always something of a mystery, considering the agricultural and urban runoff it endures from all other sides.

The Río Pizote (Long-Tailed Raccoon River) and Río Medio Queso (Half Cheese River) form the eastern and western boundaries of the preserve, home to 18 rivers, 2000 people, 81 amphibians, 42 mammals and almost 400 species of bird – the big draw. During the rainy season, this is a region of tiny cascades and waterfalls; in the dry season – the northern winter – pools of water grow still and shrink around an increasing concentration of migratory waterfowl.

Sleeping & Eating

La Esquina del Lago (☎ 505-823 5233; www.nicaraguafishing.com; packages per person US$1250-5000) Unfished since the Somoza era, it was only a matter of time before the neighbors noticed that these tarpon-infested waters were a prime spot for some serious ecotourism (the website includes a trilingual San Carlos fishing report). Plush package deals at this lodge, just 2km from San Carlos, include transportation from San José or Managua international airports, lodging, fishing and side trips to Solentiname and the Río San Juan.

Reserva Esperanza Verde (☎ 583 0354; leyko@ibw.com.ni; r per person incl 3 meals US$30) Nearby, this reserve protects 5000 hectares of humid tropical forest, and makes a fine day trip from San Carlos (US$20 per person, four-person minimum), including private *panga* transport, breakfast, guide and trail access, which can be arranged through Hotel-Cabinas Leyko (☎ 583 0354) in San Carlos. Alternatively you can spend the night in one of its simple, solar-operated rooms, which have bathroom and mosquito nets. The owners offer a number of tours, through the enormous trees and rare orchids, and along the Costa Rican border. They offer one intriguing night option where you'll fish for those huge river shrimp (US$10, including cooking and eating your catch).

Centro Ecológico de Los Guatuzos (☎ 270 5434, 583 0139; www.fundar.org.ni; dm US$12) Geared primarily to scientists and students, this tropical research station welcomes regular visitors to its dorms, and also rents tents. Breakfast is served on-site, and you can arrange other meals (US$2 to US$3) in advance with local families. The classic wooden center also makes a great day trip (more accessible from Solentiname than San Carlos) and offers several activities, including a two-hour guided hike on Las Guatuzos Trail (US$5 per person), which can be combined with a trek through the jungle canopy on a hanging bridge for US$1 more. Add a tour of the butterfly, turtle and alligator farms and the entire adventure will still set you back only US$11. Don't skip the tours (US$11) of Río Papaturro in wooden canoes – at night to look at alligators, during the day to watch the birds.

Getting There & Away

Private *pangas* to Reserva Esperanza Verde, about 20 minutes from San Carlos, run US$30 to US$50 round-trip, which can be arranged more cheaply through **Hotel-Cabinas Leyko** (☎ 583 0354; leyko@ibw.com.ni) in San Carlos. There's no public transportation, although you could theoretically take any Los Chiles, Costa Rica-bound boat – but you'd have to pay the full US$10 ticket, and explain why you don't need your passport stamped.

It costs around US$130/240 one way/round-trip to Río Papaturro and the Centro Ecológico de Los Guatuzos, including a four-hour wait. It's cheaper (US$45 round-trip) to rent a boat in Solentiname. There are also collective boats from San Carlos to Papaturro (US$4, four hours) at 7am Tuesday, Wednesday and Friday, returning to San Carlos from Río Papaturro at 7am Monday, Tuesday and Thursday.

RÍO SAN JUAN

Aztec traders used this route as early as the 1200s to ship goods between the oceans, but it was not until 1521, when Cacique Nicarao told the conquistadors that Cocibolca had a 'drain' to the Atlantic, that Spaniard Diego de Machuca ran the rapids all the way to the sea. This is still the dream trip, made legend by British pirates and history by Mark Twain, down the marvelous, mysterious Río San Juan.

There are not many places like this left in the world, you know. And rich men have been plotting to broaden this river, deepen it, straighten it into something more suitable for their mercantile whims, for almost 500 years. The thundering volcanoes and murmuring rapids may not thwart them forever.

The towns of Boca de Sábalos and El Castillo, as well as the beautiful jungle resorts strung between them, have easy access, with public boats daily. But to go into the vine-hung wilderness of jaguars and macaws, through the Indio-Maíz to the end of the river, takes commitment.

Boca de Sábalos

pop 1000

Most tourists breeze by this unassuming little town en route to nearby resorts or more tourist-friendly El Castillo. This has left it a rather unsullied shrimping village, appealing if you're eager to get off the beaten path and into the jungle. You could easily do Sábalos as a day trip between San Carlos and El Castillo – just take the morning boat into town, then catch the second boat out in the afternoon. Not that there's a lot, exactly, to do.

At the confluence of the Río San Juan and Río Sábalos (Tarpon River), you can watch the two grand rivers collide from the breezy back porch of Hotel Sábalos, over a platter of the best river shrimp in town. Another, smaller tributary effectively splits the town in half, with the inexpensive *hospedajes* (guesthouses) and main (only) road on one side, and a smaller community, threaded by a slender paved footpath through the pretty homes and gardens, on the other. It's one córdoba (US$0.06) to cross the canal in a dugout canoe.

And that one main road heading north, into the rain forest? That dirt trail penetrates the Reserva Biológica Indio-Maíz, which is technically off-limits. Here, however, there are several small, accessible communities actually inside the reserve – 4WD taxis are lined up at the dock.

SIGHTS & ACTIVITIES

Koma Rico, right by the dock, serves as the de facto tourism office, and can find guides

RIVER OF CONTENTION Tim Rogers

The Río San Juan is a fluid border in every sense. It forms a 180km natural border between the southern jungles of Nicaragua and Costa Rica's northern frontier, and also provides the central artery to remote communities where daily travel from one country to the other is as easy as, well, crossing a river. It is one of only a number of border rivers in the world that's owned exclusively by one country.

Nicaragua's territorial claim to the river, mixed with historical – and sometimes paranoid – suspicions of Costa Rica's intention to steal it, makes the Río San Juan a symbol of national unity. Although most Nicaraguans have never actually seen the river that connects Lago de Nicaragua to the Caribbean Sea, the mere mention of its hallowed waters prompts patriotic citizens to stand up a little straighter and quickly blink the mist from their eyes.

Since the 1520s, the river has been a route for trade and/or attack by groups as diverse as the Zambos, Miskitos, the Spanish and British Crowns, pirates, separatist leaders, North American adventurers, Costa Rican coffee farmers and – most recently – sportfishers and tourists.

Long eyed as an ideal location for the construction of an inter-oceanic canal (there is currently a project afoot to build a shallow-draft barge canal), the Río San Juan has long played a central role in the oftentimes-tumultuous history of Nicaragua and Central America.

The current contention over the river is a re-release of an old classic: Costa Rica's navigational rights granted by a mid-19th-century treaty, which states clearly that the river is Nicaragua's property, but that Costa Rica can use it to transport commercial 'objects.'

The vague wording remained a nonissue for much of 150 years until the late 1990s, when the Costa Rican government of then-President Miguel Angel Rodriguez decided it would no longer allow Nicaraguan troops to randomly board and search Costa Rican vessels on the river. That's when the historical revisionism started, as both sides offered different versions of what was meant by the treaty's mention of 'objects.'

for the hot springs and other trips. The three resort-style hotels also arrange tours. Day-trippers will probably want to stick close to town, perhaps hiking to Sábalos Lodge or north on the main road, or renting dugout canoes at the dock for exploring mellow river tributaries.

Marena (☎ 583 0179; pmsmaren@ibw.com.ni), which is just uphill from the city center, can arrange guides and free lodging in the Reserva Biológica Indio-Maíz – if you have scientific credentials and send them a Spanish-language request several weeks in advance. The five-hour hiking trail to the lodge begins in Las Maravilles, 20km (taxi US$35, 45 minutes) from Sábalos.

Also near Las Maravilles, **Aguas Calientes Escalara** are unimproved thermal waters that vary in temperature from steaming hot to mild, and are situated along a cool river not far from the road – perfect. Take a taxi or have Intur in El Castillo (p278) arrange a guided trip, including transportation and a tour of Las Maravilles.

Reserva Privada El Quebracho (☎ 583 0035; fdrio@ibw.com.ni; admission US$3.50), with 129 *manzanas* bordering the Reserva Biológica Indio-Maíz, offers a peek at the region's

very big trees, very small frogs, beautiful rivers and wealth of wildlife without risking karmic whiplash from sneaking in. Near Buena Vista (taxi US$30, 45 minutes), it offers guided hikes and horseback rides along two trails through orchid-carpeted primary forest, plus accommodations (dorm including three meals US$15).

You can also (theoretically) arrange tours of **Finca Reforestal de Cacao Indio-Maíz** (☎ 583 0179), a 425-hectare, communally owned cocoa plantation, for US$12 per person. The office, which appeared to still be getting organized, is just uphill from Marena.

SLEEPING & EATING

Budget lodging is very basic and located in town. Less convenient and much more comfortable are three of the best hotels on the river, one in town, the other two just downstream. Just tell the *colectivo* driver where you're staying and he'll drop you off. Most hotels offer breakfast, but ask about other meals. There are a few simple *comedor* and *fritanga* (sidewalk barbecue) setups downtown.

Hospedaje y Comedor Katiana (☎ 583 0178; r per person US$4) The best of the cheapies, clean,

Costa Rica insisted that objects included firearms – a necessary tool of the trade for 19th-century merchants. Nicaragua said that gun-toting Ticos would not be permitted in Nicaragua, and argued that tourists brought by Costa Rican tour operators could only be considered 'objects' if the intention were to sell them as slaves (also illegal).

Unable to agree on any meaningful solution, in 2002 the two governments decided to shelve the issue for three years, effectively dumping the problem on the next administrations.

Flash forward to 2005: the three-year truce ends and the two countries' quaint yet politically weak presidents decide to do a little muscle flexing over the river. Costa Rican President Abel Pacheco announced in September that his government would take its case before The Hague. Nicaraguan counterpart Enrique Bolaños responded by accusing Costa Rica of having a 'historic appetite' for the Río San Juan, and slapped a new visa tax on all Costa Ricans to raise money for Nicaragua's legal defense.

Nicaragua's Foreign Minister took the issue a step further by pondering aloud his country's historic claim to Guanacaste, the northern province of Costa Rica that annexed itself to Costa Rica in the mid-1900s. If Costa Rica was going to start questioning old treaties, perhaps Nicaragua would too. Average Nicaraguan citizens also jumped on the nationalistic bandwagon. T-shirts appeared saying 'What's the problem little Tico? The Río San Juan is 100% Nicaraguan.' And otherwise leveled-headed citizens started talking openly in bars (usually after several rums) about taking up arms to defend the river against the Costa Ricans, who were probably busy watching soccer games rather than plotting an invasion.

A bumper sticker in Nicaragua reads: 'The Río San Juan is not a topic of discussion.' And discussion, as warned, has only made a potentially messy situation actually messy.

Tim Rogers is editor of the Nica Times (www.ticotimes.net/nicatimes)

polished-wood rooms, a nice porch and passable bathrooms make this a winner. Only some rooms have windows.

Hotel Sábalos (☎ 892 0176, 820 0494; www .hotelsabalos.com.ni; r per person US$10, s/d with view US$15/24) A one-córdoba (US$0.06) canoe trip across a smaller tributary, it's fun just getting to this beautiful lodge, which is a good deal on very comfortable accommodations. Spotless, attractive rooms have hot-water bathrooms, great beds and pretty furniture, and for a few extra dollars you get a permanent breeze, lots of light and a view of the two massive rivers meeting for the first time. It also has the best restaurant (meals US$4 to US$10) in town.

Sábalos Lodge (☎ 583 0046; www.sabaloslodge .com; dm per person US$6, d US$20-35, r per person incl 3 meals US$35) Not quite 1km downstream, this is exactly what you dreamt your jungle adventure would be like when you were a little kid: plush bamboo cabañas with tastefully chosen mosquito netting, hammocks everywhere and an enigmatic jungle river meandering through the luxuriant tropical gardens right out front. Also rents kayaks (US$10 per day), horses and bikes (US$5 per day), and serves meals (US$4 to US$12).

Monte Cristo River Lodge (☎ 583 0197, 839 7558; www.montecristoriver.com; d incl 3 meals US$45-60) More comfortable, these are big, clean, very civilized cabins in paradise, with great beds and one with a hot-water bathtub; there's even a Jacuzzi (let him know that you're coming and the English-speaking owner, Augustin, will heat it up for you). The 120-*manzana finca* grows coffee, fruit and cocoa, some of which you may be able to sample, and there are horses and other animals that kids are sure to get a kick out of. The lodge specializes in birding and sportfishing packages, but can arrange almost anything, including waterskiing. You can make reservations in San Carlos, right across from the post office.

Soda Hermanas Rosales (set plate US$1.25; ☙ 7am-8pm) It's worth the walk to this small restaurant, uphill from Marena, where your *comida corriente* (with drink) is served atop checkered tablecloths.

Koma Rico (dishes US$1.25-6) This is the town favorite; it's right by the dock, serving Nicaraguan-style tacos, *comida corriente* and, most importantly, river shrimp. It's a fine spot to sit and relax while you wait for your boat.

GETTING THERE & AWAY

From San Carlos, boats leave for Boca de Sábalos (US$3.50, 1½ hours, 8am, noon and 3pm Monday to Saturday, 6am and 2pm Sunday). The last boat may be cancelled. From Boca de Sábalos, boats leave for San Carlos (US$3.50, 1½ hours, 5:30am, 7:30am and 2:30pm Monday to Saturday, 6:30am and 3:30pm Sunday), El Castillo (US$1.25, 30 minutes, 7:15am, 9:15am and 4:15pm Monday to Saturday, 8:15am and 3:15pm Sunday) and San Juan de Nicaragua (US$11, 6½ hours, 7:15am Tuesday and Friday).

El Castillo

You've already seen so much beauty by the time you round that last curve on the mighty Río San Juan, tucked-in egrets hung from the misty morning jungle like lanterns on either side, that it's hard to imagine what might yet leave you in awe. Then you'll hear the roar of Raudal El Diablo (Devil's Rapids), bane of pirates for five centuries and nature's own announcement of this postcard-perfect Spanish fortress atop an emerald-green hill, weathered rock hewn into ancient arches that will forever guard the honor of its distant mistress, Granada.

Encircling the base of El Forteleza's pedestal, like brightly colored skirts, are scores of fresh-painted wooden buildings jutting out over the rushing water, all connected by tidy paved walkways. The town is easy to navigate; from the town dock, with a wonderful Intur office, go upstream, downstream, or climb the hill to the fortress.

There is an **Internet café** (per hr US$2.50; 7am-9pm), just west of Soda Carolina, where you can make international calls.

EL FORTELEZA

Properly known as **El Forteleza de la Limpia Pura e Inmaculada Concepción** (admission US$2; 8am-noon & 1-5pm), this photogenic fortress was constructed between 1673 and 1675, commissioned after Granada was sacked three times in five years. The stunning views over Raudal El Diablo were key – they slowed precocious pirates down just long enough to aim the enormous cannons their way.

Proto-feminist folk-hero Rafaela Herrera was only 19 years old when her father, the fortress commander, was critically wounded in a 1762 battle with a British fleet. Herrera stepped into command (evidently wearing a nightgown) and successfully repelled the pirates, in some versions herself shooting the cannon that sank the lead ship.

Then, in 1780, 22-year-old Brit Horatio Nelson set out to conquer the edifice, with boundless optimism and no maps. It took two hungry weeks to travel the route he'd provisioned two days for, and worse, they drank the water. The Brits were victorious despite their weakened state, as the Spanish were eager to leave – their fortress, as Nelson soon discovered, had become a breeding ground for malarial mosquitoes. Within a few months, the bull sharks had grown fat on British bodies and the Spanish were able to walk back into the abandoned fort.

The well-designed fortress was also used by William Walker's filibusterers in 1857, and both the Sandinistas and Contras during the 1980s; in one terrible battle, more than 100 Sandinistas were killed in a single night.

Restoration of the fortress began in 1993, and today the resurrected armament houses a solid museum, with informative Spanish-language displays. Your entry fee includes a tour by the enthusiastic staff, but you'll have to pay extra (US$2/4 camera/video) to take photos of the incredible views from up top.

TOURS

Conveniently right across from the dock, El Castillo's incredibly useful Intur office arranges a variety of guided tours in conjunction with Auracaria (see the boxed text, p262). Make reservations a day in advance, although the city tour (US$6; 3hr) can be arranged the same day. In addition to a variety of guided hikes and *panga* trips, tours (priced per person in a group of four) include:

Alligator Night Tour (US$40; 2hr) No swimming.

Canoe Tours (US$35-55; 3-4hr) Explore different rivers in wooden canoes.

El Gavilán Community Tour (US$8; 5hr) Visit a small river town and watch tortillas being made in a wood-fired oven.

Horseback tour to the Costa Rican border (US$10; 3hr) Explore the jungles, farms and *fincas* on horseback.

Sarnoso Canyon (US$95; 4hr) Rapids and gold mines, together at last.

There are several private operators with signs up in town; most tours have a two-person minimum. Pulpería El Puerto, right by the dock, offers **finca tours** (per person US$10) that include a *panga* ride, 2km hike and two hours on horseback. About 200m east of the dock, Angel Alfonso Tapia offers another **horseback tour** (per person US$10) through Comunidad Gavilán and a private *finca*.

El Mariposario (admission US$1; ☑ 10am-noon & 1-4pm) You could also flutter by for a tour of this butterfly garden, run by a local women's collective.

Tour in Canoa (seylaobregon@yahoo.com) Across from the police station, Seyla leads treks downstream in traditional wooden canoes, where you'll be picked up by a motorized *panga*. You could take the Río La Juana (per person US$30, three hours) or the more serious Río Bartola (per person US$25). She also rents the canoes (US$8 for two hours).

SLEEPING
There are a handful of very basic but clean, pleasant *hospedajes* lining the waterfront, with a couple of solid midrange options a bit inland; only one has private bathrooms. A new midrange hotel, **Victoria** (☎ 583 0188; r with/without bathroom incl breakfast US$15/10) was slated to open in 2006.

Hospedaje y Pulpería El Universal (r per person US$3.50) With a wonderful waterfront porch overlooking the rapids and clean wooden rooms with shared flush toilets, this is the best of the cheapies.

Hotel Richardson (r per person US$10) With the only private bathrooms in town, not to mention some great murals, it was a darned shame they were remodeling (including new mattresses!) at press time.

Hotel Albergue El Castillo (☎ 583 0182; herrerajoe25@yahoo.es; r per person with/without balcony incl breakfast US$15/10) This is the best hotel in town, with gorgeous hard-wood rooms, fabulous furniture, great lighting and, if you spring for the extra US$5, an amazing balcony with stunning views over the river and town. All with shared bathrooms. The restaurant (US$4 to US$8) is also tops, and has a great view.

EATING
Grab a coffee or fruit juice at the juice stand next to Intur, or head to one of several *sodas* (simple cafés) lining the waterfront, most serving both cheap set plates and pricier seafood dishes.

Soda Carolina (comida corriente US$2, shrimp US$10; ☑ 6:30am-8:30pm) This wonderful spot has great service, excellent fruity beverages and a plant-packed upstairs dining area where you can enjoy a meal while watching the rain fall.

Soda Vanessa (fast food US$1-3) Two blocks east of the docks, this place specializes in cheap eats – burgers, *pintos* – served up with a million-dollar view over the roaring rapids.

Restaurante Daryzu (seafood US$2-8) Or, go upscale another block downstream at this solid seafood joint.

If you continue east across Puente de las Tortugas (Turtle Bridge), you'll come to a group of riverfront ranchos serving seafood and cold beer.

GETTING THERE & AWAY
From El Castillo, collective boats leave for Boca de Sábalos (US$1.25, 30 minutes, 5am, 7am and 2pm Monday to Friday, 2pm and 5pm Sunday), with continuing service to San Carlos (US$4, two hours).

Refugio Bartola & the River Eastward
About 15 minutes downriver from El Castillo, **Refugio Bartola** (☎ 880 8754, 289 3448; www.refugiobartola.com; r per person with/without 3 meals US$50/20) is simpler than the other river lodges. But it's not really about the big, clean rooms with two beds and built-in furniture, or pleasant thatched-roof restaurant (breakfast US$5, other meals US$10). It's the location.

Sure, it's inconvenient to catch a San Juan de Nicaragua–bound boat (El Castillo boats don't come quite this far) or rent a private *panga* (US$25) in El Castillo. But it's worth it to hike the four trails – ranging from one to eight hours in length – through primary rain forest, right on the border of the Reserva Biológica Indio-Maíz. Nonguests pay US$5 per trail to hike by themselves, plus an extra US$20 per group for an English-speaking guide, which is recommended. Wooden canoes seating eight can be rented for US$5 a day.

The refuge, at the confluence of the Caño Bartola and Río San Juan, also marks your entry into the wildest part of the journey – well, on the Indio-Maíz side, anyway. The Costa Rican side of the border rolls primarily into ranchland. Keep your passport handy, as you may need to show it to Nicaraguan or Costa Rican authorities.

About an hour further along from the mouth of the Río Sarapiquí, the San Juan Delta begins to weave through the wetlands, meeting up with the almost-as-enormous Río Colorado. Birding becomes increasingly more interesting, and fishing even better – but note that you have officially entered the bull sharks' territory, so no swimming.

You'll pass the rusting, wrecked steamship that made an impression on Mark Twain when he came through, and finally enter the expansive Bahía San Juan. That rusting hulk rising from the waters is an old dredger owned by Cornelius Vanderbilt's Transit Company, which kept the shipping lanes open for would-be gold prospectors en route to San Francisco. The dilapidated dock to the south marks what's left of Greytown and old San Juan del Norte, founded on what was then the mouth of the Río San Juan, now a sandy extension of dry land. Continue to cross the bay to the mouth of the remarkable Río Indio, where you'll reach the very last stop of all, San Juan de Nicaragua.

San Juan de Nicaragua (San Juan del Norte)

Though it's one of the Americas' oldest European cities, this damp monument to human perseverance has one of its newest names. Until 2003 it was known as San Juan del Norte, which (if you look at a map) doesn't make much sense…unless it was all a conspiracy involving those dastardly Costa Ricans (see the boxed text, p276)! Hence the change.

Many visitors to this little-touristed spot will wonder, perhaps out loud, why Costa Rica (or anyone else) would want it. But when it was founded in 1539, with the far more poetic moniker San Juan de las Perlas (Saint John of the Pearls), this was the future 'most important port on the Atlantic.' Its strategic significance, along with the promise of an inter-ocean canal, attracted British attention. In 1848 it was seized by Jamaican Governor Charles Grey (in the name of the Miskito Kingdom), who modestly renamed it Greytown. This was actually rather appropriate, given that it's the rainiest spot (over 5000mm annually) in the hemisphere.

Although the promised canal was not forthcoming, the river remained the fastest route between New York and San Francisco. And as the Gold Rush geared up, Greytown became a pleasantly seedy little boomtown, with whorehouses, gambling halls and hotels hewn of mahogany and precious cedar. Between 1851 and 1868, more than 155,000 travelers passed through.

After the canal was built in Panama, and Greytown was ceded to an independent Nicaragua – reclaiming its original name of San Juan – investment stopped and the once attractive Victorian town slipped into decay. The town was already in shambles when Sandinista leader turned Contra commander Edén Pastora, aka 'Commandante Cero,' burned it to the ground in 1982; subsequent efforts to rebuild were dashed to devastation by Hurricane Juana in 1988. The current site of SJDN has only been used since the early 1990s.

San Juan de Nicaragua remains a backwater, and while residents are hopeful that tourism will take off, their main economic activities involve fishing and, this being the Caribbean, narco-trafficking. Use the one **public phone** (☎ 506-384 7054), on the Costa Rican network, to contact anyone in town. Water and electricity may go off without notice, so carry a flashlight at night and shower when you can.

SIGHTS & ACTIVITIES

The must-see attraction is the swampy remains of **Greytown** – basically, a windmill, a few cement building foundations and four very interesting cemeteries: one for the British (including those members of Horatio Nelson's doomed campaign who were not fed to the sharks), another for Catholics, a third for North Americans and the last allegedly for Freemasons from St John's Lodge. Guide Hedley Acton Thomas Barss, or Chalí, who knows everyone in town, comes well recommended.

Also worth seeing is **Laguna Azul** (Blue Lagoon), where you can swim in relative safety, although people-eating bull sharks could theoretically cruise right in. Also be sure to check out the geographic oddity of the **Río Indio**, which flows parallel to the Caribbean coastline, at times separated from the sea by only a few hundred meters of sandy beaches and virgin jungle.

And, of course, there is some of the best **tarpon fishing** in the world.

The small Marena office, Restaurante Orquídea or Hotel Paraíso Virgen can arrange the following Intur-approved guided tours:

Fishing on Fish Creek (4 people US$80; 4hr) Recently 'discovered' by every sportfishing magazine in existence, this region is the newest, hippest place to catch enormous tarpon in the Americas, which is why so many sportfishers are willing to pay the big bucks at the Río Indio Adventure Lodge. But you could just hook up a boat and some bait with these guys.

Regional Tour (6 people US$50; 4hr) See the four Greytown cemeteries, hike a short jungle trail, visit the rusting remains of the dredges of Cornelius Vanderbilt, then finish up on a broad sandy beach near beautiful Laguna Azul.

SJDN City Tour (per person US$6; 2hr) Wander through town, meet the movers and shakers, and learn a bit about the region's rich culture, quirks and all.

Wetlands Tour (6 people US$60; 4hr) Take a *panga* through the delta and Laguna Azul to look for manatees, then head up the Atlantic coast.

SLEEPING & EATING

In addition to the official places, you can arrange **homestays** (r per person US$3-8), and several private cooks also offer meals – give them a few hours' notice.

Hotel El Británico (r per person US$4) Has simple wooden rooms with OK shared bathrooms, which are just fine for some adventurers.

Hotel Paraíso Virgen (r per person with fan US$10, d with air-con & TV US$35; 🔊) Also known as Melvin's place, this better (but still somewhat run-down) option offers bathrooms with 24-hour water, electrical generator and an on-site restaurant (meals US$3 to US$12), about seven blocks from the dock.

Restaurante Orquídea (meals US$2-10; 🕐 all day) The town's only official restaurant serves seafood and less expensive options; it's also the de facto tourist office and can arrange homestays, guides and private transportation. It's across the street from Discoteca Fantasy, the hottest (only) dance spot in town.

Río Indio Adventure Lodge (🕿 in Costa Rica 506-296 4948, in the US 866-593 3176; www.rioindiolodge .com; all-inclusive s/d US$250/400; 🔊) One of the best sports lodges in Central America, this wonderfully plush fishing center is just south of SJDN. Package deals include all manner of fishing expeditions and inter-esting side trips, as well as transportation from San José, Costa Rica, or Managua International Airport. Almost 80% of this Tico-owned hotel's clients come through Costa Rica, via the Río Colorado, spending thousands of dollars that don't end up in Nicaraguan pockets. This is not to criticize the lodge – which employs plenty of Nicaraguans and is a great addition to the river's attractions – but merely to explain (at least in part) why Nicas are so overprotective of the potential tourism gold mine that is the Río San Juan, which they as yet lack sufficient resources to develop properly.

GETTING THERE & AWAY

The San Juan de Nicaragua air strip may begin getting regular flights before this book is off the shelves, but don't count on it.

Make boat reservations at the San Carlos municipal dock, just east of the ferry terminal, in advance for San Juan de Nicaragua, particularly if you plan to catch the always-crowded boat in Boca de Sábalos or El Castillo. The last scheduled boat to or from El Castillo is often cancelled, particularly on Saturday. Travel in the morning.

Two boats leave from San Carlos for San Juan de Nicaragua (US$15, eight hours, 6am Tuesday and Friday) stopping in Boca

---

BORDER CROSSING: TO BARRA DEL COLORADO, COSTA RICA

There is a little-used – and somewhat sketchy – border crossing between Costa Rica and Nicaragua on the Río Colorado, used primarily by upscale fishing resorts and pricey packaged tours. Begin at the immigration post at San Juan de Nicaragua, where they will hopefully stamp your passport. From there, you'll need to hire a private *panga* (around US$140, 1½ hours) to Barra del Colorado, Costa Rica.

There are no roads connecting Barra del Colorado, with one relatively inexpensive hotel (and several swanky fishing lodges), to the rest of Costa Rica, but there is an airport with daily flights to San José and regular boat service to Puerto Limón. Both towns have Costa Rican immigration offices, where you will be expected to explain why you crossed the border way the heck out here.

de Sábalos at 7am and El Castillo at 8:30am. These return from San Juan de Nicaragua at 4:30am Thursday and Sunday.

NICARAGUA DIRECTORY

ACCOMMODATIONS

Ranging from five-star resorts with an infinite number of pools to windowless shacks with shared latrines, you really have your choice of accommodations in Nicaragua. Well, you have your choice in more expensive and developed A-list destinations (Managua, Granada, León, San Juan del Sur, Corn Islands), anyway; top-end places start to thin out a bit as you head for the interior.

Luxury accommodations, where they exist, can be a good deal – the most expensive resort in the country (p156) clocks in at US$150 to US$200 per person, which certainly isn't for everyone, but is a steal compared to Costa Rica. Boutique hotels (with doubles going for US$50 to US$70), concentrated in Managua, generally have fewer than 10 rooms, and are creatively decorated with lots of little luxuries; **Small Hotels** (www.centralamerica-smallhotels .com) has a list of great options. Tour agencies may be able to get a third off rack rates in top-end and midrange hotels, so be sure to ask.

There's a good midrange option, with clean, modern rooms, private bathroom, 24-hour electricity and running water, hot water and/or air conditioning (this varies with elevation) and a nice setting or neighborhood, in every major town, even in isolated spots like Las Minas and Nueva Guinea. They tend to cost US$20 to US$35 for a double; tack on US$10 to US$15 for an A-list destination. Solo travelers usually get a 20% discount, tops, in this category. Also note that hotels in the midrange and top-end categories have a 15% tax tacked onto the cost.

The budget hotels, sometimes called *hospedajes*, are inexpensive compared to the rest of Central America. You can almost always get your own clean wooden room, with sheets and sometimes a window or piece of furniture, with shared bathroom, for under US$4 per person per night. Double that and you get a bigger room and private bathroom; prices are higher in A-list destinations, where there are always cheap dorm beds (US$3 to US$6 per person) if you're on a shoestring. In less-developed regions, you may be using bucket-flush toilets and bucket showers in this price range. Budget travelers should always bring candles and flashlight (torch), just in case. If there's no mosquito net, just ask.

In rural areas without much development, there may not be signed guesthouses, but almost all small towns have families who rent rooms. Ask at the *alcaldía* (mayor's office) for leads on weekdays, or at any open business on weekends. Some communities have formalized homestays through Spanish schools (you don't need to be a student – just ask at the school) or as part of community-based alternative tourism, such as at Reserva Natural Miraflor (see p197).

Camping is available in a few private and natural reserves, and is also allowed free on most less-developed beaches. Budget hotels and private residences often let you pitch a tent out back.

ACTIVITIES

Nicaragua has almost unlimited opportunities for outdoor activities, but almost nowhere to rent or buy equipment, so come prepared. Sports with particular promise for development (once there's money invested) include **windsurfing**, with aficionados already testing the waters in Lago

---

LOVE HOTELS

Many Nicaraguan hotels aren't for travelers – they're for lovers. Sometimes called motor hotels, they generally have walled-in parking lots to discourage prying eyes, cheesy names ('Eternal Bliss,' 'Garden of Eden'), private bathrooms, flavored condoms and very special cable TV, and they may also arrange prostitutes.

They are not generally unsafe, although they may be loud (not just the sex; think romantic '80s ballads blasting from well-stocked bars), and most will bemusedly provide rooms for tourists, if you're (ahem) desperate. Note: the low price advertised outside is probably for three hours; make sure to get quotes for 'the whole night.'

de Nicaragua, Laguna de Apoyo, Corinto, Lago de Managua (yech!) and Lago Xiloá; and **whitewater rafting**, although at present you'll be running one of Nicaragua's thousand rivers in wooden canoes, which you'll carry around the Class IVs yourself. And there are some sports you really can't do anywhere else, such as **volcano surfing** (see p178) – you know you want to.

More developed activities include the following.

Canoeing & Kayaking

With all these rivers and lakes, it's no wonder that canoeing and kayaking adventures are becoming more popular. Some of the most easily accessible options include kayaking the Isletas of Granada (p118), the Río Istiam and islets around Isla de Ometepe (p141), Reserva Natural Isla Juan Venado (p176), near León, and down the Río San Juan (p278) in wooden canoes on a guided tour.

Serious adventurers can arrange to take wooden canoes on any number of rivers, including the Río Coco from Wiwilí (see the boxed text, p219), right into the heart of Bosawás.

Diving & Snorkeling

With 1040km of coastline, most of it untainted with overdevelopment, it's no wonder that people are interested in getting all wet. The best Pacific diving is between December and April, but the Caribbean's clear anytime – and don't forget those crater lakes! Divers have only just begun to exploit Nicaragua's watery riches, and the best-known dive sites are in the Corn Islands (p255) and San Juan del Sur (p150), with lower visibility but much easier access from the tourist trail. You can also dive Laguna de Apoyo (see p102), a crater lake with brownish fish and a steep, creepy drop to the bottom. For a list of Nica diving outfits, see the boxed text, p257.

Hiking

Perhaps inspired by neighboring Costa Rica, Nicaragua is building beautiful trails through its parks and reserves. Some of the most interesting and easily accessible are at Reserva Natural Miraflor (p197), Reserva Natural Cerro Musún (see the boxed text, p242) and Somoto Canyon (p205).

The climbs with the real cachet, however, are any of the dozens of volcanoes, including the Maribios Chain (p177), Volcán Cosigüina (p189) and the volcanoes of Isla Ometepe (p138).

Guides are usually recommended for hikes in all but the best developed natural parks and reserves, particularly for the volcanoes; count on US$6 to US$20 per group, more for private reserves. Most towns also have free trails to area swimming holes, crosses and other shrines, or even hot springs; Matagalpa (p209) is a standout, but feel free to ask at Intur, the *alcaldía* or even your hotel about other options.

Surfing

Nicaragua has some of the best (and least-crowded) surfing in the world. See p45 for coverage of Nicaragua's best-developed adventure sport.

BUSINESS HOURS

Most official government offices, including Intur, Marena and all *alcaldías* (mayors' offices), your three main sources of tourist information, are generally open from 8am to noon and 1:30pm to 5pm; Intur is usually open until noon Saturday and Sunday. Many other businesses, including corporate offices and many stores, also take an extended lunch hour. Banks, notably, do not.

Restaurants have widely varying hours, but in general, simple *comedores* (basic and cheap eateries) are open from about 6am until 8pm, and nicer restaurants may close from 3pm to 5pm. No matter what time a steam-table buffet is officially open, it's best to go in just as meal time begins (around 11:30am or 5pm). Discos usually don't get going until at least 9pm, later in Managua.

If a museum, cultural center or other office isn't open when it 'should' be, ask around to see if anyone in the neighborhood knows where the caretaker is.

CHILDREN

Nicaragua, like all Latin American countries, is relatively easy to travel around with children, despite the lack of infrastructure. Parents rarely pay extra for hotels, transportation or other services for youngsters small enough to fit in a lap comfortably, and even complete strangers will make an effort to accommodate and entertain children.

That said, bathrooms can be very unsanitary, bus rides long and bumpy, and disposable diapers difficult to find outside of major cities – stock up and consider carrying cloth diapers if you're planning to be in a rural area for a while.

COURSES

Most population centers have a Casa de Cultura (House of Culture) where you can enroll in all sorts of classes – painting, folkloric dance, makeup and hair care – dirt cheap, often for less than US$1 per class, or US$6 per month. Classes will almost certainly be conducted in Spanish, although in more touristy areas like Granada and San Juan de Sur there may well be someone who can help you in your native tongue.

Nicaragua is also a good place to learn Spanish, although it's a bit more expensive than Guatemala, which is a favorite among budget-minded backpacking students. Classes cost US$100 to US$120 for 20 hours of instruction at a respected school, and usually include study materials and field trips; homestays, with three meals daily, are arranged for US$60 per week. Prices tend to drop if you register for more than a week. Independent teachers will come to your hotel for US$5 per hour, and can also usually arrange homestays, if not field trips.

There are several schools in sunny San Juan del Sur, where you can also arrange surfing lessons, as well as in Granada, Laguna de Apoyo, León and Estelí.

DANGERS & ANNOYANCES

Despite the fact that Nicaragua has the lowest crime rate in Central America, lower than the US or Europe (or El Salvador, for that matter), as a 'wealthy' foreigner you will at least be considered a potential target by scam artists and thieves. Make sure they pick a different tourist by staying alert and taking precautions against theft and mugging. Several areas are considered dangerous enough to merit their own warnings, including Managua (p73), with big-city problems; San Juan del Sur (p148), with bohemian tourist-industry problems; and most of the Caribbean Coast, with serious cocaine-trafficking problems that you should stay well away from.

Always play it extra safe in the rural Caribbean Coast, undeveloped nature reserves and anywhere that infrastructure is limited and communications weak. Even if it's expensive or seems silly, consider taking precautions if recommended by a reliable source – hey, if they think two guides is better, maybe there's a reason. For tips on not being a target tourist, see the Safety chapter (p472).

DISABLED TRAVELERS

Before you put this book down and decide to instead go somewhere with actual wheelchair ramps, find a copy of **Beyond Boundaries Nicaragua** (www.bbc.co.uk/ouch/tvradio /beyondboundaries), a British reality-TV series that sends 11 disabled trekkers *overland* (the wheelchair got up to five punctures per day!) from Pearl Lagoon, using machetes to get through the woods, all the way to San Juan del Sur, including a climb up active Volcán Concepción.

Inspired? Unfortunately, there are few regular services for disabled travelers. But because the war left so many people in wheelchairs and otherwise disabled, people are used to mobility issues and will work with you. Still, it's easiest to go through a tour company: try **Tours Nicaragua** (www .toursnicaragua.com) and **Go with Wheelchairs** (www .gowithwheelchairs.com).

EMBASSIES & CONSULATES

Check at www.embajada-online.com for complete listings of all Nicaraguan consulates and embassies overseas, and all embassies and consulates in Nicaragua.

Embassies & Consulates in Nicaragua

All these offices are in Managua.

Costa Rica (Map p78; ☎ 266 3986; fax 266 3955) From the Montoya statue, two blocks south, one block east.

Denmark (☎ 268 0250) From Rotonda El Güegüense, one block west, two blocks north, and a half a block west.

El Salvador (☎ 276 0712; Av del Campo 142, Las Colinas)

France (☎ 222 6210; fax 228 1057) It's 1½ blocks west of El Carmen church.

Germany (☎ 266 3918) From Rotonda El Güegüense, 1½ blocks north.

Guatemala (☎ 279 9609; fax 279 9610; Carr a Masaya Km 11.5) There is also a consulate in León.

Honduras (☎ 279 8233; fax 279 8228; Carr a Masaya Km 12.5)

Mexico (☎ 278 4919; Carr a Masaya Km 4.5) One block east of the Carratera, contiguous with Optica Matamoros.

Netherlands (☎ 266 6175) From the canal it's 2½ blocks north, one block west.

Panama (☎ 266 8633; No 93 Colonia Mántica) From the main fire station, head one block west.

USA (Map p70; ☎ 266 6012, 266 6038 after hours; Carr Sur Km 4.5)

Nicaraguan Embassies & Consulates Abroad

Austria (☎ 403 1839; 113350.2341@compuserve.com; Ebendorferstrasse, 10-3-12, 1010 Vienna)

Costa Rica (☎ 506-223 1489, 222 2373; embanic@racsa .co.cr; Av Central 2540, Barrio La California, Frente al Pizza Hut, San José) There's another consulate in Liberia.

France (☎ 1 45 00 41 02; fax 1 45 00 96 81; Ave Bugeaud, 75116 Paris)

Germany (☎ 228 362 505; fax 228 354 001; Konstant-instrasse 41, D-53159 Bonn/2) Also covers Switzerland.

Japan (☎ 00813 34990400; nicjapan@gol.com; Kowa Bldy 38, Rm 9034 – 12-24, Nishi – Azabu, Minato-Ku Tokyo 106)

Mexico (☎ 5 540 5625; fax 5 520 6960; Prado de Norte 470, Colonia Lomas de Chapultepec, CP 11000, Delegación Miguel Hidalgo, Mexico DF)

Netherlands (☎ 70 306 17 42; fax 70 306 17 43; Sumatrastraat 336, 2585CZ The Hague)

Spain (☎ 91 555 5510; fax 91 555 5737; Paseo La Castellana 127, 10-B, 28046 Madrid)

Sweden (☎ 468 667 1857; fax 468 662 4160; Sandhamnsgatan 40-6 tr, 11528 Stockholm) Also covers Denmark, Finland and Norway.

UK (☎ 171 409 2536; fax 171 409 2593; 36 Upper Brook St, London W1Y 1PE)

USA (☎ 202 939 6570; fax 202 939 6545; 1627 New Hampshire Ave NW, Washington, DC 20009) Also covers Canadian citizens.

FESTIVALS & EVENTS

Every town has its *fiestas patronales,* or pa-tron saint–day festivities, which could run for a week or, in the case of Masaya's San Jeronimo extravaganza, three months – and most towns have two patron saints. Fes-tivities vary, but count on parades, folkloric dance, all-night vigils, bullfights (killing the bull is illegal in Nicaragua) and live music, including marching bands (and fireworks) at 5am. Sweet.

National Baseball Championship Series (March 26– April 4) Nicaragua's national pastime comes to a head.

San Marcos (April 24, San Marcos) The saints of Carazo get together in San Marcos for the department's biggest party.

Palo de Mayo (May, Bluefields) A little more sparkle than you may be used to around the big pole.

Virgen del Carmen (July 16, San Juan del Sur) Carmen blesses boats around the bay.

Santa Ana (July 26, Nandaime) For more than 400 years, ever since she saved Nandaime from Volcán Mombacho, this saint's had one of the country's best parties.

International Fishing Tournament (September 14–15, San Carlos) How big was that tarpon again?

San Jerónimo (September 30, Masaya) The longest party of the year; for more Masaya mayhem, see p96.

Noche de Agüizotes (last Friday in October, Masaya) Even cooler than Halloween.

Carnaval Mitos y Leyendas (November 1, León) Same concept, wider variety of costumes.

Lavada de la Plata (December 6, El Viejo) Wash the Virgin's silver while you pray.

La Gritería (Día de la Purísima Concepción) (December 7) Nicaragua's most important Catholic holiday; if anyone asks, 'Quien causa tanta alegria?', just answer, 'La concepción de Maria!', and you might get a treat.

GAY & LESBIAN TRAVELERS

As in most of Latin America, gay and les-bian travelers will run into fewer problems if they avoid public displays of affection, and – if there's a giant Catholic altar in the hotel lobby – by asking for two beds and pushing the m together. That said, lots of Nicaraguan gays and lesbians flaunt their sexuality, so you probably won't have much problem figuring out the scene.

Get started at **Fundación Xochiquetzal** (☎ 249 0585; xochiquetzal@alfanumeric.com.ni), a gay and lesbian advocacy group, or try www.gay .com or www.gaydar.co.uk, both with lots of Nica members. There are a handful of gay and lesbian bars in Managua (p83), while Matagalpa has a gay-friendly option in Grupo Venancio (p213). We've also heard stories that Masaya's San Jerónimo festival, which features a famous folkloric dance in drag, 'Las Negras,' has a camp com-ponent involving a 'Miss' Masaya beauty contest – but you might want to confirm this with someone on the ground before showing up in your vintage RuPaul.

HOLIDAYS

National holidays are as follows:

New Year's Day (January 1) Shops and offices start closing at noon on December 31

Semana Santa (Holy Week; Thursday, Friday and Saturday before Easter Sunday) Beaches get packed, hotel rates skyrocket and everything is closed – make sure you have a place to be

Labor Day (May 1)

Mother's Day (May 30) No one gets away with just a card – more things close than at Christmas

Anniversary of the Revolution (July 19) No longer an official holiday, but many shops and government offices close anyway

Battle of San Jacinto (September 14)

Independence Day (September 15)

Día de los Difuntos (November 2) All Souls' Day

La Purísima (December 8) Immaculate Conception

Navidad (December 25) Christmas

INSURANCE

Travel insurance is always a good idea, and your travel agent or **STA Travel** (www.statravel.com) should be able to hook you up. Keep in mind, however, that Nicaragua has cheap, decent-quality health care (a doctor's visit is only US$6), so you're really only going to need travel insurance in the case of a big emergency. Make sure your bill covers emergency helicopter evacuation, full coverage for lost luggage, and other options.

INTERNET ACCESS

Internet access on the Pacific Coast is cheap (US$0.70 to US$1.25 per hour), fast, air-conditioned and widely available in towns with more than 15,000 people. The Caribbean Coast has slower, more expensive Internet, which is most certainly not widely available. Catch up on email before you head to the Atlantic.

INTERNET RESOURCES

CIA Factbook (www.cia.gov/cia/publications/factbook) Statistics and information.

IBW Internet Gateway (www.ibw.com.ni) A solid portal; also check out Xolo (www.xolo.com.ni) and Ideay (www.ideay.net.ni).

Intur (www.intur.gob.ni) The official government website is in English and Spanish, with lots of cheerful, vague information and an awesome photo gallery.

Latin American Network Information Center (www.lanic.utexas.edu/la/ca/nicaragua) An excellent portal with academic and tourism-oriented offerings.

Lonely Planet (www.lonelyplanet.com) A good online overview of the country for travelers.

Manfut (www.manfut.org) A veritable cornucopia of photos, history, myth, articles, important phone numbers and much, much more, at this huge, messy, wonderful site covering every last corner of the country.

Marena (www.marena.gob.ni) The official site of Nicaragua's system of national parks and protected areas, this site has detailed and accurate Spanish-language information about almost all of its protected areas, but no accessibility details.

Nica Living (www.nicaliving.com) Expat network and chat room with answer-filled archives to your oddest inquiries.

US Library of Congress (lcweb2.loc.gov/frd/cs/nitoc.html) Statistics and information.

LEGAL MATTERS

Nicaragua's police force is professional and visible, and not particularly corrupt by Central American standards. Some people advocate slipping traffic cops a 100-córdoba (US$6) bill with your ID to smooth out minor traffic violations, but that could always backfire, and if you get caught with drugs or committing a more serious crime, it won't be that easy to get away from the law.

People coming to Nicaragua to invest in land should talk to other expats (www.nicaliving.com is fun) and get a lawyer before handing over one red cent for that beautiful beachfront property. Between the various wars, revolutions and redistributions, there could easily be two or three parties with legitimate claims to any piece of property. Do your homework, don't rush to buy, and observe all formalities.

MAPS

Most Intur offices have regional and city maps, which are sometimes too cutesy for their own good, but can get you around town. All car-rental places have good, simple country maps; even if you aren't renting a car, stop by and ask for one.

Marena Central (Ministry of the Environment & Natural Resources; ☎ 263 2830; www.marena.gob.ni; Km 12.5 Carr Norte; ☒ 8am-4pm Mon-Fri), in Managua, has the entire country in topo maps for about US$3 per sheet, plus several colorful brochure-type maps it will let you have for free. Bring your ID to access the library.

Ineter (Nicaragua Institute for Territorial Studies; Map p70; ☎ 249 2768; frente Imigración Extranjera; ☒ 8-11:30am & 1-4pm Mon-Fri), in Managua, has the best selection of maps in the country. Most are out of print, but bring a computer disc and they'll upload the files. The website offers free maps, but they don't scale.

InMonica (www.inmonica.com) has lots of free, downloadable maps of Nicaragua that are easier to read than Ineter's.

Guía Mananic (US$6) is a little book with an OK pull-out political country map and poorly marked but accurate maps of all department capitals.

International Travel Maps Nicaragua (US$6) is the most detailed road map available, but don't trust it completely for secondary roads, which may be incorrect – confirm with a local.

Surf Maps (www.surfmaps.com) updates its solid surf map (US$8) regularly, so log on to learn about the latest discoveries.

MONEY

Nicaragua's currency is the córdoba (C$), sometimes called a 'peso' or 'real' by locals, or a 'cord' by expats. Córdobas come in coins of C$0.25, C$0.50, C$1 and C$5, and bills of C$10, C$20, C$50, C$100 and C$500. Bills of C$100 and larger can be difficult to change; try the gas station.

US dollars are accepted almost everywhere, unless they are worn or damaged. All prices in this book are given in US dollars, as costs in córdoba are more likely to fluctuate with the exchange rate. That said, córdobas are usually easier to use, particularly at smaller businesses and anywhere off the beaten track, where people might not know the exchange rate or have easy access to a bank. Always keep at least 200 córdoba on you, preferably in smaller bills, just in case. And remember, even where people are happy to take your dollars, they may cheerfully charge you a fraction more by rounding that exchange rate up.

ATMs, Banks & Traveler's Checks

ATMs (*cajeros automatícos*) are by far the easiest way of carrying money in Nicaragua. They are available in most major towns and tourist regions, with the glaring exceptions of Isla Ometepe and the Corn Islands. Most smaller towns have a regular bank (no ATM), which probably won't do credit-card advances or cash traveler's checks. Most ATMs operate on the Visa/Plus system, but BAC (Banco America Central), located in most Pacific population centers and Esso stations, also accepts MasterCard/Cirrus

debit cards. BanPro is another good bet. Most banks charge US$2 per transaction, on top of whatever your bank charges.

Many towns don't have banks or ATMs, but almost all have **Western Union** (www.westernunion.com) outlets. Traveler's checks are inconvenient, and may be changed at only some banks, for a steep fee. Leave them at home.

Coyotes

Moneychangers, or *coyotes*, are regularly used by locals to change córdoba for US dollars at about the same rates as the banks. *Coyotes*, who flash wads of cash at markets, on plazas or close to regular banks, are generally honest, but you should know the exchange rate and about how much to expect back in the exchange. *Coyotes* may also exchange certain other currencies, including euros, pounds, Canadian dollars, Honduran lempira and Costa Rican colones, for a much larger fee.

Coyotes at border crossings are much less likely to be honest (don't trust their calculators, either). Stay on your toes and avoid changing much money.

Credit Cards

Visa and MasterCard are widely accepted throughout Nicaragua – even at tiny little *pulperías* (corner stores) in the middle of nowhere – and you can almost always count on midrange hotels and restaurants to take them. In places where electricity is unreliable – for instance, most of the Caribbean Coast – credit cards may not be widely accepted, so be prepared.

Tipping & Bargaining

Tipping is expected for table service in Nicaragua, and restaurants usually include a 10% tip in the bill. Small and/or rural eateries may not include the tip, so leave behind a few coins, if you have them. You should almost always tip guides, as that's often their only salary. Tipping is optional but appreciated at hotels.

Bargaining is not really part of Nicaraguan culture, so if it's part of yours, consider toning it down. A few back-and-forths at an outdoor market or over a hotel room is acceptable; much more and it's just annoying.

Neither of these rules apply to unregulated taxis (as opposed to taxis with rates set by their unions) – so die-hard hagglers can sharpen their claws on these guys. Ask locals what you should be paying, then bargain hard before you get in the car. You should only tip a taxi driver if service was exceptional, which sometimes happens.

SOLO TRAVELERS

Solo travelers in the midrange and luxury categories will pay about 80% of a double-room price, which is annoying. Budget hotels, on the other hand, often offer per person rates on basic rooms, under US$5 with shared bathroom, around US$10 for private bathroom. Because many destinations are accessible primarily on guided tours, and those tours usually have a two- or three-person minimum, your best strategy is to stay flexible and ask at various outfitters if a group is already going somewhere.

TELEPHONE

Nicaragua's calling code is 505. From outside the country, dial 00505 plus the number as it's listed in this book. When calling between cities from within Nicaragua, just add 0 to the number. Several payphones accept Enitel calling cards, sold at gas stations, Enitel offices and some stores in C$50 and C$100amounts. You can also make calls (three-minute minimum) from Enitel offices, available in almost every town. Many homes and businesses 'rent' their phone, which is usually expensive and unable to call cellphones. Direct calls abroad using Enitel are also expensive, but any Internet café or a private booth at Llamadas Heladas, a chain of calling centers, are much cheaper.

TOURIST INFORMATION

Intur (Nicaraguan Institute of Tourism; Map p78; ☎ in Managua 222 3333; www.intur.gob.ni) government tourism office has branches in most major cities, which range from fully equipped, professional offices to private homes with one employee. They can always recommend hotels and activities (but not make reservations) and point you toward guides. Larger Inturs sell maps, give away bilingual guide booklets, have stacks of notebooks full of articles and clippings about the region, and can arrange all sorts of adventures.

Cantur is the other official tourist information outfit, with offices in San Carlos,

San Juan del Sur, Ticuantepe and other spots. In addition to offering stacks of brochures, they can also usually make reservations for hotels and guided tours.

Marena Central (Ministry of the Environment & Natural Resources; ☎ 263 2830 in Managua) administers Nicaragua's national parks and other protected areas, and sometimes – but definitely not always – offers tourist services, including guides and accommodations. It can help with access for scientists and researchers, and has stacks of data on the reserves that each specific office manages.

Alcaldías, or mayor's offices, are your best (sometimes only) bet in small towns without a real tourist office (ie most of Nicaragua). Although tourism is not the mayor's primary function, most will help you find food, lodging, guides and whatever you might need, on weekdays only. On weekends, try asking at hotels, *pulperías* or restaurants. In indigenous communities, there may not be a mayor, as many still have councils of elders. Instead, ask for the judge *(juez* or *wihta),* who probably speaks Spanish and can help you out.

VISAS

Visitors from most countries can stay in Nicaragua for 30 or 90 days without a visa, as long as they have a passport valid for the next six months, proof of sufficient funds (US$200 or a credit card) and, theoretically, an onward ticket (rarely checked). Most border crossings are relaxed. Citizens of Afghanistan, Albania, Angola, Armenia, Bolivia, Bosnia-Herzegovina, Cameroon, China, Colombia, Croatia, Cuba, Dominican Republic, Ecuador, Egypt, Ghana, Haiti, India, Iran, Jordan, Kenya, Liberia, Libya, Mali, Montenegro, Mozambique, Nepal, Nigeria, North Korea, Pakistan, the Palestinian Territories, Peru, Rumania, Serbia, Sierra Leone, Somalia, Sri Lanka, Sudan, Syria, Ukraine, Vietnam and Yemen must have a visa to enter Nicaragua. The **Nicaraguan Foreign Ministry** (www.cancilleria.gob .ni) has more specifics.

The **immigration office** (Direccion de Migración y Extranjeria; Map p70; ☎ 265 0014; ⏱ 8-11:30am & 1:30-3pm Mon-Fri) in Managua can extend your visa for up to three months, for around US$25 per month. Alternately, you could leave the country for 72 hours, which automatically renews your visa.

WOMEN TRAVELERS

All of Nicaragua (with the exception of Bluefields and the Corn Islands) was researched by a solo female traveler, who had no real problems, unless you count *piropos* (catcalls) as a problem. Nicaragua is not particularly dangerous for women, but you know the drill: dress conservatively (knees should be covered, though shoulders are OK), especially when in transit; avoid drinking alone at night; and – this is the hard one – reconsider telling off the catcalling guy, as he might become violent. Sigh. The Caribbean Coast is more dangerous in general, so all this goes double there.

WORK & VOLUNTEERING

Nicaragua is one of the poorest countries in the hemisphere, with almost 50% of its adults unemployed or underemployed. Thus, finding a job in Nicaragua is difficult. Backpacker-oriented businesses may offer you under-the-table employment, usually in exchange for room and board, but this is mostly about extending your vacation.

Volunteer opportunities, on the other hand, are common. Spanish schools in León, Granada, San Juan del Sur and Estelí always know about volunteer opportunities, or check with any *alcaldía* (mayor's office).

Centro Girasol (p213) This yummy café helps disabled kids and can help you find volunteer opportunities in Matagalpa.

Donna Tabor (☎ 552 7113; donnatabor@hotmail .com) Can arrange a variety of volunteer opportunities in Granada; two-week commitment required, restaurant experience possibly put to good use.

Habitat for Humanity (www.habitat.org) Talk to them before you come about several home-building projects, most of them concentrated in the Northern Highlands.

Potters for Peace (www.potpaz.org) Spanish-speaking ceramicists can visit as part of a social-justice oriented tour, or stay and work with Nicaraguan potters.

Quetzaltrekkers (p169) Help children by climbing volcanoes. Really.

Seeds of Learning (www.seedsoflearning.org) Sends work brigades with an educational focus to Nicaragua and El Salvador.

Selva (p185) Located close to Chinandega, this group organizes volunteers to protect nesting turtles from poachers.

TRANSPORTATION IN NICARAGUA

GETTING THERE & AWAY

Nicaragua is accessible via two international airports and six major border crossings (and two sketchy ones) with Honduras and Costa Rica. International buses and flights leave Managua several times daily for El Salvador.

Air

Nicaragua's main international hub is **Managua International Airport** (MGA; ☎ 233 1624/28; www.eaai.com.ni; Km 11 Carr Norte), a small, manageable airport that doesn't get many flights, although this is improving. It's worth checking into fares from much busier Juan Santamaria Airport in San José, Costa Rica, four to six hours by bus from the Nicaraguan border, or the international airport in Liberia, Costa Rica, just two hours by bus from Peñas Blancas. Nature Air makes two daily flights from San José and Liberia, Costa Rica, to tiny Granada International Airport (p126). Recently reapproved for international flights, at press time Big Corn Island still only had domestic services.

The following airlines fly in and out of Nicaragua, and have offices in Managua. All airlines (except Aerocaribbean) also have offices at Managua International Airport, which can be reached by the second (233 or 263) phone number given in each listing.

Aerocaribbean (airline code CBE; ☎ 270 4134; Bosques de Altamira, frente el Cine 158; hub Havana) One flight Saturday to Havana, Cuba.

American Airlines (Map p70; airline code AAL; ☎ 266 3900, 233 1624/28; www.aa.com; 3c sur Plaza España; hub Dallas-Fort Worth) Daily flights to Miami.

Atlantic Airlines (airline code FLI; ☎ 222 5787, 233 3103; www.atlanticairlines.com; 2½c arriba del Busto

---

> **DEPARTURE TAX**
>
> Departure tax is a whopping US$32 for international flights and US$2 for internal flights, payable in cash (córdobas or US dollars) only. Overland (or over-river) travelers save a bundle, as it's only US$2 to leave Nicaragua, and US$7 to come back when you start to miss it.

José Martí; hub Managua) One daily flight to Tegucigalpa, Honduras, and daily services to Bluefields and the Corn Islands.

Continental Airlines (airline code COA; ☎ 278 7033, 263 1030; www.continental.com; Edificio Ofiplaza 5, piso 2; hub Newark) Daily flights to Houston, Texas, with international connections.

Copa Airlines (airline code CMP; ☎ 267 0045, 233 1404; www.copaair.com; Km 4.5 Carr Masaya; hub Panama City) Daily flights to Guatemala City; San José, Costa Rica; San Salvador; and Panama City.

Grupo Taca (Map p70; airline code RUC; ☎ 266 3136, 263 1929/31; www.taca.com; Plaza España; hubs San Salvador and San José, Costa Rica) Daily flights throughout Latin America.

Iberia (airline code IBE; ☎ 266 4440, 233 1624/28; www.iberia.com; Plaza España; hub Madrid) Daily flights to Madrid and throughout Europe, connecting through Miami six times weekly.

La Costeña (☎ 263 2142; hub Managua) The major internal carrier has regular service to Bluefields, Corn Islands, Las Minas, Bilwi and Waspám.

Sol Air (☎ 268 3928, 233 1624/2584; Plaza España) Honduran carrier has daily flights to Miami, San Pedro Sula and Tegucigalpa.

Land & River
BORDER CROSSINGS

The Potosí and San Juan de Nicaragua crossings are basically for *adventureros* with deep pockets, or actual pirates. The rest of these border crossings are solid, and there's more information in destination chapters. It's US$7 to enter Nicaragua, US$2 to leave. Costa Rica is free coming and going, while Honduras charges US$3 entry and free exit.

Sipoá to Peñas Blancas, Costa Rica (boxed text, p159) The main border crossing to Costa Rica is a 1km stroll through mellow border weirdness; it's fast and efficient if your arrival doesn't coincide with an international bus.

San Carlos to Los Chiles, Costa Rica (boxed text, p265) Or, take an easy, breezy, gorgeous river boat ride down the egret-lined Río Frio.

San Juan de Nicaragua to Barra, Costa Rica (boxed text, p281) This expensive river adventure is usually arranged by fancy fishing lodges, but you could theoretically do it yourself.

Potosí to La Union, El Salvador (p190) Even sketchier, you could rent a boat and follow the old international ferry route across the Gulf of Fonseca.

Guasale to Choluteca, Honduras (boxed text, p187) The fastest route from Nicaragua, an easy cruise north from lovely León.

Somoto to Choluteca, Honduras (boxed text, p187) High-altitude crossing is almost as close to El Salvador, and comes with an amazing granite canyon.

Ocotal to Tegucigalpa, Honduras (boxed text, p428) See the sunny Segovias and Honduran capital, at this major, businesslike border.

Waspám to Puerto Lempira (boxed text, p237) Challenging but definitely doable, this takes you through the Mosquitia on Central America's biggest river, then a three-hour truck ride to the Miskito capital of Honduras.

BUS

Comfy international buses have reclining seats, air-conditioning, televisions, bathrooms and sometimes even food service, and are definitely safer for travelers with bags. But it's always cheaper – and more convenient in high season (November to April), when you may need reservations for international buses – to take local buses and cross yourself.

Several bus lines serve destinations throughout Central America, including San Salvador, and all of them are convenient to Barrio Martha Quezada in Managua, and have offices or stops elsewhere in the country. Check those sections for costs and schedules.

Del Sol Bus (☎ 270 2547; San Salvador US$25) One bus leaves Managua daily, stopping in Estelí.

King Quality (Map p78; ☎ 228 1454) Service-oriented line charges a few dollars more for plusher buses and food service; there are offices in Managua, Estelí and León.

Tica Bus (☎ 222 3031, Managua; www.ticabus.com) The most popular carrier serves national capitals and major cities from Panama City to the Mexican border, including El Salvador (US$25, one bus daily). In addition to the sparkling new Managua terminal, there are offices in Rivas, Matagalpa, Estelí, León, Ocotal and Chinandega; check those sections for more information.

Transnica (Map p78; ☎ 270 3133; 1c west of Esso) This smaller company serves San José, Costa Rica and San Salvador, among other destinations. There are stops in Managua, Rivas, Estelí and León.

CAR & MOTORCYCLE

You can only drive across one border crossing to Costa Rica, at Sipoá/Peñas Blancas. To Honduras, you can drive across the borders at Guasule, Somoto/El Espino and Ocotal/Las Manos.

Sea

There are no official border crossings by sea. Although you can theoretically cross the Golfo de Fonseca to El Salvador, this is not a regular crossing (you'll need to hire a private boat) and you should talk to immigration in Managua (p72) or San Salvador (p315) before attempting it.

If passport stamps are not a huge concern, there are five international ports administered by ENAP (the National Port Company), where you could catch a cargo ship: Puerto Sandino and Corinto on the Pacific, and El Rama, El Bluff (close to Bluefields) and Bilwi on the Atlantic.

Tours

Most tour offices are based in Granada, León, Matagalpa or Managua. Scores of international tours come up with a simple Internet search, or try these.

Careli Tours (☎ 278 6919; www.carelitours.com) Recommended Swiss company that runs tours in several languages to lots of destinations.

Ecotours Nicaragua (☎ 268 5299; Crowne Plaza 2c sur ½c abajo Av Bolívar, Managua; www.centralamericaexcursions.com) Offers nature-based tours.

Gray Line (☎ 266 6134; www.graylinenicaragua.com) Offers plush, all-inclusive day trips (US$45 to US$90) beginning in Managua, and ending up on yachts, in canopy tours and wandering through colonial cities.

GETTING AROUND

Pacific and Central Nicaragua are blessed with a newly paved highway system and (usually) good dirt roads to most destinations covered in this book, which are easy to see using public buses, rental cars or even bikes. The Caribbean side, however, is linked to this grid by only a few terrible roads; access is usually easier (or in rainy season, possible) by plane and/or boat.

Air

Most domestic flights are based at Managua International Airport; its occasionally chaotic domestic offices are just west of the international terminal. Other airports, many of which are little more than dirt strips outside of town (or in Siuna's case, in the middle of town), include Waspám, Bilwi (Puerto Cabezas), Las Minas (Siuna, Bonanza, Rosita), San Carlos, Bluefields and Big Corn Island. On the Pacific Coast, airports in Granada, Montelimar and near Chinandega allow charter flights.

There are two domestic carriers, **Atlantic Airlines** (☎ 222 5787; www.atlanticairlines.com.ni), with daily domestic flights to Bluefields and the Corn Islands, and **La Costeña** (☎ 263 2142; www.flylacostena.com), with regular services to Bluefields, Corn Islands, Las Minas, San Carlos, Bilwi and Waspám. Try to make reservations in advance, particularly for Managua–San Carlos and Managua–Bilwi flights, and show up early to confirm, or they may give away your seat. Domestic flights use tiny planes where weight is important and bags necessarily get left behind, so keep all necessities in your carry-on luggage. Domestic departure tax is US$2, payable in córdobas or US dollars only.

NICARAGUA ROAD DISTANCE CHART (km)

	Bilwi (Puerto Cabezas)	El Rama	Estelí	Granada	León	Managua	Matagalpa
El Rama	680 (1day 4hr)						
Estelí	498 (1day 2hr)	372 (9hr)					
Granada	576 (1day 1hr)	312 (8hr)	166 (3hr)				
León	650 (1day 2hr)	385 (9hr)	141 (2hr 30min)	138 (2hr 30min)			
Managua	557 (1day)	292 (6hr)	148 (2hr 30min)	45 (1hr)	93 (1hr 30min)		
Matagalpa	428 (1day 2hr)	353 (8hr 30min)	71 (1hr 15min)	148 (2hr 30min)	219 (4hr)	130 (2hr)	
San Juan del Sur	644 (1 day 3hr)	400 (9hr 30min)	256 (5hr)	96 (1hr 30min)	216 (4hr 30min)	141 (2hr 30min)	233 (4hr 30min)

Bicycle

Nicaragua gets a big thumbs up from long-distance cyclists for its smooth, paved roads and wide shoulders. Bicycles are the most common form of private transport in the country, and not only is infrastructure designed to accommodate them, drivers are used to seeing bicycles on the road and usually act courteously. There are also lots of opportunities for mountain biking – just find a dirt road.

Renting bicycles is difficult outside Granada, San Juan del Sur, Ometepe and León, but your hotel can probably arrange it. Rental bikes tend to be cheap, Chinese cruisers that need TLC, so test your options.

Boat

Many destinations are accessible only, or most easily, by boat. In places without regular service, you will need to hire your own private *panga*, or light boat. Prices vary widely, but you'll spend about US$50 to US$100 per hour for four to six people; tour operators can usually find a better deal. Many public boats are collective, and only leave when full – which could be tomorrow. It's easy, if not cheap, to hire boat transport up and down the Pacific Coast. On the Atlantic side, it's much more difficult.

Bluefields (p253) Boats leave daily for Pearl Lagoon and El Rama, and twice weekly to Big Corn Island. Boats run between Big Corn and Little Corn twice daily.

El Rama (p249) Boats leave several times daily to Bluefields.

Granada (p126) Connected by twice-weekly ferry service to Isla Ometepe and San Carlos; it's more convenient to get to Ometepe via San Jorge, with almost hourly boat service to the island.

San Carlos (p265) This boat transportation hub has regular service to Granada, the Solentiname Islands, Río San Juan, the scenic border crossing to Costa Rica and several natural reserves.

Waspám (p239) The gateway to the Río Coco. You can arrange private boats up and down the river, including the Honduran border crossing.

Bus

Bus service in Nicaragua is excellent if basic. Public transport is usually on old Bluebird school buses – Canadian and US visitors can keep an eye out for their old district! – which means no luggage compartments. Try to avoid putting your pack on top of the bus, and instead sit toward the back and put your bag with the sacks of rice and beans; you could also keep it on your lap. Chances are the bus will be too crowded to keep it on the seat next to you.

Pay your fare after the bus starts moving; this is a good place to change large bills. You may be issued a paper 'ticket' on distance buses – don't lose it, as that'll be an excuse to charge you again. Some bus stations, including Mayoreo in Managua, allow you to purchase tickets ahead of time; this does not guarantee you a seat. And while buses generally cruise around town before getting under way, you're more likely to get a seat by boarding the bus at the station or terminal.

Bus stations, often huge, chaotic lots next to markets, may seem difficult to navigate, particularly if you don't speak much Spanish. Fear not! If you can pronounce your destination, the guys yelling ('Managuamanaguamanagua!') will help you find and board your bus. Note that taxi drivers may lie about bus schedules, safety and more; just ignore them.

COSTS & CLASSES

Buses cost about US$1 per hour, 30km to 40km, a bit more for *expreso* buses, sometimes called *directos*, which only stop in major destinations and shave a few minutes off your trip. *Ordinarios* or *ruteados* stop for anyone on the side of the road, which makes them slightly less safe and more time-consuming.

More comfortable microbuses cost about 25% more, and are available for most major routes, with vans leaving 'when full' (about 10 people). On the other extreme, many rural destinations connected to large cities by really bad roads use covered military trucks with bench seats (sometimes called *ruteados*), which cost about the same as a regular bus.

Car & Motorcycle

Thanks to former President Bolaños' 'one kilometer per day' paving program, Nicaragua has some of the best roads in Central America, most of them empty because so few people can afford private cars. Driving is a wonderful way to see Pacific and Central Nicaragua, but it's best to use public transport on the Caribbean side, as roads are just terrible.

DRIVER'S LICENSE

Your home driver's license is good for 30 days from entering the country. After that, you technically need an international or Nicaraguan license. This is rarely checked by rental-car companies, but traffic cops will check and write tickets.

HIRE

Renting a car in Nicaragua is relatively inexpensive, with sedans as low as US$20 per day, including taxes and mandatory insurance. In rainy season, if you plan to go off major roads, get a 4WD, which will cost anywhere from US$35 to US$120 per day. Rental companies require a driver's license and major credit card, and most want you to be at least 25 years old. Renting a car at Managua International Airport costs 15% extra, so consider taking a taxi to an off-site office.

By law, you must purchase basic insurance (US$10 per day), which usually has a whopping US$1500 deductible and does not cover flat tires. You'll be recommended supplemental insurance for another US$10 to US$15 per day, but your credit card probably already covers this; call them to make sure. Double-check your tires, including the spare, and the jack, and don't be afraid to ask for newer equipment if you think there's a problem. There is a comprehensive list of rental car agencies in the Managua chapter (p87)

PURCHASE

If you're sure you want a car, first make sure that parts are available for the car: Toyota, Nissan and Hyundai are good choices. Gas prices are about the same as in Western Europe, so if you won't need to go off paved roads often, consider a more fuel-efficient sedan.

Locals often sell cars informally, but foreigners should definitely pay a lawyer to write up an *escritura,* or sales history, then register the ride at Administración de Rentas, with offices in all department capitals. You'll need emissions and equipment checks (about US$30), a Nicaraguan driver's license and mandatory car insurance (US$70 to US$100 per year). Importing a car less than five years old is possible; **Nicaraguan Customs** (www.dga.gob.ni) has details in Spanish.

If this seems like a lot of red tape, read *My Car in Managua,* by Forrest Colburn, who bought a car here in 1985. You'll be grateful for the new system.

CITY DRIVING

Driving in Managua (heck, driving period) is not recommended after dark; even if you've rented a car, consider taking taxis instead. Other sizeable towns, including Granada, León, Matagalpa and Estelí, are mazes of unsigned one-way streets that prove a boon to police officers in search of a bribe. Be careful!

ROAD CONDITIONS

There are no up-to-date maps showing real road conditions, which change every rainy season anyway. Always ask locals if you aren't sure. Older paved roads, particularly those in the Northern Highlands, are often horribly pockmarked with axle-cracking potholes. One tactic is to get behind a local driver who knows the road, and follow them swerve for swerve. Keeping an eye on older tire tracks is also helpful.

You'll often see people with shovels pointing to a dirt-filled pothole, which they just fixed for free. They're asking for one córdoba (US$.06) from you, a good way to keep both your car and your karma clean.

During rainy season, roads flood, wash away and close. Some roads are never recommended for casual drivers, including the Río Blanco–Puerto Cabezas road and the Juigalpa–San Carlos road, two of the worst in the country. And, no matter what your map says, the road from Nueva Guinea to Bluefields is ox-cart only.

ROAD RULES

Nicaragua's traffic laws are pretty standard and universally ignored, a boon to cops on the make. Officers may wave you over to and accuse you of something as vague as 'poor driving.'

Never initiate a bribe – you may get an honest officer who just wants to give you a warning. If a bribe…er…traffic fine is requested, and you don't speak much Spanish, it may be prudent to just pay it and be done with the whole sorry mess. If you do speak conversational Spanish, consider pointing out that it's illegal to pay a fine on the spot, then asking for the officer's name and badge number. This is called 'bluffing' and could make things worse, so use your best judgment. If you do get a ticket, pay it at any BAC or BanPro bank.

Hitchhiking

Hitchhiking is very common in Nicaragua, even by solo women – just stick out your thumb. Foreign women, particularly those carrying all their bags, should think twice before hitchhiking solo – remember that to some people, you look like a bag of money with tits. Never hitchhike into or out of Managua.

You should always offer to pay the driver, which will almost always be refused. Do what Nica hitchhikers do and leave a few coins behind.

Taxi

Almost all taxis in Nicaragua are *colectivos*, which stop and pick up other clients while taking a possibly circuitous route to your destination. They can get crowded.

Managua taxis are unmetered and notorious for ripping off tourists (see the boxed text, p74), and taxis at major border crossings may also overcharge, given the chance. Most city taxis have set in-town fares, usually US$0.70. Ask a local how much a fare should cost before getting into the cab.

Hiring taxis between cities is a comfortable and reasonable option for midrange travelers. Prices vary widely, but expect to pay US$10 for every 20km. As taxi quality varies widely, try to choose a comfortable, reliable-looking vehicle for longer trips.

El Salvador

You're going to El Salvador. People ask why. You tell them about the surfing, the hiking, and the museums, and they've already stopped listening. You mention being interested in the civil war and they turn around and ask you: 'Isn't it dangerous there?'

You remind them the war has been over since 1992, for more than a decade. Over longer than the war in Guatemala, in fact, and didn't your sister just spend two weeks learning Spanish in Antigua?

'But what about gangs?'

You point out that it's not as if gang members hang out on every street corner. That more tourists get robbed in Mexico or Costa Rica than they do in El Salvador. They shake their head. No, there was an article in *Newsweek*. They're not convinced.

And they may never be. You'll return with photos of cloud forests in Parque Nacional Montecristo-El Trifinio or the moonscape on top of Volcán San Miguel. You learned to surf on the best waves in Central America. You caught a funk band at a boho bar in San Salvador. You went hiking in Perquín with a guerrilla-turned-tour guide, who told you about the war as it was: terrifying, thrilling, boring, inspiring, confusing, sad. You ate pupusas in a city park, watching little boys chase pigeons.

It's hard to understand a place like El Salvador before you go. All you see are the shifting grounds: the gangs, the long war, the refugees. You don't see the broad valleys, the sudden volcanoes, the black-sand beaches, the stories told with a laugh, the people who tell them. Like a colonial church, bright blue, battered by earthquakes, El Salvador is still standing.

FAST FACTS

- **Area** 21,040 sq km (smallest in Central America)
- **Capital** San Salvador
- **Country Code** ☎ 503
- **Money** US dollar
- **Number of Animal Species** 897
- **Phrases** *Guanaco* (Salvadoran); *cabal* (right on); *Quiubo?* (How's it going?)
- **Population** 6,704,932 (most densely populated in Central America)
- **Shoreline** 307km
- **Visa** in advance US$30; tourist cards at the border or airport US$10 (for more see p461)

HOW MUCH?

- **Surfboard rental** US$10 per day
- **Museum admission** US$2–3
- **Two-hour bus ride** US$0.90
- **Internet access** US$1 per hour
- **Típico breakfast** US$1.50

LONELY PLANET INDEX

- **Gallon of gas** US$3
- **Liter of bottled water** US$0.85
- **Bottle of Suprema beer** US$1
- **Souvenir T-shirt** US$10
- **Bean and cheese pupusa** US$0.35

HIGHLIGHTS

- **Surfing** (p45) World-class sand point and right hand cobblestone breaks make surfing on the western Pacific coast tough to beat
- **Ruta de las Flores** (boxed text, p357) A string of charming western towns – visit Juayúa for the hiking and Ataco for the colonial setting
- **San Salvador** (p311) The cultural heart of the country, with a hopping nightlife, top-notch museums, and a packed events calendar
- **Perquín** (p442) A longtime stronghold of the FMLN; hikes offer incredible natural beauty and sobering sites related to the civil war
- **Suchitoto** (p377) A laid-back colonial town with magnificent views and a burgeoning arts scene
- **Off the beaten track** (p375) The backdoor to Parque Nacional El Imposible starts in Tacuba and is a long, gorgeous hike that's mostly downhill

CLIMATE & WHEN TO GO

El Salvador has a tropical climate with only two seasons: *verano*, or dry season (November to April), and *invierno*, or wet season (May to October). Almost the entire annual rainfall occurs during the rainy season and at night. Temperatures are based mostly on elevation in El Salvador. The coastal areas are the hottest, averaging between 22°C and 32°C throughout the year; the central areas vary dramatically throughout the year, from 19°C in the coldest months to 38°C in the warmest; and the mountainous areas are always cool, with temperatures averaging between 12°C and 23°C.

The best time of year to visit is at the beginning or end of the dry season, when it doesn't rain every day and the roads are in good shape; also, you avoid the holidays – Christmas, New Year's Eve, and Semana Santa – which means the prices aren't inflated and you'll have the sights to yourself.

HISTORY

El Salvador was inhabited by Paleo-Indian peoples as early as 10,000 years ago, and their intriguing paintings (the earliest of which date from 8000 BC) can still be seen and marveled at in caves outside the towns of Corinto (p451) and Cacaopera (p449), both in Morazán.

The Olmecs were the first advanced Meso american civilization, and are believed to have lived in present-day El Salvador as early as 2000 BC. The 'Olmec Boulder,' a sculpture of a giant head found near Casa Blanca in Western El Salvador, is very similar to those found in Olmec centers in Tabasco, Mexico, and suggests their early presence and influence here.

In fact, El Salvador was an important trading center, and its archaeological remains show evidence of a number of influences, including Teotihuacán and Pipil Mayan in the west, and Lenca, Chorti and Pok'omama in the east. The step pyramid ruins at Tazumal, San Andrés and Casa Blanca (and the surrounding area, much of it unexcavated) have evidence of more than 3000 years of nearly-constant pre-Hispanic occupation, and they exhibit more than a dozen distinct building phases. Though not nearly as grand as ruins in other countries, they have good museums and are worth a short visit.

When the Spanish arrived in the 16th century, the country was dominated by the Pipils, descendants of Náhuatl-speaking Toltecs and Aztecs – both Mexican tribes. It is thought that the Pipil came to central El Salvador in the 11th century, just after the Maya dynasty collapsed. They called the land Cuscatlán, which means Land of Jewels, and built their capital – now known as Antiguo Cuscatlán – outside San Salvador. Their culture was similar to that of the Aztec, with heavy Maya influences, a maize-based agricultural economy that supported several cities, and a complex culture that pursued hieroglyphic writing, astronomy and mathematics. They spoke Nahua, a dialect related to Náhuatl. Tazumal, San Andrés and Joya de Cerén all show signs of a Pipil presence.

Spanish Rule & Independence

The Spanish conquistador Pedro de Alvarado arrived in the region in 1524. He founded the colony's first capital near present-day Suchitoto (p377) before it was moved to it present location a few years later. After a year-long struggle against the Pipil, the Spaniards prevailed and laid claim to the land, sowing plantations of cotton, balsam and indigo. Throughout the 1700s agriculture soared, with indigo leading as the number-one export. A small group of the landowning elite – known as 'the fourteen families,' though in truth there were more – controlled virtually all of the

colony's wealth and agriculture, and used enslaved indigenous people and Africans to work the land.

In 1811, Father José Matías Delgado organized a revolt against Spain, but it was quickly quelled. The seed had been planted, however, and 10 years later, on September 15, 1821, El Salvador and the rest of the Central American colonies won independence from Spain. They initially joined Mexico, but in 1823 withdrew to form the Federal Republic of Central America. (Mexico sent troops to pacify its new additions, even occupying San Salvador, but to no avail.) Manuel José Arce was made president and Father Jose Matías Delgado wrote the constitution. Many streets in El Salvador are named after Delgado and Arce.

But cultural and regional rivalries doomed the Central American Republic. Perhaps more importantly, the same wealthy clique still controlled the majority of the land, and though the new constitution abolished slavery, more and more indigenous Salvadorans were left landless and

PRIMERA PONIENTE WHAT?

El Salvador's street numbering systems looks complicated, but is in fact so easy and so useful, you'll never look at street names the same way again.

First, every city has a parque central (central park). It is located at the intersection of the main calle (street) and the main avenida (avenue). The main street and avenue usually have names, which change on either side of the parque central. All other streets are numbered in relation to the two main arteries.

Here's how it works: calles always run east–west, avenidas always run north–south, including the main ones. All of the avenues west of the main avenida have odd numbers – 1a Av, 3a Av etc. All of the avenues east of there are even: 2a Av, 4a Av etc. Which means if you are looking for 5a Av, you know it is west of the parque central. Now, remember, somewhere the main calle cuts 5a Av (and all avenidas) in half. The section of 5a Av that is north of the main calle is called 5a Av Norte, the section south of it is 5a Av Sur. So if you have an address that is 5a Av Sur 100, you at least know it is west of the central parque (three blocks west to be exact) and that it's south of the main calle.

The exact same thing goes for calles: odd calles are north of the main calle, even ones south of it. And where the calles are divided by the main avenida, the eastern side is, say, 4a Calle Oriente (abbreviated Ote) and the western side is 4a Calle Poniente (abbreviated Pte).

So with any street and cross street – 5a Av Sur at 4a Calle Pte – you know precisely where it is located; in fact, you don't technically need the direction indicators, because 5a Av Sur cannot possibly intersect with 4a Calle Ote, nor will 4a Calle Pte ever cross 5a Av Norte – details, details! In large cities, like San Salvador, there are inevitably some angled streets – like Blvd de los Heroes – or neighborhoods where the numbers don't match up precisely, like the bizarre Calle Sexta Decima (Sixth Tenth St) south of Parque Cuscatlán. And you do have to remember details like 25a Av Sur being only a block from 23a Av, but 25 blocks from 24a Av! But overall, it's an intuitive system, and one that saves travelers from dragging out their guidebooks on busy corners to find out where the heck 'Maple St' is.

EL SALVADOR

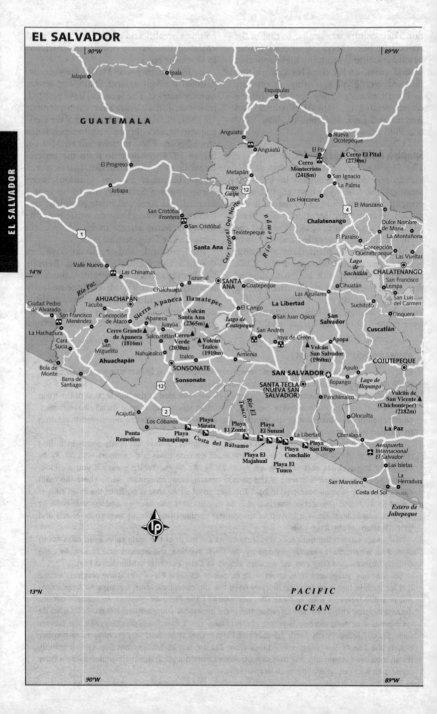

EL SALVADOR

90°W

89°W

GUATEMALA

Jalapa
Ipala
Esquipulas
Anguiatú
Anguiatú
Nueva Ocotepeque
El Poy
Cerro El Pital (2730m)
El Progreso
Metapán
Cerro Montecristo (2418m)
San Ignacio
La Palma
Jutiapa
Lago Güija
12
Los Horcones
El Manzano
San Cristóbal Frontera
San Cristóbal
Texistepeque
Chalatenango
Dulce Nombre de María
La Montañona
El Paraíso
Concepción Quezaltepeque
Las Vueltas
Santa Ana
Lago de Suchitlán
CHALATENANGO
14°N
Valle Nuevo
Las Chinamas
Tazumal
SANTA ANA
Coatepeque
Las Aguilares
Cihuatán
San Francisco Lempa
Río Paz
Chalchuapa
Ilamatepec
El Congo
La Libertad
Suchitoto
San Luis del Carmen
Cinquera
AHUACHAPÁN
Tacuba
Volcán Santa Ana (2365m)
Lago de Coatepeque
San Juan Opico
San Salvador
Ciudad Pedro de Alvarado
Concepción de Ataco
Apaneca
Juayúa
San Andrés
Cuscatlán
San Francisco Menéndez
Cerro Grande de Apaneca (1816m)
Cerro Verde (2030m)
Volcán Izalco (1910m)
Joya de Cerén
Volcán San Salvador (1960m)
Apopa
COJUTEPEQUE
La Hachadura
Cara Sucia
San Miguelito
Nahuizalco
Armenia
Apulo
Lago de Ilopango
Bola de Monte
Ahuachapán
Izalco
SONSONATE
SAN SALVADOR
Ilopango
Volcán de San Vicente (Chichontepec) (2182m)
Barra de Santiago
Sonsonate
SANTA TECLA (NUEVA SAN SALVADOR)
Panchimalco
Acajutla
Los Cóbanos
12
2
Playa Mizata
Playa El Zonte
Playa El Sunzal
La Libertad
Olocuilta
Comalapa
La Paz
Punta Remedios
Playa Sihuapilapa
Costa del Bálsamo
Playa San Diego
Aeropuerto Internacional El Salvador
Playa El Majahual
Playa Conchalío
Playa San Marcelino
Las Isletas
La Herradura
Playa El Tunco
Costa del Sol
Estero de Jaltepeque

PACIFIC

OCEAN

13°N

90°W

89°W

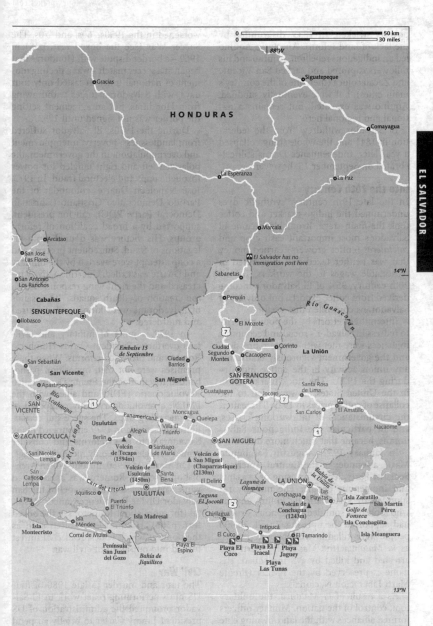

poverty stricken. In 1833, disgruntled by the lack of land reform, Anastasio Aquino led an indigenous rebellion. Aquino and his followers captured and sacked San Vicente and Zacatecoluca (then one of the country's main cities), but were eventually subdued. Aquino was executed, but remains a national and regional hero.

El Salvador withdrew from the federation in 1841 and the whole thing collapsed a year later. Independence Day is still celebrated on September 15, however.

Into the 20th Century

In the late 19th century, synthetic dyes undermined the indigo market and coffee took the main stage. It quickly became El Salvador's most important cash crop and *cafétaleros* (coffee growers) earned money that was neither taxed nor distributed in reasonable wages to the workers. By the 20th century, 95% of El Salvador's income derived from coffee exports, but only 2% of Salvadorans controlled that wealth.

Intermittent efforts by the poor majority to redress El Salvador's social and economic injustices were met with severe repression, and the government vigorously eradicated any union activity in the coffee industry during the 1920s. The stock-market crash in the United States, however, led to the collapse of coffee prices in 1929. Thereafter, the circumstances of the working classes, and in particular the indigenous Salvadorans, became that much more difficult.

In January 1932, Augustín Farabundo Martí, a founder of the Central Americán Socialist Party, led an uprising of peasants and indigenous people. The military responded by systematically killing anyone who looked or sounded indigenous, or who had supported the uprising. In all, 30,000 people were killed in what became known as *la Matanza* (the Massacre). Martí was arrested and killed by a firing squad. His name is preserved by the FMLN (Frente Martí Liberación Nacional).

As a result of *la Matanza*, the military took control of the nation. Military officers formed alliances with the land-owning elite who controlled the nation's purse strings. Few native traditions survived, and the peasants and farm workers continued to be repressed. They – and later, the Catholic Church – grew disgruntled as the economy

worsened in the 1950s, '60s, and '70s. The Soccer War (see the boxed text, p38) in 1969 – a border dispute with Honduras that began at a soccer match – was a fleeting moment of national unity. It lasted only four days, with Salvadoran forces withdrawing from Honduras, but an agreement setting the border was not signed until 1992.

During the 1970s, El Salvador suffered from landlessness, poverty, unemployment and overpopulation. In the government, the polarized left and right tangled for power through coups and electoral fraud. In 1972, José Napoleon Duarte, cofounder of the Partido Democrático Cristiano (Christian Democrat Party; PDC), ran for president, supported by a broad coalition of reform groups. His victory was denied amid allegations of fraud. Subsequent protests and a coup attempt were averted by the military and Duarte was exiled. Guerrilla activity increased and the right wing responded with the creation of 'death squads.' Thousands of Salvadorans were kidnapped, tortured and murdered.

In 1979, a junta of military and civilians overthrew President Carlos Humberto Romero and promised reforms. When these promises were not met, opposition parties banded together as the Frente Democrático Revolucionario (FDR) and allied with the FMLN, a revolutionary army composed of five guerrilla groups. The successful revolution in Nicaragua in 1979 encouraged many Salvadorans to seek reforms and consider armed struggle as the only means of change.

On March 24, 1980, the outspoken Archbishop Óscar A Romero was assassinated while saying mass in the chapel of the San Salvador Divine Providence Cancer Hospital (for more about Romero, see the boxed text, p305). His murder is often seen as the point at which widespread civil unrest turned into out-and-out civil war.

Civil War

The rape and murder in late 1980 of four US nuns performing relief work in El Salvador prompted the administration of US president Jimmy Carter to briefly suspend military aid to the Salvadoran government. But, when newly elected Ronald Reagan took office in 1981, unnerved by the success of Nicaragua's socialist revolution, his administration pumped huge sums into the moribund Salvadoran military (over US$500 million in 1985), prolonging the conflict. Guerrillas gained control of areas in the north and east, and the military retaliated by decimating villages. In 1981, the US-trained Atlacatl Battalion exterminated over 750 men, women and children in El Mozote, Morazán (see p448). As many as 300,000 citizens fled the country.

In 1982, Major Roberto D'Aubisson, founder of the extreme-right Arena party, became president of the legislative assembly and enacted a law granting the legislative body power over the national president. D'Aubisson created death squads that sought out trade unionists and others who supported PDC-proposed agrarian reform. The FMLN continued its offensive by blowing up bridges, cutting power lines, destroying coffee plantations and killing livestock – anything to stifle the economy. When the government ignored an FMLN peace proposal, the rebels refused to participate in the 1984 presidential elections, in which Duarte was elected over D'Aubisson. For the next few years the PDC and FMLN engaged in peace talks unsuccessfully. Death squads continued their pillaging, and the guerrillas continued to undermine the military powers and jeopardize municipal elections.

Nearing the End of the War

Hope for peace appeared in 1989, when the FMLN offered to participate in elections if the government agreed to postpone them for six months, to ensure the polls were democratically run. Their calls were ignored; in March of that year, Alfredo Cristiani, a wealthy Arena businessman, was elected president. The FMLN responded by intensifying its attacks and, on November 11, launched a major offensive on the capital. In retaliation, the military killed an estimated 4000 'leftist sympathizers.' Among them were six Jesuit priests, their housekeeper and her daughter, who were brutally murdered at the Centro Monseñor Romero at the Universidad Centroamerica. Today the center (p323) displays personal effects of the six priests, and of Romero and Father Rutilio Grande, as well as graphic photos of the murder scene – a recommended but deeply troubling visit.

In April 1990, UN-mediated negotiations began between the government and the FMLN. Among the first agreements was a human-rights accord signed by both parties in July 1990, but violations continued to occur. Violent deaths actually increased in 1991, the year that a UN mission arrived in the country to monitor human rights.

On January 16, 1992, an agreement – or rather a compromise – was finally signed. The ceasefire took effect on February 1. The FMLN became an opposition party, and the government agreed to various reforms, including dismantling paramilitary groups and death squads and replacing them with a national civil police force; land was to be distributed to citizens and human-rights violations investigated. In return, the government granted amnesty to those responsible for human-rights abuses.

During the course of the 12-year war, an estimated 75,000 people were killed and the US government gave a staggering US$6 billion to the Salvadoran government's war effort. Land distribution actually worked, although it was a bureaucratic process involving loans to El Salvador by the United States Agency for International Development (USAID). Unpaid loans were forgiven in 1997.

Current Affairs

El Salvador's FMLN has proven to be a model example of a former guerrilla organization successfully joining the formal political process. The left-wing party scored large victories in the 2000 and 2003 congressional elections, though without quite winning a majority. The FMLN's firebrand style has not worked on the presidential level however, where Salvadorans have elected the right-wing Arena candidate twice in a row, most recently Antonio Elías Saca in 2004.

This may have something to do with the current national obsession: crime and gangs. Saca won the presidency in large part for his 'Super Mano Dura' anti-gang plan, a tougher but more legally savvy version of the previous administration's 'Mano Dura' policy (see the boxed text, p302). The policies have had at least a short-term impact on murder rates, which for most average Salvadorans outweighs the serious human rights concerns declaimed by the left.

In October 2005, Hurricane Stan plowed into Mexico's gulf coast, sending torrential rain across southern Mexico and Central America. Most of the deaths and damage occurred in Guatemala; in El Salvador, the

MARA SALVATRUCHA

Mara Salvatrucha, considered by some to be the most dangerous criminal gang in the Americas, emerged in the 1980s from the poor, tough streets of Los Angeles, California. Its earliest members were Salvadoran, the children of refugees fleeing a US-sponsored civil war. The gang, also known as MS-13, formed in opposition to the 18th Street gang, which had roots in the Mexican barrios of Chicago, but in LA morphed into a Central American gang called Mara 18, or M-18. Today, the two gangs have around 100,000 members between them, mostly in El Salvador, Honduras, Guatemala, Nicaragua, Mexico and the United States.

The word *mara* comes from *marabunta*, a species of swarming ant, and is slang for 'gang'. *Salvatrucha* is a melding of *Salva*doreño and *trucha*, or trout, which represents cleverness. Beyond petty crime and thuggery, the *maras* are involved with Mexican and Colombian drug cartels and in the traffic of illegal immigrants at the American and Guatemalan borders. Mara 18 even has its own website: www.xv3gang.com. In January 2005 the FBI opened a major task force to deal with the Salvatruchas, and some experts have claimed (but never proven) a connection to Al Qaeda.

The rapid growth of *maras* can be traced to the 1990s, when a crackdown on LA gangs and new immigration laws resulted in tens of thousands of non-citizen gang members being deported to Central America and Mexico. Mara Salvatrucha and M-18 quickly took root, especially in El Salvador, where the end of the civil war had left a ruined economy, a lack of civilian police enforcement, and easy access to guns.

Mara members are known for their extensive tattooing, even on the face, and the gruesomeness of their attacks – machetes are popular weapons, and police have found the heads of victims in plastic bags on public benches. The vast majority of attacks are on opposing gang members, but a few incidents – like a 2004 assault on a public bus outside San Pedro Sula, Honduras, that killed 28 people – have provoked fear and calls for immediate action.

Honduras and El Salvador were the first countries to adopt anti-gang policies known as 'Mano Dura,' or 'Hard Hand.' The policies made tattoos, hand signals and writing graffiti crimes of 'illicit association,' punishable by up to 12 years behind bars. Prisons swelled beyond capacity and abuse allegations mounted. In 2003, a fire at a Honduran prison killed 68 suspected M-18 members, but an investigation found at least 59 had in fact been killed by the guards. Human-rights groups warned that off-duty officers formed vigilante groups reminiscent of government-sponsored 'death squads' of the not-so-distant past.

In El Salvador, courts overturned the more draconian measures and police have made tangible steps to improve community outreach and purge corruption. But an unnerved public continues to support hard-line policies, including sending Salvadoran troops along with police on neighborhood patrols.

Central American countries have also called on the US to stop deporting known gang members but to no avail – some 20,000 felons were sent to Central America between 2000 and 2004. And yet *maras* remain active (and are in some cases stronger) in Los Angeles, Chicago, and the suburbs of Washington DC, plus smaller cities like Durham, NC and Omaha, Neb.

For safety tips while traveling in El Salvador see p456.

official death toll was 69, with thousands left homeless by flooding and mudslides. The storm came just days after Volcán Santa Ana (aka Ilamatepec) erupted, triggering landslides that killed two, left hundreds homeless and blanketed downwind areas in thick ash, damaging coffee trees and other crops.

The Salvadoran economy grew only 2.5% in 2005 and was expected to perform the same in 2006. Though positive, it was the third-lowest growth rate in Latin America, which was itself behind other developing regions. For the first time in recent memory, El Salvador had to solicit temporary foreign workers (around 10,000 in all, mostly from Honduras and Nicaragua) for its all-important coffee and sugarcane harvests. This despite 6% unemployment (and widespread underemployment). Some experts speculate that remittances from family members working in the US are slowly eroding El Salvador's famously strong work ethic: agricultural wages are so low, and the work so physically demanding, it may not seem worth the effort to people receiving even modest monthly checks from abroad.

THE CULTURE
The National Psyche

Most people who have been to El Salvador rate its people as the best part of the country. Straight-talking, strong-minded and hard-working, Salvadorans have a powerful sense of justice and few are shy about expressing their opinion. At the same time, most travelers find Salvadorans to be extremely helpful and almost universally friendly (save the gun-toting gang members, who nevertheless show a certain charm when interviewed in the media). If you look confused, it wouldn't be out of character for a stranger to stop and ask if you need any help. And because so many Salvadorans have spent time in the USA, or have family there, quite a few speak basic or fluent English. The civil war still looms large in the psyche of many Salvadorans, as it must; not only are the memories too searing to forget, but many war-time leaders (and their disciples) remain in positions of power. At the same time, Salvadorans are genuinely dismayed to learn that many foreigners know little about El Salvador *other* than war, and they will eagerly talk up their country's parks, volcanoes and beaches.

Lifestyle

With a strong work ethic, Salvadorans have quickly raised their country from the wreckage of civil war to near the top of Central America's economic ladder. (US$2.3 billion annually in remittances from the US, or 15% of the national GDP, help considerably.) But poverty and unemployment still persist, with more than 30% of the population below the poverty line, mostly in rural areas. That said, El Salvador enjoys the highest minimum wage in Central America (about US$150 per week) and is notably more prosperous than neighboring countries. Well-to-do Salvadorans travel to Guatemala to visit the Maya ruins or to Honduras to scuba dive.

The average family has three children and both parents typically work outside of the house. Help with childcare is shared among extended family members, often falling to grandparents who have retired or work from within the home. Marriage is not as prevalent as in other Central American countries; it is not unusual to meet couples that live together in common-law unions or children who were born out of wedlock.

Education is an important part of the culture – the literacy rate is just over 80%. Even in rural communities, school lessons are heard over the radio for those children who live too far from school to attend, or for those adults who weren't able to go to school as children.

Drug use is not uncommon. Marijuana is seen in bigger cities; cocaine and crack use also is on the rise.

DO'S & DONT'S

In general, Salvadorans are very accepting people, especially in bigger cities and in towns that are used to foreigners. Still, being polite and showing respect is an important aspect of the culture and there are a few things you can do – or not do – to fit in a little better. See p22 for more tips on responsible travel.

■ Do say 'buenos días' (good morning) or 'buenas tardes' (good afternoon) when you begin a conversation or enter someone's establishment.

■ Do shake hands and say 'mucho gusto' (nice to meet you) the first time you meet someone.

■ Do dress neatly. Salvadorans are very conscious of appearances, and always wear clean, pressed clothing.

■ Don't speak loudly. Salvadorans speak their minds, but they do so quietly.

■ Don't wear tank tops, shorts or hats into churches.

■ Don't refer to the country as 'Salvador'. We know Oliver Stone and Joan Didion did it, but it doesn't mean Salvadorans like it. Keep the 'El' in front.

DISTANT FAMILIES

A photo by Salvadoran photographer Carlos Henríquez shows the living-room wall of an ordinary Salvadoran family. On it are a picture of Jesus, a poster of Spiderman and a framed portrait of a family member. The photo's title is 'The Three Heroes of El Salvador: Jesus, Spiderman and the Distant Brother.' Around two million Salvadorans – a quarter of the total population – live outside El Salvador, mostly in the USA, especially in the Los Angeles and Washington, DC areas. And, while those who left in the '70s and '80s were fleeing repression and civil war, today Salvadorans go abroad for the express purpose of supporting families back home.

Their jobs tend to be modest – construction and service work – but the impact of emigrant Salvadorans is anything but. Salvadorans send home a whopping US$2 billion to US$2.5 billion every year, or 16% of El Salvador's gross domestic product. Most is sent by individuals – a typical emigrant sends US$280 at least eight times per year – but there are also hundreds of hometown associations in the US that collect money to build schools, parks and so on in El Salvador. Hundreds of thousands of Salvadorans return for brief visits every year, making up about a quarter of the country's tourist traffic. And they return to the US carrying about $450 million dollars of 'nostalgia commerce' – things they can't find abroad, especially food items – which amounts to about 10% of El Salvador's total exports. (The cabin of any San Salvador–Los Angeles flight is full of cardboard buckets of Pollo Campero, a favorite Salvadoran fried chicken – not to eat on the plane, but as a gift for homesick family and friends.)

Salvadoran president Tony Saca has joined other Latin American leaders in urging the US to adopt sweeping immigration reform, especially for undocumented workers. As a whole, Salvadorans have a fairly high rate of legal status, thanks to amnesty programs issued to war refugees and following disasters like the 2001 earthquakes. But the president understands – like spouses, children, siblings and elderly parents across El Salvador – the importance, even heroism, of every distant brother – and sister – working abroad.

Population

El Salvador has roughly 6.7 million people. Salvadorans show more European physical traits than many other Latin American populations, due largely to the brutal repression of indigenous peoples and the small African influence. (The import of enslaved Africans was drastically reduced after a major slave rebellion was uncovered, and narrowly averted, in 1625.) Today, the vast majority of the population is definitely *mestizo* (a mixture of Spanish and indigenous) but fair skin and blue or green eyes are not uncommon. The racial figures are necessarily inexact, but the population breakdown is roughly 90% to 94% mestizo, 1% to 5% indigenous, and 1% to 9% of white European descent.

SPORTS

Soccer is El Salvador's national sport of choice. The **Federación Salvadoreña de Fútbol** (www.fesfut.org.sv) oversees the country's professional and 'minor league' teams, but there are scores of regional, school-based and local teams and tournaments. In San Salvador, Estadio Flor Blanca (35,000 capacity) and Estadio Cuscatlán (80,000) host

the country's largest games, though Santa Ana, San Miguel and San Vicente have large stadiums as well.

Auto racing is surprisingly popular as well. El Jabalí is El Salvador's modern Formula One racecourse, located 30km south of San Salvador on the highway to the airport. It hosts national and international races before crowds tens of thousands strong.

RELIGION

El Salvador, like many Latin American countries, has seen the explosive growth of evangelical Protestant churches. The fiery sermons, miracle healing, and doomsday proclamations of many such congregations appeal to those weary of the perception of many, that the country is gripped by insurmountable poverty, violence and rural decline. Yet the country remains more than 80% Roman Catholic, and has a long tradition of 'liberation theology' (see the boxed text, opposite). Before and during the civil war, priests and missionaries were outspoken critics of government repression; many, like Archbishop Óscar A Romero, were killed for their beliefs.

ARTS
Literature

Poetry is arguably El Salvador's strongest and most beloved literary tradition. Its present incarnation can be traced to the writing of Francisco Gavidia (1863–1955) and his Nicaraguan contemporary, the great Rubén Darío (1867–1916; see the boxed text, p35). Gavidia, for whom poetry was just one of many genres he undertook, was the first to voice a strong Salvadoran identity in his work. One poet influenced by those early masters was Margarita del Carmen Brannon Vega (1899–1974), better known by her pseudonym Claudia Lars. Well ahead of her time, Lars wrote spare, bold, often erotic poetry, and is widely considered one of El Salvador's foremost poets. Even more iconoclastic was poet Roque Dalton; born in San Salvador in 1933, Dalton's early work was didactic and rhetorical –

he admitted as much – but radical enough (at least in its Marxist leanings) to have him arrested and sentenced to death by El Salvador's ruling military government. He escaped execution, but vowed to perfect his craft so, if he ever were executed for his writing, it would be for good cause. Dalton was exiled several times, spent many years in Cuba, and finally returned to El Salvador in disguise to join the revolutionary movement growing in the 1970s. In 1975, Dalton was tragically executed by his own guerrilla leaders, who accused him of being a CIA spy. A prolific writer, Dalton's *Taberna y Otros Lugares* (1969) is often cited as his master work and few Salvadoran children get through school without studying at least some of his writings.

Salvador Efraín Salazar Arrué, writing under the pen name of Salarrué, is one of the country's most famous prose writers

EL SALVADOR

SAN ROMERO

Monseñor Óscar Arnulfo Romero y Galdámez served as El Salvador's archbishop from February 1977 until March 24, 1980, when he was gunned down by a military assassin while giving mass in San Salvador. Killed for his criticism of government repression, he was, and remains, a powerful symbol of 'liberation theology,' a precept which arose in the mid-1960s and which calls on Christians to work for social and economic justice. Liberation theology is especially strong among Latin American Catholics – Jean-Bertrand Aristide of Haiti, 1980 Nobel Peace Prize winner Adolfo Pérez Esqivel and Nicaragua's Ernesto Cardenal (see the boxed text, p267) are all adherents.

Though Jesuits have long practiced a form of liberation theology, the concept is commonly associated with the 1968 conference of the Latin American episcopate, held in Colombia, at which bishops decried the growing gap between rich and poor. But even before that, the Catholic Church was changing, epitomized by the declarations of the Second Vatican Council (1965; aka Vatican II) and Pope Paul VI's critique of economic exploitation in his 1967 'Populorum Progressio,' in which the pontiff implied that the poor may even be justified in armed struggle. (He later modified that position.)

Father Romero did not start out as a liberationist. He was conservative and bookish, and his elevation to archbishop disappointed progressives and pleased the Salvadoran elite. But just three weeks after the appointment, Romero's close friend, Father Rutilio Grande, a Jesuit priest and outspoken proponent of human rights, was murdered by a military death squad. Romero underwent a profound transformation, and eventually became one of the country's most prominent (and fearless) critics of government repression. He denounced death squads in radio addresses and from the alter, he confronted Pope John Paul II over the Vatican's support of the Salvadoran government, and he wrote to US president Jimmy Carter to halt arms shipments to El Salvador's military. Romero called on soldiers to disobey orders that were contrary to Christian teaching, and was threatened with death and arrested numerous times. Yet he refused bodyguards, saying 'If I die, I will rise in the Salvadoran people.'

He was right: more than two decades after his murder, Monseñor Romero's image and words appear throughout El Salvador and Latin America, in murals and sculptures, poems and songs, T-shirts and graffiti. A cause for sainthood was opened in 1997 and is ongoing; some say it's been delayed because of Romero's association with liberation theology. No matter – many Salvadorans already refer to their fallen archbishop as *San Romero*.

EL SALVADOR

FERNANDO LLORT

Born in San Salvador on April 7, 1949, Fernando Llort Choussy is El Salvador's most famous painter. Internationally acclaimed, he is known for inspiring the folk art that is created in the mountain town of La Palma, Chalatenango. His style is characterized by brightly colored country scenes painted with an almost childlike simplicity; and it is seen on everything – from keychains and pencil holders to tablecloths and furniture.

It was while studying in France that Llort began to discover this style – being in a foreign country moved him to express his cultural identity. Upon returning to El Salvador in the early 1970s, Llort moved to La Palma, a town in northern El Salvador where he had vacationed as a child. Inspired by the isolation and the mountain beauty, Llort's style began to take shape. He started the Centro de Desarrollo Integral (Center for Integral Development), a place for community members to learn about art, and La Semilla de Díos (The Seed of God; see p392), his workshop that has now become a successful artists' cooperative.

Llort lived in La Palma until 1979, when the imminent war forced him to return to San Salvador. He still continues to visit La Palma's artists to advise them about different designs and techniques. Llort also has a gallery in San Salvador called El Arbol de Dios (God's Tree; see p339), where his artwork is exhibited. His work also has adorned the facade of the Metropolitan Cathedral in San Salvador since 1998 (see p318).

Llort works in oil, acrylics, inks, ceramics, textiles and metal engravings. His works of art have been acquired by the White House, the Vatican, the UN and many private museums, and by several heads of state.

(though he wrote poetry, too). His *Cuentos de Barro* (Tales of Mud), published in 1933, is said to mark the beginning of the modern Central American short-story genre.

For more information about these and dozens more Salvadoran writers, see **Concultura** (www.dpi.gob.sv), the country's official arts and culture board, which has the latest version of its excellent *Diccionario de Autoras y Autores de El Salvador* (Dictionary of Authors of El Salvador) posted on its website.

Music

El Salvador is not known for a distinctive music style; it has not created a genre that is known as particularly Salvadoran. Instead, music is defined by what is produced by others; when you walk into a bar or you turn on the radio, you'll hear Spanish rock (mostly from Mexico and Spain), *ranchera* (from Mexico), *merengue* and *bachata* (from the Dominican Republic), *cumbia* (from Colombia), *nueva canción* (from Chile), reggae (from Jamaica), *reguetón* (from Puerto Rico and Panama), and English-language rock (mostly from the US and UK).

Still, the music scene in El Salvador – and particularly in San Salvador – is thriving. On Thursdays, check out the newspaper *El Diario de Hoy*, where you'll see listing upon listing of Salvadoran bands that are playing around the country. Among the standard favorites, you'll also find that techno, heavy metal and funk are all styles embraced and developed by younger Salvadoran musicians. For what's new – and what's hot – on the Salvadoran music scene, check out www.musica.com.sv.

Theater & Dance

There isn't much of a professional theater or dance scene in El Salvador. San Salvador's Teatro Nacional (p319) is an architectural and artistic gem – the fresco in the main hall's cupola ceiling is spectacular – but it has been closed for 'reconstruction' for the better part of a decade. Teatro Presidente (p339) has occasional performances, including theater, but its line-up is fairly traditional. The Teatro Luis Poma (p339) is a much smaller theater, but has a more varied and contemporary schedule.

As for dance, the **Teatro de Danza Contemporánea de El Salvador** (☎ 202 362 4218 in Washington, DC) is one of few repertory dance groups in the country, but it performs mostly in the United States, where it is a registered nonprofit organization. However, travelers can occasionally see dances that have been performed for centuries by local communities, and are today part of religious holidays.

The most popular dances include *Danza de los Moros y Cristianos* (Moors and Christians dance), which simulates the battles that took place in Spain between these two religious groups, complete with swords and masks. In *Danza del Torito* (Little Bull's Dance), one dancer disguises himself as a bull with horns and a long tail and several others dress as bullfighters, the fight begins with taunting chants that are sung to the beat of a drum and a flute. *Danza de los Chapetones* (Dance of the Rosy Cheeked) involves 13 dancers – 12 dressed as Spanish noblemen with fancy suits and hats, and the last dressed as the Spanish queen, complete with crown and a white dress. The dance is set to a waltz with exaggerated moves which get sloppier and sloppier as the queen distributes *chicha*, a sweet liquor that's made in rural homes, to the noblemen.

Crafts

El Salvador does not have a large variety of *artesanías* (crafts), but those that are made are distinctive and often of high quality.

Sorpresas (literally, 'surprises') are intricate miniatures that are mounted in a hollow clay egg; you lift the lid and – surprise! – there's a scene. *Pícaras* are similarly sized and shaped, but inside you'll find pornographic scenes. Both are from Ilobasco, just east of San Salvador (see the boxed text, p439).

In the 1970s, Fernando Llort (see the boxed text, opposite) taught the people of La Palma to imitate his distinctive, colorful, almost childlike painting style. Today, most of the town creates wooden objects in the Llort style.

Distinctive and beautiful, the black pottery that comes from Guatajiagua is seen throughout the country. Household items and decorative pieces are made without the wheel, and are colored using a special process.

Añil, or indigo artwork, is fast growing into a favorite *artesanía*. Workshops in the western part of the country, like **Casa Blanca** (☎ 2408 0039; Carr Santa Ana-Ahuachapán Km 74.5; admission US$2.86, parking US$1.14; ☒ 9am-4:30pm Tue-Sun) are great places to learn about indigo's history and how crafts are made. Clothing, linens, purses and other items made of cloth are dyed solid or with patterns. Students learn the techniques for creating a variety of designs; they're easy to learn but take practice to master.

The best and cheapest places to buy Salvadoran crafts are in the towns where they're made. If you're short on time, or your travels don't take you to those places, you'll find high-quality crafts in San Salvador; the boutique Nahanché (p339) is an excellent place to find a unique piece. Another good option is the Mercado Nacional de Artesanías (p340).

ENVIRONMENT
The Land

It's no wonder that El Salvador is known as the Land of Volcanoes; two volcanic ranges run east to west across the country, adding drama to almost every vista, and sometimes to daily life. Several remain technically active, mostly quiet but at times grumbling, shaking, and even spewing ashes. Evidence of volcanic activity is seen on the western coast, with its remarkable black sand beaches and volcanic rock bottoms. In the far north, mountain ranges take over where the volcanoes end and there are pine and oak trees, jagged rock formations and cloud forests.

The Río Lempa is the country's main river and it effectively cuts the country in half. The land around it is broad and fertile. Several lakes and freshwater lagoons are also sprinkled throughout the country. Although it is the only Central American country that does not touch the Caribbean, El Salvador has a Pacific coastline measuring more than 300km. This coastline is home to mangrove forests, estuaries and tropical dry forests.

Wildlife

El Salvador was drastically deforested over the 20th century, as the result of overpopulation and overcultivation of the land. As a result, many species of plants and animals ceased to exist in the country. However, national parks and protected lands still retain good biological diversity.

ANIMALS

Over 800 species of animals exist in El Salvador. Of those, almost half are butterflies – you'll see them in most of the country, fluttering about in all shapes and sizes. Birds are the next most abundant creatures, with about 330 resident species (another 170 are migratory); among those visitors may see are quetzals, toucans, herons, kingfishers,

brown pelicans, egrets, parakeets and sand-
pipers. The remaining mammal species
number under 200, and are mostly seen in
national forests and preserves – opossums,
anteaters, porcupine, agoutis, ocelots, spider
monkeys and white-tailed deer are among
the animals that can be spotted.

In all, about 90 species are in danger
of extinction in El Salvador. Endangered
animals include marine turtles, armadillos
and more than 15 types of hummingbird. In
order to help prevent their disappear-
ance, do not purchase products made from
their shells or feathers. The pet trade also
has had a major impact on the numbers of
certain birds.

PLANTS

With so much of the land cultivated, few of
the original plants still exist. In fact, only
about 2900 types exist in the entire country. Small stands of balsam trees survive
along western Pacific coast (dubbed the
Costa del Bálsamo, the Balsam Coast), and
mangroves line the many estuaries. Bosque
Montecristo and El Imposible harbor the
greatest variety of indigenous plants in their
small areas, and Cerro Verde has a good
variety of vegetation. Plants in these areas
include mountain pine, oak, fig, maguey,
ferns and orchids.

National Parks & Protected Areas

El Salvador only has four official national
parks, but you can visit a number of locally
or privately administered reserves, some of
which are detailed on the opposite page.

Turicentros

The Instituto Salvadoreño de Turismo
(ISTU) created 14 of these recreational
complexes between the late 1950s and the
1970s, the majority near lakes and natural
springs or in forests. Most have swimming
pools, restaurants, and cabins that hold
little more than a picnic table and chairs.
These *turicentros* (tourist centers) are all
close to a town and often are crowded on
weekends. The prices are roughly the same
for all: US$0.80 admission, US$0.70 parking, and US$4 cabin rental (day use only).
Most are open 8am to 4pm.

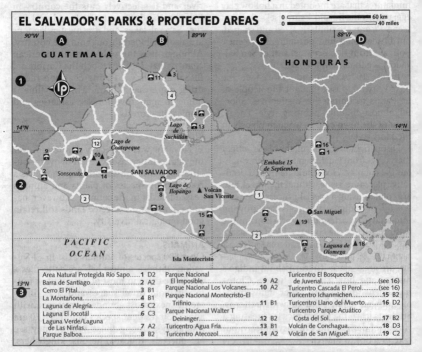

EL SALVADOR'S PARKS & PROTECTED AREAS

Area Natural Protegida Río Sapo......**1** D2	Parque Nacional
Barra de Santiago...........................**2** A2	El Imposible..............................**9** A2
Cerro El Pital................................**3** B1	Parque Nacional Los Volcanes........**10** A2
La Montañona................................**4** B1	Parque Nacional Montecristo-El
Laguna de Alegría..........................**5** C2	Trifinio...................................**11** B1
Laguna El Jocotál...........................**6** C3	Parque Nacional Walter T
Laguna Verde/Laguna	Deininger..............................**12** B2
de Las Ninfas.............................**7** A2	Turicentro Agua Fría....................**13** B1
Parque Balboa...............................**8** B2	Turicentro Atecozol.....................**14** A2

Turicentro El Bosquecito
de Juvenal.............................(see 16)
Turicentro Cascada El Perol...........(see 16)
Turicentro Ichanmichen.................**15** B2
Turicentro Llano del Muerto..........**16** D2
Turicentro Parque Acuático
Costa del Sol..........................**17** B2
Volcán de Conchagua..................**18** D3
Volcán de San Miguel..................**19** C2

PARKS & RESERVES IN EL SALVADOR

Major Park or Natural Area	Feature	Activities
Parque Nacional Los Volcanes (aka Parque Nacional Cerro Verde; p353)	volcano crater forest; beautiful vistas, emerald toucanets, jays, woodpeckers, motmots, and hummingbirds	birdwatching, hiking
Parque Nacional El Imposible (p375)	tropical mountain forest; endangered flora and fauna, rivers, waterfalls and vistas	birdwatching, wildlife watching, hiking, swimming, camping
Parque Nacional Montecristo-El Trifinio (p360)	cloud forest; spider monkeys, pumas, anteaters, porcupines, agoutis and several bird species	birdwatching, wildlife watching, hiking, camping
Parque Nacional Walter T Deininger (p397)	dry tropical forest; deer, raccoons, paca and motmot	birdwatching, wildlife watching, hiking
Area Natural Protegida Río Sapo (p444)	dry tropical forest reserve; rivers, waterfalls, white breasted hawk, swallow-tailed swift, buffy-crowned wood partridge	hiking, birdwatching, swimming, camping
Barra de Santiago (p405)	mangrove forests, estuaries, and beaches; yellow-naped parrots, white-fronted parrots and caimans	boat tours, birdwatching, beachcombing, swimming
Cerro El Pital (p392)	El Salvador's highest peak; beautiful views, pine forest, motmots, quetzals	birdwatching, hiking
Lago de Suchitlán (p377)	man-made reservoir with lush islands and gorgeous vistas; bird migration zone	boat tours, birdwatching
Laguna de Alegría (p430)	hot spring-fed lake in a volcano crater; agoutis, ocelots and coatis	hiking, wildlife watching
Juayúa Environs (p363)	dramatic waterfalls and lush coffee plantations near Juayúa	hiking, swimming, rappelling, mountain biking
Laguna El Jocotál (p429)	freshwater lagoon; migratory bird sanctuary, black-throated blue warblers, Audobon's warblers	Boat tours, birdwatching

Environmental Issues

Measuring less than 21,000 sq km, El Salvador is the smallest of the Central American countries – it's only about the size of Massachusetts (USA). It also is the most densely populated, with approximately 245 people per sq km. Overpopulation and the exploitation of the land for export crops (such as coffee, sugar and cotton) are the main culprits behind the deforestation of the land. As it stands, about 17% of El Salvador is covered by forests. However, only about 2% to 5% is primary, including 0.5% of national-park land; the rest is secondary forest, scrubland, and, perhaps surprisingly, shade trees planted by coffee plantations.

Deforestation and unplanned urban sprawl intensify the effects of the other major environmental issue: natural disas-

ters. Straddling a string of volcanoes and within reach of powerful Caribbean hurricanes, El Salvador has been repeatedly pummeled by Mother Nature. In 1998, Hurricane Mitch killed thousands of people in neighboring Honduras and Nicaragua, while El Salvador suffered extensive flooding and some 200 fatalities. Over 70,000 were left homeless; damages were most acute in the lower Río Lempa region.

On January 13, 2001, El Salvador was rocked by an earthquake measuring 7.6 on the Richter scale; 268 houses were buried in landslides and only 518 bodies were found. Exactly one month later, on February 13, 2001, another earthquake – this time measuring 6.6 on the Richter scale – struck, sending more homes and buildings tumbling to the ground. In all, 1159 people died, 8122

EL SALVADOR

EL VOLCÁN ILAMATEPEC

Just after 8:30am on October 1, 2005, Volcán Santa Ana in western El Salvador – the country's largest volcano – erupted for the first time in over a century. The 2381m volcano, also known as Ilamatepec, shot out rocks the size of cars and sent a plume of smoke and ash almost 15km into the sky. A rainwater lake that had collected in the volcano's crater instantly boiled and spilled over the lip. The shaking caused mudslides that destroyed coffee fields on the volcano's slope and killed two coffee pickers.

A 4km radius around the volcano was declared a 'red alert' zone – by 1pm over 2250 people had been evacuated from the immediate area and several thousand more in surrounding villages were warned to leave.

The eruption of Ilamatepec highlights a problem peculiar to countries like El Salvador. The slopes of volcanoes have rich volcanic soil and their high altitudes (and cooler temperatures) make them ideal for growing crops like coffee. Only three of El Salvador's 21 known volcanoes are classified as active: Santa Ana, San Miguel and Izalco. While Izalco is recognizable by its jet-black (and totally lifeless) cone, Santa Ana and San Miguel volcanoes both have extensive agricultural cultivation on all sides. This most recent eruption prompted familiar calls to restrict planting (and temporary worker housing) on the slopes of active volcanoes. But that idea seems to have little traction – within days of the eruption, even as scientists warned of another eruption coming (it never did), workers were back at the fields, readying for the harvest just a month away.

---

were wounded, and over 276,000 homes were damaged or destroyed.

In October 2005, the eruption of Santa Ana volcano and torrential rains from Hurricane Stan, just two days later, combined to unleash scores of landslides. Some of the worst damage – and greatest loss of life – was in poor areas built on step slopes or along rivers (and in some cases both).

Experts agreed that all the disasters were worsened by prior environmental damage, especially deforestation and overbuilding. Before the 2001 earthquakes, environmental groups had issued increasingly dire warnings about those very issues for a house-filled hillside in the wealthy neighborhood of Santa Tecla. When the earthquake hit, that same slope collapsed, burying dozens of houses and untold numbers of people in a suffocating wall of mud.

FOOD & DRINK
Staples & Specialties

Beans, rice and tortillas are staples of the Salvadoran diet, although chicken is a close fourth and fish is prevalent on the coast. Pupusas are a national classic – thick tortillas stuffed with *frijoles* (beans), *queso* (cheese), *chicharrón* (pork rinds) or *revuelto* (literally, 'scrambled' – a mixture of all three); all are served with a thin tomato sauce and *curtido* (pickled vegetables). *Tamales* (cornmeal stuffed with chicken, meat or vegetables) also are quite popular – if you get one with chicken or meat, chew carefully as bones are often not removed. *Panes* (French bread sliced open and stuffed with chicken, lettuce, tomato sauce and *curtido*), *yuca* (boiled, then fried *yucca* served with tomato sauce and *curtido*), and *nuegados* (balls of ground yucca fried and served with syrup) also are Salvadoran favorites.

Typical chicken dishes include *pollo dorado* (roasted chicken), *pollo encebollado* (chicken stewed with onions and vegetables) and *sopa de gallina india* (hen soup with vegetables). On the coast, you'll always find *cocteles de camarón* (shrimp cocktail), *concha* (conch) and *calamar* (squid). *Mariscada* (fish stew with chunks of lobster, crab and shrimp) also is a very popular seaside dish.

Classic desserts are *quesadilla* (a spongey cake made with cheese) and *helado* (ice cream made with seasonal fruits).

Drinks

Seasonal fruits are the base of two types of drinks: *refrescos/frescos* (fruit drinks made with water) and *licuados* (fruit drinks made with milk). Eateries often offer several varieties and encourage combinations that aren't on the menu. *Limonada* (lemonade) and *horchata* (a rice drink made with water) often fall within the *fresco* listings.

Gaseosas (soft drinks) and *agua purificada* (purified water in bottles or bags) are always on the menu; coffee (*café*) and hot chocolate (*chocolate*) are typically drunk for breakfast or dinner.

Local beers include the popular *Pilsener* and the lighter *Suprema*. Two sugarcane-based liquors – *Tic Tac* and *Torito* – also are favorites on weekends.

Where to Eat & Drink

Restaurants, cafeterias, *pupuserías*, *comedores* (cafeteria-style eateries), *panaderías* (bakeries), markets and food stands are the typical places where you'll find food and drinks. Supermarkets or corner stores also are good places to stop if you're just looking for a quick snack like drinkable yogurt, dried fruit or chips.

Most *pupuserías* and street stands start serving food around 4pm; restaurants, cafeterias and *comedores* typically begin service at 7am, with closing times that vary from 3pm to 10pm. Market stands open at 5am and usually close up by 3pm.

Bigger cities also have bars, coffee shops, and discotheques that serve beer, wine, and cocktails.

Vegetarians & Vegans

Vegetarians and vegans will have a tough time in El Salvador. Yes, there are pupusas, but mostly they're prepared with lard. Same goes with most fried foods. Your best bet it to stick to restaurants that cater to tourists; vegetarians and vegans will typically find salads, fruit plates, pasta dishes and steamed vegetables. Chinese restaurants are also a good bet. Not surprisingly, San Salvador has the most options.

Eating with Kids

Salvadoran restaurants welcome children; restaurants and restaurant-goers expect them to be around – they're part of people's families, after all. Junior menus are offered at higher-end restaurants, and kitchens often are willing to prepare something simple if your little ones have very particular tastes. Also, feel free to ask for smaller portions – that's easy enough to do.

Habits & Customs

Most Salvadorans go to an open-air market every day to buy fresh produce, dairy products and grains. They also enjoy three meals a day. The first is *desayuno* (breakfast), eaten before 9am and typically consisting of eggs (fried with tomato sauce or scrambled with onions and bell peppers), refried beans or *casamiento* (refried beans combined with rice), fried plantain, cheese, thick cream, tortillas and coffee. *Almuerzo* (lunch), eaten before 2pm, is the largest meal of the day. It typically consists of a soup, salad, main dish (beef or chicken, typically roasted or stewed with vegetables), rice and beans, and a small dessert like fresh sliced fruit. *Cena* (dinner) is eaten by 10pm and is the smallest meal of the day – either *panes* or a short stack of pupusas with a *fresco* or *gaseosa*.

SAN SALVADOR

pop 1.8 million (metropolitan area) /
elevation 621m
San Salvador is a powerhouse; the cultural and cosmopolitan heart of the country. A confident, intellectual and lefty place that's captured in its knock-out museums, heady cultural centers, war memorials, urban-hipster bars and coffee-shops-turned-artsy-film-venues. And it's a town that makes itself heard: the rush of cars on six-lane avenues, the hum of people in glittery malls, the exchange of coins on a packed commuter bus. It has a pulse.

Most travelers don't expect to find themselves in this city; reports of gang violence and stories of a brutal war that ended long ago color their perceptions before they even arrive. Like any major city, it definitely has its bad sides. Visitors should avoid Soyapango, the gangland on the east side of town (there really is no reason for travelers to be there anyhow) and should visit the *centro* only during daylight hours when it is bustling with activity. And it's no beauty – if San Salvador were a woman, you'd say she has a good personality. Make that a great personality. Because despite San Salvador's lack of colonial grandeur, it has a cosmopolitan class that's hard to find anywhere else in Central America. Explore the city – you may not snap many photos, but it may well become a highlight of your trip.

HISTORY

San Salvador was founded in 1525, by the Spanish conqueror Pedro de Alvarado, about 30km to the northeast of where it

SAN SALVADOR

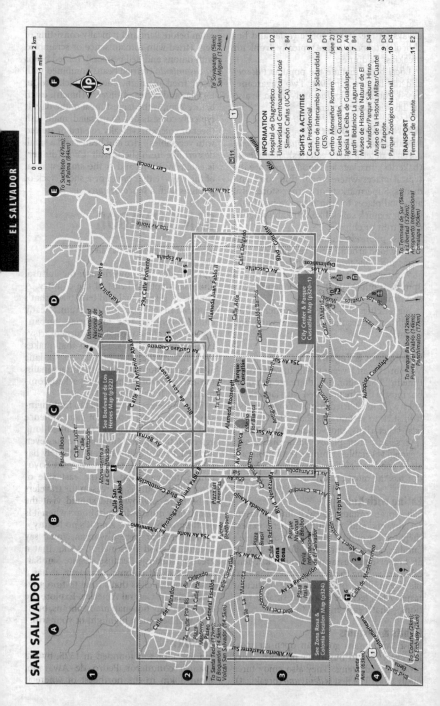

INFORMATION	
Hospital de Diagnóstico....................	1 D2
Universidad Centroamericana José	
Simeón Cañas (UCA).....................	2 B4

SIGHTS & ACTIVITIES	
Casa Presidencial............................	3 D4
Centro de Intercambio y Solidaridad	
(CIS)..	4 D1
Centro Monseñor Romero..........	(see 2)
Escuela Cuscatlán...........................	5 D2
Iglesia La Ceiba de Guadalupe.........	6 A4
Jardín Botánico La Laguna...............	7 B4
Museo de Historia Natural de El	
Salvador/Parque Saburo Hirao........	8 D4
Museo de la Historia Militar/Cuartel	9 D4
El Zapote.......................................	9 D4
Parque Zoológico Nacional..............	10 D4

TRANSPORT	
Terminal de Oriente........................	11 E2

now stands, near Suchitoto. It was moved to its present site three years later, and declared a city in 1546. It was in San Salvador in 1811 that Father José Matías Delgado first called for Central American independence; once achieved, San Salvador was the capital of the united Provinces of Central America from 1834 until El Salvador's own independence in 1839. It has been the capital of El Salvador since then.

Natural disasters have plagued the city, including more than a dozen major earthquakes (and hundreds of smaller ones). San Salvador was destroyed by tremors in 1854 and 1873, by the eruption of Volcán San Salvador in 1917, and by floods in 1934. The earthquake of October 10, 1986 caused considerable damage, and the most recent on January 13, 2001, contributed its share too.

From assassinations to student protests, San Salvador was also a flashpoint in El Salvador's long civil war. In November 1989 the Farabundo Martí National Liberation Front's (FMLN) 'final offensive' brought some of the war's bitterest fighting into the city streets. To quell the attack, government forces bombed neighborhoods thought to harbor guerrillas and their supporters; hundreds of civilians and soldiers on both sides died. The attack and counterattack left parts of the city in shambles, and proved that neither the government nor the guerrillas would win the war militarily. The stalemate lasted another 26 months before the peace accords were negotiated and signed in Mexico City in January 1992.

The declining economy during the war sparked internal migration from the countryside to the city, mostly by poor families and laborers; today over a quarter of the population of El Salvador inhabits the metropolitan area of the capital (whose residents are called *capitalinos*). Though San Salvador produces nearly 65% of the national GDP, unemployment is high and people do whatever they can to get by – vendors of all ages ply the streets and major intersections, selling everything from candy to cell-phone chargers. On buses, vitamins and other supplements are sold with special vigor and creativity.

CLIMATE

San Salvador weathers rainy and dry seasons like the rest of the country. Rain tends to fall in the late afternoon or evening,

which can complicate bar hopping but is otherwise less intrusive than you might expect. The temperature varies significantly during the year, reaching 38°C (100°F) in the warmest months and dropping to 19°C (66°F) in the coolest ones.

ORIENTATION

San Salvador sits in a large bowl, with steep hills and volcanoes on several sides. To the northwest is Volcán San Salvador, which has a high pointed peak (El Picacho) and a large lower crater (El Boquerón) (p344). Most of the city is flat, save the upscale Colonia Escalón area, which creeps up the volcano's flank. Poorer neighborhoods edge up a series of hills along the city's southern border. At the top of one of those hills is Puerta del Diablo (p344), a huge rock outcropping with views of the city, Panchimalco (p344) and the Pacific Ocean.

San Salvador follows a grid system that starts at Plaza Barrios (Map pp320–1). Two main roads intersect and change names there, dividing the city into four quadrants. The road that runs north–south along the plaza is called Av España (northside) and Av Cuscatlán (southside). The east–west road is called Calle Delgado (eastside) and Calle Arce (westside). All the numbered avenues and streets in the city ascend and descend from here.

Avenidas (avenues) run north–south, and are designated 'Norte', if they fall north of Calles Delgado, and Arce or 'Sur' if they are south of it. The avenues also are odd numbered west of Avs España and Cuscatlán, and even numbered east of it. It's confusing at first, but actually quite useful: '11 Av Sur' is south of Calles Delgado and Arce, and west of Avs España and Cuscatlán.

Calles (streets) run from east to west and are similarly ordered, using 'Oriente' (east; abbreviated 'Ote') and 'Poniente' (west; abbreviated 'Pon' or 'Pte') to indicate which side of Calle España/Av Cuscatlán they fall. Also, the streets are even numbered south of Calles Delgado and Arce, and odd numbered north of it. The odd-even thing can be tricky whether streets or avenues – it's easy to forget that 25 Av is only one block from 27 Av and more than 25 blocks from 26 Av!

There are a few thoroughfares that have names instead of numbers. Many of these run diagonally, like Blvd de los Héroes and

SAN SALVADOR IN...

One Day

First thing, head to the **Museo Nacional de Antropología David J Guzmán** (Anthropology Museum; p323). From there walk to the **Museo de Arte de El Salvador** (Museum of Modern Art; p323), or take a taxi to sunny **Parque Cuscatlán** (p319) to check out the **Sala Nacional de Expositiones** (p320) and the sobering **Monumento a la Memoria y La Verdad** (p319). After a bite to eat, the **Museo de Arte Popular** (p321) makes a good afternoon stop. Follow up with a long dinner along **San Antonio Abad** (p333) and end your day with a cold Suprema at one of the nearby **bars** (p337).

Three Days

On day one check out the **Museo Nacional de Antropología David J Guzmán** (Anthropology Museum; p323) and **Museo de Arte de El Salvador** (Museum of Modern Art; p323), and then head to **Parque Cuscatlán** (p319) to check out the sights. On day two, visit the **Museo de Arte Popular** (p321) and the **Hospital La Divina Providencia** (p323), then take a bus or taxi to Universidad Centroamericana José Simeon Cañas (UCA) to see the searing **Centro Monseñor Romero** (p317). You may be spent – at least emotionally – so either call it a day, or look into a film at the **Centro Cultural de España** (p339) or take in some music at **La Luna** (p338). Day three is for outside the city, either **Panchimalco** (p344) and **Puerta del Diablo** (p344), or the archeological sites **Joya de Cerén** (p356) and **San Andrés** (p356).

Alameda Araujo. Others are just big streets, like Alameda Juan Pablo II or Av Venezuela. A few have numbers *and* names: 25 Ave Norte is commonly called Av Gustavo Guerrero, 11 Calle Pte is known as Calle El Mirador and 79 Ave Sur turns into Blvd Hipódromo once it hits the Zona Rosa.

More than anything, proper signage is the most vexing issue – it's getting better, but is still spotty in places. If you don't see a street sign, check to see if it's painted on the curb.

Maps

The best places to find city maps are the **Centro Nacional de Registros** (Map pp320-1; ☎ 2261 8716; www.cnr.gob.sv; 1a Calle Pte; ⏰ 8am-noon & 1-4pm Mon-Fri), and the **Corsatur** (Corporación Salvadoreña de Turismo; ☎ 2243 7835; corsatur@salnet.net; Av El Espino 68, Urb Madreselva, Santa Elena, Antiguo Custcatlán; ⏰ 8am-12:30pm & 1:15-5pm Mon-Thu, 8am-12:30pm & 1:15-4pm Fri) or in hotels throughout the city (p327). For more details, see p458.

INFORMATION
Bookstores

Bookmarks (Map p324; ☎ 2224 4669; www.bookmarks .com.sv; Centro Comercial Basiliea, Blvd del Hipódromo; ⏰ 9am-7pm Mon-Sat, 10am-6pm Sun) This bookstore has a fantastic selection, though it's somewhat smaller than La Casita's.

La Ceiba Libros (Map p322; ☎ 2261 0008; Metrocentro, 1st fl, Blvd de los Héroes; ⏰ 9am-7pm Mon-Sat, 10am-5pm Sun) You'll find a good selection of Spanish-language books here, especially if you're interested in Salvadoran history and literature.

La Maya Hatcha (Map p322; ☎ 2260 3638; Metrocentro, 1st fl, Blvd de los Héroes; ⏰ 10am-7pm) A decent option if you're hankering for a thick English-language novel – classic or trashy – for the road.

Librería La Casita (Map p324; ☎ 2224 6103; www.la casitaonline.com, in Spanish; Plaza San Benito, Calle La Reforma; ⏰ 9am-7pm Mon-Sat) Hidden in a small shopping center is arguably the best English-language reading selection in town. It has rows and rows of reading material, from fashion magazines to highbrow literature, plus a huge guidebook section in case you left yours behind.

Cultural Centers

Alliance Française (Map pp320-1; ☎ 2260 5807; www .afelsalvador.com, in French & Spanish; 51a Av Norte 152; ⏰ 8am-12:30pm & 2:30-7pm Mon-Thu, 8am-12:30pm Fri, 8am-4pm Sat) Although primarily a French-language school, this center offers a wide range of weekly events to the public. Saturday programming is particularly popular, as it often includes spoken word, dance and music performances.

Casa de la Cultura de la Colonia Centroamérica (Map p322; ☎ 2260 2882; Calle Gabriela Mistral 533; ⏰ 7:30am-5pm Mon-Fri, 8am-noon Sat) This center offers music, art, and fitness classes that typically run for six weeks (US$13 to US$35). Occasional films and performances also are programmed, and weekend excursions to Copán, Honduras, are in the works.

Casa de la Cultura del Centro de San Salvador
(Map pp320-1; ☎ 2212 2016; 1 Calle Pte 822; ⊗ 8am-4pm Mon-Sat) This cultural center offers a number of courses, including painting, guitar and pottery. Most are several months in duration – best for people volunteering or taking Spanish classes in town. Art exhibits and semi-regular cultural events are also regularly scheduled.

Centro Cultural de España (Map p324; ☎ 2275 7526; Calle La Reforma 166; ⊗ 9am-5pm Mon-Thu, 9am-2pm Fri) A well-funded Spanish cultural center that offers a great variety of weekly events, including concerts, talks, dance performances, films…even puppet shows! It also boasts a small but excellent modern art gallery.

Emergency

Police (Map p322; ☎ 2261 0630, 911; Calle Berlín; ⊗ 24hr)

Immigration

Immigration Office (Direccíon General de Migración y Extranjería; Paseo General Escalón Map p324; ☎ 2202 9650; Galerías Escalón, street level; ⊗ 9am-5pm Mon-Fri, 9am-1pm Sat; City Center Map pp320-1; ☎ 2221 2111; Centro de Gobierno, 9a Calle Pte & 15a Av Norte; ⊗ 9am-5pm Mon-Fri, 9am-1pm Sat) Both offices deal with visa renewals and other immigration matters.

Internet Access

Internet cafés are a dime a dozen around San Salvador. Most charge around US$1 per hour for Internet access, and can download photos and burn them onto CDs for a couple of bucks. Many also offer telephone services.

CITY CENTER

Cíber Snack (Map pp320-1; cnr 2a Av Sur & 4a Calle Ote; per hr US$1; ⊗ 7:30am-6:30pm Mon-Sat) Enjoy a banana *licuado* (smoothie) while you check your email.

PARQUE CUSCATLÁN

Infocentros (Map pp320-1; ☎ 2502 9713; 19a Av Norte; per hr US$1; ⊗ 7am-8:30pm Mon-Fri, 7am-6pm Sat) International phone calls also available (to the US per min US$0.10, Europe per min US$0.30, Asia per min US$0.50).

BOULEVARD DE LOS HÉROES

Cyber Café Genus (Map p322; ☎ 2226 5221; Av Izalco 102-A; per hr US$1; ⊗ 9am-11pm Mon-Fri, 10am-8pm Sat & Sun) One of the only Internet cafés in town that stays open late. CD burning available (US$1.50).

PC Station (Map p322; ☎ 2257 5791; Metro Sur, Blvd de los Héroes; per hr US$1; ⊗ 7am-10pm Mon-Sat, 9am-7pm Sun) CD burning (US$2) and web-based international

phone calls (to the US per min US$0.09, Europe per min US$0.11, Asia per min US$0.14) available.

ZONA ROSA & COLONIA ESCALÓN

Infocentros (Map p324; ☎ 2223-0586; Blvd Hipódromo 324; per hr US$1.50; ⊗ 8am-7pm Mon-Fri, Sat 8am-5pm) Even Infocentros raises its prices in the Zona Rosa. Services including CD burning (US$3) and web-based international phone calls (to the US per minute US$0.10, to Mexico per minute US$0.25, to Europe per minute US$0.25 to US$0.40) are offered.

Laundry

Many hotels provide laundry service to their guests. Just be sure to ask if the cost is *por maquina* (per load) or *por pieza* (piece-meal) – nothing hurts more than having to shell out US$10 to wash a few ratty T-shirts and a pair of jeans.

Lavapronto (Map p322; ☎ 2260 1702; Av Los Sisimiles 2949; per load US$4; ⊗ 7am-6pm Mon-Fri, 7am-5pm Sat) Same-day service available.

Media

BULLETIN BOARDS

All of the following have large bulletin boards where upcoming concerts, films, talks and other cultural events are advertised:

La Ventana (Map p322; ☎ 2226 5129; cnr Calle San Antonio Abad & Av San José)

Café La 'T' (Map p322; ☎ 2225 2090; Calle San Antonio Abad 2233; ⊗ 10am-9:30pm Mon-Wed, 10am-11pm Thu-Sat)

Ximena's Guest House (Map p322; ☎ 2260 2481; www.ximenasguesthouse.com; Calle San Salvador 202)

Centro Cultural de España (Map p324; ☎ 2275 7526; Calle La Reforma 166; ⊗ 9am-5pm Mon-Thu, 9am-2pm Fri)

MAGAZINES

Travelers should pick up a copy of **Revue** (www.revuemag.com), a free English-language magazine with a small but informative section on El Salvador. Articles describe lesser-known activities around the country, and the magazine regularly reviews new accommodations and tourist sites.

Pashalua (www.pashalua.com) is a spin-off of *Revue*, focused on arts and entertainment in El Salvador. It's a terrific little magazine – most useful is the cultural events calendar for San Salvador, Suchitoto and Santa Ana. Both magazines can be found in hotels and restaurants in the area.

El Salvador Turístico is an excellent bilingual (Spanish and English) magazine, which includes a general overview of El Salvador's regions, including the country's historical and touristed sights, listings of restaurants and hotels, telephone numbers for embassies, airlines, bus terminals and car-rental agencies, and a few decent maps. It's a great complement to this guidebook.

NEWSPAPERS
San Salvador's main newspapers are **La Prensa Gráfica** (www.laprensa.com.sv, in Spanish) and the conservative **El Diario de Hoy** (www.elsalvador.com, in Spanish); check them for domestic and international news, plus entertainment listings. *El Mundo* and *El Latino* are thinner afternoon newspapers. *Más*, another afternoon newspaper, provides heavy coverage of crime and sports.

WEBSITES
In addition to the websites of the magazines and newspapers listed earlier, check out the following:

Encuentroselfaro.net (www.encuentroselfaro.net, in Spanish) Hosts online discussions every two weeks on issues in Salvadoran politics.

Musica.com.sv (www.musica.com.sv) Excellent website dedicated to the Salvadoran music scene – from weekly events to MP3 downloads.

Medical Services
CITY CENTER
Farmacia Principal (Map pp320-1; ☎ 2222 8093; Calle Delgado 227; ☽ 8:30am-8pm)

BOULEVARD DE LOS HÉROES
Farmacia Rowalt (Map p322; ☎ 2261 0515; Av Los Sisimiles; ☽ 24hr) The only 24-hour pharmacy in this neighborhood. If it looks closed, just ring the bell. Delivery available from 8am to 5pm. It's near Av Sierra Nevada.

Hospital Bloom (☎ 2225 4114; Blvd de los Héroes at Av Gustavo Guerrero/25a Av Norte; ☽ 24hr) Large public hospital specializing in treatment of children but with services for all. Expect long lines.

Hospital de Diagnóstico (☎ 2226 8878; Calle 21 Pte at 2a Diagonal; ☽ 24hr) An excellent hospital with reasonable prices.

ZONA ROSA & COLONIA ESCALÓN
Farmacia Super Medco (Map p324; ☎ 2243 3599; cnr Av La Revolución & Blvd Hipódromo; ☽ 24hr) Between 11pm and 7am use the service window on Blvd Hipódromo.

Hospital Diagnóstico Escalón (Map p324; ☎ 2264 4422; 3a Calle Pte; ☽ 24hr) One of the best private hospitals in the country, and it accepts most US and European insurance plans. Recommended by the US embassy.

Money
Banks and 24-hour ATMs are readily available throughout the capital, and issue US dollars.

CITY CENTER
Avoid withdrawing money in the city center. Your best assurance against petty crime is having (or appearing to have) nothing worth stealing.

Banco Cuscatlán (Map pp320-1; Av Cuscatlán; ☽ 9am-4pm Mon-Fri, 9am-noon Sat)

Scotiabank (Map pp320-1; 2a Calle Poniente; ☽ 9am-5pm Mon-Fri, 9am-noon Sat)

Scotiabank (Map pp320-1; Calle Arce; ☽ 9am-5pm Mon-Fri, 9am-noon Sat)

BOULEVARD DE LOS HÉROES
Scotiabank (Map p322; ☎ 2260 9038; Metro Sur, Blvd de los Héroes; ☽ 9am-5pm Mon-Fri, 9am-noon Sat)

Banco Cuscatlán (Map p322; ☎ 2212 2000 ext. 4205; Av Izalco; ☽ 9am-4pm Mon-Fri, 9am-noon Sat)

ZONA ROSA & COLONIA ESCALÓN
Banco de América Central (Map p324; ☎ 2254 9980; Paseo General Escalón; ☽ 8am-5pm Mon-Fri, 8am-2pm Sat)

Post
Correos Central (Map pp320-1; Centro Gobierno; ☽ 7:30am-5pm Mon-Fri, 8am-noon Sat) This is the main post office.

Correos Central branch office (Map p322; Metrocentro, 2nd fl, Blvd de los Héroes; ☽ 8am-7pm Mon-Fri, 8am-noon Sat)

DHL (Map p324; ☎ 2264 2708; Av Alberto Masferrer Norte; ☽ 8am-5pm Mon-Fri, 8am-noon Sat)

Tourist Information
San Salvador doesn't have an ordinary walk-up tourist office, but most of the government offices and agencies that oversee parks and protected areas around the country are located here. For how to get current information on goings-on around town, see Media (p315).

Concultura (Consejo Nacional para la Cultura; Map pp320-1; ☎ 2221 4389; www.concultura.gob.sv; Centro Gobierno, Edif A-5; ☽ 8am-4pm Mon-Fri) Oversees El Salvador's main cultural activities and sights, including museums, archaeological sites and cultural centers. General information is available at the main office, and its website is excellent.

Corsatur (Corporación Salvadoreña de Turismo; ☎ 2243 7835; corsatur@salnet.net; Av El Espino 68, Urb Madreselva, Santa Elena, Antiguo Custcatlán; ☺ 8am-12:30pm & 1:15-5pm Mon-Thu, 8am-12:30pm & 1:15-4pm Fri) Headquartered outside of town, Corsatur gives out maps, brochures and a semi-useful glossy magazine. It also has an oft-unstaffed desk at the airport, with the same materials.

ISTU (Instituto Salvadoreño de Turismo; Map pp320-1; ☎ 2222 8000; istu@mh.gob.sv; Calle Rubén Darío 619; ☺ 8:30am-12pm & 1-4pm Mon-Sat) Provides general information about El Salvador's national parks and *turicentros* (government-run recreational centers). It also oversees the Parque Nacional Walter T Deininger (p397) near La Libertad; technically you're supposed to call ISTU first to visit the park, but you can usually just show up.

Ministerio de Medio Ambiente (Map p324; ☎ 2267 6276; www.marn.gob.sv; Alameda Araujo/Carr a Santa Tecla Km 5.5; ☺ 7:30am-12:30pm & 1:30-3:30pm Mon-Fri) Manages the Parque Nacional Montecristo-El Trifinio near Metapán. You need permission to stay overnight in the park, and even daytrippers should call ahead to be sure there isn't a big group headed there at the same time. Permits are issued in person or by fax; for details see p360.

Ministerio de Trabajo (Map p324; ☎ 2298 8739; Calle Nueva Dos 19; ☺ 8am-12:30pm & 1:30-4pm Mon-Fri) Issues permits to stay at one of the four government-run workers' vacation centers, located at Lago de Coatepeque, El Tamarindo, La Palma and La Libertad. You must apply in person, and bring your passport, the number of people in your group, and exactly where and how long you want to stay. Plan your stay between Wednesday and Saturday – the centers are closed Monday and Tuesday, and are normally reserved for workers on weekends. Call ahead and the staff should be able to process the paperwork while you wait. Otherwise you may have to come back a day or two later for your approval.

SalvaNatura (Fundación Ecológica de El Salvador; Map pp320-1; ☎ 2279 1515; www.salvanatura.org, in Spanish; 33a Av Sur 640; ☺ 8am-12:30pm & 2-5:30pm Mon-Fri; phone service only Sat & Sun) The friendly, competent staff here manage Parque Nacional El Imposible (p375) and Parque Nacional Los Volcanes (p353), among other areas. Call before visiting either park; see relevant sections for details. The office has some handy brochures on its facilities and protected areas in general.

Tour Operators

Akwaterra (☎ 2263 2211, in US 410 923 0737; www.akwaterra.com) Run by Julio and Gaby Vega, an English-speaking Salvadoran couple, this outfitter offers top-notch eco-adventure tours, both 'akwa' (like surfing and kayaking) and 'terra' (including hiking, horseback riding and mountain biking). Transport and accommodations can be arranged, either on the beach or at a beautiful artsy cabin on a coffee plantation north of Juayúa (p363). The business

has no office, but does have a terrific website with detailed information. All tours can be personalized.

El Salvador Divers (Map p324; ☎ 2264 0961; www.elsalvadordivers.com; 3a Calle Pte; ☺ 9am-6:30pm Mon-Fri, 9am-1pm Sat) A friendly, professional, five-star dive shop offering all levels of scuba instruction, and fun dives in Lago Ilopango, Lago Coatepeque and in the Pacific near Los Cóbanos. Open-water courses cost US$300, two-tank fun dives US$65; multiday lake trips may include free lodging. The shop also organizes occasional excursions to Roatán, Honduras, including air travel, room, board, drinks, and between four and 10 dives (2/4 days per person US$290/599). English and Spanish are spoken; instructional material in additional languages is available.

Reyna Tours (☎ 2271 8433; www.reynatours.com, in Spanish; Puerto Bus Terminal, Local 14-A; cnr Alameda Juan Pablo II & 19a Av Norte; ☺ 8am-noon & 2-6pm Mon-Fri) Specializing in 'war tourism,' with trips near and around Cerro Guazapa, a former FMLN stronghold and the scene of bitter fighting. Tours explore the day-to-day reality of guerrilla life and warfare by visiting trenches, field hospitals and *tatús* – tunnels and underground rooms dug by rebel soldiers – preserved from the war years. Custom tours are available with prices from US$18 per person; minimum four people. Call for details (they'll often answer at night and on weekends).

Ríos Aventuras (☎ 2298 0335) El Salvador's only rafting outfit offers fun one- and two-day white-water rafting trips down various segments of the Río Lempa, Río Paz and Río Banderas. Rapids range from Class I to Class V, depending on the route you choose and the time of year. Day trips include two to three hours of rafting, breakfast, lunch, snacks and transportation. The average cost is US$60 per person for groups of up to seven; US$55 per person for eight or more.

Turismo (Map p324; ☎ 2211 8583; www.turismo.com.sv; 9a Calle Pte at 81a Calle Norte, Colonia Escalon; ☺ 8am-12:30pm & 1:30-6pm Mon-Fri) Corsatur-certified and professionally trained guides that offer customized tours to every region of El Salvador. English, German and French are spoken.

Travel Agencies

For a reliable travel agency, visit **U-Travel** (www.utravel.com; Zona Rosa Map p324; ☎ 2505 0566; Av La Revolución 3; ☺ 8am-6pm Mon-Fri, 8am-5pm Sat; Colonia Escalón Map p324; ☎ 2263 2494; World Trade Center, cnr 89a Av Norte & Calle del Mirador; ☺ 8am-7pm Mon-Fri, 8am-12:30pm Sat).

Universities

San Salvador has two major universities and a number of smaller ones. Travelers are most likely to have heard of **Universidad Centroamericana José Simeon Cañas** (UCA; Map p312; Calle de Mediterráneo), whose campus and students figured prominently in the civil war. At UCA, pronounced *oo*-ka, the Centro Monseñor Romero (p323) commemorates the assassinated archbishop and other fallen religious workers, including six Jesuit priests who were murdered at the center itself in 1989. The **Universidad Nacional de El Salvador** (Map p322; Blvd Universitario), not far from the Blvd de los Héroes area, also saw much student organization (and repression), though it now makes for a pleasant stroll. Smaller colleges include the **Universidad Tecnológica** (Map pp320-1; Calle Arce) near Parque Cuscatlán, and **Universidad Francisco Gavidia** (Map pp320-1; Alameda Roosevelt).

EL SALVADOR

DANGERS & ANNOYANCES

Crime is a serious problem in San Salvador and the country as a whole. However, the vast majority of El Salvador's violent crimes – including around 3000 murders yearly – are committed by and upon rival gang members. Assaults on tourists are extremely rare, especially in well-trafficked areas and tourist sites, where the police are quick to hustle away any suspected troublemakers. Pick-pocketing is somewhat more of a concern; always be aware of your belongings (especially on crowded buses and in market areas), and avoid flaunting cash, jewelry or other valuables. If you're going to the center of town, leave your camera at the hotel.

Taxis are safe, reliable and cheap – you can go anywhere in the city for US$3 to US$5 – so take them at night, especially if you've been drinking and/or you're un familiar with the area you're in. Blvd de los Héroes, Zona Rosa and Colonia Escalón are quite safe day and night, especially if you stick to busy streets. (The shortcut from Blvd de los Héroes to Ximena's Guest House and La Estancia should not be used at night, however.) You should not walk around the city center or the Parque Cuscatlán area after dark. As everywhere, common sense will steer you clear of almost all trouble.

Pollution is perhaps a bigger annoyance, as it's held in place by the mountains surrounding San Salvador. Thick vehicle exhaust fumes, especially from buses, can leave you with runny eyes and a sore throat. For some reason, many travelers catch a cold in San Salvador – eat right and be extra careful about germs.

SIGHTS & ACTIVITIES

City Center

A wander through central San Salvador (known to everyone as *'el centro'*) can feel like a descent into the maelstrom, with crowds pushing through sprawling markets, music blaring from every direction and buses zig-zagging around at breakneck speed. But you'll soon get your bearings, and if you like cities you'll appreciate the center's gritty vitality. Beyond the setting, there are some genuinely interesting things to see here, not the least of which is the tomb of Archbishop Romero, in the lower floor of the Catedral Metropolitana (below).

The cathedral faces the main plaza, called **Plaza Barrios** (Map pp320–1) and dedicated to a former president and crusader for the separation of church and state. There is a statue of Barrios astride a horse in the middle of the plaza, turned to face the cathedral and streaked (of course) with pigeon shit. The Palacio Nacional is on the west side of the plaza and all the trees have been removed directly in front of it – the view is clear, but the stone-paved plaza can get hot in the afternoon as a result. Plaza Barrios is where most political protests begin or end (on our last visit, a group of family members and advocates for imprisoned gang members took control of the cathedral to protest new highly restrictive incarceration laws – they left peacefully after a few days).

Two blocks east is **Parque Libertad** (Map pp320–1), with a winged statue of Liberty in the middle. This is the more pleasant of the two plazas, with islands of grass and trees, and many benches to sit on. The traffic is still loud – and this is the end of the line for a number of local bus services – but the park is as good a place as any to relax and take in the scene.

Both plazas are relatively safe, but always be aware of your surroundings and don't linger after dark. And it's probably best not to bring your camera – though you'll regret not being able to capture some of the scenes down there! Foreigners are already a rare sight downtown – you may be the only one when you visit – and it's just not worth drawing the extra attention to yourself.

CATEDRAL METROPOLITANA

San Salvador's **Metropolitan Cathedral** (Map pp320–1; 7am-7pm) faces Plaza Barrios and marks the center of the city's street grid. Completed in 1999, after years of renovation, the cathedral stands on the site of an earlier version that burned in 1956. The beige stucco building has two bell towers rising above a blue and yellow checker-patterned dome. The facade is painted with the colorful campesino motifs of La Palma painter Fernando Llort; you can see Llort's schematic paintings at his gallery, El Arbol de Dios (p339). One level beneath the cavernous nave is the tomb of Archbishop Oscar A Romero, though this is not the church he was assassinated in, as visitors sometimes mistakenly believe (that was the chapel at the Hospital La Divina Providencia; p323). Romero's tomb is the final receptacle of a steady supply of flowers, political missives and religious pilgrimages. Pope John Paul II knelt here on his visit in March 1993, and was captured in a famous photo.

IGLESIA EL ROSARIO

What appears from the outside like a dilapidated airport hangar is, in fact, one of the most intriguing churches in the country. After entering through an easy-to-miss corridor, you'll see that **Iglesia El Rosario** (Map pp320-1; 4 Calle Ote 23; admission free; ☺ 6am-noon & 2-7pm) opens into a shallow nave backed by a high brick wall and soaring arched roof above. The roof isn't a true arch, though, but a series of overhanging steps inset with a rainbow of stained-glass panels. On the walls are figures made of scrap metal, with larger, more detailed stone and metal statues displayed in the wings on either side of the main entrance. Besides the simple beauty of the place, the contrasts are striking – the modern industrial-style artwork, the quiet austerity of a church and the gritty bustle of downtown San Salvador just outside the door. Padre Delgado, the father of Central American independence, is buried here.

OTHER HISTORICAL BUILDINGS

Government headquarters until the devastation of the 1986 earthquake, the ornate **Palacio Nacional** (Map pp320-1; Calle Rubén Darío at Av Cuscatlán; ☺ 8am-5pm) occupies the west side of Plaza Barrios. Built in the early 20th century with Italian marble, the palace displays the classical style fashionable at the time. The imposing **Biblioteca Nacional** (Map pp320-1; ☎ 2221 6312; www.binaes.gob.sv; 4a Calle Ote at 2a Av

Sur; ☺ 8am-4pm Mon-Fri) is on the plaza's south end. The **Teatro Nacional** (Map pp320-1; Calle Delgado), east of the cathedral, was originally erected in 1917, but languished as a movie house for 50-odd years before being renovated in opulent style, with ornate gilt boxes and trimmings, lots of lush red velvet and a sensuous ceiling mural. West down Calle Gerardo Barrios, at 3a Av Sur, you'll see the Gothic towers of the decaying **Iglesia El Calvario** (Map pp320-1).

Parque Cuscatlán

This is a pleasant **park** (Map pp320-1; ☺ 6am-6pm Tue-Sun), with lots of benches beneath the shade of large trees. Kids play soccer on islands of grass, while women sell pupusas and other snacks from stands set up on gravel roads between them. Around the park are three excellent stops – Tin Marín children's museum (p327), the Sala Nacional de Exposiciones (National Exposition Hall) and the sobering Monumento a la Memoria y la Verdad (Monument to Memory and Truth).

This neighborhood is home to both the **Estadio Mágico González** (Estadio Flor Blanco; Map pp320-1; 49 Av Sur), where soccer games and occasional rock concerts are held, and the **Gimnacio Nacional Alfredo Piñeda** (Map pp320-1; Parque Cuscatlán), whose basketball and volleyball courts, and steep bleacher seats go largely unused. However, the park and three sites around it are well worth visiting.

MONUMENTO A LA MEMORIA Y LA VERDAD

Built in 2003, and emulating the Vietnam Memorial in Washington, DC, the **Monument to Memory and Truth** (Map pp320-1; admission free; ☺ 6am-6pm Tue-Sun) displays the names of over 25,000 people who were killed or disappeared in the repression of the 1970s and the civil war from 1980 to 1992. A number of famous names appear on the monument's austere 85m-long black granite panels – including Roque Dalton and Rutilio Grande – but the lasting power of the monument is in the staggering number of mostly faceless and (save for here) nameless men, women and children who were killed in this most brutal of civil conflicts. Notice how many died and disappeared in the war's early years, from 1980 to 1983. It's a moving and worthy stop.

EL SALVADOR

CITY CENTER & PARQUE CUSCATLÁN

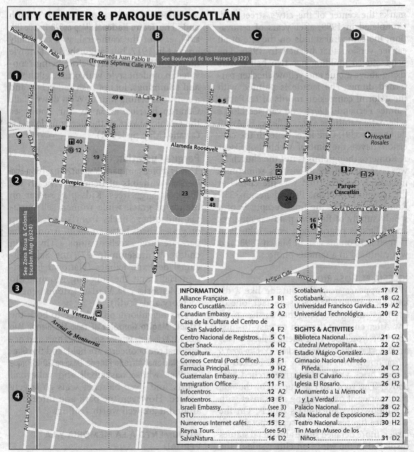

INFORMATION		
Alliance Française	1	B1
Banco Cuscatlán	2	G3
Canadian Embassy	3	A2
Casa de la Cultura del Centro de		
San Salvador	4	F2
Centro Nacional de Registros	5	C1
Cíber Snack	6	H2
Concultura	7	E1
Correos Central (Post Office)	8	F1
Farmacia Principal	9	H2
Guatemalan Embassy	10	F2
Immigration Office	11	F1
Infocentros	12	A2
Infocentros	13	E1
Israeli Embassy	(see 3)	
ISTU	14	F2
Numerous Internet cafés	15	E2
Reyna Tours	(see 54)	
SalvaNatura	16	D2

Scotiabank	17	F2
Scotiabank	18	G2
Universidad Francisco Gavidia	19	A2
Universidad Technológica	20	E2
SIGHTS & ACTIVITIES		
Biblioteca Nacional	21	G2
Catedral Metropolitana	22	G2
Estadio Mágico González	23	B2
Gimnacio Nacional Alfredo		
Piñeda	24	C2
Iglesia El Calvario	25	G3
Iglesia El Rosario	26	H2
Monumento a la Memoria		
y la Verdad	27	D2
Palacio Nacional	28	G2
Sala Nacional de Exposiciones	29	D2
Teatro Nacional	30	H2
Tin Marín Museo de los		
Niños	31	D2

Sala Nacional de Exposiciones (Map pp320-1; ☎ 2222 4959; admission free; ☑ 9am-noon & 2-5pm Tue-Sun), at the north side of Parque Cuscatlán, is an art gallery tucked in next to the Monumento a la Memoria y a la Verdad. Exhibits change frequently and are often among the best in the city.

Boulevard de los Héroes
MUSEO DE LA PALABRA Y LA IMAGEN

In its brand-new location, the **Museum of Word and Image** (Map p322; ☎ 2275-4870; 27 Av Norte 1140; www.museo.com.sv, in Spanish; admission US$2; ☑ 8am-noon & 2-5pm Mon-Fri, 8am-noon Sat) is a museum of Salvadoran writing and writers, with a heavy emphasis on the revolutionary movement of the '70s and '80s. No

surprise really – the museum's director is Carlos Henríquez Consalvi, aka 'Santiago,' the Venezuelan-born journalist who was the founder and main voice of Radio Venceremos during the war. (You're liable to see him around the museum most days.)

The museum has three small exhibit areas, through which it rotates compelling exhibits on themes such as writers (like Roque Dalton and Salarrué), the massacre of 1932, and women in Salvadoran history. Throughout the museum are terrific black-and-white photos from the war years – showing scenes such as student demonstrations, life in guerrilla camps, and just ordinary people – plus personal effects, like diaries and letters. Visitors can also watch a number of

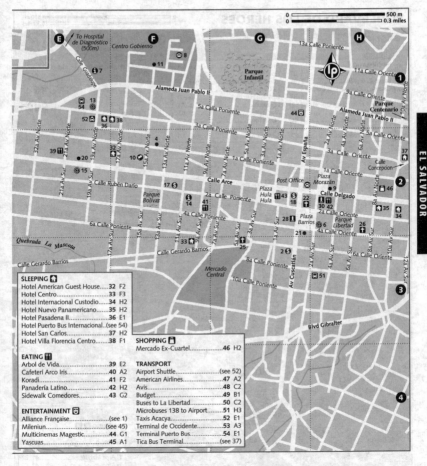

videos covering the history of the war, the founding of Radio Venceremos, as well as propaganda produced by the FMLN during the fighting, like the internationally known 'Carta de Morazán.' The sound quality isn't great, however. Finally, there's a replica of an underground clandestine radio studio; an extensive library of war-related books, documents and photos; and a small selection of books for sale at the entrance. Check the website or *Pashalua* magazine for current readings, book launches and more.

MUSEO DE ARTE POPULAR

Yet another terrific museum is the **Museum of Popular Art** (Map p322; ☎ 2274-5154; Av San Jose 125; admission US$1; ☒ 10am-5pm Tue-Fri, 10am-6pm

Sat), which showcases El Salvador's underappreciated contribution to Central American folk art. The main attraction is the Sala Dominga Herrera, which describes the evolution of '*sorpresas*,' the tiny clay figures made and sold in nearby Ilobasco. Dominga Herrera (1911–1982), the daughter of ceramic doll makers, gained modest fame for her miniature and meticulously painted creations, which she began making on a whim but have since become a cottage industry for the whole town, even the country. Classic *sorpresas* are single pieces, usually portraying a profession, domestic scene or, more recently, sexual entanglements. Contemporary artisans have gone further, creating '*procesos*' and '*cuadros*,' which portray

EL SALVADOR

BOULEVARD DE LOS HÉROS

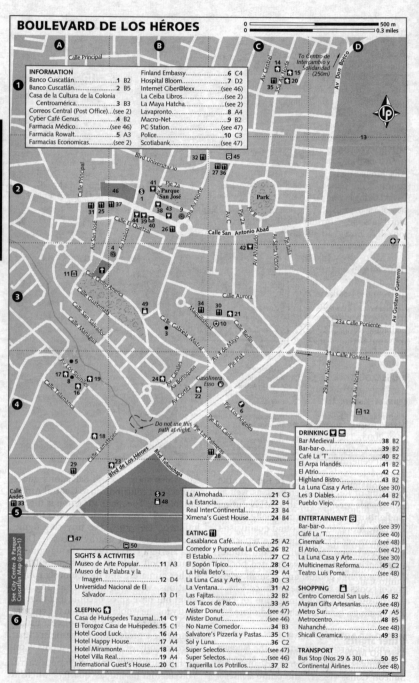

0 ——————— 500 m
0 ———————— 0.3 miles

INFORMATION
Banco Cuscatlán.....................1 B2
Banco Cuscatlán.....................2 B5
Casa de la Cultura de la Colonia
  Centroamérica......................3 B3
Correos Central (Post Office)...(see 2)
Cyber Café Genus...................4 B2
Farmacia Médico...................(see 46)
Farmacia Rowalt......................5 A3
Farmacias Economicas...........(see 2)
Finland Embassy......................6 C4
Hospital Bloom........................7 D2
Internet Ciber@lexx...............(see 46)
La Ceiba Libros......................(see 2)
La Maya Hatcha.....................(see 2)
Lavapronto...............................8 A4
Macro-Net..............................9 B2
PC Station.............................(see 47)
Police....................................10 C3
Scotiabank...........................(see 47)

To Centro de
Intercambio y
Solidaridad (250m)

Park

SIGHTS & ACTIVITIES
Museo de Arte Popular.............11 A3
Museo de la Palabra y la
  Imagen...............................12 D4
Universidad Nacional de El
  Salvador.............................13 D1

SLEEPING
Casa de Huéspedes Tazumal......14 C1
El Torogoz Casa de Huéspedes..15 C1
Hotel Good Luck.....................16 A4
Hotel Happy House..................17 A4
Hotel Miramonte.....................18 A4
Hotel Villa Real.......................19 A4
International Guest's House........20 C1

La Almohada..........................21 C3
La Estancia.............................22 B4
Real InterContinental...............23 B4
Ximena's Guest House..............24 B4

EATING
Casablanca Café......................25 A2
Comedor y Pupusería La Ceiba..26 B2
El Establo...............................27 C2
El Sopón Típico.......................28 C4
La Hola Beto's........................29 A4
La Luna Casa y Arte.................30 C3
La Ventana.............................31 A2
Las Fajitas.............................32 B2
Los Tacos de Paco...................33 A5
Mister Donut.........................(see 47)
Mister Donut.........................(see 46)
No Name Comedor...................34 B3
Salvatore's Pizzería y Pastas.....35 C1
Sol y Luna.............................36 B2
Super Selectos.......................(see 47)
Super Selectos.......................(see 46)
Taquerilla Los Potrillos.............37 B2

DRINKING
Bar Medieval...........................38 B2
Bar-bar-o..............................39 B2
Café La 'T'.............................40 B2
El Arpa Irlandés......................41 B2
El Atrio..................................42 C2
Highland Bistro.......................43 B2
La Luna Casa y Arte................(see 30)
Les 3 Diables.........................44 B2
Pueblo Viejo..........................(see 47)

ENTERTAINMENT
Bar-bar-o.............................(see 39)
Café La 'T'............................(see 40)
Cinemark..............................(see 47)
El Atrio.................................(see 42)
La Luna Casa y Arte................(see 30)
Multicinemas Reforma...............45 C2
Teatro Luis Poma...................(see 48)

SHOPPING
Centro Comercial San Luis........46 B2
Mayan Gifts Artesanías...........(see 48)
Metro Sur.............................47 A5
Metrocentro...........................48 B5
Nahanché.............................(see 48)
Shicali Ceramica......................49 B3

TRANSPORT
Bus Stop (Nos 29 & 30)............50 B5
Continental Airlines.................(see 48)

See City Center & Parque
Cuscatlán Map (p320–1)

Do not use this
path at night.

whole scenes – from emigrating to the US to complex religious festivals – and include dozens or hundreds of individual figures. The museum has some incredible pieces; if you've been underwhelmed by Salvador folk art – there is a lot of shabby work in local shops, even in Ilobasco – come here for the real deal.

Zona Rosa & Colonia Escalón
MUSEO NACIONAL DE ANTROPOLOGÍA DAVID J GUZMÁN
Absolutely one of the best museums in the country, the **Museo Nacional de Antropología David J Guzmán** (Map p324; ☎ 2243 3927; Av La Revolución; admission US$1.50; ☼ 9am-5pm Tue-Sun) is worth a solid morning's visit. It may not look like much on the outside, but once you walk through the front door, you'll find it hard to leave. Inside are two expansive floors of thoughtfully and beautifully presented exhibits on the Maya, the development of the people and land of El Salvador, the arts, religion and economy of the country…even prehistoric rock carvings and an artifact garden. The only downside of the museum is that signage is in Spanish only. It's worth bringing your dictionary.

MUSEO DE ARTE DE EL SALVADOR
San Salvador's small, well-designed **Museum of Modern Art** (MARTE; Map p324; ☎ 2243 6099; Av La Revolución; admission adult/student US$1.50/0.50; ☼ 10am-6pm Tue-Sun) opened in May 2003. The permanent exhibit, called 'Puntos Cardinales,' uses the artwork of several generations of Salvadoran modern painters to explore facets of the national consciousness. Two temporary exhibit halls feature mostly Latin American artists – a major show on Mexican muralist Álfaro Siquieros was being held when we last visited. The museum is a healthy uphill walk from the anthropology museum, and sits just behind the large Monumento a la Revolución. The museum restaurant, Punto Café (p336), is a local favorite, but isn't particularly cheap. For something less expensive, try the street stands near the parking area.

Other Sights
CENTRO MONSEÑOR ROMERO
At Universidad Centroamericana José Simeón Cañas (UCA), the **Centro Monseñor Romero** (Map p312; ☎ 2210-6675; admission free; ☼ 8am-noon & 2-6pm Mon-Fri, 8-11:30am Sat) is a small, well-organized center that pays homage to the martyred archbishop, assassinated by government agents in March 1980, and fellow priest Rutilio Grande, murdered in 1977 near the city of Aguilares. The center itself was the scene of more government atrocities in 1989, when six Jesuit priests, along with their maid and her daughter, were brutally killed, and the center burned. Four of the priests were found in the back courtyard, now a peaceful rose garden. Visitors can see photos and personal effects of each of the murdered priests, as well as of four American nuns raped and killed in December 1980. Most disturbing are a set of albums in the adjacent Sala de Afiches with photos of the Jesuits' murder scene – be forewarned, they are extremely graphic. Next door is the *capilla* (chapel), where a series of paintings on the rear wall portray victims of torture, and memorial events are occasionally held. A small selection of books, posters and T-shirts are on sale, and UCA students are usually on hand for tours and explanations, mostly in Spanish.

To get here, take bus 44. Don't get off at the main entrance; instead, wait until the smaller back entrance on Calle de Mediterreáno (ask the driver if you're unsure). From there, Centro Romero is a few minutes' walk into the campus; ask a student for directions or look at one of the posted campus maps. You can also walk to UCA from Iglesia La Ceiba de Guadalupe, which many buses (including 42 and 101) pass.

HOSPITAL LA DIVINA PROVEDENCIA
Also known as **El Hospitalito** (Map p324; Av 'B' at Calle Toluca; admission free; ☼ usually 8am-noon & 2-5pm), it was in this chapel that Monseñor Romero was assassinated by government agents, while giving mass on March 24, 1980. A man stood up at the back and fired a single shot, striking Romero in the heart and killing him instantly. The chapel, which is still in use, can be visited, and there's a plaque commemorating Romero and the assassination. Romero was giving mass at the hospital chapel because he lived his last years here, eschewing larger quarters, more prominent assignments, even bodyguards. You can tour his modest quarters, where his

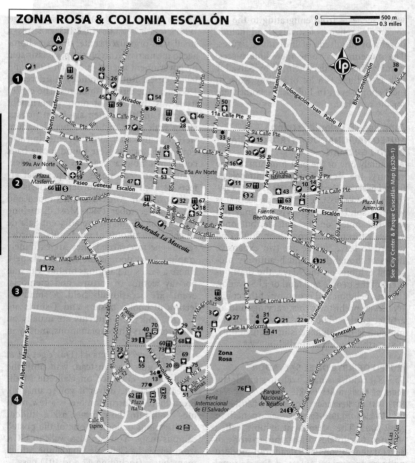

ZONA ROSA & COLONIA ESCALÓN

blood-soaked shirt and robes are displayed, as well as the typewriter he used to type his famously stirring homilies.

MUSEO DE LA HISTORIA MILITAR

For the other side of the story, head to the troubling but surprisingly interesting **Military History Museum** (Map p312; ☎ 2250 0000, ext 8800; Cuartel El Zapote, Barrio San Jacinto; admission free; ⏰ 9am-12pm & 2-5pm Tue-Sun). In a series of interconnected, barrack-like rooms, President Maximiliano Martínez is praised for the 'resolve and patriotism' with which he suppressed Communist insurgents in 1932 – some 30,000 indigenous men, women and children were killed in the process – and Colonel Domingo Monterrosa, alleged

mastermind of the massacre at El Mozote, is described as having 'written pages of glory for the history of the armed forces.' On the walls and in floor-mounted displays is an incredible array of rifles, machine guns, grenade launchers, mortars, flame throwers, radio and night-vision equipment – almost all made in the USA – as well as original copies of the 1992 peace accords. A number of military tanks, trucks, helicopters, and even the Pope Mobile used when the pontiff visited El Salvador, are also on display. But the most interesting part of the museum is a **huge relief map** of El Salvador. Completed in June 2005, and measuring 34m by 19m, the map highlights the country's rugged topography with more than a dozen volcanoes and mountains, and well-marked rivers, roads and cities nestled in between. It's well worth a visit; you can walk here from the zoo or natural history museum. A free guide service is available.

JARDÍN BOTÁNICO LA LAGUNA

Also called **Plan de La Laguna** (Map p312; admission US$0.50; 9am-5:30pm Tue-Sun), this is a lovely, cool botanical garden, at the bottom of a volcanic crater. Gravel and cement paths wind through the garden, where trees and plants are labeled and offer plenty of shade along the way. Most people arrive by car, but it's easy enough to take bus 44 from the city center or Blvd de los Héroes, and ask the driver to let you off at the right spot – it's easy to miss, so ask a couple times so he doesn't forget. From there it's a 1km downhill walk to the garden. Signage is sparse, so ask along the way if you're unsure.

COURSES
Language

Centro de Intercambio y Solidaridad (Map p322; 2235 2486; www.cis-elsalvador.org; Av Bolivar No 103 at Av Aguilares, Colonia Libertad) The Mélida Anaya Montes Spanish Language School is one of the principal programs offered by CIS, a community advocacy organization founded in 1993 by foreign and Salvadoran solidarity workers following the signing of the peace accords. Courses incorporate progressive social and political themes into assignments and discussions. Students live with local families and classes, taught by Salvadorans, are held weekday mornings. Afternoons are reserved for the school's 'Political Cultural Program,' which entails daytrips (and occasional weekend overnights) to coffee plantations, women's cooperatives, health centers, social organizations, and other sites, to give students an insight into Salvadoran life, culture and current social issues. Fees are roughly US$222.50 per week and include

THE PEACE CORPS IN EL SALVADOR

The first 20 Peace Corps volunteers (PCVs) to El Salvador arrived in 1962, a year after President Kennedy created the program. Some 1700 volunteers have served in El Salvador since, despite a 13-year hiatus during the civil war.

PCVs perform a wide variety of work, usually in association with city officials or a local organization or school. Traditional Peace Corps endeavors, like planting trees and building latrines, are becoming less common than projects like sex education classes for teenagers or setting up computer systems for city hall. Sustainable tourism has become a major focus as well.

It can be tough. Peace Corps provides basic funding and support, but many volunteers petition NGOs here and back in the US (not to mention friends and family) for support and donations. A few even pony up their own money, though volunteer wages in El Salvador – calculated according to national norms – are just US$9 per day.

Volunteers are often placed in remote communities, where change can be slow (and is not always welcome). Incoming volunteers often replace outgoing ones, so communities get 'used' to having them around, and so projects aren't interrupted. Still, many volunteers say their biggest challenge is negotiating the small-town politics and personal alliances, much of which is generations in the making.

There is certainly room to criticize the Peace Corps, from a conceptual level down to its nuts and bolts. There is something uncomfortably paternalistic, even imperialistic, about expecting local leaders to account for the opinions of a young American newcomer who is a de facto representative of the US government, but may have no real international or development experience.

But individual Peace Corps volunteers do make lasting positive impacts on their communities. Many stay long after their service is completed, working for – even heading up – independent community and environmental groups. Perhaps more enduring are the personal bonds formed after two-years of close contact. (Some PCVs even marry locals, but that's another matter altogether.) And Peace Corps volunteers can be an excellent resource to travelers (and guidebook writers), especially for tips on new and off-the-beaten-path destinations.

20 hours of classes, a homestay (including breakfast and dinner), the afternoon program and administrative costs. There's also a once-only US$25 application fee. You can also volunteer to teach English for a minimum of 10 weeks. In exchange, CIS provides training, materials, and offers half-price Spanish classes and two free weeks of the afternoon program. The school is located across the street from a high school basketball court, a half-block from the Universidad Nacional's brightly painted sports complex.

Escuela Cuzcatlán (Map p312; ☎ 2441 4726, 7850 9293; www.salvaspan.com; Pasaje Vienna 10; 1a Av Nte, btwn 17a & 19a Calles Pte) Offers Spanish classes for college credit, homestays and extracurriculars, like visiting Mayan ruins and taking salsa or surfing classes. Courses per week cost US$125, homestay per week US$90; homestay plus excursions per week costs US$150.

Culture

For more long-term courses and workshops, like yoga, pottery or reading groups, check out the **Casa de la Cultura del Centro de San Salvador** (Map pp320-1; ☎ 2212 2016; 1 Calle Pte 822; ⏰ 8am-4pm Mon-Sat) and the **Casa de la Cultura de la Colonia Centroamérica** (Map p322; ☎ 2260 2882; Calle Gabriela Mistral 533; ⏰ 7:30am-5pm Mon-Fri, 8am-noon Sat). For more details, see Cultural Centers (p314).

SAN SALVADOR FOR CHILDREN

San Salvador has a number of interesting and well-run destinations for children. The zoo, a museum (the Tin Marín children's museum is a must-see) and two kid-friendly parks should keep your little one happy and engaged. And if your children are game, don't be afraid to take them to otherwise 'grown-up' sights; children are genuinely welcome throughout El Salvador (and Latin America, for that matter.) Having a car or taking taxis could save you some tears, as a packed city bus can be intimidating for adults, let alone tiny ones. Be very alert for holes in the sidewalk and streets – many completely unmarked – as well as litter and whatever else your child may feel inclined to pick up. Remind children not to drink water from the tap, especially if it's OK back home.

Tin Marín Museo de los Niños (Map pp320-1; ☎ 2271 5147; www.tinmarin.org; Parque Cuscatlán; admission US$2; ☺ 9am-1pm & 2-5pm Tue-Fri, 10am-1pm & 2-6pm Sat & Sun) Where to start? This gem of a museum has so many interesting hands-on features, your little one may need a return trip. Roughly divided into four sections – health, environment, technology and culture – exhibits include a miniature supermarket (to learn about food groups), a huge artificial volcano (complete with smoke and red lights for lava) and a papermaking area (to learn about recycling). There's a cockpit and fuselage of a real Boeing 727 airplane, and a real VW Beetle that kids can handpaint to their heart's delight – part of an exhibit on color and senses, it looks like an Andy Warhol piece. Another kid-favorite is the Casa de Gravedad (Gravity House) – a small house built at a 23-degree angle to demonstrate balance and perspective. Add to this a butterfly cage, a puppet theatre, a mini TV studio, a huge brushable and flossable mouth, a computer area – all in all, it's a fun place to spend an afternoon. Everything's in Spanish, but that probably won't inhibit English-only youngsters. The rules are: no kids without an adult, no adults without a kid. There's a small cafeteria on-site, and shady Parque Cuscatlán (p319) – with its excellent sights – is right in front.

Parque Zoológico Nacional (Map p312; ☎ 2270 0828; Calle Modelo; admission US$0.57; ☺ 9am-4pm Wed-Sun) A surprisingly pleasant zoo near the outskirts of town, with 10 square city blocks worth of green spaces, paths, even a lagoon. Among the 144 species of animals housed here, you'll see lions, elephants and a whole host of monkeys (be sure to check out the spider monkeys who live on an island in the middle of the lagoon). It's packed with families on Sunday.

Museo de Historia Natural de El Salvador (Map p312; ☎ 2270 9228; Calle los Viveros, Parque Saburo Hirao; admission US$0.57; ☺ 9am-4:30pm Wed-Sun) Located at the far end of a shady recreational park, a stop at the Natural History Museum is a great way to spend an afternoon. It's small, but packed with information on the evolution of El Salvador's land, fauna and ecosystems. The geology and paleontology sections are particularly good. Signage is in

Spanish only. Travelers could easily combine this with a visit to the zoo, just a couple of blocks away.

FESTIVALS & EVENTS

The names El Salvador and San Salvador come from the term 'El Salvador del Mundo' (Savior of the World), a reference to Jesus Christ, the patron saint of the city and the country. The national *fiesta patronal* (patron saint festival) is celebrated during the first week of August. Schools, government offices and most businesses close for the week, and everyone goes on vacation. Anywhere with water – ocean, lakes, rivers – is inundated with Salvadoran tourists, and religious processions, street fairs and colorful parades are held throughout the country. The celebration in San Salvador is the largest and (for most people) the best.

The **Feria de Innovación Artesanal** is a national crafts fair that has been hosted by the city of San Salvador since 1996. Typically taking place in the first week of December, artisans come from all over the country to compete for prizes and to sell their work. You'll see every type of *artesanía* produced in the country at this fair: objects made of clay, wood, natural fibers, textiles, metals and leather. It's held in Parque Cuscatlán or in the Metro Sur's parking lot. Call the **Salvadoran Artisan board** (CASART; ☎ 2260-6441) for details.

SLEEPING

As El Salvador attracts more and more travelers, the number and variety of hotels has expanded. Top-end hotels have long existed here – they were popular with foreign journalists during the civil war and are now preferred by traveling businesspeople. And, befitting its reputation for being off the beaten path, San Salvador now has three hostels plus a handful of cheap hotels downtown. The main growth has been in midrange hotels, and they've expanded beyond the traditional hotel and hostel zones.

Accommodations are located in four main zones, with the city center remaining the last resort option; hotels are cheap and moderately clean but the area is a bit sketchy, especially at night. The Parque Cuscatlán area is also cheap, but somewhat safer and convenient to the main international bus terminal and airport shuttle. The

Blvd de los Héroes area has the capital's only hostels, plus several good guesthouses. There's a great bohemian bar scene nearby and two large malls with many conveniences, plus numerous bus routes pass by, making getting around easy. Colonía Escalón and Zona Rosa are two of San Salvador most exclusive neighborhoods, and are home to San Salvador's top-end, high-rise hotels. However, a number of midrange options – and easy access to buses, including two new international bus stops – make this a viable option for independent travelers with more than a backpacker's budget. The area also has a large mall and excellent museums.

City Center

It doesn't make much sense to stay in the *centro*, since safer, quieter areas are an easy bus or taxi ride away. Still, city-savvy travelers may enjoy downtown's fast pace, hectic markets and rough-around-the-edges appeal. Not surprisingly, there are no midrange or top-end options.

Hotel Nuevo Panamericano (Map pp320-1; ☎ 2221 1199; 8a Av Sur 113; r per person with air-con & TV US$7; ✖ P) We've seen this hotel go from being a dump, to a newly renovated surprise, to an aging so-so. Twenty-six rooms all have ceramic floors, high ceilings and modern but somewhat worn bathrooms. Some have saggy beds, others have three or four beds and feel cramped. Check out a few before deciding. Air-conditioned rooms are larger and have TVs, and cable was supposedly being installed.

Hotel Internacional Custodio (Map pp320-1; ☎ 2502 0678; 10a Av Sur 109; r per person with/without bathroom US$10/5) This high airy place is owned and operated by a friendly Honduran family. Rooms open onto breezy outdoor corridors and those upstairs get decent natural light. Rooms without bathrooms are tiny, while rooms with private bathrooms are large, with high ceilings and super clean sheets and pillowcases. The bathrooms are seriously grubby, though – probably the main drawback. Pop up to the top floor for a good view of downtown and the rest of the city.

Hotel Centro (Map pp320-1; ☎ 2271 5045; 9a Av Sur 410; d/tw US$15/20) A clean and relatively modern place, though it's not particularly convenient. Smallish rooms have TV (no cable) and OK bathrooms; those upstairs

get considerably more light. The hotel is near the central market, which doesn't make the area unsafe per se, but do keep your eyes open and take taxis at night. Parking is in front of the hotel – off the street but not enclosed.

Hotel San Carlos (Map pp320-1; ☎ 2222 1664; Calle Concepción 121 at 10 Av Norte; r per person US$10) The Tica bus terminal is located at this small downtown hotel, so it's convenient if you've got an early departure. The rooms are decent enough, all with bathroom and fan, though there's no hot water, air-con or TV. It's good enough for a night (or at least until the bus leaves) but neither the overall cleanliness or surrounding neighborhood are conducive to longer stays. It doesn't have any food service, but there is usually a lady selling sweet bread and *café con leche* (coffee with milk) to early-morning passengers.

Near Parque Cuscatlán

This area is west of *el centro*, but safer and mellower than downtown. The listed hotels are near the Universidad Tecnológica, meaning you'll find plenty of good inexpensive eateries and Internet cafés. It's especially convenient if you're headed out of the country – all the hotels are within walking distance of Terminal Puerto Bus (for international buses) and Taxis Acacya (which operates a convenient airport shuttle). Streets are shady and pleasantly busy during the day. It doesn't have as many conveniences as the Blvd de los Héroes area, but many city buses pass through and you can walk to a number of places nearby. It's recommended to use taxis at night.

BUDGET

Hotel Villa Florencia Centro (Map pp320-1; ☎ 2221 1706; www.hotelvillaflorencia.com, in Spanish; 3a Calle Poniente 1023; s/tw US$12/18; P) Wow – what a difference a couple of years and a good remodeling make. The location and price remain convenient, and expect new mattresses, spotless modern bathrooms and cable TV. There's a pleasant open-air common area – even free coffee some mornings – and enclosed parking. All in all, great value. It's not perfect of course: some of the rooms are tiny, and the windows in most rooms open right onto the public area and corridors – which is still preferable to facing the noisy street. Be sure not to confuse this hotel with its like-named sister establishment in the Zona Rosa (p331).

Hotel Pasadena II (Map pp320-1; ☎ 2221 4786; 3a Calle Pte 1037; d/tw US$11/16; P) Next door to Hotel Villa Florencia Centro, this place is decidedly less appealing. But on the off chance that its neighbor is full – or you can't spare the extra dollar – some rooms here are new, and the rest are at least adequate, with clean sheets and cable TV. The beds and bathrooms are hit-and-miss – see a few rooms before deciding. Not many units face the street, but avoid them as it's hard to sleep through the din. There's a simple restaurant on-site (mains US$2 to US$5; open breakfast, lunch and dinner).

Hotel American Guest House (Map pp320-1; ☎ 2222 8789; 17a Av Norte 119; r without bathroom US$10, s/d with private bathroom US$15/18) Come here for a homey atmosphere, complete with antique furniture, plants in the hallway and a no-nonsense proprietor who's been here for years. There are less than 10 rooms, all a bit shabby but not unpleasant. The shared bathrooms could use some work, however. Some rooms have high ceilings and old-world wallpaper, which would be easier to appreciate if there was more natural light, but alas… The enclosed patio restaurant (breakfast US$1.50 to US$2) is a nice place to start your day and for relaxing over a beer in the evening. Parking is in a lot around the corner.

MIDRANGE

Hotel Puerto Bus Internacional (Map pp320-1; ☎ 2217 3333; www.hotelpuertobus.com, in Spanish; Alameda Juan Pablo II; s/d/tw US$30/35/35, add US$5 to pay with credit card; Guatemalan quetzales accepted; P) Occupying the 2nd floor of Terminal Puerto Bus, this is the airport hotel of bus-bound country-hoppers. It's not five-star, but the rooms are surprisingly modern, with hot water, safety deposit box, cable TV, telephone and even complimentary bottled water. Look at a few rooms before deciding – some have saggy beds, others open onto a common sitting area. Prices include breakfast and an hour of Internet access.

Boulevard de los Héroes

This is the most popular and convenient area for travelers, especially for those on a budget. Three hostels cater to backpackers, while several small hotels are good for those willing to pay a bit more for certain creature comforts, and there's one luxury hotel for good measure. Nearby Calle San Antonio Abad has a great bar scene, and two good museums are within walking distance. Two malls offer ATMs, cinemas and other modern amenities, while buses to the city center, bus terminals, Colonia Escalón and Zona Rosa all pass through.

BUDGET

Casa de Huéspedes Tazumal (Map p322; ☎ 2235 0156; casadehuespedestazumal@hotmail.com; 35a Av Norte 3; s/d with bathroom US$20/25, with air-con US$25/30, s/d without bathroom US$18/25, with air-con US$20/28; P) Located among a small string of hotels, Tazumal is the best choice on the block – if it isn't already full. Rooms are spotless, beds are comfortable, towels are thick, every room has cable TV, there's hot water, you have 30 minutes of free Internet access per day, plus airport and bus terminal pickup, tasty and affordable meals, two homey common rooms…what more could you ask for? Oh yeah, there's laundry service (per load US$5), and three minutes of free international calls to Europe and USA.

International Guest's House (Map p322; ☎ 2226 7343; i_guesthouse@hotmail.com; 35a Av Norte 9; s/d incl breakfast US$17/28, with air-con US$20/35; P) This hotel has a mellow, artsy feel. In the main building, you'll find art and plants throughout, quiet corners to write postcards, and sitting areas to read a book or hang out with other travelers. The narrow rooms are simple but comfortable – decent beds with good linens and hot-water bathrooms. The annex is somewhat forgotten, with charmless common areas and grimy floors, but the rooms are better – sunny, new beds and renovated bathrooms (cold water only).

El Torogoz Casa de Huéspedes (Map p322; ☎ 2235 4172; eltorogoz@telesal.net; 35a Av Norte 6 & 7; s/tw incl breakfast US$20/30, r without bathroom US$15 per person;) This small hotel has a pleasant, well-maintained atmosphere. Rooms are bright and nicely decorated, and there is a refreshing pool surrounded by a pleasant grassy area. The problem is that there are only two rooms with private bathrooms; the remaining 10 share two bathrooms (pray you're not the last in line to shower) and aren't a good value for anyone other than solo travelers.

La Almohada (Map p322; ☎ 2211 8021; la-almohada@hotmail.com; Calle Berlín 220; dm US$7; ▢) The newest hostel in town, complete with 16 beds, a fully-equipped kitchen and Internet access. There is a big dining room with long wood tables and a comfy common TV room – both excellent places for socializing with fellow travelers. Cleanliness is just OK – wear flip flops in the bathrooms – but you can take hot showers and the beds are good. Service is spotty.

Hotel Happy House (Map p322; ☎ 2260 1568; www.hotelhappyhouse-elsalvador.com; Av Los Sisimiles 2951; s/d with air-con US$20/25; ▨) The Hotel Happy House would be a happier place to stay if the beds weren't so saggy. It's really the only drawback of the place: picture sunny common areas, gleaming tile floors, clean rooms and hot water, and all just a couple blocks from Metrocentro. It's good value if you can handle a sore back.

La Estancia (Map p322; ☎ 2275 3381; Av Cortés 216; dm US$6, r US$15-18; ▢) Almost too popular with Peace Corps volunteers, La Estancia has a handful of co-ed dorms and private rooms. Most are cramped, but two patios, a comfy TV room and free coffee make this a homey place. The bathrooms need a serious scrubbing, but are manageable for a night or two. Room 5 is one of the best deals in San Salvador – with bathroom, hot water, cable TV and a private patio – but it's hard to get. There's no sign – look for a distinctive purple gate half-way down the street.

Ximena's Guest House (Map p322; ☎ 2260 2481; www.ximenasguesthouse.com; Calle San Salvador 202; dm US$6-8, s US$17-19, d US$23-27, r with air-con US$10; ▨) Sad to say, but this longtime favorite has lost much of its former charm. Yes, it's got an artsy bohemian look, it's a good place to meet other travelers and it's in a great location, but the beds are old and lumpy, the linens are worn, the rooms are in sore need of a fresh coat of paint and the bathrooms…well, they're grim. Guests complain of being nickel-and-dimed on extra services like Internet access (per hour US$2), food (pupusa US$0.80), even screens on some dorm windows (US$2 extra…and you'll need them). Plus dorms don't have fans, which is a serious bummer in the heat. It's an option if you're seriously strapped for cash.

MIDRANGE

Hotel Villa Real (Map p322; ☎ 2260 1579; villarealsv@netscape.net; Av Los Sisimiles 2944; s/d incl breakfast US$25/35, with air-con US$30/40; ▨ P ▢) A handful of arches and brightly painted walls lead to a sunny courtyard at this small hotel. The bathrooms are a little cramped, but the well-maintained and clean rooms, with extras like cable TV, small desks and phones, make this is a nice midrange option.

Hotel Miramonte (Map p322; ☎ 2260 1880; www.hotelmiramonte.com; Calle Talamanca 2904; s US$35-39, d US$40-44; ▨ P ▢) Hotel Miramonte offers four floors of clean, comfortable rooms with gleaming tile floors and nice ironwork headboards. Unfortunately, some have a mildewy smell; if you have a sharp nose, check out a few before deciding. Cheaper rooms are cramped, dark, near the laundry room and, frankly, not worth the cost. The pool is squeezed in behind the parking lot and had no water in it when we passed through.

Hotel Good Luck (Map p322; ☎ 2260 1655; hotel goodluckes@yahoo.com; Av Los Sisimiles; s/d US$26/30, with air-con US$33/35; ▨ P) Just steps from Metrocentro, this hotel is a good bet. The 27 rooms are sparkling clean and have good beds, hot water and cable TV. Most have faux-wood paneling and interior facing windows, which mean they're dark but quiet. There also is a Chinese restaurant onsite that serves Cantonese and Salvadoran specialties. Service is friendly.

TOP END

Real InterContinental (Map p322; ☎ 2211 3333; www.intercontinental.com; Blvd de los Héroes; Mon-Thu s US$123-157, d US$133-168, Fri-Sun r US$85-115; ▨ ▨ P ▢ ⊠) Located across from Metrocentro, this high-rise hotel offers two categories of rooms: standard and executive; the latter includes breakfast buffet, happy hour, even a free shoe shine. On weekends, all rooms come with breakfast, a pair of movie passes and US$5 credit at the pool bar. The décor is rustic chic: carved wood armoires and TV cases, marble bathrooms, and large windows with great city or volcano views; standard rooms are smaller and somewhat less grand. The gym is well equipped, but the pool is tiny and only the men's changing room has a sauna. All told, the InterContinental compares well with the other top-end places.

Zona Rosa & Colonia Escalón

Hotels here have long catered to businesspeople; reservations are recommended during the week but look for specials on weekends. A number of smaller hotels have also opened, all offering independent travelers comfortable accommodations at midrange prices. Those staying close to Paseo General Escalón have easy access to various city buses; others may find using a taxi or car more convenient.

BUDGET

Casa de Huéspedes Australia (Map p324; ☎ 2298 6035; 1a Calle Pte 3852, Colonia Escalón; s/d US$15/22, s without bathroom US$10; ✗ P ▢) Arguably the best budget place in San Salvador. Not only is the hotel in a nice neighborhood, but the rooms are spotless, common areas are welcoming, and rooms with bathroom have hot water and air conditioning. The value is hard to beat. Rooms vary considerably in size – if that matters, check out a few before settling in.

MIDRANGE

Hotel Villa Florencia Zona Rosa (Map p324; ☎ 2257 0236; www.hotelvillaflorencia.com, in Spanish; Av La Revolución, Zona Rosa; s/d incl breakfast US$39/50) One of the Zona Rosa's best-value options, offering modern amenities, a great location and an affordable price. All 12 rooms have cable TV, telephone, tile floors and high ceilings; some have desks as well. A small open-air patio in the back, with leafy plants and a handful of tables, is perfect for breakfast. It's not to be confused with the Hotel Villa Florencia Centro (p328), its sister hotel near Terminal Puerto Bus.

Hotel Olinda (Map p324; ☎ 2263 3643; hotel olinda@navegante.com.sv; 11a Calle Pte 4134, Colonia Escalón; s/d incl breakfast US$45/50; ✗ P ▢) Brazilian owned and operated, this new hotel has spacious and well-appointed rooms, complete with mahogany furnishings, wrought-iron beds and stone inlaid floors. Common areas are comfortable, but resemble a New England gift shop at Christmas: lots of candles, crafty wall hangings and decorative dolls. A complimentary buffet breakfast is served in a pleasant dining area that overlooks a multilevel fountain, which has been mistaken for a kiddy pool (at least by one person).

Hotel Vista Marella (Map p324; ☎ 2263 4931; www.hotel-vista-marella.123.com.sv, in Spanish; Calle Juan José Cañas, Colonia Escalón; s/tw incl breakfast US$48/57; ✗ P ▣ ▢) An excellent choice, the Vista

> **THE AUTHOR'S CHOICE**
>
> **La Posada del Rey Primero** (Map p324; ☎ 2264 5245; gerencia@laposadadelreyprimero. com; Calle Dordelly, Colonia Escalón; s/tw US$42/53; ✗ ▢) A charming colonial-style hotel, with high ceilings, painted stucco walls and beautiful hand-carved woodwork that's reminiscent of an Oaxacan B&B. Rooms open onto pleasant sitting areas, with comfy chairs, tables and plenty of reading materials. Each also enjoys modern touches, like silent air-conditioners, cable TV and firm beds. The four rooms on the 2nd floor have the best view and light; the corner rooms – nos 5 and 8 – have windows on two sides. Continental breakfast is served in an attractive courtyard area on the ground floor, and there's wi-fi in the common areas. Three more rooms and a larger dining area were in the works during our visit. It's located in the swank Colonia Escalón, between 85a & 87a Avs Norte.

Marella is a comfortable hotel with 30 stylish rooms. All are ample and boast amenities like wi-fi, cable TV and hot water. A grassy courtyard with a nice garden is only outdone by the welcoming blue tile pool that lies within it; all of the hotel's hallways lead to it, and the open-air dining room opens onto it. Service is impeccable.

Hostal Verona (Map p324; ☎ 2264 6035; www.hos talverona.com; 11a Calle Pte 4323, Colonia Escalón; s/d incl breakfast US$40/60, ste US$65; ✗ P ▢) Small and pleasant, this 15-room hotel offers spotless, modern accommodations that are a bit cramped, but are equipped with excellent beds, quiet air-conditioners and minibars. The main rooms are reminiscent of a country cottage home – think pastels and lots of finely crafted trinkets.

Hotel la Posada del Angel (Map p324; ☎ 2237 7171; www.laposadadelangel-sv.com, in Spanish; 85a Av Norte 321, Colonia Escalón; s/d incl breakfast US$45/51; ✗ ▢) Ten spacious rooms make up this guest house, each with a different decorative theme and layout. Common areas include comfortable sitting rooms and a pleasant (and very green) yard with a dining area that opens onto it. All rooms have bathrooms with hot water, cable TV and telephone. An excellent option in a quiet, upscale neighborhood.

Hotel Escalón Plaza (Map p324; ☎ 2263 7480; www.escalonplaza.com; 89 Av Norte 141-B, Colonia Escalón; s/tw US$45/57) A perfectly fine mid-size hotel with friendly service and a convenient location, yet somehow lacking the charm of newer hotels in this range. Rooms are appealingly eclectic, with armchairs, table lamps, doormats and paintings; rooms 22, 24 and 25 have small balconies overlooking the pool. All have hot water, cable TV and free wi-fi (plus a desktop downstairs for the laptopless). Enjoy a beer or cocktail on the 2nd-floor patio overlooking the street, but avoid rooms on that side – a bar opposite the hotel gets very loud, especially on Friday night.

Hostal Lonigo Bed & Breakfast (Map p324; ☎ 2264 4197; www.hostal-lonigo.com; Calle del Mirador 4837, Colonía Escalón; s/d incl breakfast US$45/57; ⊠ Ⓟ ⊠) This friendly B&B (more like a small hotel) caters to businesspeople looking for a homier, less-expensive alternative to the Radisson. For travelers, it serves mainly as a back-up in case better-located hotels in this category are full. Rooms are super clean, with firm mattresses, wrought-iron headboards and small wooden writing tables; the rest of the décor is dangerously foofy. The price includes a full breakfast, and the kitchen serves simple sandwiches, salads and drinks until 11pm. Rooms 1, 2 and 4 cost less, but get street noise. There's also a small clean pool.

TOP END

Radisson (Map p324; ☎ 2257 0700; radisson@hotelsal.com; Calle del Mirador, Colonía Escalón; standard main tower US$135-165, executive US$169-185, annex US$95; ⊠ Ⓟ ⊠ ⊠ ⊠) The Radisson is literally and figuratively at the top of the heap, with classy rooms and service, and terrific city and volcano views from its high hillside location. Rooms in the five-star main tower have all the amenities you expect – security box, flat-screen cable TV, wi-fi – plus a few goodies like marble desks and a complimentary cell phone. An executive floor has additional services, including expedited check-in and afternoon tea. Suites in the three-star annex aren't bad – less modern but much larger, with separate living room and sofas – but the smell of cigarettes pervades. The pool is much better than the Hilton's, and a live duo plays nightly in the bar.

Hilton Princess (Map p324; ☎ 2268 4545; www.sansalvador.hilton.com; cnr Av Las Magnolias & Blvd Hipódromo, Zona Rosa; d/tw standard US$149/169, executive US$179/199; ⊠ Ⓟ ⊠ ⊠ ⊠) Befitting its name, the stately Hilton Princess exudes an old-world elegance that the more modern Radisson – which by many measures is an equal or better hotel – can't quite match. A marble lobby with large paintings gives way to wallpapered hallways and armchairs by all the elevators, and the bar, with overstuffed leather chairs, is befittingly called Churchill's. Rooms have thick carpet and heavy wood armoires, and some have great views of Volcán San Salvador. The Hilton caters to businesspeople, but its location in the heart of the Zona Rosa suits independent travelers well.

Sheraton Presidente (Map p324; ☎ 2283 4000; Av La Revolución, Zona Rosa; Sat & Sun US$99, Mon-Fri US$149, Sheraton Club US$179; ⊠ Ⓟ ⊠ ⊠ ⊠) The Sheraton is definitely the lesser of San Salvador chain hotels, which is not to say it's entirely bad. 'Pool view' rooms look onto the pool, yes, but most also have views of Volcán San Salvador and nice terraces. 'City view' rooms don't have the terrace or much of a view – the hotel is on a hill, but with only four stories, it barely clears the trees. The pool may be San Salvador's best though, with a waterfall and children's area, and the Museum of Modern Art (p323) is next door. Where the Sheraton trails the others is in the details – wi-fi is available but not standard, the installations are good but not great, room furniture is plain – but it's cheaper than the rest, especially if you find an online special (go to www.starwoodho tels.com and enter El Salvador in the country search option).

Hotel Mirador Plaza (Map p324; ☎ 2244 6000; www.miradorplaza.com; Calle del Mirador, Colonía Escalón; s/d US$64/69, junior ste US$76/80, ste US$82/87; ⊠ Ⓟ ⊠ ⊠ ⊠) It's impossible to miss this hotel, a stately yellow mansion near the top of Calle del Mirador. Standard rooms are fine, but junior suites are much more spacious, with kitchenette, minibar, and large terrace with views of the city, Cerro San Jacinto (look for the cable car) and double-coned Volcán San Vicente. Volcán San Salvador rises sharply behind the hotel and is visible from the amoeba-shaped pool in the back. All rooms have flat screen TVs. Unfortunately, they also share the same white tile floor as the lobby and corridors – for the price, you kind of expect carpet.

EATING

San Salvador has a large variety of restaurants, offering respite to anyone overloaded on the Salvadoran *típica* (regional specialty) that so predominates the rest of the country (...more pupusas, anyone?). Japanese, Chinese, Mexican, German – and Salvadoran – cuisines are all available, and are often not as expensive as you'd expect. There's not much of a dining *scene,* however – no Chinatown, Little Italy or a general restaurant zone as such – and you may end up going back to certain places because they happen to be close to your hotel. But if you love eating out and don't mind grabbing a bus or taxi, San Salvador won't disappoint.

City Center

There are plenty of places to eat in the city center, but few standouts. Dinner is a challenge, since most places close early.

BUDGET

Panadería Latino (Map pp320–1; Calle Delgado; mains US$2–4; ☺ 6am-7pm) So much more than a bakery, this downtown institution is popular for its huge *comida a la vista* (meal-served buffet). Just point and the servers will fill your plate from trays of lasagna, beef in salsa, steamed veggies and more, then ladle you a cupful of *horchata* (soft drink) from plastic pails at the end of the line. Fresh baked goodies are sold on the opposite side. Ovens at the front keep the place hot and sweaty.

Koradi (Map pp320–1; ☎ 2221 2545; 9a Av Sur; mains US$2–5; ☺ 7am-5:30pm Mon-Fri, 7am-5pm Sat) Everything is vegetarian at this small, easy-to-miss eatery – *tamales*, cheese pupusas, tofu pizza, veggie paella, brown rice and so on. Order from the menu or create-a-plate of fresh *comida a la vista*; try to get a table under one of the fans, as the dining area can get stuffy. Natural products and supplements are also sold.

You'll find **sidewalk comedores** (Map pp320–1; mains US$1–3; ☺ 6am-6pm) lining the streets surrounding Plaza Hula Hula, a block west of Plaza Barrios. They're all essentially the same, but everyone you ask has a personal favorite. We liked the ones on the east side of 1a Av Sur across from the park, mainly for the clean vinyl tablecloths, friendly service and mid-afternoon sun, but maybe you'll see others that call to you. Expect typical Salvadoran fare, including *panes de pollo* (chicken sandwiches), *bistec encebollada* (onion grilled beef), *sopa de res* (beef stew) and more.

Near Parque Cuscatlán

University students drive the demand here, making for a profusion of good cheap eateries.

BUDGET

Cafeterí Arco Iris (Map pp320–1; 59a Av Sur; mains US$2–3; ☺ breakfast & lunch Mon-Sat) Just down the street from Universidad Franscisco Gavidia, the menu at this small eatery changes daily – it's *comida a la vista* – but the mix always includes chicken, veggies and rice. Get there early for the best selection.

Arbol de Vida (Map pp320–1; ☎ 2222 8937; 21a Av Norte; mains US$5–7; ☺ breakfast & lunch Mon-Sat) Tasty all-vegetarian *comida a la vista* belies the charmless interior of this longtime restaurant, on the lower floor of a small commercial center. You won't be getting any Vitamin D here, but the spinach tortas, broccoli pastries and various dishes made with *carne de soya* (tofu) are certainly good for you.

Boulevard de los Héroes

The best food here is on Calle San Antonio Abad, which is convenient if you're staying at one of the hotels on 35th Ave, but somewhat of a hike if you're at one of the hostels. In that case, swallow your pride and head to chain outlets in or around the malls for something quick.

BUDGET

Comedor y Pupusería La Ceiba (Map p322; ☎ 2208 0344; Calle San Antonio Abad 721; mains US$1.50–3; ☺ breakfast, lunch & dinner Mon-Sat) A cheap no-frills eatery that is fairly convenient. Expect *comida a la vista* for breakfast and lunch – chicken *tamales* are morning faves, while roast chicken, *chili rellenos*, beef soup and shrimp tortas are popular for lunch. 0Pupusas are patted up from 5:30pm.

No Name Comedor (Map p322; Calle Berlín 264; mains US$1–3; ☺ breakfast, lunch & dinner Mon-Sat) Run out of a neighborhood home, this *comedor* offers typical Salvadoran food served cafeteria style. The place sees serious customer traffic – be sure to arrive early if you want the pick of the *tamales*.

Taquerilla Los Potrillos (Map p322; ☎ 2225 3750; Calle San Antonio Abad; mains US$1–4; ☺ 5:30pm-3am

El SALVADOR

Mon-Sat, 5:30pm-1am Sun) One of the best taco stands south of the (Mexican) border. You'll find all the classics – *tacos al pastor*, quesadillas, rows of salsas and tons of fixin's…food even comes served on Styrofoam plates. It's open late.

La Luna Casa y Arte (Map p322; ☎ 2260 2921; www.lalunacasayarte.com, in Spanish; Calle Berlín 228; mains US$2-7; ☑ noon-2am Mon-Fri, 4pm-2am Sat) A bohemian restaurant-bar in a quiet neighborhood, La Luna offers an excellent menu complete with grilled sandwiches, homemade soups, salads and various meatless meals. If you're in the mood for something small, the dessert menu and coffee bar are worth hitting up. Come here for movies (p338) and live music (p338), too.

Café La 'T' (Map p322; ☎ 2225 2090; Calle San Antonio Abad 2233; ☑ 10am-9:30pm Mon-Wed, 10am-11pm Thu-Sat) A popular bar-café at night, Café La 'T' also makes a pleasant daytime stop. Coffee is the specialty – especially latte, of course – and there is a good selection of tasty light fare, including quiche (US$3.25), granola with fresh fruit (US$2.15), or green salad with chicken and kiwi (US$3.75).

Los Tacos de Paco (Map p322; ☎ 2260 1347; Calle Andes 2931; mains US$3-6; ☑ noon-3pm & 5-10pm) Near Metrosur, this may be the most culturally enlightened taco joint you'll ever encounter. It hosts a poetry reading on Wednesday at 6pm, and has a small but good selection of books and artwork for sale. And as for the tacos…the sign says 'The Best Mexican Food in El Salvador,' which is either true or nearly true – either way, you won't be disappointed.

Casablanca Café (Map p322; ☎ 2235 1489; Calle San Antonio Abad; mains US$2-5; ☑ 7am-5pm Mon-Sat) The Casablanca has popular lunch specials and good *comida a la vista* – fresh *chiles rellenos* with a side of veggies do just fine. The dining area could use some natural light, or artificial light, for that matter, but the formica-topped tables and green ceramic-tile floor have their retro charm.

Sol y Luna (Map p322; ☎ 2225 6637; cnr Blvd Universitario & Av C; mains US$2-4; ☑ lunch Mon-Sat) A rare sight – a vegetarian restaurant! And in a breezy, sunny, comfortable setting. *Comida a la vista* is on offer, as well as à la carte soy burgers, fruit shakes and salads, and service is friendly.

El Sopón Típico (Map p322; ☎ 2260 2671; Pasaje las Palmeras 130; mains US$3-5; ☑ lunch & dinner) A

pleasant open-air restaurant in the middle of mall-land where you can get such *típica* treats as *conejo* (rabbit), *garrobo* (spiny tailed iguana), *gallo* (rooster) and *cabrito* (baby goat). The *super sopón* (super giant soup) lives up to its name, full of the meats of your choice and veggies (US$3.25). It's popular with families.

Salvatore's Pizzería y Pastas (Map p322; ☎ 2226 5574; 35a Av Norte 10; mains US$4-7; ☑ lunch & dinner) In case you had any doubts, rest assured that this cozy place is all about pizza and pasta. A dozen pasta dishes are available and the pizza combinations are just about limitless. If you're into 'shrooms, try Pasta Salvatore – spaghetti served with an awesome mushroom cream sauce. All dishes include garlic bread and a salad, and there's free delivery.

Las Fajitas (Map p322; ☎ 2225 3570; Blvd Universitario; mains US$3-6; ☑ lunch & dinner) Housed in a melon-colored building, Mexican food rules here. Well, it's more like Tex-Mex: chips and salsa, fajitas, enormous tostadas…. Call it what you like, it still tastes good.

Gasolinera Esso (Map p322; ☎ 2260 8410; Blvd de los Héroes; mains US$1.50-3; ☑ 24hr) Laugh all you want, but the freshly made sandwiches at this gas station are cheap, fast and pretty dang good. The moccachinos aren't bad either. It's close to the hostels.

Mister Donut (Map p322; ☎ 2260 3503; Metrosur, Blvd de los Héroes; mains US$2-4; ☑ breakfast, lunch &

dinner) If you can't bring yourself to eat at the gas station, this popular restaurant makes a good, quick alternative, with everything from eggs and beans to steak and Caesar salad. Plenty of donuts, too. There's another branch in **Centro Comercial San Luis** (Map p322; Calle San Antonio Abad).

For self-caterers, **Super Selectos** (Map p322; Metro Sur, Blvd de los Héroes; 8am-8pm Mon-Fri, 8am-6:30pm Sat) is a well-stocked supermarket hidden in the basement of Metro Sur. It's a good place to hit if you want to cook a meal or two back at the hostel. There's another branch in **Centro Comercial San Luis** (Map p322; Calle San Antonio Abad; 8am-10pm).

MIDRANGE

La Hola Beto's (Map p322; ☎ 2260 1810; Calle Lamatepec; mains US$5-12; lunch & dinner) Located in the middle of a string of restaurants, Hola Beto's is popular day or night. Seafood is the specialty (the nautical décor is a dead giveaway), but the menu is sprinkled with pizza, pasta and meat dishes. Service is top notch and the location – behind the Real InterContinental hotel – can't be beat.

El Establo (Map p322; ☎ 2226 9754; Blvd Universitario; mains US$6-10; lunch & dinner) This newcomer is a meat lovers' heaven. And, apparently, half of San Salvador thinks so too – the driveway is packed most nights. Portions are hefty: the *plato típico* includes a steak, Argentinean-style sausage, chicken-broth soup, refried beans, *tostones* (fried plantains), cheese, cream and garlic bread (US$7.45). Bring your appetite.

Zona Rosa & Colonia Escalón

These neighborhoods offer some of the best eating in the city. Colonia Escalón has eateries for all budgets – from open-air taco stands to upscale sushi bars – while the Zona Rosa's options fall mostly in the mid- and upper-range.

BUDGET

Dulce y Salado (Map p324; ☎ 2263 2212; 3a Calle Pte, Colonia Escalón; mains US$3-7; breakfast, lunch & dinner Mon-Sat, lunch & dinner Sun) Don't let the girlie ambiance – hanging plants, doilies galore, opera classics – stop you from sampling the excellent menu at this cozy restaurant. Light meals, including lots of vegetarian options, make up its core – salads, quiche, empanadas, and even spinach lasagna are

all offered. Mains include a choice of two salads and a fruit shake. There is also a full coffee and tea bar.

Taquería Los Tapatíos (Map p324; Paseo General Escalón, Colonia Escalón; mains US$3.50-5; 11:30am-2am) At the far western end of Paseo General Escalón at Plaza Masferrer is this large open-air taco stand, serving up great tacos, burritos and tortas stuffed with the meat of your choice: chicken, beef, pork, *adobado* (spicy marinated meat), *al pastor* (seasoned rotisserie pork). Wooden tables with benches are set up off the road, so the traffic noise can be overpowering – then again, the bustling informality is part of the charm.

No name comedor (Map p324; 93a Av Norte, Colonia Escalón; mains US$1-4; breakfast & lunch Mon-Sat) This tiny place, next to an upscale Japanese restaurant (Kamakura; p336), is popular with drivers waiting for their bosses to finish their California rolls, and one of the few budget eateries in this part of Escalón. Serving mostly *típica*, the occasional stir-fried noodles or rice-and-veggie dish does appear.

Típicos Margoth (Map p324; ☎ 2278 6632; Paseo General Escalón, Colonia Escalón; mains US$2-5; lunch & dinner) A popular cafeteria-style restaurant serving, as the name suggests, *típico*. Food is fresh and served in good-sized portions. There's occasional live music on Saturday night.

Le Croissant (Map p324; ☎ 2224 2865; 1a Calle Pte 3883, Colonia Escalón; pastries US$1-3; 7:30am-6:30pm Mon-Fri) A classic French bakery in the middle of San Salvador. Mouthwatering. Beautiful. Rich. A perfect mid-afternoon treat.

For self-caterers, **Super Selectos** (Map p324; El Paseo mall, Paseo General Escalón at 77a Av Sur, Colonia Escalón; 8am-10pm Mon-Sat, 8am-9pm Sun) is one of the only supermarkets in town with a gourmet food section.

MIDRANGE

Café Baguette Lido (Map p324; ☎ 2263 4373; Calle del Mirador 17-B, Colonia Escalón; mains US$5-10; breakfast, lunch & dinner Mon-Sat, breakfast & lunch Sun) A friendly eatery and bakery with two pages of creative sandwiches, divided between 'lite' and, well, not lite. Try the turkey breast with cottage cheese, and salmon with capers, both served on wholegrain bread; or turn the page to the pesto chicken and NY Polish sausages. All come with a side salad, fries or potato salad.

Restaurante Royal (Map p324; ☎ 2263 6989; Calle Padres Aguilar 601, Colonia Escalón; mains US$5-15;

(🕑) 11am-10pm Mon-Thu, 11am-11pm Fri & Sat, 11:30am-9pm Sun) While so many Chinese restaurants bowl you over with huge portions and no-nonsense service, the Royal lets you enjoy the experience, starting with a pleasant air-cooled dining room (the goldfish tank is spotless – that's gotta be a good sign) and culminating in tasty dishes, like garlic shrimp over rice noodles and stir-fried broccoli, mushrooms and bamboo shoots. Service is terrific, and the prices amazingly affordable.

Las Cofradías (Map p324; ☎ 2264 6148; Calle del Mirador, Colonia Escalón; buffet US$7; (🕑) dinner) This is a perfect place to head if you want to sample the full spectrum of Salvadoran fare. Every night, an all-you-can-eat buffet has 60 types of *típico* dishes and drinks: *yuca frita*, pupusas, empanadas, *tamales de elote* (corn *tamales*), *riguas* (sweet buttery corn tortillas wrapped in a corn husk), *gallina*, *chilate* (a thick corn drink served hot), *nuegados* (plantains and fried yucca with honey and cinnamon), *atole*, *horchata*…you name it, it's probably served. Food is displayed and served on traditional black pottery, which only adds to the ambiance.

Punto Café (Map p324; ☎ 2243 6706; Museo de Arte de El Salvador, Av La Revolución; mains US$6-20; (🕑) noon-11pm Mon-Sat) Located at the Museum of Modern Art, this café is popular with wealthy *capitalinos* and serves creative and pricey dishes in a sleek dining area.

Las Vacas Gordas (Map p324; ☎ 2243 3939; Blvd Hipódromo, Zona Rosa; mains US$8-22; (🕑) noon-3pm & 6pm-midnight Mon-Sat, noon-6pm Sun) There should be no mistaking that beef is the specialty at 'The Fat Cows' restaurant in the Zona Rosa. But just in case – or else to really freak out the vegetarians – black and white cow skins are used for the chair backs and as wall hangings. Choose from a dozen cuts of meat, from medallions to rib-eye, most of which can be ordered in various portions depending on your appetite and the thickness of your wallet. If your wallet is more carpaccio than filet mignon, check the menu for frequent two-for-one specials. Outdoor tables are especially pleasant, occupying a semi-shaded courtyard with plants hanging from a thick wooden trellis.

Koffee Mix (Map p324; ☎ 2243 5335; Av La Capilla 258, Zona Rosa; dishes US$2-9; (🕑) breakfast, lunch & dinner) Next to the Galería 1-2-3 art gallery, this upscale café serves only Café Illy coffee, whether in a cappuccino, frappé, latté, espresso or simple drip. You can also order fresh juices, smoothies and tea, as well as good but overpriced sandwiches – US$8.50 for salmon on a baguette. The interior is sleek and cool (in both senses); shady outdoor tables look onto the street.

TOP END
Kamakura (Map p324; ☎ 2263 2401; 93 Av Norte 61, Colonia Escalón; mains US$10-30; (🕑) noon-2:30pm & 6-10:30pm Mon-Sat) This Escalón restaurant is arguably San Salvador's finest for authentic Japanese food. The restaurant is divided into several intimate areas – a sunny front room, a back room with an open-air fountain, and another with low Japanese-style tables. The specialty is the sushi, *nigiri* and sashimi, with most fish flown in fresh from Miami. Twelve-piece rolls start at US$10.50; combo plates offer better value, ranging from US$14.50 samplers to a US$59 feast. The *plato del dia* (daily special) is served in a bamboo box and usually includes a soup, tempura, sushi, and a main dish – say, teriyaki chicken – for US$9.

Restaurante Basilea (Map p324; ☎ 2279 0833; Centro Comercial Basilea, Blvd del Hipódromo, Zona Rosa; mains US$5-20; (🕑) lunch & dinner) An upscale urban restaurant, Basilea is the place to head if you want a reliable, familiar meal. You can order such classics as coconut shrimp (US$18.50), Waldorf salad (US$6.50), or even a Philly steak sandwich (US$9.50). A pleasant outdoor eating area, complete with white wicker chairs and a koi pond, is a nice option on warm evenings.

Inka Grill (Map p324; ☎ 2230 6060; 79a Ave Sur, Zona Rosa; mains US$6-20; (🕑) lunch & dinner) Popular with *capitalinos*, this upscale Peruvian chain is a great option if you're looking for something a little different. The menu offers such mouthwatering meals as *lomo salteado* (tenderloin stir fried with tomatoes, potatoes and onion), *aji de gallina* (hen in a creamy parmesan nut sauce) and *arroz chaufa con mariscos* (fried rice with a seafood sauteé). The setting is borderline cheese ball – Inca-style doorways, replicas of indigenous art and masks – but it's easy to overlook that once the food arrives.

DRINKING
San Salvador has two main *zonas nocturnas* (nightlife areas): a string of bars on Calle San Antonio Abad catering to the bohe-

mian university set, and the Zona Rosa, which draws a younger snazzier crowd from San Salvador's upper crust. Foreigners are perfectly welcome in either scene.

Bars & Pubs
BLVD DE LOS HÉROES

La Luna Casa y Arte (Map p322; ☎ 2260 2921; www .lalunacasayarte.com, in Spanish; Calle Berlín 228; ☿ noon-2am Mon-Fri, 4pm-2am Sat) Around since 1991, La Luna is considered the mother of the hip bars found throughout the Blvd de los Heroes area. An eclectic space, it has comfortable couches, paper lanterns, a shady outdoor patio and modern artwork hanging from just about everywhere (picture floating mannequins and mammoth ants). A full menu tempts many out of having just a beer (p334), while live bands (p338) and movie nights (p338) keep the place hopping.

Les 3 Diables (Map p322; Calle San Antonio Abad; ☿ 7pm-2am Mon-Sat, 7pm-1am Sun) A lively bar attracting a diverse crowd of disaffected university students, professionals taking the edge off and Peace Corps volunteers cutting loose. There's no dance floor, but a great mix of old-school pop and alternative rock gets people moving wherever there's space. Look for drink specials from Monday to Thursday and live music on Wednesday.

Bar-bar-o (Map p322; ☎ 2257 9685; www.bar-bar-o .com, in Spanish; Calle San Antonio Abad 2237; ☿ 6pm-2:30am) A play on the expression '*Qué bárbaro*' ('How crazy!'), this place is more urban-hipster than its neighbors, with a sleek sitting area and a small dance floor. There's live music on Friday and Saturday nights from around 9pm (no cover), and a DJ before and after. Films are shown on Wednesday at 8pm.

Café La 'T' (Map p322; ☎ 2225 2090; Calle San Antonio Abad 2233; ☿ 10am-9:30pm Mon-Wed, 10am-11pm Thu-Sat) The most bohemian of the nightspots in town, Café La 'T' (*latte*, get it?) is straight out of Chiapas, with Zapatista posters, photos of indigenous coffee workers and a distinctly lefty crowd. Free films are screened on Wednesday and Thursday (7:30pm), and there's live music every other Friday (cover US$2), usually jazz or Latin American folk music. Coffee is the specialty – and it's excellent – but you can also buy beer, wine and light meals.

El Atrio (Map p322; ☎ 2226 5411; info@elatrio.com .sv; Av Alvarado 30; ☿ 10am-10pm Mon-Thu, 10am-

midnight Fri & Sat) Once in the thick of things, this longtime favorite moved to a quiet street several blocks east of the bar scene. Alternative films are shown under the stars every Monday, Tuesday and Wednesday at 7pm (free); Friday entertainment varies from live music to concert videos to just setting up telescopes to check out the stars.

Highland Bistro (Map p322; ☎ 2225 6907; Calle San Antonio Abad; ☿ 8pm-2am Fri & Sat) A raucous smoke-filled bar with two small rooms, and football shirts and movie posters instead of windows. There's live music most Fridays; expect a small cover charge.

El Arpa Irlandés (Map p322; ☎ 2225 0429; Av A; ☿ 2:30pm-2:30am Mon-Sat) The Irish-born founder of this no-nonsense pub has left, but the new management seems intent on keeping the Guinness flowing and Irish stew bubbling. There's a pool table, but most people come just to drink a few beers with friends.

Bar Medieval (Map p322; Av A; ☿ 8pm-2am Mon-Sat) Across the street from El Arpa Irlandés, this bar has a similar atmosphere.

La Ventana (Map p322; ☎ 2226 5129; Calle San Antonio Abad; ☿ until 1am Tue-Sun) A cool upscale hangout where you can down Belgian ales and German beers for around the same price as local brews. There's a pool table, good music and intriguing art on the walls. It's also a good spot for a meal (see p334).

Pueblo Viejo (Map p322; ☎ 2260 3551; Metrosur, Blvd de los Héroes; ☿ 7am-midnight) The best place for Latin dancing in town. This restaurant-club draws a somewhat older crowd, but never lacks for ambiance or energy – in fact, arrive late and you may not get a table. There's live music from 9:30pm Thursday through Saturday; no cover on Thursday, US$8 minimum consumption Friday and US$3 cover on Saturday. Meal deals start at US$11.45 and include soup, salad, a main dish with rice and veggies, dessert and a drink.

ZONA ROSA

In the Zona Rosa, bars and clubs come and go with surprising rapidity. Fortunately the area is relatively small, and you can easily follow your eyes and ears to the latest hot spot, or ask a taxi driver or area hotel bellhop. Dress to kill (so to speak). The following were the hotspots when we visited.

Rinconcitos (Map p324; ☎ 2298 4770; Blvd del Hipódromo 310, Zona Rosa) *The* place to start the night in the Zona Rosa. A two-story kara-oke bar with a decent appetizers menu and stiff drinks. Live music – typically Spanish rock – is played on weekends. Head to the 2nd floor to dance or just to kick back on the breezy terrace.

Jala La Jarra (Map p324; ☎ 2245 2486; Av Las Magnolias 206, Zona Rosa) Part of the Señor Frogs' chain, this is actually three places in one: a restaurant called Guadalajara Grill (open noon to 1am Monday to Saturday); a bar with a dancefloor called Cantina El Patrón (open noon to 2am Wednesday to Saturday); and Jala la Jarra (open 9:30pm to 2am Wednesday to Saturday, cover US$5 Friday and Saturday), the main bar and disco.

Elements (Map p324; ☎ 2263 8560; Paseo General Escalón 4850, Colonia Escalón) Near enough to the Zona Rosa to be included here, this disco-theque caters to a crowd in their early 20s, although you wouldn't guess it from the popular '80s music theme nights. The DJ also spins (current) top 40 tunes.

Gay & Lesbian Venues

Gay and lesbian travelers will find the gay nightlife scene buried. Deeply. The only openly gay places at the time of research were **Yascuas** and **Mileniun** (Map pp320–1; Condominios Juan Pablo II, Prolongación Juan Pablo II; ⏲ 9:30pm-1am Thu-Sat), two discotheques located in the same building. It's easy enough to find one if the other is slow, but that doesn't help the fact that the pickings are so slim.

Live Music

San Salvador has a terrific live music scene, from folk to funk, punk to pop and reggae to speed metal. Many bars feature local bands once or twice a week, with the best shows consistently at La Luna Casa y Arte, widely considered ground zero for live music in El Salvador. Be sure to check out **Musica.com.sv** (www.musica.com.sv) for the latest news, concerts and downloads – it's a terrific resource for everything to do with music in El Salvador.

The following venues are worth check-ing out:

La Luna Casa y Arte (Map p322; ☎ 2260 2921; www.lalunacasayarte.com, in Spanish; Calle Berlín 228; ⏲ noon-2am Mon-Fri, 4pm-2am Sat) Jazz, blues or funk Wednesday and Friday from 9pm. Cover charge is US$3 to US$6.

Les 3 Diables (Map p322; Calle San Antonio Abad; ⏲ 7pm-2am Mon-Sat, 7pm-1am Sun) A good mix of musicians play every Wednesday night. No cover charge.

Bar-bar-o (Map p322; ☎ 2257 9685; www.bar-bar-o .com, in Spanish; Calle San Antonio Abad 2237; ⏲ 6pm-2:30am) Rock, latin, groove, world music, you name it, it's probably been heard here. Bands play from 9pm Friday and Saturday. There's no cover charge.

Café La 'T' (Map p322; ☎ 2225 2090; Calle San Antonio Abad 2233; ⏲ 10am-9:30pm Mon-Wed, 10am-11pm Thu-Sat) Jazz or latin folk played every other Friday. Cover charge is US$2.

Highland Bistro (Map p322; ☎ 2225 6907; Calle San Antonio Abad; ⏲ 8pm-2am Fri & Sat) Classic rock most Fridays from around 9pm. Cover charge is US$1 to US$3.

Pueblo Viejo (Map p322; ☎ 2260 3551; Metrosur, Blvd de los Héroes; ⏲ 7am-midnight) Latin/tropical dance from Thursday through Saturday from 9:30pm to midnight. Free on Thursday; US$8 minimum consumption Friday; and US$3 cover on Saturday.

ENTERTAINMENT

Check the magazines and websites listed in the Media section of this chapter (p315) for ongoing and upcoming events.

Cinemas

Recent Hollywood films – with Spanish subtitles – dominate the cinemas. Prices vary a bit, depending on the location, but all are half-price on Wednesday. Session times are listed in both major newspapers.

Try the following cinemas:

Cinemark (Map p322; ☎ 2261 2001; Metrocentro, 3rd fl, Blvd de los Héroes) The best place to catch a movie. General admission US$3.50, US$3 for students with ID.

Multicinemas Reforma (Map p322; ☎ 2225 9588; Blvd Universitario) Tickets cost US$2.30 everyday, except Wednesday. Ask about Martes Loco specials when, on a random Tuesday, tickets cost US$1. Crazy.

Multicinemas Magestic (Map pp320–1; ☎ 2222 5965; Av España) Tickets cost US$1.75, US$1 on Wednesday. First screening is around 9:45am and the last around 6:15pm.

Cinépolis (Map p324; Galerías Escalón, Paseo General Escalón) This movie chain is opening an 11-screen megaplex here. It was still under construction when we visited.

A subset of alternative film venues (with free admission) – mostly coffee house, bars, and cultural centers – are also worth a stop. Check *Pashalua* magazine for listings, and look out for the following venues:

La Luna Casa y Arte (Map p322; ☎ 2260 2921; www .lalunacasayarte.com, in Spanish; Calle Berlín 228) Screen-ings at 8pm Monday and Tuesday.

Bar-bar-o (Map p322; ☎ 2257 9685; www.bar-bar-o .com, in Spanish; Calle San Antonio Abad 2237) Screening at 8pm Wednesday.

Café La 'T' (Map p322; ☎ 2225 2090; Calle San Antonio Abad 2233) Screening at 7:30pm Wednesday and Thursday.
El Atrio (Map p322; ☎ 2226 5411; info@elatrio.com.sv; Av Alvarado 30) Screening at 7pm Monday, Tuesday and Wednesday.
Centro Cultural de España (Map p324; ☎ 2275 7526; Calle La Reforma 166) Spanish films screened at 6pm Friday.
Alliance Française (Map pp320-1; ☎ 2260 5807; www .afelsalvador.com, in French & Spanish; 51a Av Norte 152) French films and Salvadoran documentaries shown at 7:30pm Wednesday.

Theater
Teatro Luis Poma (Map p322; ☎ 2261 1029; teatrolui spoma@gruporoble.com; Metrocentro, main entrance, Blvd de los Héroes; ⏱ 2-8pm Tue-Sun) If you're curious about San Salvador's theater scene, check out this modern play house. Yes, it's in a mega-mall, but the offerings are excellent, the setting is sophisticated and the tickets are affordable (US$5).
  Teatro Presidente (Map p324; ☎ 2243 3407; Av La Revolución, Zona Rosa) Hosts ballet, symphony, and other performances and festivals. Check local papers or *Pashalua* magazine for up-coming events.

Sports
It should come as no surprise that *fútbol* (soccer) is the biggest sport in San Salva-dor. The capitol's team **San Salvador Fútbol Club** (www.fesfut.org.sv/primeradivision.html) was formed in 2002 and joined the la Primera División del Fútbol Salvadorenó, the major league of Salvadoran soccer, straight away. Despite its youth, the team won the na-tional championship in 2003, giving *capi-talinos* something to cheer about. When at home, San Salvador Fútbol Club plays in the 80,000-seat Estadio Mágico González, also known as Estadio Flor Blanco, located west of Parque Cuscatlán.

SHOPPING
While the capital's main claim to shopping fame is Metrocentro, the largest mall in Central America, it also has a number of markets, art galleries, museum gift shops and boutiques where travelers of all tastes and budgets can find that perfect memento. Most Salvadoran folk art is represented, whether *añil* (indigo) from Chalchuapa, *sorpresas* from Ilobasco, bright bucolic paintings from La Palma or black pottery

from Guatajiagua. And you're sure to track down an 'I Love Hot Salvadoran Pupusas' T-shirt (US$17) in one of the malls.

Art
La Pinacoteca (Map p324; ☎ 2223 2808; lapinacoteca@ integra.com.sv; Blvd El Hipódromo 305; ⏱ 9am-1pm & 2-6pm Mon-Fri, 9am-1pm Sat) Whether you're in-terested in buying a high-end work of art, or just like to window shop, head to this su-perb art gallery. While showcased artwork changes regularly, there is always a good variety of paintings, sculptures, graphic art and photography on display.
  El Arbol de Dios (Map p324; ☎ 2263 9206; www.elar boldedios.com; Calle La Mascota; ⏱ 8:30am-9:30pm Mon-Sat) If you like the colorful art of La Palma, you'll love this gallery, which features works by the artist who started it all – Fernando Llort. An impressive collection of Llort's lithographs, ceramics, *tejidos* (stitchwork) and canvases are sold here. Not cheap, but they're masterpieces.
  Galería 1-2-3 (Map p324; ☎ 2275-9827; galeria123@ yahoo.com; Av La Capilla 258; ⏱ 8:30am-12:30pm &, 2:30-6pm Mon-Fri, 8:30am-12:30pm Sat) A small upscale gallery selling modern paintings and sculp-tures by mostly Central American artists. It's next to Koffee Mix café; ring the bell to get in.

Handicrafts
Nahanché (Map p324; ☎ 2245 2045; Centro Comercial Basiliea, Blvd del Hipódromo; ⏱ 9am-7pm Mon-Sat, 11am-5pm Sun) Hands down, this boutique of-fers the best selection of Salvadoran *arte-sanías* (handicrafts) in town; you'll find everything from brilliant indigo place mats to intricate miniature figurines. Items are pricey but the craftsmanship can't be beat. A sister store is located in **Metrocentro** (Map p322; ☎ 2260 3603; Blvd de los Héroes; ⏱ 9am-7pm Mon-Sat, 10am-5pm Sun), although the quality simply isn't the same.
  Shicali Ceramica (Map p322; ☎ 2226 4843; Calle Centro América; ⏱ 8am-5pm Mon-Fri, 8am-4pm Sun) Beautiful ceramics are sold at this neigh-borhood pottery workshop that was created by Acogipri, an association that is dedicated to bettering the lives of handicapped people in El Salvador. In fact, almost every item is created on-site by beneficiaries of the as-sociation.
  Mayan Gifts Artesanías (Map p322; ☎ 2261 0051; Metrocentro, 3rd fl, Blvd de los Héroes; ⏱ 9am-8pm) Not

the classiest of gift shops, but once you dig through the shiny key chains and loud T-shirts, you'll find a decent assortment of black clay pottery and colorful *artesanías*.

Markets

Mercado Nacional de Artesanías (Map p324; Alameda Araujo; 9am-6pm) A couple of dozen stands sell the gamut of Salvadoran crafts in this outdoor market: miniatures, colorful wood creations, black pottery, indigo dresses… you name it, they've probably got it. Shop around a bit before you buy – the quality varies quite a bit. It's located behind the Feria Internacional de El Salvador.

Mercado Ex-Cuartel (Map pp320-1; Calle Delgado; 7:30am-6pm Mon-Sat, 7:30am-2pm Sun) This army barracks-turned-public market has three sections: shoes, clothes and *artesanías*. The first two areas are aimed mainly at locals, although travelers can find decent leather sandals and cool soccer shirts (not to mention puffy pink dresses). The best *artesanía* products here are the hammocks, which hang from high hooks like fresh laundry, in many colors, sizes and varieties.

Shopping Centers

Metrocentro (Map p322; Blvd de los Héroes; 8am-8pm) Imagine walking into a three-story, 10-wing jungle of clothing and jewelry stores, shoe stores, department stores, bookstores, electronics stores, Internet cafés, cell-phone offices, music stores, sporting-good stores, furniture stores, banks, pharmacies, nail salons and restaurants, and then throw in a city hall outpost, play house, multiscreen cinema, airline office, post office, hardware store, supermarket, countless parking spaces, taxi stops, bus stops, escalators galore….and any number of specialty shops (maternity, chocolates, loud T-shirts) and you've got Metrocentro. Said to be the largest mall in Central America. It's mammoth. It's overwhelming. And it's almost always filled with teenagers checking each other out. It's a mall. But it's convenient and safe, and you'll find almost anything you need.

Metro Sur (Map p322; Blvd de los Héroes; 9am-7pm) The runt of the mall pack sits two floors high and has a remarkable number of Internet cafés – half a dozen at last count. You'll also find a handful of teen-wear boutiques, sporting-good stores and even a supermarket. The manageable size makes it

great place to check email, make a quick ATM stop or grab a bite to eat. A pedestrian bridge connects it to Metrocentro if you're looking for more of everything.

Galerías Escalón (Map p324; Paseo General Escalón; 8am-8pm) San Salvador's poshest mall, with three air-cooled levels of upscale clothing and jewelry stores, electronics stores and cell-phone offices, all the major banks and a new Cinépolis mega-cinema. Even the food court is fancy-pants, with sushi, shwarma and bagel joints, alongside the usual major outlets. And whereas the other malls have scads of Internet cafés packed with chat-crazy, game-playing kids, there's only one here – tucked in a quiet nook of the women's clothing section of Siman department store.

GETTING THERE & AWAY
Air

El Salvador's main international airport, and a major Central American hub, **Aeropuerto Internacional Comalapa** (SAL; ☎ 2339 8264) is located 50km southeast of San Salvador. Airline offices in San Salvador are listed below; they also have offices at the airport. Many of the phone numbers listed are for central call centers and may be open longer hours.

American Airlines (Map pp320-1; ☎ 2298 0777; Edificio La Centroamericana, Alameda Roosevelt; 8am-6pm Mon-Fri, 8am-noon Sat)

Continental Airlines (Map p322; ☎ 2207 2040; Metrocentro, 2nd fl, Blvd de los Héroes; 8am-6pm Mon-Fri, 8am-noon Sat)

Copa Airlines (Map p324; ☎ 2209 2672; World Trade Center I, cnr 89a Av Norte & Calle del Mirador; 8am-6pm Mon-Fri, 8am-noon Sat)

Delta Air Lines (Map p324; ☎ 2275 9292; World Trade Center I, cnr 89a Av Norte & Calle del Mirador; 8am-5:30pm Mon-Fri, 8am-11am Sat)

TACA (Map p324; ☎ 2267 8222; Galerías Escalón, street level, Paseo General Escalón; 8am-8pm Mon-Fri, 8am-5pm Sat, 9am-5pm Sun)

United Airlines (Map p324; ☎ 2279 3900; Galerías Escalón, street level, Paseo General Escalón; 8:30am-6:30pm Mon-Fri, 9am-1pm Sat)

Bus

San Salvador has three main terminals for long-distance domestic buses: **Terminal de Oriente** (Map p312; Alameda Juan Pablo II) is used by buses serving all eastern and some northern destinations; **Terminal de Occidente** (Map pp320-1; Blvd Venezuela) serves all western destinations, including most of the Guatemalan border crossings; and **Terminal de Sur** (Autopista a Comalapa), also known as Terminal San Marcos, serves destinations to the south and southeast, and is several kilometers south of the city center.

All three terminals are busy and hectic. They're not unsafe, per se, but keep an eye on your bags and pockets – and on buses pulling in and out! Some destinations have different categories of service, so be sure you know what bus you're getting on. 'Directo' sounds nice but is usually standard stop-and-go service known as 'ordinario.' 'Especial' buses have air-con, reclining seats and TV, and are well worth the small extra cost. They also make fewer stops (or none at all), which is not only faster but safer – though relatively rare, most bus crime occurs when a 2nd-class bus picks up an unsavory character mid-route.

TERMINAL DE ORIENTE

To get to this terminal, take bus 9, 29 or 34 from the city center; bus 29 or 52 from Blvd de los Héroes; bus 7C or 34 from Terminal Occidente; or bus 21 from Terminal de Sur. Most buses coming from the city center drop you on the opposite side of a busy roundabout. Use the pedestrian walkway to cross – it's safer and leads right into the terminal.

The following destinations are served by buses departing from Terminal de Oriente:

Chalatenango Bus 125 (US$0.90, two hours, every 10 minutes from 4am to 6:40pm).

Cojutepeque Take an ordinary San Vicente bus (US$0.40, one hour).

El Amatillo (Honduran border) Bus 306 or 346 (*directo* US$3, four hours, every 30 minutes from 3:45am to 3:45pm; *super especial* US$5, four hours, 5:20am, 11:40am and 2:20pm); or take any San Miguel bus and transfer to bus 330.

El Poy (Honduran border) Bus 119 (US$1.60, three hours, every 30 minutes from 4am to 4pm).

Ilobasco Bus 111 (US$0.70, 1½ hours, every 10 to 15 minutes 5am to 8pm); some Sesuntepeque-bound buses (bus 112) also enter Ilobasco.

La Palma Take an El Poy bus (US$1.50, 2¾ hours, every 30 minutes from 4am to 4pm).

La Unión Bus 304 (*directo* US$3, four hours, every 30 minutes from 4:30am to 4pm; *especial* US$5, three hours, 1pm).

San Francisco Gotera Bus 305 (US$3, 3½ hours, 6:40am, 12:30pm and 2:33pm); or take any San Miguel bus and transfer to bus 328.

San Miguel Bus 301 (*directo* US$2.10, 2½ hours, every 10 minutes from 3am to 5:10pm; *super especial* US$4, two hours, 7am, 8am and every 40 minutes from 11am to 3pm).

San Sebastián Bus 110 (US$0.68, 1½ hours, every 20 minutes from 5:30am to 7pm).

San Vicente Bus 116 (*directo* US$0.83, 1½ hours, every 10 minutes from 4:40am to 9pm; *especial* US$0.83, one hour, 6am, 6:20am, 6:40am, 7am, 4:20pm, 5pm, 5:30pm and 6pm).

Santa Rosa de Lima Take an El Amatillo bus, or any San Miguel bus, and transfer to bus 330.

Sesuntepeque Bus 112 (US$1, two hours, every 15-30 minutes from 4:20am to 6pm).

Suchitoto Bus 129 (US$0.66, 1½ hours, every 20 minutes from 4:35am to 8:15pm).

Usulután Bus 302 (US$1.50, 2¾ hours, 7am and 8am); or use Terminal de Sur.

TERMINAL DE OCCIDENTE

From the city center, bus 34 will drop you in front of the western terminal; from Blvd de los Héroes take bus 44 down 49a Av Sur, get off at Blvd Venezuela and walk a few blocks west to the terminal. From Terminal de Oriente, take bus 7C or 34; both buses return to Terminal de Oriente but bus 7C is fastest, notwithstanding the fact you catch it heading *west* on Blvd Venezuela.

The following destinations are served by buses departing from Terminal de Occidente:

Ahuachapán Bus 202 (*directo* US$1, 2¼ hours, every 10 minutes 4:50am to 7:10pm; *especial* US$2, one hour, every 20 minutes from 7am to 6pm).

Cerro Verde Take an ordinary Santa Ana bus to El Congo (US$0.80, 40 minutes), transfer to bus 248.

Joya de Cerén Bus 108 to San Juan Opico (US$0.52, 1¼ hours, every 10 minutes from 5:30am to 8pm).

La Hachadura Take 205 to Sonsonate, transfer to bus 259.

La Libertad Bus 102 (US$0.55, one hour, every 10 minutes from 4:30am to 8pm). Note: the bus passes in *front* of the western terminal, not inside; alternatively catch it at its terminal on 37a Av Norte near the Gimnacio Nacional, or at Iglesia La Ceiba de Guadalupe.

Lago de Coatepeque Take an ordinary Santa Ana bus to El Congo (US$0.80, 40 minutes); transfer to bus 248.

Las Chinamas Take bus 202 to Ahuachapán, transfer to bus 263.

Los Cóbanos Take 205 to Sonsonate, transfer to bus 257.

Metapán Bus 201A (*directo* US$2.50, 1¾ hours, every 30 minutes from 6am to 6:30pm).

Ruínas de San Andrés Take ordinary Santa Ana bus to ruins turnoff (US$0.80, 25 minutes).

San Cristóbal Bus 498 (US$1.25, three hours, 4:10pm, 4:50pm and 5:20pm Monday to Friday, plus 7:20am Monday and Friday and12:20pm Saturday).

Santa Ana Bus 201 (*directo* US$0.80, 1¼ hours, every 10 minutes from 4am to 8:10pm; *especial* US$1.25, one hour, every 20 minutes from 6am to 7:40pm).

Sonsonate Bus 205 (*directo* US$0.70, 1½ hours, every three to 10 minutes from 4:20am to 8pm; *especial* US$1, 1¼ hours, every 15 minutes from 5:30am to 7pm).

TERMINAL DE SUR (TERMINAL SAN MARCOS)

To get to Terminal de Sur take bus 26 or microbus 11B from the city center, or bus 21 from Terminal Oriente. From Terminal de Sur, bus 11-B is the most convenient, stopping at the city center and then on Alameda Juan Pablo II – handy if you're headed to the Blvd de los Héroes, Colonia Escalón or Zona Rosa areas. Buses 26 and 'A' also work if you're just going to the city center.

The following destinations are served by buses departing from Terminal de Sur:

Costa del Sol Bus 495 (*calle vieja* US$1.10, 2½ hours, every 30 minutes from 6am to 6pm; *calle nueva* US$1.10,1½ hours, 8am and 4pm only).

Puerto El Triunfo Bus 185 (US$1.50, two hours, 9:05am, 11:10am, 12:50pm, 1:35pm, 2:10pm and 5:30pm); or take an ordinary Usulután bus to Jiquilisco turnoff and transfer to bus 363.

Usulután Bus 302 (*directo* US$1.50, 2½ hours, every 10 minutes from 4am to 4:55pm; *especial* US$2, 1½ hours, 8am, 9:10am, 11:15am, 12:35pm, 1pm, 1:30pm, 2pm, 2:40pm, 3pm and 4:25pm).

Zacatecoluca Bus 133 (*via calle vieja* US$0.68, 1½ hours, every 10 minutes from 4:30am to 8:10pm; *via calle nueva* US$0.68, one hour, every 10 minutes from 4:30am to 8:10pm).

INTERNATIONAL BUSES

A number of bus lines offer international bus service throughout Central America. It's highly recommended that you use 1st-class service for safety as much as comfort. Some companies offer two classes (usually 'executive' and '1st class') on a single split-level bus. All quoted prices are one way.

King Quality/Comfort Lines Terminal Puerto Bus (Map pp320-1; ☎ 2271 3330, 2271 1361; Juan Pablo II); Zona Rosa (Map p324; ☎ 2257 8997; Blvd del Hipódromo) Service to Guatemala City (Comfort US$22, five hours, 7:30am and 1:30pm; first/'King' class US$26/33, five hours, 6am and 3:30pm), Tegucigalpa (first/'King' class US$28/41, six hours, 6am and 1:30pm), San Pedro Sula (first/'King' US$28/41, six hours, 5am and 12:30pm), Managua

(first/'King' US$28/42, 10½ hours, 11:30am) and San José, California (US$48, 18 hours, 3:30am). Buses depart from Terminal Puerto Bus and pass its Blvd del Hipódromo office 30 minutes later.

Pullmantur (Map p324; ☎ 2243 1300; www.pullmantur.com, in Spanish; Hotel Sheraton Presidente; Av La Revolución, Zona Rosa) Service to Guatemala City (executive/1st class US$26/41, 4½ hours, 7am and 3pm Monday to Saturday, 8:30am and 3pm Sunday) and Tegucigalpa (executive/1st class US$27/45, 6½ hours, 2:15pm).

Second Class (Map pp320-1; ☎ 2217 3300; Terminal Puerto Bus, Alameda Juan Pablo II) Groups of five 2nd-class bus lines rotate days to provide daily service to Guatemala (standard US$10, five hours, hourly 4am to 3pm; executive US$13,five hours, 6am and 4:30pm) and Tapachula, Mexico (US$43, 10 hours, 6am).

Tica Bus (www.ticabus.com) Hotel San Carlos (Map pp320-1; ☎ 2222 4808; Calle Concepción 121); Zona Rosa (Map p324; ☎ 2243 9764; Blvd Hipódromo) Service to Guatemala City (US$11, five hours, 6am), Tegucigalpa (US$15, six hours, 5:30am), Managua (US$25, 11 hours, 5am) and San José, California (US$42, 18 hours, 3am). For San Pedro Sula (US$23, nine hours) take Tegucigalpa bus and transfer; for Panama City (US$61, 36 hours) take San José bus and transfer. Buses depart from Calle Concepción and pass its Blvd del Hipódromo office approximately 15 minutes later.

Car & Motorcycle

Rental cars from well-known chains average US$50 to US$60 per day for an ordinary car: pretty pricey, especially factoring in gas prices. Ask around and check for weekend, long-term or web-only specials. Local companies are significantly cheaper – starting around US$25 per day – but less formal in their operations and service. This doesn't make them unreliable, per se, but factor in your ability to handle a breakdown or other situation should it arise – for example, how good is your Spanish? Do you have a cell phone? How much luggage do you have?

It's typically cheaper to rent in the city rather than at the airport, where agencies include an 11% surcharge. Recommended car-rental agencies include the following:

Alamo/UNO (Map p324; ☎ 2211 2111; Blvd del Hipódromo 426; ⏰ 7am-6pm Mon-Fri; 8am-5pm Sat, 8am-noon Sun)

Avis (Map pp320-1; ☎ 2261 1212, airport 2339 9268; www.avis.com.sv, in Spanish; 43a Av Sur 127; ⏰ 8am-6pm)

Budget (Map pp320-1; ☎ 2260 4333; www.budget.com.sv, in Spanish; 1a Calle Poniente 2765; ⏰ 9am-1pm & 2-6pm Mon-Fri, 8am-noon Sat)

Quick Rent a Car (☎ 2229 6959; www.quickrentacar.com.sv, in Spanish) Offers hotel or airport pick up/drop off.

GETTING AROUND
To/From the Airport

Shuttles operated by **Taxis Acacya** (Map pp320-1; ☎ 2271 4937, airport 2339 9282; cnr 19a Av Norte & 3a Calle Poniente) are the best way to get to and from the airport. The trip costs US$3 and takes 40 to 45 minutes. In San Salvador, shuttles leave from the Taxis Acacya lot in the city center, behind Terminal Puerto Bus, at 6am, 7am, 10am and 2pm. From the airport, departures are at 9am, 1pm and 5:30pm.

Bus 138 (actually a microbus) passes the airport on its way to and from the city center (US$0.60, 45 to 60 minutes, every 10 minutes). Going to the airport, catch the bus at its terminal (Map pp320–1; a vacant lot) just south of Plaza Barrios. Note that the bus does *not* enter the airport terminal area, and that the stop is very easy to miss. Remind the driver and/or his assistant several times to let you off at the airport – you'll feel obnoxious but it's a whole lot better than missing your stop – and your flight! Going from the airport into San Salvador, bus 138 passes the same stop going the opposite direction. Exiting the airport, cut through the parking lot to the highway (about 75m away), where there's a small bus shelter. Take bus 138 all the way to its terminal south of Plaza Barrios. From there, a taxi anywhere will cost US$3 to US$4, or you can walk two blocks north and one block east (right) to Parque Libertad, where bus 30 heads to Blvd de los Héroes, passing the Parque Cuscatlán area along the way.

A taxi to or from the airport costs US$20 – don't bother bargaining.

Car & Motorcycle

Exploring San Salvador by car is no more difficult or dangerous than doing likewise in any other busy Central American city. The roads are mostly well maintained, and stoplights and street signs are generally obeyed, at least on major roads. Be aware that many streets are one way, indicated by a street sign or an arrow painted on the pavement. Avoid driving through the city center area – the traffic is unreal during the day and it's unsafe at night. In general, it's quicker to take the large thoroughfares, even if the distance is greater, than to cut through narrow city streets where you may get mired in traffic or street markets. Bus,

microbus and taxi drivers are notoriously aggressive – give them a wide berth.

Public Transportation

San Salvador's extensive bus network, from large smoke-spewing monsters to zippy microbuses, can get you just about anywhere you need to go. Fares cost US$0.17 to US$0.23.

Buses run frequently from 5am to 7:30pm daily; fewer buses run on Sunday. Between around 7:30pm and 8:30pm they become less frequent and finally stop; the microbuses run later, until around 9pm. After 9pm you'll have to take a taxi.

In the city center, it may be faster to walk a few blocks away from Plaza Barrios to catch your bus, as traffic in the city center is hopelessly snarled most of the time. But if you have bags, it's safer and easier to get on a bus as soon as possible.

Key routes include the following:

Bus 9 Goes down 29a Av Norte alongside the Universidad de El Salvador, then it turns east toward the city center, heading past the cathedral and up Independencia past Terminal de Oriente.

Bus 26 Passes Plaza Barrios and Parque Zoológico on its way to Terminal de Sur (Terminal San Marcos).

Bus 29 Goes to Terminal de Oriente via the city center. Pick it up at the large stop between Metrocentro and Metrosur.

Bus 30 Heads downtown and is the best way to get to and from bus 138 to the airport. Pick it up behind Metrocentro or at Parque Libertad in the city center.

Bus 30B A very useful route, especially from Blvd de los Héroes. The bus goes east on Blvd Universitario, by Universidad Nacional, then southwest down Blvd de los Héroes to Metrocentro. From there, it goes west along Alameda Roosevelt, past the El Salvador del Mundo monument and continues west along Paseo General Escalón past Galerías Escalón. It turns south at 79a Av and continues along Blvd del Hipódromo to Av La Revolución, passing through the Zona Rosa and near the art and anthropology museums, then returns on Alameda Araujo, Roosevelt and 49a Av Sur back to Metrocentro.

Bus 34 Runs from Terminal de Oriente to Metrocentro then down to the Zona Rosa, turning around right in front of the Museo de Arte de El Salvador (MARTE). Passes Terminal de Occidente on its return.

Bus 42 Takes you to the anthropology museum and La Ceiba de Guadalupe. The bus goes west along Calle Arce from the cathedral and continues along Alameda Roosevelt. At El Salvador del Mundo, it heads southwest along Alameda Araujo, passing the Mercado Nacional de Artesanías and Museo Nacional de Antropología David

J Guzmán, and continues down the Carr Panamericana, passing Iglesia La Ceiba de Guadalupe.

Bus 44 The bus to take to the Terminal de Occidente and Universidad Centroamericana José Simeon Cañas (UCA). The route heads southwest on Blvd de los Héroes past Metrocentro and continues south on 49a Av Sur. For the Terminal de Occidente, get off at Av Venezuela and walk a few blocks west. The bus continues along a roundabout route, eventually passing the lower and then upper entrances to UCA – the latter, on Calle de Mediterráneo, is more convenient. The bus turns around, passing the upper UCA entrance again before turning at Iglesia La Ceiba de Guadalupe and heading up Alameda Araujo, past Metrosur and continuing downtown.

Bus 52 Has two different routes – one heads straight down Paseo General Escalón, the other cuts up Calle del Mirador, passing the Raddison before turning left down Av Alberto Masferrer Norte. Both return along Paseo General Escalón and can be picked up at Metrosur.

Bus 101 Goes from Plaza Barrios in the city center, past Metrosur, past the Museo Nacional de Antropología David J Guzmán, past Iglesia La Ceiba de Guadalupe and on to Santa Tecla.

Taxi

Taxis are plentiful in San Salvador, though they're not metered, so negotiate a price before you climb in. Fares are cheap – a ride around the city should cost US$3 to US$4 during the day and US$4 to US$5 at night. Be sure the license plate of the taxi begins with an 'A,' indicating it's a registered and licensed taxi (as opposed to a guy who has just painted his car yellow). Licensed drivers are not only trained but, in theory, can be held accountable for any problems that arise. If you don't spot a taxi passing by at the moment you want one, try calling **Taxis Acacya** (☎ 2271 4937) or **Acontaxis** (☎ 2270 1176).

AROUND SAN SALVADOR

EL BOQUERÓN

Quezaltepeque (Volcán San Salvador) has two peaks. The higher peak, at 1960m, is called Picacho. The other, Boquerón (Big Mouth), is 1893m high and has a second cone within its crater – 45m high and perfectly symmetrical – formed in 1917. A paved road to the top makes it a fairly easy, though slow, ride up. Once there, you'll find a landscaped park with fantastic views into the craters and over San Salvador – just try and ignore the trash you see around you.

To get here from San Salvador, take bus 101A or B to Santa Tecla from Iglesia La Ceiba de Guadalupe. From there, bus 103 departs from 6a Av Sur to the village of Boquerón. The bus is sporadic, but pickups depart from the same place. Get an early start, as the trip will take around two hours.

PARQUE BALBOA

Just 12km south of the city center, **Parque Balboa** (admission US$0.69) is one of the most popular parks around San Salvador. Close to 28 hectares are preserved for family fun; you'll find a few trails to take some quick walks, a skating rink, playgrounds and some pre-Columbian–style sculptures. And although plenty of families bring picnics, there also are a sprinkling of eateries that sell cheap eats – pupusas, chicken dishes and burgers. The best time to come is on a Saturday or Sunday afternoon, when the park is filled with *capitalinos* enjoying their day off.

To get here, take bus 12, the 'Mil Cumbres' bus, from the east side of the Mercado Central on 12a Calle Poniente – it'll drop you off at the entrance. If you're driving, take the highway toward the airport and exit at Planes de Renderos; from there, just follow the signs on the main road until you arrive.

PUERTA DEL DIABLO

Two kilometers past Parque Balboa is **Puerta del Diablo** (Devil's Door). Two towering boulders, reputedly a single stone split in two in a storm in the 1700s, form this lookout. Once an ominous place – during the war this was an execution point, the cliffs offering easy disposal of the bodies – it is now considered a pleasant place to spend a weekend afternoon. When it's clear, the views of Volcán Chichontepec (p435), the Pacific coastline and Lago de Ilopango are fantastic.

To arrive by bus or car, follow the same directions for Parque Balboa (above) and just keep going south on the main road until it ends. Be sure to take a full-size bus 12 – the small ones don't go all the way to Puerta del Diablo.

PANCHIMALCO

Toltec immigrants founded this quiet, culturally proud town, situated in a lush valley 17km south of San Salvador. The baroque church, **Iglesia de Santa Cruz** (Main Plaza) was completed in 1725 by indigenous craftsmen; it has some interesting woodwork inside, including an indigenous Jesus Christ.

A pair of cultural centers along the main drag are also worth a stop: the **Casa de la Cultura de Panchimalco** (☎ 2280 8767; Calle Antigua; ⏰ 8am-5pm Mon-Fri) has a small exhibition area showcasing traditional dance costumes, *artesanías* and paintings; while **Casa Taller Encuentros** (☎ 2280 6958; Calle Antigua 18B; ⏰ 8am-5pm Mon-Sat) offers art workshops to locals and also exhibits paintings in it's front room. Both host cultural events that are open to the public, including music concerts and dance performances.

Panchimalco is renowned for its religious festivals, particularly **Palm Sunday**, when residents parade through the streets bearing decorated palm fronds. Another famous celebration is the **Feria Cultural de las Flores y las Palmas** (Cultural Festival of the Flowers and Palm Fronds), which has been held in early May since 1980. The festival features palm artistry, live music, folk dancing and fireworks.

Bus 17 departs for Panchimalco from Av 29 de Agosto, on the south side of the Mercado Central in San Salvador (US$0.30, 40 minutes).

WESTERN EL SALVADOR

Western El Salvador is a beautiful part of the country, and a must for an El Salvador itinerary. Three of the country's six tallest volcanoes are here, including the stark black cone of Volcán Izalco and the hulking Volcán Santa Ana (p353), its sides crisscrossed with coffee trees. Santa Ana (p346) is one of El Salvador's most appealing large cities, while small colonial towns and indigenous villages pepper the famed Ruta de las Flores (p357). Rounding out the region's attractions are the exuberantly blue Lago de Coatepeque (p352), the country's best archaeological sites, and three national parks with hikes for all experience levels and vistas that will make your heart stop. And, unlike many other parts of El Salvador, traveling here is a breeze, with frequent

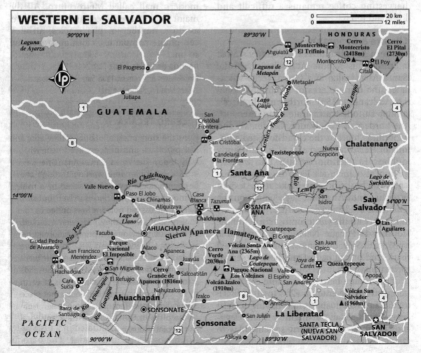

WESTERN EL SALVADOR

public transportation, well-maintained roads, recommended guided excursions, charming hotels that don't cost an arm and a leg, and even camping. Local residents are open and gracious, and are increasingly accustomed to foreign travelers.

Western El Salvador is the country's main coffee-growing region, having eclipsed Alegría and San Vicente in overall production. You'll quickly learn to recognize the waxy leaves of coffee trees, and taller trees planted in huge grid patterns to block the wind. However, for all that coffee has brought the region (and country) in jobs and income, it has also been the vehicle of tremendous division and inequality. In January 1932, indigenous coffee workers mounted a short-lived uprising against slave-like working conditions, killing around a hundred landowners and officials; in response the Salvadoran army systematically killed some 30,000 indigenous peasants, especially around the western towns of Izalco, Nahuizalco and Juayúa, in what is now known as La Matanza (The Slaughter). Working conditions have improved immensely since then, but harvesting coffee remains a difficult and low-paid job.

Climate & Geography

Western El Salvador is the country's most mountainous region. At its heart are the Santa Ana, Izalco and Cerro Verde volcanoes, the centerpieces of Parque Nacional Los Volcanes (p353). Further north, there's a high-altitude triumvirate of another sort: the borders of El Salvador, Guatemala and Honduras meet at the cloud-forested summit of Cerro Montecristo, at a point aptly dubbed El Trifinio (p360). The western region also includes Lago de Coatepeque (p352), a beautiful crater lake at the foot of Volcán Santa Ana, and Lago Guija, on the Guatemala–El Salvador border, and numerous rivers. In the westernmost corner of the country is Parque Nacional El Imposible (p375), El Salvador's most famous national park, and one of its last and best-preserved primary forests.

The climate here can be quite cool, with temperatures averaging 12°C to 20°C (54°F to 68°F). You'll appreciate having a light sweater, especially at night in high elevations and during the rainy season (May to November).

SANTA ANA
pop 181,131

A shining star, Santa Ana is the only major city in El Salvador that is overwhelmingly colonial, with a shady plaza, grand old buildings and a striking Gothic cathedral. Add to that a decent selection of accommodations, a lively food and bar scene, and big-city services, and Santa Ana makes a fine place to spend a couple days – or, better yet, a base for exploring the western corners of the country.

Orientation

Santa Ana's central park is called Parque Libertad, with its intriguing Gothic cathedral on the west side, national theatre on the north and city hall to the east. Most restaurants and services are clustered around the city center, and south along Av Independencia, one of the main roads in and out of town. The main bus terminal is on 10a Av Sur, a long 14-block walk from the city center.

Information

Like San Salvador, Santa Ana has a large modern mall called Metrocentro. All the major banks have offices and ATMs there, as do a number of pharmacies, airlines, cell-phone companies, clothing stores and so on.

Agencia de Viajes Turex (☎ 2441 1046; turex@navegante.com.sv; 1a Av Sur; ◷ 8am-noon & 2-6pm Mon-Fri, 8am-noon Sat)

CERRO TECANA

As the story goes, a long long time ago, a Pipil prince and princess lived near what is today known as Santa Ana. One day, as the couple were walking through the countryside, they were attacked by a rival tribe member. The prince survived, but alas, his princess did not. She was buried in the very spot where they had been attacked. From that day on, the prince mourned his princess. Everyday he'd walk to her grave and leave a small mound of earth. He went so many times – thousands and thousands of times – that the small mounds of earth took shape as a small hill. Today that place is called Cerro Tecana. It can be seen from the plaza in Santa Ana. Just ask any local to point it out.

SANTA ANA

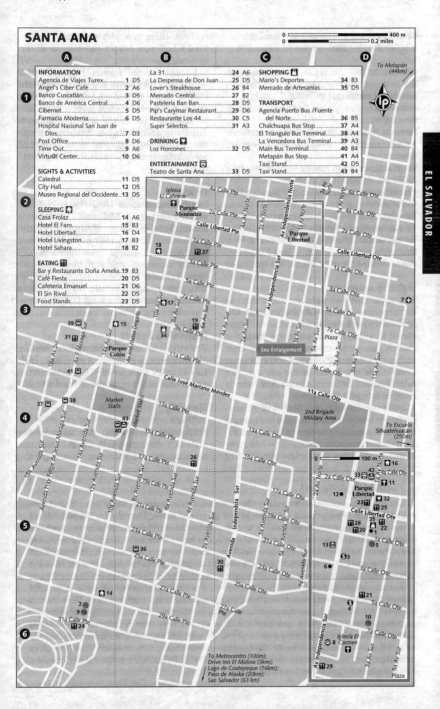

INFORMATION
Agencia de Viajes Turex..............1 D5
Angel's Ciber Café.......................2 A6
Banco Cuscatlán..........................3 D5
Banco de América Central...........4 D6
Cibernet......................................5 D5
Farmacia Moderna......................6 D5
Hospital Nacional San Juan de
   Dios.......................................7 D3
Post Office...................................8 D6
Time Out.....................................9 A6
Virtu@l Center..........................10 D6

SIGHTS & ACTIVITIES
Catedral....................................11 D5
City Hall....................................12 D5
Museo Regional del Occidente...13 D5

SLEEPING
Casa Frolaz...............................14 A6
Hotel El Faro.............................15 B3
Hotel Libertad...........................16 D4
Hotel Livingston........................17 B3
Hotel Sahara.............................18 B2

EATING
Bar y Restaurante Doña Amelia..19 B3
Café Fiesta.................................20 D5
Cafeteria Emanuel.....................21 D6
El Sin Rival................................22 D5
Food Stands..............................23 D5

La 31...24 A6
La Despensa de Don Juan..........25 D5
Lover's Steakhouse....................26 B4
Mercado Central........................27 B2
Pastelería Ban Ban....................28 D5
Pip's Carymar Restaurant...........29 D6
Restaurante Los 44....................30 C5
Super Selectos...........................31 A3

DRINKING
Los Horcones.............................32 D5

ENTERTAINMENT
Teatro de Santa Ana..................33 D5

SHOPPING
Mario's Deportes.......................34 B3
Mercado de Artesanías..............35 D5

TRANSPORT
Agencia Puerto Bus /Fuente
   del Norte................................36 B5
Chalchuapa Bus Stop.................37 A4
El Triángulo Bus Terminal..........38 A4
La Vencedora Bus Terminal........39 A3
Main Bus Terminal.....................40 B4
Metapán Bus Stop.....................41 A4
Taxi Stand.................................42 D5
Taxi Stand.................................43 B4

EL SALVADOR

Banco Cuscatlán (☎ 2489 4876; Av Independencia Sur at 3a Calle Ote; ⏲ 8:30am-5pm Mon-Fri, 8:30am-noon Sat)

Cibernet (☎ 2447 7746; 1a Calle Ote at 1a Av Norte; per hr US$0.80; ⏲ 8:30am-6pm Mon-Fri, 8:30-5pm Sat)

Farmacias Económicas (☎ 2440 2877, 2530 2530; Metrocentro; ⏲ 9am-7pm Mon-Sat & 10am-6pm Sun) Home delivery available.

Farmacia Moderna (☎ 2448 1212; Av Independencia Sur at 3a Calle Pte; ⏲ 8am-7pm Mon-Fri, 8am-6pm Sat, 8am-noon Sun)

Hospital Nacional San Juan de Díos (☎ 2447 1555; 3a Calle Ote; ⏲ 24hr)

Post Office (Av Independencia Sur; ⏲ 7:30am-5pm Mon-Fri, 7:30am-noon Sat)

Time Out (☎ 2440 4765; 10a Av Sur; per 90min US$1; ⏲ 8am-9pm Mon-Fri, 9am-7pm Sat & Sun)

Virtu@l Center (☎ 2441 3553; 7a Calle Ote at 3a Av Norte; per hr US$0.60; ⏲ 8:30am-12:30pm & 2-7pm Mon-Fri, 8:30am-12:30pm & 2-6pm Sat, 9am-1pm Sun)

Sights & Activities

The most notable sight in Santa Ana is its large neo-Gothic **Catedral de Santa Ana** (⏲ 7am-12:30pm & 2:30-7pm), which was completed in 1913. Ornate moldings cover the church's entire front, and the inside's high arches create a sense of peace and spaciousness. Inside is a figure of the city's patron saint, Nuestra Señora de Santa Ana, who is feted in late July (see right).

Built over 53 years, the **city hall** (Av Independencia Sur; ⏲ 8am-5pm Mon-Fri) has one of the most beautiful colonial facades in the country. There's not much to see inside – just rows of offices and lines of people – but if you're

curious, there is a pleasant center courtyard where you can sit and take in all the movement.

Located in the former Banco Central de Reserva, the **Museo Regional del Occidente** (☎ 2441 1215; Av Independencia Sur; admission US$0.34; ⏲ 9am-noon & 1-5pm Tue-Sun) gives a good historical overview of the west, including a display of archaeological artifacts. An entire room is also dedicated to the history of Salvadoran money – great for numismatic buffs.

Courses

Escuela Sihuatehuacán (☎ 2441 4726, 7850 9293; www.salvaspan.com; Calle E Polígano N 2, Urbanización El Milagro) Spanish classes are offered by the week, month or semester here. Home and hotel stay is available, plus there's thrice-weekly excursions and activities, from visiting Tazumal to learning salsa dancing. Instruction and materials per week costs US$125, homestay per week US$90; homestay plus excursions per week US$150.

Festivals & Events

The city's annual **Fiesta Patronal**, celebrating Nuestra Señora de Santa Ana, is held each July 17 to 26, with parades, live music in the city center and, yes, a special mass or two.

Sleeping

BUDGET

Hotel Livingston (☎ 2441 1801; 10a Av Sur; r/tw US$15/20, r with air-con US$30; ✆ Ⓟ) Dramatic headboards and spacious rooms are the

---

TEATRO DE SANTA ANA

Just west of Santa Ana's cathedral is the renaissance-style **Teatro de Santa Ana** (☎ 2447 6268; 2a Calle Pte at Av Independencia Sur; admission US$0.50; ⏲ 8am-noon & 2-6pm Mon-Fri, 8am-noon Sat), an opulent building constructed with the funds from a special export tax on coffee beans. It opened its doors in 1910, and was the symbol of wealth and high culture in the west. Sweeping marble staircases, stained-glass windows, parquet floors, bronze statutes of Roman gods...it even opened with the opera *Rigoletto*, which was performed by an Italian opera company. In 1933, following a national trend, the theater was converted into a movie house. It deteriorated quickly, fixtures and artwork disappeared, even the stage curtain was stolen. The theater remained in disrepair until 1979, when Santa Ana residents decided to renovate it to its original glory. More than 25 years later, through private donations and events, the theater is 80% redone: original items, like statues, chandeliers, chairs, and (yes!) the stage curtain, have been recovered; the facade has been painted its original mint green and murals have been restored; a modern lighting and sound system was donated by the Japanese government. Today cultural events – concerts, plays, spoken word performances – are held weekly (US$1 to US$3). Tours of the theater are given upon request – ask at the box office.

signature of this renovated hotel. Rooms are spotless, with couch, dresser, small table, TV and bathroom; some have air-conditioning. The neighborhood (near the main bus terminal) is a little sketchy, but it's a good choice if you have an early bus or don't plan on venturing out after dark.

Casa Frolaz (☎ 2440 5302; www.casafrolaz.com; 29a Calle Pte; US$7 per person; **P**) The only dorm in town and one of the best in the country, Casa Frolaz is an eat-off-the-floor–clean type of place. It's in the home of Javier Díaz, a descendant of one of the oldest families in the country, who also happens to be a great host. Two common areas – a cozy book-filled living room and a leafy garden with hammocks and chairs – are ideal for relaxing. Guests also have use of a sunny kitchen and a cranky washing machine (per load US$2.50). Two dorms have seven twin beds and one bathroom between them. The only downside is the long walk into town.

Hotel El Faro (☎ 2447 7787; 14a Av Sur; s without bathroom US$8, r/tw US$11/15; **P**) Located on a quiet street, El Faro has 11 clean rooms, most windowless but all with fantastic landscape murals inside and out. They open onto a colorful courtyard and even have music piped in (don't worry, each room also has an off switch). Room 10 has hot water. Service is super friendly and same-day laundry service (per load US$3) is available.

Hotel Libertad (☎ 2441 2358; joval@navegante.com.sv; 4a Calle Ote; r/tw US$12/20; **P**) The main draw is the location – just a block from the cathedral. Otherwise, rooms are worn and dark, and bathrooms have cold water only and no toilet seats. It's a manageable choice if you prefer easy access to the city's sights.

MIDRANGE

Hotel Sahara (☎ 2447 8865; hotel_sahara@yahoo.com; 3a Calle Pte; s/d/tw incl breakfast US$35/38/45; **P** 🐾 🖧) Although located in a sketchy neighborhood, Hotel Sahara is considered the best in town. It offers pleasant rooms, with niceties like in-room coffeemaker and complimentary bottled water. Rooms facing the street are sunny but can get loud; interior rooms are darker but quieter: pick your poison. Ask for a room with a mini-split air-conditioner rather than a loud older unit. Check out the roof-top terrace –

the 360-degree view includes the cathedral, and goes all the way around to Volcán Santa Ana.

Eating

BUDGET

Cafeteria Emanuel (☎ 2448 2575; 5a Calle Ote; mains US$1-2; 🕒 breakfast & lunch Mon-Sat) A spotless eatery near Iglesia El Carmen, serving four different *típica* (regional specialties) main dishes: chicken, beef, pasta and a vegetarian option. After 3pm, Salvadoran *antojitos* – irresistible snacks like empanadas, *pastelitos* (small meat pies) and *platano y nuegado* (plantains and fried yucca smothered in honey with a dash of cinnamon) – are served. Two thumbs up.

La 31 (☎ 2440 4080; 31a Calle Pte; mains US$1-3; 🕒 dinner) A big busy *pupusería* within walking distance of the Casa Frolaz (left) – the owner Javier often joins guests there for a late-night snack. Pupusas come in many varieties, including chicken and *loroco* (squash).

Café Fiesta (☎ 2441 1871; 1a Calle Ote; mains US$1.50-3; 🕒 breakfast, lunch & dinner Mon-Sat) Possibly the biggest disco ball in all of El Salvador – at least the biggest one hanging next to a life-size poster of Pope John Paul II – is the centerpiece of this popular restaurant. Get here early to get the best of the *típico* dishes, which are served cafeteria-style. Pupusas are also patted out all day – an unexpected treat. Note: the disco ball is activated during private parties only.

Pip's Carymar Restaurant (☎ 2441 3935; Av Independencia Sur; mains US$2-10; 🕒 breakfast, lunch & dinner) A cafeteria-style restaurant with a fast-food feel, which serves just about every standard Salvadoran meal going, and then some. Great grilled chicken, pupusas or even just a slice of pizza are standard options. Indoor and outdoor seating is available.

Pastelería Ban Ban (☎ 2447 1865; Av Independencia Sur; mains US$0.50-2.50; 🕒 8am-7pm) A good bakery just south of Parque Libertad, Ban Ban serves up fresh pastries, simple sandwiches, and coffee all day. Air-conditioning and a children's playroom are big pluses.

El Sin Rival (☎ 2447 3277; Calle Libertad Ote; cones US$0.50-0.75; 🕒 10am-9pm Mon-Fri, 9am-9pm Sat & Sun) What started out as a two-tub street cart in 1953, has become a collection of great ice-cream shops – truly 'without rival.' It boasts 16 homemade sorbets made with natural ingredients – no chemicals or colorants here. *Mora* (blueberry) and *tres leches* (sweet milk) are the original flavors from the street-cart days, and are still local favorites.

A row of **food stands** (1a Av Norte; mains US$1-2; ⏲ 7am-late night) are set up along the eastern edge of the plaza almost daily. It's busiest at lunchtime and on weekend evenings, but you can get a burger, chicken sandwich or fries any time.

For self-caterers, **La Despensa de Don Juan** (Calle Libertad Ote at 1a Av Norte; ⏲ 8am-8pm) and **Super Selectos** (Av F Moraga Sur; ⏲ 8am-9pm) are full-service supermarkets. There's another at **Metrocentro** (⏲ 8am-10:30pm).

The sprawling **Mercado Central** (8a Av Sur; ⏲ 7am-5pm) has everything you could want: produce, dairy products, animals (whole or in parts), herbal medicines, clothes, jewelry, toys. It's in a seedy part of town, though, so watch out for pickpockets.

MIDRANGE

Lover's Steakhouse (☎ 2440 5717; 4a Av Sur at 17 Calle Pte; mains US$8-20; ⏲ lunch & dinner) Don't leave Santa Ana without treating yourself to a dinner at Lover's. The menu ranges from Italian to Chinese, but the specialty is meat and seafood. Dishes are amazingly affordable – a whole roast rabbit or a huge rice and seafood plate for US$10, and steaks starting at US$8 – though specials are pricier at US$16 to US$20. A rambling dining area includes an open-air courtyard, complete with tiki torches, and beers come with your pick of no less than 34 different *bocadillos* (appetizers), from ceviche to wontons to Buffalo wings.

Restaurante Los 44 (☎ 2440 5789; Av Independencia Sur; mains US$6-20; ⏲ lunch & dinner) Smaller and somewhat less charming than Lover's, Los 44 is still a reliable place for a steak, and is closer to the city center. The front room and a little nook left of the door have a nicer ambiance than the long sterile back room. There's live music – well, a guy with a mic and keyboard – on Friday, Saturday and Sunday.

Bar y Restaurant Doña Amelia (☎ 2447 0435; 6a Calle Pte at 9a Av Sur; mains US$4-12; ⏲ lunch & dinner) Other than the tiled walls and the black light over the bar, the ambiance is actually rather pleasant: tablecloths, air-con, lively music (unless there's a game on the big-screen TV), even plastic flowers. Steak is the specialty and comes in large portions with soup and salad.

Paso de Alaska (☎ 2448 1206; Carr Santa Ana-Sonsonate Km 83; mains US$4-15; ⏲ 7am-7pm Tue-Sun) This good, friendly restaurant is located in Los Naranjos, El Salvador's highest town, in the shadow of Volcán Santa Ana and at the top of a scenic mountain pass between Santa Ana and Sonsonate (Hwy CA-12). The climate is cool, and you can see all the way to the ocean from the upper-level dining area. Hamburgers and sandwiches leave something to be desired – better to go with a typical lunch plate, like a quarter chicken with rice and garlic bread (US$5). Follow signs from the highway.

Drinking & Entertainment

Drive Inn El Molino (☎ 2447 2029; 25 Av Sur; ⏲ 11am-late) When it gets going, this is one of Santa Ana's best nightspots, with drink specials, great music and late-night table dancing. When it's dead, though, it's really dead. You'll need to take a taxi there – ask the driver if he knows if there's much *movimiento* (action) before heading out. It's located on the old San Salvador highway, behind a Texaco gas station.

Los Horcones (☎ 2484 7511; 1a Av Norte; ⏲ 10am-2am) A classic dive bar in the heart of Santa Ana, complete with *palapa* (thatched palm-leaf roof shelter) and gnarled tree trunks for tables. Balconies overlook the main park and have incredible views of the Gothic cathedral next door. Disco beats and Saturday-night beer specials provoke occasional table dancing.

Teatro de Santa Ana (☎ 2447 6268; 2a Calle Pte at Av Independencia Sur; ⏲ 8am-noon & 2-6pm Mon-Fri, 8am-noon Sat) Despite ongoing renovations, this opulent theater hosts concerts, dance performances and plays. Tickets typically cost US$1 to US$3. Stop by to pick up a schedule of events.

Cinemark (☎ 2440 7657; Av Independencia at 35a Av Pte) Six screens of Hollywood flicks; tickets cost US$3, before 3pm US$2.25, all day Thursday US$1.25.

Shopping

Mercado de Artesanías (1a Av Sur; ⏲ 8:30-6 Mon-Sat) A decent handicrafts market in the heart of town, selling items like indigo T-shirts, Llort-inspired letters and black clay pots from Guatajiagua. You have to dig a little for the good stuff, but it's there.

Mario's Deportes (2411 6852; 9a Calle Pte; 8am-12:30pm & 2-6pm Mon-Fri, 8am-5pm Sat, 8am-noon Sun) Great for that Selección Nacional jersey or other Central American sports paraphernalia you've been searching for.

Getting There & Around
BUS
Most buses leave from the **main bus terminal** (10a Av Sur at 15a Calle Pte), is socked in on all sides by market stalls; it takes buses at least 15 minutes just to get through the congestion. A few buses leave from outlying stops, mostly around El Triángulo, a busy triangular intersection a block west of the terminal.

Bus 248 to Parque Nacional Los Volcánes leaves from **La Vencedora bus terminal** (2440 8453), a block west of Parque Colón. Remember that, in order to make the 11am guided hikes (see p353), you must catch the bus from Santa Ana by 8:30am.

Buses from Santa Ana travel to the following destinations (for international bus travel to Guatemala and Belize, see the boxed text, below):

Ahuachapán Bus 210 (US$0.44, 1¼ hours, every 10 minutes from 4am to 8:20pm). This passes Casa Blanca, but not Tazumal; for Tazumal, take a Chalchuapa bus.

Anguiatú (Guatemalan border) Take bus to Metapán and transfer (US$1.10).

Chalchuapa/Ruínas de Tazumal Bus 218 (US$0.30, 30 minutes, every 10 minutes from 6:15am to 7:15pm), departs from southwest corner of El Triángulo.

Juayúa Bus 238 (US$0.75, one hour, 6:40am, 9:30am, 12:20pm, 4:20pm, 5:30pm and 6:10pm).

Lago de Coatepeque Bus 220/242 (US$0.40, 1¼ hours, every 30 minutes from 6am to 5:25pm).

Las Chinamas (Guatemalan border) Take any Ahuachapán bus and transfer.

Los Naranjos Take any bus 216 (*not* bus 209) toward Sonsonate (US$0.50, 45 minutes).

Metapán Bus 235 (US$0.85, 1¼ hours, every 20 minutes from 5am to 5:30pm), catch on cnr Av F Moraga Sur & 13a Calle Pte.

Parque Nacional Los Volcánes (Cerro Verde) Bus 248 (US$0.85, 1¾ hours, departs from La Vencedora bus terminal at 7:30am, 8:30am, 10:15am, 11:20am; 12:20am, 1:40pm, and 3:30pm, last bus returns at 5pm) Reconfirm departure times, as they may change once the park reopens following the eruption in 2005.

San Cristóbal (Guatemalan border) Bus 236 (US$0.48, one hour, every 20 minutes from 5:30am to 9pm).

San Salvador Bus 201 (*directo* US$0.80, 1½ hours, every 19 minutes from 4:15am to 7pm; *especial* US$1.25, 11¼ hours, every 20 minutes from 4:20am to 6pm); all buses also stop at Metrocentro in San Salvador.

Sonsonate (via Los Naranjos) Bus 216 (weekday/weekend US$0.65/0.75, 1¼ hours, every 20 minutes from 4:30am to 6pm).

Sonsonate (via El Congo) Bus 209, (US$0.65, *ordinario* 1¾ hours, *directo* 1¼ hours, every 20 minutes from 5:10am to 5:30pm), departs from La Vencedora bus terminal.

CROSSING THE BORDER

Getting to El Progreso, Guatemala
The border at San Cristóbal is open 24 hours. From Santa Ana, take bus 236 (US$0.48, one hour, every 20 minutes from 5:30am to 9pm). Buses on the other side of the border go to El Progreso. The last bus back from San Cristóbal is at 6pm.

Getting to Guatemala City
You can buy ordinary and *especial* bus tickets to Guatemala City from **Agencia Puerto Bus** (2440 1608; 25a Calle Pte; 4:30am-5pm) – *especial* is well worth the extra US$2.50. Ordinary buses (US$9, four hours) leave hourly from 5am to 4pm, except 7am; *especial* buses (US$11.50, 3½ hours) leave at 7am and 5:30pm only.

Another option is to head to Las Chinamas, where you can pick up 1st-class buses en route from San Salvador to Guatemala City.

Getting to Santa Elena, Belize
Agencia Puerto Bus also sells tickets for the **Fuente del Norte** (2298 3275) bus line from Santa Ana through Guatemala to Santa Elena, Belize (US$25,nine hours). Daily departure is at 8:30am, with intermediate stops at Río Hondo (US$12), Río Dulce (US$15), Puerto Barrios (US$15) and Flores, El Petén (US$25).

TAXI
There are taxi stands on the plaza, Metrocentro mall and on 10a Av Sur, adjacent to the main bus terminal. If you hail one on the street, be sure to see that the license plate starts with the letter 'A,' denoting an official taxi. Agree on the rate beforehand; rides in town cost around US$4.

LAGO DE COATEPEQUE

On the eastern slope of Volcán Santa Ana, Lago de Coatepeque is a clean, sparkling blue volcanic crater lake, 6km wide and 120m deep, surrounded by green slopes. The Cerro Verde, Izalco and Santa Ana volcanoes loom above the lake. It's a popular weekend retreat for San Salvador's well-to-do, many of whom have private homes along the lakeshore – and obstruct public access to the water! But it's very quiet midweek and, with a couple of different hotel options, makes for a peaceful getaway.

The **police** (☎ 2441 6176; ☼ 24hr) are located across from Amacuilco Guest House; uphill, then first right.

Sights & Activities

Boat trips are possible on the lake – expect to pay US$12 to US$50 for a tour of 30 minutes to several hours. Ask at **Hotel Torremolinos** (☎ 2441 6037; Calle La Benicá) or **Restaurante Rango Alegre** (☎ 2441 6071), next to Amacuilco Guesthouse. Rain in the winter and afternoon winds in the summer mean you should begin any excursion early.

Sleeping & Eating

Amacuilco Guest House (☎ 2441 6239, 7822 4051; Calle La Bendición; campsites per person US$3, hammock per person US$3, dm per person US$6-7, r without bathroom US$13-18, r/t with bathroom US$23/26; ☼ ℗ ☐) A laid-back atmosphere, affordable rooms, and a long covered jetty with hammocks, tables and beautiful views make this a popular spot for backpackers and off-duty Peace Corps volunteers. Most rooms have smooth wood floors and plenty of light; some have good views. That said, many of the beds are actually cots and there's a somewhat run-down feel – it's best for travelers who don't sweat the details. Canoes, guided hikes, visits to local communities and even Spanish classes (US$100 per week, including three hours' daily instruction, food and lodging, Monday to Friday) are also available.

The restaurant (mains US$3 to US$5; open breakfast, lunch and dinner) serves simple comfort food, including a few vegetarian dishes. Service can be extremely slow. It's 2km past Centro de Obreros Constitución.

Hotel Torremolinos (☎ 2441 6037; Calle La Benicián; hoteltorremolinos@gmail.com; r/tw US$25/35; mains US$4-20; breakfast, lunch & dinner; ℗ ☼) Gorgeous views and well-tended grounds make eating at the Torremolinos very worthwhile. Tables are arranged along the terrace of the main building and on a two-story high pier. Seafood is the specialty – try the *crema de cangrejo* (crab soup) – or the chicken and beef dishes. Live (and lively) music is played Sunday afternoon from 1:30pm (US$1 per person cover charge). If you're tempted to stay, the 16 rooms are clean, with formica floors, fans and hot-water bathrooms. Two pools and direct access to the lake make cooling off a cinch. It's 400m past Amacuilco Guest House.

Nantal Hostal & Restaurante (☎ 2473 7565; Carr al Cerro Verde Km 53.5; r person US$8; mains US$5-10) On a ridge high above the lake, Nantal is a stylish restaurant with four rooms and nice lake views. The garden at the entrance and a comfortable bar-café are highlights, especially the latter for its sofas and paintings. Rooms are small but adequate, with high ceilings and opening onto a narrow outdoor corridor with wicker chairs and a view of the highway.

Near the beginning of the road around the lake, Centro de Obreros Constitución is a large government workers' center, with lake access and several pools. Remodeled cabins each have four single beds, a table and a decent bathroom. Bring linens and a mosquito net. For a free permit to stay here, visit the **Ministerio de Trabajo** (Map p324; ☎ 2298 8739; Calle Nueva Dos 19; ☼ 8am-12:30pm & 1:30-4pm Mon-Fri) in San Salvador. For details, see p317.

Getting There & Around

Buses 220 and 242 leave Santa Ana for Lago de Coatepeque every half hour (p351); the bus descends the long scenic road from El Congo to the lakeshore, then bears left past Centro Obreros Constitución, Amaquilco Guest House and Hotel Torremolinos, in that order. Buses return to Santa Ana every half hour until 6pm. To San Salvador, take bus 220 to El Congo and transfer to bus 201.

PARQUE NACIONAL LOS VOLCANES

Parque Nacional Los Volcanes is one of the gems of El Salvador, encompassing three major volcanoes (Cerro Verde, Volcán Izalco and Volcán Santa Ana) and thousands of acres in the heart of the country. A paved road leads all the way to the visitor center, accessible by car or bus from San Salvador or (better) from Santa Ana. You can climb Volcán Izalco or Volcán Santa Ana in a day – although not on the same day, because of the way tours are arranged – or take a short stroll on a nature loop in the forested area around the visitor center. For a little more adventure, there are areas for camping in another part of the park, and guided hikes up the volcanoes from there. Before 2003, the park was called simply Parque Nacional Cerro Verde, and most Salvadorans still use that name; in fact, you may get some strange looks using the new name.

The Volcanoes

Cerro Verde (2030m) is the oldest of the park's three main volcanoes: it formed 1.5 million years ago and hasn't erupted in 25,000 years. The visitor center is in the middle of its crater, filled with thick forest and barely recognizable as a volcano.

Volcán Izalco is the youngest volcano in the group – and one of the youngest in the world. Before February 1770 there was nothing there but a hole in the ground, from which columns of black sulfuric smoke would occasionally rise. Then the hole started burping rocks and lava, and a cone began to form. In no time (geologically speaking) the cone had grown to prodigious size, and today it stands 1910m high. Izalco continued to erupt well into the 20th century, sending out smoke, boulders and flames – an impressive sight by night or day – earning it a reputation as 'the lighthouse of the Pacific.' In 1957, after erupting continuously for almost two centuries, Izalco stopped. It's still classified as active, but has only hiccupped once more, in 1966. Today the perfect cone, black and bare, stands devoid of life in an otherwise fertile land.

It had been even longer since Volcán Santa Ana (2365m) erupted – more than a century – but in October 2005 the largest of the park's volcanoes (also known as Ilamatepec, or 'Mother Hill') awoke dramatically, spewing rocks, ash, and gas (although no lava). Landslides triggered by the eruption killed two coffee pickers and forced the evacuation of thousands. It was a rainy late-winter morning, and the ash – which rose in a cloud thousands of meters high – later fell wet and thick, blanketing areas downwind (mostly to the west, including the Ruta de Las Flores) with a centimeter or more of sulphurous mud, killing large swaths of coffee trees. Scientists expected another, possibly larger, eruption soon after, but it never materialized. Still, several small earthquakes made it seem – to residents and Lonely Planet guidebook writers – that something was still grumbling deep in the old girl's belly.

Hiking

The park was closed for months following the eruption of Volcán Santa Ana, but will reopen once scientists give the go-ahead. Climbing either volcano requires sturdy shoes – near the top of both, especially Volcán Izalco, loose volcanic rock makes climbing slow and laborious. Volcán Izalco is perhaps the more dramatic peak, and is very popular for that reason. But Volcán Santa Ana is some 400m higher – it's the third-highest point in the country, in fact – and the barren windy summit affords a spectacular view, with the crater sinking hundreds of meters to one side, and Lago de Coatepeque lying even further below on the other.

Assaults used to be a major problem here, but the park service has instituted a mandatory guide service, and has posted tourist police along the trails and even at the summits. Crime has dropped dramatically, but you should still not attempt to climb the volcanoes alone. Guided hikes to Volcán Izalco (four hours, US$1) and Volcán Santa Ana (four hours, US$1.79) begin at 11am only, meaning you can't do both in one day, unfortunately. You also don't want to arrive late!

A short and easy nature trail (40 minutes) starts and ends in the parking lot. Observation points offer good views of the lake and Volcán Santa Ana. The park is a major bird sanctuary, with many migratory species passing through, including emerald toucanets, jays, woodpeckers, motmots, and 17 species of hummingbird.

Sleeping & Eating

Most people visit Cerro Verde as a day trip, and there are only limited camping facilities around the visitor center area itself. For something more isolated, two sectors of the park – San Blas and Los Andes – have rustic cabins and camping facilities.

San Blas is a small community perched on a high saddle between Cerro Verde and Volcán Santa Ana. **Campo Bello** (☎ 2271 0853) has round, no-frills cement 'igloos' with private bath, which sleep up to four people. Nearby, **Casa de Cristal** (☎ 2483 4713) is somewhat nicer – at least it's made from wood. Both were closed following the October 2005 eruption, and were yet to reopen when this book went to print. Definitely call ahead, to confirm they're open and to check current prices; camping may be possible. From San Blas you can join up with the guided groups that depart from the Cerro Verde visitor center and pass nearby. San Blas is a corner known as 'Desvío al Cerro Verde' on the road between El Congo and Cerro Verde – take bus 248 and ask the driver to drop you off.

A rough road leads 13km from San Blas to Los Andes, on Volcán Santa Ana's northern skirt. The **campground** (2 adults US$35, 2 adults & 2 children US$45, incl entrance fee) has five wooden platforms that are equipped with modern tents with cushions, and additional areas for those with their own equipment (per night US$2, plus one-time per person entrance fee US$6). There are toilets, open-air grills and – if you call ahead – simple meals can be cooked for you by a local woman. Trails lead to the top of Volcán Santa Ana and the park ranger at Los Andes can serve as a guide.

There is no public transportation to Los Andes, and you will need a 4WD to get there. The 13km access road begins just before 'Desvío a Cerro Verde' and San Blas, about 7km after 'Desvío El Pacún' on the road between El Congo and the Cerro Verde visitor center.

The San Blas facilities are managed by a local **cooperative** (☎ 2483 4713, 2483 4679). For information on Los Andes, contact or visit **SalvaNatura** (Fundación Ecológica de El Salvador; Map pp320-1; ☎ 2279 1515; www.salvanatura.org, in Spanish; 33a Av Sur 640, San Salvador; ✆ 8am-12:30pm & 2-5:30pm Mon-Fri, phone service only Sat & Sun) in San Salvador (for details, see p317). The website www .complejolosvolcanes.com also has a great deal of information about services in and around the park, plus background information and photos.

Getting There & Around

It's imperative you get to the park by 11am because the guided hikes leave only once a day. The easiest, surest way is to make the trip from Santa Ana, where bus 248 goes all the way to the entrance (see p351). The last bus normally leaves the park at 5pm, but always confirm this with the bus driver when you arrive in the morning, as service can vary. Otherwise, you can catch a bus to El Congo (last one at 5pm) and transfer to a Santa Ana bus (or one for San Salvador, if that's your destination). Verify these times when you get to the park, especially if you think you'll be there late.

From San Salvador, you run the risk of missing a connection and therefore the hike. Leave early. Take any bus to Santa Ana and disembark at El Congo on the Carr Panamericana; walk uphill to the overpass and catch bus 248. Ask to be sure you're in the right place.

If you're driving, Parque Nacional Los Volcánes is 67km from San Salvador along the Sonsonate route, or 77km by the more scenic Carr Panamericana toward Santa Ana.

IZALCO

pop 20,927

Izalco is built on a slight slope – the lower edges of the Volcán Izalco and Volcán Santa Ana, the skirt hem, as it were, of those two ever-present sentinels – overlooking the town from the north. Izalco was an indigenous community and important trading center long before the Spanish arrived; it was here that some of the worst violence of the January 1932 massacre of indigenous people, known as La Matanza (The Slaughter), took place. The killings followed a failed peasant/communist uprising and one of the rebel leaders, José Feliciano Ama, was executed in Izalco's main plaza. The massacre drove most of the trappings of traditional indigenous life – clothing, language, ceremonies – into nonexistence, but Izalco is one of a handful of Salvadoran towns that retain a powerful indigenous character. *Cofradías*, a form of community government born of Catholic and indigenous religious traditions, are still utilized here.

Orientation

Av Morazán is Izalco's main road and commercial center, extending from the highway, past the official parque central (main plaza) and up to Parque Dolores, where most of the activity is. The main plaza is a pleasant leafy place, bordered on one side by the *alcaldía* (mayor's office) and the Iglesia Nuestra Señora de la Asunción on the other. Av Morazán continues another five blocks to Parque Dolores. There's much more movement here than in the main plaza, especially at night when the *pupusodromo* gets fired up. Buses also leave and drop off here, adding to the bustle.

Information

Cíber Space (☎ 2453 5597; Av Morazán 28; per hr US$0.50; ☺ 10am-10:30pm) Just south of Parque Dolores.

Farmacia Vida Nueva (☎ 2453 5086; Av Morazán 33; ☺ 8am-7pm Mon-Sat; 8am-5pm Sun)

Police (☎ 2453 5069; 1a Calle Ote at 2a Av Norte; ☺ 24hr)

Post Office (Pasaje Asunción at 2a Calle Ote; ☺ 8:30-noon & 2-5pm Mon-Fri, 8am-noon Sat) Across from Iglesia Asunción.

Unidad de Salud (☎ 2453 5019; 9a Calle Ote 60; ☺ 7am-5pm Mon-Fri, 7:30am-3:30pm Sat & Sun) This hospital treats non-Spanish speakers. It's located four long blocks east of Parque Dolores.

Sights

Izalco has one of the country's largest and best-preserved collections of *imaginería*, handcarved painted wood figures representing saints and religious figures. Many are on display in the town's two churches; many more are in private collections or stored away until special festivals are held in their honor. Indeed, the town holds a number of religious festivals, which can be fascinating for their fusion of Catholic and indigenous rites. Semana Santa and Día de los Muertos are especially intriguing.

One of the oldest churches in El Salvador, **Iglesia Nuestra Señora de la Asunción** (Av Morazán btwn Calle Libertad & 2 Calle Ote; ☺ 8am-noon & 1:30-7pm Tue-Sun) dates from the mid-1500s. The original structure was destroyed in the devastating earthquake of 1773, which also leveled much of Antigua, Guatemala. A new church was built alongside the ruins of

the old one, and together they make a short interesting stop. The bells of the original church have been preserved and are Izalco's most prized relic. They are enclosed in the white cement *campenario* (kiosk) near the entrance.

The broad steps and tall pale facade of **Iglesia Dolores** (Av Morazán & 9 Calle Pte) are more grand than its interior, but then that's the case of many churches. At the end of evening services, worshippers pour out of the church into the plaza in front, filling the pupusa stands and marveling at the thousands of chattering swallows that spend the night in the park's trees.

Everyone says that **Turicentro Atecozol** (admission US$0.80; ☺ 8am-5pm), seven blocks east of Iglesia Dolores, is the best tourist center in the country – which, let's be honest, isn't necessarily a big achievement. But this swimming park really is quite nice, with a half-dozen natural-ish pools filled with spring water, and a huge waterslide that the kids will enjoy.

Sleeping & Eating

Izalco has one recommendable hotel, and just a handful of places to eat.

La Casona de Los Vega (☎ 2453 5951; casonalelosvega@yahoo.com; 2 Av Norte 24; s/d incl breakfast without bathroom US$20/30; Ⓟ) This grand old home is over a century old, and once took up the entire block. It has since been partitioned; the part used for the hotel today was where the carriages pulled in, and is now a pleasant courtyard surrounded by rooms and a broad corridor. The rooms were likely used by servants; accordingly, they are small with tiny windows. There's one room with bathroom for US$35. The price is high for what you get – some competition would help.

Pupusadromo Izalqueño (Av Morazán at 9a Calle Pte; pupusas US$0.35-0.50; ☺ dinner) Women bend over a row of wood-burning stoves here, patting out pupusas for the scores of people who fill picnic tables set up in front. It's a classic Salvadoran dining experience, and cheap to boot. A hot chocolate or coffee helps wash it all down.

Restaurante Familiar El Chele (☎ 2453 6740; Calle La Violeta Caserío; mains US$4-12; ☺ breakfast, lunch & dinner) A lovely countryside setting surrounds the tables at this hacienda-style restaurant. House specialties include *gallo* *en chicha* (rooster marinated in sweet moonshine), *conejo asado* (grilled rabbit) and *coctel de concha* (conch cocktail), all prepared fresh. A sad zoo of sorts – more like a collection of captured animals held in too-small cages – is set up at the back. And while the restaurant is tops, the three rooms are musty and dark with saggy beds. Horseback riding tours are available.

Little Chicken (Av Morazán at 7a Calle Pte; mains US$2-4; 8am-7:30pm) This modest fast-food outlet should probably be called Little Farm Animal, as you can get burgers and hot dogs, as well fried chicken. It's OK for a quick meal.

If you enjoy wandering around markets, you'll like the **Mercado de Izalco** (5a Calle Pte; 7am-4pm), a rambling indoor market that spills out onto the streets around it. You'll see everything from women haggling over chicken's feet to little boys eyeing plastic toy trucks. It's great for buying fresh produce and breads.

Getting There & Around

Bus 53A connects Izalco to nearby Sonsonate (US$0.35, 20 minutes) departing from Parque Dolores at the end of Av Morazán. There is no direct service from San Salvador; instead, take any Sonsonate-bound bus and get off at the Izalco turnoff (US$0.70) on the highway, from where you can either walk or catch bus 53A entering town (US$0.20 from the turnoff). Returning to San Salvador, go back to the Izalco turnoff and catch bus 205 from Sonsonate.

RUÍNAS DE SAN ANDRÉS

In 1977, a step pyramid and a large courtyard with a subterranean section were unearthed in this **archaeological site** (admission US$3; 9am-5pm Tue-Sun), which was inhabited by Maya people between AD 600–900. Experts believe up to 12,000 people lived at San Andrés and that the city held sway over the Valle de Zapotitlán, and possibly the neighboring Valle de las Hamacas, where San Salvador is now situated. The Pedernal Eccentrico, an exquisitely carved obsidian blade now displayed in the Museo Nacional de Antropología David J Guzmán (p323) in San Salvador, was found here.

The ruins are interesting and peaceful, if not terribly impressive, and the museum is small but excellent. Quite a bit of restoration

has been performed to protect the original structures, and protective walls cover much of the original stone and brick. The main pyramid is sometimes called the Campana San Andrés, because of its bell shape. A trench in front of Estructura 3 shows how the platform was built with hundreds of thousands of adobe bricks. Another dozen or so mounds are yet to be unearthed.

The ruins are about 300m north of the highway, 33km west of San Salvador in the Valle Zapotitán. Take the Santa Ana bus 201 from San Salvador's Terminal de Occidente, and get off at Km 33, where there's a small black sign for the ruins. If you're combining this with a visit to Joya de Cerén (below), visit Joya de Cerén first – the bus goes all the way to the ruins – then catch any bus on the highway the short distance to San Andrés. A small outdoor *comedor* (a basic cheap eatery) serves pupusas and other *típica*.

JOYA DE CERÉN

Often called the Pompeii of America, **Joya de Cerén** (admission US$3; 9am-5pm Tue-Sun) is the ruins of a small Mayan settlement, buried under some 6m of volcanic ash following the eruption of the Laguna Caldera volcano in AD 595. No human remains were found, suggesting the residents had time to escape, but they were obviously in a hurry because they left behind a wealth of everyday items, the kind seldom found at sites that were abandoned more systematically. Discovered by accident in 1976, Joya de Cerén has provided archaeologists with invaluable clues into how and what early peoples planted for their crops, how they built their homes, and cooked and stored their food. It was named a UN World Heritage Site in 1993.

The main compound, consisting of four or five small structures, is protected by a tall mesh fence; you can peer through but not enter. It's somewhat underwhelming, but not uninteresting. The on-site museum, recently expanded and remodeled, has a good collection of artifacts and models of the villages. One of the most compelling pieces is a small dish where you can see fingerprints smeared in the remains of an interrupted meal.

The site is 36km west of San Salvador; take bus 108 from Terminal de Occidente and get off after crossing the bridge over the

RUTA DE LAS FLORES

The winding mountain road that links Sonsonate to Ahuachapán has been dubbed Ruta de Las Flores (Route of the Flowers). Thirty-six kilometers long, it's a dramatic ride that traverses the heart of El Salvador's coffee country, and is known for its natural beauty, charming towns and cultural traditions. Flowers, as the name suggest, are also found on this road; the cool mountain climate and the rich soil are favorable to growers, and nurseries dot the route. The only time you're likely to see lots of 'wild' flowers is in May, when coffee blossoms cloak the volcanoes like white skirts.

The route is easy to navigate – the roads are in great condition and the buses pass frequently. If you're in a car, don't hesitate to pull off the road at the many vista points, or at a stand selling homemade honey in recycled bottles. La Ruta de las Flores is perfect for wandering about, and its popularity will come as no surprise. Look out for the following highlights:

■ Nahuizalco (p362) A Pipil village specializing in wicker *artesanía* (handicrafts) and furniture; stop by the gift shop at CEDART for a sampling of the town's work.

■ Juayúa (p363) A charming mountain village with a popular weekend food fair – munch on *yuca* (steamed and fried sweet potato topped with *curtido,* a mixture of pickled cabbage and carrots, and hot sauce) as you stroll the cobblestone streets. Or stay the night at the hip Hotel Anáhuac, a hostel with a dorm and a handful of private rooms.

■ El Jardin de Celeste (p370) Spend the night in a comfortable cabin, enjoy a tasty meal or just admire the flowers at this charming, lush nursery and coffee farm between Apaneca and Ataco.

■ Ataco (p369) A colonial town with a strong indigenous presence; similar to how Antigua, Guatemala, was before tourism hit big.

RUTA DE LAS FLORES

Río Sucio. If you're combining this with a trip to San Andrés, come here first – you'll do less walking.

RUÍNAS DE TAZUMAL

The ruins of **Tazumal** (☎ 2408 4295; admission US$3; ⏰ 9am-5pm Tue-Sun) are the most important and impressive in El Salvador, although they do not compare to the grandeur of sites in Guatemala, Honduras and Mexico. There's a fine museum, though, and the shops outside the ruins sell some of the country's best clay replicas of Mayan masks, statues and other artifacts. A trip here also can be combined with an even more interesting stop at nearby Casa Blanca

(p358); both are located on the outskirts of Chalchuapa, 13km west of Santa Ana on the way to Ahuachapán.

Tazumal, which means 'pyramid where the victims were burned' in Quiche, is just one of six known sites in a 10-sq-km archaeological zone, much of which remains unexcavated. The area has been occupied almost continuously for over 3000 years, possibly longer. It was an important trading center (especially for cacao, obsidian and ceramics), and structures and artifacts here show influences ranging from Olmec to Teotihuacán to Pipil. The main interruption to human settlement here came in AD 260, when the eruption of the Ilopango volcano prompted a mass evacuation of the entire zone. People slowly reoccupied the area, however, and the most active period of construction was AD 400 to 680, during which a strong Teotihuacán influence is evident.

You used to be able to climb Tazumal's main pyramid and other structures, but they were closed after being damaged in the 2001 earthquakes. The obtuse cement covering – placed there by early restorers to protect the stone and simulate what the structures looked like with their original stucco cap – is set to be removed by 2009. The museum displays bowls, urns, figurines and other artifacts that are evidence of, among other things, an active trade reaching as far as Panama and Mexico. One of the most important artifacts uncovered is a lifesize statue of Xipe-totec, a Nahua god of fertility and war. The figure is covered in what appears to be scales, but are believed to represent pieces of human skin that were evidently cut from sacrificial victims as a tribute. Other finds – including the Estela de Tazumal, a 2.65m-high basalt monolith inscribed with hieroglyphics – are at the Museo Nacional de Antropología David J Guzmán (p323) in San Salvador.

Bus 218 comes from Santa Ana, 14km (45 minutes) away (for full transport details see p351). A sign on the main road through Chalchuapa points toward the ruins, a five-minute walk from the highway. If driving from Santa Ana, stay right at the fork in the road, continuing toward Ahuachapán, then turn left at the Texaco station in Chalchuapa. The ruins are at the end of the road.

CASA BLANCA

An excellent three-part complex, **Casa Blanca** (☎ 2408 0039; Carr Santa Ana-Ahuachapán Km 74.5; admission US$2.86, parking US$1.14; ◐ 9am-4:30pm Tue-Sun) is an archaeological site, a museum and an indigo workshop sitting across from the town of Chalchuapa. The **archaeological ruins** are fairly impressive. They are thought to be the remains of a purely ceremonial site – as no evidence of domestic occupation has been found – dating to the Late Pre-Classic period (roughly 400 BC to AD 250). The site was built on a massive artificial platform, 2m high and extending a whopping 240m by 220m. The platform is now itself several meters underground, visible only in a covered trench that is the first

stop of a guided tour of the site. Three of six pyramid-like structures have been excavated; standing a modest 10m to 11m high, they were constructed by covering packed earth with a layer of stone and then a layer of stucco. What appears to be a cement cap is, in fact, the original stucco – incredible considering the severity of heat, rain and humidity it has resisted. Only the color is gone – archaeologists believe the pyramids were originally a rich orange.

The small but excellent **museum** in the main building has informative and very well-presented exhibits on the Maya and Pipils, including a section on pre-Colombian musical instruments. Another section gives a detailed history of indigo, its importance to indigenous people as a magical and divine color, and its value to Europeans as a dye. A small gallery exhibits impressive examples of indigo-tinted fabrics from around the world. Signage is in Spanish only.

A popular **indigo workshop** also offers classes on different indigo dyeing techniques. Classes are offered on Wednesday and Saturday for beginners (US$4, six hours) and involve learning the Shibori technique, a Japanese style that uses twist ties to make designs. Advanced students are taught on Thursday and Sunday (US$10 per kg of cloth used, six hours) and focus on batik, an Indonesian technique using beeswax. Classes are open to the public – just be sure to call a few days in advance to reserve a spot.

From Santa Ana, bus 218 to Chalchuapa and bus 210 to Ahuachapán both pass Casa Blanca, which is just off the main highway at the entrance to town. You can combine a visit here with one to Ruínas de Tazumal – a long walk (but short ride on bus 218) away, on the other side of Chalchuapa.

METAPÁN

pop 18,857

This medium-sized mountain town near the Guatemalan border is the nearest access point to Parque Nacional Montecristo-El Trifinio (p360), one of the country's most inaccessible (but beautiful) parks. The park is closed from May to November to let animals breed, and when it is open you need a 4WD vehicle to get there. The town is pleasant enough, but if you don't think you'll go to the park, there's not much reason to stop.

Information

Farmacia Económica (☎ 2402 3788; Carr principal; 8am-7pm Mon-Sat) Next to the Supermercado de Todo.

Farmacia El Milagro (☎ 2442 0078; 4 Av Sur at 15 de Septiembre; 7am-12:30pm & 1:30-5pm) Near Hotel Christina.

Fusión Ciber Café (☎ 2442 4029; 2 Av Sur; per hr US$0.60; 9am-9:30pm)

Hospital Nacional Metapán Arturo Morales (☎ 2442 0184; Carr principal; 24hr) Located 400m south of the entrance to town.

Scotiabank (☎ 2402 0039; Av Ignacio Gómez) Exchanges traveler's checks but not foreign cash; has a 24-hour ATM.

Tu Metapán (www.tumetapan.com.sv, in Spanish) A decent website on the town.

Sleeping & Eating

Hotel California (☎ 2442 0561; s/tw US$8/10; P) Metapán's best budget option is a five minute walk out of town, 500m north of the bus terminal on the highway. Live it up in medium-sized rooms, with bath-room and fan. The beds are aging but adequate – same goes for the linens and toilet (the shower-curtain bathroom door is a bit of a killjoy). It's quite a walk into town, but you'll get good views of El Trifinio along the way. If you're headed to the Guatemalan border, buses pass in front.

Hotel Christina (☎ 2442 0044; 4a Av Sur btwn Calle 15 de Septiembre & 2a Calle; r/tw with fan US$12/15, r/tw/q with air-con & TV US$18/23/35;) Walk three blocks downhill from the bus terminal for these modern, though somewhat stuffy rooms, all with clean bathrooms. Those fac-ing the street are noisier, especially in the morning when the stalls outside start setting up, but they get better light and ventilation. Three rooms on the top floor share a nice, large terrace with tables and hammocks overlooking a busy street.

Hotel San José (☎ 2442 0556; Carr a le Frontera; r/tw/tr US$34/39.50/45.50; P) Right at the turnoff to Parque Montecristo, this is with-out question Metapán's top hotel – so nice you may forget you're in grubby Metapán. Thirty-four spotless modern rooms have hot-water bathrooms, cable TV, new beds, even complimentary bottled water. Rooms 303, 305, 403 and 405 have large enclosed balconies; rooms 201, 309 and 409 also get better light.

Pollo Sheriff (☎ 2402 0918; Carr a la Frontera; mains US$1.50-5; 6am-10pm) A basic fried-chicken

---

> ### GETTING TO CHIQUIMULA, GUATEMALA
>
> From Metapán, microbuses run every half hour to the border at Anguiatú (open 24 hours). There is no fee or visa requirement to enter Guatemala for most nationalities. Once on the Guatemalan side, buses run frequently to Chiquimula (one hour, last bus at 5:30pm) and from there to Guatemala City (three hours, last bus from Chiquimula at 3:30pm). In El Salvador, the last bus from the border to Metapán is at 6:30pm. You can also easily use this route to reach Nuevo Ocotopeque or Copán Ruínas, Honduras, saving you the long, albeit scenic, trip over the mountains to El Poy.

eatery right across from the bus terminal. Ask about the daily specials, which generally involve getting free items when you order something else.

Supermercado De Todo (Carr a la Frontera; 7am-7pm) Next to the Hotel San José, this is the best place to stock up on supplies for trips into Parque Nacional Montecristo-El Trifinio, though it's often understocked.

Getting There & Around

Metapán's bus terminal is a large dirt lot on the main highway, across from the entrance to town. San Salvador buses are modern *espe-ciales*, with air-con, video and restroom. There are two departures daily over the mountains to Citalá, near the Honduran border crossing at El Poy – a long, gorgeous ride. A rickety bus follows a mostly unpaved road past diz-zying precipices, thick forest and incredible vista points. For once you may not mind the bus' snail-like pace. Buses from Metapán travel to the following destinations:

Anguiatú/Guatemalan border Bus 235 and microbuses (US$0.50, 30 minutes, every 30 minutes from 5:30am to 5:35pm); last bus from border at 6:30pm.

Citalá/Honduran border Bus 463 (US$2, three hours, 5am and noon only).

San Salvador Bus 201A (US$2.50, 1¾ hours, 5:40am, 6:30am, 8:30am, noon, 1pm and 3:15pm); or take any Santa Ana bus to Santa Ana's Metrocentro mall, where you can transfer to a San Salvador bus.

Santa Ana Bus 235 (US$0.85, *ordinario* 1½ hours, *directo* one hour, every 15 to 30 minutes from 4:15am to 6:30pm); or take bus 201A to Santa Ana's Metrocentro, and take a cab or local bus into town (US$1.25, 50 minutes).

PARQUE NACIONAL MONTECRISTO-EL TRIFINIO

At the top of Cerro Montecristo – 2418m above sea level – the borders of El Salvador, Honduras and Guatemala all converge at a point called El Trifinio. All three countries have designated their respective wedge's protected areas – on the Salvadoran side Parque Nacional Montecristo-El Trifinio is one of the country's most spectacular natural areas, an isolated and pristine cloud forest with excellent hiking and camping options. This is the most humid region in the country, with 2000mm annual precipitation and 100% average relative humidity. Oak and laurel trees grow to 30m, and leaves intertwine to form a canopy impenetrable to sunlight. The forest floor provides a habitat for abundant unique plant life, including orchids, mushrooms, lichens, mosses, and tree ferns up to 8m tall. The temperature averages between 10°C and 15°C.

Animals seen (albeit rarely) include spider monkeys, two-fingered anteaters, porcupines, spotted and hooded skunks, pumas, red and gray squirrels, wild pigs, opossums, coyotes and agoutis. The forest is also home to at least 87 bird species, including quetzals, green toucans, woodpeckers, hummingbirds, nightingales, white-faced quail and striped owls.

Parque Nacional Montecristo-El Trifinio is administered by the **Ministerio de Medio Ambiente** (Environmental Ministry; Map p324; ☎ 2267 6259, 2267 6276; www.marn.gob.sv, in Spanish; Alameda Araujo/Carr a Santa Tecla Km 5.5; ☒ 7:30-12:30am & 1:30-3:30pm Mon-Fri) in San Salvador. Admission is US$6 per day for foreigners, plus US$1.15 per vehicle, which you pay whether you hire a truck or drive your own. Permission is required to stay in the park overnight, and it's recommended you call ahead even for a day trip to be sure a large group isn't headed there at the same time. You can apply in person or download the permission form at www.marn.gob.sv/patrimonio/fmontecristo.doc and return it by fax (2267 6246). You'll need to provide a fax number where you can receive the signed permission – many photocopy or Internet shops have fax service. Be sure to include the names of everyone in your group.

Be aware that the area above Los Planes is closed from May to November, the breeding season of the local fauna.

Hiking

Several hiking trails begin from a spot called Los Planes (approx 1900m), a grassy clearing around 22km from Metapán in a bowl at the foot of Cerro Montecristo. Two trails lead about 1km each to wooden observation towers with views of the park and surrounding area. But the trail you're probably looking for is the one to the top – a tough 7km ascent through thick, dripping cloud forest. At the top is a plaque marking the borders of the three countries, and terrific views into each one. A number of smaller hikes are also possible from Los Planes, though they're not as well marked. Ask your truck driver or the owner of the small shop at Los Planes for directions.

Sleeping & Eating

You can camp at Los Planes, which has an area for tents, plus grills, tables and toilets. A small store sells snack foods, but you should plan on bringing all supplies, including water, from Metapán. You need advance permission from the Ministerio de Medio Ambiente (left) to spend the night in the park.

Getting There & Away

Montecristo's pristine quality has almost everything to do with its inaccessibility. There's no regular bus service, and it takes an experienced driver with a 4WD truck to navigate the long rough road to the entrance.

Francisco Monterrosa Figueroa (☎ 2402 2805) is a local bus driver who, given a day's notice, is almost always free to drive travelers to and from the park. For day trips, he charges US$45 to pick you up at your hotel in the morning and wait in Los Planes until you're ready to return. If you want to camp, it's US$85 for him to drop you there and return a day or two later. If Monterrosa isn't available, try asking other pickup drivers parked near the turnoff for the park.

This is definitely the recommended method. Buses do leave from the turnoff to the cantón of San José (US$0.40, 30 minutes, 7am, 10am, 11am, noon, 1:30pm, 3pm, 4pm, 6pm and 7pm), located about 10km from Metapán; pickups make the same trip, but don't usually start until about noon. Half-way to San José is a spot called 'La Pluma,' where you must stop and pay your entrance fee at the national park kiosk there. You'll have to convince the bus driver (and passengers) to wait for you, and hope the ranger lets you by – technically you are not allowed past there without a private vehicle. If you do get as far as San José, it's a tough 11km to Los Planes – start early.

SONSONATE
pop 66,201

The Guatemalan border, Parque Nacional El Imposible, Ruta de las Flores, Puerto La Libertad, Los Cóbanos…almost all the top spots in western El Salvador and the western pacific coast have Sonsonate in their flight path, which makes it all the more depressing that Sonsonate is so depressing. The city center isn't so bad, at least during the day. Beyond the city center, though, the streets turn chaotic and not a little dangerous, as Sonsonate boasts one of El Salvador's more intractable gang problems. You are almost certain to pass through, but other than a vivid Semana Santa celebration, it is a city with relatively little to offer most travelers.

Orientation

Chances are you're just passing through Sonsonate, in which case you'll see one of its best features…drum roll…the new bus terminal! It's huge and airy, with great *licuado* (fresh fruit drink, blended with milk or water) stands and women selling home-cooked food – just don't miss your bus. The new bus terminal is 2km east of the city center – the road starts out as Paseo 15 de Septiembre but turns into Calle Obispo Marroquín, a few blocks before hitting the parque central (central park). The main north–south street is Av Morazán/Av Rafael Campos. To orient yourself in town, the church is on the east side of the parque central.

Information

Banco Cuscatlán (☎ 2489 4895; Calle Obispo Marroquín near 4a Av Norte; ☯ 8:30am-5pm Mon-Fri, 8:30am-noon Sat) Exchanges foreign currencies but does not cash travelers checks. Has a 24-hour ATM.
Farmacia Fernández (☎ 2451 0465; Calle Obispo Marroquín btwn Av Rafael Campos & 2 Av Sur; ☯ 8am-6pm Mon-Fri, 8am-5pm Sat, 8am-12:30pm Sun) Consultations with a doctor (US$2) available daily from 8am to noon.
Hospital Nacional Sonsonate (☎ 2451 0200; 3 Calle Pte btwn 3 & 5 Avs Norte; ☯ 24hr) Large public hospital.

Infocentros (☎ 2429 1497; 3 Calle Pte btwn 1 Av Norte & Av Morazán; per hr Thu & Fri US$0.80, per hr Sat-Wed US$1; ☯ 8am-6pm Mon-Sat)
Police (☎ 2450 2421; 5 Calle Pte btwn 1 Av Norte & Av Morazán; ☯ 24hr)
Post Office (1 Av Norte btwn 1 & 3 Calles Pte; ☯ 8am-5pm Mon-Fri, 8am-noon Sat)
Scotiabank (☎ 2451 0977; Av Fray Flavio Muchi btwn 2a Calle Ote & Calle Obispo Marroquín; ☯ 8am-4pm Mon-Fri, 8am-noon Sat) Cashes travelers checks. Has a 24-hour ATM.

Sleeping & Eating

Sonsonate's best hotel is several blocks from the city center – the place to go if you just want to crash somewhere nice for the night. Hotel Orbe is less special, but perfectly fine, and closer to services like Internet access and banks.

Hotel Plaza (☎ 2451 6626; 9a Calle Ote at 8a Av Norte; s/d US$35/40; ⓟ 🐾 🏊) A fountain greets you as you step from the blazing sun into the cool, tile-floored lobby of this hotel. The décor is very '80s, but the rooms are spacious and clean; all have good beds and cable TV. A well-tended pool is surrounded by a pleasant grassy area, and there's even a decent restaurant on-site (mains US$2 to US$7; open breakfast, lunch and dinner). It's the go-to choice if you can swing it.

Hotel Orbe (☎ 2451 1517; 4a Calle Ote at Av Flavio Muchi; r US$8, r/tw with TV US$12/16, r/tw with air-con & TV US$16/20; ⓟ 🐾) In business for over 35 years, the Hotel Orbe is very clean but somewhat worn. It has 36 rooms with good beds and scrubbed floors, and is located close to the city center. On hot nights, air-con is definitely worth the extra four bucks. Service is friendly.

La Casona (3 Calle Pte btwn 1 & 3 Av Norte; mains US$1.50-4; ☯ breakfast & lunch Mon-Sat) Whether it's the sound and smell of fresh pupusas sizzling on a hot grill, or the great old building where they're being served, there's something almost irresistible about this place. A haven of simple charm in a rather charmless city, and the food (including fresh *comida a la vista*, a meal-served buffet) is tasty to boot. Too bad it's not open for dinner.

Jugos, Licuados y Más (1 Av Norte btwn 1 & 3 Calles Pte; ☯ 7am-6pm Mon-Sat) A hole-in-the-wall juice bar with a couple of wood tables and a blender, just up from the post office. It serves freshly squeezed juice and great *licuados* for under US$1 – heaven on a hot day.

EL SALVADOR

Just down the street from the Hotel Plaza, a string of **food stands** (7a Calle Ote at 10a Av Norte; mains US$1-2; 🕑 5-10pm) open for business in the evenings to sell pupusas, burgers and sandwiches. Good for fast eats.

Getting There & Around

The bus terminal is 2km east of Sonsonate's center. To get into the city center, take a taxi or bus 53C from just outside the terminal. To get back, you can catch the same bus from the parque central. For San Salvador, always take the *especial* service: it's faster and safer, since it doesn't pick up passengers along the way. Note there are two different buses to Santa Ana: bus 216 via Los Naranjos is beautiful and more direct, but take bus 209B if you want to connect to Parque Nacional Los Volcánes (and remember that hiking tours there start at 11am – plan accordingly).

The following are destinations served from Sonsonate:

Ahuachapán Bus 249 (US$0.83, two hours, 36km, every 15 minutes from 4:15am-6:05pm).

Apaneca Take any Ahuachapán bus (US$0.60, 50 minutes).

Ataco Take any Ahuachapán bus (US$0.70, one hour).

Barra de Santiago Bus 285 (US$1, 1¼ hours, 10:30am and 4:30pm); or take any La Hachadura bus to turnoff and transfer to pickup.

Cara Sucia Take any La Hachadura bus (US$0.45, 30 minutes).

Izalco Bus 53A (US$0.35, 20 minutes); catch outside new bus terminal.

Juayúa Take any Ahuachapan bus (US$0.45, 30 minutes).

La Hachadura Bus 259 (US$0.83, 1¾ hours, 58km, every 10 minutes from 4:30am-7:30pm).

La Libertad Bus 287 (US$1.25, 2½ hours, 76km, 6:15am and 3:45); or take any La Perla bus and transfer to bus 192 (last bus at 5pm).

La Perla Bus 261 (US$0.80, 1½ hours, 51km, 5:45am, 9:55am, 10:55am, 11:15am, 12:30pm, 3pm, 4:25pm, 5pm); or take La Libertad bus.

Los Cóbanos Bus 257 (US$0.42/0.52 weekday/weekend, 40 minutes, 24km, every 30 minutes from 5:15am to 6pm); last return bus 6pm.

Los Naranjos Take any Santa Ana bus 216 (US$0.65; 40 minutes).

Nahuizalco Bus 53D (US$0.45, 30 minutes; catch outside new terminal); or take any Ahuachapán bus and walk from turnoff (500m).

Parque Nacional Los Volcánes Take any Santa Ana bus 209B via El Congo to El Pakún turnoff (*ordinario* US$0.65, 1½ hours; *directo* US$0.65, 40 minutes) and transfer to bus 248 from Santa Ana.

GETTING TO GUATEMALA CITY

The international border post at **La Hachadura** (☎ 2420 3631) is open 24 hours on both sides, although crossing at night is rarely a good idea. Bus 259 from Sonsonate drops you right at the border; Salvadoran and Guatemalan immigration windows are side by side at the far end of the complex. Once you enter Guatemala, the bus stop is a further 1km down the road; walk or catch a bicycle taxi for around US$0.50. Buses leave there for Guatemala City (US$5, three to four hours, last bus at 3pm) every half hour via Chiquimulilla and Esquintla. Headed the other direction, the last bus to Sonsonate leaves La Hachadura at 6pm.

Parque Nacional El Imposible Take any La Hachadura bus to Puente Ahuachapío or Cara Sucia (US$0.45, 30 minutes).

San Salvador Bus 205 (*directo* US$0.70, 1½ hours, every five minutes from 3:30am to 6:40pm; *especial* US$1, one hour, every 15 to 20 minutes from 4:30am to 5pm) 70km.

Santa Ana Bus 216 (US$0.65, 1¼ hours, every 20 minutes from 4:30am to 6pm) via Los Naranjos.

Santa Ana Bus 209B (*ordinario* US$0.65, two hours, 7:30am, 8:30am, 10:30am, 12:20pm, 1:40pm, 3:30pm; *directo* US$0.65, 1½ hours, 4:40am, 5:35am, 7am, 9:15am, 11:55am, 12:55pm, 1:45pm, 4:30pm) via El Pakún and El Congo.

NAHUIZALCO

North of Sonsonate, Nahuizalco is a quiet village specializing in wicker baskets and furniture. Nahuizalco has a large and long-standing indigenous population, and you occasionally see women in traditional Pipil clothing – including colorful wraparound skirts – in the market and elsewhere.

There are *artesanía* stores and family workshops on almost every street in town. Shop around or, if you're running short on time, check out the shop at **CEDART** (☎ 2453 1336; 3a Calle Pte 3; 🕑 8am-noon & 1-5pm Mon-Fri, 10am-noon & 1-4pm Sat & Sun), a government-sponsored organization that helps artisans develop their craft and business; it carries an excellent sampling of local artwork.

Bus 53D (US$0.45, 30 minutes) goes from Sonsonate's new bus terminal all the way into Nahuizalco's center. Otherwise, bus 249, from Sonsonate or Juayúa, will drop you at the highway turnoff; it's about 500m into town.

JUAYÚA

Juayúa (pronounced 'why-*you*-uh') is awesome – no two ways around it. Besides attractive colonial architecture, a pleasant central plaza, and a historic church – gotta have one of those – Juayúa also hosts a wildly successful weekend *feria gastronómica* (food festival), when local and invited restaurateurs serve terrific food at tables set up around the parque central. The event draws scads of local and international tourists, and has been copied by towns throughout El Salvador – though none quite equal it. Around Juayúa are excellent hiking and other eco-outdoorsy activities, from rappelling down waterfalls to mountain biking in private *fincas* (coffee plantations). For something less sweaty, you can take a tour of a coffee processing plant or – if you come midweek – simply soak in Juayúa's small-town charm.

History

Juayúa's happy vibe contrasts with the events of the not-so-distant past. It was here, as well as Salcoatitán and Izalco, that an ill-fated Communist/indigenous uprising was plotted and carried out. Government troops responded with bloody and indiscriminate zeal, killing tens of thousands of indigenous people in a matter of days. Generations of indigenous people subsequently eschewed trappings of their native culture, especially clothing and language, for fear of standing out. Juayúa has not retained or recovered its indigenous character to the degree other affected towns have, though a quiet pride still pervades.

Orientation

Streets follow a standard grid pattern here, though street signs are sometimes lacking. Luckily, just about everything you're looking for is within a couple blocks of the town center – wandering around town slightly lost is not an entirely bad thing.

Information

Cyber & Equipment (☎ 2452 2769; 1a Av Norte; per hr US$0.75; ⏰ 8:30am-1pm & 2-9pm) Located half a block north of the plaza; sometimes open until 11pm.

EL SALVADOR

JUAYÚA

| | 0 | 100 m |
| 0 | 0.1 miles |

INFORMATION
Cyber & Equipment.....................1 C2
Farmacia Cristo Negro.................2 C3
Farmacia Don Bosco....................3 D2
Hotel Anáhuac..........................(see 10)
Hotel-Posada y Restaurante
El Mirador...........................(see 11)
Juayutur Kiosk...........................4 C2
Police......................................5 C1
Scotiabank................................6 A2
Unidad de Salud de Juayúa.........7 B2

SIGHTS & ACTIVITIES
Tempo del Señor de Juayúa.......8 B2

SLEEPING
Casa de Huespedes Doña
Mercedes.............................9 D3
Hotel Anáhuac.........................10 B1
Hotel-Posada y Restaurante
El Mirador...........................11 B2
Laura's Casa de Huespedes......(see 12)

EATING
Laura's Comida a la Vista...........12 D2
Pupsería Doña Cony..................13 D3
Restaurante Pollo Rico...............14 D2
Taquería La Guadalupana..........15 D2
Tienda San José.......................16 C2

TRANSPORT
Weekday Bus Stop....................17 C2
Weekend Bus Stop...................18 A2

Farmacia Cristo Negro (☎ 2452 2954; Calle Monseñor Oscar Romero; ⏱ 8am-9pm) Open daily, but ring the bell if the doors are closed, as the proprietors live on-site.

Farmacia Don Bosco (☎ 2452 2017; 2 Av Sur at 2 Calle Ote; ⏱ 8am-noon & 2-6pm) Founded in 1942 by the present owner's father, this is one of the oldest businesses in town and worth a peek inside. All the old apothecary bottles are still on display, making it as much a museum as a place to get medicine.

Hotel Anáhuac (☎ 2469 2401; hotelanahuac@tikal.dk; 5a Av Norte at 1a Calle Pte) Offers custom tours, led by the English-speaking owners.

Hotel-Posada y Restaurante El Mirador (☎ 2452 2432; 4a Calle Pte 4-4; ⏱ 7am-7pm) Laundry service for guests and nonguests; wash and dry per load US$4; same day service if you drop off in the morning.

Juayutur (⏱ 9am-5pm Sat & Sun) Juayúa's tourist agency dispenses information about the town and area excursions at its kiosk on the east side of the plaza. The kiosk is closed Monday to Friday, but you can contact its coordinator, **Edgar Antonio Álfaro** (☎ 2469 2387, 77461167; edarya_antony16@yahoo.com) to arrange tours midweek (for details, see below). Most guides speak Spanish only.

Police (☎ 2452 2455; 1 Av Norte; ⏱ 24hr)

Scotiabank (☎ 2452 2007; Calle Monseñor Oscar Romero; ⏱ 8am-4pm Mon-Fri, 8am-noon Sat) Still no ATM, but one is reportedly in the works. The teller should be able to withdraw cash against your credit card in a pinch (Visa only). Exchanges traveler's checks, but no foreign currency.

Unidad de Salud de Juayúa (☎ 2452 2089; Calle Monseñor Oscar Romero; ⏱ 7:30am-3:30pm) Medical service one block west of the plaza, diagonally opposite the rear of the church.

Sights

Juayúa's white-washed church – the **Templo del Señor Juayúa** – is famous for its crucifix: the 'Cristo Negro,' carved by Quirio Cataño in the late 16th century and displayed prominently at the back of the nave. It is the object of a great deal of worship and pilgrimage – you can climb a set of stairs behind the altar for a closer look. On your way out, don't miss the beautiful stained-glass windows along the walls, representing the 14 stages of the cross.

Tours

Juayutur (⏱ 9am-5pm Sat & Sun), on the east side of the plaza, offers around 10 organized tours that vary from easy to hard, adventurous to educational, half-day to all day (per person US$3 to US$6). There are a

half-dozen trained guides, although **Edgar Antonio Álfaro** (☎ 2469 2387, 7746 1167; edarya_antony16@yahoo.com), the team's young energetic leader, handles most tours himself. Most trips are best taken in the morning, so try calling or stopping by a day or two before to make arrangements.

The cool folks at **Hotel Anáhuac** (☎ 2469 2401; hotelanahuac@tikal.dk; 5a Av Norte at 1a Calle Pte) offer similar tours for similar prices, and they speak English. Following are some of Juayatur's more popular routes.

Chorros de la Calera A massive underground river pours out of hundreds of fractures in the three long cliffs, each about 10m high and ranging from 30m to 70m long. A cement retaining wall below one of the falls creates a nice swimming area, though the water is frigid. Edgar can also guide you through two half-submerged tunnels – they're 30m and 50m long, the water is chest level (roughly 1.25m) and at one point you're in pitch darkness – definitely not for claustronyctohydrophobics of the group. The site is only 1.5km from town, but a few assaults have been reported in this area, so always go with a guide (and never enter the tunnels unaccompanied).

Ruta de las Siete Cascadas The name pretty much says it all: the Route of Seven Waterfalls follows the Río Bebedero downriver past the waterfalls, which vary in height and drama (three are over 50m high), until you reach Chorros de Calera. Bring two pairs of shoes, one for walking in and along the river, the other for the hike out.

Rapel Mojado A 2km hike through coffee fields brings you to the top of the highest of the seven waterfalls on the previous Ruta de las Siete Cascadas tour, some 70m up. And it's not called 'wet rappel' for nothing – water from the falls pours all around you as you lower yourself down. Most people take five to 15 minutes to reach the bottom; you can do it twice if you don't mind the hike back to the top. An instructor and (ahem) paramedic accompany every trip (per person US$25).

Tur de Café First you'll visit a *finca* where you can pick your own coffee berries. Then you head to a working *beneficio* (processing plant), where you can see how the red flesh is stripped away, the bean dried and toasted (when it finally starts to smell like coffee), and how it's then bagged up for market or export. The tour ends with a cup of fresh brew. Held from November to January.

Sleeping

Hotel Anáhuac (☎ 2469 2401; hotelanahuac@tikal.dk; 5a Av Norte at 1a Calle Pte; dm per person US$7, r with bathroom per person US$15; 🖳) Owned and operated by two accomplished musicians, this is an artsy, homey and very cool place to crash: a renovated colonial home with one dorm and five private rooms that open onto a large courtyard garden with hammocks. Private rooms are very comfortable and have windows that open onto the cobblestone street, skylights in hot water bathrooms and beautiful *azulejo* (decorative tiles) floors; the dorm has three bunk beds, high ceilings and a shared cold-water bathroom. Guests have access to a small common kitchen, and welcoming sitting rooms decorated with indigenous and bohemian art. There's also free Internet access. Tours of the area are organized and led by the owners, too.

Hotel-Posada y Restaurante El Mirador (☎ 2452 2432; www.elmiradorjuayua.org; 4a Calle Pte 4-4; s/d/tw US$12/15/28; P) You'll find 19 spotless and spacious rooms here, with bathrooms (hot water US$2 extra), good beds and cable TV. All open onto an enclosed courtyard and a set of stairs that lead to a rooftop restaurant that has a great view of Juayúa and the volcanoes beyond. Look for the huge mural half a block from the main plaza – the entrance is unmistakable. Staff speak English.

Casa de Huespedes Doña Mercedes (☎ 2452 2287; cnr 2a Av Sur & 6a Calle Oriente; d with/without bathroom US$25/23; P) A friendly guesthouse with five clean, mid-sized rooms, all with cable TV, fan and hard beds. Two rooms share a bathroom in the hallway, while another two have an internal foyer and bathroom between them. Room 4 looks onto a small interior courtyard, while room 5 is the only one with a bathroom.

Hotel-Posada El Encanto (☎ 2452 2187; www .hotelelencanto.com; r with fan US$30, tw/ste with aircon US$40/45; P 🌐) Located on the road to Santa Ana, this is a charming colonial-style inn with eight rooms. Each is decorated a bit differently from the others, but all have hot water, cable TV and high ceilings. The suite is probably the best room in all of Juayúa: spacious, with mezzanine-level beds, a cozy living room, a huge terrace with a view of the red roofs below, and an impressive picture window overlooking the volcanoes of Izalco and Santa Ana. Comfortable sitting areas, including one with a fountain and another in a small garden, make good places to relax. Continental breakfast is included.

La Escondida Bed & Breakfast (in San Salvador ☎ 2263 2211; www.akwaterra.com; Finca El Portezuelo, Calle Real Km 6; campsites per person US$8, 2-3 incl breakfast US$55, 4-6 US$95, 7-10 US$125, add approx US$5 per person Fri-Sun; P) A spacious brightly painted home in the middle of a private coffee plantation, 6km by rough road from Juayúa. It's owned and overseen by the folks at Akwaterra, one of El Salvador's coolest tour operators. It has four bedrooms, three hot-water bathrooms, three fireplaces and a full kitchen. From here you can organize a plethora of outdoor excursions, including mountain biking, horseback riding, hiking and coffee tours. Reservations are required. Camping equipment is also available for rent.

If you arrive on a weekend and the hotels listed are full, two other options are **Hotel Juayúa Inn** (☎ 2469 2109; 6a Av Pte; r US$15-35; P 🌐), with second-rate rooms but a fantastic view of the area's volcanoes, and **Laura's Casa de Huespedes** (☎ 2469 2151; Av Daniel Cordón Sur 1-3; d/t incl one meal US$20/30), with so-so 1st-floor rooms and one good 2nd-floor room, plus lots of windows and a narrow wraparound terrace.

Eating & Drinking

Juayúa hosts a hugely successful *feria gastronómica* every Saturday and Sunday. Stands start serving food around 10:30am and keep running until the last visitor leaves.

Taquería La Guadalupana (☎ 2452 2195; 2a Calle Ote; mains US$1.75-5; 🕐 lunch & dinner Tue-Sun) Classics like *tacos al pastor* (seasoned rotisserie pork; three for US$1.75) and chicken mole (US$3.50) are served along with burritos, nachos, fajitas and other Tex-Mex faves. The daily special (US$2.50) is a bargain, consisting of a large main dish, rice, salad and a drink. The restaurant has two floors and – lest you forget you're eating Mexican food – little caricatures of jalapeños, sombreros and tomatoes dance along the brightly painted walls.

Restaurante Pollo Rico (☎ 2452 2383; 2 Av Sur; mains US$3-8; 🕐 lunch & dinner) What started as a simple chicken stand in 1990, has over the years become a Juayúa institution. Chicken is still the specialty, but the menu has grown to include *cabrito adobado* (chili-marinated goat), *tenquiques* (wild mushrooms, served grilled, in soup or ceviche), and even grilled frog's legs – they *taste* like chicken, right? Upstairs is a patio and great view of Volcán Santa Ana.

Tienda San José (☎ 2479 2349; Main Plaza, 2a Calle Pte; mains US$2-5; ☉ 8:30am-11pm Mon-Fri, 8:30am-midnight Sat & Sun) Inside this ordinary chips-and-soda minimart hides a surprisingly pleasant dining area with a sunflower motif and picnic tables. Friendly service and large plates of well-prepared *típica* make this a good choice. In the evening it becomes a popular meeting spot for locals and travelers alike.

Laura's Comida a la Vista (☎ 2469 2151; Av Daniel Cordón Sur 1-3; mains US$1.25-4; ☉ 7am-8pm Mon-Sat, 7am-3pm Sun) This long narrow restaurant is especially popular for breakfast, but is busy most mealtimes. As the name implies, it's all *comida a la vista*, all the time – choose from various dishes displayed in steam trays. It's nothing fancy, but the food is homemade and consistently good.

Pupsería Doña Cony (2 Av Sur at 6 Calle Ote; pupusas US$0.35-$0.40; ☉ 5-10pm) You can't go wrong at this busy *pupusería*, which many say is the best in town. It's especially handy if you're staying at Doña Mercedes's across the street.

Hotel-Posada y Restaurante El Mirador (☎ 2452 2432; 4a Calle Pte 4-4; mains US$1.50-5; ☉ breakfast & lunch) A rooftop restaurant with one of the best views in town: a (low-flying) bird's-eye view of Juayúa and the volcanoes in the distance. *Típica* is served cafeteria-style, and during the high season there's live music on weekend afternoons.

Getting There & Around

During the week bus 249 comes and goes from the east side of the main plaza. On Saturday and Sunday the bus stop is four blocks west, at the entrance of town across from the Scotiabank. Buses travel through Juayúa every 15 minutes for Sonsonate (US$0.45, 45 minutes), Apaneca (US$0.35, 20 minutes), Ataco (US$0.35, 30 minutes) and Ahuachapán (US$0.70, one hour). The first bus to Sonsonate passes Juayúa at 4:15am, and the one to Ahuachapán at 5:15am; the last in both directions is at around 7pm. For Santa Ana (US$0.45, 40 minutes) bus 238 goes direct and leaves a few blocks west of the parque central at 5am, 6am, 7am, 9am, 2pm and 4pm. If there are enough passengers, additional departures at 8am and 10am are added. Otherwise, take a bus to Sonsonate or Ahuachapán and connect there.

APANECA

Situated in the Sierra Apaneca Ilamatepec, Apaneca (1450m) is the second-highest town in El Salvador, after Los Naranjos. It is also one of the more pleasant, with cobblestone streets, a cool climate and a mellow ambiance. There's not much to do in Apaneca: a couple of low-impact hikes and some flower nurseries are the main attractions. Active travelers will probably get more out of a place like Juayúa or Tacuba, with their many eco-tourism options, but Apaneca is perfect for those with time to spare and a soft spot for small-town life. The town's beautiful Iglesia San Andres Apóstol was one of the country's oldest churches (dating back over 400 years) before the January 2001 earthquake reduced it to rubble.

Orientation

It's all but impossible to get lost in Apaneca. The only confusing thing is that, coming into town from Ahuachapán, you're actually facing north, rather than south as you might think. The main road, 1a Calle, runs along the east side of the parque central, and the church is on the north side. Av Central is a block over.

Information

There are no banks or ATMs in Apaneca, and the clinic has only nursing staff. For a doctor (and the money to pay for one), head to Ahuachapán.

Alcaldía (mayor's office; ☎ 2433 0442; Main Plaza; ☉ 8am-12:30 & 2-5pm Mon-Fri)

Caseta Información Turística (Tourist Information Booth; Main Plaza; ☉ 9am-6pm Sat & Sun)

Cybercafé Apaneca (☎ 2433 0367; 3a Av Sur; per hr US$0.75; ☉ 8am-11pm) Behind the school; also burns CDs for US$1.

Farmacia Sagrado Corazón 2 (Av Central Sur; ☉ 8am-8pm Mon-Sat, 8am-noon Sun)

Police (☎ 2433 0347; ☉ 24hr) Two blocks north and one block east of the parque central.

Unidad de Salud (Clinic; ☎ 2433 0006; ☉ 7:30am-3:30pm Mon-Fri) One block east of the police station.

Sights & Activities

The folks at the tourist information kiosk can give you information and arrange for guides to any of Apaneca's sights. José Douglas Areval directs the guide service, and can be found at the *alcaldía* if he's not at the tourist information booth. That said, guides aren't really necessary – all of the hikes are along (fairly) well-marked roads and paths, and there are usually people along the way who can keep you on target. Crime here is extremely rare.

Laguna Verde is a deep and cold crater lake with a distinctive aqua-green color, hence the name. It's 4km northeast of town, mostly uphill, and makes for a very pleasant, if not particularly spectacular, excursion. Swimming is not recommended; a few people have drowned, reportedly because of whirlpools caused by the lake's currents. Just past Apaneca on the highway headed toward Sonsonate is a turnoff to 'Villas Suizas'; turn there, then bear right at the first chance. You'll pass Villas Suizas on your right, while the road veers slightly left and uphill. Follow this road the entire way – regular cars won't get far, but 4WDs often make it up.

Laguna de las Ninfas is swampy, full of reeds and lily pads, and generally not as interesting as Laguna Verde. The hike there is nice enough, with good views of Apaneca and the surrounding countryside. To get there take the same turnoff from the highway to Villa Suizas, but stay left (instead of bearing right to Laguna Verde) and follow the signs. It's about 2km further.

Chichicastepeque is the official name of the 1816m-high mountain overlooking Apaneca from the south, but everyone in town calls it *el cerro grande* (the big hill). Bristling with communication antennae, it's not exactly a journey into the wild, but the summit affords outstanding views of the area. There are a number of roads and paths to the top, as the hillside is covered with coffee fields. Start by going to the southern end of Av Central. Go left a block, then right, though a neighborhood called Regalo de Díos. Following the road, always opt for the uphill path.

Tours

Vivero (plant nursery) tours make for a mellow, interesting afternoon. **Vivero Alejandra** (☎ 2433 0310; mains US$0.50-2; ☼ 7am-4pm) is a short walk from the center of town, on the highway at Apaneca's southern entrance, and is one of the nicer *viveros* to visit. Come for the flowers and rare plants, but stay for the great little café, serving coffee, quesadillas, and homemade strawberries and cream.

Other nice *viveros* include **Vivero Santa Clara** (☎ 2433 0559; ☼ 7:30am-5pm), a small nursery across the street from Vivero Alejandra, **Las Flores de Eloisa** (☎ 2433 0415; Carr Apaneca-Ataco Km 92.5; ☼ 7am-6pm) and **El Jardín de Celeste** (☎ 2450 5647; Carr Apaneca-Ataco Km 92.5; ☼ 7am-6pm); for more details on Las Flores de Eloisa and El Jardin de Celeste, see p370.

Hotel & Resort Santa Leticia (☎ 2298 2986; www .coffee.com.sv; Carr Sonsonate-Ahuachapan Km 86.5), a hotel, restaurant and coffee plantation 2km south of Apaneca, offers a guided tour of its small **archaeological park** (admission US$5, 45 minutes). Located in the middle of a coffee field, you'll see a few artifacts, including two pot-bellied figures carved from huge basalt boulders that weigh between 6350kg and 9525kg. Experts speculate that the 2000-year-old sculptures were created by an early Maya group, possibly in deference to their rulers. This tour also can be combined with a visit to the 230-acre **coffee plantation** (admission US$30, four hours), which is offered with advanced notice only. Visitors walk through the coffee fields and learn about the growing and cutting of different beans, before being driven to the processing plant to watch the beans being weighed, cleaned, dried and, finally, roasted. The best time of year for the tour is October to March. To get here, catch any bus headed toward Juayúa and Sonsonate, and ask the driver to let you off in front.

Sleeping

Apaneca has two budget guesthouses in town, and two upscale options on the highway at the town's entrance. There are also some great accommodations in nearby Ataco, and on the road between the two towns.

CENTRAL APANECA

Hostal Rural Las Orquídeas (☎ 2433 0061; 4 Calle Pte btwn 1 Av Sur & Av Central; s/tw US$12/17; ℗) There's seven rooms here, all smallish, but very clean with hot water and brightly painted walls; some are cheerier than others. A covered corridor and grassy interior courtyard have hammocks, chairs, and a ping-pong table for you and your travel partner to determine, once and for all, who is the champ of all champs. It's two blocks south and a half-block east of the parque central – look for signs.

EL SALVADOR

EL SALVADOR

Hostal Magaña (☎ 2433 0268; Av Central btwn 4 & 6 Calles Sur; s/d US$17/20) A new, very private guesthouse around the corner from Las Orquídeas. There are just two rooms, both large with two beds, bathroom, and use of the kitchen and dining room. The owners live upstairs.

Hotel y Restaurante Las Cabañas de Apaneca (☎ 2433 0500; www.lascabanasdeapaneca.com; Carr Sonsonate-Ahuachapán Km 90.5; r/tw US$40/50; P ▢) This charming hillside establishment is owned by an artist, and it shows – original artwork in the dining room, sculptures in the garden, bold colors throughout, and chic décor. Fifteen rooms are scattered along several hillside ridges, each slightly different from the next. All are very clean, with hot-water bathrooms and great views of a lush valley that extends below like a full green skirt. Breakfast is included and served in the hotel's sunny restaurant.

OUTSIDE APANECA

Hotel & Resort Santa Leticia (☎ 2298 2986; www .coffee.com.sv; Carr Sonsonate-Ahuachapán Km 86.5; tw US$68, cabañas US$73; P ▢ ▣) Surrounded by lush grounds and coffee fields, this place is perfect if you like nature right outside your door and modern conveniences inside. Eleven rooms and eight cabañas are built around two solar-heated pools. All have attractive and colorful décor, shabby-chic furnishings, and bathrooms with hot water and handpainted tiles. Each room also has a porch with a hammock, chairs and a table. Cabañas are bigger and a little quieter. Breakfast is included, and served in a lodge-like restaurant. Tours of the coffee plantation and of a small archaeological site on the property also can be arranged (p367).

Eating

Salvadoran food rules in Apaneca, ranging from market stalls to upscale gourmet.

Mercado Saludable (1 Calle Norte; mains US$1.50-3; ⏱ 6:30am-8pm) Facing the parque central and something of a community meeting point, this market has around a dozen little eateries. All serve inexpensive *típica*, like eggs, beans, *atole* and coffee in the morning, and roast chicken, pupusas and beef soup in the afternoon and evenings.

Restaurante Típicos Texixal (☎ 2433 0035; 1a Av Norte at 4a Calle Ote; mains US$1.50-7; ⏱ breakfast, lunch & dinner Tue-Sun) Expect large plates of *típica* at this gaudy purple and white restaurant, a block south of the plaza. The *plato del día* (daily special) is just US$1.50 and includes a main dish, rice and salad. Not to be confused with the popular *plato típico*, which comes with better cuts of meat, soup and fried bananas for US$5.

La Cocina de Mi Abuela (☎ 2433 0100; 1a Av Norte at 4a Calle Ote; mains US$7-11; ⏱ lunch & dinner Sat & Sun) This is considered one of the best restaurants in the country, and is a major reason why so many people make the long drive from San Salvador to Apaneca. The menu includes high-quality meats and classic Salvadoran fare prepared especially well. The desserts are great.

Hotel y Restaurante Las Cabañas de Apaneca (☎ 2433 0500; Carr Sonsonate-Ahuachapán Km 90.5; mains US$2-9; ⏱ breakfast & lunch Mon-Fri, breakfast, lunch & dinner Sat & Sun) Sky lights, exposed brick, sculptures and indigenous art help to create the welcoming ambiance at this popular restaurant. Live music on weekends (12:30pm to 4pm) and good service round it out. *Gallina asada para cuatro* (grilled hen for four) comes with rice, vegetables and salad for only US$22 – perfect for small groups. Be sure to check out the impressive sculpture garden.

Hotel & Resort Santa Leticia (☎ 2298 2986; Carr Sonsonate-Ahuachapan Km 86.5; mains US$4-12; ⏱ breakfast, lunch & dinner) Located 2km south of Apaneca, the restaurant in this upscale hotel offers a reliable menu, with several international dishes (pasta, soups, salads and seafood) along with standard Salvadoran fare. Meals are served in a lodge-like atmosphere, complete with wood paneling and heavy furniture.

Getting There & Around

Like all the other towns along the Ruta de Las Flores, Apaneca is served by bus 249, which runs northward to Ataco (US$0.25, 10 minutes) and Ahuachapán (US$0.45, 40 minutes) and southward to Juayúa (US$0.35, 20 minutes) and Sonsonate (US$0.60, 50 minutes). Buses pass every 30 minutes, stopping a block north of the plaza; the last north-bound bus passes at 7:30pm, the last southbound at 8pm. Microbuses pick up and drop off at the plaza; they cost the same and are slightly faster, but serve Ataco and Ahuachapán only.

ATACO

Ataco is one of El Salvador's most picturesque colonial towns, with its brightly-painted homes, cobblestone streets, and the indigenous character of an Antigua, Guatemala or Copán, Honduras. Yet Ataco (its complete name is Concepción de Ataco) receives a fraction of the visitors that those towns, or even nearby Juayúa or Suchitoto, do. Part of the reason is location: Ataco is fairly isolated from all three of western El Salvador's large cities. But another reason must be the town itself, which has been decidedly reticent about opening its doors to visitors. This is changing, however, with the inauguration of a tourist information kiosk and a fledgling guide service, and Ataco is well worth visiting, provided you tread lightly. Most travelers here find locals friendly, though somewhat reserved, perhaps wary of the changes that outsiders (national or international) may bring.

Orientation

Ataco is easy to navigate and charming enough that even getting lost is not a bad thing. The parque central (main plaza) is at Av Central and 1 Calle Pte – the church is on the east side and *alcaldía* on the west. Calle Central intersects Av Central a block south of the plaza, and the streets follow the standard grid pattern from there. There's a handy tourist brochure with a map available at the tourist information kiosk at the entrance of town and tourist office next to the *alcaldía*.

Information

Farmacia Union (☎ 2450 5050; 2a Av Sur 3; ☷ 8am-noon & 2-7pm)

Laundry (☎ 2450 5175; Café Casa Bambú; 8a Av Sur at 2a Calle Ote; ☷ 3-10pm Mon-Fri, 8am-6pm Sat & Sun) Wash, dry and iron: per 12 items US$3.

Medical Office (☎ 7756 7142; 8a Av Sur; ☷ 24hr) Ring the bell or call after regular business hours; English is spoken.

Police (☎ 2450 5590; 6a Calle Ote at 4a Av Sur; ☷ 24hr)

Post (Main Plaza, Av Central Norte; ☷ 8am-noon & 2-5pm Mon-Fri, 8am-noon Sat)

Tourist Information Kiosk (☷ 7am-7pm Sat & Sun) Located at the entrance to town.

Tourist Office (☎ 2450 5021; Main Plaza, Av Central Nte; ☷ 8am-5pm Mon-Fri)

ATACO

0 _____ 200 m
0 _____ 0.1 miles

To Ahuachapán (6km)

To Cielito Lindo (1km)

To El Jardin de Celeste (4.5km); Alicante Montaña Hotel (5km); Las Flores de Eloisa (6km); Apaneca (8km)

Sights & Activities

May 3rd is the **Día de las Cruces** (Day of the Crosses) celebration, which in Ataco was traditionally held at **Cruz del Chico**, a large cross just outside of town. However, participation started to decline, so the celebration was moved to **Cruz Cielito Lindo**, which is closer to the town center and more visible – not so easy for those of flagging faith to say they didn't know it was happening. The festival is interesting to see if you're in town. Otherwise both crosses make for pleasant walks with good views.

Ataco also has a nascent guide service, made up of a half-dozen friendly young guys who can lead you to sights further afield. Some options include **Salto de Chacala**, a 50m waterfall on the Río Matala, and **Chorros del Limo**, an upwelling of water that forms a broad pool, which is good for swimming – if you can stand the cold. The cost isn't well defined, but US$3 to US$7 per person seems fair. Some tours require a 4WD, which none of the guides have, but they can be rented from a local for around US$15.

Sleeping

Ataco has some gorgeous colonial homes, the kind with colorful facades, high stucco walls and sunny central courtyards. It's only a matter of time before charming B&Bs open up here, like in other colonial towns. For now the options in town are still fairly modest, but three great *posadas* can be found on the highway nearby.

CENTRAL ATACO

Quinta El Carmen (☎ 2298 4187, 2450 5669; quintaelcarmen@yahoo.com; Carr Ahuachapán-Sonsonate Km 97; r incl breakfast with/without bathroom US$50/40, ste US$80; P ✕) A real gem, this converted townhouse has common areas decorated with indigenous and colonial-era artifacts, and a pink stucco fountain in the sun-splashed interior corridor. There are just three rooms and one suite; the beds are comfortable, the bathrooms modern and spotless (the suite's bathroom is enormous), and details like fresh flowers, rocking chairs and wood-framed mirrors exude understated class. It's very private, yet just a short walk from Ataco's center. Advance reservations are recommended, especially on weekends. Horseback riding and coffee tours can be arranged.

La Posada de Don Oli (☎ 2450 5155; 1a Av Sur; r US$25 & US$35; P) More popular as a restaurant than a hotel, the Don Oli has only three rooms: two small ones and a larger six-person unit. The small rooms feel cramped, with a queen bed and two bunks. The bathrooms are unexpectedly quaint with decorative ceramic tiles, but so small that the sink is on the outside. Pricey for what you get.

El Mesón de San Fernando (☎ 2413 0169; 1a Calle Pte; r Mon-Fri US$20, Sat & Sun US$25, without bathroom per person US$10) These are clean, but utterly charmless rooms, occupying a long low cinder-block building. The yellow and blue paint helps, but only so much. Rooms with bathrooms have hot water and tile floors; shared bathrooms are in a detached cinder-block structure and are acceptably clean. What redeems the place are the large garden, good restaurant and friendly hardworking proprietors.

Café Casa de Bambú (☎ 2450 5175; 8a Av Sur at 2a Calle Ote; r without bathroom US$15; P ⬚) Two small rooms with one bed apiece are squeezed into the 2nd floor of this restaurant. Both are small and closed in – two people in one room may feel crowded. Bathrooms are clean and have hot water. The rate includes one meal of your choice – breakfast, lunch or dinner – served in the pleasant dining area below. It's owned and operated by a local doctor, who lives and practices on-site (p369).

OUTSIDE ATACO

El Jardin de Celeste (☎ 2450 5647; Carr Sonsonate-Ahuachapán Km 94; r US$38, r with TV US$45, tw/ste US$45/60; P) Set in an expansive nursery and coffee farm, the accommodations here are among the best in the region. Ten spotless and modern cabins each have wood-beam ceilings, nice tile bathrooms, and a large porch with hammocks and chairs; they're decorated simply but lovingly, with regional textiles and art, and always fresh flowers. The suite is worth the extra cash; it has a living room, bedroom and a kitchenette – the canopy bed and the huge wraparound porch are pluses. A great restaurant (mains US$3 to US$11; open breakfast, lunch and dinner), with indigenous art, heavy handcarved furnishings and wonderful aromas wafting out from the kitchen, makes a great place to start (or end) your day. Vegetarian meals, a children's menu and a mean Hungarian goulash (among the other international dishes) are pleasant surprises.

Las Flores de Eloisa (☎ 2433 0415; Carr Sonsonate-Ahuachapán Km 92.5; r US$20-26, tw US$30; **P**)) Just down the highway, this smaller version of El Jardin de Celeste (the owners are related) offers seven cabins set on the edge of a lush nursery. Each cabin has two rooms, each with hot-water bathroom, good beds and, of course, fresh flowers. A small garden café (mains US$2 to US$4; open breakfast and lunch) serves *típico*, sandwiches and desserts.

Eating & Drinking

El Mesón de San Fernando (☎ 2413 0169; 1a Calle Pte; mains US$2-10; ☯ lunch & dinner Fri-Sun) Salvadoran comfort food is the specialty at this family-run restaurant and hotel. Try *gallo en chicha* (US$5), a viscous soup made of chicken, vegetables and *chicha* (a traditional Salvadoran liquor made of fermented corn), or *sopa de pata* (US$3) made of cow hooves, cabbage and other veggies, all slow-cooked into a thick stew. Indoor and outdoor eating areas are both airy and pleasant, and the service is friendly.

Fonda y Vivero Restaurante (☎ 2450 5020; 1a Av Sur; mains US$1-3; ☯ breakfast, lunch & dinner) An open-air courtyard filled with plants, indigenous art and lots of wood tables make up this homey eatery. Specialties include *pupusas de champiñones y queso* (mushroom and cheese) and *chorizo con frijoles* (sausage with beans, plantains and cream). If you just want a snack (or dessert), try the *quesadilla* (US$1), a fluffy cheese cake that's typically served with coffee.

La Posada de Don Oli (☎ 2450 5155; 1a Av Sur; mains US$6-15; ☯ lunch & dinner Sat & Sun) This place has a great dining area, with hot-pink walls, garden view and ceramic tiles embedded in the dark wood tables. The food is decent but overpriced; then again, the main clientele are wealthy weekend warriors from the capital.

Café Casa de Bambú (☎ 2450 5175; 8a Av Sur at 2a Calle Ote; mains US$3-5; ☯ 3-10pm Mon-Fri, 8am-1am Sat, 8am-6pm Sun) A sunny eatery with indigenous art, serving Salvadoran and Mexican meals. A bamboo-laden sitting room and a rooftop terrace make good places to have a drink and sit a while, too. Try the *pato en naranja* (duck marinated in orange juice) for something a little different (US$4).

Diconte-Axul (☎ 2450 5030; 2a Av Sur at Calle Central; mains US$0.60-2; ☯ 8am-6pm) This great little gift shop is also a fine place to get a cappuccino and a pastry. Tables and chairs are set up in the shop and in a lush garden – perfect to sit and write postcards.

A rambling **market** (2a Av Sur; ☯ 8am-6:30pm) makes for a fascinating walkabout, and is a great place to stock up on fresh fruits, veggies and breads.

Shopping

Diconte-Axul (☎ 2450 5030; axulartisans@hotmail.com; 2a Av Sur at Calle Central; ☯ 8am-6pm) A bohemianhip giftshop selling artwork made on-site, such as textiles, hand-dyed T-shirts, paintings and colorful household objects. Customers can watch artisans at work – just be sure to ask before you snap a photograph. Look for the building with the huge mural. A good coffee shop is also on-site.

Getting There & Around

Bus 249 stops in Ataco on its way north to Ahuachapán (US$0.35, 15 minutes), and south to Apaneca (US$0.25, 10 minutes), Juayúa (US$0.45, 30 minutes) and Sonsonate (US$0.70, one hour). There is also microbus service to and from Ahuachapán (US$0.30, 15 minutes) and Apaneca (US$0.25, 10 minutes). Both the buses and microbuses operate roughly 7:30am to 7:45pm, and pass every 15 to 30 minutes. All buses should drop off and pick up at the corner of 2a Calle Ote and 4a Av Sur; however, the road was under construction at the time of publication, so double-check that you're in the right spot.

AHUACHAPÁN

pop 38,633

A smaller safer version of Sonsonate, a hub for all sorts of places but not much of a destination itself, Ahuachapán is at the beginning (or end) of the Ruta de las Flores, and within easy reach of Tacuba (and great excursions into El Imposible), the Guatemalan border, Tazumal and Casa Blanca archaeological sites, and Santa Ana further on.

Orientation

Ahuachapán has two large plazas that are five blocks apart and connected by Av Menéndez, a busy commercial street running roughly north–south.

EL SALVADOR

Information

Centro Médico Ahuachapán (☎ 2413 4700; Prolongación 6 Calle Ote; ☼ 24hr) Located on the eastern outskirts of town; some English is spoken.

Ciber Café Cetcomp (☎ 2413 3753; 2a Av Sur at 1a Calle Pte; per hr US$0.55; ☼ 9am-8pm Mon-Fri, 9:30-8:30 Sat, 10am-9pm Sun)

Farmacia Central (☎ 2443 0158; 2a Av Sur btwn Calle Gerardo Barrios & 1a Calle Ote; ☼ 8am-9pm Mon-Sat, 9am-noon & 5-7pm Sun)

Police (☎ 2443 0911; 2 Calle Ote btwn Av Menendez & 1 Av Norte; ☼ 24hr)

Post Office (1a Calle Ote at 1a Av Sur; ☼ 8am-5pm Mon-Fri, 8am-noon Sat)

Scotiabank (☎ 2443 0400; Av Menéndez at 4 Calle Pte; ☼ 8am-4pm Mon-Fri, 8am-noon Sat) Changes AmEx and Visa traveler's checks, but not foreign currency.

Tours & Aventuras (☎ 2422 0016; www.elsalvadorvacations.com.sv; 2 Av Norte 2-4; ☼ 8am-noon & 2-6pm Mon-Fri, 8am-noon & 2-5pm Sat & Sun) Friendly travel agency offering tours of sights within the area.

Sights

Plaza Concordia (3a Calle Pte btwn Av Menendez & 4a Av Norte) is definitely the more appealing of Ahuachapán's two plazas, with lush gardens and tall palm trees that provide plenty of shade. A central kiosk is occasionally used to stage free concerts and events.

The town church, **Nuestra Señora de Asunción**, sits on the eastern side of Plaza Concordia. The interior is pleasant, with *azulejo* floors and a wood ceiling, and the blue-and-white facade has a stained-glass Virgin Mary looking out from under a well-maintained belltower.

Ahuachapán is famous for its intense geothermic activity – pits of steaming mud and water can be found throughout the surrounding area. **Los Ausoles** is the largest and most famous of these sites, 'discovered' by Spanish explorers in the 16th century and known by many as *los infernillos* (the little hells). A power plant that uses tubes to capture super-heated underground vapor was built in 1968, and now provides some 10% of El Salvador's electricity. Tourists can visit the undeveloped areas, where the water bubbling up is hot enough to poach an egg. **Tours & Aventuras** (☎ 2422 0016; www.elsalvadorvacations.com.sv; 2 Av Norte 2-4; ☼ 8am-noon & 2-6pm Mon-Fri, 8am-noon & 2-5pm Sat & Sun) offers an educational three-hour tour of the area, or you can contact recommended local guide **Carlos Alvarado Martínez** (☎ 2413 3360).

Sleeping & Eating

Hotel Casa Blanca (☎ 2443 1505; www.casablancaahuachapan.com, in Spanish; 2a Av Norte at Calle Gerardo Barrios; s/d US$20/30, s with air-con US$35, d with air-con US$45-50; P ⊠ 🖳 ⌨) Located just a few blocks from Plaza Concordia, the Casa Blanca is a colonial home transformed into a comfortable hotel. Eight clean rooms hold two beds, a desk, cable TV and hot-water bathroom. Although all are well maintained, the rooms with air-conditioning are in better shape – just be sure to ask for a mini-split air-conditioner (they're quieter than the older models). A tranquil courtyard is the centerpiece of the hotel, with tables, chairs and a tiny pool. If you plan to go for a dip, let the management know, so that they can clean and fill the pool.

Hotel San José (☎ 2413 0033; 6 Calle Ote 1; r with fan per person US$8, with air-con US$24; ⊠ P) A rambling no-frills hotel on the south side of Parque Menéndez. The fan rooms are a decent option for budget travelers, but couples and midrangers may as well pay a bit more for a room at the Casa Blanca. Some rooms are cleaner than others.

La Estancia (☎ 2443 1559; 1a Av Sur btwn Calle Gerardo Barrios & 1a Calle Ote; mains US$2-4; ☼ breakfast & lunch Mon-Sat) An airy mansion-turned-restaurant that makes for a good breakfast or

---

GETTING TO GUATEMALA CITY

The border post at **Las Chinamas** (☎ 2401 3601) is open 24 hours a day, but avoid crossing outside of daylight hours. Two bus lines go to the border from Ahuachapán: large bus 263 (US$0.50, 40 minutes, every 15 minutes from 6am to 5pm) and smaller Ruta 11 buses (US$0.50, 30 minutes, every five to 10 minutes from 4:50am to 7:40pm). Pick up either one at the northwest corner of Parque Menéndez. Once across the border, walk 300m to the bus stop for the onward service to Guatemala City via Cuilapa. Second-class 'La Humilde' buses leave almost constantly, but most travelers prefer to wait for a 1st-class Melva, Mermex or Tica bus (US$3), which pass roughly every half hour from 5am to 7pm. They are faster and safer than 2nd-class buses and much more comfortable, with bathroom, air-con and reclining seats. King Quality and Pullmantur buses do not stop.

lunch spot, serving cafeteria-style *típica*. Get here early for the best pickin's.

Restaurant Mixta 'S' (☎ 2443 1471; 2a Av Sur at 1a Calle Pte; mains US$2-3; breakfast, lunch & dinner) Popular with locals and travelers alike, the specialty here is *mixtas* – delicious pitas stuffed with pickled veggies, salsa and meat or cheese. The fruit shakes are tasty too, and come in 26 flavors. Service is friendly and fast.

For self-caterers, **Supermercado De Todo** (8 Calle Pte; ⏰ 7am-8pm) is a big busy supermarket on the northside of Parque Menéndez.

Drinking
Brisas de Santa Monica (☎ 2443 0470; Carr a Las Chinamas Km 101; cover US$4; ⏰ disco 9pm-3am Fri & Sat) Ahuachapán's best nightspot is actually few kilometers north of town on the banks of the Laguna del Llano. But get this: you can call the club and they will send a microbus to pick you up at your hotel and return you in the wee hours, totally free of charge. Sweet! Staff are friendly and bilingual.

Getting There & Around
Buses line up along Av Menéndez at 10a Calle Ote. Microbuses to Apaneca leave from the highway turnoff, but regular buses are usually faster and leave more frequently. Buses for the Guatemalan border at Las Chinamas leave from 8a Calle Pte, at the northwest corner of Parque Menéndez. The following destinations are served from Ahuachapán:

Apaneca Take any Sonsonate bus (US$0.45, 40 minutes).
Ataco Take any Sonsonate bus (US$0.35, 25 minutes).
Juayu'a Take any Sonsonate bus (US$0.70, 55 minutes).
Las Chinamas Bus 263 (US$0.50, 40 minutes, every 15 minutes from 6am to 5pm); or Ruta 11 (US$0.50, 30 minutes, every 10 minutes from 4:50am to 7:40pm).
San Salvador Bus 202 (*ordinario* US$1, 2¼ hours, every 10 minutes from 3:30am to 5pm; *clase-A* US$1.40, 1½ hours, every 15 to 20 minutes from 4:45am to 7:30am daily and 3pm to 5:15pm Sunday only; *especial* US$2, 1¼ hours, every 15 minutes from 5am to 6am daily, and 10:30am, 11:30am, 12:30pm and 1pm Friday to Sunday).
Santa Ana Bus 210 (US$0.45, one hour, every 10 minutes from 4:10am to 7:15pm); alternatively take the faster San Salvador bus, get off at Metrocentro and catch a local bus into town.
Sonsonate Bus 249 ($0.83, two hours, every 15 minutes from 4:30am to 6pm).
Tacuba Bus 264 or Ruta 15 (US$0.50/$0.60 weekday/weekend, 40 minutes, every 15 to 30 minutes from 5:30am to 7pm) Note: Ruta 15 until 4:30pm only.

TACUBA
Tacuba is surrounded by mountains and volcanoes, the land draped with forests and coffee plantations, and crisscrossed with rivers, trails and dirt roads. Fourteen kilometers west of Ahuachapán, it lies on the northern edge of Parque Nacional El Imposible, and along the rolling Guatemalan border. Tacuba is also one of El Salvador's poorest regions, and until the last few years tourist traffic here was little more than a trickle. But a freshly paved road, a gang problem brought under control and the almost single-handed work of one local guide have turned Tacuba into one of El Salvador's most rewarding eco-tourism destinations. As a growing stream of travelers continue to make their way here, many crossing over from Guatemala, it seems likely more infrastructure will emerge. A **Spanish school** (Escuela Tlocopan; ☎ 2417 4202) was in the works just when this book went to print – look for it on Av Cuscatlán, four blocks from the plaza.

Information
Tacuba has no banks or ATMs.
Centro Escolar (per hr US$1; ☎ 7am-6pm Mon-Fri) The school computer center has the fastest Internet connection in town and is open to the public.
Compucentro Tacuba (☎ 2417 4641; 2 Calle Ote & 2 Av Sur; per hr US$0.75; ⏰ 8am-6:30pm Mon-Sat, 8am-noon Sun) Next to the police station.
Farmacia La Providencia (☎ 2417 4241; Av Cuscatlán 16; ⏰ 8am-12:30pm & 2-6:30pm)
Police (☎ 2417 4676; 2 Calle Ote btwn Av Cuscatlán & 2 Av Norte; ⏰ 24hr)
Unidad de Salud (☎ 2417 4303; ⏰ 7am-4pm Mon-Fri, 8am-noon Sat) Located at far southern (uphill) end of main street, three blocks past turnoff to Manolo's place.

Sights
Tacuba's **historic colonial church** survived, with serious damage, the 1773 earthquake that destroyed Antigua, Guatemala. It used to be open to visitors, but the 2001 earthquakes damaged it even further and the ruins are now technically off-limits, surrounded by a chain-link fence. The guard will usually let you in to look around – if you can find him. If you can't, Manolo González at Imposible Tours can usually arrange a visit.

Tours
Imposible Tours (☎ 2417 4268; www.imposibletours .com; Hostal de Mamá y Papá) is a one-man operation run by Manolo González, a kinetic

Tacuba native who can arrange or guide just about any outdoor activity you want, from hiking and birdwatching to horseback riding and mountain biking. Most are wholly or partly in Parque Nacional El Imposible, and cost around US$15 per person, including transport, lunch, entrance fees and an evening trip to *la ceiba de los pericos*, a 600-year-old tree where thousands of parrots roost every night, all squawking to high heaven. Manolo has over a dozen planned tours, and can customize them to the type, duration and difficulty you prefer. His most popular tours include the following:

Montehermoso A six-hour hike down (and sometimes through) the Río Guayapa to 'El Salto,' a gorgeous 75m waterfall within Parque Nacional El Imposible. A deep clear pool is perfect for swimming and, for the brave, a stomach-lurching leap from partway up the cliff. After swimming and lunch, it's a one- to two-hour hike up and out, along a different path.

Tacuba to San Benito A moderately strenuous transect of Parque Nacional El Imposible, passing through dense forest and by several spectacular vista points, skirting Cerro El Leon and ending at the San Benito visitors center (opposite). This hike is longer and more isolated than any of those from the visitors center, but because the mountains are higher near Tacuba, it's mostly downhill.

Tacuba to Cara Sucia A newer hike, following the original road used by early coffee farmers to take their harvest to market. You'll descend past several terrific view points to Cara Sucia on the Carr Litoral, where Manolo has a return truck waiting. A convenient option is to load your bags in the truck before leaving so you can head straight to Guatemala or La Libertad.

Carita de Palmera Most trips can be extended to include a night at a family home on the beach near Cara Sucia, allowing you to spend the next day boogie-boarding, horseback riding or just hanging out. You can say your goodbyes from there, or return with Manolo via the Ruta de las Flores. Two-day trips cost US$35 per person, including transportation, lodging and three meals.

Festivals & Events

Tacuba's **fiestas patronales** (patron saint celebrations) are held in honor of Saint Mary Magdalene yearly from July 17 to 22. The festivities include parades, traditional dances, live music, fireworks, mechanical toys, sporting events, and even a beauty queen.

Sleeping & Eating

Hostal y Restaurante Miraflores (☎ 2417 4746; miraflores@hotmail.com; 2a Av Norte at 7a Calle Ote; r without bathroom US$15; P) Three spotless rooms

with fans make up this small hotel; each opens onto a green courtyard that doubles as a flower nursery. The shared bathroom has cold water only and needs a scrub, but all in all it's a decent place to stay. A good restaurant on-site (mains US$1.50 to US$3; open breakfast, lunch and dinner) serves *típico*, along with a good selection of Italian, Mexican and Chinese dishes.

Hostal de Mamá y Papá (☎ 2417 4268; www .imposibletours.com; hammock US$3, r with/without bathroom per person US$6/5) Run by – who else? – Manolo González out of the González family home. Mamá, Papá, and Manolo all live here; three older rooms have multiple beds; newer rooms have stone floors, queen-size beds, hot-water bathroom and wood paneling for a rustic-cabin look. Above them is a platform with an awesome view over town and into Guatemala. A great all-you-can-eat breakfast is just US$2, and water, coffee and fruit are always available.

La Cabaña de Tacuba (☎ 2417 4332; www .lacabanadetacuba.com; r/tw US$30/45; P ☻) Twelve rooms on sprawling grounds make up this midrange hotel. The rooms are simple but clean, and have hot-water bathrooms; most also have outdoor hammocks that overlook a cross-shaped pool. The main building houses a welcoming reading room, as well as a good restaurant (mains US$4 to US$10; open breakfast, lunch and dinner) that specializes in French and Salvadoran cuisine. Tours of the area – on foot, horse or bicycle – can be arranged. To get here follow signs from the entrance of town. Ask here about **Juanimar** (Av Cuscatlán 23; r per person US$10), a converted colonial home in town with rooms for rent.

Sol de Media Noche (☎ 2417 4239; mains US$1.50-4; ☼ 6:30am-5pm Mon-Sat) One of several vegetarian restaurants owned and operated by a Salvadoran Hindu sect. The all-veggie menu includes tasty carrot tortas and brown rice. Smiling gurus peer down from pictures on the walls. It's two blocks past the plaza.

No Name Pupusería (2a Calle Ote; mains US$0.35-1; ☼ 4-10pm) Next to the police station near Av España, this *pupusería* is the top dog in tiny Tacuba. Locals flock here daily to fill up on the mouthwatering pupusas that are patted out as soon as night falls.

Getting There & Around

Bus 264 and smaller Ruta 15 buses (week-day/weekend US$0.50/$0.60, 40 minutes, 5:30am to 7pm) come and go from Ahuach-apán to Tacuba's main plaza.

PARQUE NACIONAL EL IMPOSIBLE

Decreed a national park in 1989, El Im-posible is a tropical mountain forest be-tween 300m and 1450m above sea level in the Apaneca Ilamatepec mountain range. The park is named for the perilous gorge through which coffee growers once labored to move their crop from the northern *fincas* to the port of Acajutla. Many mules and crews fell to their deaths attempting to cross the gorge via makeshift tree-trunk bridges. The notoriously treacherous journey gave the park its name; when bridges were finally built a plaque was installed to mark the occasion. Still there, the plaque famously reads: '*Mayo 1968 – dejó de der imposible*' (May 1968 – it's no longer impossible).

The majority of the park is original for-est, the remains of a threatened ecosystem and habitat for an extraordinary variety of plant and animal life. Nearly 400 kinds of trees grow in the area, and endangered animals, such as pumas, tigrillos, wild boar, king hawks and black-crested eagles, are protected here. Eight rivers flow through Imposible, providing the watershed for Barra de Santiago and other mangrove for-ests along the coast.

Orientation & Information

The park's main entrance is at the small hamlet of San Benito. Theoretically you are supposed to stop by the San Salvador office of **SalvaNatura** (Fundación Ecológica de El Salvador; Map pp320-1; ☎ 2279 1515; www.salvanatura.org, in Spanish; 33a Av Sur 640, San Salvador; ⏰ 8am-12:30pm & 2-5:30pm Mon-Fri, phone service only Sat & Sun) to pay your entry fee and to arrange for a guide. You can also just call – even on weekends, when a guard should be available – and the office will radio a guide. You can pay at the park when you arrive. If all else fails, you can just show up – weekends are busy, but there's usually space and guides on weekdays. Sal-vaNatura is opening a second entrance and visitors center at San Francisco Menéndez. Still under construction when we passed through, this entrance will have a paved access road and be geared to a slightly less

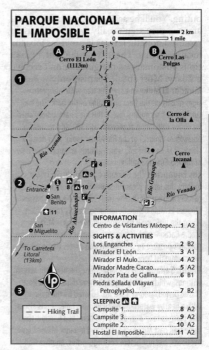

PARQUE NACIONAL EL IMPOSIBLE

0 — 2 km
0 — 1 mile

INFORMATION
Centro de Visitantes Mixtepe.....1 A2

SIGHTS & ACTIVITIES
Los Enganches 2 B2
Mirador El León 3 A1
Mirador El Mulo.........................4 A2
Mirador Madre Cacao................5 A2
Mirador Pata de Gallina............6 B1
Piedra Sellada (Mayan
　Petroglyphs)...........................7 B2

SLEEPING 🏠 🏡
Campsite 1..................................8 A2
Campsite 3..................................9 A2
Campsite 2................................10 A2
Hostal El Imposible...................11 A2

adventurous crowd. Entrance fees per per-son cost US$6 and parking is US$3.

You can also enter the park through the 'back door,' starting in the town of Tacuba and hiking south to the visitors center. **Im-posible Tours** (☎ 2417 4268; www.imposibletours.com; Hostal de Mamá y Papá) is a one-man operation offering a number of recommended hikes starting from the northern edge of the park (for details, see p373). The best time to visit is October to February, as the rainy season hinders travel.

Just past the gate at San Benito is the **Centro de Visitantes Mixtepe**, a small solar-powered visitors center. There's a mildly interesting little museum with exhibits on local his-tory and on plants and animals found in the park, as well as books and other gifts for sale. There's also a lookout tower with views of the ocean, and restrooms.

Hiking

The park has three primary hikes, none ter-ribly difficult. The trails merge and intersect at various places, so it is possible to com-bine two or more destinations on the same outing. You'll be assigned a guide when you arrive – they aren't really necessary, but are required nonetheless, as it provides jobs for local residents. There is no fee, but a US$5 tip is customary as the guides don't receive a salary. Most speak Spanish only.

Mirador El Mulo An easy 1km trail with interpretive signs mostly on the flora and fauna of the park. The trail cuts through secondary forest, this area having been used for coffee cultivation as recently as 1980, and passes the *nacimiento* (source) of the Río Ahuachapío. Your destination is El Mulo overlook, which affords an impressive view of the Río Guayapa valley.

Los Enganches The Guayapa and Venado rivers join to form this large, pleasant swimming hole, a nice place to relax and eat lunch. The trail (3.5km one way) passes Mirador El Mulo before descending steeply to the rivers. Along the way you'll pass another overlook – Mirador Madre Cacao – with views of the southeastern part of the park. It's possible to see agoutis and coates (large rodent-like mammals) here.

Piedra Sellada This is a large stone, etched with Mayan writings, which archaeologists believe dates to the Post Classic period, around 1500 AD. Located by the river, with a nearby waterfall and swimming hole, this is also a nice place to take a break. To get here, you'll follow the same trail past Mirador El Mulo and Mirador Madre Cacao overlooks, but just before Los Engcanches, another trail cuts upriver about 1km to Piedra Sellada.

Cerro El León A more challenging hike up one of the park's tallest mountains, with great vista points. From the visitors center the trail makes a steep 1km descent to the Río Ixcanal, a narrow river in a lush, humid gorge. Crossing the river you climb the other side, known as Montaña de los Águilares, through dense forest to the summit of Cerro El León (1113m) and a 360-degree panoramic view. Return by the different route, along the narrow ridge between the Ixcanal and Guyapa river valleys. It's an 8km circuit; budget several hours and bring plenty of water.

Sleeping & Eating

Hostal El Imposible (☎ 2411 5484; 0.8km before park entrance; 1-2 people Mon-Thu US$34, Fri-Sun US$45.50, per person extra US$5.65; 🔌 ℗) Everything is eco-friendly here – from the solar-power lights and organic waste composting to erosion barriers and certified eco-friendly lumber. Five A-frame wood cabins are spread widely down a long steep hillside, lending each a sense of privacy. Cabins each have a double bed, two bunk beds and a hot-water bathroom. They're ample but not huge, and each has a pleasant patio. At the bottom of the hill is a small stone swimming pool filled with spring water. At the top of the

hill is the reception and parking area, and an excellent little restaurant (dishes US$2 to US$6; open 7am to 7pm). The menu is creative, both in its content (banana pancakes, yogurt and granola, barbecue rabbit, even *gazpacho*) and for the images of local creatures printed on its pages.

Inside the park are three large **camping areas** (free with entrance; limited tent rental US$5-7) each with latrines and outdoor grills. There are no showers, but you can rinse off in the nearby Río Ahuachapío if you don't use soap. Campsites 1 and 2 can be reached by car, but 3 is more isolated and can be reached by trail only (1km). Small fires are allowed; bring drinking water and a sleeping bag.

Getting There & Around

From Sonsonate, catch bus 259 toward La Hachadura and the Guatemalan border (see p362) and get off at Cara Sucia. From there, a bus leaves daily at 11am and a pickup truck at 2pm (both US$0.90, one hour). If you think you might miss the bus or pickup in Cara Sucia, you may be able to cut them off by being dropped off at Puente Ahuachapío (Ahuachapío Bridge), a few kilometers east of Cara Sucia. If the pickups have already passed, you can take a bus or pickup up from Cara Sucia or the Ahuachapío bridge to El Refugio (US$0.60, 45 minutes, every 30 minutes 7am to 5pm), one of the intermediate towns on the road to the park. From there you may be able to hitch a ride, but it's likely you'll have to walk the rest of the way, about 5km mostly uphill.

To return, the bus leaves Parque Nacional El Imposible at 5:30am and the pickup at 7am. Otherwise, walk back to El Refugio and catch a bus or pickup there – the last one leaves at 2:30pm. Remember, you can also visit the park from the northern side, via the town of Tacuba (p373).

NORTHERN EL SALVADOR

A short bus ride from San Salvador are the small towns of northern El Salvador and the Chalatenango department. Suchitoto (opposite) is the honey pot of the area, and possibly the country, attracting hundreds of visitors every week with its colonial

good looks, laid-back attitude and artsy bohemian style. La Palma (p389), up the road, has less flair than Suchitoto, but shares its artistic leanings – Salvadoran painter Fernando Llort (p306) taught his style and technique to local artisans, who now earn their livings creating the colorfully painted wood crafts that are so well known in El Salvador and abroad. Throughout the area are great hiking opportunities and lush mountain views, including those from the summit of Cerro El Pital, El Salvador's highest (but most easily climbed) mountain (p392).

During the civil war the north saw intense fighting between the Salvadoran military and the Farabundo Martí National Liberation Front (FMLN) guerrillas. Villages here, including Suchitoto, bore the brunt of the military's *tierra arrasada* (scorched earth) campaign, in which entire towns, communities and farms were destroyed. Salvadorans fled en masse to Honduras, where 'temporary' camps just across the border became home to thousands of refugees for more than a decade, and became the source of tension between the two countries. Many refugees returned as the war wound down, and after the signing of the 1992 Peace Accords. Others, especially those who fled to the USA, have never returned – it is not uncommon to find Salvadoran immigrants who not only still haven't gone back themselves, but who in some cases refuse to allow their children to visit either. Those who did return formed new towns, like El Manzano (p389), so refugees and former combatants whose hometowns were destroyed would have a place to call home.

Climate & Geography

The northern region has the greatest elevation change of anywhere in El Salvador, rising from the broad river valley north of San Salvador (now a reservoir called Lago Suchitlán) to the country's highest point, Cerro El Pital, near the Honduran border. The climate follows in lockstep, from the warm low-lying areas of Aguilares and Cihuatán, commonly reaching 23°C (73°F), to the higher and cooler towns of La Palma and San Ignacio, which fall to 12°C (53°F). If you are camping on top of El Pital, it can get downright cold – you'll need several layers and a good sleeping bag.

SUCHITOTO

Suchitoto, 47km north of San Salvador, is a great little town, with colonial buildings and cobblestone streets. A cultural capital during the heyday of the indigo trade, it is now experiencing something of an arts revival. An art and food festival is held every weekend, a February arts and culture festival brings in world-class music and dance groups, and there's a concert, performance or art exhibit practically every week.

Suchitoto overlooks the Embalse Cerrón Grande, also known as Lago de Suchitlán, which visitors often enjoy for its boat rides. A bird migration zone, as many as 200 species have been spotted around the lake. Thousands of hawks and falcons fill the skies as the seasons change, and birds of all sorts nest in the relative safety of its islands.

Southwest of Suchitoto stands the massive Volcán Guazapa, also known as Cerro Guazapa, a dormant volcano whose steep, forested flanks protected an FMLN stronghold during the war years. Bomb craters

EL SALVADOR

EL SALVADOR

SUCHITOTO

0 — 200 m (Approx)
0 — 0.1 miles

To Casa Museo de Alejandro
Cotto (50m); Centro Turístico
Puerto San Juan (800m);
Boats/Ferry to San Francisco
Lempa (800m)

To Salto El Cubo (1.5km)

Parque San Martín

Calle Francisco Morazán

Teatro Las Ruinas

Parque Centenario

Iglesia Santa Lucía

To Hospital Nacional Suchitoto (75m); Aguilares (19km); San Salvador (47km)

To La Bermuda 1525 (5km); San Martín (28km)

Calle Dr Pío Romero Bosque

Casacada Los Tercios (2.5km)

SLEEPING 🏠
Dos Gardenias Hostal	**11** D2
Hotel Posada Altavista	**12** B2
Hotel y Restaurante El Obraje	**13** C3
La Posada de Suchitlán	**14** A1
La Villa Balanza	(see 20)
Los Almendros de San Lorenzo	**15** B2
Restaurante Vista Conga	(see 21)

EATING 🍴
El Tejado	**16** D2
Hotel y Restaurante El Obraje	(see 13)
La Bella Esquina	**17** B2
La Casa del Escultor	**18** A3
La Fonda del Mirador	**19** D1
La Posada de Suchitlán	(see 14)
La Villa Balanza	**20** B2
Los Almendros de San Lorenzo	(see 15)
Restaurante Vista Conga	**21** D2

DRINKING
La Fonda del Mirador	(see 19)
Restaurante Vista Conga	(see 21)
ZukaFé y Bar	(see 11)

SHOPPING 🛍
Galería de Arte Lucia Cañas	**22** B2
Galería de Arte Shanay	**23** C3
La Casa del Escultor	(see 18)

TRANSPORT
Buses to San Salvador & Aguilares	**24** B3

INFORMATION
Café Artex	**1** B3
Clínica Médica Asistencial	**2** B3
Clínica Orden de Malta	**3** B2
Cyber Café El Gringo	**4** A2
Farmacia Santa Lucía	**5** B3
Hotel y Restaurante El Obraje	(see 13)
Infocentros	**6** B2
Police	**7** B2
Post Office	**8** B2
Tourism Office	**9** B2

SIGHTS & ACTIVITIES
Centro Arte para La Paz	**10** B2

and rebel field camps are still visible, not to mention terrific views of the San Vicente and San Salvador volcanoes. Walking and horseback tours can be arranged in Suchitoto or through Reyna Tours (p317) in San Salvador.

Indigenous Yaqui and Pipil groups settled the surrounding river region about a thousand years ago. Spanish explorers arrived in the 16th century, establishing their nascent colony's first capital in 1528, just outside of present-day Suchitoto. More recently some of the earliest fighting of the civil war began in Suchitoto, accompanied by much destruction and emigration. Visitors today will find the town has rebounded very well.

Orientation

Suchitoto's church, Iglesia Santa Lucia, stands on the east side of Parque Centenario, the town center. Signs to the lake lead you a block east of the park, left onto 3a Av Sur, then down, down, down to the water (about 1km; it's steep in places). You can also follow the street that forms the park's western edge (Av 15 de Septiembre); it merges with 3a Av Sur several blocks down.

Parque San Martín is two blocks to the west and two blocks to the north of the town center. The Spanish International Cooperation Association (AECI) is planning to install new street signs all over the town.

Information

EMERGENCY

Police (☎ 2335 1141, 2335 1147; Av 15 de Septiembre at 4 Calle Pte; ☽ 24hr)

INTERNET ACCESS

Café Artex (☎ 2335 1440; Calle Francisco Morazán at 1a Av Sur; per hr US$1; ☽ 8am-9pm) You can connect your laptop and order a cappuccino, cocktail and dessert.

Cyber Café El Gringo (☎ 2335 1770; 8a Av Norte 9; per hour US$1)

Infocentros (☎ 2335 1739; Calle Francisco Morazán at Av 5 de Noviembre; per hr US$1; ☽ 8am-6pm Mon-Fri, 8am-5pm Sat & Sun) At the southwest corner of Parque Centenario. Printing and CD burning available.

LAUNDRY

Hotel y Restaurante El Obraje (☎ 2335 1173; 2a Calle Ote; per small/large load US$4/6; ☽ 8am-8pm) Laundry service available daily. Same-day service if you drop your clothes off early.

MEDICAL SERVICES

Clínica Médica Asistencial (☎ 2335 1781; 1a Calle Pte 5; ☽ 8am-4pm Mon-Fri, 8am-noon Sat)

Clínica Orden de Malta (4 Calle Pte 8; ☽ 7am-3pm Mon-Fri)

Farmacia Santa Lucía (☎ 2335 1063, 7101 2950; Calle Francisco Morazán at Av 5 de Noviembre; ☽ 8am-noon & 2-6pm)

Hospital Nacional Suchitoto (☎ 2335 1062; Calle Cementerio; ☽ 24hr) Located outside of town, with a 24-hour emergency room.

MONEY

There is still no bank or ATM in Suchitoto, despite concerted efforts by the tourism office to attract one. This has got to change at some point, but bring plenty of cash just in case.

POST

Post Office (Av 15 de Septiembre; ☽ 8am-noon & 1-5pm Mon-Fri, 8am-noon Sat)

TOURIST INFORMATION

Tourism Office (☎ 2335 1782; www.suchitoto-el -salvador.com; Calle Francisco Morazán at 2a Av Norte; ☽ 8am-noon & 1-4pm Wed-Sun) Professional and friendly office, with information on sights, activities and cultural events in Suchitoto.

Sights & Activities

The tourism office can give you additional info on most excursions in the area.

Salto El Cubo is a somewhat larger waterfall (about 15m) than Cascada Los Tercios (below) and has water year-round. A pair of pools has been formed at the base of the falls – climb from the lower one to the upper, hemmed in by rocks with the water crashing down from above. To get there, take Calle Francisco Morazán west out of town; it turns to dirt before reaching the trailhead. A narrow path descends steeply to the falls. To return, continue on the same trail, which climbs through the trees and has some excellent lake views before reaching town, near the Hotel Villa Balanza. The first leg takes about a half-hour, the second about double that. You can also go the reverse direction; all should be well marked by the time you read this, thanks to the tourism office and a local Peace Corps volunteer. Wear good shoes, as the trail has some rocky sections.

Considering **Casa Museo de Alejandro Cotto** (☎ 2335 1140; Calle al Lago; adult/child US$4/1; ☽ 2-6pm Sat & Sun) is one of the most expensive museums in the country, you'd think this place would be spectacular. It's not. It's a

---

LOS TERCIOS WATERFALL

Cascada Los Tercios is a small waterfall that tumbles over a cliff of tightly packed hexagonal stone spires, a geological oddity related to volcanic activity. The falls are a bit underwhelming when the water is low (often), but the rock formation is interesting enough, as is getting there. To visit, go south on the road in front of Iglesia Santa Lucia; it curves left, down and up again, before intersecting with a main road at a soccer field. Turn left and continue for about 1.5km. Right after a smoking garbage dump, look for a gate on your left. Enter here or continue to the next house, where one of the kids can guide you – either way, you pass through the family's property, so be sure to greet them, a simple *buenas* (good morning or good afternoon) or *con permiso* (literally, 'with permission') is nice. You can also combine a visit with a tour of the lake (p380) – ask your boat captain to let you off at the trail for the *cascadas* (waterfalls), walk up to the road, turn right and walk another four to five minutes. If you reach the dump, you've gone too far.

EL SALVADOR

private collection of antiques, musical instruments, fine paintings and books displayed in a rambling colonial-era home. If you like poking around – and don't mind dropping the cash – this may be worth your while. Alejandro Cotto, a Salvadoran filmmaker born in Suchitoto, may even be there to show you around. Look for the museum just past the turnoff to the lake.

Tours

René Barbón, the young English-speaking owner of **Restaurante Vista Conga** (☎ 2335 1679; vistacongasuchi@yahoo.com; Pasaje Norte 8) leads excellent eco-tours around the area. A waterfall tour (per person US$6, minimum four people) is a 3½-hour trek along – and sometime in – a frigid river that tumbles over four different waterfalls. Two are massive – 42m and over 100m – while the others, at 7m and 12m, are jumpable if you have the nerve.

A highly recommended Cinquera tour (per person US$15, entrance US$3, minimum four people) visits both Cinquera town and the nearby national forest. The tour offers hiking; great views; a stop at a reconstructed guerrilla campsite, including *tatús* (trenches and underground rooms used by guerrillas as field hospitals and air-raid shelters), kitchen, barracks etc; and a fascinating talk with Don Paulito, a former guerrilla sympathizer. Mountain biking tours of various difficulties (per person US$5 to US$7) are also available. All tours should be arranged at least a day in advance, preferably more.

Boat tours of the lake and its various islands can be arranged at the new **Centro Turístico Puerto San Juan** (☎ 2310 8736; admission US$0.50, parking US$1), about 1km north (downhill) from the center of town. What used to be a grubby dirt lot is now an attractive modern structure, complete with eateries, *artesanía* vendors and a walkway overlooking the water. The tourism office have managed to convince the boat operators to establish fixed prices, which are charged per boat (up to 10 people). Tours range from 45 minutes (US$15) to six hours (US$75), and visit a combination of islands, sights and lakeside villages, including Isla del Burro, San Luis Carmen and Isla Los Pájaros. You may be able to combine a boat tour with a visit to Cascada Los Tércios (p379) – ask to be dropped at the trail.

Volcán Guazapa (also known as Cerro Guazapa), towering to the southwest of Suchitoto, was an FMLN stronghold during the war. Today you can see bomb shells, craters and *tatús,* plus views of San Salvador and San Vicente volcanoes. You can visit by horse (per person US$18, six hours) or on foot (one to three people US$15, four to 10 people US$20, six hours); the tours are operated by an independent cooperative, and the quality (vegetation cleared, *tatús* maintained, horses not depressed) depends greatly on who's in charge at the time. Check with the tourism office for details.

City tours can be arranged by the tourism office, and visit up to 32 historical buildings and sites in and around Suchitoto. Price depends on the length of tour and number of people.

Festival & Events

The tourism office's website, **Suchitio – de Oficina Municipal de Tourisma** (www.suchitoto-el-salvador.com), as well as other websites listed in this section, are excellent resources for upcoming events.

Held every weekend, **Feria Artesenal 'Así es mi Tierra'** ('This is My Land' arts festival) includes live music, food stands, performances, painters, sculptors, and stands displaying and selling *artesanía,* natural medicine, hammocks and more.

The long-running **Festival Internacional Permanente de Arte y Cultura**, held every weekend in February, brings top national and international artists and artwork to Suchitoto for a month of artistic celebration. The festivities include parades, expositions, live performances and presentations.

Taking place in August, the **Festival de Maíz** (Corn Festival) stems from pre-Columbian rituals associated with harvesting corn. It features residents of outlying communities marching in processions to the church, bearing corn to be blessed and donated, followed by a special Mass. In the plaza, food stands sell traditional corn-based foods, like tortillas, *atole* and *tamales*. In a modern addition, festival-goers elect a festival king and queen from among local young people.

Sleeping

BUDGET

Hotel y Restaurante El Obraje (☎ 2335 1173; 2a Calle Ote; r without bathroom US$21, with air-con US$23, r with bathroom & air-con US$27; ❄) A very welcoming place near the parque central, El Obraje rents three spotless rooms, each named after a famous writer and opening onto a leafy passageway. The rooms are tiny – really tiny – but have firm beds and share a clean bathroom. Hammocks and couches in the hotel's courtyard make a great place to relax. A hearty breakfast is also included in the rate and is served in the popular restaurant at the front of the building. It's located across the street from the church.

La Villa Balanza (☎ 2335 1408; Parque San Martín; r without bathroom US$10) An eclectic establishment decorated with war-relics-turned-sculptures, La Villa Balanza offers the best value for budget travellers. Although the restaurant is the focus of the place, a handful of small but comfortable rooms are tucked into the building. Each is well kept, nicely decorated and share a clean bathroom. If calling to reserve a room, make sure you don't book one in the building across the street: they're grim – dirty walls, scuzzy bathrooms and saggy beds. Not good. And not worth US$10.

Dos Gardenias Hostal (☎ 2335 1868; www .gaesuchitoto.com, in Spanish; 3a Av Norte 48; r per person US$10) Originally called Casa de los Mestizos, this used to be *the* backpacker spot in Suchitoto, but the new ownership seems to be resting on past laurels. Dos Gardenias definitely looks the part – with a mango-shaded courtyard, an artsy lounge bar and a young go-with-the-flow atmosphere. But below the surface, the rooms are grubby, the bathrooms neglected and service is reluctant at best. If you can do without the scene, Villa Ballanza and El Obraje are cleaner and better value.

Restaurante Vista Conga (☎ 2335 1679; Pasaje Norte 8; campsites per person US$3, tent rental US$3) Primarily a place for meals and tours (see opposite), Vista Conga has space for three or four tents on a grassy platform at the back of a large lot, with awesome views right from your tent flap.

MIDRANGE
Hotel Posada Altavista (☎ 2335 1645; Av 15 de Septiembre 8; r/tw without bathroom US$15/25, tw with bathroom & air-con US$35-45; P) In the heart of town, this hotel is hard to miss. But once you step inside it is totally unremarkable – no-frill rooms with firm beds and cleanish bath-

rooms. It's just a simple hotel that knows it's in a great location, and charges for it.

TOP END
Los Almendros de San Lorenzo (☎ 2335 1200; www .hotelsalvador.com; 4a Calle Pte 2B; r incl breakfast US$80-90, ste US$100-120; P ❄ 🖳) Without a doubt this is one of the best places to stay in El Salvador. A posh boutique hotel set in a restored 200-year-old home, high-end Salvadoran art, antique and modern furnishings, custom-made doors and several gurgling fountains set the scene for six immaculate rooms. All have high ceilings, large tile bathrooms and classy, simple décor. The suites – one with its own fountain, the other distributed over two floors – are worth every extra cent. In addition to rooms that are hard to leave, guests can lounge in a luxurious library, at the well-tended pool, or in the lush garden. A fine restaurant and hip lounge bar only complete the experience.

La Posada de Suchitlán (☎ 2335 1064; www .laposada.com.sv, in Spanish; 4a Calle Pte; d incl breakfast US$58, tw US$64-68, tw with air-con US$70-75; P ❄ 🖳) Overlooking Lago de Suchitlán, this colonial-style posada has the best views of any hotel in town. Rooms are divided in two sections – older ones that open onto a beautiful garden courtyard and newer ones with dramatic views of the lake. All have high ceilings, tile bathrooms, good beds and simple décor; the older ones are worn but comfortable nonetheless. Breakfast is served at a pleasant open-air restaurant.

El Tejado (☎ 2335 1769; 3a Av Norte 58; d/tw US$45/60; ⏰ 10am-5pm Tue-Fri, 10am-6pm Sat & Sun; ❄ 🖳 P) Most people come here for the day to use the swimming pool and hammocks, and to eat at the large, open-air restaurant. But El Tejado's two rooms – seven more are being built – are actually quite nice. Opening onto a small courtyard near the heavy wood front doors, and well apart from the restaurant and pool area, rooms have yellow walls, new comfortable beds and cable TV. There are small wooden tables and chairs, and the passageway in front has colonial period pieces. The price includes a full Salvadoran breakfast for two, and free use of the swimming pool and hammocks (the pool is US$3 otherwise). Checkout is 10am – ouch.

La Bermuda 1525 (☎ 2225 5103; www.labermuda .com; Carr Suchitoto-San Martín Km 34.5; s/d US$40/50;

EL SALVADOR

(☉ Mon-Fri) The first colonial city in El Salvador was founded near this spot in 1525, and served as the capital until being moved to present-day San Salvador in 1528. Today, the remnants of a colonial-era hacienda – several of the buildings were destroyed during the war – serves as a lovely hotel and restaurant. Five rooms (another two are being built) have working fireplaces, antique furniture and *azulejo* (traditional decorative tile) floors, and include a full breakfast. La Bermuda hosts regular cultural events, especially music and dance, and has a small museum and gift shop with rotating displays of colonial and pre-Columbian artifacts.

Eating

At weekends, you'll find various local specialties on the plaza, including *fogonazo* (sugarcane juice) and *riguas* (sweet buttery corn tortillas wrapped in a corn husk).

BUDGET

La Bella Esquina (☎ 2335 1110; Av 15 de Septiembre 12 at 4a Calle Ote; mains US$1-3.50; ☉ breakfast, lunch & dinner) A 'beautiful corner' indeed, which you can enjoy from a window table at this friendly eatery. Fresh *comida a la vista* (meal-served buffet) includes beef soup, baked chicken and other Salvadoran fare. For breakfast, look for eggs, beans or *tamales*; the weekend speciality, as at most restaurants, is *sopa de gallina india* (wild hen soup).

La Villa Balanza (☎ 2335 1408; Parque San Martín; mains US$2-9; ☉ breakfast, lunch & dinner Tue-Sun) War relics transformed into art pieces are the main draw to this pleasant open-eatery. The *típico* (regional specialities) is good, the service is excellent, but the biggest reason people come here is to be surrounded by the historical art and artifacts from the war, including the shell of a 340kg bomb found in Cinquera. At the entrance is a sculpture of a giant scale *(la balanza)* weighing a stack of tortillas against a bomb.

Hotel y Restaurante El Obraje (☎ 2335 1173; 2a Calle Ote; mains US$3-12; ☉ breakfast, lunch & dinner) A popular restaurant in the heart of town, El Obraje serves up classic Salvadoran dishes. Take a look at the floors – covered with gorgeous tiles that were imported from Europe in the 1840s. Apparently the tiles were shipped along with those in the Iglesia Santa Lucia.

El Gringo (☎ 2335 1770; 8a Av Norte 9; mains US$2-6; ☉ dinner Fri-Wed) The gringo here is Robert Perry Brozmorán, an amiable California native who has lived and worked in El Salvador for over a decade. The business started out as an Internet café, but he recently started offering food as well. The menu is mostly Mexican and Tex-Mex, including fajitas, tacos, burritos and *chimichangas*. Full bar service often keeps the place open well past 10pm.

Restaurante Vista Conga (☎ 2335 1679; vista congasuchi@yahoo.com; Pasaje Norte 8; mains US$4-10; ☉ breakfast & lunch Wed-Fri & Sun, breakfast, lunch & dinner Sat) The owner, a young English-speaking San Salvador transplant, sure knows how to pick a spot: down a sometimes muddy road, a heavy wooden door opens onto a lush garden, giving way to fantastic views of the surrounding hillsides. Tables are set up in an open corridor; favorite dishes include a chorizo platter, *lomo de aguja* (filet mignon) and, of course, *sopa de gallina india*. Dinner service is by appointment. It's just off the road to the lake, near where Av 15 de Septiembre and 3a Av Norte merge.

MIDRANGE

Virtually all the higher-end hotels also have recommendable restaurants.

La Fonda del Mirador (☎ 2335 1126; Calle al Lago; dishes US$5-10; ☉ lunch & dinner) On the road to the lake, this Suchitoto institution has spectacular views of Lago de Suchitlán far below. The open air–dining room has exposed beams and a low-slung clay tile roof, with ferns hanging here and there. The food is great – *gallo en chicha* (chicken marinated in homemade moonshine) is a weekend favorite, and the *boca colorada filete* (fillet of smapper) is prepared with a homemade salsa of arrayan, mamey and tamarindo – all local fruits. The *ensalada marinera* (seafood salad, US$4) is a meal in itself.

La Casa del Escultor (☎ 2335 1836; 2a Av Sur 26A; mains US$7-14; ☉ lunch Sun) An eclectic restaurant set in the workshop of sculptor Miguel Marino, this is the place to come if you want a feast for your eyes and just a plain ol' feast. Every Sunday a classic Argentinean meal is prepared – choice meats, chicken and vegetables grilled on a large wood-burning grill – and served at tables that are surrounded by spectacular pieces of art. Clients start arriving around noon, and before you can say *choripan*, the place is packed. Meals are hearty; the smallest includes two types of meat, sausage links, grilled vegetables, potatos and a salad (US$7) – plenty for one person with a big appetite. The place is also open to the public during the week, when it functions as a workshop and gallery.

Los Almendros de San Lorenzo (☎ 2335 1200; www.hotelsalvador.com; 4a Calle Pte 2B; mains US$6-12; ☯ breakfast, lunch & dinner) The classiest restaurant in town, the menu in this glass-enclosed restaurant has a good variety of international favorites: salmon in lemon broth with cilantro (US$12), escargot with garlic and garden herbs (US$11), grilled chicken (US$8), and a variety of salads (US$4 to US$6). All are presented with an elegant flair. If you're in the mood, enjoy a cocktail or after-dinner drink at the understated lounge bar just a few steps from the dining room.

La Posada de Suchitlán (☎ 2335 1064; www .laposada.com.sv, in Spanish; End 4a Calle Pte; mains US$3-10; ☯ breakfast, lunch & dinner) Going head to head with La Fonda del Mirador for the best view in town, this place definitely holds its own. Diners enjoy the glorious view almost anywhere in the expansive, colonial-style dining room. Meals are based on Salvadoran dishes, but you'll also find a few international options. It's especially busy on weekends, when *capitalinos* drive up to take it all in.

El Tejado (☎ 2335 1769; 3a Av Norte 58; mains US$6-8; ☯ breakfast & lunch Tue-Sun) Travelers with kids may appreciate the large enclosed grounds here, with hammocks and a clean swimming pool within view of the main dining area (pool per person US$3). Service is excellent, and meals, mostly large meat and chicken plates, are perfectly fine. The dining area boasts yet another stunning view, this one over the valley to the south, with the end of the reservoir way off in the distance.

La Bermuda 1525 (☎ 2225 5103; www.labermuda .com; Carr Suchitoto-San Martín Km 34.5; mains US$4.50-13; ☯ breakfast, lunch & dinner Fri-Mon) Spanish and criollo food is the specialty here, owing to his hacienda's location near the original colonial capital of El Salvador. Try the aromatic *lomo de cerdo español* (Spanish-style pork chop) or grilled *cordoñiz* (quail). The hacienda grows many of its own herbs and vegetables and even brews indigenous liquors, including *chicha* and *chaparro* (both made from corn), and others fermented from nance, cashew fruit and coconut.

Drinking

Harlequín (☎ 7930-4417; ☯ 7pm-1am Fri-Sun) Suchitoto's go-to bar and nightspot features film nights, great music and frequent drink specials. It was about to change locations when we visited, but it's too good to leave out – ask at the tourism office for the latest.

ZukaFé y Bar (☎ 2335 1868; 3a Av Norte 48; ☯ 7:30am-9pm) Located inside Dos Gardenias Hostal, the name is a contraction of 'café' and 'Zuka', the name of the little dog running around barking. Rotating art exhibits and cool music (including occasional live performances on Saturday) make this a good place for drinks and meeting other travelers. The food and service is only so-so. Free art-house type movies play every Thursday at 7pm.

La Fonda del Mirador (☎ 2335 1126; Calle al Lago; dishes US$5-10; ☯ 7am-1am Fri-Sun) This popular restaurant has long had a full bar, and now the owner is planning to push all the tables aside and use the dining area as a dance floor. There isn't really room for a live band, but the right DJ could make things interesting. The view on a full-moon night ought to be sublime.

Restaurante Vista Conga (☎ 2335 1679; vista congasuchi@yahoo.com; Pasaje Norte 8; ☯ to 6pm Wed-Fri & Sun, to midnight Sat) This place has a full bar, a cool clientele and is open late on Saturday. The owner, René, also organizes huge boat parties about once a month – he rents the ferry, hires a DJ, brings tons of food and drink, and invites up to 200 people, who tool around the lake for a couple hours, dancing and partying. It costs US$4 to US$10, depending on what's included – just food, or food and drinks. Email to get on the invite list.

Entertainment

Centro Arte para La Paz (☎ 2335 1080; www .centroartex.org; 6a Av Nte at 4 Calle Pte) Occupying a full city block, this former school – that has stood closed for the last 25 years – is being renovated and reopened as an arts and performance space, emphasizing 'a culture of peace.' Not yet fully opened when we visited, it promises to be an important addition to Suchitoto's already vibrant arts and culture scene. Plans include a 300-person theatre for live shows, film screenings and more; an outdoor garden and performance space; studios for art classes; and a media and digital resources center. The website is very professional, and includes an up-to-date events calendar.

Shopping

Galleria de Arte Lucia Cañas (☎ 2335 1008; Av 15 de Septiembre at 4a Calle Pte; ✆ 9am-5pm Sat & Sun) This beautiful colonial-era home houses an eclectic collection of paintings for sale and old photographs of Spanish émigres. Occasionally, music recitals also are hosted here. Open weekends only, it's a pleasant stop on your stroll through town. If you want to lounge awhile, you can enjoy a glass of wine in the shady courtyard.

La Casa del Escultor (☎ 2335 1836; www .miguelmartino.com; 2a Av Sur 26A; ✆ 7am-10pm Wed-Sat) This is the gallery and workshop of the talented sculptor Miguel Martino. Most of the week you'll find him working on his next pieces while surrounded by some of his beautiful – and finished – creations. On Sunday the workshop is transformed into a popular Argentinean restaurant.

Galería de Arte Shanay (3a Av Norte at 2a Calle Ote; ✆ Sat & Sun) Owner and artist Víctor Manuel Sanabria exhibits his realism-style paintings and those of his students in this gallery behind the church. Curios and antiques also are sold.

Getting There & Around

BOAT

Boats take passengers from Suchitoto across the reservoir to San Francisco Lempa (per person US$5, 20 minutes). A car ferry (per person US$1, per car US$4) makes the same trip, albeit less frequently and less quickly. From the pier on the other side, it's about 500m up to the bus stop for Chaletenango. Although this route is shorter, it is almost always quicker to get to Chaletenango by bus via Aguilares. Then again, the boat is more fun.

BUS

Buses to Terminal de Oriente in San Salvador (US$0.80, 1½ hours, every 15 to 20 minutes from 4am to 6pm) leave from the corner of 1a Calle Pte and 4a Av Sur, a block

west of Parque Centenario. If you're headed north, catch bus 163 to Aguilares (US$0.68, 45 minutes, every 40 minutes from 4:45am to 6:10pm) and transfer to a bus to Chalatenango (bus 125) or to Las Palmas and El Poy (bus 119). On the return, the last bus from Aguilares to Suchitoto leaves at 6:15pm.

CAR

If driving to San Salvador, consider going west from Suchitoto to Aguilares and then south on Hwy CA-4. This brings you into the city from the north – follow signs to Hospital Bloom if you're headed for the Blvd de los Héroes or Colonia Escalón areas – instead of from the east through more dangerous and congested areas, like Soyapongo and the *centro*.

CINQUERA

pop 500

Twenty kilometers southeast of Suchitoto, this charming little mountain town saw heavy fighting during the civil war. Like so many small communities in former guerrilla strongholds, Cinquera was a ghost town until the end of the war, after military raids forced residents to abandon their homes and bombing virtually destroyed it. It has slowly repopulated in the years since.

ARDM (☎ 2389 5732; ardmcqr@yahoo.com; ✆ 8am-4pm Mon-Fri) is Cinquera's municipal reconstruction and development association, and its de facto tourist office. Staff can provide you with a guide (per group US$8) to explain the town's history and show you its sights, including the massive bomb casing used in place of a church bell, and a mural and wall with the names of people killed during the conflict. Many of those working as guides were guerrilla sympathizers, and have fascinating personal accounts of those years as well. It's best to call ahead, especially if you'll be arriving on a weekend when the office is closed.

About 1km from town is **Montaña de Cinquera** (admission US$3), a private forest reserve with interpretive trails, natural springs and waterfalls (great for swimming), an observation tower and an area for camping (per person US$2).

Two buses from Suchitoto stop in Cinquera (US$0.70, 45 to 60 minutes) at 9am to 9:30am and 2:30pm to 3pm daily, on their

RUINAS DE CIHUATÁN

Cihuatán was founded along the banks of the Río Guazapa around the end of the first millennium, in the aftermath of the collapse of Maya city-states across Mesoamerica. Like many Postclassic cities, it was probably composed of various ethnic groups, who joined in commerce and common defense in a deeply unstable period. The city flourished, and quickly become one of largest pre-Columbian cities between Guatemala and Peru. However, in the 10th century, just a century after its founding, Cihuatán was sacked and burned by as-yet-unknown raiders.

The ancient city's existence was first noted in a German traveler's diary in 1878, and it was partially excavated in 1925 and 1954. In the 1970s, archaeologist Karen Olsen Bruhns identified scores of unexcavated structures and – after a 20-year hiatus during the Salvadoran civil war – returned in the 1990s to continue work. A brief history of the site, is available at www.cihuatan.org.

All of El Salvador's ruins are modest, and **Ruínas de Cihuatán** (admission US$3; 9am-4pm Tue-Sun) more so than others. Visitors can see two ball courts, a rambling defensive wall, and a low pyramid-like mound in one of two ceremonial centers. The rest is left to the imagination and future excavation. But the site is peaceful, with birds tweeting in the trees, and makes a good place to relax with a picnic lunch. As one traveler put it, 'it's like a really nice park with some old stuff in it.' With any luck, it will be much more than that in coming years.

From the Terminal de Oriente in San Salvador, take bus 119 toward Chalatenango and get off about 4km beyond Las Aguilares; ask the driver to let you off at Las Ruinas. It's a 900m walk to the site.

---

way to Ilobasco (from Suchitoto US$1.20, two hours; from Cinquera US$0.70, one hour). There is only one return bus, however, at 12:30pm. **Restaurante Vista Conga** (2335 1679; vistacongasuchi@yahoo.com; Pasaje Norte 8) in Suchitoto does interesting tours here as well (see p380).

CHALATENANGO

pop 16,254

The first thing you notice upon arriving in 'Chalate' is the huge military garrison on the plaza. FMLN guerrillas controlled the regional capital during the early part of the war, and the government established a major military presence here to rein in revolutionary activity. The scars have faded – at least on the surface – and Chalatenango hums with activity. The only reason you'll find yourself here is if you're headed to the nearby villages; it makes a decent base to explore the area or to spend a night if the last bus leaves without you.

Orientation

The parque central is divided by 3a Av, with the church on the east (uphill) side and a small plaza with benches on the west (downhill) side. A huge army barracks stands north of the parque central, while most buses pick up and drop off on 3a Av south of the park. The exceptions are buses

to Arcatao, which leave at the top of Calle Morazán, near the turnoff to the local *turicentro* (tourist center), and those to San Francisco Lempa and San Luis del Carmen, which leave east of the main stop. The primary east–west street is Calles San Martín and Morazán, which borders the church and is packed solid with market stalls – it's hard to see it's a street, in fact. The main north–south street, at least in name, is Avs Fajardo and Libertad, although 3a Av is, in fact, a busier and more useful street.

Information

Banco Cuscatlán (2335 2113; 4a Calle Pte near 6a Av Sur; 8am-4:30pm Mon-Fri, 8am-noon Sat) Traveler's checks are cashed for a small commission; there's no charge for foreign-currency exchange. It has one 24-hour ATM.

Cibercafé @halate On line (2301 1882; 1a Calle Ote at 5a Av Norte; per hr US$0.80; 8am-9:30pm Mon-Sat, 9am-1pm Sun) Offers fast Internet connection and CD burning (US$1.50).

Farmacia Vista Bella (2335 2726; 3a Av Sur at 6a Calle Pte; 7am-6pm Mon-Sat, 7am-5pm Sun) Well-stocked pharmacy on the main drag.

Hospital Nacional Dr Luis Vasquez (2335 2156; 2a Calle Pte; 24hr) A long uphill walk – go four blocks east on 2a Calle Pte, take a hard right at a tiny chapel (the street has no name) and continue up, up, up until you reach the hospital. The entrance is to the left, around a long bend.

EL SALVADOR

Police (☎ 2302 7200; 1a Calle Ote btwn Av Fajarda & 2a Av Norte; ☉ 24hr)

Sights & Activities

The **Iglesia de Chalatenango**, with its squat bell tower and blindingly-white exterior, stands on the east side of the parque central, a stone's throw from the military garrison.

A 20-minute walk from the parque central, **Turicentro Agua Fría** (US$0.80; ☉ 8am-5pm, pools 8am-3:30pm, waterslides 10am-noon & 2-3:30pm) has picnic tables in a pleasant park, kept cool by lush foliage. Three pools are the main attraction, one nearly Olympic-sized, with a huge artificial rock island and slide in the middle. The pools are not replenished in the dry season, when groundskeepers simply chlorinate the hell out of what water's already there. A *cafetería* serves beer, soda and simple meals. To get here, go up Calle Morazán (east) about 400m and turn left at the big sign.

Cerro La Peña is a viewpoint affording panoramic views of the Cerrón Grande reservoir, and beyond to Suchitoto. The hike starts just before the Turicentro Agua Fría and takes about 1½ hours to reach the top. There are a number of roads and paths that will take you to the top – ask passersby as you go.

Sleeping & Eating

Hotel La Ceiba (☎ 2301 1080; 1a Calle Pte near 5a Av Norte; s/d US$12-15; ✄) The only decent hotel in town is this two-story place behind the military garrison. Rooms are simple but clean; all have cable TV and bathrooms that are separated by a divider that doesn't quite reach the ceiling. It's a quiet hotel except on those random Saturdays when a discotheque in the basement blasts *cumbias* into the wee hours of the night. Service is friendly.

Restaurante El Paraíso (☎ 2325 4432; 1a Calle Ote at Av Fajardo; mains US$2-5; ☉ 9:30am-9pm) Chalate's top restaurant isn't exactly paradisiacal – could be the exhausted tile floor or the ever-present smell of cigarettes – but it serves great food for remarkably low prices. *Pollo a la turquesa* is a chicken breast with a zingy sauce; beef and chicken taco plates are hefty and a bargain at US$2.40. Other notable menu items include beef liver with onions, or (for those who don't like liver) beef tongue with onions. A tall slushy lemonade goes nicely with either.

Comedor Carmary (☎ 2335 2362; 3a Av 12; dishes US$2-4; ☉ breakfast & lunch Mon-Sat) Popular with locals, this cafeteria serves excellent *comida a la vista*, including several non-meat choices. Arrive early for meals as the best pickin's go fast. The fruit drinks in tall glasses are especially refreshing.

Hamburguesas Camir (4a Calle Pte near 6a Av Sur; mains US$0.75-1.25; ☉ breakfast & lunch) A simple eatery, with plastic tables and chairs, that offers burgers, sandwiches and fruit shakes. Menu items sell out relatively quickly; if you want more than fries, arrive by late morning. Cool papaya *licuados* (fresh fruit drink, blended with milk or water; US$0.60) are especially good.

For self-caterers, **Despensa Familiar** (6a Calle Pte at 3a Av Sur; ☉ 7am-7pm) is a good supermarket in the heart of town. Look for the bright yellow and green building.

An **open-air market** (☉ 5am-1pm) is held around the church and down the main street every day. You'll see fruits and vegetables of all shapes and colors, breads and grains, dried fish and meats, clothing, shoes, toiletries and lottery tickets…great if you're craving apples, or need toothpaste or a brand-new set of rulers.

Getting There & Around

Buses to San Salvador (bus 125, US$0.90, two hours, every 10 minutes from 3:30am to 5:40pm) come and go from the corner of 3a Av Sur at 6a Calle Pte, across from the Despensa Familiar supermarket. For La Palma and El Poy, on the Honduran border, take bus 125 to El Amayo (the highway intersection) and transfer to bus 119.

Bus 542 goes to San Francisco Lempa (US$0.75, 45 minutes), where you can catch boats to Suchitoto, and continues to San Luís del Carmen (from Chalatenango US$0.85, one hour); it leaves at 10:15am, 11:30am, 1:30pm, 3pm and 5:45pm from opposite Funerales La Nueva Protección – from the main drag, go two blocks east on 4a Calle Pte, turn left on Av Libertad and then turn right after a large hardware store. There's also one bus 125 from San Salvador that continues all the way to San Luís Carmen, passing the San Salvador stop at around 9:30am.

For Concepción Quezaltepeque (US$0.35, 20 minutes, every 30 minutes from 6:30am to 5pm) take bus 300B from the 3a Av Sur bus terminal. For Dulce Nombre de María, take bus 125 to the turnoff, where you can pick up the 124 from San Salvador. From there, you can catch a pickup for the last 10km to El Manzano.

For La Montañona, the bus to Petapa (bus 295, 11:15am) and to El Carnizal (bus 542, 12:30pm) both pass the turnoff, and both leave from 3a Av Sur between 1a and 3a Calles Pte. Ask the driver to drop you at *desvio a La Montañona* (La Montañona turnoff; US$1, two hours); from there it's a 5km to 6km uphill climb to the village. The road is very steep – 4WDs with good traction should make it, but most ordinary cars cannot.

Bus 508 goes to Arcatao (US$1.15, two hours, hourly from 7am to 5:30pm) via San José Las Flores, leaving Chalate from a stop on Calle Morazán in front of Iglesia El Calvario, about 400m east (uphill) of the parque central. Arrive early to get a seat.

SAN FRANCISCO LEMPA

This small friendly town is the transit point between Chaletenango and Suchitoto, and the small town of San Luis del Carmen further down the lakeshore. It has a pretty colonial church and many houses made of adobe – geologically stable, it is one of only a few areas in the country where adobe buildings haven't been reduced to rubble by earthquakes. The boat pier is 500m from the center of town, where the buses pass.

Restaurante Tao Tao (☎ 2399 3118; mains US$3-6; ☯ 6am-9pm) is a restaurant, a watering hole, an office for boat tours and transportation services, a town landmark, a de facto tourist office and a proud owner of a Rock-Ola jukebox – there's not much in San Francisco Lempa that this family-run establishment doesn't have some connection to. Stop here if you're interested in a tour of the lake, or need info on getting to and from any of the surrounding towns. The food's not bad, either.

Hacienda Grande (☎ 2375 1447) is a 'big hacienda' indeed, with hiking trails and horseback riding through beautiful terrain, plus camping (per person US$1), an eatery (mains US$2 to US$3), and a swimming pool. A local Peace Corps volunteer has been collaborating with the owner on an organic gardening project, which green-thumbed travelers may find interesting.

Hacienda Grande is located 2km north of San Francisco Lempa, along the lakeshore. It's a pleasant 45-minute walk, or you can get there by boat from either San Francisco Lempa (US$10, 15 minutes) or Suchitoto (US$20, 40 minutes); prices are negotiable.

Buses between Chalatenango and San Luis del Carmen stop in San Francisco Lempa (for details, see opposite and p388). The road in either direction is gorgeous. For Suchitoto, passenger boats (per person US$5) and the car ferry (per person $1, per car US$6) leave from the pier; you can negotiate boat transportation to other locations too, including San Luis del Carmen and Hacienda Grande.

SAN LUIS DEL CARMEN

Way off the beaten path is the tiny lakeside village of San Luis del Carmen, reachable by boat from Suchitoto or by bus from Chaletenango. There are some simple hikes around town and canoe trips are a possibility, though the main attraction here is a peek into the lives of rural Salvadorans – men fishing or bringing their harvest into town on horseback, women grinding corn with *metates* made of volcanic pumice. A number of houses are made of adobe with clay tile roofs, and the church facade dates to the 1880s. (If it's open, you can climb the church's exterior tower.)

All around town are great views of Volcán Guazapa, Volcán San Salvador and, of course, the lake. San Luis del Carmen was not always a lakeside village though – women and children used to walk to Suchitoto to sell homemade soap and other products – but in 1977 the Río Lempa was dammed and the gorge flooded, and a number of families had to be relocated as their land and homes were slowly swallowed by the new reservoir.

Sights & Activities

From San Luis del Carmen there are a few short excursions. About 2km away is **Santa Cruz**, another small lakeside community, where you may be able to rent a canoe for paddling around the lake. Ask for fisherman **Nahum** (☎ 7934 8213, 2354 7162) or **Lito Fibrian** (☎ 2354 7157). To get there, follow the road from the church, past the health clinic and school. The road is paved, but quite steep and exposed – bring water plus a hat or umbrella to protect you from the sun. Another hike is to **Las Pilas**, four springs set in volcanic rock that make for nice swimming. The path can be hard to follow, though, and somewhat muddy after rain – ask at the *alcaldía* (mayor's office) in San Luis del Carmen for directions or a guide.

Festivals & Events

San Luis del Carmen's **patron saint festival** takes place during the third week of December, and is well known for its rodeo, held in the town's *plaza de toros* (bull ring). Contact the *alcaldía* (☎ 2354 7020) for more information.

Sleeping & Eating

There are no accommodations or restaurants in town, though the smoothie shop a block west of the church is worth a stop. A few stands sell snacks, but consider bringing your own lunch.

Getting There & Around

There are six buses daily from Chaletenango to San Luis del Carmen – for details, see p386. Return buses leave San Luis's parque central at 5:40am, 6am, 7:10am, 11:45am, 12:45pm (continues to san Salvador) and 2:30pm.

San Luis can be reached from Suchitoto by passenger boat (US$6 to US$7, 20 minutes) or by ferry (US$1, 30 minutes). If there are no boats around, call or ask around for boat drivers **Raul** (☎ 7985 0469) or **Facundo** (☎ 7842 8326). You can also try **Restaurante Tao Tao Boat Service** (☎ 2399 3118) in San Francisco Lempa (see p387).

Be aware that during the rainy season (May to October) the lakeshore can become choked with a fast-growing water plant commonly known as *lechuga* (literally, 'lettuce') making boat travel impossible.

That said, the rainy season is the best time to visit, when the vegetation is at its most lush. November and December see changing colors.

ARCATAO

This quiet mountain village lies almost due east of Chaletenango, at the end of a beautiful winding road near the border of Honduras. An FMLN stronghold, then and now, the walls around town have stenciled pictures and quotes by guerrilla and religious leaders, from Compañera Ana to Monseñor Romero. It is also home to a Jesuit community and religious center, operated in the liberation theology model. The town church, Iglesia San Bartolomé, stands right in the middle of the main plaza, and has a wide nave with cloth runners strung crosswise. Most services, such as they are in this tiny town, are located around the plaza. The local **health clinic** (☎ 2354 8012), with a pharmacy next door, is a block away.

The local **Jesuit order** (☎ 2354 8009; bartolome 2408@yahoo.com) can receive occasional guests, and can even set up guided tours of the town, *tatús* and other remnants of the war. Definitely call or email ahead – it's not their primary mission.

Sleeping & Eating

Centro de Formación Mártires de Sumpul (☎ 2354 8006; per person US$3) Used for teachers' conferences and other large events, the barrack-like rooms here are available for independent travelers when there isn't a group visiting. Simple cement-block rooms, with wood-frame beds and sloped ceilings, are clean and spare. Large shared bathrooms have cold-water showers – which are OK in the lowlands, but up in the mountains they're painful.

Getting There & Around

Arcatao is served by bus 508 from Chaletenango (US$1.15, two hours) – for details, see p386. The same bus returns to Chaletenango hourly from 5am to 4pm, although the 4pm run is occasionally cancelled. Buses come and go from the main plaza.

CONCEPCIÓN DE QUEZALTEPEQUE

To the northwest of Chalate is the City of Hammocks, Concepción de Quezaltepeque. A hammock-making center, the whole village is engaged in the activity – you'll even see women threading them along the side of the road. Once created from henequen, today's hammocks are made of cotton, nylon or sedalina (an imported synthetic material). They cost US$30 to US$120, with the price based on the material, the length, width and weave thickness of the hammock. Many townspeople have also have branched out to crochet and macramé *artesanías*.

The main street is lined with stores; you're bound to find a hammock that you like after looking at a few. A good place to start is **Artesanías Quezaltecas** (☎ 2331 2001; Calle Principal; ☻ 6am-9pm), which carries an excellent variety; it's next to the *alcaldía*. Another good place to buy one is at the annual **Festival de Hamacas**, which is held every November 10 to 12.

To arrive, take bus 300B from Chalatenago (US$0.35, 20 minutes, every 30 minutes from 5:30am to 3:15pm). To return to Chalate, catch the bus on the main drag, three blocks south of the plaza.

LA MONTAÑONA

A pine forest reserve at 1600m, La Montañona offers excellent views, pre-Columbian rock carvings and several *tatus*, including one used by a clandestine guerrilla radio station – Radio Farabundo. You can stay in the small village here; a rustic cabin has simple beds (per night around US$5), and a local woman Teresa Avilar cooks up basic meals. Call **Cesar Alas** (☎ 7723 6283) before going; he oversees the lodging and also acts as a guide to the area.

Getting There & Around

From Chaletenango, the bus to Petapa (bus 295, 11:15am) and to El Carnizal (bus 542, 12:30pm) both pass the turnoff to La Montañona – for details, see p386. From the turnoff, it's a steep 5km or 6km climb to the village. The road is steep and unrelenting – pack light! You'll need a 4WD to drive there.

EL MANZANO

pop 100

Ten kilometers north of the small town of Dulce Nombre de María, is an even smaller town known as El Manzano, a cooperative community established after the signing of the Peace Accords in 1992, and populated by former FMLN combatants. The road there is rough but beautiful, winding through hills with views of valleys dotted with volcanoes and pine-laden hillsides.

Sights & Activities

From the town, two **hiking** trails make pleasant day trips: one climbs a low bare hill known as La Tortilla, for the way it looks from afar. A moderately difficult 45- to 60-minute hike – the last portion is especially steep – earns you great views into

nearby Honduras. The other trail leads in the opposite direction to a no-name *mirador*; it's an easier hike, with views of Lago Suchitlán and Volcán Santa Ana beyond. The area also has numerous bomb craters, and you can even find scattered spent gun casings. A local guide can show them to you, and describe the history of the community and the fighting here.

Sleeping & Eating

There are no hotels or restaurants per se, although the community is building simple cabins for overnight visitors and you can arrange to eat with a local family. Camping is also a possibility if you have equipment. The *tienda* (store) in the middle of town serves as a community meeting area and informal visitor's office – stop there when you arrive for info on sleeping and eating, and the standard prices for both.

Getting There & Around

From Chalatenango, take bus 125 and ask the driver to drop you at the *desvio* for Dulce Nombre de María. Bus 124 (originating in San Salvador's Terminal de Oriente) passes on its way to Dulce Nombre, or there may be pickups or private vehicles you can get a ride with. From Dulce Nombre, hitch a ride with a pickup for the last 10km into El Manzano – the entrance is marked 'Parque Ecológico El Manzano.' From there, it's a short walk into town. Start early, as you never know how long you'll have to wait between legs.

LA PALMA

elevation 1200m

Surrounded by verdant mountains and bathed in fresh mountain air, La Palma may be 84km north of San Salvador, but it's well worth the climb, and it's a must if you're heading into Honduras via El Poy. Stay here for easy access to the area's hiking and outdoors options, without giving up amenities like Internet access, banking facilities, a grocery store and a variety of restaurants. To get even further away, consider staying in nearby San Ignacio, or one of the several great country lodges nearby.

Wherever you stay, definitely spend an hour or two perusing La Palma's famous *artesanía* stores. Painter Fernando Llort moved to La Palma in 1972, and developed

EL SALVADOR

EL SALVADOR

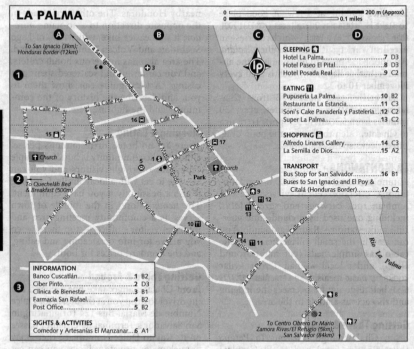

LA PALMA

0   200 m (Approx)
0   0.1 miles

To San Ignacio (3km);
Honduras border (12km)

Carr a San Ignacio & Honduras

Church

To Quecheláh Bed
& Breakfast (500m)

Park

Church

Calle Independencia

Calle Gerardo Barrios

Río La Palma

To Centro Obrero Dr Mario
Zamora Rivas/El Refugio (5km);
San Salvador (84km)

---

an art trend that today represents El Salvador around the world. Llort's childlike images of mountain villages, campesinos or images of Christ are painted in bright colors on anything from seeds to church walls. He taught some residents in La Palma how to create the same images and soon began a cooperative that churned out dozens of painted artifacts, from crosses to key rings to napkin holders. Today 75% of the village makes a living by mass-producing this art, none deviating too far from the traditional drawings or colors.

Orientation

Two one-way streets cut through the center of town: 2a Av Sur, which runs northwest towards the border, and Calle Gerardo Barrios/Av José Matías Delgado, which runs southwest toward San Salvador. The main plaza is located between the two, about half way through town. Almost every listing is on one of these two streets.

Information

Banco Cuscatlán (☎ 2305 9331; Calle Gerardo Barrios at 1a Calle Pte; ☙ 8:30am-12:15pm & 1-4pm Mon-Fri,

8:30am-12:30pm Sat) Traveler's checks cashed and foreign currencies exchanged. It has one 24-hour ATM.

Ciber Pinto (☎ 2335 9001; Calle de Espina 83; per hr US$1; ☙ 8am-8pm) Speedy Internet connections.

Clínica de Bienestar (☎ 2305 8469, after hours 7848 7413; ☙ 8am-4pm Mon-Fri, 8am-noon Sat) Health clinic within walking distance of the center of town; it's just off 2a Av Sur.

Farmacia San Rafael (☎ 2305 8477; Calle Gerardo Barrios at 1a Calle Pte; ☙ 7am-12:30pm & 1:30-6pm) Offers basic medical facilities and toiletries.

Post Office (1a Calle Pte; ☙ 8am-noon & 2-5pm Mon-Fri, 8am-noon Sat)

Sights & Activities

There is great hiking in this area, though most is easily undertaken from the small town of San Ignacio (p392), a few kilometers north of La Palma. If you're interested in guided hikes, contact José Samuel Hernández, a friendly and very knowledgeable local who owns the **Comedor y Artesanías El Manzanar** (☎ 2305 8379; Carr La Palma-El Poy Km 85; ☙ 7am-8pm Tue-Sun). Trips are reasonably priced – a three-hour hike costs around US$10 to US$15 for a group of four people. Look for Samuel at the restaurant.

Sleeping

La Palma's hotel situation leaves something to be desired. The best place (a B&B) is a long and winding walk from town. The central options are all budget, but only one has genuinely appealing rooms and only a handful at that. The rest are a compromise.

Quecheláh Bed & Breakfast (☎ 2305 9328; quecheláh@navegante.com.sv; s/d without bathroom US$26/39, extra person US$15; **P**) The best lodging in town is a private house turned B&B. Three simple, quaint rooms have wood-frame beds, brown ceramic floors and high sloped ceilings, and share a large clean hot-water bathroom. Two rooms have views of the hillside opposite. The price includes a full breakfast, taken in the front dining area or at tables set under the trees on a sunny rise behind the house; lunch and dinner can be arranged for extra. A sunken living room is nice for reading or drinking coffee, and a small bar area has sofas and a full liquor selection. The price is higher than you'd expect for a room with a shared bathroom, but the main drawback is its distance from the town center – most visitors arrive by car, otherwise take one of the red mototaxis (US$0.50).

Hotel La Palma (☎ 2305 9344; hotellapalma@yahoo .com; 2a Av Sur; r per person US$11.50) Right at the entrance of town, this hotel sure looks like a charming mountain retreat. And it is – as long as you get the right rooms. The lower rooms (ask for *los cuartos de abajo*) are cozy – alright, tiny – with ochre ceramic tiles, a low sloped ceiling and clean modern bathrooms. A front passageway has hammocks and tables, overlooking the hotel's clean pool, and beyond that the Río La Palma. Some of the lower rooms look onto the parking lot, however, which can be noisy on weekends. Worse are the 16 rooms in two large A-frame buildings up the hill from the entryway: they're musty and plain, with aging bathrooms.

Hotel Paseo El Pital (☎ 2335 9344; r with bathroom per person US$10; **🐾 🖳 P**) The advantages of this big purple hotel are all followed by a 'but': rooms are spacious, with cable TV and minifridge, but the sagging beds and musty smell are hard to handle (covering the shower drain with a plastic bags helps a little). You can spend time in a hammock or armchair on the front patio, but the view is of the driveway and restaurant area. It's conveniently located and the service is friendly, but it's probably not your first choice.

Hotel Posada Real (☎ 2335 9009; Calle Gerardo Barrios; r per person US$6-8; **P**) Not exactly the regal setting the name implies. Rooms have cable TV, hot water (usually) and come with breakfast, but are also small with grubby walls and bathrooms, and old beds. All open onto a long open-air courtyard, the first part of which doubles as a breakfast area and parking lot. Back rooms are less well maintained, but you can open windows to freshen them up a bit (no fan). The best part of the hotel is the upstairs covered terrace, with hammocks and chairs, and a view of Peña Cayaguanca (p393).

Centro Obrero Dr Mario Zamora Rivas/El Refugio (admission free; 🕒 8am-4pm) These are adjacent government-run properties about 5km south of town. The Centro Obrero (Workers' Center) is one of four such facilities in the country, where you can stay for free with prior permission from the **Ministerio de Trabajo** (Map p324; ☎ 2298 8739; Calle Nueva Dos 19; 🕒 8am-12:30pm & 1:30-4pm Mon-Fri) in San Salvador (for details, see p317). This one offers 15 remodeled cabins and a couple of swimming pools, with various well-marked trails through protected forest areas, and a somewhat sad mini zoo at El Refugio.

Eating

Restaurante La Estancia (☎ 2335 9049; Calle Gerardo Barrios 35; mains US$2-8; 🕒 breakfast, lunch & dinner) A huge mural depicting a farming scene is on the back wall of this pleasant sit-down restaurant. *Típica* is the focus, but salads, sandwiches and burgers round out the menu nicely. If in doubt, try the *pollo a la estancia*, (chicken fried in red wine) – it's the house specialty.

Pupuseria La Palma (☎ 2335 9063; Calle Gerardo Barrios near Calle Libertad; mains US$1-4; 🕒 breakfast, lunch & dinner) A handful of tables occupy a small dining area in this simple and clean pupusa shop, located across from the Telecom office. It's often busy with local residents, even on weekdays, which must be a good sign.

Restaurante del Pueblo (mains US$2-5; 🕒 breakfast, lunch & dinner) This eatery serves a variety of soups and sandwiches, and a good *plato típico* (bananas, beans, cheese, cream). It's down the road from the Hotel La Palma.

EL SALVADOR

Soni's Cake Panadería y Pastelería (2a Av Sur; pastries US$0.25-1; ☺ 7:30am-6:30pm) Freshly baked pastries – served warm if you stop in early (take-out only).

For self-caterers, **Super La Palma** (2a Av Sur; ☺ 7:30am-8pm) is a small but decent supermarket near the center of town, half a block south of the church.

Shopping

La Semilla de Dios (☎ 2335 9098; coopsem@unete .com; 3a Calle Pte at 5a Av Norte; ☺ 8am-noon & 1-4pm) Employing over 40 artists, this cooperative offers some of the highest-quality Llort-inspired artwork in the country. Most of the items are exported to the USA and Europe, but extras are made and sold at their gift shop. Items change as orders do – wallets, embroidered blouses, and tables were on sale when we passed through – but you'll always find classics such as letters, jewelry boxes, and pencil holders. Free tours of the workshop also are offered.

Alfredo Linares Gallery (☎ 2335 9049; Calle Gerardo Barrios; ☺ 8am-5pm) The only gallery in town displays lithographs and paintings by Salvadoran artist Alfredo Linares. Works are pricey for the quality (US$50 to US$1000), but beauty is in the eye of the beholder – stop in and decide for yourself.

Getting There & Around

You can pick up San Salvador–El Poy buses anywhere along the two main roads through town, simply wave your hand for the driver to stop.

Bus 119 runs every half hour from San Salvador's Terminal de Oriente to the El Salvador–Honduras border at El Poy, stopping at La Palma (US$1.50, three hours) and San Ignacio (US$1.60, 3¼ hours); some buses enter San Ignacio, others drop you at the turnoff. The last bus to San Ignacio and El Poy (weekday/weekend US$0.50/0.60, 30 minutes from La Palma) trundles through at 7pm; the last bus to San Salvador leaves El Poy at 4:15pm.

Buses for Cerro El Pital and Miramundo leave from San Ignacio – for details, see p394.

SAN IGNACIO

The neighboring village of San Ignacio is even smaller and quieter than La Palma – some travelers prefer it for that

---

> **GETTING TO SAN PEDRO SULA OR COPÁN RUINAS, HONDURAS**
>
> The bus from La Palma drops you about 100m from the El Salvador–Honduras border, where you pay nothing to leave El Salvador, but US$3 to enter Honduras. From **El Poy** (Immigration office ☎ 2335 9402; ☺ 24hr) you can take a bus or collective taxi to Nueva Ocotepeque, Honduras. From there, buses leave hourly to San Pedro Sula. For Copán Ruinas, transfer at La Entrada.
>
> The last bus to El Poy from La Palma (bus 119, US$0.50, 30 minutes) leaves at 7pm. The last bus south from El Poy (and continuing to San Salvador) leaves around 4:15pm.

---

reason alone. But it is also closer to most of the hiking options in this area – and the border – making staying here a logical as well as an aesthetic choice.

Orientation & Information

The main plaza is the heart of the town; it's located two blocks east of the highway on Calle Municipal (north side) at Av Baden Powell (east side). All of the listings here are on the main plaza, or just north or east of it.

Alcaldía de San Ignacio (☎ 2335 9320; Main Plaza, Calle Municipal; ☺ 8am-noon & 1:30-4:30 Mon-Fri) Staff at the city hall offer informal but good information on sights within the area, and can assist with contacting hiking guides.

Unidad de Salud (☎ 2352 9212; Av Rivoli; ☺ 8am-4pm Mon-Fri) Small clinic with limited resources. A pharmacy also is on-site.

Sights & Activities

Cerro El Pital (2730m) is the highest peak in El Salvador, but thanks to an access road, it is one of the easiest to hike. From La Palma, a steep dirt road winds up the mountain-side to the small community of Río Chiquito – diesel buses make the trip but private cars, even 4WDs, may have trouble passing the steepest sections. From Río Chiquito, a smaller, mostly dirt road leads up to a large grassy area near the top – it takes about 1½ hours to hike through the thickening cloud forest. The grassy area, which has terrific views, is actually private property and you must pay a US$2 entrance fee. From here, there are two smaller trails, each about

1km. One leads to the actual **summit**, where a cement block marks El Salvador's highest point. The other trail leads to **Piedra Rajada**, a huge rock cloven down the middle. A narrow log bridge spans the 25m chasm between the two pieces, with a cable installed for balance. It is a nerve-wracking passage, which you should only attempt with good shoes and in dry weather. You can stay the night, either in a comfortable hotel near Río Chiquito or in a tent at the top – for details, see right.

Peña Cayaguanca is the large rock that can be seen protruding from the top of a forested hilltop northeast of La Palma. It actually lies right on the Honduras–El Salvador border, and a plaque on top marks the dividing line. The view from here is terrific, taking in La Palma, San Ignacio, Citalá and Nuevo Ocotepeque, Honduras. Climbing Cayaguanca is a popular excursion for locals and visitors alike. In fact, many bring a little wood and build a fire to heat up their lunch, and make an afternoon out of it. Which is not to say it's an easy hike: it takes about two hours, and good shoes and long pants are definitely recommended for contending with brush and rocks on the trail. The trail begins in the small community of El Rosario, a few kilometers north of San Ignacio.

Humberto Regalado (☎ 2352 9138) owns and maintains the trail, and serves as the primary guide (per person US$1.50). If you can't track him down, try Niña Solya at **Tienda de Niña Solya** (☎ 2325 9138) in town. Humberto also maintains a small **swimming pool** (admission US$1), with a changing room and bathrooms – a perfect way to cool off after hiking up and back. Nearby is a test farm used to study eco-friendly farming techniques, like worm composting and organic fertilizers; those who are interested can request a tour.

There are hotel and camping options in El Rosario (see right). For a guide on these and other excursions, contact **José Samuel Hernández** (☎ 2305 8379; Comedor y Artesanías El Manzanar, Carr La Palma-El Poy Km 85; ☻ 7am-8pm Tue-Sun) in La Palma. For details, see p390.

Sleeping & Eating

CENTRAL SAN IGNACIO

Posada de Reyes (☎ 2335 9318; Calle Municipal; r with/without air-con US$25/20; **P** ☒ ☒) A welcome surprise, the Posada de Reyes is a colonial-style hotel with a lush garden and a well-maintained pool, one block north of the main plaza. Guests choose from 10 comfortable rooms, each with high ceilings, tile floors, two full-size beds and bathroom. Hot water and cable TV are welcome amenities, especially for the price. It's one of the best-value options around.

Posada San Ignacio (☎ 2352 9419; Main Plaza, Calle Municipal at Av Rivoli; r with/without bathroom US$15/10; **P**) Rooms are simple but clean, with bathrooms in good condition. Those who end up in a shared-bathroom situation will discover that their rooms are dark and musty, the toilets are on the edge of manageable, and the shower is a rusty pipe cemented into a grimy wall. A decent on-site *comedor* (a basic and cheap eatery; mains US$2 to US$5, open breakfast, lunch and dinner) is a plus.

El Polletón Comedor y Pupusería (☎ 2352 9075; Av Baden Powell; mains US$2-3; ☻ breakfast, lunch & dinner) Good food and excellent service are served up at this modest eatery. Salvadoran meals and, as the name suggests, pupusas are prepared fresh throughout the day. Food is served cafeteria-style and eaten at one of several wooden picnic tables in the spotless dining room.

For self-caterers, **Mini-super Las Delicias** (☻ 6:30am-8pm Mon-Sat, 6:30am-noon Sun) is a decent supermarket that makes a good pit stop before a day of hiking. Look for the sign on the highway; it's at the northern entrance to town.

OUTSIDE SAN IGNACIO

There are a number of excellent accommodations outside of San Ignacio proper, including near Cerro El Pital and Peña Cayaguanca.

El Pital Highland (☎ 2259 0602; pital20@yahoo.com; r/tw US$50/60, cabaña US$70/105) Three hundred meters up the El Pital access road from Río Chiquito (the road is still paved to there, so most cars can make it), the Highland is the best of a couple options here, with cool details, like a row of boots used as flower planters. Comfortable woodsy rooms have hot-water bathrooms; cabañas are larger, with separate living room and bedroom(s), refrigerator, and even a fireplace. The hotel restaurant, Sol y Luna (mains US$5 to US$15), serves a wide variety of Salvadoran dishes, with pleasant indoor and outdoor seating. The hotel and restaurant are normally open weekends only; the hotel can be opened mid-week by request. Reservations are recommended. Camping is possible at the grassy area on top (per person with a tent US$4, tent rental US$12)

Parador de Compostela (☎ 2263 3461; r US$40) Four comfortable cabañas have hot-water bathrooms here. Located on the road into El Rosario and near the Peña Cayaguanca trailhead, this hotel has 15 acres of landscaped grounds and forest – ask about trails and horseback-riding tours (per half hour US$5). There's a restaurant (mains US$6 to US$12) open on weekends only. Camping is also a possibility: Humberto Regalado rents a large tent (per night US$5), which can be set up on the Peña or on a nice little rise closer to town.

Hostal Miramundo (☎ 2230 0437; www.hostal miramundo.com; r or cabaña US$45) A short distance past Río Chiquito, this hotel may have the best view of any lodging in El Salvador. Perched on a ridge in the aptly named Miramundo community, it seems as if the whole country is spread out below you. Eight large rooms sleep up to four people, with wood-paneled walls, firm beds, and matching bedspreads and window curtains. Three newer cabañas are for couples or solo travelers, and come with bathroom, double bed and cable TV. You can hike from trails right outside the hostel by day, and practice your crooning with the hotel karaoke machine by night. No joke. From San Ignacio, bus 509 travels twice daily – typically the 9:30am and 12:30pm departures, but double check with the driver – to Los Planes instead of Las Pilas, passing Miramundo (US$1.25, one hour) along the way. Otherwise you can walk from Río Chiquito to Miramundo – it's only about 2km and is very scenic. Buses return to San Ignacio at roughly the same times.

Cabañas Prashanti (☎ 2352 9304; Carr Troncal del Norte Km 88.5; cabins US$50-70; P) Perfect for travellers looking for an outdoorsy place that isn't a resort, three log cabins set in a clearing at the foot of the mountains make up Cabañas Prashanti. Each is spacious – sleeping five to seven people – and come with fully equipped kitchenettes, small living rooms, and porches with comfy chairs that just say 'relax.' The views are worth a thousand words. Be sure to stock up on groceries before you arrive. Look

for the entrance about 500m north of San Igancio.

Entre Pinos (☎ 2335 9312; www.hotelentrepinos .com, in Spanish; Carr Troncal del Norte Km 87.5; campsites per person US$6, r Mon-Thu US$37, Fri-Sun US$44, r with air-con Mon-Thu US$60-68, Fri-Sun US$72-83, deluxe Mon-Thu US$82, Fri-Sun US$99, bungalows Mon-Thu US$86, Fri-Sun US$105; ✂ P 🖳 🖳) Just 500m south of San Ignacio, this mountain resort is reminiscent of *Dirty Dancing* – without the private dance lessons. Instead you'll find a slew of activities anchored around outdoor fun – hiking, horseback riding, tennis, swimming, basketball, volleyball, even 4WD-ing alongside mountain cornfields. The rooms, unfortunately, are somewhat hit or miss. The cheaper ones and the bungalows aren't worth the cost – they're worn and musty; the others are very comfortable and well kept, with gleaming tile floors, good beds and terraces – some even with a fireplace. Camping is also a great option, although you'll need to bring your own gear. Rates include continental breakfast, which is served in the main lodge's classy restaurant (mains US$6 to US$12; open breakfast, lunch and dinner). The restaurant serves a good variety of international dishes and is open to the public.

Getting There & Around

Bus 119 passes by the town center every half hour, headed for the border at El Poy (US$0.25, 15 minutes) and, in the opposite direction, La Palma (US$0.25, 15 minutes). For El Rosario, take any El Poy–bound bus and get off at the large sign for Parador la Compostela; its 200m to the hotel, and between 1km and 2km to town. The last bus to El Poy passes around 7:15pm, the last to La Palma at 4:30pm. You can also catch them on the highway.

Bus 509 passes Río Chiquito and the turnoff to El Pital (US$1.10, 45 minutes) and continues to Las Pilas; it leaves Calle Cayaguanca in San Ignacio (at the corner where women sell fruits and vegetables) at 7am, 9:30am, 12:30pm, 2:30pm and 4:30pm, and returns at the same time.

EL POY/CITALÁ

The border crossing at (actually a neighborhood of the town of Citalá) is very mild as border towns go. There's a **health clinic and pharmacy** (☎ 2335 9482; ☺ 24hr) on the main plaza, next to Telecom.

BORDER CROSSING: TO NUEVA OCOTEPEQUE, HONDURAS

The Salvadoran immigration desk at El Poy is open 24 hours, the Honduran one from 4am to 10pm. Both sides of the border are safe and mellow, as border areas go. There's no tax to leave El Salvador, but you may have to pay US$3 to enter Honduras. On the Honduran side, taxis and buses for Nueva Ocotepeque leave frequently from a stop 200m from the border; from there connect to buses to Santa Rosa de Copán and onward.

Hotel y Restaurante Monte Cristo (☎ 2325 5541; Av Maximiliano Hernández 1; r/tw US$6/8) is the best place to crash for the night if you get stuck. Rooms are basic but clean, with cold-water bathrooms and cable TV – the double rooms are larger and have better light, and may be worth the extra US$2 even if you're solo. The restaurant (mains US$1.25 to US$3; open 7am to 9:30pm) has a surprisingly pleasant dining area in the back, with wood tables on a shady open-air platform.

In El Poy, a man named José Pineda uses a special spicy sauce to make awesome grilled chicken at an open-air stand at the turnoff to Citalá on the main highway. A quarter-bird plus rice and tortillas costs US$2 – a steal. Otherwise, a string of *pupuserías* line the highway between there and the border.

Bus 119 leaves from a terminal several blocks south of the border to La Palma (US$0.50, 30 minutes) and continues to San Salvador (US$1.60, three hours, 4am to 4:15pm). Bus 463 to Metapán (US$2, three hours, 5am and noon) follows a beautiful winding road over the mountains. It leaves from Citalá, a few blocks past (and up the hill) from the main plaza. To get to Citalá, take a bicycle taxi (US$1, five minutes) from the border crossing area.

WESTERN PACIFIC COAST

El Salvador boasts some of the best surfing waves in Central America, even the world, and surfers have long made up the bulk of foreign travelers here. At least a dozen named waves – and scores of nameless ones – break right and left, fast and slow, over rock and over sand, all along the coast. Some of the most popular breaks can get crowded on weekends, but there are plenty of spots within easy reach that are blissfully traffic-free.

Non-surfers have a few options here, not the least of which is learning to surf; numerous surfing outfits and independent instructors offer individual and group lessons. Black-sand beaches have a certain allure, though most travelers discover they prefer 'normal' beaches, where the sand is thicker and softer. The western Pacific coast's best sandy-brown beaches are in Los Cóbanos (p404), which also has the country's best open-water diving. This is also where El Salvador's first all-inclusive resort is located – a sign of things to come? Even further west is Barra de Santiago, a quiet fishing village on a spit of land between the ocean and a bird-filled estuary, with the very beginnings of tourist infrastructure (p405).

The western Pacific coast is known as the Costa del Bálsamo, for its once vibrant (but quickly fading) balsam oil trade (see the boxed text, p405). Acajutla, a large and rather seedy city west of Los Cóbanos, was once the country's main commercial port, but it has seen its freighter traffic decline as La Union's, in the east, increases. This trend will likely accelerate once Puerto Cutuco, a mega-port being built southeast of La Union, opens for business.

Rural areas here are often hit hard by storms and other natural disasters, as the steep coastal bluffs (which have been heavily deforested) can be unstable. Many communities were isolated for days or weeks following the earthquakes in 2001 and Hurricane Stan in 2005, when landslides blocked the highway and secondary roads. None of which should prevent you from coming, however, as the western Pacific coast, with its winding coastal roads and dramatic ocean overlooks, remains one of the country's most beautiful regions.

Climate & Geography

The coast is predictably hot and humid, though not as much as the eastern coastal areas. Temperatures hover in the mid-20s°C to low 30s°C (77°F to 89°F); while,

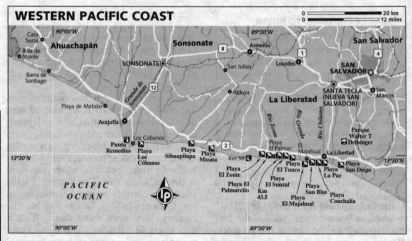

WESTERN PACIFIC COAST

EL SALVADOR

for surfers, water temperatures average 27°C to 30°C (80°F to 86°F).

The geography here is dramatic – the shoreline zig-zags around small inlets and sharp promontories, fringed by rocky or black-sand beaches and backed by high bluffs. The coastal highway winds its way along the tops of the bluffs, passing through five tunnels between La Libertad and Playa Sihuapilapa, where the terrain finally flattens out.

Dangers & Annoyances

Travelers should be extra cautious in La Libertad, where pickpocketing, robbery and even assault are persistent problems. A long-standing drug trade is largely to blame – needless to say, travelers who buy and use drugs here not only contribute to the problem, but also frequently become crime victims themselves. And, unlike elsewhere in El Salvador, the police may not be on your side. You're likely to spend at least some time in La Libertad, if only to change buses or buy groceries. You needn't be especially concerned during the daytime, as long as you stay alert to your surroundings and belongings, but definitely plan to be inside (or somewhere else) by dark.

Also, avoid walking alone on the beach, and never leave anything unattended, whether a camera, shirt or shoes – it will likely disappear. Most surfers carry only their board and enough money for bus fare. This goes for the entire coast.

LA LIBERTAD

pop 20,677

Many people think of El Salvador as dangerous and chaotic. For 90% of the country, it's a bogus reputation, but for La Libertad, it's pretty accurate. And, as it happens, La Libertad is the one place in El Salvador that receives a steady flow of foreign visitors, so the negative stereotype is constantly being reinforced.

La Libertad does have flashes of gritty vitality – the market, early-morning surfers, lone fishermen plying the rocky shoreline – but the overall atmosphere is that of a grimy and decaying port town. La Libertad has a serious drug problem, which is the cause of most theft and assaults here. Foreigners are occasionally targeted; sometimes it's random, but usually the victim was buying or using drugs. Follow normal precautions – like not walking around at night or leaving valuables on the beach – and you should be fine.

There are also a number of beach lodges west of La Libertad that are safe and popular. They don't have Punta Roca on their doorstep – La Libertad will always have that – but can be a good alternative to staying in town.

Orientation

La Libertad fronts a small bay. The right (west) side of the bay is Playa La Paz, with Punta Roca breaking just beyond it. A pier juts into the bay from the center of the beach and is worth visiting – it's full of fish, some freshly caught, others dried and diced, all emitting a pungent, salty smell. The plaza is two blocks back; the market and main bus stop is northeast of there – a block over and a block up.

Information

EMERGENCY
Police (☎ 2335 3046; Calle El Calvario; ☺ 24hr)

INTERNET ACCESS
Infocentros (☎ 2346 0253; 4a Av Norte & 1a Calle Pte; per hr US$1; ☺ 8am-6pm Mon-Fri, 8am-4pm Sat) Located at the back of the open-air Centro Comercial Porteña.

Freedom Net Shop (☎ 2246 1626; 2a Calle Pte; per hr US$1; ☺ 9am-8pm Mon-Sat, 9am-5pm Sun) Located below Hotel Surf Club Inn, on the 1st floor of Centro Comercial Miramar Plaza.

MEDICAL SERVICES
Centro Médico Moises (☎ 2335 3531; Calle Gerardo Barrios; ☺ 7am-6pm Mon-Fri, 7am-noon Sat) A recommended private clinic; located across from Banco Agrícola.

Unidad de Salud Puerto La Libertad (☎ 2335 3934, 2335 3745; ☺ 24hr) Located 100m down the road to Playa Conchalía, just west of the town center.

Farmacia Libertad (☎ 2335 3308; Calle El Calvario; ☺ 7:30am-8pm Mon-Sat, 8am-noon Sun)

MONEY
Incredibly, there is no ATM that accepts foreign debit cards in La Libertad.

Banco Agrícola (Calle Gerardo Barrios; ☺ 8am-4:30pm Mon-Fri, 8:30am-noon Sat) Changes AmEx traveler's checks only.

POST
Post Office (2a Calle Ote btwn 2a & 4a Avs Norte; ☺ 8am-noon & 12:45-4pm Mon-Fri, 8am-noon Sat)

SURFBOARD RENTAL & REPAIR
Hospital de Tablas de Surf (☎ 2335 3214, 7944 3632; 3a Ave Norte 27-8; ☺ 7am-4pm) Repairs cracks, dings and leg ropes (US$3 to US$40); rents boards (per hour US$2.50, per day US$12, per day for three days or more US$10); and buys and sells used boards (US$100 to US$250). Surf lessons also available. The local surfer proprietor and family live on-site, so just knock if it's closed.

TELEPHONE
Freedom Net Shop (☎ 2246 1626; 2a Calle Pte; ☺ 9am-8pm Mon-Sat, 9am-5pm Sun) Can place web-based phone calls (per minute to USA and Canada US$0.15; per minute to Europe and Australia US$0.20 to US$0.40).

Sights & Activities
Four kilometers east of La Libertad along the Comalapa road, **Parque Nacional Walter T Deininger** (admission US$0.80; ☺ 7am-noon & 1-5pm) was named after the German settler who donated his lands to El Salvador. It consists of two types of forest: *caducifolio*, which sheds its leaves in summer, and *galería*, which retains its foliage year-round. A well-maintained 18km trail skirts the park; you must be accompanied by a ranger. Signs point out trails to the Río Amayo (Mystery Cave) and a lookout point offering views of the whole park down to the sea that fringes the forest. Deer, raccoons and the endangered *tepezcuintle* (paca) can be spotted in the park, as well as many bird species, including the *torogoz* (blue-crowned motmot), El Salvador's national bird.

To visit Parque Deininger, you are supposed to obtain a permit from **ISTU** (Instituto Salvadoreño de Turismo; Map pp320-1; ☎ 2222 8000; istu@mh.gob.sv; Calle Rubén Darío 619, San Salvador; ☺ 8:30am-12pm & 1-4pm Mon-Sat) in San Salvador five days before your arrival. However, you can almost always simply show up and the guard will let you in. The guide service is US$11.50. From La Libertad, the park is a 15-minute bus ride away.

La Libertad's **church** (MainPlaza) has a sad corrugated cement exterior surrounded by a high steel fence – it's surprisingly easy to miss. The inside is a slight improvement, with a high nave, evidently sealed with varnished plywood. Wooden pews fill the interior, and small statues adorn the walls. Mass is held daily at 6pm, plus 7am, 9am and 11am on Sunday.

The closest **beach** to the capital, La Libertad fills up with city dwellers on weekends. In the rainy season (March to October) the beach is rocky, covered with large black boulders, and the riptide, along with the possibility of sewage, makes the water uninviting. In the dry season the rocks get covered in sand, but the boulders are still whipped by the waves. **Playa San Diego** (p400) and **Playa San Blas** (p401) are the best beaches for, well, beachgoing. They are broad and flat, with grey-brown sand, and stretch for kilometers.

Surf classes are offered by a number of instructors and outfits around town, either per-hour or on a package basis. From November to February, most beginners are

EL SALVADOR

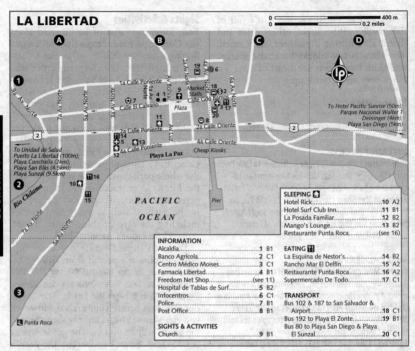

LA LIBERTAD

taken to Playa La Paz (in front of the Restaurant Punta Roca), where there's sandy beach and easy waves. During the rest of the year Playa La Paz turns rocky, so Playa El Sunzal – usually accessed through Playa El Tunco – is the go-to spot. Advanced classes can be taught anywhere, depending on the student's ability.

Sleeping

Since it's not a good idea to be walking around much at night, be sure to pick a hotel where you won't mind spending long evenings.

BUDGET

Hotel Surf Club Inn (☎ 2346 1104; 2a Calle Pte; r US$12, with air-con US$20; ✗ 🖳) Air-conditioned rooms are surprisingly clean and comfortable, with tile floors, wood table, chairs and armoire, a sofa and a small refrigerator – it's a good deal. Fan rooms have more space to store gear, but are definitely dumpier. This isn't an area you want to wander around past dark, but there's an Internet café open until 8pm on the 1st floor. A large *turicen-*

tro (tourist center) with a swimming pool is being built across the street, which may enliven the area and improve security.

Mango's Lounge (☎ 2346 1626; info@central surfroad.com; 4a Calle Pte; r without bathroom per person US$10; 🖳) Four small simple rooms come with TV and surfboard racks here. A homey lounge on the 1st floor has couches, tables and four computers with Internet access – it's a good place to kick back and relax. Overall, it's great value, especially for solo travelers.

Hotel Rick (☎ 2335 3542; 5a Av Sur; r US$25; ✗ 🅿) Although the rooms are somewhat shabby, they're clean and boast bathrooms, cable TV and decent beds. Not a bad deal considering the hotel is across the street from the town beach. Be sure to ask for a room on the 2nd floor – they're much brighter and, if you're lucky, you'll have an ocean view.

La Posada Familiar (☎ 2335 3552; www .hotellaposadafamiliar.com.sv, in Spanish; 3a Av Sur at 4a Calle Pte; s/d with bathroom US$10/15, s/d without bathroom US$8/10, r with bathroom & air-con US$20; 🅿 ✗) You'll find small rooms in need of a serious scrub at this old-timer. Most have hammocks right outside the doors and all open onto a pleasant courtyard – a great place to hang out after everyone's back from surfing. It's OK if every penny counts.

MIDRANGE
Hotel Pacific Sunrise (☎ 2346 2000; www .hotoleselsalvador.com; Calle El Obispo at Carr Litoral; s/d /ste US$45/57/68; P 🐕 🏊) This is the nicest place to stay in La Libertad: rooms have a chain-hotel feel, with matching bedspreads and curtains, industrial carpeting, alarm clocks, telephone, cable TV, and even bottled water. Beds are comfortable, rooms are spotless, bathrooms have hot water, silent air-conditioning units let you sleep – it's a haven. A private bridge leads guests directly to the town beach and, for those who prefer chlorine, there's a well-maintained pool with a view of the parking lot. It's located at the eastern edge of town.

Restaurante Punta Roca (☎ 2335 3261; www .puntaroca.com.sv; 5a Av Sur at 4a Calle Pte; r US$40; P 🐕) This popular restaurant has two large units over the kitchen, they're somewhat rough around the edges, but are comfortable – especially by La Lib standards. They share a large terrace strung with hammocks, overlooking the beach and almond trees. Each room has a front area with dining table, small fridge, floor-to-ceiling windows and plenty of room for surfboards, plus a large bedroom in back with three beds. The bathroom, installed in the corner, has one-way mirror walls – no one can see in, but you can see out. A little trippy. It's often full, but is worth asking about.

Eating
Restaurante Punta Roca (☎ 2335 3261; 5a Av Sur at 4a Calle Pte; mains US$4-10; 🕐 breakfast, lunch & dinner) American Bob Rotterham has been here forever, and his son is one of the best surfers in Central America. The restaurant is a Libertad institution – the country's most famous wave, which breaks just up the beach from here, is named after the restaurant, not the other way around. There are superb views of the ocean and the food doesn't disappoint: try the *mariscada* (seafood soup), shrimp cocktail or *filete pizziola* – a fish filet covered in Italian tomato sauce, mozzarella cheese and oregano, and then baked.

La Esquina de Nestor's (cnr 2a Calle Pte & 3a Av Norte; mains US$3-4; 🕐 10am-10pm) Run by a friendly Mexican-Salvadoran couple, this spot serves up authentic Mexican seaside holiday fare: tacos (shrimp, beef and *al pastor* pork), gorditas, tostadas and more. It's a tiny restaurant – lime green on the outside, red tile floor inside – with nice light from doors and windows on two sides.

Rancho Mar El Delfín (☎ 2335 3361; 5a Av Sur; mains US$2-6; 🕐 breakfast, lunch & dinner) One of a string of oceanside eateries that serve seemingly identical meals – seafood dishes and *típico* (regional specialties) – Rancho Mar is a particularly good place to get a big breakfast before heading out to the beach.

Supermercado De Todo (Calle Gerardo Barrios btwn 4a & 6a Av Norte; 🕐 7am-7pm) A large supermarket where you can stock up on canned foods, bottled water, munchies and more.

Getting There & Away
La Libertad doesn't have an official bus terminal, but most of the local and long-distance buses line up at designated spots in the market and traffic-choked northeast corner of town. Buses from La Libertad travel to the following destinations:

La Perla Bus 192 (US$0.45, every 30 minutes from 7am to 5:30pm).

San Salvador Bus 102 (US$0.55, one hour, every five minutes from 4:30am to 7pm).

Sonsonate Bus 287 (US$1.25, 2½ hours, 1:45pm only); or take any La Perla bus and transfer to bus 216 (US$0.80, 1½ hours, seven departures daily).

Getting Around
Surfers are welcome to take boards onto all local buses here. Bus 80 has two routes: east to Playa San Diego (US$0.30, 15 minutes, every 30 minutes from 5:40am to 6pm) and west on the Carr Litoral to Playa El Sunzal (US$0.25, 30 minutes, every 15 minutes from 4:30am to 6pm), passing the turnoffs to Playas Conchalía, San Blas, El Majahual and El Tunco along the way. Buses line up on 4a Ave Sur, between Calle Gerardo Barrios and 2a Calle Oriente – ask which direction the bus is going before getting on.

For beaches further west – Playas Palmarcito, El Zonte, Km 59 and Km 61 – take bus 192 (see above). For Playas Mizata and Sihuapilapa, take a Sonsonate bus.

Both bus 192 and westbound bus 80 pass the corner of 3a Av Norte and Calle

El Calvario on their way out of town, in case you don't feel like walking all the way to the market/bus area.

BEACHES NEAR LA LIBERTAD

The coastal expanse between La Libertad and Playa Sihuapilapa is known as 'la Costa del Bálsamo.' It derives its name from the balsam trees whose dye was once extracted by thousands of *balsameros* (balsam workers). Today only a handful of balsam workers remain (p405) and the main cash crop is now cotton.

From La Libertad, the road winds west above a rocky coast with many sheltered coves and sandy beaches (most are private). Weekend hordes head for Playas Conchalío and El Majahual, the latter a wide swath of black sand bordered by endless seafood shacks and parking lots. Independent travelers will probably prefer beaches a bit further on. You can really take your pick – they stretch uninterrupted for more then 50km.

Bus 80 goes as far as Playa El Sunzal. Beyond that, take the less frequent bus 192.

Playa San Diego (Km 30)

Four kilometers east of La Libertad, Playa San Diego is a long, broad swath of flat, gray sand, backed by private homes that are empty most of the week. There are two roads parallel to the beach – a dirt road closest to the water and a paved road a block inland. Both end at La Bocana, where two rivers empty in the ocean, forming the San Diego estuary. There, a gaggle of restaurants compete mightily for your business, offering cheap beer and fish plates.

The estuary is popular for swimming and wading, though God knows what's dumped in the water upstream. You can walk west along the beach and find nice spots to lay out a towel, but be cautious of strong waves and undertow if you swim. It's best not to come alone, or to leave your stuff unattended. There are public passageways every couple of hundred meters, cutting from the beach to the coastal roads. Bus 80 goes to La Bocana and back – catch it in on the paved road.

Half a kilometer from the highway and 200m from the beach, **Restaurante Costa Brava** (☎ 2345 5698; Calle a Playa San Diego; mains US$3-10; ⊗ 8am-6pm) is a modest restaurant-club that is the best of the bunch in Playa San Diego. Two large clean pools have spray nozzles embedded along the sides – it's like swimming in a city fountain without all the pennies. Hammocks cost US$1 a day, and the friendly owners serve good, basic meals, like a quarter-chicken or shrimp with rice. A day visit is free if you spend US$5 or more per person on food or drinks. Three simple rooms, each with two beds, large TV and air-con (to be installed), can be rented for the day (US$25) or for 24 hours (US$30). Bus 80 passes frequently.

TOP FIVE SALVADORAN SURF BREAKS

El Salvador has dozens of named breaks along more than 300km of coastline. All the best waves here break right, whether they're zippy point breaks or long clean waves that peel off forever. Top picks include the following:

Punta Roca A no brainer – this is the best wave in the country *and* Central America. It's rocky bottom makes it fast and strong, but still perfectly shaped and long enough for 15 maneuvers or more. World class – it's often compared to Jeffrey's Bay in South Africa.

Las Flores A fast sandy point break in El Salvador's 'Wild East', which is best at low tide. A picture-perfect set up, with a hollow take-off from a palm-filled point ending on a black-sand beach. A ride of 300m isn't impossible (at least for the wave). It's compared to Rincón in Santa Barbara, California.

Punta Mango Also in the east, Punta Mango is shorter, stronger and more vertical than Las Flores, and is best reached by boat. In fact, some people prefer Punta Mango for its aggressiveness. It's compared to El Capitan in Santa Barbara, California, but is not so elusive.

Km 59 A powerful right-hand point break, accessible through private property. It's short, but hollow, and you'll have it to yourself.

Playa El Sunzal The old standby. Not as crazyman as others, but it's waves are consistently big and you'll appreciate it when everything else is flat. The deep water break holds its shape through thick and thin.

Playa San Blas (Km 39.5)

The gate at the highway makes this look like a private development, which it is, but not exclusively. The long attractive beach, possibly the best after Los Cóbanos, is better for relaxing than for surfing. Three hotels set along the coastal road are all good-value options.

Straight out of a Caribbean island picture book, the brightly colored clapboard **Hotel Restaurant Surf & Sol** (☎ 2310 6560; www.surfysol .com; Playa San Blas; r with/without bathroom US$50/35; P X R) is one of the most charming places on the coast. Four rooms share three full bathrooms in the main building; all are spotlessly clean, have eclectic décor, and open onto a common room with a fantastic ocean view. One room sits apart from the rest – it has a bathroom and a small terrace, but considering the number of shared bathrooms in the other section, it's not really worth paying the extra US$20 for your own. A garden courtyard with hammocks and two pools perfect this oceanfront hotel. A restaurant (mains US$3 to US$13; open breakfast, lunch and dinner) specializing in seafood dishes also keeps customers happy. Staff speak English.

Opened in 2005, the small, low-key hotel and beach club **Sol Bohemio** (☎ 2338 5158; www .solbohemio.com; Playa San Blas; r US$25; X R P) has owners who definitely have the right idea, but were still working out some kinks when we passed through. The upsides include a well-tended garden, a clean (albeit teeny-tiny) pool and easy access to one of the area's best beaches. Clean stylish rooms have *azulejo* (decorative tiles) floors and large TVs (with cable), but they were stuffy – even damp – especially in the rainy season; air-con definitely helps dehumidify things. A 2nd floor with three new rooms, all with bathroom, is in the works; they're sure to have better ventilation. Day use is free, with at least US$6 per person consumption at the restaurant, where options include hamburgers (US$3.50), jalapeño chicken (US$6.75), or shrimp or conch cocktail (US$5 to US$7). Call ahead, as the remodel may alter the prices.

Manicured grounds leading to a nice stretch of beach are the highlights of **Hotel Bello Sol** (☎ 2313 9485; Playa San Blas; s/d without bathroom US$30/40, r with bathroom US$50; P X R). The rooms are just OK – whitewashed cinder-block walls with fluorescent lights and cold-water bathrooms. It seems expensive, but rooms are clean and just steps from the ocean. An oceanfront restaurant on-site (mains US$4 to US$17; open breakfast, lunch and dinner) serves decent seafood and pasta dishes.

Life is still sweet, and the food good, at **La Dolce Vita II** (☎ 2346 0136; mains US$7-17; ⏰ 8:30am-6pm), the smaller, mellower version of the original Dolce Vita restaurant in La Libertad. The specialty is seafood pasta – try the *penne mare e monti*, prepared with a shrimp, mushroom and wine cream sauce. It's rather overpriced, unfortunately, but there aren't many restaurants to choose from in San Blas. Two small pools offer relief for kids (and parents), and there's direct access to the beach. It's next to Hotel Bello Sol.

Playa El Majahual (Km 40.5)

The least appealing of the seaside villages, Playa El Majahual's restaurants are crammed too tightly along the jet-black sand. On the upside, your hotel choices include a water park or a pool in the shape of a guitar.

Ever wonder what it would be like to have Marine World to yourself? Well, **Parque Acuático El Pacifico** (☎ 2310 6505; hotelelpacifico .com.sv; r with/without air-con US$25/12-15; P X R) gives you the chance to find out. An impressive aquatic park – complete with four pools, two huge slides and water jungle gyms – also doubles as a hotel. Clients stay in tiny cinder-block rooms that are clean but cramped; ask for one with a remodelled bathroom, as they're slightly bigger. The room rate covers 24-hour use of the park – giving you free reign of the place once the daytrippers have left! It's open to the public from 8am to 6pm daily; day passes cost US$3 per adult and US$2 per child.

Hotel Santa Fe (☎ 2310 6508; Carr Litoral; s/d US$12/15, with air-con US$20/25), on a small rise opposite the entrance to town, has an appealing exterior with quiet tables set up under almond trees. Rooms don't have as much character, though they're fairly clean, with high ceilings and decent beds. Most of the bathrooms could use a scrub, and many have thin curtains instead of doors. Look at a few before deciding. There are two pools, one for kids and the other in the shape of a guitar. Rock on.

Playa El Tunco (Km 42)

This is the most developed of the beach communities west of La Libertad. The narrow access road has several hotels along its side, and ends in a cluster of beachside restaurants. A broad beach means you can walk to four different breaks: El Sunzal, El Sunzalito, La Bocana (the locals' wave) and La Bocanita.

Papaya's Lodge (☎ 2389 6231; www.papayasurfing .com; Centro El Tunco; s US$8, d with/without bathroom US$14/12; ◫ ℗) is a small hotel run by Jaime 'Papaya' Delgado, a down-to-earth guy who grew up here and is a local surfing legend. Rooms are simple, fairly clean, and aimed squarely at backpackers and surf bums. Guests are free to use the kitchen, and there's an open-air common area with TV, sofas and a computer for checking email (per hour US$2). Delgado lives and runs a surfshop on-site, plus he offers surfboard rental and repair, surf lessons and pretty much anything surf related. There's a small book exchange, and discounts for long stays.

There are four large, airy rooms with tile floors and high ceilings at the beachside **Tortuga Surf Lodge** (☎ 2389 6125; www.tortugasurflodge .net; El Tunco access road; r with/without bathroom US$20/25, r with bathroom & air-con US$45; ℗ 🍴). Each is kept clean and tidy. An on-site restaurant (mains US$3 to US$5; open breakfast, lunch and dinner) keeps guests well fed, and also provides a welcoming sitting area. A large balcony with a great view and an ocean-side deck also make good alternatives. It's a mellow and comfortable spot that fills up on the weekends – perfect if you like being near the scene but not in it. Look for the sign pointing down a small dirt road as you head to the main beach.

Roca Sunzal (☎ 2389 6126; www.rocasunzal.com; 50m from beach; r/tw Mon-Thu US$25/30, Fri-Sun US$30/35, r/tw with air-con Mon-Thu US$40/45, Fri-Sun US$50/55, ste Mon-Thu US$100, Fri-Sun US$125; ℗ 🍴 ◫ 🍴) is the most upscale of the hotels here, with impressive grounds 50m from the town beach. It has two crystal-clear pools in the middle of a manicured garden and a two story *palapa*-roof restaurant (mains US$4 to US$15; open breakfast, lunch and dinner). Rooms are simple but clean, with tile floors, good beds, and balconies or terraces. One is located off

the restaurant, which makes for late nights and early mornings when the restaurant is hopping – if you like to sleep, ask for a room in the main building. Suites – two bedroom apartments with nice furnishings, Jacuzzi tubs and great views – can accommodate up to six people and offer excellent value. Breakfast is included in all rates, except the fan-only rooms, which is a bummer.

Just 25m from the beach, **Hotel los Surfeadores** (☎ 2389 6054; 25m from beach; r without bathroom US$10), is all about the shared balcony; it has a picture-perfect view of the Río Tunco, the black-sand beach and early morning surfers riding the waves. Otherwise, it's very basic: three small clapboard rooms, with a bed, window and a fan. Period. The bathroom is on this side of sketchy – wear flip-flops. It's located above Restaurante Erika, 25m from the beach.

The listed rates at **Ta'kea Nikal** (☎ 2288 7424; Calle a El Tunco; r US$70; 🍴 ℗ 🍴) are a bit inflated, but it's a new hotel and hopefully the owner will have rethought his prices by the time you read this. It's worth checking out the six rooms (four upstairs and two down), which have private bathroom, cable TV, two new beds and cheery yellow interiors. All have large windows and the upstairs rooms have huge views of the Bocanita surf break in front, and Peña El Tunco – El Tunco's famous rock formation – to the right. Downstairs rooms don't have the vista, but are larger and open onto a nice little maguey- and driftwood-filled garden. There is also a small deep pool, a long leafy garden area and plenty of protected parking. It's two doors up from Tortuga Surf Lodge.

The most popular place in El Tunco, **Restaurante Erika** (☎ 2389 6054; mains US$3-6; 🕑 breakfast, lunch & dinner) is a laid-back family-run restaurant, 25m from beach. Fresh seafood meals are the specialty – the ocean is just steps away after all – and come steaming to the tables. If you can't decide what to order, try the *pescado al ajillo*, a thick fillet of fish sautéed in garlic – it's brilliant. Chicken and beef dishes are also offered, and the *típico* breakfast can't be beat.

Cafetería Brian (mains US$1-3; 🕑 breakfast, lunch & dinner) is a small eatery at the end of the road, 30m from the beach, serving up *licuados* and burgers. It's good for a quick meal after a morning on the waves.

Km 43.5

The western Pacific Coast's best hotel has a beach of its own.

One of the few boutique hotels in the country, **Casa de Mar** (☎ 2389 6284; www.casademarhotel .com; r US$102, tw US$136-170; P X ▣ ⊠) has 10 spacious rooms in five colorful buildings. Each room is different – in layout and décor – but all are modern and very classy, with understated furnishings, luxurious linens and original art. All have patios and terraces with dramatic ocean views. A tropical garden, with stone-inlayed paths and several cascades, runs through the property, while a crystalline pool overlooking a black-sand beach takes center stage. Breakfast is included in the rate and is served in a beachside lounge.

Located at Casa de Mar, the excellent open-air restaurant **Café Sunzal** (mains US$9-17; ☺ lunch & dinner) sits at the top of the property. Dishes are Salvadoran-Asian fusion – classic meals with a creative twist. *Camarones Caribeños* (curry shrimp topped with coconut, bacon and pineapple, served over rice, US$12) are a popular choice. The views from above are stunning, and the service can't be beat.

Playa El Sunzal (Km 44.5)

This is a quiet road-side cluster of homes and businesses, including three inexpensive hotels and a couple of eateries. It's good for those who just want to surf and sleep, as it's well removed from the scene at La Libertad and, increasingly, El Tunco. The hotels are also among the few budget places with plenty of securely gated parking. A dirt road runs from the highway, behind Santa Cecelia and Surfer's Inn, and continues a further 300m down to the beach. One itchy guest had dubbed the road Dengue Alley – bring bug repellent. The break here is the western edge of Punta Sunzal, which surfers also access from El Tunco.

Rancho San Patricio (☎ 2389 6107; Carr Litoral; r with/without bathroom US$15/12; P ⊠) has the most appealing rooms around for the price – too bad there are only two of them. The friendly owners of this roadside *rancho* (restaurant with rooms to rent) say they're planning to build more units; until then cross your fingers that one is free when you get here. Rooms are mid-sized, and have high sloped ceilings, white stucco walls

and wood dressers, which is nice if you're staying a while. The room without a bathroom shares the toilet and shower by the pool – a wee drag. Both rooms open onto an open-air sitting area, with a TV and DVD player, and nothing beats a dip in the small clean pool after a day in the salt water. The restaurant serves basic meals. It's on the north side of the highway, across from Santa Cecelia.

Surfer's Inn (☎ 2389 6266; Carr Litoral; camping with/without electrical hook up US$2.50/2; s/d US$8/12, per person in groups of 3 or more US$5; P) has very small cinder-block rooms – good for one person, a bit cramped for two plus bags and boards – but they're clean and new, and come with bathroom. A large window in each room lets in decent light; room 4 is on a 2nd-floor platform and has windows on all sides – unsurprisingly, it's often taken. A grubbier older room sleeps six people with space for a small mountain of gear. Guests can use the kitchen, and there's a place to handwash clothes.

Santa Cecelia (☎ 2389 6048; www.santaceceliarooms .com; Carr Litoral; r per person US$5; P) has five rooms occupying an aging A-frame building set in the middle of a large leafy plot next to the Surfer's Inn. Rooms are much larger than next door, but the shared showers and toilets are grimy, and the walls could use a good scrub. It's about what you'd expect for the price, but the property is pleasant, and filled with mango, ceiba, guancaste and chilamate trees – mangos start dropping in March or April. The kitchen is theoretically open to guests, but it's use doesn't appear to be encouraged.

Playa El Palmar (Km 50)

Many locals and surfers know this as Palmarcito, though technically that's the name of the beachside *colonia* (neighborhood) rather than the community as a whole. The break is fairly popular and the beach – which shares a small bay with the upscale Atami beach club – is decent. There's just one hotel; the turnoff is west of Puente El Palmar – look for signs.

Peaceful, isolated **Hotel Ver-Mar** (☎ 2310 6689; r US$10, per person in groups of 3 or more US$5; X ⊠ P), in a residential neighborhood 500m from highway, has disappointing rooms, starting with the so-so shared bathrooms. Two singles are small and musty, even for US$10. There's more breathing room in two larger rooms, each with a pair of bunks and a twin bed (all saggy), and a fifth room with bathroom and space for four people (US$25). White-painted cinder-block walls don't scream luxury, but the grounds are some consolation – featuring hammocks, shaded chairs and a small decent pool – and the beach and a couple of food stands are just 200m down the road. The owners can arrange surfboard rental and lessons with a neighborhood surfer.

Playa El Zonte (Km 53)

This is less developed than El Tunco, and boasts two excellent accommodations options, though the wave can get busy at times.

Horizonte Surf Resort (☎ 2323 0099; saburo surfcamp@hotmail.com; d/t without bathroom US$15/20, r with bathroom US$30, r with 3/6 beds & bathroom US$30/60; ✕ ☒ ℗) is one of the best places around, though volleyball teams and other groups of six get the best value. Everyone's favorite room is a split-level, six-bed suite facing the ocean, with wood floors and wall-to-wall windows, providing great breeze and views. Other units are perfectly comfortable, if less memorable, with good beds and clean bathrooms. A few are quite small: the rooms without bathrooms have high blue ceilings, which you could try pretending are the sky and not the lid of a glorified cement box. (The shared bathrooms, however, are amazingly agreeable.) Perks include a welcoming pool, an outdoor bar/TV/common area and cheap surfboard rentals. Surf lessons and tours are also available.

Esencia Nativa (☎ 2302-6258, 7737 8879; esencianativa@yahoo.com; s/d without bathroom US$9/14, s/d with bathroom US$15/18, r with bathroom & air-con US$25; ℗ ✕ ☒) has five well-maintained, colorful rooms that help make this a very cool place to stay. Add common lounging areas with paperbacks, surfing magazines and games, a welcoming kidney-shaped pool, a palm-tree studded garden with hammocks and chairs, and a great restaurant (mains US$2 to US$7; open breakfast, lunch and dinner), and it's a beach haven. If that isn't enough, try surfing lessons (per hour US$10) which include a surfboard and a bilingual (English/Spanish) instructor. Laundry service

(per load US$3) is offered to guests and nonguests alike.

Lest you get enticed by the appealing-looking signs on the highway and road into El Zonte, the only redeeming feature of **Rancho Escondido** (☎ 2313 7535; r US$10) is the nice woman who attends it – use it as a last resort. Three rooms have three beds each.

Playa Mizata (Km 87)

There are no accommodations at Mizata, but it's a good, seldom-visited surf spot with both right and left breaks, and a few shacks serving simple meals under a stand of shade trees. Coming from La Libertad, look for a large sign on a curve reading 'Entrada Mizata.' The road down to the beach is only 100m, but those in a car should watch for some muffler-hungry rocks.

Playa Sihuapilapa (Km 90)

This long flat beach extends almost perfectly straight for kilometer after kilometer, backed by private homes. There are no accommodations here, nor many good waves, but it's a nice enough stretch of sand for a wander, or to find a spot to lay out a towel and read a book. As always, avoid going alone or leaving belongings unattended, and be cautious of the undertow. From La Libertad, the signs for Sihualilapa start at around Km 88, but the best beach access is past a large red gate at Km 90. The gate is often locked, but you can easily walk around it. If you're bussing it, ask the driver to drop you in front. If you're driving, look for an entrance marked 'Kari' at Km 89.5, follow the dirt road to the right (west) and continue 500m to the path leading to the beach.

Los Cóbanos

A series of small coves and bays have western El Salvador's best beaches – with thick beige (almost white) sand hemmed in by large rocky points. Los Cóbanos also has El Salvador's best diving, around the only major coral formation on the American side of the Pacific Ocean. It's not a reef, but thousands of rocky heads, covered in coral. And where did the rocks come from? From the sky, scattered like bird-seed during a long-ago volcanic eruption. To get here, take bus 257 from Sonsonate

EL SALVADOR

THE LAST OF THE BALSAMEROS

The aromatic oil known as Balsam of Peru – used in cosmetics, shampoos, perfumes and skin lotions – is not from Peru at all, but two small regions of El Salvador's western Pacific coast. In fact, it is only here that balsam trees (common throughout Latin America) produce the unique and prized substance. Thousands of families have worked in the balsam trade, which dates to pre-Hispanic times. In fact, the western Pacific coast was (and is) known as la Costa del Bálsamo (the Balsam Coast).

Balsameros (balsam workers) burn the trees' bark just enough to release the oil without killing the tree. The oil is soaked up using strips of cloth, which are then boiled and pressed to release the red-black oil. The men must climb high into the trees, using only rope and their bare hands and feet, to reach as much fresh bark as possible. It's an amazing sight: men dangling from ropes, holding torches or swinging between trees to remove the soaked fabric.

But it's a dying trade – only about 400 men still harvest balsam. A group in the town of Atiluya, with help from a Peace Corps volunteer, have begun offering fascinating **balsam tours** (☎ 7787 0272; per person US$2), including hiking through the balsam forest, seeing the presses and watching men work high in the trees. A small museum/visitor center displays tools and photos, with explanations in Spanish and English.

Balsam season is from November to May. To visit, call at least a day in advance, so one of the workers will be waiting for you. to get here, take bus 205 from San Salvador to the turnoff for San Julian, from where you can catch a pickup to San Julian and then another (or bus 800) to Atiluya. Budget 1¾ hours from San Salvador. It's much easier in a car.

(US$0.42, 40 minutes, every 30 minutes from 5:15am to 6pm). The bus stops at the parking lot in the middle of the village.

An upscale beachfront hotel in the middle of a small fishing village, **Los Cobanos Village Lodge** (☎ 2420 5248; www.loscobanos.com; Punta Remedio; dm per person US$15, r Mon-Fri US$45, Sat & Sun US$70; P ☒) has eight spacious rooms in two thatch-roof buildings, with hip beachy décor, whitewashed walls, and polished wood or clay tile floors. All have a small living room with a mini refrigerator, coffee maker and toaster oven. Each also has a balcony or terrace – room 7 has the best ocean view. All rooms have two twin beds, except for the dorm, which has four. Breakfast is included and is served at the poolside restaurant (mains US$4 to US$8; open breakfast, lunch and dinner). Hammocks are strung near the pool and kayaks are available for guest use. Snorkeling, diving (see p44) and fishing tours also can be arranged.

Club de Golf & Villas Las Verenaras (☎ 2420 5000; www.lasverenaras.com; Carr a Los Cóbanos Km 88.5; small villa per week/weekend US$119/153, large villa per week/weekend US$96/119; ☒ ☒ P ☒ ☒) is an exclusive golf resort with eight small villas (room for two adults and a child) and 20 large villas (room for six people) set on sprawling carefully manicured grounds.

Villas are fully furnished, with everything from kitchen utensils to Internet access, and have pleasant terraces and airy living areas. There's a small market on-site, but many guests staying several days bring groceries. The golf course (green fees US$20; open 6am to 7pm) is the newest of just three courses in the country; it's got nine holes and you go around twice, using different tee offs, to complete the full 5420 yards. Las Verenaras is well suited for families – with a beach club (a new marina plus snorkeling and scuba trips are planned), a country club (tennis, horseback riding etc) and waterslides in two of the resort's four pools.

On the way to the beach, the open-air **Restaurante Marsolie** (☎ 2273 5017; Calle Principal; mains US$3-9; ☘ 8am-5pm Tue-Sun) offers good seafood dishes and snacks alongside a crystal-clear pool. Customers can take a dip while they wait for their meals or just enjoy the lively atmosphere. It's popular with families.

Barra de Santiago

The protected estuary and mangrove forest reserve of Barrio de Santiago is teeming with birds, crocodiles, turtles, fish and plant life. Residents of the small fishing village here are still unused to travelers, but more and more tour guides are organizing trips to this area, and a handful of beachfront lodging options have already popped up.

Run by the same people as Ximena's Guest House (p330) in San Salvador, **Capricho Beach House** (☎ 2260 2481; ximenas@navegante.com.sv; Final Calle Principal; cabin per person US$7, r with fan & without bathroom per person US$10, d/tr/q with bathroom & air-con US$35/40/45; ✷ P) has a newish main house with three bedrooms, and a rustic adobe cabin with a thatched roof. An outdoor grill and kitchen can be used by guests. The owners can arrange for various excursions, from canoe trips into the estuary and mangrove forest, to deep sea fishing (per hour US$27). Advance reservations are required for lodging and excursions.

There are a few simple *comedores* (basic, cheap eateries) around Barrio de Santiago.

From Sonsonate's new bus terminal, direct Barra de Santiago buses leave at 10am and 4:30pm and drop you a short walk from Capricho Beach House; the return buses are at 4:30am and 11:30am. If you miss the direct bus, you can take any La Hachadura bus from Sonsonate and get off at the turnoff; from there, pickups shuttle back and forth to the village. Ask the bus driver to take you all the way to Capricho – you may have to pay a little extra – otherwise it's a solid 45-minute walk.

EASTERN PACIFIC COAST

Packed with day-trippers on weekends and holidays, but deserted the rest of the time, you could say this region has two personalities: the partier who likes beer, loud music and crowds, and the loner who just wants to relax in a hammock or look for shells undisturbed. The majority of foreign travelers prefer the latter, though a Sunday visit to a popular beach like El Cuco (p417) is as much a cultural experience as any museum or religious festival.

The eastern Pacific coast begins at the Costa del Sol (opposite), just west of the mouth of the Río Lempa, which has served as a natural border since pre-Columbian times – dividing Maya and Lenca communities in the east from Pipiles in the west. It ends at the large busy Golfo de Fonseca (p419) shared by El Salvador, Honduras and Nicaragua (the closest thing to a shared border that the two countries in this guidebook have). Though hotter and more humid than the west, the east boasts world-class surfing near Playa El Cuco, up-and-coming beach areas like Playa El Espino (p418), and some off-the-beaten-path adventure opportunities in places like Bahía de Jiquilisco (p410), Isla Montecristo (p409) and Isla Meanguera (p419). Lodging and food can be expensive – expect to pay twice as much on the coast as you would inland – but a couple of resorts do

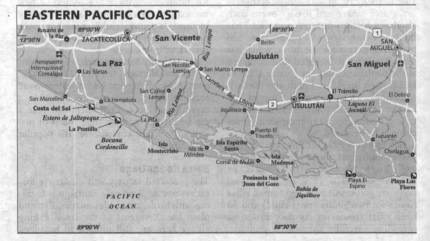

EASTERN PACIFIC COAST

deliver on the promises that their high prices seem to make.

La Unión (p412) is the eastern Pacific coast's largest city, a desultory place with little appeal of its own. However, many buses along the coast come and go from there, and it's the jumping-off point for trips to the islands in the Golfo de Fonseca. La Unión has siphoned away much of El Salvador's commercial boat traffic from Acajutla, in the west, and will soon be home to the country's largest port, Puerto Cutuco. Word is that even cruise ships will be stopping there – a first for El Salvador.

Climate & Geography

The eastern Pacific coast is predictably hot and humid – even more so than the western coastal areas. Temperatures hover in the high 20s°C to mid 30s°C (82°F to mid 95°F); for surfers, water temperatures average 27°C to 30°C (80°F to mid 86°F). The geography here is mostly flat, with expansive grey-sand beaches, sleepy fishing villages, and tangled estuaries and bays. Outside of La Unión stands the impressive Volcán de Conchagua (p414), with views of the Pacific and the dramatic rocky islands of the Golfo de Fonseca.

Dangers & Annoyances

Avoid walking alone or leaving items unattended on beaches here – local crime tends to be opportunistic and occurs mostly to those who make themselves easy targets.

La Unión is somewhat seedy and Puerto El Triúnfo (on the mainland side of Bahía de Jiquilisco) is downright dodgy, with persistent drug and gang problems. You don't need to skip them altogether – both are gateways to interesting places – but do use common sense and avoid being out at night.

COSTA DEL SOL

The first string of beaches you hit from San Salvador, Costa del Sol is on a thin peninsula with the Pacific on one side and an estuary on the other. Being so close to the capital, most of the beachfront is taken up with private homes and hotels. As you drive down the coastal road, all you'll see are walls. If you come down for the day, choose between paying for a day pass at one of the nicer hotels or driving to the tip of the peninsula where beach shacks and food stands open onto the beginning…or rather, the end of the beach.

Orientation & Information

There is one road on the Costa del Sol that travels the length of the peninsula. If you're driving, reset your odometer when you start down the road as fancy homes with signs look like hotels from the outside. There are no services out here; for medical care, Internet access or laundry facilities, head back to the capital.

Sights & Activities

The Costa del Sol has beautiful **beaches**, but getting to them can be harder than you'd think. All the hotels listed in this section have beach access; some of the top-end hotels are diligent about clearing the trash and seaweed that washes onto shore, and their beaches are more pleasant for the effort. Of course, all non-military beaches in El Salvador are public, and you can walk along the water until you find a spot you like, whether you're a hotel guest or not. There's beach access via a small beachside community at Playa Los Blancos (Km 64) near the Hotel Haydee Mar.

The huge **Turicentro Parque Acuático Costa del Sol** (☎ 2338 2050; Blvd Costa del Sol Km 63.5; adult US$0.80, seniors & children free, parking US$0.69; ☽ 7am-4pm) spans both sides of the highway, connected by a pedestrian bridge. Independent travelers may prefer something more, well,

EL SALVADOR

independent, but those with kids or just out for an easy day trip will appreciate having ready access to the beach, swimming pools, play areas, bathrooms, cheap eateries, parking, and rentable chairs and tables (US$2).

Boat excursions in the estuary can be arranged at La Puntilla, including birdwatching at Isla las Garzas, sailboat admiring at Isla Cordoncillo and visiting ocean beaches at Isla Tasajera. Excursions cost around US$20 for up to 12 people if you approach the boats yourself – if you're led there by a local, the boatman has to pay him (and charge you) a US$10 commission. Which means, don't ask where the boats are or mention that you want to take a trip! They're impossible to miss – long boats with outboard motors and sunshades are moored on the beach directly behind the bank of seaside restaurants. They're out there by 8am; to go earlier, or simply reserve a boat, call boat operator **Esteban Pineda** (☎ 2375 1290) after 6pm.

On the Estero de Jaltepeque side, **Aqua Fun** (☎ 2338 0384, 7850 4419; http://aquafundelsol.com; Blvd Costa del Sol Km 77.5) is a new watersports club offering rentals of all kinds, including jet skis (per hour/day US$60/395), kayaks (per hour US$20) and fishing rods with spinner reels (per day US$12). Deep-sea fishing trips cost US$1550 for a five-person, eight-hour excursion; US$100 per extra person (up to two people). Its website is quite sophisticated, with photos, online reservations, and tons of info on the area and El Salvador.

Sleeping

The Costa del Sol's two budget hotels are nearly side by side, so you can easily compare them and choose the one you prefer. Otherwise take your pick of the top-end places. All have easy access to broad windswept beaches.

Mini Hotel y Restaurante Mila (☎ 2338 2074; Playa Los Blancos, Blvd Costa del Sol Km 64; r without bathroom US$15, r with bathroom & fan/air-con US$20/29, tw US$40; ✖ ☱ P) Smaller and tidier than the Haydee Mar next door, rooms here have modern newly tiled bathrooms and the walls are painted twice a year to prevent peeling. The English-speaking owners are building a small 2nd-floor restaurant-bar area that, when completed, will be a great place to watch the sunset over nearby

houses and the ocean beyond. It also has a small pool.

Hotel Haydee Mar (☎ 2338 2046; Blvd Costa del Sol Km 64; r with fan/air-con Sat & Sun US$18/40, Mon-Fri US$15/25; ✖ P ☱) The Haydee Mar's two swimming pools are it's biggest attraction – one has little nooks with a table and umbrella in the middle and underwater benches with jets to massage your back. Rooms are definitely showing their age – some upstairs units have large windows and good ventilation, and open onto a wide corridor with tables where breakfast is served. Others are musty and dark, with stinky plumbing.

Hotel Pacific Paradise Costa del Sol (☎ 2338 0156; www.hotelpacificparadise.com, in Spanish; Blvd Costa del Sol Km 75; r US$86, ste US$184; ✖ P ☱ ☲) This hotel screams late '70s – lots of flower prints and dark, heavy furniture – but the rooms are comfortable enough, with good beds, clean bathrooms and balconies. The grounds are nicely maintained, the beach is expansive and free of debris, and the pool's clear waters are especially tempting. Breakfast is included and served either beachfront – under a huge *palapa*-roofed structure – or indoors in a dark, air-conditioned dining room. Day passes are available, too: use of the facilities costs US$10/8 per adult/child; add in a ceviche plate and lunch with a drink for US$20/12, plus an afternoon snack (on Sunday only) for US$25/15.

Tesoro Beach (☎ 2335 1447; tesorobeach@telesal .net; Blvd Costa del Sol Km 69.5; r/ste per person all inclusive US$125/200; ✖ P ☱ ☲) The remnants of this hotel's glory days are obvious as soon as you step onto its beachfront grounds – a grand lobby with marble floors, a mural and impressive chandeliers; two aquamarine pools with bridges, benches and palm trees; an amphitheatre lined with Romanesque pillars – but look just a bit closer and you'll see that the paint is peeling, grass is overgrown, the flowers are plastic and the beach, well, it's somewhat neglected. The rooms are decent, though dated, with two queen beds, red tile floors and a balcony. Suites have separate living rooms, views of the beach and, in three cases, have private outdoor pools. Frankly, the rack rate is over the top, even if it includes all you can eat and drink; there seems to be some denial that the hotel's heyday has come and gone. Fortunately, there are frequent specials and all-inclusive day passes aren't bad (US$35/20 adult/child), considering you get a good lunch and all the domestic liquor and beer you want.

Hotel Bahía del Sol Marina y Yacht Club (☎ 2338 0001; www.bahiadelsolelsalvador.com; Blvd Costa del Sol Km 78.5; r with/without Jacuzzi US$147/118, tw with Jacuzzi US$250, 3bdrm townhouse US$300; ⓟ ⓧ ⓡ ⓛ) The Costa del Sol's most exclusive resort, owing mainly to its marina, which is popular with cruisers and anglers. Room prices include all meals; cruisers staying onboard get a 30% discount on meals and drinks, plus free use of the pool, beach club etc. Rooms are clean and attractive – the square Jacuzzis set in an outdoor kiosk are a nice touch, especially nice lit up at night. Day passes (available 8am to 5pm) are a good deal – US$20 includes US$15 in food or drink credit. The hotel hosts an annual Marlin fishing tournament, usually in September; ask about deep sea fishing trips and other excursions.

Eating

Just a few restaurants service this entire coastline. If you're looking for cheaper eats with a view, head to La Puntilla, where you'll find a handful of rustic eateries.

Comedor Ruth (Playa Los Blancos, Blvd Costa del Sol Km 64; mains US$2-4; ⓧ breakfast & lunch) A friendly eatery in what appears to be the middle of the coastal road, across from the Hotel Haydee Mar. Fried fish and chicken are prepared in an open-air grill and kitchen, and served piping hot at plastic covered tables.

Restaurante Yessenia (☎ 2338 2578) and **Restaurante KennyMar** (☎ 2338 2576) are side-by-side and virtually identical restaurants in San Marcelino, the beachside community located right where the road bends east (left) along the coast and becomes Blvd Costa del Sol. You'll be harangued by waiters from both eateries as you step out – someone is going to be disappointed. Seafood is the specialty, though you can order just about any standard Salvadoran dish here. Both are open 7am to 9pm, and dishes cost US$5 to $15. The beach here is popular with residents in the area, more for its convenience than its quality.

For self-caterers, **Supermercado Costa del Sol** (☎ 2338 2589; Blvd Costa del Sol Km 57.5; ⓧ 8am-6pm Mon-Fri, 7am-7pm Sat & Sun) is a decent supermarket with a little bit of everything – water,

toiletries, canned food, dairy products, and fresh fruits and vegetables.

Getting There & Around

Bus 193 covers the Costa del Sol and inland, from La Puntilla up to Zacatecoluca (US$1, 1½ hours, every 30 minutes from 4:30am to 5:15pm) and back again. Bus 193E continues to San Vicente (US$1.50, 2¼ hours, 8:30am, 8:35am, 3pm and 3:35pm), while bus 495 goes to Terminal de Sur in San Salvador (US$1.25, 2½ hours, every 30 minutes from 6am to 2:45pm). Calle Nueva buses are faster.

ISLA MONTECRISTO

Hundreds of pelicans and egrets nest around this pristine (but very hot) island and estuary, where the Río Lempa meets the Pacific Ocean. During the war the island and its cashew plantation were abandoned, and then taken over by the FMLN. After 1992 it was resettled by area farmers taking advantage of the post-war land transfer program. The community was evacuated in 1998, when Hurricane Mitch flooded the lower Río Lempa, and again in 2005 following Hurricane Stan. It is now inhabited by a couple of dozen families growing organic *mariñones* (cashews) as an export crop. On the mainland is the fishing community of La Pita, where the area's tourism services are based.

Hostal Lempa Mar (☎ 2310 9901, 2632 2084; www.gbajolempa.net; r US$15; ⓟ) is operated by a local development group and includes four simple cabins, with a double bunk and individual bed in each, plus tile floors and high ventilated ceilings. Each has a comfortable terrace with a hammock and share a bathroom. The restaurant serves basic homemade meals (US$3 to US$8). It's in La Pita, right where the buses turn around, and is impossible to miss.

Boat tours (up to 15 people, US$20 to $30) include a visit to the mouth of the estuary, passing through narrow 'canyons' in the trees, and a trip to Isla de Montecristo proper, with its cashew plantations. The basic tour lasts about 40 minutes, but can be extended to 1½ hours by visiting another community, with a fishing cooperative, in Estero Jaltepeque, the next estuary over. Ask, too, about renting **traditional canoes** to explore the mangroves, going **fishing** with a local fisherman using traditional methods, and **hiking** possibilities. There is also a small **museum** focusing on the war period.

Note that the hotel is open Wednesday to Sunday, and tours are only available those days. There is talk of remaining open all week, but it's best to call ahead if you're thinking of arriving on Monday or Tuesday.

La Pita and Isla Montecristo are at the end of a 22km road connecting the Carr Litoral and the coast. The first 10km are paved, the last 11 are not – ordinary cars can usually make it, though the road can get pretty rough in the rainy season. Bus 155 (US$0.70, 40 minutes) leaves from the Texaco gas station in San Nicolas Lempa at roughly 6am, 7am, 10:30am, 11:30am, 12:30pm, 1:30pm, 5pm and 5:30pm. There are also pickups (same price) that leave from the Texaco gas station every 40 minutes throughout the day. To return, catch any of the buses or pickups back to San Nicholas Lempa.

BAHÍA DE JIQUILISCO

Shielded from the ocean by the long thin Península San Juan del Gozo, Jiquilisco Bay is studded with mangrove-fringed islands, and is home to thousands of pelicans, gray egrets and other water birds. The peninsula has terrific beaches on both sides. Bay beaches have calm water and views of inland volcanos, while those on the ocean side are arguably the best in the country – kilometer after kilometer of glorious white sand, shaded by palm trees, pounded by heavy surf and virtually deserted. After years of relative disinterest, the government and foreign NGOs (with help from Peace Corps volunteers) are finally investing in development here, especially in terms of eco-tourism. The infrastructure is still very basic, but fledgling projects – from mangrove and bird tours to turtle projects and home stays – are a sign of what's to come.

Puerto El Triunfo, the traditional access point to the bay, is a seedy port town whose reputation for gangs and general unpleasantness surely explains why so few people visit the area. Things improve immensely across the bay, where the small fishing communities of **Corral de Mulas** and **Isla de Méndez** are reasonably accessible, by boat and bus respectively, and have the most 'to do.'

Punta San Juan, the eastern tip of the peninsula, has gorgeous beaches and a number of upscale private homes, but is hard to reach affordably. Inside the bay, **Isla Espíritu Santo**, also known as Isla Jobal, has interesting coconut groves and processing facilities, and **Isla Madre Sal** has decent beaches, but getting there and back remains a problem.

Puerto El Triunfo

A grim town known for its delinquency, you must pass through here to access the Bahía de Jiquilisco. If you can help it, don't stop as you head toward the pier to catch your boat.

INFORMATION
Farmacia Popular (☎ 2663 6061; ⏱ 7am-noon & 2-9pm) Around the corner from ISSS.
ISSS (☎ 2663 6038; ⏱ 24hr) A public hospital two blocks north of Hotel El Jardín.
Police (☎ 2663 6300; ⏱ 24hr) Located at entrance to the pier area.

SLEEPING & EATING
Hotel El Jardín (☎ 2663 6089; Calle Principal; r US$12, with air-con US$17; ⊠ P) Unfortunately, the only hotel in town has been operating for 20 years, and it shows. Rooms are pretty grim – you should avoid sitting on the toilet at all costs – though the sheets are clean. It is also the sort of hotel that charges by three-hour increments – use it as your last resort. It's half a block from the bus station.

Cheap food (including fresh fish, pupusas and *licuados*) is served at a dozen or more **pier eateries** (⏱ breakfast, lunch & dinner) at the end of Calle Principal. Tables and chairs are set up in two well-kept structures that overlook the bay, which makes having a meal a surprisingly pleasant experience.

GETTING THERE & AROUND
The Puerto El Triunfo bus stop is a half-block south of Hotel El Jardín and a short distance from the pier. For San Salvador and San Miguel, it's often quicker to take any bus to the turnoff on the Carr Litoral and transfer there. Buses from Puerto El Triunfo travel to the following destinations:
San Miguel Bus 377 (US$1.35, 2½ to three hours; every 40 minutes from 4am to 3pm); or take any Usulután bus and transfer.
San Salvador Bus 185 (US$1.50; two hours, 4am, 4:30am, 5am, 6:30am, 7:15am and 3:15pm).

Usulután Bus 363 (US$0.52, one hour, every 10 minutes from 4am to 5:30pm).

Corral de Mulas

Deserted beaches and a peek into small-town Salvadoran life have long been the main attractions here. An ambitious tourism development project was underway at the time of research; it was scheduled to be completed in 2007. The area will remain a work in progress, of course, and a certain amount of uncertainty is part of the appeal.

ORIENTATION

Corral de Mulas has several parts, all stretched along the peninsula. El Icaco is a small *caserío* (outlying neighborhood) where most of the tourism-related development is taking place, and for that reason most travelers will prefer to disembark here. The main community is divided into Corral de Mulas I and Corral de Mulas II – the latter has a reputation for being somewhat dangerous and is best avoided. If arriving by boat, ask the driver to drop you at any of these areas.

SIGHTS & ACTIVITIES

The long **bay beach** in front of El Icaco has a beautiful view of the bay and Isla Madresal directly across, with San Vicente, Usulután and San Miguel volcanoes looming behind. The community is building three covered, floating platforms here, to be reached by swimming or boat, where visitors will be able to read, swim, relax or enjoy a picnic lunch. Be sure to ask about *marea roja*, or 'red tide,' a toxic algae bloom that spreads through the bay once or twice a year for about a week, during which time swimming is not a good idea.

The **ocean beach** has thick white sand, swaying coconut trees and a glorious, deserted island feel. The surf is powerful – it mellows out somewhat at low tide and in the dry season, but definitely think twice about swimming here. In the dry season the beach provides a pleasant 15-minute walk, zig-zagging through and around cow pastures and private homes. During the rainy season it's another story though, requiring an hour's slog through muddy roads and water up to your knees – possibly your waist – in places. Don't forget the bug repellent, as the mosquitos can be vicious.

A **turtle nursery** and **mangrove tours** are also planned in El Icaco. Both are more established in Isla de Méndez (below), but are worth asking about here.

SLEEPING & EATING

There were no accommodations in Corral de Mulas or El Icaco at the time of research. As tourism grows in the area, it seems likely like that some form of lodging – whether homestays, hostels, hotels or camping – will pop up here. Ask at the *alcaldía* (mayor's office) in Puerto El Triunfo for the latest info. As for eating, you'll find a few modest *comedores* (basic and cheap eateries) and markets in the village.

GETTING THERE & AROUND

Corral de Mulas can be reached by boat from Puerto El Triunfo. Passenger boats leave fairly regularly in the morning; the fare is US$2 per person with at least five or six passengers. By late morning and throughout the afternoon you may have to wait an hour or more for a boat to fill up; the last boat leaves Puerto El Triunfo around 4:30pm – but given there's no lodging, you'll probably be heading out there early, anyway. Getting back is trickier, as the only scheduled departure is at 6am and many of the passenger boats that come from Puerto El Triunfo don't return. Your best bet is to arrange with a boat operator to pick you up in the afternoon; the standard fare is US$15. This is actually a roundtrip fare – they've got to come out to get you before taking you back. It's worth asking in the morning, before you get on a passenger boat, if any boat driver is willing to take you across and wait in Corral de Mulas (many live there) until you're ready to return; that way you save the passenger boat fare and there's no confusion as to when and where you'll be picked up. Of course, be sure everyone is clear on the terms – if the driver makes two roundtrips, he'll be expecting US$30.

Isla de Méndez

Deeper in the bay, Isla de Méndez is another pleasant fishing village with a modest but growing tourism trade. Like Corral de Mulas, it has great beaches and some basic eco-tourism options, but being further east means it can be reached by bus instead of boat. You can also stay over night here – with a private family for now, though hostels are being built.

INFORMATION

The local community development group, **Adesco** (☎ 7727 3453), oversees all things tourist related. María Antonia de la Paz was the latest contact person, but anyone there should be able to help. The office was near the soccer field, but may have moved – ask for directions.

SIGHTS & ACTIVITIES

Like Corral de Mulas, the **bay beach** here has calm shallow water and good inland views, while the **ocean beach** features soft sand, tall palms and giant waves. Access to the ocean beach is dependent on the season – an easy half-hour walk in the dry season, a long muddy march in the rainy season.

Boat trips in the bay are interesting and beautiful, though pricey for travelers not in a group. Destinations include area mangroves, and Palacio de las Aves, an island where hundreds of water birds flock to spend the night. Trips cost around US$35 per boat.

SLEEPING & EATING

You can stay with a local family in Isla de Méndez (per person US$10), which is a great way to see how ordinary Salvadorans live. The system is agreeably informal: you may or may not get a private room, and the price may or may not include breakfast or

---

TURTLE PRESERVATION

The Isla de Méndez community has a growing turtle preservation project. Turtle-egg collectors (who would normally sell their catch to locals and restaurants) are paid to give eggs or point out fresh nests to the project organizers. The eggs are monitored until they hatch, 40 days after being laid, and the baby turtles released to the ocean. Travelers can participate in any part of the process, whether checking nests at night, transferring eggs or releasing newly hatched turtles. The main difficulty is that turtle season (August to November) coincides with rainy season, making getting to and from the ocean tough and muddy.

---

dinner. The families genuinely enjoy hosting foreigners, and it's common for family members to join their guests at the beach or while just exploring town. It's best to call **Adesco** (☎ 7727 3453) before you arrive, but it's not required.

Two hostels were being built at the time of research. Call ahead or inquire at Adesco for more information.

GETTING THERE & AROUND

Isla de Méndez is 30km by road from San Marcos Lempa, a small town on the Carr Litoral about 11km west of the Jiquilisco/Puerto El Triunfo turnoff. Bus 368 leaves from there for Isla de Méndez (US$1, 1¼ hours) at 1pm and 2pm daily; return buses leave Isla de Méndez at 5:30am and 6am. You'll need a 4WD to drive there yourself, especially in the rainy reason – the last 15km are unpaved and quite rough in places, including crossing a small river just west of Isla de Mendez. The road is being improved (and a bridge built), but it will probably be some time before ordinary cars can make the trip.

LA UNIÓN

pop 24,354

La Unión is a hot and seedy town that is engulfed by blocks of drab, chaotic market stalls, which exude an air of menace at night. There's not much redeeming about this town. Actually, the best thing about it, is that you can leave; La Unión is a hub for the beaches just south (see p416) and it's also the primary embarkation point for the islands in the Golfo de Fonseca (p419). For some respite from the heat, you also can head to Conchagua (p414), a pleasant village built on the imposing volcano of the same name.

A new deep sea port – Puerto Cutuco – is in the works just outside of town and is expected to receive cruise ships; it's a long-awaited project, and one that is expected to bring much-needed revenue into this region. The inauguration was planned for 2005, but that year came and went. No firm date for its opening has been rescheduled. Perhaps when it is, La Unión will undergo a face-lift.

La Union has no real sights. The morning bustle at the main dock is mildly interesting though, especially at low tide when boatmen and passengers transport their

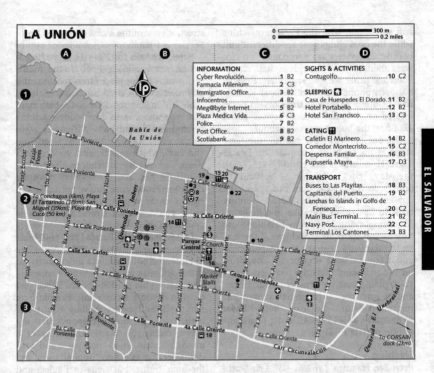

LA UNIÓN

0 .... 300 m
0 .... 0.2 miles

INFORMATION			SIGHTS & ACTIVITIES		
Cyber Revolución	1	B2	Contugolfo	10	C2
Farmacia Milenium	2	C3			
Immigration Office	3	B2	**SLEEPING**		
Infocentros	4	B2	Casa de Huespedes El Dorado	11	B2
Meg@byte Internet	5	B2	Hotel Portabello	12	B2
Plaza Medica Vida	6	B2	Hotel San Francisco	13	C3
Police	7	B2			
Post Office	8	B2	**EATING**		
Scotiabank	9	B2	Cafetín El Marinero	14	B2
			Comedor Montecristo	15	C2
			Despensa Familiar	16	B2
			Pupusería Mayra	17	D3
			TRANSPORT		
			Buses to Las Playitas	18	B3
			Capitanía del Puerto	19	B2
			Lanchas to Islands in Golfo de		
			Fonseca	20	C2
			Main Bus Terminal	21	B2
			Navy Post	22	C2
			Terminal Los Cantones	23	B3

EL SALVADOR

gear across the mud flats in make-shift wheelbarrows.

Orientation

La Unión is no trouble to navigate by foot, as long as you remember that the water is always to the north. By car it can be a little trickier, as a number of streets are one way, or else clogged by market stalls. Also, the highway was redesigned so traffic to and from Puerto El Cutuco – which will eventually be heavy – bypasses the city instead of going through it. If arriving from San Miguel, you now pass through a huge roundabout and are fed, eventually, onto Calle General Menéndez on the *east* side of La Unión, not the west as you'd expect.

Information

Cyber Revolución (☎ 2604 4815; 1a Calle Pte; per hr US$1; ⊗ 8am-5pm) Download photos and burn CDs for US$2.

Farmacia Milenium (☎ 2604 1672; Calle General Menéndez; ⊗ 6am-8:30pm)

Immigration Office (☎ 2604 4375; Av General Cabañas at 7a Calle Pte; ⊗ 6am-10pm) Next door to the post office – look for the sign that says 'Control Migración.' You must stop here if you're arriving or departing by boat from Nicaragua or Honduras.

Infocentros (☎ 2604 1950; 1a Calle Pte; per hr US$1; ⊗ 8am-5:30pm Mon-Fri, 8-noon Sat)

Meg@byte Internet (☎ 2604 0163; 1a Calle Pte; per hr US$1 Mon, Wed & Fri, per 75min US$1 Tue & Thu, per 90min US$1 Sat; ⊗ 9am-7pm Mon-Fri, 9am-noon Sat)

Plaza Medica Vida (☎ 2604 2065; Calle General Menéndez; ⊗ 24hr) A decent hospital near the center of town.

Police (Centro de Gobernación; Av General Cabañas; ⊗ 24hr)

Post Office (☎ 2604 4002; Av General Cabañase; ⊗ 8am-5pm Mon-Fri, 8am-noon Sat)

Scotiabank (☎ 2604 1919; 1a Av Norte at 1a Calle Ote; ⊗ 8am-4pm Mon-Fri, 8am-noon Sat) A second branch is a half-block north. Exchanges traveler's checks.

Tours

A booze cruise, er...sorry, a souped up **car ferry** (☎ 2604 2222; www.contugolfo.com, in Spanish) plies the Golfo de Fonseca (adult/child US$10/5) every Saturday and Sunday from 10am to 3pm. Passengers can eat, drink, and even sit in the blow-up kiddie pool and sing along with the karaoke machine while the boat chugs past six different gulf islands. The views are gorgeous – no two ways about it – and the ride is, well, cheap. Food and drink are sold separately. Reserve a spot by phone and meet the boat 30 minutes before departure at the Corsain dock, located on the road to Las Playitas, about 1km past the huge new roundabout.

On one Saturday per month, the ferry stops at the town of Amapala, on Isla El Tigre, Honduras (adult/child US$15/7.50); the day trip is longer – 8:30am to 6pm – so that passengers can spend the day enjoying the beaches before heading back to La Unión, karaoke mic in hand. More importantly, you may be able to use this as transport to Honduras – there is an immigration post at the Amapala pier, and frequent boat service to Coyolitos, on the mainland. Tell the ferry operators your plan when you reserve your ticket, and be sure to go through Salvadoran immigration before you leave. **Hotel Mirador de Amapala** (☎ 504 795 8643) is an overnight option on Isla El Tigre.

Sleeping

Hotel San Francisco (☎ 2604 4159; Calle General Menéndez; r US$15, d/tw with air-con US$30/35; ✷ P) Accommodations surround two leafy courtyards at this quiet hotel. Rooms are spacious and spotless; each with a hammock and cable TV, and some with shared balconies. Located on the quiet end of the street, it's one of the nicest options in town. Service is friendly.

Hotel Portobello (☎ 2604 4113; 1a Calle Pte at 4a Av Norte; r with air-con US$20; P ✷) In the middle of downtown, this place offers spacious and airy rooms with shared balconies. Each has cable TV, a hammock, a clean bathroom (the type whose walls don't quite reach the ceiling) and decent beds. Air-con is available in every room, but only between 7pm and 7am, which makes for a good night's sleep and sweaty afternoons. The location is the best and worst thing about the place – great because you've got La Unión right outside your front door, awful because you've got La Unión right outside your front door.

Casa de Huespedes El Dorado (☎ 2604 4724; Calle San Carlos 2-2 at 2a Av Norte; s/d/tw US$7/8/10; P) The El Dorado is built around a quiet courtyard with gardenias and mango trees, offering respite from the market-choked streets just outside. Rooms have a fan, double bed, hammock and pretty grubby cold-water bathrooms. The beds are spongy, but the sheets clean. It attracts something of a mixed clientele – that toothpaste and condoms are for sale here implies some by-the-hour traffic, but signs in English and Spanish exhorting guests to preserve the hotel's 'clean reputation' suggests the hotel has not given in entirely. There are no twin rooms, but you can ask for an extra bed to be added. You can also handwash and line-dry your clothes here.

DETOUR: CONCHAGUA

Just 6km from La Unión is the pleasant village of Conchagua, a small town nestled on the volcano by the same name. It's the sort of place where there are flower gardens in the plaza, everyone knows each other and kids play in the streets. Unfortunately, there is no hotel, but relaxing in the shady plaza or wandering along the small streets is a nice way to spend an afternoon.

Dating to 1693, the small blue and white **church** is said to be the second-oldest in El Salvador; the interior is nondescript, but it's worth a stop. If you're hungry, food stands sell burgers, pupusas and ice cream on the main plaza. The one restaurant – **Cafetín Villa Central** (☎ 2680 3483; mains US$2-8; ☼ lunch & dinner Wed-Mon) – also serves good *típica* in its open-air restaurant.

Although climbing the 1243m **Volcán de Conchagua** is prohibited (the top is privately owned), plans to develop a tourist center were in the works when we passed through. **Codeca** (☎ 2659 5320; ☼ 8am-4pm Mon-Fri), a Morazán-based community organization, was developing five hectares of land on the volcano. By the time you read this there should be two trails (1.5km and 6km, both roundtrips), three lookout points, a restaurant, and accommodations ranging from campsites (per person US$2) and rustic rooms (US$10) to cabins with bathroom (US$25). At the time of research, the 6km road up from Conchagua was only drivable with a 4WD vehicle. Call Codeca or stop by Conchagua's **alcaldía** (☎ 2680 3334; main plaza) for more information.

Eating

Pupusería Mayra (☎ 2604 2065; Calle General Menéndez; mains US$1-2; ⊗ dinner) Hopping every night of the week, this eatery offers fresh pupusas and huge sandwiches for just a few coins each. Pupusas are made in a leafy courtyard, while customers wait on colorful wood benches or in two spotless dining rooms. It's across the street from the Hotel San Francisco, and open late.

Cafetín El Marinero (Av General Cabañas at 3a Calle Pte; mains US$2-6; ⊗ breakfast & lunch) Come here for good, cheap breakfasts and lunches in a homey setting. The menu varies according to what's available, but always includes fish and shrimp dishes. The *licuados* are especially nice, as is the sunny wrap-around patio.

For self-caterers, **Dispensa Familiar** (1a Av Norte; ⊗ 7am-7pm Mon-Sat, 7am-6pm Sun) is a full-on supermarket on the parque central, complete with fresh produce, dairy products and toiletries.

Getting There & Around
BUS

La Unión has two bus terminals, or rather two empty lots where buses come and go. The **main bus terminal** (3a Calle Pte) is used by long-distance buses. The other bus terminal is called **Terminal Los Cantones** (Calle San Carlos at 4a Av Sur) because it serves the *cantones* (outlying neighborhoods and nearby towns). Buses for Las Playitas (bus 418; US$0.55, 30 minutes, 8am, 11am and 3pm) leave from 4a Calle Ote. Buses from La Unión travel to the following destinations:

Conchagua Bus 382A (US$0.25, 15 minutes, 7:50am,10:30am, 12:10pm; 3:30pm and 4:50pm; departs Terminal Los Cantones).

El Amatillo (Honduran border) Take any Santa Rosa de Lima bus to San Carlos (US$0.90, one hour) and transfer to bus 330.

El Embarcader/Buenavista Take any El Tamarindo bus (US$0.65; 35 minutes; departs Terminal Los Cantones).

El Tamarindo Bus 383 (US$0.90, 1¾ hours, every 20 minutes from 4:30am to 5:30pm; departs Terminal Los Cantones).

Intipucá Bus 339 (US$0.90, 1¼ hours, 6am, 7:20am, 9:25am, 10:25am, 11:10am, 1:15pm, 2:25pm and 4:05pm; departs Terminal Los Cantones).

Playa Jagüey Take any El Tamarindo bus (US$0.90, 1½ hours; departs Terminal Los Cantones).

Playa Las Tunas Take any El Tamarindo bus (US$0.70, one hour; departs Terminal Los Cantones).

San Miguel Bus 324 (*ordinario* US$0.85, 1¼ hours, every 10 minutes from 4:15am to 5:50pm; *especial* US$1, 55 minutes, 5:50am, 6:20am, 6:45am and 4:15pm).

San Salvador Bus 304 (*ordinario* US$3, four hours, every 30 minutes from 3:30am to 2:30pm; *especial* US$5, three hours, 4am, 6am and 12:30pm); or take any bus to San Miguel and transfer.

Santa Rosa de Lima Bus 342 (US$0.90, 1½ hours, every 15 minutes from 4am to 5:30pm).

BOAT

While boats come and go to all the islands, the only regular passenger boat service is to Isla Meanguera (US$2.50) and to Isla Zacatillo (US$2). Boats leave La Unión just once a day, usually between 10am and 10:30am, and don't return until 5am the following day (which makes day trips impossible unless you hire a boat). The odd schedule is due to the fact that the passenger boats primarily serve island residents, who take the early boat into town to shop and conduct other business, and catch the mid-morning boat back home. An all-day private charter to Meanguera will cost around US$60 for the roundtrip. It is a much shorter trip from Las Playitas, but boat operators there are wise to the prices in town and charge about the same, especially for foreigners.

There are very infrequent services from La Unión to Coyolitos, Honduras, some direct, some stopping in Isla Meanguera. Prices vary widely – we were quoted between US$10 and US$60 – and you may have to wait days or weeks before a boat actually goes. **Hotel El Mirador** (☎ 2648 0072) on Isla Meanguera (p420) sometimes arranges onward transportation if enough guests and locals want it – call to see if any trips are planned. Otherwise consider going by land via El Amatillo – it's not too thrilling, but neither is hanging out in La Unión. In theory, it's is also possible to take a boat all the way to Potosí, Nicaragua, but transport is even less frequent and non-Central Americans may have visa complications trying to enter Nicaragua this way.

At the pier, a navy post – really just a sailor with a clipboard behind a desk – oversees all boat traffic; ask there for the day's departures, including the name of the boat and the time it will leave. Officers at the **Capitanía del Puerto** (☎ 2406 0348; 7a Calle Ote at 1a Av Nte; ⊗ 24hr) can also answer most questions.

TAXI

If you need a taxi, you'll find plenty lined up in front of the Hotel Portabello on 1a Calle Pte at 4a Av Norte.

BEACHES NEAR LA UNIÓN

There's a string of popular beaches on the ocean side of a small finger of land southwest of La Unión, and around the corner from Volcán de Conchagua. They are so-so by most traveling beachgoers' standards, but closer than Playa El Cuco or Playa El Espino, and often are empty midweek.

From La Unión, bus 383 passes all the beaches in this area on its way to and from Playa El Tamarindo; the last return bus leaves Playa El Tamarindo at 5pm. You can ask the bus 383 driver to drop you at the coastal village of El Embarcadero/Buenavista, and catch a *lancha* (boat) across the small inlet directly to Playa El Tamarindo (US$0.25) – a pleasant little shortcut.

Playa El Tamarindo

The most popular of the beaches here, Playa El Tamarindo wraps around the tip of the peninsula and includes both ocean and bay-side beaches. The ocean beach forms a long curving indentation; on the bay side, boats shuttle day-trippers back and forth from a pier off the Carr Litoral, and a number of modest *comedores* serve fried fish and other beach grub.

Tropitamarindo (☎ 2649 5082; Playa El Tamarindo; r incl breakfast US$65; ☒ 🆒 Ⓟ) The smallest of the Trópico Inn hotels is also the least impressive, with just six plain rooms and a sad little triangular pool squeezed next to the restaurant. The grounds are pretty enough though – consisting of a grassy palm-shaded area giving way to a windy beach on a long curving bay. The rooms have high-ish ceilings and cable TV, but for the price you expect something a bit more charming. Day use makes more sense – US$10 per person minimum consumption, with easy transport to and from La Unión.

Playa Jagüey

Few people come to this broad gray sandy beach with moderate surf. At the town of Jagüey – there are no signs, so ask the bus driver to let you off – a local road descends from the highway to a grassy parking lot, next to which a small access road leads to the beach. A number of large private homes front the beach, but you are free to lay out a towel anywhere you like. There are no facilities here, save for a few small *bodegas* in town, selling chips and soda.

Playa El Tunas

The beach here is pleasant enough, with the area's best sleeping and eating options. The road into town descends steeply to the water, where restaurants crowd a small patch of sand. To your right (west) the beach is less busy, spreading wide and flat a 100m or so to the mouth of an estuary. At low tide you can wade across the channel to a rustic deserted beach beyond. Caution: cross only at low tide and return well before the tide returns. The current can be extremely strong and the sandy bottom unstable.

Hotel Torola Cabaña Club (☎ 2681 5528; www .hoteltorola.com; r US$78-102; tw US$88; ☒ Ⓟ 🆒) Thirty rooms – some old, others renovated – make up this beachfront hotel 6.5km from town. Rooms are overpriced for what you get – but then again, what's new in this part of the country? Older rooms are smallish, dark and worn, but renovated rooms are a bit better, with nice furnishings and decent views. Neither have hot water. Notwithstanding the drawbacks, the Torola is a popular place to stay because of its well-kept grounds, its direct access to the beach and its decent **restaurant** (mains US$4-15; ☯ breakfast, lunch & dinner). Visitors also often just come for the day to enjoy relaxing in the sun without the steep price tag. Day passes cost US$7 per adult, and US$4 per child.

Hotel Bar y Restaurante Las Tunas (☎ 2681 5515; r/tw US$50/60) Something about the bright yellow paint, treeless lot and manicured look make this feel like a paper house glued to a fake background (and whoever set the price had to be dreaming). But it's real, with a huge restaurant dining area and a perfect two-story box with rooms overlooking a perfect little pool. Rooms are comfortable, though plain – those on the 2nd floor get better light and views of the rocky shore beyond. Staying at a restaurant and bar is always a gamble, especially for light sleepers and on weekends, but things are pretty mellow midweek. It's 200m east of Playa Las Tunas proper.

Rancho Las Tunas (☎ 2526 5542; Playa Las Tunas; mains US$4-10; ⏰ 7am-8pm) Of course, you're going to eat here – out of all the restaurants crammed onto the beach, this one is perched on a rock protruding into the water, with waves crashing all around. The dining area itself is pretty drab – plastic tables and chairs set on raw concrete – though mariachis occasionally enliven the scene. The menu is what you expect: pick a meat – fish, pork, beef, chicken – and a style – fried, grilled, *encebollado* (covered in onion), *entomatado* (covered in tomato) – then add rice and salad, and voila, lunch is served.

Playa El Cuco

As you may have gathered by now, most of El Salvador's beaches are of the broad gray-brown variety – not the stuff of Caribbean fantasies, but attractive in their own right. El Cuco is no exception. At low tide it's an impressive 100m wide – a flat expanse of gray sand fringed by palm trees, stretching for miles. San Migueleños flock to Playa El Cuco on weekends, anxious to escape the sometimes bruising inland heat, but on weekdays it's virtually empty.

INFORMATION

Centro de Internet El Cuco (☎ 2619 9229; Main Plaza, Calle Central; per hr US$1; ⏰ 8am-7pm) The only Internet café in town.

Consultorio Médico (☎ 2610 9877; ⏰ 7:30am-5:30pm Mon-Fri, 7:30am-noon Sat) Next door to the pharmacy.

Farmacia Divina Providencia (☎ 2619 9098; ⏰ 7am-10pm) Opposite the bus stop.

SIGHTS & ACTIVITIES

The **beach** right in front of El Cuco proper is choked with beachside food shacks, hammocks, moored boats and – on weekends – thousands of people. For more wiggle room, walk well down the beach… or drive! Its legal here and very popular.

Eastern El Salvador's best **surfing** is at Playa Las Flores, 3.2km west of Playa El Cuco. While La Libertad and the Costa del Bálsamo remains El Salvador's premier surf destination, more and more surfers are making their way here, where the water is cleaner and the waves even less

crowded – in fact, a few can only be reached by boat. All of the eastern breaks are right-hand; the best are Punta Mango and Las Flores – both truly world-class waves – plus El Toro, La Vaca and Punta Bongo. **Punta Mango Surf Tours** (☎ 2236 0025; www.puntamango.com) has turned this area into a full-fledged surf destination, hosting guests at its private – and super awesome – Las Flores Surf Camp. **Jungle Surf Tours** (☎ 2245 1482, 7886 2367; www.junglesurf tours) operates a more modest surf hostel that can be reserved by individuals and walk-ins. Camping is also possible on the beach.

The best waves are from March to November, when the water's warm, the faces average 4ft to 8ft and waves break cleanly for up to 200m. To get to Playa las Flores, bear right at the entrance to town up a steep, rocky incline, after which the road flattens out and is paved.

SLEEPING & EATING

Hotel Pacific Paradise El Cuco (☎ 2502 2678; www.hotelpacificparadise.com, in Spanish; Calle al Esterón; bungalow Mon-Thu US$86, Fri-Sun US$100, s/d all inclusive per person US$115/81; ✴ P ✴ 🖳) Without a doubt, this is *the* place to stay if you can swing the price tag. You'll find nine spotless and modern bungalows on beautifully manicured beachside grounds; each has two small bedrooms, gleaming tile floors, a cozy living room, a nice front porch and satellite TV. The beach is well tended and free of debris; two pools – both with a mosaic-tile design on the floor – have lounge chairs and umbrellas. There also are beachside and poolside life guards, a rare service in this part of the world. A full breakfast is included in the rate, although guests can choose the all-inclusive plan, which includes three meals with a drink. Day passes are available (adult/child, US$10/8), which can be upgraded to include a welcome ceviche plate, lunch and, on Sunday, a mid-afternoon snack (Monday to Saturday US$20/12, Sunday US$25/15). This place books up fast – reservations are recommended at least two weeks in advance. It's located 4.5km east of town.

Tropiclub Hotel (☎ 7730 8675; cabaña US$39, ste US$65; P ✴ ✴) Two appealing pools, set in a well-tended beachside garden with sky-high palm trees, are the best features of this hotel, along with the expansive beach right in front. The cabañas are somewhat run-down though – *palapa*-roofed, brick-floored and with a bathroom that's separated by a brick wall that doesn't quite reach the ceiling. All have a queen-size bed, a bunk bed and a hammock, so while somewhat cramped, each easily sleeps five people. Suites are nicer – brighter, bigger and more modern – but also less clean. Day passes are available (US$10 per adult, or US$5 per child under six) for use of the facilities, and they can also be used as a credit at the on-site restaurant (mains US$3 to US$15; open breakfast, lunch and dinner). It's located 2.4km east of town.

Hotel Cucolandia (☎ 2619 9190; Main Plaza, Calle Central; r US$70; 🞰 🅿) The only hotel in town that doesn't charge by the hour, Cucolandia instead overcharges by the night. Charmless but clean rooms have tile floors, interior-facing windows and worn linens. A rooftop terrace complete with hammocks and a view of the Pacific is the only nice touch. It's one block from the beach.

Hotel Cucolindo (☎ 2619 9012; r with/without bathroom US$28/18, cabaña US$40) The only decent cheapie around, the Cucolindo offers 11 basic, clean but somewhat worn rooms, most set in cinder-block buildings in a beachside garden. Those located in the main house all share an outdoor bathroom (no fun at 3am) and have to contend with bats who seem to like flying indoors (*really* no fun at 3am). The beach has *palapas* for guest use, and is definitely one of the best tended on this coastline – two huge pluses. It's 1.5km east of town.

Hotel-Restaurante Leones Marinos (☎ 2619 9015; s/d with fan US$30/40, with air-con & TV US$40/50; 🞰 🅰 🅿) A hundred meters from the bus terminal, Leones Marinos is the best and largest of a string of hotel-restaurant-beach club establishments on the coastal road east of town. Rooms are overpriced (no surprise), but relatively clean and modern, which can't be said for other hotels on this strip. Innumerable hammocks swing between palm trees and in a breezy corridor near the beach, and the two pools, including a kids' area, are fairly well maintained. The day pass (US$4) is a good deal.

Rancho Amor del Mar (☎ 7789 6312; grinaco@yahoo.com; Calle al Esterón; per day/week US$150/900; 🞰 🅿) This comfortable and modern five-bedroom house, 5km east of town, is owned and operated by a friendly American family and makes a terrific getaway for a family or group of friends. It's got everything: a pool, Jacuzzi, fully-equipped kitchen, gas BBQ grill, screened living area, two hot-water bathrooms, even a washer and drier. Guests are given a cell phone to use, and airport pickup can be arranged if you're staying a week or more. The owners run a restaurant (Federico's) from their home a few hundred meters down the road – it's usually just open for dinner, but breakfast and lunch can be arranged. The owners have a number of additional projects planned, including a second rental property, camp sites, turtle preservation ideas, and mangrove tours – call or email for the latest info.

GETTING THERE & AROUND

Bus 320 to/from San Miguel (US$0.95, 1½ hours, every 30 minutes from 4:30am to 4:30pm) is El Cuco's lone bus service. It boards at the intersection of the highway and the coastal road, just north of the central plaza. For La Unión take bus 320 to El Delirio turnoff (US$0.70, 55 minutes) and transfer.

East of El Cuco, a dirt road called Calle al Esterón hugs the coast for about 5km, passing several hotels and private homes before bumping into a small community along the namesake *esterón* (large estuary). The road turns north, crosses a brand-new bridge and makes a steep, rocky ascent to the town of Intipucá. Pickups go up and down the hill occasionally – you may have to ask around – while buses shuttle between Intipucá and La Unión (bus 339; US$0.90, 1¼ hours, six to eight departures daily).

There are plans to pave the coastal road from El Cuco all the way to Playa El Espino, which would open up a huge swath of otherwise isolated coastline. For now, you can reach Playa Las Flores, but it's rough and isolated after that.

Playa El Espino

Long considered one of the best beaches in the country, Playa El Espino was for many years one of the most isolated as well, reachable only by a rough two-hour truck ride. But with the road freshly paved and frequent bus service from Usulután, it's become a hot 'new' spot, with decent hotels and a nice beach drawing a large weekend crowd. On weekdays the place is practically empty.

ORIENTATION
The road to Playa El Espino dead-ends at the beach and a small cluster of hotels and day spots. About 50m before the water, a marked dirt road turns right (west) toward the Arcos del Espino area, with a smattering of private homes and at least one good hotel.

SIGHTS & ACTIVITIES
All along the beach are *ranchos* (beach cabañas), which can be rented for the day for around US$5. They typically include hammocks, a table, chairs, and use of the shower and toilet. They also vary considerably in quality, though not much in price. The most appealing here are Las Cabañas de Irene and El Jaguar Cabaña Restaurant.

SLEEPING & EATING
Hotel Arcos del Espino (☎ 2608 0686; El Espino center; r $50; P 🍴 🖭) A two-story pink facade – you can't miss it – marks the entrance to the Arcos del Espino. Once inside, you'll see the long, cinder-block building that houses its 20 rooms. Though charmless, they're comfortable enough – tile floors, two queen-size beds and a hammock. A large, welcoming pool is the centerpiece of the place, and a simple restaurant (mains US$3 to US$10; open breakfast, lunch and dinner) serves *típica* and has an ocean view.

Pacific Dreams Hotel (☎ 2608 0785; tw US$60, ste US$100; P 🍴 🖭) A hella-long water slide leading to a refreshing pool is the most prominent feature of this hotel. The six rooms are less notable – they're a bit cramped but clean. The two suites are worth taking a look at, if only to gawk at the enormous bathrooms, which are almost the size of a regular room. Each sleeps four people, and comes with a Jacuzzi and cable TV. All rooms have access to individual roof-top patios, each with hammocks, a table and chairs, and a view of the Pacific. It's 1.5 blocks from the entrance to town.

Restaurante y Cabañas Mirage (☎ 7885 7014; El Espino center; r US$25; restaurant 🕒 US$8am-8pm Sat & Sun) At the back of a somewhat worn restaurant and day-use area are two large newly built rooms, each with TV, two beds,

a hammock, minifridge and clean modern bathrooms. One of the rooms shares its bathroom with the owners' private room, though she isn't there most of the time. In fact, during the week the place is deserted, save a lone attendant. It's next to Hotel Arcos del Espino.

La Estancia de Don Luís (☎ 2610 5745; Calle Arcos del Espino; r US$50; 🍴 🖭 P) Modern comfortable rooms, beautifully manicured grounds and friendly service make these are the best accommodations in town. About 1.3km west of the road into town, the hotel has four rooms and three more being built, all with firm new beds, tile floors and modern bathrooms. They face a broad grassy lot, with a large, immaculately maintained swimming pool and an open-air restaurant area, featuring a pool table. The hotel is open to day visitors and has a number of *glorietas* (shaded kiosks), which can be rented for US$30 per day, including use of the pool, hammocks, beach and grounds (you can bring you're own food as well).

GETTING THERE & AROUND
Buses 351 and 358/358B from Usulután reach the coast and turn right (west) toward Hotel Arcos de Espino, going as far as (and past) La Estancia de Don Luis; for details see the Usulután section (p432). Buses return on the same route, leaving Playa El Espino at roughly 5:30am, 6am, 7am, 8am, 9am, 11:30am, 12:45pm and 4:30pm. Bus 351 goes directly to Usulután (US$1.25, 1½ hours), while bus 358B goes to Jucuarán – transfer at the Jucuarán turnoff for bus 358 to Usulután.

GOLFO DE FONSECA
The Gulf of Fonseca is a stunning inlet with lush volcanic islands, small fishing villages and black-sand beaches. Sailed first by a European – Gil González de Ávila – in 1522, it soon became a haven for pirates. In fact, they terrorized the villages so often during the 16th and 17th centuries, that the Spanish crown, unable to protect the gulf, forced islanders to leave altogether. The area was not resettled until the 20th century.

Today the 1810 sq km gulf is shared by El Salvador, Honduras and Nicaragua. El Salvador controls five islands plus a few very big rocks. The most important of the lot is **Isla Meanguera**, the southernmost isle,

SIR FRANCIS DRAKE'S BOOTY

According to legend, the master naviga-
tor and privateer Sir Francis Drake made
a stop in the Golfo de Fonseca during his
famous 16th-century circumnavigation of
the world. He had just spent the better half
of a year plundering and pillaging Spanish
towns and ships in South America – it is
said he captured over 26 tons of silver in
that time. As he sailed by the volcanic Isla
Meanguera, he decided to stop. Locals say,
before he went on his way, he left some of
his booty stashed on the island.

which was long the subject of territorial
disputes with Honduras and Nicaragua; in
1992 an international court declared it part
of El Salvador. It's the only island in the gulf
with lodging.

Hotel Paraíso de Meanguera (☎ 2648 0145; r/
tw US$12/15) has decent rooms with a ham-
mock, cable TV and bathroom. Meals are
provided upon request; a typical dish will
include fresh shrimp, lobster or crab for
just US$3.

Hotel El Mirador (☎ 2648 0072) was undergoing major renovation at the time of
research – before it had a dozen small and very
rustic rooms with fans, but it may well turn
into the best hotel on the island, with modern amenities and a restaurant. It's easy
enough to compare the hotels – when you
get to the ferry landing, anyone you ask can
point you in the right direction.

Food can be found at several small eateries in town; fresh seafood rules the menu,
although you can always find pupusas.
Playa Majahual, one of the best beaches on
the island, is a 45-minute walk from the
village or a US$1 boat ride away.

The other islands range from mediocre
to decent. A tiny island called Meanguerita,
or **Isla de los Pájaros**, is the best if you're into
birdwatching. Located directly in front of
Isla Meanguera, it's a nature reserve and
home to hundreds of birds. **Isla Zacatillo**
is the closest island to the mainland. Just
2.4km from La Unión, it has numerous
coves with sandy beaches, but it's no tropical dreamscape. Just south, **Isla Martín Perez**
is uninhabited and great if you're looking
for solitary beaches. Finally, mountainous
Isla Conchagüita offers good opportunities for

hiking. Locals also say that prehistoric rock
carvings can be seen on the way to Playa
Brava, a black-sand beach an hour's walk
from the village.

A boat leaves and returns to La Unión
once a day for Isla Meanguera and Isla
Zacatillo, and returns every morning at
5am – for details, see p415. To get to the
lesser-travelled islands, you can either hire
a private boat from the mainland or negotiate with fishermen on one of the main
islands.

Nicarao Tours (☎ 2274 4556; graguimar@hotmail
.com) offers one- and two-day tours (per
person US$80 to US$120) to Isla Zacatillo
and Isla Martín Pérez, including guide, simple lodging, and bus and boat transportation from San Salvador.

La Ruta del Zapamiche (☎ 2228 1525 in San
Salvador; www.larutadelzapamiche.com) also con-
ducts multi-day trips to the islands, from
a two-day backpacker tour to a nine-day
'eco-cultural' expedition (US$55 to US$400
per person for groups of four). Activities
include staying and fishing with local families, exploring the beaches and protected
areas, and learning about the islands' colonial and pre-Colombian history.

EASTERN EL SALVADOR

El Salvador's eastern interior is the least
explored of all of its regions. Though San
Miguel (p422) is the country's second-
largest city (and an important commercial
and transportation hub), the area has no
hook – no national parks, no surfing spots,
no phenomenal museums. But what eastern El Salvador does have is pockets of
possibilities – a vibrant nightlife in San
Miguel, appealing mountain towns, challenging volcano ascents, and artisan communities whose wares are sold throughout
the country. The east is a historically vital
economic and agricultural zone, with
cotton, sugarcane, cattle and, of course,
coffee.

Most people visit the eastern interior on
their way to or from areas with more obvious tourist appeal, like Morazán and the
Pacific coast. And there's nothing wrong
with that. So as you're flying by on that
painted Blue Bird bus, consider stopping to
smell the flowers in Alegría (p429) or watch

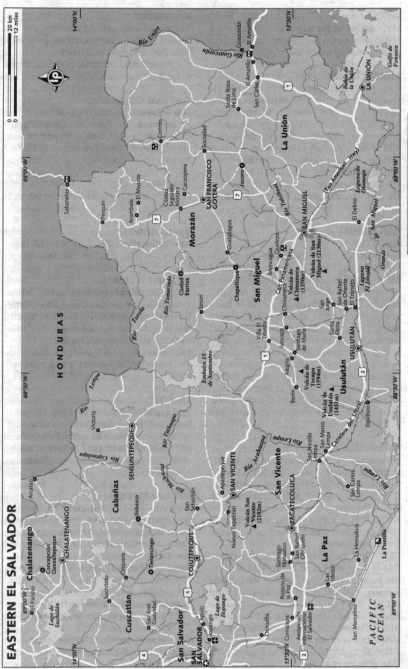

EASTERN EL SALVADOR

artists at work in Ilobasco (p438). Heck, even sitting in the plaza in Sesuntepeque (p440) is a nice way to spend an afternoon after a week of beach-hopping.

Climate & Geography

Eastern El Salvador's most remarkable feature is the string of volcanoes jutting up from the otherwise broad flat valley: Volcán San Vicente (aka Chinchontepec), Volcán de Usulután, Volcán de Tecapa and Volcán de San Miguel (aka Chaparrasique), among many other smaller ones. The climate is similar to San Salvador, with the temperature dropping into the teens in the rainy winter season and pushing 40°C (104°F) in the dry summer season.

SAN MIGUEL

pop 181,819

San Miguel, one of El Salvador's largest cities, is the main hub for the eastern half of the country. Founded in 1530, it still shows signs of Spanish influence in its colonial-style buildings and central plazas. It has a few park areas, too, and its cathedral is in better shape than most, though like other Salvadoran cities it's choking on its own smog. The market spills out of its central area onto many streets, adding some excitement to the active city – active, that is, until the sun sets bright-orange and then it's downright dead. When the city center shuts down, make sure you're where you want to be.

Orientation

The heart of San Miguel is its parque central (central park), Parque David J Guzmán, with the cathedral on its east side. The area east of the park is clogged with traffic by day and is rather dangerous by night – there's no avoiding it, though, as the bus terminal and several hotels are to be found there.

West of the central park, the neighborhoods are quieter and better kept, and include pleasant Parque Gerardo Barrios and Capilla Medalla Milagrosa, a cozy chapel set in a shady park. Av Roosevelt – which is really just the Carr Panamericana – curves along the western and southern edges of town; this is where you'll find most of San Miguel's nightclubs, as well as Metrocentro, a large modern mall.

Information

There are no calling centers in San Miguel – phone booths are as good as it gets. Buy a Ladatel or a Telefónica card to place a call; coin-operated phones are hard to find.

CULTURAL CENTERS

Casa de Cultura (☎ 2660 2968; 1a Calle Ote 206; ☼ 8am-noon & 2-5pm Mon-Fri, 8am-1pm Sat) Organizes cultural events like drama, dance, spoken word and music concerts. It's worth stopping by to check out the bulletin board or to talk to a representative.

EMERGENCY

Police (☎ 2661 2033; 10a Av Sur at 11 Calle Ote; ☼ 24hr)

IMMIGRATION

Immigration office (Migración; ☎ 2660 0957; 15a Calle Ote at 8a Av Sur; ☼ 7:30am-3:30pm Mon-Fri)

INTERNET ACCESS

Centro Cibernético Avanzado (Metrocentro, Av Roosevelt near 2a Av Sur; per hr US$1; ☼ 7:30am-8:30pm)

Ciber Kafe.com (☎ 2661 1213; 6a Calle Ote 101; per hr US$1; ☼ 8am-5pm Mon-Fri, 8am-noon Sat) Offers fast connections and CD burning (US$1 to US$2.50).

Infocentros (☎ 2661 1633; 6a Calle Pte; per hr US$1; ☼ 7am-6pm Mon-Sat, 8am-noon Sun) A quiet and cool Internet café.

LAUNDRY

Lava Rapido (☎ 2661 7543; 6a Av Norte 510; per load US$3.25; ☼ 8am-7pm) This is one of the only self-service laundromats in the country. Wash and dry your clothes, or, for an extra buck, treat yourself to full service. Detergent and softener cost extra, of course. Very friendly service.

MEDICAL SERVICES

Climesam (☎ 2661 1047; 4a Calle Pte 407; ☼ 7am-5pm) Private medical group with 19 doctors, ranging from internal medicine to general surgery to dentistry.

Farmacia Central (☎ 2661 1084; 4a Calle Pte at Av Monseñor Romero; ☼ 7:30am-6pm Mon-Sat)

Farmacia El Progreso (☎ 2661 1098; 4a Calle Ote at 6a Av Norte; ☼ 7:30am-6pm Mon-Fri, 8am-noon Sat) A well-stocked pharmacy in the city center.

Hospital Clínica Laboratorio San Francisco (☎ 2661 1991; 5a Av Norte) Private hospital with 24-hour emergency room.

Hospital de Especialidades Nuestra Señora de la Paz (☎ 2661 0001; Av Roosevelt Sur) Has a 24-hour emergency room.

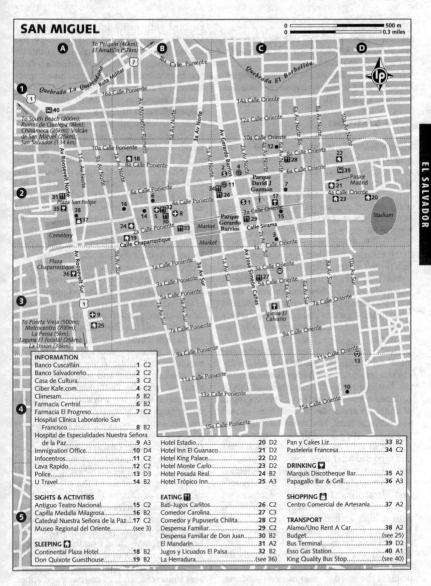

SAN MIGUEL

EL SALVADOR

MONEY

Banco Cuscatlán (☎ 2678 4502; Av Gerardo Barrios at 4a Calle Pte; ⏰ 8:30am-5pm Mon-Fri, 8:30am-noon Sat) This bank exchanges travelers checks, as well as euros, quetzales and, if you're lucky, lempiras. It has one 24-hour ATM.

Banco Salvadoreño (☎ 2661 4880; Av Gerardo Barrios at 6a Calle Pte; ⏰ 8:30am-1pm & 1:45-4pm Mon-Fri, 8:30am-noon Sat) This branch will cash a maximum of US$500 in travelers checks per day, but there's no currency exchange. It has one 24-hour ATM machine.

POST

Post Office (4a Av Sur at 3a Calle Ote; ⏰ 8am-5pm Mon-Fri, 8am-noon Sat)

EL SALVADOR

TRAVEL AGENCIES

Continental Airlines (☎ 2667 8558; www.continental
.com; Metrocentro, Av Roosevelt near 2a Av Sur; ☼ 8am-
5:45pm Mon-Fri, 8am-noon Sat)

U Travel (☎ 2661 6341; www.utravel.com.sv, in Spanish;
4a Calle Pte 500 at Av Monseñor Romero; ☼ 8am-5:30pm
Mon-Fri, 8am-12:30pm Sat)

Sights & Activities

Facing Parque David J Guzmán, **Catedral
Nuestra Señora de la Paz** (☼ 7am-7pm) is San
Miguel's cathedral and dates from the 18th
century. It was heavily damaged during the
civil war.

Just around the corner from the main
plaza sits the **Antiguo Teatro Nacional** (☎ 2660
7480; 2a Calle Ote at 6a Av Sur; admission free; ☼ 8am-
4pm Mon-Fri). Opened in 1909, this neoclassical building was converted into a movie
theater during the silent-film era, and later
functioned as the Telecom building and a
public hospital. At the time of research it
was undergoing a slow renovation – there
were no stage lights and only plastic chairs
– but music concerts and spoken-word performances are held often, and typically free
of charge.

Don't waste your time at the **Museo Regional del Oriente** (☎ 2660 2968; 1a Calle Ote 206;
admission free; ☼ 8am-noon & 2-5pm Mon-Fri, 8am-1pm
Sat). Located inside the Casa de Cultura, it
contains a small collection of photographs
of churches and colonial buildings, as well
as a bit of pottery. Few items have descrip-
tive signs – it's a good thing it's free.

Built in 1904 by an order of French nuns
and modeled after their church in Paris, the
small Gothic-style **Capilla Medalla Milagrosa**
(7a Av Norte at 4a Calle Pte) is one of San Miguel's
best attractions. It's a sublime place, set
in the middle of large tree-filled grounds,
with a high arched ceiling (painted baby
blue) and famously gorgeous stained windows. The altar is populated with flowers
and statues of saints, most prominently the
Virgin Mary, who has a neon crown and
displays the words – also in neon – *María,
concebida sin pecado, rogad por nos que
recurrimos a vos* (Mary, conceived without sin, pray for us who have recourse to
thee). The saying comes from the namesake
'Miraculous Medal,' which was forged in
1830 after Mary twice appeared to a young
French nun named Catherine Laboure. The
medal and innumerable replicas have been

credited with many miracles, and helped
foment (along with other apparitions) the
intense worship of 'la Virgin' so common
today, especially in Latin America where
she nearly overshadows Jesus. Small quiet
masses are held at 5pm on Sundays

Also known as Volcán de San Miguel,
Chaparrastique is the 2130m volcano towering southwest of San Miguel. It's a real
behemoth, and climbing it requires some
advance planning (and should be done only
in the dry season). First, you'll need a police escort, usually arranged through the
Chinameca police station (☎ 2665 0074; fax 2665
1014), whose jurisdiction the volcano falls
into. Two weeks' notice is preferred, but
with some friendly pleading you may be
able to get an escort, usually two to three
officers, within a couple of days. You'll have
to fax a written request with the date and
names of the people in your group. There
is no fee, but definitely bring food for all
(say, tamales for breakfast and pupusas for
lunch) and extra water. The road up begins
near a coffee plantation in the community
of Placitas, off the Carr Panamericana – the
police will guide you. Most people leave
their car with the guards at the plantation
entrance and continue by foot, following
the road up a steep and seemingly endless
series of switchbacks through coffee fields.
Footpaths used by workers cut straight
up through the waxy trees – a shorter but
tougher route. Near the top coffee plants
give way to thick grass and scrub trees and
then a barren moonscape – the last 1km
or so (about 45 minutes) is very steep and
rocky, and you'll be clambering up on all
fours for much of it. At the top are stunning views of eastern El Salvador, its hills,
coastline and patchwork of farms and plantations. The crater is hundreds of meters
deep, with brown, black and white stria-
tions on the walls, and a jumble of boulders
at the bottom. It can be cold and windy on
top, yet intensely bright – bring a sweatshirt
and sunscreen, and, of course, good shoes.
Up and back, budget eight to nine hours.
Theoretically, you can get permission from
the plantation to drive all the way to the
beginning of the last, hardest section. It's
not safe to leave your car there unattended,
but one of the police escorts may be happy
to stay behind. It's worth asking about if
you aren't up for the whole climb.

Festivals & Events

San Miguel's **Fiesta Patronal** in honor of the Virgen de la Paz is held every November and is an occasion for religious processions, as well as the creation of enormous and colorful sawdust carpets. The final celebration – a city-wide party known as **Carnaval** – is held on the last Saturday of November. Starting at sun down and continuing until sun up, parades wind their way through the streets, more than three dozen bands play *cumbia, bachata, reguetón* and *merengue* (you name the Latin music, it's probably played), and people dance the night away. Food stands and liquor booths sell provisions all night. The party typically starts on Av Roosevelt, but the entire city ends up partying before too long.

Sleeping

San Miguel's best traveler hotel is a midrange option right across from the bus terminal, which is so convenient you may overlook the fact that, well, it's right across from the bus terminal. Gritty and eerily abandoned after dark, the bus terminal area is not safe to walk around at night. Hotels on the other side of Parque David J Guzmán are in a better area – and nearer San Miguel's nightlife – but a pain to walk to with your bags; best to spring for one of the taxis that line up by the dozen at the bus terminal. A number of San Miguel's hotels fill up on weekdays, so calling ahead is a good idea.

BUDGET

Hotel Monte Carlo (☎ 2660 2737; 4a Calle Ote 610; s/d US$7/10, r with air-con US$15; ❄ P) You'd think the purple-and-yellow paint job would have been enough. Nope. The 40 rooms at this hotel are swathed and swaddled in gold lamé. Frankly, all that's missing is the disco ball. Nevertheless, this is the best of the cheapies – renovated rooms with tile floors, good beds and cable TV. Top-floor rooms get the best light. Be sure to ask if *Dance Fever* re-runs are still playing.

Hotel Estadio (☎ 2660 2734; 4a Calle Ote 628; s/d US$6/8, r/tw with air-con US$12/14; ❄ P) Behind the bus terminal and next to the stadium, the Estadio offers 21 worn but clean rooms. Most are tiny but all have bathroom and TV. During the day use the back exit of the bus terminal to get here. It's good for a night or two.

Don Quixote Guesthouse (☎ 2661 2718; 2a Calle Pte 507; s/d incl breakfast US$10/15; ❄) The young English-speaking attorney who operates the Don Quixote with his wife is passionate about San Miguel and will happily expound on the city's past or present. The guesthouse is also their home, and it's not uncommon for one or both to share meals with guests. There are just three basic rooms, with large, sloped wood ceilings, cable TV, and red-and-yellow tile floors. Rooms are a bit dark, but homey, and two have air-con. All open onto a narrow, leafy courtyard, and rates include a full Salvadoran or American breakfast (a Spanish restaurant is planned). It's far from the bus terminal, but in a safer area.

MIDRANGE

Hotel King Palace (☎ 2661 1086; www.hotelking palace.com, in Spanish; 6a Calle Ote 609; s US$20-26, deluxe tw US$26-35; ❄ P 🖥 ⌨) Offering five-star service, there's no doubt that this is the best place to stay in town. Recently renovated rooms have modern furnishings, gleaming tile floors and comfortable beds with nice linens. Deluxe rooms are worth the extra few dollars for the renovated bathrooms, large windows, silent mini-split air-con and flat-screen TVs. A well-maintained pool with a small fountain sits in the middle of the hotel; if you're on the 1st floor, the pool is literally steps away. Also, there are two broadband computers for cheap and fast Internet connections, a good restaurant serving three meals a day and a basic rooftop gym in case you want to work out between pupusa runs. Best of all, the hotel is directly across the street from the bus terminal; be sure to make a reservation on weekdays, as the hotel is often booked solid with business travelers.

Hotel Inn El Guanaco (☎ 2261 8026; 8a Av Norte at Pasaje Madrid; s/d US$20/30; ❄ P) A quiet street and hot water is what distinguishes this hotel from the rest in the city center. Rooms are spacious, bathrooms are clean and the common room is welcoming. The onsite restaurant serves up tasty Salvadoran meals, too. The only problem with this hotel is having to walk past the gun shop down the street to get to it. It's an excellent second choice if the Hotel King Palace is booked.

Hotel Posada Real (☎ 2661 7174; 7a Av Norte at 2a Calle Pte; r/tw/tr US$22/26/38; ❄ P) This large

EL SALVADOR

two-story pink hotel is west of the city center, a long walk from the bus terminal, but in a much nicer area once you get there. Downstairs rooms are musty and windowless; upstairs rooms 9 to 11 and 14 to 16 have large windows and views onto the street. All have bathrooms, good beds, white tile floors and cable TV, and there's a wraparound patio on the 2nd floor. It's clean, if not spotless, and offers good value.

Continental Plaza Hotel (☎ 2661 5077; 8a Calle Pte 512; s/d/tw/tr incl breakfast US$25/30/40/45; ❌ ⌘ ℗ ▯) Popular with business travelers, it can be hard to get a room during the week, especially Wednesday through Friday, at this newer hotel west of the city center. And no wonder – the rooms are spotless and modern, all with good beds, cable TV, and colorful curtains and bedspreads; a full Salvadoran breakfast is included. Rooms 209 to 212 have the best light; one deluxe room (US$35) has more space and a four-poster bed. Internet access is available in the reception area. It's comparable to the King Palace – it depends on whether you want to be near the bus terminal.

Hotel Trópico Inn (☎ 2661 1399, 2661 1800; Av Roosevelt Sur 303; s/d incl breakfast US$47/57; ❌ ⌘ ℗ ▯ ❌) This large modern hotel is a long way from the city center and even further from the bus terminal, but right in the thick of San Miguel's nightlife and convenient to the highway if you have a car. Rooms are clean and comfortable, though rather frenetic in their décor, and each has cable TV and telephone. The hotel has a large garden and pool area, with plenty of chairs and shade for lounging.

Eating

A number of restaurants have *comida a la vista* (meal-served buffet) for breakfast and lunch; show up early when the trays are full and the food is fresh.

Comedor y Pupusería Chilita (☎ 2661 1176; 8a Calle Ote 802; mains US$2-4; ❌ breakfast, lunch & dinner Mon-Sat) One of the most popular restaurants in San Miguel, this open-air place offers a good variety of meals – from a steamed vegetable and beet salad to a hefty grilled steak dish. Repeat diners are the main clientele, but everyone leaves full and happy. After 4pm, steaming pupusas are served up from the side entrance.

El Mandarín (☎ 2669 6969; Av Roosevelt Norte 407; mains US$4-9.50; ❌ 10am-9pm) Laminated tables with conference-room chairs are arranged in straight lines, four deep, at this popular Chinese hotel-restaurant. The dining room is a bit worn, but clean, and maintained in arctic conditions by industrial-strength air-con. Like so many Chinese restaurants in Latin America, service is lightning quick, if not exactly warm, and the portions enormous. Two can share a plate of shrimp chow mien, a side of wontons and two beers for under twelve dollars.

La Herradura (☎ 2660 4783; Plaza Chaparristique, Av Roosevelt Sur; mains US$10-20; ❌ 11am-10:30pm) Specializing in high-quality imported meat and seafood, this is a favorite of wealthy San Migueleños and considered by many to be the best restaurant in town. The rib eye, surf and turf, and *parrillada* are classics; the *punta jalapeña* is a spicy alternative, served with chorizo, potatos and veggies. Service is excellent. It's located off-street in a small commercial center.

Pan y Cakes Liz (2a Calle Pte; dishes US$1-3) Not much to look at, but an oasis of friendly service in the hectic streets just west of the market. Fill your tray with good *comida a la vista*, including eggs, tamales, plantains, beans and coffee – as with most buffet-style places, it's best to come during (or slightly before) the morning and noon rush, when the food is freshest.

Comedor Carolina (Av José Simeón Cañas; mains US$2-4; ❌ breakfast & lunch) A popular – and packed – lunchtime favorite, Carolina's serves fresh *comida a la vista*. Salvadoran dishes change daily but you can always be assured of a vegetable, chicken and meat dish. Arrive early for the best selection of food and a seat under a fan.

Bati-jugos Carlitos (☎ 2661 0606; 1a Av Norte; mains US$1-5; ❌ breakfast & lunch Mon-Sat) Crowded and friendly, this tiny restaurant is known for its huge variety of *batidos* (shakes) and *jugos* (juices) – 45 in all. In addition to being a great place to get a drink, it's also good for tasty and cheap sandwiches, burgers and chicken plates. Two thumbs up.

Jugos y Licuados El Paisa (4a Calle Pte; ❌ 7:30am-5pm Mon-Sat) A great juice and *licuado* (fresh fruit drink blended with milk or water) shop. In case you don't know the name of your favorite fruit, there are painted wooden examples mounted on the wall over the counter.

Pastelería Francesa (☎ 2661 8054; 1a Av Norte; pastries US$1-2; ⏲ 7am-6pm Mon-Sat, 7am-noon Sun) With nonstop air-con, booths galore and a steady stream of fresh pastries, this bakery is great place for a mid-afternoon sugar fix.

La Pema (☎ 2667 6055; mains US$5-12; ⏲ 10:30am-4:30pm) This San Miguel institution is famous for its *mariscada* – creamy seafood soup, served with a mallet to crack shellfish and two thick cheese tortillas. It's not cheap and it's a trek to get there – 5km along the road to Playa El Cuco – but it's worth the effort and expense.

For self-caterers, **Despensa Familiar** (Av José Simeón Cañas near 2a Calle Ote; ⏲ 7am-6pm Mon-Sat, 7am-5pm Sun) and **Despensa de Don Juan** (5a Av Nte; ⏲ 8am-8pm) are large central supermarkets where you can stock up on veggies, fruit or sandwich fixin's.

Drinking & Entertainment
NIGHTCLUBS
San Miguel has a half-dozen clubs on Av Roosevelt, most between Metrocentro and *el triángulo*, the triangle intersection of Av Roosevelt and the highway. The intersection used to be ground zero of San Miguel's nightlife, and a few old standbys (and at least one new club under construction when we passed through) keep the area alive, but its reputation for petty crime and prostitution was one reason the party moved elsewhere. The drawback is that you can no longer safely or conveniently walk from one club to the next – with a few exceptions, you need to take a taxi (US$2). Always ask the bartender to call a taxi for you – this is a common request – and remember that legitimate taxis have license plates starting with an 'A.' A number of robberies have been committed by men posing as taxi drivers outside nightspots. Clubs are liveliest Friday and Saturday nights, getting busy by 9pm to 10pm; all close around 2am.

Papagallo Bar & Grill (☎ 2661 0400; Plaza Chaparrastique, Av Roosevelt Sur; cover US$5) it attracts a slightly older and wealthier crowd than the other clubs, but by no means is this place dull. A large hardwood floor and strong air-con make for fun dancing, and there's an outdoor patio area if you need a breather. Live concerts are held occasionally.

South Beach (Carr Panamericana; cover US$5) One of the newer clubs located just north of the triangle (on the highway), South Beach plays a mix of salsa, *reguetón* and techno, and cultivates a somewhat wilder reputation by hosting wet T-shirt contests and other events. It has one large dance floor, a balcony level and air-con.

Marquís Discotheque Bar (☎ 2669 8931; Av Roosevelt Norte 405; cover US$4) A gay-friendly (but not gay-exclusive) bar and disco at the back of Plaza San Felipe, a small commercial center. The light is very dim and there's not much seating, but the music – a mix of techno and hip-hop – should keep you on your feet. Drinks are cheaper here than elsewhere.

Puerta Vieja (☎ 2660 0263; Av Roosevelt Sur 802) Most people come here to have a few drinks before heading somewhere for dancing, preferably somewhere with air-con. There is a small dance floor here, though, and all sorts of music finds its way to the turntable.

CINEMAS
Cinemark (☎ 2667 1364; Metrocentro, Av Roosevelt near 2a Av Sur) Three screens show Hollywood fare. Tickets US$2.50 before 12:30pm, US$1.75 on Wednesday and US$3.50 all other times.

Shopping
San Miguel's **market** (⏲ 6am-6pm), west and southwest of Parque Gerardo Barrios, makes for fascinating exploration; it's a labyrinthine journey through Salvadoran small commerce. Several square blocks of indoor and outdoor stands are connected by long, sometimes winding corridors, the sections distinguished by what is predominantly sold there. Wandering through you will see shoes, machetes, pots and pans, bootleg CDs, electronics, hardware goods, soccer shirts, rough-hewn wood tables, hammocks, a small amount of *artesanía*, fruit, vegetables, whole plucked chickens and slabs of meat hanging from hooks. In the food section, smoke hangs low in the air and grease-spattered stands, packed with diners during meal hours, are attended by women in aprons cooking up pupusas, *panes de pollo* (kaiser rolls stuffed with chicken), tripe soup, roast chicken, grilled beef and more.

At **Centro Comercial de Artesanía** (☎ 2669 7577; Av Roosevelt Norte at 4a Calle Pte; ⏰ 8am-5pm Mon-Sat), one stand – just one! – sells beautiful indigo shirts, hemp-paper products and handmade ceramics. The rest sell tourist kitsch, most with 'El Salvador' emblazoned across them, plus perennial favorites, like the toilet-paper holder with a dry corncob mounted behind a piece of glass and the words 'In case of emergency, break glass' written next to a small hammer on a string. Wow.

Getting There & Around

BUS

Local buses 90-B and 13 go to and from Parque David J Guzmán and the Metrocentro mall. Buses 88 and R3 go west from the bus terminal and Parque Guzmán to Av Roosevelt and the hospital.

San Miguel's **bus terminal** (☎ 2660 2722; 6a Calle Ote) used to be shiny and new, and the best in the country. A few years later it's gotten a bit drab, and the area's never been too nice. It's still better than most, with clearly marked bus lanes, several restaurants and shops, including a pharmacy, an ATM and decent public bathrooms. Buses from San Miguel travel to the following destinations:

Cacaopera Bus 337; US$1.05, 2½ hours, 11am and 12:10pm

Corinto Bus 327; US$1.80, two hours, every 35 minutes from 5am to 5pm

El Amatillo (Honduran border) Bus 330; US$1.75, 1½ hours, every 10 minutes from 3:50am to 6pm

El Cuco Bus 320; US$0.95, 1½ hours, every 30 minutes from 5:30am to 4pm

El Tamarindo Bus 385; US$1.25, 1½ hours; hourly from 5am to 5pm

La Unión Bus 324; US$0.95, 1¼ hours, every 10 minutes from 4:30am to 6pm

Marcala (Honduras) Bus 426; US$3.50, 5½ hours, 4:40am and 11:40am

Perquín Bus 332; US$1.50, three hours, 9:50am, 10:20am, 11:30am, 12:40pm, 1:40pm and 3:20pm; or take any San Francisco Gotera bus and transfer to a pickup

Puerto El Triunfo Bus 377; US$1.50,two hours, hourly from 5:20am to 5pm

San Salvador Bus 301; *ordinario* US$2.10, three hours, every 15 minutes from 3am to 4:30pm; *especial* (no aircon) US$3, two hours, 9am, 10am, 1pm and 2:30pm; *super* (air-con and video) US$4, two hours, 5am, 6am, 7am, 8am, 2pm and 3pm

Usulután Bus 373; US$1, 1½ hours, every 10 minutes from 4:10am to 6:20pm

For international bus travel to Honduras, Nicaragua and Costa Rica, see the boxed text, below.

CROSSING THE BORDER

Arrive early for the following bus trips – all international buses originate in San Salvador and the times listed are approximately when the bus will pass San Miguel. Prices indicated are for one-way travel.

Getting to Tegucigalpa, Honduras

For Tegucigalpa (US$27, five hours), 1st-class buses operated by **King Quality** (☎ in San Salvador 2271 1361) stop at the **Esso gas station** (☎ 2669 5687; Av Roosevelt at Ruta Militar; ⏰ 24hr) at about 8am and 3:30pm daily. Buy tickets at the Esso gas station in person at least a day in advance.

Otherwise, take bus 330 to the border at El Amatillo, where a bridge crosses a pretty river into Honduras. From there, buses leave amid a jam of 18-wheeler trucks, headed to Choluteca (US$1.50, 2¼ hours) and to Tegucigalpa (US$2, 3½ hours); the last bus to both leaves at 5:30pm. Entering El Salvador, the last bus from El Amatillo to San Miguel is at 6:30pm.

Getting to Managua, Nicaragua

King Quality also operates buses to Managua, Nicaragua (US$27, nine hours), stopping at the same Esso gas station at 7:30am and 1:30pm. Alternatively, at El Amatillo there are microbuses that zip across the southern tip of Honduras to the Nicaraguan border town of Guasaule (US$4, two hours), where you can connect to buses to León and Managua.

Getting to San José, Costa Rica

King Quality buses to San José (US$47, 19 hours) stop at the Esso gas station at 5:30am.

CAR

Alamo/Uno Rent A Car (☎ 26796 0188; Av Roosevelt Norte; ☻ 8am-6pm Mon-Fri, 8am-4pm Sat) Very friendly, professional service.

Budget (☎ 2682 1062; Av Roosevelt Sur 303; ☻ 8am-6pm Mon-Fri, 8am-4pm Sat) Located at Hotel Trópico Inn.

AROUND SAN MIGUEL
Quelepa

Located 8km north of San Miguel are the **Ruínas de Quelepa**, a ceremonial center that was inhabited by the Lencas between the 2nd and 7th centuries AD. An archaeological team from Tulane University excavated the site between 1949 and 1959 and found objects like fine clay pottery, figurines with wheels, and tools, which revealed advanced artistic activities, as well as trading with indigenous groups in Mexico, Honduras and Belize. Unfortunately, the ruins were buried again to prevent looting. Today the structures – more than 40 ceremonial platforms with multilayered terraces, access ramps and short stacks of stairs – look like small grassy mounds in the middle of a vast cornfield.

There's really not much to see or appreciate if you're not an archaeology buff, though you may enjoy tromping out there – over the river and through the corn, so to speak. Before going, stop by Quelepa's **Casa de la Cultura** (☎ 2682 0144; ☻ 8am-noon & 2-5pm Mon-Fri, 8am-1pm Sat) to see a handful of artifacts, including clay urns, stone metates and figurines of women and monkeys, some with paint still showing. Ask about a guide to the ruins (it's easy to miss); either a Casa employee or a police officer is usually available to show you the way. From San Miguel's cathedral, take bus 90G to Moncagua (US$0.35, 30 minutes, every 30 minutes from 6:30am to 5pm, last bus back 5pm) and ask to be let out at the village of Quelepa. There's no bus service on Sunday.

Laguna El Jocotál

Laguna El Jocotál, at Carr del Litoral Km 132, is one of the largest bird sanctuaries in the country, hosting 214 species of birds, 101 of which are migratory. As you stumble over women washing clothing, and random piles of trash, you'll find that the best bird-watching is from inside a boat. Trips are run by any local with a canoe or row boat; a tour typically costs US$5 per person. To arrange a ride, simply head to the lagoon. Paddlers will find you. October to March is the best time of year to visit since the migratory birds are in the country. To get there, take bus 373 from San Miguel to Usulután and ask the driver to let you off; if you're driving, look for the big red-and-white 'Centro Escolar Borbollón' sign at Km 132 on the highway just west of the entrance.

ALEGRÍA
elevation 1593m

High in the mountains, Alegría is an unsung gem and one of El Salvador's most picturesque towns. Once the heart of El Salvador's coffee country – a distinction that now belongs to Santa Ana – Alegría has transformed itself into the country's flower-growing capital and is a very fine place to visit. Around 230 flower *viveros* (nurseries) fill porches, fields and backyards throughout town, and you are welcome to visit most of them.

Orientation

Alegría is organized around its parque central (central park), which is flanked by 1a Av Norte (west side) and Av Camillo Campos (east side), 3a Calle Pte (south side) and 1a Calle Pte (north side). The church is on the southwest corner. Most of the listings in this section are on the west and north side of the park and continue down the steep slope north.

Information

Alegría has no bank or ATM.

Ciber Café Casa Vieja (☎ 2628 1168; 1a Av Norte at Calle Alberto Masferrer; per hr US$0.80; ☻ 10am-7pm) An Internet café that actually serves coffee, located on the parque central.

Police (☎ 2668 1016; 4a Av Sur btwn 1a & 3a Calles Pte; ☻ 24hr)

Tourist Office (☎ 2628 1087; 1a Av Norte at 1a Calle Pte; ☻ 8am-noon & 1-4pm) A kiosk on the parque central offering basic information about sights, nurseries and accommodations. Guided tours of the area can be arranged with advanced notice. A small display of colonial era and pre-Colombian artifacts are also on-site.

Unidad de Salud (☎ 2628 1100; ☻ 7:30am-4pm Mon-Fri, 7:30am-noon Sat)

Sights & Activities

Alegría is famous for its flowers and you can visit a number of *viveros* around town – there's no fee, just knock. You'll see plenty just walking around, though the tourist office may have a map to give you. The city's **vivero municipal** is near the exit to Berlín.

Two kilometres east of town, **Laguna de Alegría** (admission US$0.25; 8am-4pm) is an attractive crater lake on Volcán de Tecapa. Its waters are said to be medicinal, but the overpowering smell of sulphur might just stop you from confirming it. It's an easy walk from town.

Don't miss the beautiful view from the **Mirador de los Cien Grados** – a vista point at the top of 100 steps found on the western edge of town. Take Calle Manuel Enrique Araujo toward Berlín and look for the steps before the road splits.

If you're a fan of philosopher Alberto Masferrer, you can walk by the **house** (Calle Alberto Masferrer at 1a Av Sur) he lived in, a bright orange and green building one block east of the parque central. It is not open for public viewing, but there are two small plaques outside commemorating him.

Sleeping & Eating

The hotels and eateries are pleasant and easy to find in this tiny town. Many are on the parque central or just a stone's throw away from it.

Casa de Huéspedes La Palma (2628 1012; 1a Av Norte near Calle Alberto Masferrer; dm US$10) Opening onto a pleasant garden, this guest house offers simple, clean and very pink dorm rooms with twin-size beds. Guests have kitchen privileges, and hot-water bathrooms are a welcome surprise.

Restaurante y Vivero Cartagena (2628 1131; 4a Calle Pte near 1a Av Norte; mains US$4-10; breakfast, lunch & dinner) What started out as a small nursery has now become a haven for weekend warriors. And it's all about the view; one of the best in the country, in fact. From here, you'll see the green valley below cut by the Río Lempa and extending north, north, north until it hits the gray mountains. It's simply breathtaking. Cartagena has an open-air restaurant serving delicious *típico* meals – try the specialty, *gallo en chicha* (rooster in a sweet marinade prepared with olives, plums and carrots). It also has a handful of modern stand-alone cabins (US$45 to US$50) that sleep four people, and feature big porches, good beds and clean bathrooms; and an enormous nursery that is spread out throughout the lush grounds. A great stop, even if it's just for a drink. To get here, look for the signs around the parque central and walk north.

Merendero Mi Puelito (2628 1038; dishes US$3.75-5; 7am-7pm) The oldest restaurant in town is still one of the best. On the south side of the park, this friendly family-run spot has a loyal clientele. The dining area is cool and quiet, virtually buried in a thick garden. Steaks are the house specialty, and they're delicious. The owner, Margarita Marroquín, often gives foreign visitors small gifts, like keychains with 'El Salvador' written on them, as mementos.

Restaurante La Fonda de Alegría (2628 1010; end of Av Golgata; mains US$3.25-11; 9am-9pm) The restaurant name is written in Llort-like wooden letters over a stucco arch. A leafy, open-air dining area has several nooks and crannies with just a few tables each and separated by tall plants. The menu is mostly quality *típica*, from pupusas to *mariscada*, a traditional cream soup made of crab, lobster, fish and shrimp. There's full bar service from noon to 9pm, and a trio of musicians often plays on weekend afternoons. It's a block from the entrance to the Cartagena, and opposite El Calvario church and a tiny park of the same name.

Restaurante El Portal (parque central; mains US$3-10; 9am-9pm) It feels a little like a hunting lodge inside this park-front restaurant, with wood tables and benches, wood A-frame roof, and wood logs burning in the kitchen. Might as well order the *conejo asado* (grilled rabbit) and be done with it. Service is friendly.

Ciber Café Casa Vieja (2628 1168; 1a Av Norte at Calle Alberto Masferrer; 10am-7pm) It's hard to miss this eatery – a red-roofed building on the parque central with rows and rows of pinewood tables and a breezy porch. Internet service is offered, along with good coffee (US$0.40) and an array of freshly baked pastries (US$1). It's a great spot to kick back for a while.

Getting There & Around

Bus 348 goes southwest to Berlín (US$0.40, 15 minutes, every 30 to 60 minutes from 7:30am to 6pm) and southeast to Santiago de María (US$0.40, 10 minutes, every 45 to 60 minutes from 5:40am to 6pm). From Santiago de María, bus 362 goes south to the Carr Litoral and Usulután (US$0.60,

45 minutes, every 10 minutes from 4:15am to 4:45pm) or north to Villa El Triunfo (US$0.30, 15 minutes, every 10 minutes from 4:30am to 5pm) along the Carr Panamericana; microbuses also shuttle between Santiago de María and Villa El Triunfo. The same buses also make the return route – from either main highway, catch a bus to Santiago de María and follow the signs a few blocks to the stop for bus 348 to Alegría (last bus at 5:40pm). There is one direct bus to San Salvador daily at 5am (US$2, 2½ hours); otherwise catch bus 301 on the Carr Panamericana.

BERLÍN
pop 11,000

Watching the steady increase of visitors to Alegría, a tourism development group called **Adestur** (☎ 2663 2058; Calle Dr Antonio Guandique), is hoping to entice visitors just 10 minutes further to Berlín. Unfortunately, this town has only a few things going for it: the hotel, the museum and its history. Once a coffee-producing community, it became a military hub during the war before being sacked by the guerrillas (you can still see the bullet holes in some walls around town). Although it might make a decent pit stop, Berlín still has a long way to go. Cleaning up the parque central would help.

Orientation & Information

Berlín's church is on the east side of the parque central, the police station is on the south side and the hotel is just a few blocks northeast.

Farmacia Modelo (☎ 2663 2190; Av José Simeon Caña; ☻ 8am-noon & 2-6pm) A half-block south (uphill) from the parque central.

Police (☎ 2663 2220; ☻ 24hr) Faces the parque central.

Scotiabank (1a Calle Pte; ☻ 8am-4pm Mon-Fri, 8am-noon Sat) On the parque central.

Western Union/Internet Café (☎ 2663 3262; per hr US$1; ☻ 8am-9pm Mon-Sat, 9am-9pm Sun) A half-block west of the parque central.

Sights & Activities

Adestur is offering **hiking** as its main attraction to draw tourists to Berlín. The surrounding hillsides offer fine views – La Cruz is an hour's walk from town and is the traditional pilgrimage site on **Día de la Cruz** (Day of the Cross; May 3), and the

45-minute hike to Los Pinos offers great views of Bahía de Jiquilisco.

Steam from superheated underground water is used to generate electricity at **La Geo Berlín** (☎ 2211 6850; www.lageo.com.sv, in Spanish; Km 107 Hwy btwn Mercedes Umaña & Berlín; ☻ by appointment only), the huge geothermal plant outside of town, providing power – and jobs – for much of the region and beyond. Free tours of the plant (around three hours; Spanish only) explain the process from beginning to end. Arrange tours at least a day in advance, preferably more. There's a similar plant in Ahuachapán (p372).

An informal **museum of Berlín** in the home of a local family offers a modest but fascinating look at the town's past. Most of the pieces are from around the turn of the 20th century, including photographs, antique typewriters and household items, even original birth certificates, handwritten on lined paper and dated 1886. A few excellent Lenca artifacts, plus photos and items from the civil war, round out the collection. The house itself is an artifact, carved out of the former worker's quarters of a Berlín coffee plantation. To arrange a visit, call **Julio Rivas** (☎ 2663 2020) or ask about 'la casa de Ruth Quinta Zelaya' at city hall, which is around the corner from the police station and – get this – adjacent to a prison for female members of Mara 18. Hard to miss.

Sleeping & Eating

La Casa Mia Hostal (☎ 2663 2027; 3a Calle Ote 8; r without bathroom per person US$12; **P**) A diamond in the rough, La Casa Mia is one of the few redeeming places in Berlín. A colonial-style house turned hotel, it is a labyrinth of rooms – some filled with beautiful antiques and original Portuguese tile floors, others renovated, modern rooms with little charm but comfortable nonetheless. Check out the children's bedroom upstairs – at about 150cm (5ft), it's reminiscent of that 'half-floor' in the film *Being John Malkovich*. A welcoming courtyard with lots of plants and chairs is just one place to relax; two indoor common rooms, with couches, tables, cable TV, even a ping-pong table, also make a great place to kick back. Bathrooms need some attention – they're showing some wear – but they're clean and have hot water. Meals are lovingly prepared upon request. Tours of the area available – ask for details.

La Cocina de Doña Silvia (☎ 2663 2267; 2a Calle; mains US$1.25-5; ◷ 6:30am-8:30pm) Around the corner from the *alcaldía* (mayor's office), and popular with officials there, Doña Silvia serves fresh *comida a la vista* from steam trays, while diners crowd around laminated tables with wood benches, beneath pictures and promotional posters of El Salvador. Doña Silvia's husband, Aurelio Bonilla, is one of the organizers of Adestur, Berlín's fledging tourist development and guiding service.

Getting There & Around

An informal stop a half-block east of the parque central is the turn-around point for bus 348, which goes from Berlín to Alegría (US$0.40, 20 minutes) and Santiago de María (US$0.70, 35 minutes). Some continue to Usulután (US$1.10, 1¼ hours); those that don't can drop you at the right stop. The first bus leaves Berlín at 5:50am, the last at 6pm, departing every 45 to 60 minutes. To San Miguel or San Salvador, catch a bus from Santiago de María down the hill to Villa El Triunfo, on the Carr Panamericana, and transfer there.

USULUTÁN

pop 45,854

Situated at the foot of Volcán de Usulután (1451m), this busy departmental capital is a pleasant enough stop on your way across the country. It has many of the modern conveniences you expect – Internet access, pharmacies, a market – plus a great parque central that's perfect for people-watching. It also makes a good overnight stop if you don't make the last boat to the villages in Bahía de Jiquilisco or if the sun will set by the time you get to Playa El Espino.

Orientation & Information

Arriving from San Salvador or anywhere to the west, get off at *centro* (center) to avoid the walk back. The hotels are northeast of there.

Banco Cuscatlán (☎ 2678 4582; 2a Calle Ote near Av Dr Guandiquil; ◷ 8:30-5pm Mon-Fri, 8:30am-noon Sat) One of several banks on the parque central. Cashes travelers checks and has one indoor 24-hour ATM.

Cyber Planet (4a Calle Ote btwn 2a & 4a Avs Norte; per hr US$0.50; ◷ 8:30am-6pm Mon-Sat, 8:30am-noon Sun) Cheap, fast Internet connections. CD burning (US$2), too.

Farmacia Central (☎ 2662 1032; 4a Calle Ote near 4a Av Norte; ◷ 7am-6:30pm Mon-Sat, 7am-6pm Sun) One well-stocked pharmacy in a string of many.

Hospital Metropol (☎ 2624 6733; 4a Calle Ote near 2a Av Norte; ◷ 24hr)

Post Office (2a Av Sur at Calle Dr Grimaldi; ◷ 8-11:45am & 2-5pm Mon-Fri, 8am-noon Sat)

Sleeping & Eating

Hotel Florida (☎ 2662 0540; 4a Calle Ote btwn 6a & 8a Avs Norte; s/d US$8.50/14, with cable TV US$11.50/17, r with cable TV & air-con US$24; ❄ Ⓟ) Simple but very clean rooms distributed between two seemingly endless buildings. The best rooms are those on the upper floors, facing the parking lot – they're quiet, get decent sunlight and have individual hammocks for relaxing right outside your door. All meals are available from the small kitchen/*comedor*.

Tortas Lito's (☎ 2624 4926; Calle Dr Federico Penado at 1a Av Norte; mains US$2-3; ◷ 10am-8pm) A purple dining room with long tables, a large-screen TV and about a dozen overhead fans set the scene for this popular Mexican restaurant. You can order such classics as *sopes*, tacos, enchiladas and, of course, tortas. Once you place your order, just sit back and relax; meals can take awhile. Delivery is available. It's located one block west of the parque central.

Pastelería Trigo Puro (☎ 2662 0630; Calle Dr Federico Penado 8; mains US$2-3; ◷ 8am-5:30pm Mon-Sat) A sunny bakery selling a good variety of freshly made baked goods and Salvadoran fare, served cafeteria-style. Breakfast is especially hearty. It's next to Tortas Lito's and a half-block west of the parque central.

Mercado de Usulután (4a Av Norte btwn 2a & 4a Calle Ote; mains US$1-2.50; ◷ 6am-3pm) Picture a big, gray warehouse. Add rows and rows of picnic tables. Now throw in dozens of women making fresh Salvadoran meals on portable gas stoves – grilled chicken, fried eggs, *casamiento* (rice and beans mixed together), pork stew, beans. Add a steady stream of customers and a few dogs and you're in the *mercado*. If your stomach is up for it, it's definitely a great way to start your day.

Getting There & Around

Usulután's main bus terminal is 1.5km east of the parque central. To get there costs US$2 in a taxi. Buses for Puerto El Triunfo and Playa El Espino leave from separate lots, also on the highway but closer to town. San Miguel buses use a terminal west of Usulután proper. Fortunately, almost all buses pass through town on their way out, so you don't have to go to the various terminals to catch them. (Of course, you're more likely to get a seat if you do.) Buses to San Salvador, Puerto El Triunfo and Alegría all take 4a Calle west through town, picking up passengers along the way. The terminal for San Miguel buses is west of town; buses pick up passengers all along 1a Calle Ote, a block south of the parque central, plus in front of the main bus terminal. Buses from Usulután travel to the following destinations:

Alegría US$0.95, one hour; take any Berlín bus, or take any Santiago de María bus and transfer

Berlín Bus 348; US$1.10, 1¼ hours, every one to 1½ hours from 6am to 4pm

La Unión Take any San Miguel bus and transfer

Playa El Cuco Take any San Miguel bus to El Delirio (US$0.70) and transfer to bus 320

Playa El Espino Bus 351/358; US$1.10, 1½ hours, 6:20am, 9:30am, 10:30am, 11:30am, 12:30pm, 1:40pm and 2:40pm; catch from a small lot 100m west of the main bus terminal, or if you take bus 358, transfer to bus 358B at turnoff to Jucurán (one hour)

Puerto El Triunfo Bus 363; US$0.50, one hour, every 10 minutes from 4:25am to 5:30pm; catch on 4a Calle Ote or at small lot east of town, across highway from Despensa de Don Juan supermarket

San Miguel Bus 373; US$0.70, 1½ hours, every 10 minutes from 3:50am to 6pm

San Salvador Bus 302; *directo* US$1.50, 2½ hours, every 10 minutes from 3:20am to 4:30pm; *especial* US$2, 1½ hours, every 30 minutes from 5:10am to 8:50am, plus 11:25am, 1pm and 2:15pm (or take bus 302C; US$2.50, three hours, 12:15pm and 1:45pm; arrives at Terminal del Ote via Santiago de María)

San Vicente Bus 417; US$1.25, 2¼ hours, 8:20am, 10am, 11am, 11:40am, 2:20pm and 4pm

Santiago de María Bus 392C, 35, 348 or 349; US$0.75, 40 minutes

Villa El Triunfo/Carr Panamericana Bus 349; US$0.82, one hour, every 15 minutes from 4:30am to 5:30pm

Zacatecoluca US$0.65, 1½ hours; take any San Vicente or San Salvador bus except bus 302C

ZACATECOLUCA

pop 35,199

Zacatecoluca is a bustling little city that makes a good overnight stop if you can't make it to your destination by sunset. There's little to do here, but the hotel is

good and you can catch up on your emails. Some use it as a jumping-off point for trips to Costa del Sol.

Orientation

The main drag, Av José Matias Delgado, runs north–south, from the Carr Litoral to the parque central and beyond. The church is located on the north side of the parque central with most places listed here, including the bus terminal, found south of it toward the highway.

Information

Computer Center (☎ 2334 2988; 1a Av Norte at 1a Calle Pte; per hr US$0.75; ☑ 8:30am-7pm Mon-Sat, 9am-6pm Sun) Cheap but sluggish Internet access.

Farmacias Económicas (☎ 2334 3999, 2530 2530; Av Villacorte; ☑ 8am-5:30pm Mon-Sat, 8am-1pm Sun)

Hospital de Especialidades La Paz (☎ 2334 4450; 3a Calle Ote near Av José Matías Delgado; ☑ 24hr)

Police (☎ 2334 1690; Av José Matías Delgado btwn 5a & 7a Calle Pte; ☑ 24hr) Located behind the bus terminal.

Post Office (3a Av Sur btwn 1a Calle Pte & Calle Nicola Peña; ☑ 8am-5pm Mon-Fri, 8am-noon Sat)

Scotiabank (☎ 2334 0102; Av Villacorte at Calle General Rafael Osorio; ☑ 8am-4pm Mon-Fri, 8am-noon Sat) Cashes traveler's checks, but does not exchange foreign cash. Has an exterior ATM.

Sights & Activities

The only sight in town is the **Catedral Nuestra Señora de los Pobres**, a renovated colonial-era cathedral dedicated to Saint Lucia. Toward the back and up a small set of stairs, you'll find her image – a glass-enclosed doll standing alongside images of the Virgin Mary and Jesus. All around and inside the case are letters, flowers, candles and mementos all asking or thanking the saints for their help. Be sure to wait until the altar is empty before you ascend the staircase.

About 1½km south of town is the largest *turicentro* (tourist center) in El Salvador, **Ichanmichen** (admission US$1.50; ☑ 8am-6pm). It is a shady place in a tropical forest filled with cedar and conacaste trees that migratory birds seem to like. Twelve clean pools and a restaurant make it an easy place to spend a day.

Sleeping & Eating

Hotel Primavera (☎ 2334 1346; Av Vicente Valicorta 20; r with fan/air-con US$8/15; ❄ Ⓟ ⓪) This kitschy motel features two floors of rooms, each with gleaming tile floors, good beds and clean bathrooms. All have cable TV and access to a huge games room, complete with board games, a ping-pong table, foosball, even a covered pool with a Jacuzzi. Be sure to check out the multi-tiered fountain in the parking lot. Service is friendly.

Pupusería y Comedor Magdy (Av Villacorte at 1a Calle Pte; mains US$1-3; ☺ breakfast & lunch) Don't you get cravings for pupusas in the morning? Although pupusas are considered an afternoon food, this small shop on Zacate's main drag pats 'em up from the wee hours. Eggs, beans and other regular breakfast foods are also available. Service is a bit begrudging; other *pupuserías* (places that sell pupusas) on this street are open at night.

Sorbetería Estrella Polar (☎ 2334 0785; 5a Calle Ote at Av Narciso Monterrey; dishes US$1-3; ☺ 7am-6pm) An unlikely place to find a vegetarian meal, this open-air ice-cream parlor serves up soy-based dishes and sautéed vegetables every weekend between 11:30am and 3pm. Throw in a banana milkshake and you've got yourself a good lunch. Ice cream is served all week.

An **open-air market** (☺ 7am-6pm) is held in and around the parque central daily. Here you'll be able to stock up on fruits, veggies, clothes, and loads and loads of toys. Don't be surprised if vendors touch (or grab) your arm as you walk past their stand – it's customary.

For self-caterers, **Despensa Familiar** (3a Calle Ote at Av José Matías Delgado; ☺ 7am-7pm Mon-Sat, 7am-6pm Sun) is a fully stocked supermarket just south of the parque central.

Getting There & Around

Zacate's bus terminal is on Av Villacorte south of the parque central, directly across from the Hotel Primavera. Most buses pull into the actual terminal area, but some buses at certain hours (especially the San Vicente and Costa del Solo routes) stop on the street behind the terminal, Calle Jose Matías Delgado, only. Ask when you get there where you should be waiting. The San Vicente bus has its own stop on 2a Calle Ote between 5a and 7a Avs Norte; catch Ususulatán buses on the highway (Carr Litoral) south of town. For San Salvador, note that there are three options: bus 133 is the early-morning *especial*; bus 133A is ordinary service via the new

highway; and bus 133B is ordinary service on the old highway, and is the slowest of the three. All cost the same and go to San Salvador's Terminal de Sur (San Marcos). Buses from Zacate travel to the following destinations:

Aeropuerto Internacional Take bus 133A to airport turnoff at Comalapa and transfer to microbus 138

Costa Del Sol/La Puntilla Bus 193; US$1, 1½ hours, every 30 minutes from 4:45am to 4:40pm

San Salvador Bus 133 *especial* US$0.68, 50 minutes, 5am, 5:20am, 5:35am, 5:50am and 6:10am; bus 133A US$0.68, one hour, every 10 minutes from 3:40am to 6:10pm; bus 133B US$0.68,1½ hours, every five minutes from 3:30am to 8pm

San Vicente Bus 177; US$0.60, 45 minutes, every 15 minutes from 5am to 6pm; catch at 2a Calle Ote between 5a and 7a Avs Norte; or bus 193E from Costa del Sol passes Zacate four times daily

San Miguel Take any Usulután bus and transfer to bus 373

Usulután Bus 302; US$0.70, 1½ hours, last bus approximately 5:30pm; catch on the Carr Litoral south of the bus terminal

SAN VICENTE

pop 34,921

At the foot of the twin-peaked Volcán San Vicente in the Jiboa Valley, San Vicente is a small, mellow city worth a short stop. The approach to town is memorable, with the town's landmark clock tower – sort of a small, cartoon version of the Eiffel Tower – nestled amid green hills and agricultural lands. You used to be able to climb the tower for a good view, but it was closed after being damaged in the 2001 earthquakes. In fact, the top looks ready to topple over at any time, with cracks in the support columns and an obvious list. Also notable – and also closed after the 2001 earthquake – is Iglesia El Pilar, a beautiful colonial church. Built in the 1760s, it is one of the oldest in the country. Neither had reopened when we visited, which makes one wonder if their closure is now permanent.

Orientation

For landmarks, remember that the cathedral is on the east side of the parque central and the Hotel Central Park on the west side. Outbound buses stop at the northeast corner of the parque central, while a military base takes up an entire square block southwest of the parque central.

EL SALVADOR

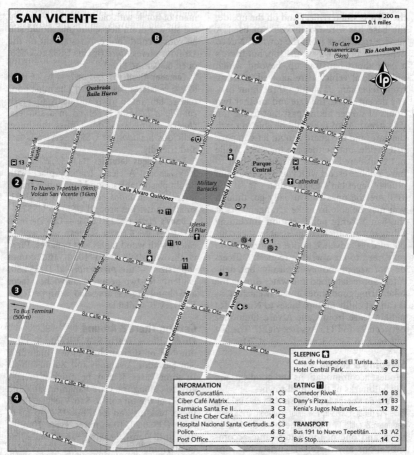

SAN VICENTE

0 ——— 200 m
0 ——— 0.1 miles

Information

Banco Cuscatlán (☎ 2393 5422; 2a Av Sur; ⊗ 8:30am-5pm Mon-Fri, 8:30am-noon Sat) This bank cashes travelers checks, and has one 24-hour ATM machine.

Ciber Café Matrix (☎ 2393 1909; 2a Calle Ote; per hr US$0.75; ⊗ 8am-8pm) Fourteen bathroom-like stalls serve as workstations.

Fast Line Ciber Café (☎ 2393 6726; 2a Calle Ote; per hr US$0.85; ⊗ 9am-9pm) One block west of Ciber Café Matrix.

Farmacia Santa Fe II (☎ 2393 1701; 4a Calle Ote; ⊗ 24hr) Ring the bell for service after 9pm. Delivery is available.

Hospital Nacional Santa Gertrudis (☎ 2393 0261; 2a Av Sur at 4a Calle Ote; ⊗ 24hr) Located next to a strikingly mint-green church.

Police (☎ 2302 7300; 1a Av Norte at 3a Calle Pte) One block west of the parque central; can also help arrange for an officer to accompany you up the volcano.

Post Office (Calle Alvaro Quiñonez near Av JM Cornejo; ⊗ 8am-5pm Mon-Fri, 8am-noon Sat)

Sights & Activities

Also known as Volcán San Vicente, **Chichontepec** (2182m) is the distinctive double-peaked volcano southwest of town. It's makes for a moderately difficult climb, mostly through coffee plantations that stretch much of the way up the mountainside (including one owned by former president Alfredo Cristiani.) At the summit is a small military outpost, several communications antennae, even a helicopter pad, but

EL SALVADOR

the view is still terrific. (And on the upside, the base has a restroom you can use.) A service road leads from the town of Nuevo Tepetitán all the way to the top, but there's a gate about half-way up, beyond which only official vehicles are allowed. Starting from Tepetitán, its about a three-hour hike at a decent clip to the gate and another two hours of slower hiking past that to the top (it's steep). A 4WD should be able to reach the gate, and the guard should let you park just inside, but neither are for sure. While not considered terribly unsafe, it's best to have a police escort with you. Officers from Nuevo Tepetitán's **police station** (☎ /fax 2396 3353) are the ones who usually go, though you may be able to make arrangements at the San Vicente police station (including filling out an official request; at least as couple of days' advance notice required). You may need to fax a written request. Officers do not accept money, typically, but definitely appreciate food and water during the hike. Bring good shoes and a sweatshirt, as it can get chilly on top. Buses to Nuevo Tepetitán leave from Calle Alvaro Quiñonez between 9a and 11a Avs (see right). The last bus back to San Vicente leaves at 7:15pm.

Sleeping & Eating
Modest accommodations and good eats are the hallmarks of this small town.

Casa de Huespedes El Turista (☎ 2393 0323; 4a Calle Pte 15 at 1 Av Sur; r without bathroom US$8, with bathroom & cable TV US$10) The best option in town and one of the better-value accommodations anywhere, El Turista has nine small, tidy rooms surrounding a compact cement courtyard/parking area. Potted plants stand around the sides and laundry hangs breezily from lines strung overhead. Rooms on the 2nd floor get more light. Attached bathrooms are extremely clean, complete with doilies on the toilet seat and tank. (The shared bathroom is another story, however.)

Hotel Central Park (☎ 2393 0383; Av JM Cornejo; r/tw with fan US$12/15, with air-con US$15/25; ✸) Its location on the parque central – with a fine view of the same from a 2nd-floor terrace – is the best feature of this otherwise nondescript, overpriced hotel. Rooms open onto a reasonably pleasant courtyard and passageway, but are toothpaste green and suffer from serious Stinky Bathroom Syndrome, a common ail-

ment of hotels with old plumbing. Covering the shower drain helps, but this should still be your second choice. A restaurant on the 1st floor serves *típica* (mains US$2 to US$6, open 6:30am to 8pm).

Comedor Rivolí (☎ 2393 0492; 1a Av Sur; mains US$2-4; ❤ breakfast, lunch & dinner) The most popular restaurant in town and justly so. Fresh *comida a la vista* is served in a spotless, cheery dining area; don't miss the huge, delicious *licuados* for US$1. Service is fast and friendly.

Kenia's Jugos Naturales (1a Av Sur; mains US$1-2; ❤ 7am-5pm) A clean, friendly place with bright plastic tables. Good for a quick snack, juices and *licuados* cost US0.75 to US$1, small sandwiches around US$1 to US$2.

Dany's Pizza (☎ 2393 6998; 4a Calle Pte; mains US$2-7; ❤ lunch & dinner) A clean and well-lit eatery with wood tables and benches. Pizza is thrown daily from 10am and comes supersized – the *pizza normal* (US$4.80) is plenty for two people. Sandwiches, tacos and hamburgers are also whipped up. Delivery is available.

Getting There & Around
Direct buses reach San Vicente from a number of surrounding cities, including San Salvador, Usulután and Zacatecoluca. In some cases, it may be quicker to take any bus along the Carr Panamericana and get off at the turnoff to San Vicente. From there, pickups and local bus 157 zip up to town (US$0.20, 10 minutes, every 10 minutes until 9pm). Leaving San Vicente, the bus terminal is a dirt lot at the corner of 8a Calle Pte and 15 Av Sur, a long 10 blocks uphill from the parque central. Fortunately, all buses (except for bus 191 to Tepetitán) pass by the parque central on their way out of town, or you can beat the crowd by getting on a few blocks early – the corner of 6a Calle Ote and 2a Av Sur is a good spot. Again, you may save time by taking a pickup (or any passing bus) to the Carr Panamericana and catching a passing bus from there. Buses from San Vicente travel to the following destinations:

Alegría Take any eastbound bus from the Carr Panamericana and transfer at Villa El Triunfo

Costa del Sol Bus 193E; US$1.50, 2¼ hours, 5am, 6am, noon and 1pm; or take any Zacatecoluca bus and transfer

Ilobasco Bus 530; US$0.60, one hour, 6:50am, 11am and 4pm

WHITE CORN

It's said that the corn that we eat comes from one woman's sacrifice.

As the legend goes, in the ancient city of Cinaca-Mecallo, a chieftain's daughter went to the river to bathe. As she stepped into the cool water, she heard a divine voice asking her to follow it. Fascinated, the young woman left the river, following the beautiful sound. It led her to a cave where she saw a man whom she'd heard about her whole life – El Señor de los Murciélagos, 'The Bat Man.' She was mesmerized by him, gave herself to him and became pregnant.

When her son was born, the town was starving; a plague of rats had eaten all of the corn. The chieftain was convinced that the gods were punishing them for his daughter's indiscretion. He told her that if she didn't find seeds to plant, her child would be sacrificed.

The young women walked for miles, searching high and low for seeds. Exhausted and anguished at finding none, she collapsed near the river. When the young women awoke, she found herself in The Bat Man's cave. She told him about her son's fate. He looked at her and in the same voice that she had heard at the river, told her to return to her town and ask the townspeople to clear the fields. He then said she should pull her teeth out and plant them in the dirt as if they were seeds.

The young women did as The Bat Man instructed. The corn stalks grew and at harvest, as the ears were pulled back, everyone saw that the corn was brilliantly white, just as the young woman's teeth had been.

Isla Montecristo/La Pita Bus 158; US$1.75, two hours, 4:30am and 12:30pm; or take any Zacatecoluca bus to Carr Litoral, transfer to any eastbound bus to San Nicholas Lempa and transfer again to a La Pita-bound bus or truck

Nuevo Tepetitán Bus 191; US$0.34, 20 minutes, every 30 minutes from 5am to 6:45pm; catch bus on Calle Alvaro Quiñonez between 9a and 11 Avs Norte

Puerto El Triunfo Take any Usulután bus and transfer at the Jiquilisco turnoff

San Miguel Take bus 301 from the Carr Panamericana; US$1.50, 1½ hours, every 10 minutes, last bus at 6:30pm

San Salvador Bus 116; *ordinario* US$0.83, 1½ hours, every 10 minutes from 3am to 7pm; *directo* US$0.83, 5:25am, 5:50am, 6:10am, 6:50am, 4:10pm, 4:45pm and 5:20pm; or take bus 301 from the Carr Panamericana; US$0.75, 40 minutes, every 10 minutes, last bus at 6pm

Usulután Bus 417; US$1.25, 2½ hours, 4:45am, 6:15am, 7:05am, 7:45am, 11:30am and 1:30pm

Zacatecoluca Bus 177; US$0.60, 50 minutes, every 15 minutes from 5:30am to 6pm

COJUTEPEQUE

pop 48,611

You could whiz by Cojutepeque on the highway and never notice – there are almost no signs for the town on the San Salvador side. But local leaders are trying to change that, following Juayúa's example by hosting a food festival every Sunday. The event is held at the top of Cerro de los Pavas, which is easily Cojutepeque's best feature: a conical hill with a handful of trails and narrow roads leading through thick trees to a clearing on top, where there are great views and an important religious shrine. The remainder of the town is unremarkable.

Orientation

Cojutepeque is organized around two parks. The parque central (the one with the banks) is located on the north side of town at the corners of Av Santa Ana (west side) and 3a Calle (south side). The other, Parque Francisco Menéndez (the one with the basketball court), is located two blocks south on Av Santa Ana. To head to Cerro de Pavas, take Av Jos Rivas (one block west of Av Santa Ana), which will become Av Contreras and will lead you straight up the Cerro de Pavas.

Information

Banco Cuscatlán (☎ 2372 5499; Av Santa Ana near 1a Calle Ote; 🕑 8:30am-5pm Mon-Fri, 8:30am-noon Sat) Faces the parque central. Has one 24-hour ATM.

Cybermania (☎ 2372 5979; Plaza Centro, Av Santa Ana near 1a Calle Ote; per hr US$0.80; 🕑 8am-7pm) Decent Internet speed and offers cheap CD burning (US$1).

Farmacia Genesis (☎ 2372 2015; Plaza Centro, Av Santa Ana near 1a Calle Ote; 🕑 7am-7pm)

Hospital Guadalupano (☎ 2372 0453, 2372 0003; Calle Dr Mario Zamora at 3a Av Norte) Consults available 10am to noon and 3pm to 6pm; emergency room open 24 hours.

Police (☎ 2372 7500; 7 Av Sur near 4a Calle Pte; 🕑 24hr)

Sights & Activities

Cojutepeque is best known for **Cerro de las Pavas** (Hill of the Turkeys; admission free; ☏ 9am-6pm), which has an outdoor shrine to the Virgen de Fátima brought here from Portugal in 1949. The shrine attracts a steady stream of religious pilgrims, especially on May 13 (Día de la Virgen). Be sure to take a look at the stone wall around the shrine – it's covered in small plaques, made of marble, stone or ceramic, and placed there by the faithful as thanks for having their prayers answered. Also at the top of the hill are three fine **miradores** (lookouts), with views of Lago Ilopango, Cerro Guazapa, Volcán San Vicente and more, plus a **mini-zoo**, with spider monkeys, raccoons, turkeys and other creatures in too-small enclosures.

On Sunday the town hosts a popular **Feria de la Cocina Cojutepeque** (admission free; ☏ 9am-6pm) at the top of Cerro de las Pavas, with food vendors from around town, plus tables, music and simple *artsanía*.

The walk up Cerro de las Pavas is a pleasant one, with two different roads circling up the hill beneath a thick canopy of trees. Footpaths, known as *los zig zags*, also wend their way to the top. It's easy to be confused but almost impossible to get lost. The area is considered very safe, with guards patrolling and plenty of foot traffic. On foot or in a car, follow Av Contreras to the end and follow the signs; it's 1km from the foot of the hill to the top.

Sleeping & Eating

Cojutepeque has no recommendable hotels, as most people come on a day trip. If you're here on Sunday – the best day to visit – definitely eat up at the Fería de la Cocina Cojutepeque on top of Cerro de las Pavas.

Restaurante Coeri (2a Av Sur btwn 1a & 3a Calle Pte; mains US$1.50-2.50; ☏ 6am-6pm) Could be the *comida a la vista*, could be the friendly service, but this simple restaurant gets crowded during breakfast and lunch, which is always a good sign. It's right on the main drag south of the parque central.

Just east of the church, **food stands** (1a Calle Ote at 4a Av Sur; ☏ 7am-8pm) sell Salvadoran *típica* – you should find tacos, sandwiches, ice cream and even a juicery.

For self-caterers, **Despensa Familiar** (3a Calle Ote at 4a Av Sur; ☏ 7:30am-7:30pm) is a decent su-

permarket selling basic foodstuffs and toiletries. It's on the parque central.

Getting There & Around

Buses leave from around Parque Francisco Menéndez. Buses to San Salvador (bus 113, US$0.40, two hours, every five minutes from 4:10am to 7:50pm) leave from the southwest corner of the park at 2a Av Sur and 3a Calle Pte. However, it is much faster to take bus 113 only as far as El Pino (US$0.20, five to 10 minutes) and catch bus 301 from San Miguel, preferably an *especial*. Buses to San Rafael (bus 515, US$0.20, 55 minutes, every 10 minutes from 6am to 6:30pm) leave from the northwest corner of the park at 2a Av Norte at 5a Calle Pte; from there transfer to buses for Ilobasco (bus 111) or Sesuntepeque (bus 112). For San Miguel, take bus 515 to 'La Curva,' where you can pick up bus 301 coming from San Salvador; again, preferably the *especial*.

ILOBASCO
pop 23,070

One of the principle ceramic centers in pre-Colombian times, Ilobasco is still recognized as a key city for the production of ceramics. The reason? The clay is top-notch and the 80 families who produce the crafts are talented. The main road into town – Av Carlos Bonilla – is lined with a string of *artesanía* stores selling everything from intricate clay *sorpresas* (literally, surprises; miniature scenes hidden in a clay egg) to huge bundles of ceramic fruit. You'll see a fair share of plastic keychains, too. Shops are typically open from 8am to 5pm, a little later on weekends. You can easily spend an afternoon walking along the strip, looking at the incredible variety of crafts for sale.

Ilobasco is right in the middle of the country, about midway along the scenic well-maintained route between Cojutepeque and Siguatepeque. A mostly dirt road heads west from Ilobasco, reaching Cinquera and eventually Suchitoto.

Orientation

Av Carlos Bonilla, the main road into town, runs east–west. The parque central is located one block south on 1a Calle (south side) and 2a Av (west side). Most listings are located on the main drag or around the parque central.

Information

Banco Cuscatlán (☎ 2329 4320; Av Carlos Bonilla near Calle Bernardo Perdomo; ☽ 8:30am-5pm Mon-Fri, 8:30am-noon Sat) Has one 24-hour ATM.

Ciber Café Ilobasco (☎ 2384 4543; 3a Av Norte at 6a Calle Pte; per hr US$1; ☽ 9am-10pm)

Farmacia San Miguel (☎ 2332 2190; 3a Calle Ote at 4a Av Norte; ☽ 7am-7pm) Facing the parque central, this is a well-stocked pharmacy.

Hospital Nacional de Ilobasco (☎ 2384 3211; end of 4a Calle Pte; ☽ 24hr)

Infocentros (☎ 2332 2686; Av Carlos Bonilla 25; per hr US$1; ☽ 8am-5pm Mon-Fri, 8am-3pm Sat) Located inside Cedart (below).

Police (☎ 2384 2256; 4a Calle Pte near 3a Av Sur; ☽ 24hr)

Post Office (2a Av Norte near 1a Calle Ote; ☽ 8am-5pm Mon-Fri, 8am-noon Sat)

Sights & Activities

If you're short on time or if window shopping isn't really your thing, head straight to **Cedart** (☎ 2332 2116; Av Carlos Bonilla 25; ☽ 8am-5pm Mon-Fri, 9am-4pm Sat & Sun). This center offers classes to aspiring artists, maintains a small exhibit outlining the development of ceramic art in Ilobasco, and also has an excellent gift store. Plus, if you see a style of craftmanship in the store that you like, just ask the sales clerk to point you in the direction of the artist's workshop or store. More likely than not, it's within a couple of blocks of the town center.

Sleeping & Eating

There are slim pickin's in town for hotels and eateries. Following are the best of the small lot available.

TÍPICA OR PÍCARA?

Sorpresas (surprises) are tiny, detailed scenes and figures in little oval shells about the size of a walnut. The outside may be designed as a walnut, egg, apple, orange or anything round. Open one up to view a delightful little scene of daily life set around a village. A savvy artist in Ilobasco added a new dimension to the surprise: a naked couple in the throes of sexual passion. Even though the priest in town condemns the making of these, and at one point made the stores remove their heathen goods, the '*pícara*' (sinful) *sorpresas* are still hot sellers (so to speak), albeit tightly wrapped in paper.

Hotel Ilobasco (☎ 2332 2563; 4a Calle Pte; r per person US$12; ℗) Four long blocks west of the main drag, this hotel is the only decent place to stay in town. Prices are inflated for what you get, though – rundown rooms with faded wallpaper and hit-or-miss cleanliness. Service, at least, is friendly.

Italyan Pizza (☎ 2332 2663; Av Carlos Bonilla btwn 4a & 6a Calles Pte; mains US$1.50-6; ☽ lunch & dinner) One of the most popular places to eat, this modest restaurant offers a simple menu – pizza, sandwiches and tacos. Food comes out hot and fast, and somehow always manages to hit the spot. *Licuados* are good, too. Tables are jam-packed at dinnertime.

Restaurant Mi Bocadito (☎ 2820 5218; Av Carlos Bonilla 25; mains US$2.50-4; ☽ lunch & dinner Wed-Mon) A family-run restaurant serving up good-sized, freshly made Salvadoran classics, like grilled chicken with rice, avocado sauce and *chirmol* (US$2.50), and garlic shrimp with rice (US$3). The service is somewhat gruff but the prices make up for it.

For self-caterers, **Supermercado de Todo** (Av Carlos Bonilla near 1a Calle Pte; ☽ 7am-7:30pm) is a decent supermarket half a block west of the parque central. Look for the tall orange-and-white telephone antenna across the street.

Getting There & Around

There is no one central bus terminal in Ilobasco. Bus 111 leaves from the corner of 7a Calle Ote and 2a Av Norte and goes to San Salvador (US$0.70, 1½ hours, every 10 minutes from 3:40am to 6:10pm), stopping in Cojutepeque (US$0.35, 35 minutes) along the way. A faster way to get to the capital is to take bus 111 just to the highway intersection at San Rafael and transfer there to a westbound bus 301, preferably an *especial*. This is the same (and only) way to get to San Miguel, instead catching an eastbound bus 301 on the other side of the highway. Buses going to Sesuntepeque (bus 529, US$0.60, 45 minutes, approximately 7am, 8am, 10:30am, 11am, 11:30am, 12:30pm, 1pm, 2:30pm and 3:30pm) leave from the southeast corner of the parque central at 1a Calle Ote and 4a Av Norte; those heading to San Vicente (bus 530, US$0.68, one hour, 5:50am, 8:50am and 1:50pm) leave from the other side of the parque central on 3a Calle Ote near 4a Av Norte.

EL SALVADOR

SESUNTEPEQUE

pop 17,267

Looking at it on the map, Sesuntepeque looks moored in the middle of nowhere; you'd imagine a gritty hard-luck town. The Cabañas state capital *is* in the middle of nowhere – no normal travel itinerary would lead you here – which only makes Sesuntepeque's friendly air and tidy appearance all the more surprising. A well-tended parque central, Parque Luciano Hernández, is surrounded by low neat buildings, including a number of good places to eat Due north, one man is working hard to turn the town of Victoria into an eco-destination, which would give people an active reason to make the trip here. For now, it's probably the nicest town most travelers will never see.

Information

Banco Cuscatlán (☽ 8:30am-5pm Mon-Fri, 8:30am-noon Sat) Located on the northwest corner of Parque Luciano Hernández. Has an ATM.

Farmacia La Esperanza (☎ 2382 2985; 4a Calle Ote at 4a Calle Sur; ☽ 7am-6pm Mon-Sat, 7am-noon Sun) Run by a young, friendly, Lonely Planet–reading pharmacist.

Hospital Nacional Sesuntepeque (☎ 2382 0844; 10 Av Norte near 4a Calle Ote; ☽ 24hr) There are also many private clinics and laboratories on 10 Av Norte near the hospital entrance.

Infocentros (☎ 2382 1283; 2nd fl, 1a Calle Ote at 2a Av Norte; per hr US$1; ☽ 8am-7pm Mon-Fri, 8am-5pm Sat) On the north side of Parque Luciano Hernández.

Police (☎ 2382 2961; Calle Dr Velasco btwn 1a & 3a Avs Sur; ☽ 24hr)

Post Office (4a Av Sur btwn 2a & 4a Calles Ote; ☽ 8am-4pm Mon-Fri, 8am-noon Sat)

Scotiabank (☽ 8am-4pm Mon-Fri, 8am-noon Sat) Located on the southwest corner of Parque Luciano Hernández. Has an ATM.

Sights & Activities

Sesuntepeque's **Parque Luciano Hernández** is unique for its elaborate artificial fountain, with fresh water burbling out of clay pots and gushing down a sloping rock formation. Fake birds and real plants complete the effect. In fact, the entire park is remarkably manicured and clean, with a pretty kiosk in the middle and palms and pine trees lending broken shade to the benches and walkways.

Basketball games are held at a spectator complex, complete with bleachers, at the top of Calle Dr Velasco near Iglesia El Cal-vario. Sesuntepeque's boys basketball team was the national champion in 2005, and the games are usually very well attended.

Victoria is a small town 9km due north of Sesuntepeque. An ambitious project by a Sesuntepeque doctor, Dr Oscar Antonio Henríquez, aims to turn Victoria into the next big eco-tourism destination with his hotel-restaurant-nightclub-resort **Victoria Cabaña Club** (☎ 2389 3319; Calle Principal; ☽ 10am-10:30pm Thu-Sun). The restaurant (mains US$5 to US$9) has been operating since 2003, serving everything from hamburgers to salmon at covered, open-air dining areas with memorable views of the blue-green landscape. Private cabins, camping areas, basketball court, swimming pool and nightclub are all planned, plus rafting, hiking and rappelling excursions. It was still an idea when we visited, but the bulldozers obviously meant business – call ahead for the latest.

Victoria is indeed a beautiful area, which you can appreciate from **El Mirador**, a roadside vista point just south of Victoria, and from **Cerro Ocotillo**, a 1012m hill just beyond town. Volcán San Vicente and Volcán Izalco, and Cerro Guazapa near San Salvador, are visible on clear days. El Mirador can be reached by car or bus; Cerro Ocotillo has a road to the top (but no bus service) and can also be climbed by foot. Victoria Cabaña Club was considering offering short walking tours.

Sleeping & Eating

Sesuntepeque has a number of good eating options, all facing Parque Luciano Hernández, but no recommendable hotels. Victoria Cabaña Club will be a welcome addition when completed.

El Merendero (☽ 6am-9pm; mains US$1-3) This is the large structure on the east side of Parque Luciano Hernández, where a line of stalls sell mostly pupusas – in fact, it used to have the much cooler name of El Pupusodromo – plus tamales, fried chicken, coffee and chocolate. The tables in front have a more pleasant view, if all you want are fresh juice and a bag of chips.

Coctelería Costa del Sol (1a Calle Ote; mains US$1-10; ☽ 8am-7pm) A family of Costa del Sol transplants brings classic beach food to the mountains at this low-key eatery facing Parque Luciano Hernández. Cocktails are made from fish, shrimp, conch, squid, plus all the sauces and goodies, starting at just US$1. Hamburgers and sandwiches are also available.

El Gran Portal (☎ 2382 2861; 1a Calle Ote; mains US$5-12; ☺ 10am-10pm) Sesuntepeque's top restaurant faces Parque Luciano Hernández and has an attractive interior, with rust-colored walls, sloped ceiling and a long heavily varnished wood bar along one side. The main clientele are those up for a day from San Salvador, so dishes are accordingly overpriced. The Especial Gran Portal includes chicken, steak and shrimp, plus two side dishes, like yucca and guacamole, for US$10.

Getting There & Around
Buses line up at a busy intersection on 2a Av Sur near 6a Calle Pte, right where the highway enters town. Buses head to Ilobasco (bus 529, US$0.60, 45 minutes, every 30 minutes from 3:30am to 5:30pm) and San Salvador (bus 112, US$1, two hours, every 15 to 30 minutes from 3:30am to 5:30pm). For Victoria (US$0.35, 20 minutes, every 15 minutes from 6am to 6pm) take bus 181 or a microbus on 1 Av Norte near 3a Calle Pte.

MORAZÁN DEPARTMENT

Morazán Department, occupying the northeast corner of the country, has always been poor, at least monetarily speaking. It was a stronghold of the Farabundo Martí National Liberation Front (FMLN) during the war, in no small part because the farmers naturally rallied to the guerrillas' call for land reforms. But serving as a rebel stronghold earned Morazán the ire of government forces, and some of the war's worst fighting – and atrocities – took place here. Even communities that remained neutral suffered terrible persecution and destruction.

Whether despite that history or because of it, Morazán is now a favorite destination among many foreign travelers in El Salvador. Perquín (p442) is the crown jewel, with an excellent museum about the war and a well-organized tourist office. The town itself

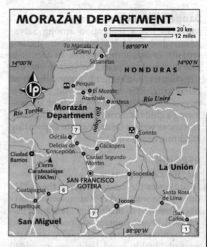

is charming and cool, and the surrounding area offers great hiking among forest-clad hills, crashing waterfalls and brilliant blue skies. Morazán boasts the country's cleanest river, the Río Sapo, with well-maintained camping facilities nestled in the trees along its banks. Given more time, you can visit Morazán's smaller towns, like Cacaopera and Guatajiagua, or Ciudad Segundo Montes, which are fascinating in their own right, whether for indigenous influence, strong artistic traditions or simply for their small-town charm.

Climate & Geography
The highland areas of Morazán share the same mountain range – and the same climate – as other northern regions, like La Palma (p389) and Metapán (p358). Temperatures average 12°C to 20°C (53°F to 68°F), but can get unexpectedly cold at night, especially in the rainy reason (May to November). The Río Torola divides the state into almost even halves, and was an important division during the war, when the FMLN controlled the northern half and the government the southern half. Guerrillas frequently bombed the bridge spanning the river, to impede government incursions into northern areas. The state's highest mountain, Cerro Cacahuatique, saw considerable fighting; today it is home to small communities of subsistence farmers, living in one of the country's most isolated and difficult-to-reach regions.

Dangers & Annoyances

Morazán has a reputation among Salvadorans as being a lawless frontier, the last redoubt of armed insurgents. In fact, it is one of the safest places to visit in the entire country, and certainly among the most interesting. The main risk you run here is getting lost on poorly marked trails – hiring a guide is recommended for that very reason, as well as being a way of supporting local tourism efforts.

PERQUÍN

pop 5500 / elevation 1117m

Perquín was the headquarters of the FMLN during the war, and is a must-see for anyone interested in that period. The guerrillas enjoyed broad popular support here and throughout northern Morazán, and the rugged, thickly treed landscape provided cover from military patrols.

Just as intriguing are Perquín's natural surroundings. All around stand low, stocky mountains, connected by broad valleys and a patchwork of subsistence farms. It's a great place to hike, swim or just chill out for a few days. Orchids and butterflies are in abundance here, and Perquín is a prime birding zone – 12 varieties of oriole have been spotted, along with the rare chestnut-headed oropendola.

Orientation

The highway enters town from the south, bumping into the parque central and the rear of the church. Most of Perquín's shops and services are on or near the park, while the museum is a just short walk uphill. Two of Perquín's hotels are back along the highway; if you're staying at one of them, ask the bus driver to let you off in front, to save having to walk back down with your bags.

Information

Ciber Digital Perquin.com (Calle Los Héroes near Av Los Próceres; per hr US$1) Operates random hours; count yourself lucky if you see it open.

Fuente de Vida Venta de Medicina (☎ 2680 4082; parque central, Av Reconstrucción at Calle La Libertad; ✆ 6am-7pm Sun-Fri) Not technically a pharmacy – that would require a license – but still selling pharmaceuticals to all.

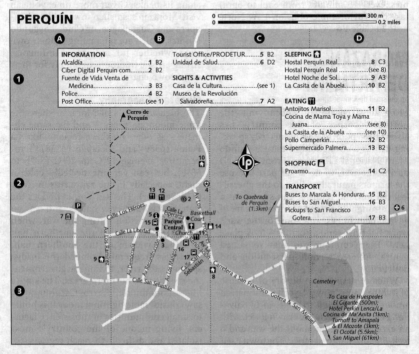

PERQUÍN

0 — 300 m
0 — 0.2 miles

INFORMATION
Alcaldía........................**1** B2
Ciber Digital Perquin com.........**2** B2
Fuente de Vida Venta de
    Medicina.................**3** B3
Police........................**4** B2
Post Office.................(see 1)

Tourist Office/PRODETUR........**5** B2
Unidad de Salud..................**6** D2

SIGHTS & ACTIVITIES
Casa de la Cultura................(see 1)
Museo de la Revolución
    Salvadoreña...................**7** A2

SLEEPING
Hostal Perquín Real..................**8** C3
Hostal Perquín Real....................(see 8)
Hotel Noche de Sol....................**9** A3
La Casita de la Abuela.............**10** B2

EATING
Antojitos Marisol.....................**11** B2
Cocina de Mama Toya y Mama
    Juana.............................(see 8)
La Casita de la Abuela ....(see 10)
Pollo Camperkin.....................**12** B2
Supermercado Palmera............**13** B2

SHOPPING
Proarmo................................**14** C2

TRANSPORT
Buses to Marcala & Honduras..**15** B2
Buses to San Miguel.................**16** B3
Pickups to San Francisco
    Gotera.............................**17** B3

Cerro de Perquín

Calle Los Héroes
Calle La Libertad
Calle La Esperanza
Basketball Court
Parque Central
Church
Av Los Ramiros
Av Democracia
Av Reconstrucción
Calle La Maira
Calle Sebastián
Calle San Sebastián

To Quebrada de Perquín (1.3km)

Carretera a San Francisco Gotera & San Miguel

Cemetery

To Casa de Huéspedes
El Gigante (500m);
Hotel Perkin Lenca/La
Cocina de Ma'Anita (1km);
Turnoff to Amapala
& El Mozote (3km);
El Ocotal (5.5km);
San Miguel (61km)

WOMEN GUERILLAS

The Museo de la Revolución Salvadoreña in Perquín has dozens of photographs taken in FMLN camps, on the battlefront and in planning sessions. In every sphere you will see women participating, some wearing fatigues and carrying AK-47s, others at strategy tables and behind microphones, still others teaching fellow guerillas how to read and write or care for the wounded. Women played a uniquely prominent role in El Salvador's revolutionary movement, stepping outside of their traditional roles as wives and mothers.

El Salvador's civil war officially broke out in 1981, following the merger of five guerilla factions that formed the FMLN in late 1980. Women made up roughly 40% of the FMLN membership, a higher percentage than in many other revolutionary movements in the region. In fact, women represented about a third of the guerrillas' armed combatants and roughly 20% of the military leadership. Radio Venceremos, the FMLN's clandestine radio station that broadcast from Morazán, had female voices on air and behind the scenes as well.

Three high-ranking women commanders participated in the peace talks of 1992. Their presence helped to assure that female soldiers, as well as noncombatant supporters, were included in combatant benefits programs. Perhaps more than any other, this aspect of the peace treaty exemplified how significantly gender relations had shifted during the war.

Upon the signing of the treaty, however, women ex-guerillas were pressured to return to roles that they had occupied before the conflict. Having performed distinctly nontraditional roles during the war – and having liked it – many women chafed at the prospect of returning to their former lives. A great many simply refused, choosing instead to pursue advanced degrees, to establish women's and environmental organizations, or to work in government agencies to help rebuild their battered country. Others embraced the prospect of entering (or returning to) the world of being a mother and spouse, though never fully relinquishing the independence they'd known as soldiers and activists.

By fighting alongside men, and later refusing to retreat to traditional roles, women of the revolutionary movement helped redefine the very nature of womanhood and women's roles in El Salvador. The war is long over, but their impact remains quite tangible.

Police (☎ 2680 4027; Calle Los Héroes; ☻ 24hr)

Post Office (parque central, Av Reconstrucción at Calle La Libertad; ☻ 8am-noon & 1-4pm Mon, Tue, Thu & Fri) Look for the small desk inside the *alcaldía* (mayor's office).

Tourist Office/Prodetur (☎ 2680 4086; prodeturperq uin@navegante.com.sv; parque central, Av Reconstrucción at Calle La Libertad; ☻ 8am-5pm Mon-Fri, 8am-2pm Sat) Very helpful tourist office located next to the *alcaldía*. Information is available on sights and services within the area, and guided hikes and tours are also organized (see p444).

Sights

Just west of the parque central, the **Museo de la Revolución Salvadoreña** (☎ 2610 6737; Calle Los Héroes; admission US$1.20; ☻ 8am-4:30pm Tue-Sun) is an excellent museum that charts the causes and course of the armed struggle with photos, posters, weapons and histories of those who served and died in action. Weapons range from high-tech hardware to homemade bombs and mines. Behind the main building are the remains of the downed helicopter that carried Lieutenant Colonel Domingo Monterrosa, head of the

notorious Atlacatl Battalion, to his death. The studios of the FMLN's clandestine station Radio Venceremos (We Shall Prevail Radio) are also here; an elaborate hoax involving a radio transmitter rigged with explosives was what brought Monterrosa's helicopter down. Exhibits are in Spanish and English; tours of the museum are led by former guerrillas in Spanish only. Local crafts, books and T-shirts are sold in the museum's shop.

Festivals & Events

Perquín's *fiestas patronales* (patron-saint festivals) are held on January 22 (San Sebastian) and August 15 (Virgen de Tránsito). But they are very low key compared to the town's biggest annual event.

In August 1992 (August 1 to 7) Perquín hosted its first **Festival del Invierno** (Winter Festival) to celebrate the signing of the Peace Accords just seven months earlier. The idea was to demonstrate to the country that Perquín had embraced peace and was now safe and open to all. (Even today many Salvadoran's think of Perquín as dangerous and unruly – in fact, it's one of the safest places in the entire country.) The festival has been held yearly since, and has grown into one of the most anticipated and well-attended events in Morazán. Not surprisingly, it has a distinctly bohemian character, with a largely college-age crowd and an emphasis on art and music. A number of well-known groups have performed here – the famed Ballet Garífuna from Honduras has performed for several years in a row. Hotels are booked solid well in advance, and even good camping space can be a challenge to find.

Activities

Southeast of Perquín, the Río Guaco and Río Talchiga tumble over several picturesque waterfalls before meeting southeast of Perquín to form the Río Sapo, considered the cleanest river in El Salvador. An agreement between landowners and the local environmental organization has set aside 6000 hectares (about 14,826 acres) to create the **Area Natural Protegida Río Sapo** (Sapo River Protected Natural Area).

Perquín's tourism and environmental-protection organization, **Prodetur** (☎ 2680 4086; prodeturperquin@navegante.com.sv; parque central, Av Reconstrucción at Calle La Libertad; ☺ 8am-5pm Mon-Fri, 8am-2pm Sat), operates the eco-hostel, Eco Albergue de Río Sapo (p446), in the Río Sapo protected area, and offers guided hikes there and around Perquín. Guides are local residents, many of them former guerrilla members, and have ample information on the area as well as fascinating accounts of the war years; most speak Spanish only. The longer hikes are best begun early in the morning to avoid the heat and (more importantly) afternoon rains. Stop by the Prodetur office when you arrive to arrange a tour for the following day; or call ahead if you're only visiting for a day. If you stay at the eco-hostel, the guide will stay there as well, giving you an early start for the next day's excursions.

Fees are US$15 per group (up to 15 people) for eight hours – with planning, it's possible to take more than one hike, in which case you should treat your guide to lunch. The city tour alone costs US$5 per person. Following are some of the most popular hikes and tours:

Cerro el Pericón–El Mozote This three-hour hike is the most popular of Prodetur's tours. It starts in Perquín and climbs Cerro el Pericón, the summit of which affords fine views of the Río Sapo and the surrounding valley. Descending the other side, you reach the Río Sapo protected area and eco-hostal. After stopping for a snack and possibly a swim – it's cold! – continue to El Mozote to see the monument to the 1981 massacre. From there it's possible to walk to the highway (about 10km along a dirt road, through the town of Arambala) or you can wait for bus, which passes at 12:45pm. At the highway, hop on one of the frequent pickup trucks for the last 3km back to Perquín.

Cerro Gigante A 6km loop starts behind the Gigante Casa de Huepedes El Gigante and passes a number of historical and war-related sights. You pass the Pueblo Viejo (Old Town), where Perquín was originally located, and a Lenca cemetery where stones are used to mark graves instead of crosses. Doubling back you pass a container used by the UN to store weapons following the signing of the Peace Accords. The trail climbs Cerro Perón, in the shadow of Cerro Gigante, then returns to the starting point, passing a guerrilla hospital on the way. Though this can all be done solo, but a guide helps bring the history to life.

City Tour This walking tour of Perquín focusses on events that took place here during the war. Most of the sights are right around the parque central, including the Casa de la Cultura (formerly a military barracks) and the church. You'll also visit the Museo de la Revolución Salvadoreña and Cerro de Perquín (entrance fees not included). A nice option following lunch and a longer tour in the morning.

There are also walks you can do without a guide.

Cerro de Perquín This is the small hill that rises behind town, with a pretty view from the top. Prodetur is planning to install interpretive signs along the easy 1km trail to the summit, explaining some of the natural and historical significance of the area. There is also talk of charging a US$0.35 entry fee. Look for the trail opposite the entrance to the Museo de la Revolución Salvadoreña, near a public parking lot.

Llano del Muerto Three side-by-side *turicentros* (tourist centers; admission to each US$1, all open 7am to 4pm) along the Río Guaco make this area a popular destination for daytrippers from San Miguel and San Francisco Gotera, though it tends to have less appeal to nature-seeking backpackers and independent travelers. Turicentro Cascada El Perol (☎ 2654 2090) is the best of the three, mainly for its namesake *cascada* (waterfall) and the swimming hole beneath it. (Water level is lowest February to April.) It also has swimming pools and simple eateries, like its neighbors Turicentro El Bosquecito de Juvenal (☎ 2690 4082) and Turicentro Llano del Muerto (☎ 2661 3363). Most people drive to Llano del Muerto; walking there takes about two hours from Perquín or you can catch the 6:45am bus to

Marcala, Honduras, and ask the driver to let you off. The same bus passes by going the other direction at around 1:30pm.

Quebrada de Perquín A small natural swimming hole with a modest waterfall. It's right at the intersection of two dirt roads that see very little traffic but still detract from the scene. It's a pleasant, if steep, descent and a long climb back up. Follow the road past Perquín's cemetery just south of town. May be dry February through April.

Sleeping
CENTRAL PERQUÍN

Hotel Noche de Sol (☎ 2680 4273; Av Los Ramírez; dm/r per person US$5/10; **P**) The young couple who run this hotel are not the type of live-in hosts to fade into the background when guests are around. With a kid (or two?), pool table and a penchant for rock music, this is a great place if you like to *convivir* (hang out) but not for those looking for a quiet hideaway. The two-story pink-and-white building has two dorm rooms with four bunks each downstairs, and two private rooms upstairs, all large and gleaming, though rather plain. There's one common bathroom on each floor, also very clean. Guests are free to use the kitchen, TV and DVD player. There's a great view from the 2nd floor.

La Casita de la Abuela (☎ 2680 4314; Calle Los Héroes; r per person US$10) Nine basic but very clean rooms make up this humble home-turned-hotel. All have good queen-size beds with colorful bedspreads and share one bathroom. About half of the rooms are divided by plywood walls, which means you can hear your neighbor breathing – rough if you're a light sleeper or end up with an over-laugher next door. Water is scarce, too – it's only available in the early morning; be sure to shower by 8am. By far, the best rooms are on the 2nd floor; each is spacious and has cement walls. Room 9 also has a private balcony with a glorious view of the mountains. If you arrive and the hotel appears closed, walk a couple of blocks west to the *artesanía* (handicrafts) store by the same name, where the namesake *abuela* (grandmother), Doná Alba, should be there to help you. A popular eatery is also located on the ground floor of the hotel.

Casa de Huespedes El Gigante (☎ 2680 4037; r/t US$12/17; **P**) From lumber mill to guest house, this long log building has been partitioned into a dozen fairly comfortable but very plain cubicles, each with fan, small table and one or two firm beds. Large common bathrooms are at one end of the building. The Gigante is Perquín's first hotel; everything is clean but starting to show its age. It's located in the trees a short distance off the highway – look for the large roadside sign about 500m south of town.

Hostal Perquín Real (☎ 2680 4158; r per person US$5; **P**) The hotel's restaurant, Cocina de Mama Toya y Mama Juana, is one of the better eateries in town. However, the rooms open right onto the dining area, which is awkward going to and from the shared bathroom. And speaking of the bathroom, don't forget your flip-flops: the toilet is scuzzy (there's only one for six rooms and the restaurant), and the shower is actually a big plastic drum with cold water and a dipper. That's a real shame because the rooms themselves, save for proximity to the restaurant and a few saggy beds, are spacious and clean, and not bad for the price. It's located at the south entrance of town.

OUTSIDE PERQUÍN

Hotel Perkin Lenca (☎ 2680 4046; www.perkinlenca .com; Carr a Perquín Km 205.5; s/d US$12/20, cabins s/d/tr/q US$40/50/63/100; **P** 🖳) Easily Perquín's most comfortable and modern lodging, the Perkin Lenca has eight cozy private cabins, each with sloped wooden ceilings, bright interior, oak paneling and a small porch with hammocks and superb views. Rooms were still being completed when we visited, but will have bathrooms and share an open-air common area. All bathrooms are spotless and have hot water, a huge plus. The beautiful hillside grounds practically explode with leafy and flowering plants, and include a small sitting area by a natural spring, working coffee plants and a huge organic garden. Owner and Delaware native Ronald Brenneman is a carpenter by trade and built houses for Salvadoran refugees in Honduras during the war before settling here.

El Ocotal (☎ 2680 4190; Carr a Perquín Km 201; cabins US$30-50; **P** 🐾) If the Perkin Lenca is full, this is the next best thing, with eight pleasant A-frame cabins spread through tree-filled grounds. Though lacking the little details that make the Perkin Lenca so appealing, cabins still have firm beds, hot water, TV and small porches. There's a clean good-sized pool near the entrance. Located 3.5km south of town off the highway, it may look empty if you arrive midweek at night, but there should be a guard there at all times.

Eco Albergue de Río Sapo (☎ 2680 4086; admission US$0.70; campsites/dm per person US$3.50/6; **P**) Decent dorms and well-maintained campgrounds are open to the public inside the Sapo River Protected Natural Area. Dorms are basic – bunk beds in an adobe building with a corrugated tin roof – but comfortable. Two campgrounds are tucked into the forest near the Sapo River; the sites are very well maintained and have communal fire pits for cooking and late-night hanging out. Guests without gear can rent tents (tents sleeping two to five people from US$3 per person) and sleeping bags (US$1) from Prodetur. As the name suggests, the Eco Albergue is also eco-friendly, with gray-water recycling, spring-fed showers and no electricity (bring extra candles and matches). Probably the best thing about staying here is having direct access to half a dozen hikes, two rivers with good swimming holes and a handful of waterfalls. Prodetur guides are always on-site to lead guests around the reserve; in fact, each group of travelers is *required* to hire a guide (US$15 per day) to take them to the site and to stay with them for the length of their visit. Carry in your own food or prepare to walk 3km to the nearest village for your meals. In a country where backcountry camping is still novel, this is a one-of-a-kind experience.

Eating
CENTRAL PERQUÍN
Cocina de Mama Toya y Mama Juana (☎ 2680 4158; mains US$3-7; ☼ 6am-9pm) Nothing fancy here, just good fresh *típica* (regional specialities) served in a clean comfortable setting at decent prices. It's part of the Hotel Perquín Real – or rather the hotel is part of the restaurant, as the latter was open first – and its rooms open onto a dining room with rows of wood tables and benches. It's an open-air setting, so be sure to bundle up in the winter months. It's at the south entrance to town.

Antojitos Marisol (mains US$2-4; ☼ breakfast, lunch & dinner) On the south side of the parque central, this is a classic greasy spoon. Handwritten menus and a few printed addendums ('Pilsner $1') are taped to the wall at the head of each of the long wooden tables, which have benches and tablecloths. The walls are aqua-green and the florescent lights are about as unflattering as light can be, yet it's somehow appealing – anyway, it's one of only two places in town open late. Beers come with small glasses and simple *botanas* (appetizers); a chicken burger and fries costs US$2, a plate of grilled meat with rice and salad US$2.50, and awfully good pupusas cost US$0.35 to US$0.45

La Casita de la Abuela (☎ 2680 4314; Calle Los Héroes near Av Próceres; mains US$0.35-2; ☼ breakfast & lunch) A popular eatery located on the ground floor of the hotel of the same name. This is a good place to get a good-sized *típico* breakfast and midday pupusas. The relative cleanliness inspires confidence, too.

Pollo Camperkin (☎ 2680 4006; Calle Héroes; mains US$2-4; ☼ breakfast, lunch & dinner) *Comida a la vista* (meal served buffet) is prepared daily at this modest cafeteria – there is typically a chicken dish (as the name suggests), vegetables and beans. Arrive early for each meal to get the best pickin's. Around sunset pupusas are served up hot and fresh.

Supermercado Palmera (☎ 2680 4006; Calle Los Héroes; ☼ 7am-8pm Mon-Sat, 7am-1pm & 4-8pm Sun) is a modest grocery store, good for stocking up on fruit and dried goods for long hikes.

OUTSIDE PERQUÍN
La Cocina de Ma'Anita (Hotel Perkin Lenca, Carr a Perquín Km 205.5; mains US$4-9; ☼ breakfast, lunch & dinner) Perquín's best hotel also has its most formal restaurant, though the huge A-frame dining area is more ski-lodge than mountain bistro. Tables along the front windows get nice morning light and have overhead lamps on henequen cords for nighttime. The owner may install booths, which would class it up a bit. The food is reliable and good, but not spectacular, ranging from taco salad to chicken with mango chutney to a four-person *parrillada* (platter of grilled meat, sausage and chicken). Afterward, head up to the much cozier bar for drinks.

El Ocotal (☎ 2680 4190; Carr a Parquín Km 201; mains US$2-7; ☼ breakfast, lunch & dinner) A pleasant eatery at the top of a forested hill, where wood tables and benches are set in an open-air dining room with a small bar – the view of the trees below is nice. *Típica* is the specialty – *gallina india asada* (grilled hen) is a favorite among regulars – but you always can order a burger and fries, too. Bring a sweater at night.

Shopping

Proarmo (☎ 2680 4290; Av Los Próceres; ◷ 8am-4pm) Opened in 2004, this cooperative specializes in *artesanías* made in Morazán. You'll find a wide assortment of crocheted items (hats, belts, bags, jewelry); there is also a smattering of wood, clay and henequen crafts. It's all kind of kitschy but it's got a lot of heart.

Getting There & Around

The CA7 north of San Miguel to the Honduran border is in good shape. Bus 332 runs from San Miguel to Perquín (US$1.50, 2½ hours) several times daily, or you can also take the more frequent bus 328 to San Francisco Gotera (US$0.70, 1½ hours) and hop on a pickup the rest of the way (see p428 and p451 for details). The last bus back to San Miguel is at 4pm; the last pickup to San Francisco Gotera leaves at 5:40pm, but you have to catch the 5pm to make the last San Francisco Gotera–San Miguel bus.

Buses to Marcala (Honduras) start in San Miguel and pass through Perquín twice

RUTA DE LA PAZ

More than any other place in El Salvador, Morazán is known for having been a guerrilla stronghold during the war. You may discover that your hiking guide is a former guerrilla or that the woman cooking your meals had done the same thing for soldiers-in-training during the war. La Ruta de la Paz (The Peace Route) is a collection of several communities in Morazán, many of which played central roles in the conflict. Calling it the Peace Route obviously evokes that history, which is, after all, what draws most travelers here.

But a number of the towns are better known for their archeological or artistic treasures, and visiting them highlights the fact that 'peace' is more than 'not war' but the space for all the riches of an area to be appreciated. Residents along the Ruta de la Paz are friendly, if generally reserved. For all the international attention paid to Morazán, it is (and always has been) an area of mostly small towns and subsistence farms. Travelers should by all means ask questions about the war, but also about present-day life and current issues; life goes on, after all, and no one wants to be seen as merely a relic of the past. Look out for these towns along the route:

- **Perquín** (p442) The center of La Ruta de la Paz. Not only was Perquín the main FMLN stronghold, it is the easiest of the towns to reach, and has the best variety of lodging, food, sights and activities.

- **Arambala** (p448) and **El Mozote** (p448) The sites of heavy bombing and the war's most notorious massacre.

- **Cacaopera** (p449) Known for its strong indigenous presence. This town has a good Maya-Kakawira museum and a number of interesting hikes, including to caves with prehistoric paintings.

- **Corinto** (p451) Connected to Cacaopera by a scenic and newly paved road, Corinto has a large shallow cave that is covered in prehistoric paintings, while a twice-weekly market is a feast for the eyes, ears and nose.

- **Guatajiagua** (p452) A town known for its distinctive black-clay pottery.

daily. See the boxed text on p450 for details and important issues about this border crossing.

EL MOZOTE

Once a town hidden in the lap of the northern hills, El Mozote is now a destination for those paying homage to the hundreds of men, women and children here and in surrounding villages who were massacred by government troops over the course of three days in December 1981. A simple iron silhouette of a family is backed by a brick wall on which wooden boards hang with the names of the victims. For more details, see the boxed text, below.

The turnoff to El Mozote is 3km south of Perquín, and the town lies about 10km from el pavimentado (the paved road). From Perquín, you can walk or take a pickup to the turnoff, and catch a Joateca-bound bus that passes there at 8am and stops in El Mozote The same bus stops at El Mozote on the return journey at 12:45pm, and can drop you at the turnoff. Some travelers take the bus in and walk out, or vice versa. On the way

you'll pass through **Arambala**, a village that stood empty for years after being decimated by air raids.

There are no restaurants or eateries in El Mozote, but on your way back to the highway, **Comedor Gloria** (☎ 2680 4252; mains US$2-4; ☾ breakfast & lunch Mon-Sat) is worth a stop. A spotless and pleasant cafétería on Arambala's parque central, it offers good *comida a la vista;* you'll always find meat, pasta, bean and rice dishes. Service is friendly, too.

CUIDAD SEGUNDO MONTES

More a loose collection of communities than an actual city, Ciudad Segundo Montes sees very few visitors. A foundation and community center near the highway is the main 'attraction,' and you can certainly meander down the tree-lined dirt roads, but the best reason to stop here is to learn more about Ciudad Segundo Montes' troubled but fascinating origin.

Until 1980 mass and militant resistance to government repression was centered in the cities. But between the prospect of facing a US-backed military following

---

MASSACRE AT EL MOZOTE

Early on the morning of December 11, 1981, soldiers from the elite US-trained Atlacatl battalion of the Salvadoran armed forces roused residents from their beds and hustled them to the center of town. Men and women were separated and locked in various places, including the church and convent. For the entire day, and into the next and the next, soldiers terrorized and executed everyone they captured, often to sadistic extremes – women and girls were marched into the hills to be raped, infants were speared with bayonets, a group of children was locked in the church and machine gunned through the windows. Many of the bodies were left to rot, others were burned along with the village houses. In all, at least 767 people were killed.

In the days before the massacre, guerrillas had warned residents in the area to evacuate in advance of an expected government attack. However, a local leader in El Mozote had been assured by army officers that the villagers would be safest in town. In fact, hundreds of people from outlying villages had come to El Mozote (which had only about 20 families normally). Perhaps more importantly, the people of El Mozote did not consider themselves targets – they had never extended special help to the guerrillas, and they were mostly Protestants in a region where pro-guerrilla sentiment came mainly from Catholics. The government had long (and correctly) suspected the guerrillas received vital logistical support from certain local residents, whether openly or clandestinely. But it remains a mystery why soldiers, led by the army's most storied officer Colonel Domingo Monterroso, chose El Mozote to 'drain the ocean to catch the fish.'

The massacre was extensively reported by the FMLN's clandestine radio station, but its reports were brushed off as propaganda. Even after reporters from the *New York Times* and *Washington Post* visited the site and interviewed two surviving eyewitnesses, the Salvadoran and US government refused to admit anything other than ordinary fighting had occurred. It wasn't until more than a decade later, following the 1992 Peace Accords, that exhumations confirmed a massacre had taken place. Of the 143 victims uncovered, 131 of them were children.

For the definitive account of the incident, read Mark Danner's *The Massacre at El Mozote*.

Reagan's election in the US, and a failed offensive in January 1981 that was intended by urban militants to split the military and spark a popular uprising, guerrillas fell back to more defensible positions in the countryside. The army followed them there, sparking a mass exodus of the rural poor. Many flocked to the cities, others fled across the border to Honduras where huge refugee camps were established. The camps were intended to be temporary; then again, the war was supposed to be short-lived. Tens of thousands of Salvadorans spent a decade or more as refugees in Honduras.

Cuidad Segundo Montes (named after one of the six Jesuit priests murdered at San Salvador's Universidad Centroamericana José Simeon Cañas in 1989) is made up of former refugees from one of the largest camps, Colomoncagua, which had, at its peak, around 8000 Salvadorans.

Some former refugees lived in Morazán before the war, other started here afresh. They are bound here by their common ordeal, and talking with residents about their lives, present and former, casts a unique light on the armed conflict.

Any bus traveling between San Francisco Gotera and Perquín passes right by. Let the driver know where you're going, as the entrance is easy to miss.

Sights & Activities
In the camps, makeshift schools helped improve literacy from 10% to 85%, according to local leaders; the same self-reliance is evident at **Fundación Segundo Montes** (☎ 2680 5574, in San Salvador 2260 2710; segmontes@integra.com. sv), which coordinates a number of economic development projects, including bottling, candy-making and garment production. The foundation used to host large conferences, and had a modest hostel and organized guided history tours for guests. That business has since declined, and leaders are seeking to attract more day-to-day tourism. (The opening of Puerto Cutuco near La Union may create a steady flow of short-term visitors to Morazán, a possibility everyone seems to view with a mixture of hopefulness and nervous dread.) Projects in the works here include a hostel, restaurant and museum, as well as eco-historical tours in the surrounding area – a butterfly enclosure is already open. Such projects

are sure to take years to develop, but they should be fascinating when they're finally realized. In the meantime interested travelers can always stop by the foundation's public center, where you can see a number of the community projects and ask if any of the others are available.

CACAOPERA
pop 10,484 / elevation 520m
Cacaopera – 'Place of Cacao' – is one of just a handful of towns in El Salvador that retains a distinct, if subdued, indigenous character. It was built along the Río Torola in the heart of Morazán, and the town's original inhabitants would have been well positioned for agriculture and trade. Cacao cultivation has faded, along with many other pre-Hispanic traditions, but many in the town remain committed to preserving their ancient heritage. Cacaopera has a fine Casa de Cultura, a local indigenous community center (which is not really designed to receive tourists), an excellent museum and a rustic hotel. The town celebrates a number of intimate festivals and ceremonies, many of them stemming from pre-Colombian practices. The people in the *alcaldía* are friendly and helpful, and the small parque central outside the *alcaldía* doors has a bright, low-key atmosphere.

Orientation
Cacaopera's parque central is perched on a bluff of sorts, flanked by the city hall, market and Casa de Cultura. The museum is on the main road headed downhill from the park, well outside of town. Some streets in town are steep and winding, and few are named; fortunately, locals are happy to dispense directions.

Information
Alcaldía (☎ 2651 0244, 2651 0206; ☼ 8am-noon & 1-4pm Mon-Fri) Located on the parque central.
Post Office (Calle Principal; ☼ 8am-noon & 2-5pm Mon-Fri, 8am-noon Sat)
Unidad de Salud (☎ 2654 0212; Calle El Calvario; ☼ 8am-4pm Mon-Fri) Public clinic with an on-site pharmacy.

Sights & Activities
The excellent Kakawira cultural center, **Centro de Interpretacion Eco-Cultural Maya-Kakawira** (☎ 2651 0251; winaka@terra.com; admission US$1;

EL SALVADOR

GETTING TO MARCALA, HONDURAS

There's a twice-daily bus service to Marcala, Honduras, from San Miguel (US$3.50, five hours, 4:40am and 11:40am), which you can also board in Perquín (US$2.50, three hours, approximately 6:30am and 1:30pm). The bus stops at Honduran immigration, where a 30-day tourist card costs US$2. However, due to a border dispute, there is no Salvadoran immigration or customs post there. This is immaterial if you're not planning to return to El Salvador on this trip; however, if you are planning to re-enter El Salvador, even through another entry point, you may be fined or barred entry for having left without passing immigration. If you enter El Salvador here, you will be in the country illegally and could be fined when your status is discovered – even if you go directly to the immigration office in San Miguel or San Salvador. The only sure alternative is to exit/enter through another location, ie El Amatillo. Local businesspeople and tourism officials are pushing the Salvadoran government to open a border control, so far to no avail.

9am-3pm), was created by a local community leader, Miguel Ayala, to study, preserve and teach the history and language of his people. The center functions as a school for local children, an educational ethnographic museum (signage in Spanish only) and hostel. Guided **hikes** during the dry season (December to April) can also be arranged and include countryside tours to two different sets of pre-Colombian petroglyphs: Unamé (4km away) and Yarrawalaje (15km). Guide fees are US$10 per group. The center is located at a Kakawira ceremonial site, at the end of a rocky path that starts 1.5km north of the parque central on a paved road; ask for Miguel Ayala or the *museo* as you go along.

The blue-and-white building a block up the hill from the church is the **Casa de la Cultura** (admission free; 8am-noon & 2-5pm Mon-Fri). A modest photo exhibit show scenes from the town's many religious festivals, and there are indigenous artifacts and artwork on display. It hosts occasional events and presentations (often dance) and has a small library.

The **municipal market** (6am-9pm), alongside (and over) the *alcaldía*, has a small selection of *artesanías*, including hammocks, along with fruits, veggies and other supplies. Many stores close between noon and 1pm (or 2pm) and on Sunday.

Sleeping & Eating

Centro de Interpretacion Eco-Cultural Maya-Kakawira (2651 0251; winaka@terra.com; dm US$5) A very rustic hostel built at the Kakawira cultural center. Dorms have several bunk beds, no electricity, no running water, and buckets for toilets. Bathing (without soap) is permitted in the nearby Río Torola. Occasionally meal service can be arranged,

but guests should come prepared to cook their own meals on the wood-burning stove and fire pit. It's roughing it for sure, but the experience of staying in an indigenous community in the Salvadoran foothills is priceless. See p449 for how to get here.

Comedor Juanita (mains US$2-3; 6:30am-8:30pm) One of a number of small eateries on the 2nd floor of the municipal market. All serve pretty much the same thing – plates of grilled beef, fried chicken or baked fish accompanied by rice and salad; pupusas in the afternoons; and eggs and beans in the mornings. Juanita's faces the front and has nice light and a view of the plaza.

Getting There & Around

Buses go daily to Cacaopera, making it relatively easy to check out. From San Miguel, direct buses to Cacaopera (bus 327, US$1.05, 2½ hours) leave the main terminal at 11am and 12:10pm, and leave Cacaopera on the return trip at 5:30am and 6am. Or take any bus to San Francisco Gotera and switch to bus 337A to Cacaopera (US$0.55, one hour, every 30 to 45 minutes), or the reverse to return. Both buses run all day – the last bus from San Francisco Gotera to Cacaopera leaves at 6:40pm, and the last return bus leaves Cacaopera around 4pm. From Cacaopera, bus 337A to San Francisco Gotera (US$0.55, one hour) departs half-hourly from 5am to 4pm and returns half-hourly from 6am to 6:30pm.

SAN FRANCISCO GOTERA
pop 18,000 / elevation 280m

As a gateway to the upper reaches of Morazán, San Francisco Gotera held strategic importance to both sides in the armed conflict, and a number of bloody street battles took place here. The military maintained a major base in Gotera (as it is commonly known) but suffered frequent attacks by guerrillas operating in the surrunding FMLN-controlled area. Despite its tumultuous past, there's not a whole lot to do or see in San Francicso Gotera these days. Most travelers simply pass through on their way to or from Perquín. It does have a good hotel, though, if you find yourself here around sunset and need a place to crash for the night.

Orientation

From San Miguel, the highway feeds onto Av Norberto Cruz/Morazán, San Francisco Gotera's main northbound avenue. Choked with people, cars and vendors, the avenue cuts up through town, passing Parque La Concordia, the town's central park, before rejoining the highway toward Perquín. Most hotels, restaurants and services are a few blocks north of the park. Southbound traffic, including buses to San Miguel, uses 2a Av, a block east.

Information

Clínica Médica San José (☎ 2664 0160; Av Morazán; ✹ 9:30am–noon Mon-Sat) Across from the hotel Arco Iris and next to Farmacia Versailles.

Club Digital Cíber Café (☎ 2654 3173; Av Morazán; per hr US$1; ✹ 8am-7pm) Opposite hotel Arco Iris.

Farmacia Versailles (☎ 2654 0169; Av Morazán; ✹ 7am–noon & 1-5pm Mon-Sat) Next to Clínica Médica San José and opposite hotel Arco Iris.

Sleeping & Eating

Hotel San Francisco (☎ 2654 0066; Av Morazán 29; r US$5-8, r/tw with air-con US$12/15; P ✹) The best of the two options in town, this is a simple, clean hotel. Rooms are small and a little worn but comfortable nonetheless. Those on the 2nd floor get good sunlight.

Arco Iris (☎ 2654 0492; Av Morazán 25; r US$5, tw with air-con US$8-11; P ✹) A decent second choice if Hotel San Francisco is full. Rooms are simple but in sore need of an update; even a coat of paint would help. Check out a couple before committing to one – they're all relatively clean, but most beds are on the saggy side.

Comedor Brenda Susana (Av Morazán 25; mains US$2-4; ✹ 7am-5pm) A hole-in-the-wall eatery attached to the Arco Iris. Six wood tables are squished into a small square dining area with high ceilings. Service is friendly and meals are what you expect – eggs and tamales in the morning, then in the afternoon grilled or roasted beef, chicken or pork served with rice and salad.

Pollo Campestre (☎ 2671 1000; Av Morazán; mains US$2.50-6; ✹ 7am-9pm) Some pooh-pooh fastfood chains as inauthentic, but look around and you'll see that eating here is a real treat for many working Salvadorans. Besides, sometimes the red-and-yellow plastic seats, picture menus and chirpy uniformed service are a welcome anaesthetic after a long day. Not to be confused with the takeout-only Pollo Campero just up the street. It has a huge children's playground.

Getting There & Around

Bus 328 to San Miguel (US$0.70, one hour) barrels down San Francisco's main southbound drag every 10 minutes until 7pm. Bus 337 goes to Cacaopera (US$0.55, one hour) from 6am to 6:40pm, roughly every 40 to 60 minutes. Pickups line up at the top of Av Morazán, at the northern exit of town, bound for Perquín (US$0.50, one hour).

CORINTO

pop 4000 / elevation 820m

A couple of kilometers outside this small border town are an impressive set of cave paintings, dating back thousands, perhaps tens of thousands, of years. Occupying a high overhanging cliff, they are one of El Salvador's best prehistoric sites – or at least among those you can reach without too much trouble!

Corinto is also well known for its international market. If you can combine a visit to the cave paintings and the market, you've done well. There's not a whole lot else to do here, and you definitely don't want to spend a night in the local hotel. Two roads lead to Corinto, one from the highway, the other from Cacaopera. Both are quite scenic – if you can, come in on one and leave by the other.

Orientation

The heart of Corinto is its large parque central, at the intersection of Corinto's two main streets: Calle Morazán/Pablo Aquilar and Av Rubén Darío/Gustavo Guerrero. Just about everything in Corinto is on the park or one of those two streets. As a reference, the church is on the east side of the park.

Information

Ciber Café Galaxy (☎ 2658 1202; parque central; per hr US$1; ☽ 8am-7pm) Across from the church, on the south side of the parque central.

Clinica Medica Padilla (☎ 2658 1061; 4a Calle Ote at 4a Av Norte; ☽ 8am-4pm) Health clinic next to the pharmacy.

Farmacia Santa Elena (☎ 2658 1061; 4a Calle Ote at 4a Av Norte; ☽ 7am-9pm) A well-stocked pharmacy.

Police (☎ 2658 1219; Av Gustavo Guerrero; ☽ 24hr)

Sight & Activities

Also known as Gruta de Corinto, **Gruta de Espiritu Santo** (admission free; ☽ 9am-4pm Tue-Sun) is the city's main tourist attraction and an important archaeological site. The *gruta* (cavern) is a large overhanging cliff (40m by 5m), where several dozen pictographs are painted on the rock face. (Pictographs are paintings, as opposed to petroglyphs, which are engravings.) The paintings use red, yellow and brown paint, and depict animals like deer, turtles, spiders, crabs and birds. Some also show human figures, holding hands or wearing large headdresses, and a few negative handprints, made when the painter pressed his or her hand to the wall and blew paint over it, creating a silhouette. A number of images are 10m or more above the ground – considering the overhang, it seems the painters must have constructed a scaffolding or ladder of some sort. The site was studied in the 1970s by archaeologists Wolfgang Haberland and Manuel López; they determined the paintings dated to Paleo-Indian times, over 10,000 years ago, but that later engravings and other evidence suggested the cave had been used as a shelter, perhaps by bands of hunters, during the Late Classic period (roughly AD 600–800) and as far as the Post Classic period (after AD 1000).

The site is northeast of Corinto; from the parque central, take Calle Pablo Escobar east two blocks to 4a Av Norte, tun left and follow the signs. The road is unpaved and rough in places, but an ordinary car can make it if you go slowly. Otherwise, it's an easy enough walk – the road forks a few times, so ask passersby as you go.

Every Wednesday and Sunday, hundreds of people, sometimes thousands, come to Corinto's **international market** from surrounding neighborhoods and cities, like San Francisco Gotera and San Miguel, and from across the border in Honduras, to buy and sell mostly domestic products, though there's a little of everything. Sunday is the busier day, but Wednesday is when livestock is sold, always making an interesting scene. The **main market** (☽ 8am-4pm) is just south of the plaza and open daily; on Wednesday and Sunday stalls spread all the way to (and around) the parque central.

Sleeping & Eating

Hotel & Restaurant Corinto (☎ 2658 1263; 4a Av Nte at 4a Calle Ote; r/tw US$6/12, s with bathroom US$10; **P**) God forbid you have to stay the night here. The rooms are humid and dirty, the bathrooms worse. Rooms with a shared bathroom are preferable – the bathroom itself isn't better, but at least it's not stinking up your room. Rooms have cable TV, which is some solace. It's located two blocks east and a block north of the park. If you do get stuck in Corinto, ask around if another hotel has opened before heading here.

Pollo Silvestre (☎ 2658 1496; 1a Calle Ote at Av Rubén Darío; mains US$2-3; ☽ 7am-10pm) Bright clean restaurant with a high-ceiling dining area filled with plastic tables with benches. Chicken is the specialty, of course, served fried, breaded or grilled, but fish, beef and pork are also on the menu. It's located a half-block east of the parque central.

Getting There & Around

All buses come and go from the parque central area. Bus 782 (US$1, hourly from 5am to 4pm) covers the windy, newly paved road between Corinto and Cacaopera, while bus 327 goes to and from San Miguel (US$0.80, 4am to 4:15pm).

GUATAJIAGUA

pop 7500 / elevation 260m

The name Guatajiagua comes from a Lenka Potón expression meaning 'Valley with Tobacco Cultivation,' formed by the words *gua* (tobacco), *ta* (cultivation) and *yagual* (valley). Today most farmers here grow beans, corn and pineapple, but the town is known for something different altogether: black pottery. One local sculptor is internationally known for his clay figures, and many townspeople are involved in the making of clay plates, bowls and vases, which can be found in *artesanía* markets around the country. A special process tints the clay dark brown or, done thoroughly enough, charcoal black.

Most days, Guatajiagua's streets are quiet and its market sleepy. The road on either side of Guatajiagua – east to San Francisco Gotera and west to Chapeltique – should be paved by the time you read this. That will surely increase the number of San Migueleños who come here to shop, but it's hard to imagine Guatajiagua as anything but a peaceful little town.

The main road bends around Guatajiagua's central park, where the church, city hall and market are all located. Most restaurants and shops, including Cedart, are west of the park, on the road toward Chapeltique.

The **patron saint festival** is held on January 17 to 20 in honor of San Sebastián Mártir.

Information

Alcaldía (☎ 2658 6216; parque central; ☻ 8am-noon & 1-4pm Mon-Fri)

Police (☎ 2658 6223; Calle Principal; ☻ 24hr)

Unidad de Salud (Calle Principal; ☻ 7am-4pm Mon-Fri) Located near the exit to Chapeltique.

Sights & Activities

Most people come to Guatajiagua to shop for local pottery in various home workshops. A nearby waterfall makes a pleasant hike and swim, if you have extra time.

Sarbelio Vásquez Garcia is Guatajiagua's most famous sculptor; he won an international art prize in Spain in 2001 and served on national artisan's committees. He is best known for his *clameme*, a black clay figure of a man kneeling to lift a heavy basketful of *artesanías*. He makes them in many sizes and degrees of elaboration, and they can be found in *artesanía* stores throughout the country – a must for any collection of Salvadoran folk art. You can also see (or buy) them at his home workshop, a short walk from the city center. Ask someone in the *alcaldía* to call to make sure that he's at home. Another sought-after sculptor is Pacita García, whose workshop is on the road toward San Francisco Gotera.

If you want to look at a good selection of local artists' works, check out **Cedart** (☎ 2658 6441; Calle Principal; ☻ 8am-5pm Mon-Fri, 8am-noon Sat), a government-sponsored community center that provides assistance to local artists. A small gift shop has beautiful examples of some of the best work in Guatajiagua. If you like one object or style in particular, let a clerk know; she will likely point you in the direction of the artist's workshop.

La Cascada del Salto (Waterfall of the Waterfall) is the somewhat redundant name of a local – er – waterfall. Most people just call it El Salto; by any name, it's a nice enough spot to visit, with the 10m falls forming a small swimming hole. Located in the neighborhood of Caserio Los Llanitos, it's just a half-hour's walk along the Río Pueblo from the city center; just about anyone can point you in the right direction.

Sleeping & Eating

Guatajiagua's first hotel was in the works when we visited; ask at the *alcaldía* for the latest info.

Las Cocinas (☻ 6am-5pm) These are commonly referred to as 'The Kitchens' by everyone in town; they are a handful of open-air food stands just outside the market building facing the parque central. They're especially popular for breakfast, including eggs, beans, beef soup, coffee, atole – all the classic Salvadoran sunrise food.

El Merendero Buena Vista (mains US$1.50-3; ☻ breakfast, lunch & dinner) A simple restaurant serving *típica*. You can't miss it – it's on a prominent corner on the main road, about a block east (downhill) from the parque central.

Getting There & Around

Getting to and from Guatajiagua should be immensely easier and faster once the road is paved. The frequency and duration of the bus route may change, though probably less than you'd think.

From Guatajiagua, you can catch a bus to San Francisco Gotera (bus 410, US$0.80, one hour, hourly from 5:30am to 4:30pm) or go via Chapeltique to San Miguel (bus 326, US$1, 1¼ hours, hourly).

EL SALVADOR DIRECTORY

ACCOMMODATIONS

El Salvador has a better selection of hotels than you might guess – though casual tourism is still nascent, there's a steady flow of business travelers. All large cities and towns have at least a couple of recommendable hotels in the budget and midrange categories; upper-end hotels are mostly in San Salvador, though you'll find a smattering in Suchitoto, La Libertad and elsewhere on the coast. Small towns are less predictable – some receive mostly daytrippers from San Salvador or San Miguel, so there's little demand for accommodations (nor pressure to make them decent or affordable).

El Salvador has fewer hostels than other Central American countries, but the idea is catching on. San Salvador now has three dorm accommodations – up from one a few years ago – and there are others in Santa Ana, Juayúa, Perquín, Los Cóbanos and Lago Coatepeque.

Camping areas and *eco-albergues* (rural lodges) are appearing in El Salvador's popular outdoors destinations, including most national parks. Camping supplies are another story – best to come well equipped. There's a handful of higher-end mountain retreats, for those who want to be in the countryside but aren't keen on latrine toilets.

You can stay for free at *centros de obreros* (government workers' centers), huge compounds designed to give workers and their families a place to relax on the weekend. Sounds good, except there are only four in the country – at Lago de Coatepeque, El Tamarindo, La Palma and just outside La Libertad – and you have to go in person to the appropriate office in San Salvador to reserve a spot. See p316 for details.

Room rates don't change much season to season, except during the summer holiday (August 1 to 6), when hotels in popular towns fill up fast.

ACTIVITIES
Diving

El Salvador has two diveable crater lakes and one of the only large coral formations on the American side of the Pacific Ocean. While the sites are mildly interesting, the overall diving experience is far better and less expensive in nearby Honduras and Belize. Lago Ilopango has the best lake diving, including a large underwater hill called La Caldera, the top of which is at about 10m. One side drops almost vertically 175m, the other side is a rocky slope with numerous thermal vents known as *vapores* ('steamers') – the water flowing from them is extremely hot, distorting the cooler lake water. Visibility averages 6m to 9m, water temperature around 77 degrees Fahrenheit (25°C).

Los Cóbanos, south of Sonsonate near the western port town of Acajutla, has El Salvador's best ocean diving. A sloping shelf contains hundreds of boulders ejected from an ancient volcanic eruption, now covered in coral. There are about 350 significant promontories, and untold smaller and unexplored ones, spread over 160 sq km. They range from 1m to 5m in diameter and are found at depths ranging from 3m to 60m. They are home to numerous fish, eels, lobsters and turtles, plus at least four shipwrecks in 9m to 18m of water, including a huge hybrid steam and sail ship that sunk around 1890. The major drawback here is the visibility, which can reach 9m or fall to less than 1m, with an unpredictable current. December to February has the best conditions (and whales are in the area at the same time), but getting a good day is still mostly luck.

See p317 for diving-tour operators based in San Salvador.

Hiking

El Salvador has some excellent hiking, despite serious deforestation. Parque Nacional El Imposible (p375), near the border with Guatemala, offers the best combination of easy accessibility and rewarding hikes through primary forest. The Ruta de las Flores, especially the town of Juayúa, also has excellent guided hiking trips, mostly half-day excursions to nearby lakes and waterfalls. Further north, Parque Nacional Montecristo-El Trifinio (p360) is much harder to access and accordingly more pristine; the main hike there leads you through cloud forests to the beak of Cerro Montecristo and the point at which El Salvador, Guatemala and Honduras all meet. The park is known for its wildlife and is closed during mating season, which is from May to November. Parque Nacional Los Volcanes (p353) has two climbable volcanoes and is a beautiful, if sometimes crowded, destination. El Pital (2730m) is El Salvador's highest peak and also one of the easiest to climb. It's accessible via the northwestern towns of La Palma and San Ignacio (p392). The northeastern state of Morazán, including the town of Perquín, has a cool climate and fine hiking, and, as a longtime stronghold of the FMLN, has interesting and sobering sites related to the civil war.

Surfing

El Salvador has arguably the best surfing in Central America, and is among the top spots in the world. Punta Roca, an awesome right-hand point break, and the country's best wave, is in Puerto La Libertad (p396), a short drive due south from San Salvador. Punta Roca can get busy, but west of La Libertad are a string of world-class waves with very little traffic, especially midweek. A number of small beachside communities have surfer lodges, which many foreigners prefer to La Libertad proper (which is rather seedy). Even less trafficked are the eastern beaches, accessible through the beach town of El Cuco; many of the breaks are reachable only by boat. Several surfing outfits have set up private surf camps there, offering all-inclusive week-long surf safaris. The main drawbacks to El Salvador's surfing scene are the dearth of left-hand breaks and the unpleasantness of La Libertad. Surf lodges and private instructors offer surf classes for all levels. The following places offer lessons.

Akwaterra (☎ 2263 2211; www.akwaterra.com)

Epic Surfing Adventures (☎ 7890 4751, ☎ 888-669-7873 in USA; www.epicsurfingadventures.com)

Horizonte Surf Resort (☎ 2323 0099; saburosurfcamp@hotmail.com; Playa El Zonte)

Hospital de las Tablas (☎ 2335 3214, 7944 3632; 3a Ave Norte 27-8 btwn 2a & 4a Calles Pte, La Libertad)

Jungle Surf Tours (☎ 2245 1484 or 310-544-1942 in USA; www.junglesurftours.com)

K59 Surf Tours (☎ 2235 0432; www.k59surftours.com)

Papaya Surf Tours (☎ 2389 6231; www.papayasurfing .com; Playa El Tunco)

Punta Mango (☎ 2236-0025, ☎ 888-899-8823 in USA; www.puntamango.com)

Punta Roca Surf Resort (☎ 2335 3261; www .puntaroca.com)

For more information about surfing in El Salvador, see p45.

BUSINESS HOURS

Businesses generally operate 9am to 6pm weekdays, and government offices from 8am to 4pm. Some government offices and small shops close at lunchtime, between noon and 2pm, but this practice is fading. Banks are open 8am to 4pm or 5pm weekdays; most are open Saturday morning as well. Restaurants serve dinner early, and 4pm is pupusa (cornmeal mass stuffed with cheese or refried beans) hour.

CHILDREN

El Salvador isn't a bad place to bring children, as long as they are amenable to the uncertainties of traveling in an off-the-beaten-path area. San Salvador has an excellent children's museum, natural-history museum and zoo, and many of the hiking and other outdoors activities are short enough for youngsters to tackle.

Also, as in most Latin American countries, children are welcome almost everywhere; you'll find business owners and tour operators generally unfazed by their presence. In some cases, you may even be treated better if you're traveling with youngsters

COURSES

A number of universities and church groups organize student trips to El Salvador, but there are a handful of schools based in El Salvador itself where travelers can take courses, mostly to learn Spanish. The best is the Centro de Intercambio y Solidaridad (p325) in San Salvador. Another option in San Salvador is Escuela Cuscatlán (p325), which has a sister school, Escuela Sihuatehuacán (p348), in Santa Ana.

CUSTOMS

Salvadoran border officials are among the most scrutinizing in the region. They will actually check your passport for previous entry and exit stamps, and may well search your bags. Carry your passport with you in all border areas, even if you don't plan on crossing, as there are a number of police checkpoints (mostly looking for drugs). It's not necessary to keep it on you in the interior.

DANGERS & ANNOYANCES

Crime shouldn't deter travelers from El Salvador any more than it does from Guatemala, Honduras or the rest of Central America. Despite a reputation for violence, attacks on tourists are rare. Take common-sense precautions: carry as little as possible on day trips, avoid carrying flashy cameras, expensive watches and jewelry, and make copies of your credit cards and important documents. Take taxis after dark, especially if the streets are deserted. This is particularly important in San Salvador, San Miguel, Sonsonate, La Unión and La Libertad. Most volcano climbs are best done with a police escort, partly for safety and partly so you don't get lost on unmarked and intersecting trails. The service is free, but you must request it by telephone or in person at least a day in advance (and preferably more) Officers are friendly and trustworthy.

Of course, violence does occur. Two major *maras* (gangs) operate in the country: Mara 18 and Mara Salvatrucha, also known as MS-13 (see the boxed text, p302). El Salvador has a disturbingly high murder rate, but the vast majority of victims and perpetrators are affiliated with a gang. Travelers are unlikely to encounter any gang members as they are concentrated in neighborhoods with no outside appeal, and because the police patrol most tourist areas. Still, travelers should avoid traveling at night and should never resist a robbery – it's not worth it.

DISABLED TRAVELERS

There are plenty of disabled people in El Salvador, but little is done to make their lives (or yours) any easier. There are virtually no wheelchair-friendly buses, few well-maintained ramps and handrails, and few services for the visually and hearing impaired. However, disabled travelers (like all travelers) will find Salvadorans friendly and eager to help. See p468 for some helpful websites.

EMBASSIES & CONSULATES
El Salvador Embassies & Consulates Abroad

For a complete list, go to www.rree.gob.sv /website/embajadas.html.

Argentina (☎ 0054 11 4325 0849; Calle Suipacha 1380, 2nd fl, Buenos Aires)
Australia (☎ 61 3 9867 4400; Level 3, 499 St Kilda Rd, Melbourne 3004)
Belgium (☎ 0322 733 0485; Ave de Tervueren 171, 2nd fl 1150, Brussels)
Brazil (☎ 055 61 364 4141; Shis QL 10, Conjunto 01, Casa 15, CEP 71630-100, Brasilia) Consular representation also is found in Salvador, Bahia.
Canada (☎ 613 238 2939; 209 Kent St K2P, 1Z8, Ottawa, Ontario) Consular representation also is found in Toronto, Montreal and Vancouver.
Chile (☎ 0562 233 8324; Calle Coronel 2330, 5th fl, Oficina 51 Providencia Santiago de Chile)
Colombia (☎ 0571 349 6765; Carrera 9, 8015 Ofic, 503, Edif El Nogal, Bogota)
Ecuador (☎ 0593 22 433 070; Edif Portugal, Av Republica de El Salvador 130, 11th fl, Quito)
France (☎ 033 147 20 4202; 12 Rue Galilée 75116, Paris)
Germany (☎ 49 30 206 4660; Joachim-Karnatz-Allee 47, 10557 Berlin)
Israel (☎ 0972 2672 8411; 4 Avigail, Apto 4 Abu-tor, Jerusalem 93551)
Italy (☎ 039 06 807 6605; Via Gualtiero Castellini 13, Scala B, Int 3, 00197 Roma) Consular representation also is found in Milan.
Japan (☎ 081 3 3499 4461; Kowa 38, Bldg 803 Nishi Azabu, 4 Ch Tokyo 106)
Mexico (☎ 5281 5725; Temístocles 88, Col Polanco 11560, México DF) Consular representation also is found in Monterrey, Nuevo León and Tapachula, Chiapas.
Peru (☎ 0511 440 3500; Av Javier Prado Oeste 2108, Lima)
South Korea (☎ 082 2753 3432; Samsung Life Insurance Bldg 150, 20th fl, Taepyungro 2-KA, Choong-Ku, Seoul 100-716)
Spain (☎ 034 91562 8002; Calle General Oraá 9, Quinto Derecha 28006, Madrid)
Sweden (☎ 0468 765 8621; Herserudsvagen 5a, 5th fl, 181 33 Lindingo, Stockholm)
Taiwan (Republic of China) (☎ 0886 2 2876 3509; 9, 2F, Lane 62, Tien Mou West Rd Shih-Lin 111, Taipei)
UK (☎ 044 207 436 8282; Mayfair House, 3rd fl, 39 Great Portland St, London W1W7JZ)
USA (☎ 202 387 6511; 2308 California St, NW, Washington, DC 20008) Consular representation also is found in Nogales (AZ), Los Angeles (CA), San Francisco (CA), Washington (DC), Coral Gables (FLA), Duluth (GA), Chicago (ILL), Boston (MA), Elizabeth (NJ), Las Vegas (NV), Brentwood (NY), New York City (NY), Dallas (TX), Houston (TX) and Woodbridge (VA).
Venezuela (☎ 058 212 959 0817; Centro Comercial (Cuidad Tamanaco CCCT) Torre C, 4th fl, 406 Caracas)

Embassies & Consulates in El Salvador

Australia does not have an embassy in El Salvador, but Australians can get basic assistance at the local Canadian Embassy.

New Zealand and the UK do not have consular representation in El Salvador. All of the following are in San Salvador.

Argentina (Map p324; ☎ 2263 3580; Calle El Mirador 5546, Col Escalón; 🕑 9am-2pm Mon-Fri)

Belize (☎ 2248 1423; Calle El Bosque Norte 704, Col La Lima IV; 🕑 8am-noon,1-5pm Mon-Fri, 8am-noon Sat)

Brazil (Map p324; ☎ 2298 7888; Blvd del Hipódromo 132, Col San Benito; 🕑 8am-2pm Mon-Fri)

Canada (Map pp320-1; ☎ 2279 4655; Alameda Roosevelt at 63a Av Sur, Torre A; 🕑 8:30am-noon Mon-Fri)

Chile (Map p324; ☎ 2263 4268; Pasaje Bella Vista 121 near 9a Calle Pte, Col Escalón; 🕑 8:30am-12:30pm Mon-Fri)

Colombia (Map p324; ☎ 2263 1936; Calle El Mirador 5120, Col Escalón; 🕑 8:30am-1pm, 2-4pm Mon-Fri)

Costa Rica (Map p324; ☎ 2264 3863; Calle Cuscatlán 4415, Col Escalón; 🕑 8am-12:30pm Mon-Fri) Some services are available until 4pm

Dominican Republic (Map p324; ☎ 2263 1816; Av Républica Federal de Alemania 163, Col Escalón; 🕑 8:30am-2pm Mon-Fri)

Ecuador (Map p324; ☎ 2263 5258; Pasaje Entre Pinos 241, Col Escalón; 🕑 8am-1pm, 2-4pm Mon-Fri)

Finland (Map p322; ☎ 2261 1113; Calle Gabriela Mistral 375; 🕑 8am-noon, 1-5pm Mon-Fri)

France (Map p324; ☎ 2279 4016; www.embafrancia.com.sv; 1a Calle Pte 3718, Col Escalón; 🕑 8:15am-noon Mon-Fri)

Germany (Map p324; ☎ 2247 0000; www.san-salvador.diplo.de; 77a Av Norte at 7a Calle Pte, Col Escalón; 🕑 9am-noon Mon-Fri)

Greece (Map p324; ☎ 2263 3402; 77a Av Norte btwn 5 Calle Pte & Pasaje Istmania; 🕑 9am-1pm Mon-Fri)

Guatemala (Map pp320-1; ☎ 2271 2225; 15a Av Norte btwn Calles Arce & 1a Calle Norte, Col Escalón; 🕑 9am-noon, 2-5pm Mon-Fri) Afternoons open for document pick-up only.

Honduras (Map p324; ☎ 2263 2808; 89a Av Norte btwn 7a & 9a Calle Pte, Col Escalón; 🕑 8:30am-12:30pm, 2-4:30pm Mon-Fri)

Israel (Map pp320-1; ☎ 2211 3434; Alameda Roosevelt at 63a Av Sur, Torre Telefónica; 🕑 9am-noon Mon-Fri)

Italy (Map p324; ☎ 2223 4806; Calle La Reforma 158, Col San Benito; 🕑 9am-noon Mon-Fri)

Japan (Map p324; ☎ 2264 6100; World Trade Center 1, 6th fl, Calle El Mirador at 89a Av Norte, Col Escalón; 🕑 8am-noon, 2-5:30pm Mon-Fri)

México (Map p324; ☎ 2243 0445; Calle Circunvalación at Pasaje 12, Col San Benito; 🕑 8am-noon Mon-Fri)

Netherlands (Map p324; ☎ 2298 2185; 1a Calle Pte 3796, 2nd fl, Col Escalón; 🕑 9am-1pm Mon-Fri)

Nicaragua (Map p324; ☎ 2263 8789; Calle El Mirador btwn 93a & 95a Av Norte, Col Escalón; 🕑 8am-12:15pm Mon-Fri)

Panama (Map p324; ☎ 2245 5410; Gran Plaza Bldg, 2nd fl, Blvd del Hipódromo, Col San Benito; 🕑 8am-4pm Mon-Fri)

Peru (Map p324; ☎ 2259 8080; Calle Mirador 217, Col Escalón; 🕑 9am-12:30pm Mon-Fri)

South Korea (Map p324; ☎ 2263 9145; 5a Calle Pte btwn 75a & 77a Av Norte, Col Escalón; 🕑 8am-12:30pm, 1:30-5pm Mon-Fri)

Spain (Map p324; ☎ 2257 5709; Calle La Reforma 164, Col San Benito; 🕑 9am-1pm Mon-Fri)

Switzerland (Map p324; ☎ 2263 7485; Paseo Escalón at 85 Av Sur; 🕑 8am-noon Mon-Fri) This is an honorary consulate only.

Taiwan (Map p324; ☎ 2263 1330; Av La Capilla 716, Col Escalón; 🕑 8am-12:30pm, 2-5:30pm Mon-Fri)

USA (☎ 2278 4444 ext 2628; www.sansalvador.usembassy.gov; Blvd Santa Elena Final, Col Antiguo Cuscatlán, La Libertad; 🕑 8am-3:30am Mon, Tue, Thu & Fri, 8am-noon Wed)

Venezuela (Map p324; ☎ 2263 3977; 7a Calle Pte 3921, Col Escalón; 🕑 8:30am-noon Mon-Fri)

FESTIVALS & EVENTS

Festival Internacional Permanente de Arte y Cultura (February) A month-long celebration in Suchitoto that brings national and international artists to town. The festivities are held every weekend and include parades, expositions, live performances and presentations.

Feria Cultural de las Flores y las Palmas (May) A flower and palm festival held in Panchimalco with palm artistry, live music, folk dancing and fireworks.

Festival del Invierno (August) An art and music festival held the first week of the month in Perquín. Artists from all over of the country and region come to perform their music or to exhibit their work. Popular with the college-aged and boho crowd.

Festival de Maíz (August) Suchitoto's Corn Festival, which stems from pre-Colombian rituals associated with harvesting corn. Religious processions, a special mass and a street party are held.

Festival de Hamacas (November) A hammock festival held in the middle of the month in Concepción Quezaltepeque; a street fair, and a huge variety of hammocks are sold in the main plaza.

Feria de Innovación Artesanal (December) A three-day national crafts fair held in San Salvador.

Feria Artesanal 'Así es mi Tierra' (weekly) An arts festival that's held every weekend in Suchitoto; food is served, live music is played and several stands sell *artesanías* and artwork.

Feria Gastronómica (weekly) A popular food fair held every weekend in Juayúa. Stands start serving regional food around 10:30am and keep running until the last visitor leaves.

Feria de la Cocina Cojutepeque (weekly) A smaller food fair held every Sunday at the top of the Cerro de las Pavas, sometimes with live music and *artesanía* stands.

GAY & LESBIAN TRAVELERS

Little tolerance is given to openly gay men or women. Some hotel managers will simply refuse to rent a room with one bed to two men, and public displays of affection will instantly attract disapproving stares. In San Salvador, the area around Blvd de los Héroes has cultural centers and clubs that, being more bohemian, are also more tolerant. **Entre Amigos** (Between Friends; ☎ 225 4213; entreamigos@salnet.net; Av Santa Victoria No 50 near Blvd de los Héroes) is the most established gay organization in the country and is dedicated mostly to HIV/AIDS outreach.

HOLIDAYS

Each city, town and village has a festival for its patron saint during the year called a *fiesta patronal*. The country celebrates its patron saint the first week of August; most banks, government offices and universities are closed, and tourist sites and borders are crowded. Holidays include:

New Year's Day (January 1)
Semana Santa (Holy Thursday to Easter Sunday)
Labor Day (May 1)
Corpus Christi (first week in June)
Festival of El Salvador (August 1-6)
Independence Day (September 15)
All Souls' Day (November 2)
Cry of Independence Day (November 5)
Virgen de Guadalupe Day (December 12)
Christmas (December 25-31)

INTERNET ACCESS

The Salvadoran government has opened dozens of Internet cafés called Infocentros, from the capital to the tiny mountain towns. Most have air-con and fast connections, and charge US$1 an hour. Privately run Internet cafés are also common and mostly have the same prices and services.

INTERNET RESOURCES

El Diario de Hoy (www.elsalvador.com) The link to the Spanish-language newspaper *El Diario de Hoy*; particularly good for a schedule of cultural events.
El Salvador by Bus (www.elsalvadorbybus.com) Website aimed at backpackers with links to hostels, bus routes and activities. Spanish and English.
El Salvador en Imagenes (www.4elsalvador.com)

Extensive photo library and background information on sights and attractions. Spanish and English links.
El Salvador Turismo (www.elsalvadorturismo.gob.sv) Corsatur's official website offers links to tourist sights, officialdom, and cultural events in the entire country. Spanish only, although an English-language link is in the works.
iExplore (www.iexplore.com/dmap/El+Salvador) English-language website with general information and recommendations on traveling to and around El Salvador.
La Prensa Gráfica (www.laprensa.com.sv) The Spanish-language website for one of El Salvador's major daily newspapers.
Latin America Network Information Center (www.lanic.utexas.edu/la/ca/salvador) Comprehensive lists of Salvadoran sites, arranged by topic.
Surfer El Salvador (www.surfer.com.sv) Description of the Western Pacific surfing scene. Spanish and English links.
Tim's El Salvador Blog (http://luterano.blogspot.com) A handy private blog with current news items and commentary about El Salvador, all in English.

LEGAL MATTERS

Law enforcement is strict and effective, from beat cops to border officials. Police are entitled to stop buses and search people and bags, and do so with some frequency, often helped by army soldiers. Bribes are not the norm here, as in some other countries – if you're arrested it's better to cooperate and call your embassy. That said, even minor offences can carry jail time, and there's little your embassy can do if you have, in fact, committed a crime.

MAPS

With a general lack of tourists comes a general lack of good, readily available maps. Corsatur (p317) and the Ministry of Tourism produce similar glossy maps, with San Salvador on one side and either the country or additional cities on the other. They are for sale (or handed out free) in various hotels and tourist offices.

At the other extreme, the **Centro Nacional de Registros** (Map pp320-1; ☎ 2261 8716; www.cnr.gob.sv; 1a Calle Pte; ☼ 8am-noon, 1-4pm Mon-Fri) has extremely detailed, high-quality maps of the entire country and most municipalities. Map-lovers will swoon over the huge (1.5m by 0.95m) full-color official country map; if US$36 is your food budget for the week, there's a smaller version (0.62m by 0.40m) for just US$2.30. City maps (called *planos urbanos*) run to about US$5; the big

San Salvador map is US$12. You can also get maps of the states, or booklets called *monografías departamentales* which have maps and statistical info about each state; some haven't been updated since the Reagan years. The CNR is located south of the Metrosur shopping center; buy maps at the *Atención a cliente y comercialización* desk on the second floor of Module 1.

MONEY

In January 2001, El Salvador adopted the US dollar as official currency, a change known as the *dolarización*. The previous currency (the colón) technically still exists, but you'll probably never see or use one.

ATMs

ATMs (*cajeros automáticos*) can be found in most cities and towns, especially those that receive a fair number of travelers. (The glaring exceptions are Suchitoto, Perquín and La Libertad.) Banco Cuscatlán, Scotia-bank, and Banco Atlántida have the largest network of ATMs, and most accept major foreign debit cards. It used to be that ATMs only accepted cards with Plus/Visa symbols, but Cirrus/Mastercard debits cards now generally work as well. If the machine doesn't take your card, you may be able ask the teller inside the bank. Or if your bank at home charges exorbitant foreign ATM fees (and your debit card has a Visa or Mastercard symbol) you can usually avoid the fee by going into the bank and using your debit card to take out a cash advance, as if it were a credit card. For this to work be sure to say it is a *tarjeta de crédito* not a *tarjeta de débito*. The malls in San Salvador, Santa Ana and San Miguel all have multiple ATMs, and are a secure place to withdraw cash. In town, some banks place their ATMs in small locking cabins, which are preferable to those right on the street. In all cases, be aware of your surroundings and avoid withdrawing money at night.

DOLARIZACIÓN

In January 2001, El Salvador became the third Latin American country to phase out its currency, the colón, and adopt the US dollar as its sole legal tender (the others are Panama and Ecuador). If it succeeds in controlling inflation and promoting growth, it is likely other Central American countries will follow suit (Guatemala has already made dollars legal currency alongside its own quetzales).

Dollarization was opposed by the FMLN and others on the left, but more than a decade of Arena control of the presidency kept the plan on track. The colón was pegged to the US dollar in 1994 (at 8.75 to the dollar) and strict controls put in place to avoid inflationary creep: bus fares, for example, were converted to the nearest penny, resulting in strange fares, like US$0.23 for most urban routes. Most people complain that prices went up, but admit it wasn't drastic. Today, all transactions are in dollars – even the word 'quarter' has been adopted (sounding more like *cuoda* when Salvadorans say it) though 'penny', 'nickel' and 'dime' have not.

Dollarization makes certain sense for a country like El Salvador, which is already deeply entangled in the US economy. Fifteen percent of its GDP is in remittances from the United States, and fully two thirds of its exports go to US buyers – dollars are certainly not new to most Salvadorans. A dollar economy ought to ease those and other international transactions, and eventually boost outside investment.

A loss of economic autonomy is one argument against dollarization. With US trade deficits so high, and the euro and yen rising as 'safe' international currencies, being tied to the US dollar may be risky. Likewise, if neighboring currencies fall against the dollar Salvadoran products suddenly become more expensive, hurting exports. The Salvadoran workforce has proven nimble enough to adjust to changing markets, but a few red flags are appearing – growth was just 2.5% in 2005 and for the first time in a long time the country had to import guest workers to pick coffee and cut sugarcane.

Another argument against it is a loss of national sovereignty and identity. The US already looms large in the lives of most Salvadorans; the adoption of US money strikes more than a few Salvadorans as, well, weak. And many see no coincidence that El Salvador is the only Central American country with troops still in Iraq.

EL SALVADOR

Tipping & Bargaining

A 10% tip is expected at restaurants, but it is not customary to tip taxi drivers. Bargaining isn't as common in El Salvador as in other Central American countries. A little back-and-forth is common with taxi drivers and market shopkeepers, but hard bargaining, á la Guatemala, can seem a bit rude.

Cash

Bring US dollars, preferably in US$20 bills and smaller. There is no need to buy, carry or use the old Salvadoran currency – even ATMs distribute dollars. Banco Cuscatlán, Scotiabank and Banco Atlántida change travelers checks; only Banco Cuscatlán exchanges non-US currency, like euros or quetzals. You can also change Honduran lempira and Guatemalan quetzals at the respective borders.

Credit Cards

Credit cards are usually accepted without an additional fee in modern malls, high end hotels and upscale stores, but smaller establishments often add a 6% to 12% surcharge. Visa cards encounter the least resistance, though Mastercard is very widely-accepted now as well; American Express is much more hit-and-miss.

Traveler's Checks

Many people find travelers checks less convenient and no more secure than using debit cards. You may consider bringing a couple of hundred dollars in TCs, as an emergency stash should your debit card be lost or stolen; you can always re-deposit unused checks into your bank account when you return home. Most Banco Cuscatlán, Scotiabank and Banco Atlántida branches change traveler's checks (passport required); American Express checks are best. There are also Western Union offices in most towns, even tiny isolated ones – hello, remittances!

POST

There are two rates for sending mail internationally: airmail and express mail. Letters sent by airmail to the USA should arrive in 10 days (US$0.50), to Europe and Asia in up to 15 days (US$0.65). Letters sent by express mail to the USA should take five days (US$1), to Europe and Asia 10 days (US$1.20). FedEx and DHL also have offices in large cities for urgent deliveries worldwide.

SOLO TRAVELERS

As in most of the world, people traveling alone in El Salvador will find themselves paying a little extra for it. Rooms rates are not cut in half for solo travelers, and guided tours typically have a minimum fee that is based on a party of four.

And while traveling alone can be fun and safe, it is especially important for solo travelers to avoid traveling after dark, to not walk in isolated areas, to refuse drinks from people you don't have a good reason to trust (even if they are cute), and to be aware of their belongings at all time.

TELEPHONE

The country code when calling El Salvador from abroad is ☎ 503; there are no internal area codes. In May 2005, all phone numbers had an eighth digit added at the beginning – '2' for land lines and '7' for cell phones. Some brochures and business cards still have seven-digit numbers listed; land lines used to begin with digits 1-6, and cell phones 7-9, to which you should add '2' or '7' accordingly.

There are virtually no public calling centers in El Salvador though a number of Internet cafés offer web-based calling. For local calls, public phone booths are everywhere – street corners, gas stations, in the back of restaurants and at upscale hotels. Two different phone companies – Telecom and Telefónica – have competing phone booths. Telecom's booths, with their yellow plastic cabins, are by far the most common. Telefónica's booths are lime green. Both operate with prepaid cards; you insert the card chip-side first and the phone reads how much credit you have. (Not to be confused with prepaid cards for cellphones, which are thin and have a code you reveal by scratching off the grey film.) Telecom phones accept *tarjeta Ladatel* (Ladatel cards) which are sold at corner stores, pharmacies, and supermarkets; same goes for Telefónica cards. Local and international dialing instructions should be printed in English and Spanish on a chart inside the phone cabin. Coin-operated phones are rare but gaining popularity, no doubt helped by El Salvador's adoption of US dollars and coins as the official currency.

TOURIST INFORMATION

There are few tourist information offices in El Salvador, and even fewer that provide more than general brochure-type info. Perquín and Suchitoto have the best offices, both professional, friendly and genuinely helpful. Other towns, like Juayúa and Apaneca, have kiosks in their main plazas that are open on weekends. Certain hotel owners and tour operators are also reliable sources of information – we've noted this wherever applicable.

The national tourism entities are in San Salvador (details are on p316), though they are not really worth your time. Corsatur is inconveniently located near the US Embassy and gives out maps, brochures and fliers; they also publish a glossy magazine containing some useful information. It also has a desk at the international airport, open from 10am to 5:30pm, but it's often unmanned. The Instituto Salvadoreño de Turismo has very general information about El Salvador's national parks and turicentros. Concultura manages El Salvador's major museums, archaeological sites, and cultural centers. General information is available at the main office, but its website (www.concultura .gob.sv) is much more useful.

VISAS

Citizens of the USA, Canada, Australia, New Zealand, South Africa, Switzerland, Norway, Japan, Taiwan, Brazil, Argentina, Mexico, other Central American countries, Israel, UK and other EU member countries do not need an advance visa, but must purchase a single-entry tourist card for US$10 when entering the country. It is typically good for 30 days, but you can request up to 90 days – be sure to ask when you step up to the immigration counter. You are technically required to have a return or onward ticket, but this is rarely checked. Note that the new Salvadoran tourist card is a large sticker which takes up a full page of your passport – be sure you have plenty of free space! For those who do need visas, the cost is US$30.

If you leave El Salvador by land and return within your original allotted time, you are not supposed to have pay the US$10

again. Officials at some border crossings may still try to charge you – throwing a fit probably won't help, but respectfully explaining what you were told when you got your tourist card and asking the officer to double check the rule shouldn't hurt. The provision is relatively new (and very few tourists make use of it) so in many cases officers are simply unaware of the rule.

If you lose your visa or tourist card, or want to extend your stay, go to the Salvadoran **immigration office** (Dirección General de Migración y Extranjería; Map p324; ☎ 2202 9650; Galerías Escalón, street level, Paseo General Escalón; ⟨Y⟩ 9am-5pm Mon-Fri, 9am-1pm Sat).

WOMEN TRAVELERS

Foreign women may be approached by men more often than at home, but such behavior is generally harmless. Although traveling alone here presents a challenge, solo women are unlikely to encounter any dangerous situations if they take ordinary precautions. A good way to reduce unwanted attention is to ignore the hissing sounds or catcalls, don't make eye contact, and wear clothes that are appropriate to the locale (ie avoid shorts everywhere but the beach, and cover up more in rural areas).

VOLUNTEERING

El Salvador has many opportunities for people interested in volunteering while on vacation or as a vacation.

Centro de Intercambio y Solidaridad (☎ 2235 2486; www.cis-elsalvador.org; Blvd Universitario near 39 Av Norte, San Salvador) Offers Spanish classes to tourists and English classes to low-income and activist Salvadorans, always with a strong emphasis on progressive politics. CIS has positions for volunteer English teachers (10-week minimum) and has information about NGOs working on various issues, including community development, gang intervention, the environment and more. During national elections, you can volunteer with CIS's well-respected international election observer mission.

Catholic Relief Service El Salvador (☎ 410 625 2220, 800 736 3467; www.catholicrelief.org; 209 West Fayette Street, Baltimore, Maryland, USA) A charitable organization that helps staff and coordinate social service projects with local churches, parishes, health clinics, cooperatives, government ministries and NGOs. Projects range from agriculture and community-health efforts to microfinancing and emergency aid.

Caracen International (Central American Resource Center; ☎ 2274 8332; caracen@cyt.net; Residencial

Tehuacan Sur, Senda los Eliseos 32, San Salvador) A nonprofit humanitarian organization that provides legal assistance and social services to Salvadorans within and outside of their country. It is based in Washington DC but has offices in San Salvador, Los Angeles, San Francisco, Houston and New York City.

TRANSPORTATION IN EL SALVADOR

GETTING THERE & AWAY

El Salvador's immigration officials are more discerning – and the border procedures more sophisticated – than those of most other Central American countries. They're fair, but they *do* scrutinize entry and exit stamps, so avoid cutting corners.

Entering El Salvador

Entering El Salvador is a relatively painless procedure. Salvadoran immigration officials are well-known to be efficient, polite and professional. They are also more scrutinizing than in most Central American countries, carefully checking all entry and exit stamps (so don't overstay your visa!). The procedures are the same whether you enter the country at an airport or at a border: visitors must present their passport, fill out a simple tourist card and pay a US$10 entrance fee.

Air

El Salvador's international airport, **Aeropuerto Internacional Comalapa** (SAL; ☎ 2339 8264), is located about 50km southeast of San Salvador. It is a major Central and Latin American hub, and a gateway to and from North American cities like Los Angeles,

---

DEPARTURE TAX

There was a US$27.14 departure tax to fly out of San Salvador's international airport at the time of research, and this will likely increase to US$30. This tax is not included in the price of the ticket, though plans were in the works to do so. It is payable in cash only, at a booth in line for ticketing desk. You will not be able to clear immigration – or even check in for your flight – until you have paid it.

New York and San Francisco. The following airlines fly to and from San Salvador, and have offices in the capital

American Airlines (Map pp320-1; airline code AA; ☎ 2298 0777; Edificio La Centroamericana, Alameda Roosevelt at 59a Av Sur; ☒ 8am-6pm Mon-Fri & 8am-noon Sat; hub Dallas-Fort Worth)

Continental Airlines (Map p322; airline code CO; ☎ 2207 2040; Metrocentro, 2nd fl; ☒ 8am-6pm Mon-Fri, 8am-noon Sat; hub Houston)

Copa Airlines (Map p324; airline code CM; ☎ 2209 2672; World Trade Center I; 89 Av Norte & Calle El Mirador; ☒ 8am-6pm Mon-Fri, 8am-noon Sat; hub Panama City)

Delta Air Lines (Map p324; airline code DL; ☎ 2275 9292; World Trade Center I, 89a Av Norte & Calle del Mirador; ☒ 8am-5:30pm Mon-Fri, 8am-11am Sat; hub Atlanta)

TACA (Map p324; ☎ 2267 8222; airline code TA; Galerías Escalón mall, street level; ☒ 8am-8pm Mon-Fri, 8am-5pm Sat, 9am-5pm Sun; hub San Salvador)

United Airlines (Map p324; airline code UA; ☎ 2279 3900; Galerías Escalón mall, street level; ☒ 8:30am-6:30pm Mon-Fri, 9am-1pm Sat; hub Chicago/O'Hare).

Land

BUS

There are three first-class international bus lines connecting El Salvador to other Central American capitals. There are also a number of second-class bus lines, but it is highly recommended you take a first-class line, as much for safety as for comfort. The second-class buses stop more often, and make much easier targets for would-be bandits in El Salvador or another country.

See p342 for details of San Salvador–based bus companies serving international destinations.

Guatemala

Border crossings to Guatemala are La Hachadura, Las Chinamas, San Cristóbal (all in the west) and Anguiatú (north of Metapán). Ordinary buses make it just to the border; international buses continue to Guatemala City.

Ordinary buses to the Guatemalan border crossings all leave San Salvador from the Terminal de Occidente (p341), connecting through Sonsonate, Santa Ana, Ahuachapán or Metapán.

For La Hachadura take bus No 205 to Sonsonate, transfer to bus No 259 to the border; for Las Chinamas take bus No 202 to Ahuachapán (from Santa Ana use bus

210) and transfer to bus No 263; and for San Cristóbal take bus No 498 at 4:10pm, 4:50pm and 5:20pm Monday to Friday, plus 7:20am on Monday and Friday only, and Saturday at 12:20pm. There's no service on Sunday. For Anguiatú take bus No 201A direct, or 201 to San Salvador and transfer to No 235. In Metapán transfer to a microbus to the border.

Pullmantur has two daily buses to Guatemala City (executive/first-class US$26/41, 4½ hours, 7am and 3pm Monday to Saturday, 8:30am and 3pm Sunday), while Tica Bus has just one bus daily (US$11, five hours, 6am), passing its Zona Rosa stop a half-hour later. King Quality/Comfort Lines has first-class service to Guatemala City on Comfort Lines (US$22, five hours, 7:30am and 1:30pm) and the slightly more upscale King Quality (first/'King' class US$26/33, five hours, 6am and 3:30pm). Second-class buses leave Terminal Puerto Bus for Guatemala City (standard US$10, five hours, every hour 4am to 3pm; executive US$13, five hours, 6am and 4:30pm).

Honduras

Border crossings to Honduras include El Poy, El Amatillo and Sabanetas/Perquín. Note that there is no Salvadoran immigration post at the Sabanetas/Perquín border. This means your passport will not be stamped when you leave El Salvador – no big deal if you're not planning to return this trip, but it could cause complications

if you are. It is not recommended to enter here until an official immigration post is established, as you risk being fined for entering illegally.

Ordinary buses to the Honduran border at El Poy leave from the Terminal de Oriente in San Salvador every half-hour from 4am to 4pm (Bus No 119). Buses to El Amatillo (No 306 or 346) leave frequently from the Terminal de Oriente in San Salvador and from San Miguel. There is twice-daily service to Marcala, Honduras, via Perquín and Sabanetas.

Pullmantur buses leave every day for Tegucigalpa at 2:15pm (executive/first-class US$27/45, 6½ hours). King Quality has services there at 6am and 1:30pm (first/ 'King' class US$28/41, six hours, 6am and 1:30pm), and San Pedro Sula at 5am and 12:30pm (first/'King' US$28/41, six hours). Tica Bus has a once-daily service to Tegucigalpa at 5:30am (US$15, six hours). You can transfer to a San Pedro Sula bus from there, but it's quicker and cheaper to take the direct King Quality bus.

Nicaragua

From the Honduran side of the El Amatillo crossing, you can take microbuses across the southern tip of Honduras to the Nicaraguan border town of Guasaule (US$4, two hours). From there, connect to buses to León and Managua.

King Quality has one daily departure to Managua (first/'King' US$28/42, 10½

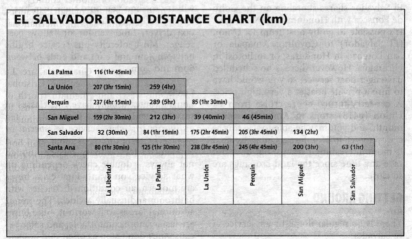

EL SALVADOR ROAD DISTANCE CHART (km)

	La Libertad	La Palma	La Unión	Perquín	San Miguel	San Salvador
La Palma	116 (1hr 45min)					
La Unión	207 (3hr 15min)	259 (4hr)				
Perquín	237 (4hr 15min)	289 (5hr)	85 (1hr 30min)			
San Miguel	159 (2hr 30min)	212 (3hr)	39 (40min)	46 (45min)		
San Salvador	32 (30min)	84 (1hr 15min)	175 (2hr 45min)	205 (3hr 45min)	134 (2hr)	
Santa Ana	80 (1hr 30min)	125 (1hr 30min)	238 (3hr 45min)	245 (4hr 45min)	200 (3hr)	63 (1hr)

hours, 11:30am) as does Tica Bus (US$25, 11 hours, 5am).

Costa Rica & Panama

King Quality has a once-daily service to San José, Costa Rica (US$48, 18 hours, 3:30am). The Tica Bus to San José (US$42, 18 hours, 3am) continues to Panama City (US$61, 36 hours).

Mexico

The Tica Bus that runs to Guatemala City continues to the Mexican border at Tapachula, Chiapas. From San Salvador, the trip takes 12 hours and costs US$23 one way. There's also second-class service to Tapachula from Terminal Puerto Bus (US$43, 10 hours, 6am)

CAR & MOTORCYCLE

If you drive your own vehicle into El Salvador, you must show a driver's license (an international driving permit is accepted) and proof that you own the car. You must also fill out extensive forms. Car insurance is both available and advisable but is not required – you should double check at the border in case this has changed. Vehicles may remain in El Salvador for 30 days. Those travelers wishing to stay longer should leave the country and drive back in rather than attempt to deal with the Transport Ministry.

Sea

El Salvador shares shoreline on the Golfo de Fonseca with Honduras and Nicaragua. It's possible to go by boat from La Unión (El Salvador) to Coyolito, Amapala or San Lorenzo in Honduras, or to Potosí in Nicaragua. However there is no scheduled passenger boat service, so you would have to hire a private boat at a very high price. A car-ferry-turned-booze-cruise from La Unión (p413) stops in Amapala once a month, and you may be able to use this as a way to get to Honduras. Going by boat is more interesting, perhaps, but does not save any time since the land crossings are so close.

GETTING AROUND
Air

There is no regular domestic air service in El Salvador.

Bicycle

It is possible to bike around El Salvador – a mountain bike or all-terrain bike is recommended as roads can be rough in places. Western El Salvador is best overall, in terms of the quality of road, the amount of traffic, temperature and humidity, and possible routes – come prepared for some serious climbing! All the challenges of biking in a developing country apply here – be aware of narrow shoulders, heavy trucks and varying road conditions.

Boat

You'll need to use a boat to get around the Bahía de Jiquilisco in eastern El Salvador for any trips in the Golfo de Fonseca, near La Unión. There is a passenger boat and car ferry service across Lago Suchitlán, connecting Suchitoto to Chalatenango (though taking the bus is usually faster). Otherwise, water transportation is rare.

Bus

El Salvador has an extensive intercity bus service, which uses mostly old American school buses painted in vivid multicolored designs. Most of the bus terminals are chaotic and dirty, as is the area around them. Information about routes and timetables is rarely posted, but anyone in the terminal can point you in the right direction. As with everywhere else in Central America, it can be hard to determine which bus on any given route is leaving first – often men will try to shoo you onto their own bus – but try following the crowd, or asking a taxi driver, food vendor or fellow passenger. Most intercity bus service begins between 4am and 5am and ends between 6pm and 7pm.

CLASSES

Longer routes usually have two classes of service: regular service is usually called *ordinario*; first-class service is *especial* or *super*. The term *directo* is often used as a euphemism for ordinary service, though not always – double check depending on what service you want. First-class buses are modern, air-conditioned coaches with bathroom and usually a video. The minor additional fare is well worth it – the buses are faster, more comfortable, and safer because they don't stop as often mid-route.

COSTS

There are no ticket offices or reservations; purchase your ticket on the bus after you're seated. Fares are very cheap, usually US$0.40 to US$1.50, with a few US$2 to US$4 fares on longer *especial* routes. Weekend fares are 25% higher on some routes

Car & Motorcycle

Driving around the country allows you to see more in less time and offers opportunities to see small villages with infrequent bus service, but navigating through areas where roads and turnoffs are not marked can be frustrating. Gas can be found in the smallest villages but it's not cheap; a gallon of regular unleaded is over US$3.

DRIVERS LICENSE

Foreign drivers should carry a valid drivers license from their country of residence at all times.

HIRE

Travelers can rent vehicles in San Salvador and at the international airport, as well as in San Miguel. Check out their respective Getting There and Away sections for more information.

INSURANCE

You always should get automobile insurance when you rent. Agencies typically make it easy by including coverage in the daily rate. However, American Express, Visa and Mastercard often offer insurance if you use your credit card to pay for the rental. Doing so could save you at least US$10 per day but certain restrictions apply: coverage does not usually extend to pick-up trucks and may not include driving on dirt roads or rentals longer than 15 days.

ROAD CONDITIONS

Although El Salvador's major highways and main city streets are paved, be prepared for an occasional pot hole or con-

struction site – they always seem to come when you least expect them and they can do numbers on your shocks (not to mention your nerves). Villages and back roads often are made of dirt with pebbles, and sand roads rule coastal villages. Children at play, drying corn, fruit stands or herds of cow or pigs also take over highways and streets – be sure to drive slowly and be ready to use your horn if necessary.

ROAD RULES

Outside of major cities, driving is relatively basic – get in the habit of lightly honking, especially when passing or before driving on a blind curve. Also watch for signals from other cars, usually a hand waving to pass or to turn. Police checkpoints are set up at random to slow the flow of traffic or to search trucks for illegal goods. You'll almost always find checkpoints near border crossings or outside of cities.

In major cities, the flow of traffic is faster and more congested. Drivers are seemingly less aware of one another – drive defensively and don't hesitate to use your horn if necessary. Theft is also a problem in cities – be sure to park in a garage or in an otherwise protected lot and avoid driving in areas of ill repute.

Hitchhiking

Hitching a ride in El Salvador isn't advisable and, in fact, it's not really necessary considering that buses and collective pick-ups go just about everywhere in the country. However, if you do opt to hitch, be sure that you give (or at least offer) a small payment when you get off.

Taxi

Taxis are found in most cities in El Salvador; none have meters, so you should agree upon a price before you get in the car. Also, to assure that you're not getting a ride from a random driver in a yellow car, take a look at the license plate; all registered cabs have plates that begin with the letter 'A'.

REGIONAL DIRECTORY

Regional Directory

CONTENTS

Although this little chapter is designed as your one-stop shop for information about your destinations, be sure to turn to the directories for Nicaragua (p282) and El Salvador (p454) for more detailed, country-specific information.

Almost all prerecorded videos sold in the region (most of them bootlegs) use the NTSC image registration system, incompatible with the PAL and Secam systems.

ACCOMMODATIONS

Although there are excellent, modern hotels in Managua and San Salvador, as well as in upscale beach towns and colonial centers, in most major towns your choices will be between basic and midrange options. Hostels are relatively rare outside the main tourist magnets, but you can usually find basic rooms for US$3 to US$5 in Nicaragua, US$6 to US$8 in El Salvador. Midrange hotels can be expensive for what you get (particularly for solo travelers, who usually pay almost as much as a couple), but if you need the extra amenities (hot water, air-conditioning, 24-hour running water) there's usually one in every town. Official campsites are few and far between, but you're usually welcome to pitch your tent on private property, though you should always offer to pay. For country-specific information, check the directories

PRACTICALITIES

- Electrical current and plugs are the same as in the US and Canada: 110V AC, 60Hz in outlets accepting two flat-pronged plugs.
- Both Nicaragua and El Salvador officially use the metric system, but *libras* (pounds) may still be used in markets, and *galones* (US gallons) at gas stations – although here the equivalent in liters is also usually given. Also common are two colonial Spanish measurements, *manzanas* (0.70 hectares or 1.74 acres), useful if you're investing in land, and *varas* (0.70 meters or 33 inches), often used in lieu of meters for giving directions (100 *varas* to one block). For more conversion information, see the inside front cover.
- Bilingual tourist guides are available in hotels and tourist offices. In El Salvador, look for *Pashalua* (www.pashalua.com) and *El Salvador Turístico*, while Nicaragua's tourist board publishes small, bilingual destination-specific glossy booklets; also look for the English-language quarterly *Between the Waves*. El Salvador's major newspapers include the liberal *La Prensa Gráfica* (www.laprensa.com.sv) and the conservative *El Diario de Hoy* (www.elsalvador.com); in Nicaragua, there's the relatively right-wing *La Prensa* (www.laprensa.com.ni) and the more liberal *Nuevo Diario* (www.elnuevodiario.com.ni).
- Just because your hotel room has a cable TV doesn't mean you'll get to watch Simpsons reruns in English: there are several different cable packages, and the most common has primarily Spanish-language programming, including CNN, *en Español* only. In more expensive hotels, cable with English-language offerings include the BBC, DW Journal (also in German) and CNN in English.

for Nicaragua (p282) and El Salvador (p454).

ACTIVITIES

Although El Salvador has a stunning array of outdoor attractions, ranging from waterfall rappels (p363) to fuming Parque Nacional Los Volcanes (p353), much larger and less populated Nicaragua has the larger playground – its (officially) protected wilderness areas clocking in at almost the exact acreage of all of El Salvador.

See the Nicaragua & El Salvador Outdoors chapter (p43) for much more information about outdoor activities, from sea-turtle watching to the region's spectacular surfing, but also check the Environment sections, which have a rundown of parks and protected areas for both Nicaragua (p63) and El Salvador (p307).

Diving & Snorkeling

Diving is beginning to gain popularity in both countries, and Nicaragua's Corn Islands' site is world class. There are also interesting dives on the Pacific Coast (though visibility varies with the season and weather), as well as dives into crater lakes – the fish are less flashy, but the earth's open maw on one side and perhaps a few fumaroles on the other should make up for it.

Hiking & Trekking

Both countries have hikes that range from 1km interpretive trails for the whole family, to multiday treks into the mountains – not to mention plenty of volcano climbs. For most treks longer than a few hours, you'll probably be required (or strongly recommended) to hire a guide or, on some El Salvador hikes, request a free police escort. Guides, except at some private reserves, are

usually very inexpensive (US$6 to US$15 per day, per group) and generally well worth the cash because of safety issues. In less developed wilderness areas, at least let the ranger station or *alcaldía* (mayor's office) know where you'll be, and when you expect to return.

Surfing

See p45 for a special section on some of the best (and least crowded) surfing in the world – the region's best-developed adventure sport.

CLIMATE CHARTS

Thanks to altitude variations and microclimates, you can usually find agreeable weather somewhere no matter the time of year, but be mindful of hurricane season, which officially runs from June to November. The worst storms usually make landfall in October and November.

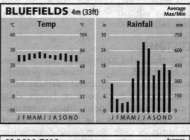

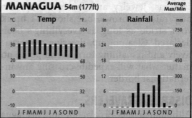

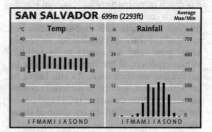

COURSES

Although neither country can quite match Guatemala for cheap Spanish classes, there are still plenty of fine spots to learn the subjunctive tense, including San Salvador and Santa Ana in El Salvador, and, in Nicaragua, León, Estelí, Granada, Laguna de Apoyo and San Juan del Sur; you could also take Miskito Waspám.

You can also try surfing lessons, which can be arranged as either pricey package deals, including three meals and airport pickup, or on the spot with a local guide, who may be able to throw in a day's surfboard rental with your lesson. In El Salvador, head to La Libertad and the beaches west of there (like Playa El Tunco, Playa El Zonte) for private instruction on some of Central America's best waves. Higher-end surf camps are popping up on El Salvador's east coast, near Playa El Cuco. The top spots to bust your chops in Nicaragua include San Juan del Sur – also with Spanish schools – Playa Pie de Gigante and Salinas.

CUSTOMS

Customs is a bit stricter in El Salvador than in Nicaragua, but wise travelers generally won't have to worry about anything other than lines at most borders. Drugs, drug paraphernalia, weapons, fruits, vegetables and any artifacts are forbidden. Large amounts of cash or expensive items like cameras, jewelry and laptop computers may raise eyebrows, but shouldn't break your stride as long as everything's been declared. Cleaning up, dressing conservatively and remaining formal and polite no matter what will expedite crossing any international border.

DISABLED TRAVELERS

Although neither El Salvador nor Nicaragua has much infrastructure for disabled travelers, both countries have a disproportionate number of people with mobility issues because of the wars and landmines, so people know how (and are eager) to be helpful. While experienced travelers may be able to get around on their own, it's still better to go with a tour; see the Disabled Travelers sections for both countries (p284 and p456) for more information, or try some of these sites.

Access-Able Travel Source (www.access-able.com) Although their great searchable Central American database doesn't include specific El Salvador or Nicaragua listings, it does have links to several agencies that could arrange tours or at least point you in the right direction.

Mobility International USA (www.miusa.org) Works with Seeds of Change sending brigades to Nicaragua and El Salvador.

National Information Communication Awareness Network (www.nican.com.au) Offers advice to travelers from Australia and New Zealand.

For a list of services available to disabled travelers by airline, go to www.everybody.co.uk/airindex.htm.

EMBASSIES & CONSULATES

See the individual country directories for embassy and consulate lists for Nicaragua (p284) and El Salvador (p456). General embassy information can be found at www.embassyworld.com. Generally, your embassy won't be much help in emergencies where you're remotely at fault, and can't help you if you've committed a crime locally, even if such actions are legal in your own country. However, if your money and documents are stolen, it might assist with getting a new passport, but a loan for onward travel is probably out of the question. Most embassies and consulates can help you by contacting relatives or friends, or by suggesting reliable doctors, clinics and so on.

GAY & LESBIAN TRAVELERS

Neither El Salvador nor Nicaragua is particularly open to the gay scene, though it does exist; check each country for a very short list of gay bars, predictably concentrated in San Salvador and Managua. Men in particular should err on the side of caution. There is a scene, however, and you will find it. The following are good places to begin:

International Gay & Lesbian Travel Association (IGLTA; www.iglta.com) A general resource with the strength of 1200 travel-oriented companies.

Out & About (www.outandabout.com) Some Central America information.

The Gully (www.thegully.com) Politically charged gay zine in English and Spanish, with interesting Central America coverage.

Rainbow Network (www.rainbownetwork.com) The travel section has a gay guide and useful forum.

HOLIDAYS

Major holiday periods to consider when trip planning include Semana Santa (Easter Week; Palm Sunday to Easter Sunday in March or April), Christmas through New Year, and El Salvador's summer holiday (the first week in August). At these times, prices rise, hotels fill up and tourist density reaches a maximum. Consider making reservations ahead of time if you'll travel during these periods. For holiday hours and closures in each country, see the individual directories.

INSURANCE

A travel-insurance policy to cover theft, loss and medical problems is a good idea. Some policies specifically exclude dangerous activities, which can include scuba diving, motorcycling, even trekking.

You may prefer a policy that pays doctors or hospitals directly rather than you having to pay on the spot and claim later. If you have to claim later, ensure you keep all documentation. Check that the policy covers ambulances or an emergency flight home. See also the information on insurance on p286.

Worldwide cover to travelers from over 44 countries is available online at www .lonelyplanet.com/travel_services.

INTERNET ACCESS

Internet access is speedy and cheap (around US$1 per hour) throughout El Salvador and the Pacific side of Nicaragua; on Nicaragua's Caribbean Coast, things get a bit spottier. For more information and country-specific websites, see p286 and p458.

MONEY

Nicaragua uses the córdoba, but US dollars are accepted almost everywhere. El Salvador has officially adopted the US dollar as its currency. All prices in this book are in US dollars. Other currencies, including the euro and British pound, are difficult to exchange in this part of the world, so bring dollars.

ATMs (*cajeros automaticos*) are widely available in El Salvador and the Pacific side of Nicaragua, but on the Caribbean Coast you'll need cash in many destinations. Most are on the Visa/Plus system, but Master-card/Cirrus machines are becoming more popular. Try to bring two different cards,

and be sure to let your bank and credit-card companies know you'll be leaving the country, so they don't freeze your account after a US$800 withdrawal. To check out worldwide MasterCard/Cirrus ATM locations, visit www.mastercard.com; for Visa/Plus ATM locations, see www.visa.com.

Credit cards are also widely accepted (except, once again, on Nicaragua's Caribbean Coast), with Visa the favorite. With the ascendancy of debit cards, travelers checks are becoming less useful and more difficult to exchange worldwide, and Central America is no exception; consider leaving them at home or just bring US$100 or so for emergencies. **Western Union** (US ☎ +1-800-325-6000; www.westernunion.com) has offices all over both countries, and may be your best bet in case of emergencies.

Check the directories for Nicaragua (p287) and El Salvador (p459) for country-specific information.

PHOTOGRAPHY & VIDEO

Film stores, groceries and pharmacies may sell regular color film (100 or 400), but anything special, including black-and-white and *diapositiva* (slide film), should be brought from home – although you should be able to find most items (albeit expensively) in Managua or San Salvador. Videos for sale in the region conform to the NTSC image registration system. VHS and mini DV tapes are sold in film and electronics stores in most major cities.

Etiquette & Restrictions

Most people won't mind having their picture taken if you ask first, and are perhaps able to pony up a dollar for the subject's trouble. In the indigenous communities of the Nicaraguan Caribbean, people may be less inclined to pose, so respect that.

TELEPHONE

Both countries have payphones, usually operated by telephone cards (available at small stores and specific outlets) rather than local currency. See the directories of each country for more details. In both cases, it's much more expensive to make international calls using landlines than heading to the nearest Internet café, where you can make the same calls (with those awful, echoing connections) for a fraction of the cost.

DOES ANYBODY REALLY KNOW WHAT TIME IT IS?

In 2005, ostensibly to save energy, Nicaragua enacted Daylight Savings Time (DST), springing forward (GMT-5) the second Sunday in April and falling back (GMT-6) the first Saturday in November – like the US Central Time Zone. DST, which makes sense at latitudes where day length varies by five or six hours over the year, has been met with bemusement and irritation in Nicaragua, where a 1½ hour variation doesn't seem to warrant anything as drastic as changing your clocks.

Thus, la Hora Nueva (the New Hour) is not universally observed. Although official business in Nicaragua proper observes DST, the RAAS and RAAN autonomous zones do not – except for the Managua-based airlines. Moreover, private businesses and homes all over the country also ignore DST, so if it's important, ask. In many countries, this sort of temporal anarchy would lead to missed meetings, lost hair and quite possibly the end of civilization. In Nicaragua, where (as in most of Latin America) there's an already hour leeway for any appointment or meeting, it's just a minor inconvenience. Well, unless you just missed your flight.

TIME

Both El Salvador and Nicaragua are on GMT-6, or six hours behind Greenwich Mean Time, equal to Central Standard Time in the USA – and Nicaragua has even been experimenting with daylight savings time (see the boxed text, above).

TOILETS & SHOWERS

While the major population centers often offer the same services you're used to at home (with the caveat that you should never, ever, flush your toilet paper; there's a wastebasket close by), take just a few steps off the beaten path and you could run into some surprises.

If the handle doesn't seem to work, this may be your introduction to bucket-flush toilets. Look around for a plastic bucket or large bowl, and some large, water-filled receptacle nearby. Fill the bucket with about a liter of water, lift the lid of the toilet (a splash-related courtesy) and pour the water into the bowl from around chest height. Repeat as necessary. In very basic hotels, you may also be using bucket showers, which should be self-explanatory, if inconvenient.

In all but the very nicest hotels, hot water comes from an electrical device attached to the shower, colloquially called a 'suicide machine.' While electrical shocks are very rare, avoid touching the machine when the water is running. For the hottest water (probably not very hot), set the heater to 'hot' and turn on the water, then wait a couple of minutes and slowly ratchet the flow down until the low humming noise stops. Then increase water pressure just until the hum comes back on again. And that's as good as it gets.

VISAS

If you attend to one bureaucratic detail before you hit the road, it should be making sure your passport is not soon to expire (all travelers must have at least six months until their passport expires to enter either country) and verifying what visas, if any, you'll need. Visitors from Australia, Canada, the EU, New Zealand and the US do not need visas to enter Nicaragua or El Salvador. See the individual country directories (p288 and p461) for visa specifics, length-of-stay regulations and extension options.

WORK & VOLUNTEER OPPORTUNITIES

Both El Salvador and Nicaragua have high unemployment and underemployment, and thus it's very difficult to get jobs without some sort of specialty and a sponsor company. There are, however, a wide variety of volunteer gigs waiting to be filled in both countries. Most, but by no means all, volunteer positions require a minimum time commitment. From one month to three is typical, though organizations realize that there are many altruistic travelers who only have two or three weeks to vacation and are looking to spend it doing good. Consequently, shorter-term opportunities are becoming more available; connecting through your Spanish school is another option. Do your research before committing, read the fine print associated with different positions and talk to past volunteers.

Australian Volunteers International (www.austra lianvolunteers.com) Places volunteers from Australia and New Zealand in Central America and around the world.

Earthwatch (www.earthwatch.org) Offers often pricey volunteer opportunities.

Habitat for Humanity (www.habitat.org) Talk to them before you come about several home-building projects, most concentrated in the Northern Highlands.

International Volunteer Programs Association (www.volunteerinternational.org) Collects many volunteer positions in Central America.

Peace Corps (www.peacecorps.gov) Places US citizens in both El Salvador and Nicaragua for a variety of humanitarian projects.

Seeds of Learning (☎ 707 939 0471; www.seedsof learning.org; 13606 Arnold Drive, Ste 1, Glen Ellen, California, USA) A nonprofit organization that sends work brigades to El Salvador or Nicaragua to help build and equip schools.

Transitions Abroad (www.transitionsabroad.com) An excellent resource for finding paid work, contacts and volunteer positions, from planting mangroves on the Yucatán coast to educat ing sex workers in Guatemala.

Volunteer Abroad (www.volunteerabroad.com) Scores of volunteer, study abroad and internship opportunities listed by country, plus many useful resources. Paid teaching jobs and opportunities for high-school students also available.

Safety

Both Nicaragua and El Salvador have image problems dating back to their civil wars – which were bad, but certainly no worse than the 36-year bloodbath in Guatemala, which now gets droves of tourists, regardless. El Salvador is the more dangerous of the two countries (on par with Guatemala), with a gang problem (see the boxed text, p302) that rarely affects travelers but does merit a special heads up. And while Nicaragua is, according to some statistics, the second-safest country in the hemisphere (after Canada), it's also the second-poorest (after Haiti), and 'wealthy' travelers make tempting targets.

Most travelers to these countries have no serious problems; instead, they rave with some surprise about how helpful and friendly everyone is – with one minor exception. Opportunistic theft (beach towels, drying laundry) of anything left unchaperoned in a public space is more the rule than the exception.

DANGERS & ANNOYANCES

El Salvador's homicide rate, already one of the world's highest, continues to rise as gang members deported from the USA fight for turf in their unfamiliar and overcrowded homeland. Travelers are rarely the targets of these crimes, but be you sure don't get caught in the crossfire. Stay alert and avoid that scene altogether.

Both Nicaragua and El Salvador have muggers and pickpockets that do target tourists, but commonsense security measures will help you avoid most problems – see the boxed text opposite for tips. Also check out the Health chapter (p483) for hints on how to avoid those dangers.

Robbery & Theft

The most common crimes in Nicaragua and El Salvador are robbery and theft. The vast majority of these are opportunistic crimes, the unwatched beach towel or backpack. Don't leave anything you love outside and unchaperoned, particularly at the beach. Unload your car every night, and use guarded parking, particularly in Managua and San Salvador.

Pickpockets are common in many markets and on public buses, so whenever you're in a crowd be aware of where your cash is. Some travelers keep an emergency cab fare stashed in their sock or bra before going into a high-risk area, such as Managua's notorious Mercado Oriental.

Armed robbery is on the rise, so pay attention to each town's danger zones (described in most chapters, but always ask around) and don't carry anything you wouldn't readily surrender at machete point. Carjacking is covered on p474.

Police

Police forces in both countries, while certainly infested with plenty of corruption, are among Latin America's most honest. Let the cop suggest the bribe first, as you don't want to make your situation worse. For traffic offenses, it's generally better to pay the ticket rather than the bribe, which may not save you much money anyway. Your rental company will help you pay your ticket when you return the car.

Police can help you file theft reports for your insurance company, but probably won't put much effort into recovering items or arresting anyone. They're also useless in the event of a rape or assault, so ask them to take you to the women's center (there's one in every good-sized town) after reporting the incident.

Know how to contact your embassy or consulate, which can help you out of a variety of situations, but probably won't be able to loan you money, purchase plane tickets or get you out of jail if you've committed a crime. They may help you find an attorney, however.

Drugs

Both countries, and Nicaragua's Caribbean Coast in particular, are transit points for South American cocaine cartels (see p224). With the exception of a few touristed spots, such as La Libertad, San Juan del Sur and the Corn Islands, there's not much infra-

---

TIPS FOR A SAFER TRIP

There's no such thing as a risk-free trip, but then again, thousands suffer bathtub injuries annually – how much cooler is it to break your arm falling off an active volcano? Assuming you survive, of course. But there are lots of ways to reduce risk, including asking other travelers, area expats and your friendly hotel manager who or what is dangerous; they'll have the latest.

Go Native Especially when in transit, dress conservatively (no shorts; this is a good idea for men as well as women) and look local if possible; there are a fair number of blondes in both countries. Veteran travelers sometimes skip the backpack and opt for a duffel bag, just like everyone else on the bus.

Make Copies Photocopy your plane tickets, passport, drivers license, travel insurance and other documents. Store one set in your backpack (the originals should be in your moneybelt) and the other with a friend at home; make a list of important numbers (passport, credit-card companies, etc) and store them in several places as well, including your email account. Store emergency cash – US$50 is a good amount – somewhere in your backpack, perhaps sewn into the padding, and one other place – perhaps a hidden pocket (not your moneybelt, which the bad guys do know about), in your shoes or even your camera case.

Stay in Touch Make sure someone has your itinerary and knows to contact your embassy if they don't hear from you every few days.

Get a Guide If you're headed into the wilderness, pony up a few dollars for a guide; if they're required, there's probably a very good reason.

Sleep Soundly Choose a room with good security – solid construction, real locks, a night watchperson – and orientation, with well-lit windows and doors, perhaps on the second floor. Make sure your car is watched all night. Valuables are almost always safer in the hotel instead of on you.

Don't be the Weak Gazelle Muggers are looking for ATM transactees, dangling fanny packs and disoriented travelers. Leave your bag at the hotel, take taxis if you're carrying money or bags, stay alert and walk confidently enough that the bad guys take their risks elsewhere.

Stay Zen And if you do get robbed, give up the goods calmly. It's a great story for the folks back home, unless you get shot.

---

structure for marketing the stuff to travelers; it's more about moving large quantities between scary seasoned professionals, while filling the noses of addicts who take all the street risks. Both countries are really lousy places to have your holiday drug binge; you're a small fish taking big risks in a pond where you have no idea what's going on. So please be smart, or at least be careful.

Natural Threats

The Pacific Coast of both countries is known for its awesome surfing – and terrible rip currents. Even strong swimmers are sucked out to sea periodically; be sure to ask locally about rip-tides, and always be aware of your position in relation to the beach. And, while we highly recommend climbing volcanoes, remember that they are dangerous – don't descend into active craters (you could be overpowered by venting gases and pass out) or go where guides won't go. Although earthquakes, tsunamis, mudslides and other natural disasters occur here with some frequency, the most annoying problem from September to November

are hurricanes. Check the weather before traveling to the Caribbean side, and obey evacuation orders.

DANGEROUS REGIONS & RISKY BEHAVIOR

The Pacific side of Nicaragua is very safe, and with the exception of Managua, with its big-city problems (see p73), and to a much lesser extent Granada and San Juan del Sur, with tourism-related opportunistic crime, you're probably a lot safer here than back home. The Caribbean Coast is a bit sketchier – see p224.

El Salvador has a gang problem (see the boxed text, p302), San Salvador has predictable urban crime issues (p318), and you should also take extra precautions in La Libertad, Sonsonate and Puerto El Triunfo.

Women Travelers

Two out of the three authors of this book are women, and even famously sketchy regions like Las Minas were researched completely *sola* without any serious hassles. The main annoyances are *pirópos*, or catcalls, which you'll probably survive. Women should think twice before drinking alone in bars or even staying out much past dark outside major tourist haunts. Dress conservatively (it's all about capri pants), particularly when in transit, and you'll avoid a lot of annoying attention. Topless sunbathing is almost never acceptable (though breast-feeding in public usually is), and in less touristy areas, consider swimming in shorts and a T-shirt.

Drivers

For general safety tips on public transport, see the Transportation chapter (opposite). Drivers face a special set of risks, not the least of which are cows, also covered in the Transportation chapter, along with other special road hazards.

Have your rental car company remove obvious logos from the car, and try to pack it so it's not obvious (from afar, anyway) that you're tourists. Drive with your windows up in the cities, and keep valuables out of snatching distance if your windows are open. Avoid night driving – even if you have a rental car, it's often worth taking taxis after dark. Although hitchhiking is common in Nicaragua, use your best judgment about picking up hitchhikers; they are best avoided altogether in El Salvador.

Make sure your jack and spare tire are in good condition, but don't hesitate to limp 10km on the rim if your tire may have been flattened on purpose; this is common on deserted dirt roads, where you're already at a disadvantage. Driving is never recommended east of Río Blanco in Nicaragua. Carjacking is a problem in San Salvador,

Managua and the Tipitapa–Masaya highway (the shortcut between the international airport and Granada), while in 2004 several drivers were carjacked in El Salvador close to the Guatemalan border. And finally, either park your car in a private car park, or pay a guard to keep an eye on it for you.

Back Country Hikers

In both countries, it's important to get a guide for most serious wilderness adventures; in Nicaragua because of infrastructure issues, and in El Salvador because armed robberies used to occur on popular volcano climbs.

Most of Nicaragua and all of El Salvador are officially mine-free, but back-country hikers, scientists and others headed into the hinterlands should still play it safe.

Ineter (Nicaragua Institute for Territorial Studies; Map p70; ☎ 249 2768; frente Imigración Extranjera; ◷ 8-11:30am & 1-4pm Mon-Fri) in Managua and **Centro Nacional de Registros** (Map pp320-1; ☎ 2261 8716; www.cnr.gob.sv; 1a Calle Pte; ◷ 8am-noon & 1-4pm Mon-Fri) in San Salvador have maps of old mine fields. In El Salvador they're concentrated in Chalatenango, Cabañas, Cuscatlán and Ususlután; in Nicaragua, along the Honduran border in the Northern Highlands and RAAN, and on the Costa Rican border from Los Guatuzos to the Atlantic Coast. Staying on obvious trails and roads, hiring local guides and talking to area residents are the best ways to avoid stumbling into problems. The **World's Most Dangerous Places** (www.comebackalive.com/df/landmine) site has more minefield information for travelers, while **Canada's Guide to the Global Ban on Landmines** (www.mines.gc.ca) just wants to stop the things from being laid.

Transportation

CONTENTS

Perhaps the most peculiar aspect of this book is that these two countries, while close as kin, don't actually share a border. There was once a ferry between La Unión, El Salvador, and Potosí, Nicaragua, but it's been out of service for years and rumors of its resurrection, at press time, seem exaggerated.

Regardless, it's easy to get between the two countries, via an inexpensive flight or even cheaper bus ride, with the option of a layover in the Honduran capital of Tegucigalpa.

Flights, tours and rail tickets can be booked online at www.lonelyplanet.com /travel_services.

GETTING THERE & AWAY

Central America can appear bigger on a map than it really is, and many travelers overestimate distances between cities and countries. The bus ride from Managua to San Salvador, which looks pretty epic from afar, is only 11 hours including breaks and border crossings.

ENTRY REQUIREMENTS

With your passport in hand, plus visa if necessary (see p461 and p288), entering Nicaragua and El Salvador should be a

---

> **THINGS CHANGE...**
>
> The information in this chapter is particularly vulnerable to change. Check directly with the airline or a travel agency to make sure you understand how a fare (and ticket you may buy) works and be aware of the security requirements for international travel. Shop carefully. The details given in this chapter should be regarded as pointers and are not a substitute for your own careful, up-to-date research.

breeze. You fill out the normal forms, immigration officials flick through your passport and stamp it, and you're on your way. Crossing a land border, it's US$7 to enter Nicaragua and US$2 to leave. Costa Rica is free coming and going, while Honduras charges US$3 entry and you exit free. It is US$1.50 to enter Guatemala and US$1 to leave. El Salvador costs US$10 to enter, and there's no fee for leaving. If you're Salvadoran or of Salvadoran descent, it's free both ways

If there are problems, however, stay patient and polite, even – or especially – if things are taking much longer than you'd like.

AIR

Certainly the most inspirational way to arrive to the lands of volcanoes – and lakes too, in the case of Nicaragua – is by plane, where on a clear day you'll be able to get the lay of the land while the butterflies in your stomach try to assist with the landing.

Airports & Airlines

Managua International Airport (MGA; ☎ 233 1624/28; www.eaai.com.ni), just east of the Nicaraguan capital, is a small, manageable but rapidly expanding airport. Look for tickets to get cheaper and lines to get longer as Nicaragua's popularity as a tourist destination increases. Tiny Granada International Airport (p126) has two flights daily between Granada and both San José and Liberia, Costa Rica. While the airport on Big Corn Island (p259) had recently been

DEPARTURE TAXES

Departure taxes of US$27.14 in El Salvador and US$32 in Nicaragua are levied on international outbound air passengers at airport check-in. You must pay it in cash – either local currency or US dollars. In Nicaragua, domestic flights carry a US$2 surcharge that must also be paid in cash.

approved for international flights, at press time there was only domestic service; rumors about a direct flight from Miami were going around.

El Salvador's **Aeropuerto Internacional Comalapa** (SAL; ☎ 2339 8264), about 50km southeast of San Salvador, is a major Central and Latin American hub, and a gateway to and from North American cities like Los Angeles, New York, and San Francisco; because it gets more flights, it may be less expensive than Managua.

El Salvador is a regional hub, and you may be able to find special deals on fares (check weekends, when business travel lulls) if you're diligent. Underused Managua International Airport gets less traffic, and fewer special offers.

If you're flexible, it may be less expensive to book a flight into Costa Rica, which has two international airports and a lot more travelers to drive down prices. San José is four to five hours from the Nicaragua border, while Liberia is just two hours from Peñas Blancas. Inexpensive Nature Air (see below) flights connect both with Granada twice daily. Very flexible travelers could also look into Cancún, with excellent deals on international flights but no cheap connections to San Salvador or Managua; instead schedule in an extra two weeks and pick up a copy of Lonely Planet's *Guatemala, Belize & the Yucatan.* If you'd rather just fly into Managua or San Salvador, these are your airlines:

Aerocaribe (QA; in Managua ☎ 800 502 20 00; www .aerocaribe.com, in Spanish; hub Cancún)
American Airlines (AA; in San Salvador ☎ 2298 0777, in Managua 233 1624/28; www.aa.com; hub Dallas)
Atlantic Airlines (in Managua ☎ 233 3103; www .atlanticairlines.com; hub Tegucigalpa)
Continental Airlines (CO; in San Salvador ☎ 2207 2040, in Managua 263 1030; www.continental.com; hub Houston)

Copa Airlines (CM; in San Salvador ☎ 2209 2672, in Managua 233 1404; www.copaair.com; hub Panama City)
Delta Airlines (DL; in San Salvador ☎ 2275 9292; www .delta.com; hub Atlanta)
Grupo TACA (TA; in San Salvador ☎ 2267 8222, in Managua 266 3136; www.taca.com; hub San Salvador)
Iberia (IB; in Managua 233 1624/28; www.iberia.com; hub Madrid)
Nature Air (in San José, Costa Rica ☎ 506 299 6000, in USA/Canada 800 235 9272; www.natureair.com; hub San José)
United Airlines (UA; in San Salvador ☎ 2279 3900, in Mexico 800-003-0777; www.united.com; hub Los Angeles)

Tickets

Unless you're arriving from Mexico or South America, most long-distance flights to and from El Salvador and Nicaragua pass through hubs in the United States, like Miami, Houston or Los Angeles. Some travelers arrange for a day or two layover for the fun of it, but airline surcharges and increasingly tedious US visa regulations can thwart such plans.

An open-jaw ticket (eg flying into San Salvador and out of Managua) can save you the time and effort of backtracking, but can be a problem at immigration if you're asked to prove you have an outbound ticket (not common, but possible). Ticket prices may rise during Semana Santa, the Christmas holidays and the December to April high season, although these seasonal changes are less pronounced in El Salvador and Nicaragua than in their more touristed neighbors.

From Australia, New Zealand & Japan

You've got to want to come: from Sydney, American Airlines connects through Los Angeles for San Salvador or Miami for Managua, clocking in at around US$2200 round trip either way – which isn't much less than a round-the-world trip, if you were thinking of making an upgrade. **Qantas** (www.quantas.com.au) offers a flight connecting in Houston for about the same amount.

It's quite a bit cheaper to fly from Tokyo, where you stop in the USA before touching down in San Salvador for around US$1500 round trip. Try www.travel.com.au and www.travel.co.nz for online fares.

Flight Centre Australia (☎ 1300 133 133; www.flight centre.com.au); New Zealand (☎ 0800 243 544; www .flightcentre.co.nz)

STA Travel Australia (☎ 1300 733 035; www.statravel
.com.au); New Zealand (☎ 0508 782 872; www.statravel
.co.nz)

From Central America & the Caribbean

Grupo TACA, a consortium of regional airlines, is based at San Salvador's Comolapa International Airport, Central America's largest. TACA has connections with Belize City, Guatemala City, Guayaquil, Havana, Managua, Mexico City, San Pedro Sula and Tegucigalpa, among many others. Other airlines struggle to stay competitive, so look for good deals on Copa's Panama City flight.

From Managua, Copa offers service to Costa Rica, Guatemala and Panama; Atlantic Airlines has a flight to San Pedro Sula, and Aerocaribe offers one flight weekly from Havana; there are much better connections to Cuba from San José, Costa Rica. The tiny Granada airport offers flights twice daily to Liberia and San José, Costa Rica.

From Europe

The cheapest flights from Europe originate in Brussels and Madrid, connecting through various US cities on American, or Madrid on Iberia (nice if you want to avoid US visa requirements) for just under US$1000 to either San Salvador or Managua. Amsterdam also has a good connection with KLM, stopping in Houston.

It pays to look into San José flights from Europe. From Rome, for example, if you fly to MGA on the AirFrance-TACA route through Paris and Miami, you'll pay US$1500; if you fly into San José on Iberia, you can get tickets for around US$1000. To search online for cheap flights, try www.dialaflight.com and www.lastminute.com. Recommended agencies in Europe include the following:

FRANCE
Nouvelles Frontières (☎ 0825 000 747; www
.nouvelles-frontieres.fr)
OTU Voyages (☎ 0 820 817 817; www.otu.fr) Student and youth travel specialist.
Voyageurs du Monde (☎ 01 40 15 11 15; www.vdm
.com)

GERMANY
Expedia (www.expedia.de)
Just Travel (☎ 089 747 3330; www.justtravel.de)
STA Travel (☎ 01805 456 422; www.statravel.de) For travelers aged under 26.

ITALY
CTS Viaggi (☎ 06-462 0431; www.cts.it) A specialist in student and youth travel.

NETHERLANDS
AirFair (☎ 020-620 5121; www.airfair.nl)

SCANDINAVIA
Kilroy Travels (www.kilroytravels.com)

SPAIN
Viajes Zeppelin (☎ 902 384 253; www.v-zeppelin.es)

UK
Flight Centre (☎ 0870 890 8099; www.flightcentre
.co.uk)
Flightbookers (☎ 0870 010 7000; www.ebookers.com)
Journey Latin America (☎ 020-8747 3108; www
.journeylatinamerica.co.uk)
STA Travel (☎ 0870 160 0599; www.statravel.co.uk) For travelers under the age of 26.
Trailfinders (☎ 020-7937 1234; www.trailfinders.co.uk)

From South America

Although TACA has direct flights to Lima and Quito, the most convenient flights to South America are through Lacsa in San José, Costa Rica, and Copa, with transfers in Panama City, which both fly to Bogotá, Caracas, Quito and Lima. Most other connections with South America run through Miami or Cancún.

Recommended travel agencies include the following:
ASATEJ (☎ 54-011 4114-7595; www.asatej.com) In Argentina.
IVI Tours (☎ 0212-993 6082; www.ividiomas.com) In Venezuela.
Student Travel Bureau (☎ 3038 1555; www.stb.com
.br) In Brazil.
Viajo.com (www.viajo.com) Online and telephone bookings from several countries.

USA & Canada

Unsurprisingly, North Americans get the best deal, with round-trip flights to San Salvador running anywhere from US$300 to US$500 from Los Angeles, Miami or Houston, all served by a variety of carriers including American, Continental, Delta, TACA and United. TACA also offers direct flights to Chicago, Dallas/Fort Worth, JFK and Washington Dulles, but tack on another US$100 for the convenience. TACA also offers a round trip from Toronto to

San Salvador (US$500 to US$700). Managua also has daily direct flights to Miami on American and TACA averaging US$400 to US$600, and to Houston on Continental for about US$100 more.

Travel Cuts (☎ 800 667 2887; www.travelcuts.com) is Canada's national student travel agency. For online bookings try www.expedia .ca and www.travelocity.ca. The following agencies are recommended for online bookings from the USA:

Amex Travel (www.itn.net)
Cheap Tickets (www.cheaptickets.com)
Expedia (www.expedia.com)
Lowest Fare (www.lowestfare.com)
Orbitz (www.orbitz.com)
Smarter Living (www.smarterliving.com)
STA Travel (www.sta.com) For travelers under the age of 26.
Travelocity (www.travelocity.com)

LAND
Bus
With Managua and San Salvador just 11 hours away from each other on a smooth, safe and air-conditioned international bus (and León and San Miguel much closer) these clean, comfortable buses are an excellent option between the two countries and elsewhere in the region.

Managua is the major Nicaraguan hub, with at least five international bus companies represented, four of them convenient to the budget tourist quarter. But you can easily catch buses headed south to Costa Rica and Panama from Granada, Masaya and Rivas, while León has several buses running to San Miguel and San Salvador, the shortest trip between the two countries. Buses leaving from Estelí also connect to San Salvador, as well as points north and east.

San Salvador is El Salvador's major international hub, but you can also catch buses in Sonsonate, San Miguel and Santa Ana.

Border Crossings
Most people cross at the relatively hassle-free land borders. International buses do everything but hold your hand through the process, or you can take regular buses, walk a few hundred meters at most to immigration, attend to entry formalities and connect with ongoing bus service on the other side. If you arrive in a car or motorcycle, have your paperwork in order. To expedite any border crossing, dress your best and act respectfully and deferentially.

Below are the main land border crossings between the countries in the region; see below for river crossings. Onward bus connections are usually well coordinated.

Nicaragua–Costa Rica Sapoá/Peñas Blancas (p159).
Nicaragua–Honduras From west to east: Guasaule/Choluteca (p187); El Espino/San Marcos (p204); Las Manos/Danlí (p204).
El Salvador–Honduras From west to east: El Poy/Nueva Ocotopeque (p395); Perquín (p442); El Amatillo (p428).
El Salvador–Guatemala From south to north: Ciudad Pedro de Alvarado/La Hachadura (p362); Valle Nuevo/Las Chinamas (p372); San Cristóbal/San Cristóbal (p351); Anguiatú/Anguiatú (p359).

RIVER
Nicaragua has three river border crossings, all incredibly scenic.

San Carlos to Los Chiles, Costa Rica (p265) Easy, beautiful, recommended for the whole family.
Waspám to Puerto Lempira, Honduras (p237) Challenging but definitely do-able.
San Juan de Nicaragua to Barra, Costa Rica (p281) Expensive; you must arrange everything in advance.

INTERNATIONAL BUSES SERVING NICARAGUA & EL SALVADOR

Company	Local Telephone	Website	Areas Served
Pullmantur	El Salvador ☎ 2243 1300	www.pullmantur.com	San Salvador, Guatemala City, Tegucigalpa
Tica Bus	El Salvador ☎ 222 4808 Nicaragua ☎ 222 3031	www.ticabus	Panama, Costa Rica, Nicaragua, El Salvador, Honduras, Guatemala, Mexican border
King Quality/ Comfort Lines	El Salvador ☎ 2271 3330 Nicaragua ☎ 228 1454	no website	Costa Rica, Nicaragua, El Salvador, Guatemala
Transnica	Nicaragua ☎ 270 3133	www.vianica.com/go /profile/1-Transnica.html	Costa Rica, Nicaragua, Honduras, El Salvador
Del Sol Bus	Nicaragua ☎ 270 2547	no website	Nicaragua, El Salvador

TEGUCIGALPA, SAN MARCOS & CHOLUTECA, HONDURAS

Going overland between El Salvador and Nicaragua, you have to pass through Honduras (obviously) but rapid bus service to and from the borders means you can easily make the trip in a day, or even a couple of hours. Leaving El Salvador, cross at El Amatillo, where minibuses leave every 45 minutes for the Nicaraguan border at Guasaule (US$4.75, 1¾ hours, last departure 10pm); there are no stops, making this the fastest route by far. To get to the border at El Espino, take an ordinary bus to Choluteca (US$1.75, two hours, every 25 minutes, last at 4:30pm) and transfer to a San Marcos bus (US$1, 1½ hours, every 60 to 90 minutes, last at 6:15pm). From there, it's another 10 minutes by taxi or bus to the border. Coming from Nicaragua, follow the same routes in reverse; the last minibus from Guasaule to El Amatillo leaves at 10pm, the last bus from Choluteca to El Amatillo is at 4:30pm.

If you need just to stay the night, the most logical stop is Choluteca. **Hotel Santa Rosa** (☎ 782 0355; Av La Rosa btwn Calles Paz Barahona & Williams; s/d US$4.75/7.50, with air-con US$11/14.50) is a clean reliable option opposite Mercado San Antonio. From Choluteca, frequent buses go to Tegucigalpa (*ordinario* US$2.75, 3½ hours; direct US$7, 2½ hours) and beyond.

If you actually want to stay a while, the most charming town in southern Honduras is San Marcos, near the Nicaraguan border at El Espino. There, stay at **Hotel Shalom** (☎ 788 3268; s/d US$12/15), which has the highest perch in town and is impossible to miss. Ask at **Restaurante La Exquisita** (☎ 788 3505; ☺ breakfast, lunch & dinner) about arranging an overnight at the owners' coffee farm in Duyusupo, with excellent hiking opportunities into the nearby Ojochal wildlife refuge.

SEA

The only potential (legal) sea crossings are at the Gulf of Fonseca. From La Unión, in El Salvador, there's a very infrequent ferry service that goes to Coyolitos, in Honduras, as well as the opportunity to rent a boat to Potosí, in Nicaragua, which according to rumors will offer an official international ferry between them in the future. If you decide to use this option, make sure that you arrange everything in advance at immigration in Managua and/or San Salvador.

GETTING AROUND

AIR

Only Nicaragua has domestic flights, most based out of Managua, plus one flight daily between Bilwi and Bluefields. For more info see p291.

BICYCLE

Both Nicaragua and El Salvador have considerable potential as road-biking destinations – they have beautiful paved roads with wide shoulders, plus populations who use, and are used to seeing, bicycles absolutely everywhere, most definitely including on the Interamericana/Carr Pan-americana.

BOAT

Boats are not an important part of the Salvadoran transportation system, although there is a scenic route from Suchitoto across the Cerrón Grande to San Francisco Lempa, and you'll need a boat from Puerto El Triúnfoto get to Corral de Mulas and around the Bahía de Jiquilisco. La Union offers a variety of boat trips around area islands, and may provide service to Honduras.

Nicaragua, however, relies on boats for travel around Lake Nicaragua and throughout the humid Caribbean Coast. Major boat routes include El Rama to Bluefields, down the Río Escondido, the only way to the Corn Islands if you'd rather not fly. Isla Ometepe (and its 500 sister islands) can only be reached by boat, with almost hourly, one-hour ferries from San Jorge and twice-weekly, four-hour trips from Granada, which continue for nine hours across the lake to San Carlos and the Río San Juan, a region almost entirely (and only) navigable by boat. You'll also rely on boats for side trips from Bluefields, Bilwi and Waspám, while in San Juan del Sur, boat taxi is often the best way up and down the coast.

Public boats are affordable – the trip from Granada to San Carlos costs US$6 for first class – but schedules can be erratic or inconvenient, and private *pangas* (light

TRANSPORTATION

boats) can easily cost more than US$100 per day. When relying on boat transport, always get there early and see if you need to sign your name to a list; if you can buy tickets ahead of time, that may be a good idea. And please remember that these aren't Disney rides – the Ometepe Ferry sank just after this book was researched. Everyone was fine, but please wear your life preserver.

BUS

Buses in Nicaragua and El Salvador range from ultra-comfortable international cruisers – which you can take within either country if you don't mind paying premium prices for reclining seats, food service, air conditioning and bathrooms – to old Bluebird school buses, many modified to take on roads that would make a Sherman tank blanche. Bus transportation is one thing that's cheaper in El Salvador, but regular buses in both countries usually cost under US$1 per hour, while speedy microbuses cost a bit more. While you should always try to purchase tickets for international buses in advance, most local buses don't even give you that option (but when they do, there's usually a good reason). Pay when you get on the bus, or after it starts moving.

Buses are generally safe in both countries, although the city buses in Managua are best avoided unless you're comfortable with a little urban mayhem. It's always safer to take a *directo* or *expreso* bus, which doesn't stop as often as an *ordinario* or *ruteado*, and international buses are the safest.

Classes

Both countries have a hierarchy of classes with different and potentially, misleading names. In El Salvador, regular service is usually called *ordinario*; first-class service is *especial* or *super*. The term *directo* is often used as a euphemism for ordinary service, though not always – double check depending on what service you want. First-class buses are modern air-conditioned coaches with a bathroom and usually a video.

Nicaraguan buses are rarely so plush, and the only difference between *ordinarios* or *ruteados*, the cheaper buses, and *expresos* or *directos*, it that the latter only stop in major destinations, which shaves a few minutes off your trip. More comfortable microbuses

cost about 25% more, and are available for most major routes, with vans leaving 'when full' (about 10 people).

CAR & MOTORCYCLE

Driving in Nicaragua and El Salvador allows you to go where you want to go, when you want to go. Whether you bring your own vehicle or hire one upon arrival, it's worth thinking carefully about whether driving here is for you (look at the boxed text, below; and remember, buses are generally safe, economical and efficient).

Driver's License

Foreign drivers should carry a valid drivers license from their country of residence at all times, which is (technically) only good for 30 days after entering the country. An international driver's license is required after that, and is recommended at all times.

SHOULD I BE DRIVING?

Are you traveling alone? Cost, liability issues and endurance limits tip the scales against driving for most solo travelers.

Do you have language or mechanical facility? Spanish-speaking drivers will be better able to resolve problems, while any off-the-beaten-track breakdown will likely require some repair work by you. Bikers, especially, should know how to fix their ride.

Are you traveling during the rainy season? Flooding and washouts are common in Nicaragua from May to November, and roads to more isolated spots are often in disrepair any time of year. Consider renting a 4WD.

Do you have gear? Anything unwieldy, like a kayak, photo equipment or surfboard may make driving a car the most convenient alternative. Get a car with a trunk - backpacks on the back seat invite break-ins

Are you at least 25 years old? In both countries, the person renting a vehicle usually has to be at least 25, or pay a much higher rate, often from a less reputable company.

Do you have a major credit card? Rental agencies usually require a credit card or large cash deposit. And some credit cards include rental car insurance, which can save you money. Folks driving their own vehicles will want one too, for that 'oh shit!' scenario.

Hire

Renting a car is almost twice as expensive in El Salvador (US$40 to US$60 per day for an ordinary car) than in Nicaragua (US$25 to US$40 per day) – you've got to love pro-tourism tax breaks. If you plan to use dirt roads, particularly in the rainy season, you're going to want a 4WD, which ups the final total even more. Both countries have gas prices more on par with Europe's than the United States' (US$3 to US$4 per gallon); keep this in mind while figuring your final bill. Always check several companies, and don't be afraid to quote your lowest offer; there's usually wiggle room. Avoid renting at either airport, where stiff surcharges can add 11% to 15% to your bill.

CHINANDEGA
Budget (☎ 341 1663)
Dollar (☎ 341 2303)

GRANADA
Hertz (☎ 552 8103; sergiouca@yahoo.com)
Alamo (☎ 552 2877; www.alamonicaragua.com)
Dollar (☎ 552 2947; www.dollar.com.ni)
Budget (☎ 552 2323; www.budget.com.ni)

MANAGUA
Alamo (airport ☎ 233 3718; Managua ☎ 270 1939; alamo@cablenet.com.ni)
Avis (☎ 233 3011; avisnic@cablenet.com.ni)
Best (☎ 263 3242)
Budget (☎ 266 6226; www.budget.com.ni)
Dollar (☎ 266 3620; www.dollar.com.ni)
Exotic (☎ 233 4695; www.exoticrentacar.com.ni)
Hertz (☎ 233 1237; www.hertz.com.ni)
Lugo (☎ 263 2368; www.lugorentacar.com.ni)
National (☎ 270 1968; www.nationalnicaragua.com)
Nicaragua (☎ 250 2114; www.nicarentacar.com)
Payless (☎ 233 1329; www.payless.com.ni)
Targa (☎ 222 4824; rentacar@ibw.com.ni)
World (☎ 263 1011; worldrentacar@cablenet.com.ni)

MATAGALPA
Budget Rent-A-Car (☎ 772 3041)
Dollar Rent-A-Car (☎ 772 4645)

SAN MIGUEL
Alamo/Uno Rent A Car (☎ 2679 0188)
Budget (☎ 2682 1062)

SAN SALVADOR
Budget (☎ 2260 4333; www.budget.com.sv)
Alamo/UNO (☎ 2211 2111)

Avis (☎ 2261 1212, 2339 9268; www.avis.com.sv)
Quick Rent a Car (☎ 2229 6959; www.quickrentacar.com.sv)

Insurance

You are required to get basic insurance and will be asked to consider supplemental insurance to cover the deductible. If you're paying with a credit card, your agreement probably includes free supplemental car insurance, so ask before paying another US$10 to US$15 per day.

Road Rules

Road rules in both countries are similar to the United States, in terms of driving on the right side of the street, obeying standard international signs and pulling over when a corrupt cop notices that you're in a rental and wants to accuse you of, say, 'poor driving.' There is no system of paying fines or tickets on the spot, and your rental company can help you pay them later. But if you'd rather pay the bribe, at least pretend you don't speak any Spanish – make 'em work for it.

Note that Salvadoran police are decidedly less corrupt than those in Nicaragua and other Central American countries. It is rare to be pulled over for no reason; the most common mistake foreign drivers make is going the wrong way on a one-way street. If it wasn't clearly marked (very possible) you can and should plead your case, always respectfully.

In cities, unsigned one-ways, overstuffed markets spilling out into the streets, and traffic circles, perhaps a new trick for some, make things challenging even in broad daylight. Avoid driving in cities at night, which can be dangerous; even if you have a rental car, consider taking a taxi after hours.

Road Hazards

While city driving can be sketchy – keep an eye out for those unsigned one-way roads and traffic circles – rural driving has hazards all its own.

Cattle Red flags mean cows ahead (unless its election time), so slow down. After making eye contact with the cowboy or cowgirl in charge, aim sloooowly for the side of the herd with the lowest cattle density; make your way through without honking, and keep an eye on younger, more impetuous cows and unruly individuals with Y-shaped yokes (that's their punishment) around their necks.

TRANSPORTATION

Checkpoints Police and/or military checkpoints are common, especially near borders. Officers are looking for drugs and illegal immigrants, and most tourist-looking people will be waved through. If stopped, you'll have to produce your passport, driver's license and vehicle registration; in rare instances, they'll search your car. Be patient and cooperative.

Potholes and Pothole Repair People Axle-snapping potholes are just part of the fun, so try to get behind someone who obviously knows the road, and follow their tracks. In Nicaragua, you may see people pointing to a dirt-filled pothole and pointing into the air. That means, 'I just filled in this pothole, please give me a coin.' It's worth keeping small change in your ashtray.

Rivers Always ask locals first before crossing any rivers you can't see the bottom of. No locals? Get out and check. If you feel confident your car can pass, aim slightly upstream and punch it; don't stop for anything.

Hitchhiking

Hitchhiking is much more common in Nicaragua than in El Salvador, even by solo women. That said, hitching is always potentially dangerous, so you should use your best judgment and go in pairs whenever you can't avoid hitching completely.

LOCAL TRANSPORTATION

Local transport comes in a variety of shapes and sizes; ramble off the beaten track and you'll almost certainly need to rely on horses and/or motorized canoes, or else your own two feet. Horse carriages are common in Masaya and Southwest Nicaragua, while covered trucks take over on roads where even mighty Bluebirds can't go.

Bicycle

Bicycles are often the most common form of public transportations, dominating the thoroughfares alongside drivers used to catering for (not to mention seeing) two-wheelers. Maddeningly, it's difficult to find bicycle rental places outside the main tourist centers, and even then quality tends to be poor. So ask at your hotel or, in smaller towns, the *alcaldía* (mayor's office) to see if they can arrange a private rental. And off you go.

Boat

Boats are rarely used for transportation in El Salvador, which has only one major river system and is primarily a dry tropical forest ecosystem. Nicaragua's lakes and vast Atlantic lowlands, however, rely on boats as transport between cities and within regions.

This can get expensive. The Río San Juan region has cheap public boats; on some routes, only three times a week. If you don't have time, tack another US$100 onto your bill for a private boat. The indigenous beach towns north of Bluefields are the same – day trips are out for Pearl Lagoon unless you spring for a private *panga*, and if anyone figures out a cheap way to Rama Key, please email us!

In towns, where you just need to use private canoes to cross smaller rivers, fees are typically less than US$0.50 for the ride, and worth it just for the views.

Bus

Almost all population centers have some sort of public bus system. In major cities, crowded buses are a favorite haunt of pickpockets, so be aware (this goes triple in Managua) of your surroundings and belongings. In smaller cities and rural regions, public buses may be less formal, perhaps a local with a minivan who drives back and forth along one particular route, and who may not be feeling well that day. In general, where you need a bus you'll find one; ask locals about routes and destinations, and hold on as they pull you into whatever vehicle flies by.

Taxi

Taxis are found in cities and towns throughout both countries, and are almost never metered. In El Salvador, official taxis have a license plate that begins with 'A' and are usually painted yellow; in Nicaragua, taxis should have a red license plate. In many towns, especially in El Salvador, small three-wheeled 'mototaxis' or 'motos' are a new, and usually cheaper, option for short rides. All should have a photo ID posted, and you should check the photo against the actual driver's mug. Agree on a fare before getting into the taxi (ask locals what you should be paying; there's often a set fare, at least in daytime), particularly in Managua (see the boxed text, p74), San Salvador, or anywhere with a lot of tourist traffic.

Almost all taxis in Nicaragua are *colectivos*, which will offer to pick you up while already packed with people; this is why they usually cost around US$0.70 to anywhere. Using taxis between cities is a comfortable and reasonable option for midrange travelers, in Nicaragua at least; prices double in El Salvador.

Health Dr David Goldberg

CONTENTS

Travelers to Central America need to be concerned about food- and water-borne, as well as mosquito-borne, infections. Most of these illnesses are not life-threatening, but they can certainly ruin your trip. Besides getting the proper vaccinations, it's important that you bring along a good insect repellent and exercise great care in what you eat and drink.

BEFORE YOU GO

Since most vaccines don't produce immunity until at least two weeks after they're given, visit a physician four to eight weeks before departure. Ask your doctor for an international certificate of vaccination (otherwise known as the yellow booklet), which will list all the vaccinations you've received. This is mandatory for countries that require proof of yellow fever vaccination upon entry, but it's a good idea to carry it wherever you travel.

INSURANCE

If your health insurance does not cover you for medical expenses abroad, consider supplemental insurance. Check the Subway section of the **Lonely Planet website** (www.lonely planet.com/subwwway) for more information. See also the **US State Department website** (www .travel.state.gov) for a list of medical-evacuation and travel-insurance companies. Find out in advance if your insurance plan will make payments directly to providers or reimburse you later for overseas health expenditures.

MEDICAL CHECKLIST

- antibiotics
- antidiarrheal drugs (eg loperamide)
- acetaminophen/paracetamol (Tylenol) or aspirin
- anti-inflammatory drugs (eg ibuprofen)
- antihistamines (for hay fever and allergic reactions)
- antibacterial ointment (eg Bactroban) for cuts and abrasions
- steroid cream or cortisone (for poison ivy and other allergic rashes)
- bandages, gauze, gauze rolls
- adhesive or paper tape
- scissors, safety pins, tweezers
- thermometer
- pocket knife
- DEET-containing insect repellent for the skin
- permethrin-containing insect spray for clothing, tents and bed nets
- sunblock
- oral rehydration salts
- iodine tablets (for water purification)
- syringes and sterile needles

RECOMMENDED VACCINATIONS

The only required vaccine is yellow fever, and only if you're arriving in El Salvador or Nicaragua from a yellow-fever-infected country in Africa or South America. However, a number of vaccines are recommended. Note that some of these are not approved for use by children and pregnant women – check with your physician.

Bring medications in their original containers, clearly labeled. A signed, dated letter from your physician describing all medical conditions and medications, including generic names, is also a good idea. If carrying syringes or needles, be sure to have a physician's letter documenting their medical necessity.

HEALTH

RECOMMENDED VACCINES

Vaccine	Recommended for	Dosage	Side Effects
hepatitis A	all travelers	1 dose before trip; booster 6-12 months	soreness at injection site headaches; body aches
typhoid	all travelers	4 capsules by mouth, 1 taken every other day	abdominal pain; nausea; rash
yellow fever	required for travelers arriving from a yellow-fever-infected area in Africa or the Americas	1 dose lasts 10 years	headaches; body aches; severe reactions are rare soreness at injection site; low-grade fever
hepatitis B	long-term travelers in close contact with local population	3 doses over 6 months	soreness at injection site; low-grade fever
rabies	travelers who may have contact with local population with animals and may not have access to medical care	3 doses over 3-4 weeks	soreness at injection site; headaches; body aches
tetanus/ diphtheria	all travelers who haven't had booster within 10 years	1 dose lasts 10 years	soreness at injection site;
measles	travelers born after 1956 who've had only 1 measles vaccination	1 dose	fever; joint pains; allergic reactions
chickenpox	travelers who've never had chickenpox	2 doses 1 month apart	fever; mild case of chickenpox

ONLINE RESOURCES

There is a wealth of travel health advice on the Internet. For further information, the **Lonely Planet website** (www.lonelyplanet.com) is a good place to start. A superb book called *International Travel and Health*, which is revised annually and is available online at no cost, is published by the **World Health Organization** (www.who.int/ith/). Another website of general interest is **MD Travel Health** (www.mdtravelhealth.com), which provides complete travel health recommendations for every country, and is updated daily, also at no cost.

It's usually a good idea to consult your government's travel health website before departure, if one like the following is available:

Australia (www.dfat.gov.au/travel/)
Canada (www.hc-sc.gc.ca/pphb-dgspsp/tmp-pmv /pub_e.html)
UK (www.doh.gov.uk/traveladvice/index.htm)
United States (www.cdc.gov/travel/)

FURTHER READING

For further information, see *Healthy Travel Central & South America*, also from Lonely Planet. If you're traveling with children, Lonely Planet's *Travel with Children* may

be useful. The *ABC of Healthy Travel*, by E Walker et al, and *Medicine for the Outdoors*, by Paul S Auerbach, are other valuable resources.

IN TRANSIT

DEEP VEIN THROMBOSIS (DVT)

Blood clots may form in the legs during plane flights, chiefly because of prolonged immobility. The longer the flight, the greater the risk. Though most blood clots are reabsorbed uneventfully, some may break off and travel through the blood vessels to the lungs, where they could cause life-threatening complications.

The chief symptom of deep vein thrombosis is swelling or pain of the foot, ankle or calf, usually but not always on just one side. When a blood clot travels to the lungs, it may cause chest pain and breathing difficulties. Travelers with any of these symptoms should immediately seek medical attention.

To prevent the development of deep vein thrombosis on long flights you should walk about the cabin, perform isometric compressions of the leg muscles (ie contract the leg muscles while sitting), drink plenty of fluids, and avoid alcohol and tobacco.

JET LAG & MOTION SICKNESS

Jet lag is common when crossing more than five time zones, and can result in insomnia, fatigue, malaise or nausea. To avoid jet lag, try drinking plenty of fluids (nonalcoholic) and eating light meals. Upon arrival, get exposure to natural sunlight and readjust your schedule (for meals, sleep etc) as soon as possible.

Antihistamines such as dimenhydrinate (Dramamine) and meclizine (Antivert, Bonine) are usually the first choice for treating motion sickness. Their main side effect is drowsiness. An herbal alternative is ginger, which works like a charm for some people.

IN NICARAGUA & EL SALVADOR

AVAILABILITY & COST OF HEALTH CARE

Good medical care is available in San Salvador and Managua, but options are limited elsewhere. In general, private hospitals are more reliable than public facilities, which may experience significant shortages of equipment and supplies. In Nicaragua, **Hospital Metropolitano Vivian Pellas** (☎ 255 6900; www.metropolitano.com.ni; Km 9.75 Carr Masaya, Managua) is Central America's most advanced hospital. In El Salvador, **Hospital Diagnóstico Escalón** (☎ 2264 4422; 3 Calle Pte at 99 Av Norte, San Salvador) and **Hospital de Diagnóstico** (☎ 2226 8878; Calle 21 Pte at 2a Diagonal, San Salvador) are considered among the best medical centers in the country.

For an online list of hospitals and physicians in Nicaragua and El Salvador, go to the US embassy websites (www.managua .usembassy.gov and www.elsalvador.us embassy.gov).

Many doctors and hospitals expect payment in cash, regardless of whether you have travel health insurance. If you develop a life-threatening medical problem, you'll probably want to be evacuated to a country with state-of-the-art medical care. Since this may cost tens of thousands of dollars, be sure you have insurance to cover this before you depart.

Many pharmacies are well supplied, but important medications may not be consistently available. Be sure to bring along adequate supplies of all prescription drugs.

INFECTIOUS DISEASES
Cholera

Cholera is an intestinal infection acquired through ingestion of contaminated food or water. The main symptom is profuse, watery diarrhea, which may be so severe that it causes life-threatening dehydration. The key treatment is drinking oral rehydration solution. Antibiotics are also given, usually tetracycline or doxycycline, though quinolone antibiotics such as ciprofloxacin and levofloxacin are also effective.

Cholera outbreaks occur periodically in Central America, but the disease is rare among travelers. Cholera vaccine is no longer required, and is in fact no longer available in some countries, including the United States, because the old vaccine was relatively ineffective and caused side effects. There are new vaccines that are safer and more effective, but they're not available in many countries, and are only recommended for those at particularly high risk.

Dengue Fever (Break-bone Fever)

Dengue fever is a viral infection found throughout Central America. Thousands of cases occur each year in both Nicaragua and El Salvador. Dengue is transmitted by aedes mosquitoes, which bite predominantly during the daytime and are usually found close to human habitations, often indoors. They breed primarily in artificial water containers, such as jars, barrels, cans, cisterns, metal drums, plastic containers and discarded tires. As a result, dengue is especially common in densely populated, urban environments.

Dengue usually causes flu-like symptoms, including fever, muscle aches, joint pains, headaches, nausea and vomiting, often followed by a rash. The body aches may be quite uncomfortable, but most cases resolve uneventfully in a few days. Severe cases usually occur in children under the age of 15 who are experiencing their second dengue infection.

There is no treatment for dengue fever except to take analgesics such as

HEALTH

acetaminophen/paracetamol (Tylenol) and to drink plenty of fluids. Severe cases may require hospitalization for intravenous fluids and supportive care. There is no vaccine. The cornerstone of prevention is protecting against insect bites; see p488 .

Hepatitis A

Hepatitis A occurs throughout Central America. It's a viral infection of the liver that is usually acquired by ingestion of contaminated water, food or ice, though it may also be acquired by direct contact with infected persons. The illness occurs all over the world, but the incidence is higher in developing nations. Symptoms may include fever, malaise, jaundice, nausea, vomiting and abdominal pain. Most cases resolve uneventfully, though hepatitis A occasionally causes severe liver damage. There is no treatment.

The vaccine for hepatitis A is extremely safe and highly effective. If you get a booster six to 12 months later, it lasts for at least 10 years. You really should get it before you go to Nicaragua, El Salvador or any other developing nation. Because the safety of hepatitis A vaccine has not been established for pregnant women or children under the age of two, they should instead be given a gammaglobulin injection.

Hepatitis B

Like hepatitis A, hepatitis B is a liver infection that occurs worldwide but is more common in developing nations. Unlike hepatitis A, the disease is usually acquired by sexual contact or by exposure to infected blood, generally through blood transfusions or contaminated needles. The vaccine is recommended only for long-term travelers (on the road more than six months) who expect to live in rural areas or have close physical contact with the local population. Additionally, the vaccine is recommended for anyone who anticipates sexual contact with the local inhabitants or a possible need for medical, dental or other treatments while abroad, especially if a need for transfusions or injections is expected.

Hepatitis B vaccine is safe and highly effective. However, a total of three injections are necessary to establish full immunity. Several countries added hepatitis B vaccine to the list of routine childhood immunizations in the 1980s, so many young adults are already protected.

Malaria

Malaria occurs in every country in Central America. It's transmitted by mosquito bites, usually between dusk and dawn. The main symptom is high spiking fevers, which may be accompanied by chills, sweats, headache, body aches, weakness, vomiting or diarrhea. Severe cases may involve the central nervous system and lead to seizures, confusion, coma and death.

Taking malaria pills is strongly recommended for all rural areas in Nicaragua and El Salvador, except at altitudes greater than 1500m (4900ft). In Nicaragua, the risk is greatest for rural areas, around the outskirts of Managua, and during the rainy season in the northeastern lowlands. In El Salvador, the rural areas of the departments of Santa Ana, Ahuachapán and La Unión have high malaria rates. Transmission is greatest during the rainy season (June through November).

For both countries, the first-choice malaria pill is chloroquine, taken once weekly in a dosage of 500mg, starting one to two weeks before arrival and continuing through the trip and for four weeks after departure. Chloroquine is safe, inexpensive and highly effective. Side effects are typically mild and may include nausea, abdominal discomfort, headache, dizziness, blurred vision or itching. Severe reactions are uncommon.

Protecting yourself against mosquito bites is just as important as taking malaria pills (see the recommendations on p488), since no pills are 100% effective.

If you think you may not have access to medical care while traveling, you should bring along additional pills for emergency self-treatment, which you should undergo if you can't reach a doctor and you develop symptoms that suggest malaria, such as high spiking fevers. One option is to take four tablets of Malarone once daily for three days. If you start self-medication, you should try to see a doctor at the earliest possible opportunity.

If you develop a fever after returning home, see a physician, as malaria symptoms may not occur for months.

Rabies

Rabies is a viral infection of the brain and spinal cord that is almost always fatal. The rabies virus is carried in the saliva of infected animals and is typically transmitted through an animal bite, though contamination of any break in the skin with infected saliva may result in rabies. Rabies occurs in all Central American countries. Most cases are related to dog bites.

The rabies vaccine is safe, but a full series requires three injections and is quite expensive. Those at high risk for rabies, such as animal handlers and spelunkers (cave explorers), should certainly get the vaccine. In addition, you should consider asking for the vaccine if you might be traveling to remote areas and might not have access to appropriate medical care if needed. The treatment for a possibly rabid bite consists of rabies vaccine with rabies immune globulin. It's effective, but must be given promptly. Most travelers don't need rabies vaccine.

All animal bites and scratches must be promptly and thoroughly cleansed with large amounts of soap and water, and local health authorities should be contacted to determine whether or not further treatment is necessary.

Typhoid

Typhoid fever is caused by ingestion of food or water contaminated by a species of salmonella known as *Salmonella typhi*. Fever occurs in virtually all cases. Other symptoms may include headache, malaise, muscle aches, dizziness, loss of appetite, nausea and abdominal pain. Either diarrhea or constipation may also occur. Possible complications include intestinal perforation, intestinal bleeding, confusion, delirium or (rarely) coma.

Unless you expect to take all your meals in major hotels and restaurants, typhoid vaccine is a good idea. It's usually given orally, but is also available as an injection. Neither vaccine is approved for use in children under the age of two.

The drug of choice for typhoid fever is usually a quinolone antibiotic such as ciprofloxacin (Cipro) or levofloxacin (Levaquin), which many travelers carry for treatment of travelers' diarrhea. However, if you self-treat for typhoid fever, you may

also need to self-treat for malaria, since the symptoms of the two diseases may be indistinguishable.

Yellow Fever

Yellow fever no longer occurs in Central America, but many countries, including Nicaragua and El Salvador, require yellow-fever vaccine before entry if you're arriving from a country in Africa or South America where yellow fever is known to occur. If you're not arriving from a country with yellow fever, the vaccine is neither required nor recommended. Yellow-fever vaccine is given only in approved vaccination centers, which provide validated international certificates of vaccination (also known as yellow booklets). The vaccine should be given at least 10 days before departure and remains effective for about 10 years. Reactions are generally mild and may include headaches, muscle aches, low-grade fevers, or discomfort at the injection site. Severe, life-threatening reactions have been described but are extremely rare.

Other Infections

CHAGAS' DISEASE

This is a parasitic infection that is transmitted by triatomine insects (reduviid bugs), which inhabit crevices in the walls and roofs of substandard housing in South and Central America. The triatomine insect lays its feces on human skin as it bites, usually at night. A person becomes infected when he or she unknowingly rubs the feces into the bite wound or any other open sore. Chagas' disease is extremely rare in travelers. However, if you sleep in a poorly constructed house, especially one made of mud, adobe or thatch, you should be sure to protect yourself with a bed net and a good insecticide.

HISTOPLASMOSIS

Caused by a soil-based fungus, histoplasmosis is acquired by inhalation, often when the soil has been disrupted. Initial symptoms may include fever, chills, dry cough, chest pain and headache, sometimes leading to pneumonia.

HIV/AIDS

This has been reported in all Central American countries. Be sure to use condoms for all sexual encounters. Because both nations were at war, and therefore isolated, during the 1980s and early 1990s, the HIV/AIDS pandemic is only now becoming a serious problem in Nicaragua and El Salvador. In El Salvador, approximately 28,000 people – or 0.7% of the population – are living with HIV/AIDS.

LEISHMANIASIS
This occurs in the mountains and jungles of all Central American countries. The infection is transmitted by sandflies, which are about one-third the size of mosquitoes. Leishmaniasis may be limited to the skin, causing slowly growing ulcers over exposed parts of the body, or (less commonly) may disseminate to the bone marrow, liver and spleen. The disease may be particularly severe in those with HIV. There is no vaccine for leishmaniasis. To protect yourself from sandflies, follow the same precautions as for mosquitoes (right), except that netting must be finer mesh (at least 18 holes to the linear inch).

LEPTOSPIROSIS
This is acquired by exposure to water contaminated by the urine of infected animals. Outbreaks often occur at times of flooding, when sewage overflow may contaminate water sources. The initial symptoms, which resemble a mild flu, usually subside uneventfully in a few days, with or without treatment, but a minority of cases are complicated by jaundice or meningitis. There is no vaccine. You can minimize your risk by staying out of bodies of fresh water that may be contaminated by animal urine. If you're visiting an area where an outbreak is in progress, you can take 200mg of doxycycline once weekly as a preventative measure. If you actually develop leptospirosis, the treatment is 100mg of doxycycline twice daily.

ONCHOCERCIASIS (RIVER BLINDNESS)
Onchocerciasis is caused by a roundworm that may invade the eye, leading to blindness. The infection is transmitted by black flies, which breed along the banks of rapidly flowing rivers and streams.

TYPHUS
This may be transmitted by lice in scattered pockets of the country.

TRAVELERS' DIARRHEA
To prevent diarrhea, avoid tap water unless it has been boiled, filtered or chemically disinfected (with iodine tablets); only eat fresh fruits or vegetables if cooked or peeled; be wary of dairy products that might contain unpasteurized milk; and be highly selective when eating food from street vendors.

If you develop diarrhea, be sure to drink plenty of fluids, preferably an oral rehydration solution containing lots of salt and sugar. A few loose stools don't require treatment, but if you start having more than four or five stools a day, you should start taking an antibiotic (usually a quinolone drug) and an antidiarrheal agent (such as loperamide). If diarrhea is bloody or persists for more than 72 hours, or is accompanied by fever, shaking chills or severe abdominal pain, you should seek medical attention.

ENVIRONMENTAL HAZARDS
Animal Bites
Do not attempt to pet, handle or feed any animal, with the exception of domestic animals known to be free of any infectious disease. Most animal injuries are directly related to a person's attempt to touch or feed the animal.

Any bite or scratch by a mammal, including bats, should be promptly and thoroughly cleansed with large amounts of soap and water, followed by application of an antiseptic such as iodine or alcohol. Local health authorities should be contacted immediately for possible post-exposure rabies treatment, whether or not you've been immunized against rabies. It may also be advisable to start an antibiotic, since wounds caused by animal bites and scratches frequently become infected. One of the newer quinolones, such as levofloxacin (Levaquin), which many travelers carry in case of diarrhea, would be an appropriate choice.

Mosquito Bites
To prevent mosquito bites, wear long sleeves, long pants, hats and shoes (rather than sandals). Bring along a good insect repellent, preferably one containing DEET, which should be applied to exposed skin and clothing, but not to eyes, mouth, cuts, wounds or irritated skin. Products

containing lower concentrations of DEET are as effective, but for shorter periods of time. In general, adults and children over 12 should use preparations containing 25% to 35% DEET, which usually lasts about six hours. Children between two and 12 years of age should use preparations containing no more than 10% DEET, applied sparingly, which will usually last about three hours. Neurologic toxicity has been reported from DEET, especially in children, but appears to be extremely uncommon and generally related to overuse. Compounds containing DEET should not be used on children under the age of two.

Insect repellents containing certain botanical products, including oil of eucalyptus and soybean oil, are effective, but last only 1½ to two hours. Repellents containing DEET are preferable for areas where there is a high risk of malaria or yellow fever. Products based on citronella are not effective.

For additional protection, you can apply permethrin to clothing, shoes, tents and bed nets. Permethrin treatments are safe and remain effective for at least two weeks, even when items are laundered. Permethrin should not be applied directly to skin.

Don't sleep with the window open unless there is a screen. If sleeping outdoors or in an accommodation that allows entry of mosquitoes, use a bed net, preferably treated with permethrin, with edges tucked in under the mattress. The mesh size should be less than 1.5mm. Hotels will often provide a net if you ask, although it may have holes in it. If the sleeping area is not otherwise protected, use a mosquito coil, which will fill the room with insecticide through the night. Repellent-impregnated wristbands are not effective.

Snake Bites

Snakes are a hazard in some areas of Central America. The chief concern is *Bothrops asper*, the Central American or common lancehead, also called the fer-de-lance and known locally as *barba amarilla* (yellow beard) or *terciopelo* (velvet skin). This heavy-bodied snake reaches up to 2m (6½ feet) in length and is commonly found along fallen logs and other small animal runs, especially in the northern provinces.

In the event of a venomous snake bite, place the victim at rest, keep the bitten area immobilized and move the victim immediately to the nearest medical facility. Avoid tourniquets, which are no longer recommended.

Sun

To protect yourself from excessive sun exposure, you should stay out of the midday sun, wear sunglasses and a wide-brimmed sun hat, and apply sunscreen with SPF 15 or higher, with both UVA and UVB protection. Sunscreen should be generously applied to all exposed parts of the body approximately 30 minutes before sun exposure and should be reapplied after swimming or vigorous activity. Travelers should also drink plenty of fluids and avoid strenuous exercise when the temperature is high.

Water

Tap water in Nicaragua and El Salvador is not safe to drink. Vigorous boiling for one minute is the most effective means of water purification. At altitudes greater than 2000m (6500ft), boil for three minutes.

Another option is to disinfect water with iodine pills. Instructions are usually enclosed and should be carefully followed. Or you can add 2% tincture of iodine to one quart or liter of water (five drops to clear water, 10 drops to cloudy water) and let stand for 30 minutes. If the water is cold, longer times may be required. The taste of iodinated water may be improved by adding vitamin C (ascorbic acid). Iodinated water should not be consumed for more than a few weeks. Pregnant women, those with a history of thyroid disease and those allergic to iodine should not drink iodinated water.

HEALTH

TRADITIONAL MEDICINE

The following are some traditional remedies for common travel-related conditions.

Problem	Treatment
jet lag	melatonin
motion sickness	ginger
mosquito-bite prevention	oil of eucalyptus
	soybean oil

A number of water filters are on the market. Those with smaller pores (reverse osmosis filters) provide the broadest protection, but they are relatively large and are readily plugged by debris. Those with somewhat larger pores (microstrainer filters) are ineffective against viruses, although they remove other organisms. Manufacturers' instructions must be carefully followed.

Safe-to-drink, inexpensive purified water (agua pura) is widely available in hotels, shops and restaurants. Aguas Claras is a trusted brand in Nicaragua; Agua Cristal is a good brand in El Salvador.

CHILDREN & PREGNANT WOMEN

In general, it's safe for children and pregnant women to go to Nicaragua and El Salvador. However, because some of the vaccines listed on p483 are not approved for use in children and pregnant women, these travelers should be particularly careful not to drink tap water or consume any questionable food or beverage. Also, when traveling with children, make sure they're up-to-date on all routine immunizations. It's sometimes appropriate to give children some of their vaccines a little early before visiting a developing nation. You should discuss this with your pediatrician. Lastly, if pregnant, you should bear in mind that should a complication such as premature labor develop while abroad, the quality of medical care may not be comparable to that in your home country.

Since yellow fever vaccine is not recommended for pregnant women or children less than nine months old, these travelers, if arriving from a country with yellow fever, should obtain a waiver letter, preferably written on letterhead stationery and bearing the stamp used by official immunization centers to validate the international certificate of vaccination.

Dr David Goldberg MD completed his training in internal medicine and infectious diseases at Columbia-Presbyterian Medical Center in New York City, where he has also served as voluntary faculty. At present, he is an infectious diseases specialist in Scarsdale NY and the editor-in-chief of the website MDTravelHealth.com.

Language

CONTENTS

Spanish is the official language of Nicaragua and El Slavador and the main language the traveler will need. Every visitor to the country should attempt to learn some Spanish, the basic elements of which are easily acquired.

A month-long language course taken before departure can go a long way toward facilitating communication and comfort on the road. Language courses are also available in both countries (see Courses on p468). Even if classes are impractical, you should make the effort to learn a few basic phrases and pleasantries. Don't hesitate to practice your new skills – in general, Latin Americans meet attempts to communicate in their languages, however halting, with enthusiasm and appreciation.

PHRASEBOOKS & DICTIONARIES

Lonely Planet's *Latin American Spanish Phrasebook* will be extremely helpful during your trip. The University of Chicago *Spanish-English, English-Spanish Dictionary* is another exceptionally useful resource. It's small, light and has thorough entries, making it ideal for travel. It also makes a great gift for any newfound friends upon your departure.

HANDY MISKITO PHRASES

With more than 150,000 native speakers scattered along one of the Caribbean's most beautiful and untouched stretches of coastline, Miskito isn't a bad language to know for the visitor to Nicaragua. Here are a few phrases to get you started. Intrigued? Contact Dr Dionisio Melgara Brown (brownmelgara@hotmail.com), who publishes a comprehensive Spanish–Miskito dictionary and can arrange classes at his museum in Waspám.

Hello./Goodbye.	*Naksa./Aisabi.*
Yes./No.	*Ow./Apia.*
Please./Thank you.	*Plees./Dingki pali.*
How are you?	*Nakisma?*
Good, fine.	*Pain.*
Bad, lousy.	*Saura.*
friend	*pana*
Does anyone here speak Spanish?	*Nu apo ya Ispel aisee sapa?*
How much is it?	*Naki preis?*
My name is (Jane).	*Yan nini (Jane).*
What's your name?	*An maninam dia?*
Could you tell me where a hotel is?	*Man ailwis hotel ansara barsa?*
Excuse me, but could you help me?	*Escyus, man sipsma ilpeimonaya?*
I'm a vegetarian.	*Yan wal wina kalila pias.*
I feel sick.	*Yan siknes.*
I'm allergic to mangos/peanuts	*Yan siknes brisna mango/mani.*
Where is the bus station?	*Ansarasa buskaba takaskisa?*
What time does the bus/boat leave?	*Man nu apo dia teim bustaki/duritaki sapa?*
How do I get to Bonanza?	*Napkei sipsna gwaiya Bonanza?*
Is it far/near?	*Nawina lihurasa/lamarasa?*
May I cross your property?	*Sipsna man prizcamku nueewaiya?*
Are there landmines?	*Danomite barsakei?*
Where can I change dollars?	*Ansara dalas sismonaya sipsna?*
Can I smoke here?	*Yan cigaret diaya sipsna?*
Do you have a bathroom?	*Baño brisma?*

LATIN AMERICAN SPANISH

The Spanish of the Americas comes in a bewildering array of varieties. Depending on the areas in which you travel, consonants may be glossed over, vowels squashed into each other, and syllables and even words dropped entirely. Slang and regional vocabulary, much of it derived from indigenous languages, can further add to your bewilderment.

Throughout Latin America, the Spanish language is referred to as *castellano* more often than *español*. Unlike in Spain, the plural of the familiar *tú* form is *ustedes* rather than *vosotros;* the latter term will sound quaint and archaic in the Americas. Another notable difference is that the letters **c** and **z** are never lisped in Latin America; attempts to do so could well provoke amusement.

OTHER LANGUAGES

Travelers will find English is often spoken in the upmarket hotels, airline offices and tourist agencies, and some other European languages are encountered in hotels run by Europeans. On the Caribbean coast, many of the locals speak some English, albeit with a local Creole dialect.

Indigenous languages are spoken in isolated areas, but unless travelers are getting off the beaten track they'll rarely encounter them. The indigenous languages Bribri and Cabécar are understood by an estimated 18,000 people living on both sides of the Cordillera de Talamanca.

PRONUNCIATION

Spanish spelling is phonetically consistent, meaning that there's a clear and consistent relationship between what you see in writing and how it's pronounced. Also, most Spanish sounds have English equivalents, so English speakers shouldn't have too much trouble being understood.

Vowels

a	as in 'father'
e	as in 'met'
i	as in 'marine'
o	as in 'or' (without the 'r' sound)
u	as in 'rule'; the 'u' is not pronounced after **q** and in the letter combinations **gue** and **gui**, unless it's marked with a diaeresis (eg *argüir*), in which case it's pronounced as English 'w'
y	at the end of a word or when it stands alone, it's pronounced as the Spanish **i** (eg *ley*); between vowels within a word it's as the 'y' in 'yonder'

Consonants

As a rule, Spanish consonants resemble their English counterparts. The exceptions are listed below.

While the consonants **ch**, **ll** and **ñ** are generally considered distinct letters, **ch** and **ll** are now often listed alphabetically under **c** and **l** respectively. The letter **ñ** is still treated as a separate letter and comes after **n** in dictionaries.

b	similar to English 'b,' but softer; referred to as 'b larga'
c	as in 'celery' before **e** and **i**; otherwise as English 'k'
ch	as in 'church'
d	as in 'dog,' but between vowels and after **l** or **n**, the sound is closer to the 'th' in 'this'
g	as the 'ch' in the Scottish *loch* before **e** and **i** ('kh' in our guides to pronunciation); elsewhere, as in 'go'
h	invariably silent. If your name begins with this letter, listen carefully if you're waiting for public officials to call you.
j	as the 'ch' in the Scottish *loch* (written as 'kh' in our guides to pronunciation)
ll	as the 'y' in 'yellow'
ñ	as the 'ni' in 'onion'
r	a short **r** except at the beginning of a word, and after **l**, **n** or **s**, when it's often rolled
rr	very strongly rolled
v	similar to English 'b,' but softer; referred to as 'b corta'
x	usually pronounced as **j** above; in some indigenous place names **x** is pronounced as the 's' in 'sit'; in other instances, it's as in 'taxi'
z	as the 's' in 'sun'

Word Stress

In general, words ending in vowels or the letters **n** or **s** have stress on the next-to-last syllable, while those with other endings have stress on the last syllable. Thus *vaca* (cow) and *caballos* (horses) both carry stress on the next-to-last syllable, while *ciu-*

dad (city) and *infeliz* (unhappy) are both stressed on the last syllable.

Written accents will almost always appear in words that don't follow the rules above, eg *sótano* (basement), *América* and *porción* (portion).

GENDER & PLURALS

In Spanish, nouns are either masculine or feminine, and there are rules to help determine gender (there are of course some exceptions). Feminine nouns generally end with **-a** or with the groups **-ción**, **-sión** or **-dad**. Other endings typically signify a masculine noun. Endings for adjectives also change to agree with the gender of the noun they modify (masculine/feminine **-o/-a**). Where both masculine and feminine forms are included in this language guide, they are separated by a slash, with the masculine form first, eg *perdido/a*.

If a noun or adjective ends in a vowel, the plural is formed by adding **s** to the end. If it ends in a consonant, the plural is formed by adding **es** to the end.

ACCOMMODATIONS

I'm looking for ...	Estoy buscando ...	e·stoy boos·kan·do ...
Where is ...?	¿Dónde hay ...?	don·de ai ...
a cabin	una cabina	oo·na ca·bee·na
a camping	un camping/	oon kam·ping/
ground	campamento	kam·pa·men·to
a guesthouse	una casa de	oo·na ka·sa de
	huespedes	wes·pe·des
a hostel	un hospedaje/	oon os·pe·da·khe/
	una residencia	oon·a re·see·den·sya
a hotel	un hotel	oon o·tel
a youth hostel	un albergue	oon al·ber·ge
	juvenil	khoo·ve·neel

Are there any rooms available?

| ¿Hay habitaciones libres? | ay a·bee·ta·syon·es lee·bres |

I'd like a ...	Quisiera una	kee·sye·ra oo·na
room.	habitación ...	a·bee·ta·syon ...
double	doble	do·ble
single	individual	een·dee·vee·dwal
twin	con dos camas	kon dos ka·mas

How much is it	¿Cuánto cuesta	kwan·to kwes·ta
per ...?	por ...?	por ...
night	noche	no·che
person	persona	per·so·na
week	semana	se·ma·na

MAKING A RESERVATION

(for phone or written requests)

To ...	A ...
From ...	De ...
Date	Fecha
I'd like to book ...	Quisiera reservar ... (see the list under 'Accommodations' for bed and room options)
in the name of ...	en nombre de ...
for the nights of ...	para las noches del ...
credit card ...	tarjeta de crédito ...
number	número
expiry date	fecha de vencimiento
Please confirm ...	Puede confirmar ...
availability	la disponibilidad
price	el precio

full board	pensión completa	pen·syon kom·ple·ta
private/shared	baño privado/	ba·nyo pree·va·do/
bathroom	compartido	kom·par·tee·do
too expensive	demasiado caro	de·ma·sya·do ka·ro
cheaper	más económico	mas e·ko·no·mee·ko
discount	descuento	des·kwen·to

Does it include breakfast?

| ¿Incluye el desayuno? | een·kloo·ye el de·sa·yoo·no |

May I see the room?

| ¿Puedo ver la habitación? | pwe·do ver la a·bee·ta·syon |

I don't like it.

| No me gusta. | no me goos·ta |

It's fine. I'll take it.

| Está bien. La tomo. | es·ta byen la to·mo |

I'm leaving now.

| Me voy ahora. | me voy a·o·ra |

CONVERSATION & ESSENTIALS

In their public behavior, Latin Americans are very conscious of civilities. You should never approach a stranger for information without extending a greeting, such as *buenos días* or *buenas tardes*, and you should use only the polite form of address, especially with the police and public officials.

Central America is generally more formal than many of the South American countries. The polite form *usted* (you) is used in all cases in this guide; where options are given, the form is indicated by the abbreviations 'pol' and 'inf.'

Hi.	Hola.	o·la (inf)
Good morning.	Buenos días.	bwe·nos dee·as
Good afternoon.	Buenas tardes.	bwe·nas tar·des
Good evening/ night.	Buenas noches.	bwe·nas no·ches

The three most common greetings are often abbreviated to simply *buenos* (for *buenos días*) and *buenas* (for *buenas tardes* and *buenas noches*).

Bye/See you soon.	Hasta luego.	as·ta lwe·go
Goodbye.	Adiós.	a·dyos
Yes.	Sí.	see
No.	No.	no
Please.	Por favor.	por fa·vor
Thank you.	Gracias.	gra·syas
Many thanks.	Muchas gracias.	moo·chas gra·syas
You're welcome.	De nada.	de na·da
Apologies.	Perdón.	per·don
May I?	Permiso.	per·mee·so
(when asking permission)		
Excuse me.	Disculpe.	dees·kool·pe
(used before a request or when apologizing)		

How are things?

   ¿Qué tal?   ke tal

What's your name?

   ¿Cómo se llama usted?   ko·mo se ya·ma oo·sted (pol)

   ¿Cómo te llamas?   ko·mo te ya·mas (inf)

My name is ...

   Me llamo ...   me ya·mo ...

It's a pleasure to meet you.

   Mucho gusto.   moo·cho goos·to

The pleasure is mine.

   El gusto es mío.   el goos·to es mee·o

Where are you from?

   ¿De dónde es/eres?   de don·de es/er·es (pol/inf)

I'm from ...

   Soy de ...   soy de ...

Where are you staying?

   ¿Dónde está alojado?   don·de es·ta a·lo·kha·do (pol)

   ¿Dónde estás alojado?   don·de es·tas a·lo·kha·do (inf)

May I take a photo?

   ¿Puedo sacar una foto?   pwe·do sa·kar oo·na fo·to

DIRECTIONS

How do I get to ...?

   ¿Cómo llego a ...?   ko·mo ye·go a ...

Is it far?

   ¿Está lejos?   es·ta le·khos

Go straight ahead.

   Siga/Vaya derecho.   see·ga/va·ya de·re·cho

Turn left.

   Voltée a la izquierda.   vol·te·e a la ees·kyer·da

SIGNS	
Entrada	Entrance
Salida	Exit
Información	Information
Abierto	Open
Cerrado	Closed
Prohibido	Prohibited
Comisaria	Police Station
Servicios/Baños	Toilets
Hombres/Varones	Men
Mujeres/Damas	Women

Turn right.

   Voltée a la derecha.   vol·te·e a la de·re·cha

Can you show me (on the map)?

   ¿Me lo podría señalar   me lo po·dree·a se·nya·lar

   (en el mapa)?   (en el ma·pa)

north	norte	nor·te
south	sur	soor
east	este	es·te
west	oeste	o·es·te
here	aquí	a·kee
there	ahí	a·ee
avenue	avenida	a·ve·nee·da
block	cuadra	kwa·dra
street	calle/paseo	ka·lye/pa·se·o

HEALTH

I'm sick.

   Estoy enfermo/a.   es·toy en·fer·mo/a

I need a doctor.

   Necesito un médico.   ne·se·see·to oon me·dee·ko

Where's the hospital?

   ¿Dónde está el hospital?   don·de es·ta el os·pee·tal

I'm pregnant.

   Estoy embarazada.   es·toy em·ba·ra·sa·da

I've been vaccinated.

   Estoy vacunado/a.   es·toy va·koo·na·do/a

I'm allergic to ...	Soy alérgico/a a ...	soy a·ler·khee·ko/a a ...
antibiotics	los antibióticos	los an·tee·byo·tee·kos
nuts	las fruta secas	las froo·tas se·kas
penicillin	la penicilina	la pe·nee·see·lee·na

I'm ...	Soy ...	soy ...
asthmatic	asmático/a	as·ma·tee·ko/a
diabetic	diabético/a	dya·be·tee·ko/a
epileptic	epiléptico/a	e·pee·lep·tee·ko/a

| I have ... | Tengo ... | ten·go ... |
| a cough | tos | tos |

diarrhea	diarrea	dya·re·a
a headache	un dolor de cabeza	oon do·lor de ka·be·sa
nausea	náusea	now·se·a

EMERGENCIES

Help!	¡Socorro!	so·ko·ro
Fire!	¡Fuego!	fwe·go
I've been robbed.	Me han robado.	me an ro·ba·do
Go away!	¡Déjeme!	de·khe·me
Get lost!	¡Váyase!	va·ya·se
Call ...!	¡Llame a ...!	ya·me a
the police	la policía	la po·lee·see·a
a doctor	un médico	oon me·dee·ko
an ambulance	una ambulancia	oo·na am·boo·lan·sya

It's an emergency.
Es una emergencia.   es oo·na e·mer·khen·sya
Could you help me, please?
¿Me puede ayudar, por favor?   me pwe·de a·yoo·dar por fa·vor
I'm lost.
Estoy perdido/a.   es·toy per·dee·do/a
Where are the toilets?
¿Dónde están los baños?   don·de es·tan los ba·nyos

LANGUAGE DIFFICULTIES

Do you speak English?
¿Habla/Hablas inglés?   a·bla/a·blas een·gles (pol/inf)
Does anyone here speak English?
¿Hay alguien que hable inglés?   ai al·gyen ke a·ble een·gles
I (don't) understand.
(No) Entiendo.   (no) en·tyen·do
How do you say ...?
¿Cómo se dice ...?   ko·mo se dee·se ...
What does ...mean?
¿Qué significa ...?   ke seeg·nee·fee·ka ...

Could you please ...?	¿Puede ..., por favor?	pwe·de ... por fa·vor
repeat that	repetirlo	re·pe·teer·lo
speak more slowly	hablar más despacio	a·blar mas des·pa·syo
write it down	escribirlo	es·kree·beer·lo

NUMBERS

1	uno	oo·no
2	dos	dos
3	tres	tres
4	cuatro	kwa·tro
5	cinco	seen·ko
6	seis	says
7	siete	sye·te
8	ocho	o·cho
9	nueve	nwe·ve
10	diez	dyes
11	once	on·se
12	doce	do·se
13	trece	tre·se
14	catorce	ka·tor·se
15	quince	keen·se
16	dieciséis	dye·see·says
17	diecisiete	dye·see·sye·te
18	dieciocho	dye·see·o·cho
19	diecinueve	dye·see·nwe·ve
20	veinte	vayn·te
21	veintiuno	vayn·tee·oo·no
30	treinta	trayn·ta
31	treinta y uno	trayn·ta ee oo·no
40	cuarenta	kwa·ren·ta
50	cincuenta	seen·kwen·ta
60	sesenta	se·sen·ta
70	setenta	se·ten·ta
80	ochenta	o·chen·ta
90	noventa	no·ven·ta
100	cien	syen
101	ciento uno	syen·to oo·no
200	doscientos	do·syen·tos
1000	mil	meel
5000	cinco mil	seen·ko meel

PAPERWORK

birth certificate	certificado de nacimiento
border (frontier)	la frontera
car-owner's title	título de propiedad
car registration	registración
customs	aduana
driver's license	licencia de manejar
identification	identificación
immigration	migración
insurance	seguro
passport	pasaporte
temporary vehicle import permit	permiso de importación temporal de vehículo
tourist card	tarjeta de turista
visa	visado

SHOPPING & SERVICES

I'd like to buy ...
Quisiera comprar ...   kee·sye·ra kom·prar ...
I'm just looking.
Sólo estoy mirando.   so·lo es·toy mee·ran·do
May I look at it?
¿Puedo verlo/a?   pwe·do ver·lo/a
How much is it?
¿Cuánto cuesta?   kwan·to kwes·ta

That's too expensive for me.

Es demasiado caro	es de·ma·sya·do ka·ro	
para mí.	pa·ra mee	

Could you lower the price?

¿Podría bajar un poco	po·dree·a ba·khar oon po·ko
el precio?	el pre·syo

I don't like it.

No me gusta.	no me goos·ta

I'll take it.

Lo llevo.	lo ye·vo

Do you accept ...?	¿Aceptan ...?	a·sep·tan ...
American dollars	dólares americanos	do·la·res a·me·ree·ka·nos
credit cards	tarjetas de crédito	tar·khe·tas de kre·dee·to
traveler's checks	cheques de viajero	che·kes de vya·khe·ro

less	menos	me·nos
more	más	mas
large	grande	gran·de
small	pequeño/a	pe·ke·nyo/a

I'm looking for the ...	Estoy buscando ...	es·toy boos·kan·do
ATM	el cajero automático	el ka·khe·ro ow·to·ma·tee·ko
bank	el banco	el ban·ko
bookstore	la librería	la lee·bre·ree·a
exchange house	la casa de cambio	la ka·sa de kam·byo
general store	la tienda	la tyen·da
laundry	la lavandería	la la·van·de·ree·a
market	el mercado	el mer·ka·do
pharmacy/ chemist	la farmacia	la far·ma·sya
post office	la officina de correos	la o·fee·see·na de ko·re·os
supermarket	el supermercado	el soo·per·mer·ka·do
tourist office	la oficina de turismo	la o·fee·see·na de too·rees·mo

What time does it open/close?

¿A qué hora abre/cierra?	a ke o·ra a·bre/sye·ra

I want to change some money/traveler's checks.

Quisiera cambiar dinero/cheques de viajero.	kee·sye·ra kam·byar dee·ne·ro/che·kes de vya·khe·ro

What is the exchange rate?

¿Cuál es el tipo de cambio?	kwal es el tee·po de kam·byo

I want to call ...

Quisiera llamar a ...	kee·sye·ra lya·mar a ...

airmail	correo aéreo	ko·re·o a·e·re·o
letter	carta	kar·ta
registered (mail)	certificado	ser·tee·fee·ka·do
stamps	timbres	teem·bres

TIME & DATES

What time is it?	¿Qué hora es?	ke o·ra es
It's one o'clock.	Es la una.	es la oo·na
It's seven o'clock.	Son las siete.	son las sye·te
Half past two.	Dos y media.	dos ee me·dya

midnight	medianoche	me·dya·no·che
noon	mediodía	me·dyo·dee·a
now	ahora	a·o·ra
today	hoy	oy
tonight	esta noche	es·ta no·che
tomorrow	mañana	ma·nya·na
yesterday	ayer	a·yer

Monday	lunes	loo·nes
Tuesday	martes	mar·tes
Wednesday	miércoles	myer·ko·les
Thursday	jueves	khwe·ves
Friday	viernes	vyer·nes
Saturday	sábado	sa·ba·do
Sunday	domingo	do·meen·go

January	enero	e·ne·ro
February	febrero	fe·bre·ro
March	marzo	mar·so
April	abril	a·breel
May	mayo	ma·yo
June	junio	khoo·nyo
July	julio	khoo·lyo
August	agosto	a·gos·to
September	septiembre	sep·tyem·bre
October	octubre	ok·too·bre
November	noviembre	no·vyem·bre
December	diciembre	dee·syem·bre

TRANSPORT
Public Transport

What time does ... leave/arrive?	¿A qué hora sale/llega?	a ke o·ra ... sa·le/ye·ga
the bus	el bus/autobús	el bus/ow·to·boos
the ferry	el barco	el bar·ko
the minibus	el colectivo/ la buseta/ el microbus	el ko·lek·tee·vo/ la boo·se·ta/ el mee·kro·boos
the plane	el avión	el a·vyon
the train	el tren	el tren

the airport	el aeropuerto	el a·e·ro·*pwer*·to
the bus station	la estación de autobuses	la es·ta·*syon* de ow·to·*boo*·ses
the bus stop	la parada de autobuses	la pa·*ra*·da de ow·to·*boo*·ses
the train station	la estación de ferrocarril	la es·ta·*syon* de fe·ro·ka·*reel*
the luggage locker	la consigna para el equipaje	la kon·*see*·nya para el e·kee·*pa*·khe
the ticket office	la boletería/ ticketería	la bo·le·te·*ree*·ya/ tee·ke·te·*ree*·ya

A ticket to ..., please.
Un boleto a ..., por favor.   oon bo·*le*·to a ... por fa·*vor*
What's the fare to ...?
¿Cuánto cuesta hasta ...?   kwan·to *kwes*·ta *a*·sta ...

student's	de estudiante	de es·too·*dyan*·te
1st class	primera clase	pree·me·ra *kla*·se
2nd class	segunda clase	se·*goon*·da *kla*·se
single/one-way	de ida	de *ee*·da
return/round trip	de ida y vuelta	de *ee*·da e *vwel*·ta
taxi	taxi	*tak*·see

Private Transport

I'd like to	Quisiera	kee·*sye*·ra
hire a ...	alquilar ...	al·kee·*lar* ...
4WD	un todo terreno	oon *to*·do te·*re*·no
car	un auto/carro	oon *ow*·to/*ka*·ro
motorcycle	una motocicleta	*oo*·na mo·to·see·*kle*·ta
bicycle	una bicicleta	*oo*·na bee·see·*kle*·ta

pickup (truck)	camioneta	ka·myo·*ne*·ta
truck	camión	ka·*myon*
hitchhike	hacer dedo	a·ser de·do

Where's a petrol station?
¿Dónde hay una gasolinera/bomba?
don·de ai oo·na ga·so·lee·*ne*·ra/*bom*·ba
How much is a liter of gasoline?
¿Cuánto cuesta un litro de gasolina?
kwan·to *kwes*·ta el *lee*·tro de ga·so·*lee*·na
Please fill it up.
Lleno, por favor.
ye·no por fa·*vor*
I'd like (2000 colones) worth.
Quiero (dos mil colones) en gasolina.
kye·ro (dos meel ko·*lo*·nes) en ga·so·*lee*·na

diesel	diesel	*dee*·sel
leaded (regular)	gasolina con plomo	ga·so·*lee*·na kon *plo*·mo
petrol (gas)	gasolina	ga·so·*lee*·na

unleaded	gasolina sin plomo	ga·so·*lee*·na seen *plo*·mo
oil	aceite	a·*say*·te
tire	llanta	*yan*·ta
puncture	agujero	a·goo·*khe*·ro

ROAD SIGNS	
Acceso	Entrance
Ceda el Paso	Give Way
Desvío/Desviación	Detour
No Adelantar	No Passing
No Hay Paso	Road Closed
No Pase	No Overtaking
Pare/Stop	Stop
Prohibido Estacionar	No Parking
Prohibido el Paso	No Entry
Salida (de Autopista)	Exit (Freeway)
Una Via	One Way

Is this the road to ...?
¿Por acquí se va a ...?
por a·*kee* se va a ...
(How long) Can I park here?
¿(Por cuánto tiempo) Puedo estacionar aquí?
(por kwan·to tyem·po) pwe·do ess·ta·syo·*nar* a·*kee*
Where do I pay?
¿Dónde se paga?
don·de se *pa*·ga
I need a mechanic/tow truck.
Necesito un mecánico/remolque.
ne·se·*see*·to oon me·*ka*·nee·ko/re·*mol*·ke
Is there a garage near here?
¿Hay un garaje cerca de aquí?
ai oon ga·*ra*·khe ser·ka de a·*kee*
The car has broken down in ...
El carro se ha averiado en ...
el *ka*·ro se a a·ve·*rya*·do en ...
The motorbike won't start.
La moto no arranca.
la *mo*·to no a·*ran*·ka
I have a flat tire.
Tengo una llanta desinflada.
ten·go oo·na yan·ta des·een·*fla*·da
I've run out of petrol.
Me quedé sin gasolina.
me ke·*de* seen ga·so·*lee*·na
I've had an accident.
Tuve un accidente.
too·ve oon ak·see·*den*·te

TRAVEL WITH CHILDREN
Do you mind if I breast-feed here?
¿Le molesta que dé el pecho aquí?
le mo·*les*·ta ke de el *pe*·cho a·*kee*

Are children allowed?
¿Se admiten niños?
se ad·*mee*·ten *nee*·nyos

I need ...
Necesito ...
ne·se·*see*·to ...
Do you have ...?
¿Hay ...?
ai ...

  a car baby seat
  un asiento de seguridad para bebés
  oon a·*syen*·to de se·goo·ree·*da* pa·ra be·*bes*
  a children's menu
  un menú infantil
  oon me·*noo* een·fan·*teel*

a day care service
una guardería
oo·na gwar·de·*ree*·a
(disposable) diapers/nappies
pañales (de usar y tirar)
pa·*nya*·les (de oo·*sar* ee tee·*rar*)
infant formula (milk)
leche en polvo
le·che en *pol*·vo
a highchair
una silla para bebé
oo·na *see*·ya *pa*·ra be·*be*
a stroller
una carreola
oona ka·re·*o*·la

Also available from Lonely Planet:
Latin American Spanish Phrasebook

LANGUAGE

Glossary

See p41 for useful words and phrases dealing with food and dining. See the Language chapter (p491) for other useful words and phrases.

abrazo – hug
adiós – means 'goodbye' universally, but used in Nicaragua as a greeting
aguas negras – sewage
aguila – eagle
alcaldía – mayor's office
aldea – hamlet
alquiler de automóviles – car rental
apartado – post-office box
árbol – tree
ardilla – squirrel
automóvil (auto) – car
ave – bird; see also *pájaro*
avión – airplane

baño – bathroom; see also *servicio*
barrio – district, neighborhood
barro – mud
beso – kiss
bicicleta – bicycle
billete – bank note, bill
boleto – ticket (bus, train, museum etc)
bomba – gas station; short funny verse; bomb
borracho/a – drunk male/female
bosque – forest
bosque nuboso – cloud forest
bote – boat

caballeros – gentlemen; the usual sign on male-toilet doors
caballo – horse
cabinas – cheap hotel
cafétalero – coffee baron
cafétera – coffee-making machine
cajero automático – ATM
cama – bed
cama matrimonial – double bed
caminata – walk; hike
camión – truck
camioneta – pick-up truck
camiseta – T-shirt
campesino – peasant; person who works in agriculture
carretas – wooden ox carts
carretera – road
cascada – waterfall

catedral – cathedral
caverna – cave
cerro – mountain
chele/a – White/European, from 'leche,' or milk
chicle – chewing gum
chunche – literally, a 'thing'
cien metros – one city block
cigarrillo – cigarette
cochino – pig; also means 'filthy'
cocina – kitchen; cooking
colectivo – buses, minivans, or cars operating as shared taxis; see also *normal* and *directo*
colibrí – hummingbird
colina – hill
condón – condom
cordillera – mountain range
córdoba – Nicaraguan unit of currency
correo – mail service
correo electrónico – email
coyote – moneychanger
cruce – crossing
cruda – often used to describe a hangover: *'tengo una cruda'*, literally 'raw'
cuadraciclo – all-terrain vehicle (ATV)
cuchara – spoon
cuchillo – knife
cueva – cave
culebra – snake; see also *serpiente*

damas – ladies; the usual sign found on female-toilet doors
derecha – right
dios – god
directo – direct; long-distance bus that has only a few stops
doble – double (as in double room)
doble tracción – 4WD

eco-albergue – rural lodge in El Salvador
mergencia – emergency
empalme – three-way intersection
encomienda – sending packages, usually via bus
estación – station (as in ranger station or bus station); season
estero – estuary
estudiante – student

farmacia – pharmacy
fauna silvestre – wildlife
fiesta – party or festival

finca – farm or plantation
flor – flower
frontera – border
fuego – flame
futból – soccer

galón – US gallon
garza – cattle egret
gasolina – gas, petrol
gracias – thanks
gringo/a – male/female North American or European visitor (can be affectionate or insulting, depending on the tone used)
guapote – large fish caught for sport, equivalent to rainbow bass

hacienda – a rural estate
hay – pronounced 'eye,' meaning 'there is' or 'there are;' *no hay* means 'there is none'
hielo – ice
hombre – man

iglesia – church
incendio – fire
indígena – indigenous
Ineter – Nicaragua Institute for Territorial Studies
Interamericana – Pan-American Highway
Intur – Nicaraguan Institute of Tourism
invierno – winter; the rainy season
isla – island
izquierda – left

jardín – garden

kilometraje – distance in kilometers; mileage

lancha – boat (usually small); see also *panga*
lapa – parrot
lavabó – hand sink
lavandería – laundry facility, usually offering dry-cleaning services
lentes – eyeglasses
liciado – hurt
llanuras – tropical plains

machismo – an exaggerated sense of masculine pride
macho – a virile figure, typically a man
maje – slang that means 'dude,' used among men
malecón – pier; sea wall; waterfront promenade
manglar – mangrove
Marena – Nicaragua's Ministry of the Environment & Natural Resources
marías – local name for taxi meters
marimba – word xylophone
menso – dumb

mercado – market
mesa – table
meseta central – central plateau; Central Valley
mestizo – person of mixed descent, usually Spanish and Indian
migración – immigration
minisuper – small convenience store
mirador – lookout point
mochilero – backpacker (though the English word is being used more and more)
mono – monkey
mono cara blanca – capuchin monkey
mono colorado – spider monkey
mono congo – howler monkey
mono tití – squirrel monkey
motocicleta (moto) – motorcycle
muelle – dock
mujer – woman
murciélago – bat
museo – museum

Nica – Nicaraguan, male or female
niñera – nanny or babysitter
niño – child
normal – long-distance bus with many stops

Oficina de Migración – Immigration Office
ojalá – hopefully; literally, 'if God wills it'

página web – website
pájaro – bird
pañales – diapers, nappies
panga – light boat; see also *lancha*
paños – towel or rag
pántano – swamp or wetland
papel higiénico – toilet paper
parada – bus stop
parque – park
parque central – central town square or plaza
parque nacional – national park
peón – someone who does heavy unskilled labor
perezoso – sloth
perico – mealy parrot
periódico – newspaper
pirópos – catcalls
piso – floor (as in 2nd floor)
pista de aterrizaje – landing strip, tarmac
pista de baile – dance floor
plato – plate
playa – beach
posada – guesthouse
propina – tip for service
prostituta – prostitute (also shortened to the more vulgar *puta*)
puerto – port

pulpería – corner grocery store
puro – cigar (as in *un puro*)

refresco – soda or bottled refreshment
refugio nacional de vida silvestre – national wildlife refuge
repelente – bug repellent
río – river

sacerdote – priest
saco de dormir – sleeping bag
salado – frequently meant as 'tough luck;' literally 'salty'
sencilla – single room
sencillo – simple; monetary change (small bills or coinage)
sendero – trail; path
serpiente – snake; see also *culebra*
servicio – toilet; see also *baño*
servicio a domicilio – home delivery
servilleta – napkin
soda – very Costa Rican term for a simple café; you'll find these all over southern Nicaragua
sucio – dirty
supermercado – supermarket

taller mecánico – mechanic's shop
taza – cup
tenedor – fork

tepezcuinte – jungle rodent that is a relative of the guinea pig, often eaten by locals
tienda – store
tienda de campaña – camping tent
típica/o – typical; particularly used to describe food (*comida típica* means 'typical cooking')
toallas higienicas – sanitary napkins
tortuga – turtle
trago – cocktail
tú – you (informal, same as *vos*)
¡Tuanis! – Cool!
tucán – toucan

Unesco – UN Educational, Scientific, and Cultural Organization

vaso – glass
vecino – neighbor
venenoso – poisonous
verano – summer; the dry season
viajero – traveler
vino – wine
vivero – plant nursery
vos – you (informal, same as *tú*)

zancudo – mosquito
zapato – shoe
zonas – zone
zoológico – zoo

Behind the Scenes

THIS BOOK

The first edition of *Nicaragua & El Salvador* was co-ordinated by Paige Penland. Gary Chandler and Liza Prado wrote the El Salvador portions of this book. Tim Rogers, Ruth Danelia López Gaitan and Bob Olson contributed in-depth boxed texts, and the Health chapter was adapted from text by Dr David Goldberg. This guidebook was commissioned in Lonely Planet's Oakland office, and produced by the following:

Commissioning Editor Greg Benchwick, Jay Cooke
Coordinating Editor Kate James
Coordinating Cartographer Csanad Csutoros
Coordinating Layout Designer Clara Monitto
Managing Editor Jennifer Garrett
Managing Cartographer Alison Lyall
Assisting Editors Kristin Odijk, Anne Mulvaney, Alan Murphy, Craig Kilburn, Janet Austin, Pat Kinsella
Assisting Cartographers Andrew Smith, Owen Eszeki, Valentina Kremenchutskaya, Marion Byass, Jolyon Philcox
Assisting Layout Designers Cara Smith, Wibowo Rusli
Cover Designer James Hardy
Project Manager Rachel Imeson
Language Content Coordinator Quentin Frayne

Thanks to the hard-working folks at Lonely Planet's Talk2Us (especially regional representatives Haydn Ellis and Jessa Boanas-Dewes), Sally Darmody and Celia Wood.

THANKS

PAIGE R PENLAND
For this project, I needed help, and I got it. First, thanks to my mom, Wanda Olson, for taking care of the business side of my life; thanks to Beto Lizarraga and the staff of Hotel Liberia (Lety, Alexis, Manfred and Zelmira) for everything; and thanks to Keyoe Halsey for moral support. Tim Rogers, Ruth Danelia López Gaitan and Bob Olson wrote the amazing boxed texts; enjoy them.

Just a few of the others without whom this book would have sucked include: 'Miskito' Alan and Mira-sol Bowie, Felicity Butler, Robert Dull, Martin, Marta and Alyson Elliot, George and Jan Fergusen, Jessica Floyd, Lawrence Goodlive, Berman Gómez, Brice Gosnell, Leah Griffin, Jose Rene Jiron Gutierrez, Randy Haase, Regina Hurtado de Arana, Nadene at Mavericks, Johny 'Bluefields' Nixon, María Nelly Rivas, Marisol Robles-Jarquin, Manuel Ruiz, Todd Sotkiewicz, Tomi Särkioja, 'Brooklyn' Steve, Ann Thorne, Joni Valkila and family, Marielena Vanegas, Marga Luna Villalobos, John Wayne, Darren Webb, Nate Yue, and Joe, Karen and Terry from Matagalpa. And of course, to all the editors and cartographers who mash the raw manuscript into something useful, you rock.

GARY CHANDLER & LIZA PRADO

We have many, many people to thank. Thank you first to Paige Penland for pulling this mother together; to Greg Benchwick and Jay Cooke, good editors and good guys both; to cartographer extraordinaire Alison Lyall; and to all the talented editorial and production folks in Australia. We received a tremendous amount of help from Peace Corps volunteers, including John Bova, Preston Clark, Seth Colby, Laura Dane, Michelle Dulski, Christie Eastburn, Sarah Edelman,

---

THE LONELY PLANET STORY

The story begins with a classic travel adventure: Tony and Maureen Wheeler's 1972 journey across Europe and Asia to Australia. There was no useful information about the overland trail then, so Tony and Maureen published the first Lonely Planet guidebook to meet a growing need.

From a kitchen table, Lonely Planet has grown to become the largest independent travel publisher in the world, with offices in Melbourne (Australia), Oakland (USA) and London (UK). Today Lonely Planet guidebooks cover the globe. There is an ever-growing list of books and information in a variety of media. Some things haven't changed. The main aim is still to make it possible for adventurous travellers to get out there – to explore and better understand the world.

At Lonely Planet we believe travellers can make a positive contribution to the countries they visit – if they respect their host communities and spend their money wisely. Every year 5% of company profit is donated to charities around the world.

Erica Frenkel, Neil Gormley, Michael Hoffman, Bonnie Holman, Dan Holmes, Moni Johnson, Kate Kenealy, Tamar Losleben, Maria Marasigan (and her brother), Sherri Mangum, Scott Montegna, Rebecca Paskos, Elizabeth Patton, Steve Quinlan, David Reichbaum, Taki Skiadas, and Jenny Rose Tobin. Thanks also to Michael Irvine, Gesa Wedig and the many others who wrote to LP with tips about El Salvador.

We are grateful to the countless Salvadorans and expatriates we hit up for information, directions, advice and insight. Special thanks go to Marisol Galindo, Serafín Gómez, Sebastian Torogoz and Norma Rivas of PRODETUR in Perquín; Ronald Brenneman of Hotel Perkin Lenca, also in Perquín; Javier Díaz of Casa Frolazin Santa Ana; Jaime Delgado of Papaya's Lounge Playa El Tunco; and Manolo González of Imposible Tours in Tacuba.

Thank you, finally, to our families and friends – you make coming home one of the best parts of traveling.

ACKNOWLEDGMENTS

Many thanks to the following for the use of their content:

Globe on back cover ©Mountain High Maps 1993 Digital Wisdom, Inc.

SEND US YOUR FEEDBACK

We love to hear from travelers – your comments keep us on our toes and help make our books better. Our well-travelled team reads every word on what you loved or loathed about this book. Although we cannot reply individually to postal submissions, we always guarantee that your feedback goes straight to the appropriate authors, in time for the next edition. Each person who sends us information is thanked in the next edition – and the most useful submissions are rewarded with a free book. See the Behind the Scenes section.

To send us your updates – and find out about Lonely Planet events, newsletters and travel news – visit our award-winning website: **www.lonelyplanet.com/feedback**.

Note: We may edit, reproduce and incorporate your comments in Lonely Planet products such as guidebooks, websites and digital products, so let us know if you don't want your comments reproduced or your name acknowledged. For a copy of our privacy policy, go to www.lonelyplanet.com/privacy.

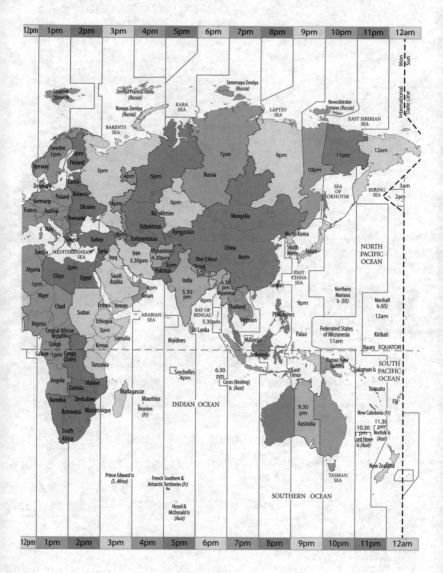